South Africa
Namibia & Botswana

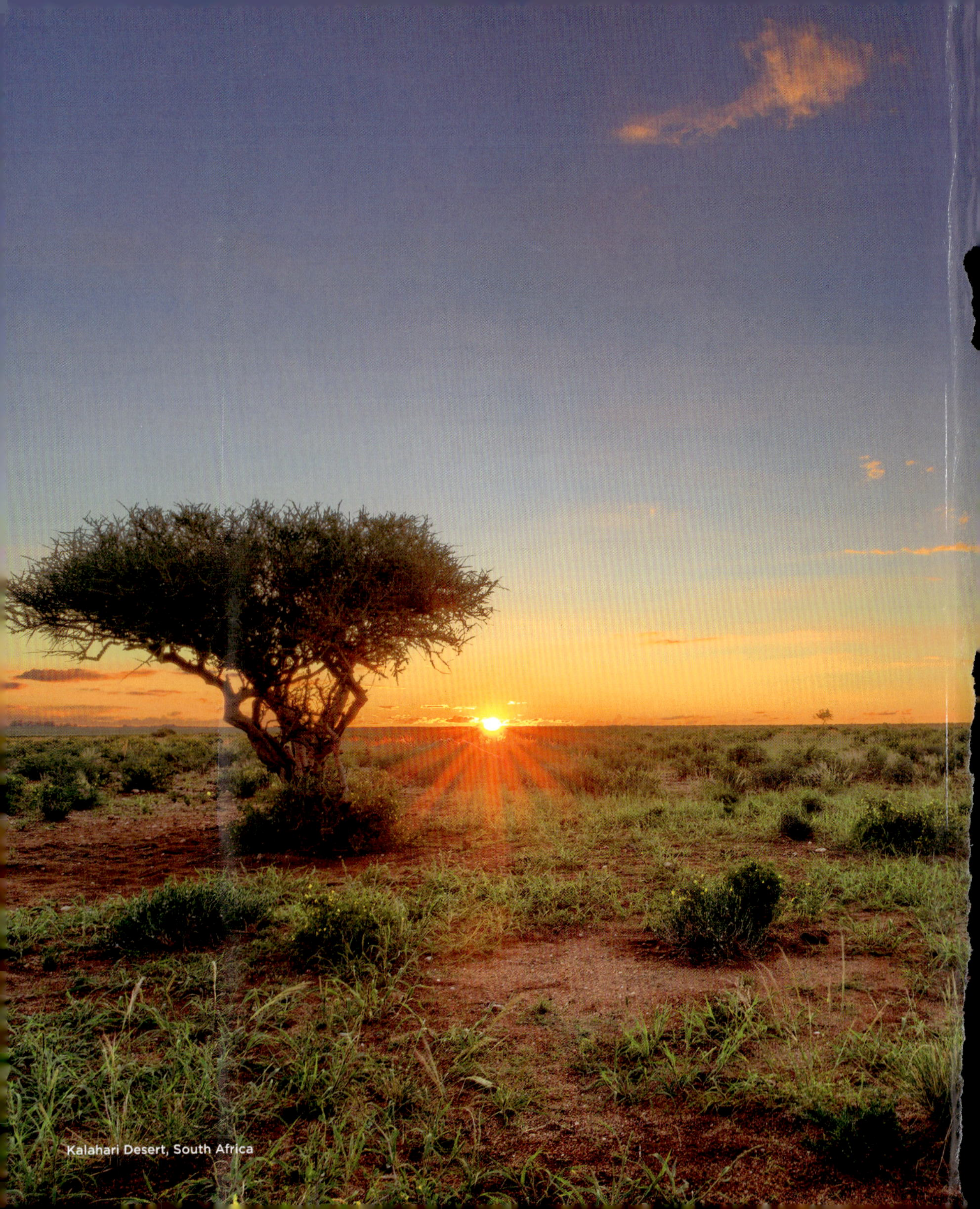

Kalahari Desert, South Africa

South Africa Namibia & Botswana

Afrique du Sud, Namibie & Botswana

Südafrika, Namibia & Botswana

Sudáfrica, Namibia & Botsuana

Sudafrica, Namibia & Botswana

Zuid-Afrika, Namibië & Botswana

Markus Hertrich

Christine Metzger

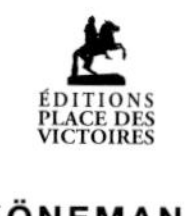

KÖNEMANN

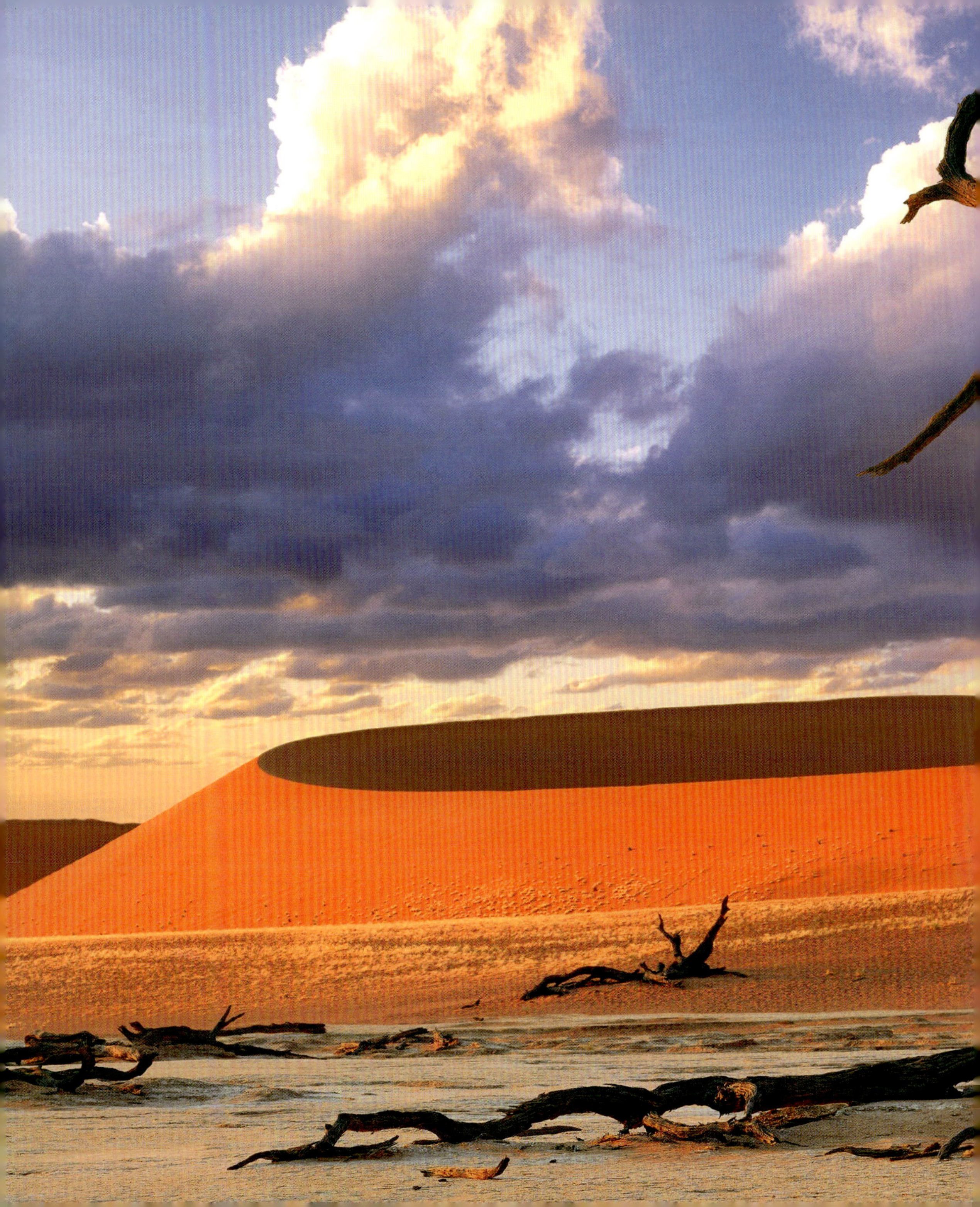

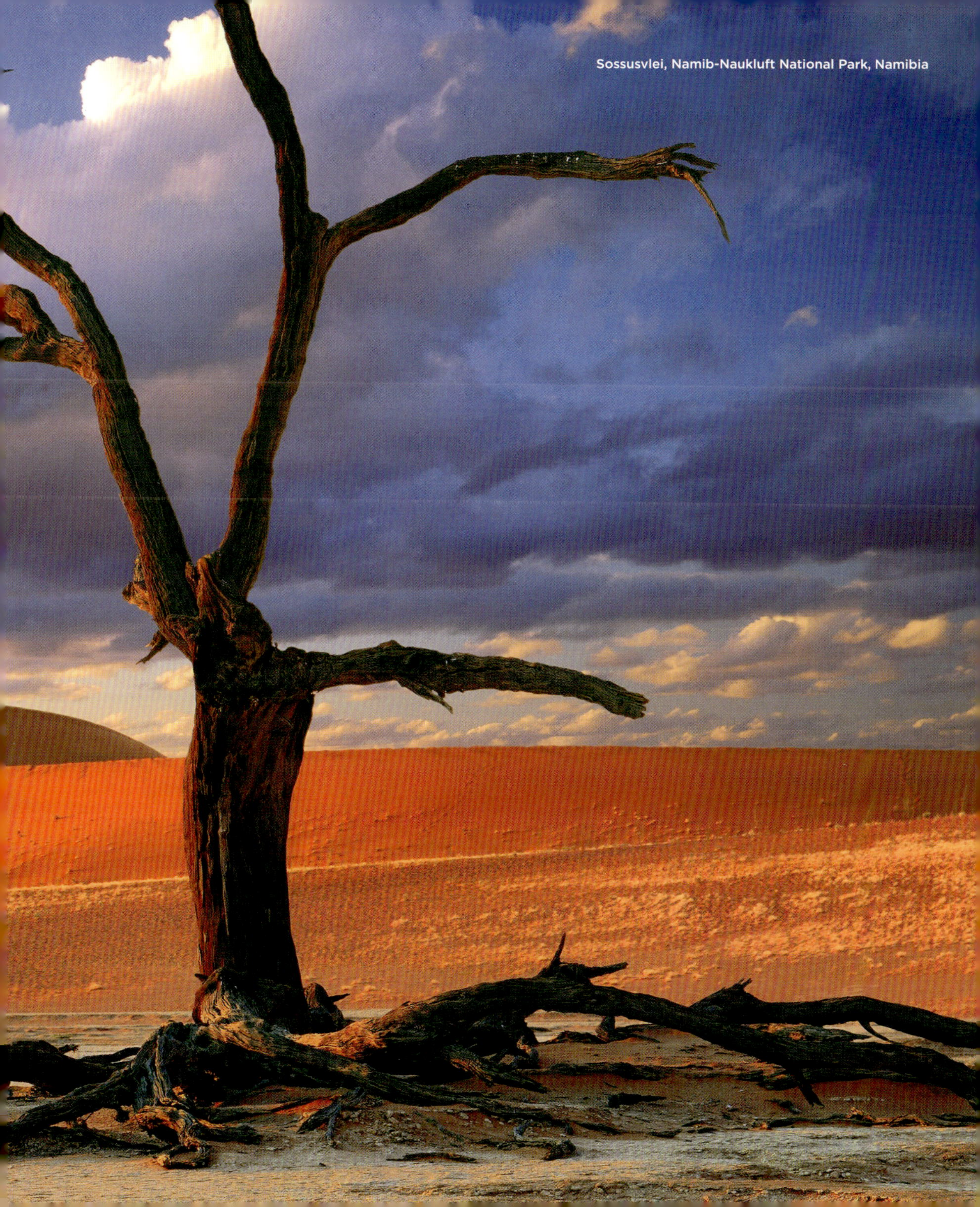

Sossusvlei, Namib-Naukluft National Park, Namibia

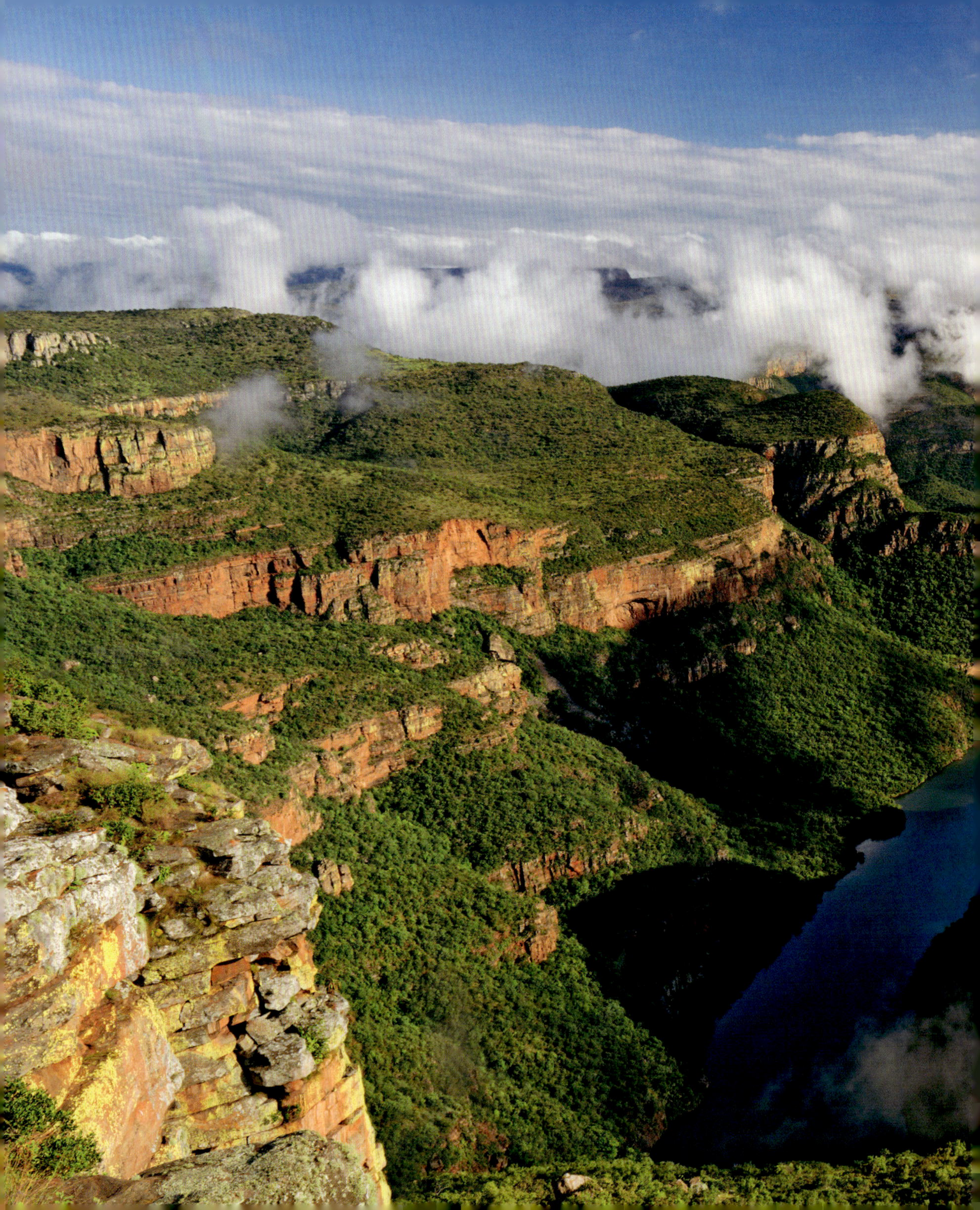

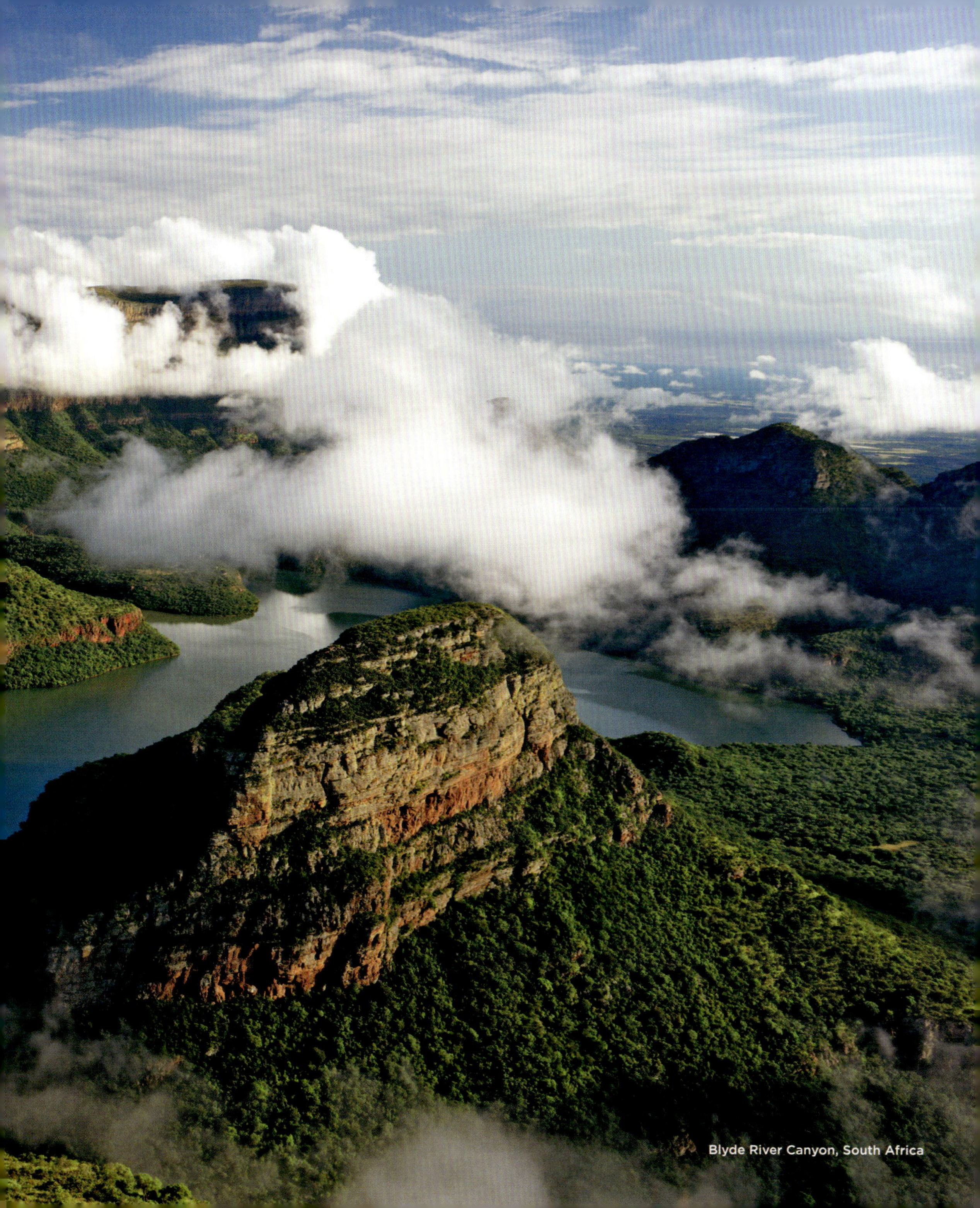

Blyde River Canyon, South Africa

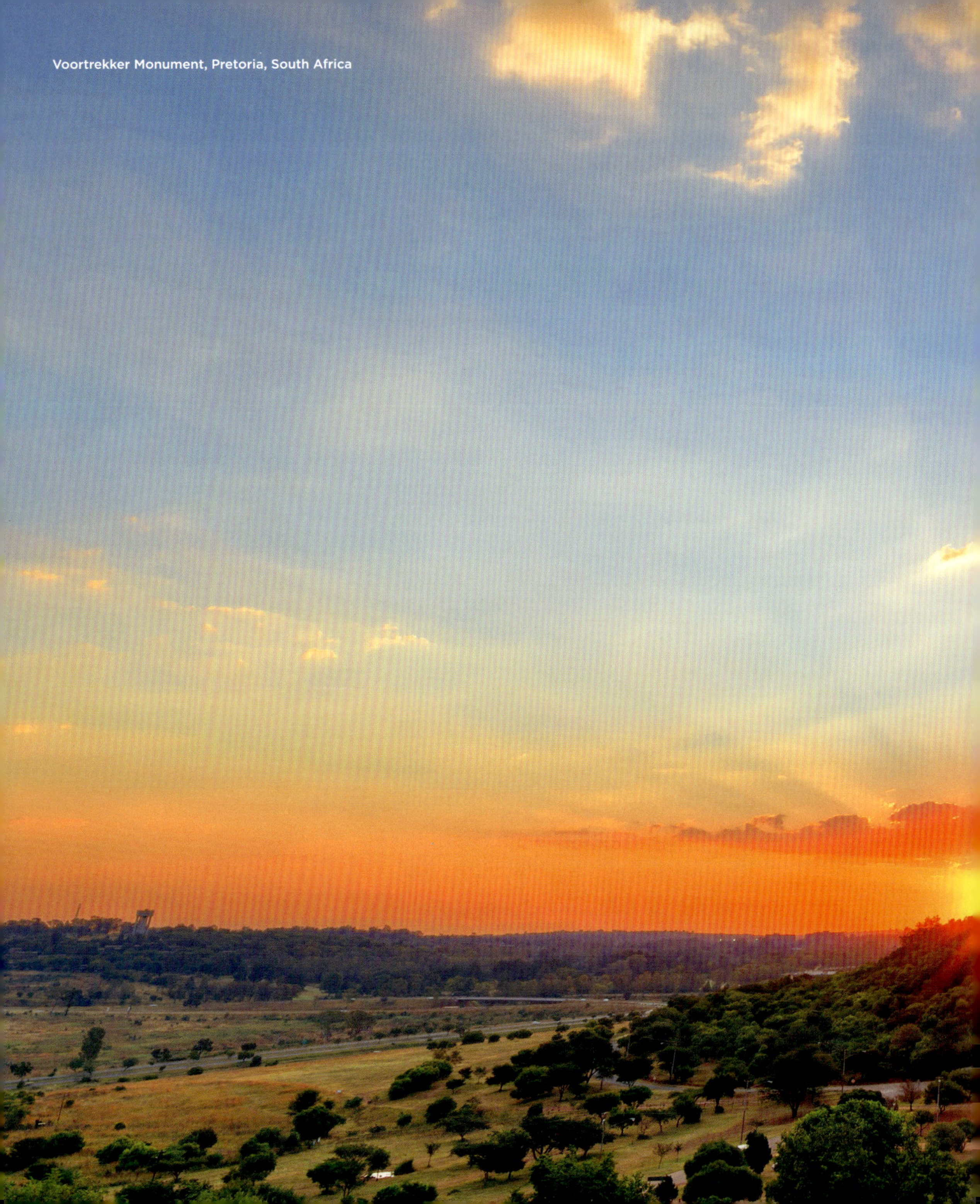
Voortrekker Monument, Pretoria, South Africa

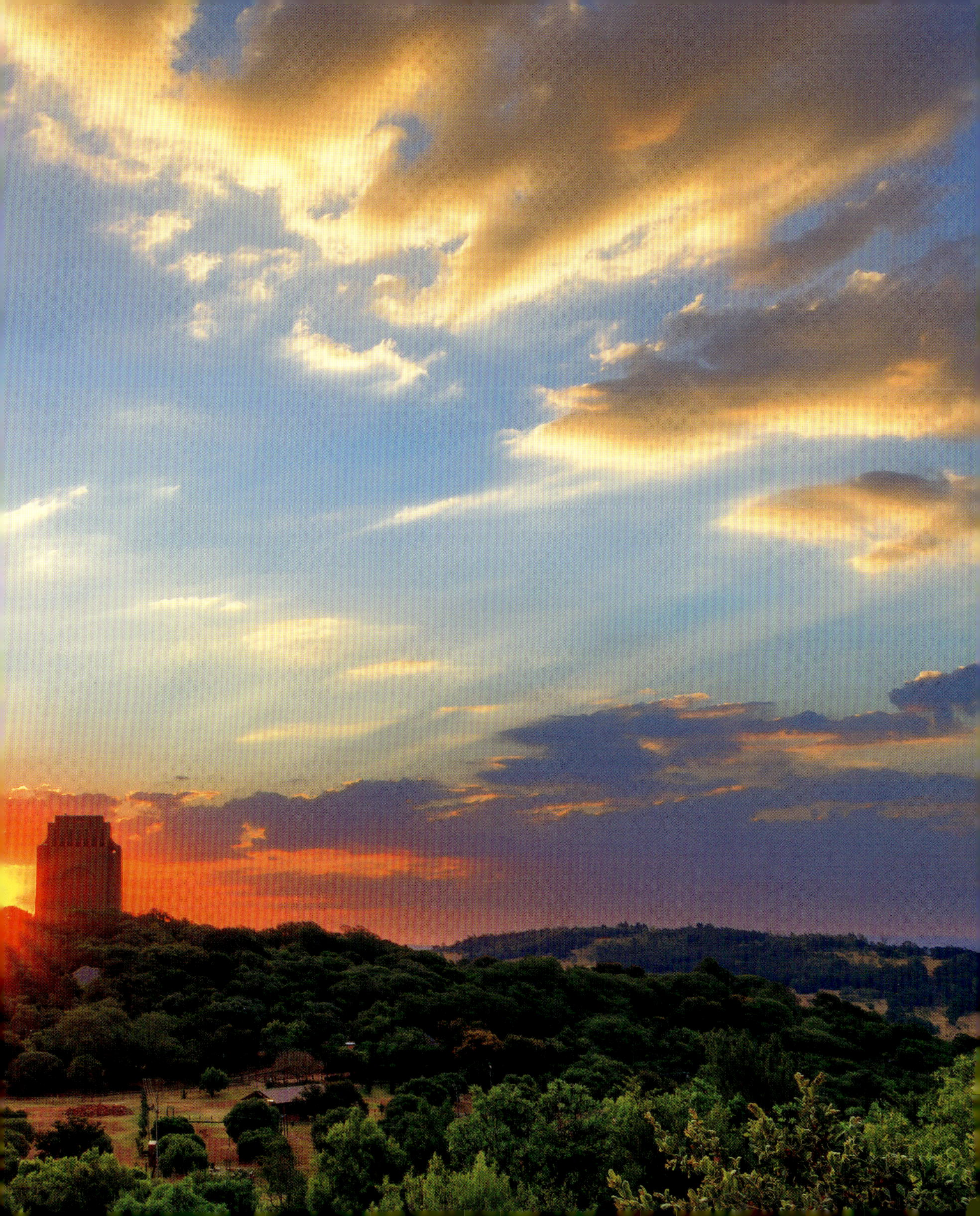

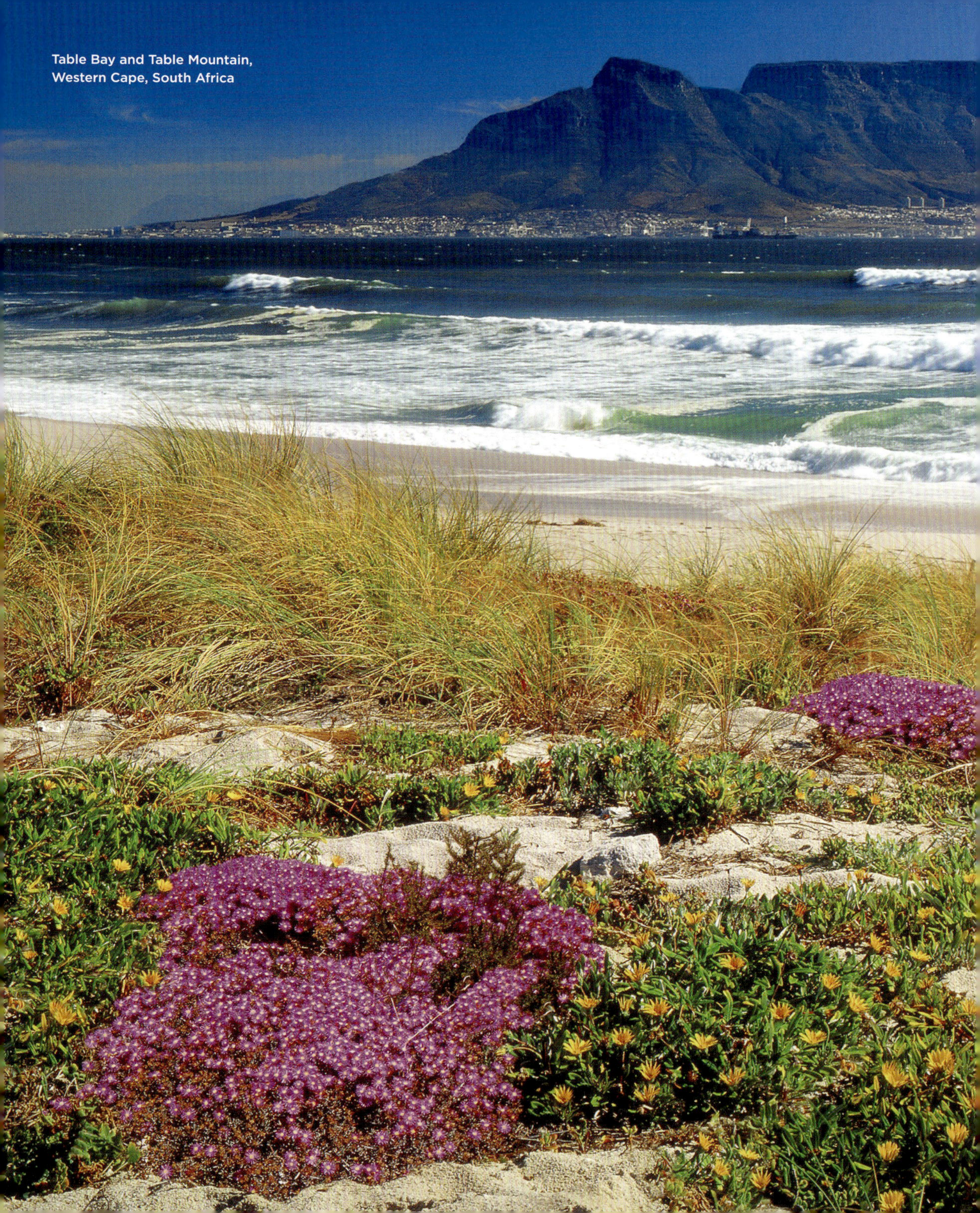
Table Bay and Table Mountain,
Western Cape, South Africa

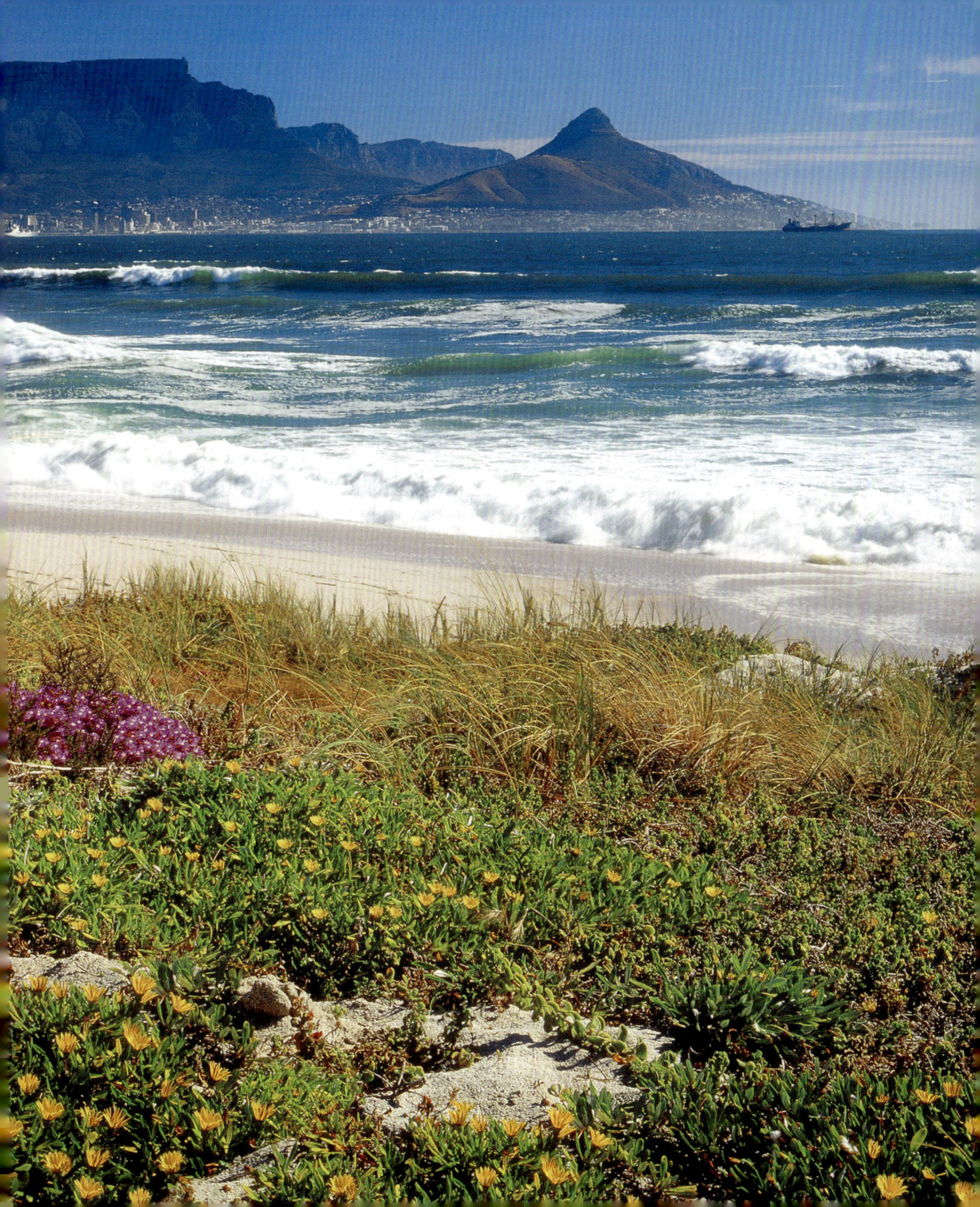

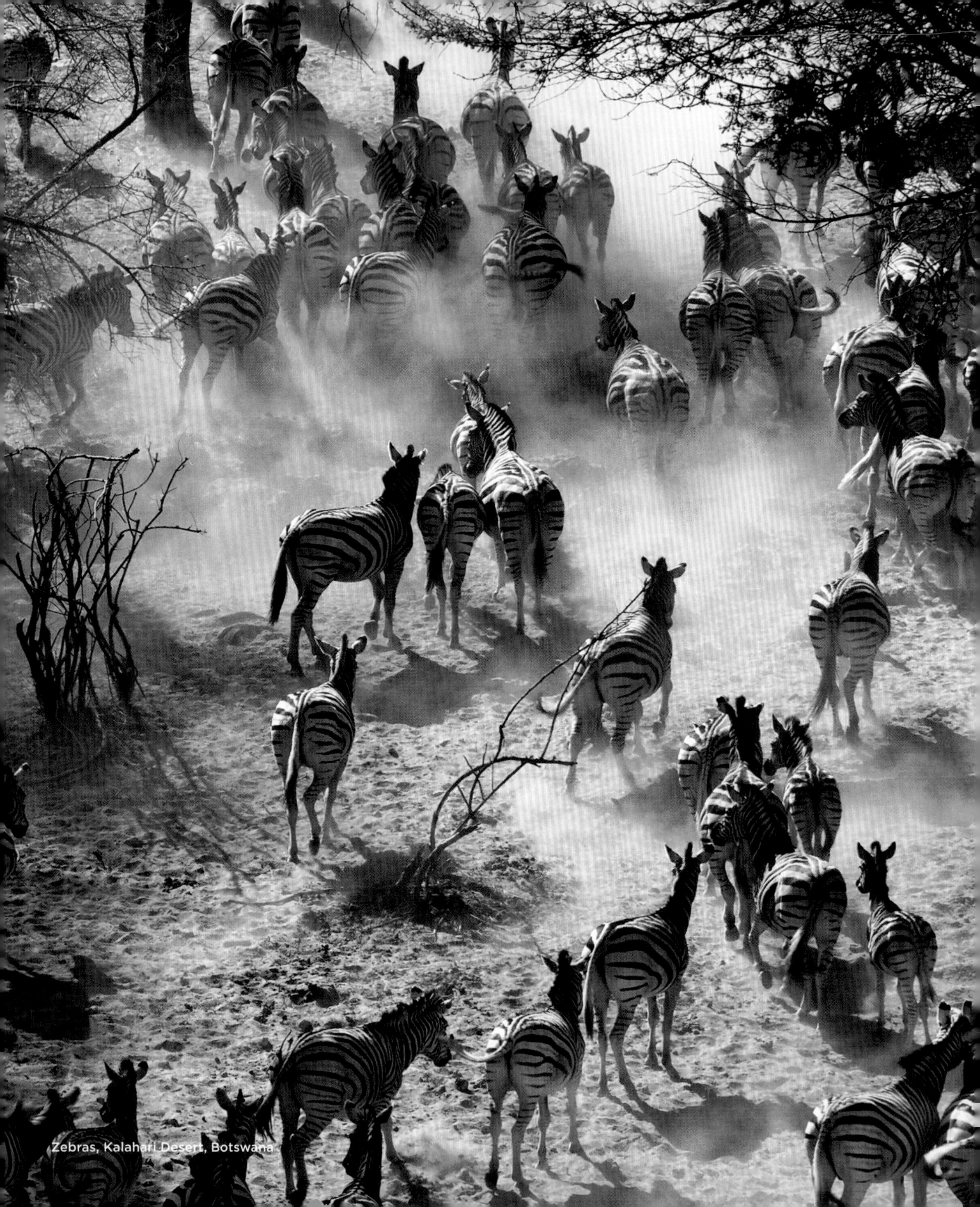

Zebras, Kalahari Desert, Botswana

Contents · Sommaire · Inhalt · Índice · Indice · Inhoud

14 Introduction
Einleitung
Introducción
Introduzione
Inleiding

18 Kaokoveld, Namibia
Le Kaokoveld
Kaokoveldwoestijn

32 Caprivi-Strip, Namibia
La bande de Caprivi
Caprivi-Zipfel
Franja de Caprivi
Dito di Caprivi
Caprivistrook

40 Etosha National Park, Namibia
Le parc national d'Etosha
Etosha-Nationalpark
Parque Nacional de Etosha
Parco Nazionale di Etosha
Nationale Park van Etosha

62 Skeleton Coast, Namibia
La côte des Squelettes
Skelettküste
Costa de los Esqueletos
Costa degli Scheletri
Skeleton Coast

70 Damaraland, Namibia
Le Damaraland

84 Waterberg Plateau National Park, Namibia
Plateau du Waterberg
Altopiano del Waterberg
Waterbergplateau

92 Namib-Naukluft National Park, Walvis Bay & Windhoek, Namibia
Le parc national du Namib-Naukluft, Walvis Bay & Windhoek
Namib-Naukluft-Nationalpark, Walvis Bay & Windhuk
Parque Nacional Namib-Naukluft, Walvis Bay & Windhoek
Parco Nazionale di Namib-Naukluft, Walvis Bay & Windhoek
Namib-Naukluft National Park, Walvisbaai & Windhoek

116 Tsau ||Khaeb National Park (Sperrgebiet) & Lüderitz, Namibia
Le parc national de Sperrgebiet & Lüderitz
Tsau-||Khaeb-(Sperrgebiet)-Nationalpark & Lüderitz
Parque nacional de Sperrgebiet & Lüderitz
Parco Nazionale Tsau-||Khaeb & Lüderitz
Sperrgebiet & Lüderitz

128 Fish River Canyon, Namibia
Le Fish River Canyon
Fish River Canyon
Cañón del río Fish

138 Chobe National Park & Tsodilo Hills, Botswana
Le parc national de Chobe & Les Tsodilo Hills
Chobe-Nationalpark & Tsodilo-Hügel
Parque Nacional de Chobe & Colinas Tsodilo
Parco Nazionale Chobe & Tsodilo Hills
Nationale Park van Chobe & Tsodiloheuvels

150 Okavango Delta, Botswana
Le delta de l'Okavango
Okavangodelta
Delta del Okavango
Delta dell'Okavango

166 Makgadikgadi Salt Pans, Botswana
Les cuvettes salées de Makgadikgad
Makgadikgadi-Salzpfannen
Salares de Makgadikgadi
Saline di Makgadikgadi
Zoutvlakten van Makgadikgadi

178 Northern Tuli Game Reserve & Mapungubwe National Park, Botswana & South Africa
La réserve naturelle de Tuli Nord & Le parc national de Mapungubwe
Northern Tuli Game Reserve & Mapungubwe-Nationalpark
Reserva de Caza del Norte de Tuli &Parque Nacional Mapungubwe
Riserva di caccia di Northern Tuli & Parco Nazionale Mapungubwe
Northern Tuli Game Reserve & Nationale Park van Mapungubwe

188 Kalahari & Gaborone, Namibia, South Africa & Botswana
Le Kalahari & Gaborone

204 Kgalagadi Transfrontier Park, South Africa & Botswana
Le parc national transfrontalier du Kgalagadi
Kgalagadi-Transfrontier-Park
Parque internacional de Kgalagadi
Parco Nazionale Transfrontaliero Kgalagadi

220 Kruger National Park, South Africa
Le parc national Kruger
Kruger-Nationalpark
Parque Nacional Kruger
Parco Nazionale Kruger
Nationale Park Kruger

246 Blyde River Canyon, South Africa
Le Blyde River Canyon
Cañón del río Blyde

258 Pilanesberg National Park, South Africa
Le parc national du Pilanesberg
Pilanesberg-Nationalpark
Parque Nacional Pilanesberg
Parco Nazionale di Pilanesberg
Nationale Parwk Pilanesberg

270 Johannesburg & Pretoria, South Africa

278 Maputaland, South Africa
Le Maputaland

292 Hluhluwe-Imfolozi Park, South Africa
La réserve d'Hluhluwe-Umfolozi
Hluhluwe-iMfolozi-Park
Parque Nacional Hluhluwe-Imfolozi
Parco Nazionale Hluhluwe-Imfolozi
Hluhluwe-Imfolozipark

300 Golden Gate Highlands National Park, South Africa
Le parc national des Golden Gate Highlands
Golden-Gate-Highlands-Nationalpark
Parque Nacional Golden Gate Highlands
Parco Nazionale Golden Gate Highlands
Nationaal Park Golden Gate Hoogland

310 Drakensberg Mountains & Durban, South Africa
Le Drakensberge & Durban
Drakensberge & Durban
Monti dei Draghi & Durban
Drakensbergen & Durban

328 Augrabies Falls National Park, South Africa
Le parc national des Chutes d'Augrabies
Augrabies-Wasserfälle-Nationalpark
Parque Nacional de las Cataratas Augrabies
Parco Nazionale delle Cascate di Augrabies
Nationaal Park Augrabies Falls

334 Namaqualand, South Africa
Le Namaqualand

342 West Coast, South Africa
Westküste
Costa Oeste
Costa occidentale

360 Cederberg Mountains & Tankwa Karoo National Park, South Africa
Les montagnes du Cederberg & Le parc national de Tankwa Karoo
Zederberge & Tankwa Karoo Nationalpark
Cederberg & Parque Nacional Tankwa Karoo
Cederberg & Tankwa Karoo National Park
Cederberg & Nationaal Park Tankwa Karoo

370 Cape Winelands, South Africa
Cape Viñedos

384 Cape Town & Table Mountain, South Africa
Le Cap et la montagne de la Table
Kapstadt und der Tafelberg
Ciudad del Cabo y la Montaña de la Mesa
Città del Capo e il Tafelberg
Kaapstad en de Tafelberg

410 Overberg, South Africa

434 Lodge

436 Garden Route & Port Elizabeth, South Africa
Garden Route & Port Elisabeth
Ruta Jardín & Puerto Elizabeth

476 Wild Coast, South Africa
La Côte Sauvage
Costa Salvaje

496 Map
Carte
Landkarte
Carta
Landkaart

498 Index

502 Photo Credits

South Africa, Namibia and Botswana

The allure of the uncontrolled forces of nature may still be experienced in southern Africa! Here in Botswana, Namibia and South Africa, these forces are united in more diverse ways than anywhere else on earth. Two oceans, which could not be more different, flow spectacularly around the southernmost tip of the continent: here, the Atlantic meets the subtropical, warm Indian Ocean with its cold force. The richness of the contrasts may be seen everywhere: in the landscape, with the angular rock formations of its sandy deserts, the almost subtropical river basins, the deep canyons or lush, green hill chains. The fauna is also extremely diverse, with many rare species which can no longer found anywhere else in the world. Preserving this paradisiacal habitat has become the task of the numerous national parks, nature reserves and game reserves in the region. Not only Nelson Mandela believed that "South Africa is the most beautiful place in the world" ...

Afrique du Sud, Namibie et Botswana

Dans le sud de l'Afrique, on peut encore contempler avec fascination la puissance de la nature à l'état sauvage ! Ici, au Botswana, en Namibie et en Afrique du Sud, les forces de la nature se combinent avec une diversité probablement unique au monde. Deux océans, on ne peut plus différents, se rencontrent de manière spectaculaire à la pointe sud du continent : l'Atlantique, avec sa froide impétuosité, et l'océan Indien, chaud et subtropical. La richesse des contrastes est visible partout, notamment au niveau des paysages, où les déserts de sable côtoient les formations rocheuses escarpées, les zones fluviales presque subtropicales, les canyons profonds ou encore les chaînes de collines verdoyantes. La faune présente également mille facettes, avec ses nombreuses espèces rares voire disparues dans le reste du monde. Préserver ce biotope paradisiaque est devenu une véritable mission pour tous les parcs nationaux, les zones protégées et les réserves naturelles de la région. Nelson Mandela n'était pas le seul à penser que « L'Afrique du Sud est le plus bel endroit au monde » ...

Südafrika, Namibia und Botswana

Die absolute Faszination wilder Naturgewalt – im südlichen Afrika ist sie noch zu erleben! Hier in Botswana, Namibia und Südafrika vereinen sich die Kräfte der Natur auf so vielfältige Weise wie sonst wahrscheinlich nirgends auf der Erde. Zwei Weltmeere, die unterschiedlicher nicht sein könnten, umströmen spektakulär den südlichsten Zipfel des Kontinents: Hier trifft der Atlantik mit seiner kalten Wucht auf den subtropischen, warmen Indischen Ozean. Der Reichtum der Kontraste zeigt sich überall: ob landschaftlich in sandigen Wüsten mit kantigen Felsformationen, fast subtropischen Flussgebieten, tiefen Canyons oder satten, grünbewachsenen Hügelketten. Überaus facettenreichen ist auch die Tierwelt mit vielen seltenen Arten, die es sonst auf der Welt nicht (mehr) gibt. Diesen paradiesischen Lebensraum zu erhalten, ist die Aufgabe zahlreicher Nationalparks, Naturschutzgebiete und Tierreservate in der Region geworden. Nicht nur Nelson Mandela glaubte, „Südafrika ist der schönste Ort der Welt" ...

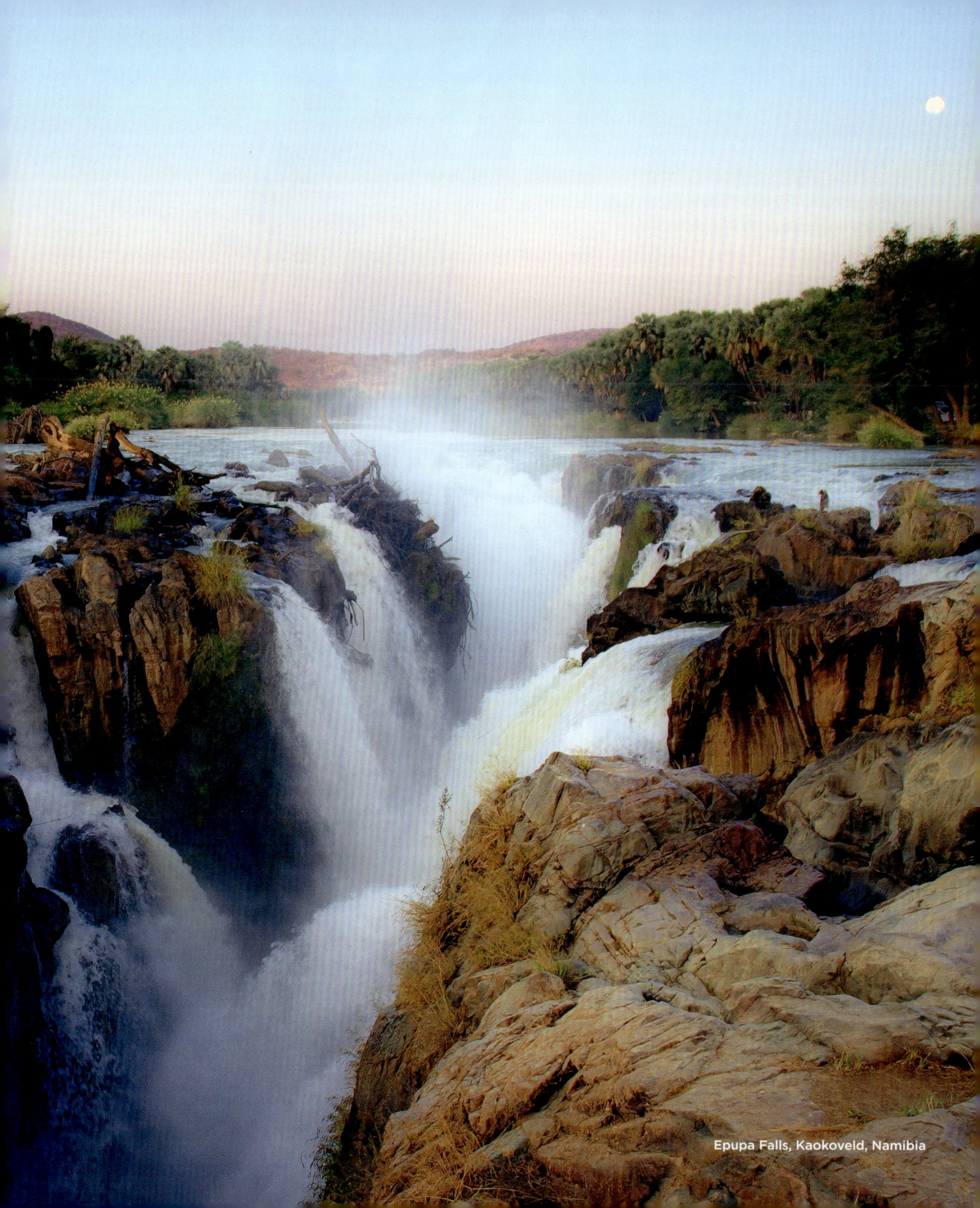

Epupa Falls, Kaokoveld, Namibia

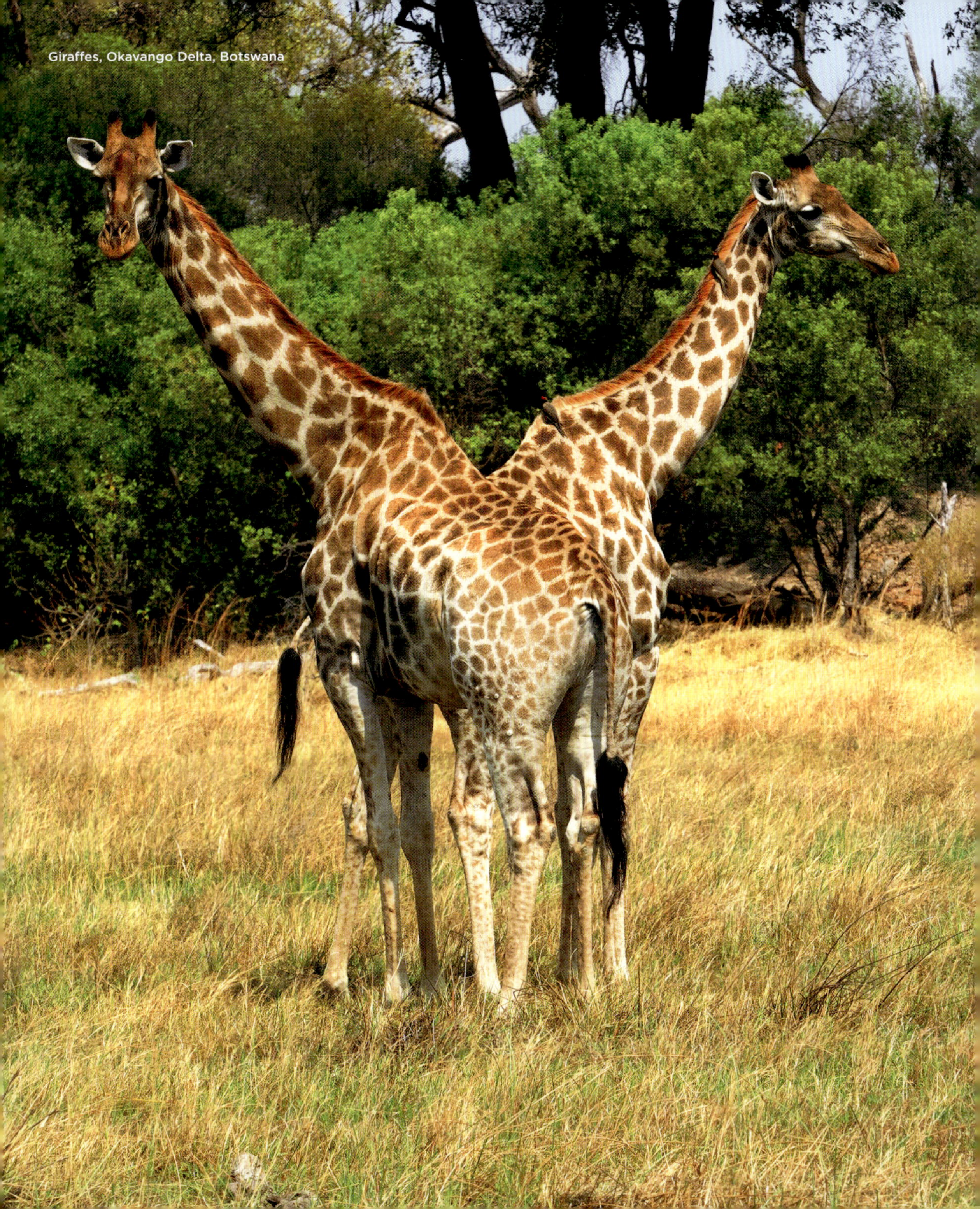
Giraffes, Okavango Delta, Botswana

Sudáfrica, Namibia y Botsuana

La fascinación absoluta de las fuerzas salvajes de la naturaleza - ¡todavía se puede experimentar en el sur de África! Aquí en Botswana, Namibia y Sudáfrica, las fuerzas de la naturaleza se unen de tantas formas distintas como en ningún otro lugar de la tierra. Dos océanos, que no podrían ser más diferentes, fluyen espectacularmente alrededor del extremo sur del continente: aquí el Atlántico, con su fuerza fría, se encuentra con el subtropical y cálido Océano Índico. La riqueza de los contrastes se puede ver en todas partes: ya sea en desiertos arenosos con formaciones rocosas angulosas, en cuencas de ríos casi subtropicales, en cañones profundos o en cadenas de colinas verdes y exuberantes. La fauna es también extremadamente diversa, con muchas especies raras que no se encuentran (ya) en ninguna otra parte del mundo. Preservar este hábitat paradisíaco se ha convertido en la tarea de numerosos parques nacionales, reservas naturales y reservas cinegéticas de la región. No sólo Nelson Mandela creía que "Sudáfrica es el lugar más hermoso del mundo" ...

Sudafrica, Namibia e Botswana

Il fascino assoluto delle forze selvagge della natura - nell'Africa meridionale si può ancora rivivere! Qui nel Botswana, nella Namibia e nel Sudafrica, le forze della natura si intrecciano nei modi più dissimili rispetto forse ad altri luoghi della terra. Due oceani, che non potrebbero essere più diversi, scorrono spettacolari intorno alla punta più meridionale del continente: qui il freddo Atlantico incontra il subtropicale, caldo Oceano Indiano. La ricchezza dei contrasti è visibile ovunque: nei deserti sabbiosi con formazioni spigolose, nei bacini fluviali quasi subtropicali, nei profondi canyon o nei lussureggianti rilievi collinari verdeggianti. Anche la fauna è estremamente varia, con molte specie rare che non si trovano (non si trovano più) in nessun'altra parte del mondo. La conservazione di questo habitat paradisiaco è diventata il compito di numerosi parchi nazionali, riserve naturali e oasi protette della regione. Nelson Mandela non era il solo a credere che "il Sudafrica è il posto più bello del mondo" ...

Zuid-Afrika, Namibië en Botswana

De absolute fascinatie van wild natuurgeweld – dat kan nog steeds worden ervaren in zuidelijk Afrika! Hier in Botswana, Namibië en Zuid-Afrika komen de krachten van de natuur op totaal andere manieren samen dan waar ook ter wereld. Twee oceanen, die niet sterker van elkaar hadden kunnen verschillen, stromen spectaculair rond het zuidelijkste puntje van het continent: hier ontmoet de Atlantische Oceaan met zijn koude kracht de subtropische, warme Indische Oceaan. De rijkdom aan contrasten is overal te zien: landschappelijk in zandwoestijnen met hoekige rotsformaties, bijna subtropische stroomgebieden, diepe ravijnen en weelderige, groene heuvelketens. De fauna is ook zeer divers, met veel zeldzame soorten die nergens anders ter wereld (meer) te vinden zijn. Het behoud van deze paradijselijke habitat is de taak van talrijke nationale parken, natuurgebieden en wildreservaten in de regio geworden. Niet alleen Nelson Mandela geloofde dat "Zuid-Afrika de mooiste plek ter wereld is" ...

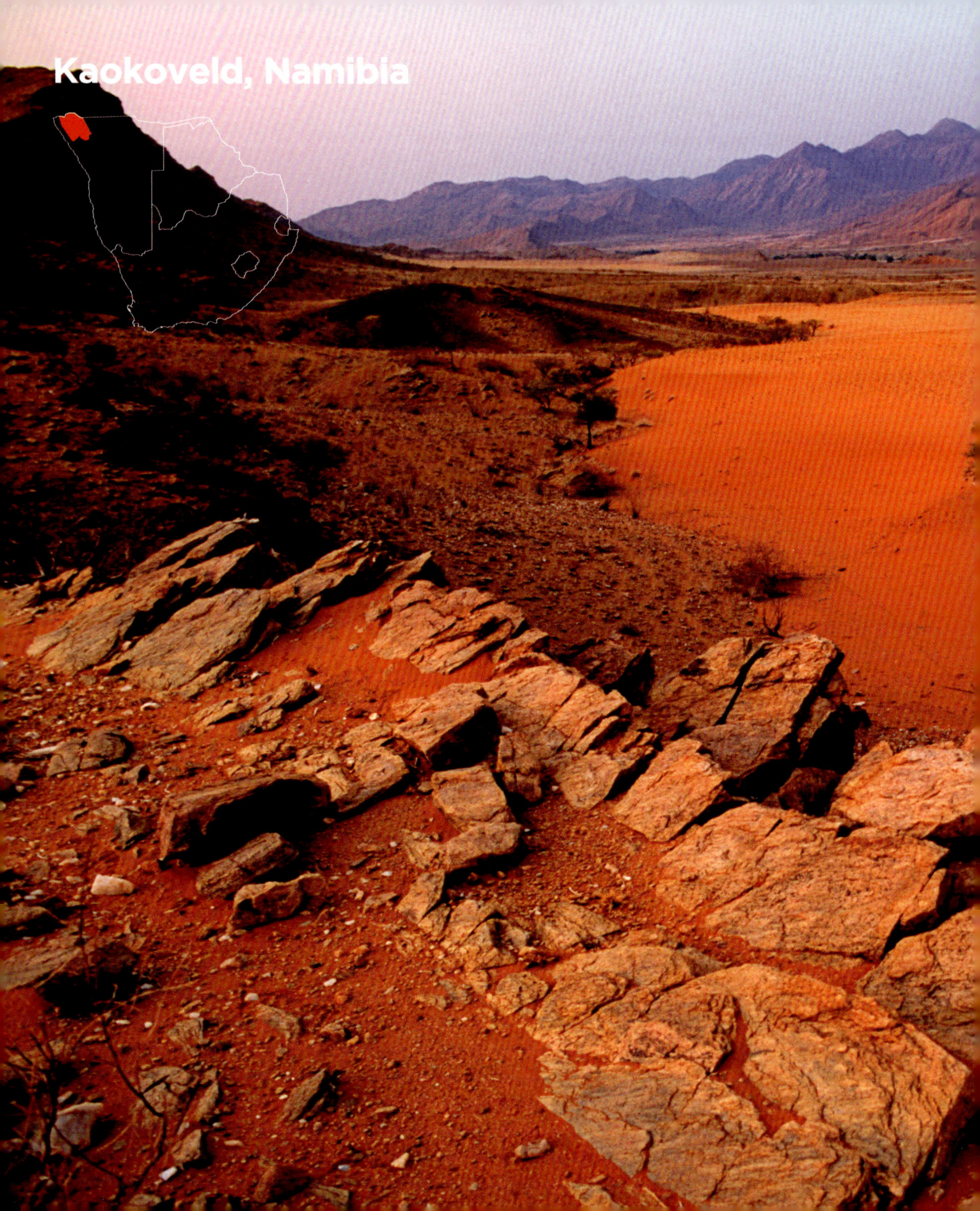
Kaokoveld, Namibia

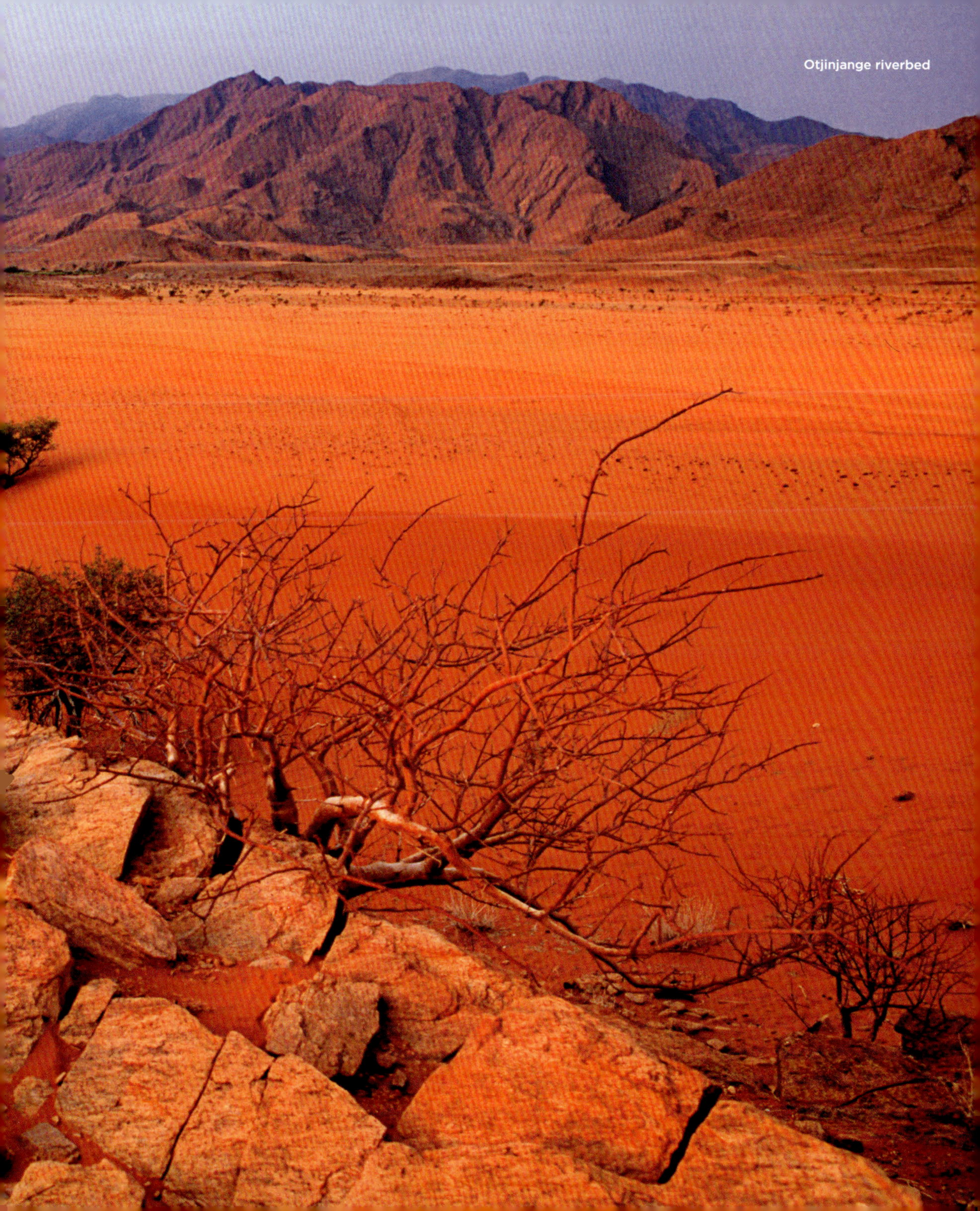
Otjinjange riverbed

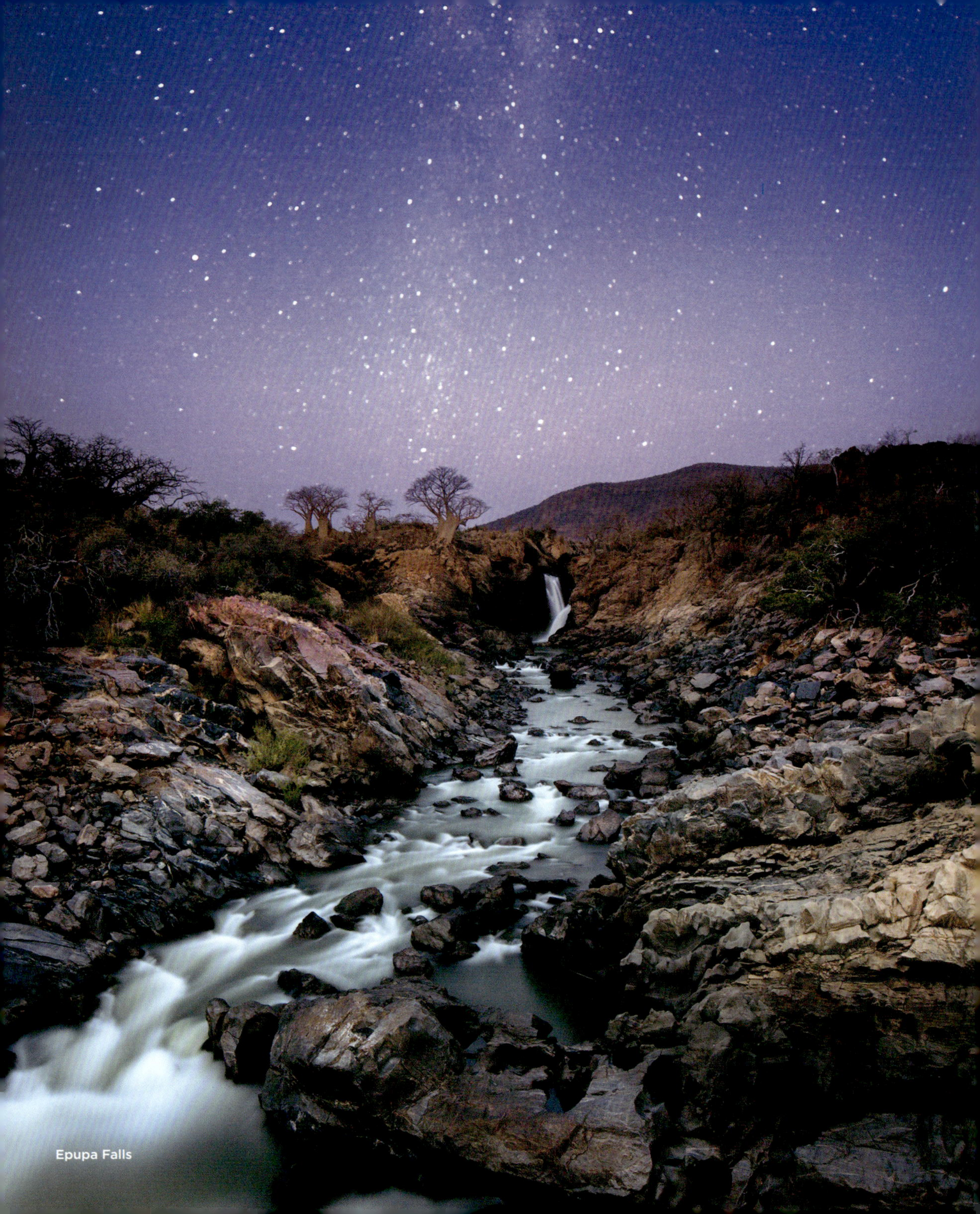
Epupa Falls

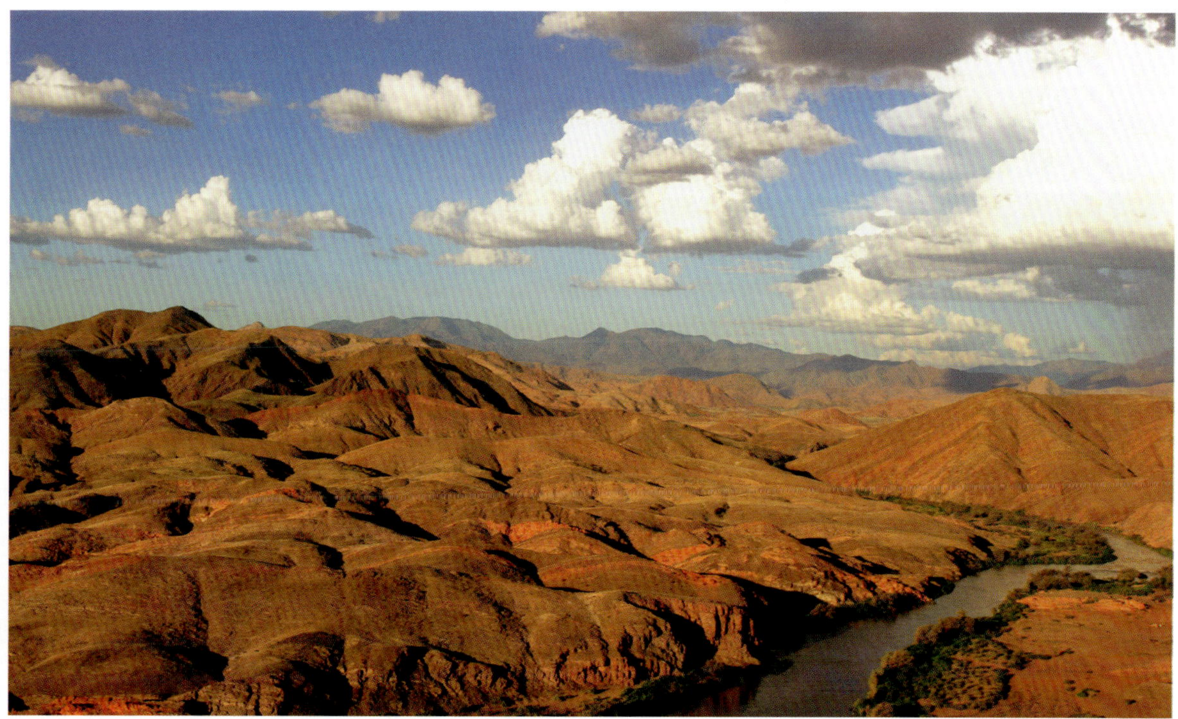

Kunene River

Kaokoveld
The Kaokoveld in northwestern Namibia is one of the few regions of Africa still largely untouched. The Herero and the Himba peoples live in this sparsely populated land. Rugged plateaus and dry valleys characterize the landscape, and the only river that flows all year round is the Kunene.

Le Kaokoveld
Le Kaokoveld, dans le nord-ouest de la Namibie, est l'une des dernières régions en grande partie inexplorées d'Afrique. Les Herero et les Himbas vivent sur ce territoire très peu peuplé. Des hauts plateaux désolés et des vallées sèches dominent le paysage dont l'unique fleuve pérenne est le Cunene.

Kaokoveld
Das Kaokoveld im Nordwesten Namibias gehört zu den wenigen noch weitgehend unberührten Regionen Afrikas. In dem dünn besiedelten Landstrich leben die Herero und die Himba. Karge Hochflächen und Trockentäler prägen das Landschaftsbild, der einzige Fluss, der ganzjährig Wasser führt, ist der Kunene.

Kaokoveld
El Kaokoveld en el noroeste de Namibia es una de las pocas zonas vírgenes que quedan de África. En esta zona escasamente poblada viven los Herero y los Himba. Yermos páramos y secos valles dominan el paisaje; el Kunene, con agua durante todo el año, es el único río.

Kaokoveld
Il Kaokoveld, situato nella Namibia nord-occidentale, appartiene ad una delle poche regioni ancora ampiamente incontaminate dell'Africa. Nell'area scarsamente popolata vivono le etnie Herero e Himba. Altipiani aridi e vallate asciutte caratterizzano il paesaggio, l'unico fiume che porta acqua tutto l'anno è il Kunene.

Kaokoveldwoestijn
De Kaokoveldwoestijn in het noordwesten van Namibië behoort tot de weinige regio's in Afrika die nog grotendeels ongerept zijn. In het dunbevolkte gebied leven de volken van de Herero en Himba. Kale hoogvlakten en uitgedroogde dalen bepalen hier het landschap; de enige rivier waarin het hele jaar door water staat, is de Kunene.

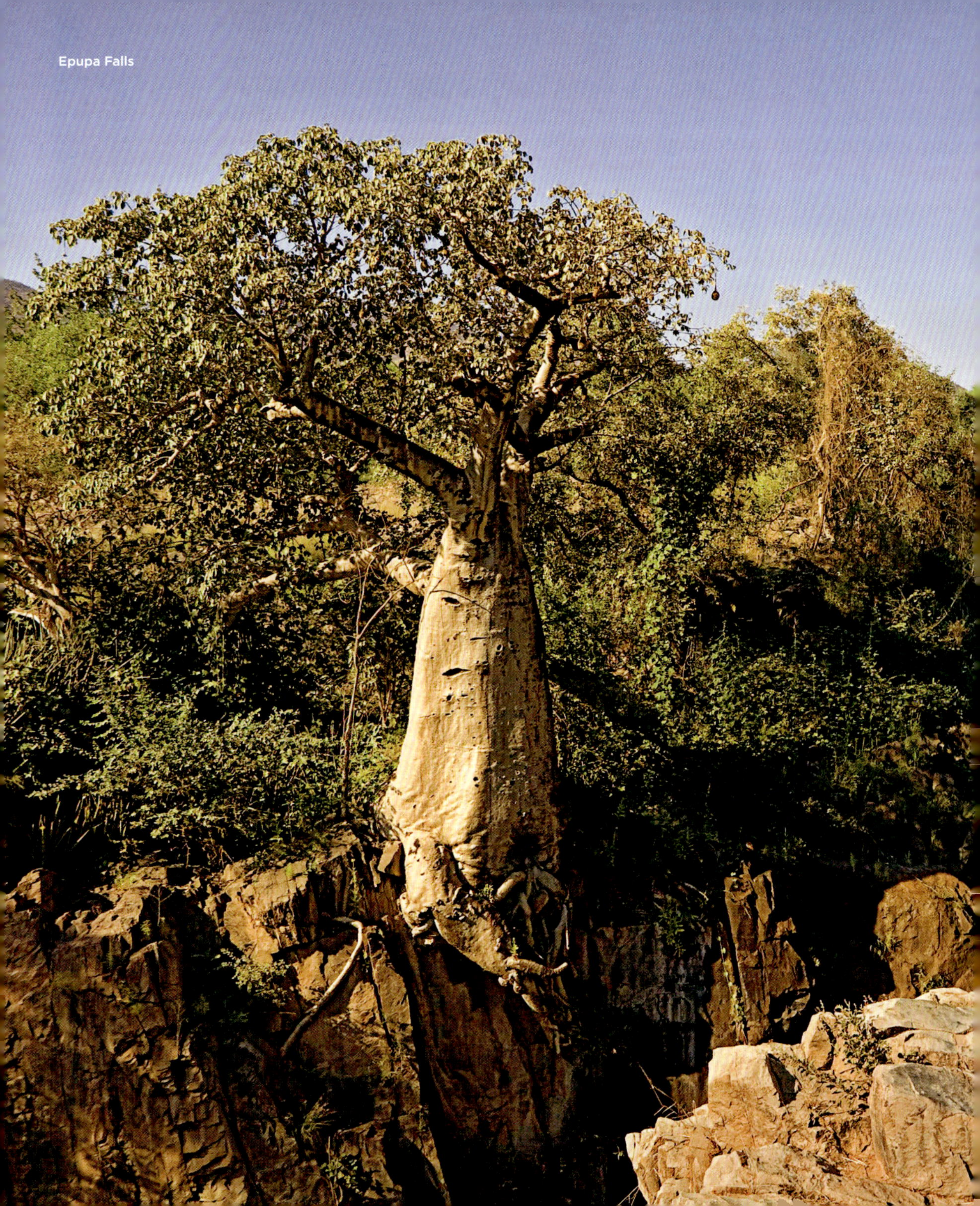
Epupa Falls

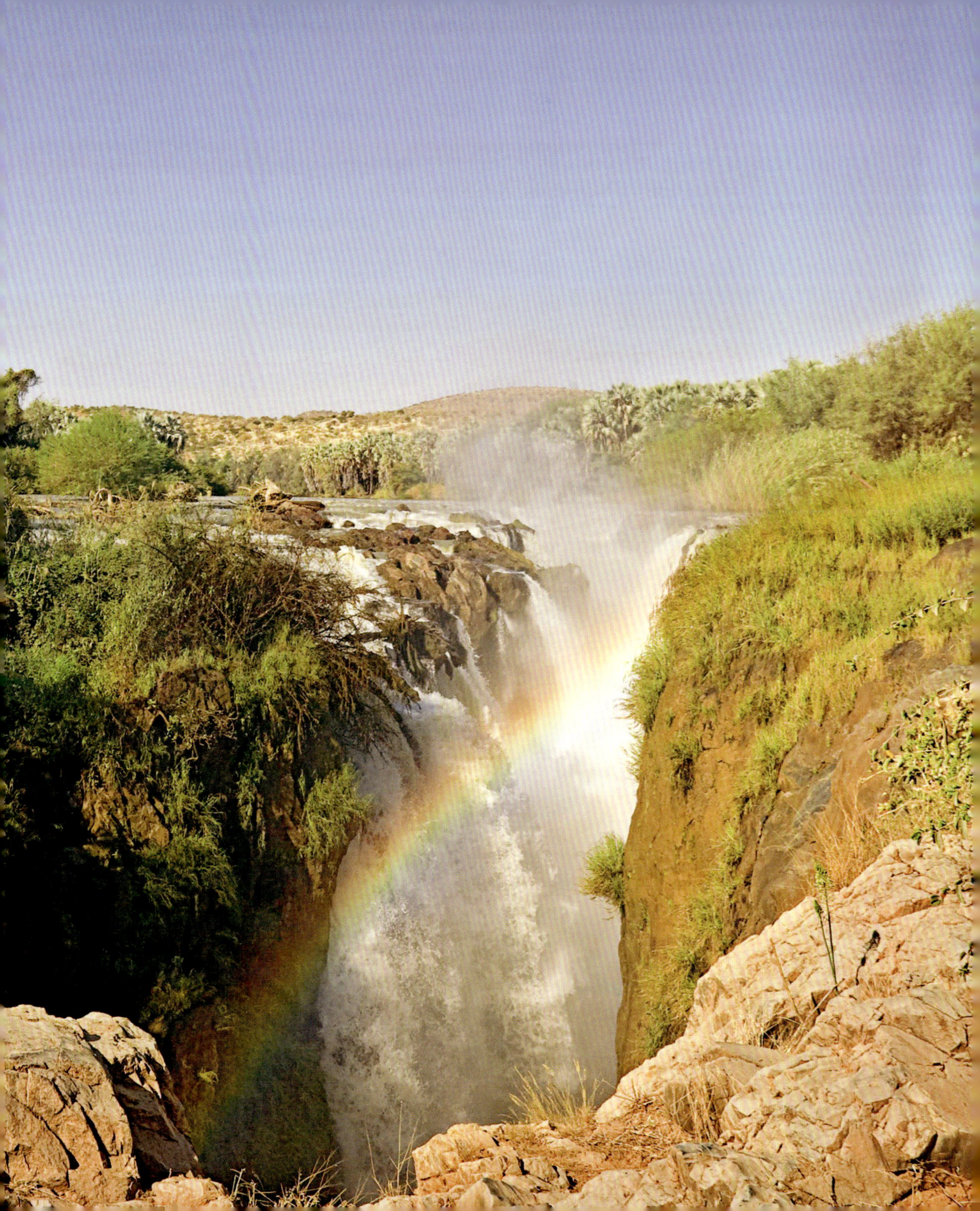

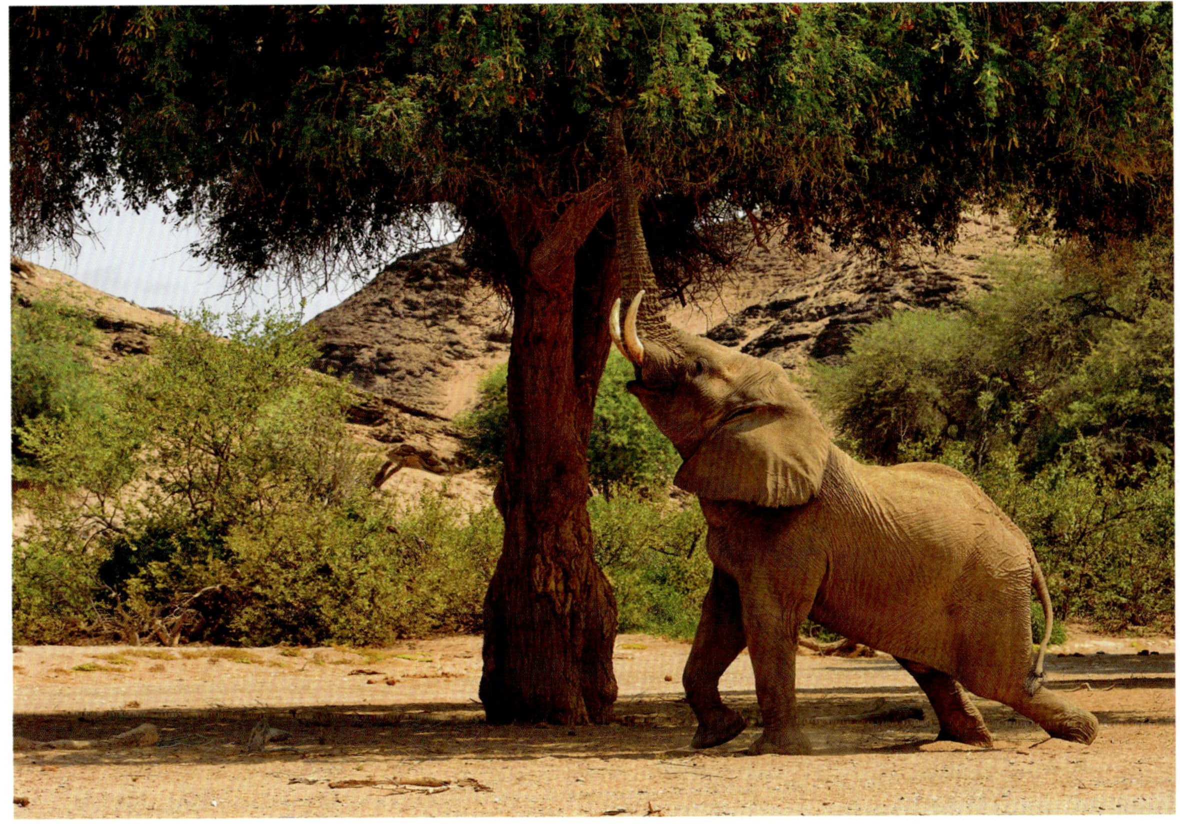

Namibian desert elephant, Hoanib

Desert elephants
The desert elephants living along the banks of the Kunene have adapted perfectly to their arid environment. Their legs are longer, they are lighter in weight and they have larger feet than other elephants. Desert elephants are also able to go for four days without drinking water, but will roam up to 70 km (43 mi) a day in search of food.

Les éléphants du désert
Les éléphants du désert qui vivent dans la région du Cunene sont parfaitement adaptés à ce milieu aride. Plus hauts sur pattes, ils sont aussi plus légers et ont de plus grands pieds que leurs congénères. Ils tiennent quatre jours sans boire. La quête de nourriture leur fait parcourir jusqu'à 70 km par jour.

Wüstenelefanten
Die in der Region Kunene lebenden Wüstenelefanten haben sich perfekt an ihre aride Umwelt angepasst. Ihre Beine sind länger, sie sind leichter und haben größere Füße als ihre Artgenossen. Sie können vier Tage ohne Wasser auskommen. Auf der Suche nach Nahrung legen sie täglich bis zu 70 km zurück.

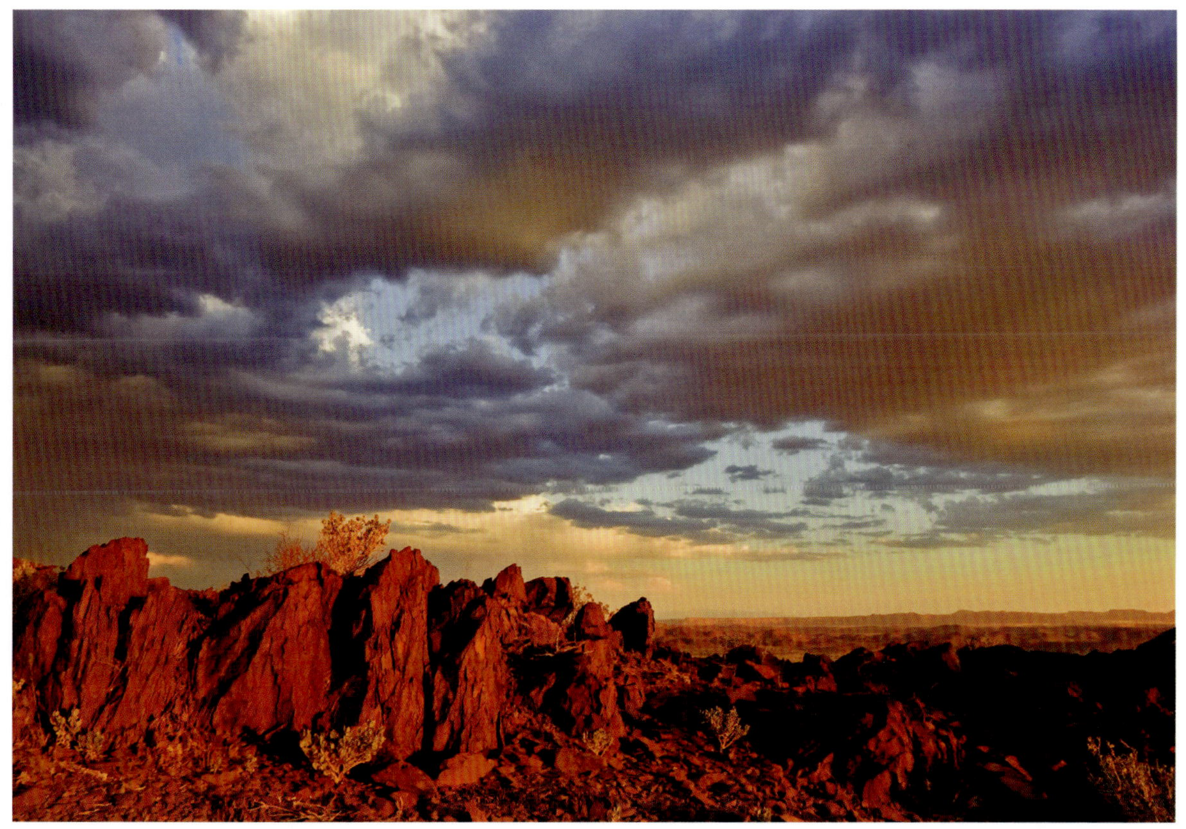

Southern Kaokoveld and Damaraland

Los elefantes del desierto
Los elefantes del desierto de la región de Kunene están perfectamente adaptados a su árido entorno. Sus piernas son más largas, son más ligeros y tienen los pies más grandes que sus congéneres. Puede llegar a subsistir durante cuatro días sin agua. En busca de comida recorren todos los días hasta 70 km.

Gli elefanti della savana
Gli elefanti della savana che vivono nella regione di Kunene si sono adattati perfettamente al suo ambiente arido. Le loro zampe sono più lunghe, sono più leggeri e hanno piedi più grandi dei loro simili. Possono sopravvivere per quattro giorni senza bere acqua. Alla ricerca di cibo possono percorrere fino a 70 km al giorno.

Namibische woestijnolifanten
De Namibische woestijnolifanten van de regio Kunene hebben zich perfect aan hun kurkdroge omgeving aangepast. Hun poten zijn langer, ze wegen minder en ze hebben bredere pootbedden dan hun soortgenoten. Ze kunnen vier dagen zonder water, en op zoek naar voedsel leggen ze soms wel zeventig kilometer af.

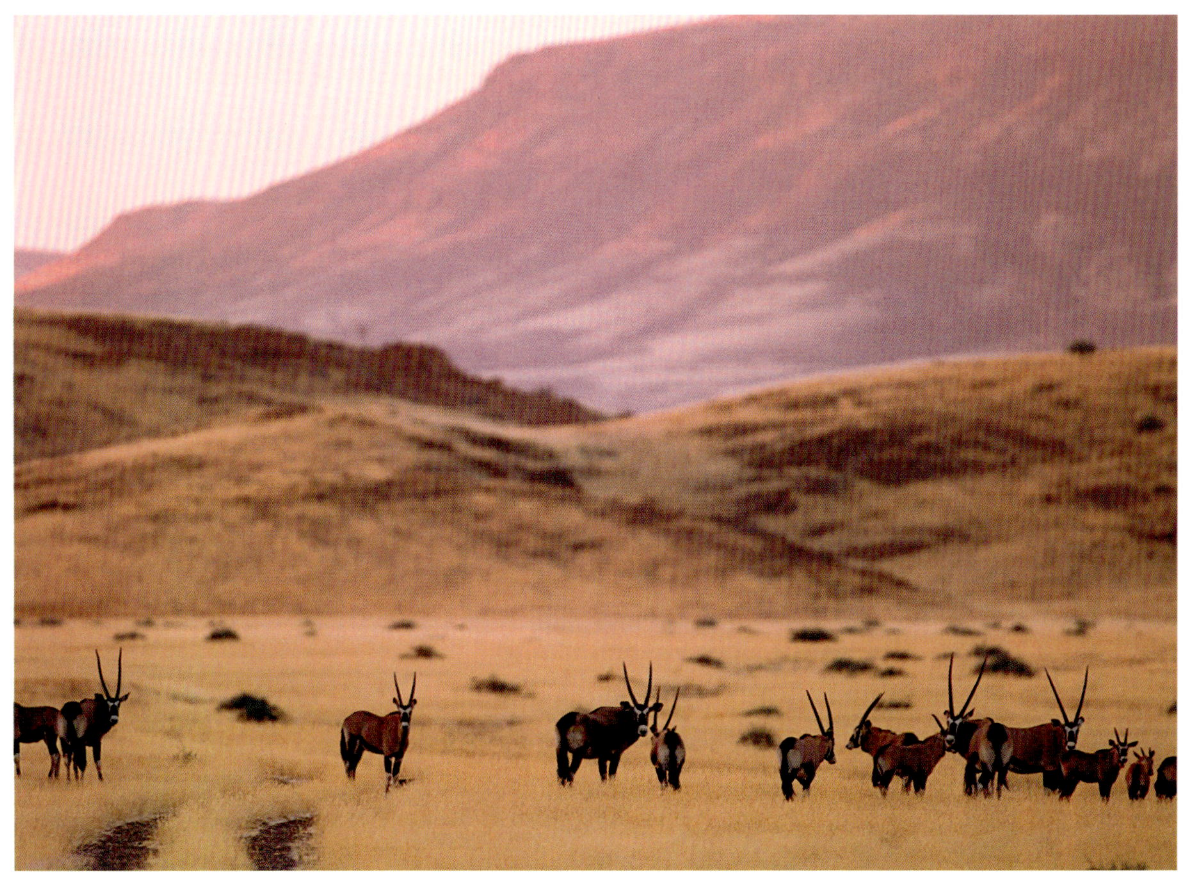

Gemsbok herd, Kaokoveld

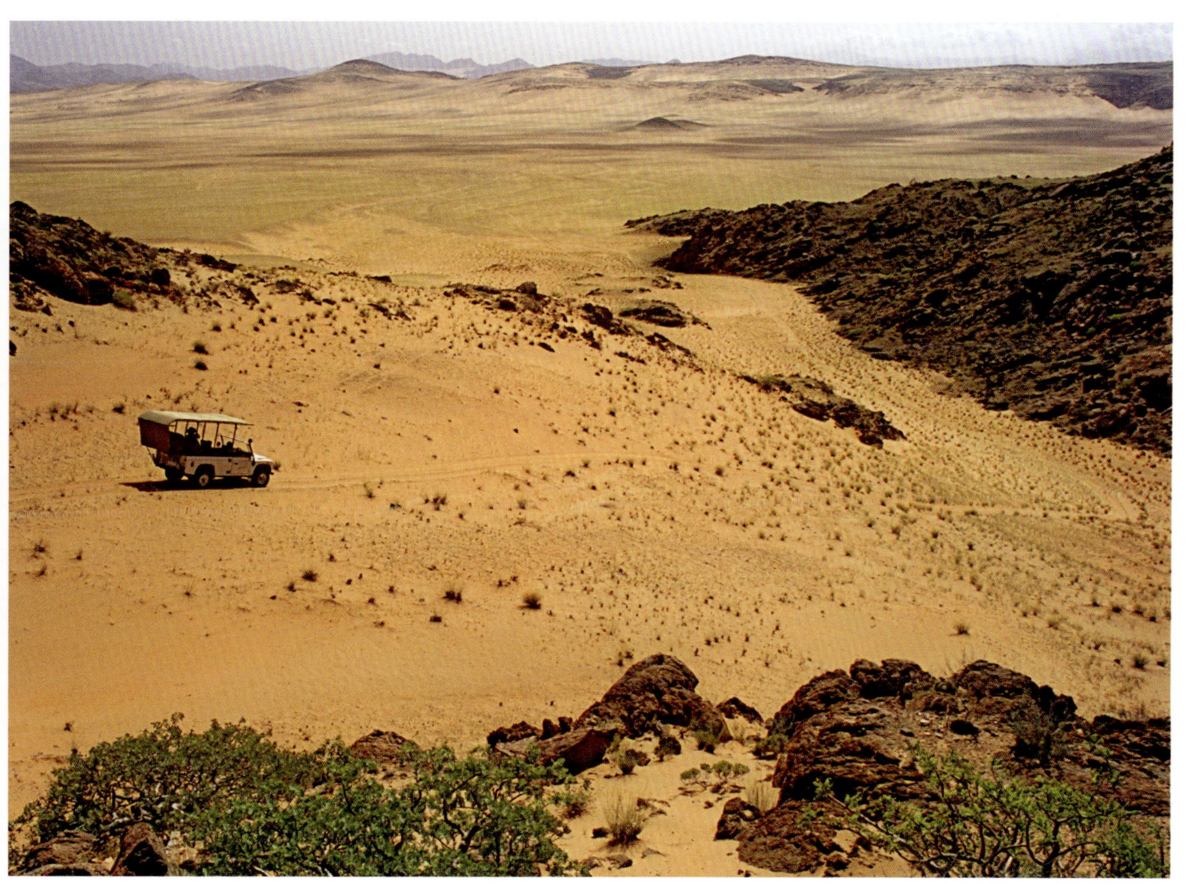

Kaokoveld

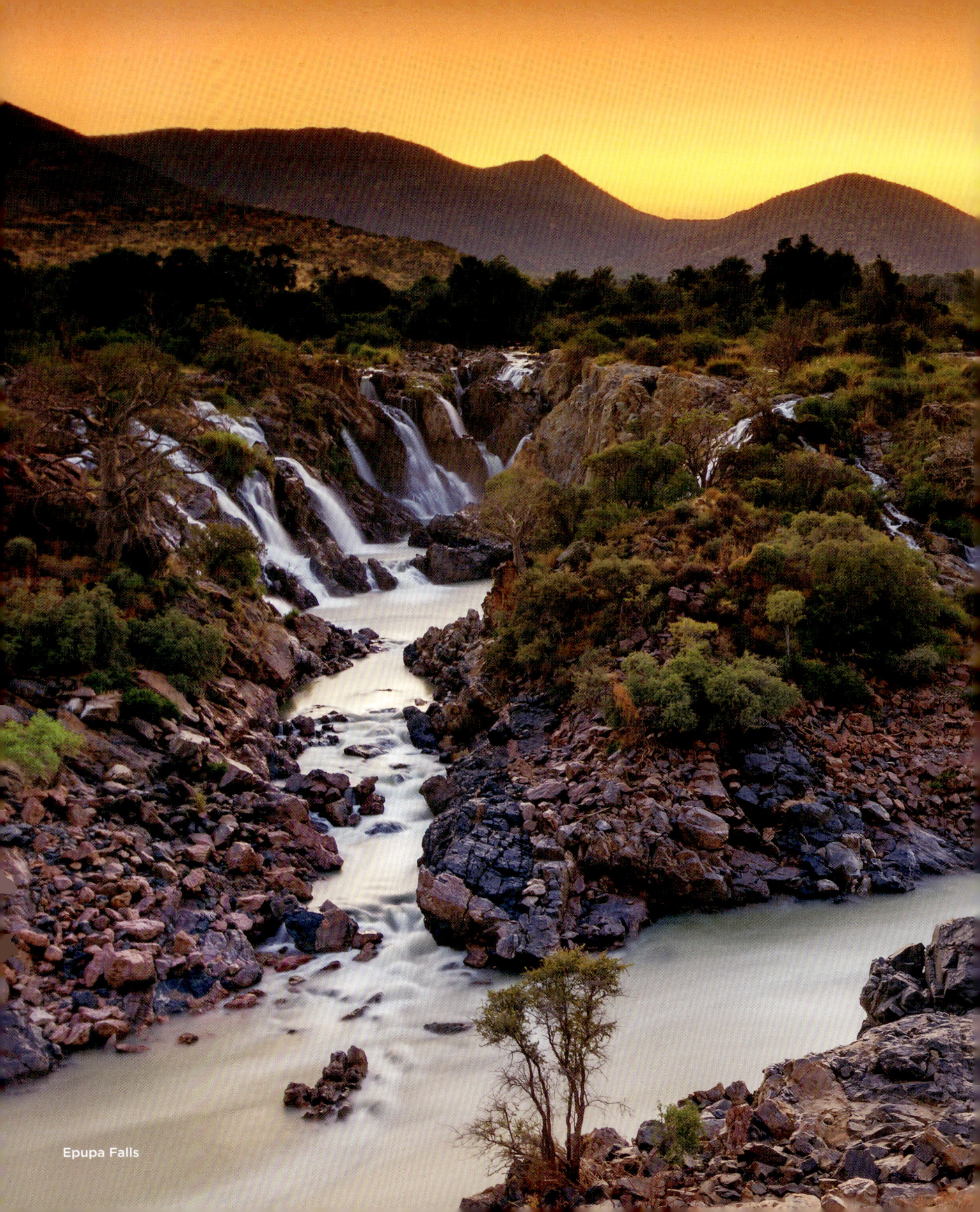

Epupa Falls

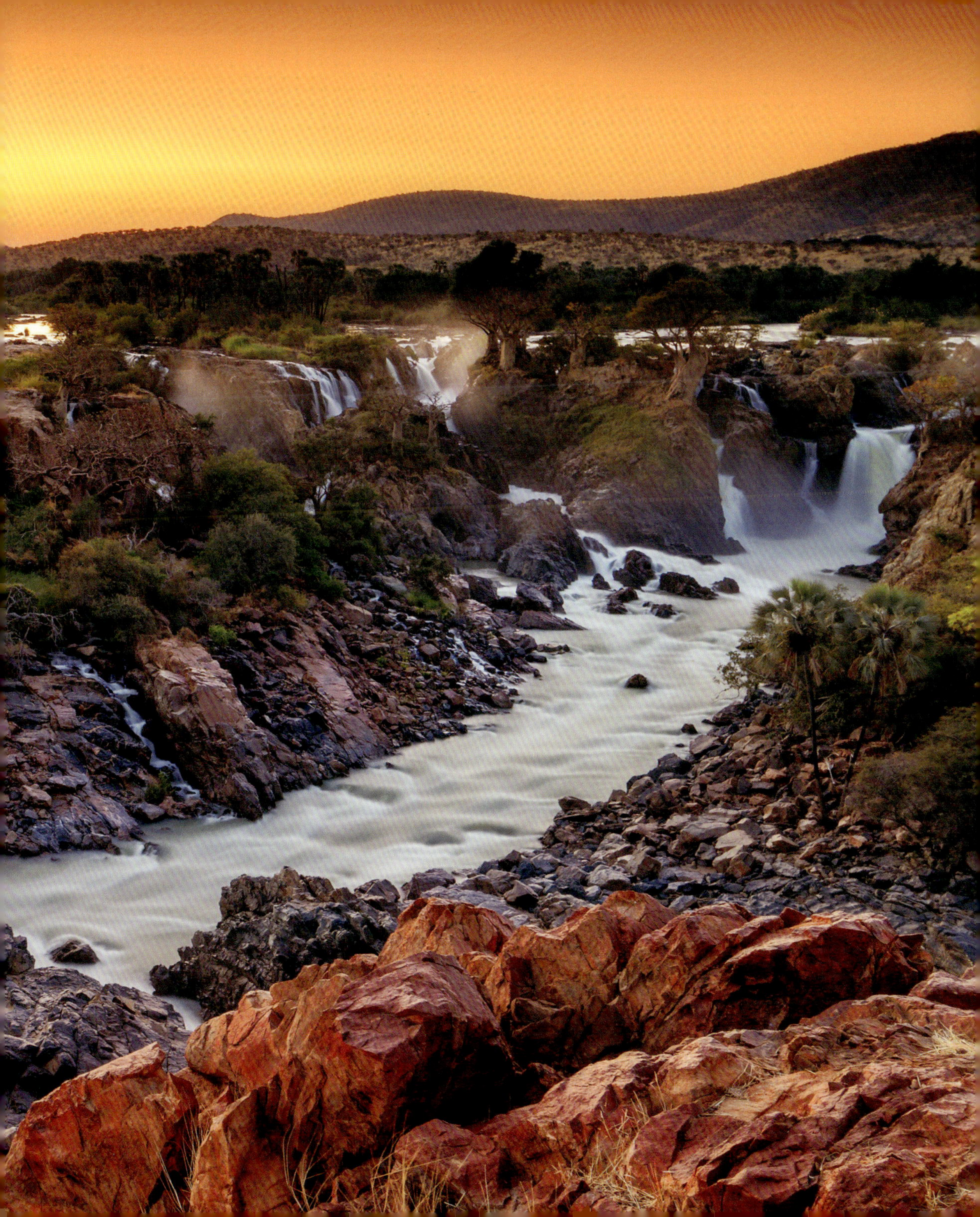

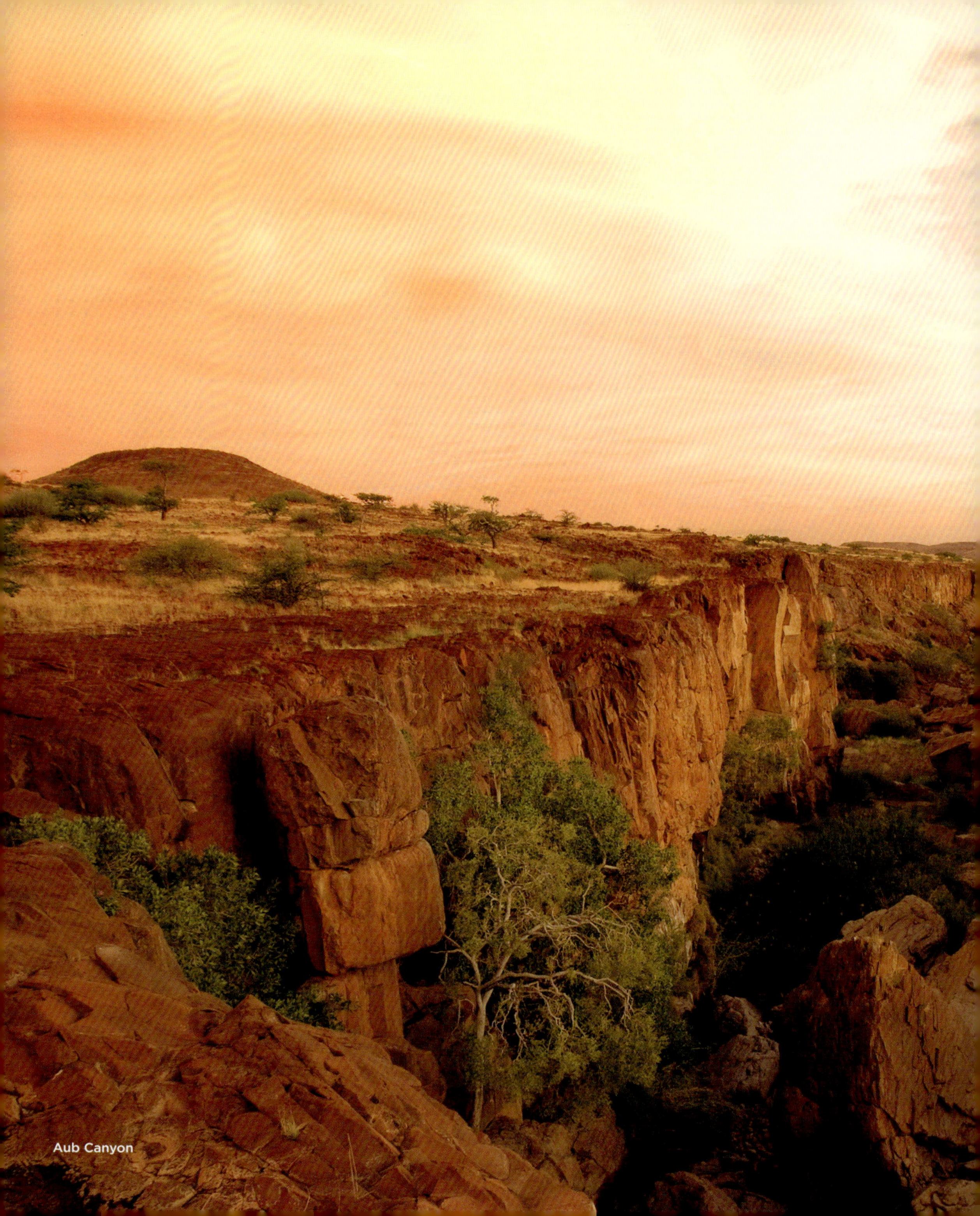
Aub Canyon

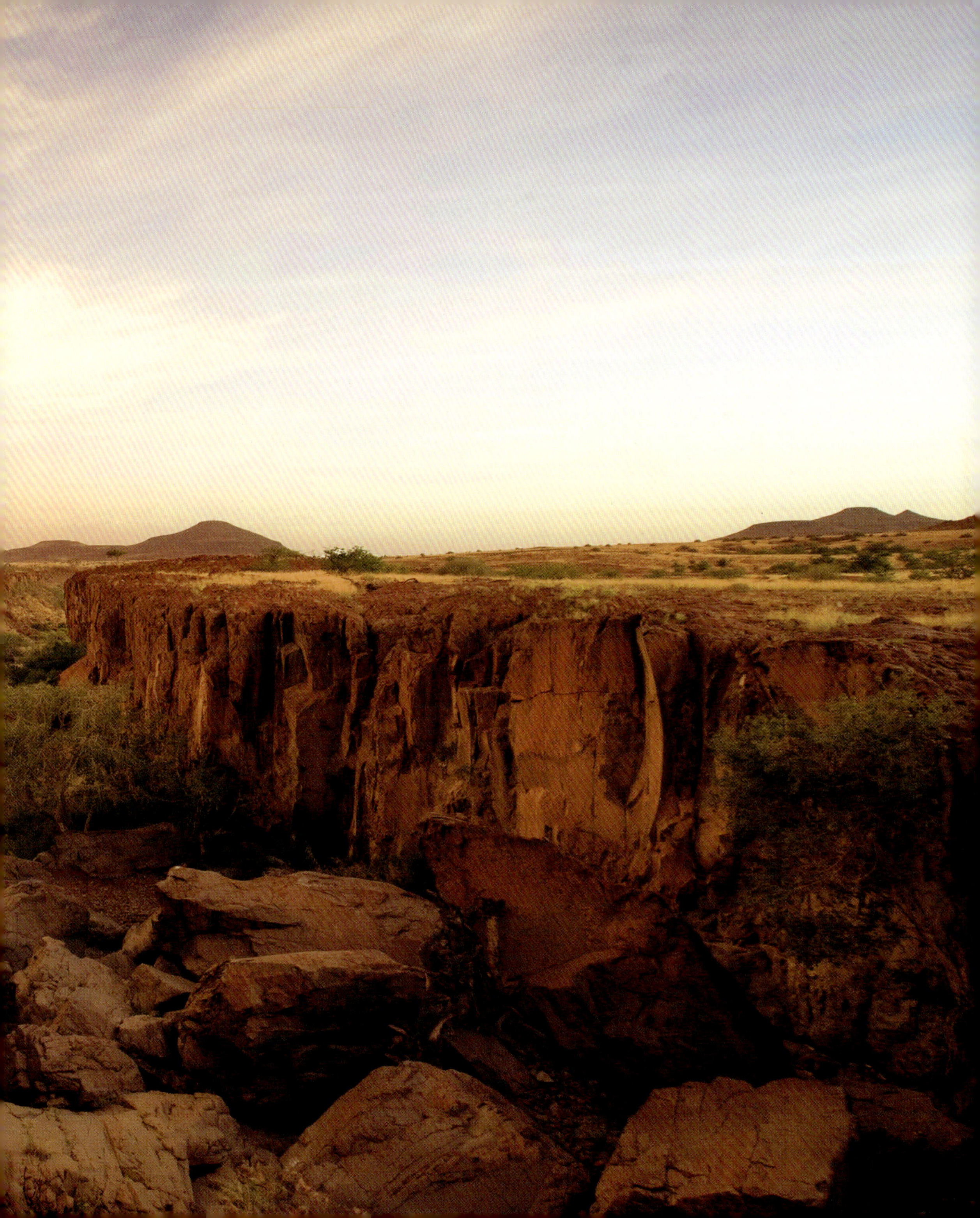

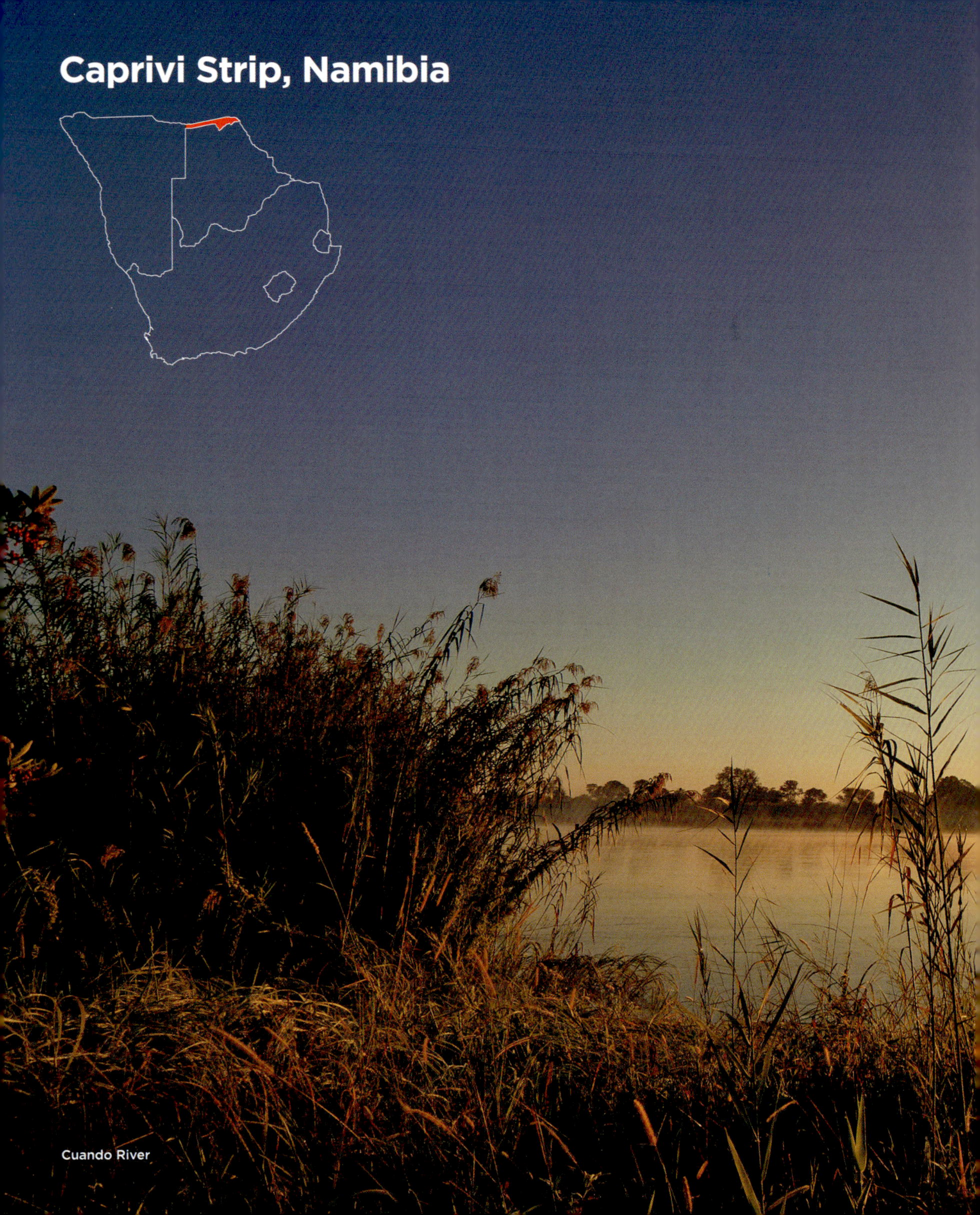

Cuando River

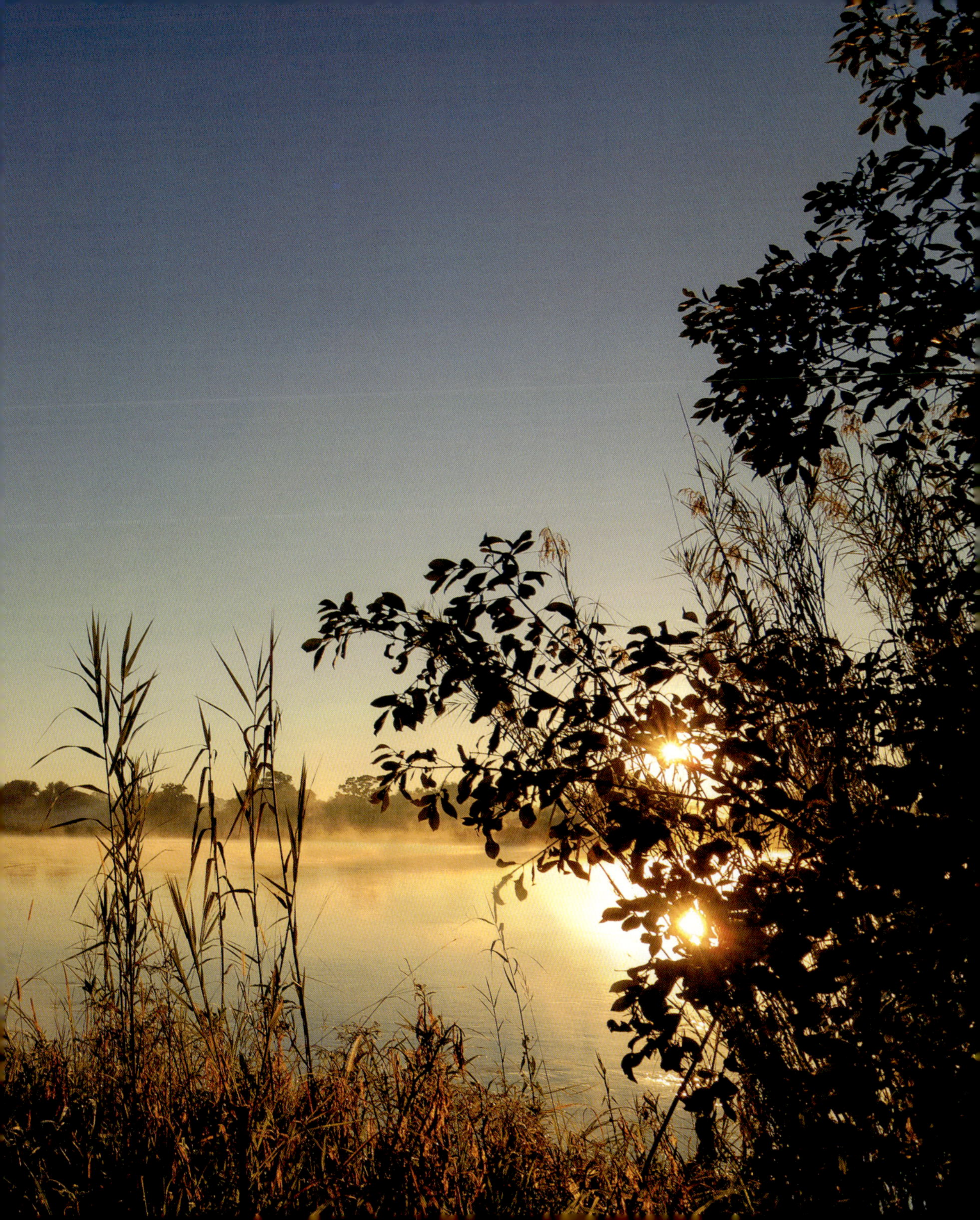

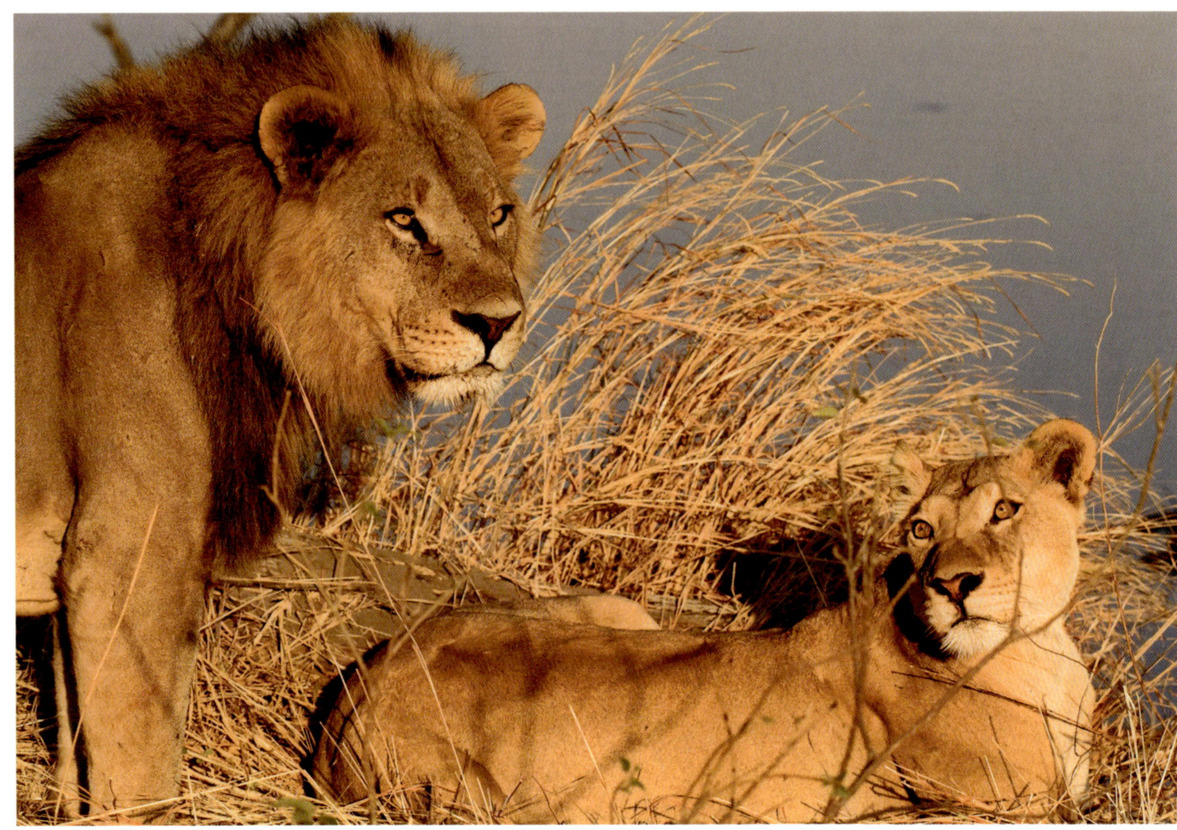

Male and female lion, Caprivi Strip

Caprivi Strip
Namibia's eastern border was drawn by the colonial powers using a ruler. However, in the north a 400 km long strip of Namibian territory juts eastwards: the Caprivi Strip. Here is Namibia at its most tropical, thanks to the presence of what is largely lacking throughout the rest of the country: water in abundance. Rivers and marshlands have created dense green forests, which are home to the many varied species thriving in this abundance.

La bande de Caprivi
La frontière orientale de la Namibie a été tracée à la règle, à part une longue bande de 400 km au nord, qui s'étire vers l'est : la bande de Caprivi. Il y règne un climat tropical. L'eau coule à profusion, contrairement au reste du pays. Rivières et marécages favorisent une végétation dense, des bois, et donc des animaux de toutes sortes venus en profiter.

Caprivi-Zipfel
Namibias Ostgrenze wurde mit dem Lineal gezogen. Nur im Norden ragt ein 400 km langer Streifen nach Osten: der Caprivi-Zipfel. Dort zeigt Namibia seine tropische Seite. Was im übrigen Land fehlt, gibt es hier im Überfluss: Wasser. Flüsse, Sümpfe und damit dichtes Grün, Wälder – und Tiere aller Art, die diesen Überfluss genießen.

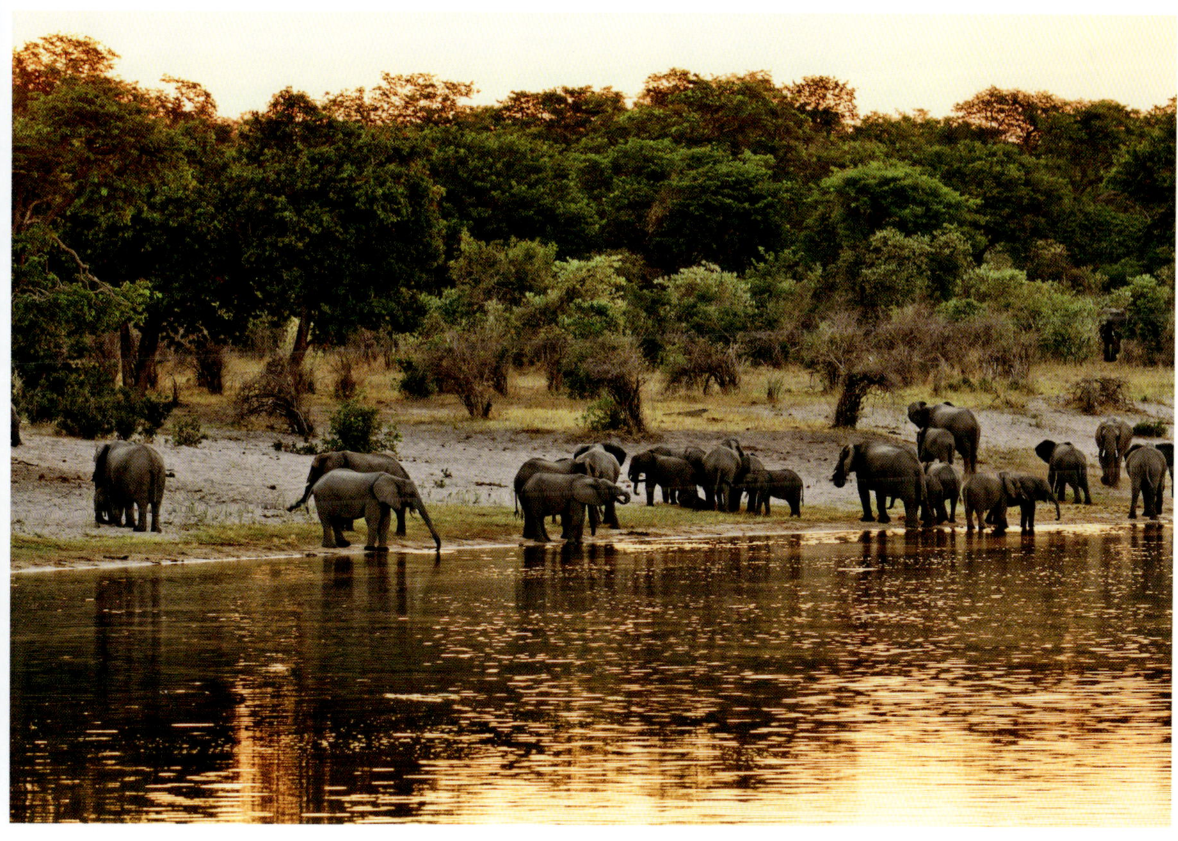

Elephants, Bwabwata National Park

Franja de Caprivi
La frontera oriental de Namibia se dibujó con regla. Justo al norte, se extiende una larga franja de 400 km hacia el este: la franja de Caprivi. Ahí Namibia muestra su lado tropical. Lo que falta en el resto del país, existe aquí en abundancia: agua. Ríos, pantanos y densos bosques verdes – y animales de todo tipo que disfrutan de esta abundancia.

Dito di Caprivi
Il confine orientale della Namibia è stato tracciato con un righello. Solo nella zona nord si estende una striscia lunga 400 km verso est: il Dito di Caprivi. Lì la Namibia mostra il suo lato tropicale. Quello che manca nel resto del paese qui si trova in abbondanza: l'acqua. Fiumi, paludi e quindi fitta vegetazione, boschi e animali di tutte le specie si godono quest'abbondanza.

Caprivistrook
De oostgrens van Namibië werd met een liniaal getrokken. Aan de noordgrens strekt zich een 400 km lange strook oostwaarts uit: de Caprivistrook. Daar toont Namibië zijn tropische kant. Wat in de rest van het land ontbreekt, is hier in overvloed te vinden: water. Rivieren, moerassen en daarmee weelderig groen en bos – en de talloze diersoorten die van deze weelde genieten.

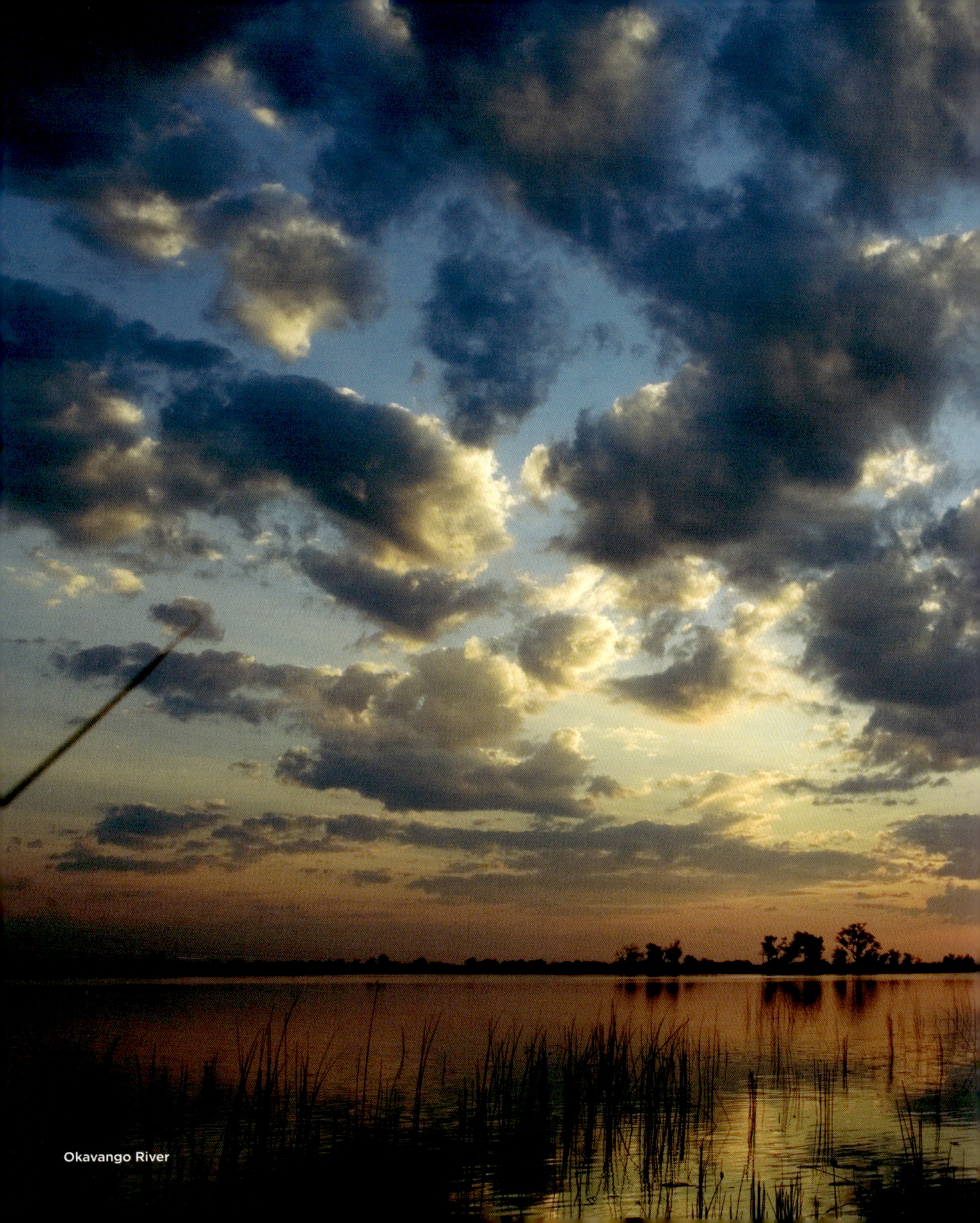

Okavango River

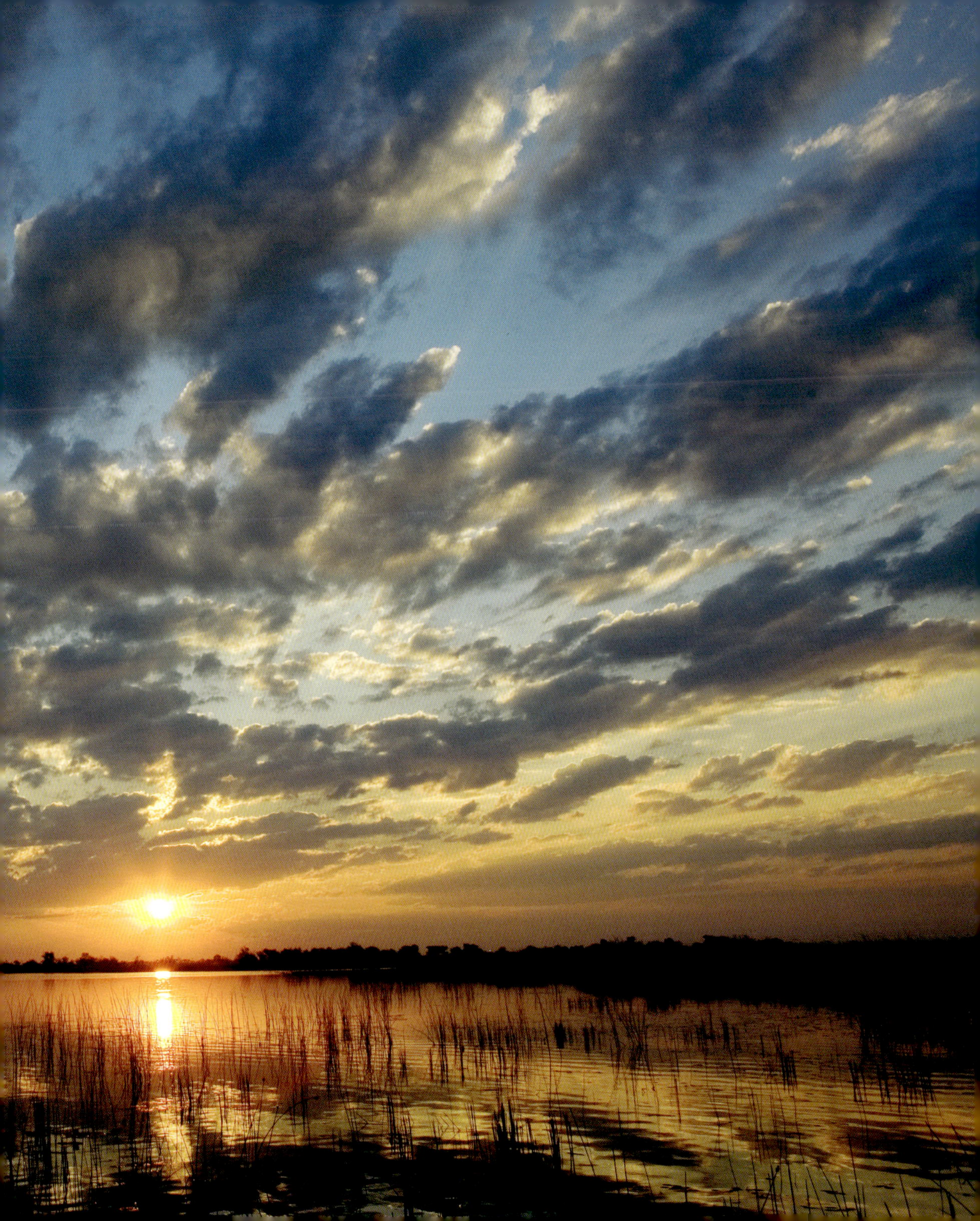

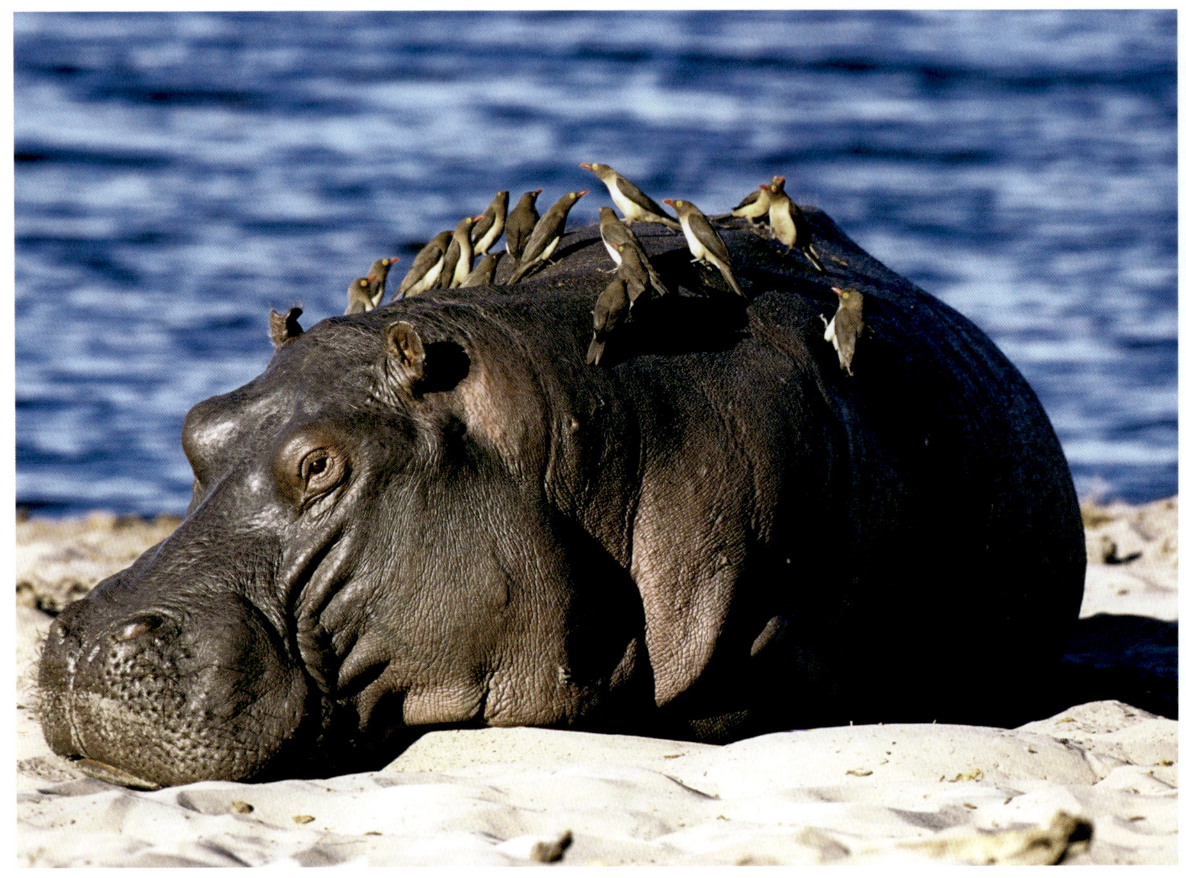

Hippopotamus with red-billed oxpeckers, Bwabwata National Park

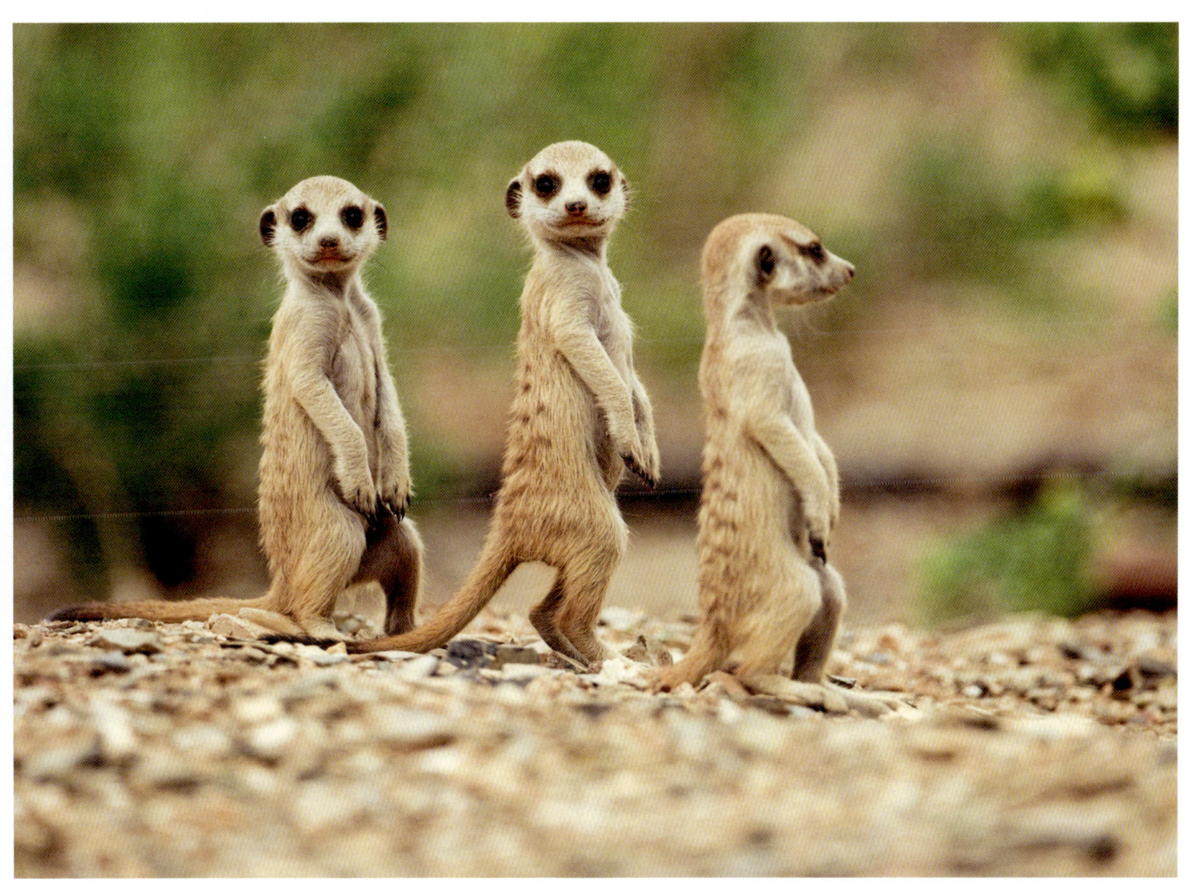

Young Meerkats, Caprivi Strip

Etosha National Park, Namibia

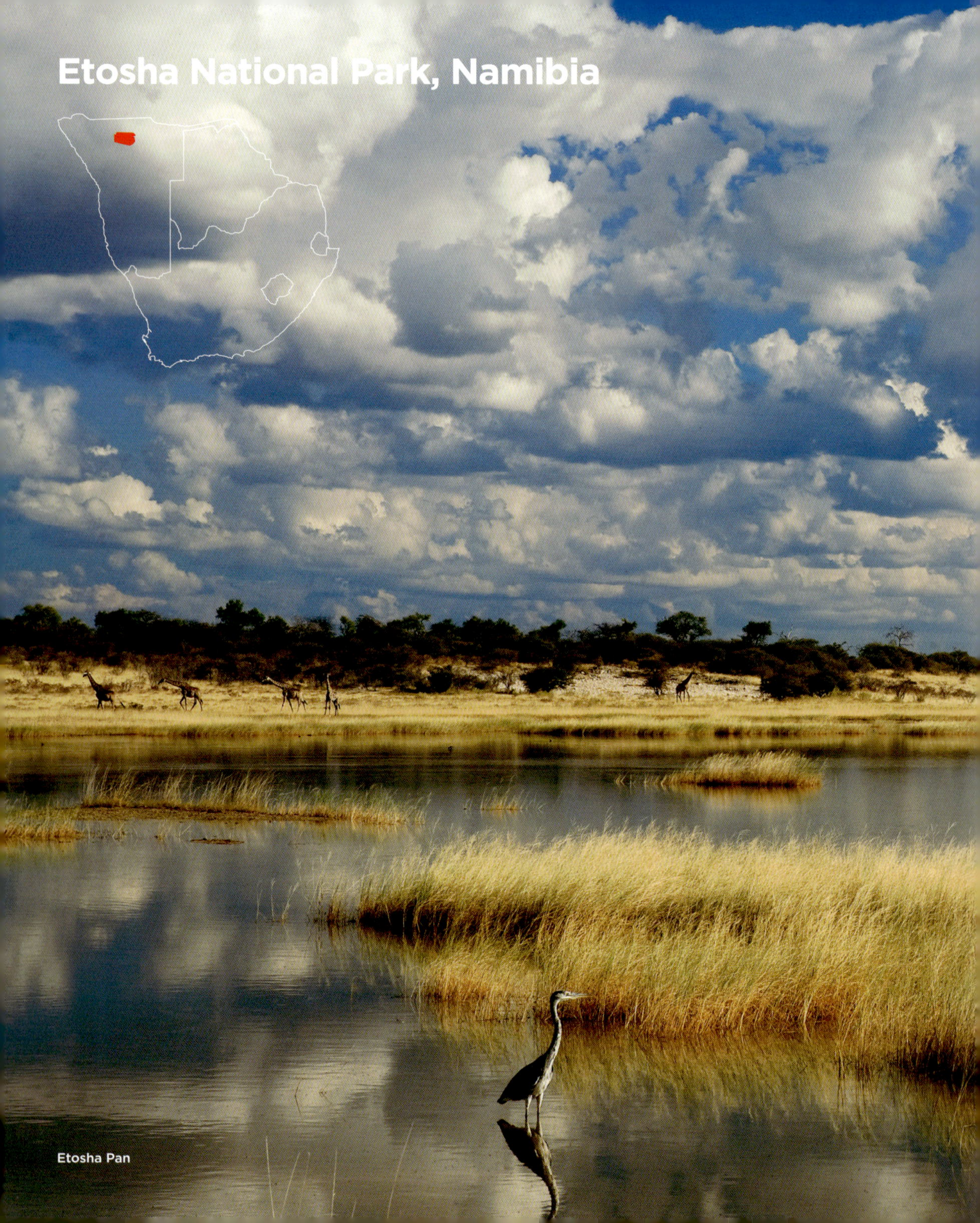

Etosha Pan

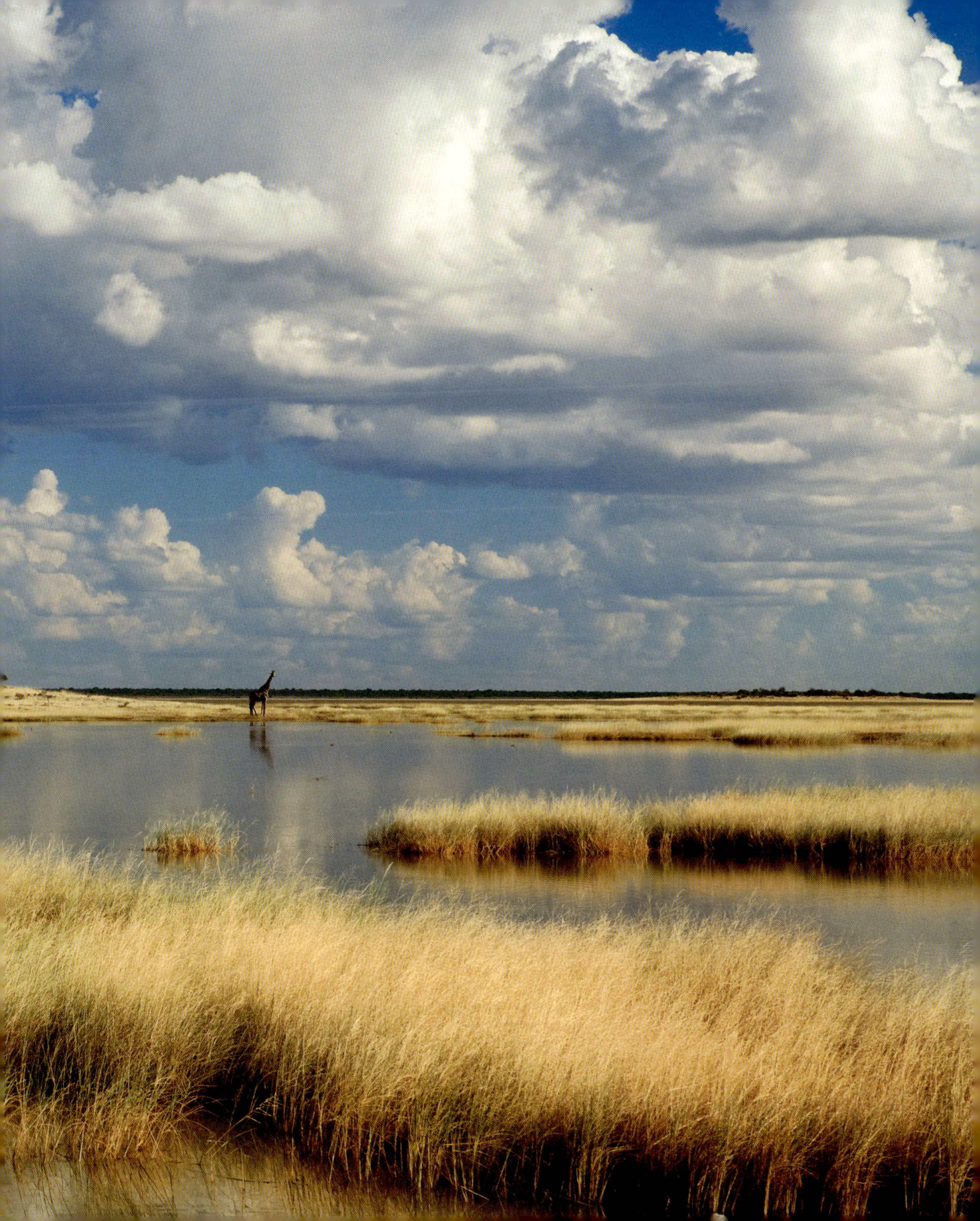

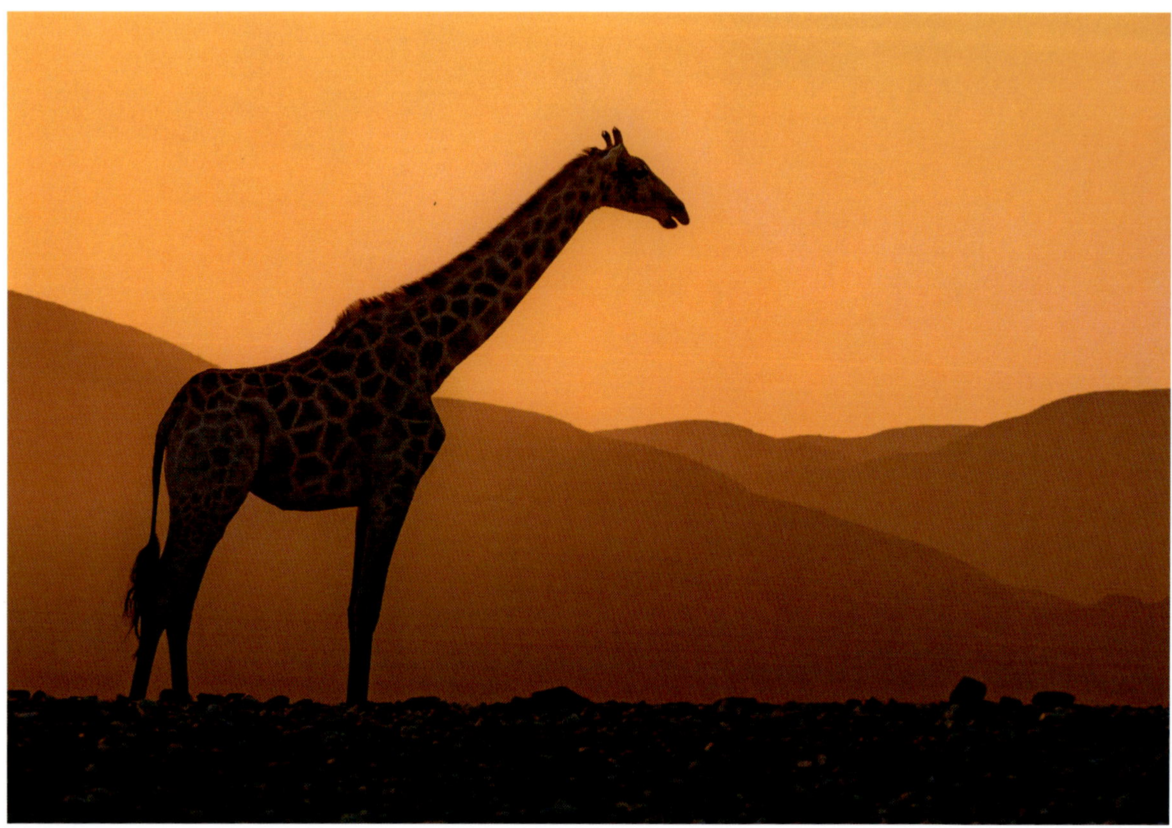

Giraffe, Etosha National Park

Etosha National Park
Etosha National Park has the most animals of any park in Namibia. Differing vegetation zones, including savannas, dry forests and grassy fields, provide habitats for mammals, birds, and reptiles. Since there are no running streams here, the animals depend on natural and artificial waterholes. Part of the park is the Etosha Pan, an endorheic salt basin.

Le parc national d'Etosha
Le parc national d'Etosha est celui qui compte le plus d'animaux en Namibie. Les zones de végétation variées – savanes, forêt sèche, herbages – sont autant d'habitats pour les mammifères, les oiseaux et les reptiles. En l'absence de cours d'eau, les animaux dépendent des points d'eau naturels et artificiels. La dépression d'Etosha, dans une partie du parc, est une cuvette argileuse et salée.

Etosha-Nationalpark
Der Etosha-Nationalpark ist der tierreichste Park Namibias. Unterschiedliche Vegetationszonen – Savannen, Trockenwald, Grasfelder – bieten Lebensräume für Säugetiere, Vögel und Reptilien. Da es keine fließenden Gewässer gibt, sind die Tiere auf natürliche und künstliche Wasserstellen angewiesen.
Teil des Parks ist die Etosha-Pfanne, eine Lehmpfanne mit Salzgehalt.

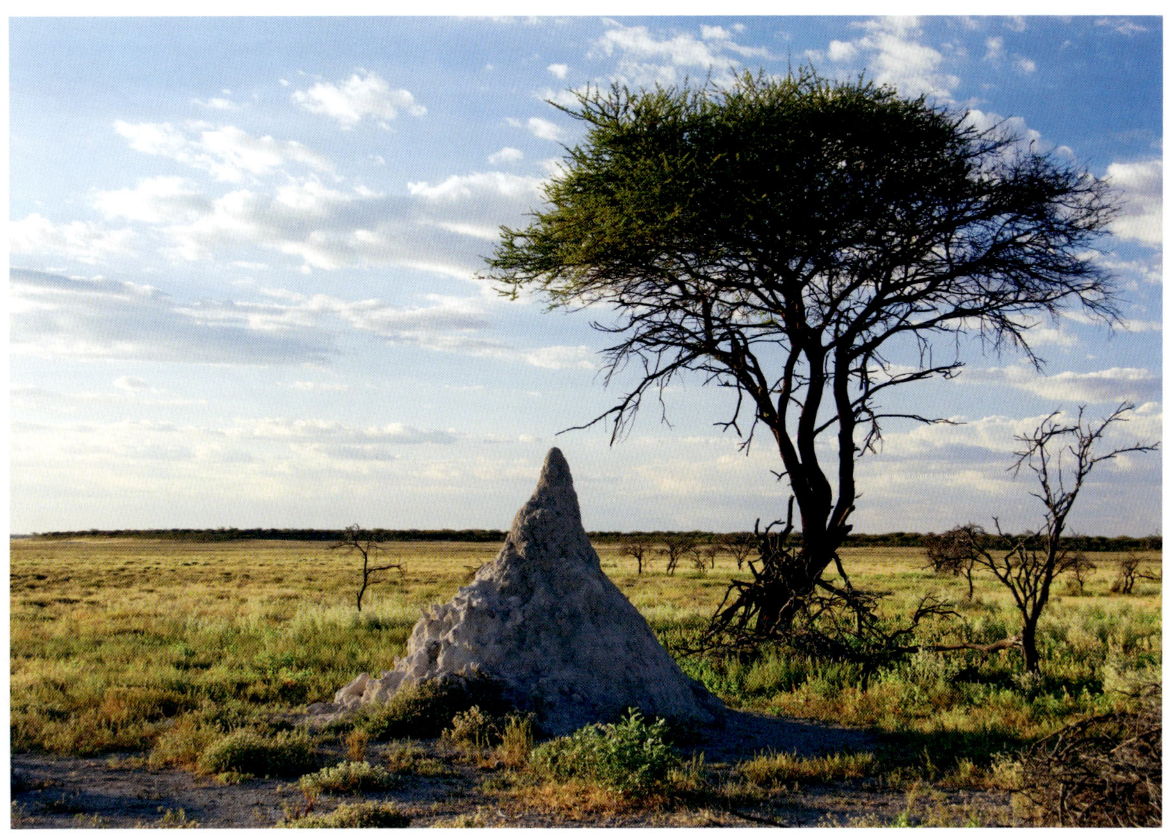

Termite mound, Etosha National Park

Parque Nacional de Etosha
El Parque Nacional de Etosha es el mayor parque de animales en Namibia. Posee diferentes zonas de vegetación –sabanas, bosques secos, campos de hierba– que ofrecen el hábitat adecuado a mamíferos, aves y reptiles. Al no haber corrientes de agua, los animales dependen de las fuentes de agua naturales y artificiales. Parte del parque es la olla salina Etosha, una olla de arcilla con contenido de sal.

Parco Nazionale di Etosha
Il Parco Nazionale di Etosha è il parco più ricco di animali della Namibia. Differenti zone di vegetazione, savana, foresta secca e campi erbosi, offrono spazi vitali per mammiferi, uccelli e rettili. Dato che non esistono corsi d'acqua gli animali si dirigono verso sorgenti naturali e artificiali. Parte del parco è la conca di Etosha, una conca di argilla che contiene sale.

Nationale Park van Etosha
Het Nationale Park van Etosha is het Namibische reservaat met de rijkste fauna. Verschillende vegetatiezones – savanne, droog bos, grasland – vormen leefgebieden voor zoogdieren, vogels en reptielen. Omdat hier geen stromende rivieren zijn, zijn de dieren op natuurlijke en kunstmatige drinkplaatsen aangewezen. Onderdeel van het park is de Etosha-zoutpan, een bekken van klei dat met zout is gevuld.

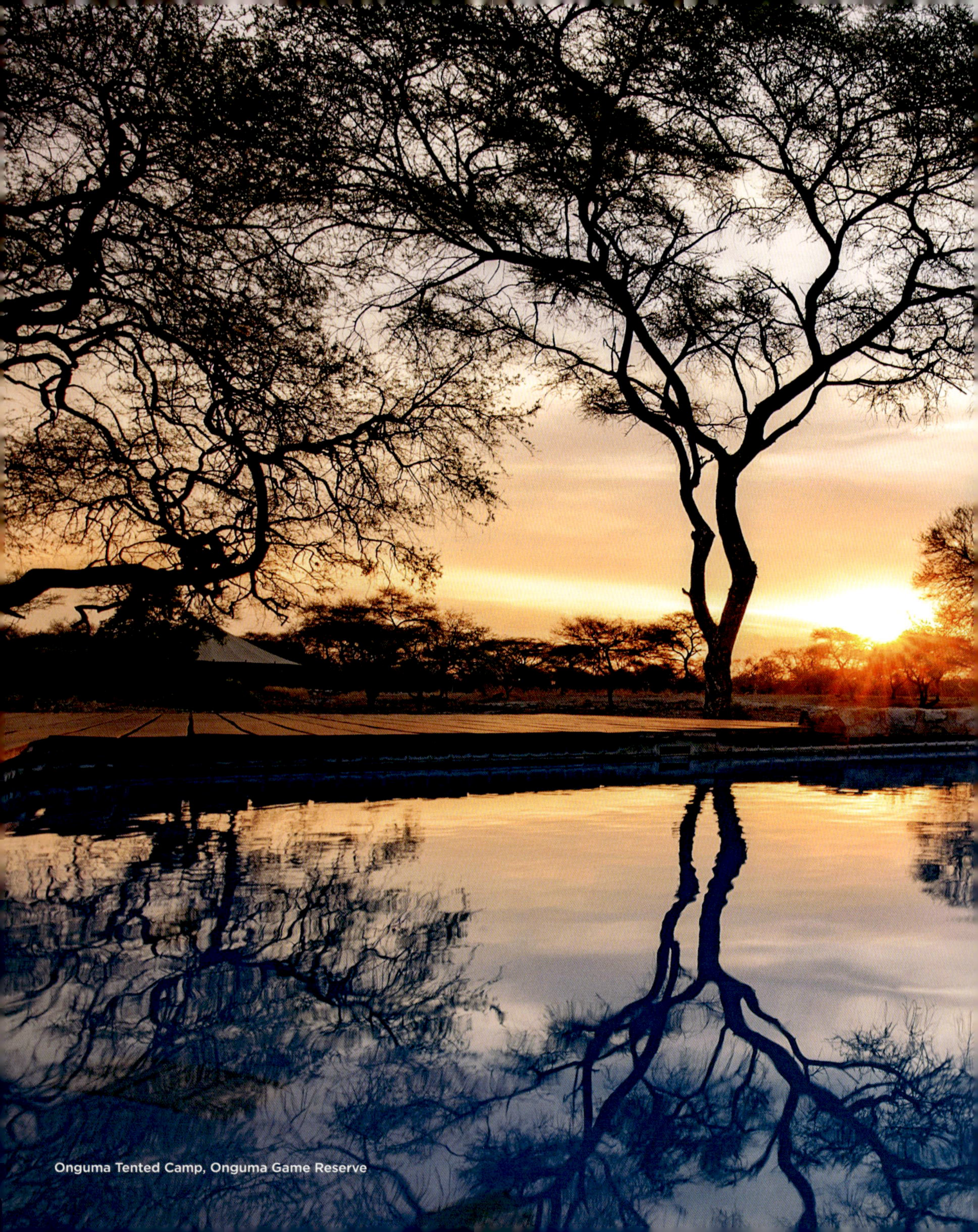

Onguma Tented Camp, Onguma Game Reserve

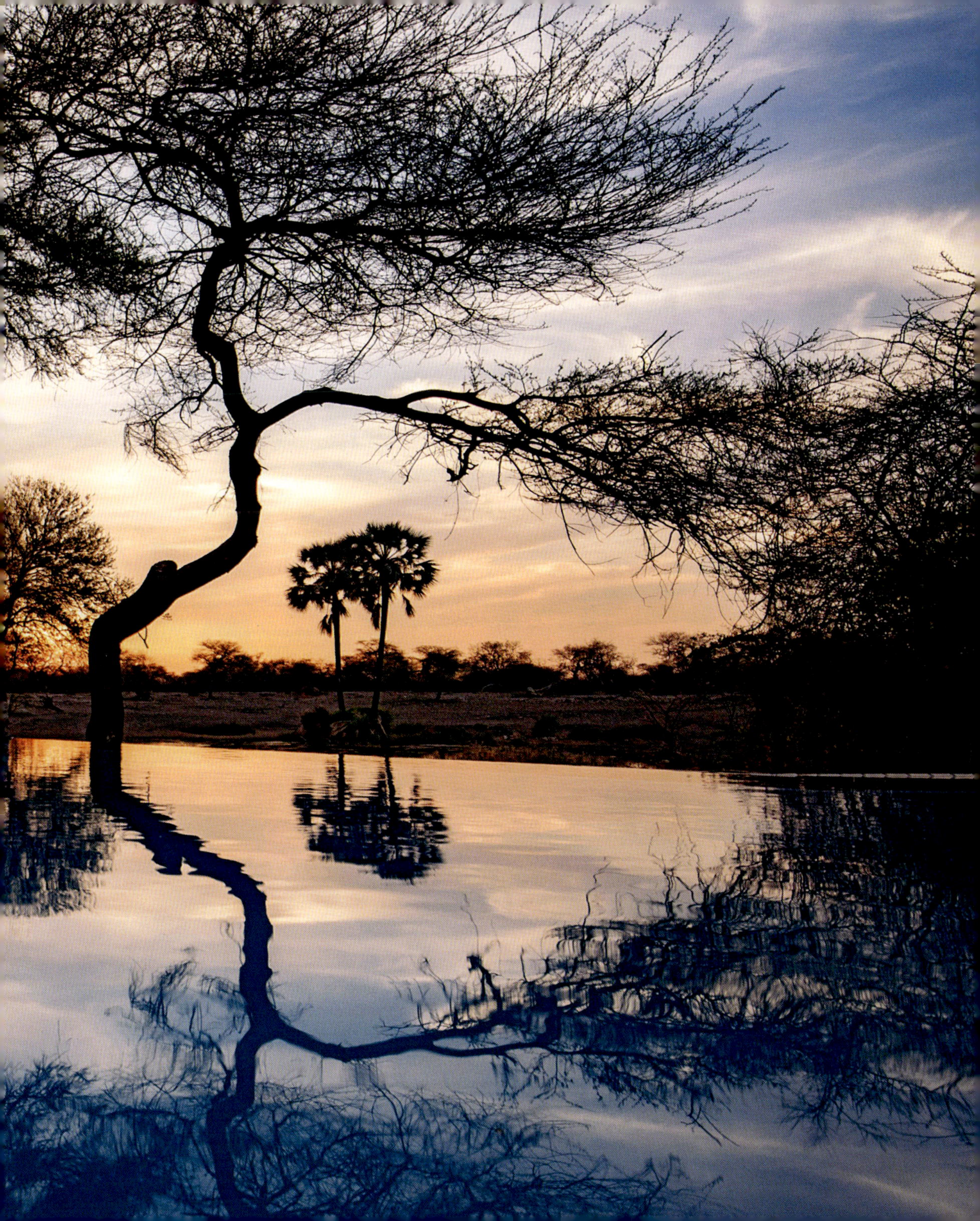

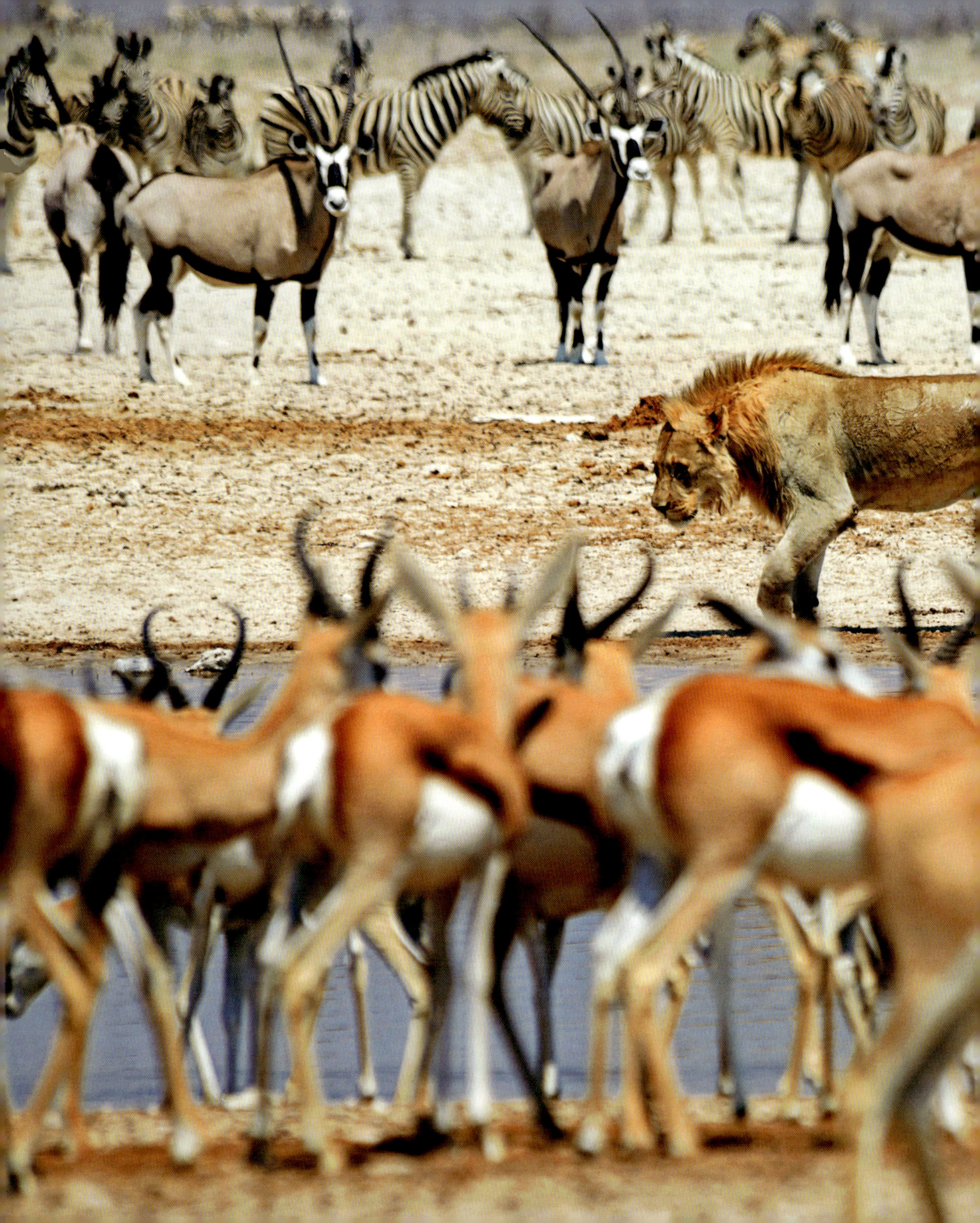

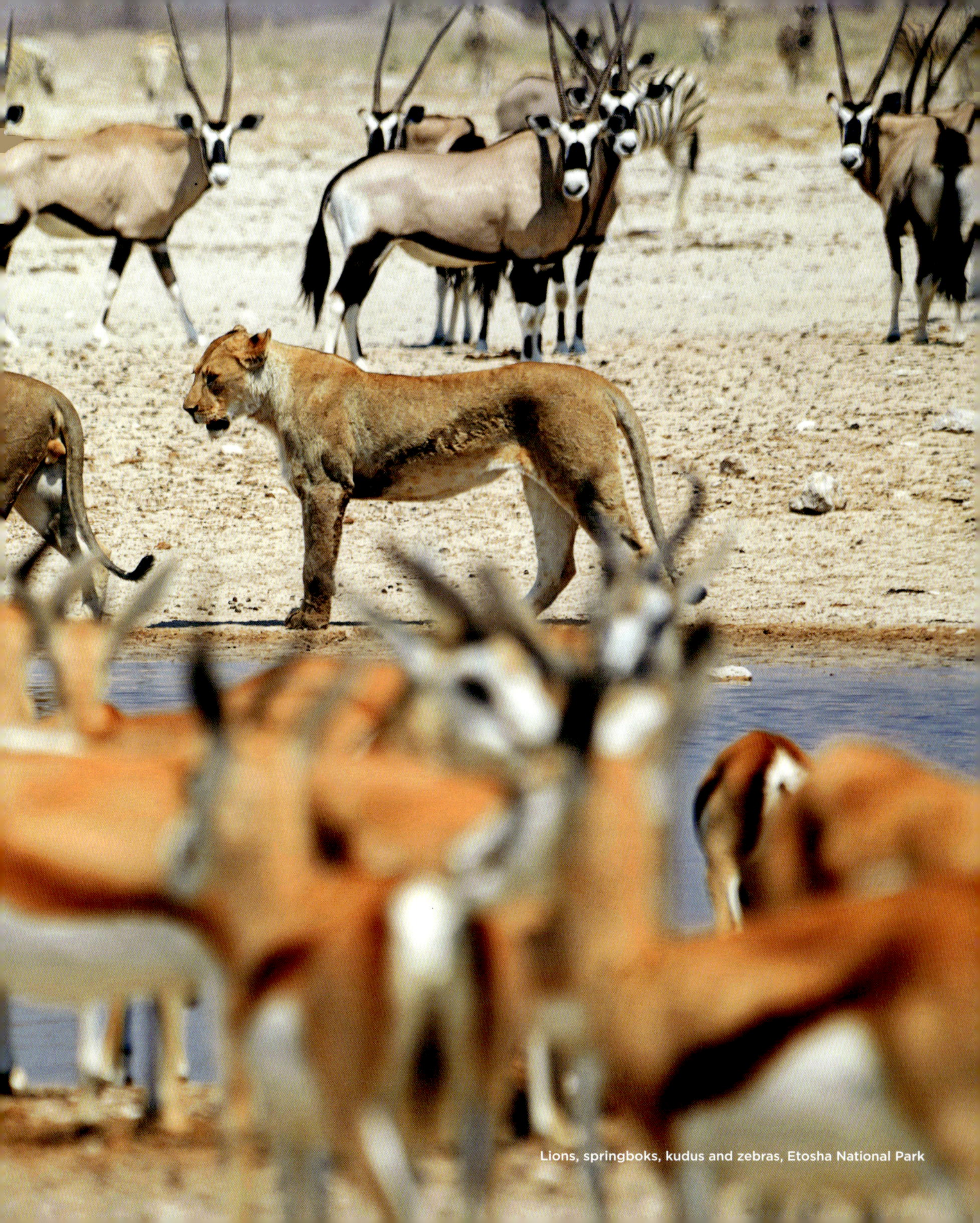

Lions, springboks, kudus and zebras, Etosha National Park

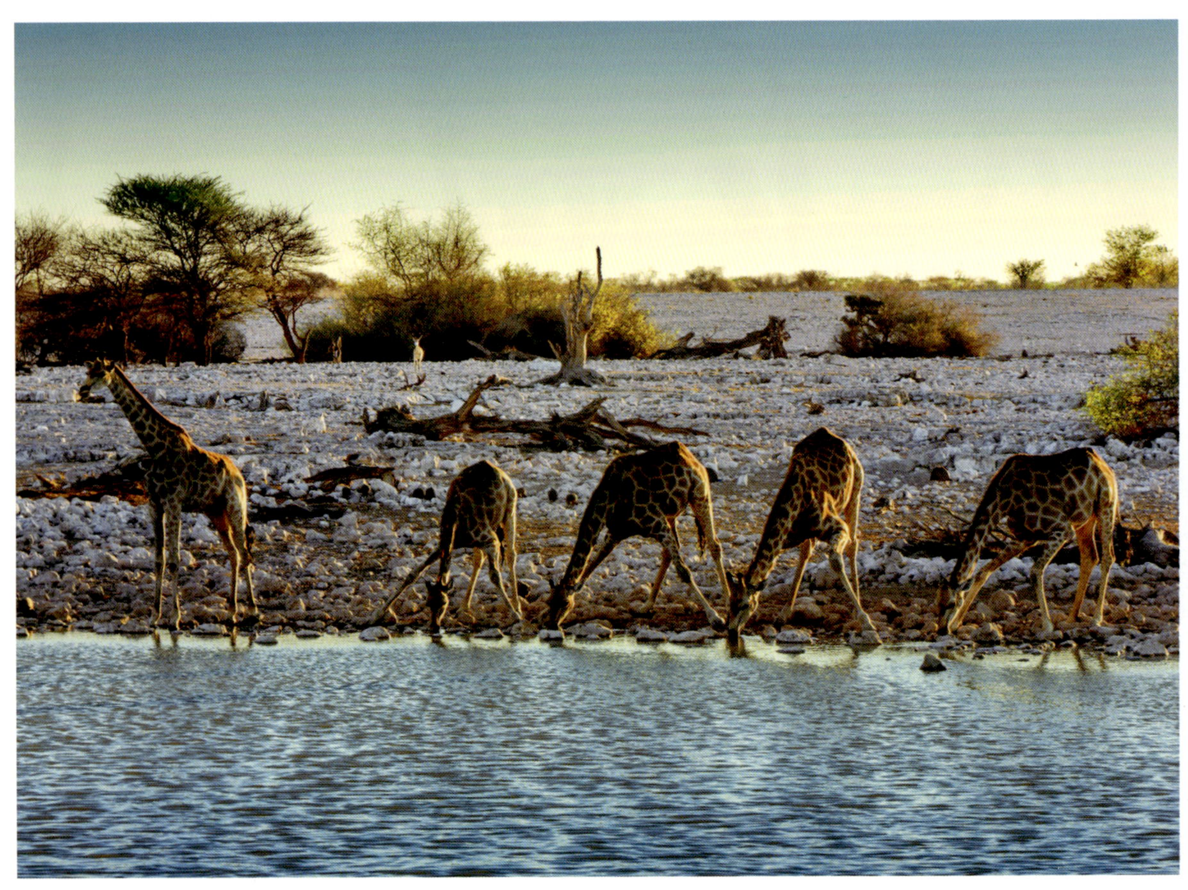

Giraffes, Okaukuejo watering hole, Etosha National Park

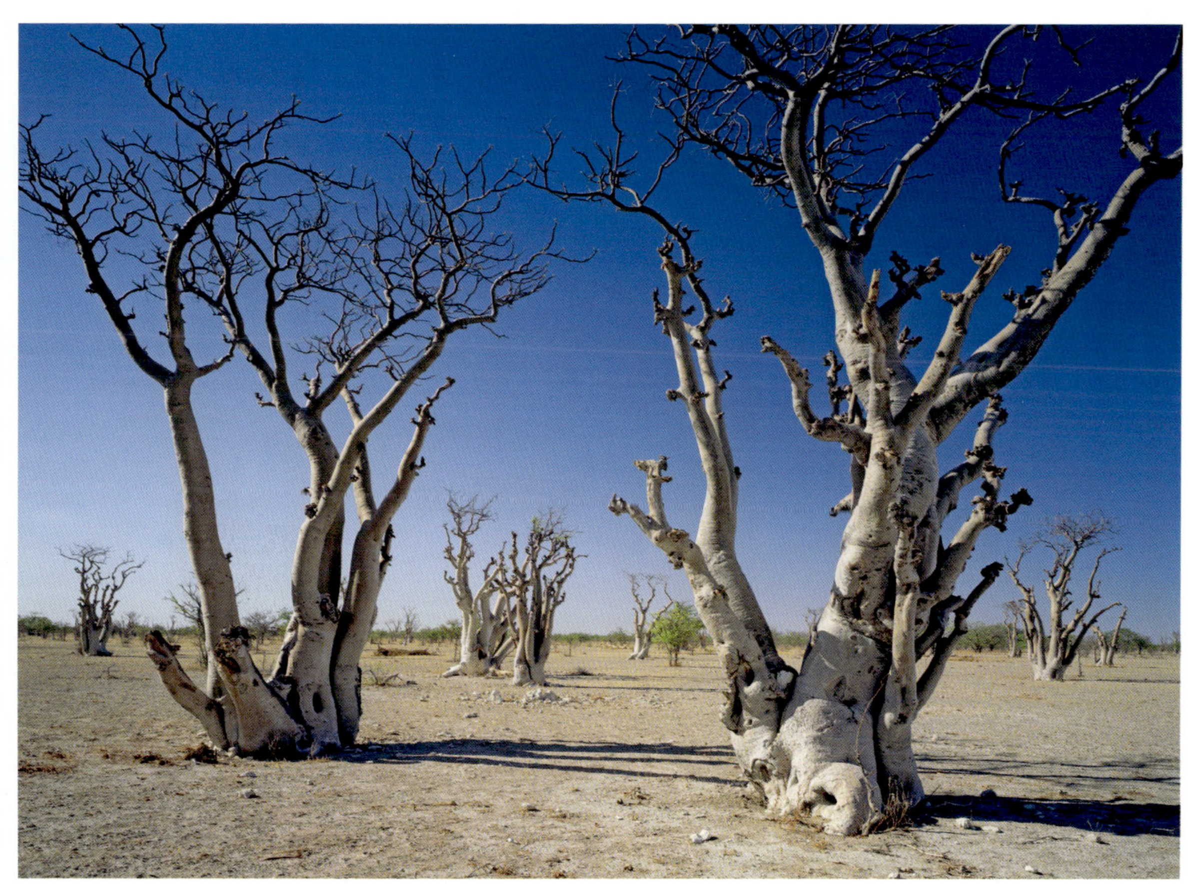

Moringa trees, Etosha National Park

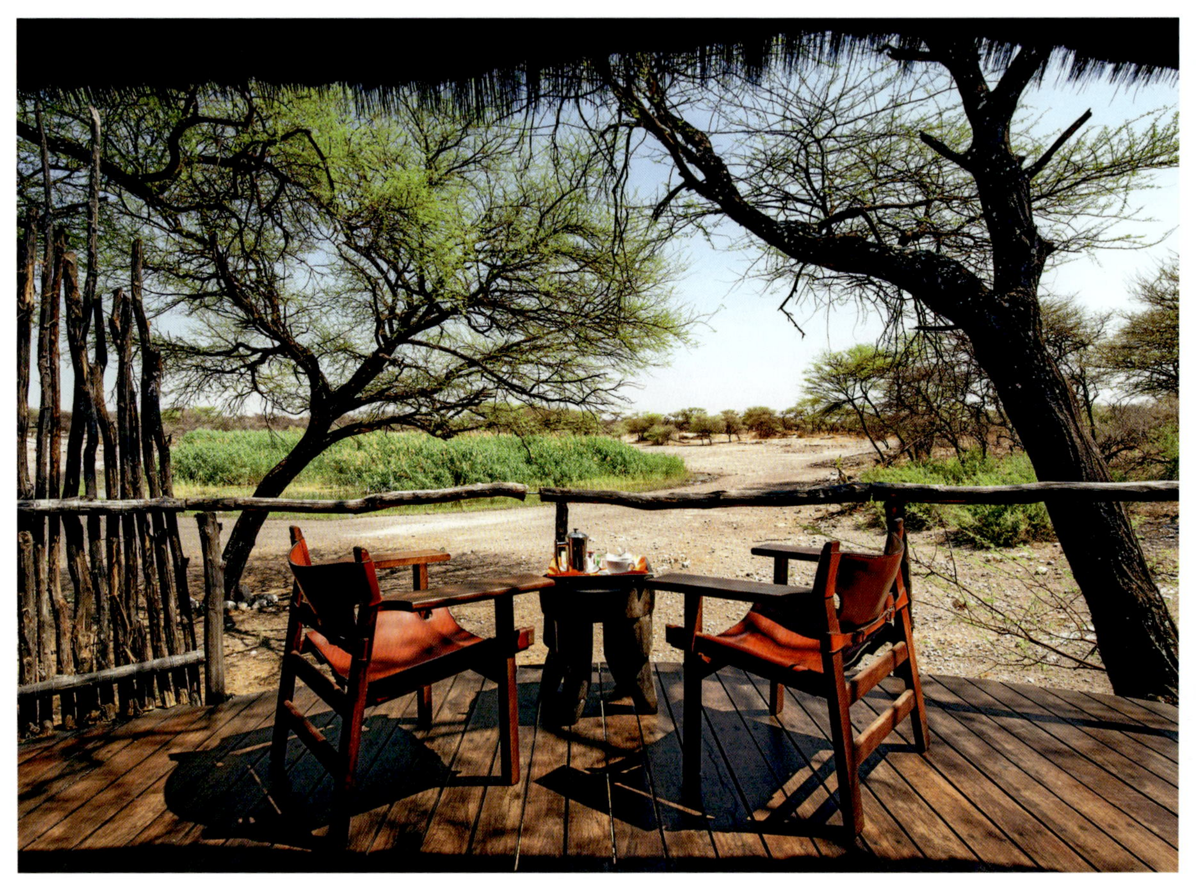

Onguma Tree Top Camp, Onguma Game Reserve

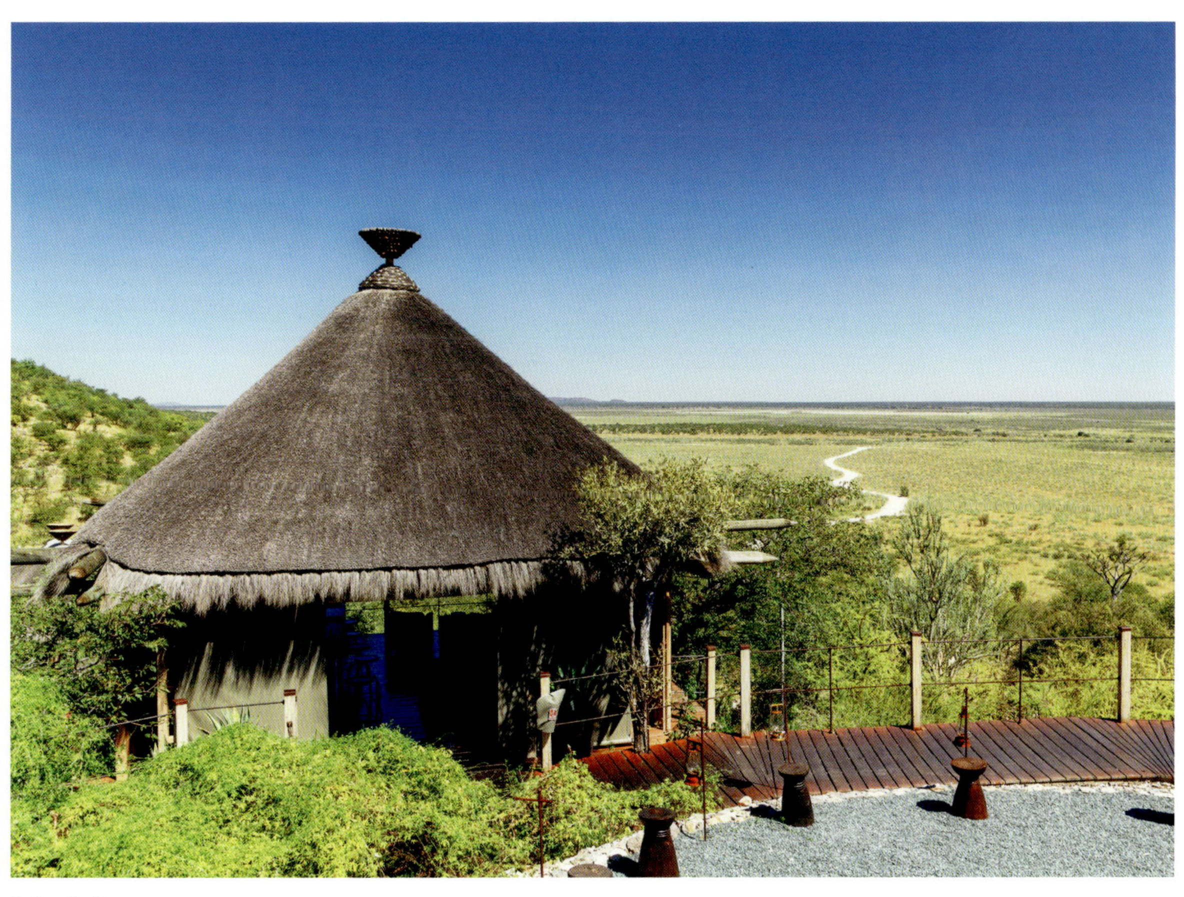

Dolomite Camp

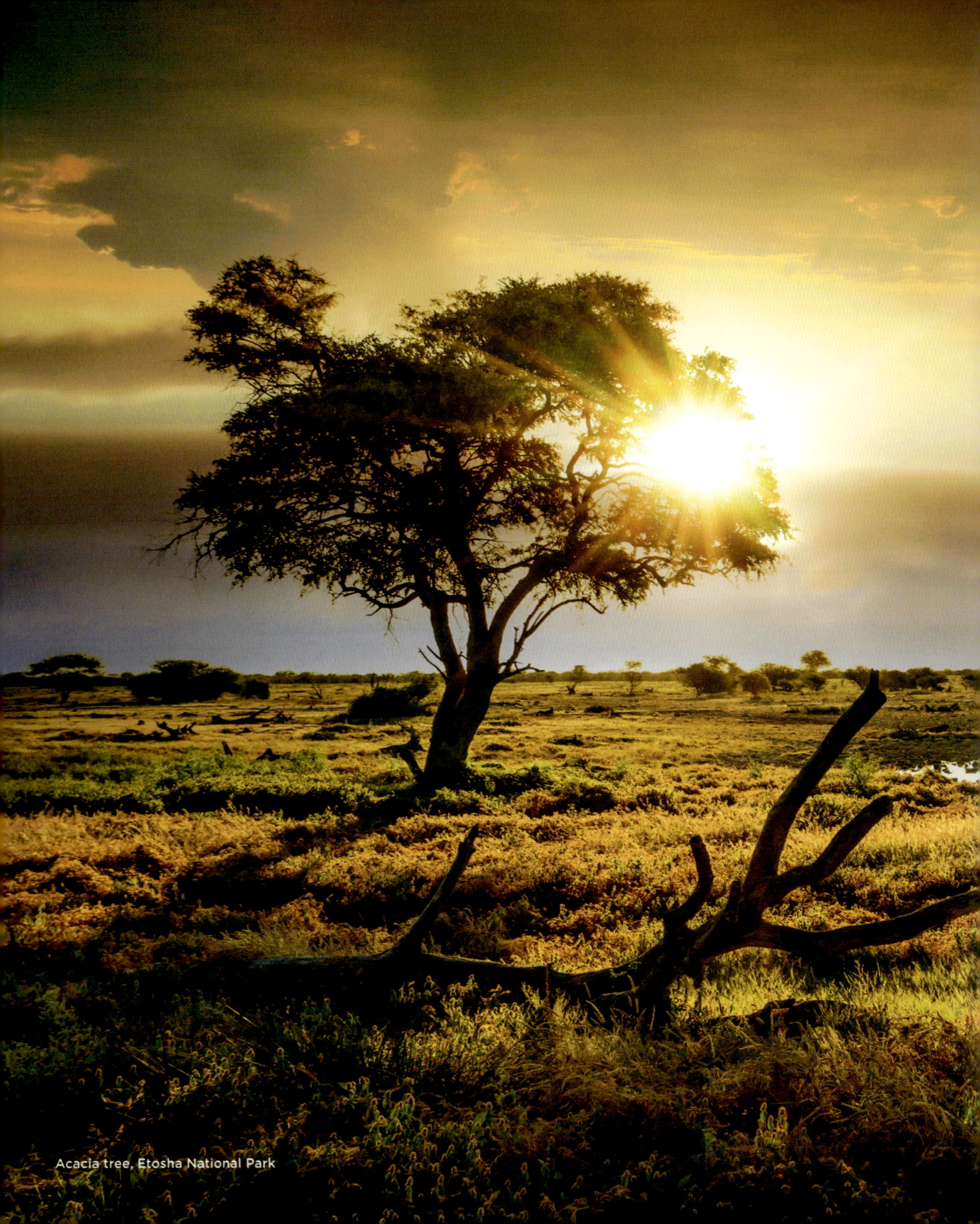

Acacia tree, Etosha National Park

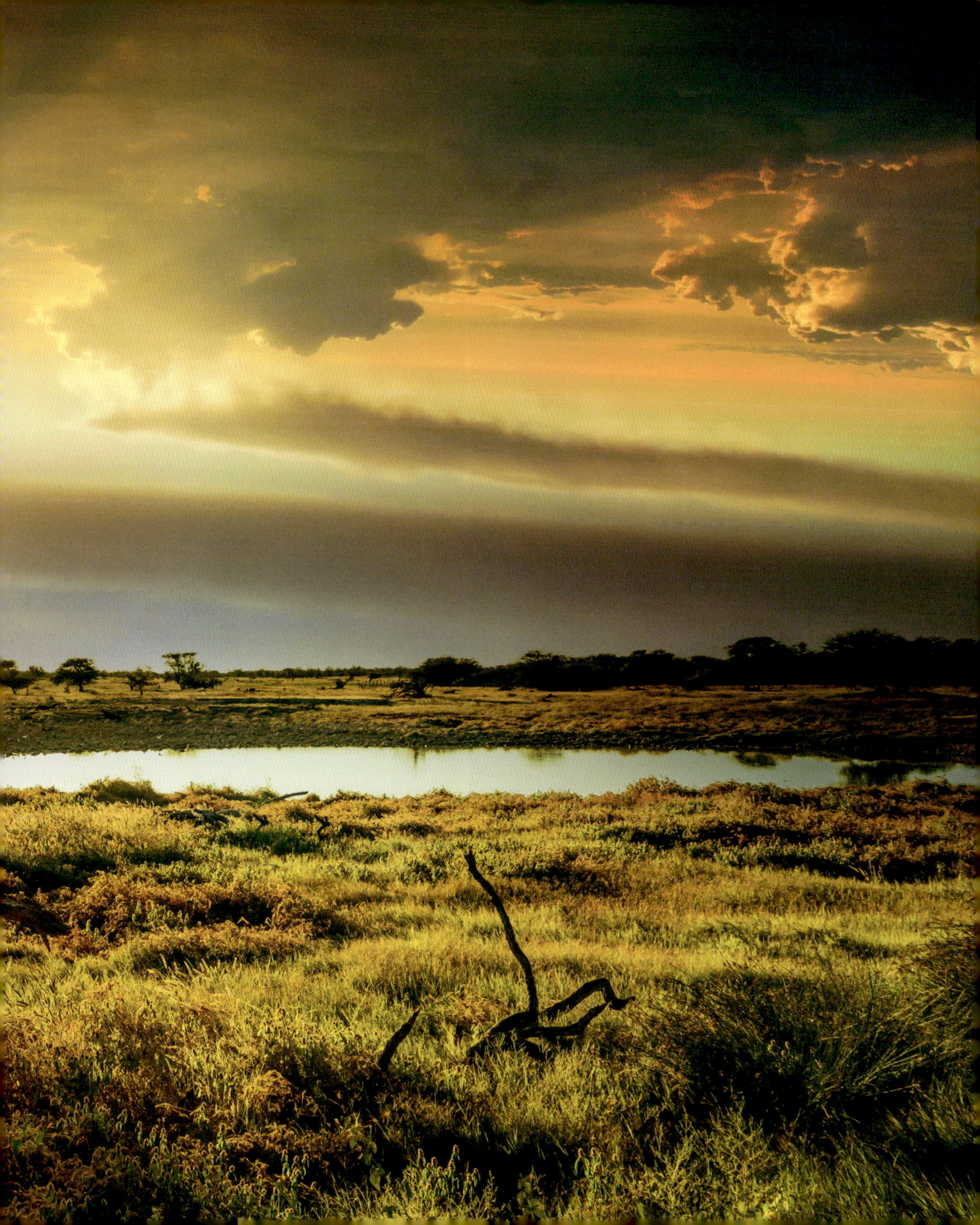

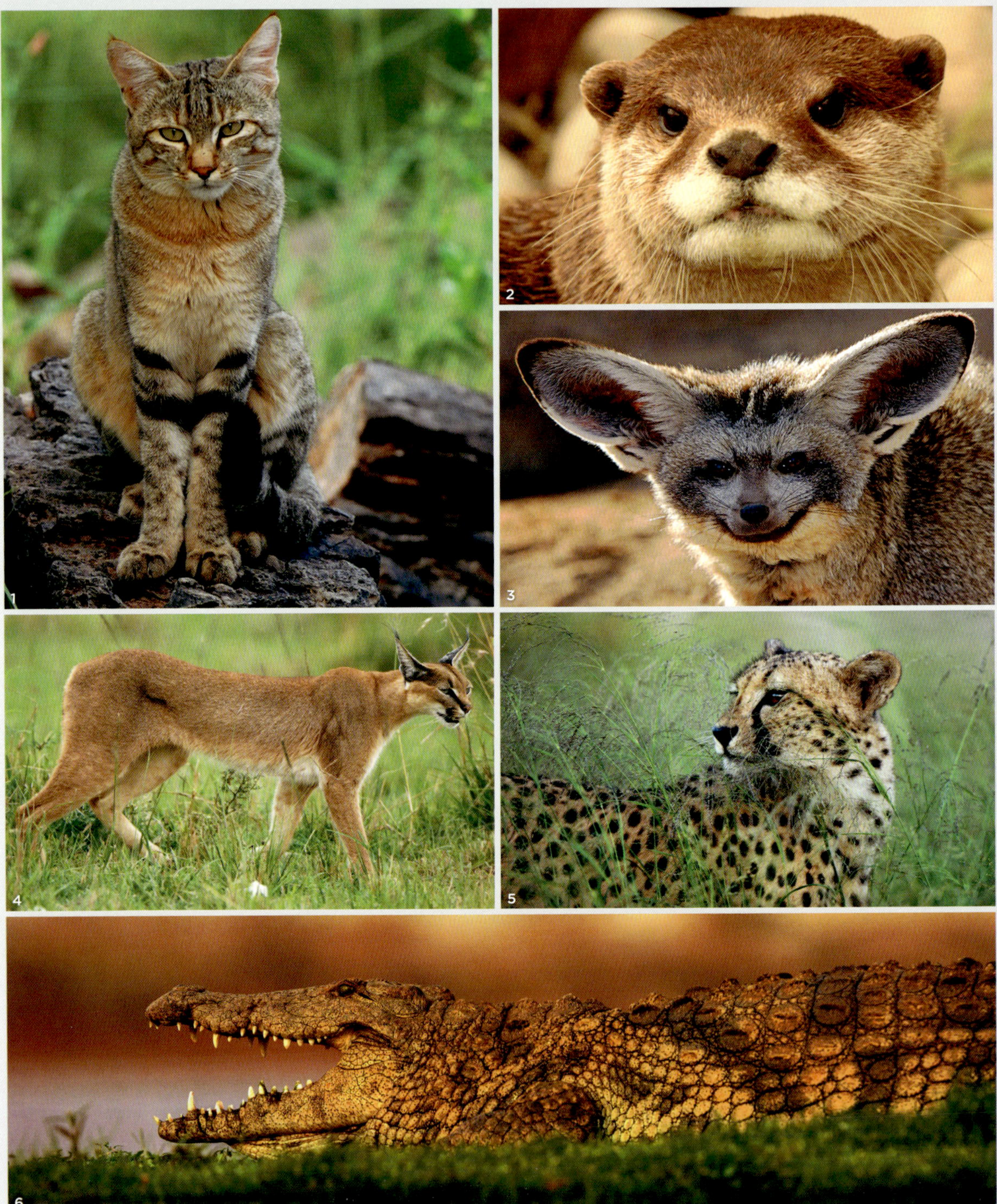
1
2
3
4
5
6

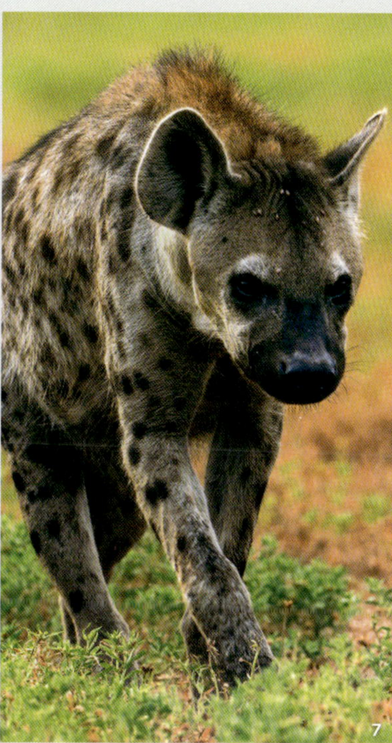

7

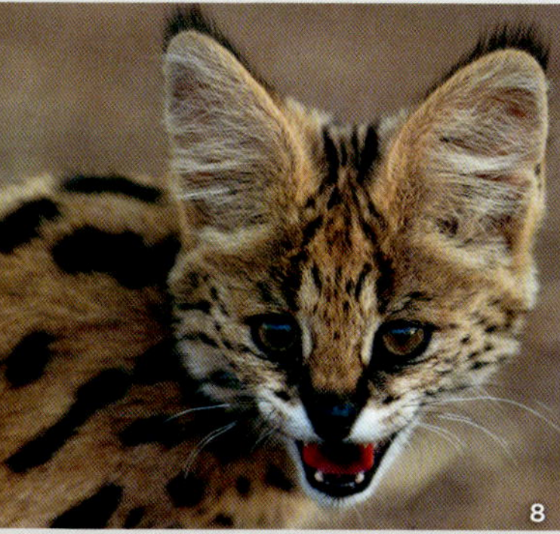

8

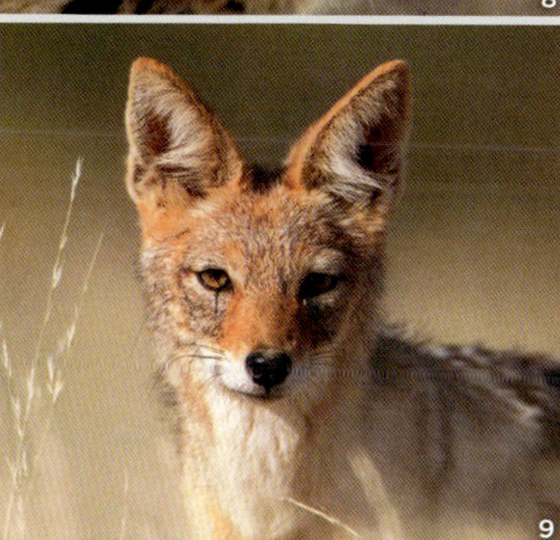

9

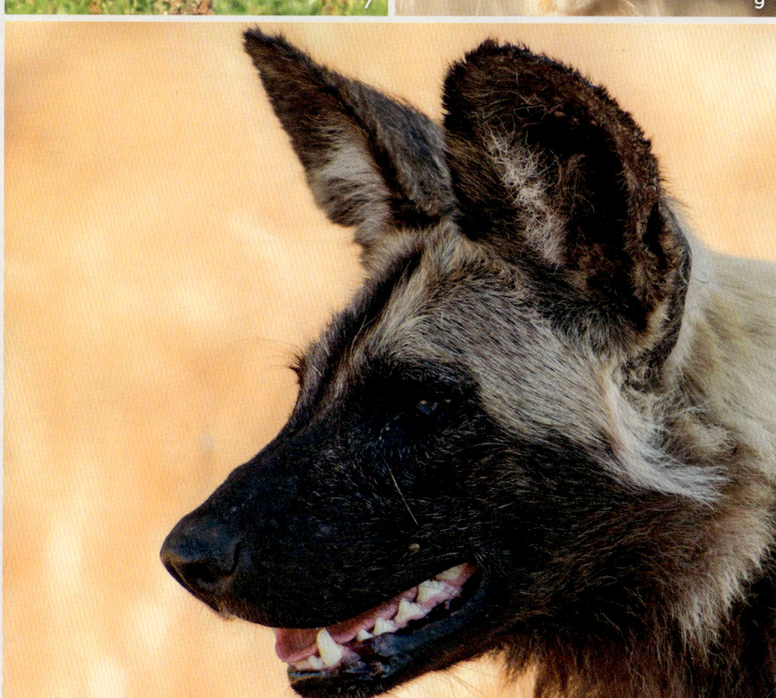

10

Carnivores

1 African wildcat
2 African clawless otter
3 Bat-eared fox
4 Caracal
5 Cheetah
6 Nile crocodile
7 Spotted hyena
8 Serval
9 Jackal
10 African wild dog

Carnivores

1 Chat sauvage d'Afrique
2 Loutres à joues blanches
3 Renard à oreilles de chauve-souris
4 Caracal
5 Guépard
6 Crocodile du Nil
7 Hyène tachetée
8 Serval
9 Chacal
10 Lycaon ou chien sauvage

Fleischfresser

1 Falbkatze
2 Kapotter
3 Löffelhund
4 Karakal
5 Gepard
6 Nilkrokodil
7 Tüpfelhyäne
8 Serval
9 Schakal
10 Afrikanischer Wildhund

Carnívoros

1 Gato salvaje africano o gato del desierto
2 Nutria sin garras
3 Zorro orejudo
4 Caracal
5 Guepardo
6 Cocodrilo del Nilo
7 Hiena manchada
8 Serval
9 Chacal
10 Licaón o perro salvaje africano

Carnivori

1 Gatto selvatico africano
2 Lontra senza unghie africana
3 Otocione
4 Caracal
5 Ghepardo
6 Coccodrillo del Nilo
7 Iena maculata
8 Serval
9 Sciacallo
10 Licaone

Vleeseters

1 Afrikaanse wilde kat
2 Kaapse otters
3 Grootoorvos
4 Caracal
5 Jachtluipaard
6 Nijlkrokodil
7 Gevlekte hyena
8 Serval
9 Jakhals
10 Afrikaanse wilde hond

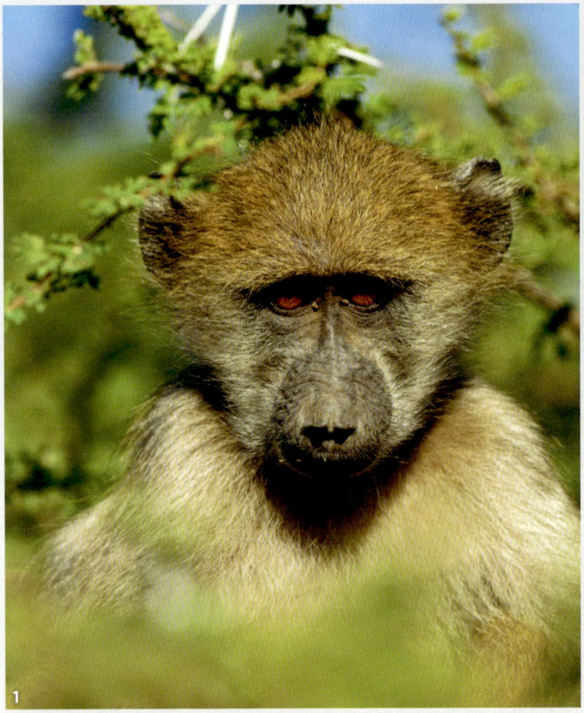

1

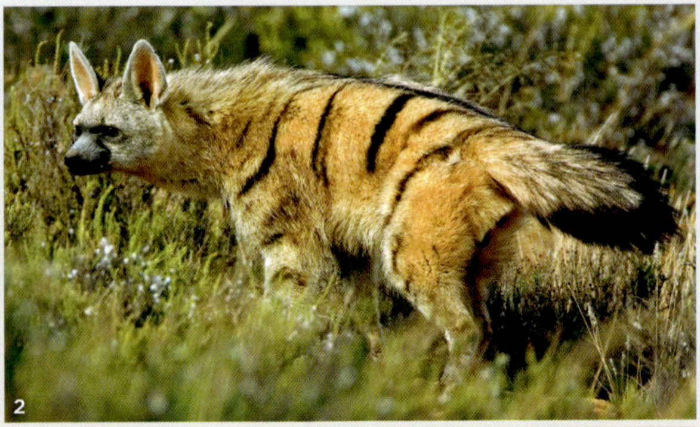

2

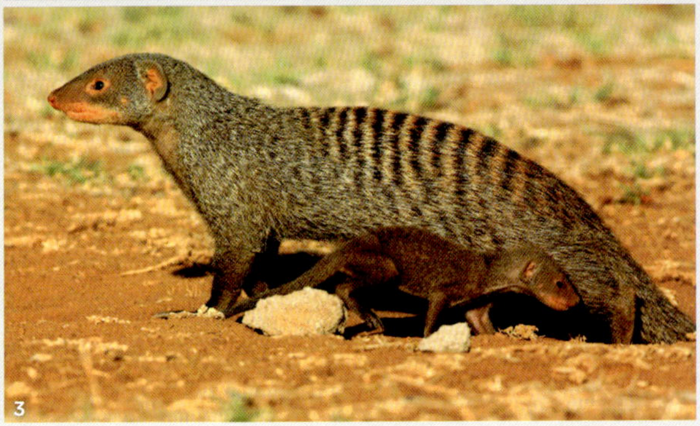

3

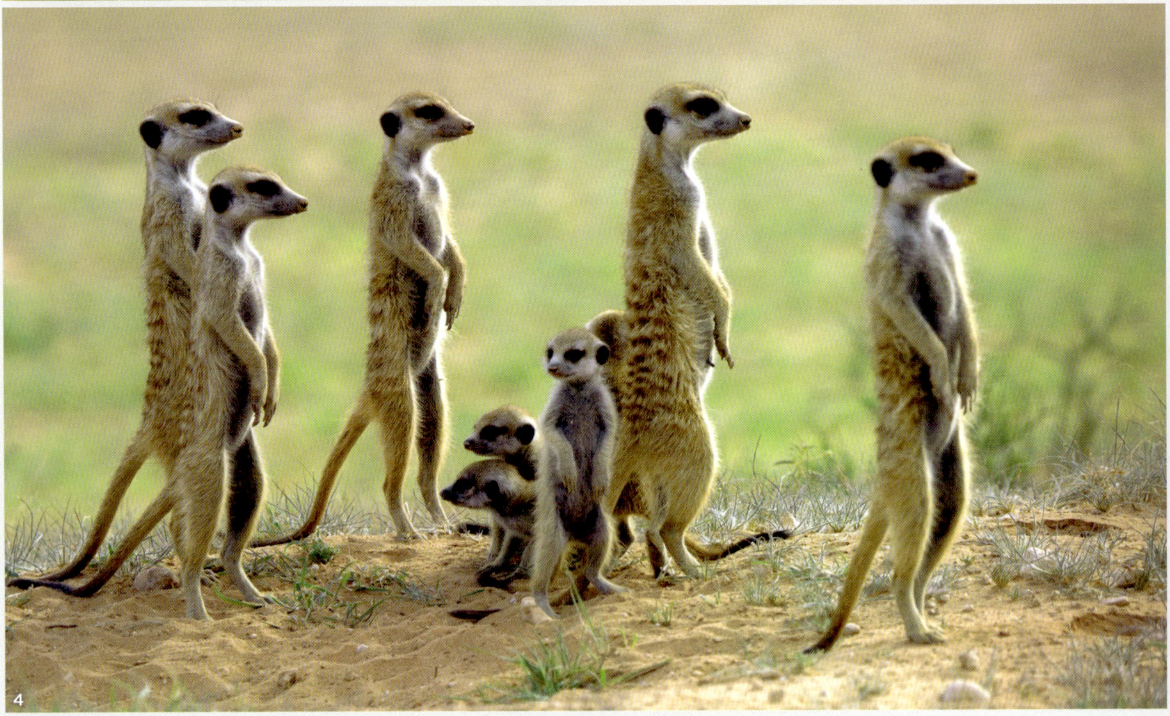

4

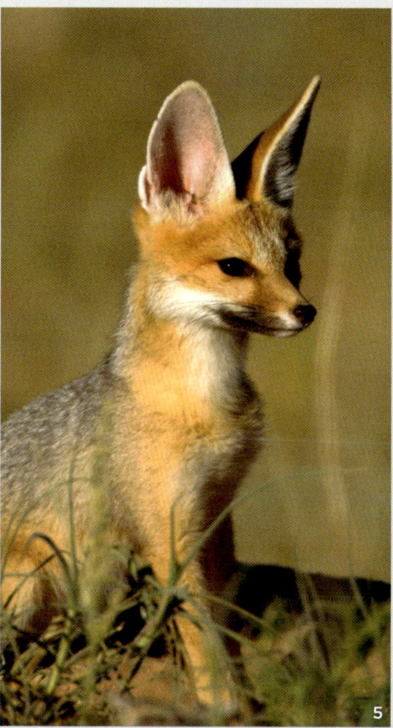

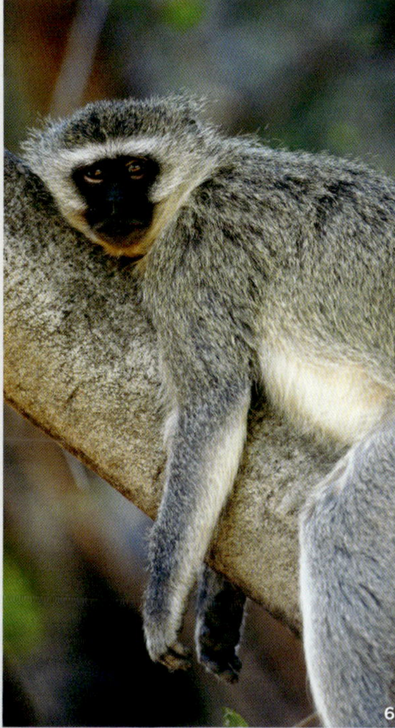

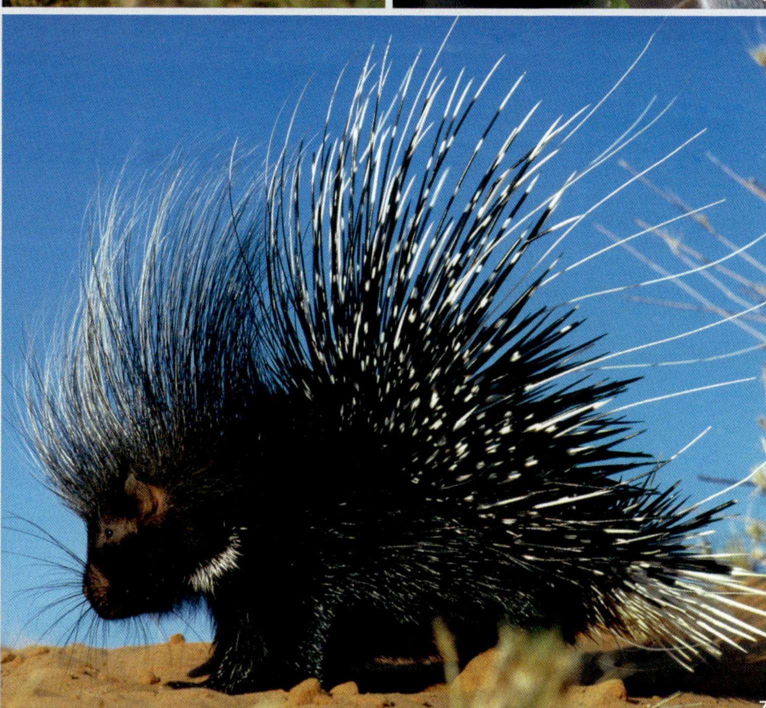

Omnivores and Insectivores

1 Chacma baboon
2 Aardwolf
3 Banded mongoose
4 Meerkat
5 Cape fox
6 Vervet monkey
7 South African porcupine

Omnivores et insectivores

1 Babouin chacma
2 Protèle
3 Mangouste rayée
4 Suricate
5 Renard du Cap
6 Vervet bleu
7 Porc-épic du Cap

Alles- und Insektenfresser

1 Bärenpavian
2 Erdwolf
3 Zebramanguste
4 Erdmännchen
5 Kapfuchs
6 Südliche Grünmeerkatze
7 Südafrikanisches Stachelschwein

Omnívoros e insectívoros

1 Papión chacma
2 Lobo de tierra
3 Mangosta rayada
4 Suricato
5 Zorro del Cabo
6 Cercopiteco verde
7 Puercoespín sudafricano

Onnivori e Insettivori

1 Babbuino nero
2 Protele
3 Mangusta striata
4 Suricato
5 Volpe del Capo
6 Cercopiteco verde
7 Istrice africano

Omnivoren en insecteneters

1 Beerbaviaan
2 Aardwolf
3 Zebramangoeste
4 Stokstaartjes
5 Kaapse vos
6 Vervet
7 Zuid-Afrikaans stekelvarken

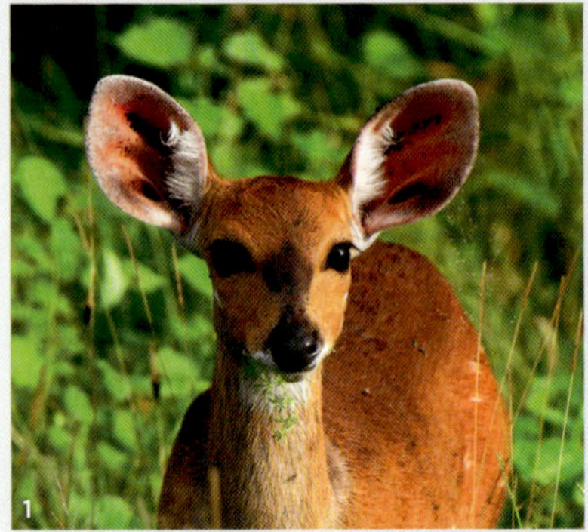

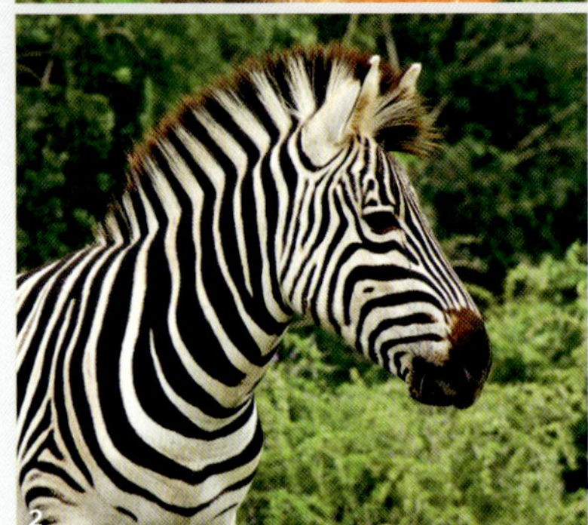

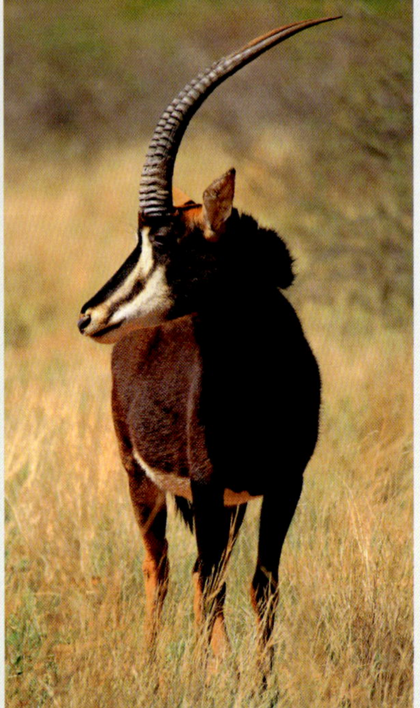

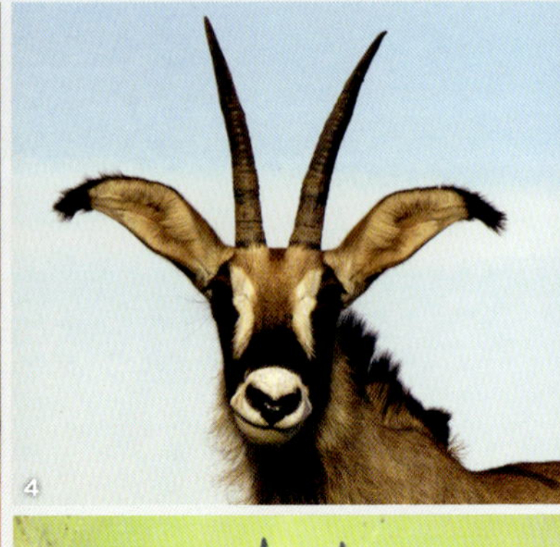

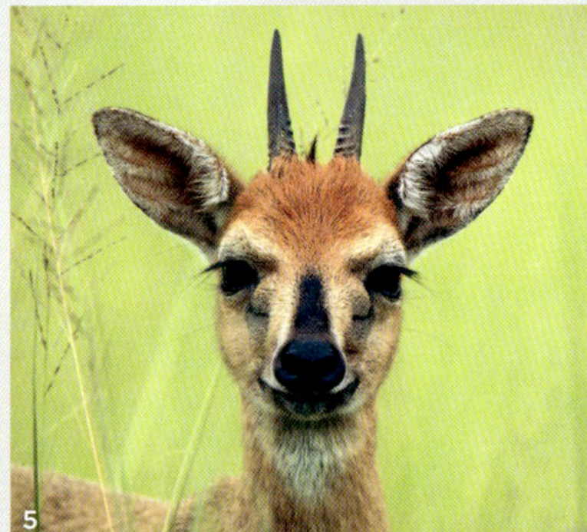

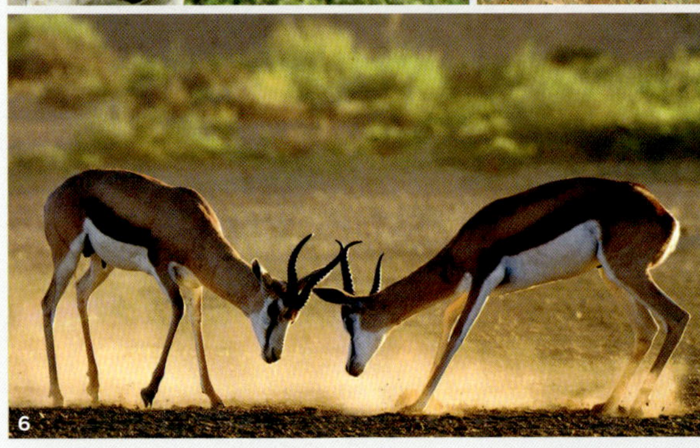

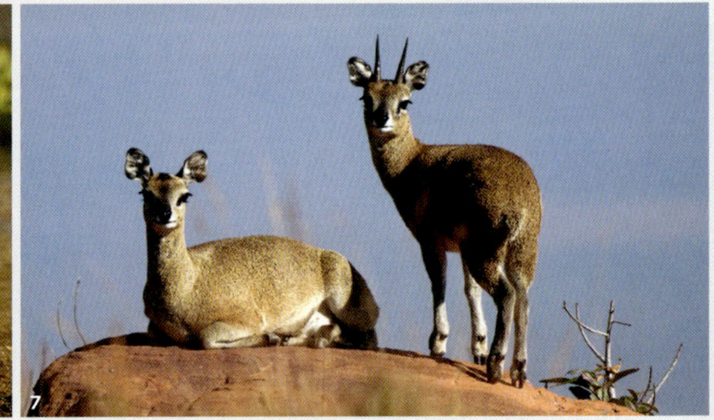

Herbivores
1 Imbabala
2 Burchell's zebra
3 Sable antelope
4 Roan antelope
5 Common duiker
6 Springbok
7 Klipspringer
8 Giraffe
9 Common eland
10 Red hartebeest
11 Impala
12 Desert warthog

Herbivores
1 Guib harnaché
2 Zèbre des plaines
3 Antilope noire
4 Antilope rouanne
5 Céphalophe de Grimm
6 Springbok
7 Oréotrague
8 Girafe
9 Éland
10 Bubale caama
11 Impala
12 Phacochère

Pflanzenfresser
1 Buschbock
2 Steppenzebra
3 Rappenantilope
4 Pferdeantilope
5 Kronenducker
6 Springbock
7 Klippspringer
8 Giraffe
9 Elenantilope
10 Südafrikanische Kuhantilope
11 Impala
12 Wüstenwarzenschwein

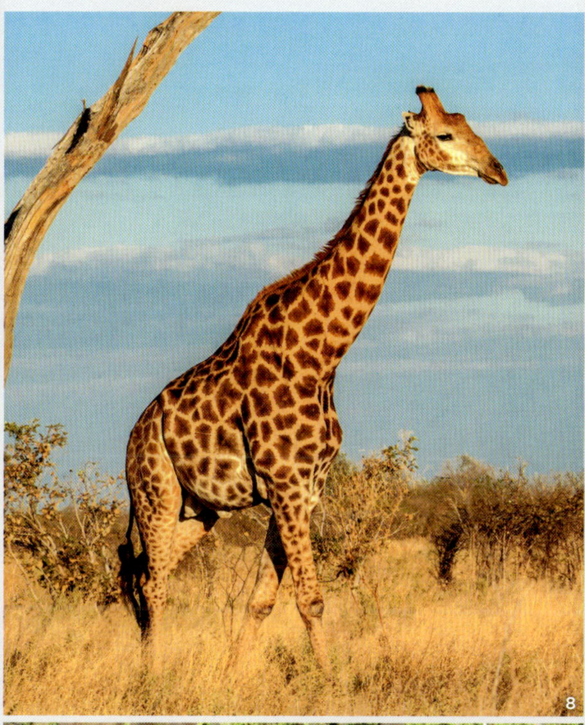

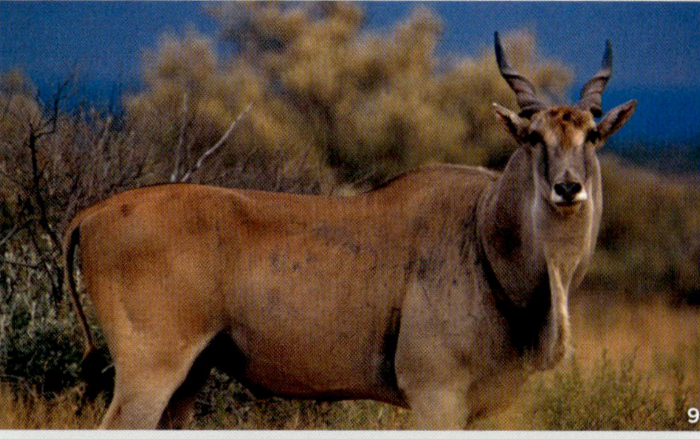

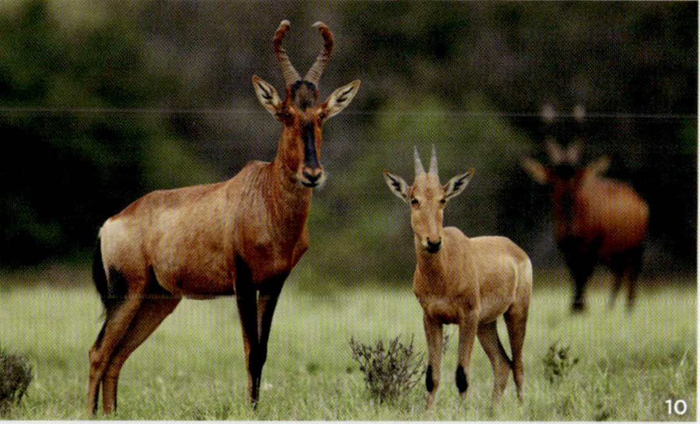

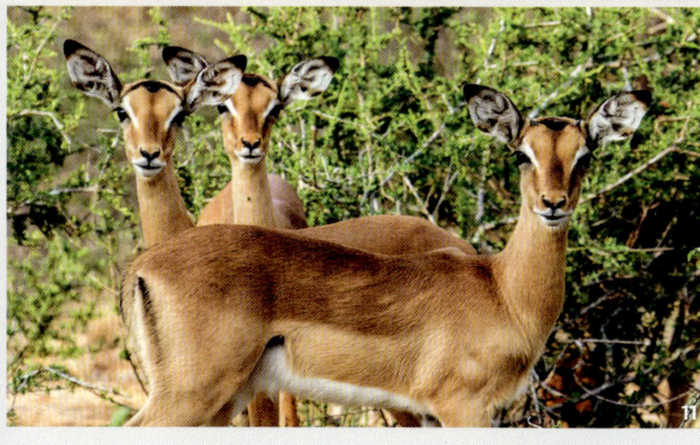

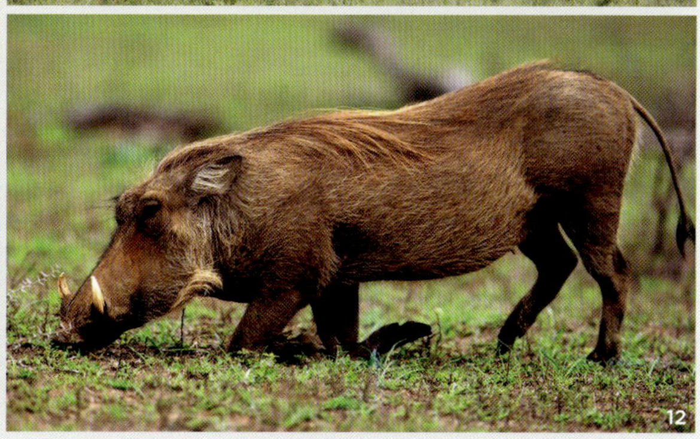

Herbívoros
1 Antílope geroglífico
2 Cebra común
3 Antílope sable
4 Antílope ruano
5 Duiker común
6 Gacela saltarina
7 Saltarrocas
8 Jirafa
9 Eland común
10 Alcélafo caama
11 Impala
12 Facóquero oriental

Erbivori
1 Tagelafo striato
2 Zebra di pianura
3 Antilope nera
4 Antilope roana
5 Silvicapra
6 Springbok
7 Saltarupi
8 Giraffa
9 Antilope alcina
10 Alcelafo rosso
11 Impala
12 Facocero del deserto

Grazers
1 Bosbok
2 Steppezebra
3 Sabelantilope
4 Roanantilope
5 Gewone duiker
6 Springbok
7 Klipspringer
8 Giraf
9 Elandantilope
10 Red hartebeest
11 Impala
12 Woestijnknobbelzwijn

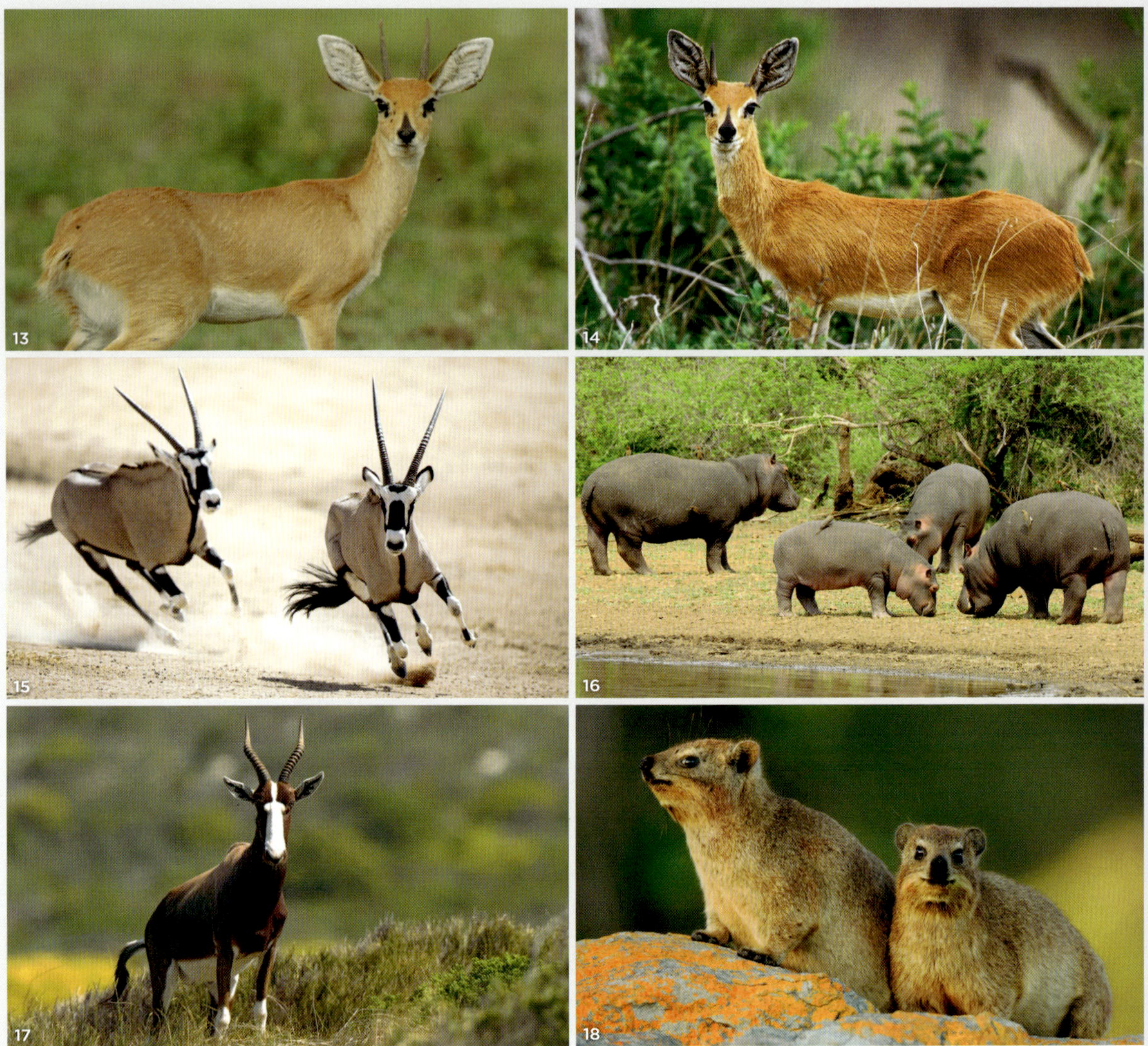

13 Oribi
14 Steenbok
15 Gemsbok
16 Hippopotamus
17 Bontebok
18 Rock hyrax
19 Blue wildebeest
20 Nyala
21 Lyre antelope
22 Greater Kudu
23 Waterbuck

13 Ourébi
14 Steenbok
15 Oryx gazelle
16 Hippopotame commun
17 Damalisque à front blanc
18 Daman du Cap
19 Gnou bleu
20 Nyala
21 Sassabi
22 Grand koudou
23 Cobe à croissant

13 Oribi
14 Steinböckchen
15 Spießbock
16 Flusspferd
17 Buntbock
18 Klippschliefer
19 Streifengnu
20 Nyala
21 Leierantilope
22 Großer Kudu
23 Wasserbock

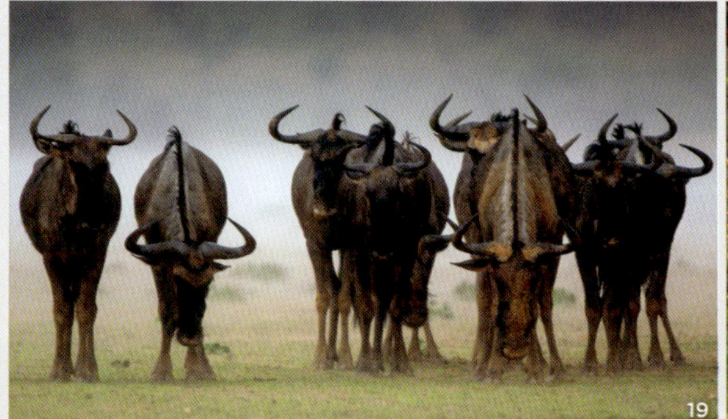
19

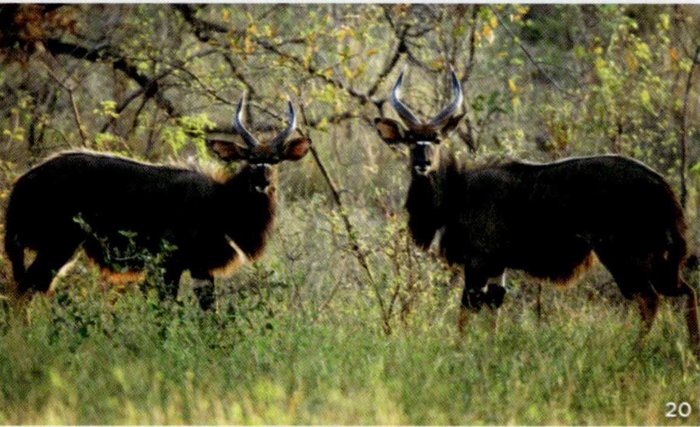
20

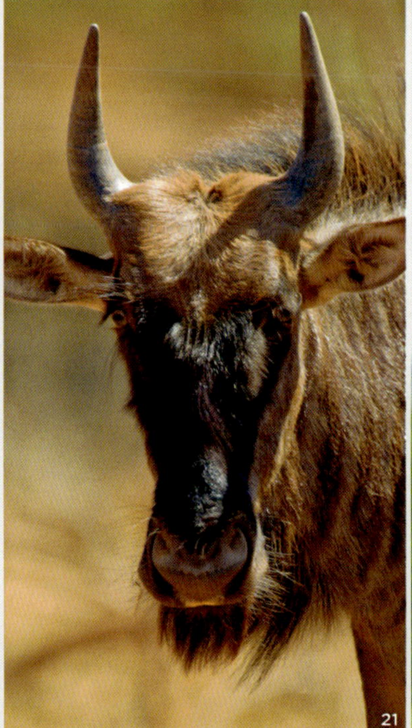
21

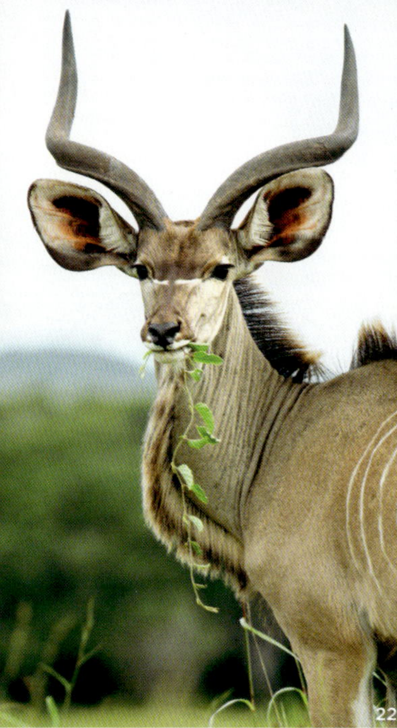
22

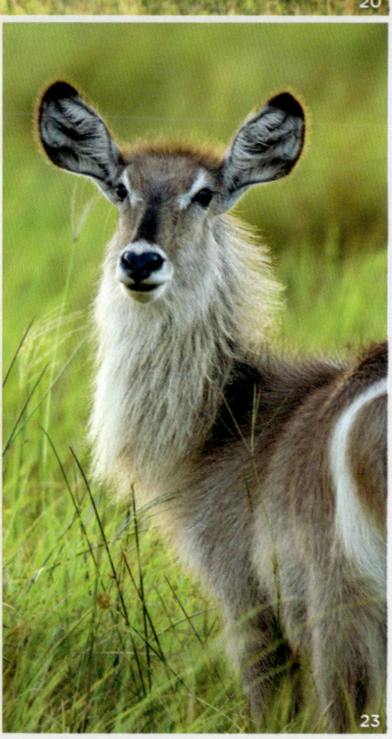
23

13 Oribí
14 Racifero común
15 Órice del Cabo
16 Hipopótamo común
17 Bontebok
18 Damán de El Cabo
19 Ñu azul
20 Niala
21 Tsessebe común
22 Gran Kudú
23 Antílope acuático

13 Oribi
14 Raficero campestre
15 Orice gazzella
16 Ippopotamo
17 Bontebok
18 Irace del Cabo
19 Gnu
20 Nyala
21 Damalisco comune
22 Kudu
23 Cobo

13 Oribi
14 Steenbokantilope
15 Gemsbok
16 Nijlpaard
17 Bontebok
18 Kaapse klipdas
19 Blauwe gnoe
20 Nyala
21 Lierantilope
22 Grote koedoe
23 Waterbok

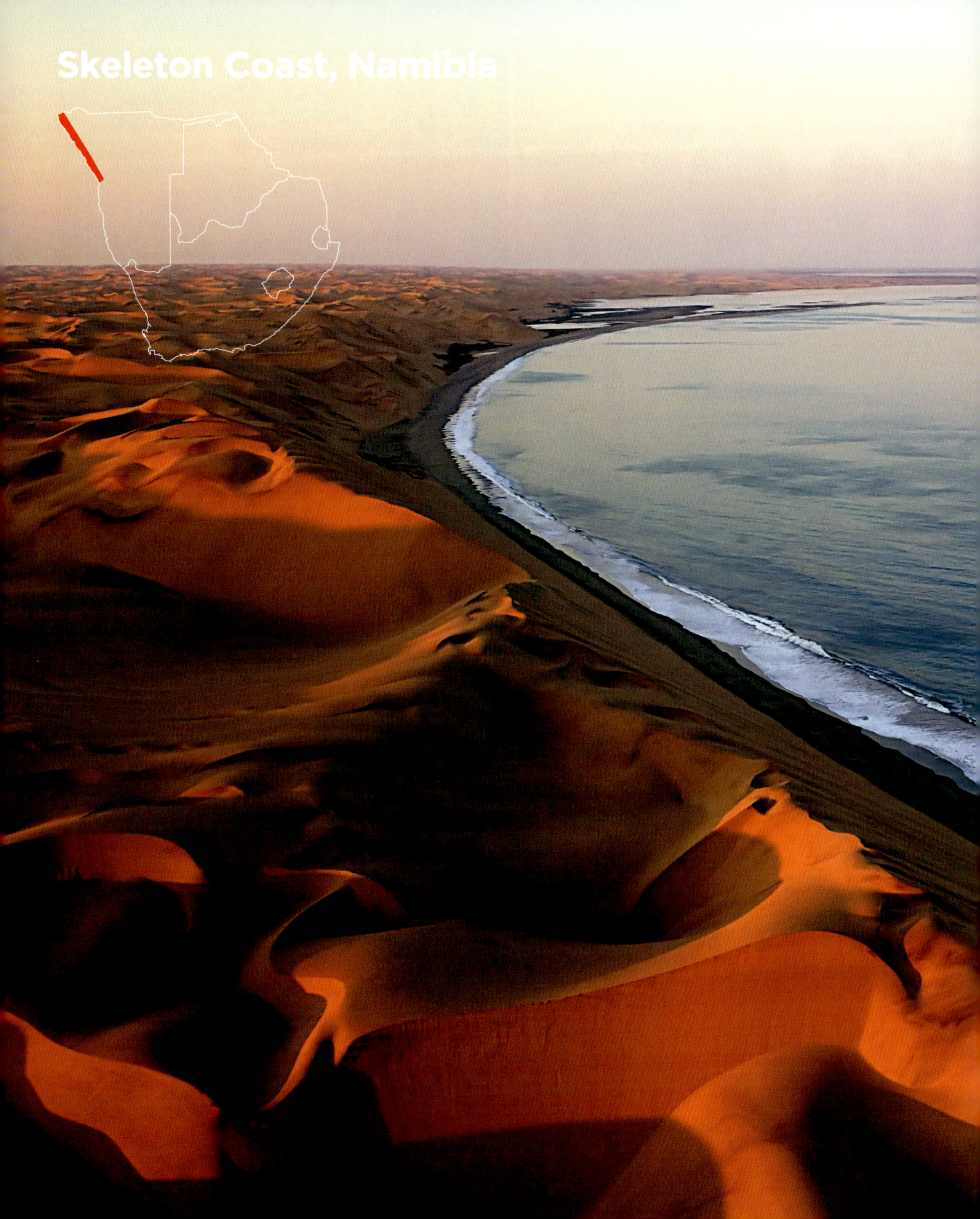
Skeleton Coast, Namibia

Skeleton Coast, Namib Desert, Skeleton Coast National Park

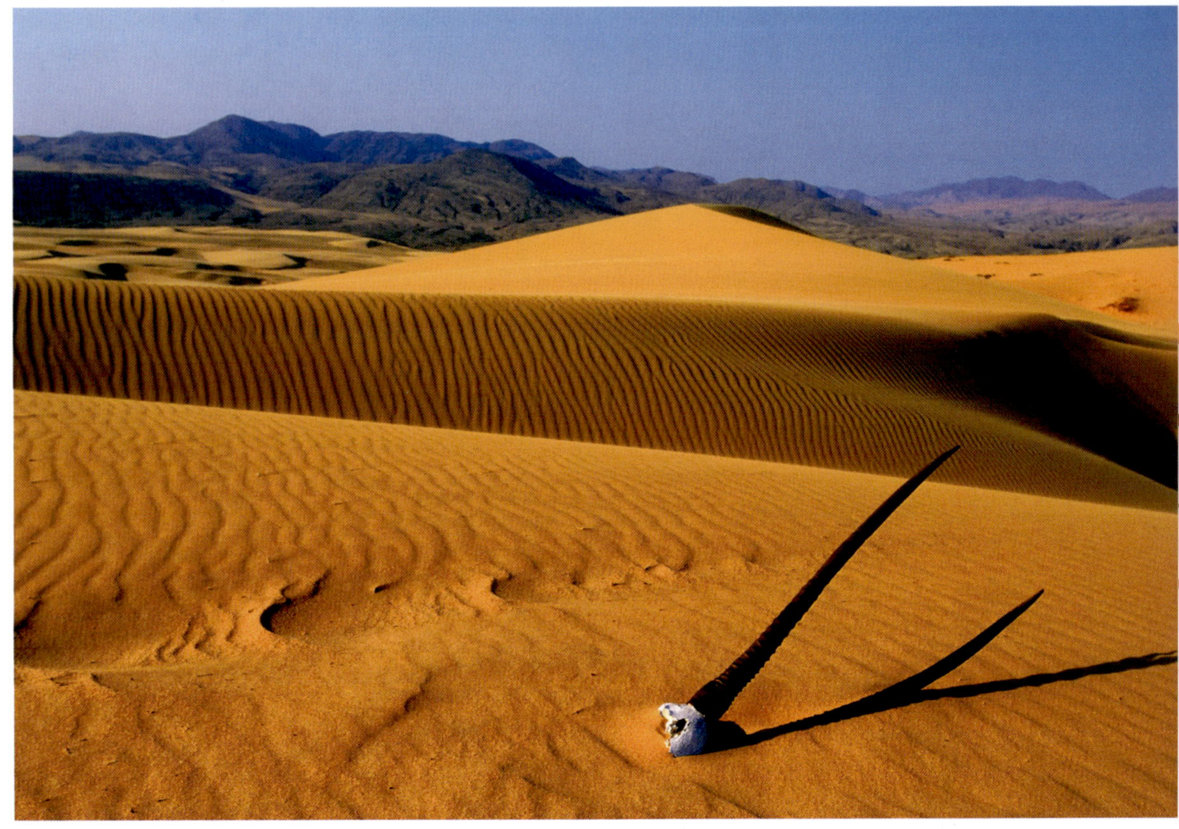

Northern Namib Desert, Skeleton Coast National Park

Skeleton Coast

The name speaks volumes, telling of the still visible shipwrecks along the coastline, as well the whale bones and human skeletons that litter these shores. The unpredictable currents and violently breaking surf have led sailors to call the northern coast of Namibia the "Gates of Hell". The Skeleton Coast is a part of the Namib Desert. The national park of the same name stretches from the Ugab River valley to the Kunene in northern Namibia.

La côte des Squelettes

La côte des Squelettes porte un nom révélateur. Il évoque des épaves qui sont encore visibles, des ossements de cétacés et d'humains. Pour les marins, la côte septentrionale de la Namibie, avec ses courants imprévisibles et de violentes vagues déferlantes, était la « porte de l'Enfer ». La côte des Squelettes fait partie du désert du Namib. Le parc national éponyme s'étend de la vallée de l'Ugab jusqu'au Cunene, dans le nord du pays.

Skelettküste

„Skelettküste" – der Name spricht Bände. Er erzählt von Schiffwracks, die noch immer zu sehen sind, von Walknochen und menschlichen Gebeinen. Unberechenbare Strömungen, heftige Brandung – für Seefahrer war die Nordküste Namibias das „Tor zur Hölle". Die Skelettküste ist Teil der Namib-Wüste. Der gleichnamige Nationalpark erstreckt sich vom Tal des Ugab River bis zum Kunene im Norden Namibias.

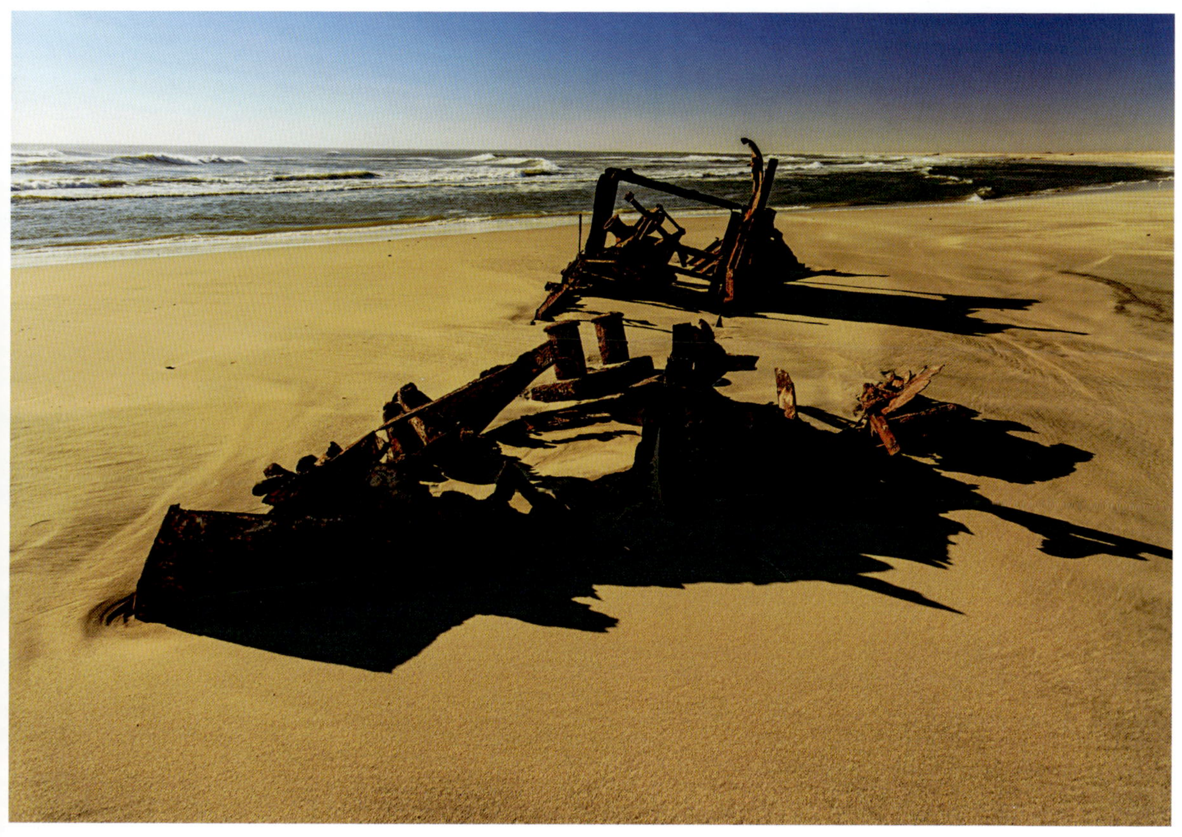

Skeleton Coast

Costa de los Esqueletos
"Costa de los Esqueletos"– el nombre lo dice todo. Habla de naufragios que aún son visibles, huesos de ballena y huesos humanos. Corrientes impredecibles, el fuerte oleaje– la costa norte de Namibia fue para los navegantes la "Puerta al Infierno". La Costa de los Esqueletos forma parte del desierto de Namibia. El parque nacional del mismo nombre, se extiende desde el valle del Ugab hasta el Kunene, en el norte de Namibia.

Costa degli Scheletri
"La Costa degli Scheletri": il nome dice tutto. Racconta di relitti di navi tuttora visibili, di ossa di balene e di resti umani. Correnti imprevedibili e forti risacche: per i navigatori la costa nord della Namibia era la "porta per l'inferno". La Costa degli Scheletri fa parte del deserto della Namibia. Il Parco Nazionale che porta il suo nome si estende dalla valle del fiume Ugab fino al Kunene nel nord della Namibia.

Skeleton Coast
De "Skeletkust" - de naam spreek boekdelen - vertelt het verhaal van (nog altijd zichtbare) scheepswrakken, walvisbotten en menselijk gebeente. Met zijn verraderlijke stromingen en zware branding was de noordkust van Namibië de "Poort van de Hel". De Skeleton Coast maakt deel uit van de Namibwoestijn. Het gelijknamige nationale park strekt zich uit van het dal van de Ugab tot aan Kunene in het noorden van Namibië.

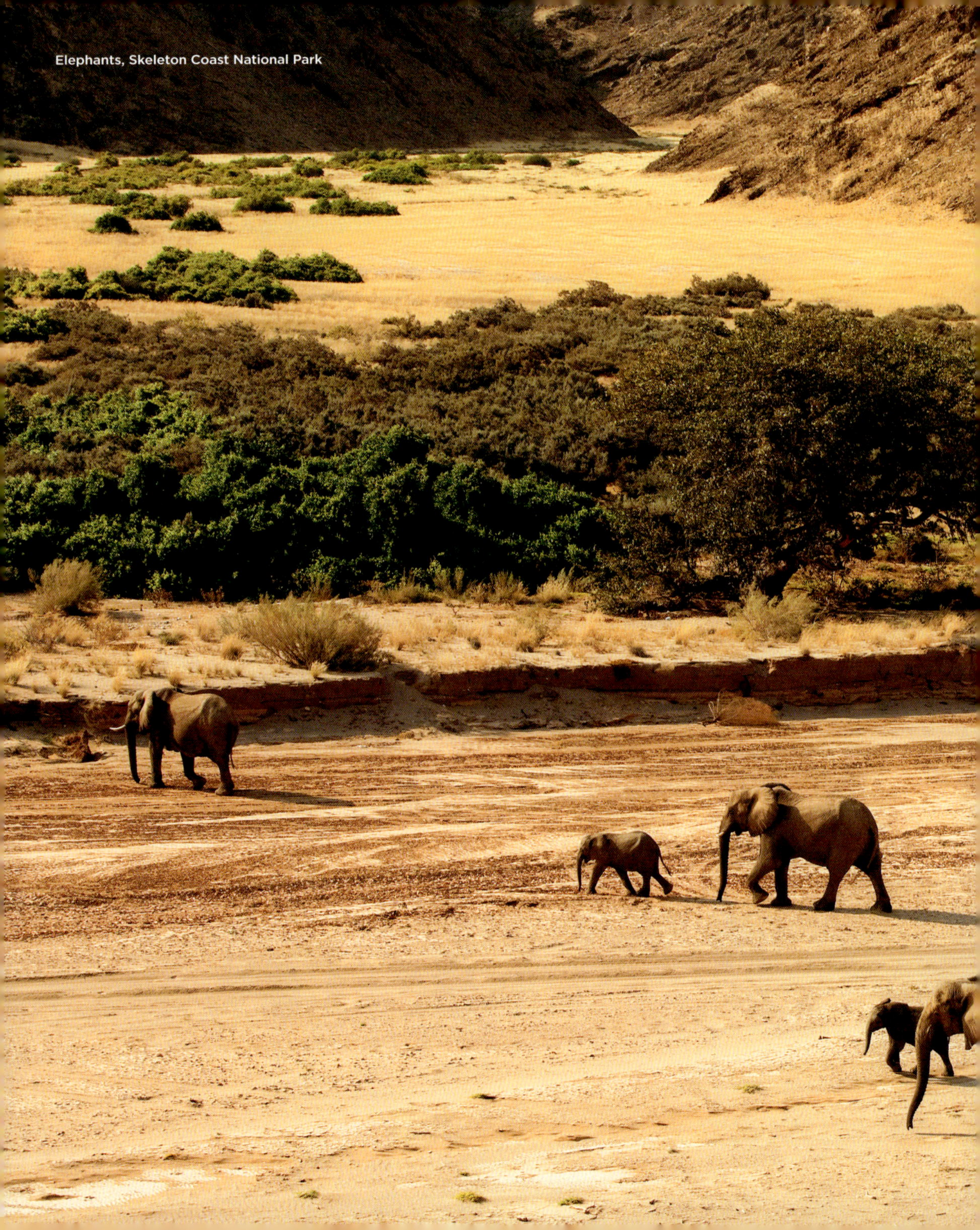

Elephants, Skeleton Coast National Park

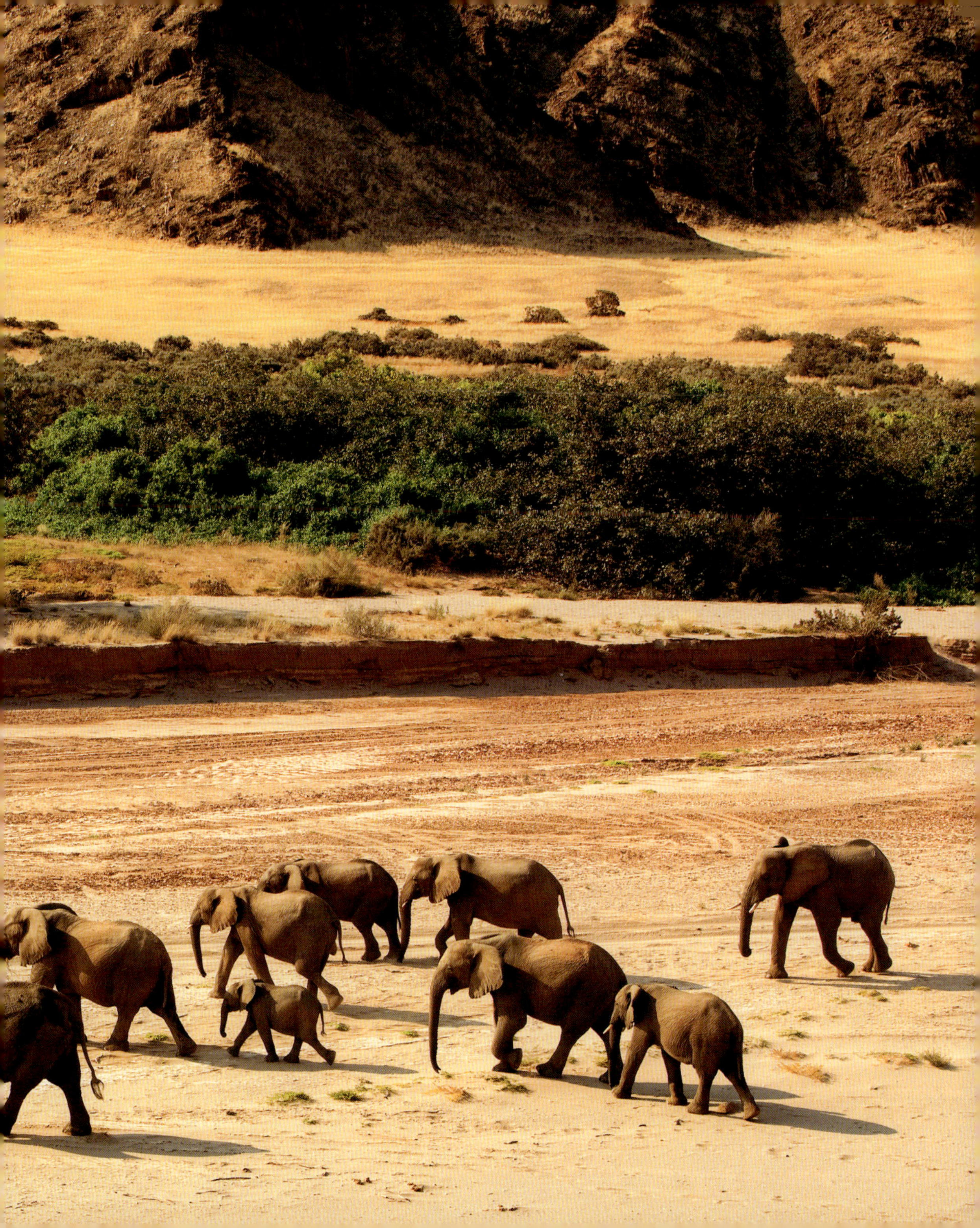

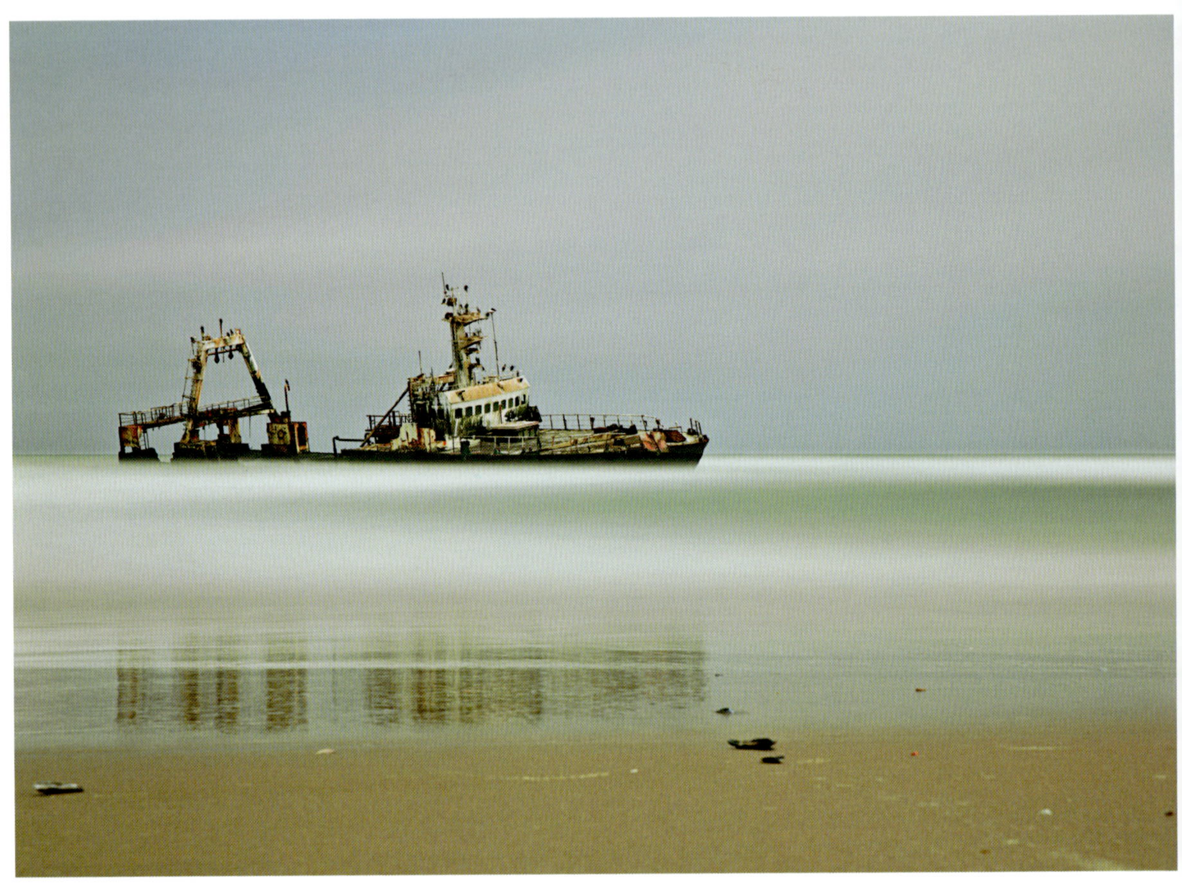

Northern Skeleton Coast

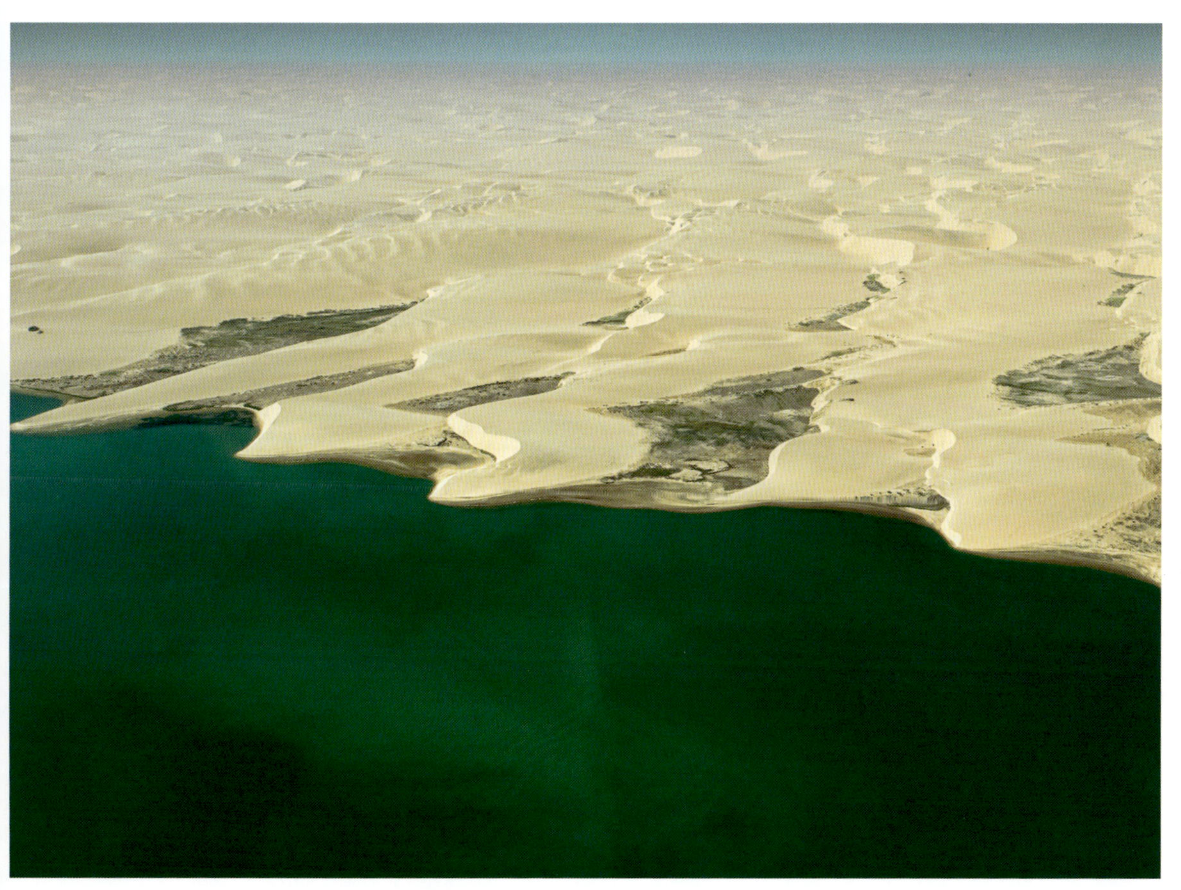

Skeleton Coast

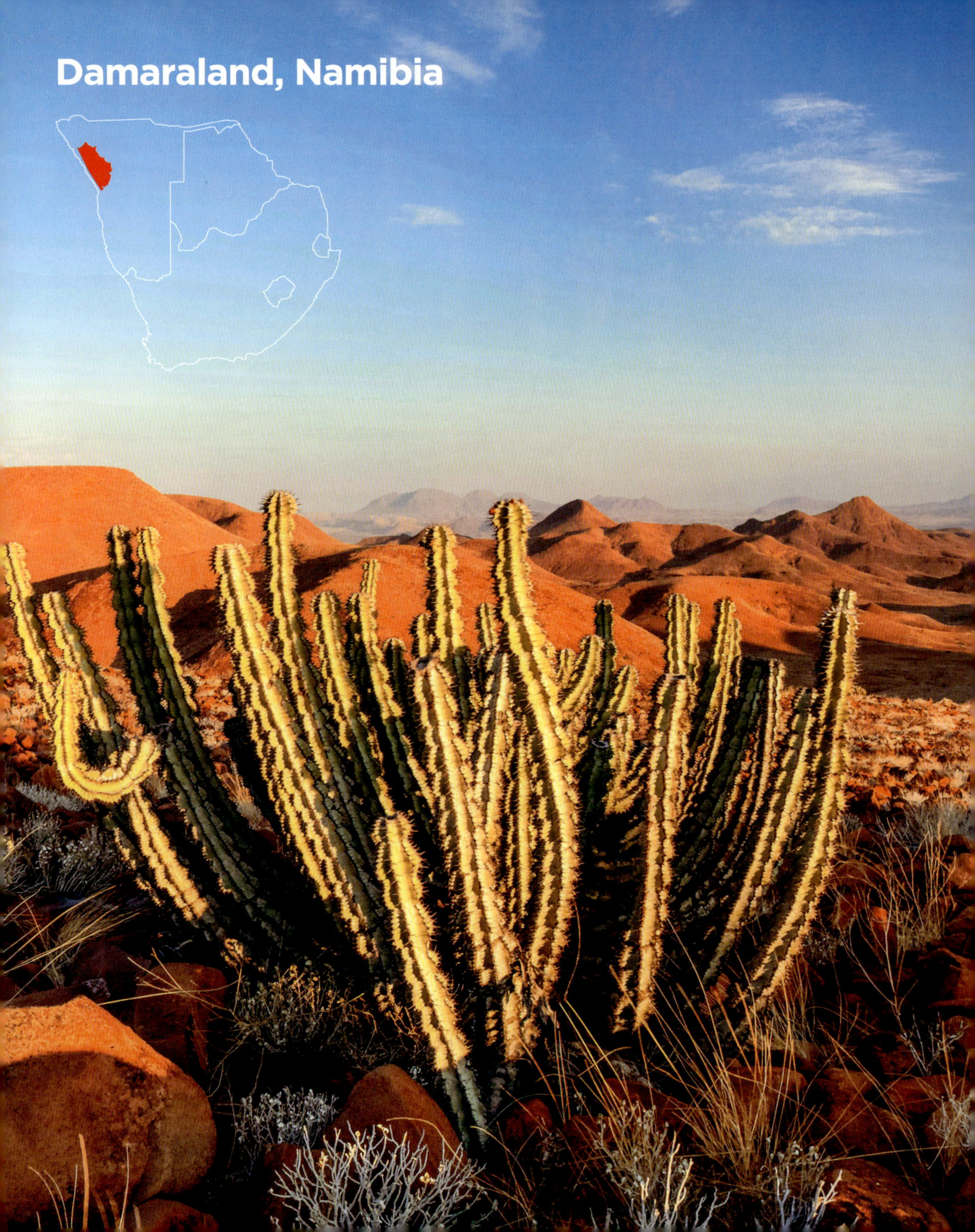
Damaraland, Namibia

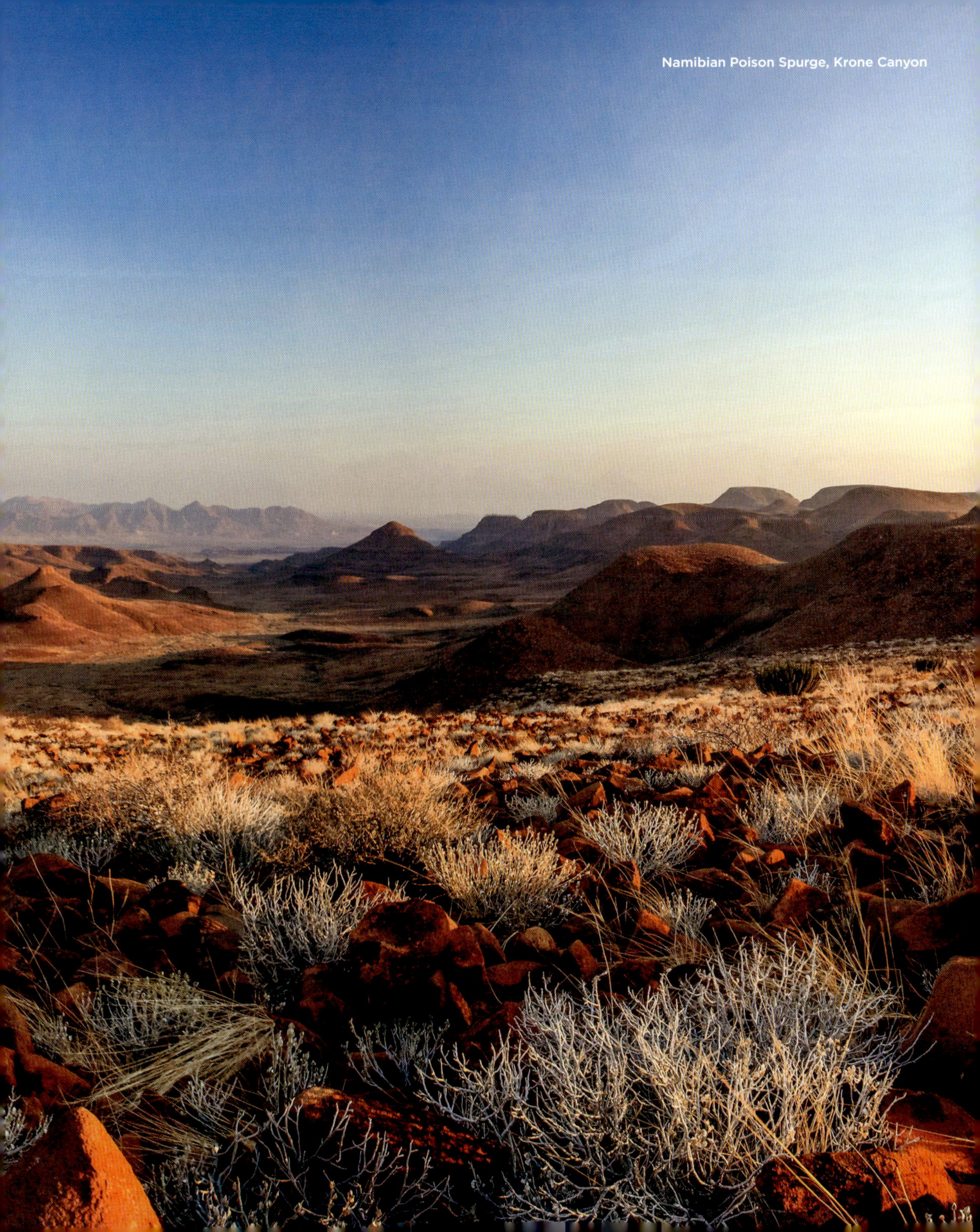
Namibian Poison Spurge, Krone Canyon

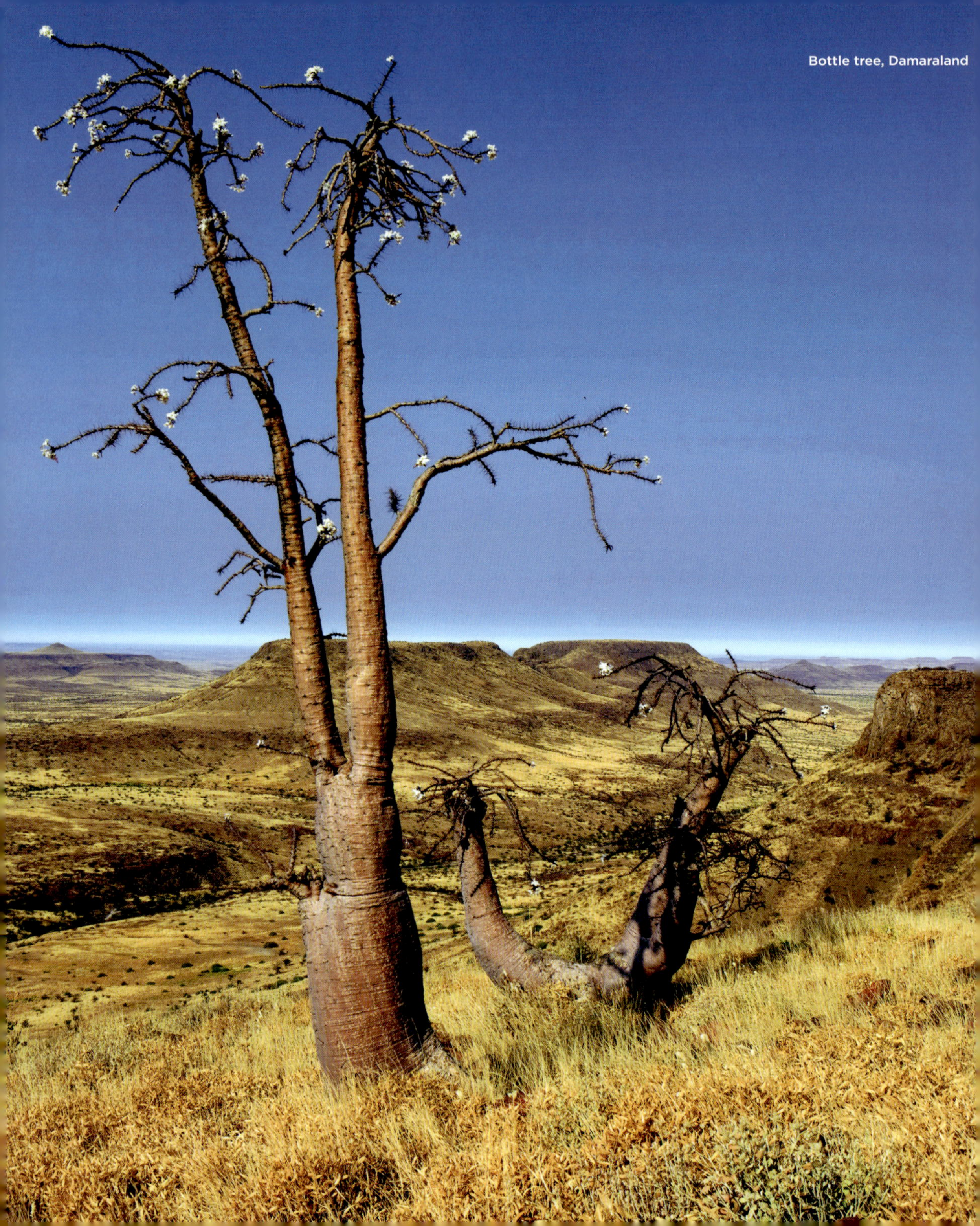

Bottle tree, Damaraland

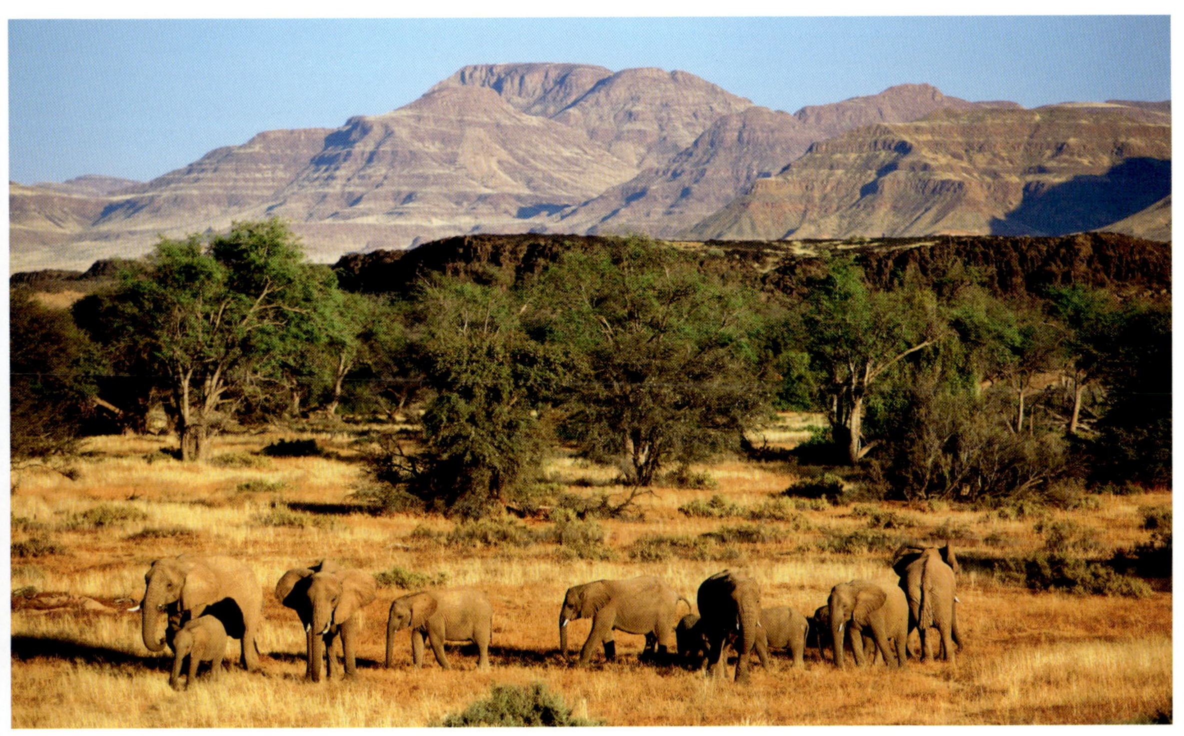

Elephants, ephemeral Huab River

Damaraland
Damaraland offers dramatic sights, with rock formations such as the *Vingerklip* (Rock Finger) (929 m · 3045 ft) and mountains such as the Spitzkoppe (1728 m · 5669 ft) dotting this barren, parched landscape, situated to the south of the Kaokoveld Desert. The rivers which once formed the region's valleys and gorges have long since dried up and only carry water after heavy rainfall.

Le Damaraland
Inhabité, couvert d'une maigre végétation et brûlé par le soleil, le Damaraland, au sud du Kaokoveld, se caractérise par des reliefs spectaculaires avec le Vingerklip (929 m) et le Spitzkoppe (1728 m). Les rivières qui ont creusé les vallées et des ravins sont depuis longtemps asséchées et ne se remplissent d'eau qu'après de fortes pluies.

Damaraland
Menschenleer, karg, ausgedörrt – das südlich des Kaokovelds gelegene Damaraland setzt sich dramatisch in Szene: Felsformationen wie der Vingerklip (929 m) und Berge wie die Spitzkoppe (1728 m) bilden Highlights im Landschaftsbild. Die Flüsse, die Täler und Schluchten geformt haben, sind längst versiegt und führen nur noch nach starken Regenfällen Wasser.

Damaraland
Desierto, árido, reseco – situado al sur de Kaokoveld, Damaraland pone el drama en escena: formaciones rocosas como el Vingerklip (929 m) y montañas como el Spitzkoppe (1728 m) dibujan hitos en el paisaje. Los ríos, valles y las gargantas que están formadas, se han secado y solo cumplen su función tras fuertes y abundantes lluvias.

Damaraland
Disabitato, arido, secco. Il Damaraland, situato a sud del Kaokoveld, entra in scena in modo drammatico: formazioni rocciose come il Vingerklip (929 m) e montagne come lo Spitzkoppe (1728 m) sono i luoghi di spicco del paesaggio. I fiumi, che hanno formato valli e gole, sono prosciugati da molto tempo e ora scorrono solo dopo forti piogge.

Damaraland
Het onbewoonde, kale en uitgedroogde Damaraland, ten zuiden van de Kaokowoestijn, is een spectaculair gebied met rotsformaties als de Vingerklip (929 m) en bergen als de Spitzkoppe (1728 m). De rivieren die hier dalen en ravijnen hebben uitgesleten, zijn allang uitgedroogd en bevatten alleen nog water na zware regens.

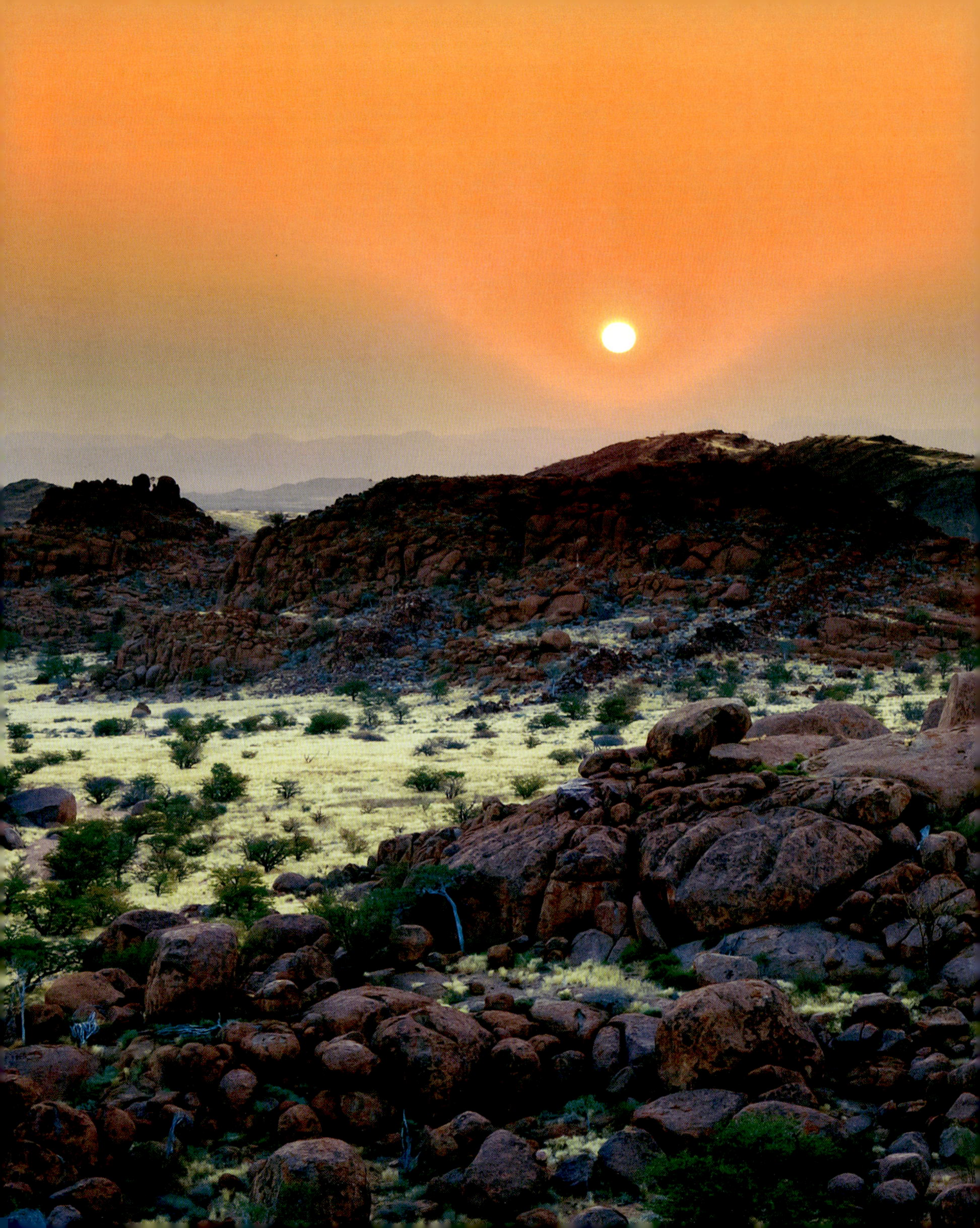

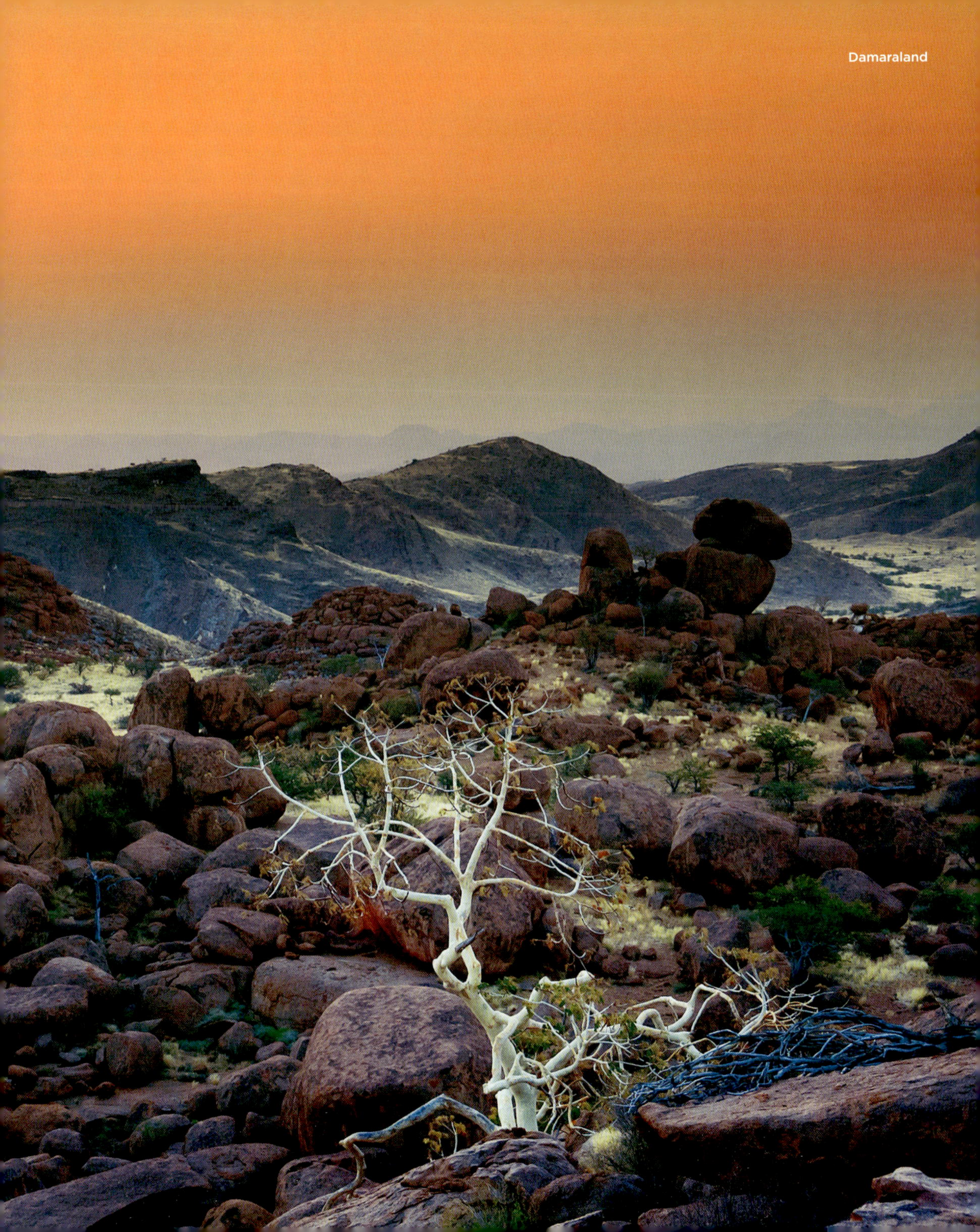
Damaraland

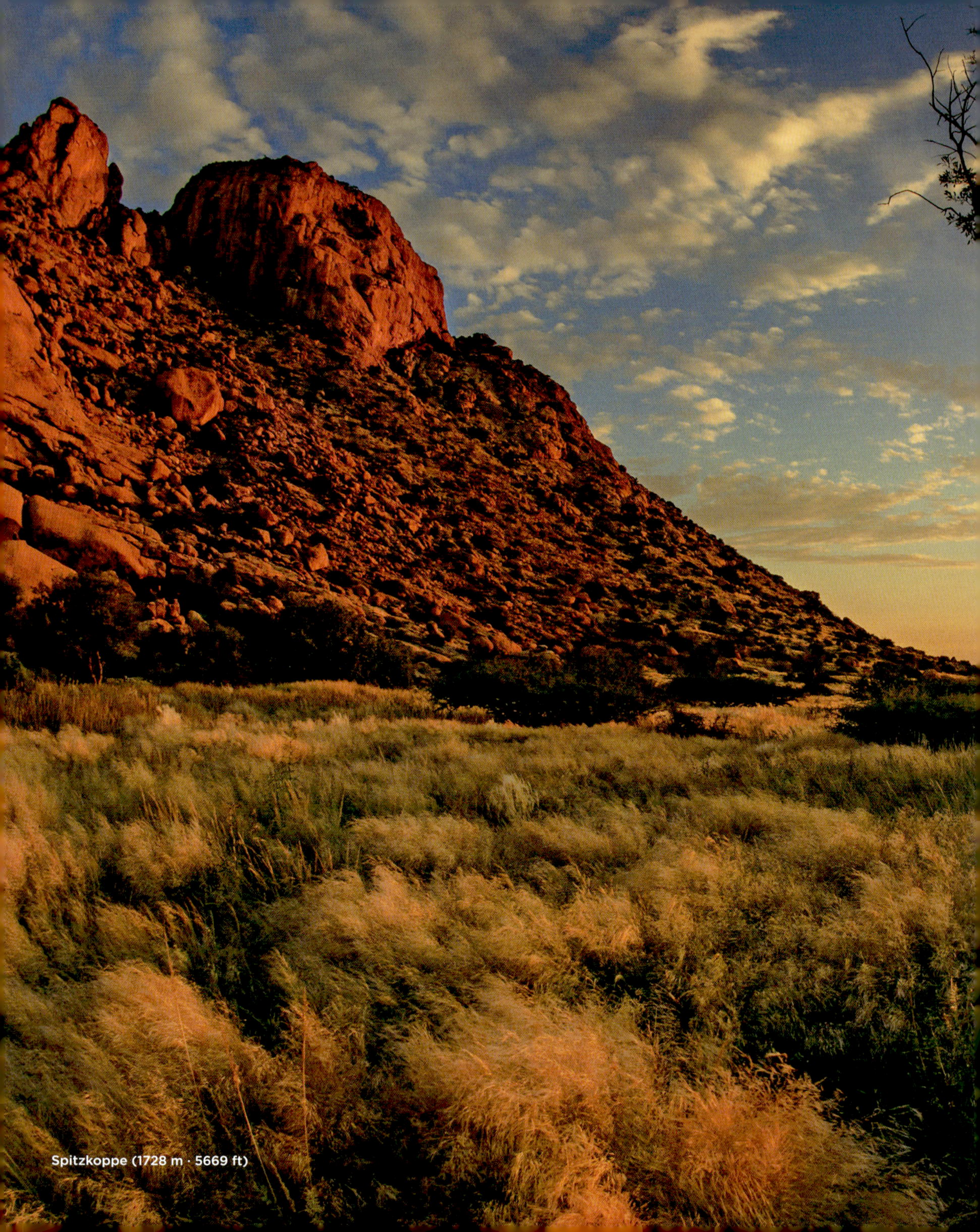

Spitzkoppe (1728 m · 5669 ft)

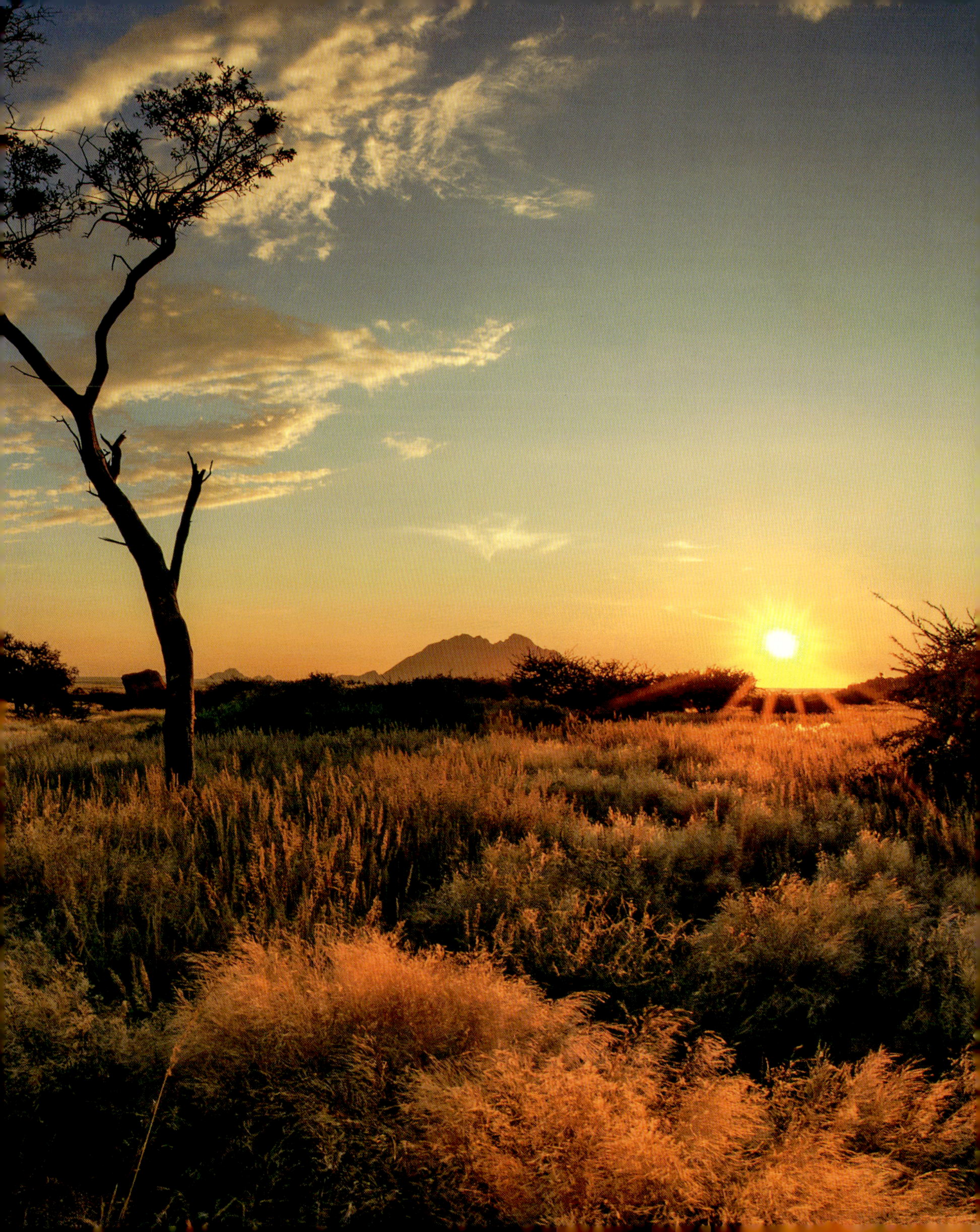

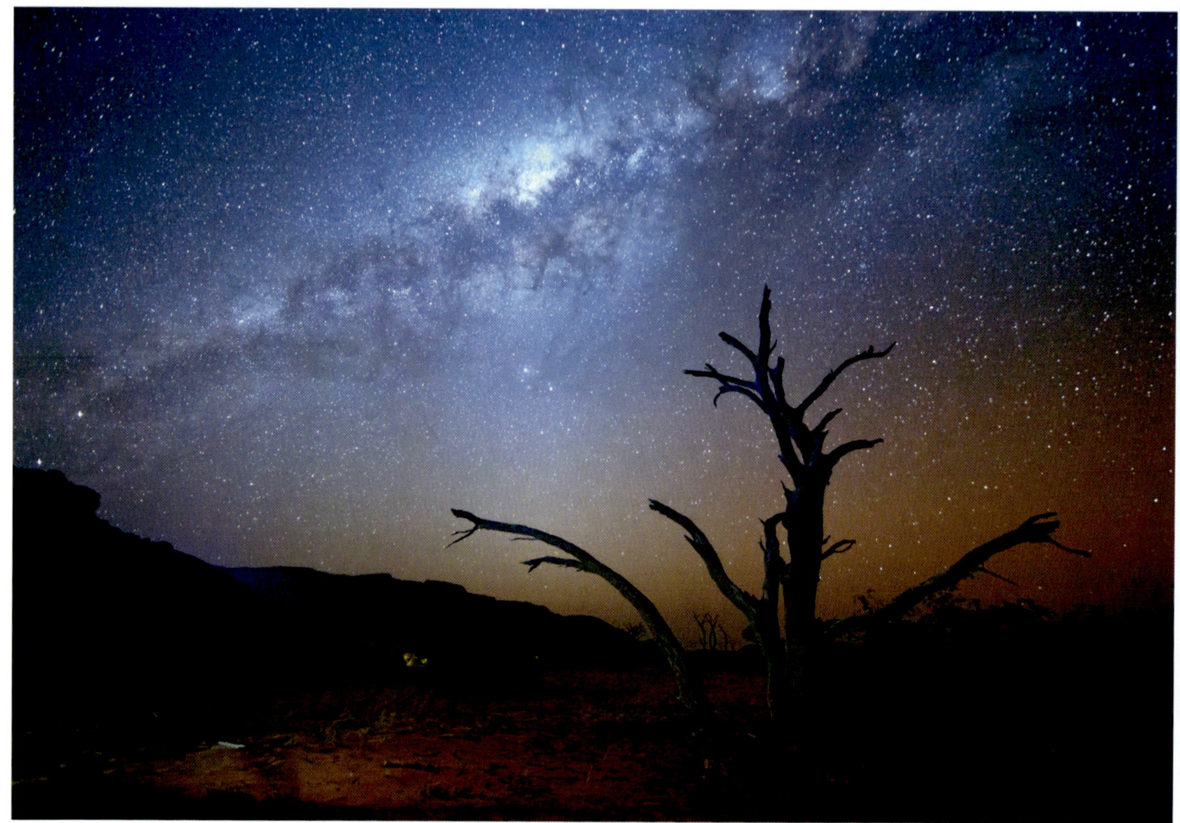

Damaraland

Milky Way
The Milky Way appears quite differently from the southern hemisphere, with the galaxy's centre being visible south of the equator, high in the sky, whereas in the north one can only see towards the periphery of the galaxy.

La Voie lactée
Dans l'hémisphère sud, la Voie lactée se présente sous un tout autre visage que celui qui est habituel dans le ciel septentrional. Son centre est mieux visible au sud de l'équateur, alors que sous nos latitudes seule apparaît la tranche de la galaxie circulaire.

Milchstraße
Die Milchstraße zeigt sich am Südhimmel ganz anders, als man sie von der Nordhalbkugel her kennt: Ihr Zentrum liegt südlich des Äquators, hier steht sie hoch am Himmel, während man im Norden nur den Rand der Galaxie sehen kann.

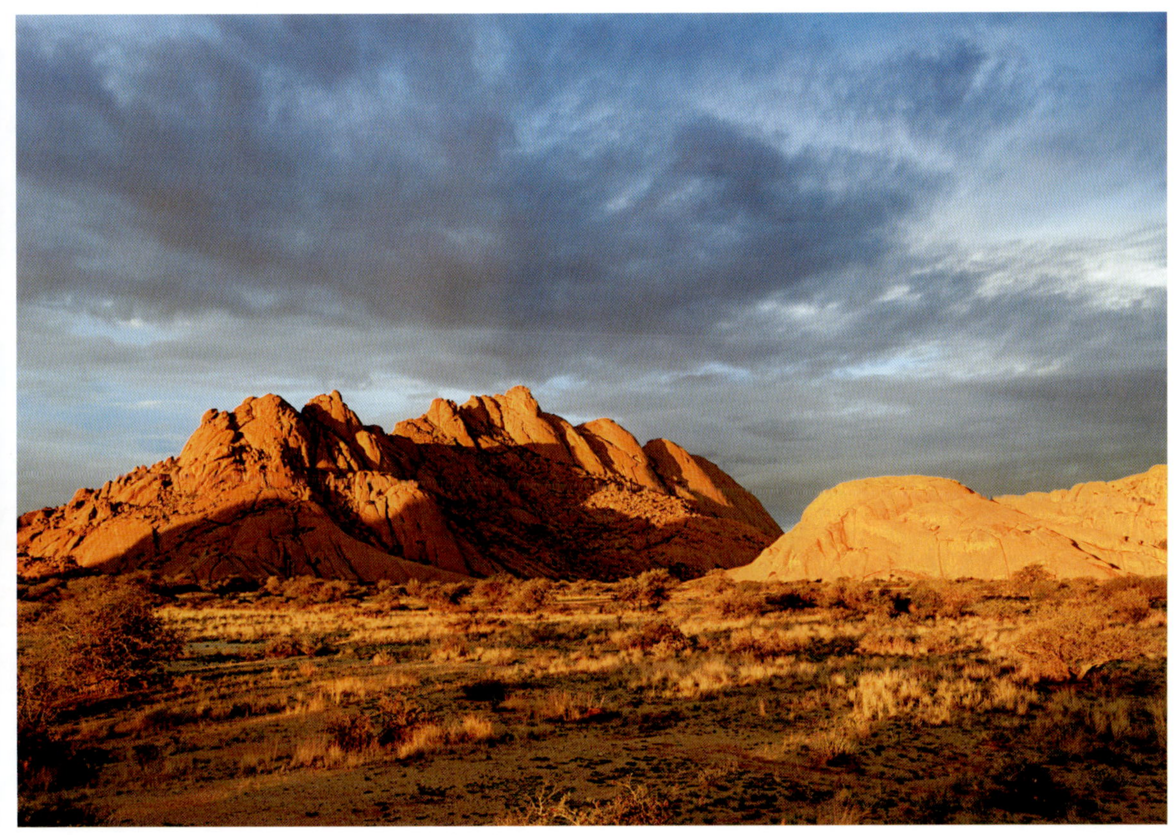

Spitzkoppe (1728 m · 5669 ft)

Vía Láctea
La Vía Láctea se ve en el cielo del sur bastante diferente a lo que conocemos en el hemisferio norte: su centro se encuentra al sur del ecuador, aquí está en lo alto del cielo, mientras que en el norte sólo se puede ver el borde de la galaxia.

Via Lattea
Nel cielo dell'emisfero sud la Via Lattea si mostra totalmente diversa da come è conosciuta nell'emisfero settentrionale: il suo centro si trova a sud dell'Equatore, qui si trova alta nel cielo, mentre nel nord si può vedere solo il margine della galassia.

Melkweg
De Melkweg ziet er aan het zuidelijke firmament heel anders uit dan wanneer hij vanaf het noordelijk halfrond wordt aanschouwd; het galactische centrum staat hier hoog aan de hemel, terwijl op het noordelijk halfrond slechts een rand van het sterrenstelsel kan worden gezien.

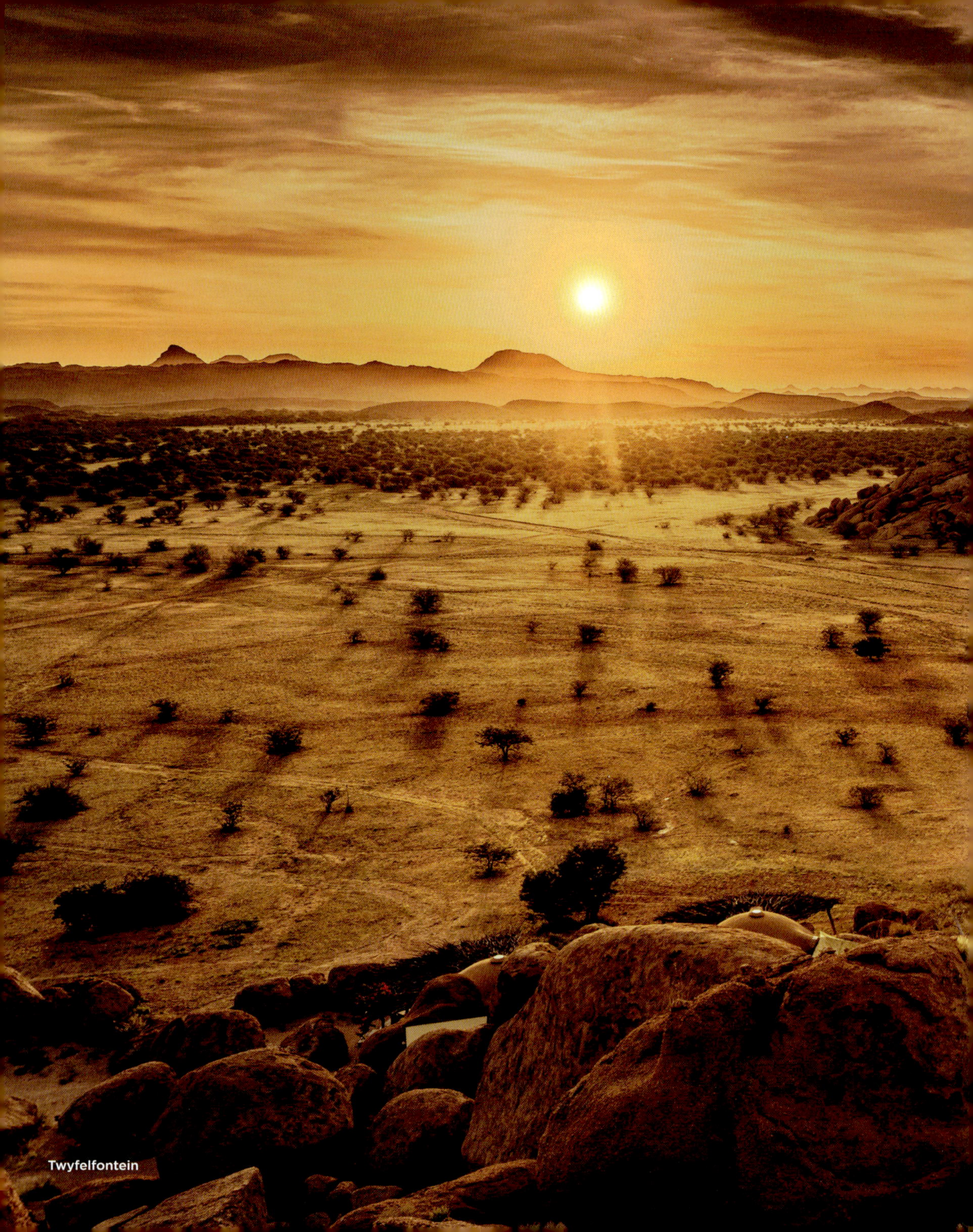

Twyfelfontein

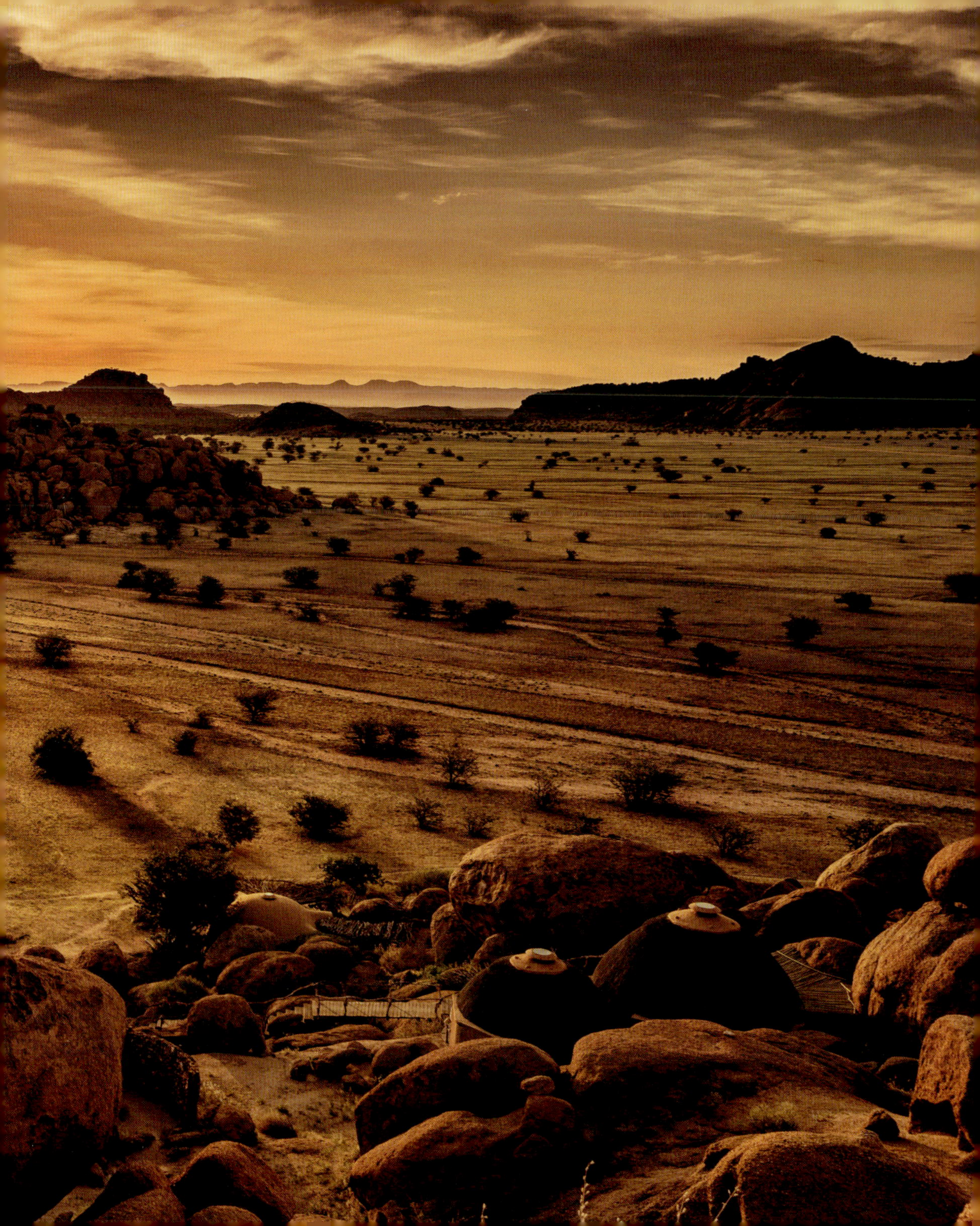

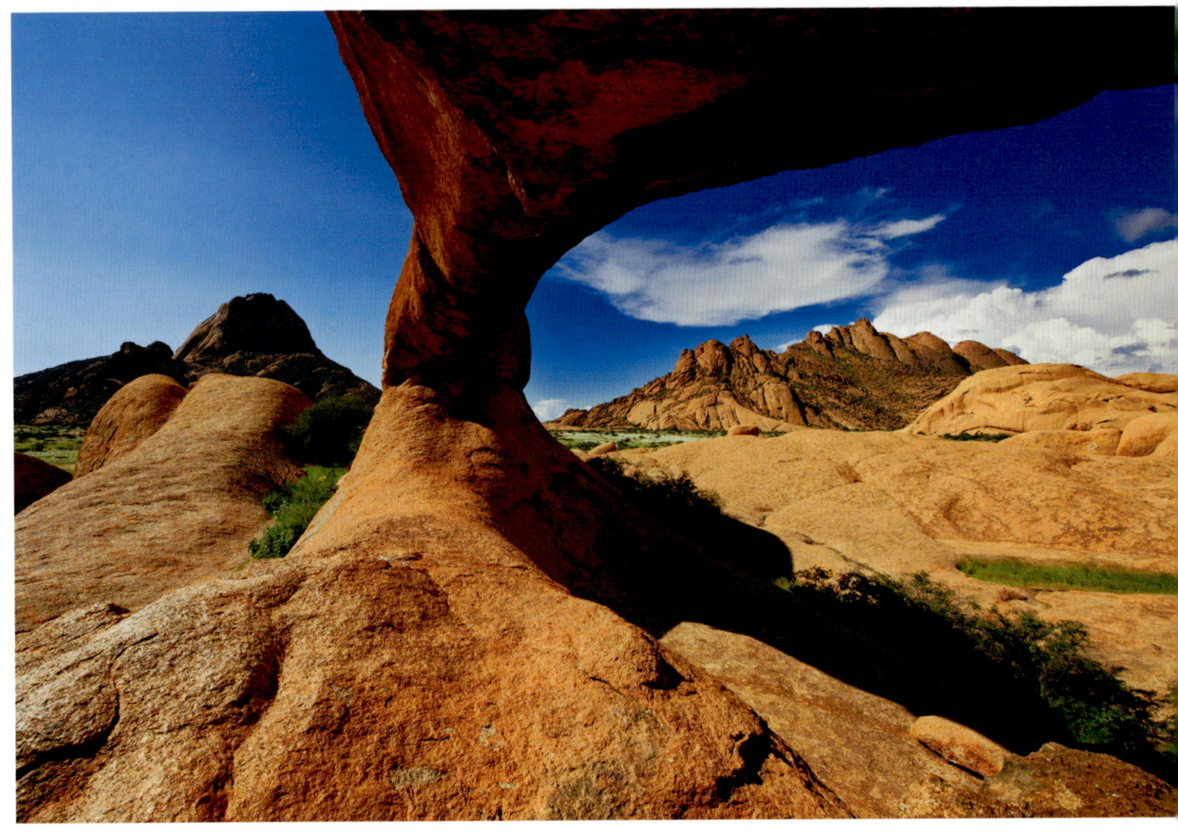

Spitzkoppe (1728 m · 5669 ft)

Spitzkoppe
The Spitzkoppe is a national monument and has been called the "Matterhorn of Namibia", due to its distinctive shape. It dates back more than a 100 million years, with the mesa rising 700 m (2297 ft) above the surrounding plain.

Le Spitzkoppe
Monument national en Namibie, le Spitzkoppe est surnommé le « Matterhorn de la Namibie » en raison de sa silhouette particulière. Sa formation remonte à 100 millions d'années. Ce plateau s'élève à 700 m au-dessus de la plaine qui l'entoure.

Spitzkoppe
Die Spitzkoppe ist ein nationales Denkmal Namibias und wird wegen ihrer markanten Form auch „Matterhorn Namibias" genannt Sie entstand vor mehr als 100 Millionen Jahren. Der Tafelberg überragt die ihn umgebende Ebene um 700 m.

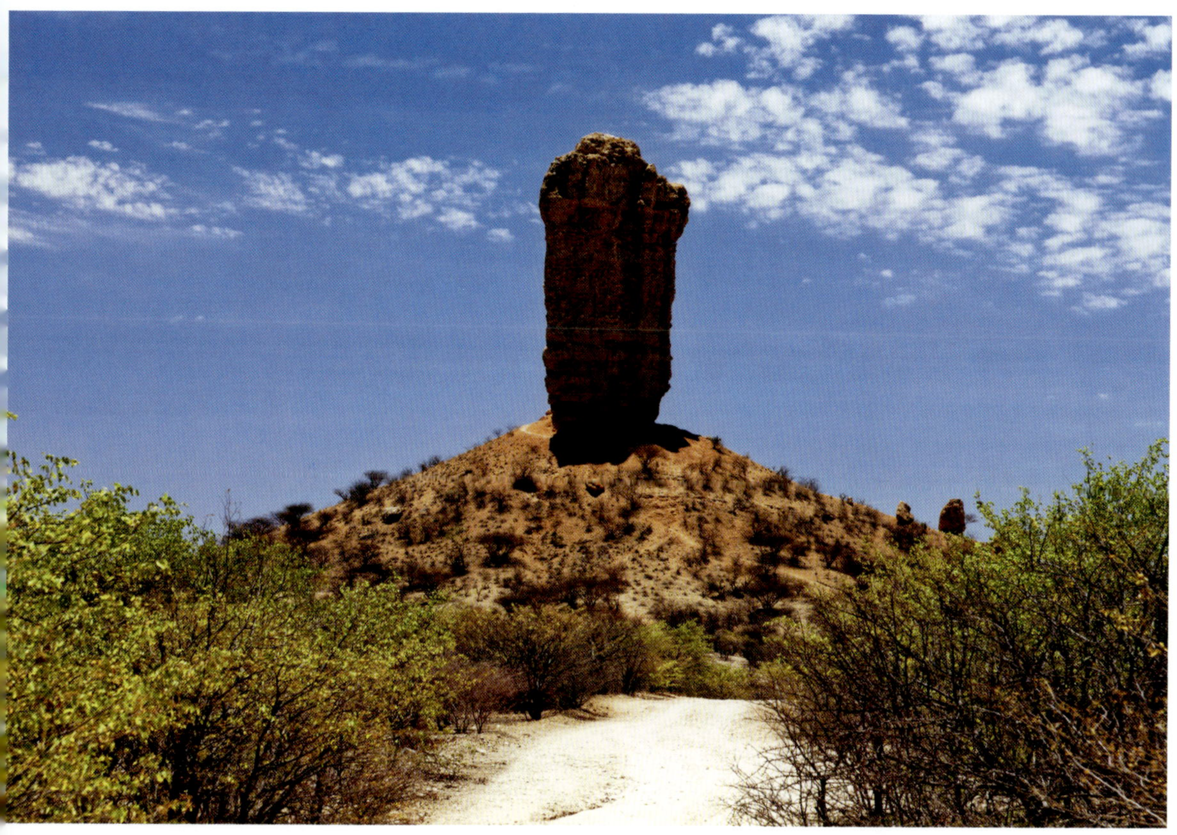

Vingerklip (929 m · 3047 ft)

Spitzkoppe
El Spitzkoppe es un monumento nacional de Namibia y se llama así debido a su forma distintiva parecida al "Cervino de Namibia". Se formó hace más de 100 millones de años. El Spitzkoppe es una meseta y se proyecta más allá del plano circundante unos 700 m).

Spitzkoppe
Lo Spitzkoppe è un monumento nazionale della Namibia e a causa della sua forma marcata viene chiamato anche "il Cervino della Namibia". Nacque oltre 100 milioni di anni fa. Lo Spitzkoppe è un monte a tavola e supera l di 700 m le pianure che lo circondano.

Spitzkoppe
De Spitzkoppe is een nationaal monument in Namibië en wordt wegens zijn markante vorm de "Matterhorn van Namibië" genoemd. De berg, die honderd miljoen jaar geleden ontstond, is een tafelberg en torent 700 m boven de omringende vlakte uit.

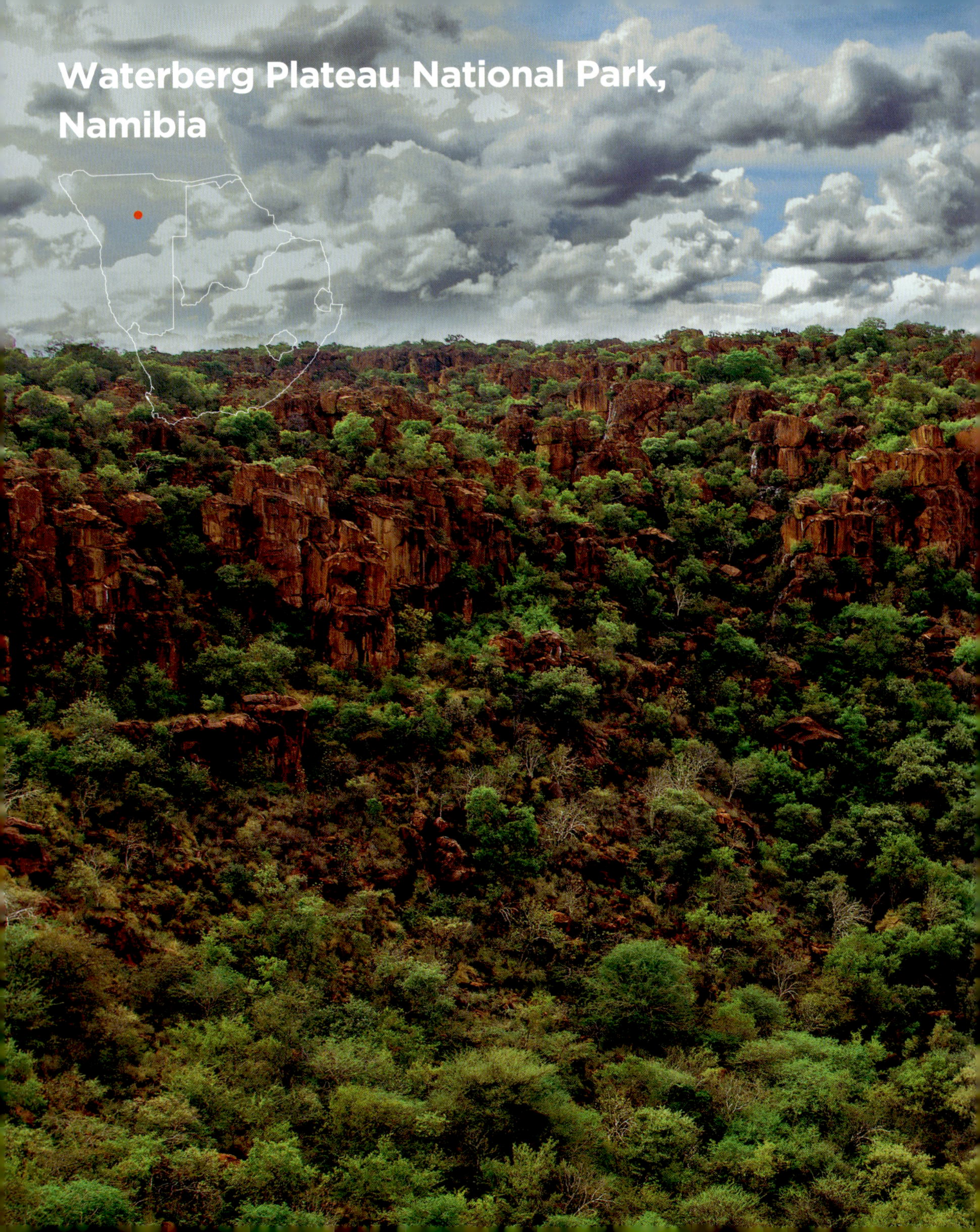
Waterberg Plateau National Park,
Namibia

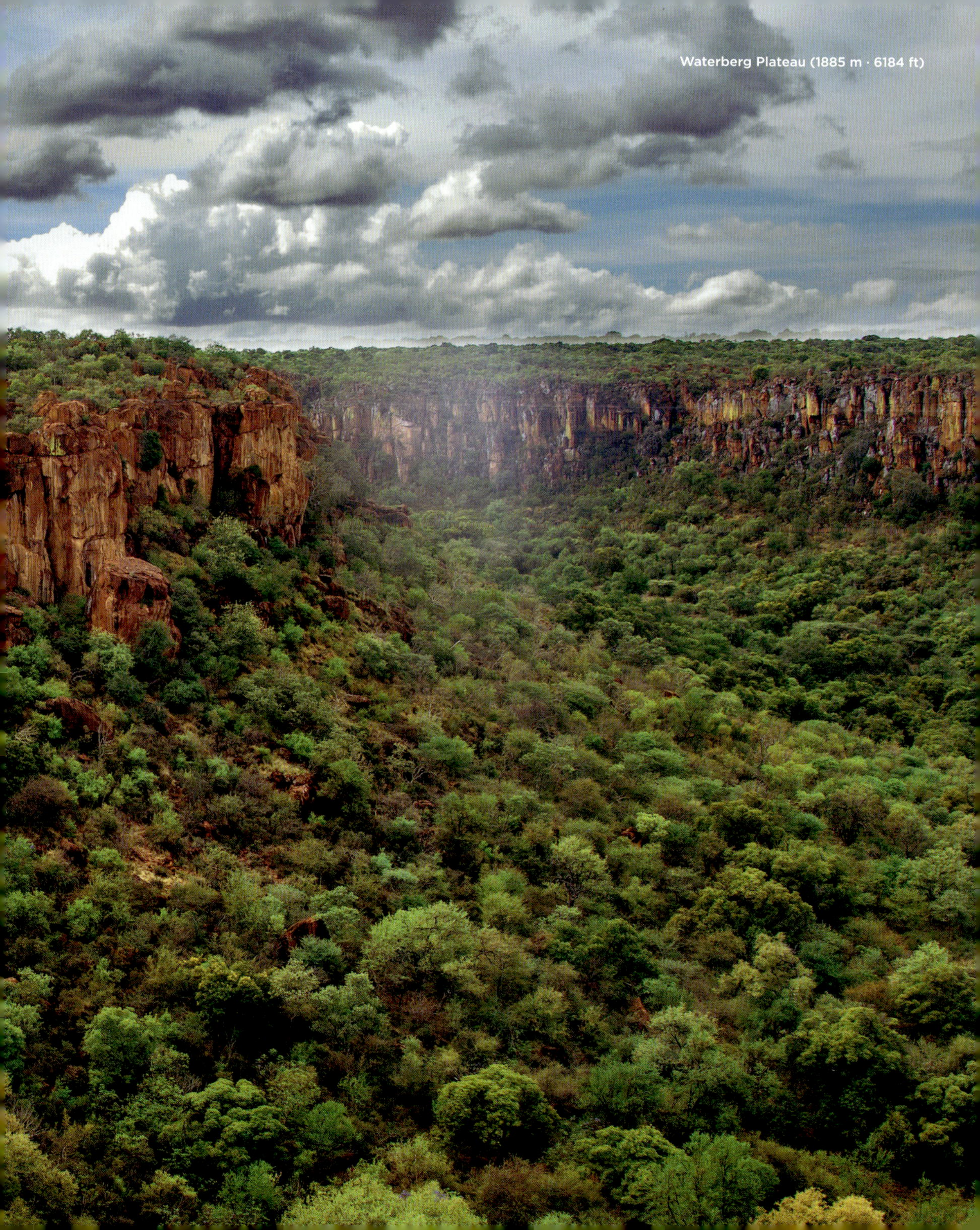
Waterberg Plateau (1885 m · 6184 ft)

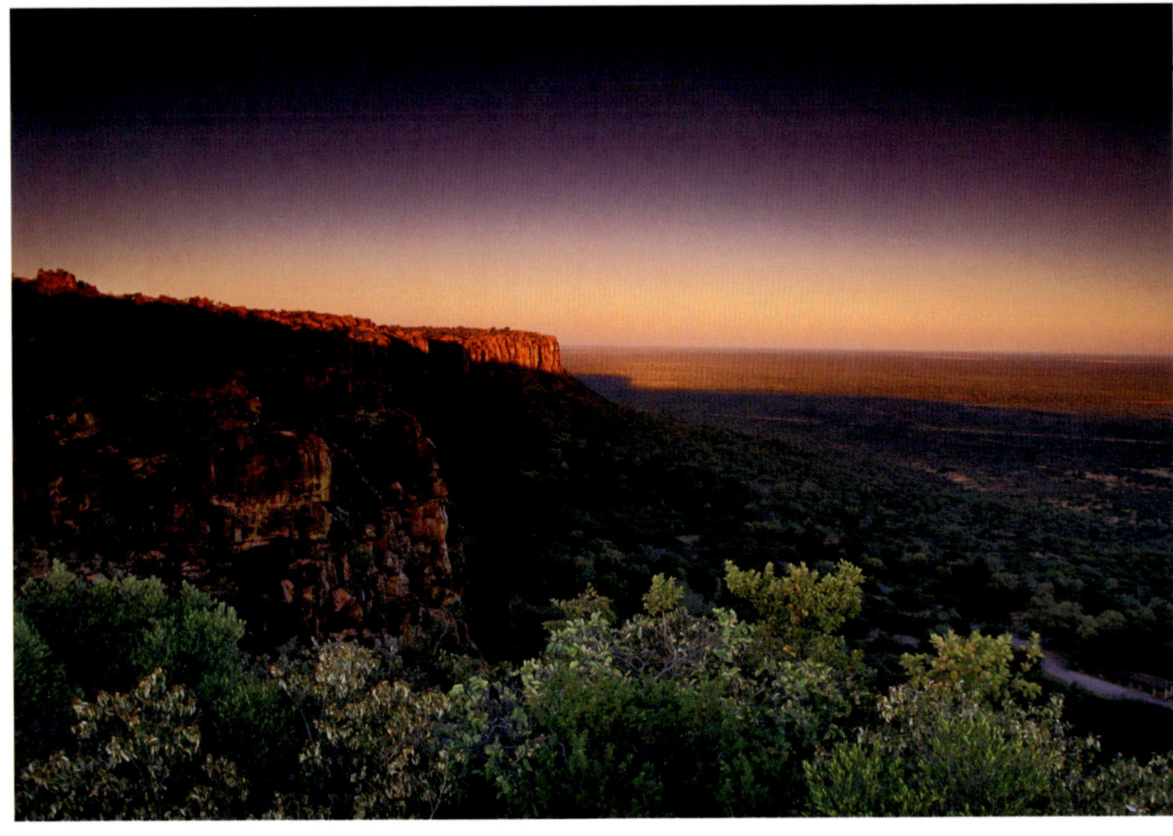

Waterberg Plateau (1885 m · 6184 ft)

Waterberg Plateau
The Waterberg is a mesa created 150 million years ago, rising 200 m (656 ft) above the Kalahari plain. The mountain is part of the Waterberg Plateau Park, whose savanna provides a home to many mammal, reptile, and bird species. It is also one of the last spots in Namibia where one may find the Cape vulture.

Plateau du Waterberg
Le Waterberg est un plateau vieux de 150 millions d'années et qui domine de ses 200 m l'étendue plate du Kalahari. Ce relief fait partie du parc national du plateau du Waterberg, dont les savanes arborée et arbustive accueillent de nombreux mammifères, reptiles et oiseaux. Les derniers vautours chassefientes y ont trouvé refuge.

Waterberg Plateau
Der Waterberg ist ein Tafelberg, der vor 150 Millionen Jahren angehoben wurde und 200 m über der ebenen Kalahari emporragt. Der Berg ist Teil des Waterberg-Plateau-Nationalparks, in dem Busch- und Baumsavanne zahlreichen Säugetieren, Reptilien und Vögeln einen Lebensraum bieten. Hier finden auch die letzten Kapgeier Namibias ihr Rückzugsgebiet.

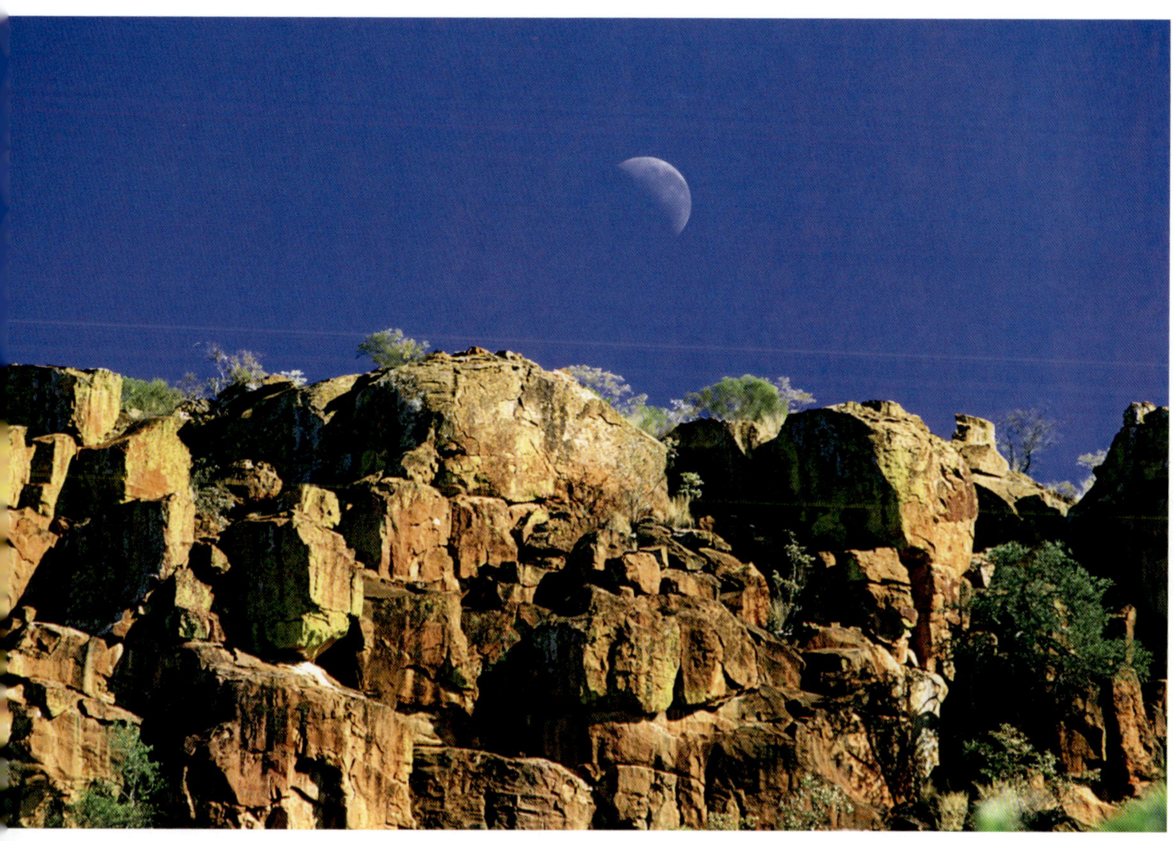

Waterberg Mountain

Waterberg

El Waterberg es una meseta que se formó hace 150 millones de años y se eleva 200 m por encima del plano de Kalahari. La montaña es parte del Parque Nacional Waterberg, los numerosos arbustos y árboles de la sabana proporcionan un hábitat a mamíferos, reptiles y aves. Aquí encuentra su refugio el último Buitre de El Cabo de Namibia.

Altopiano del Waterberg

Il Waterberg è un monte a tavola che ebbe origine 150 milioni di anni fa e svetta per 200 m sopra il piatto Kalahari. Il monte fa parte del Parco Nazionale dell'altopiano del Waterberg, nei cespugli e negli alberi della sua savana trovano lo spazio vitale numerose specie di mammiferi, rettili e uccelli. Qui trovano rifugio anche gli ultimi grifoni del Capo della Namibia.

Waterbergplateau

De Waterberg is een tafelberg die 150 miljoen jaar geleden tot een hoogte van 200 m boven de omringende Kalahari werd opgestuwd. De berg maakt deel uit van het Nationale Park Waterbergplateau, waar talloze zoogdieren, reptielen en vogels op de struik- en bossavanne leven. Hier vinden ook de laatste Kaapse gieren van Namibië een toevluchtsoord.

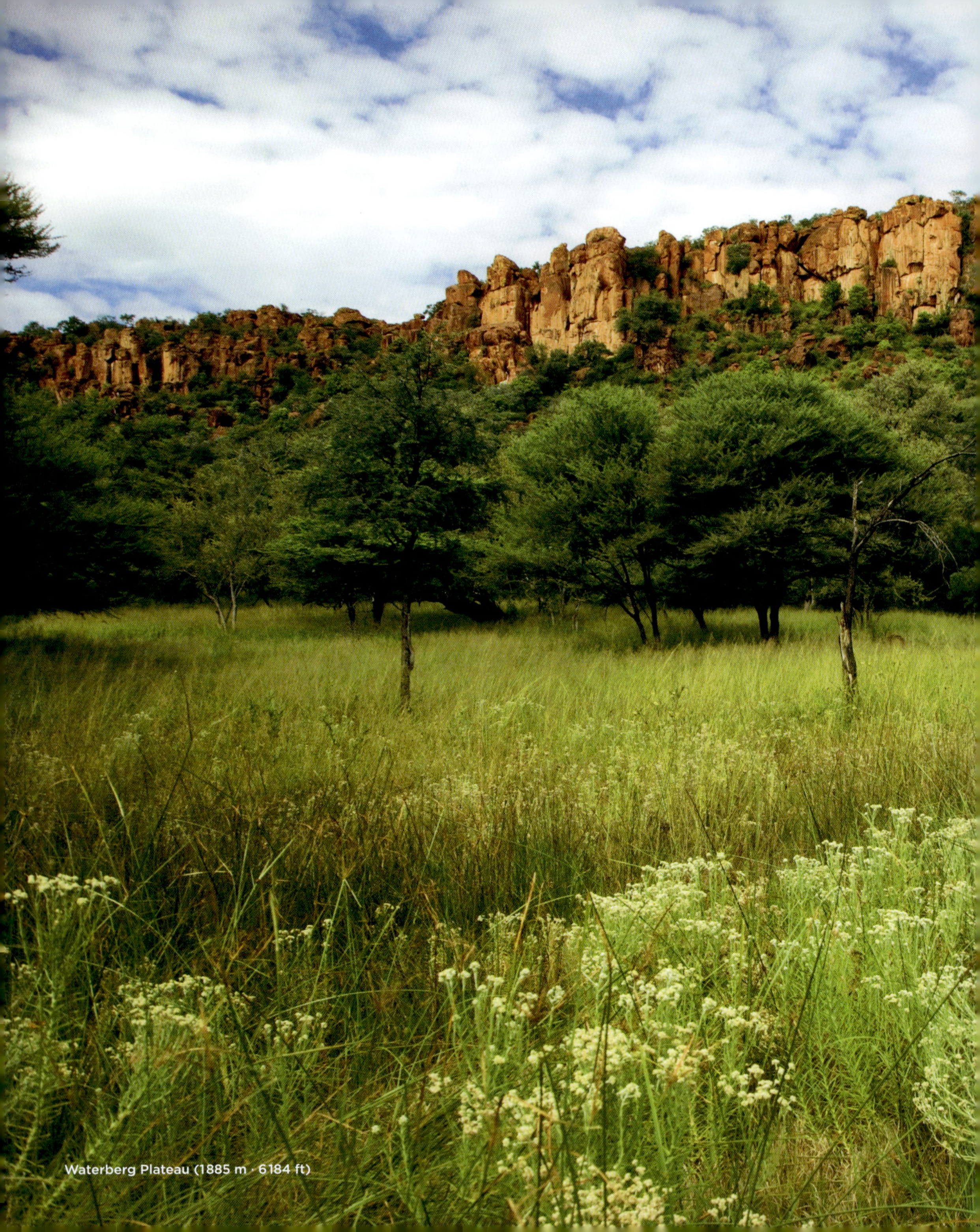

Waterberg Plateau (1885 m · 6184 ft)

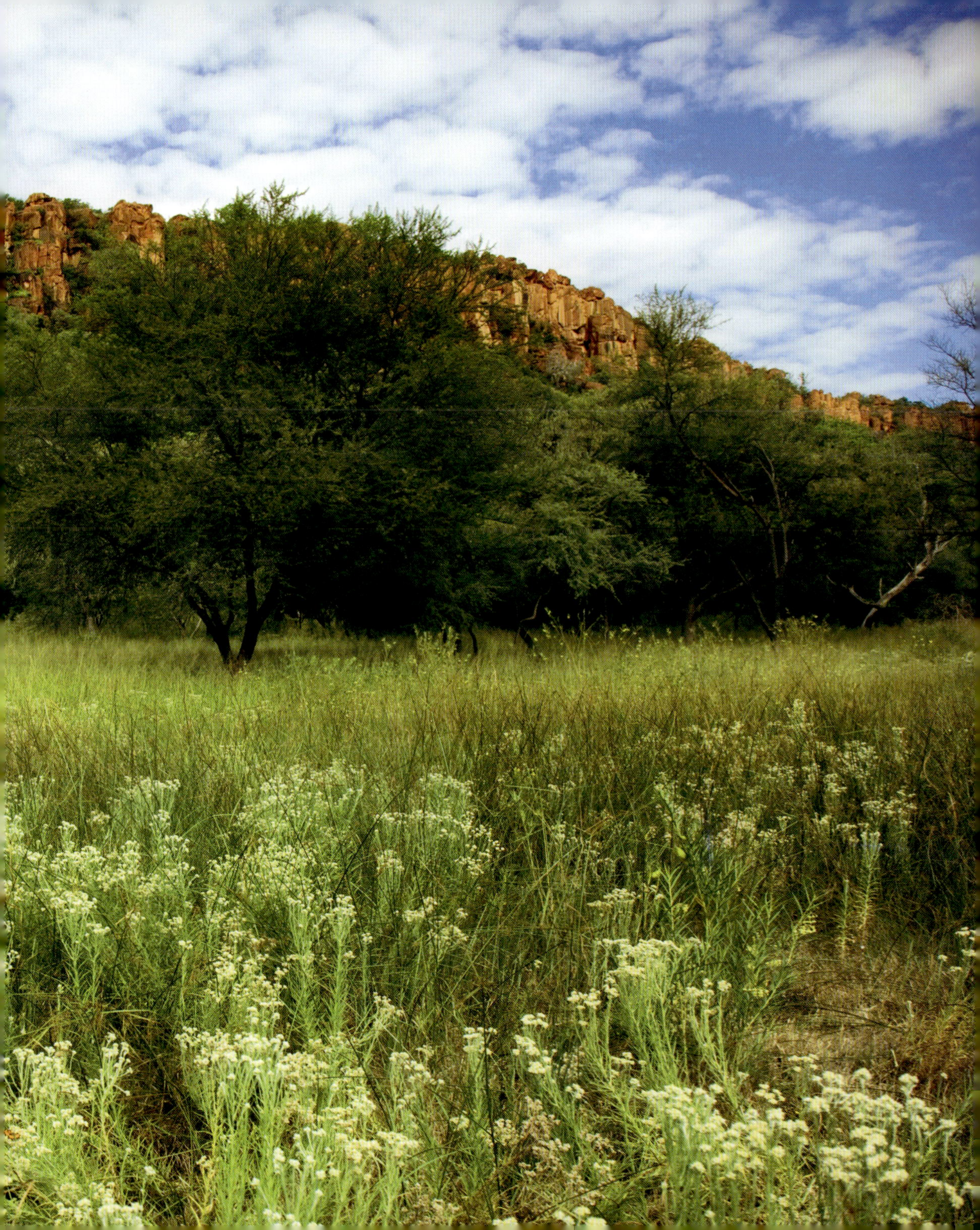

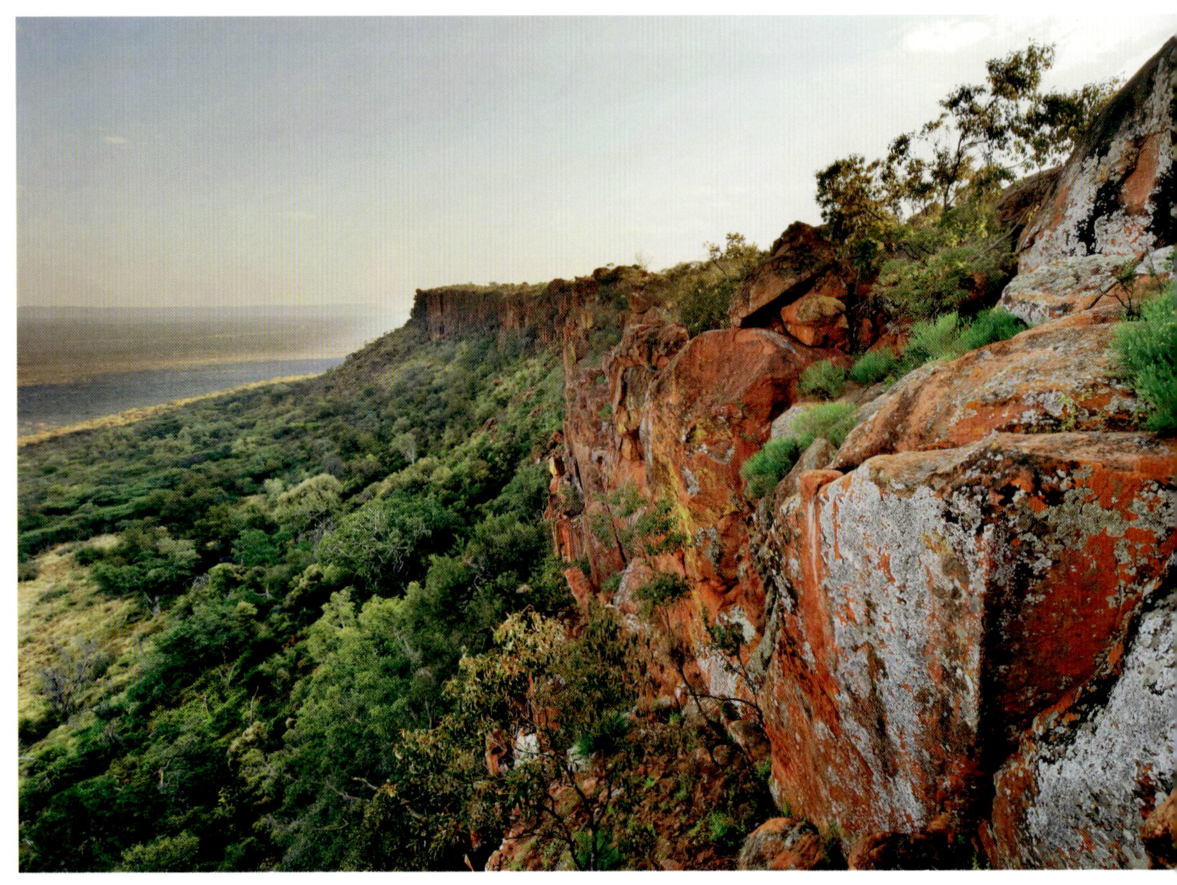

Waterberg Plateau (1885 m · 6184 ft)

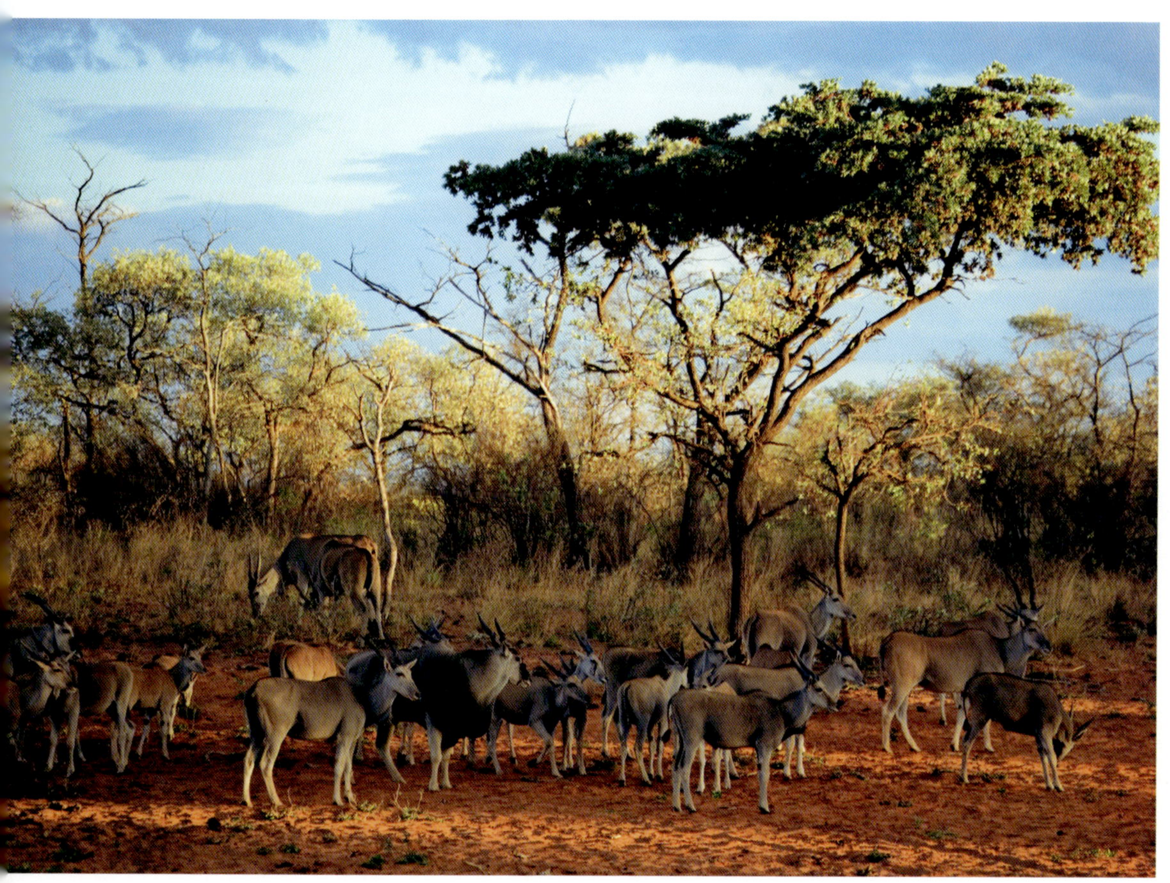

Eland antelopes, Waterberg Plateau National Park

Namib-Naukluft National Park, Walvis Bay & Windhoek, Namibia

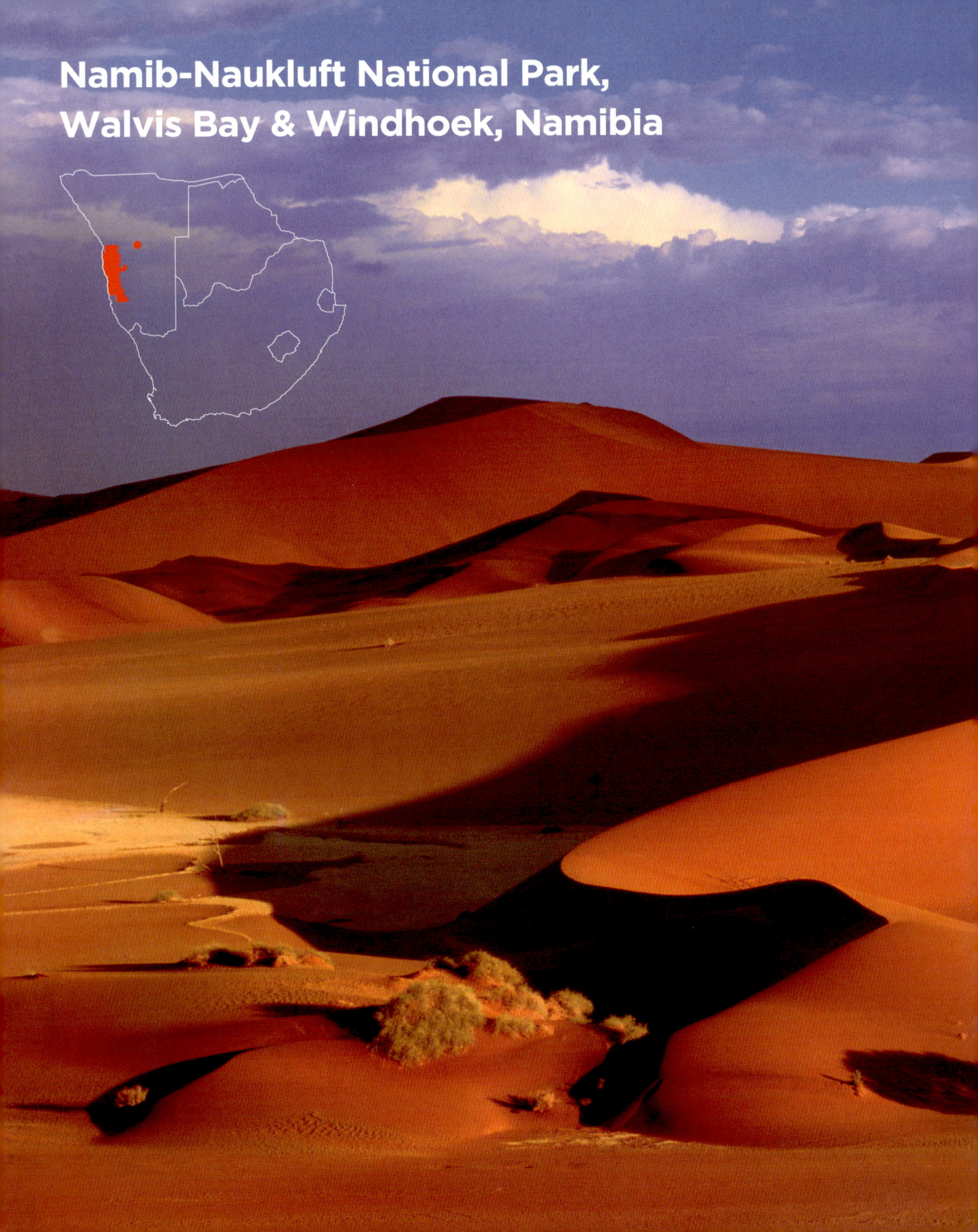

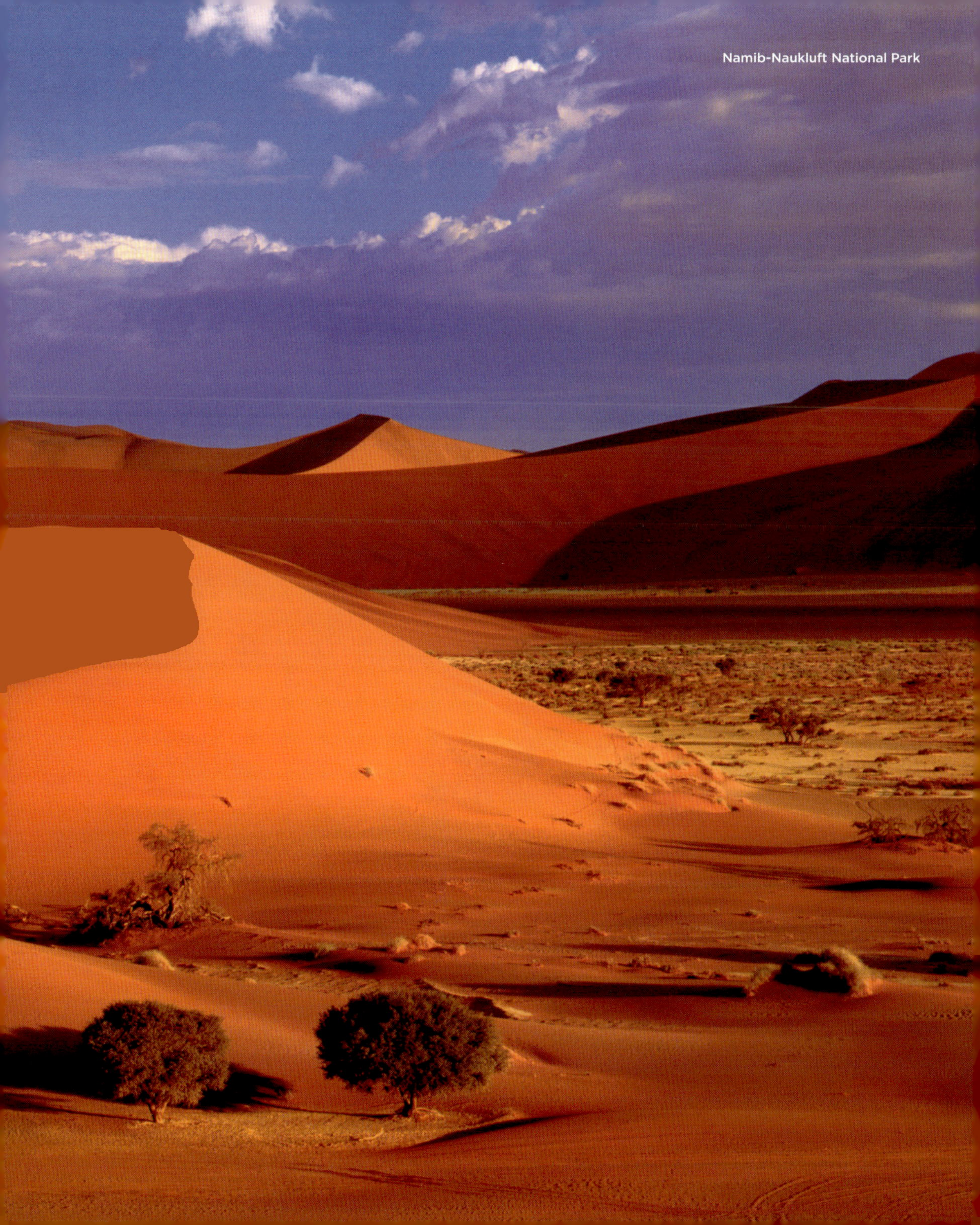

Namib-Naukluft National Park

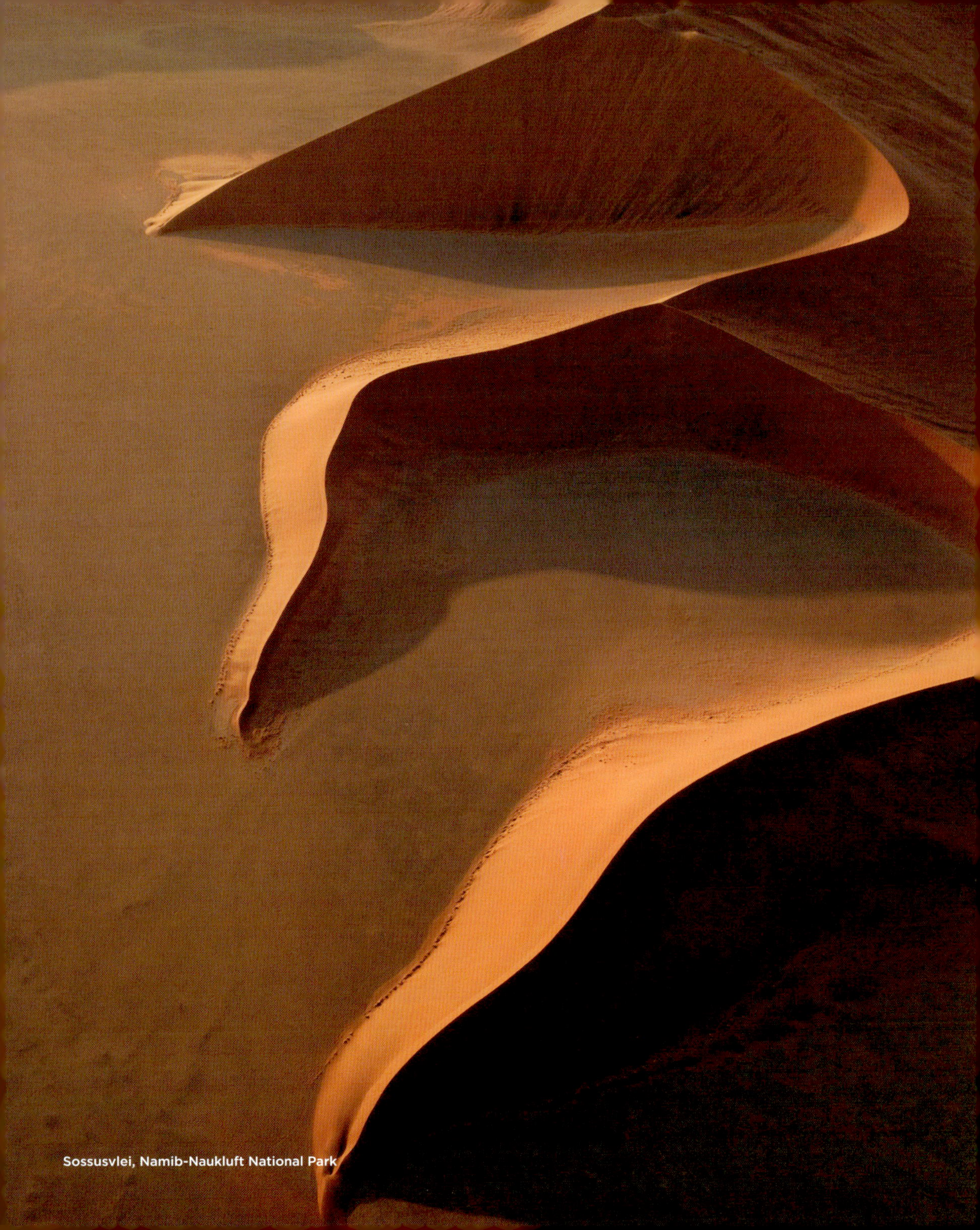
Sossusvlei, Namib-Naukluft National Park

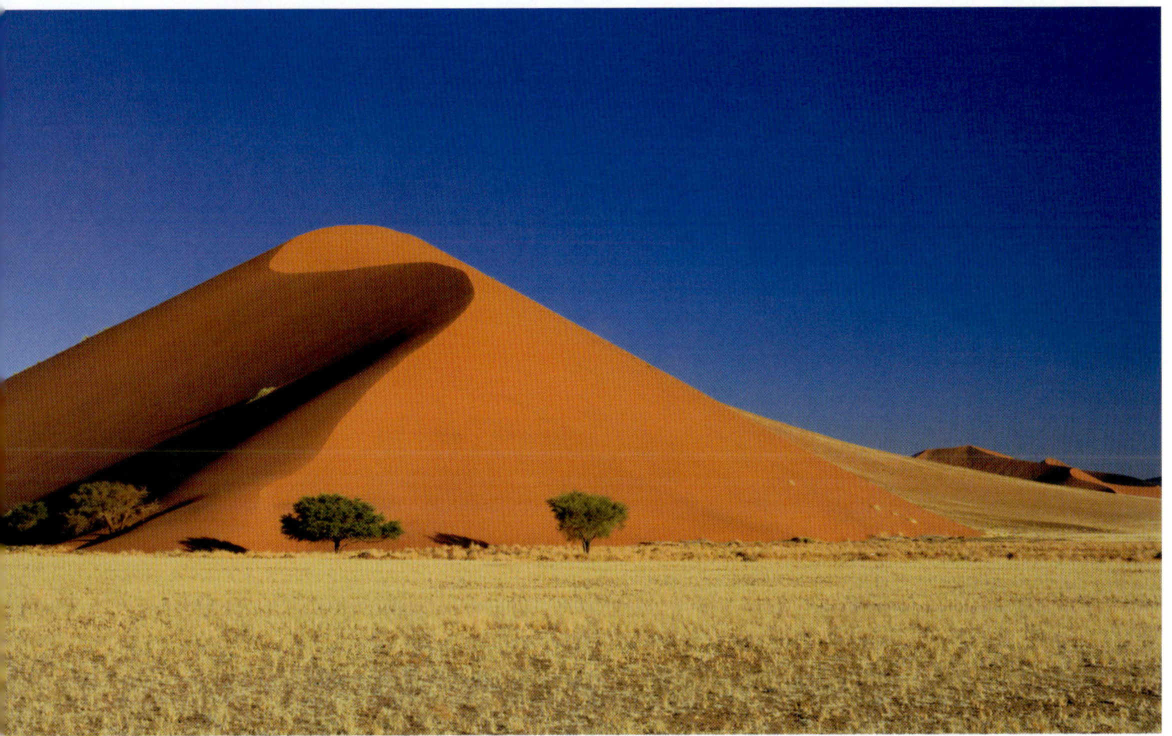

Sossusvlei, Namib-Naukluft National Park

Namib-Naukluft National Park
Dating back some 80 million years, the Namib is considered to be the world's oldest desert. Although it lies directly on the Atlantic, it is one of the driest regions on the planet. Only coastal mist provides the moisture which has allowed animals to survive this harsh climate. The deep red to golden yellow sand dunes on the edge of the Sossusvlei, a salt and clay pan, reach heights of up to 300 m (984 ft).

Namib-Naukluft-Nationalpark
Mit einem Alter von rund 80 Millionen Jahren ist die Namib die älteste Wüste der Welt. Obwohl sie direkt an den Atlantik grenzt, gehört sie zu den trockensten Regionen unseres Planeten. Einzig Küstennebel liefert die Feuchtigkeit, die den über einen langen Evolutionszeitraum angepassten Tieren das Überleben ermöglicht. Die tiefrot bis goldgelb strahlenden Dünen am Rande des Sossusvlei, einer Salz-Ton-Pfanne, erreichen Höhen bis zu 300 m.

Parco Nazionale di Namib-Naukluft
Nato circa 80 milioni di anni fa, il Namib è il deserto più antico del mondo. Sebbene confini direttamente con l'Atlantico, appartiene ad una delle regioni più secche del nostro pianeta. Soltanto la foschia costiera fornisce l'umidità che permette la sopravvivenza degli animali adatti durante un lungo periodo di tempo evolutivo. Le dune splendenti che vanno dal rosso intenso al giallo oro ai margini del Sossusvlei, una conca di sale e argilla, possono raggiungere un'altezza di 300 m.

Le parc national du Namib-Naukluft
Avec ses quelque 80 millions d'années, le Namib est le plus ancien désert du monde. Bien qu'il soit bordé par l'Atlantique, c'est l'une des régions les plus arides de la planète. Seuls les brouillards côtiers fournissent l'humidité indispensable à la survie d'animaux qui se sont adaptés au fil d'une très longue évolution. Les dunes éclatantes, rouge foncé à jaune d'or, de la cuvette salée argileuse du Sossusvlei culminent à 300 m.

Parque Nacional Namib-Naukluft
Con una edad de 80 millones de años, el Namib es el desierto más antiguo del mundo. A pesar de que limita con el Océano Atlántico, es una de las regiones más secas del planeta. Sólo la niebla costera proporciona la humedad que permite que los animales adaptados durante un largo período evolutivo sobrevivan. Las brillantes dunas de color rojo oscuro a amarillo oro en el borde de Sossusvlei, una olla de sal y arcilla, alcanzan hasta 300 m de altura.

Namib-Naukluft National Park
Met een ouderdom van tachtig miljoen jaar is de Namib de oudste woestijn op aarde. Hoewel ze direct aan de Atlantische kust ligt, behoort ze tot de droogste regio's van onze planeet. Alleen mist die vanaf zee het binnenland in drijft, zorgt voor enig vocht, waardoor dieren die zich hier gedurende lange tijd hebben aangepast, kunnen overleven. De dieprood tot goudgeel glanzende duinen aan de rand van de Sossusvlei, een bekken van zout en klei, kunnen tot wel 300 m hoog worden.

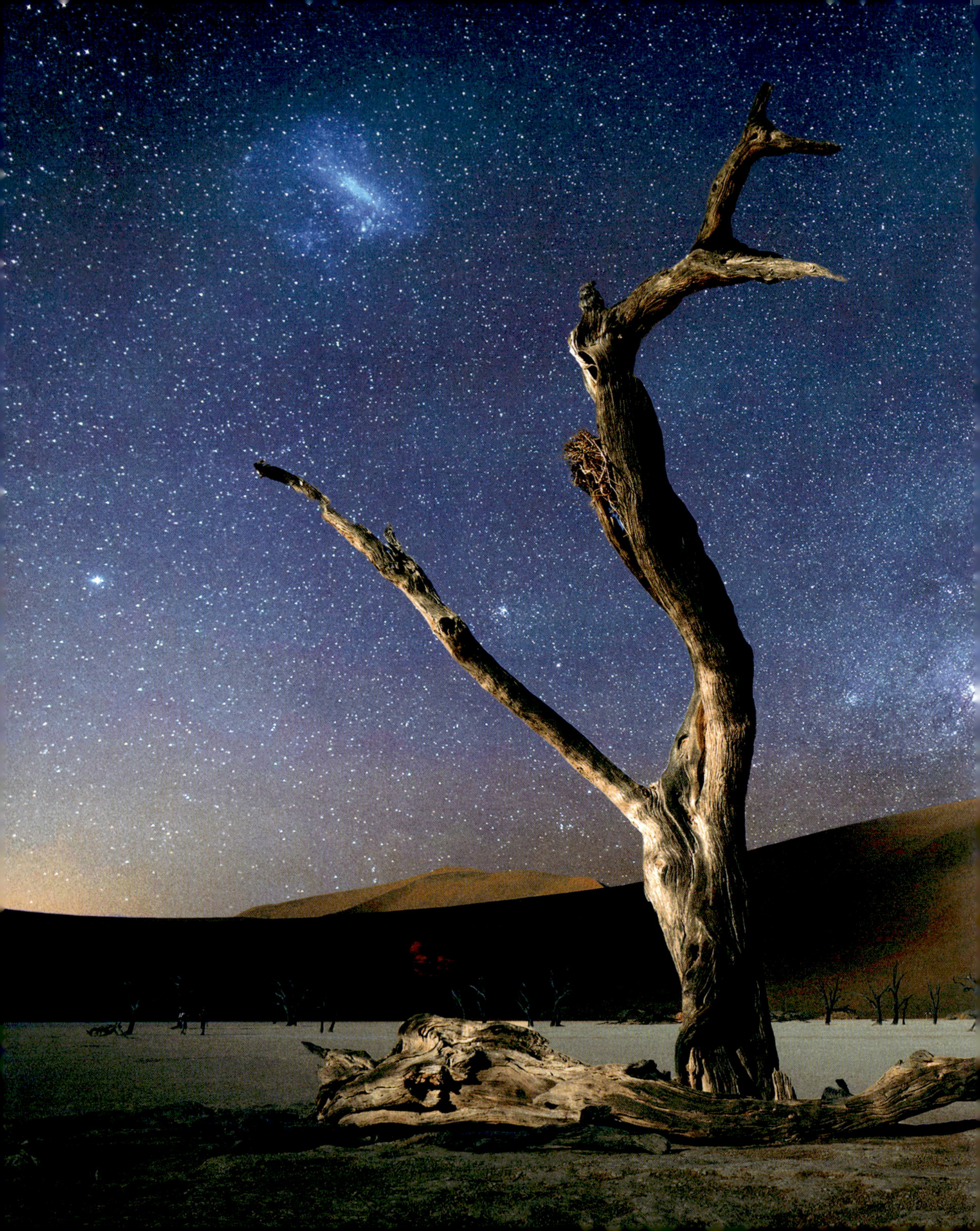

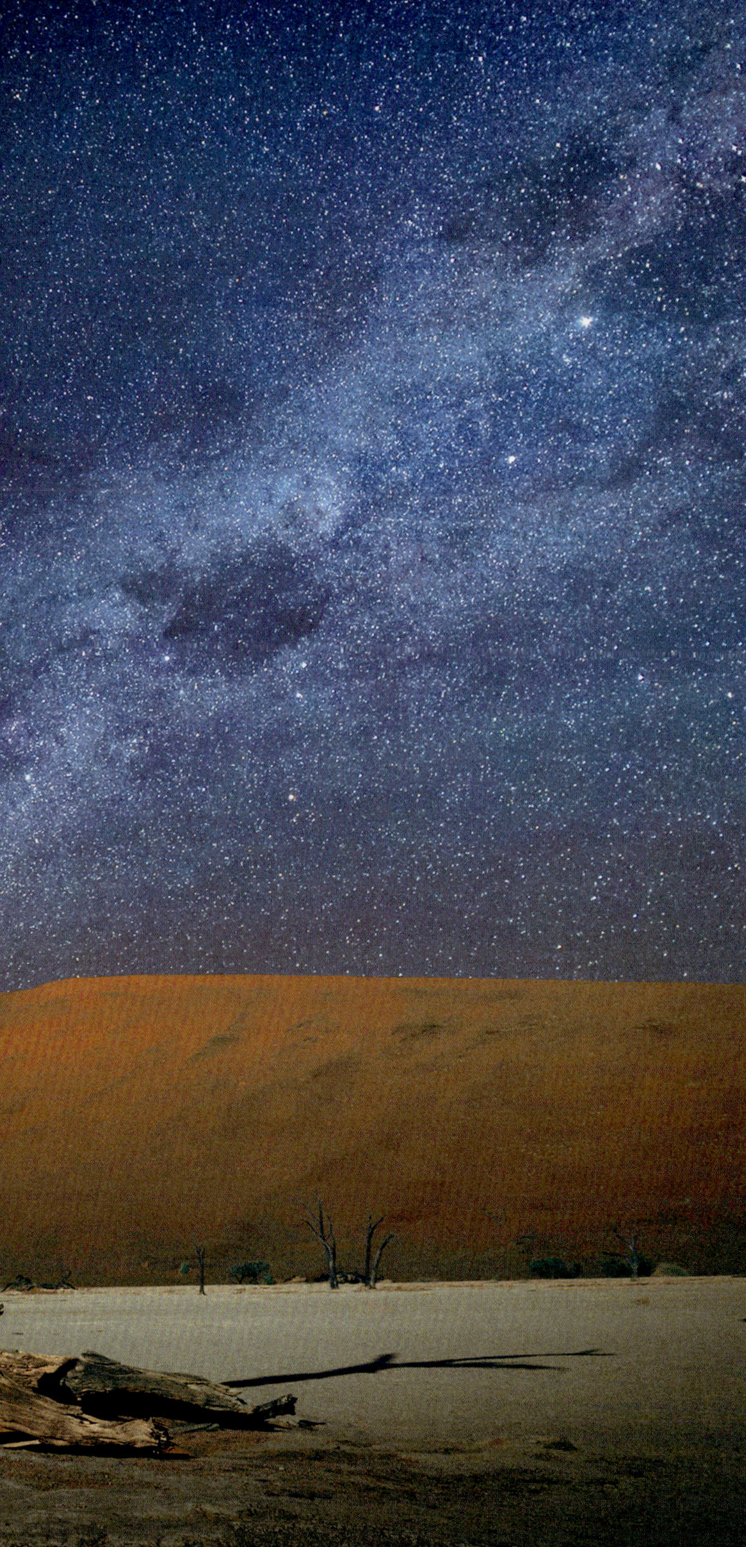

Deadvlei, Namib-Naukluft National Park

Deadvlei
Deadvlei is a clay pan enclosed by high dunes in the Namib Desert. The water that once nourished these trees has long since dried up. Some acacia here are over 500 years old. The wood is not petrified, but it cannot rot as the air contains no moisture.

Deadvlei
Le Deadvlei est une cuvette argileuse cernée de hautes dunes dans le désert du Namib. L'eau qui faisait vivre les arbres autrefois a disparu depuis longtemps. Certains acacias sont âgés de plus de 500 ans. Le bois n'est pas pétrifié et l'absence totale d'humidité ambiante l'empêche de pourrir.

Deadvlei
Deadvlei ist eine von hohen Dünen umschlossene Tonpfanne in der Namib-Wüste. Das Wasser, das die Bäume einst nährte, ist längst versiegt. Manche Akazien sind über 500 Jahre alt. Das Holz ist nicht versteinert. Es kann nicht verrotten, da die Luft keine Feuchtigkeit enthält.

Deadvlei
Deadvlei una de las ollas rodeada por altas dunas en el desierto de Namibia. Hace tiempo que el agua que antes nutría los árboles se ha secado. Algunas acacias tienen más de 500 años de antigüedad. La madera no está petrificada. No puede pudrirse porque el aire contiene humedad.

Deadvlei
Deadvlei è una conca di argilla circondata dalle alte dune del deserto di Namib. L'acqua che una volta nutriva gli alberi si è esaurita da molto tempo. Alcune acacie hanno oltre 500 anni. Il legno non si è pietrificato e non può marcire perché l'aria non contiene umidità.

Deadvlei
De Deadvlei in de Namibwoestijn is een kleibekken dat door hoge duinen wordt omringd. Het water dat de bomen hier ooit verzorgde, is allang in de ondergrond gesijpeld. Veel acacia's zijn ruim vijfhonderd jaar oud. Het hout is niet versteend, omdat het vanwege de lage luchtvochtigheid niet kan rotten.

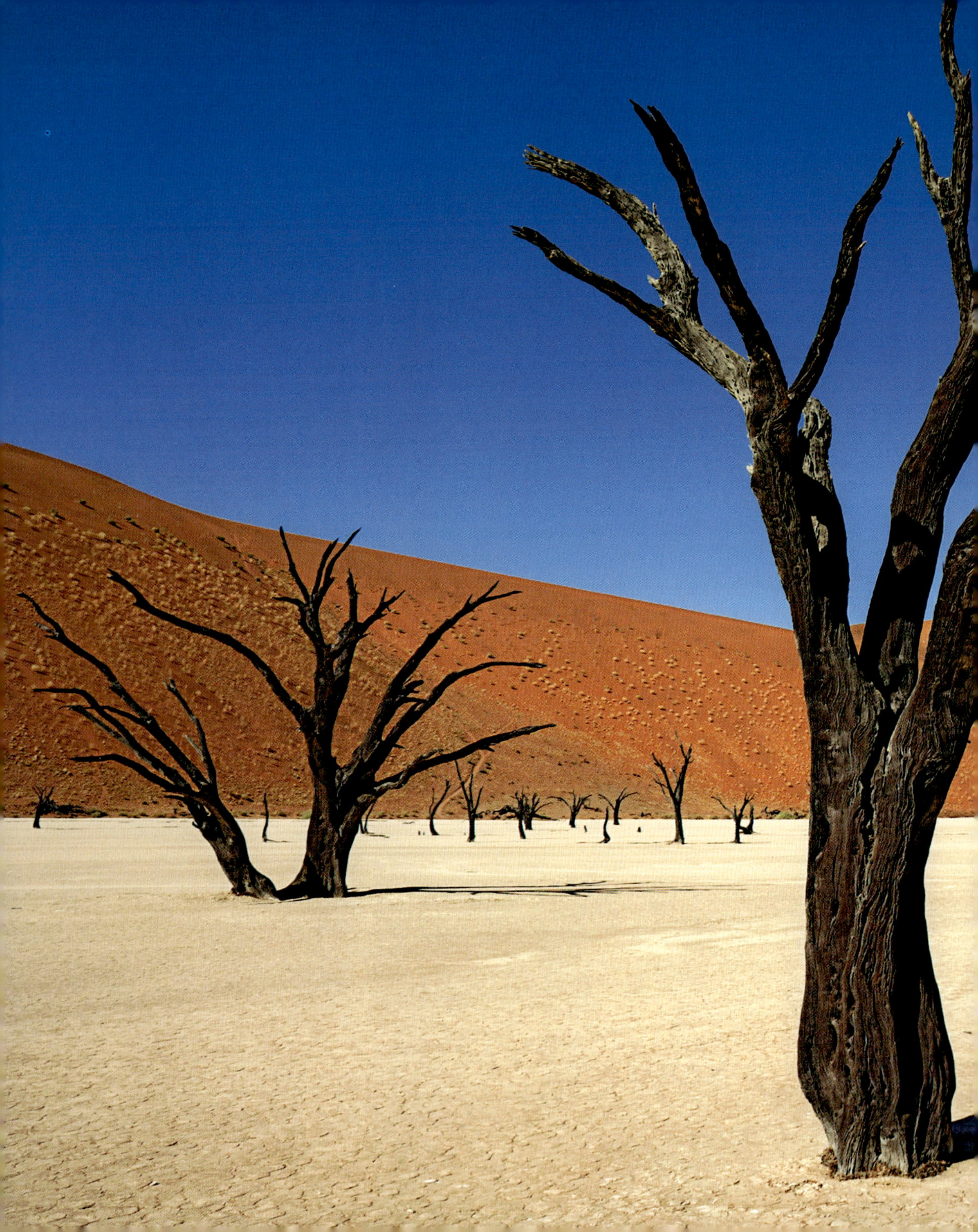

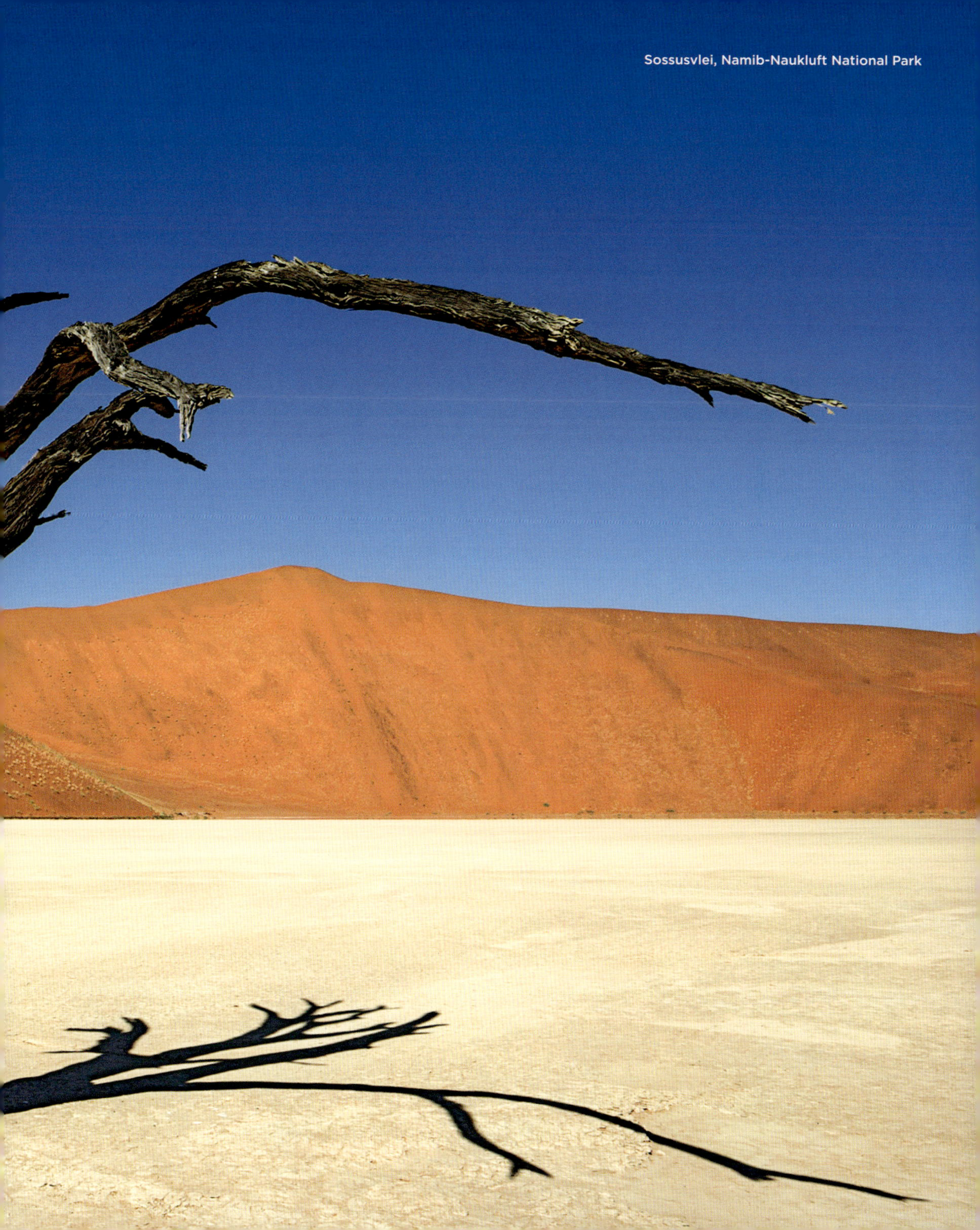
Sossusvlei, Namib-Naukluft National Park

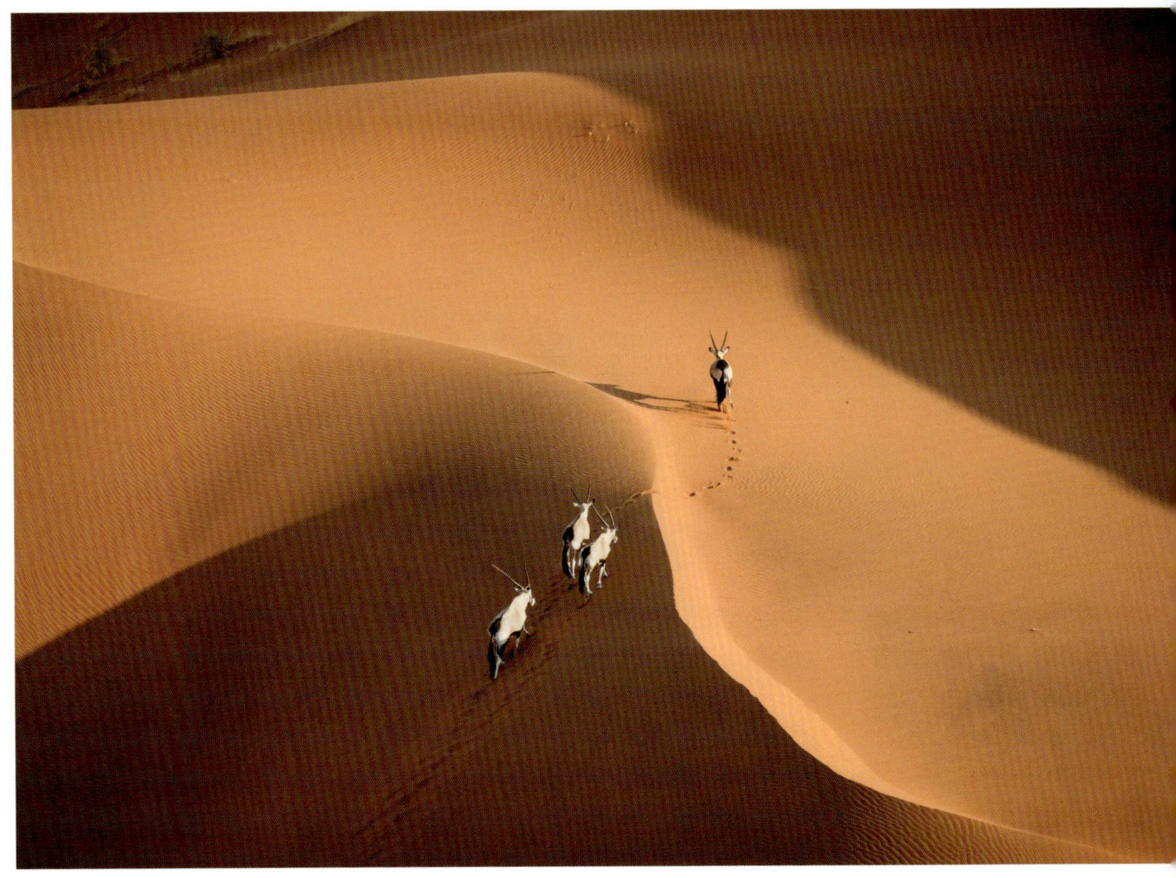

Gemsboks, Namib-Naukluft National Park

Sesriem Canyon, Namib-Naukluft National Par

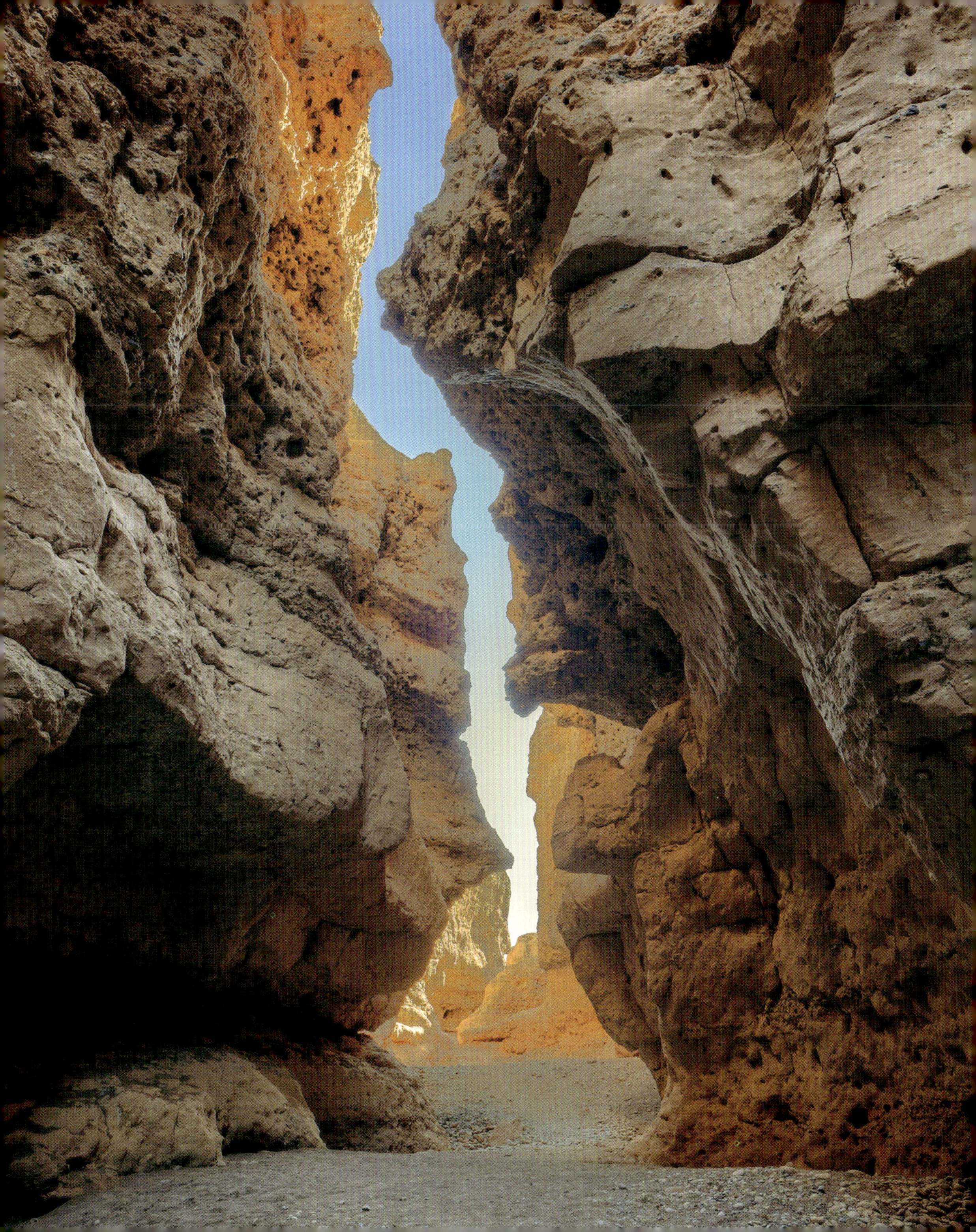

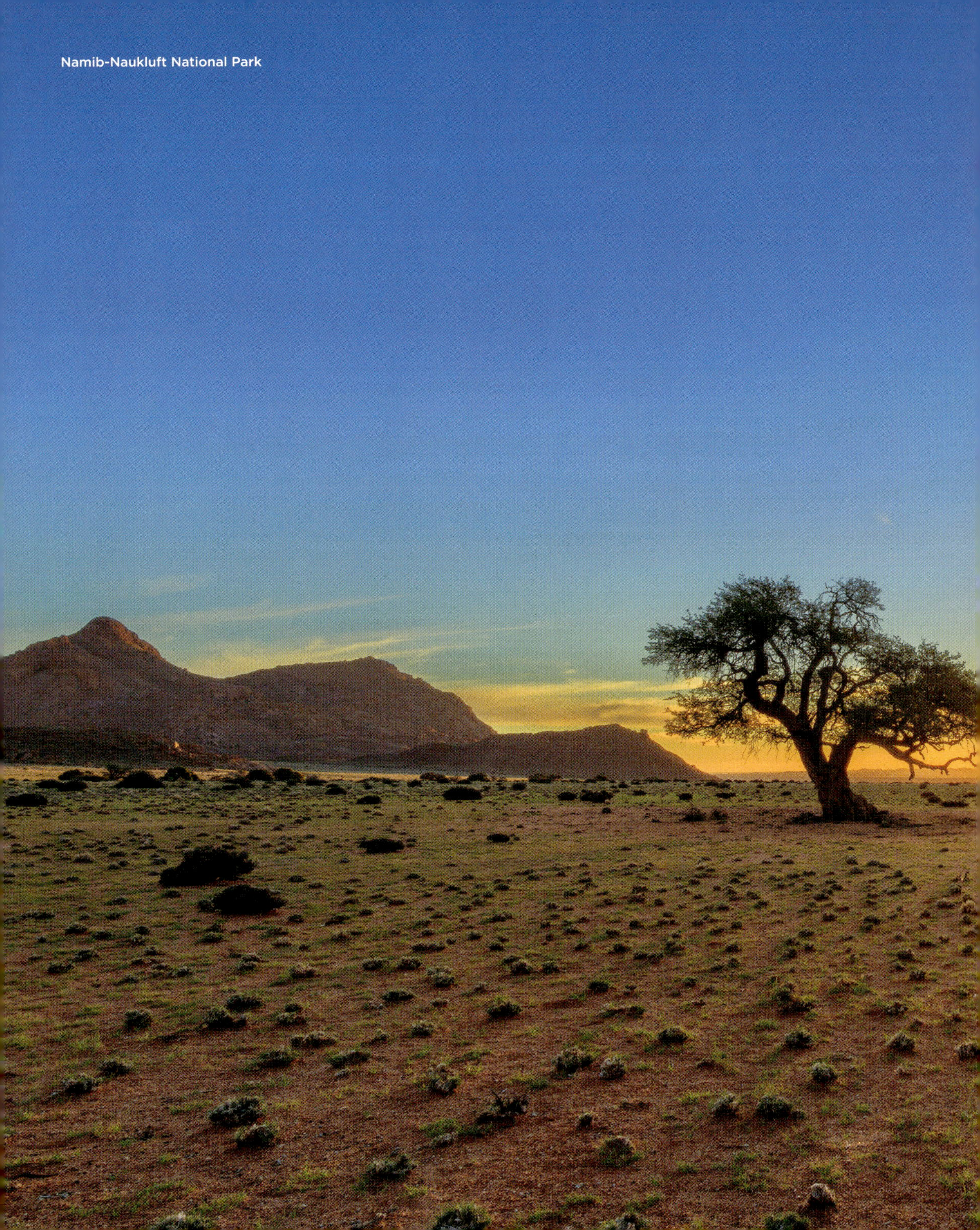

Namib-Naukluft National Park

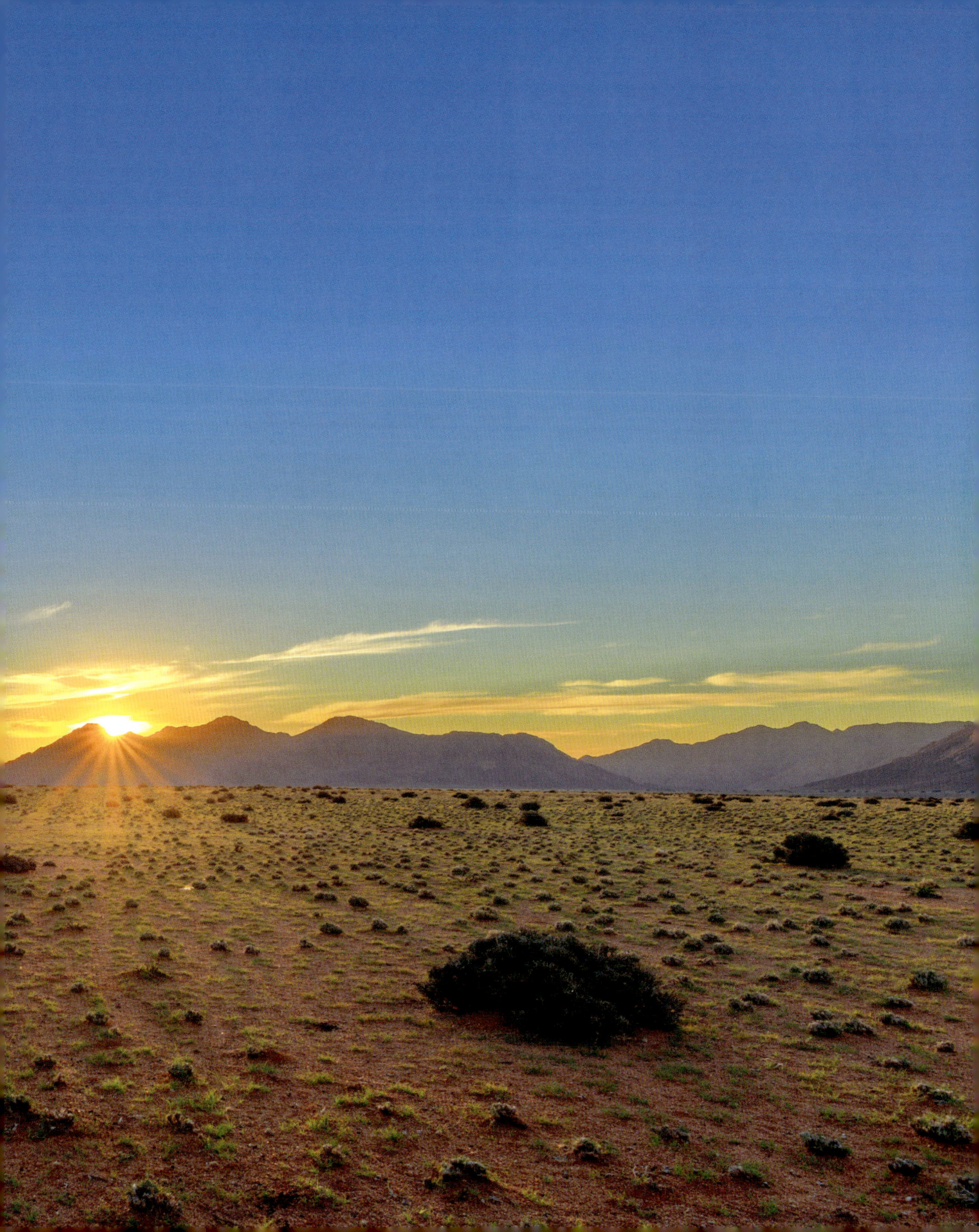

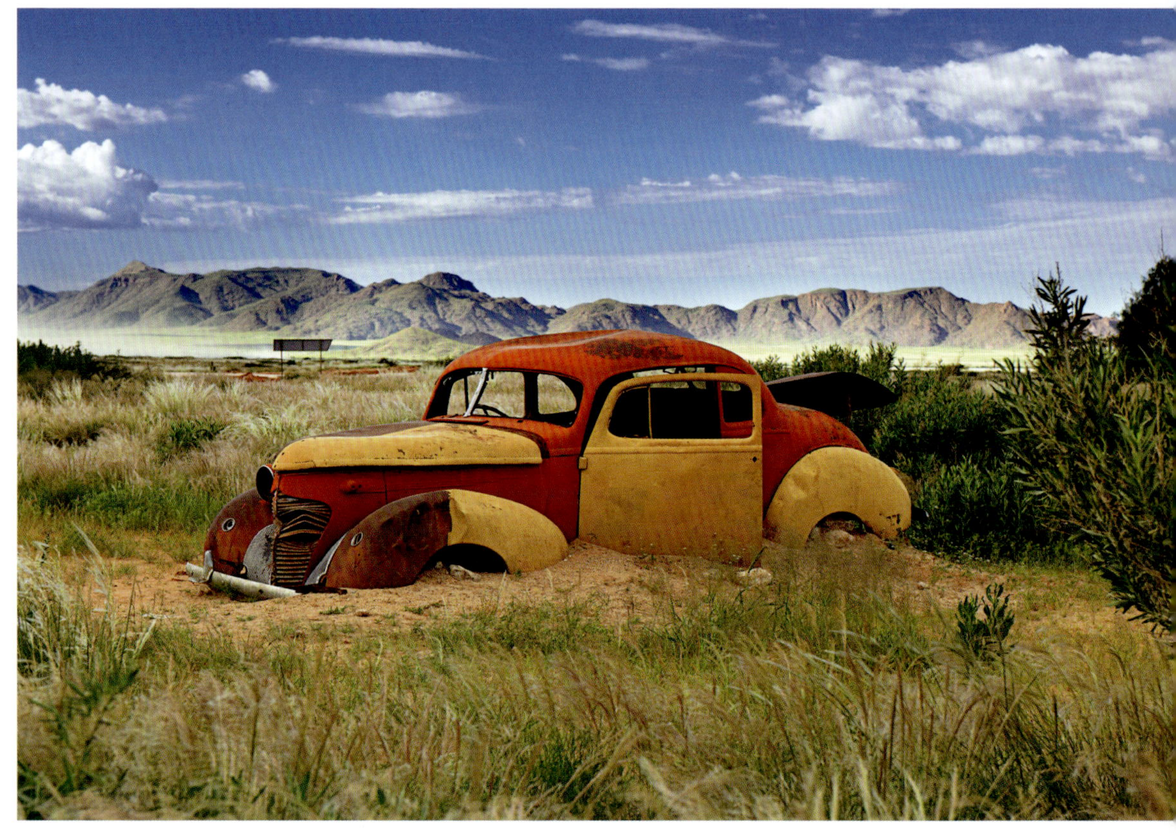

Namib-Naukluft National Park

Red Dunes
Why do the huge sand dunes in the Namib-Naukluft National Park have such intoxicating hues of orange and red? Given the unique beauty of this desert landscape, the answer is rather mundane, yet surprising: rust. The high concentration of iron in the sand oxidises to give the reddish hues and luminous characteristic of iron oxide. This is an ongoing process, which explains why the colour of the sand dunes continues to deepen.

Les dunes rouges
Pourquoi les immenses dunes du parc national du Namib-Naukluft arborent-elles des tons orange et rouges aussi fabuleux ? L'explication est pour le moins prosaïque face à la beauté exceptionnelle de ce désert c'est la rouille. Le fer présent dans les grains de sable s'oxyde et rouille. C'est aussi pourquoi la coloration rouge et la luminosité des dunes s'intensifient avec le temps.

Rote Dünen
Warum strahlen die riesigen Sanddünen im Namib-Naukluft-Nationalpark in so berauschenden Orange- und Rottönen? Die Erklärung ist angesichts der einzigartigen Schönheit dieser Wüstenlandschaft ernüchternd: Rost. Die im Sand enthaltenen Eisenionen oxidieren zu Eisenoxid. Das erklärt auch, warum mit dem Alter die Rotfärbung und damit die Leuchtkraft der Sanddünen zunimmt.

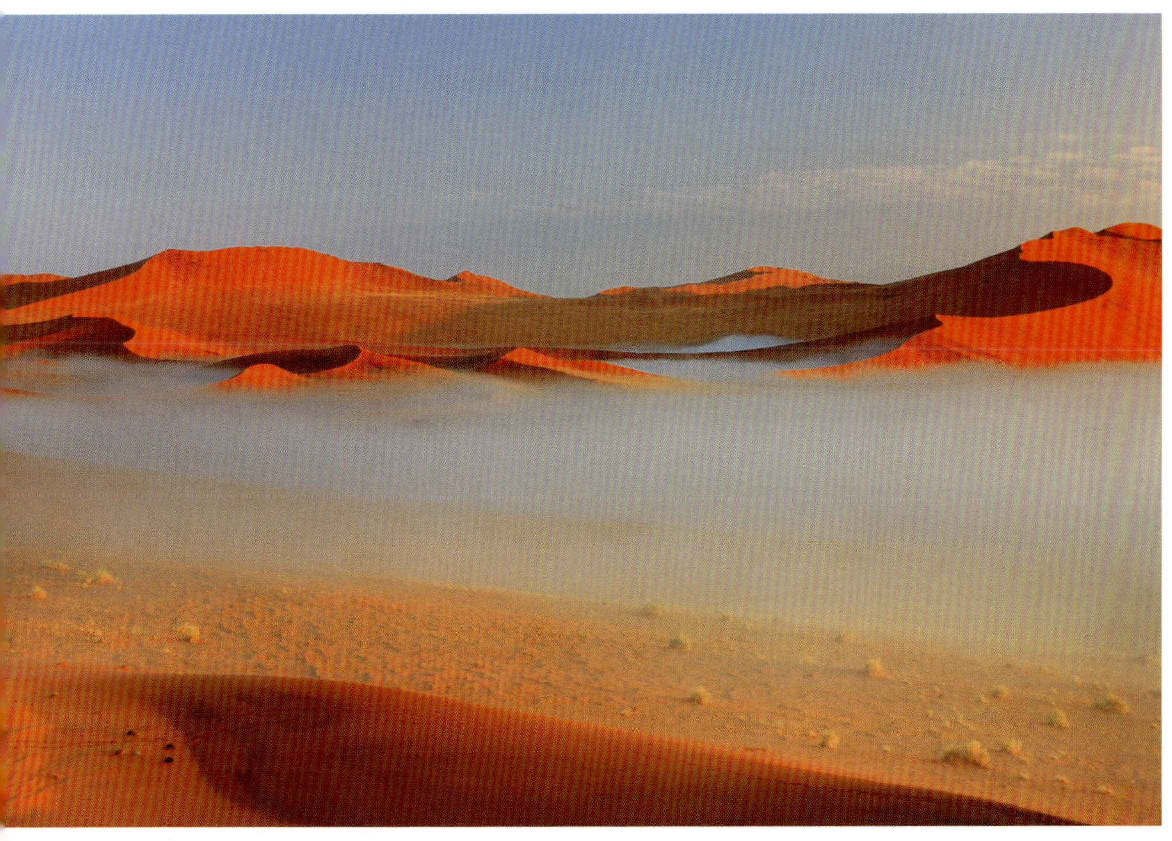

Namib-Naukluft National Park

Dunas rojas
¿Por qué brillan las enormes dunas de arena en el Parque Nacional Namib-Naukluft en tan embriagantes colores naranja y rojo? La explicación dada es algo desilusionante ante la singular belleza del paisaje del desierto: el óxido. Los iones de hierro contenidos en la arena para oxidar el óxido de hierro. Esto también explica por qué el color rojo y el brillo de las dunas de arena aumenta con la tiempo.

Deserto rosso
Perché le enormi dune di sabbia del Parco nazionale di Namib-Naukluft risplendono di sfumature arancione e rosso così stupefacenti? La spiegazione è deludente se si considera la straordinaria bellezza del paesaggio desertico: a causa della ruggine. Gli ioni di ferro contenuti nella sabbia si ossidano in ossido ferrico. Questo spiega anche perché con il passare del tempo aumenta la sfumatura rossa e quindi la luminosità delle dune di sabbia.

Rode duinen
Waarom stralen de reusachtige zandduinen van het Namib-Naukluft National Park in zulke betoverende oranje en rode tinten? Gezien de unieke schoonheid van dit woestijnlandschap is het antwoord ontnuchterend: roest. De ijzerdeeltjes die het zand bevat, oxideren tot ijzeroxide. Dat verklaart ook waarom de rode verkleuring en daarmee de lichtkracht van de zandduinen toeneemt naarmate ze ouder worden.

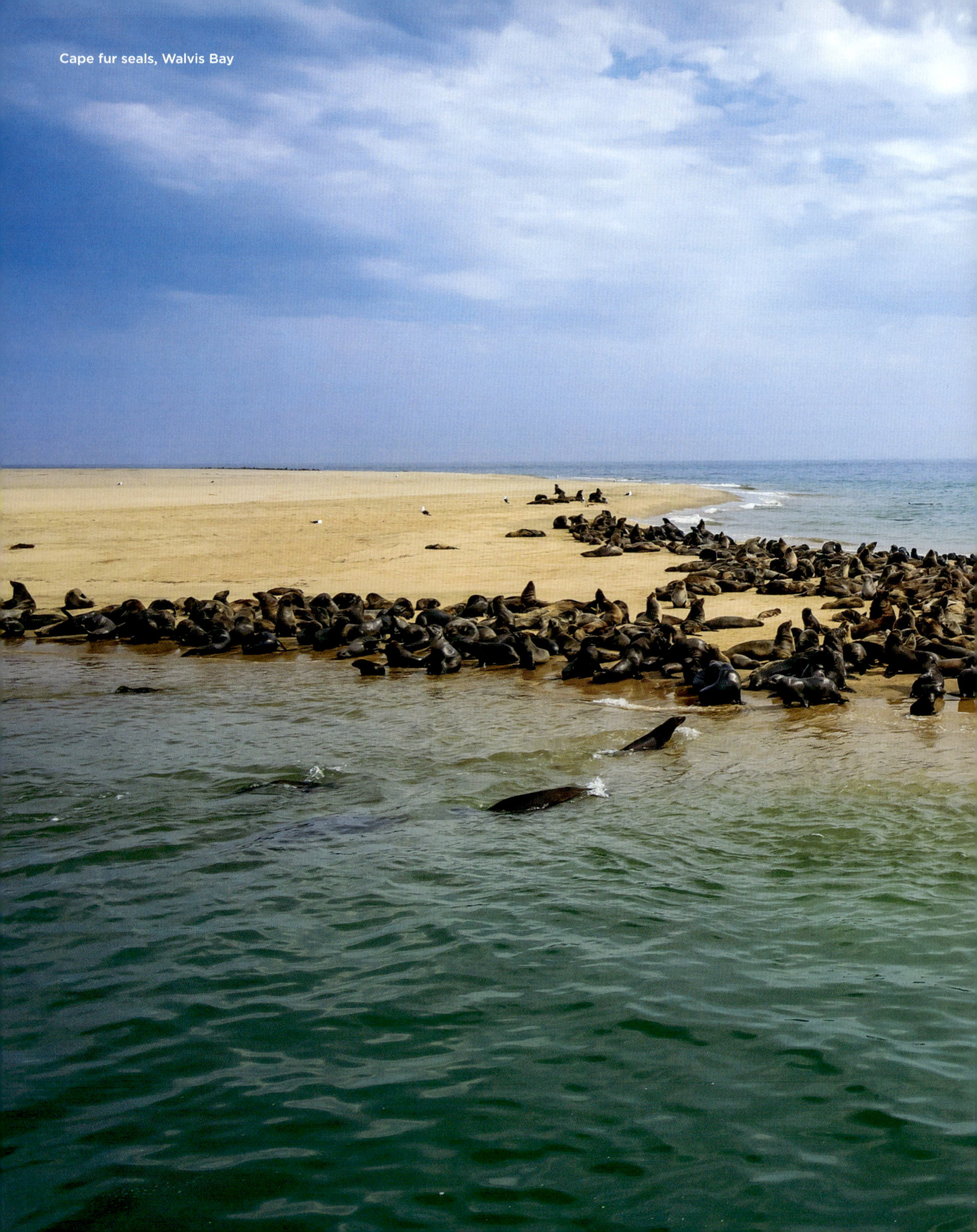
Cape fur seals, Walvis Bay

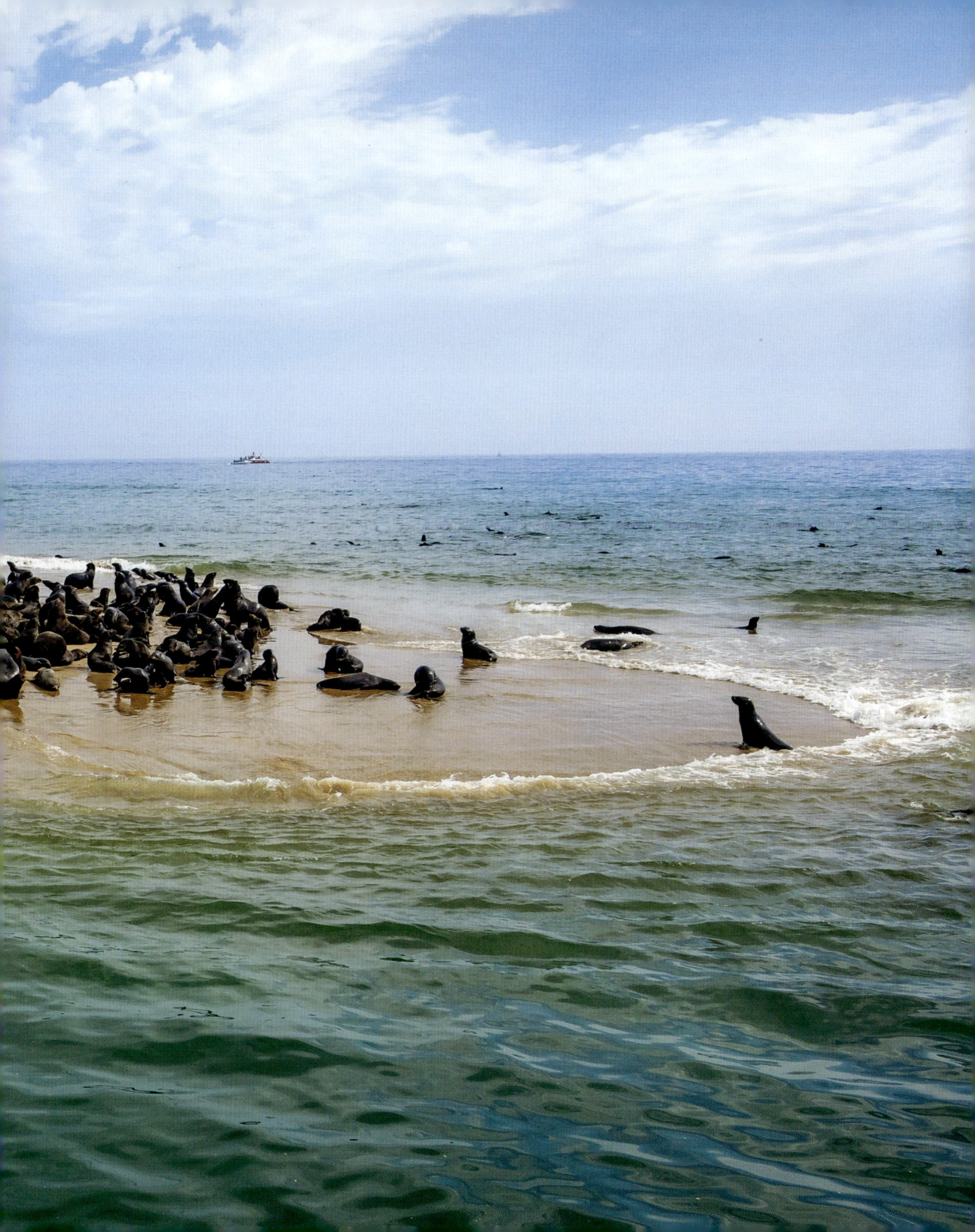

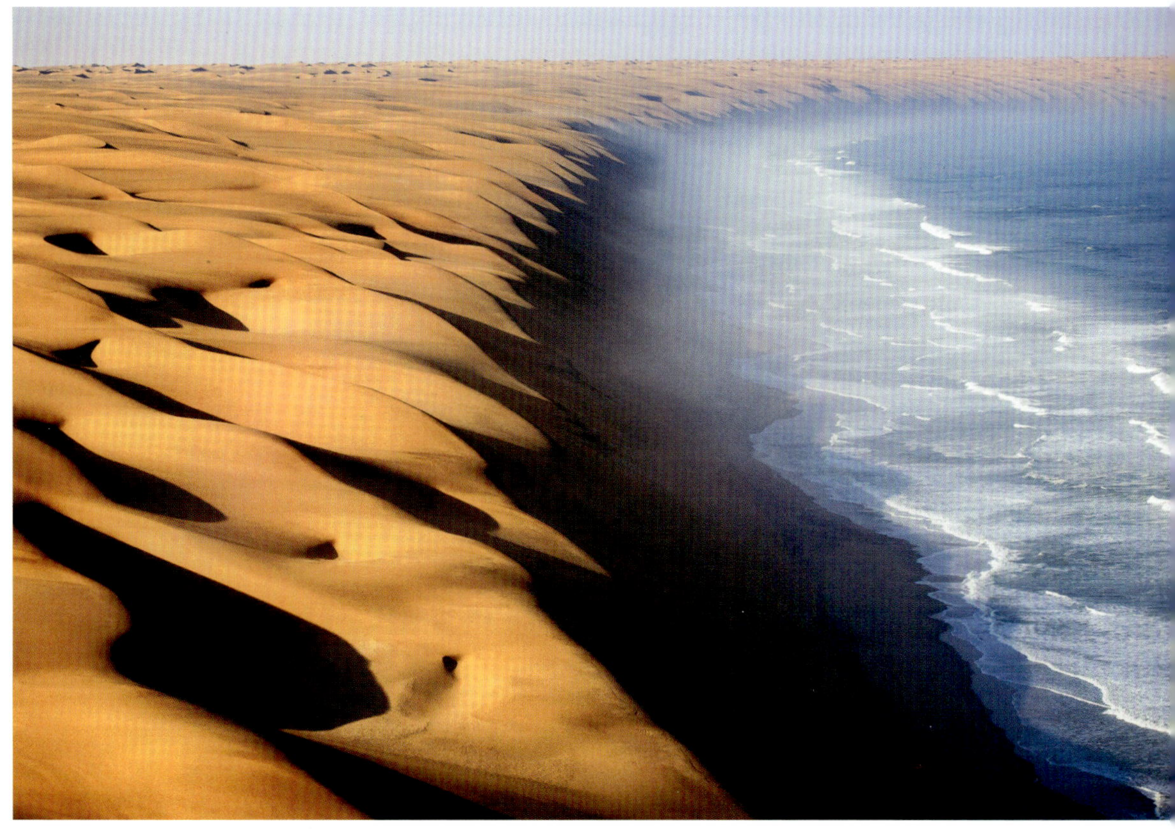

Namib-Naukluft National Park

Walvis Bay
Walvis Bay lies 30 km south of Swakopmund and is Namibia's second largest city. The vast lagoon, with its mighty sand dunes, is considered to be one of the most important wetlands in southern Africa. Seals, dolphins, pelicans and flamingos romp around in the sea and along the coast, with hundreds of thousands of migratory birds coming here to hibernate.

Walvis Bay
Walvis Bay (« la baie des baleines ») se situe à 30 km au sud de Swakopmund. Par sa taille, c'est la deuxième ville de Namibie. Avec ses dunes majestueuses, cette vaste lagune est l'une des zones humides les plus importantes du sud de l'Afrique. Dans la mer et sur la côte s'ébattent phoques, dauphins, pélicans et flamants roses, et des centaines d'oiseaux migrateurs viennent passer l'hiver ici.

Walvis Bay
Walvis Bay („Walfischbucht") liegt 30 km südlich von Swakopmund und ist die zweitgrößte Stadt Namibias. Die weite Lagune mit ihren mächtigen Sanddünen gilt als eines der wichtigsten Feuchtgebiete im gesamten südlichen Afrika. Im Meer und an der Küste tummeln sich Robben, Delfine, Pelikane und Flamingos und hunderttausende Zugvögel kommen zum Überwintern hierher.

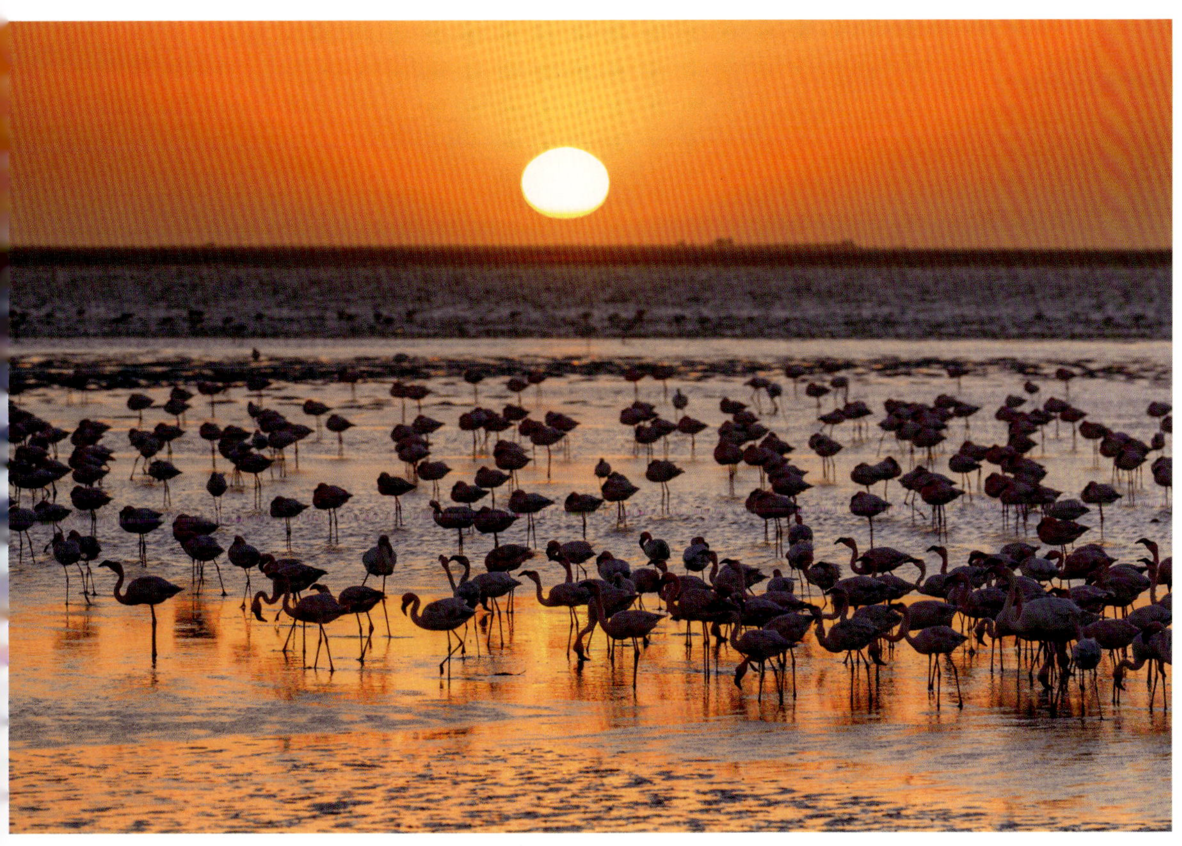

Flamingos, Walvis Bay

Walvis Bay
Walvis Bay se encuentra a 30 km al sur de Swakopmund y es la segunda ciudad más grande de Namibia. La vasta laguna con sus poderosas dunas de arena es considerada uno de los humedales más importantes del sur de África. Focas, delfines, pelícanos y flamencos juegan en el mar y a lo largo de la costa y cientos de miles de aves migratorias vienen aquí a hibernar.

Walvis Bay
Walvis Bay è situata a 30 km a sud di Swakopmund ed è la seconda città più grande della Namibia. La vasta laguna con le sue imponenti dune di sabbia è considerata una delle zone umide più importanti dell'Africa meridionale. Foche, delfini, pellicani e fenicotteri nuotano nel mare e lungo la costa e centinaia di migliaia di uccelli migratori vengono qui per passare l'inverno.

Walvisbaai
Walvisbaai ligt 30 km ten zuiden van Swakopmund en is de op één na grootste stad van Namibië. De uitgestrekte lagune met zijn machtige zandduinen wordt beschouwd als een van de belangrijkste wetlands in zuidelijk Afrika. Zeehonden, dolfijnen, pelikanen en flamingo's dartelen rond in zee en langs de kust en honderdduizenden trekvogels komen hier overwinteren.

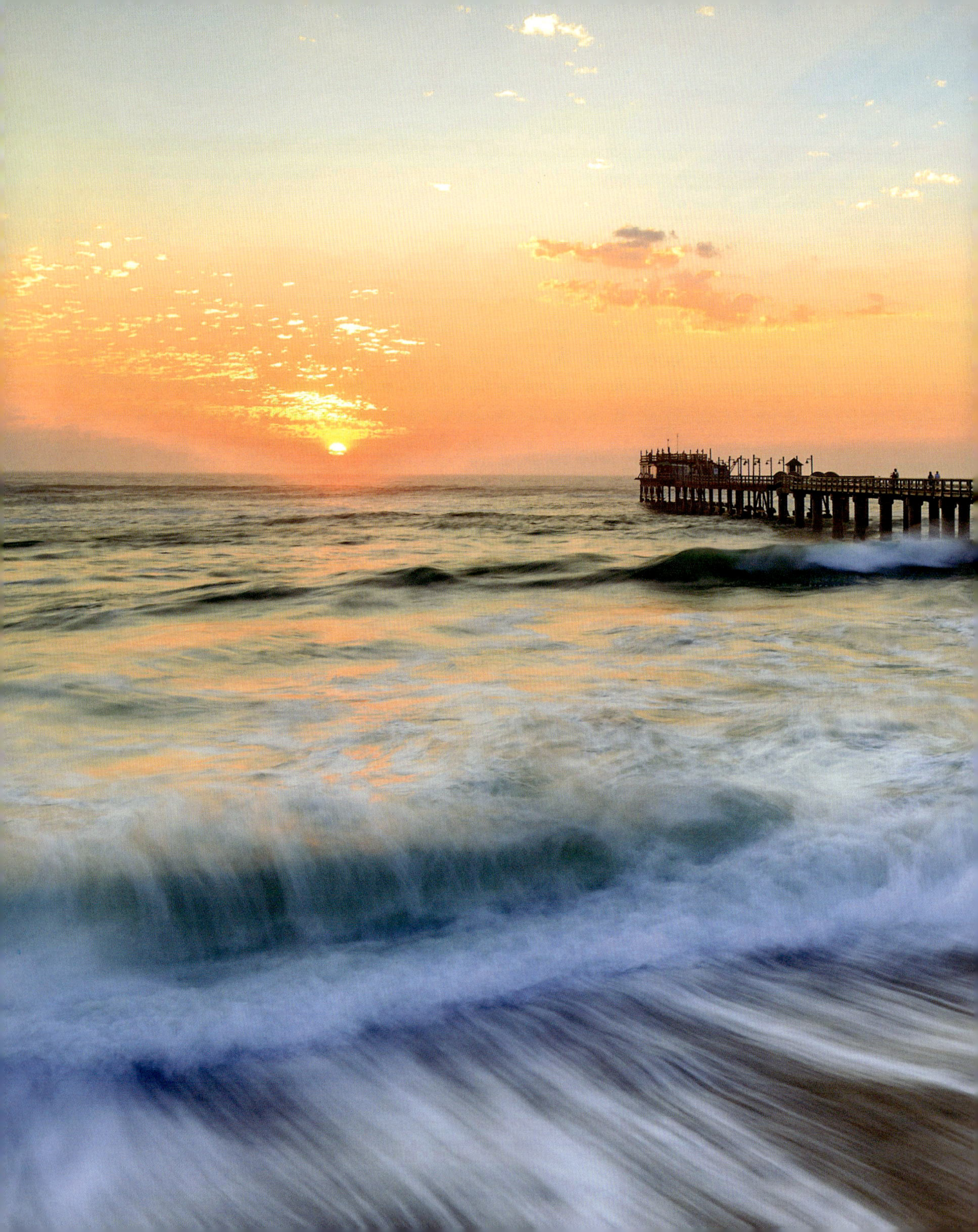

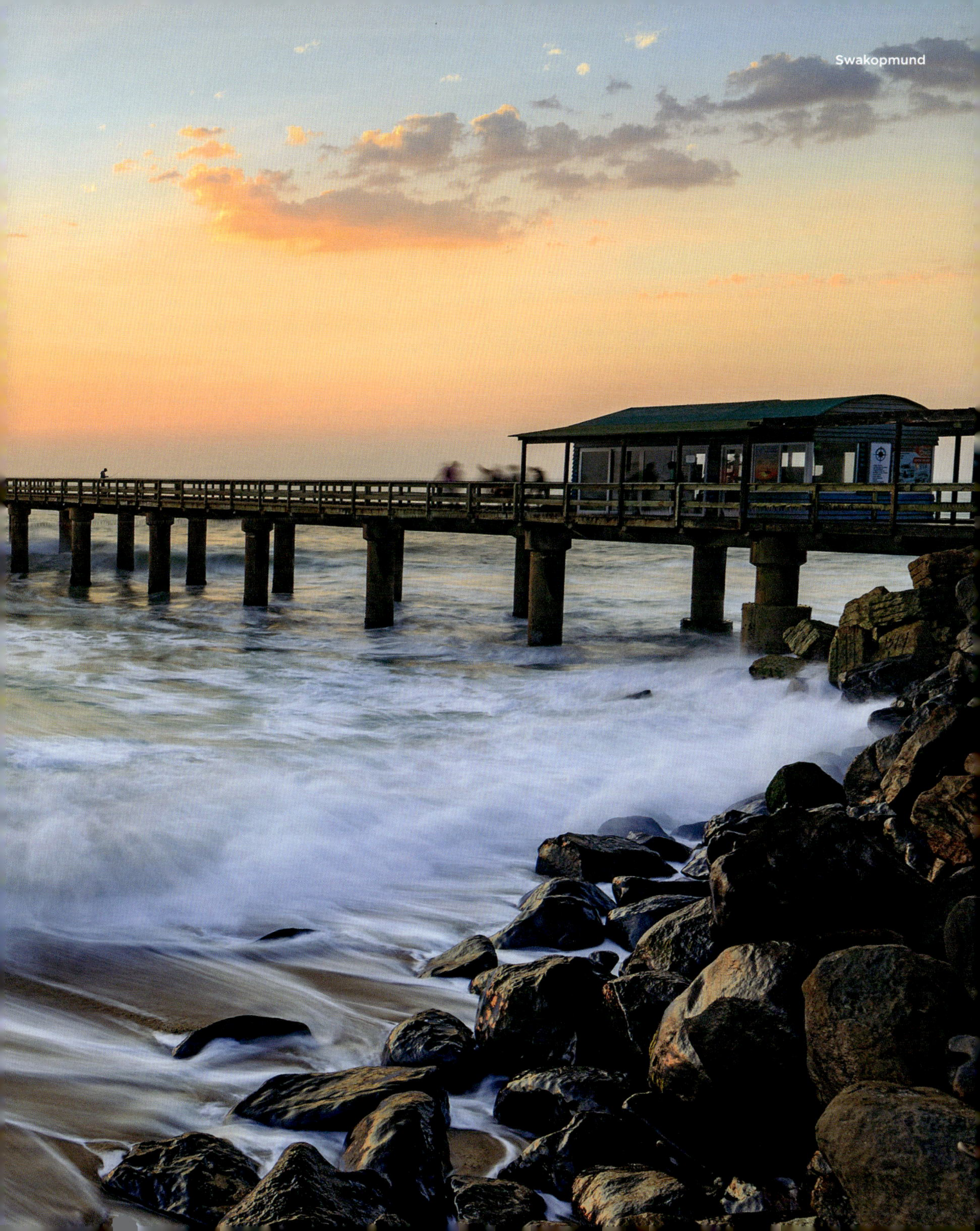

Swakopmund

Windhoek
In the interior, and at 1600 m above sea level, the capital of Namibia lies picturesquely in a valley basin. The townscape of Windhoek is very well-kept, with the influence of the Wilhelminian colonial times still evident in many parts, but nevertheless, many modern buildings dominate the city centre. The official language is English, but almost everywhere one can also communicate in German.

Windhoek
Située à l'intérieur des terres et à une altitude de plus de 1 600 m, la capitale de la Namibie est joliment lovée dans une cuvette. La physionomie de la ville est particulièrement soignée, avec des influences notables de l'époque coloniale wilhelmienne, mais aujourd'hui de nombreux bâtiments modernes dominent le centre-ville. L'anglais est la langue officielle, mais l'on peut se faire comprendre en allemand presque partout.

Windhuk
Im Landesinneren und auf 1600 m ü. NN liegt die Hauptstadt Namibias malerisch in einem Talkessel. Das Stadtbild von Windhuk ist sehr gepflegt, an vielen Stellen sind die Einflüsse wilhelminischer Kolonialzeit erkennbar, mittlerweile dominieren aber auch viele moderne Bauten das Stadtzentrum. Amtssprache ist englisch, fast überall kann man sich jedoch auch auf Deutsch verständigen.

Windhoek
En el interior y a 1600 m sobre el nivel del mar, la capital de Namibia se encuentra pintorescamente en una cuenca del valle. El paisaje urbano de Windhoek está muy bien conservado, en muchos lugares se pueden ver las influencias de la época colonial de Wilhelmina, pero con el transcurso del tiempo también muchos edificios modernos dominan el centro de la ciudad. El idioma oficial es el inglés, pero en casi todas partes también se habla alemán.

Windhoek
Nell'entroterra e a 1600 m sopra il livello del mare, troviamo la capitale della Namibia in una pittoresca conca valliva. La città di Windhoek è molto ben tenuta, in molti luoghi si possono riconoscere le influenze del periodo coloniale di Guglielmo II, ma il centro della città è dominato anche da molti edifici moderni. La lingua ufficiale è l'inglese, ma quasi ovunque è possibile comunicare anche in tedesco.

Windhoek
In het binnenland en op 1600 m boven de zeespiegel ligt de hoofdstad van Namibië schilderachtig in een dalketel. Het stadsbeeld van Windhoek is zeer goed onderhouden. Op veel plaatsen zijn de invloeden uit de tijd van keizer Wilhelm II nog te zien, maar ondertussen domineren ook veel moderne gebouwen het stadscentrum. De officiële taal is Engels, maar bijna overal kun je je ook in het Duits verstaanbaar maken.

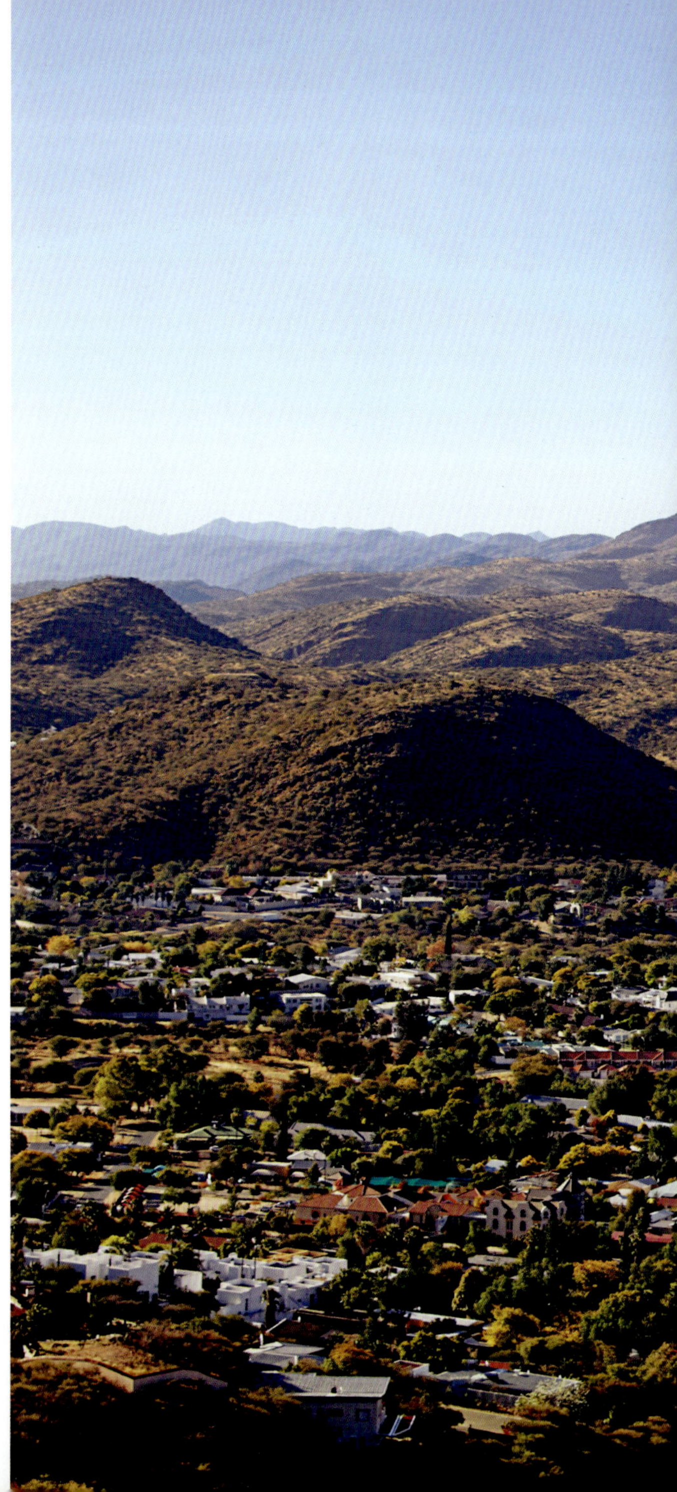

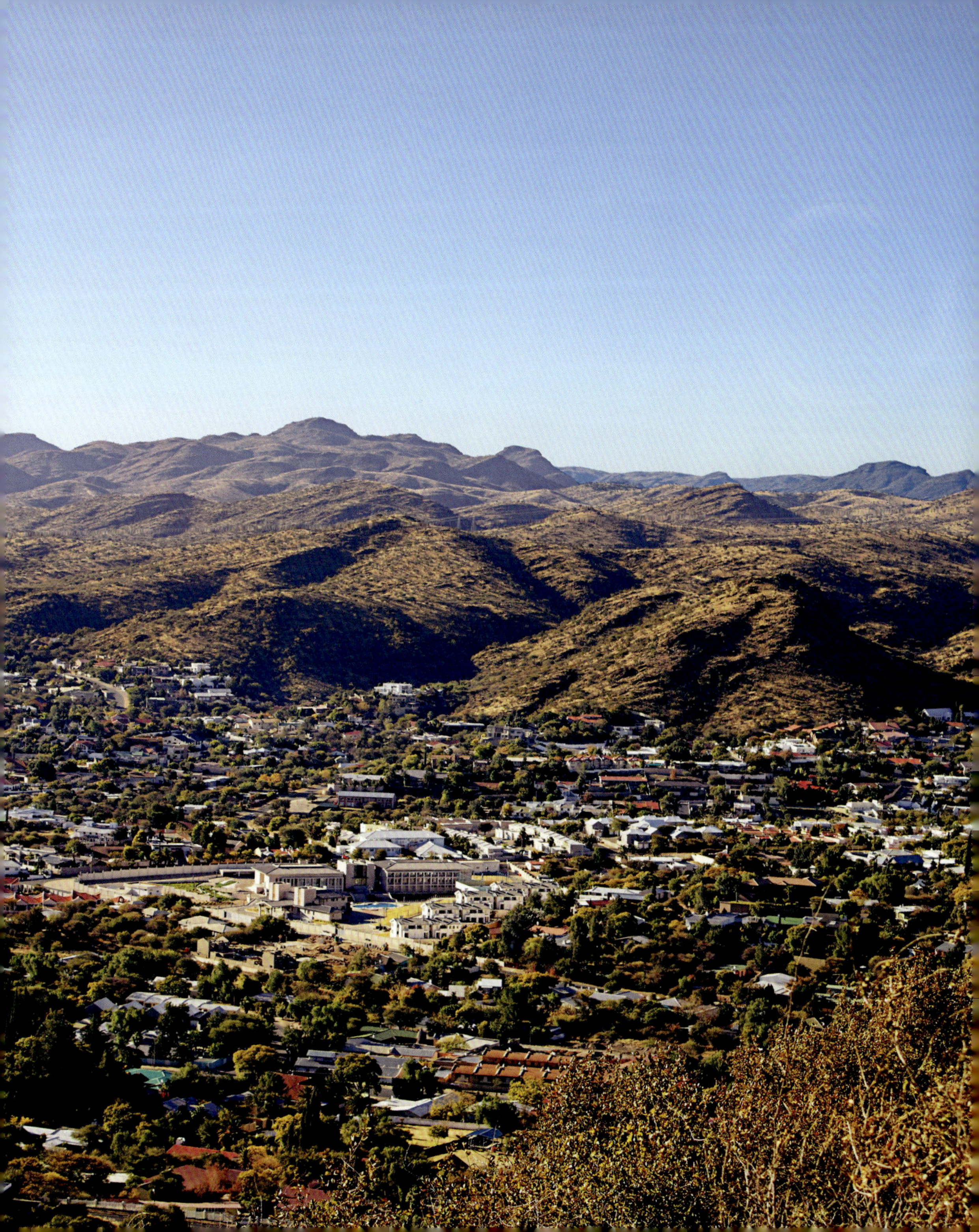

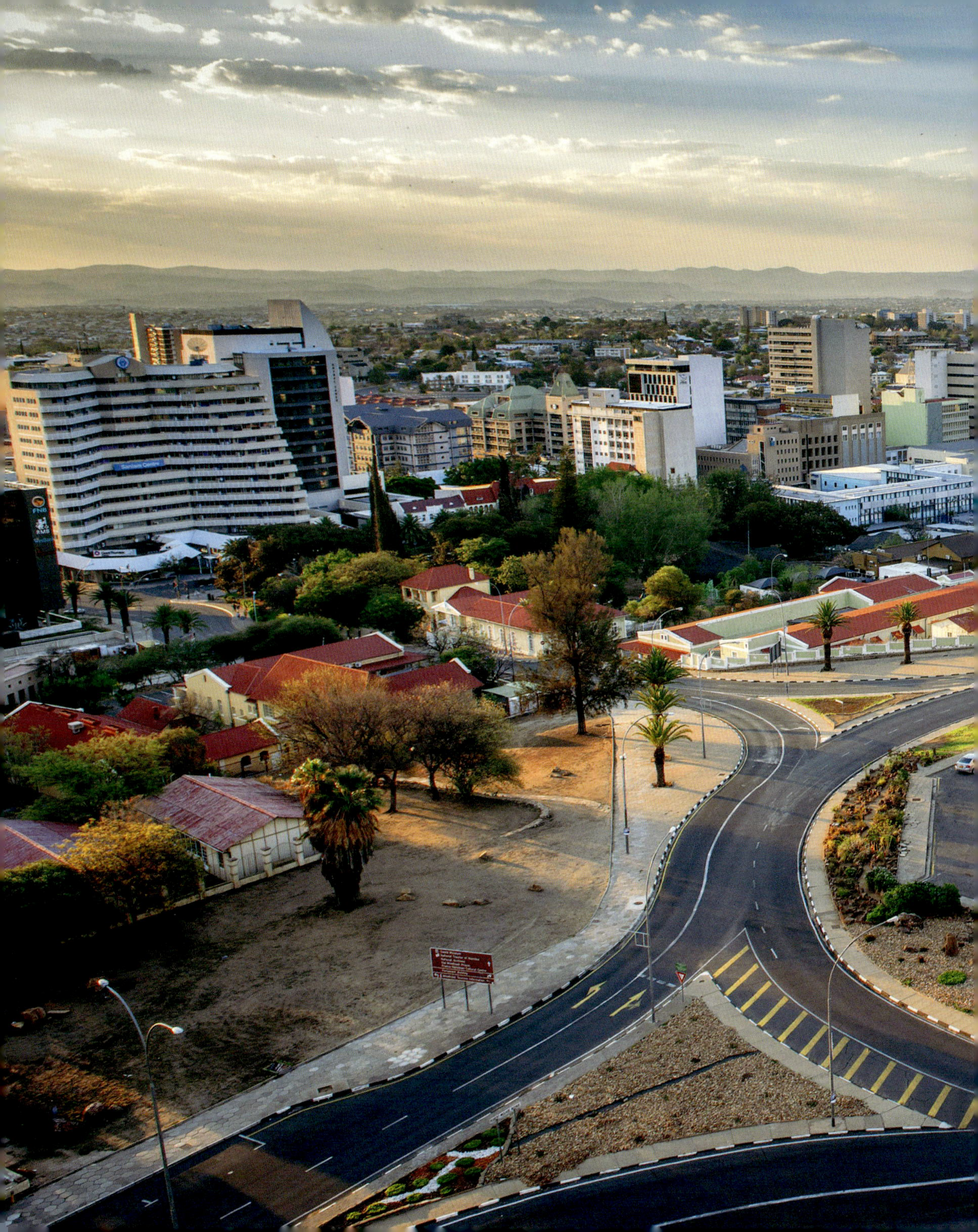
FNB

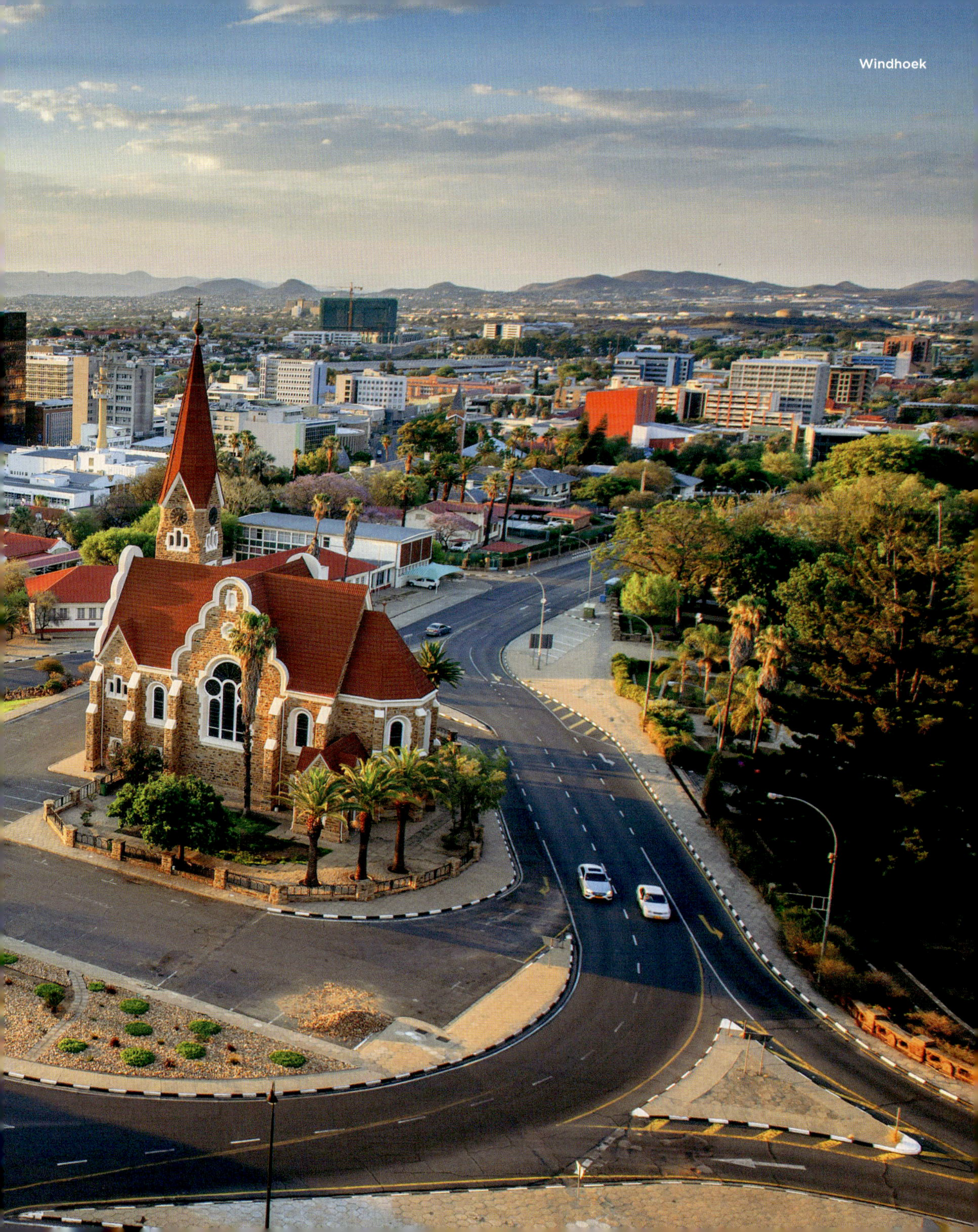
Windhoek

Tsau ||Khaeb National Park (Sperrgebiet) & Lüderitz, Namibia

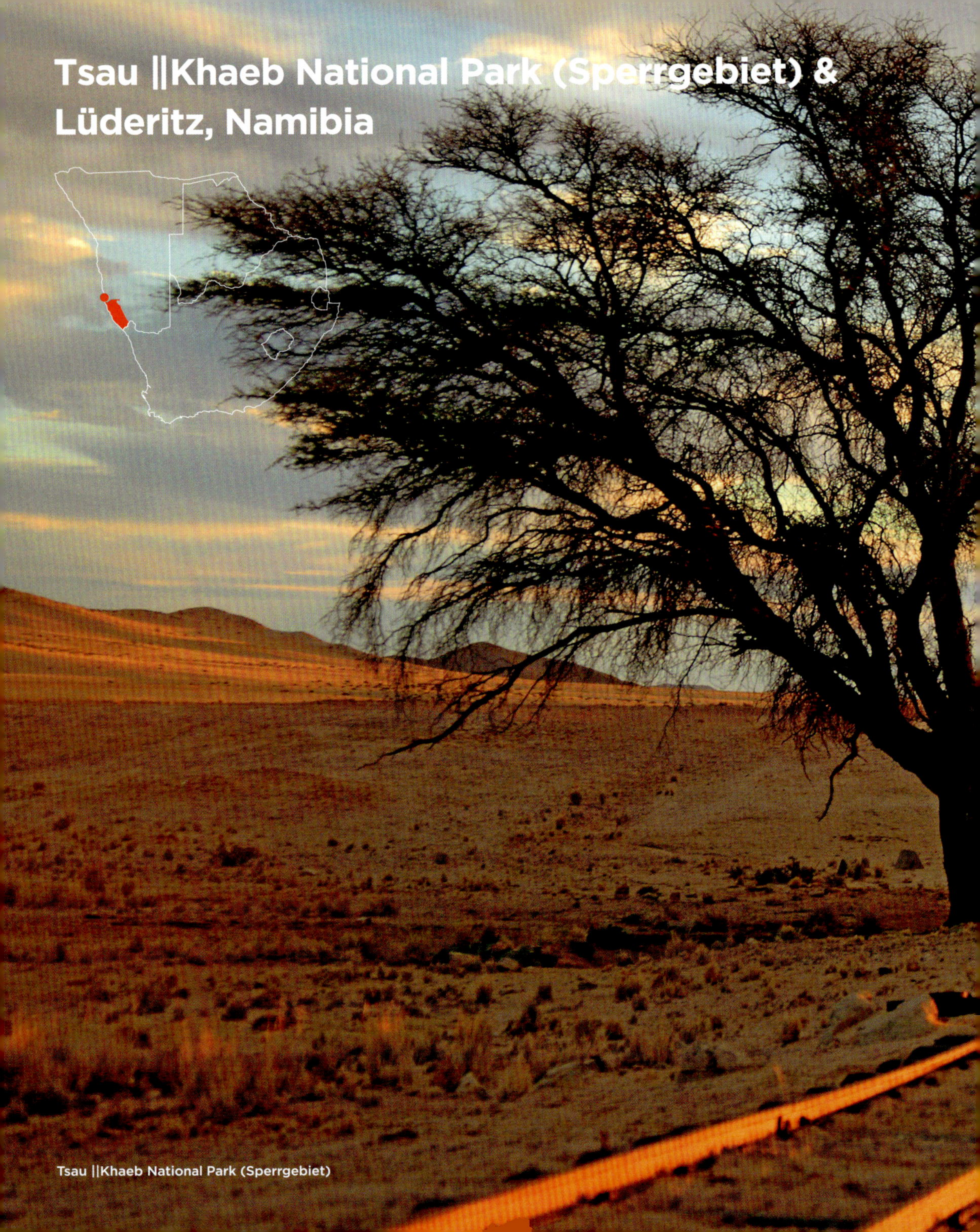

Tsau ||Khaeb National Park (Sperrgebiet)

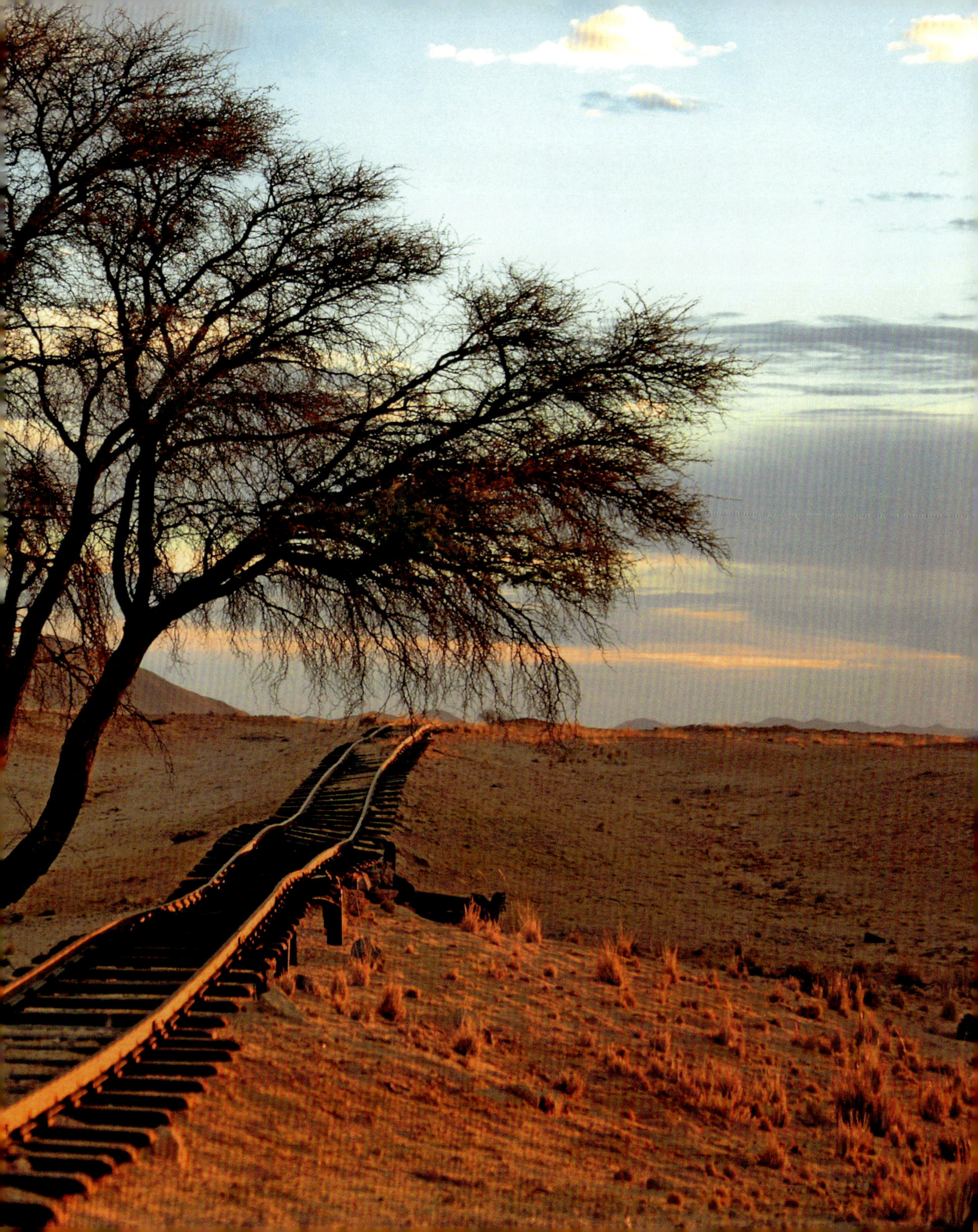

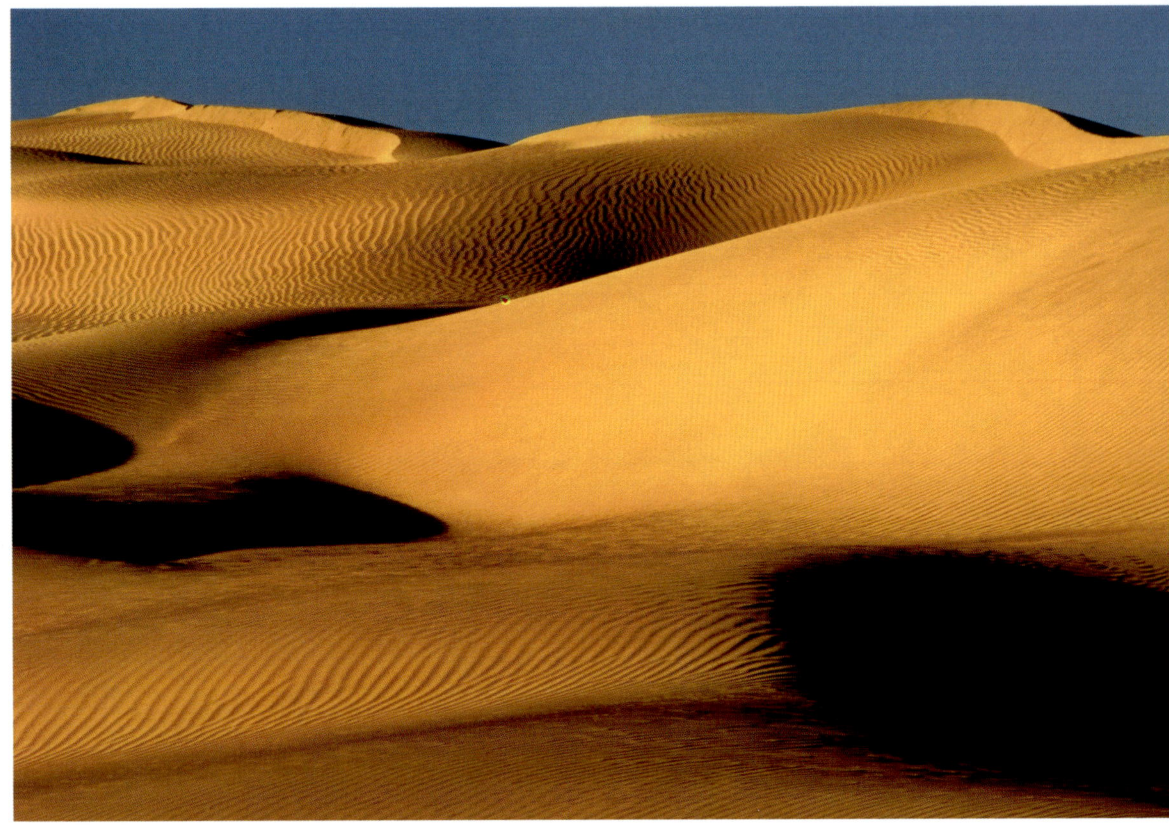

Tsau ǁKhaeb National Park (Sperrgebiet)

Tsau ǁKhaeb National Park (Sperrgebiet)
This region in the south of Namibia was closed to the public for 100 years. Following the discovery of diamonds in 1908, it was declared a restricted area. The subsequent industrial exploitation has left its mark with ghost towns and scars in the desert landscape as reminders of a not so distant past. However, some unique biotopes have survived.

Le parc national de Sperrgebiet
Pendant un siècle, cette région du sud de la Namibie est restée inaccessible : après la découverte de gisements de diamants en 1908, elle fut fermée au public. L'industrie minière a laissé des traces : les villes fantômes témoignent du passé, les cicatrices sont visibles dans certaines parties du désert. Mais les biotopes qui subsistent sont exceptionnels.

Tsau-ǁKhaeb-(Sperrgebiet)-Nationalpark
Diese Region im Süden Namibias war 100 Jahre lang nicht öffentlich zugänglich: Nach Diamantenfunden im Jahr 1908 wurde sie zum Sperrgebiet erklärt. Die anschließende industrielle Ausbeutung ließ Spuren zurück: Geisterstädte zeugen von der Vergangenheit, Teile der Wüstenlandschaft zeigen Narben. Es blieben aber auch einmalige Biotope erhalten.

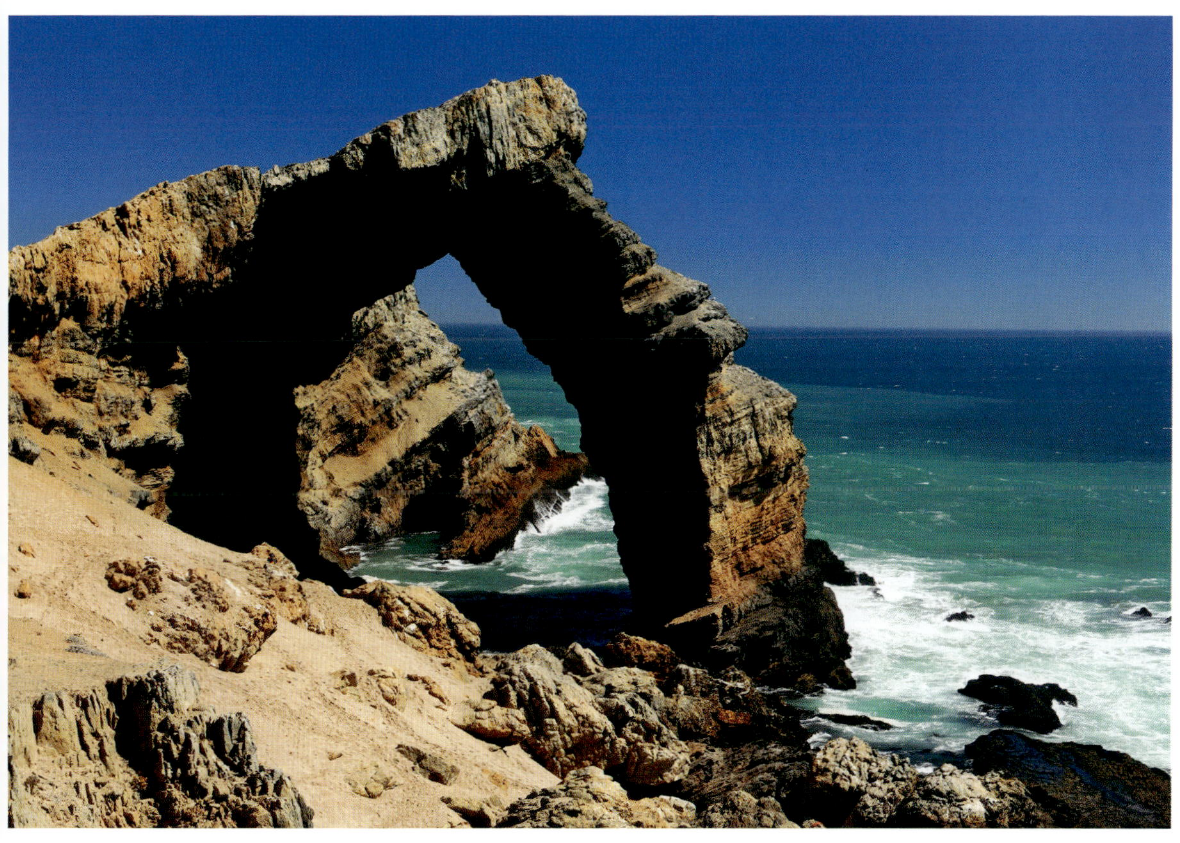

Elbow Rock, Tsau ||Khaeb National Park (Sperrgebiet)

Parque nacional de Sperrgebiet
Esta región en el sur de Namibia estuvo cerrada al público durante 100 años: después de que se encontraran diamantes en el año 1908 fue declarada área restringida. La explotación industrial posterior dejó sus huellas: ciudades fantasma testimonian el pasado, parte del paisaje del desierto paisaje muestra las cicatrices. Quedan sin embargo hábitats únicos.

Parco Nazionale Tsau-||Khaeb
Questa regione nel sud della Namibia non è stata accessibile al pubblico per 100 anni: dopo le scoperte di diamanti nel 1908 fu dichiarata zona vietata. Il successivo sfruttamento industriale ha lasciato delle tracce: le città fantasma testimoniano il passato, alcune parti del paesaggio desertico mostrano le cicatrici. Ma sono conservati anche biotopi unici.

Sperrgebiet
Dit gebied in het zuiden van Namibië was een eeuw lang verboden gebied. Nadat hier in 1908 diamanten werden gevonden, werd het tot "Sperrgebiet" verklaard. De daarop volgende industriële uitbuiting liet haar sporen na. Spookstadjes getuigen nog van dat verleden en delen van het woestijnlandschap vertonen littekens. Maar er ontstonden ook unieke biotopen.

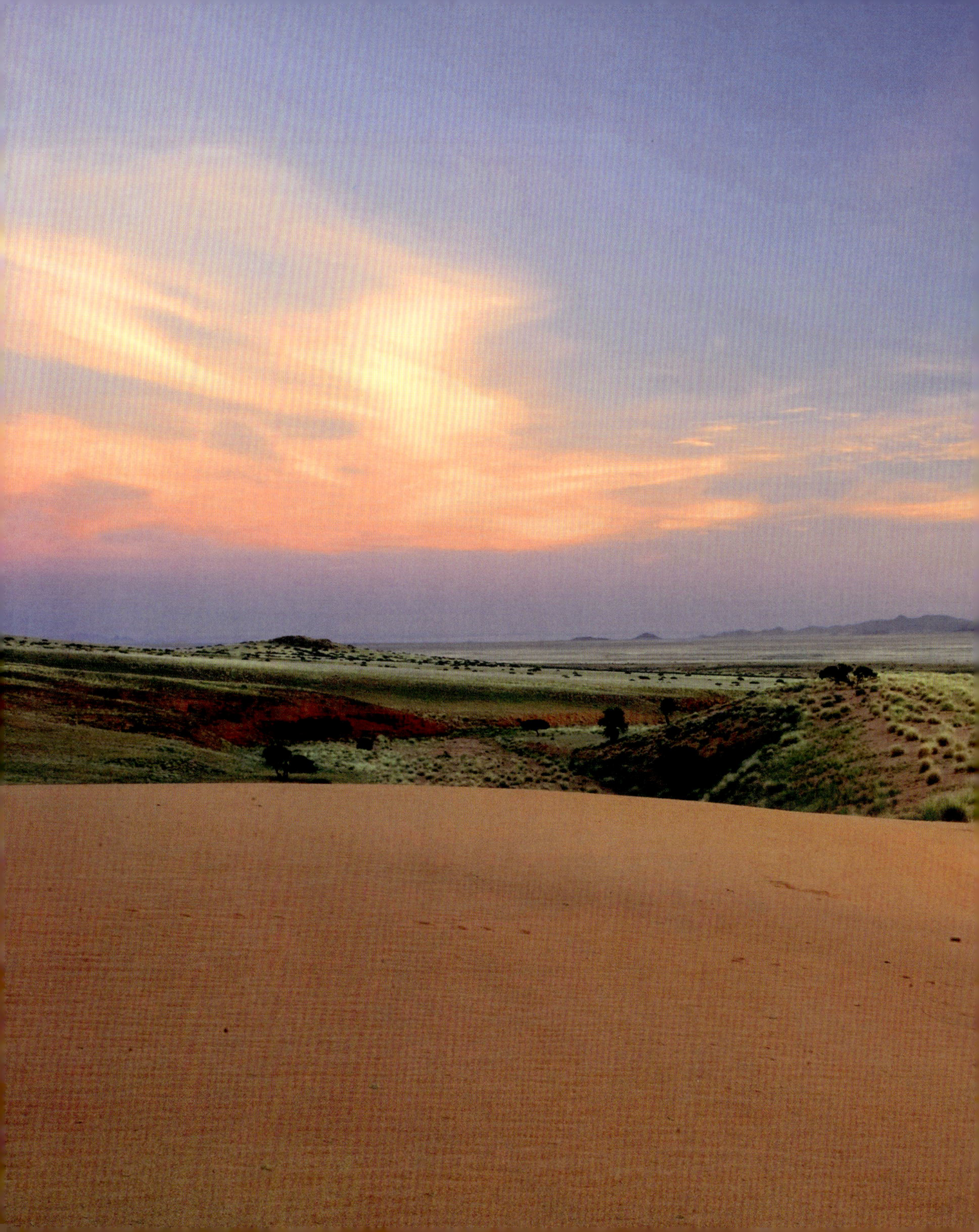

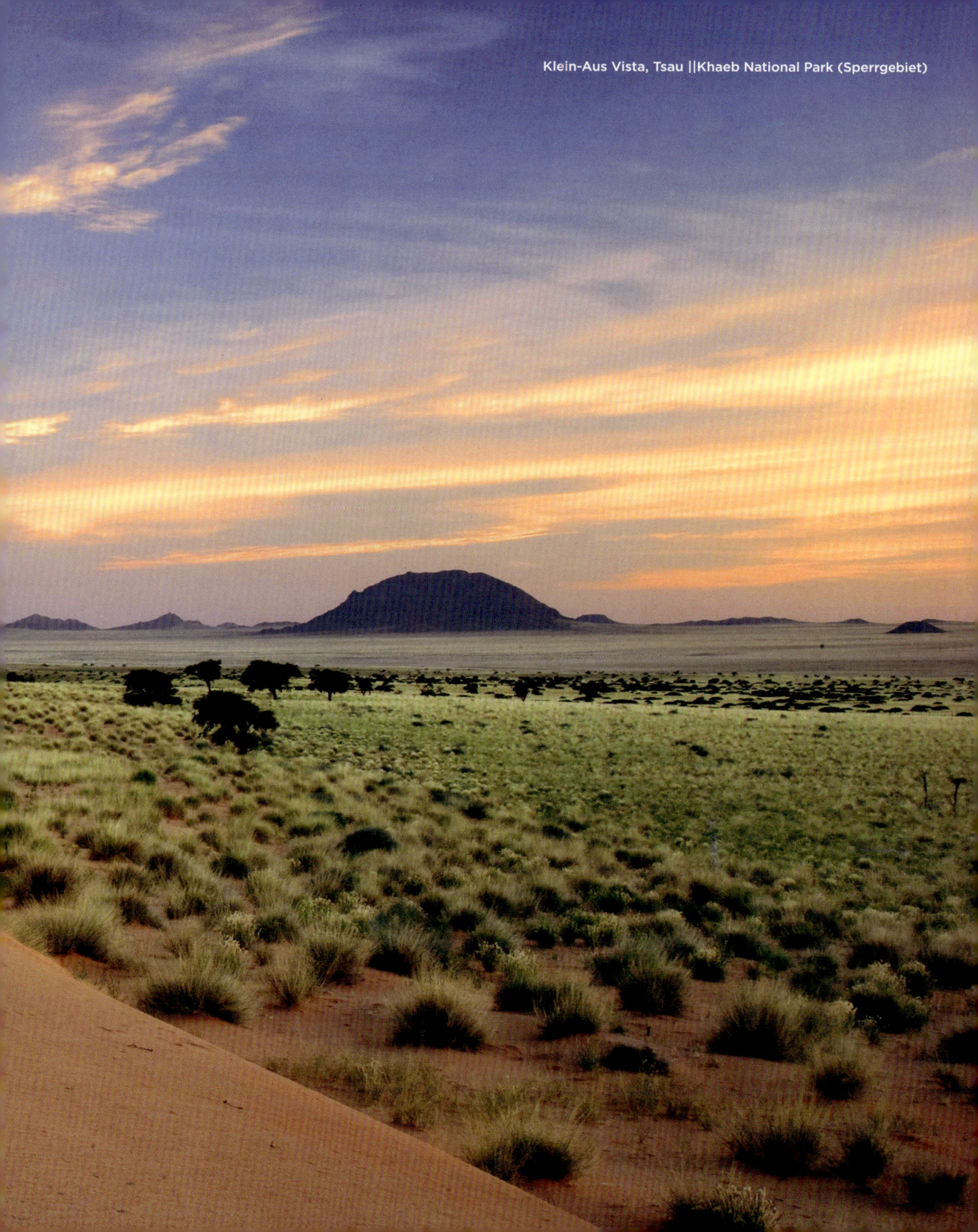

Klein-Aus Vista, Tsau ||Khaeb National Park (Sperrgebiet)

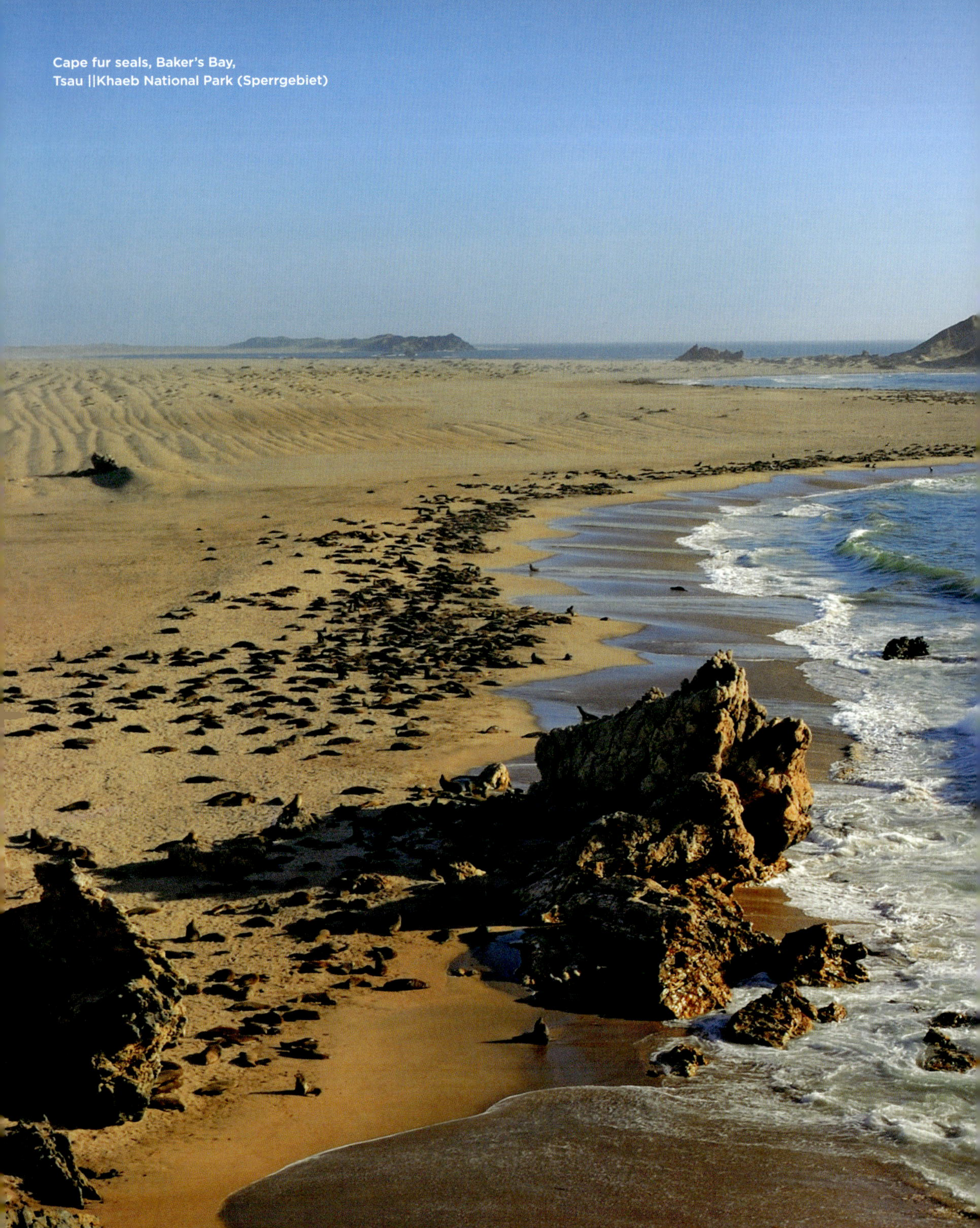

Cape fur seals, Baker's Bay,
Tsau ||Khaeb National Park (Sperrgebiet)

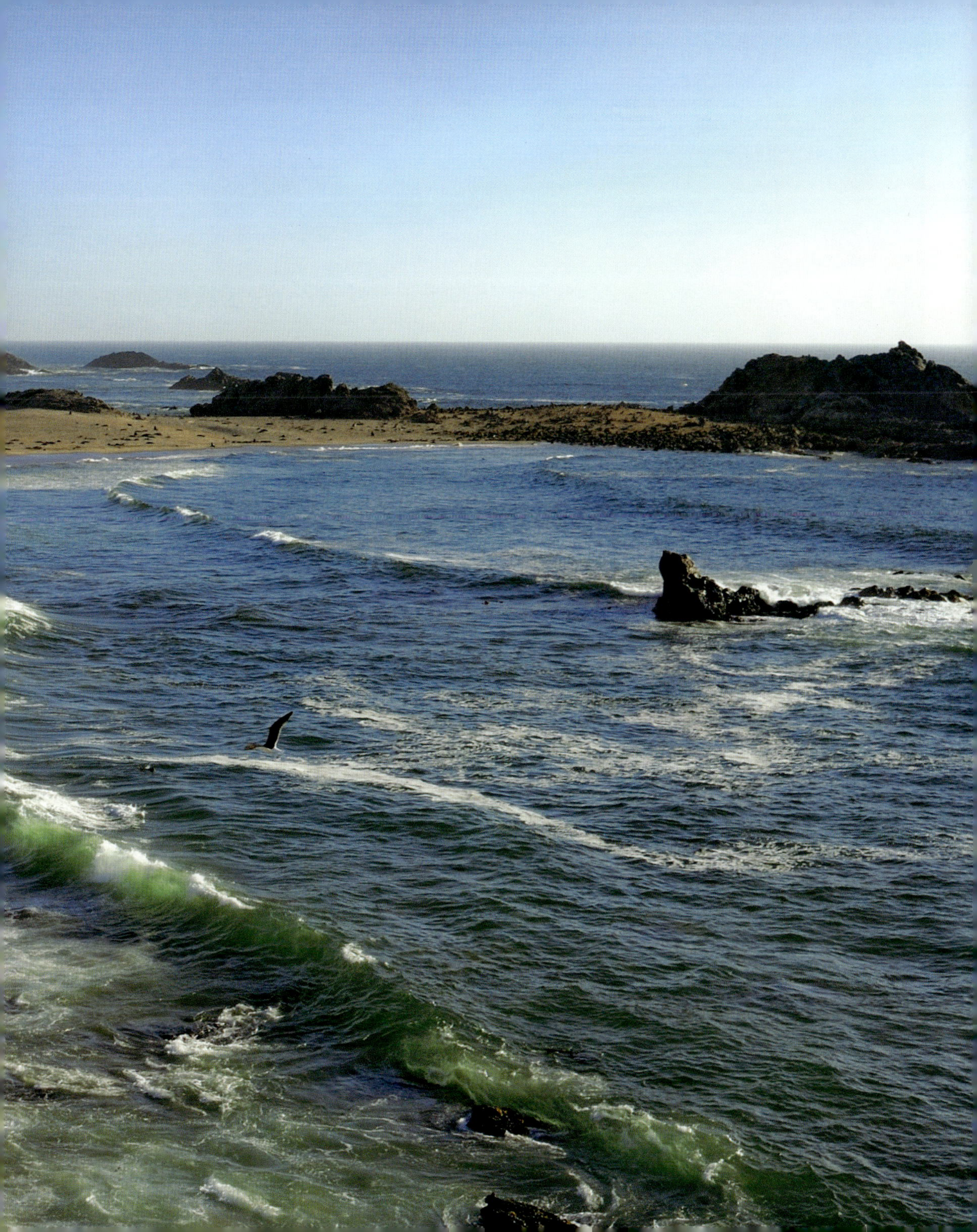

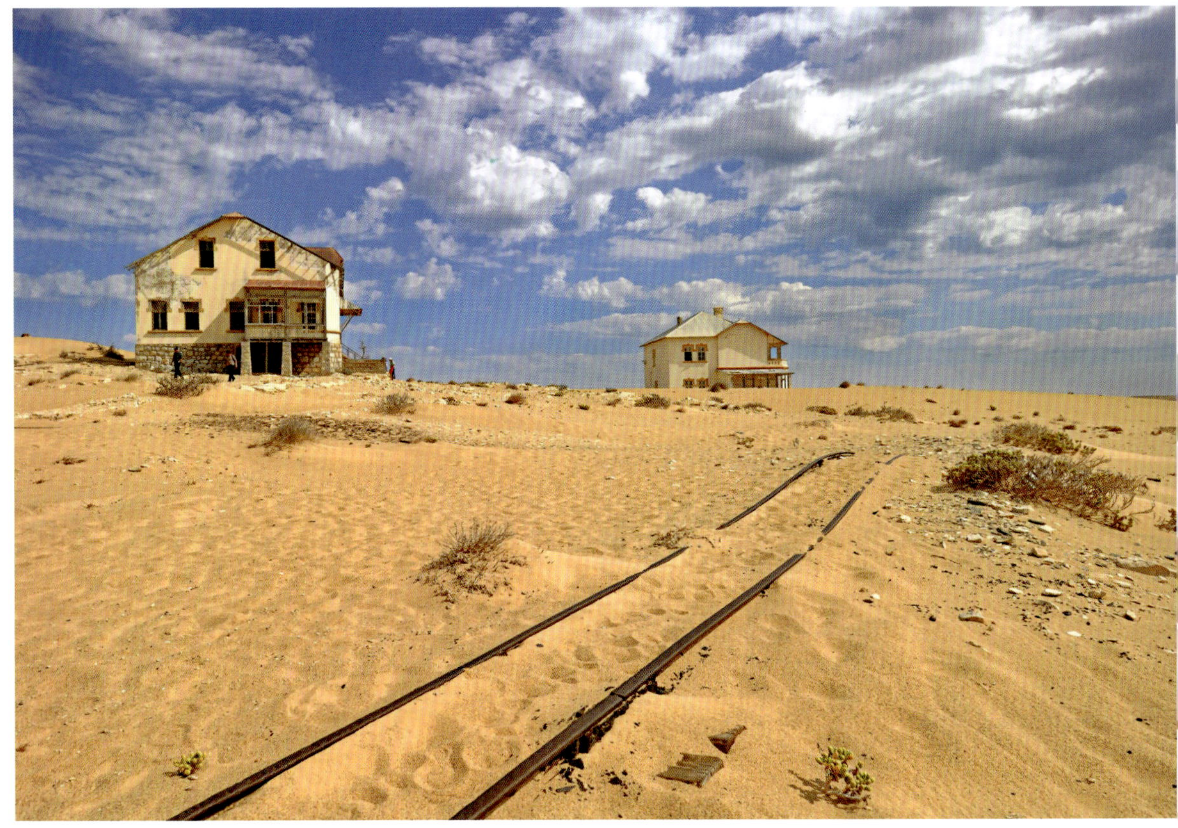

Kolmanskop, Tsau ǁKhaeb National Park (Sperrgebiet)

Kolmanskop
August Stauch's hobby was mineralogy, so he knew what he had found: a diamond in the rough. When this became known, a diamond rush broke out in the south of Namibia. In the desert, diamond-mining towns such as Kolmanskop, one of the richest settlements in German South-West Africa, sprung up. By 1919, the mines around Lüderitz had been exhausted, with Kolmanskop being finally abandoned in 1954 to become a ghost town.

Kolmanskop
August Stauch, en minéralogiste amateur, était conscient de la valeur de sa découverte, un diamant brut. La nouvelle se répandit et ce fut la ruée dans le sud de la Namibie : les mineurs construisirent dans le désert des villes comme Kolmanskop, qui fut l'une des plus riches du sud-ouest de l'Afrique, alors une colonie allemande. En 1919, les mines des environs de Lüderitz étaient épuisées, et Kolmanskop, abandonnée, n'est plus qu'une ville fantôme.

Kolmannskuppe
August Stauchs Hobby war Mineralogie und so wusste er, was er gefunden hatte: einen Rohdiamanten. Als das bekannt wurde, brach der Diamantenrausch im Süden Namibias aus: In der Wüste entstanden Diamantengräberstädte wie Kolmannskuppe, das zu den reichsten Siedlungen Deutsch-Südwestafrikas gehörte. 1919 waren die Lager um Lüderitz erschöpft, Kolmannskuppe wurde verlassen und zur Geisterstadt.

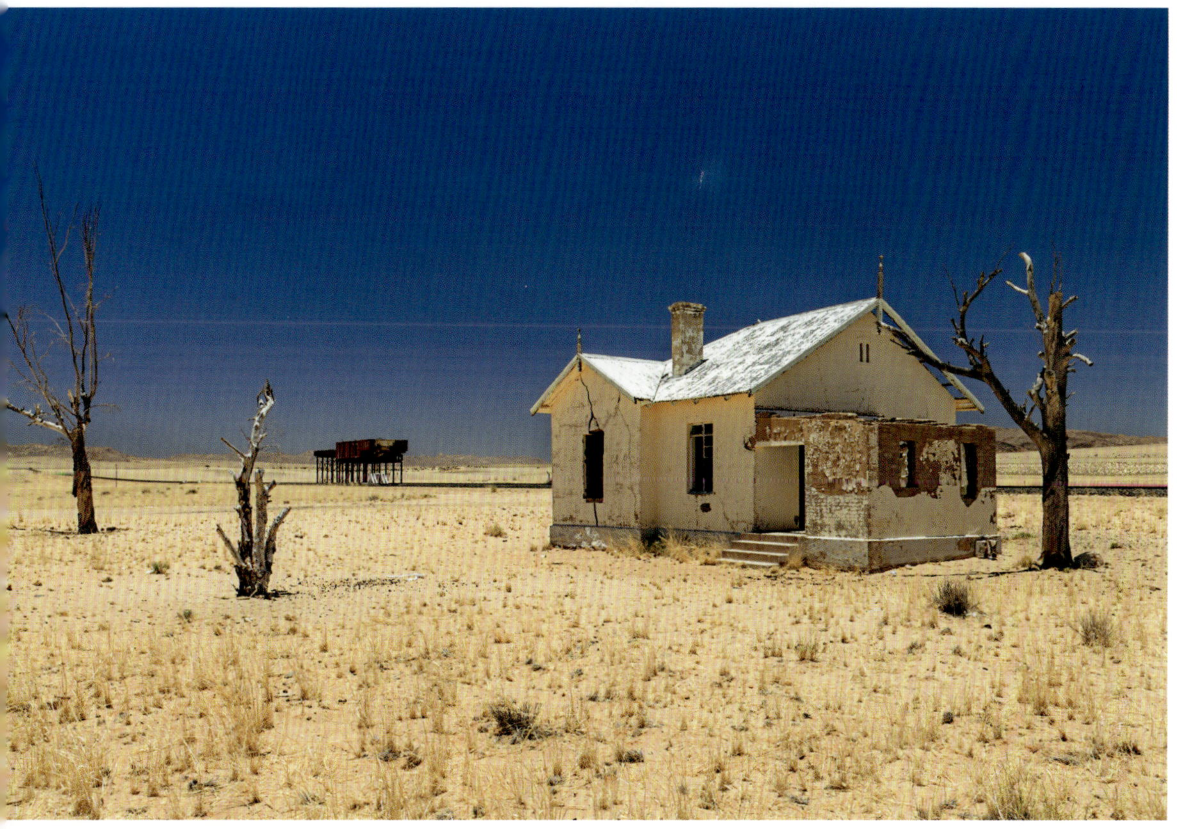

Garub, abandoned train station between Aus and Lüderitz, Tsau ||Khaeb National Park (Sperrgebiet)

Kolmanskop
La afición de August Stauch era la mineralogía y sabía lo que había encontrado: un diamante en bruto. Cuando esto se hizo público, la fiebre de los diamantes estalló en el sur de Namibia: en el desierto se crearon pueblos mineros de diamantes como Kolmanskop, que pertenecían a los asentamientos más ricos de Alemania y del suroeste de África. En 1919, el campamento alrededor de Lüderitz se habían agotado, Kolmanskop fue abandonado y un se convirtió en un pueblo fantasma.

Kolmanskop
L'hobby di August Stauch era la mineralogia e così sapeva cosa aveva trovato: un diamante grezzo. Quando questo si seppe, si scatenò la corsa ai diamanti nel sud della Namibia:nel deserto nacquero le città dei cercatori di diamanti come Kolmanskop, uno degli insediamenti più ricchi dell'Africa Tedesca del Sud-Ovest. Nel 1919 si esaurirono i giacimenti vicino Lüderitz, Kolmanskop fu abbandonata e divenne una città fantasma.

Kolmanskop
Mineralogie was de hobby van August Stauch en dus zag hij meteen wat hij had gevonden: een ruwe diamant. Toen dat bekend werd, ontstond een ware diamantkoorts in Zuid-Namibië; in de woestijn verrezen stadjes voor diamantgravers, zoals Kolmanskop, dat tot de rijkste nederzettingen in Duits-Zuidwest-Afrika behoorde. In 1919 waren de groeves rond Lüderitz uitgeput en werd Kolmanskop een spookstad.

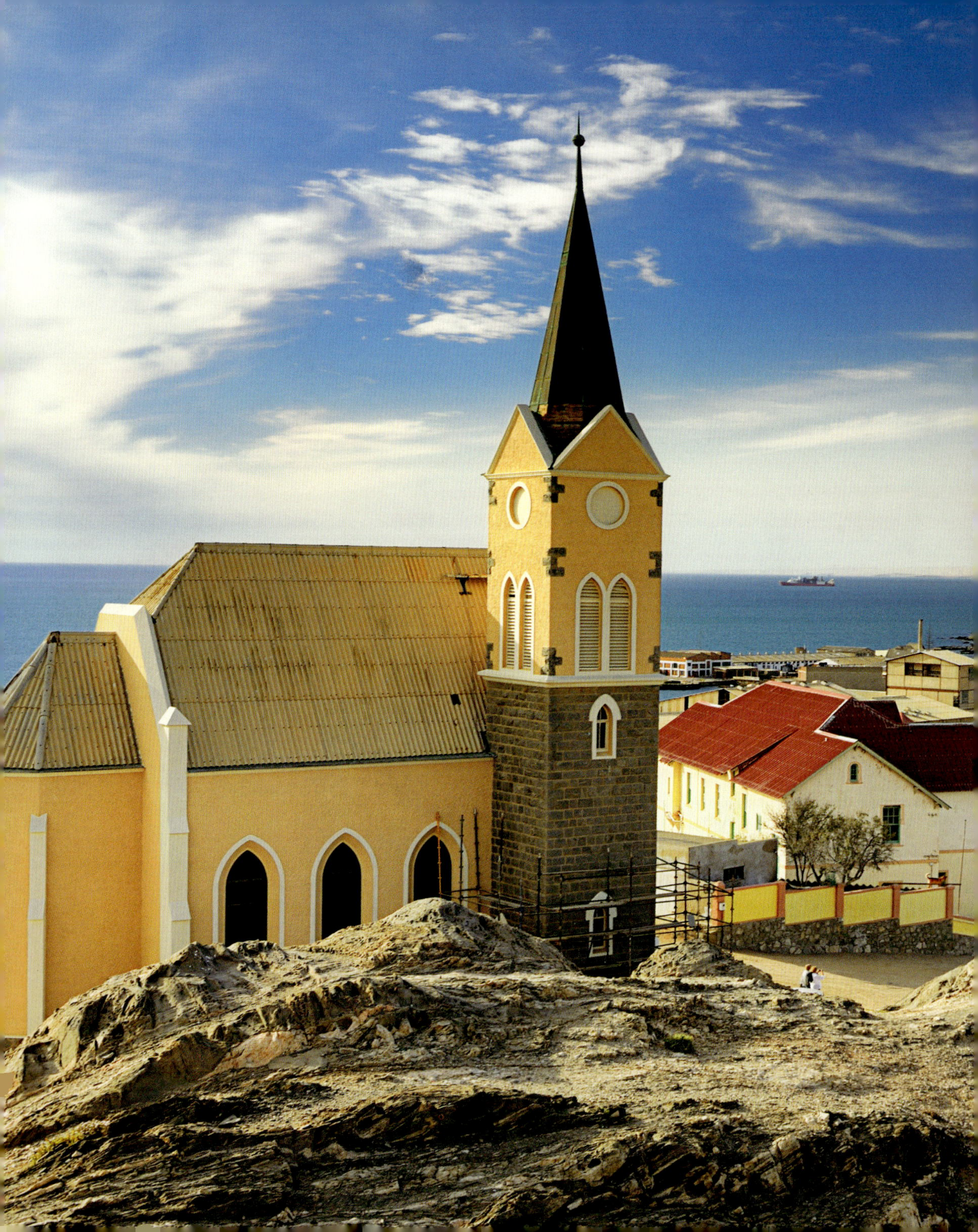

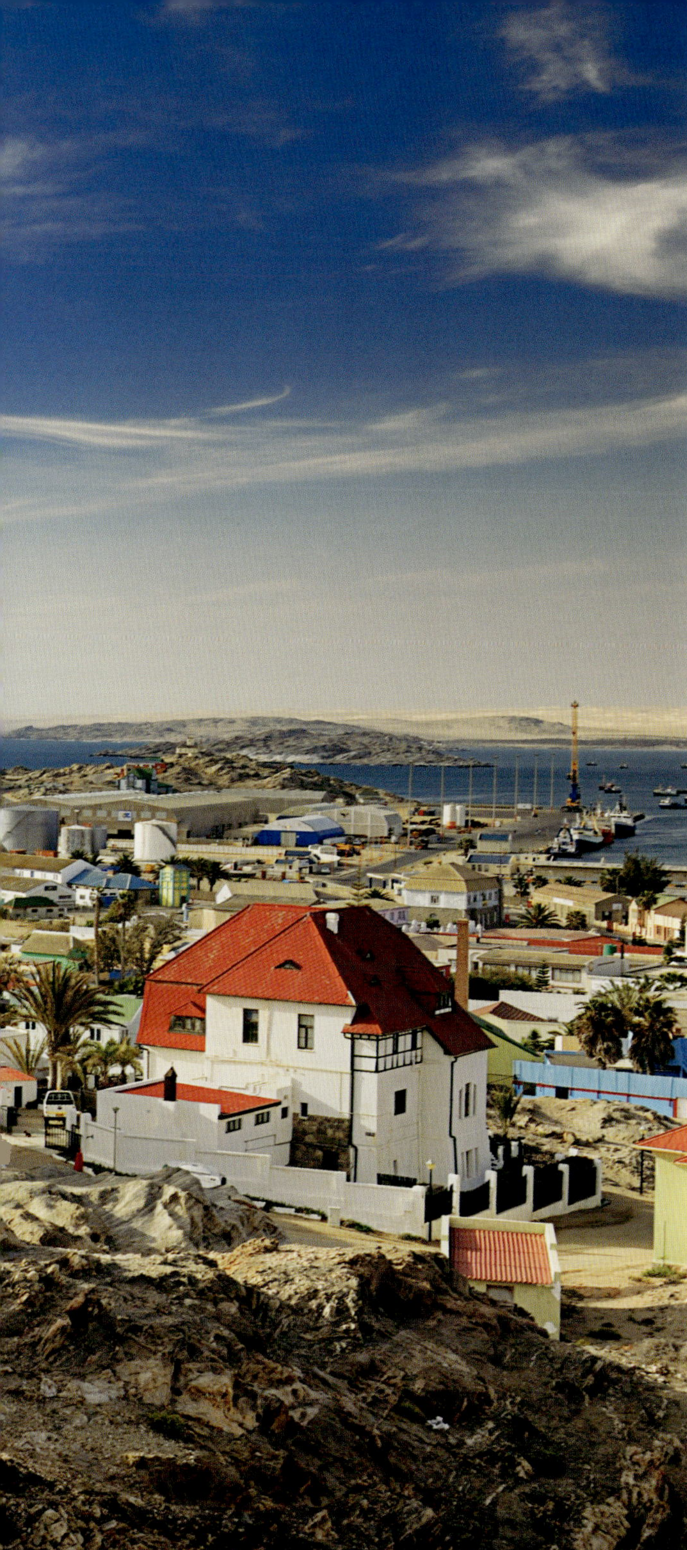

Evangelical Lutheran church on Diamond Hill, Lüderitz

Lüderitz
Today about 20,000 people live in this colourful little town on the edge of the Namib Desert. The former German founding colonial city of Namibia was built on bare coastal rock and is often exposed to stormy Atlantic winds. In the city centre are numerous lovingly maintained art nouveau buildings dating from the German colonial era.

Lüderitz
Près de 20 000 personnes vivent aujourd'hui dans cette petite ville si colorée située à la limite du désert du Namib. Cette ville, la plus ancienne de Namibie, fut édifiée sur la côté à même la roche et est souvent exposée aux vents violents de l'Atlantique. Dans le centre, on trouve nombre de bâtiments Art nouveau soigneusement entretenus, datant de l'époque coloniale allemande.

Lüderitz
Heute leben etwa 20 000 Menschen in der farbenprächtigen kleinen Stadt am Rande der Namib Wüste. Die einstige Gründerstadt Namibias wurde auf nacktem Küsten-Fels gebaut und ist oft stürmischen Atlantikwinden ausgesetzt. Im Stadtzentrum findet man zahlreiche liebevoll gepflegte Jugendstil-Bauten aus der deutschen Kolonialzeit.

Lüderitz
Hoy en día, alrededor de 20 000 personas viven en este colorido pueblecito al borde del desierto de Namibia. La antigua ciudad fundadora de Namibia fue construida sobre roca costera desnuda y a menudo está expuesta a los vientos tormentosos del Atlántico. En el centro de la ciudad se encuentran numerosos edificios Art Nouveau de la época colonial alemana.

Lüderitz
Oggi circa 20 000 persone vivono in questa splendente cittadina ai margini del deserto del Namib. Questa città della Namibia, fondata dai primi pionieri, è stata costruita su nude rocce costiere ed è spesso esposta ai venti tempestosi dell'Atlantico. Nel centro della città si trovano numerosi edifici in stile Art Nouveau di epoca coloniale tedesca ben tenuti.

Lüderitz
Vandaag de dag wonen er zo'n 20 000 mensen in dit kleurrijke stadje aan de rand van de Namibwoestijn. De eind 19e eeuw opgerichte stad is gebouwd op kale rotsen aan de kust en wordt vaak geteisterd door stormachtige Atlantische winden. In het centrum van de stad zijn tal van liefdevol onderhouden jugendstilgebouwen uit de Duitse koloniale tijd te vinden.

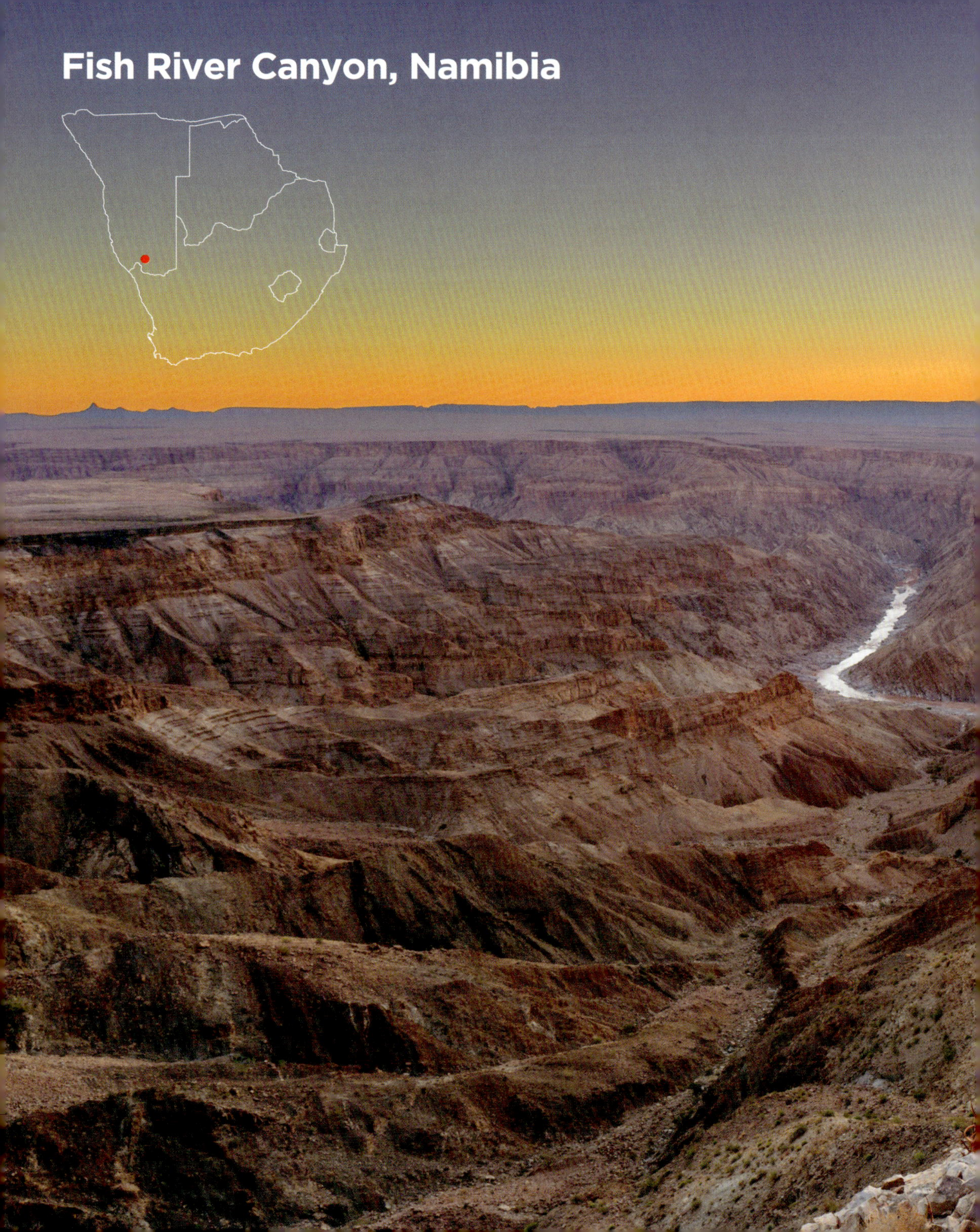
Fish River Canyon, Namibia

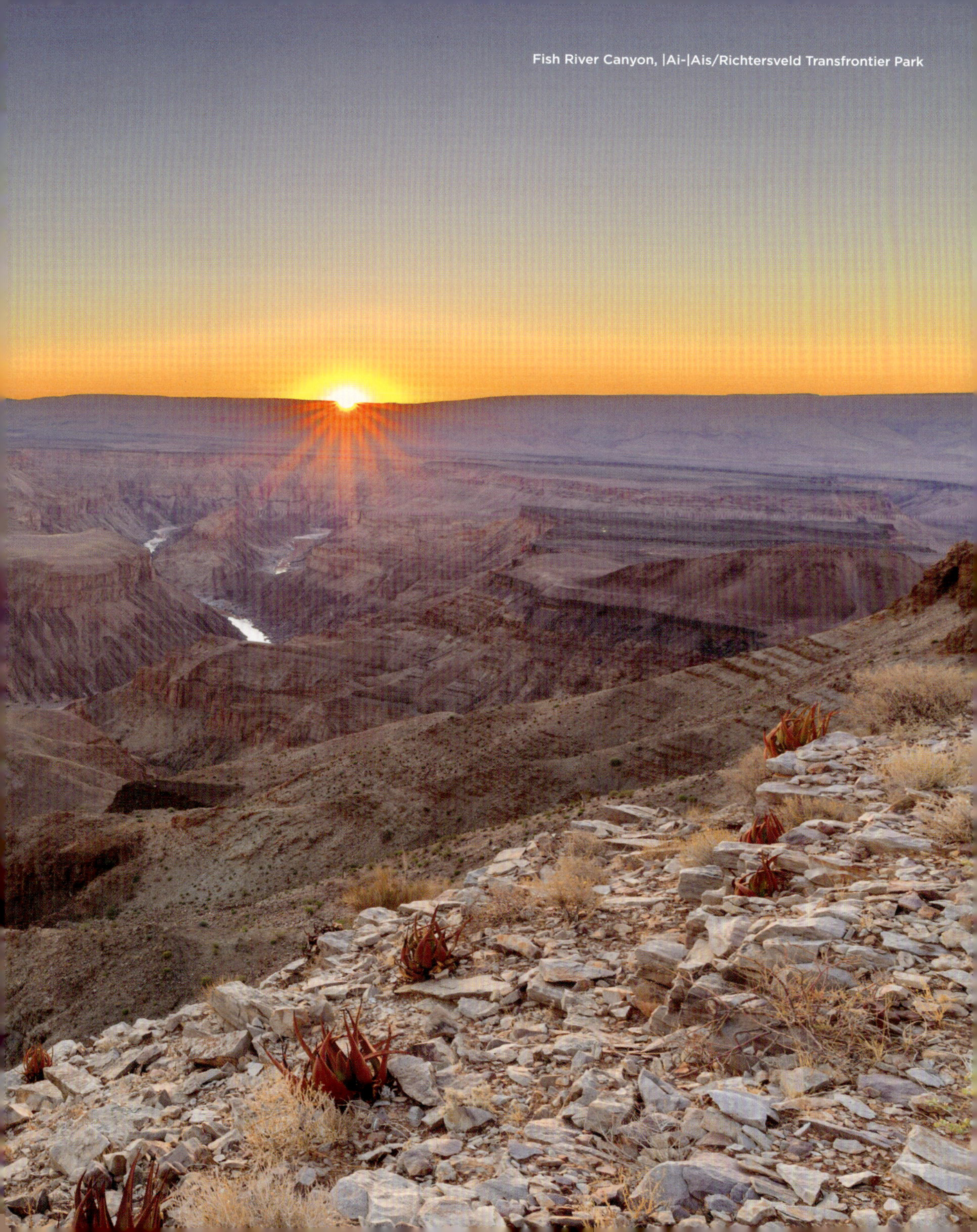
Fish River Canyon, |Ai-|Ais/Richtersveld Transfrontier Park

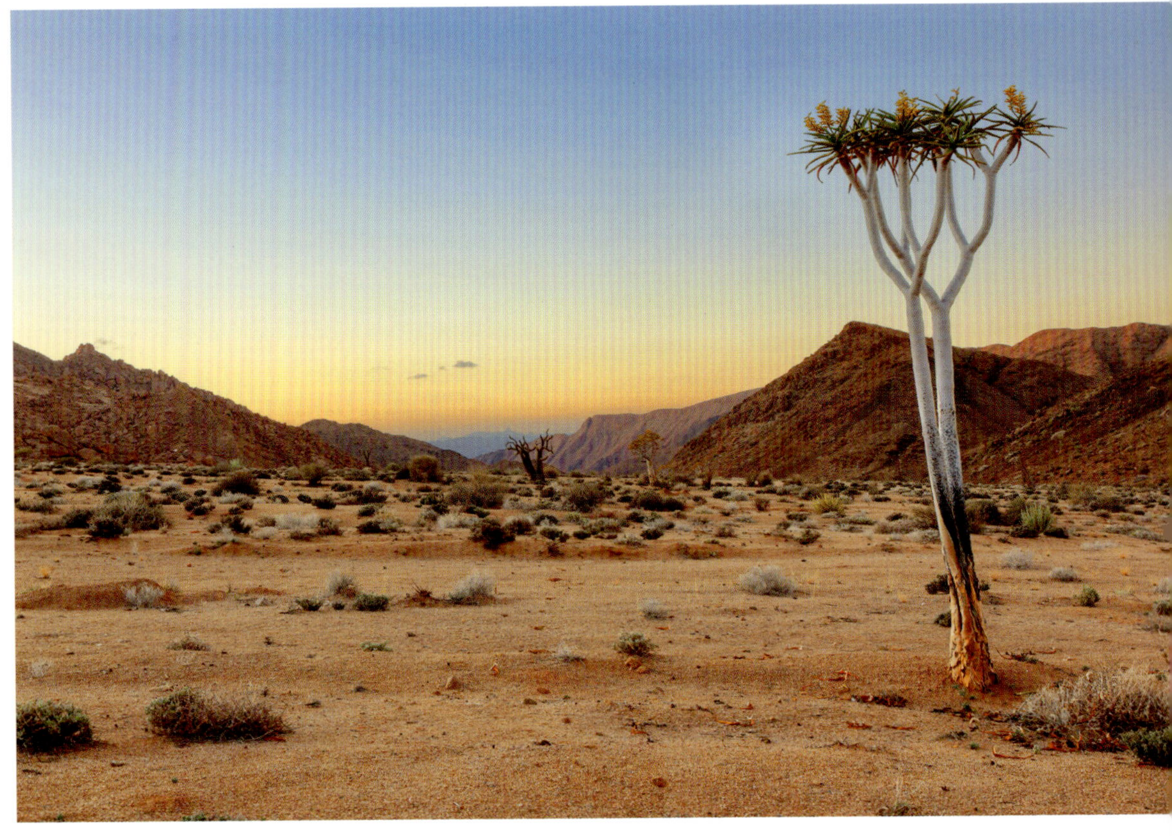

Quiver tree, Fish River Canyon, |Ai-|Ais/Richtersveld Transfrontier Park

Fish River Canyon

Fish River Canyon is located in southern Namibia, and is part of the |Ai-|Ais/ Richtersveld Transfrontier Park, which straddles the border with South Africa. The gigantic gorge is 160 km (99 mi) long, 27 km (17 mi) wide, and up to 550 m (1804 ft) deep, making it the second largest canyon in the world after the Grand Canyon in Arizona.

Le Fish River Canyon

Le canyon de la Fish River, dans le sud de la Namibie, est le clou du parc transfrontalier de l'|Ai-|Ais/Richtersveld. Ce canyon gigantesque, long de 160 km, large de 27 km et d'une profondeur atteignant 550 m est le deuxième du monde par la taille, après le Grand Canyon du Colorado.

Fish River Canyon

Der Fish River Canyon liegt im Süden Namibias und ist Teil des grenzüberschreitenden |Ai-|Ais/ Richtersveld Transfrontier Parks. Die gigantische Schlucht ist 160 km lang, 27 km breit und bis zu 550 m tief - und damit nach dem Grand Canyon (USA) der zweitgrößte Canyon der Welt.

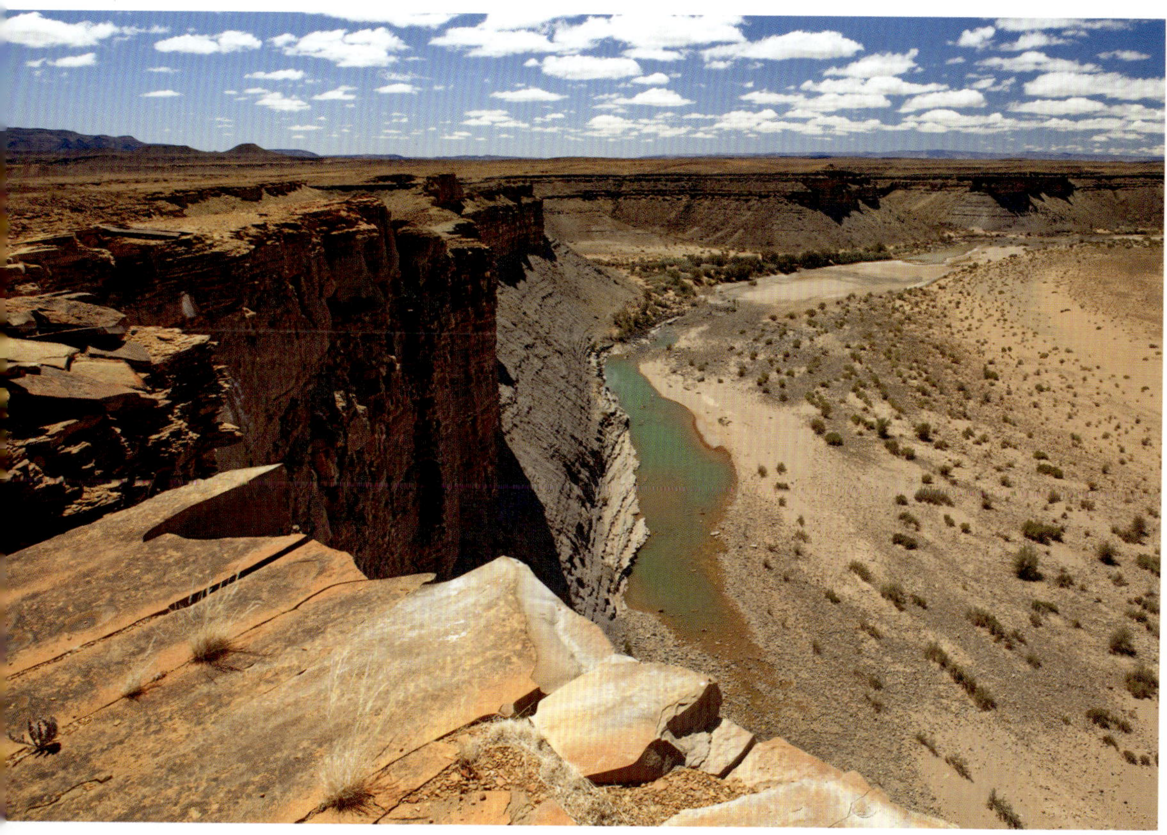

ish River Canyon, |Ai-|Ais/Richtersveld Transfrontier Park

añón del río Fish
cañón del río Fish se encuentra en el ır de Namibia y es parte del parque ansfronterizo |Ai-|Ais/Richtersveld. gigantesco cañón tiene 160 km de rgo, 27 km de ancho y hasta 550 m de ofundidad – y por lo tanto es el segundo añón más grande del mundo después del ran Cañón (EE.UU.).

Fish River Canyon
Il Fish River Canyon si trova nel sud della Namibia e fa parte del Parco transfrontaliero |Ai-|Ais/Richtersveld. La gigantesca gola è lunga 160 km, larga 27 km e raggiunge una profondità di 550 m, e quindi dopo il Grand Canyon (USA) è la seconda più grande al mondo.

Fish River Canyon
De Fish River in het zuiden van Namibië maakt deel uit van het grensoverschrijdende |Ai-|Ais/Richtersveld Transfrontier Park. De gigantische kloof is 160 km lang, 27 km breed en tot wel 550 m diep – en daarmee het op één na grootste ravijn op aarde, na de Grand Canyon in de VS.

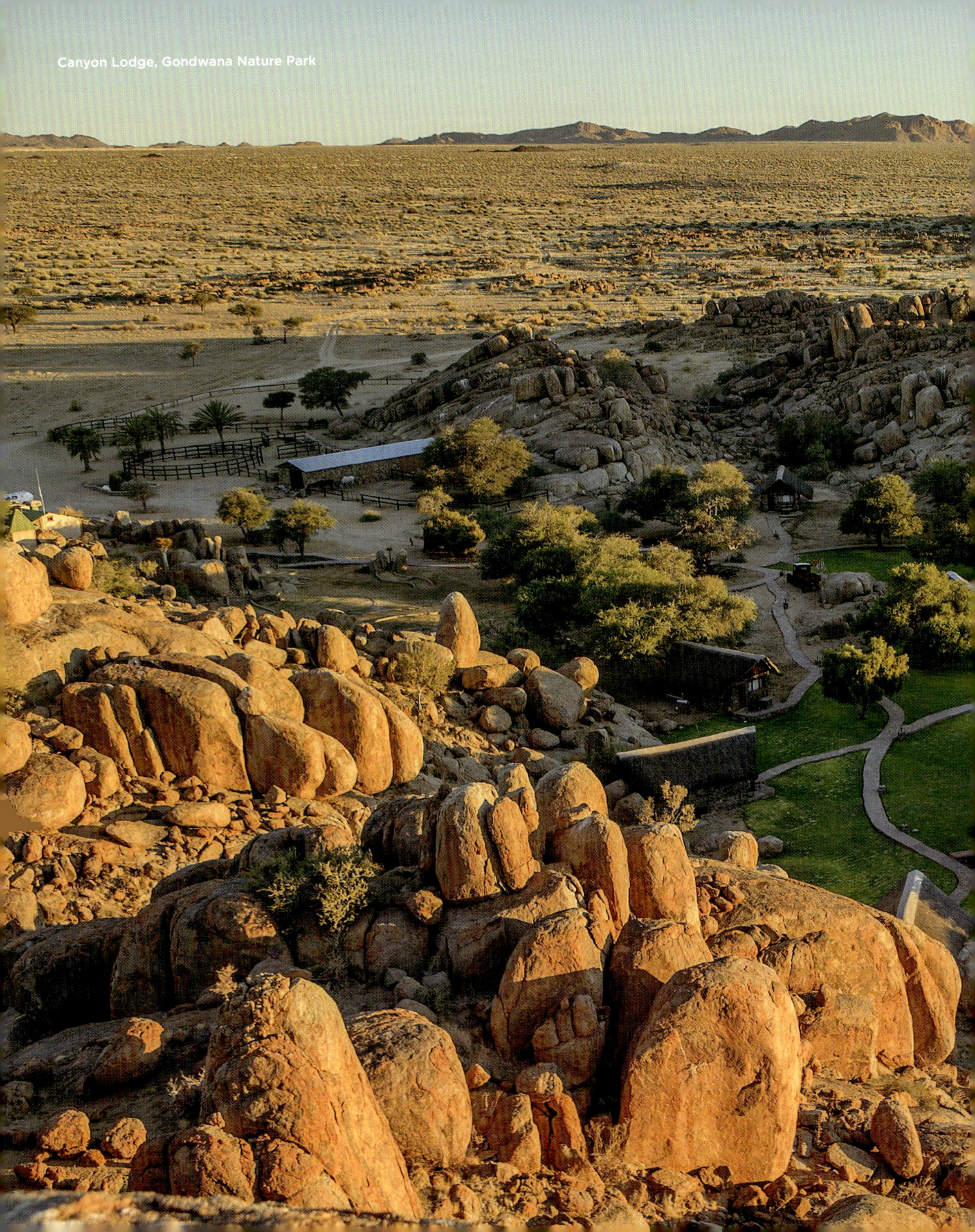

Canyon Lodge, Gondwana Nature Park

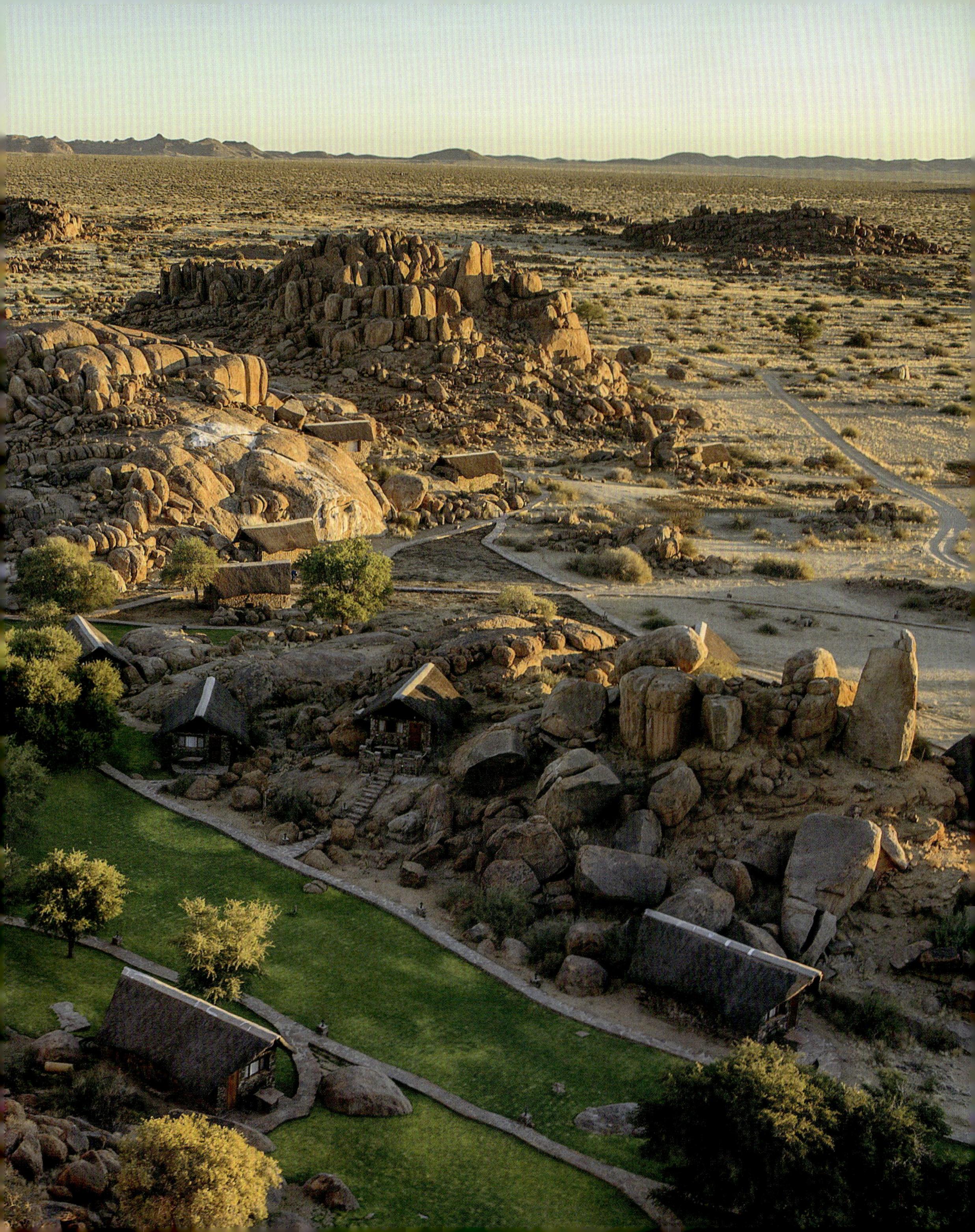

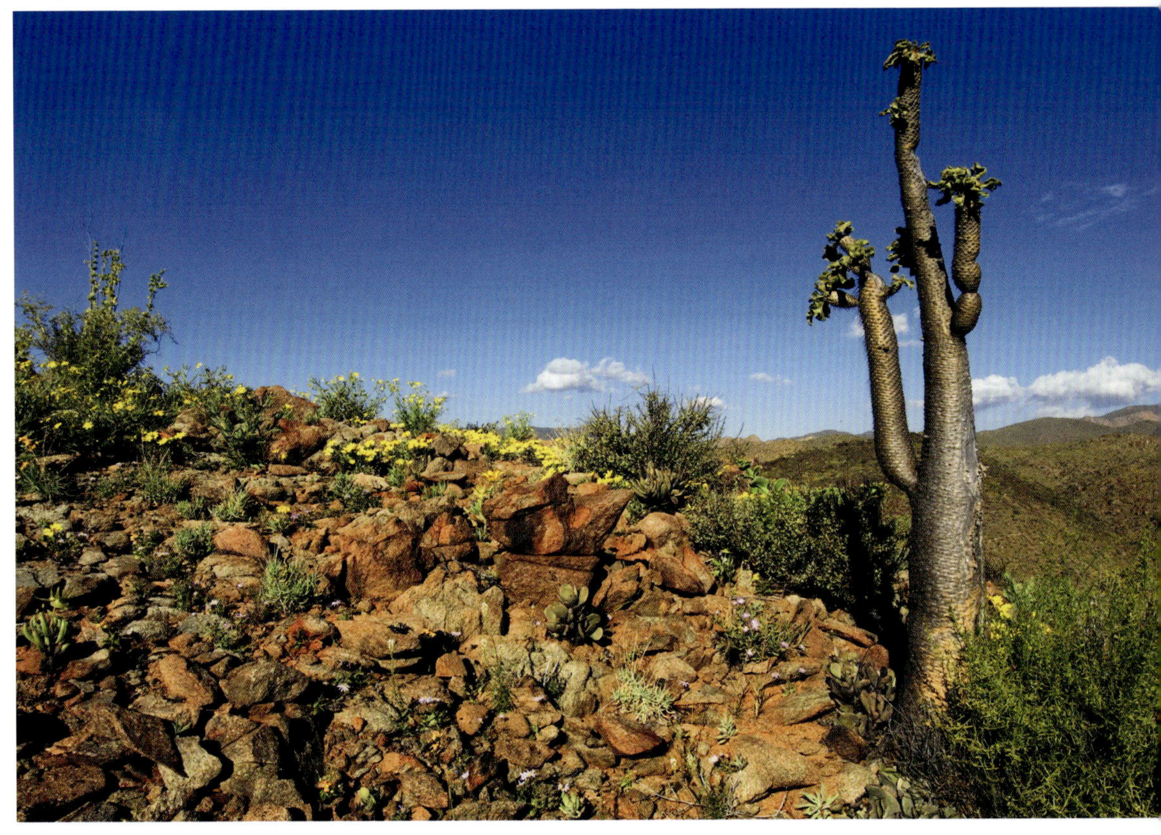

Halfmens, |Ai-|Ais/Richtersveld Transfrontier Park

Halfmens
(Pachypodium namaquanum)
The name halfmens, Afrikaans for "semi-human", may be traced back to a legend: after losing the war, the Namas were forced to leave their ancestral area. Those who looked longingly back towards their homeland eventually froze in place, their heads turned northward. The crowns of these succulents always point northward. The plant is also known as "elephant's trunk".

Demi-homme
(Pachypodium namaquanum)
Le nom de « demi-homme » (halfmens) a sa source dans une légende. Les Namas, après avoir perdu une guerre, durent quitter leurs terres ancestrales. Ceux qui tournèrent la tête pour contempler une dernière fois leur ancienne patrie, vers le nord, furent pétrifiés. Les couronnes de ces plantes succulentes sont toujours orientées au nord.

Halbmensch
(Pachypodium namaquanum)
Der Name „Halbmensch" (halfmens) geht auf eine Legende zurück: Nach einem verlorenen Krieg mussten die Namas ihr angestammtes Gebiet verlassen. Diejenigen, die sehnsüchtig Richtung Heimat zurückblickten, erstarrten, den Kopf nordwärts gewandt. Die Kronen dieser Sukkulenten weisen immer nach Norden.

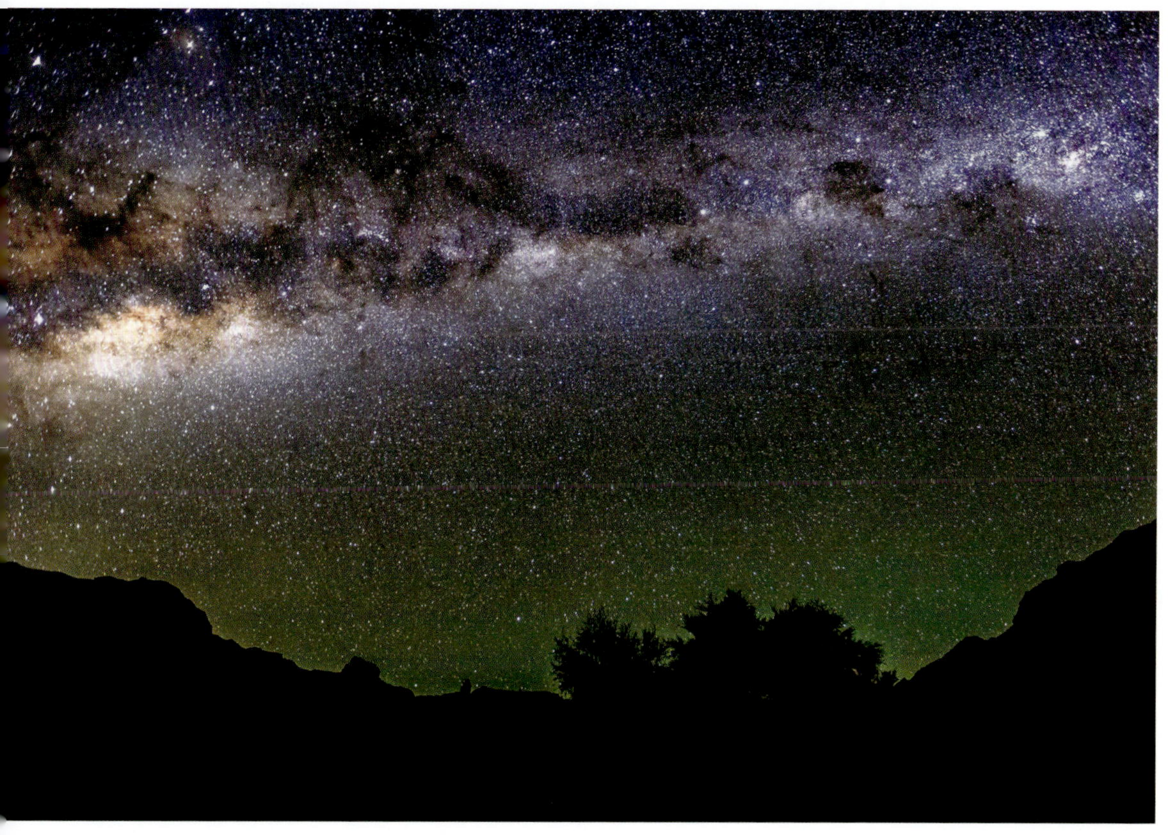

sh River Canyon, |Ai-|Ais/Richtersveld Transfrontier Park

edio hombre
Pachypodium namaquanum)
nombre de "medio hombre" (halfmens) remonta a una leyenda: después de na guerra perdida, los Namas tuvieron ue salir de su territorio ancestral. Los ue miraban hacia atrás con nostalgia, se ongelaban con la cabeza hacia el norte. as coronas de estas suculentas plantas empre apuntan al norte.

Mezzo uomo
(Pachypodium namaquanum)
Il nome "mezzo uomo" (halfmens) risale ad una leggenda: dopo aver perso una guerra, la tribù dei Nama dovette abbandonare la zona che aveva ereditato. Chi guardava con nostalgia in direzione della sua patria, veniva pietrificato con la testa rivolta verso nord. Le chiome di queste piante succulente indicano sempre il nord.

Half-mens
(Pachypodium namaquanum)
De benaming "half-mens" stamt van een legende: na een verloren oorlog moesten de Nama's hun stamgebied verlaten. Degenen die vol heimwee naar hun geboortestreek omkeken, versteenden met het hoofd naar het noorden gekeerd. De kruinen van deze vetplanten wijzen altijd naar het noorden.

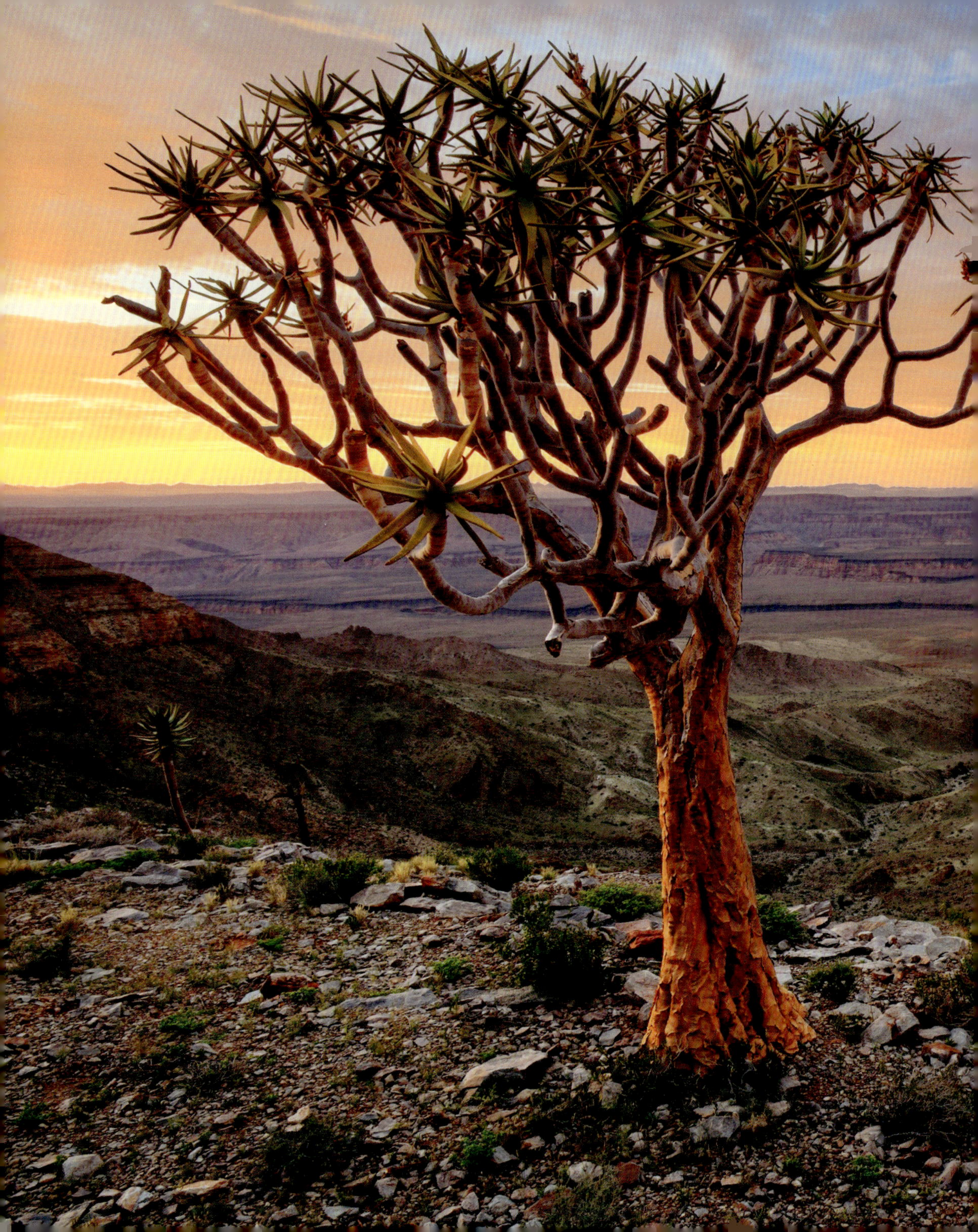

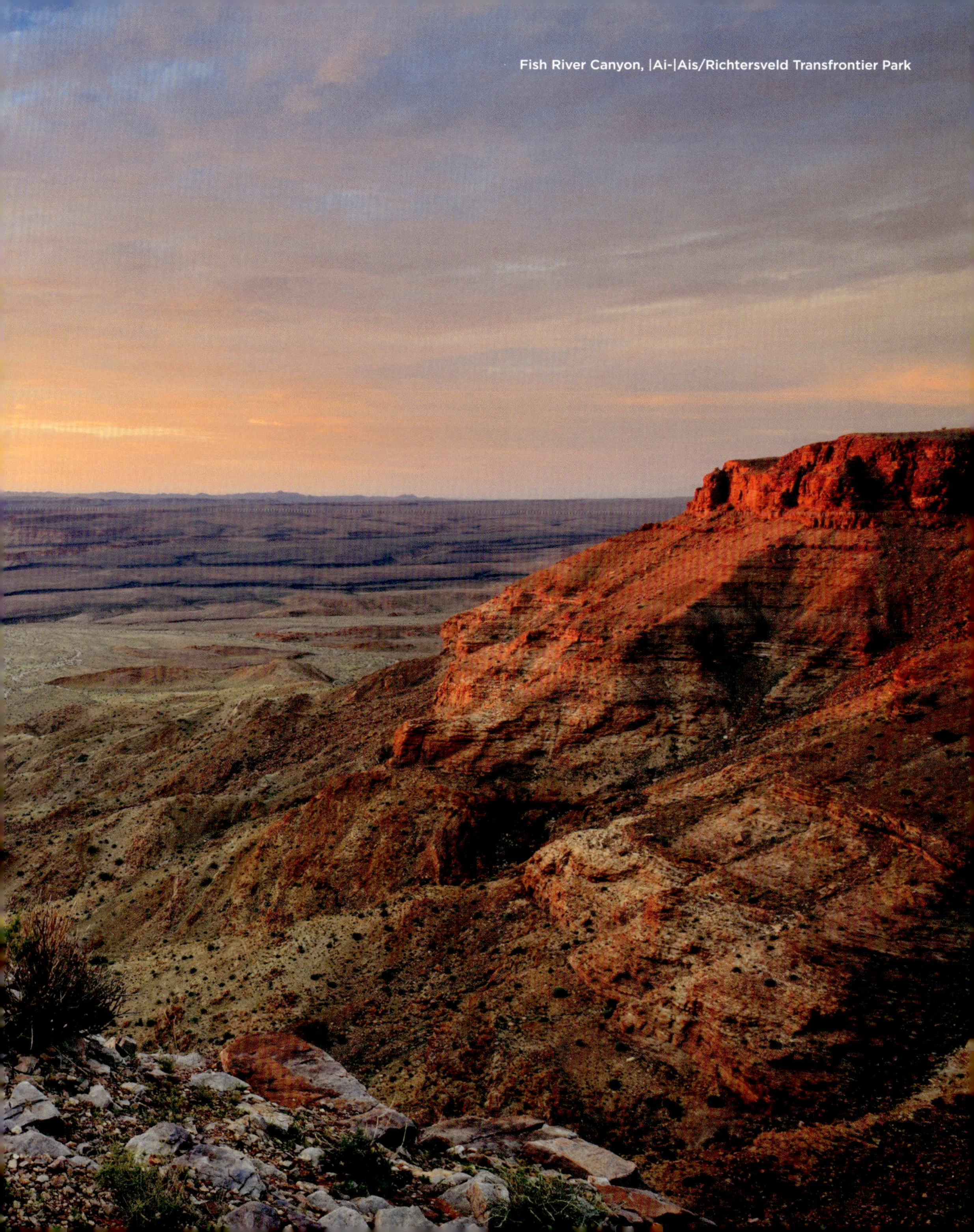

Fish River Canyon, |Ai-|Ais/Richtersveld Transfrontier Park

Chobe National Park & Tsodilo Hills, Botswana

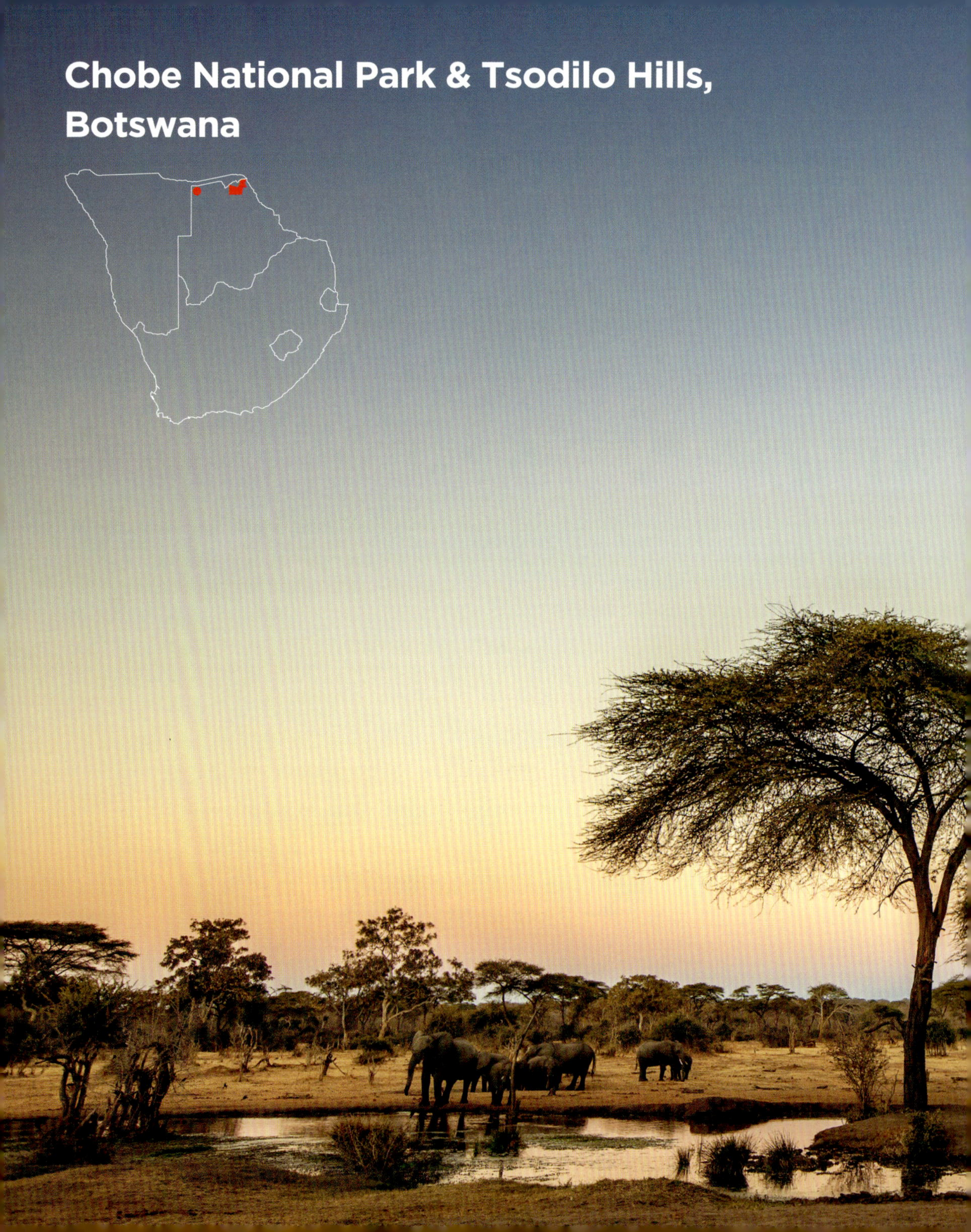

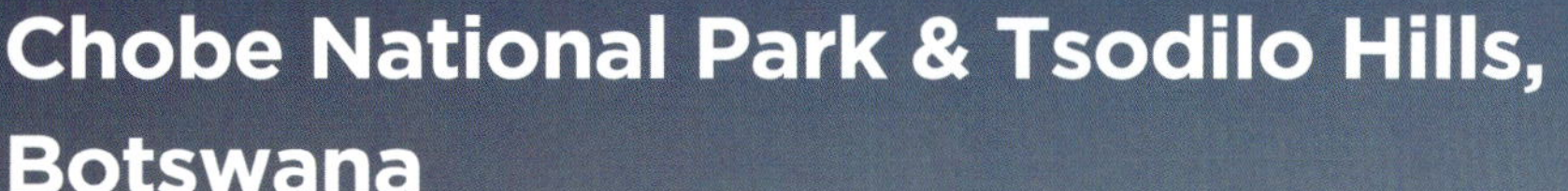

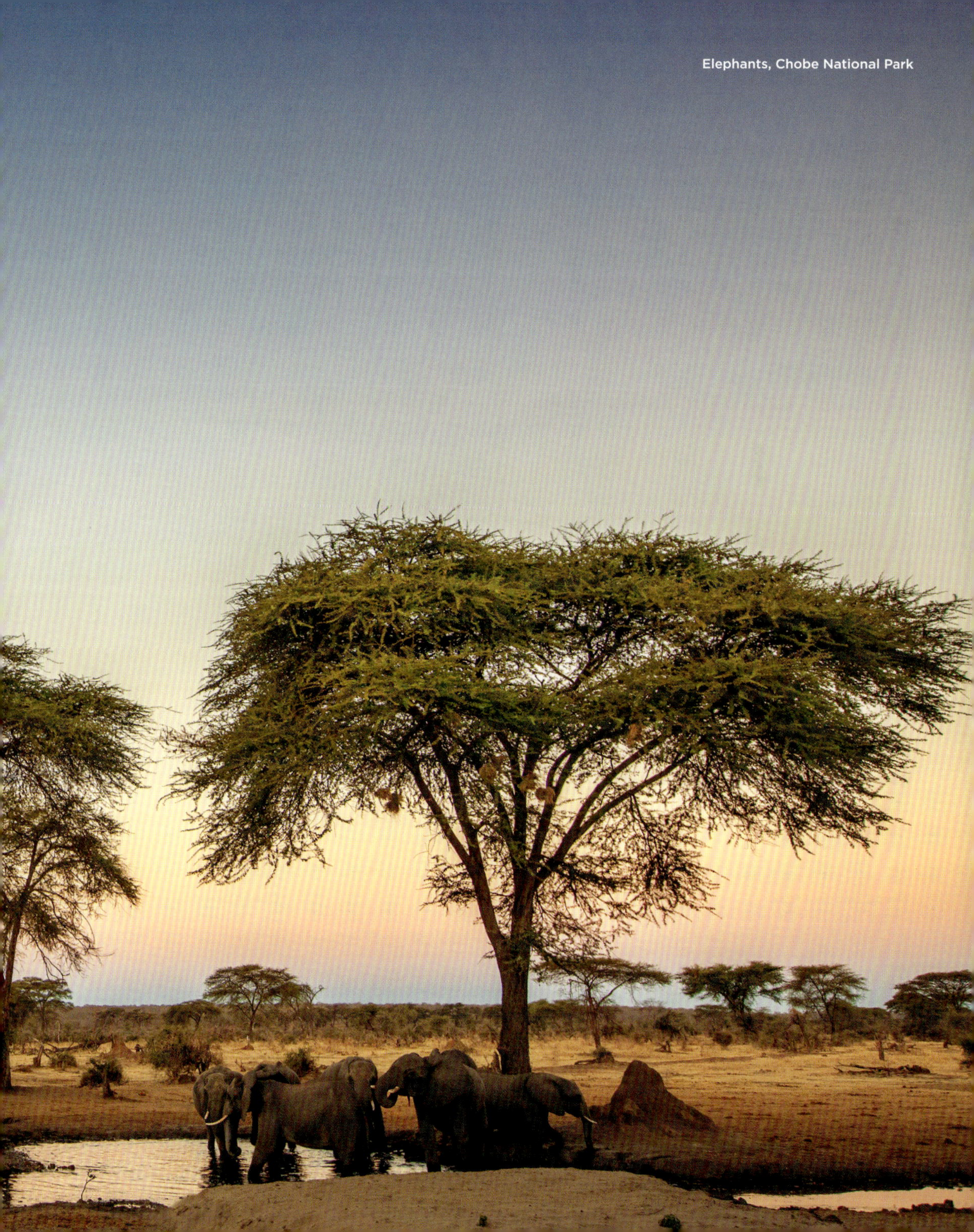
Elephants, Chobe National Park

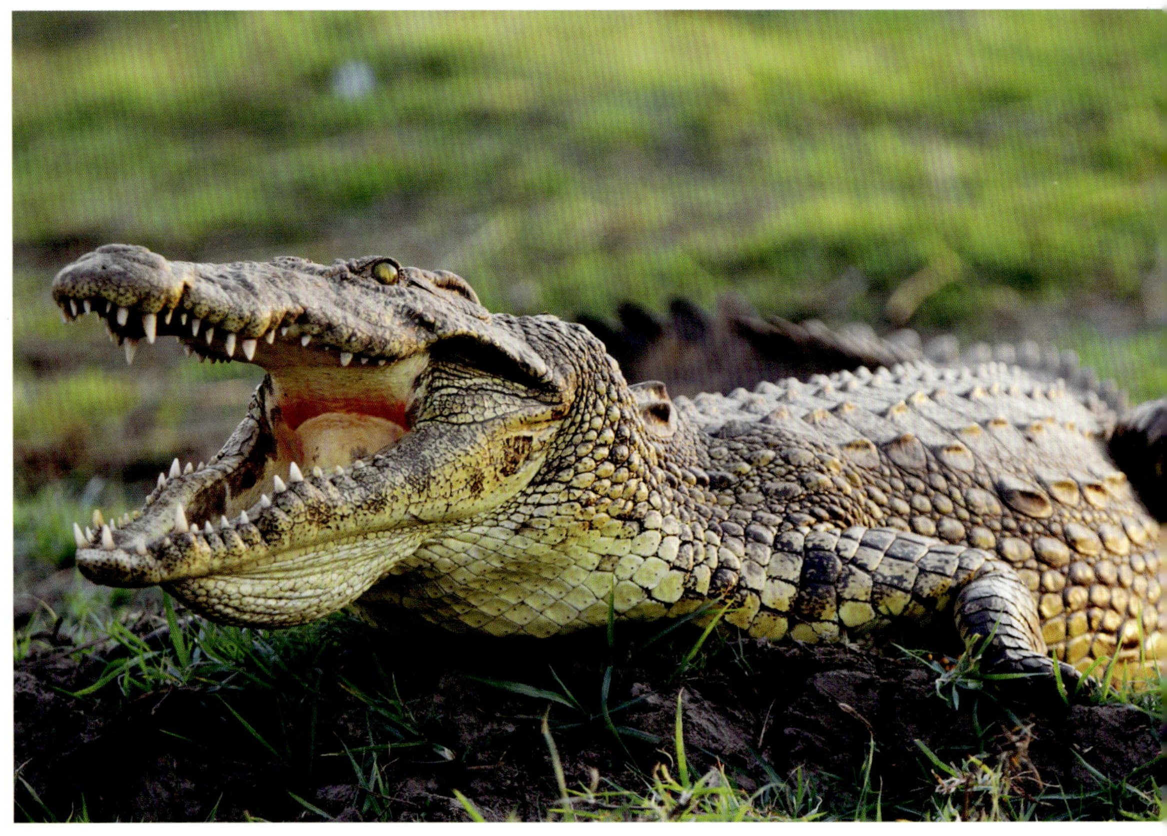

Crocodile, Chobe National Park

Chobe National Park

Chobe National Park is located in northern Botswana. It is named after the Chobe River, which flows along the northern edge of the park. Whilst the southern portion of the park is predominantly savanna, the area on the banks of the Chobe and the regions around Linyanti and the Savuti Marsh provide a habitat for diverse wildlife. Four hundred and fifty species of birds have been counted to date and Chobe National Park is also known for its large elephant and buffalo herds.

Le parc national de Chobe

Le parc national de Chobe s'étend au nord du Botswana. Il doit son nom au fleuve Chobe, qui le délimite au nord. Si les savanes dominent au sud, de nombreux animaux vivent sur les rives du Chobe, aux alentours de Linyanti et du fleuve Savuti. Dans ce parc, qui est également connu pour ses grands troupeaux d'éléphants et de buffles, on a recensé 450 espèces d'oiseaux.

Chobe-Nationalpark

Der Chobe-Nationalpark liegt im Norden Botswanas. Seinen Namen erhielt er von dem Fluss Chobe, der die Nordgrenze des Parks bildet. Während im Süden Savanne das Bild bestimmt, bieten die Uferregion des Chobe und die Regionen um Linyanti und den Fluss Savuti zahlreichen Tieren Lebensraum. 450 Vogelarten hat man gezählt, bekannt ist der Chobe-Nationalpark auch für seine großen Elefanten- und Büffelherden.

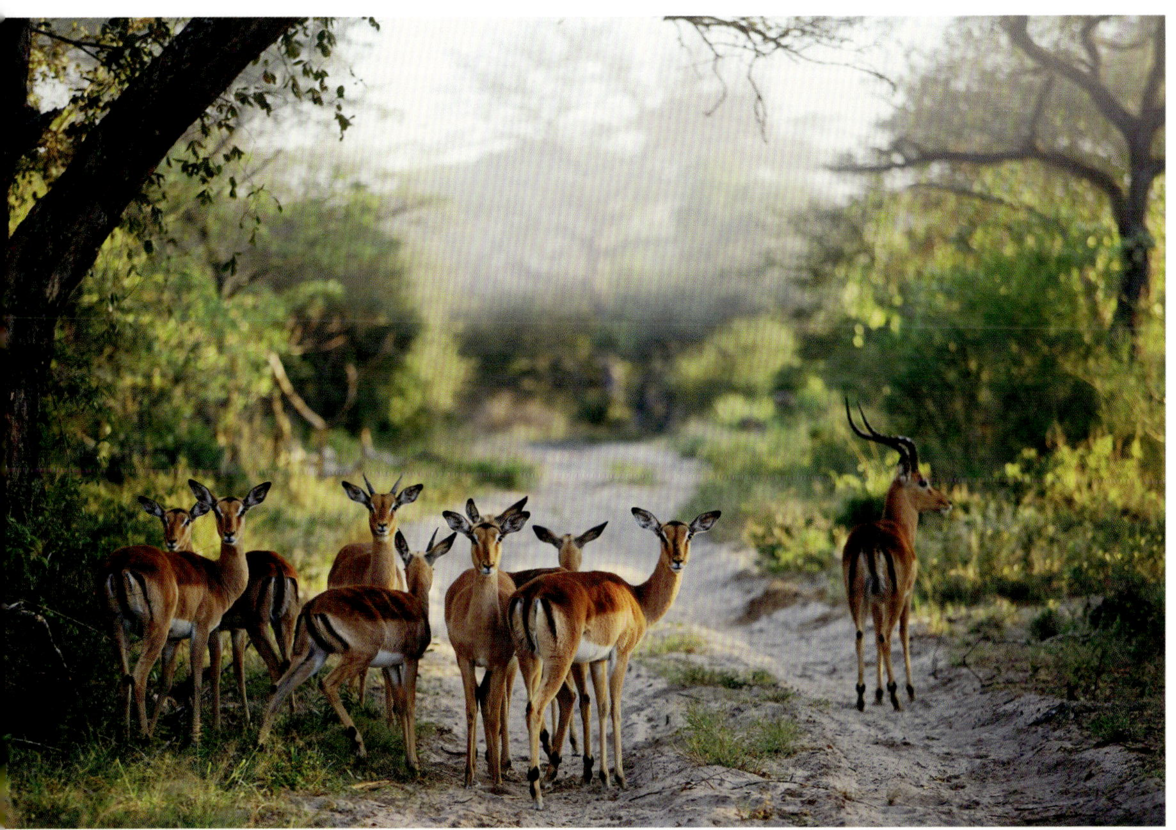

Impalas, Chobe National Park

Parque Nacional de Chobe
El Parque Nacional de Chobe está situado en el norte de Botswana. Debe su nombre del río Chobe, que forma el límite norte del parque. Mientras que al sur es la sabana el paisaje dominante, la región lateral de Chobe y las regiones alrededor de Linyanti y del río Savuti proporcionan un hábitat a numerosos animales. Han sido contadas 450 especies de aves, pero también es conocido el Parque Nacional de Chobe por sus enormes rebaños de elefantes y búfalos.

Parco Nazionale Chobe
Il Parco Nazionale di Chobe si trova nel Botswana del Nord. Prende il nome dal fiume Chobe, che delimita il confine settentrionale del parco. Mentre a sud la savana caratterizza il paesaggio, la regione rivierasca del Chobe e le zone intorno a Linyanti e al fiume Savuti offrono lo spazio vitale per numerose specie animali. Sono stati contati 450 tipi di uccelli; il parco nazionale di Chobe è conosciuto anche per le sue grandi mandrie di elefanti e bufali.

Nationale Park van Chobe
Het Nationale Park van Chobe ligt in het noorden van Botswana. Zijn naam dankt het park aan de rivier de Chobe, die de noordgrens vormt. Terwijl savanne het landschap in het zuiden bepaalt, vormen de oevers van de Chobe, de Linyanti en de Savuti een leefgebied voor talloze dieren, waaronder 450 vogelsoorten. Het Nationale Park van Chobe staat ook bekend om zijn grote olifanten- en buffelkuddes.

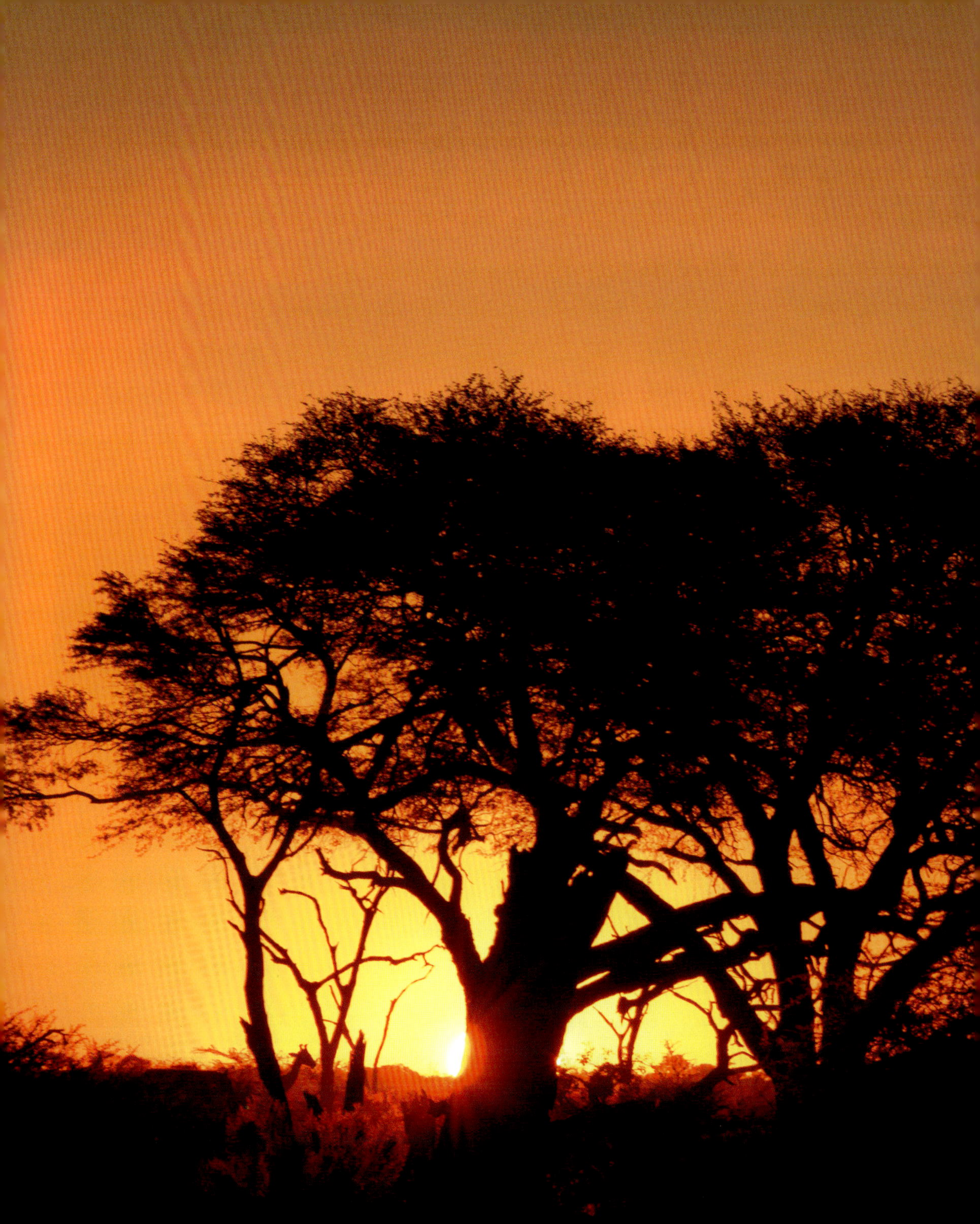

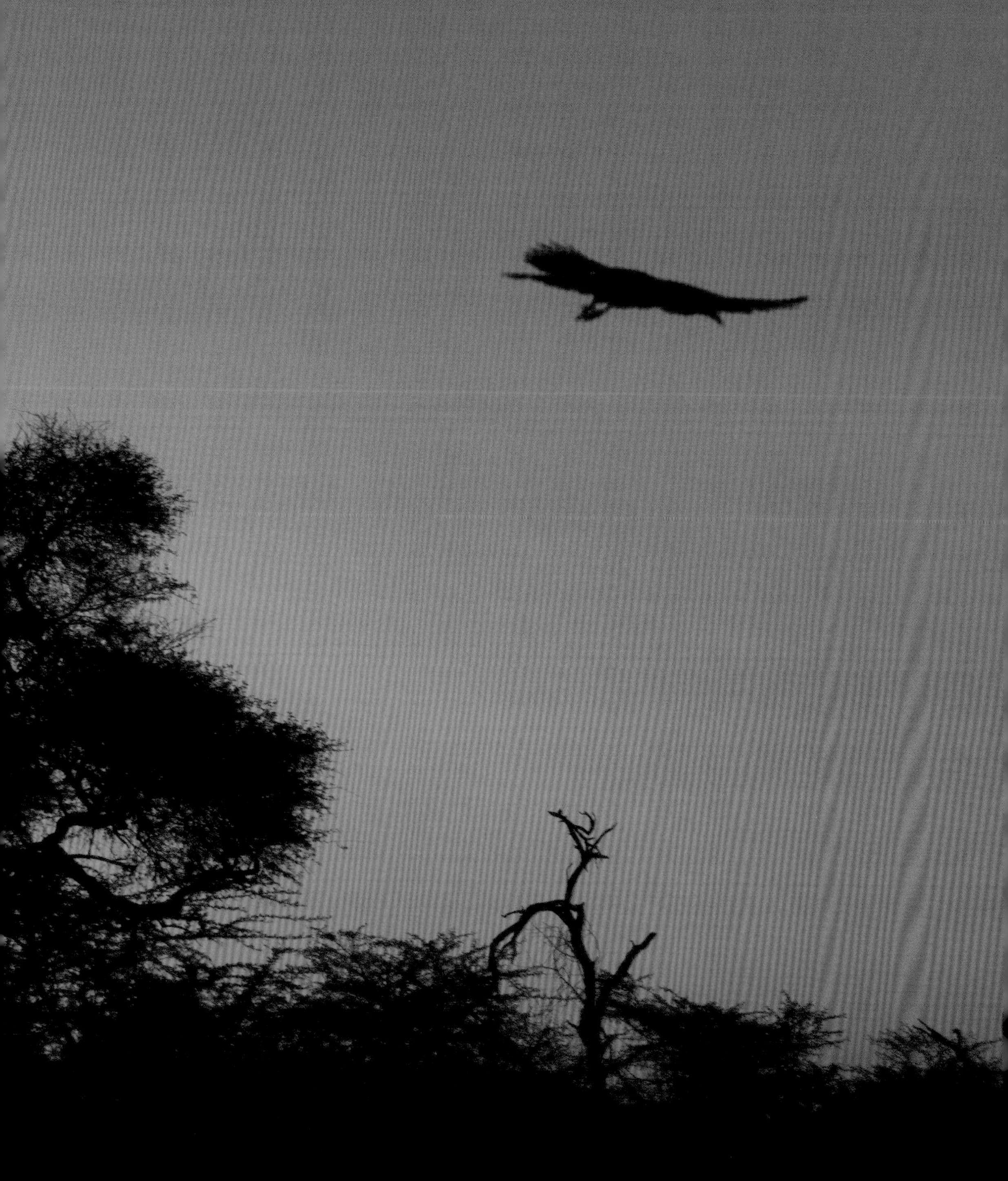

Chobe National Park

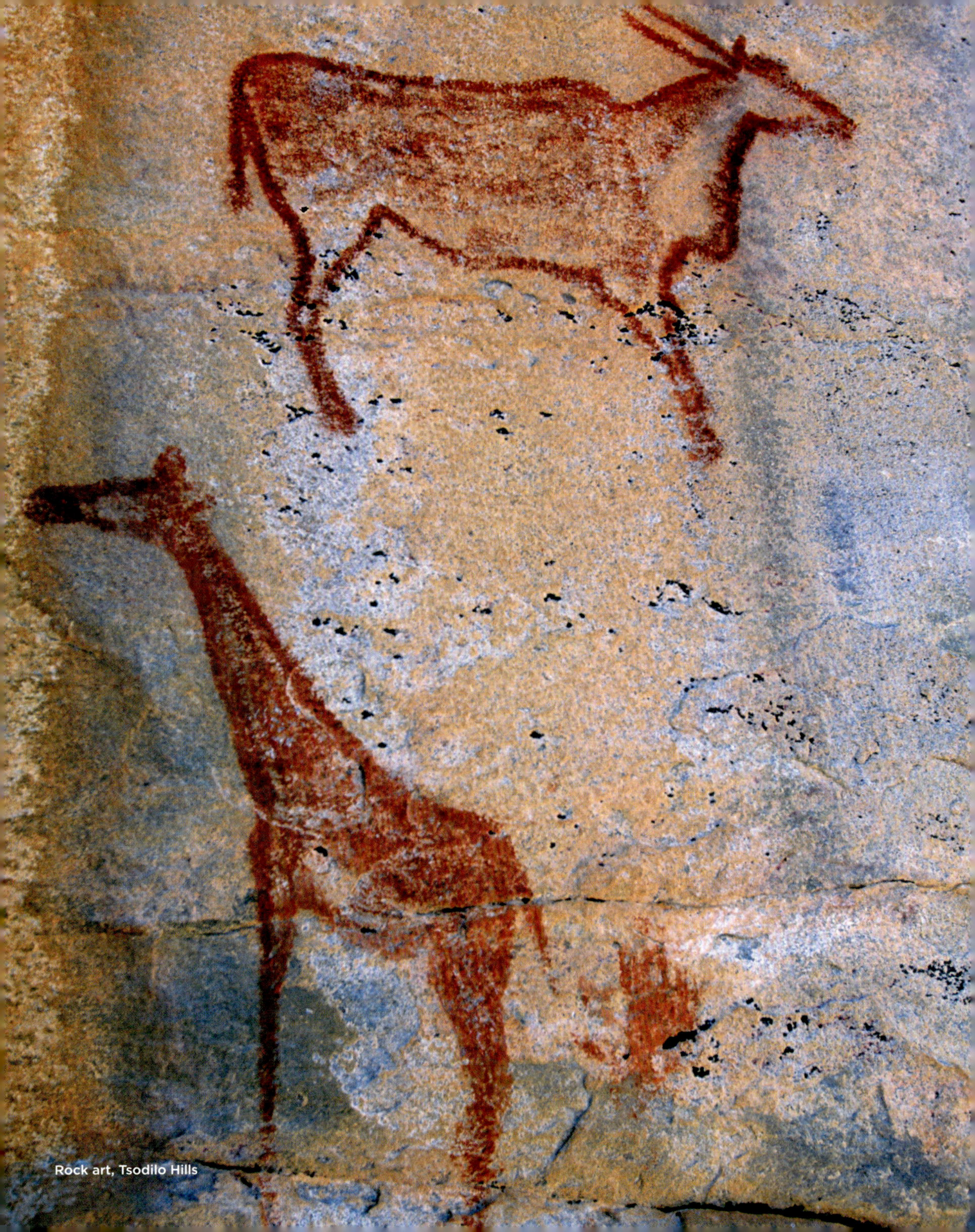

Rock art, Tsodilo Hills

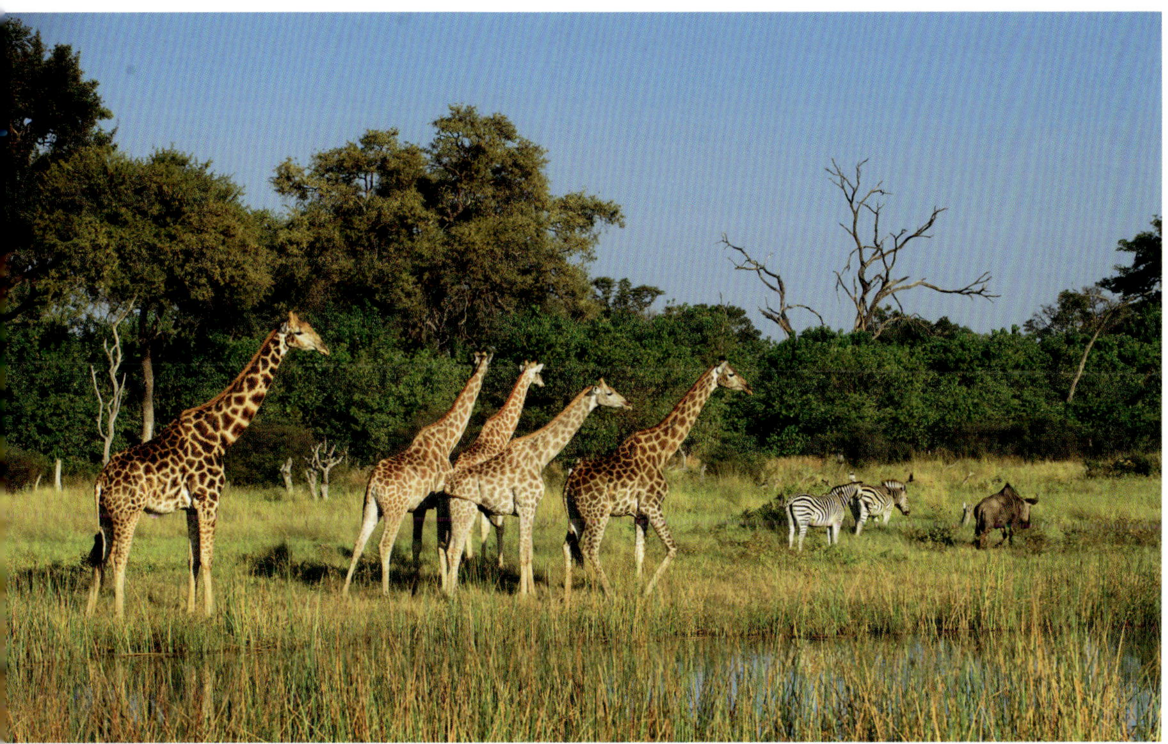

Giraffes, zebras and a gnu, Chobe National Park

Tsodilo Hills
A World Heritage site, this chain of hills in the north of the Kalahari desert has the highest density of rock paintings in the world. More than 4500 drawings, some of them dating from the 8th century, were made here by the San and Hambukushu, who still live in this region. The location is sacred to the locals as a place where the spirits of their ancestors live.

Les Tsodilo Hills
Cette chaîne de collines située au nord du désert du Kalahari arbore la collection la plus dense au monde de peintures rupestres. Plus de 4500 dessins, certains datant du VIIIe siècle, y ont été réalisés par les Sans et les Mbukushus, qui vivent toujours dans cette région. C'est un lieu sacré pour les peuples autochtones, car il abrite d'après eux les esprits des ancêtres.

Tsodilo-Hügel
Die Hügelkette im Norden der Kalahari-Wüste weist die weltweit höchste Dichte an Felsmalereien auf. Mehr als 4500 Zeichnungen, manche davon schon aus dem 8. Jahrhundert, wurden hier von den San und Hambukushu geschaffen, die immer noch in dieser Region leben. Der Ort ist den Einheimischen heilig als ein Ort, an dem die Geister der Ahnen wohnen.

Colinas Tsodilo
La cadena de colinas al norte del desierto del Kalahari tiene la mayor densidad de pinturas rupestres del mundo. Más de 4500 dibujos, algunos del siglo VIII, fueron realizados aquí por los San y Hambukushu, que todavía viven en esta región. El lugar es sagrado para los lugareños, consideradoun lugar donde viven los espíritus de los antepasados.

Tsodilo Hills
La catena collinare a nord del deserto del Kalahari ha la più alta densità di pitture rupestri del mondo. Più di 4500 disegni, alcuni dei quali del VIII secolo, sono realizzati dalle popolazioni San e Hambukushu, che vivono tuttora in questa regione. Il luogo è sacro per la popolazione che ritiene vi alloggino gli spiriti degli antenati.

Tsodiloheuvels
De heuvelketen in het noorden van de Kalahariwoestijn heeft de hoogste rotstekeningendichtheid ter wereld. Meer dan 4500 tekeningen, waarvan sommige uit de 8e eeuw, werden hier gemaakt door de San en Hambukushu, die nog steeds in deze regio wonen. De plaats is heilig voor de lokale bevolking, omdat hier de geesten van de voorouders wonen.

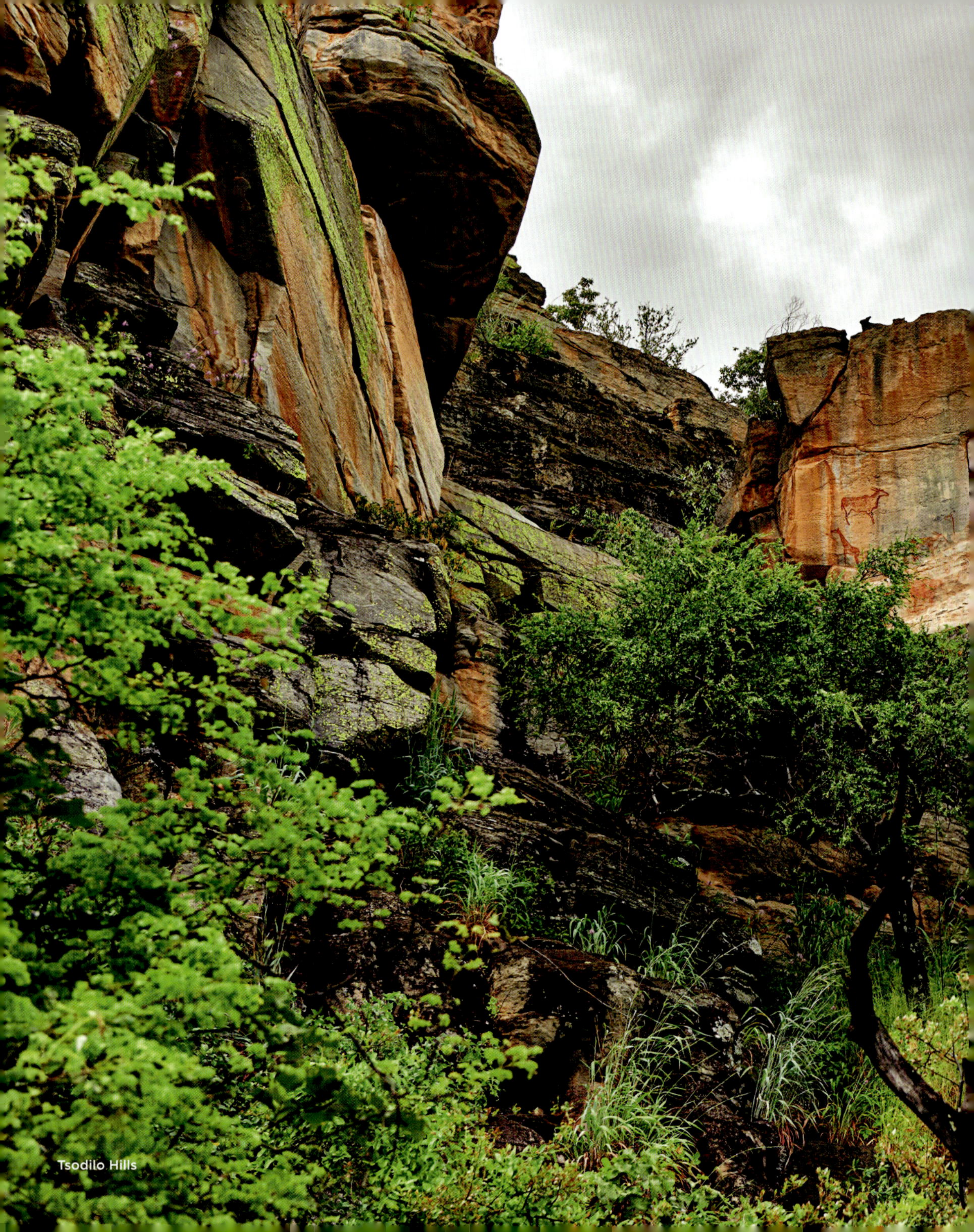
Tsodilo Hills

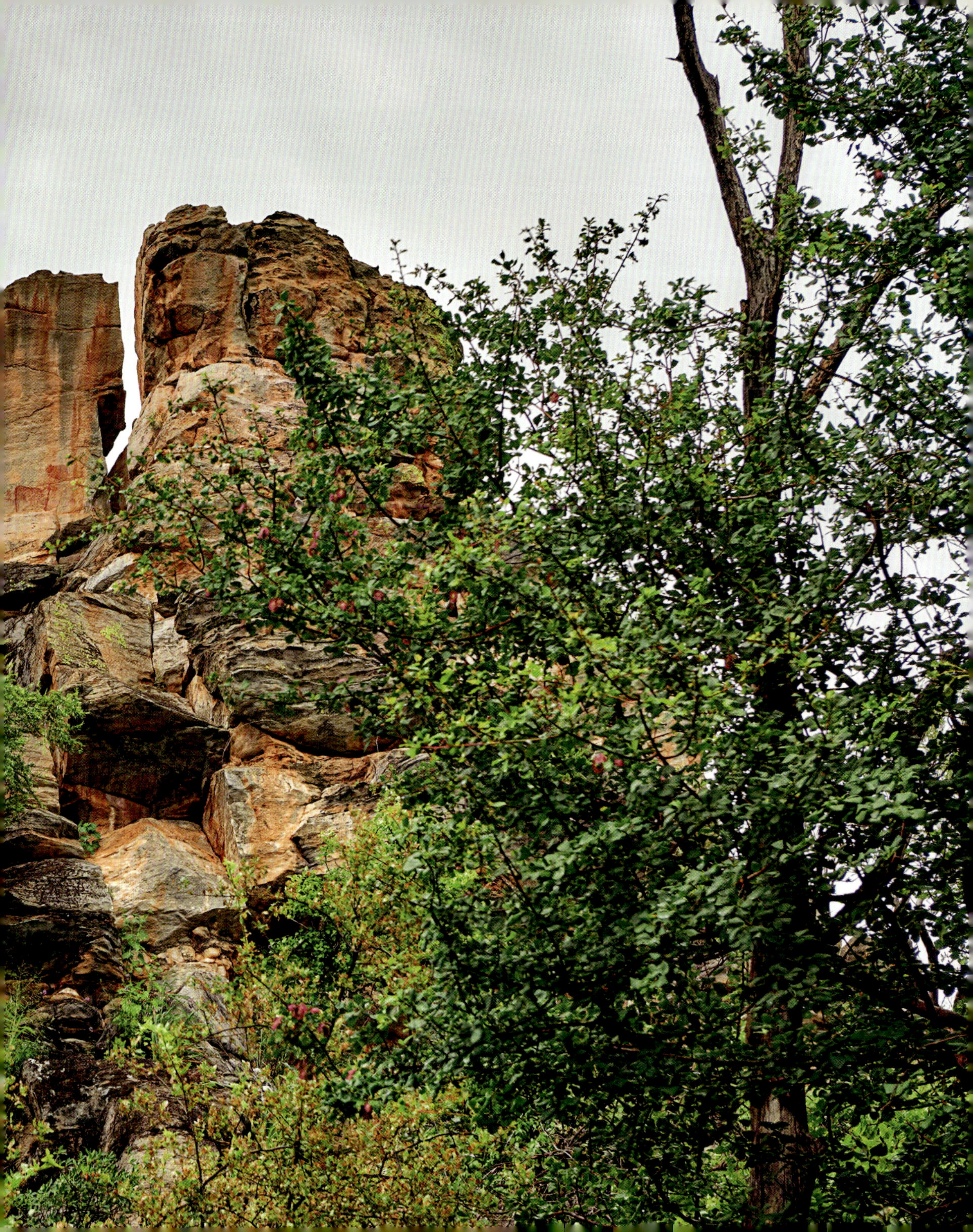

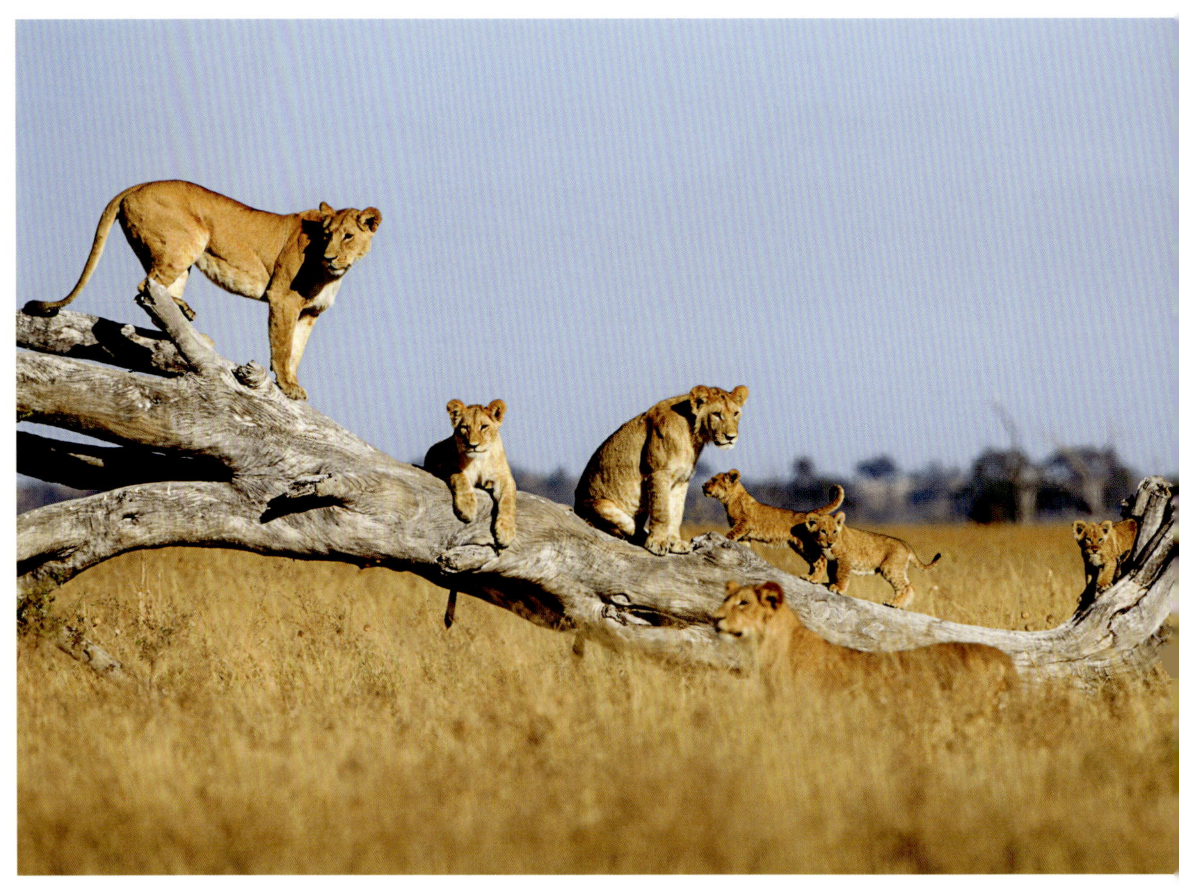

Lions with cubs, Savuti Marsh, Chobe National Park

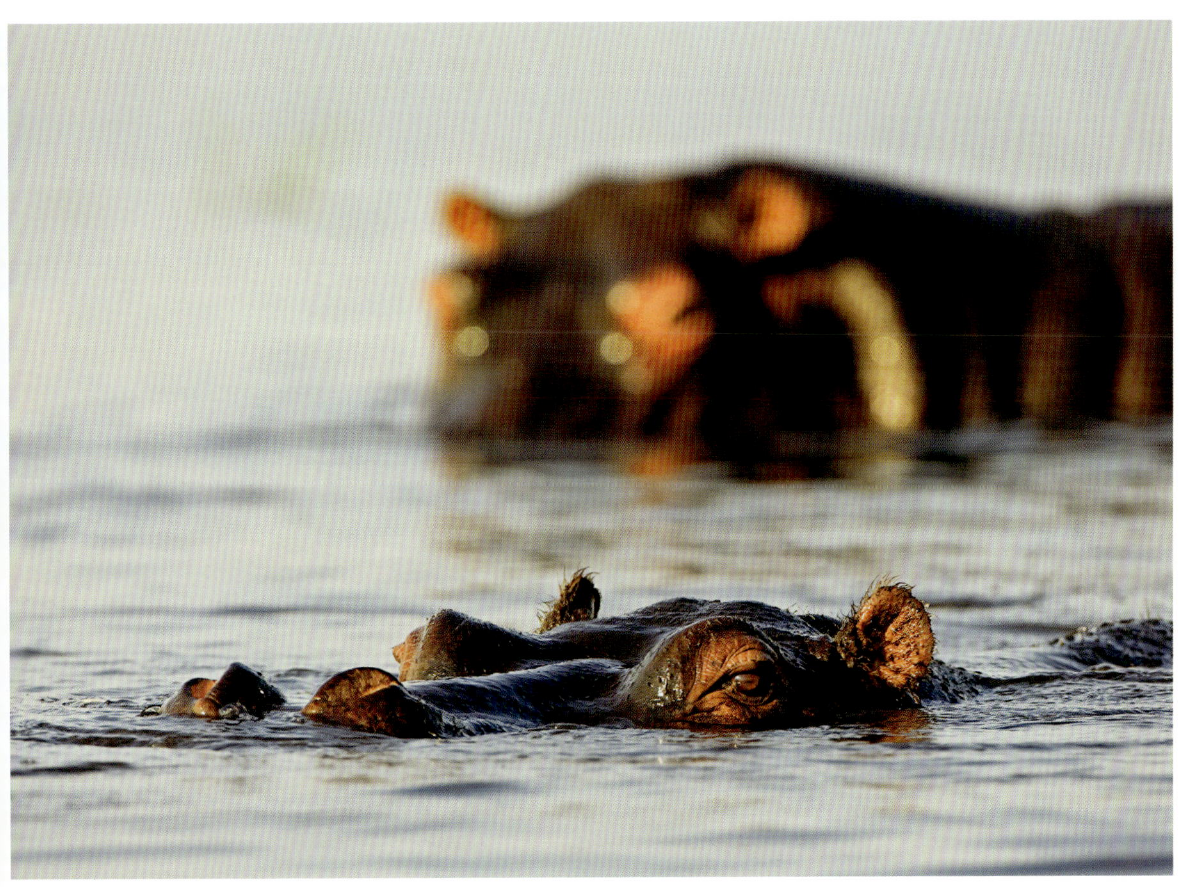

Hippos, Chobe National Park

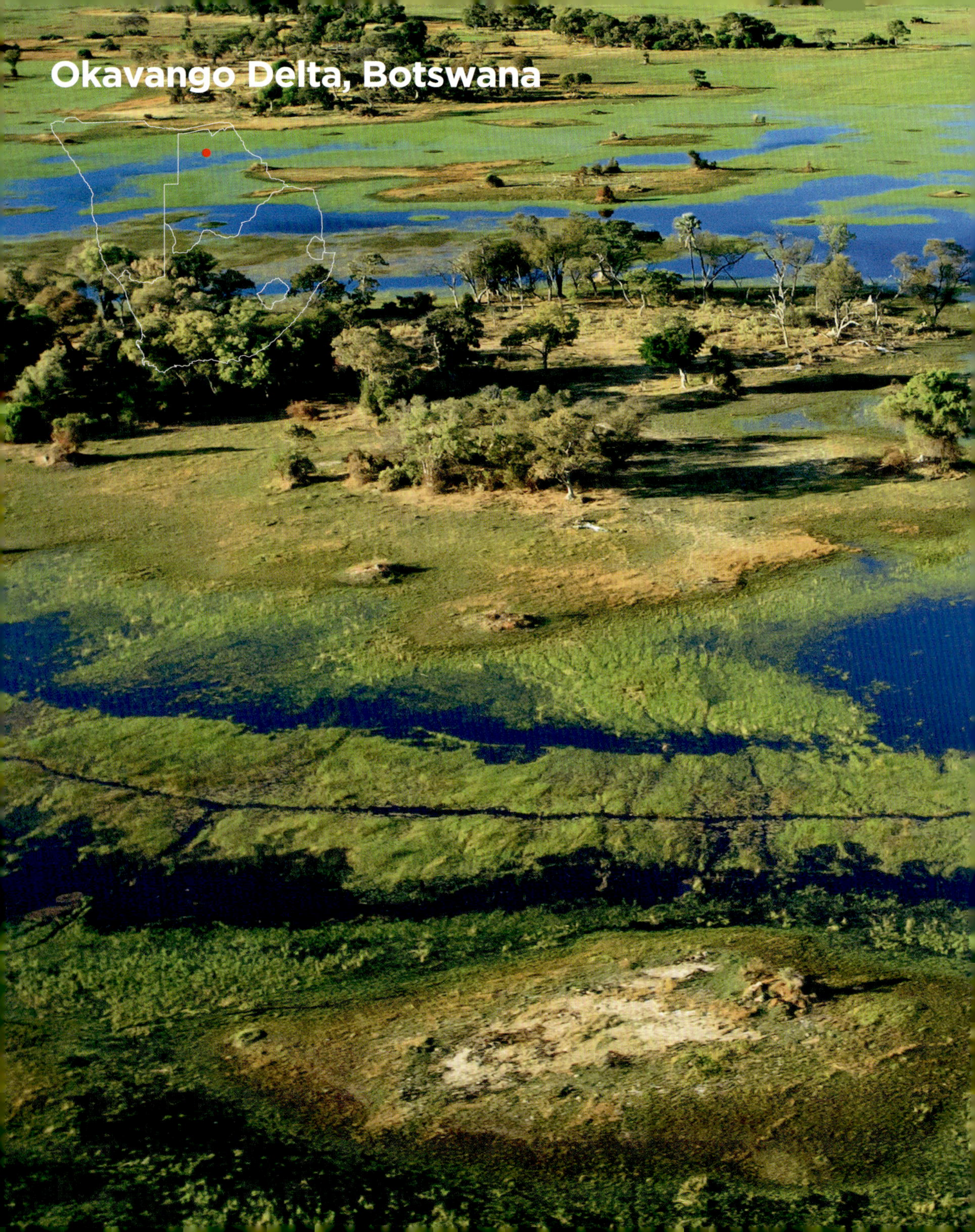
Okavango Delta, Botswana

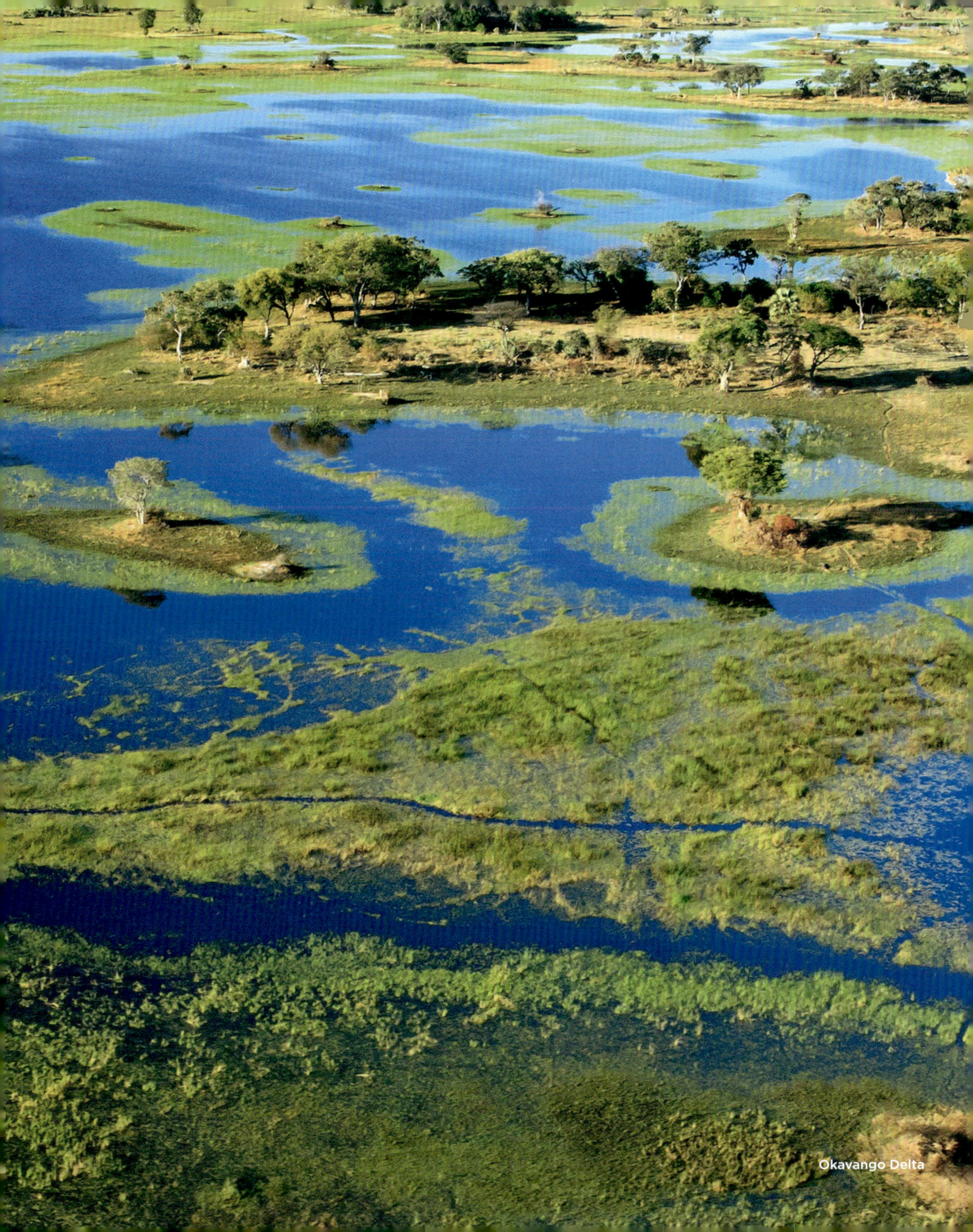

Okavango Delta

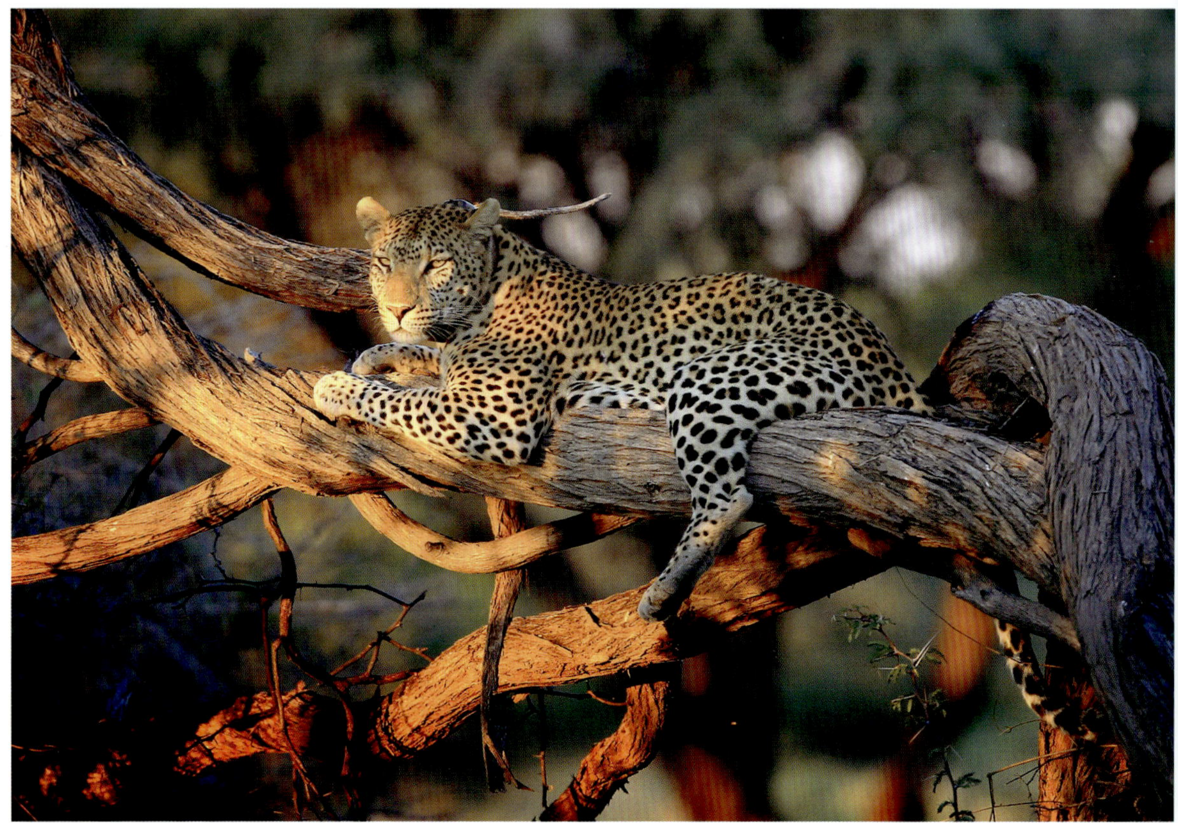

Leopard, Okavango Delta

Okavango Delta
The Okavango Delta lies in northwestern Botswana. Unlike most deltas, this 20,000 km^2 (6178 mi^2) delta does not empty into an ocean, but instead floods 12,000 km^2 (4633 mi^2) of land when it reaches its high water mark. At these times, the surrounding areas are subject to long stretches of drought, which brings many animals to the delta to find water and food.

Le delta de l'Okavango
Le delta de l'Okavango, d'une superficie de 20000 km^2 mais qui n'atteint pas l'océan, est le joyau du nord-ouest du Botswana. Quand l'eau est à son niveau maximal, elle inonde 12000 km^2 La sécheresse actuelle qui frappe les régions voisines pousse de nombreux animaux à venir s'abreuver et s'alimenter dans le delta.

Okavangodelta
Im Nordwesten Botswanas liegt das Okavangodelta. Dieses Delta – das nicht in einen Ozean mündet – ist rund 20000 km^2 groß. Wenn das Wasser seinen Höchststand erreicht, sind etwa 12000 km^2 Fläche überflutet. In den umliegenden Gebieten herrscht zu dieser Zeit Dürre und viele Tiere strömen ins Delta, um Wasser und Nahrung zu finden.

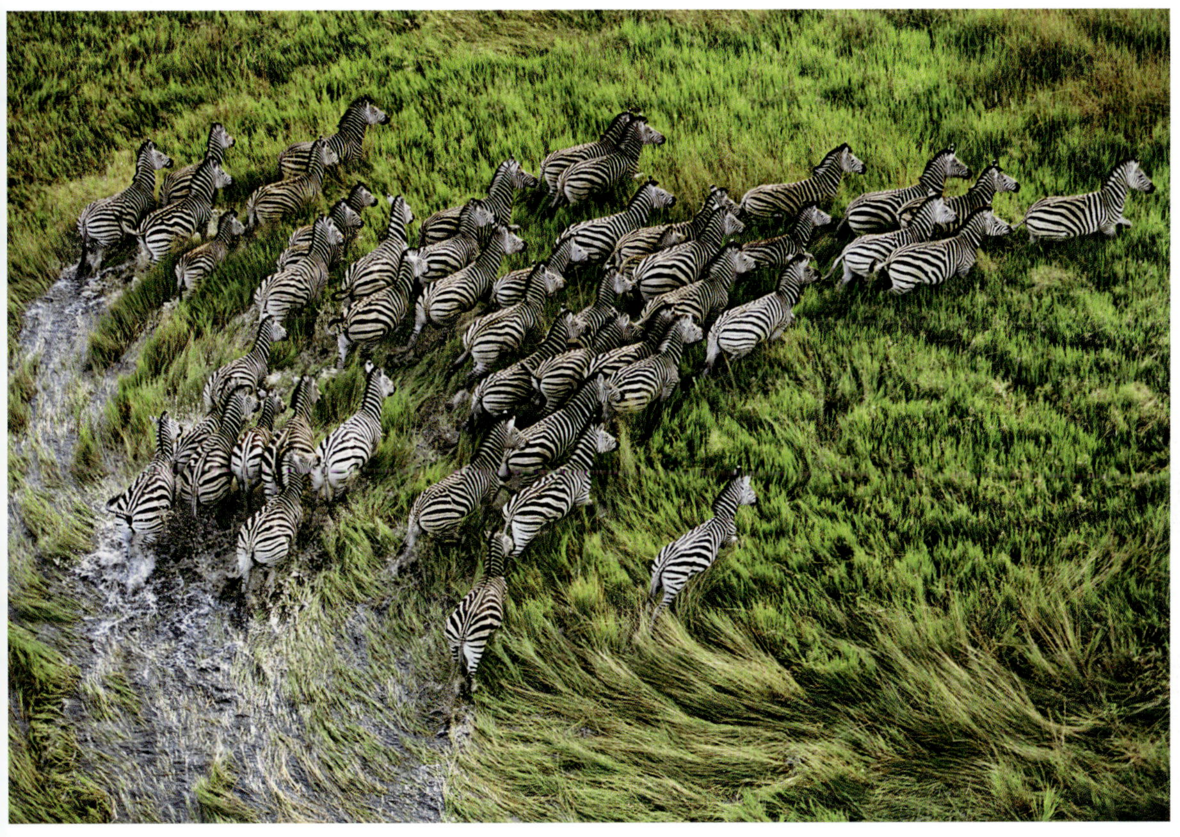

Zebras, Okavango Delta

Delta del Okavango
En el noroeste de Botswana se encuentra el delta del Okavango. Este delta -que no desemboca en un océano- tiene aproximadamente unos 20000 km². Cuando el agua alcanza su punto más alto se inundan cerca de 12000 km². En los alrededores se extiende la sequía y muchos animales acuden al delta para encontrar agua y comida.

Delta dell'Okavango
Nel nord-ovest del Botswana si trova il delta dell' Okavango. Questo delta, che non sfocia in un oceano, è grande circa 20000 km². Quando l'acqua raggiunge il suo livello massimo, inonda una superficie di circa 12000 km². Nelle regioni circostanti in questo periodo regna la siccità e molti animali si riversano nel delta per cercare acqua e cibo.

Okavangodelta
In het noordwesten van Botswana ligt de Okavangodelta. Deze rivierdelta - die nooit in zee uitmondt - is rond 20000 km² groot; wanneer het waterpeil de hoogste stand bereikt, staat een gebied van 12000 km² onder water. In het omringende gebied heerst in deze tijd droogte, waardoor vele dieren naar de delta trekken om water en voedsel te vinden

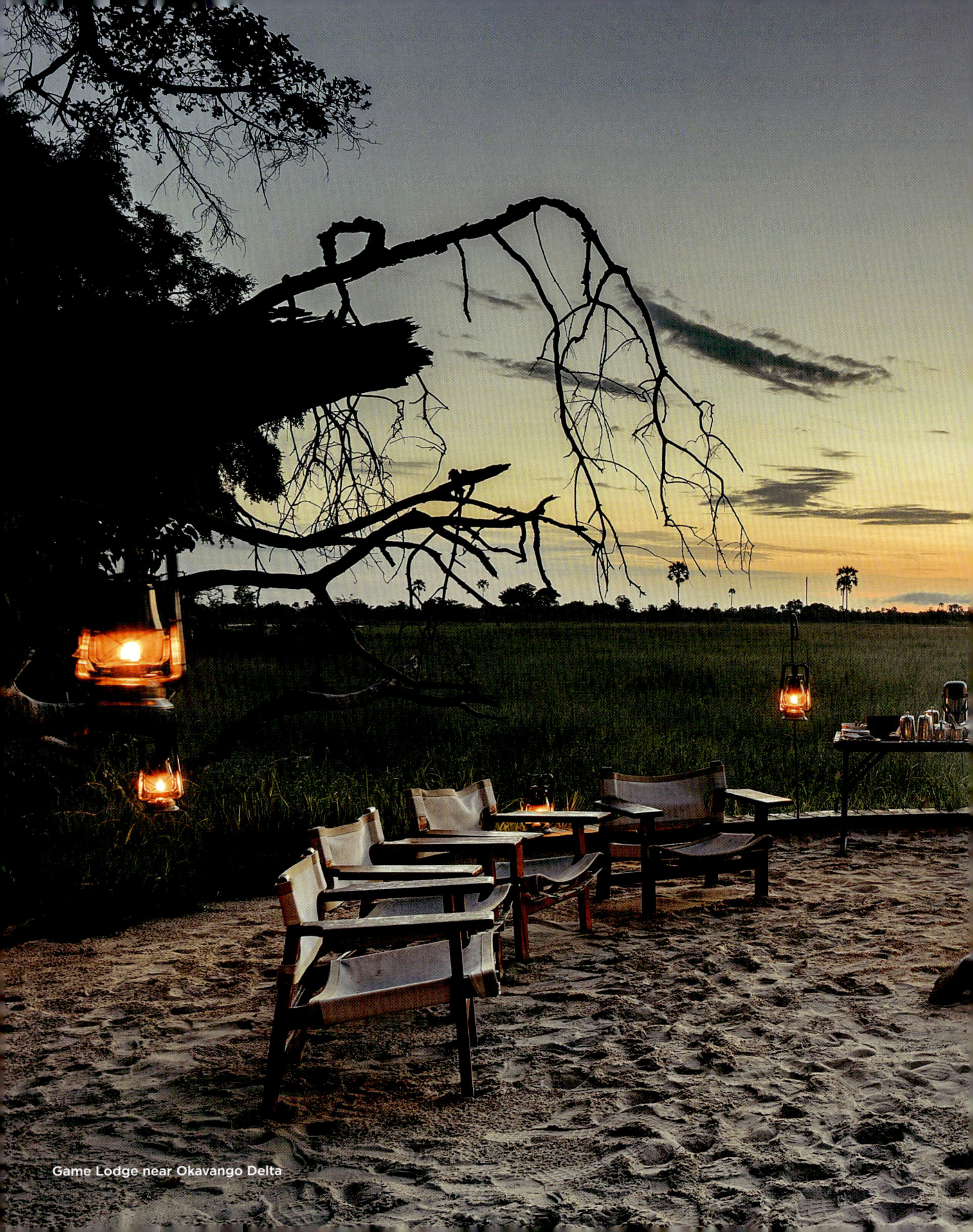

Game Lodge near Okavango Delta

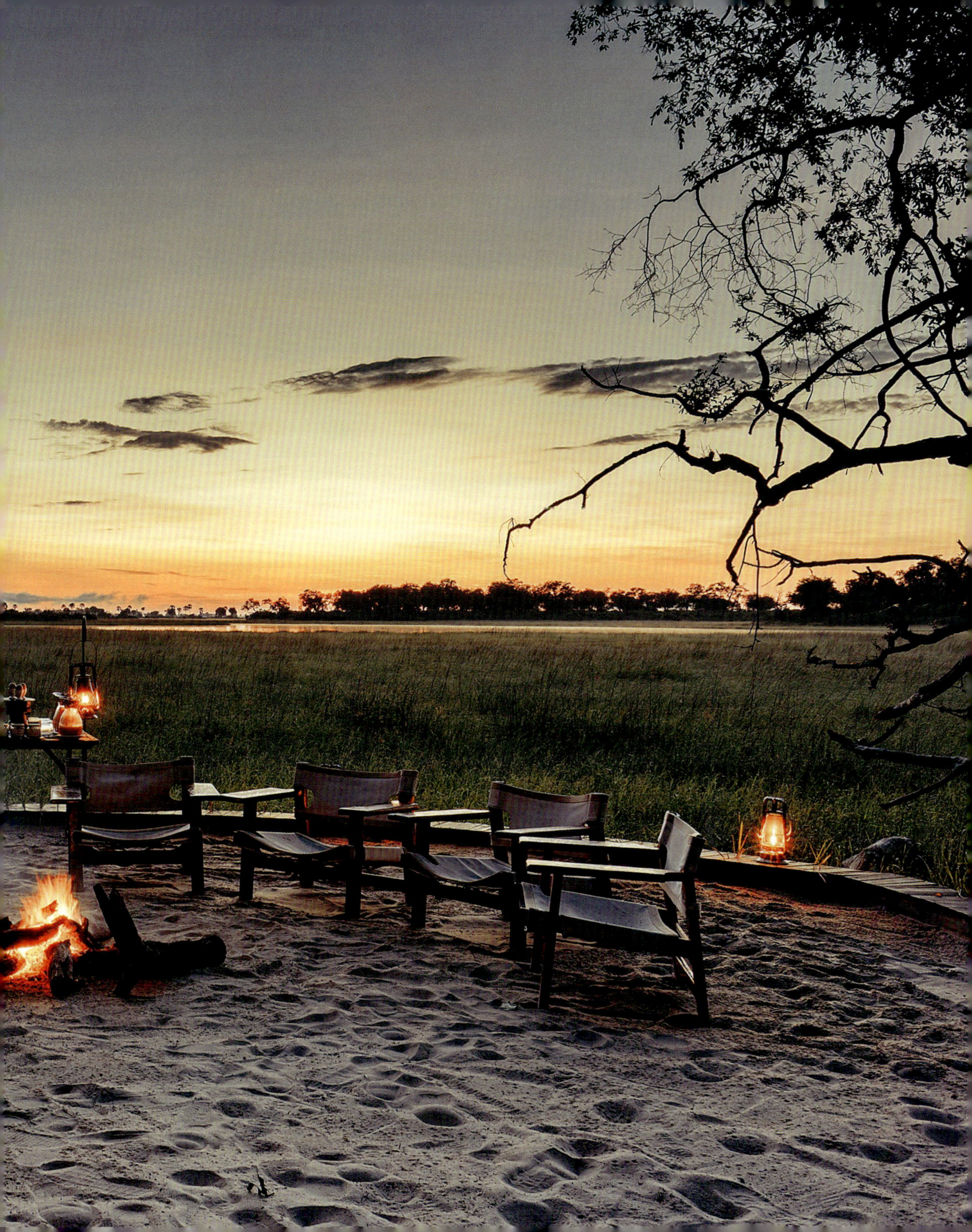

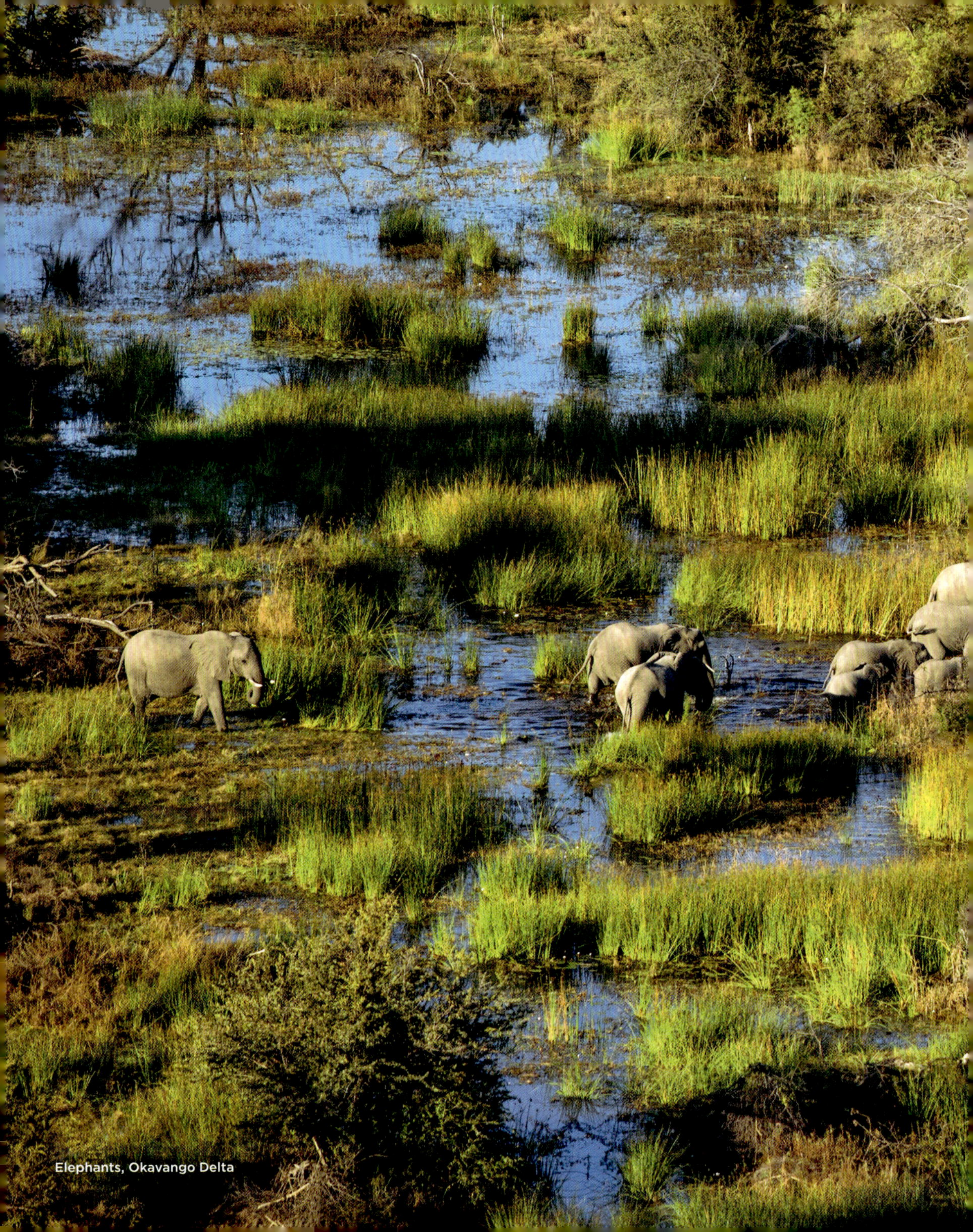

Elephants, Okavango Delta

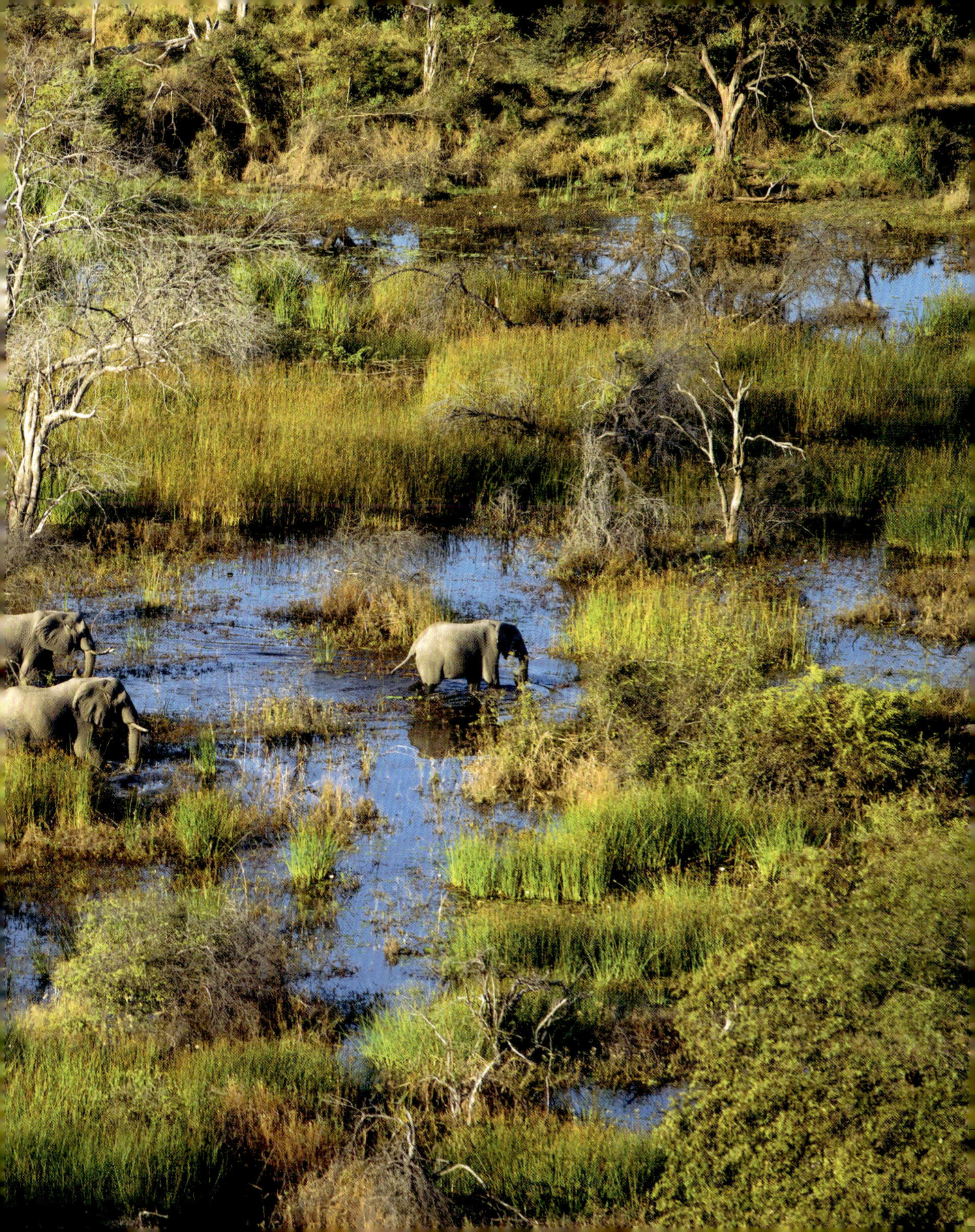

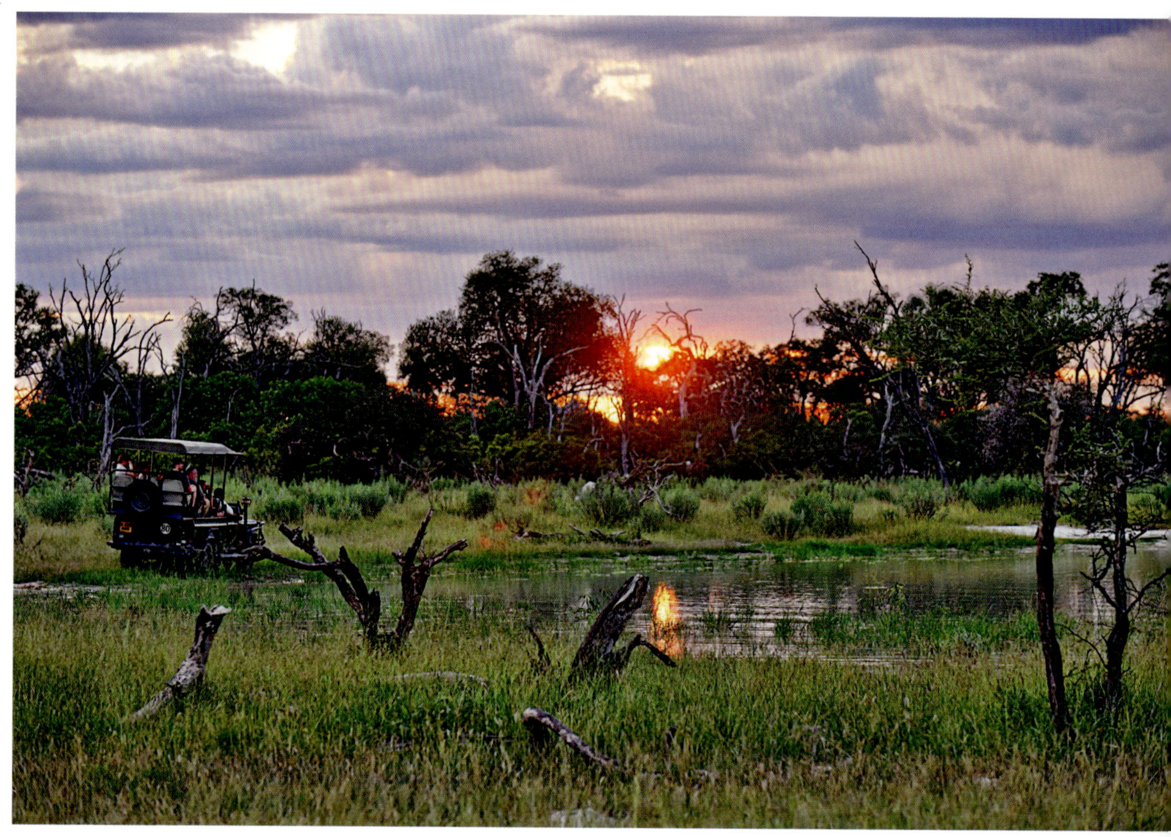

Chitabe, Okavango Delta

African wild dogs
These could be confused with hyenas and, indeed, the African wild dogs were also once called hyenas. Their fur features reddish, white, brown, and yellowish spots all over their bodies. Their habitat encompasses the entire African savanna, but the species is very endangered.

Les lycaons
On pourrait confondre les lycaons – appelés autrefois « loup peints » ou « chiens sauvages africains » – avec les hyènes. Leur fourrure est entièrement couverte de taches rouges, blanches, marron ou jaunes. Ces animaux ont leur territoire dans toute la savane africaine, mais l'espèce est gravement menacée.

Afrikanische Wildhunde
Man könnte sie mit Hyänen verwechseln – und tatsächlich wurden die Afrikanischen Wildhunde früher auch Hyänenhunde genannt. Ihr Fell weist am ganzen Körper Flecken auf: rötlich, weiß, braun, gelblich. Das Habitat der Tiere ist die gesamte afrikanische Savanne. Die Art ist allerdings stark gefährdet.

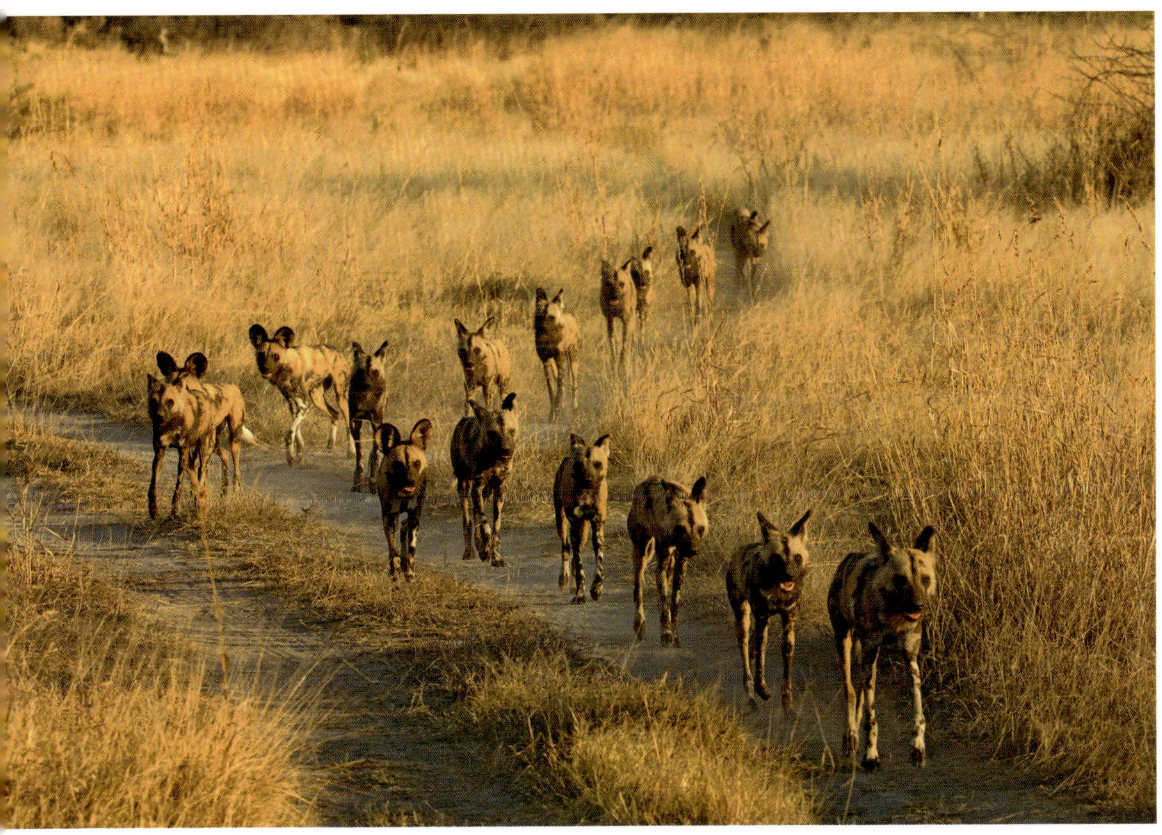

frican wild dogs, Okavango Delta

os perros salvajes africanos
e podrían confundir con hienas- y de echo los perros salvajes africanos se onocían antiguamente también como erros hiena. Su piel presenta puntos en odo el cuerpo: rojos, blancos, marrones, marillos. El hábitat de estos animales es oda la sabana africana. Sien embargo, la specie se encuentra en peligro crítico.

I cani selvatici africani
Si potrebbero confondere con le iene, e in effetti i cani selvatici africani in passato furono chiamati anche cani iena. La loro pelliccia presenta macchie su tutto il corpo: rossicce, bianche, marroni e giallognole. L'habitat di questi animali è l'intera savana africana, tuttavia la specie è a forte rischio di estinzione.

Afrikaanse wilde honde
Ze zijn eenvoudig te verwarren met hyena's, en de Afrikaanse wilde hond wordt ook wel hyenahond genoemd. Over hun hele vacht hebben de honden rode, bruine en gelige vlekken. Het leefgebied van de dieren is de hele Afrikaanse savanne. De soort wordt echter sterk bedreigd.

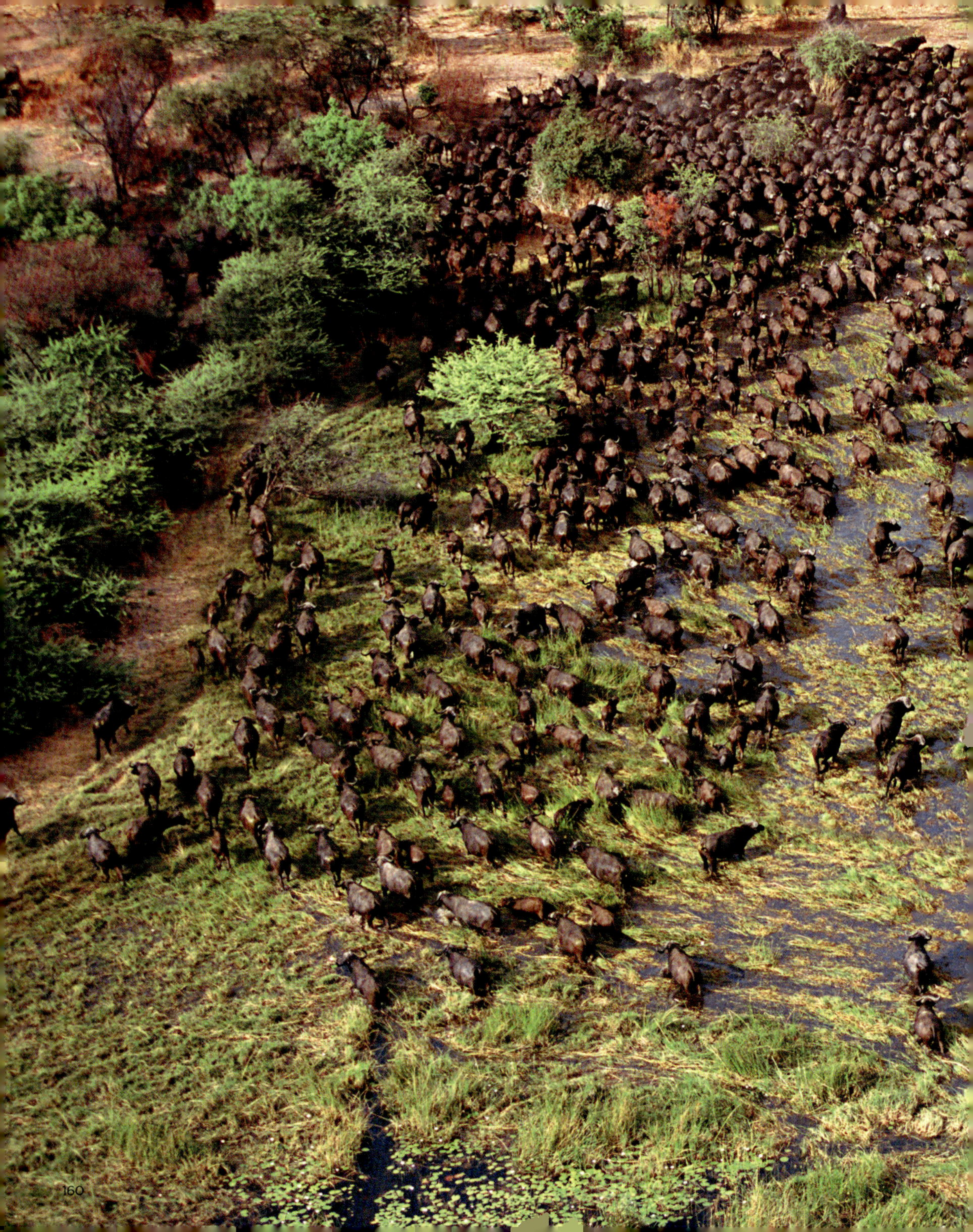

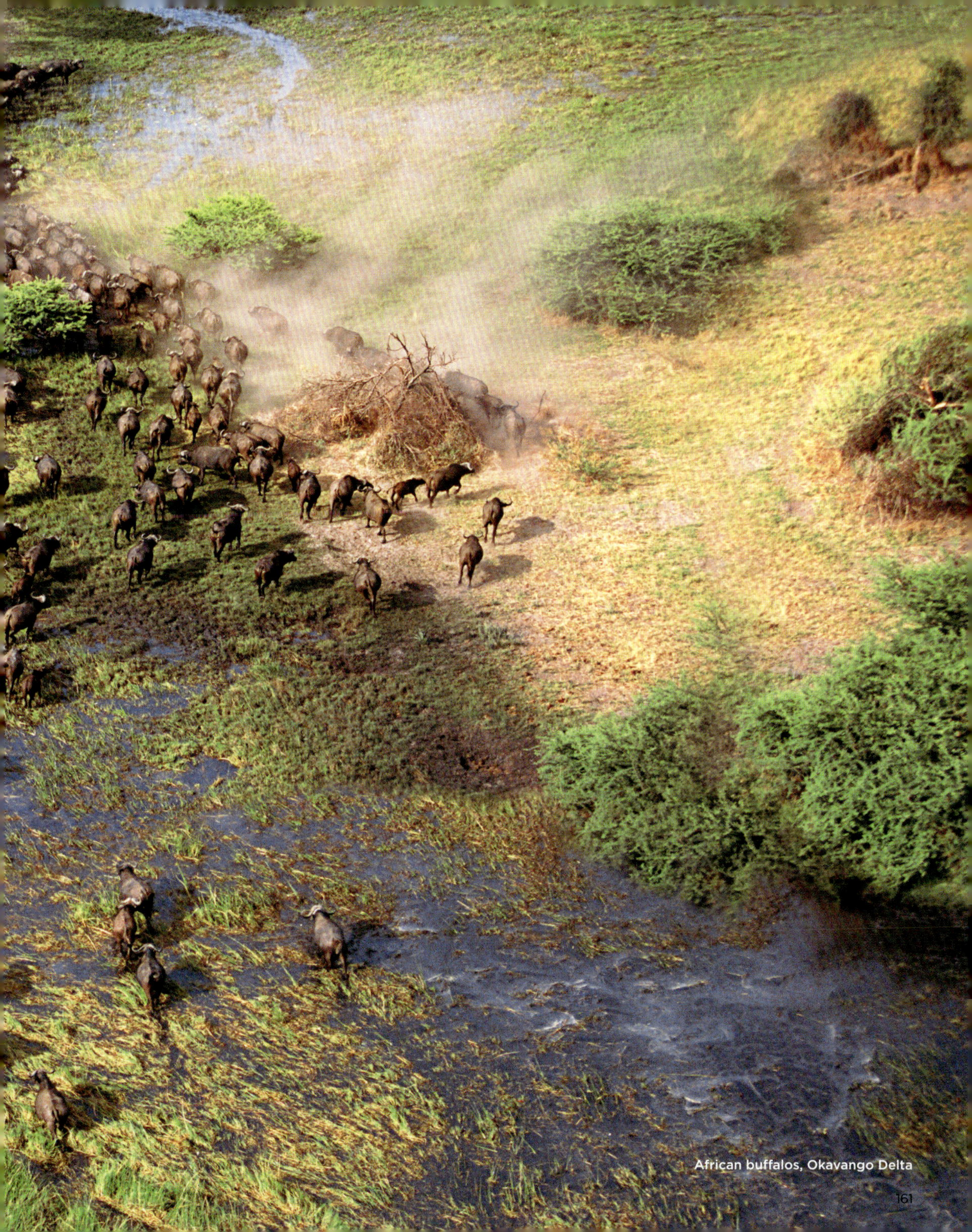

African buffalos, Okavango Delta

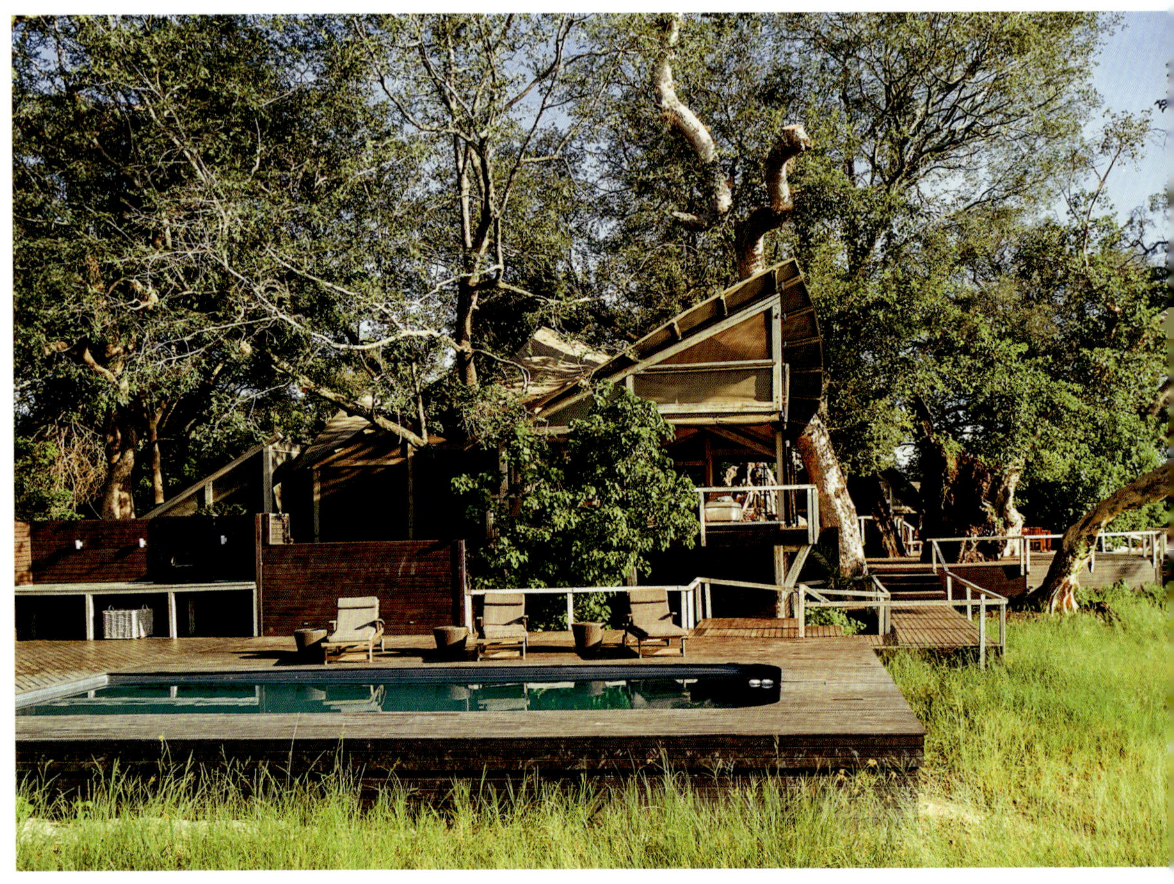

The Abu Elephant Camp, Okavango Delta

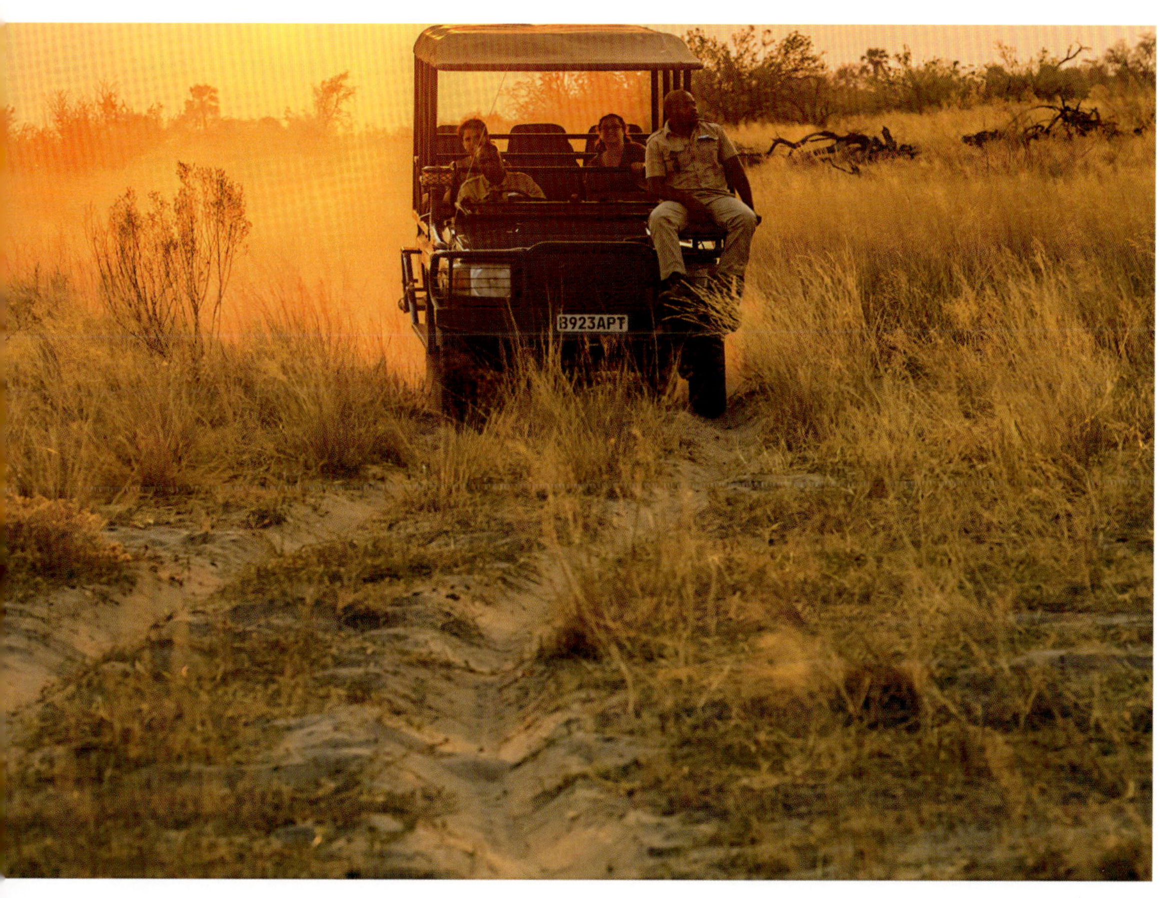

oremi Game Reserve, Okavango Delta

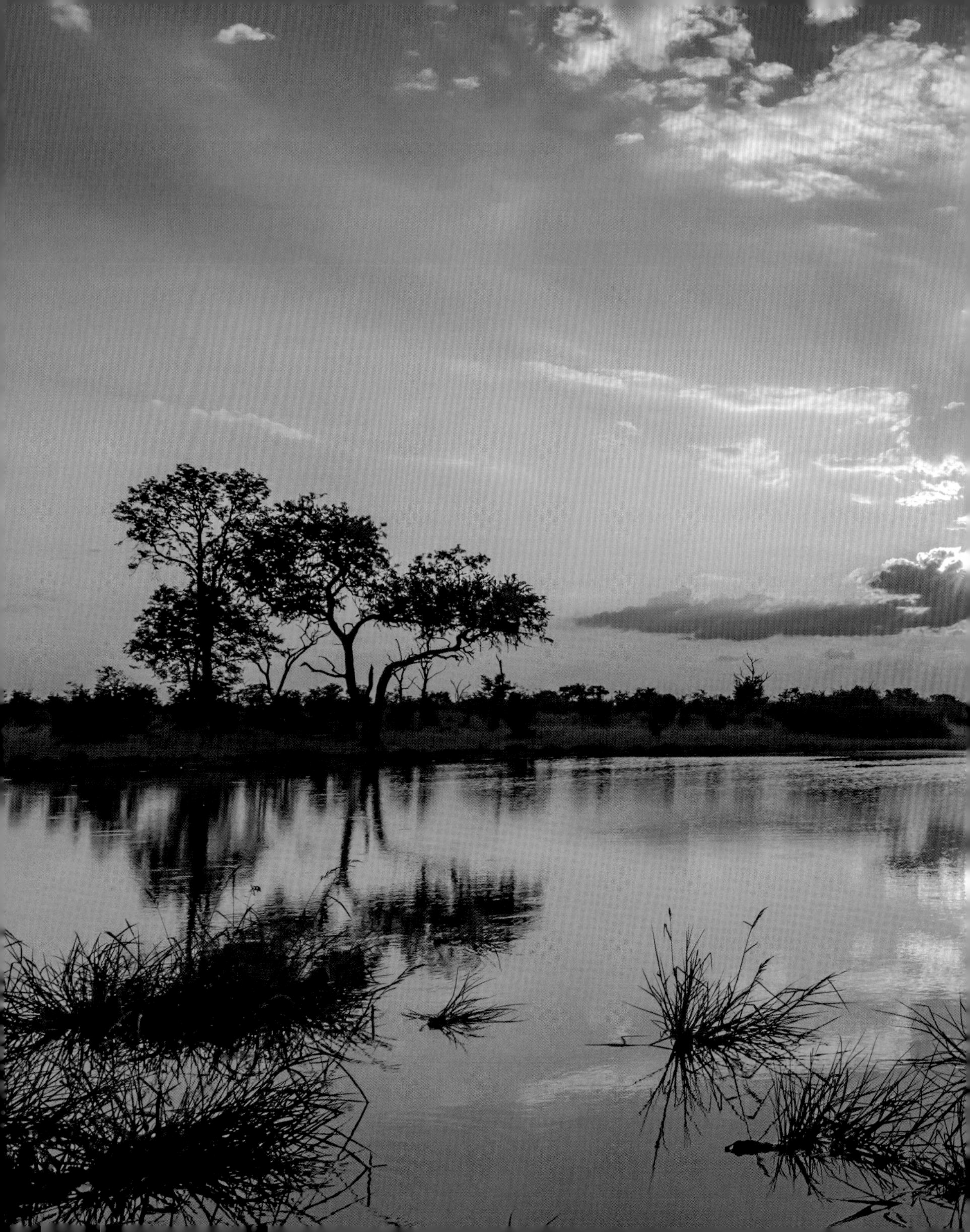

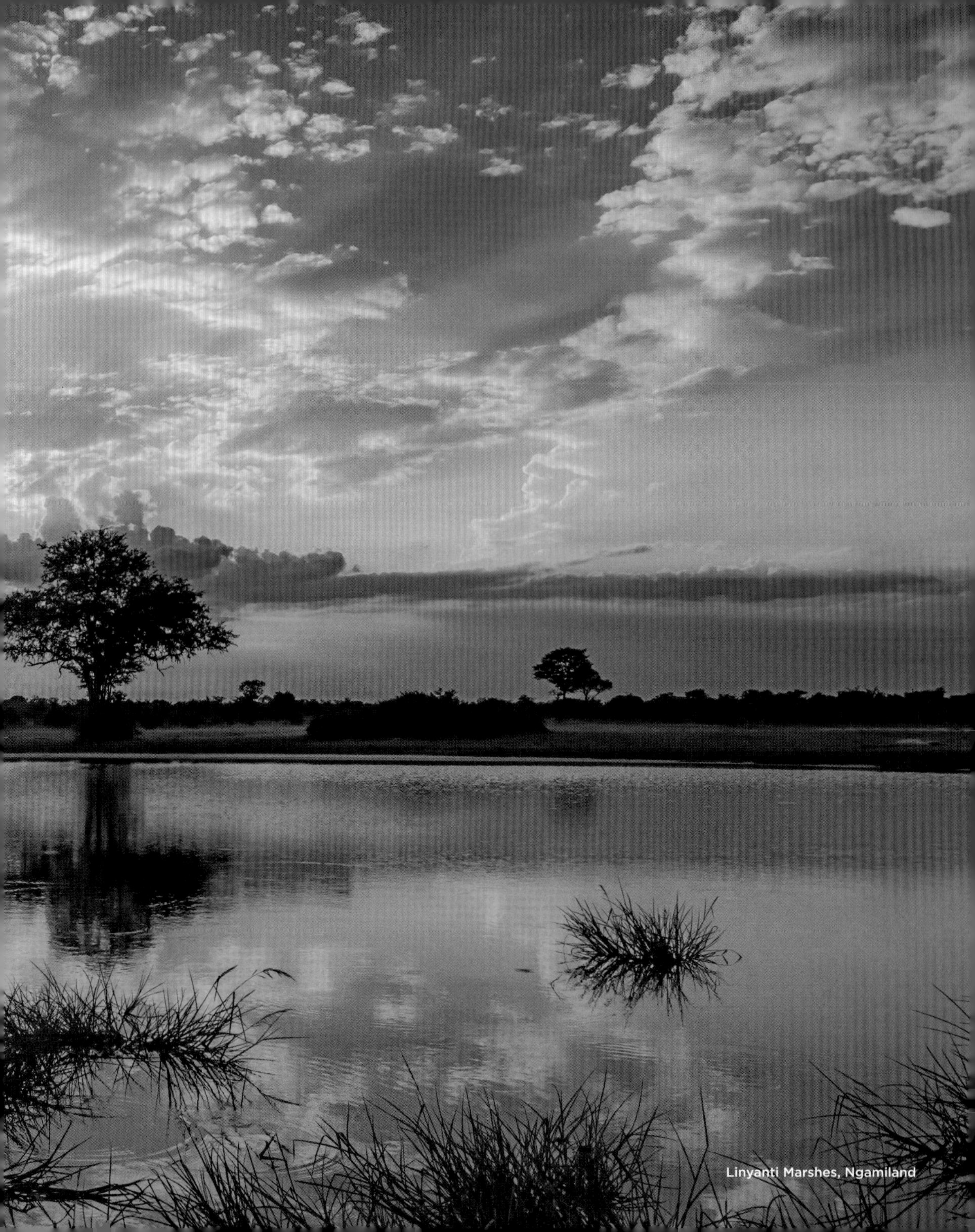

Linyanti Marshes, Ngamiland

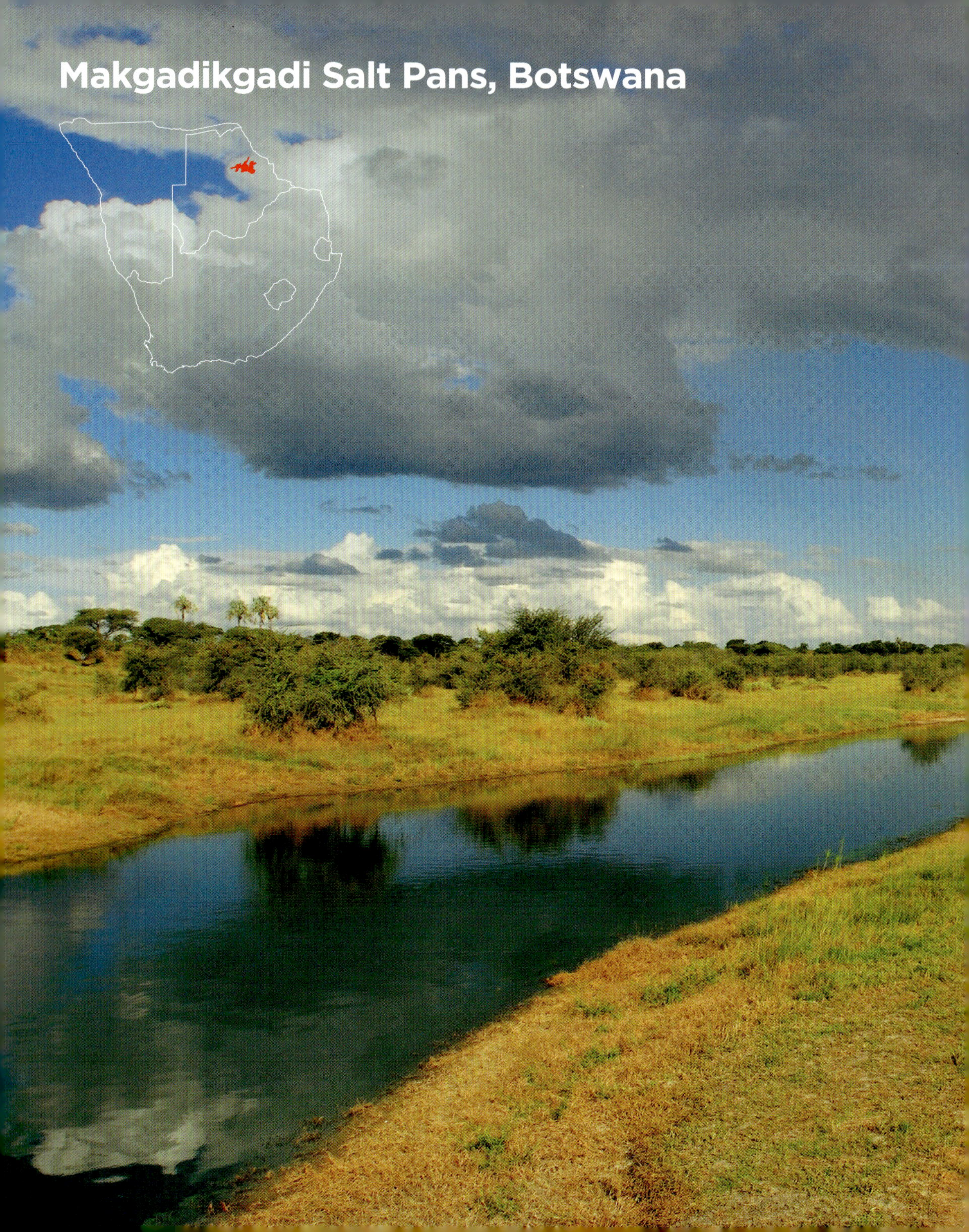
Makgadikgadi Salt Pans, Botswana

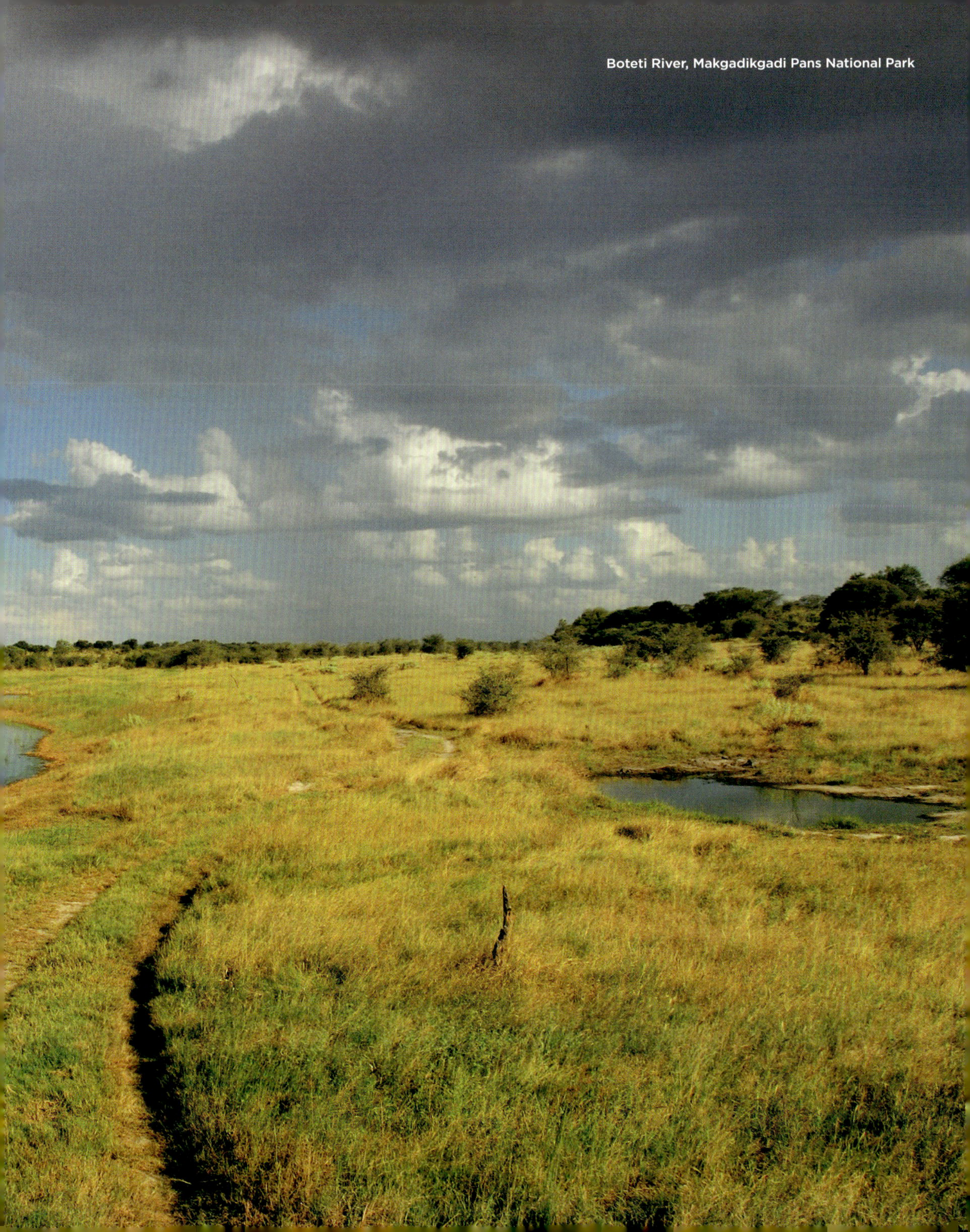

Boteti River, Makgadikgadi Pans National Park

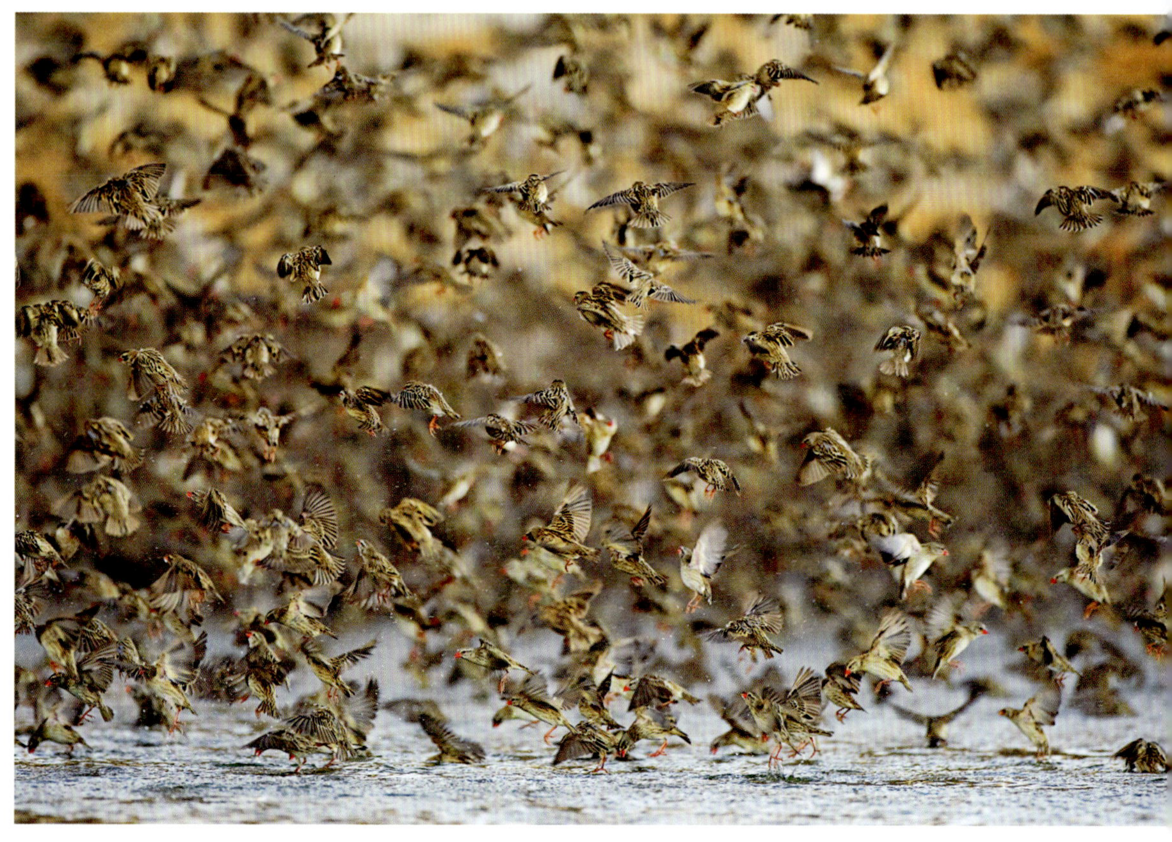

Red-billed quelea, Boteti River, Makgadikgadi Pans

Makgadikgadi Salt Pans

Makgadikgadi means „vast, lifeless land" and is a good description. The land is free of vegetation and these salt pans in the northeastern Kalahari in Botswana cover 16,000 km^2 (6178 mi^2), making it one of the largest salt deserts on earth. The edges of the salt pans are surrounded by grassy savanna and the Boteti River provides water to support life here.

Les cuvettes salées de Makgadikgadi

Makgadikgadi signifie « vaste pays sans vie ». C'est un nom bien choisi pour cette région privée de végétation et dont les cuvettes salées dans le nord-est du Kalahari, au Botswana, sont parmi les plus vastes de la terre avec leur superficie de 16 000 km^2. Les abords des cuvettes salées sont occupés par une savane herbeuse, l'eau et la vie proviennent du fleuve Boteti.

Makgadikgadi-Salzpfannen

Makgadikgadi bedeutet „ausgedehntes, lebloses Land". Beides trifft zu: Die Region ist vegetationslos, und die Salzpfannen im nordöstlichen Bereich der Kalahari in Botswana gehören mit einer Fläche von 16 000 km^2 zu den größten Salzwüsten der Erde. Die Ränder der Salzpfannen sind von Grassavanne umgeben, Wasser und damit Leben spendet der Fluss Boteti.

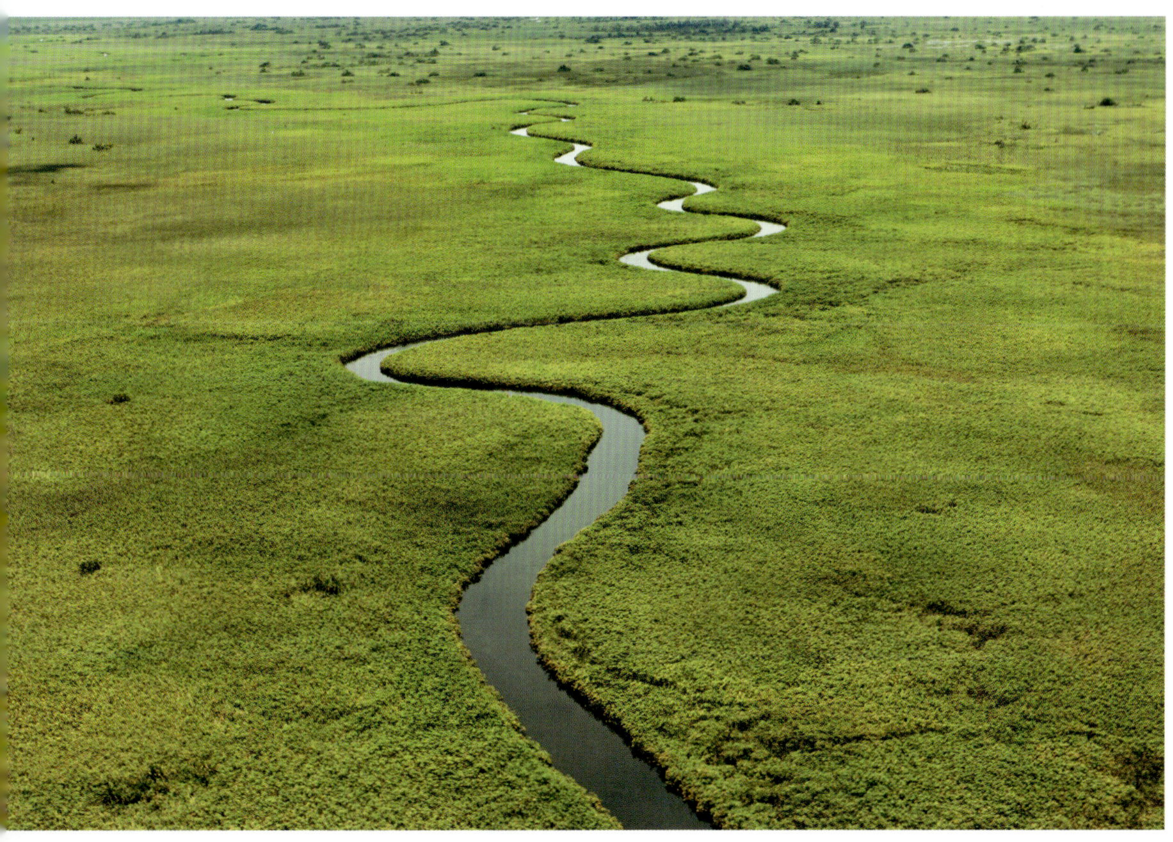

Boteti River, Makgadikgadi Pans National Park

Salares de Makgadikgadi
Makgadikgadi significa „tierra extensa, sin vida". Ambas cosas son ciertas: la región no cuenta con vegetación y los salares en la zona noreste del Kalahari en Botswana, con una superficie de 16 000 km², es uno de los mayores salares del mundo. Los bordes de los salares están rodeados por la sabana de hierba, agua y por tanto vida, ofrece el río Boteti.

Saline di Makgadikgadi
Makgadikgadi significa „vasta terra senza vita". Ed è davvero così: la regione è priva di vegetazione e le saline nella zona nord-orientale del Kalahari in Botswana appartengono ad uno dei deserti salati più grandi del pianeta, con una superficie di 16 000 km². I margini delle saline sono circondati dalla savana erbosa, e il fiume Boteti fornisce l'acqua e quindi anche la vita.

Zoutvlakten van Makgadikgadi
'Makgadikgadi' betekent 'uitgestrekt land zonder leven' en dat is terecht: de regio heeft geen vegetatie en de zoutpannen in het noordoosten van de Kalahariwoestijn in Botswana behoren met een oppervlakte van 16 000 km² tot de grootste zoutwoestijnen op aarde. De oevers van de zoutpannen worden omringd door grasland, het water (en daarmee leven) wordt aangevoerd door de rivier de Boteti.

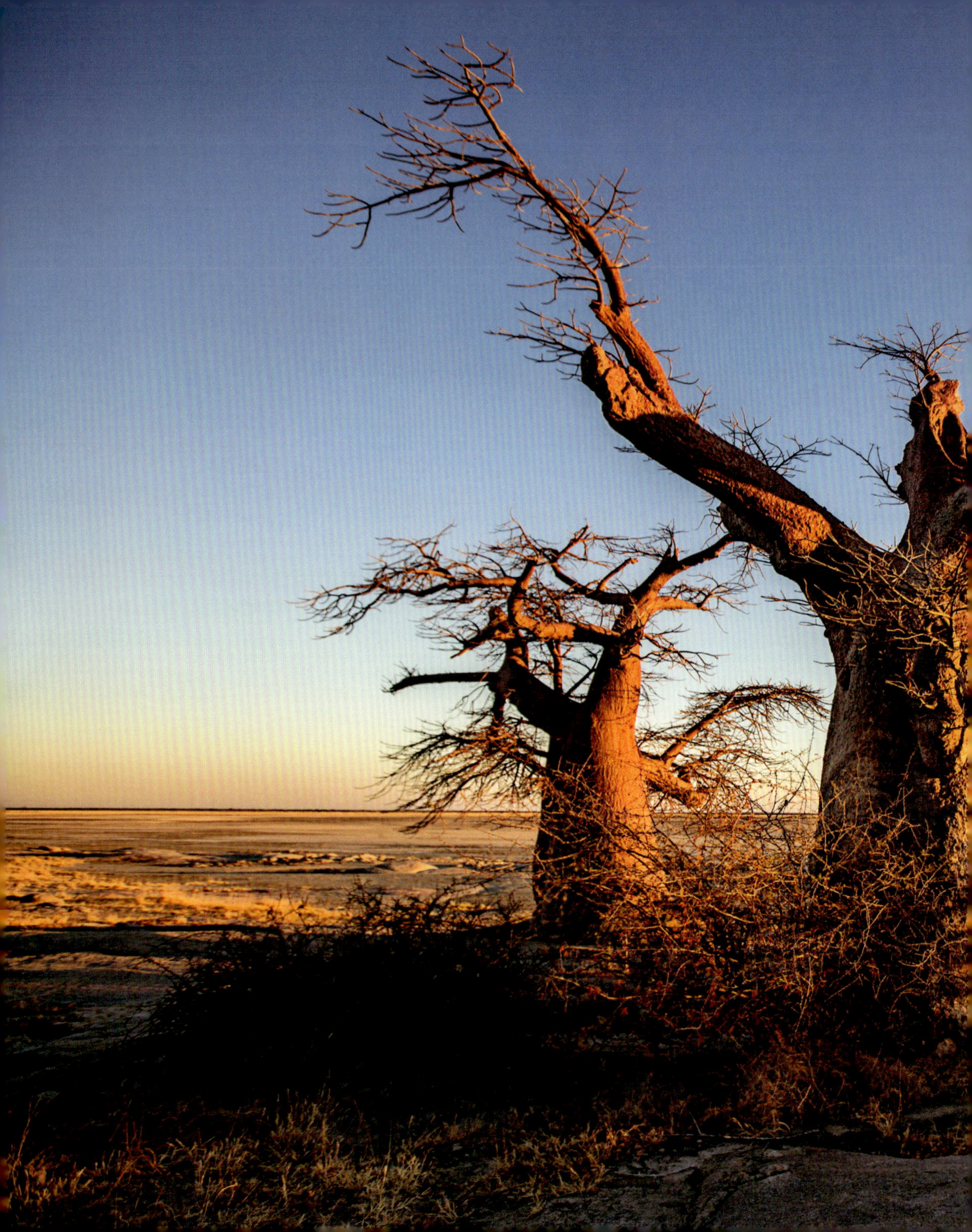

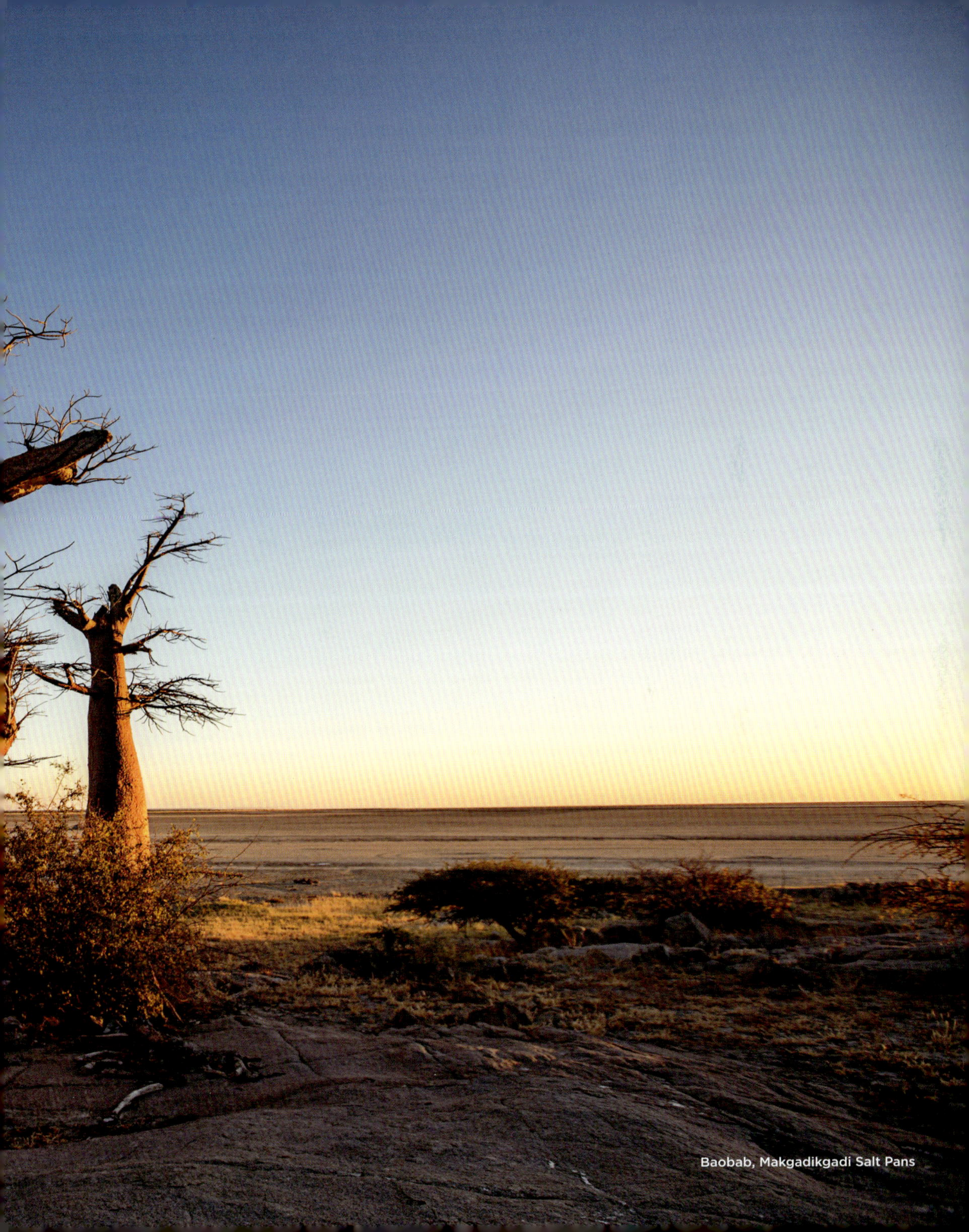

Baobab, Makgadikgadi Salt Pans

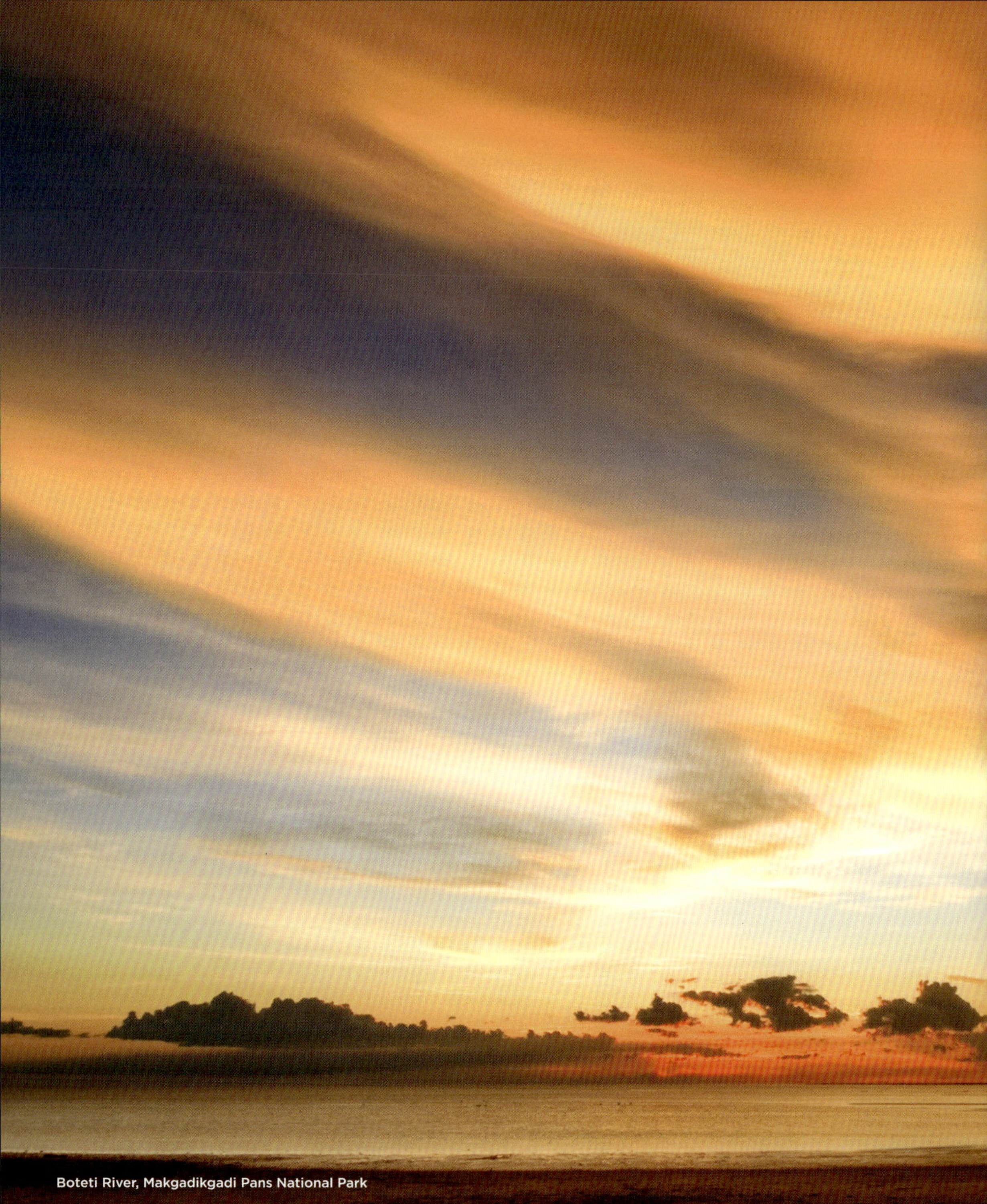

Boteti River, Makgadikgadi Pans National Park

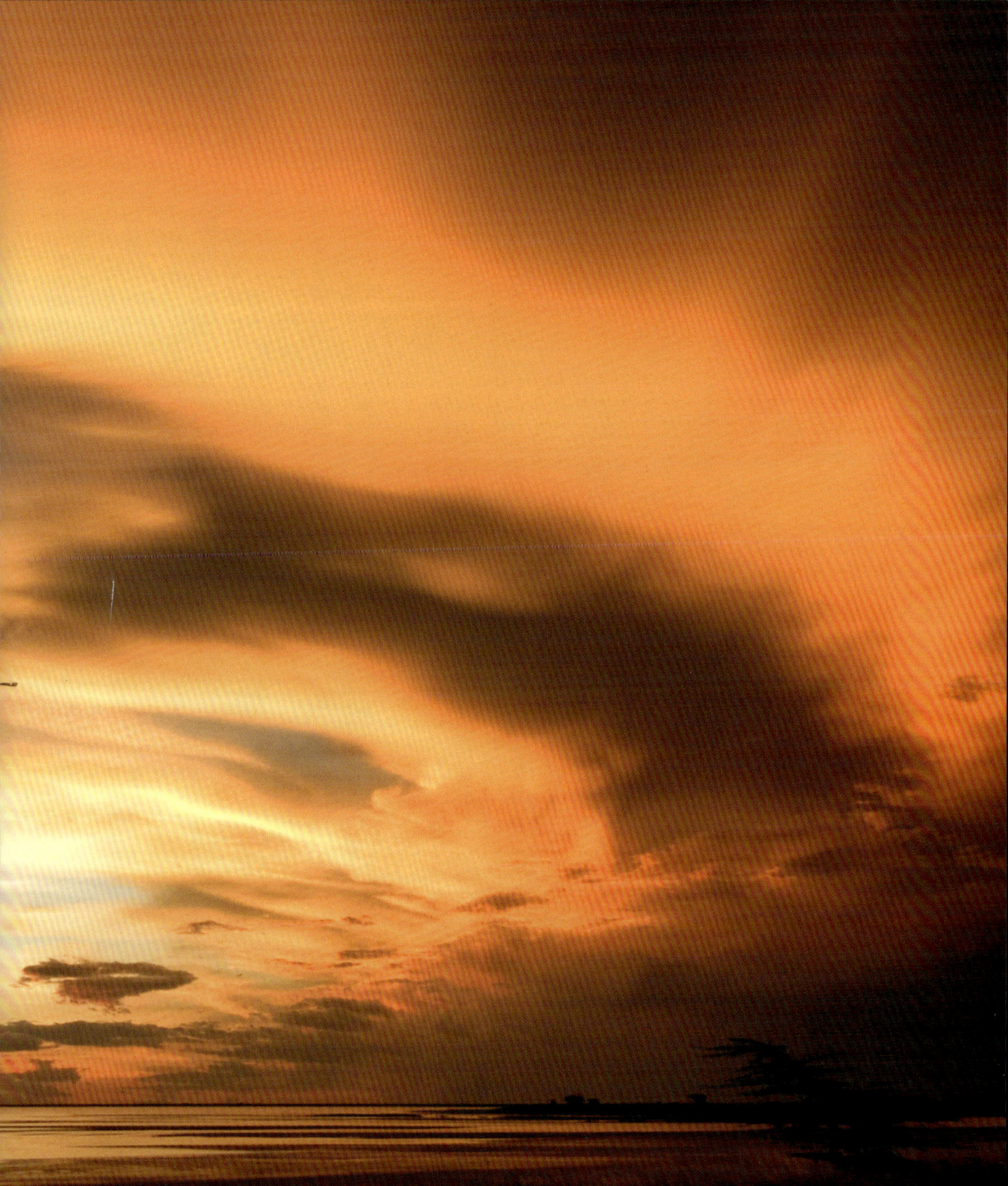

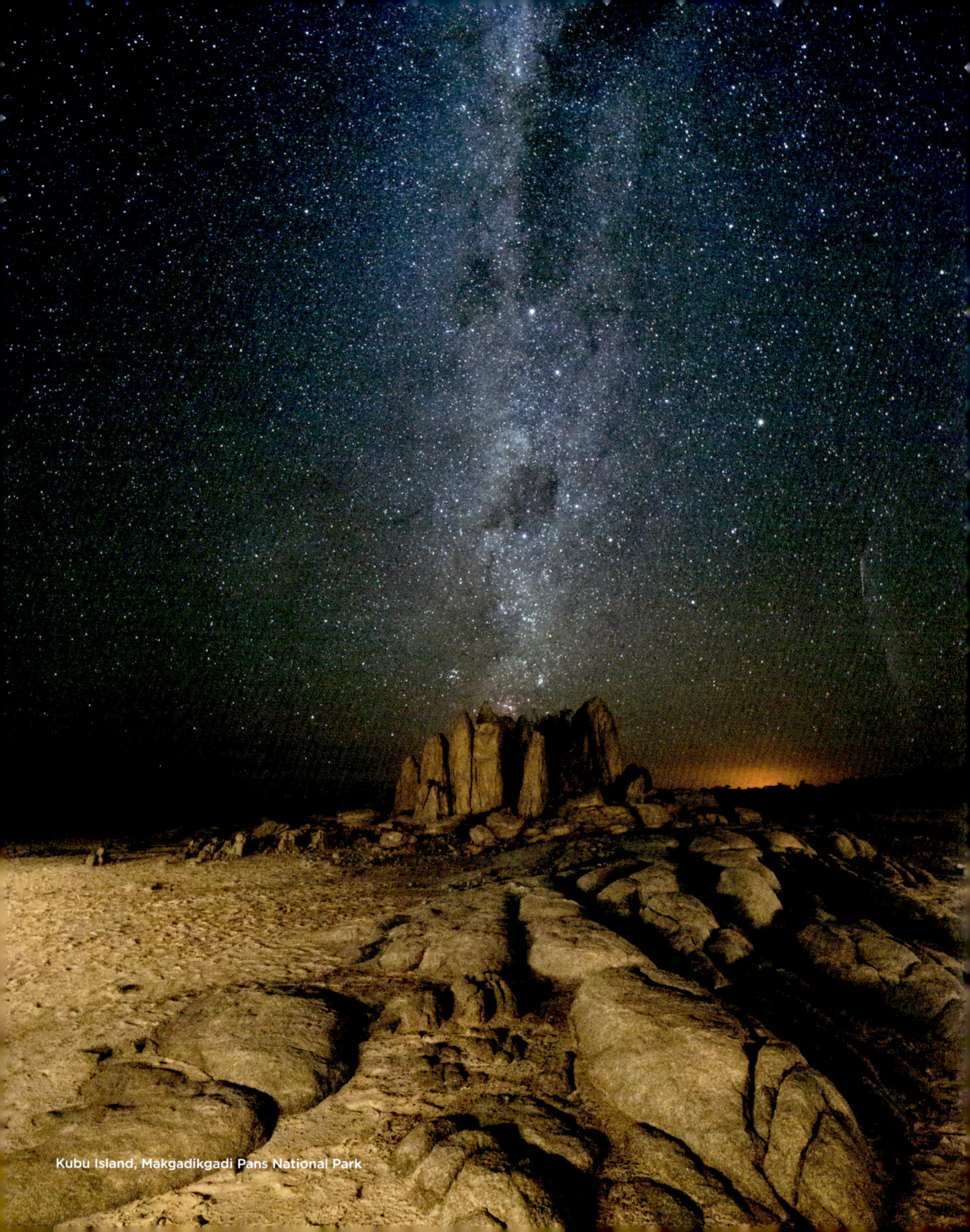
Kubu Island, Makgadikgadi Pans National Park

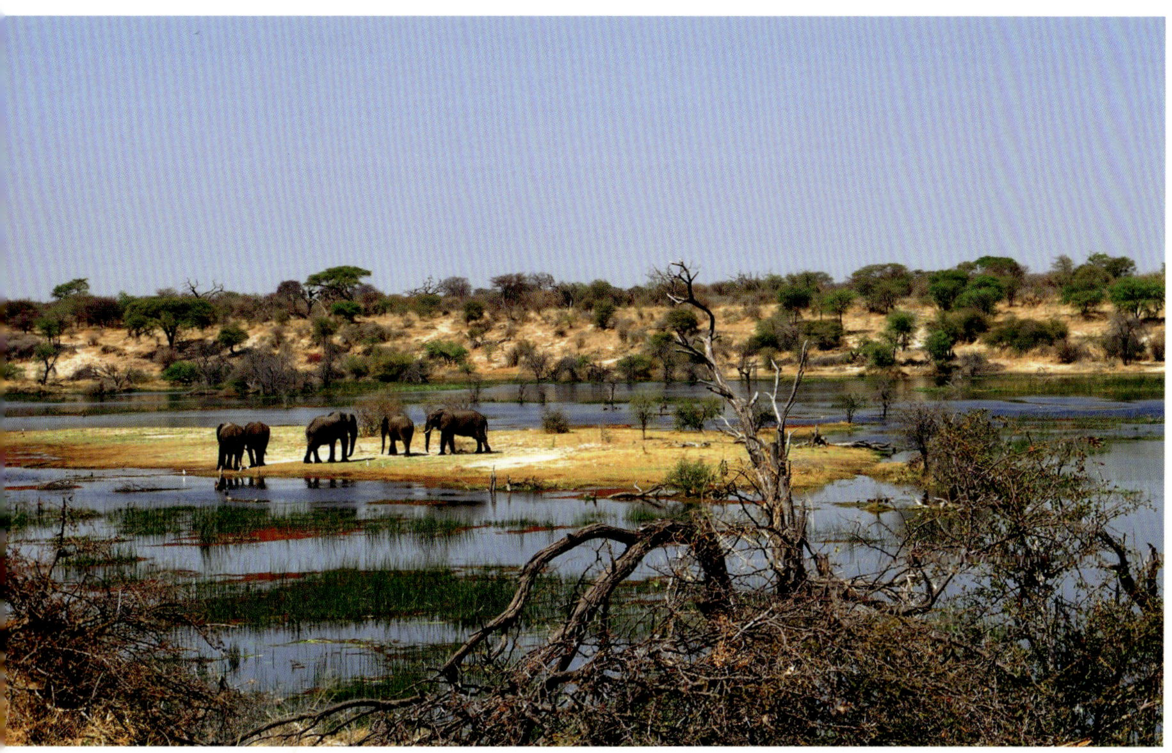

Elephants, Boteti River, Makgadikgadi Pans National Park

Starlit
The Milky Way is one of the most photographed motifs in Botswana and Namibia, where neither air pollution nor the lights of cities clouds the view of the stars.

Sternenklar
Die Milchstraße gehört zu den meistfotografierten nächtlichen Motiven in Botswana und Namibia, wo weder Luftverschmutzung den Blick trübt noch urbane Lichtquellen die Sicht beeinträchtigen.

Cielo stellato
La Via Lattea è uno dei temi notturni più fotografati di Botswana e Namibia, dove l'inquinamento atmosferico non offusca lo sguardo e le luci urbane non limitano la vista.

Ciel étoilé
La Voie lactée est l'un des motifs nocturnes les plus photographiés au Botswana et en Namibie, où le regard n'est gêné ni par la pollution de l'air, ni par l'éclairage urbain.

Cielo estrallado
La Vía Láctea es una de las escenas nocturnas más fotografiada en Botswana y Namibia, donde ni la contaminación del aire dificulta la vista ni las fuentes de luz urbanas afectan a la visibilidad.

Met heldere sterrenhemel
De Melkweg behoort in Botswana en Namibië tot de meest gefotografeerde nachtelijke natuurfenomenen, omdat de blik op de sterren noch door stedelijke lichtbronnen noch door luchtvervuiling wordt verstoord.

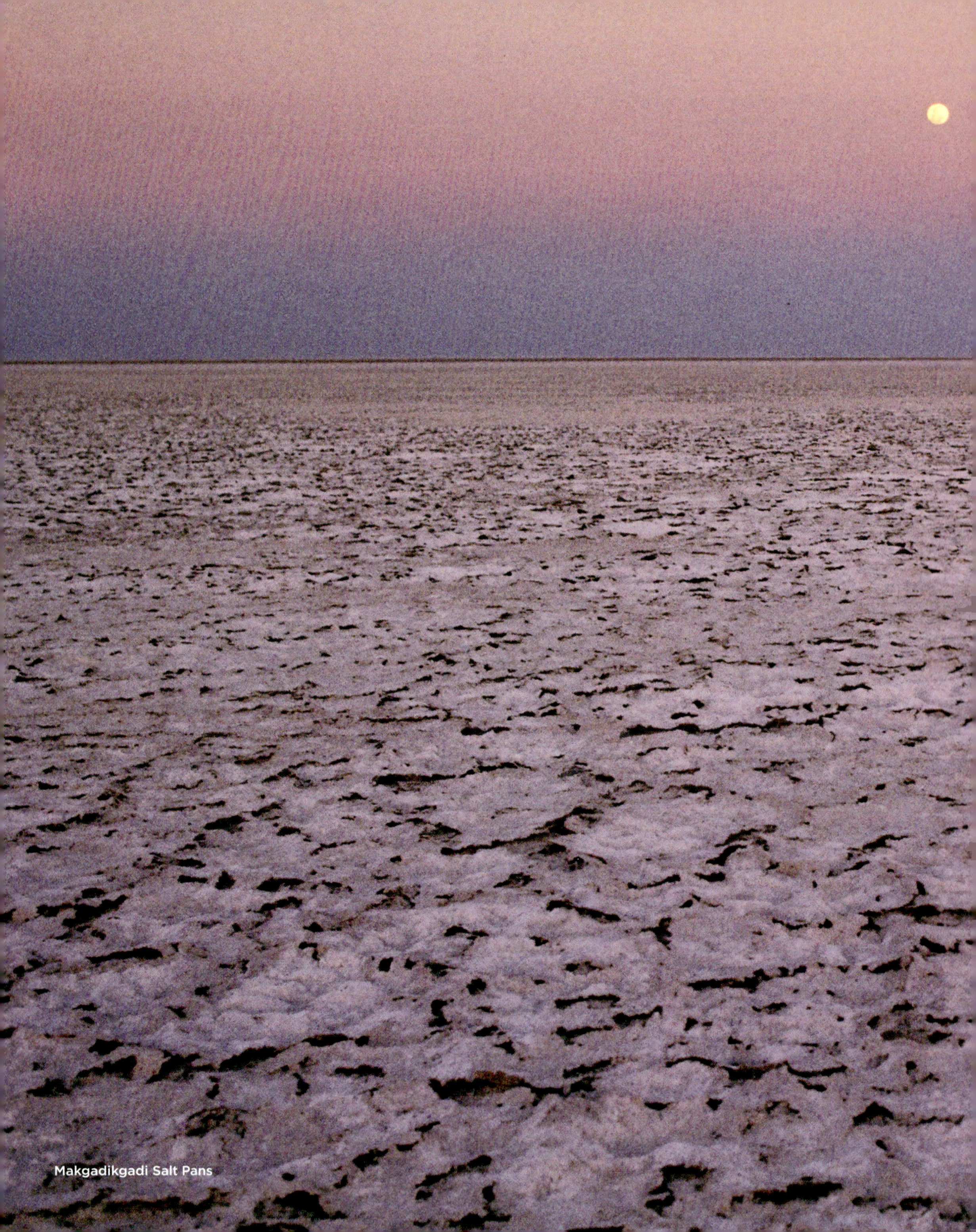

Makgadikgadi Salt Pans

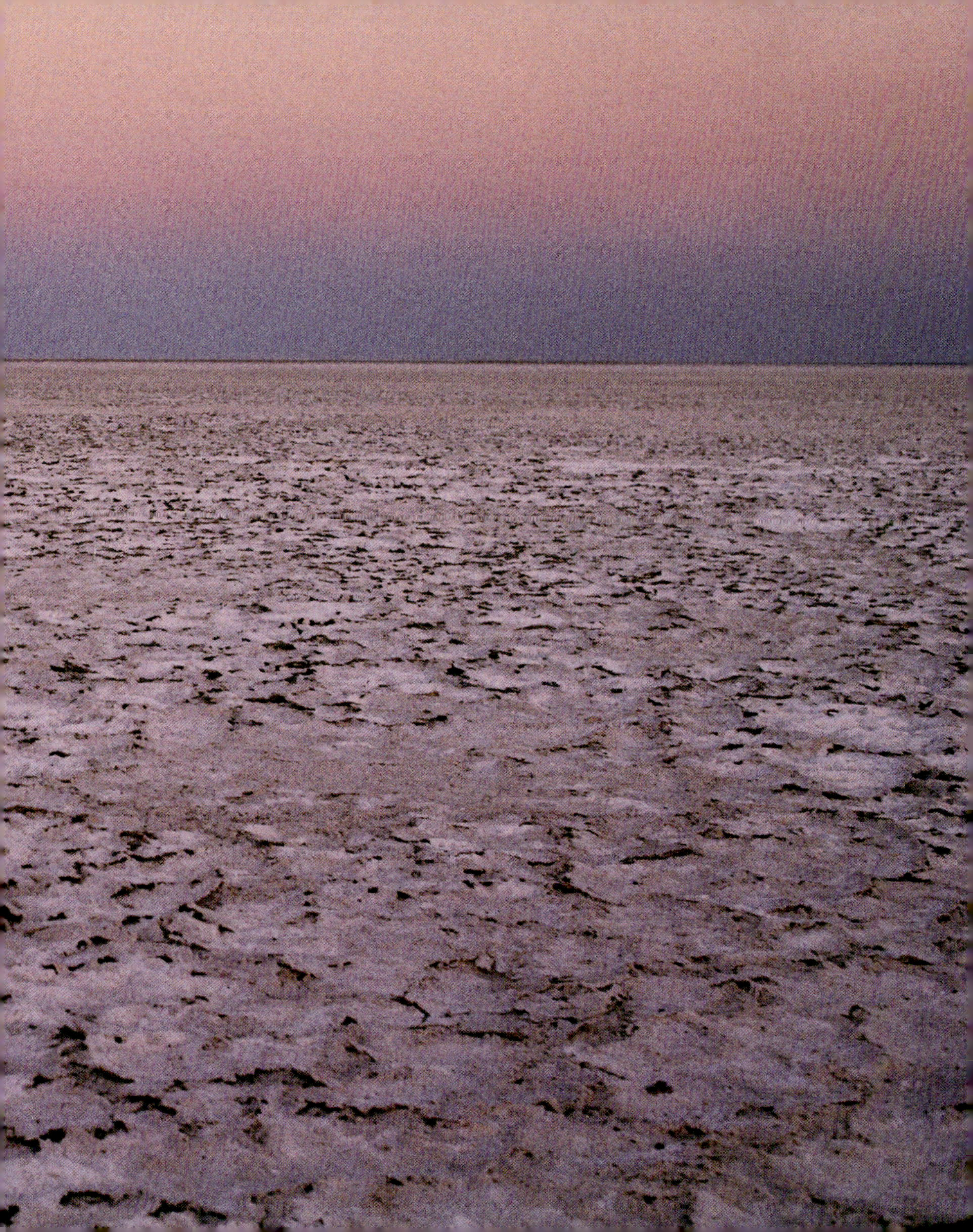

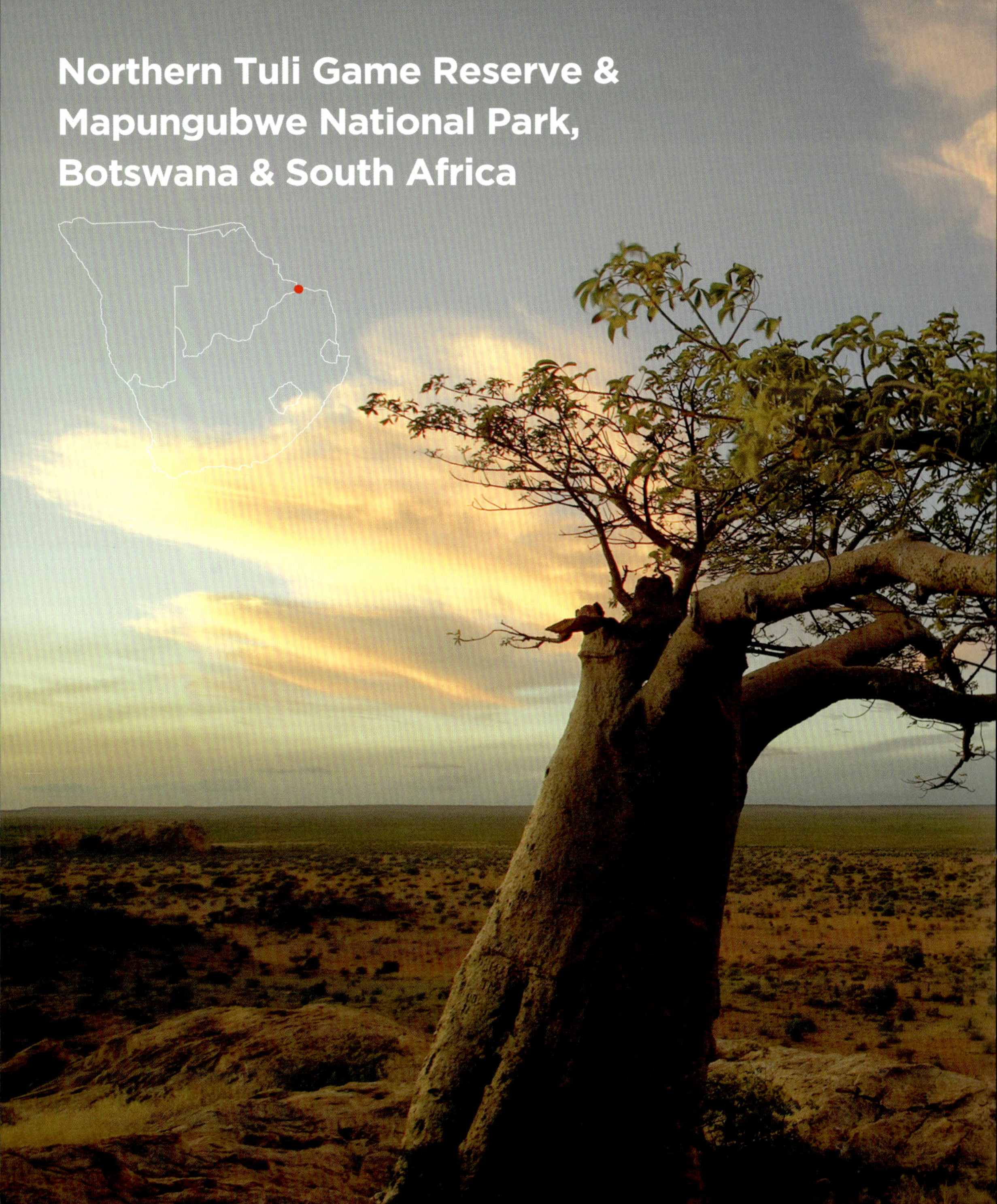
Northern Tuli Game Reserve &
Mapungubwe National Park,
Botswana & South Africa

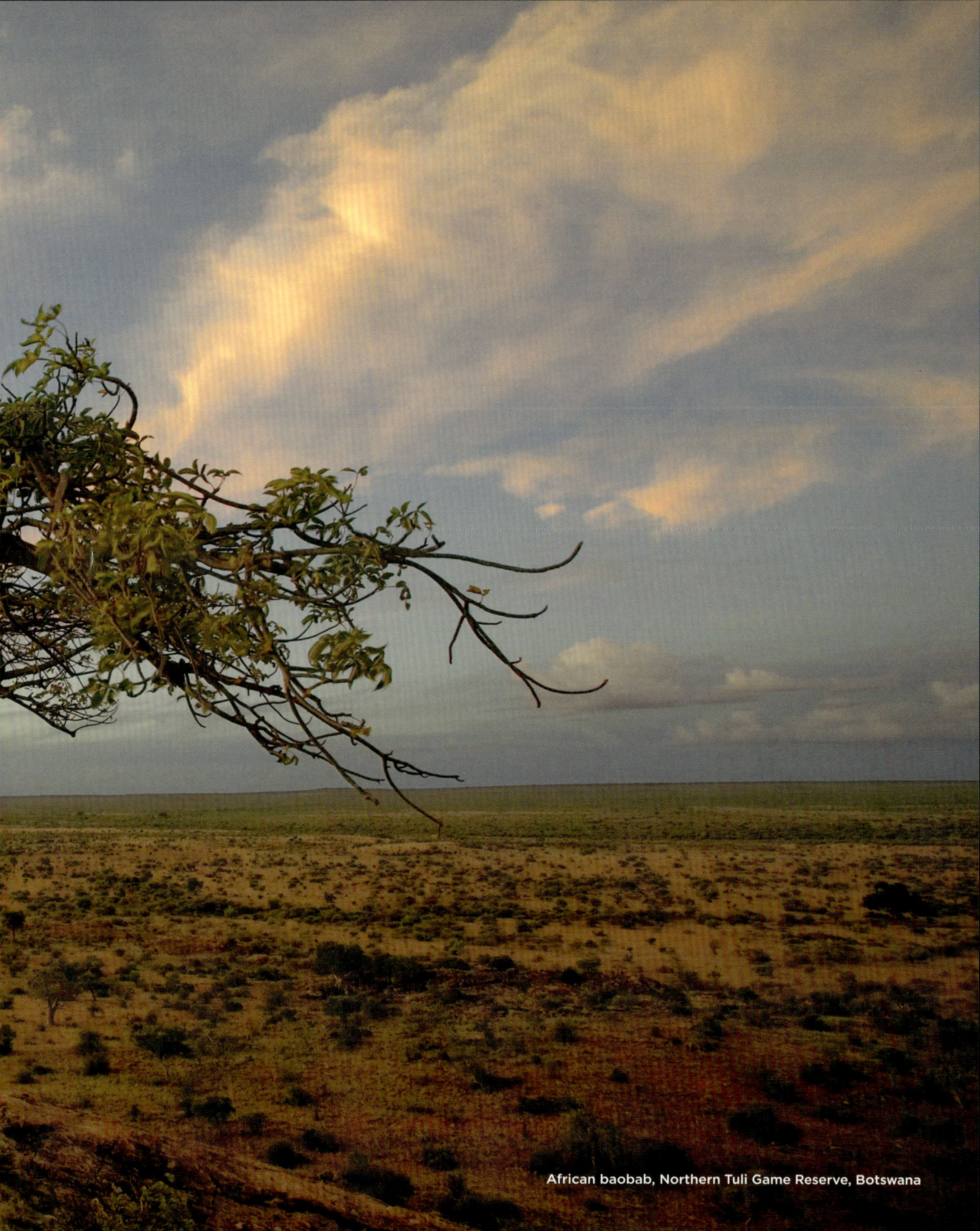

African baobab, Northern Tuli Game Reserve, Botswana

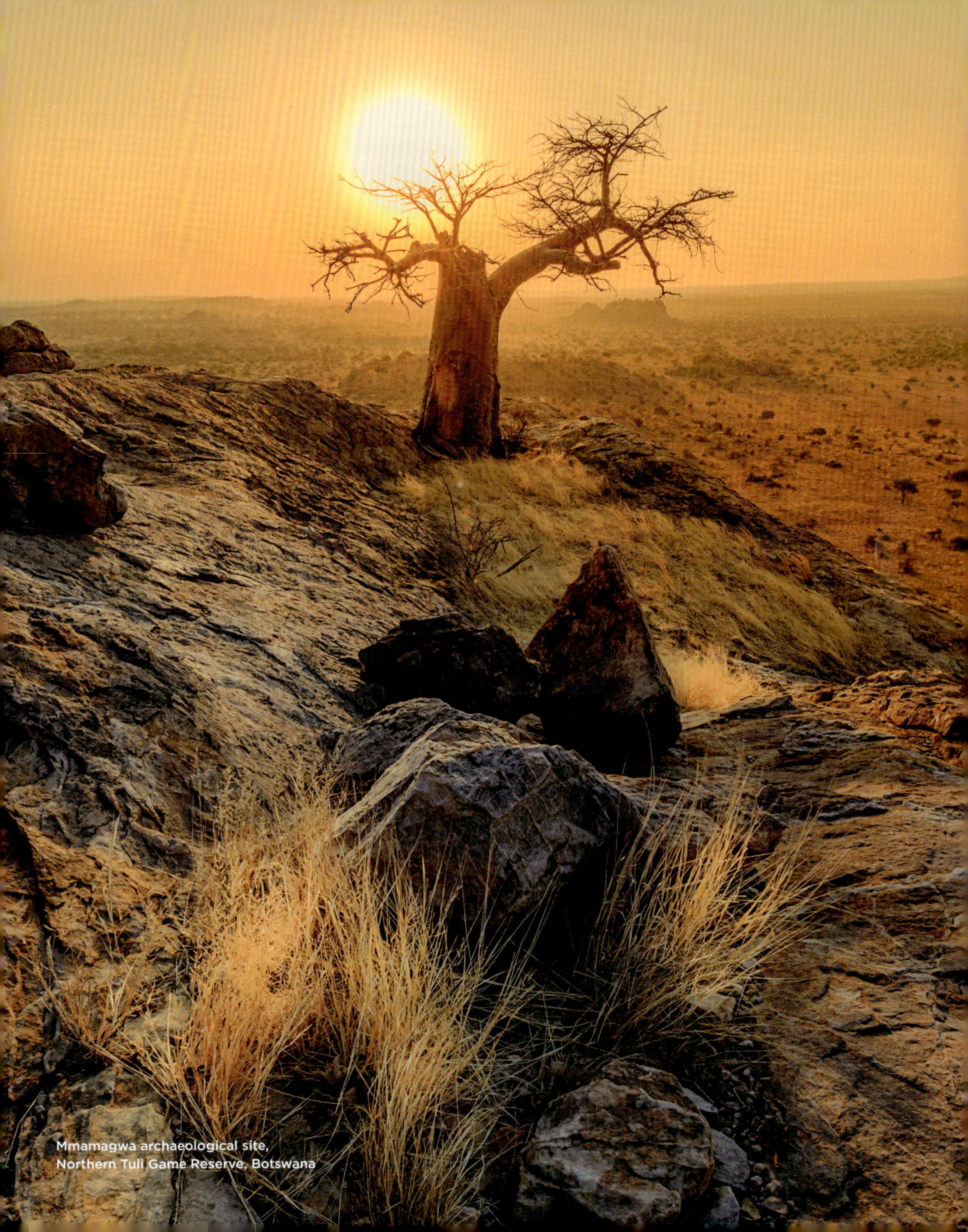

Mmamagwa archaeological site,
Northern Tuli Game Reserve, Botswana

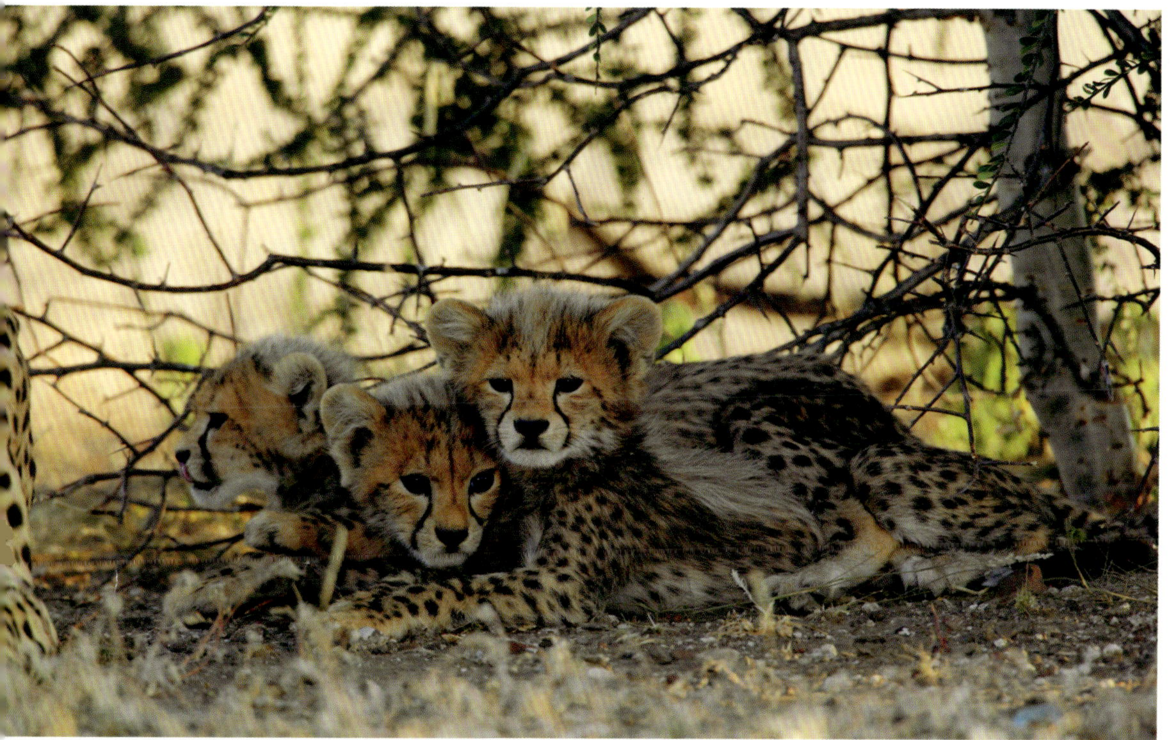

:heetah cubs, Northern Tuli Game Reserve, Botswana

Iorthern Tuli Game Reserve
he barren beauty of the Kalahari plain ıarks the landscape of the Central District. Ɔnly in the east does Botswana show ery different side, with basalt formations nd sandstone hills, forests, meadows nd swampland offering areas of green to reak up the savanna. The Northern Tuli ame Reserve houses a large population f elephants.

a réserve naturelle de Tuli Nord
a beauté austère de la cuvette du Kalahari ıarque les paysages du Central District. e Botswana se présente sous un tout utre visage dans sa partie orientale, avec es formations basaltiques et ses collines e grès impressionnantes, tandis que les prêts, les prairies et les marais posent des ccents verts. La réserve naturelle de Tuli ord abrite une abondante population 'éléphants.

Northern Tuli Game Reserve
Die karge Schönheit der ebenen Kalahari prägt das Landschaftsbild des Central District. Nur im Osten zeigt sich Botswana von einer ganz anderen Seite: Hier beeindrucken Basaltformationen und Sandsteinhügel, Wälder, Wiesen und Sumpfland setzen grüne Tupfer. Das Wildreservat Northern Tuli Game Reserve beherbergt eine reiche Elefanten Population.

Reserva de Caza del Norte de Tuli
La cruda belleza de la llanura del Kalahari caracteriza el paisaje del Distrito Central. Sólo en el este de Botswana se muestra un lado totalmente diferente: aquí impresionan las formaciones de basalto y las colinas de arenisca, bosques, praderas y pantanos ponen el punto verde. La reserva de caza del Norte de Tuli tiene una rica población de elefantes.

Riserva di caccia di Northern Tuli
L'arida bellezza del piatto Kalahari caratterizza il paesaggio del Central District. Solo nella zona est il Botswana mostra un lato totalmente diverso: qui impressionano le formazioni di basalto e colline di arenaria, boschi, prati e terreni paludosi formano macchie verdi. La riserva naturale di caccia Northern Tuli ospita una ricca popolazione di elefanti.

Northern Tuli Game Reserve
De lege schoonheid van de vlakke Kalahari bepaalt het landschap van het Central District. Alleen in het oosten toont Botswana zich van een heel andere kant, met imposante basaltformaties en zandsteenheuvels, bossen, weiden en draslanden met groene accenten. Het wildreservaat Northern Tuli Game Reserve herbergt een grote populatie olifanten.

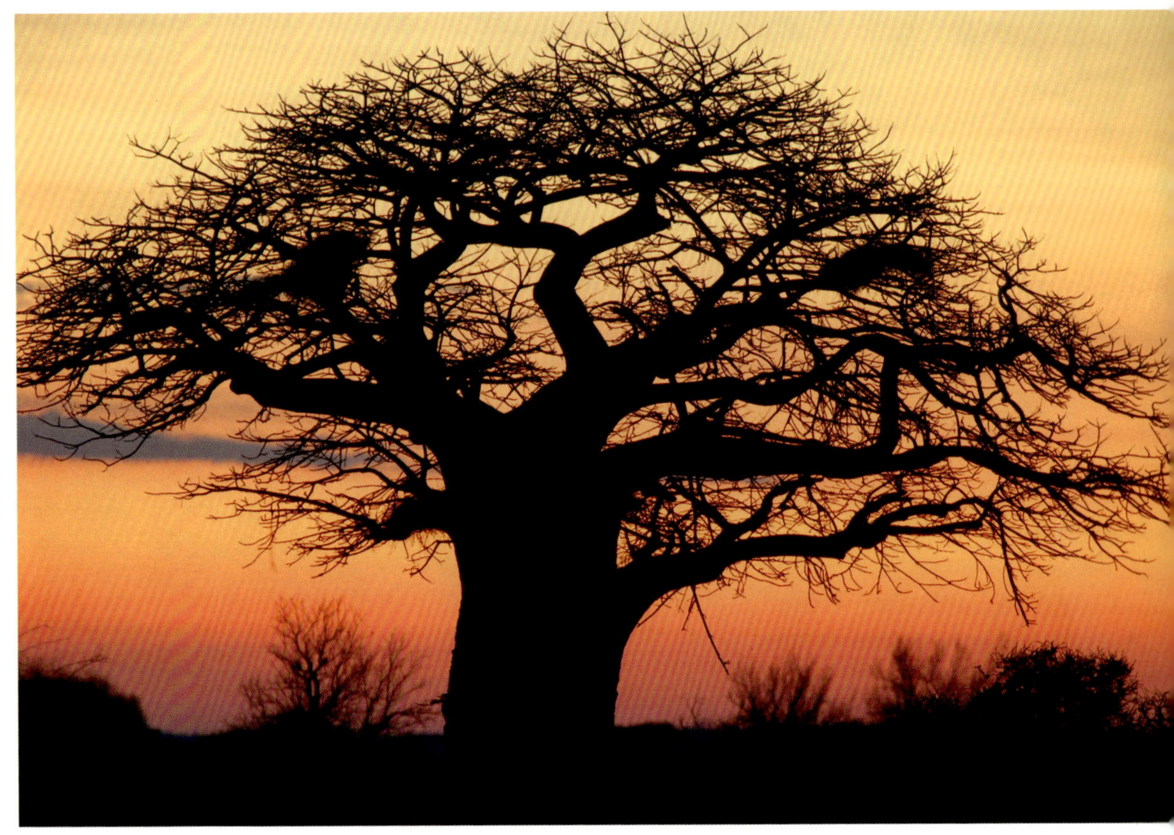

African baobab, Northern Tuli Game Reserve, Botswana

Baobab
The baobab tree is perfectly equipped for survival in regions where rain is rare: its trunk serves as a water tank. The trees may reach heights of up to 30 m (98 ft), while their trunks can be as much as 11 m (36 ft) across. If they grow that large, they can store up to 120,000 l (31,700 gallons) of water.

Baobab
Les baobabs, dont les troncs sont de véritables citernes, sont parfaitement équipés pour survivre dans des régions où les pluies sont rares. Ces arbres peuvent culminer à 30 m (98 ft) pour un diamètre pouvant atteindre jusqu'à 11 m. Ils sont capables de stocker dans les 120 000 l d'eau.

Baobab
Baobabs sind perfekt ausgerüstet für das Überleben in Regionen, in denen selten Regen fällt: Ihre Stämme dienen als Wassertanks. Die Bäume können bis zu 30 m hoch werden, ihre Stämme erreichen Durchmesser bis zu 11 m. Dort können sie bis zu 120 000 l Wasser speichern.

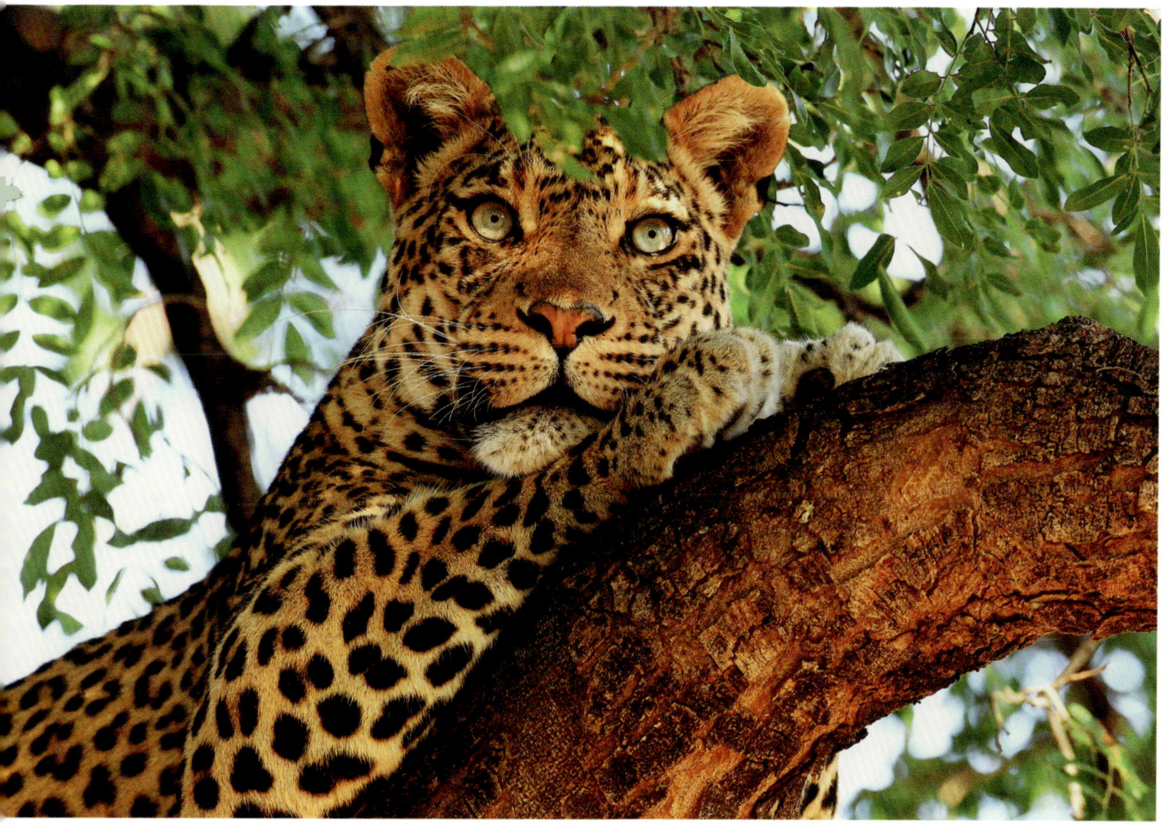

eopard, Northern Tuli Game Reserve, Botswana

aobab
os baobabs están perfectamente quipados para la supervivencia en egiones donde la lluvia cae rara vez: sus oncos sirven como depósitos de agua. os árboles pueden ser de hasta 30 m de to, sus tallos alcanzan un diámetro de asta 11 m. Allí pueden almacenar agua asta 120 000 l.

Baobab
I baobab sono perfettamente equipaggiati per la sopravvivenza nelle regioni in cui cade raramente la pioggia: i loro tronchi servono da serbatoi per l'acqua. Gli alberi possono raggiungere un'altezza di 30 m e i loro tronchi un diametro di 11 m. Lì possono immagazzinare fino a 120 000 l d'acqua.

Apenbroodboom
Baobabs zijn perfect aangepast voor het overleven in gebieden waar zelden regen valt: hun stammen dienen als waterreservoirs. De bomen kunnen tot wel 30 m hoog worden, met stammen van 11 m doorsnede waarin ze tot wel 120 000 l water kunnen opslaan.

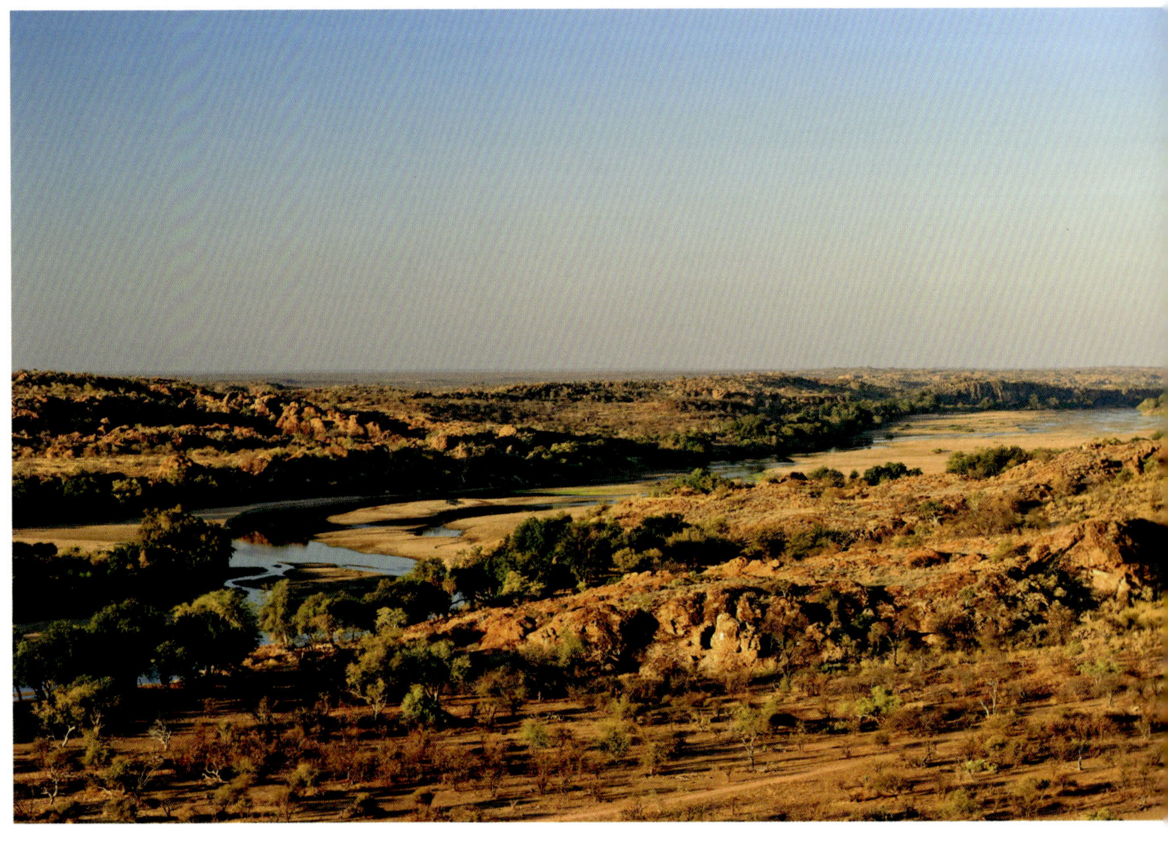

Limpopo River, Mapungubwe National Park, South Africa

Mapungubwe National Park
Mapungubwe National Park in northern South Africa impresses not only with its biodiversity, striking sandstone cliffs, and forests, but has also been named a UNESCO World Heritage site. Archaeological finds bear witness to the fact that the first kingdom in southern Africa flourished here, between 900 and 1300 AD, at the confluence of the Limpopo River and the Shashe River.

Le parc national de Mapungubwe
Le parc national de Mapungubwe, dans le nord de l'Afrique du Sud, impressionne par sa biodiversité, ses extraordinaires falaises de grès et ses forêts. Il est d'ailleurs inscrit au patrimoine mondial de l'Unesco. Des fouilles archéologiques ont établi la présence ici du premier royaume d'Afrique australe, au confluent du Limpopo et du Shashe. Sa grande époque se situe entre 900 et 1300 aprés J.-C.

Mapungubwe-Nationalpark
Der Mapungubwe-Nationalpark im nördlichen Südafrika imponiert nicht nur durch seine Artenvielfalt, markante Sandsteinfelsen und Wälder, er gehört auc zum UNESCO-Welterbe. Archäologische Funde zeugen davon, dass hier, am Zusammenfluss des Limpopo und des Shashe, das erste Königreich im südlichen Afrika lag, das zwischen 900 und 1300 v. Chr. florierte.

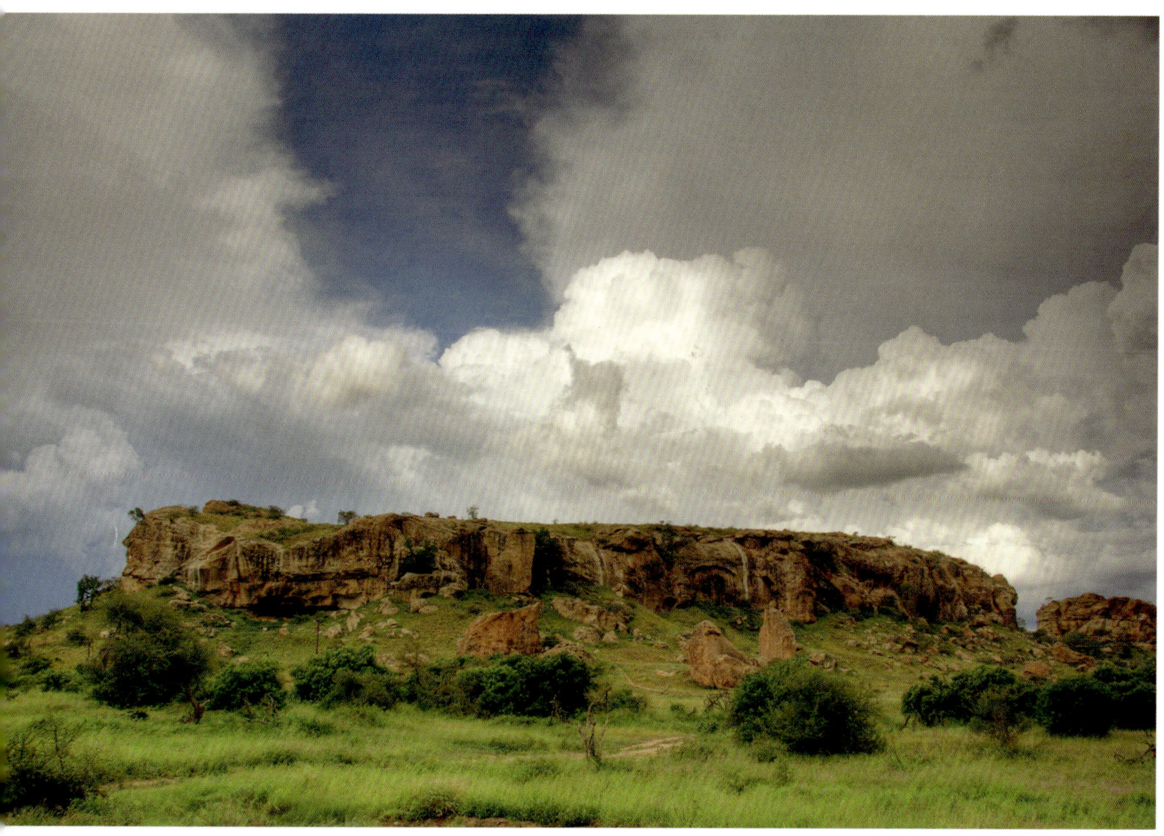

apungubwe National Park, South Africa

arque Nacional Mapungubwe
Parque Nacional Mapungubwe en el orte de Sudáfrica no impresiona sólo por u biodiversidad, sus notables acantilados e arenisca y bosques, sino que también ertenece al Patrimonio de la Humanidad. os hallazgos arqueológicos demuestran ue aquí, en la confluencia del Limpopo del Shashe, floreció el primer reino en sur de África entre el 1300 y el 900 espués de Cristo.

Parco Nazionale Mapungubwe
Il Parco Nazionale Mapungubwe nel nord del Sudafrica non si distingue solo per la sua varietà di specie, notevoli rocce di arenaria e boschi, ma appartiene anche al patrimonio mondiale dell'UNESCO. Reperti archeologici hanno dimostrato che qui, alla confluenza del Limpopo e dello Shashe, si trovava il primo regno dell'Africa del Sud, che fiorì tra il 900 e il 1300 dopo Cristo.

Nationale Park van Mapungubwe
Het Nationale Park van Mapungubwe in het noorden van Zuid-Afrika imponeert met zijn soortenrijkdom, markante zandsteenrotsen en bossen, en is dan ook een werelderfgoed van de UNESCO. Archeologische vondsten bewijzen dat rond de samenloop van de Limpopo en de Shashe het eerste Zuid-Afrikaanse koninkrijk ontstond, dat hier tussen 900 en 1300 na Chr. floreerde.

African baobab, Mapungubwe National Park, South Africa

Work of the Devil
In the dry season, the leaves fall off the baobabs and the tree crowns then look like a root system, planted upside down, which led some people to see the trees as the work of the devil.

L'œuvre du diable
Quand les feuilles du baobab tombent, à la saison sèche, la couronne fait penser à des racines. Autrefois, on y voyait l'œuvre du diable, qui aurait planté les arbres la tête en bas.

Teufelswerk
In der Trockenzeit fallen die Blätter der Baobabs ab, die Baumkronen wirken dann wie Wurzelwerk. Früher sah man hier ein Werk des Teufels: Er habe die Bäume verkehrt herum gepflanzt, glaubte man.

Obra del diablo
En la estación seca las hojas de los árboles baobab se caen, las copas de los árboles hacen el trabajo de las raíces. Antes se podía ver aquí una obra del diablo: se creía que había invertido los árboles plantados.

Opera del diavolo
Durante la stagione secca le foglie dei baobab cadono, le chiome degli alberi servono quindi da apparato radicale. In passato questa era considerata un'opera del diavolo: si pensava che avesse piantato gli alberi all'incontrario.

Werk van de duivel
In de droge maanden vallen de bladeren van de baobab af, zodat de kruinen doen denken aan wortelstelsels. Vroeger zag men hier het werk van de duivel in, die de bomen omgekeerd zou hebben geplant.

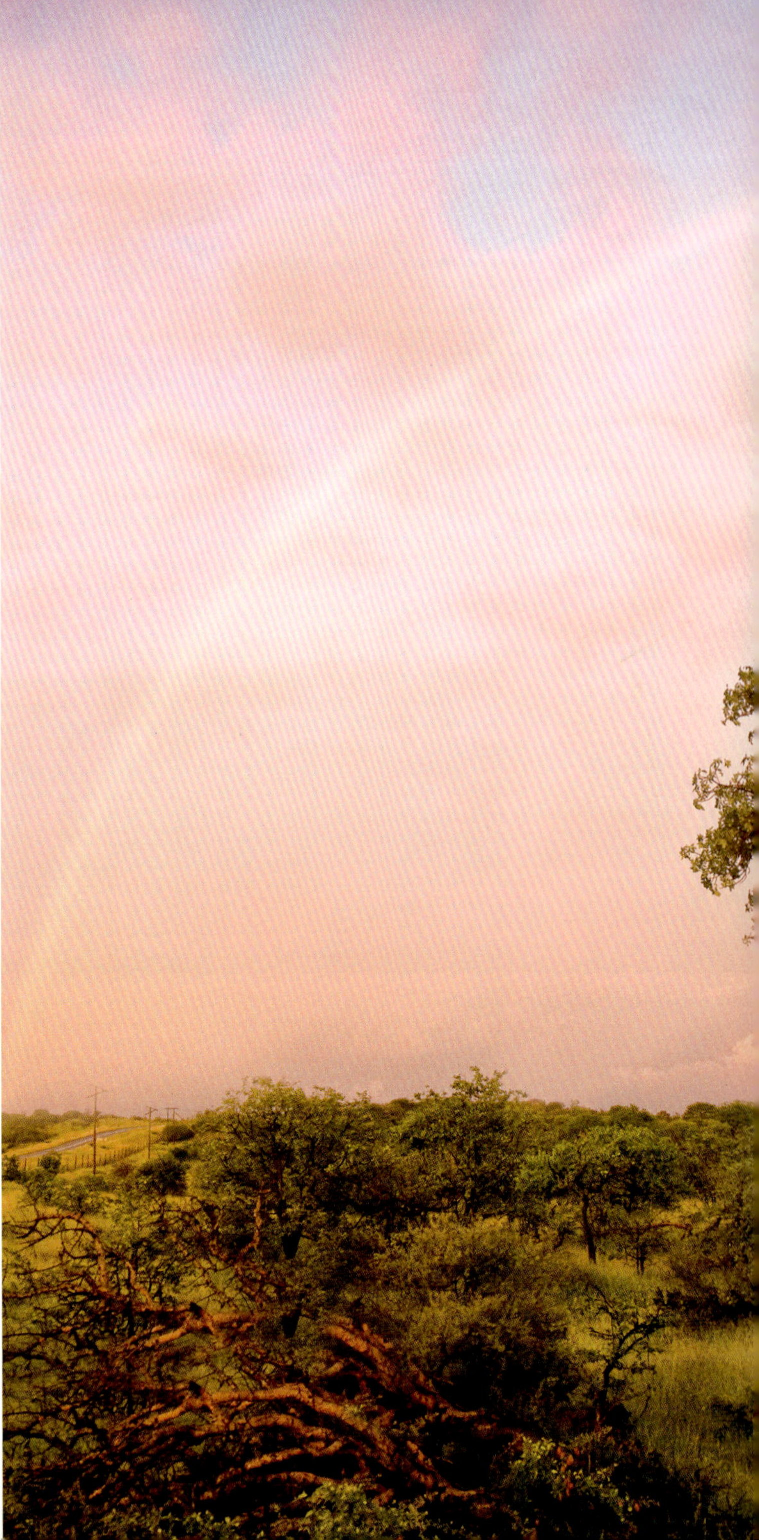

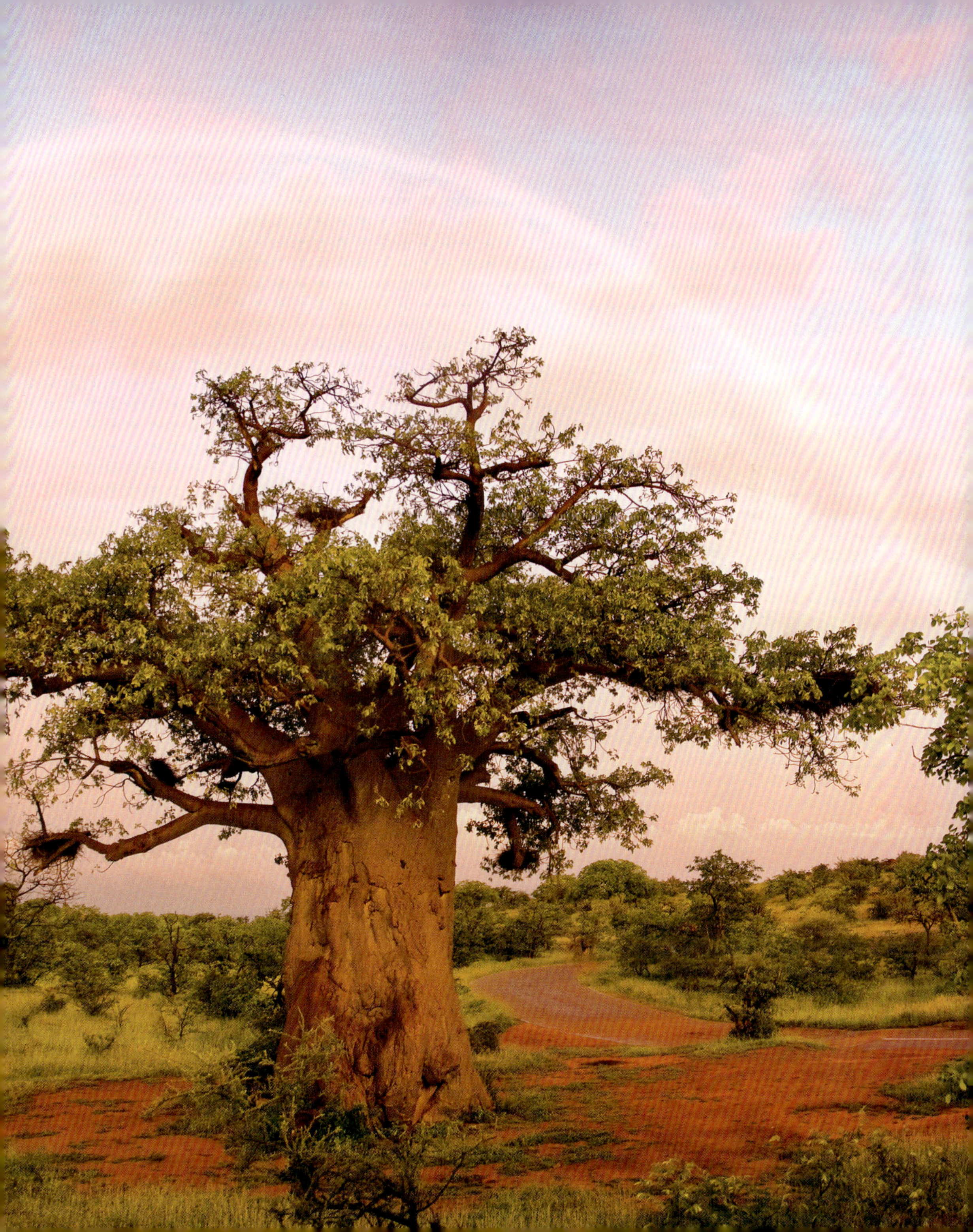

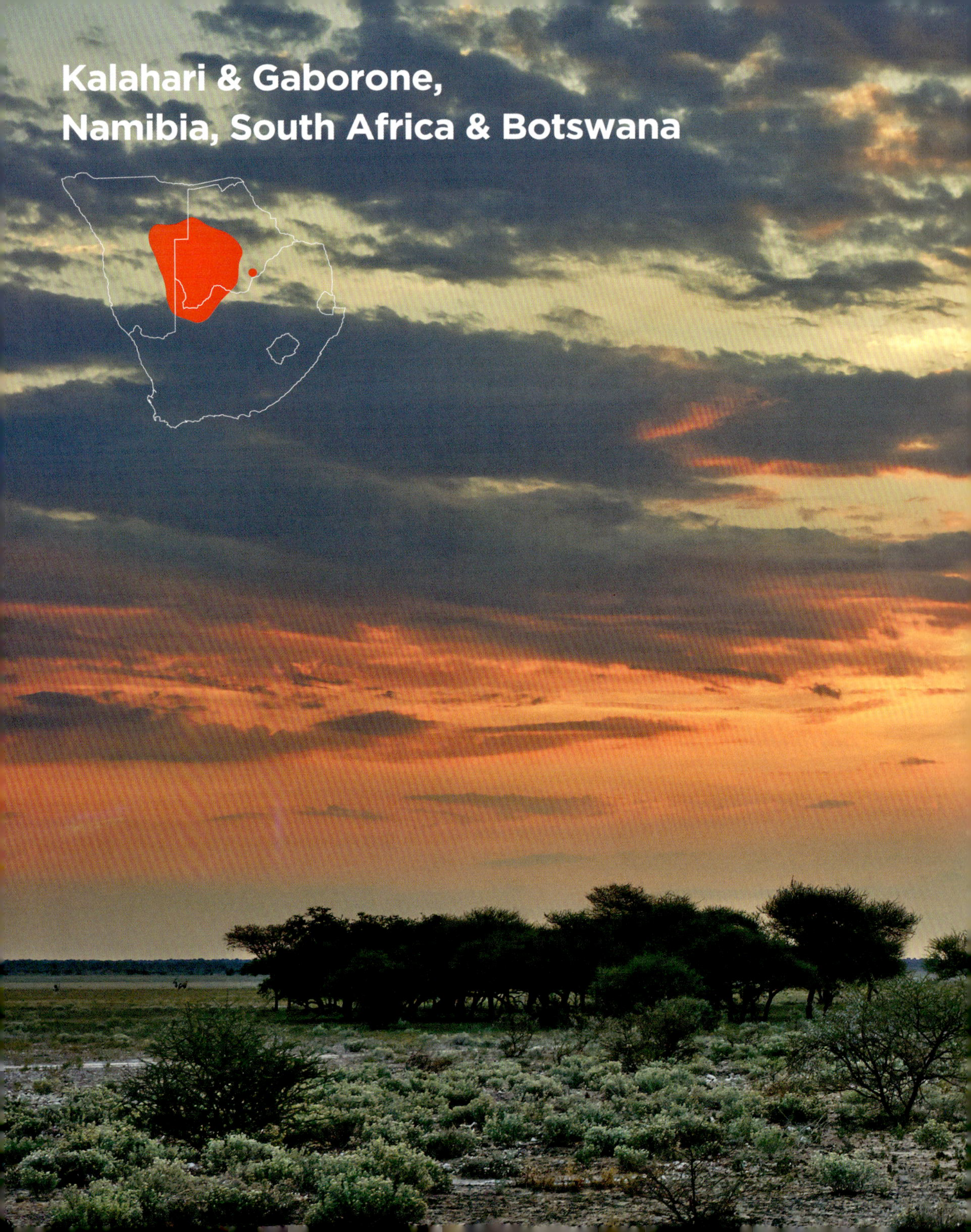
Kalahari & Gaborone,
Namibia, South Africa & Botswana

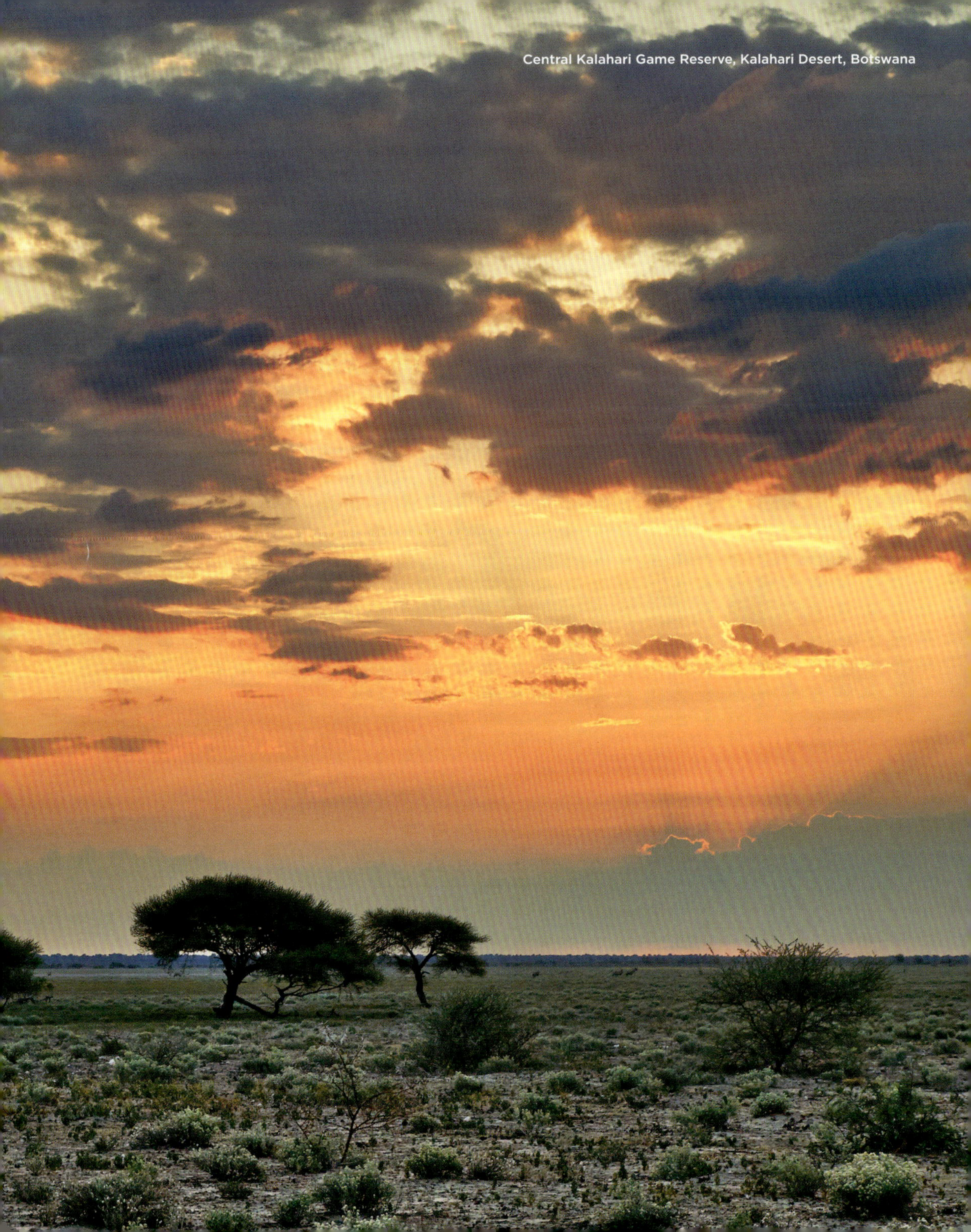

Central Kalahari Game Reserve, Kalahari Desert, Botswana

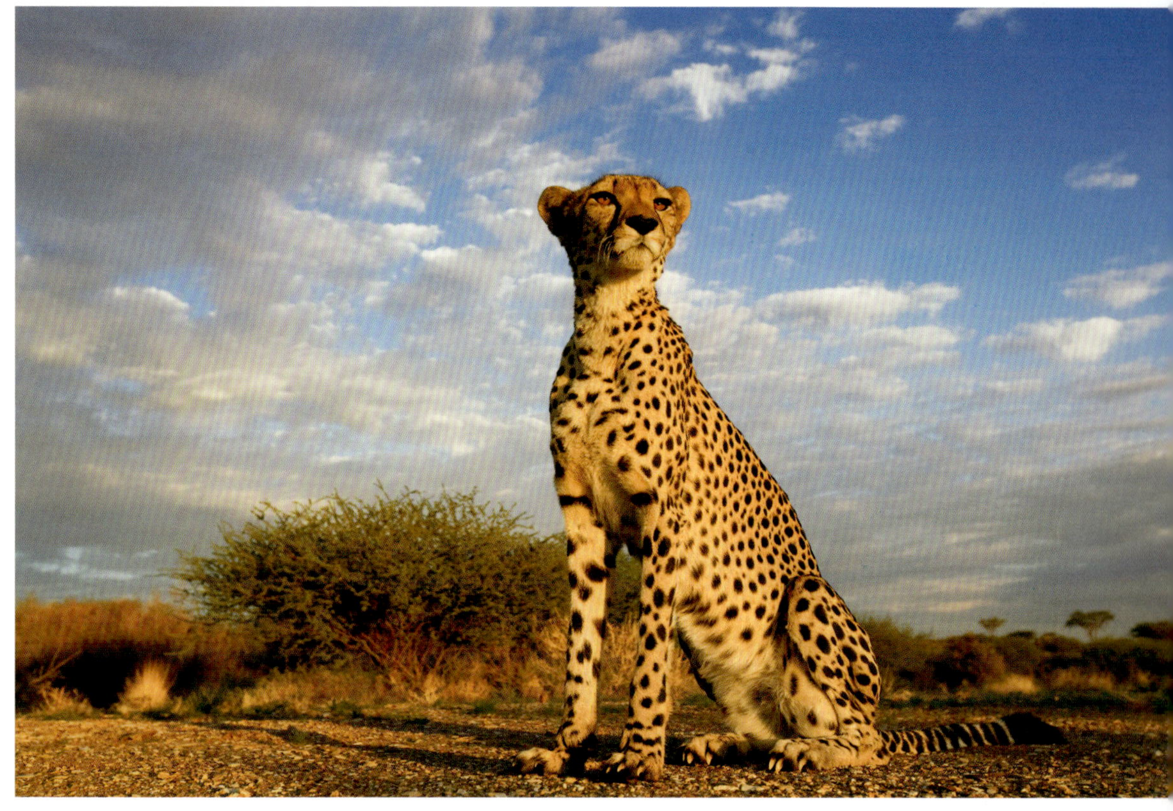

Cheetah, Kalahari Desert, Namibia

The Kalahari
The Kalahari extends from Namibia across Botswana to the Northern Cape province in South Africa. Due to its red sands in the south and west, and the yellow to grey sands in the north and east, this area has been incorrectly called a desert. In fact, the Kalahari is not as arid as the Namib, but is instead a dry, grassy and thorny shrub savanna.

Le Kalahari
Le Kalahari commence en Namibie, traverse le Botswana et rejoint la province du Cap-Nord en Afrique du Sud. Il doit sa qualification de désert à ses sols sableux, rouges au sud et à l'ouest, jaunes à gris au nord et à l'est. En fait, le Kalahari n'est pas aride comme le Namib, mais constitué de savanes sèches, herbeuses et épineuses où, selon les régions, poussent de l'herbe, des buissons ou des arbres.

Kalahari
Die Kalahari erstreckt sich von Namibia über Botswana bis in die Provinz Nordkap in Südafrika. Wegen ihrer im Süden und Westen roten, im Norden und Osten gelbe bis grauen Sandböden wird sie als Wüste bezeichnet. Tatsächlich ist die Kalahari nicht arid wie die Namib, sondern eine Trocken-, Gras- und Dornstrauchsavanne, die je nach Region Bewuchs von Gräsern, Sträuchern und Bäumen aufweist.

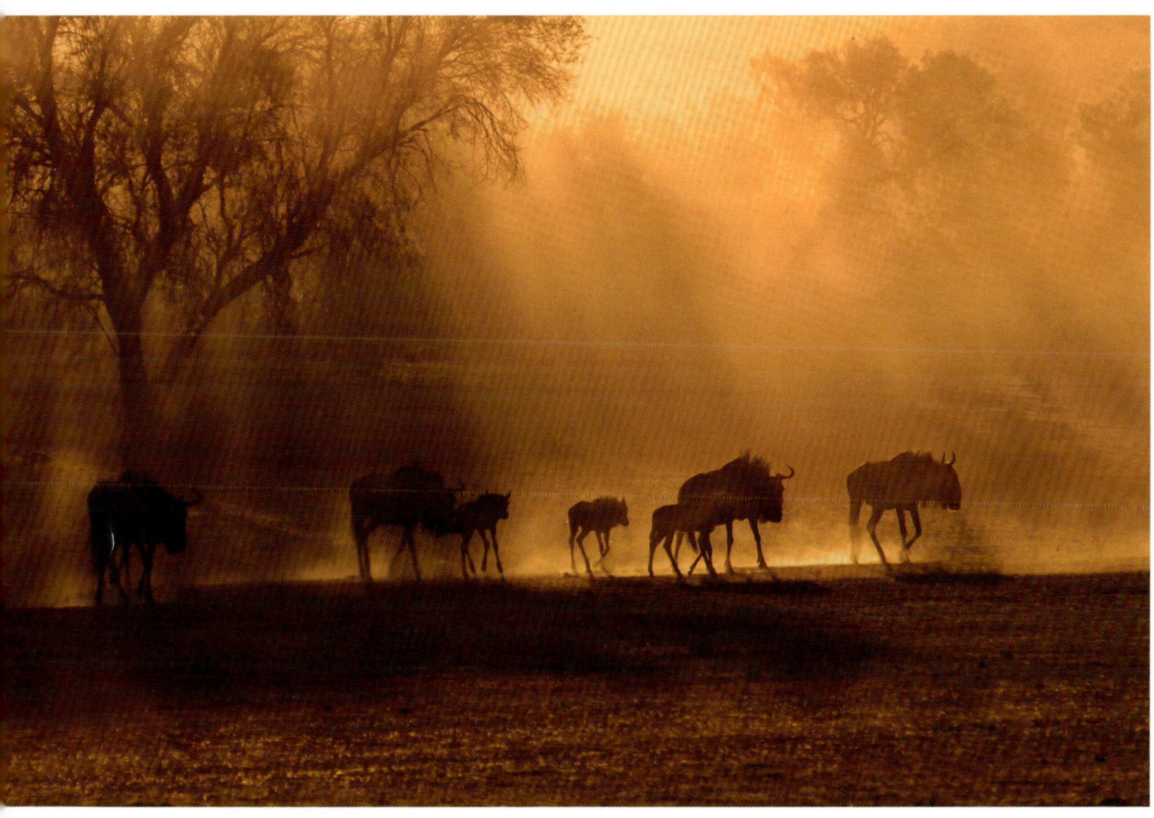

hus, Kgalagadi Transfrontier Park, Kalahari Desert, South Africa

alahari
Kalahari se extiende desde Namibia a avés de Botswana hasta el Cabo Norte Sudáfrica. Se llama desierto debido a s suelos arenosos rojos al sur y oeste, de narillos a grises en el norte y el este. De echo, el Kalahari no es tan árido como el Namibia, sino que es un lugar seco, de asto y matorral xerófilo, que tiene una egetación de praderas, arbustos y árboles función de la región.

Kalahari
Il Kalahari si estende dalla Namibia attraverso il Botswana fino alla provincia del Capo Settentrionale in Sudafrica. Viene denominato deserto a causa dei suoi terreni sabbiosi rossi a sud e ad ovest, e di colore dal giallo al grigio a nord ed est. Effettivamente il Kalahari non è arido come il Namib, bensì ha una savana secca, erbosa e cespugliosa, che a seconda della regione ospita zolle d'erba, cespugli e alberi.

Kalahari
De Kalahari strekt zich van Namibië via Botswana tot aan de provincie Noord-Kaap in Zuid-Afrika uit. Vanwege de rode zandbodem in het westen en zuiden en de gele tot grijze zandbodem in het noorden en oosten wordt dit gebied als woestijn aangeduid; maar de Kalahari is niet zo droog als de Namib, maar veeleer een semi-droge savanne met stukken grasland en doornstruiken, die al naar gelang door gras, struikgewas of bomen wordt bepaald.

Quiver tree, Keetmanshoop,
Kalahari Desert, Namibia

Quiver trees *(Aloidendron dichotomum)*
Quiver trees belong to the aloe genus and were given their name by European settlers in the 17th century. The name indicates how the plant was used: the bushmen hollowed out the branches and made quivers for their arrows from the hard bark of the tree.

L'arbre à carquois
(Aloidendron dichotomum)
L'arbre à carquois (kokerboom en néerlandais) est un grand aloès. Les Européens lui ont donné ce surnom au XVIIe siècle. Les Bochimans, en effet, évidaient ses branches et se servaient de l'écorce dure pour fabriquer leurs carquois.

Köcherbäume *(Aloidendron dichotomum)*
Köcherbäume gehören zur Gattung der Aloen. Ihren Namen erhielten sie im 17. Jahrhundert von den Europäern. Die Bezeichnung „Köcherbaum" (kokerboom) weist auf die Nutzung der Pflanze hin: Die Buschmänner höhlten die Äste aus und stellten aus der harten Rinde des Baums Köcher für ihre Pfeile her.

El aloe dichotoma
(Aloidendron dichotomum)
El aloe dichotoma pertenece al género de los aloe y fue llamado así por los europeos en el siglo XVII. El término tiene que ver con el uso de la planta: los bosquimanos ahuecaban las ramas y usaban la dura corteza del árbol como carcaj para sus flechas.

L'albero faretra
(Aloidendron dichotomum)
L'albero faretra appartiene alla specie dell'aloe. Il suo nome gli fu dato nel XVII secolo dai colonizzatori europei. La denominazione "albero faretra" (kokerboom) si riferisce all'utilizzo della pianta: i boscimani scavavano i rami e producevano le loro frecce con la dura corteccia dell'albero faretra .

De kokerboom
(Aloidendron dichotomum)
De kokerboom behoort tot het geslacht aloë. De benaming "kokerboom" stamt uit de zeventiende eeuw en werd door Europeanen gebruikt om het gebruik van de boom aan te duiden: de Bosjesmannen holden de takken ervan uit en maakten pijlkokers van de harde bast.

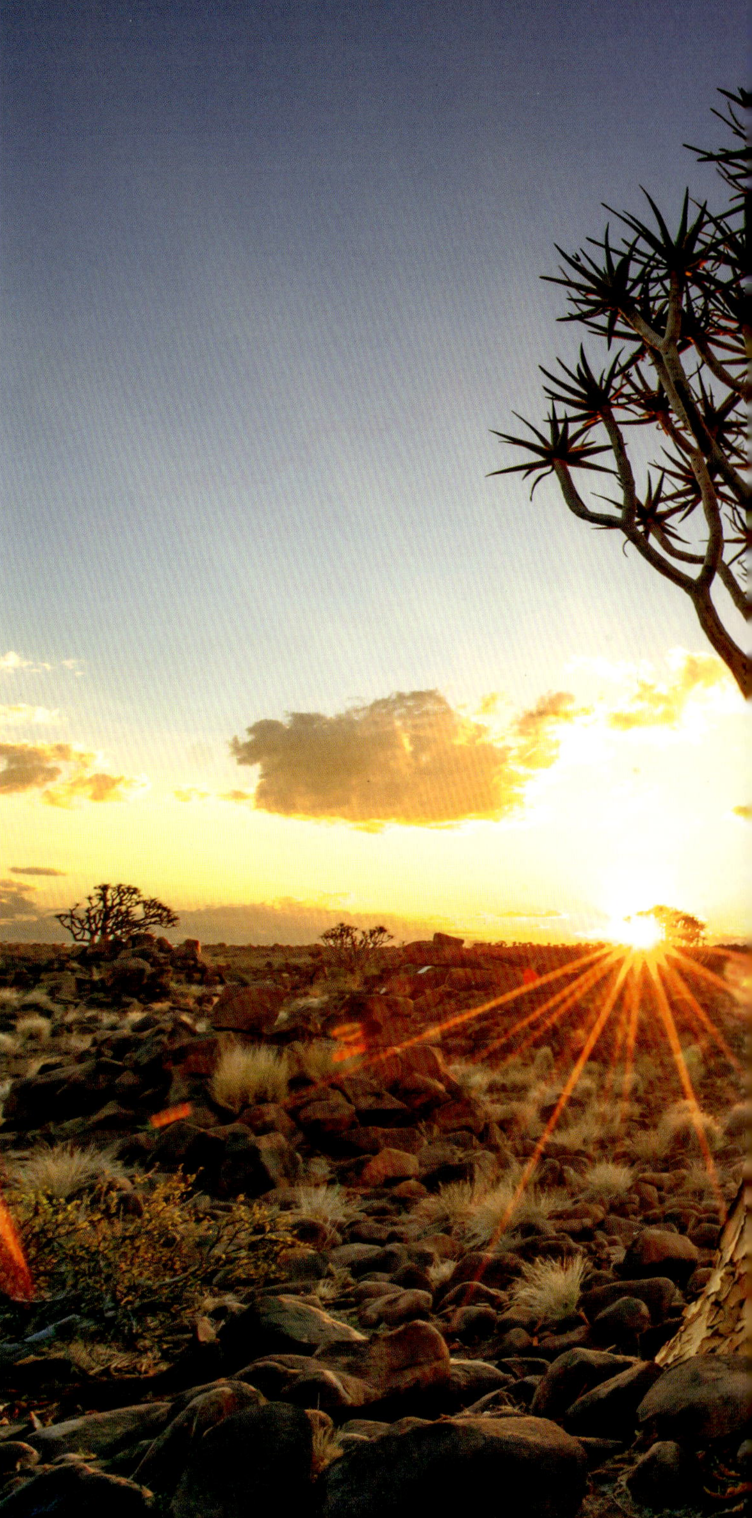

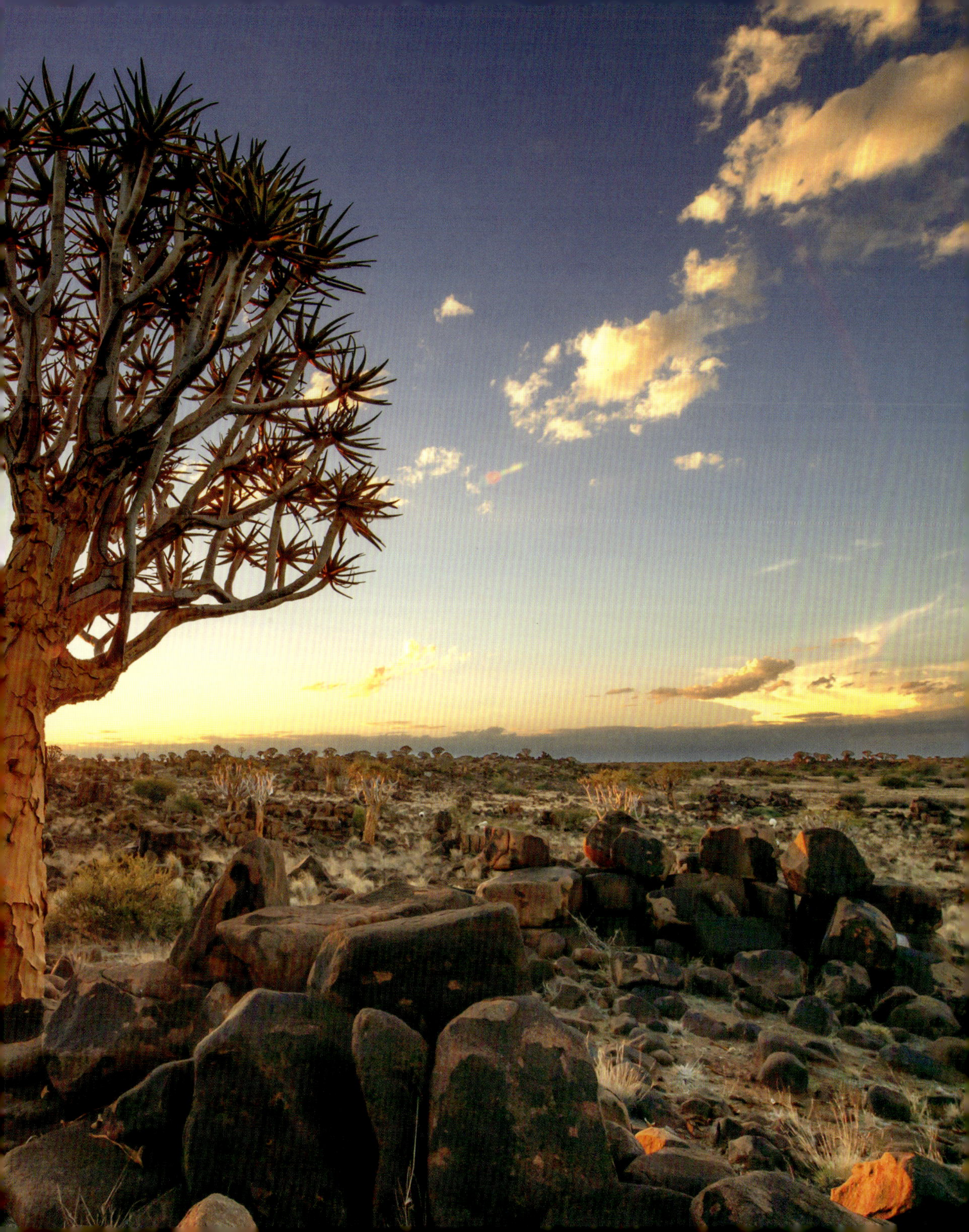

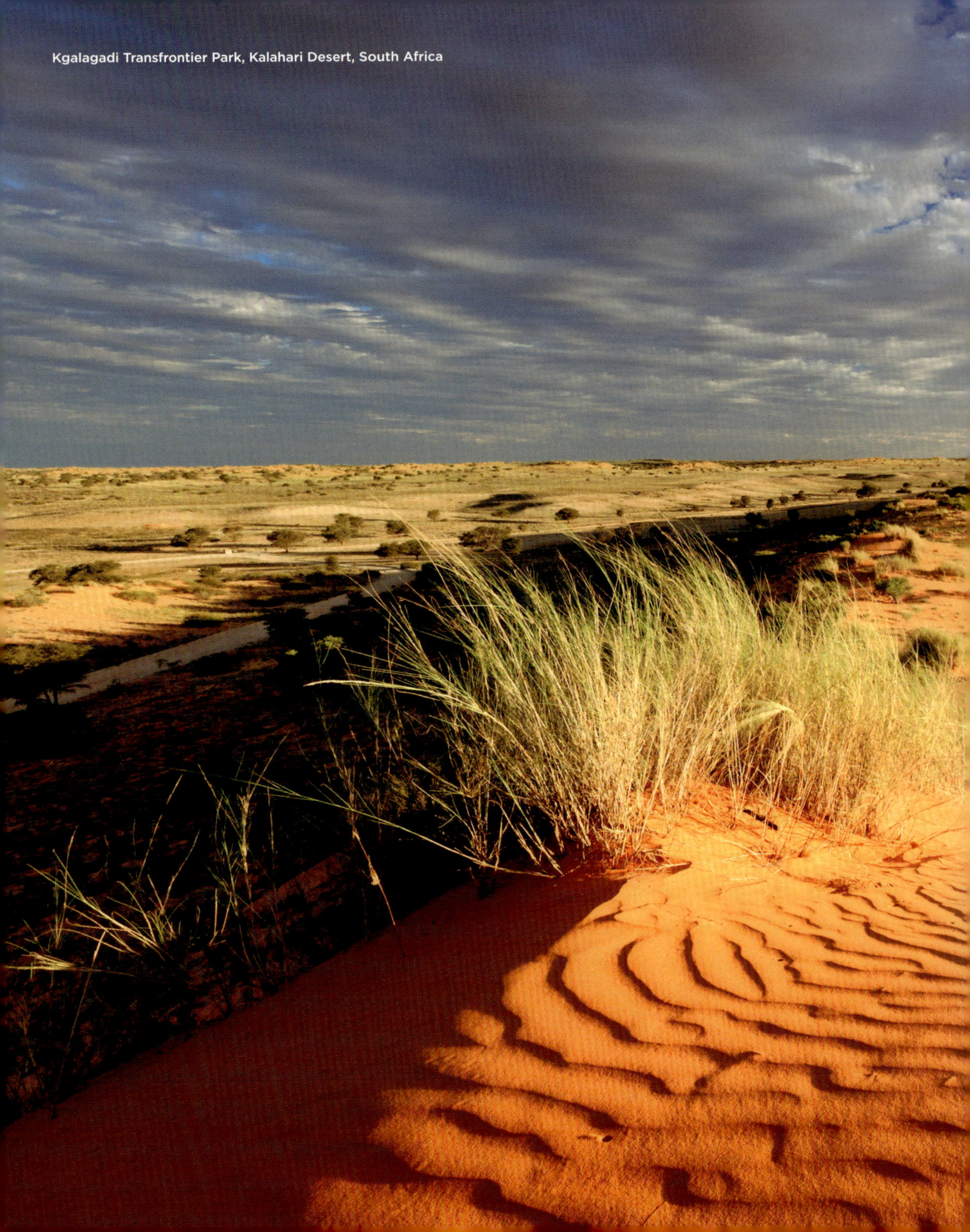
Kgalagadi Transfrontier Park, Kalahari Desert, South Africa

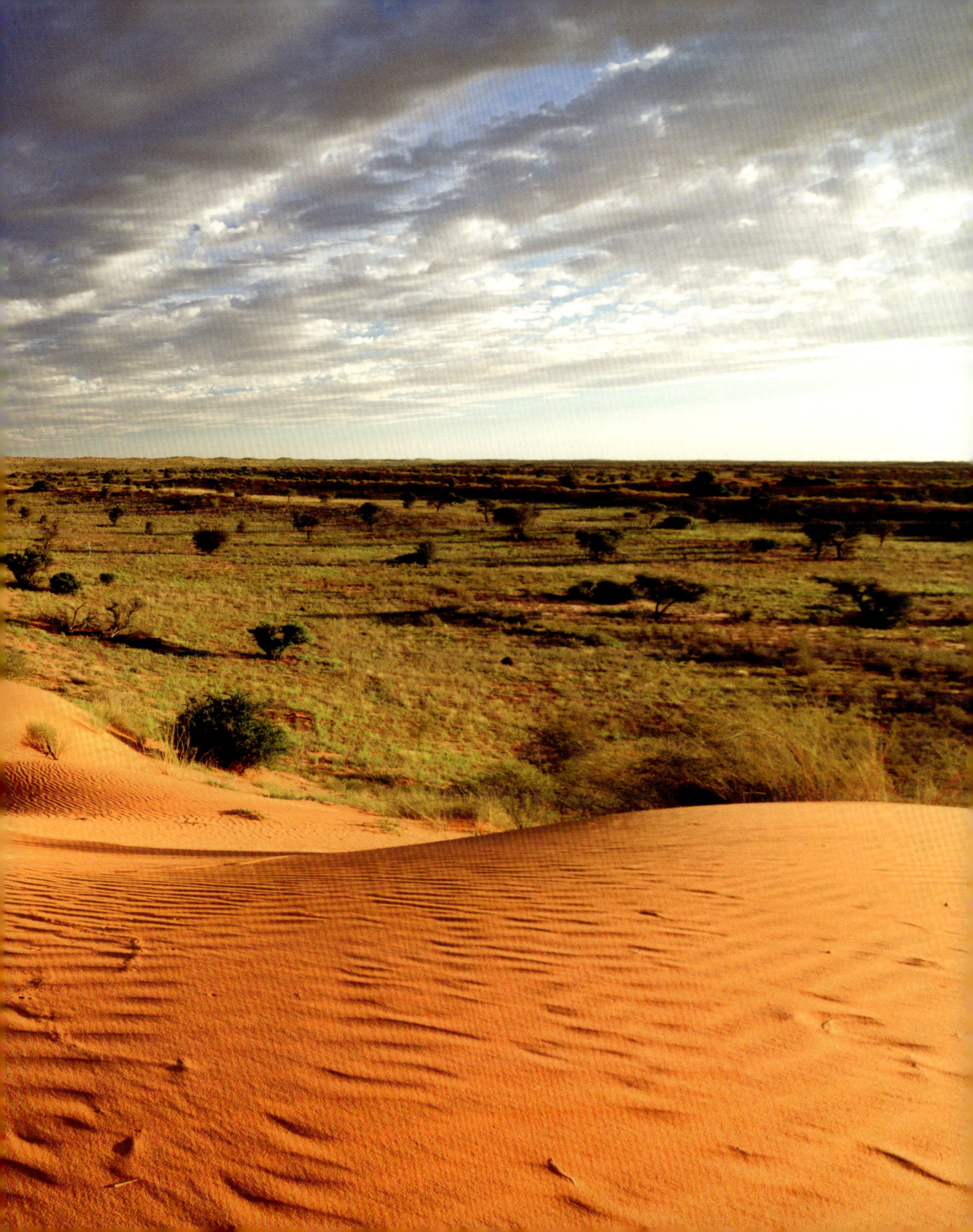

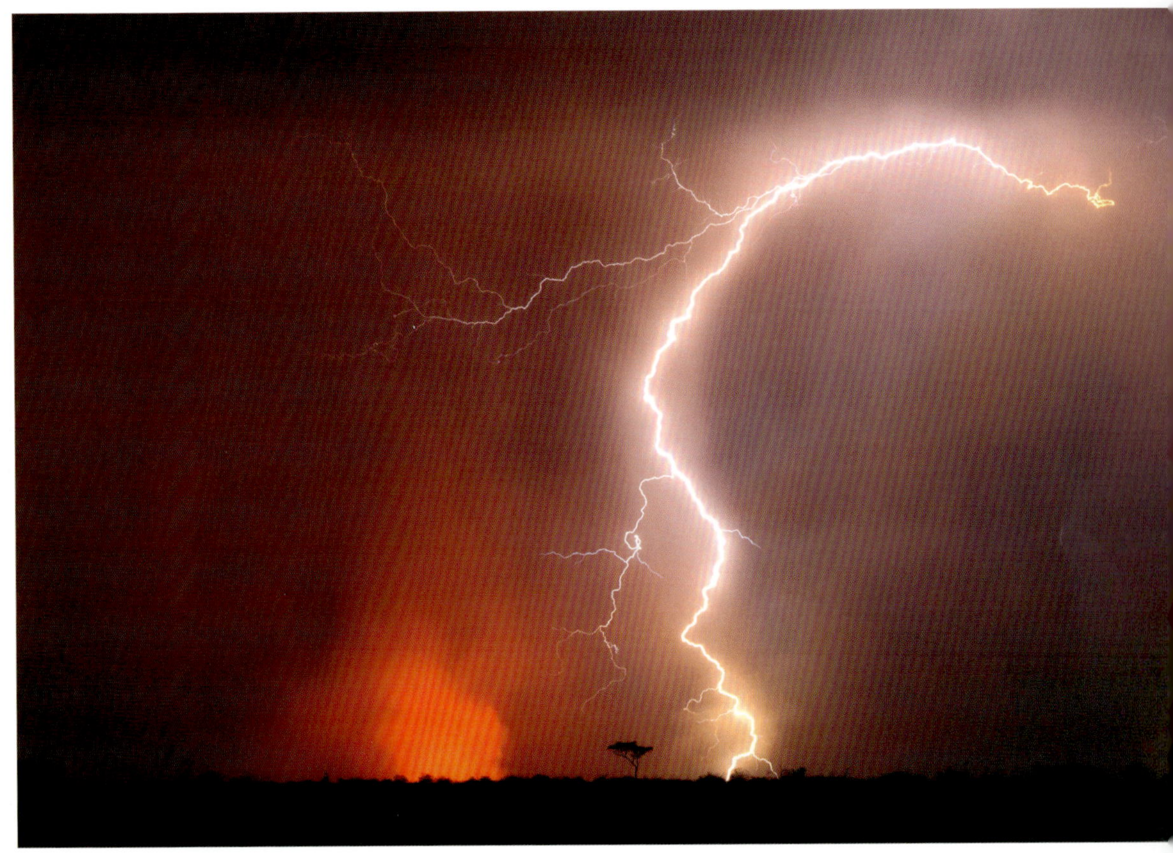

Kalahari Desert, Botswana

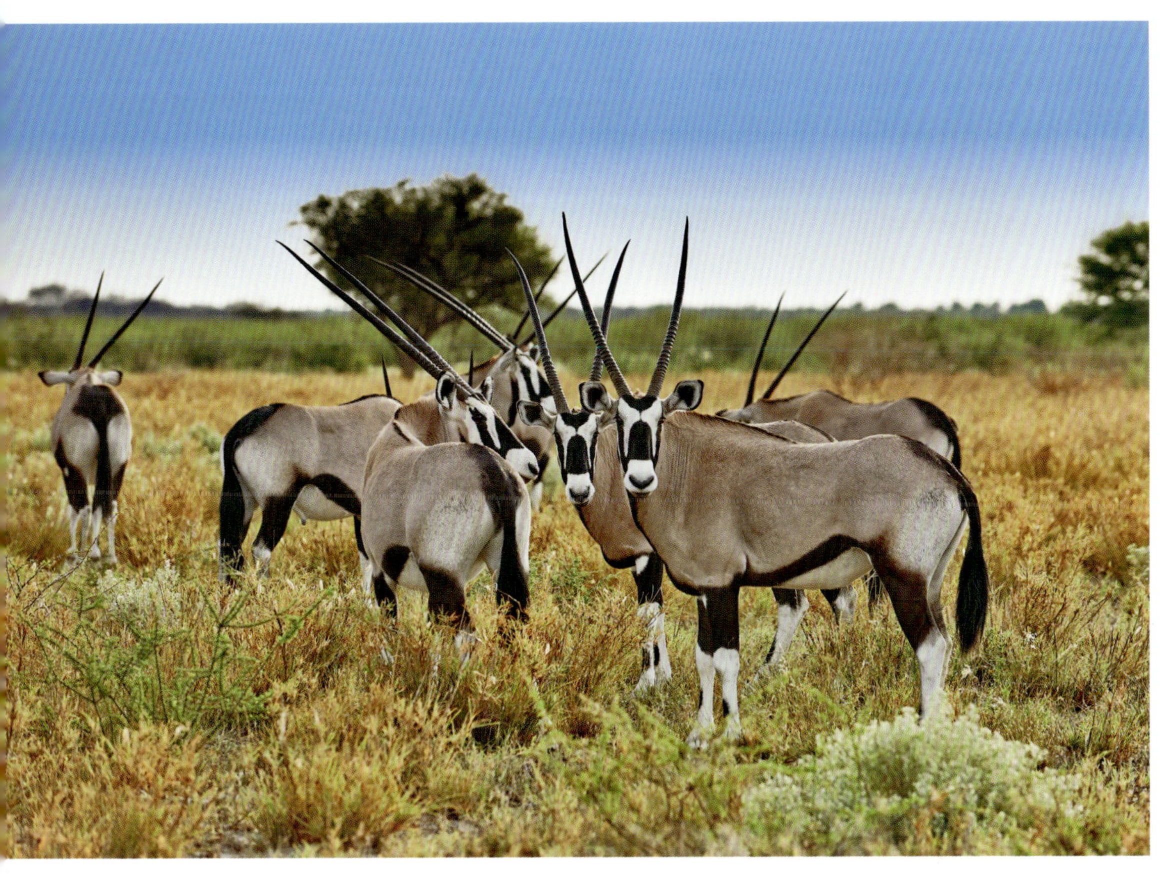

ast African oryxes, Central Kalahari Game Reserve, Kalahari Desert, Botswana

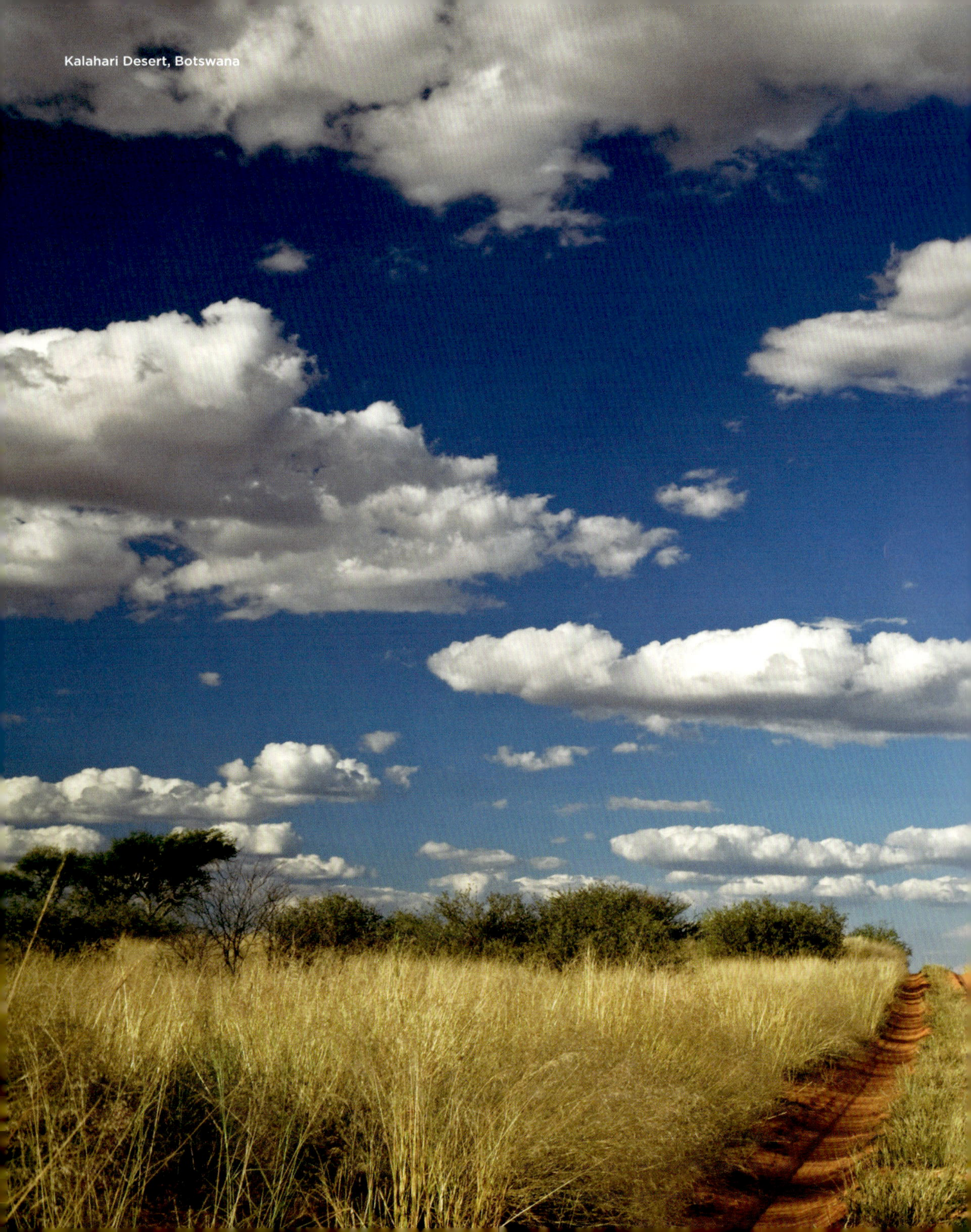
Kalahari Desert, Botswana

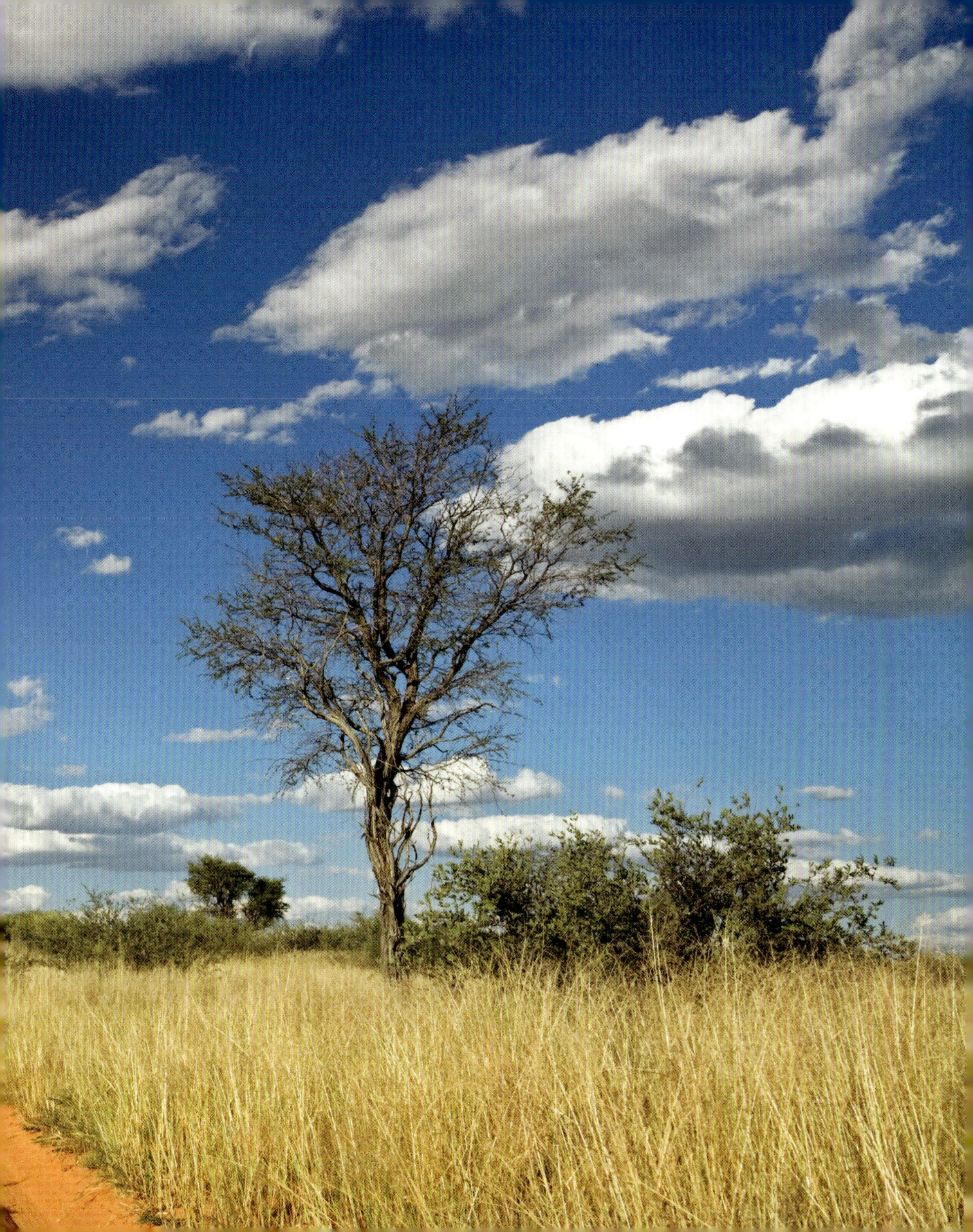

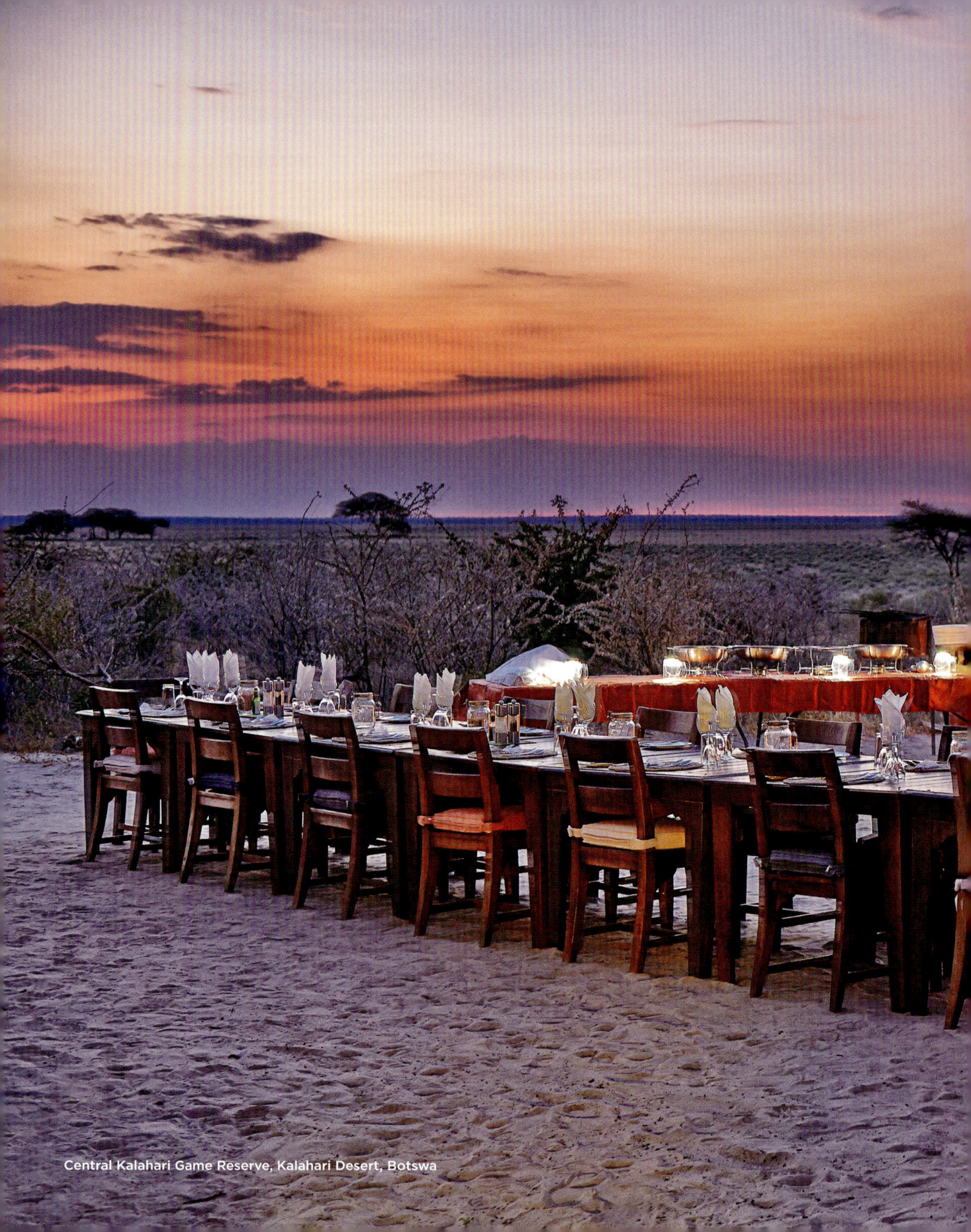

Central Kalahari Game Reserve, Kalahari Desert, Botswa

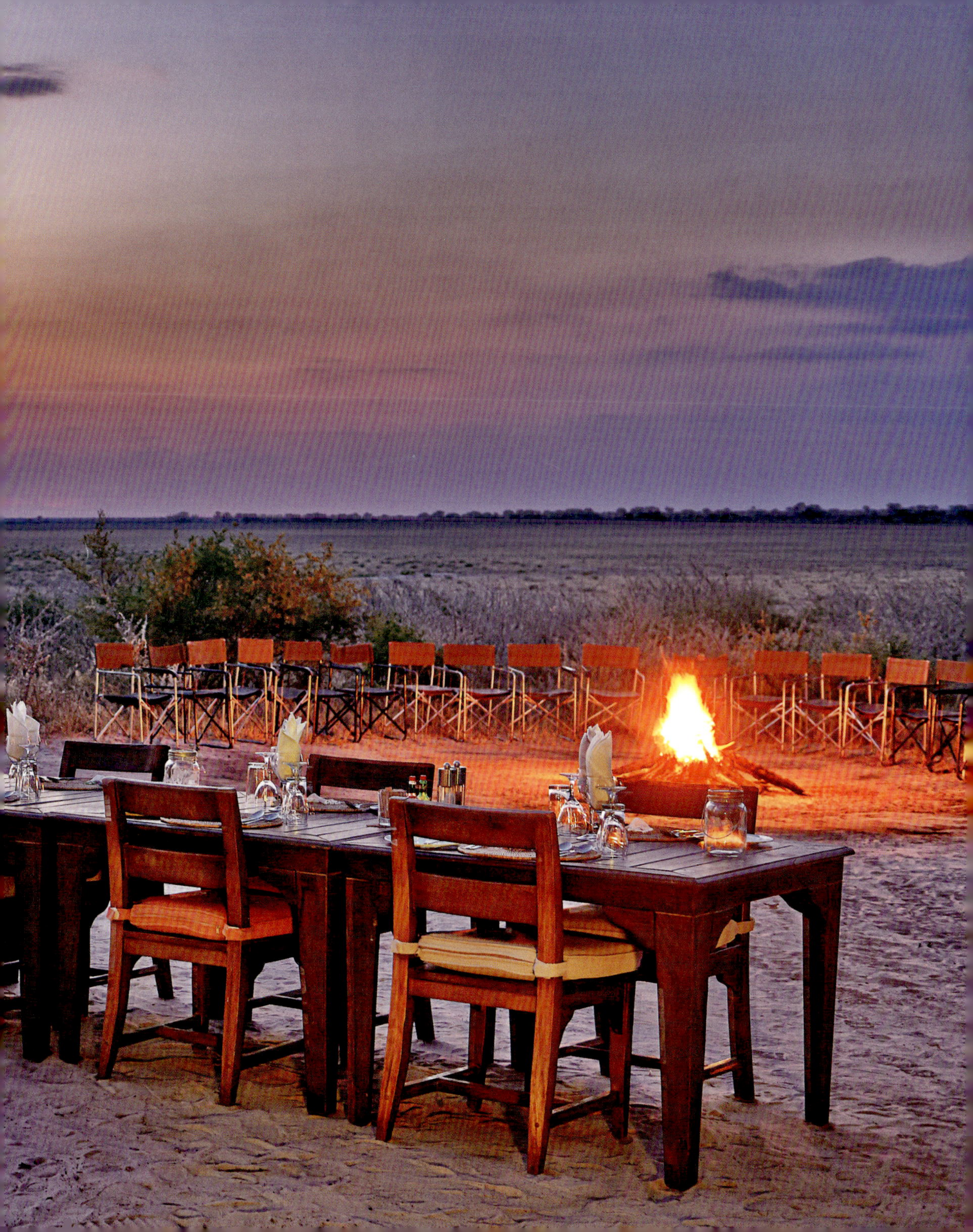

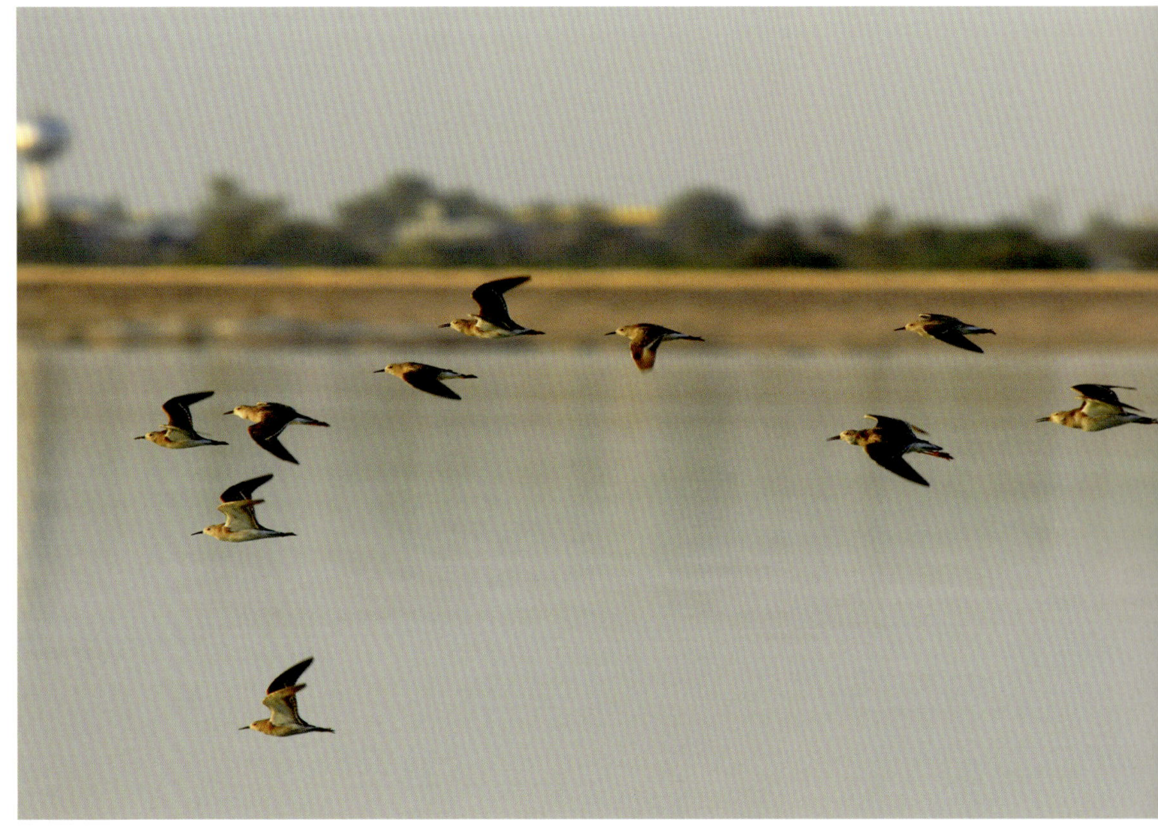

Birds near Gaborone, Botswanaa

Gaborone
The capital of Botswana is the seat of government and the centre of its economic and financial world, but with fewer than 250,000 inhabitants it is only the third largest city in the country. At the end of the 1960s, large diamond deposits were discovered in the north of the country, making Gaborone one of the fastest growing capitals in the world.

Gaborone
Avec ses 250 000 habitants, la capitale du Botswana est le siège du gouvernement et le centre de la vie économique et financière, mais n'est néanmoins que la troisième ville du pays en termes de taille. À la fin des années 1960, on a trouvé d'importants gisements de diamant dans le nord du pays, et Gaborone est ainsi devenue l'une des capitales à la croissance la plus rapide au monde.

Gaborone
Die Hauptstadt von Botswana ist Regierungssitz und Mittelpunkt der Wirtschafts- und Finanzwelt, mit knapp 250 000 Einwohnern allerdings nur die drittgrößte Stadt des Landes. Ende der 60er-Jahre wurden im Norden des Lande große Diamantenvorkommen entdeckt ur so entwickelte sich Gaborone zu einer de am schnellsten wachsenden Hauptstädte der Welt.

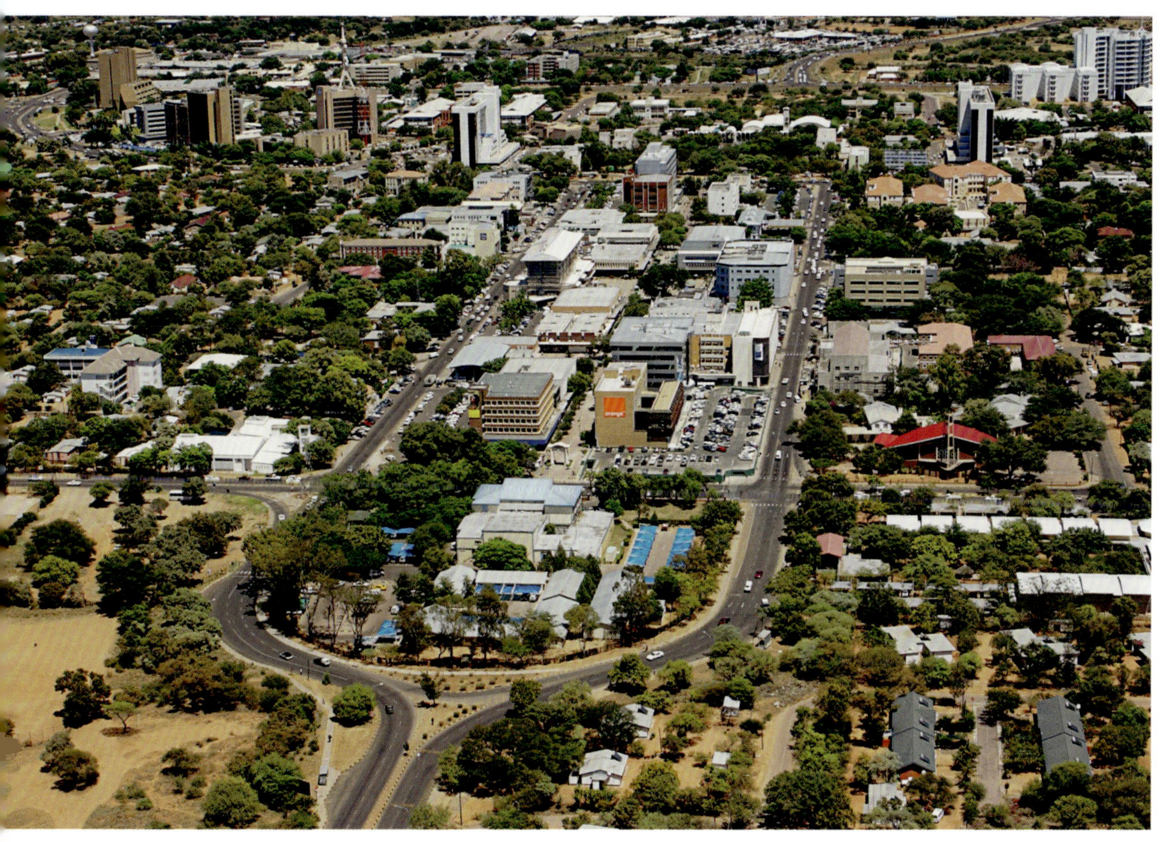

aborone, Botswana

aborone
a capital de Botswana es la sede del obierno y el centro del mundo económico financiero, pero con algo menos de 50 000 habitantes es sólo la tercera udad más grande del país. A finales de la écada de 1960 se descubrieron grandes acimientos de diamantes en el norte del aís, lo que convirtió a Gaborone en una e las capitales de más rápido crecimiento el mundo.

Gaborone
La capitale del Botswana è la sede del governo e il centro del mondo economico e finanziario, ma con poco meno di 250 000 abitanti è solamente la terza città più grande del paese. Alla fine degli anni ,60, furono scoperti enormi giacimenti di diamanti nel nord del paese, facendo di Gaborone una delle capitali dallo sviluppo più rapido al mondo.

Gaborone
Hoewel de hoofdstad van Botswana de regeringszetel en het economische en financiële centrum is, is hij met iets minder dan 250 000 inwoners slechts de op twee na grootste stad van het land. Eind jaren zestig van de vorige eeuw werden in het noorden van het land grote diamantvoorraden ontdekt, waardoor Gaborone een van de snelst groeiende hoofdsteden ter wereld is.

Kgalagadi Transfrontier Park, South Africa & Botswana

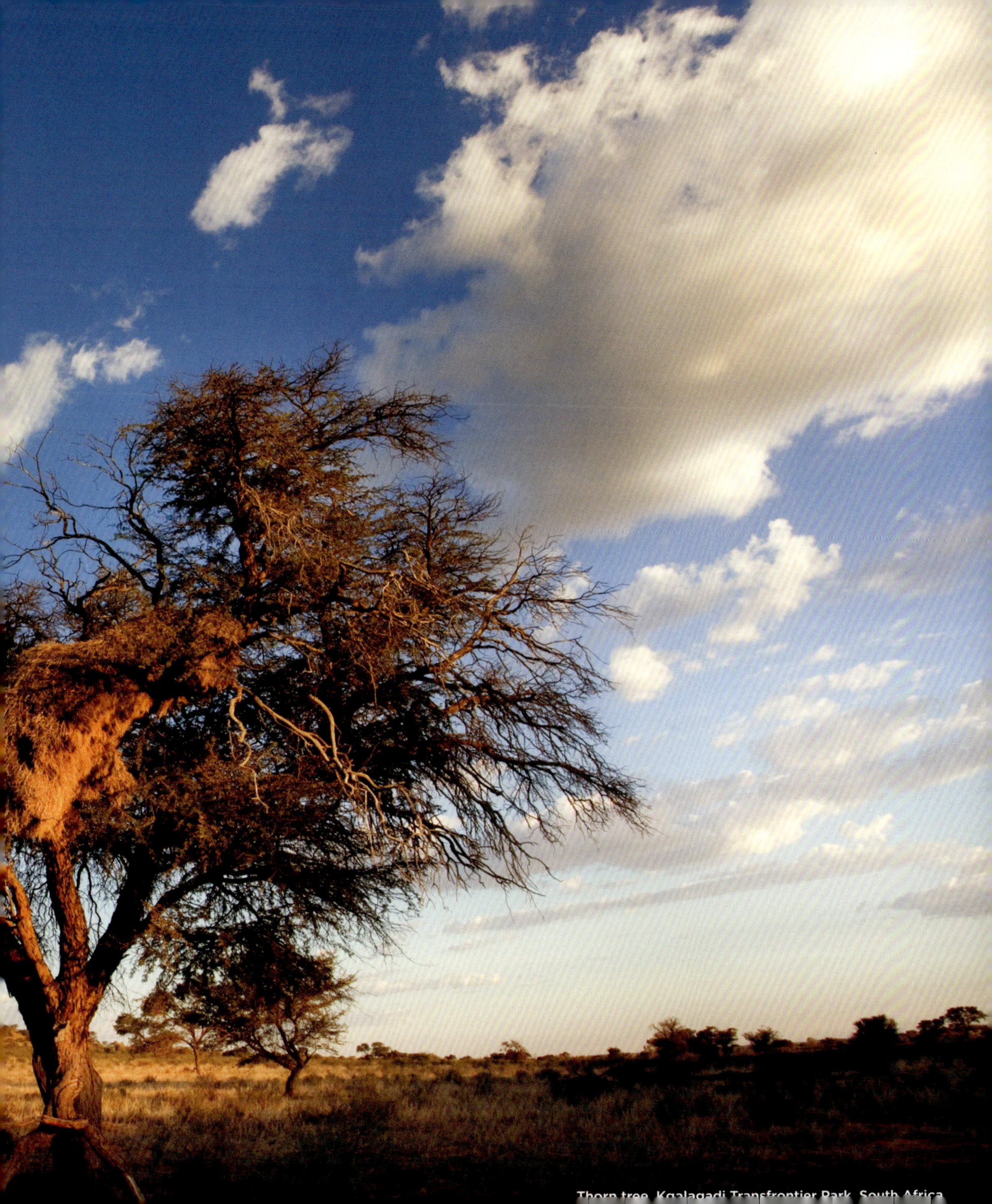

Thorn tree, Kgalagadi Transfrontier Park, South Africa

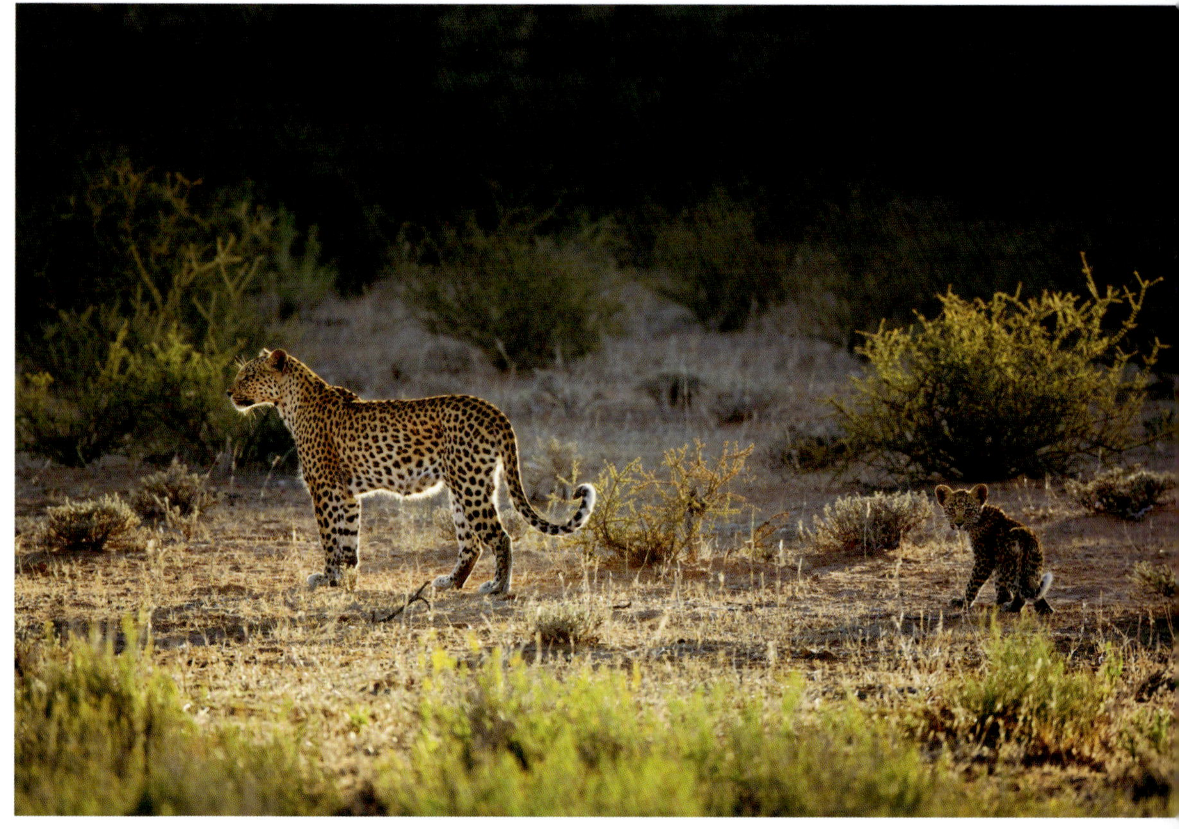

Leopard with cub, Kgalagadi Transfrontier Park, Botswana

Kgalagadi Transfrontier Park
Based on the principle that animals on the move should not have to run against fences set up by humans, this national park was set up as the first cross-border protected area in Africa. The Kgalagadi Transfrontier Park is located in the dry savanna of southwestern Botswana and South Africa's North Cape province. The 36,000 km² (13,899 mi²) park is home to a rich variety of animal species.

Le parc national transfrontalier du Kgalagadi
Les barrières installées par l'homme ne doivent pas faire obstacle aux migrations des animaux. En vertu de quoi le premier parc transfrontalier d'Afrique a vu le jour en 1999, celui du Kgalagadi qui se partage entre la savane sèche du sud-ouest du Botswana et la province du Nord-Ouest en Afrique du Sud. Une faune fabuleuse vit sur ce territoire de 36 000 km².

Kgalagadi-Transfrontier-Park
Wandernde Tiere sollen nicht an von Menschen gezogenen Zäunen scheitern. Deshalb entstand 1999 das erste grenzübergreifende Schutzgebiet Afrikas: der Kgalagadi-Transfrontier-Park, der in der Trockensavanne im Südwesten Botswanas und in der Nordkap-Provinz Südafrikas liegt. Der Tierreichtum in dem 36 000 km² großen Gebiet ist immens.

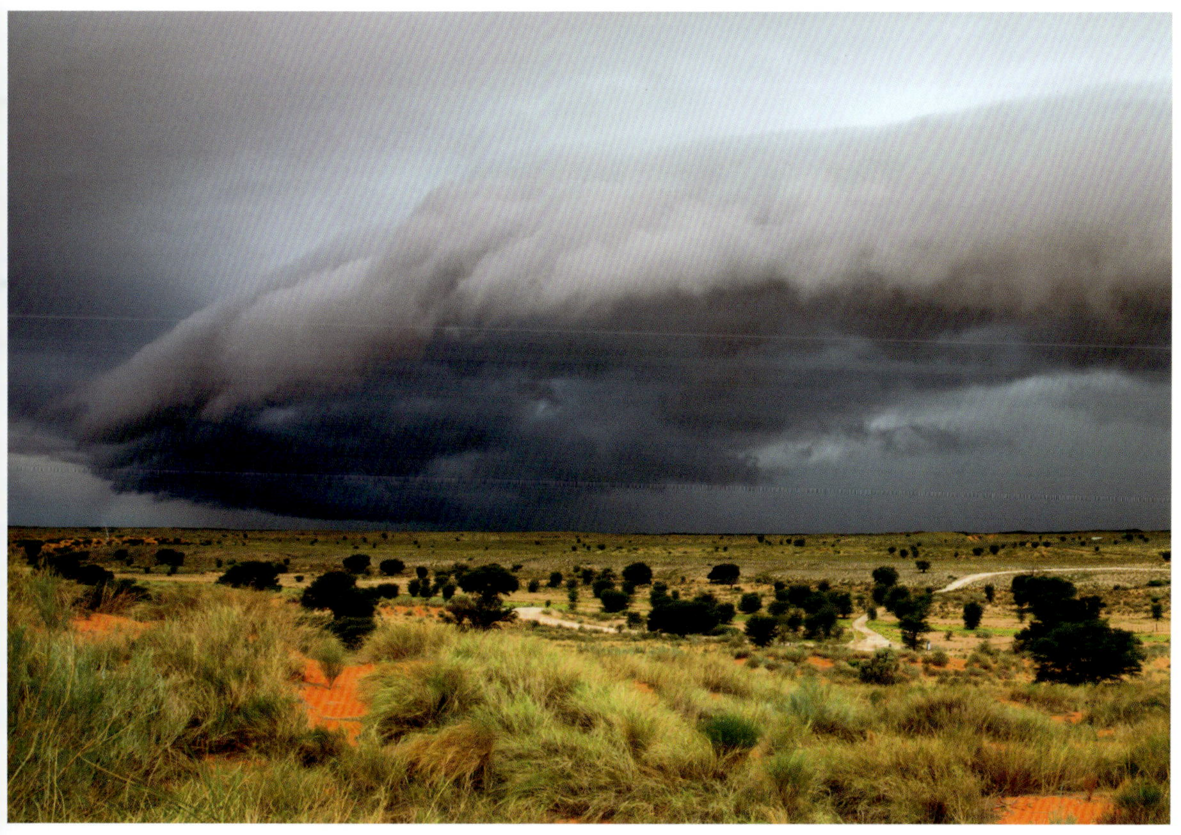

Kalahari Desert, Kgalagadi Transfrontier Park, South Africa

Parque internacional de Kgalagadi
Los animales migratorios no deben fracasar a causa de las cercas que levantan las personas. Debido a ésto surgió la primera reserva transfronteriza en África en 1999: el Parque Nacional transfronterizo de Kgalagadi, que se encuentra en la sabana seca en el suroeste de Botswana y en la provincia septentrional del Cabo de Sudáfrica. La riqueza de vida animal en esta gran área de 36 000 km^2 es inmensa.

Parco Nazionale Transfrontaliero Kgalagadi
Gli animali migratori non dovrebbero essere ostacolati dai recinti creati dagli uomini. Perciò nel 1999 fu creata la prima area protetta transfrontaliera dell'Africa: il Parco Nazionale Kgalagadi-Transfrontier, che si trova nella secca savana del Botswana sud-occidentale e nella provincia del Capo Settentrionale in Sudafrica. L'area grande 36 000 km^2 vanta un'immensa ricchezza di specie animali.

Kgalagadi-Transfrontier-National Park
Migrerende dieren zouden niet tegengehouden moeten worden door afbakeningen die door de mens zijn opgeworpen. Vandaar dat in 1999 het eerste grensoverschrijdende wildreservaat van Afrika ontstond: het Kgalagadi-Transfrontier-National Park, dat in de droge savanne van zuidwestelijk Botswana en de provincie Noord-Kaap in Zuid-Afrika ligt. Dit dierenrijk met een oppervlakte van 36 000 km^2 is immens.

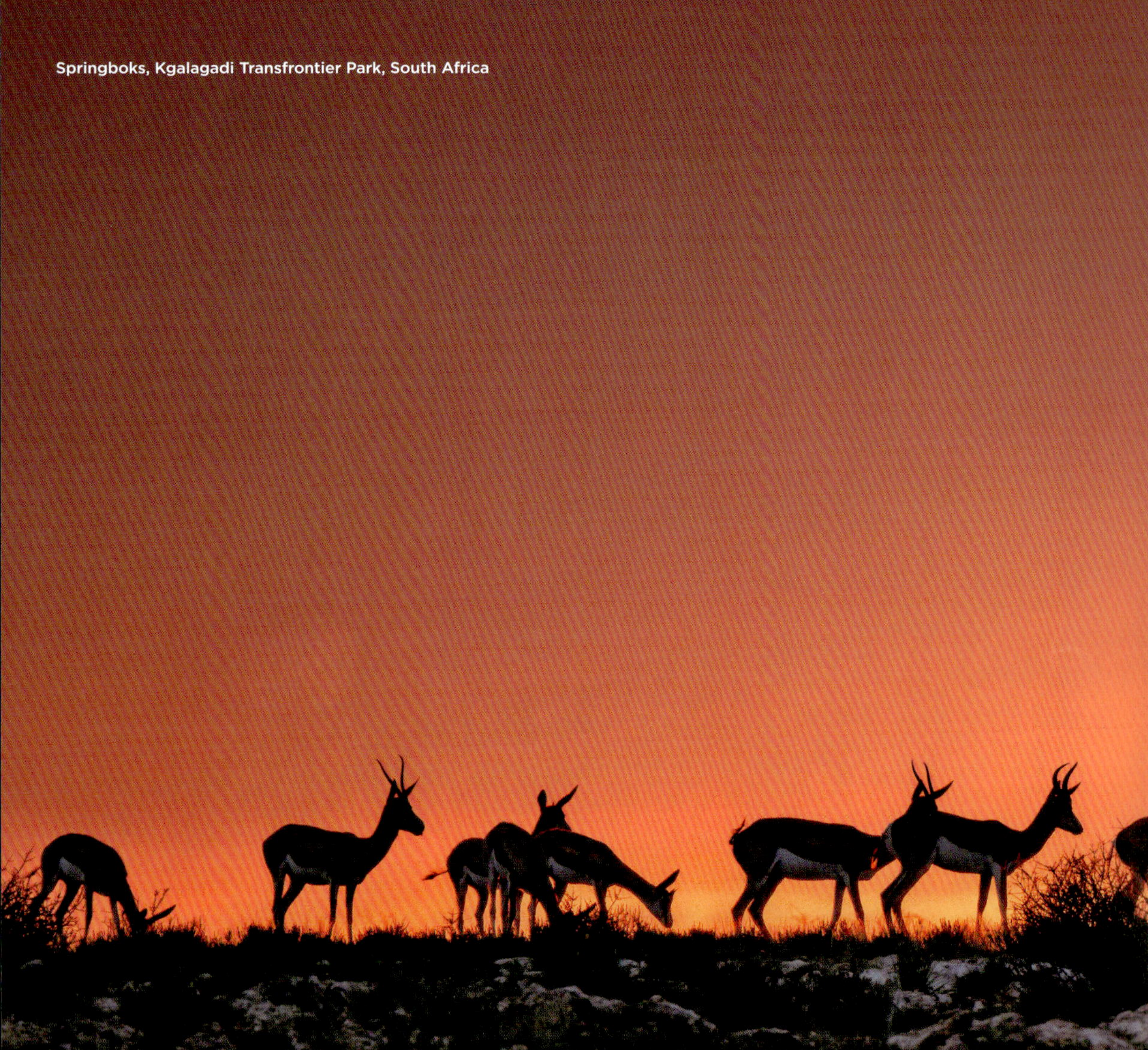

Springboks, Kgalagadi Transfrontier Park, South Africa

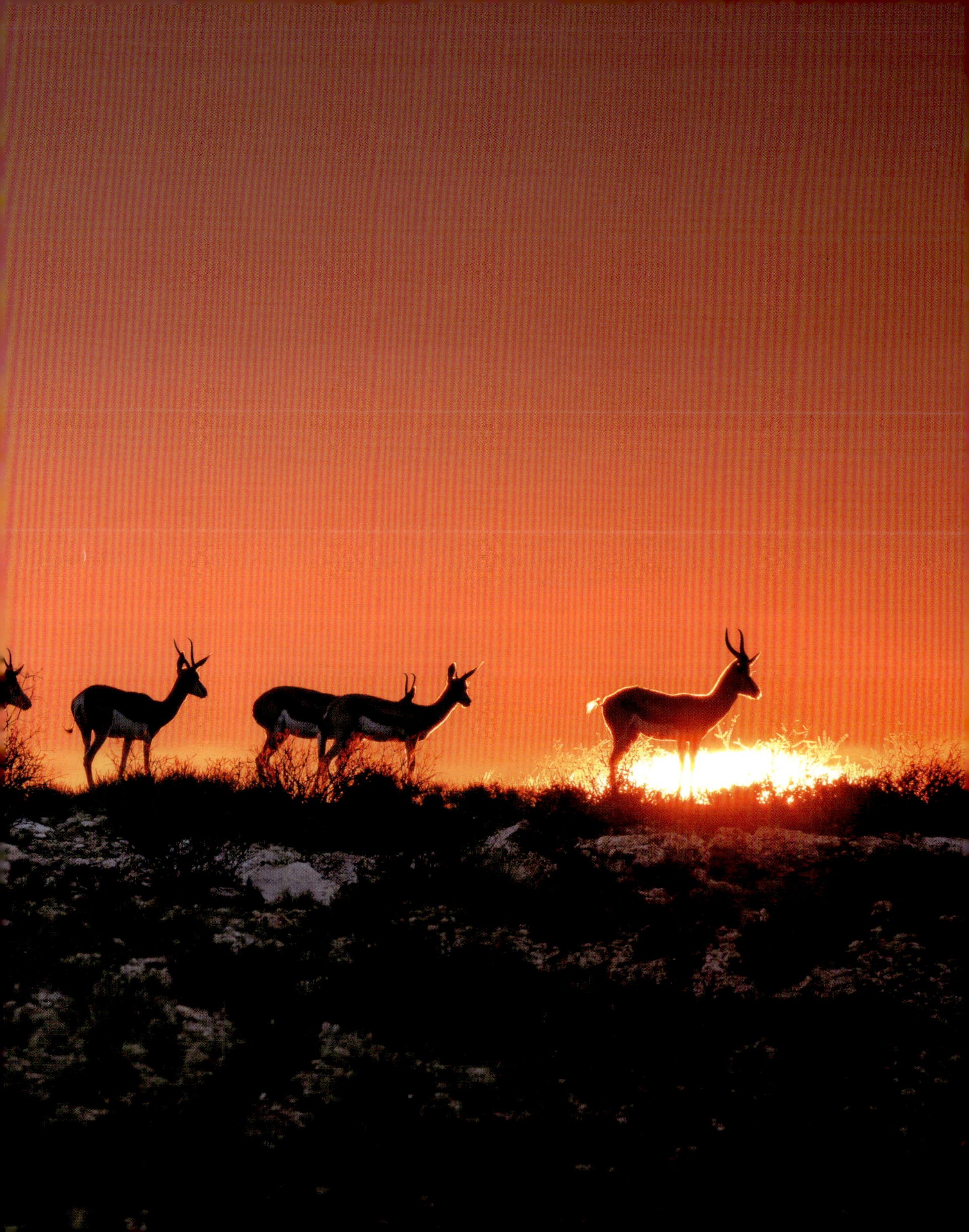

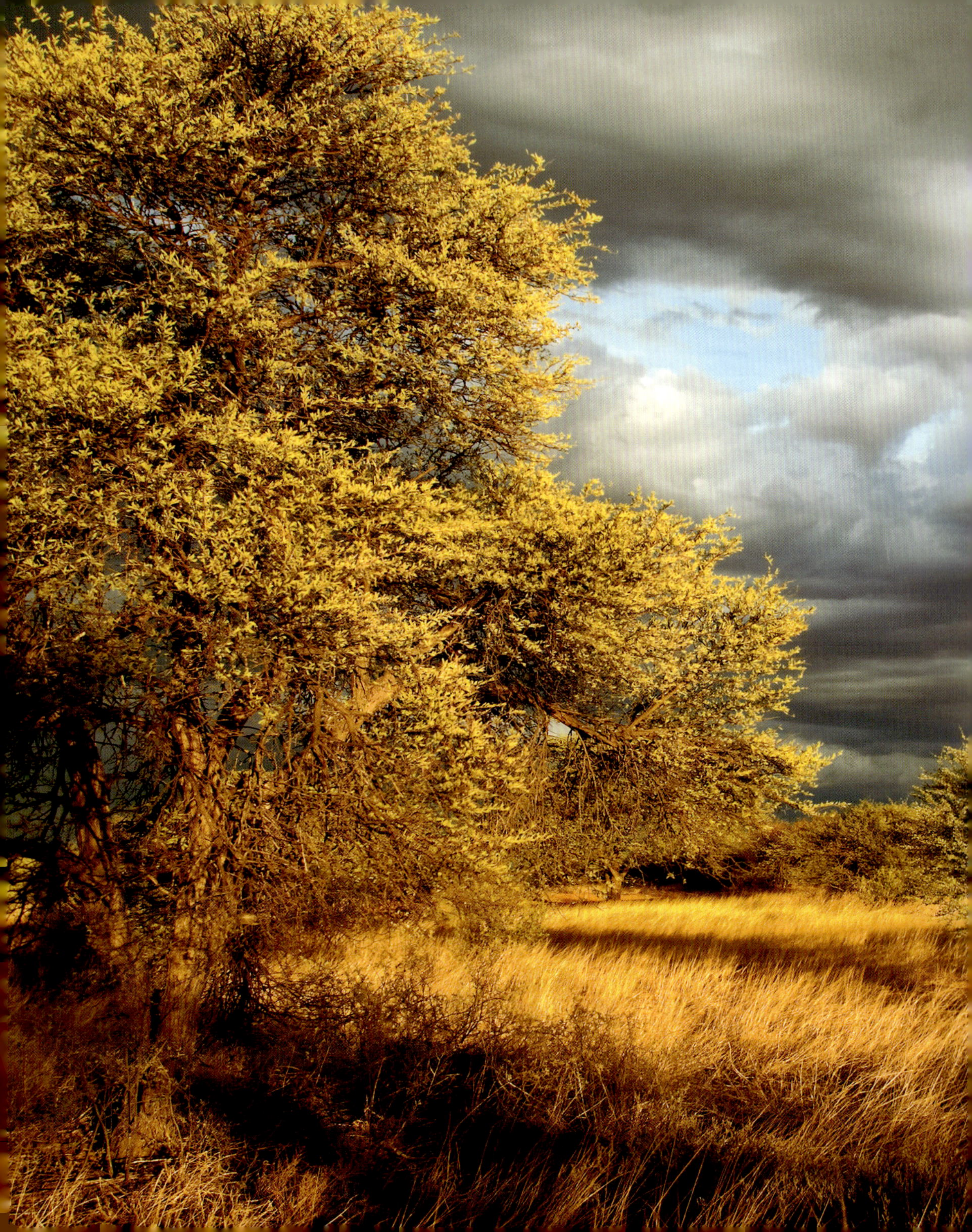

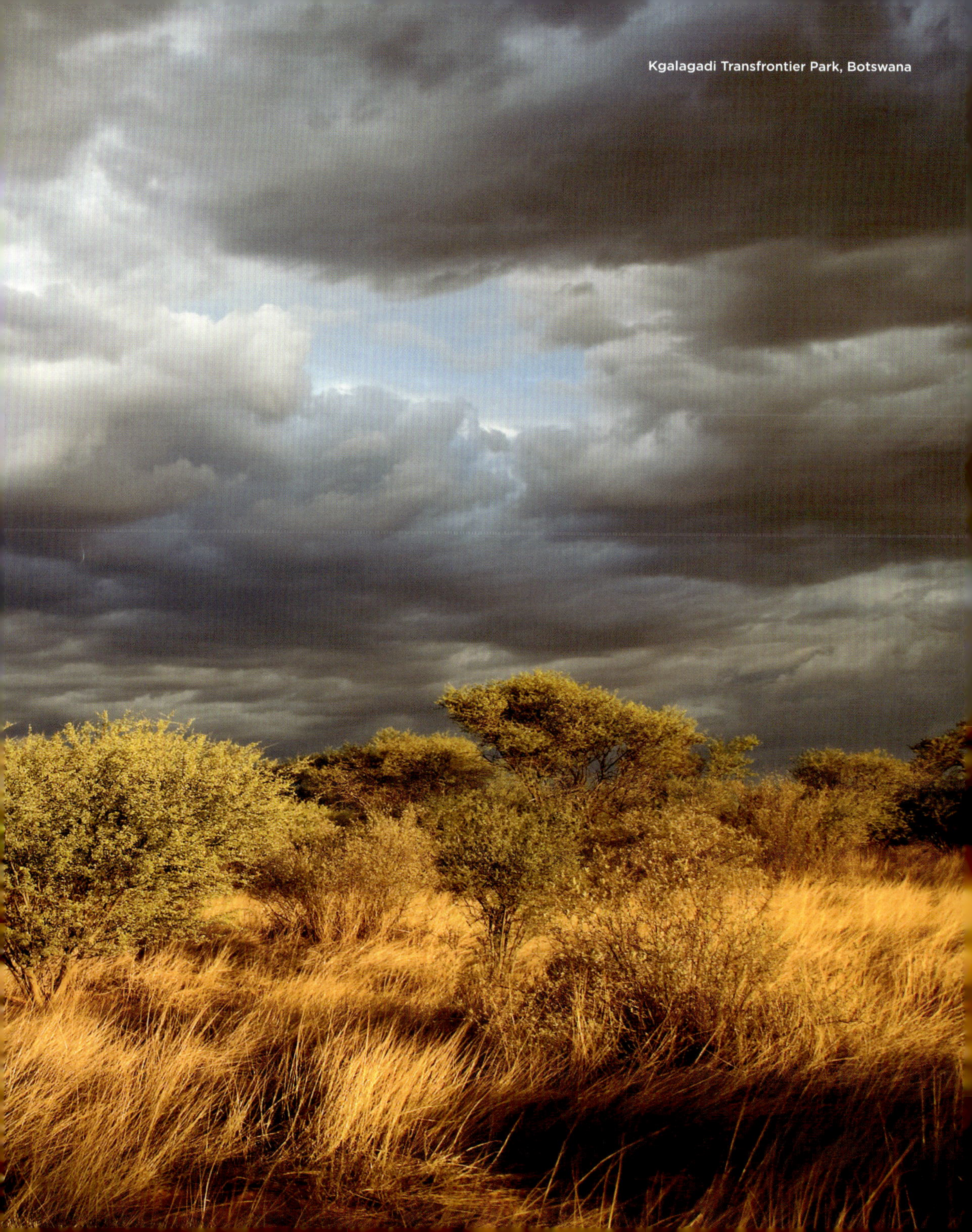

Kgalagadi Transfrontier Park, Botswana

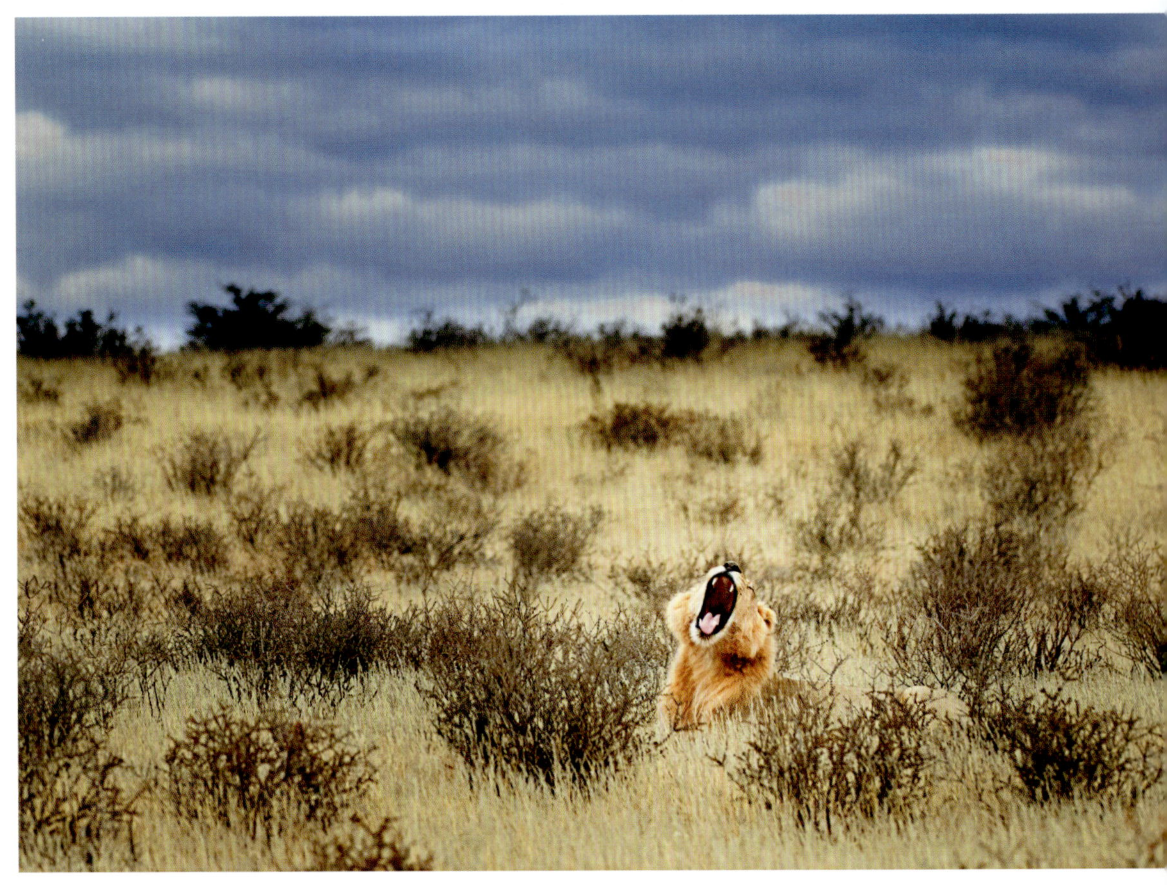

Rowing lion, Kgalagadi Transfrontier Park, South Africa

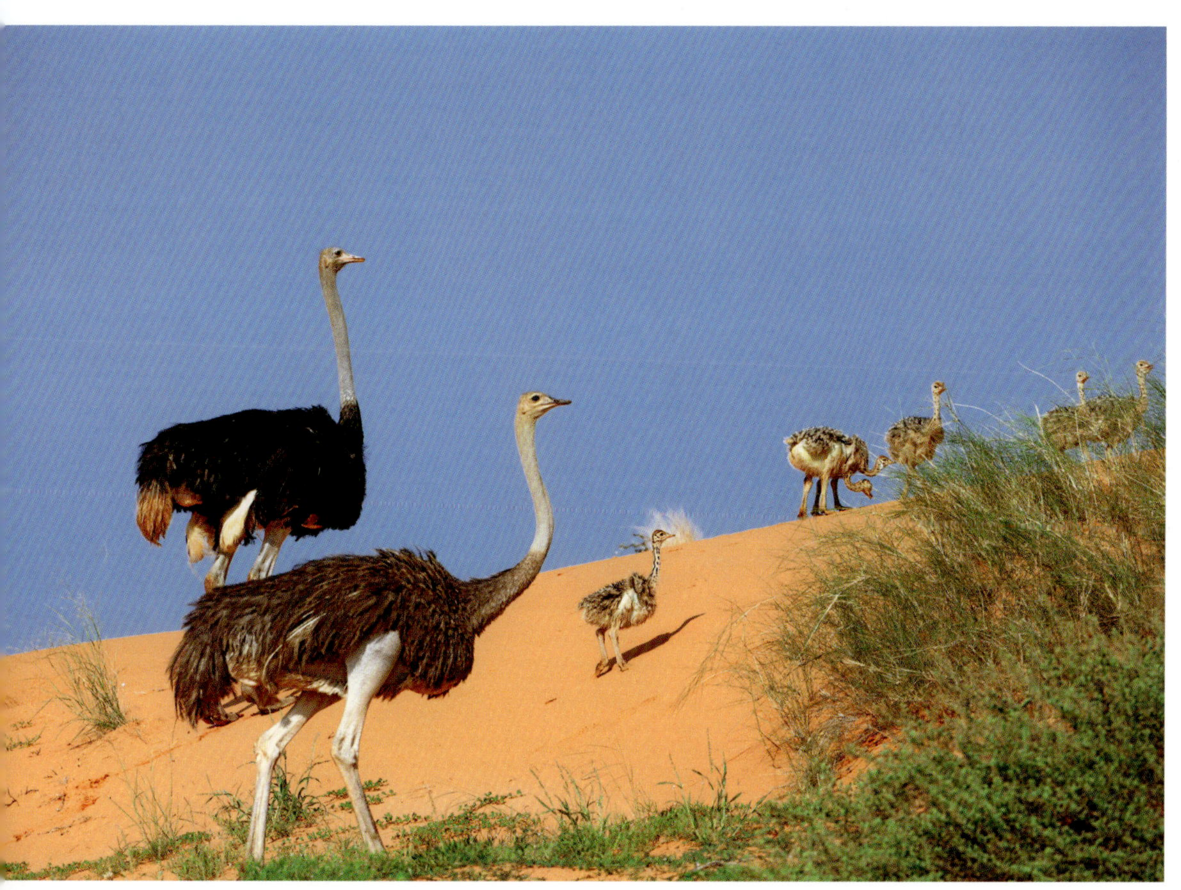

Ostriches, Kgalagadi Transfrontier Park, South Africa

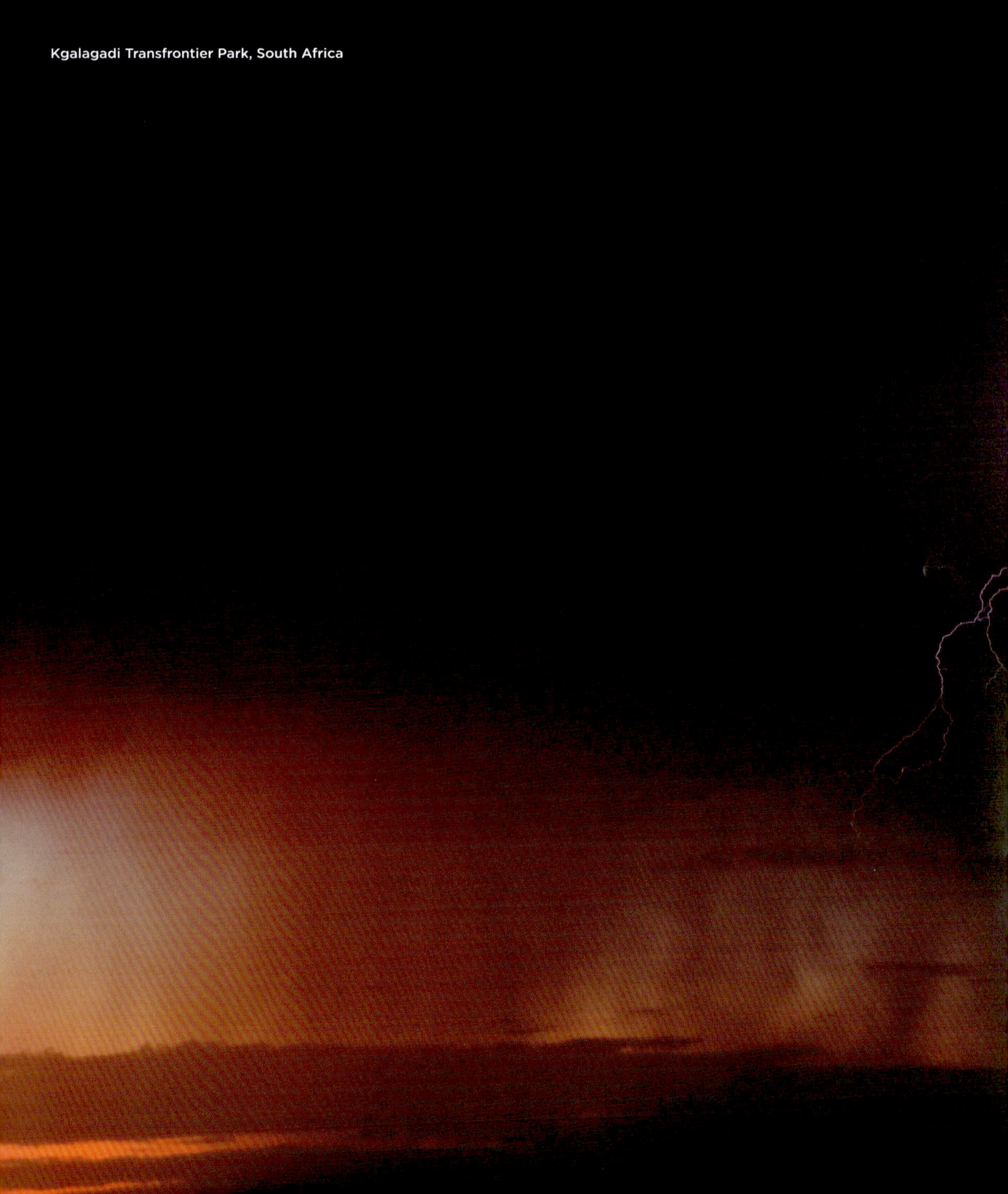

Kgalagadi Transfrontier Park, South Africa

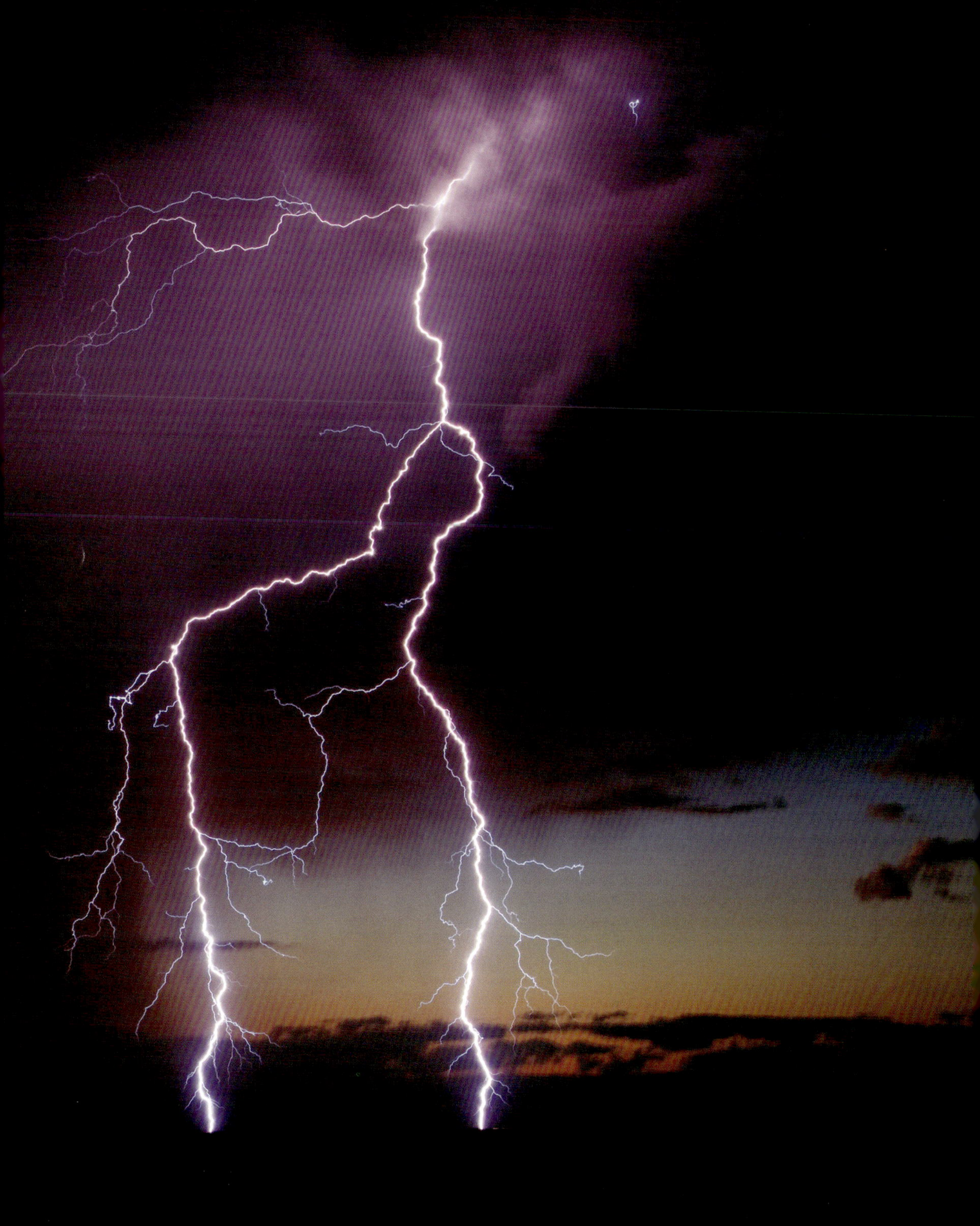

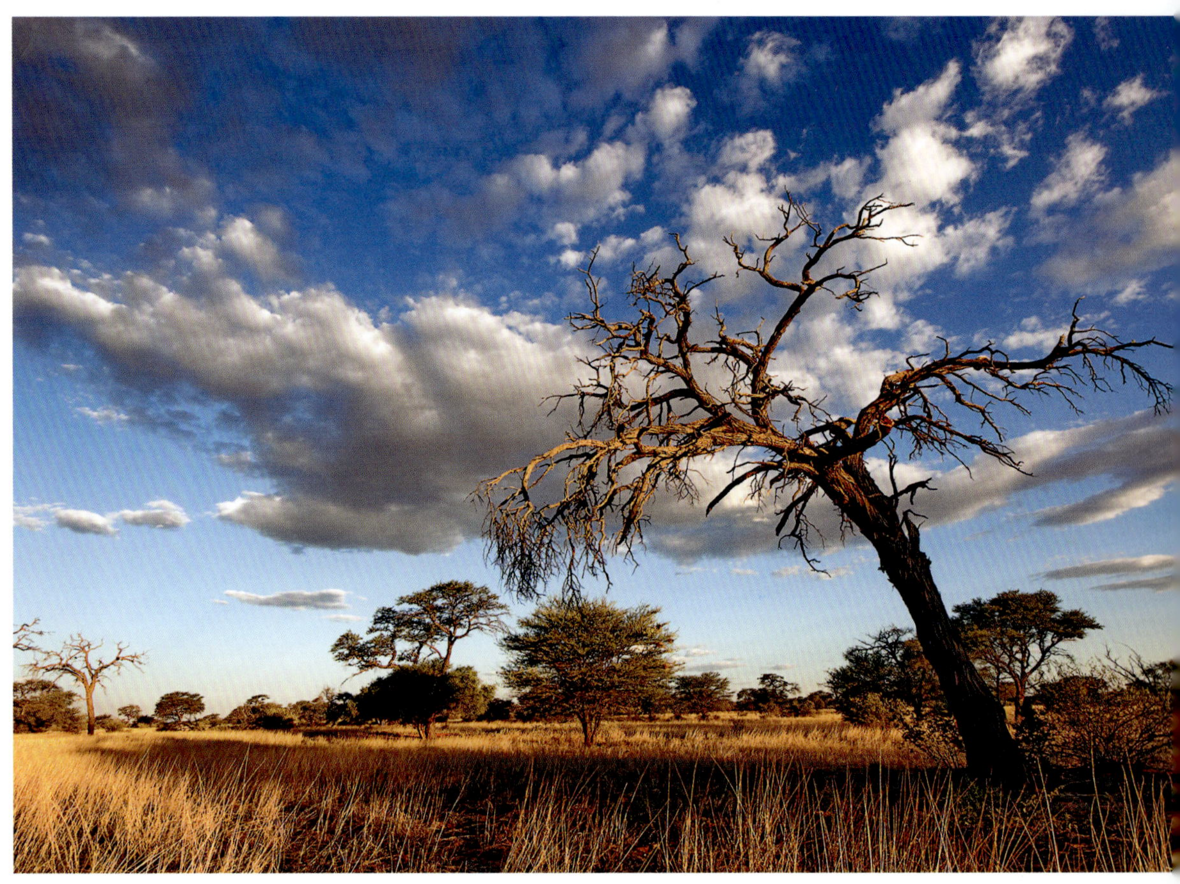

Kgalagadi Transfrontier Park, Botswana

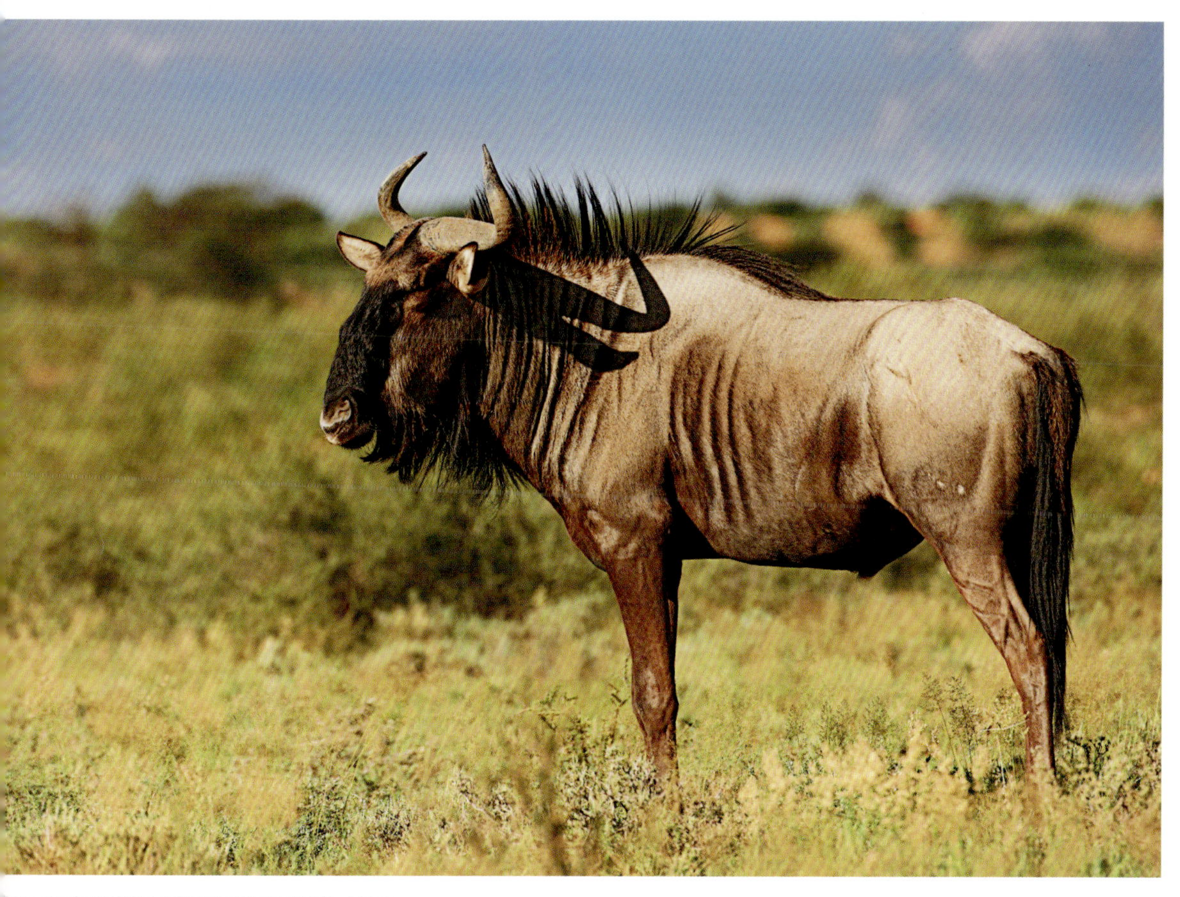

Gnu, Kgalagadi Transfrontier Park, South Africa

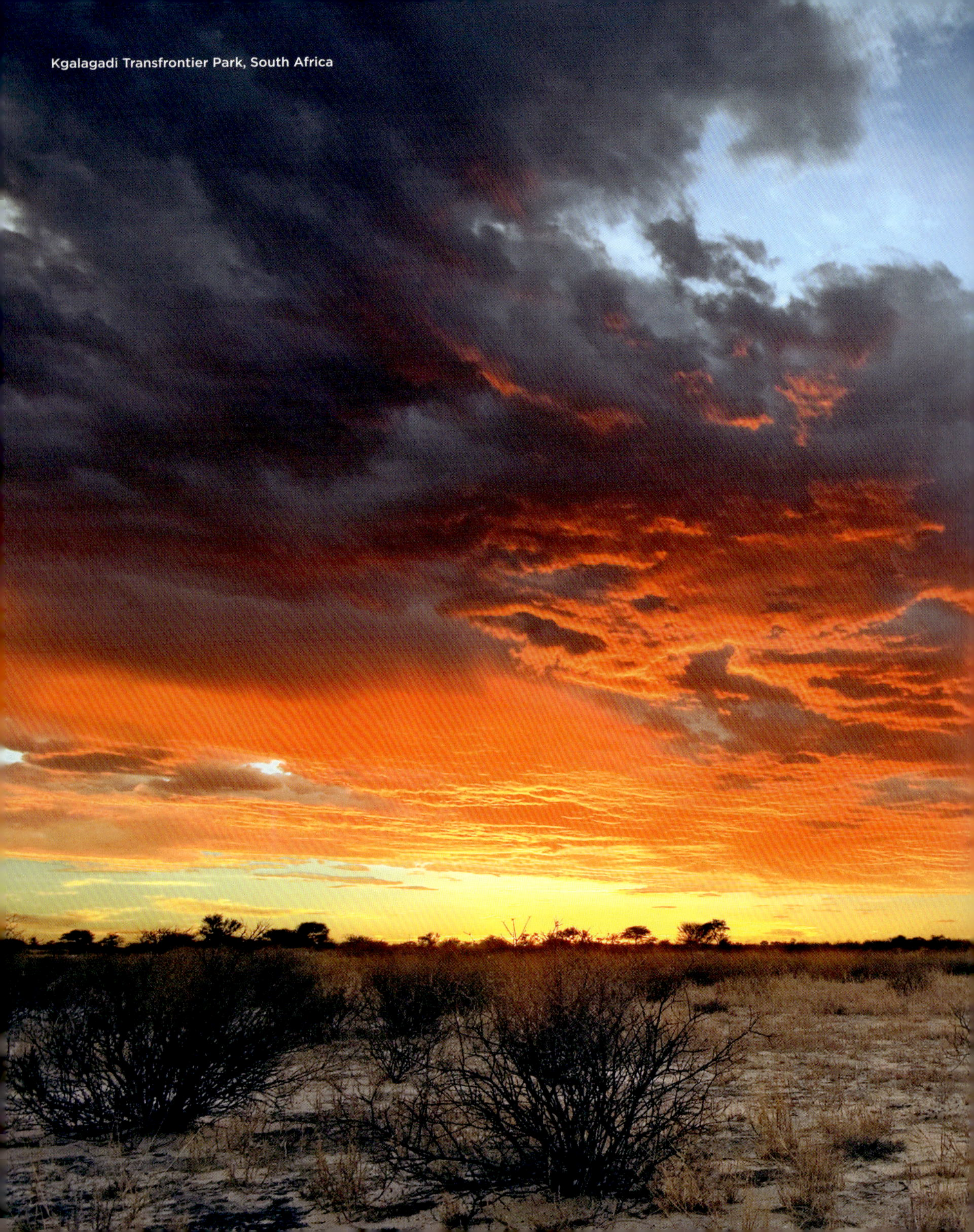

Kgalagadi Transfrontier Park, South Africa

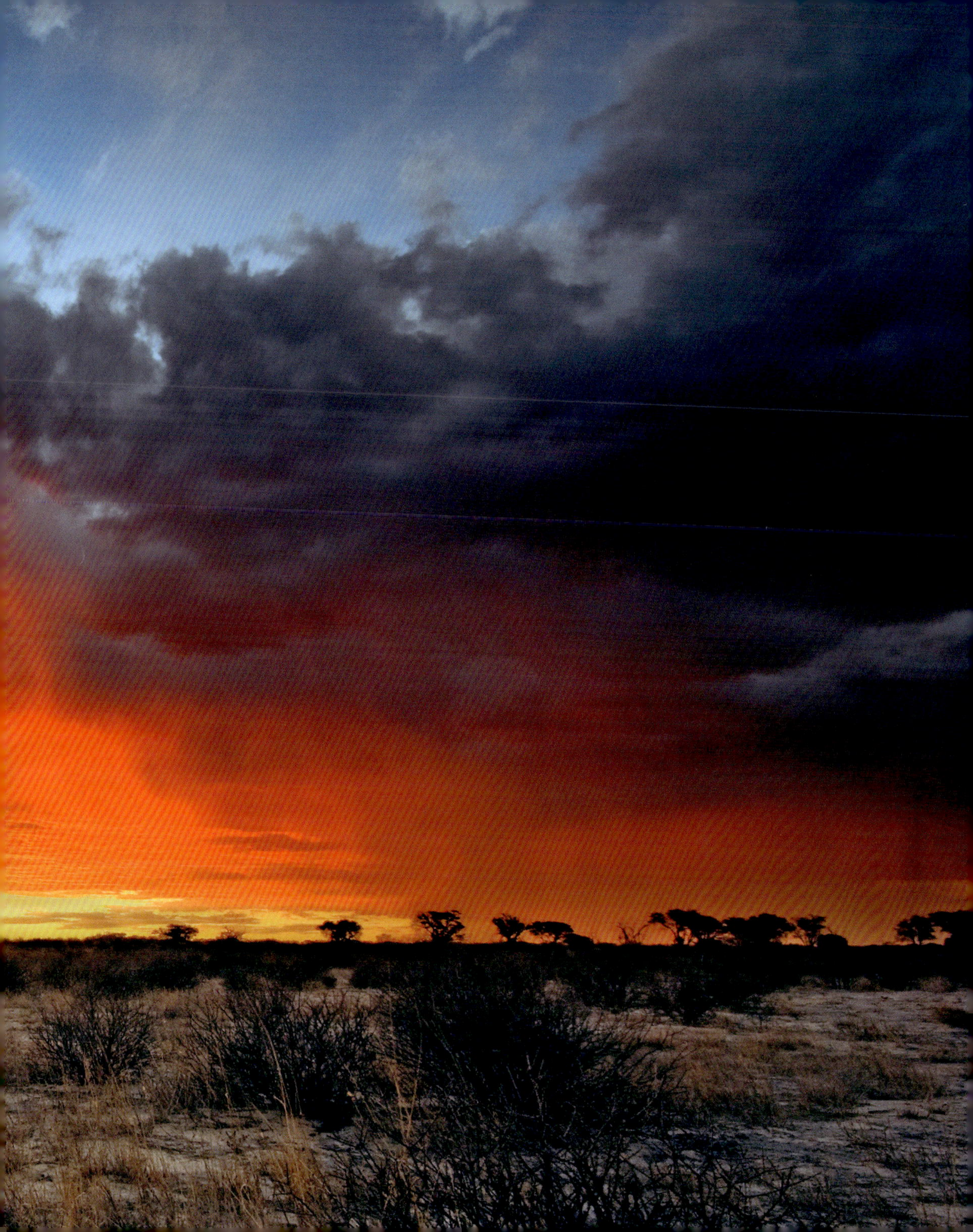

Kruger National Park, South Africa

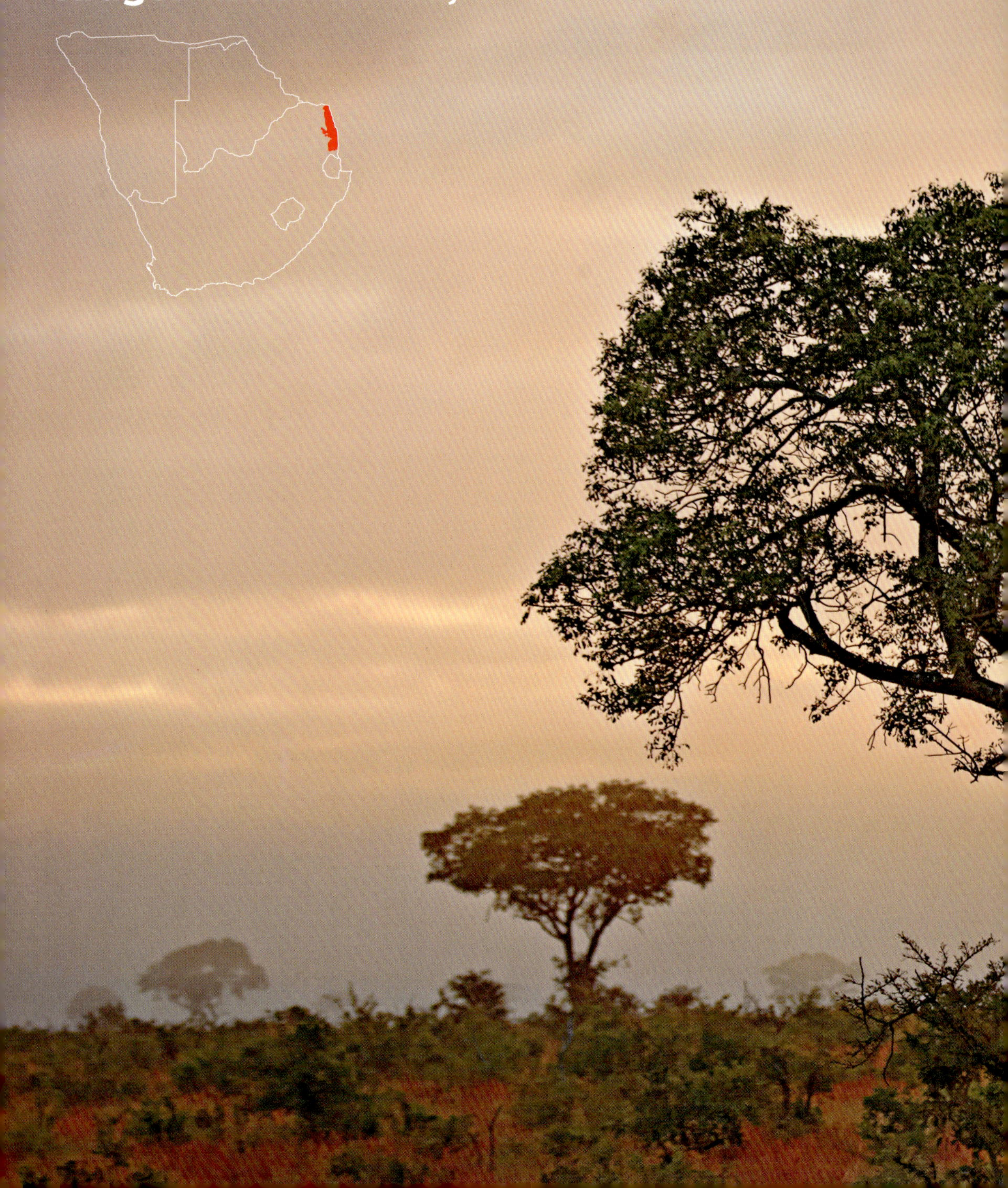

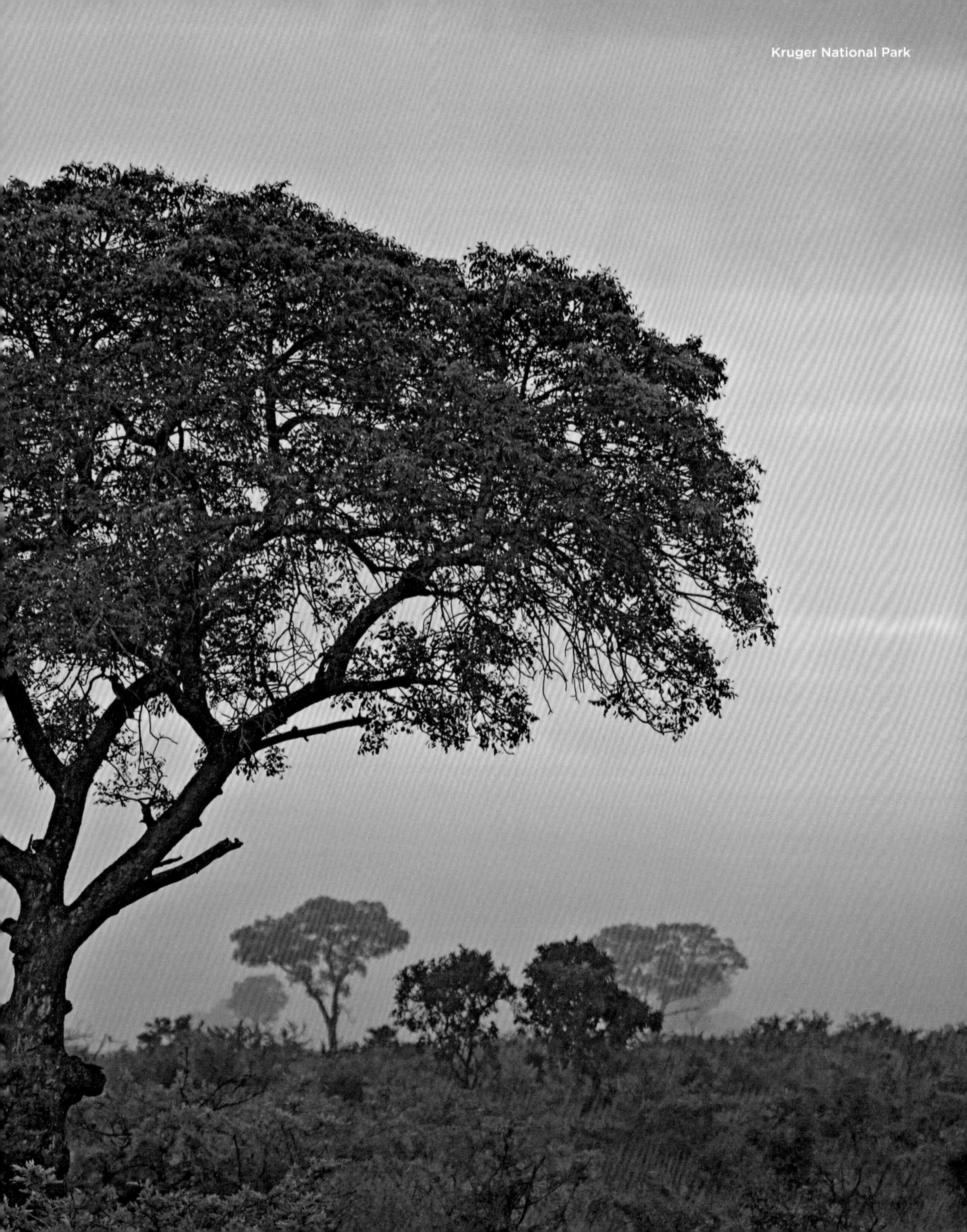

Kruger National Park

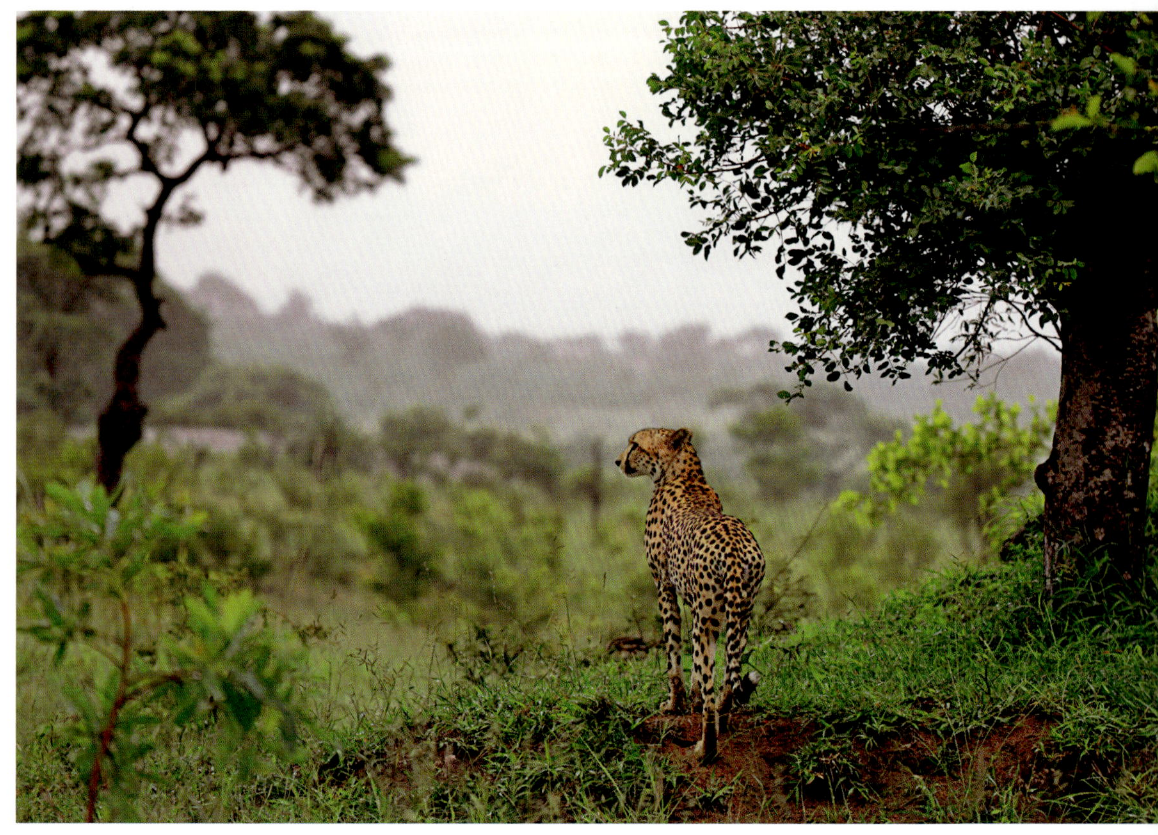

Cheetah, Kruger National Park

Kruger National Park
Kruger National Park combines many superlatives: established in 1926, it was the first area in South Africa to be placed under protection. Covering an area of 19,485 km² (7523 mi²), the park is also the largest of its kind in South Africa. It is one of the most famous wildlife sanctuaries on the continent. Visitors have good chances of catching sight of the big five: the elephant, the rhino, the African buffalo, lions, and leopards.

Le parc national Kruger
Le parc national Kruger bat plusieurs records : fondé dès 1926, il est le premier territoire sud-africain placé sous protection. D'une superficie de 19 485 km² il est le plus vaste de son genre en Afrique du Sud. C'est l'une des réserves les plus connues du continent. Ici, le visiteur a de bonnes chances d'apercevoir les Big Five : éléphants, rhinocéros, buffles, lions et léopards.

Kruger-Nationalpark
Der Kruger-Nationalpark vereint viele Superlative: Bereits 1926 errichtet, ist er das erste unter Schutz gestellte Gebiet Südafrikas. Mit einer Fläche von 19 485 km² ist der Park der größte seiner Art in Südafrika. Er gehört zu den bekanntesten Wildschutzgebieten auf de Kontinent. Die Chancen stehen gut, hier d Big Five beobachten zu können: Elefant, Nashorn, Afrikanischer Büffel, Löwe und Leopard.

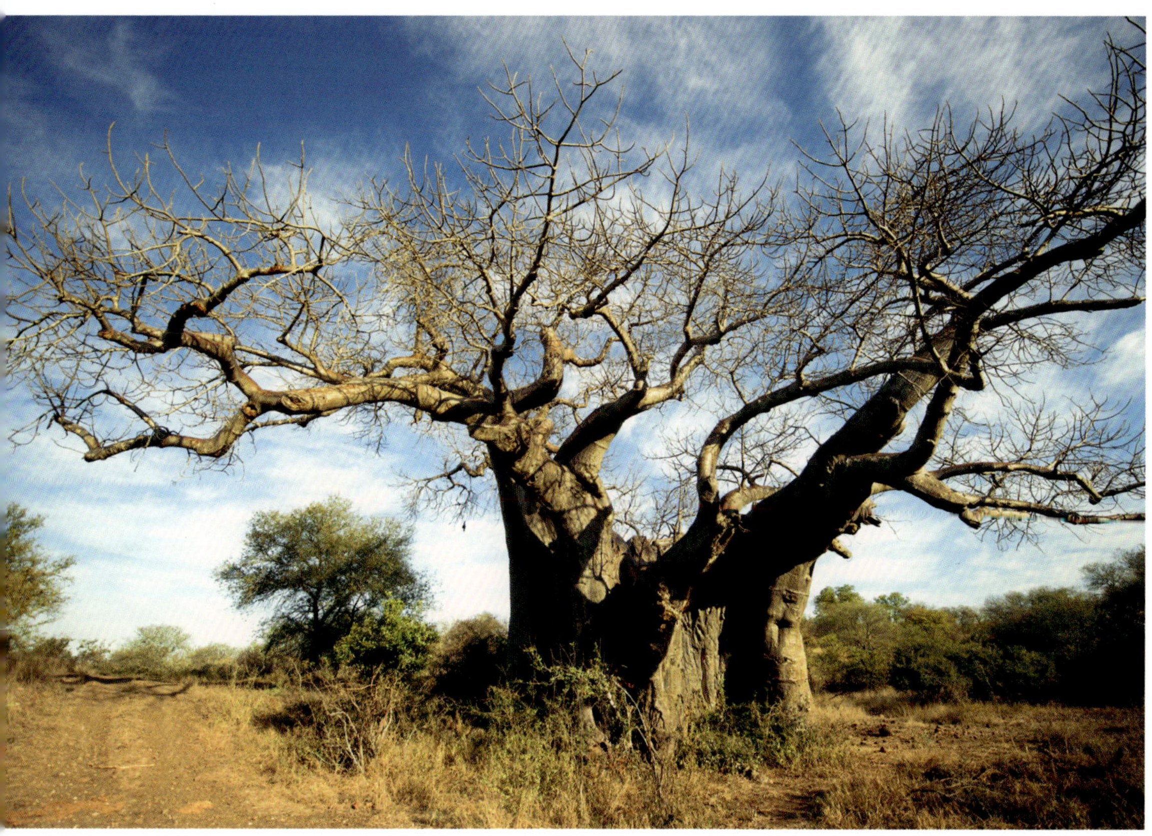

ican baobab, Kruger National Park

rque Nacional Kruger
Parque Nacional Kruger combina chos superlativos: construido en 1926, el primero que se puso bajo reserva en dáfrica. Con una superficie de 19 485 ², es el parque más grande de su tipo África del Sur. Él es una de las más nosas reservas de caza del continente. probable que se puedan observar aquí cinco grandes: elefante, rinoceronte, alo africano, león y leopardo.

Parco Nazionale Kruger
Il Parco Nazionale Kruger vanta molti primati: fondato già nel 1926, è la prima zona protetta del Sudafrica. Con una superficie di 19 485 km², il parco è il più grande del suo genere in Sudafrica. È una delle riserve naturali protette più note del continente. Vi sono buone possibilità di osservare qui i Grandi Cinque: l'elefante, il rinoceronte, il bufalo africano, il leone e il leopardo.

Nationale Park Kruger
Het Krugerpark is een park van superlatieven. Het werd al in 1926 uitgeroepen en was het eerste beschermde natuurgebied van Zuid-Afrika. Met een oppervlakte van 19 485 km² is het park ook het grootste van zijn soort in Zuid-Afrika en behoort tot de bekendste wildreservaten van Afrika. Bezoekers hebben grote kans hier de 'Big Five' te zien: olifant, neushoorn, Afrikaanse buffel, leeuw en luipaard.

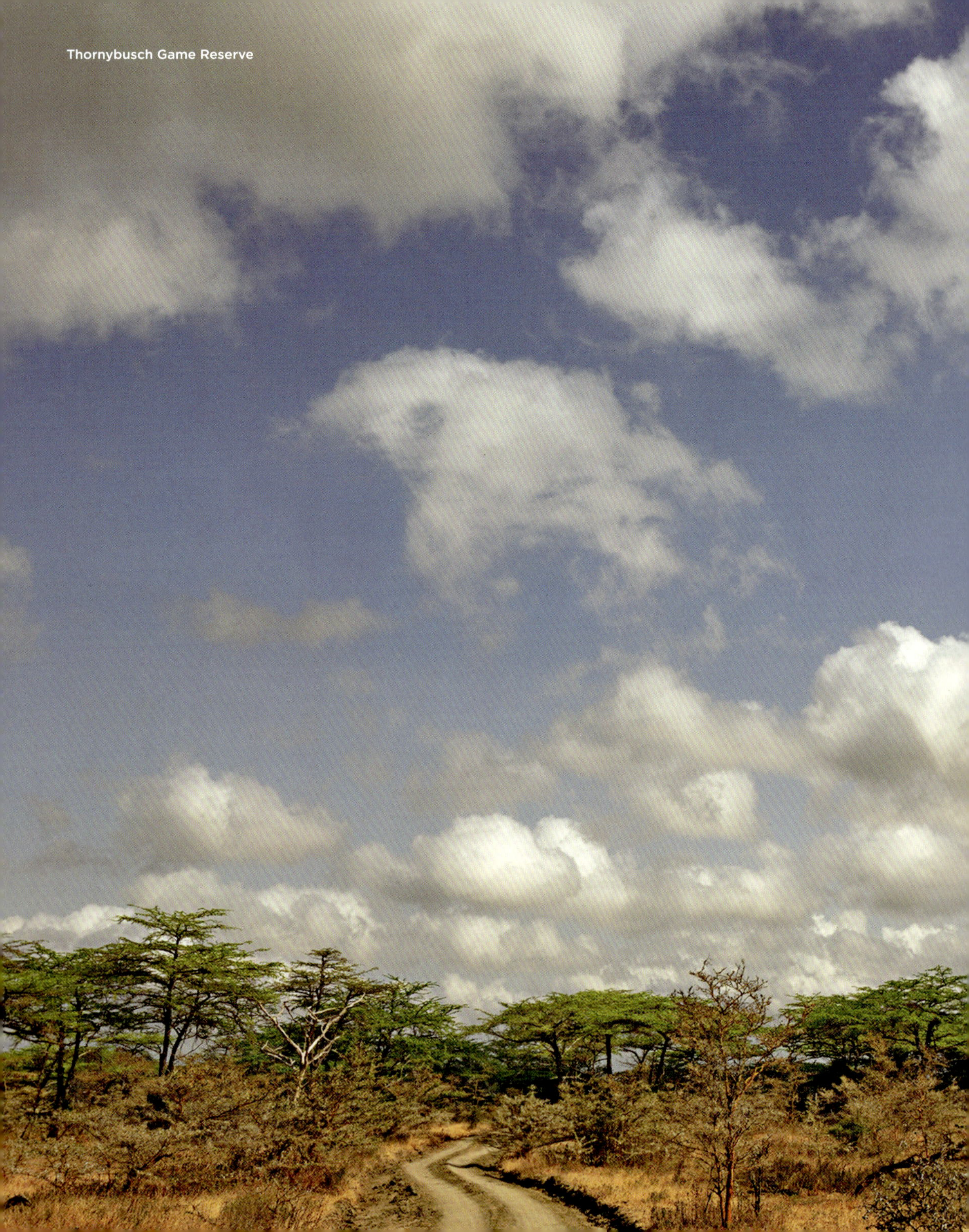
Thornybusch Game Reserve

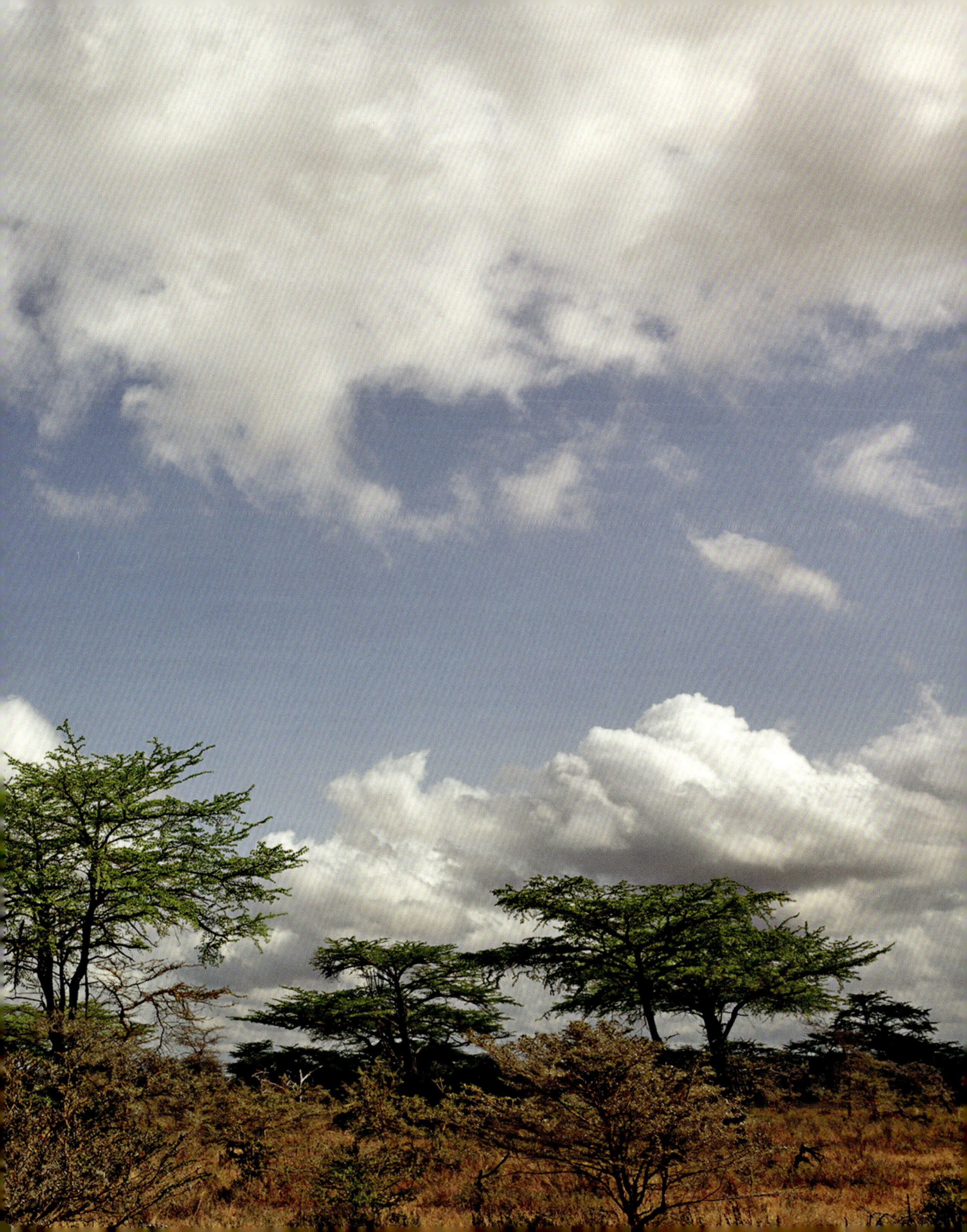

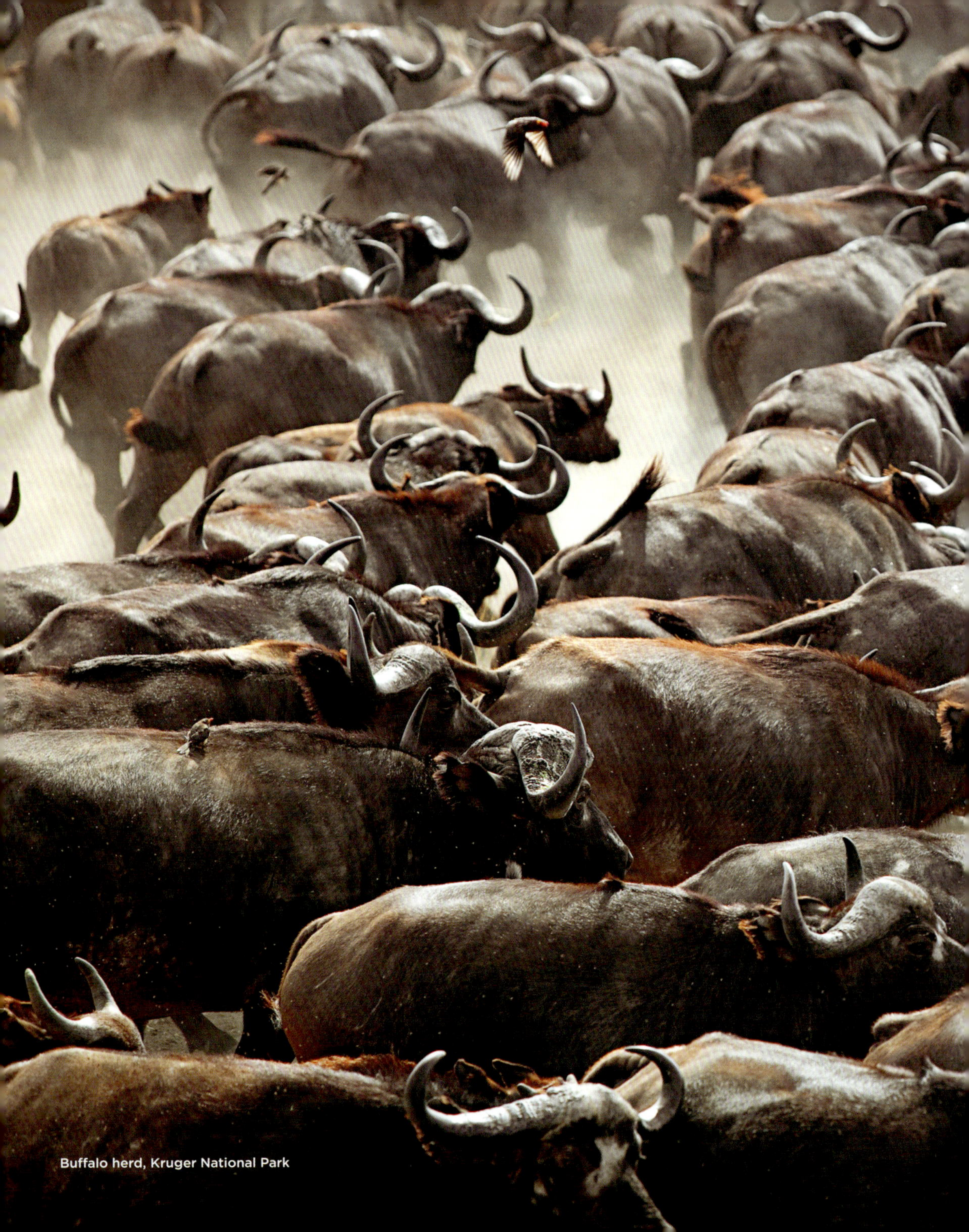

Buffalo herd, Kruger National Park

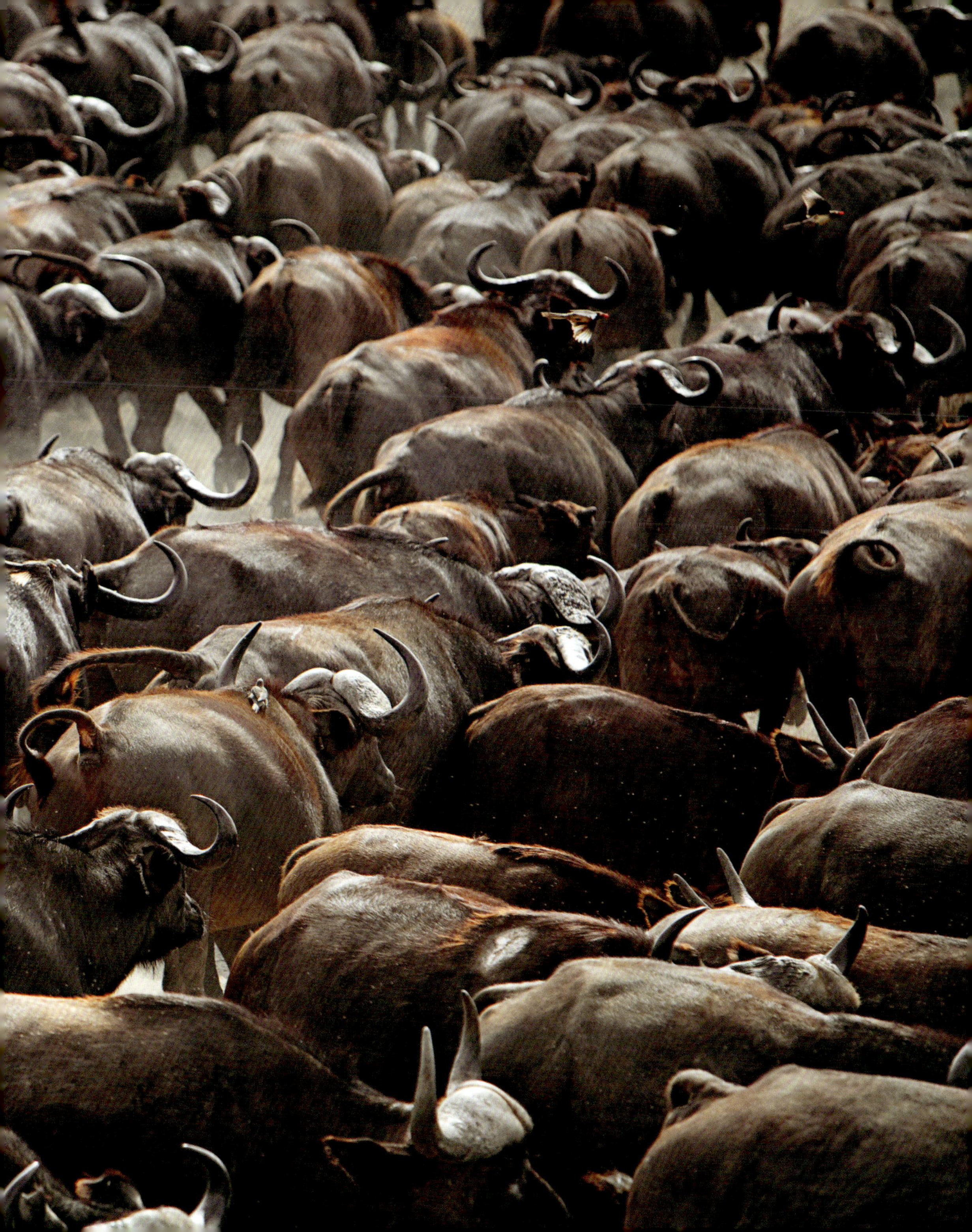

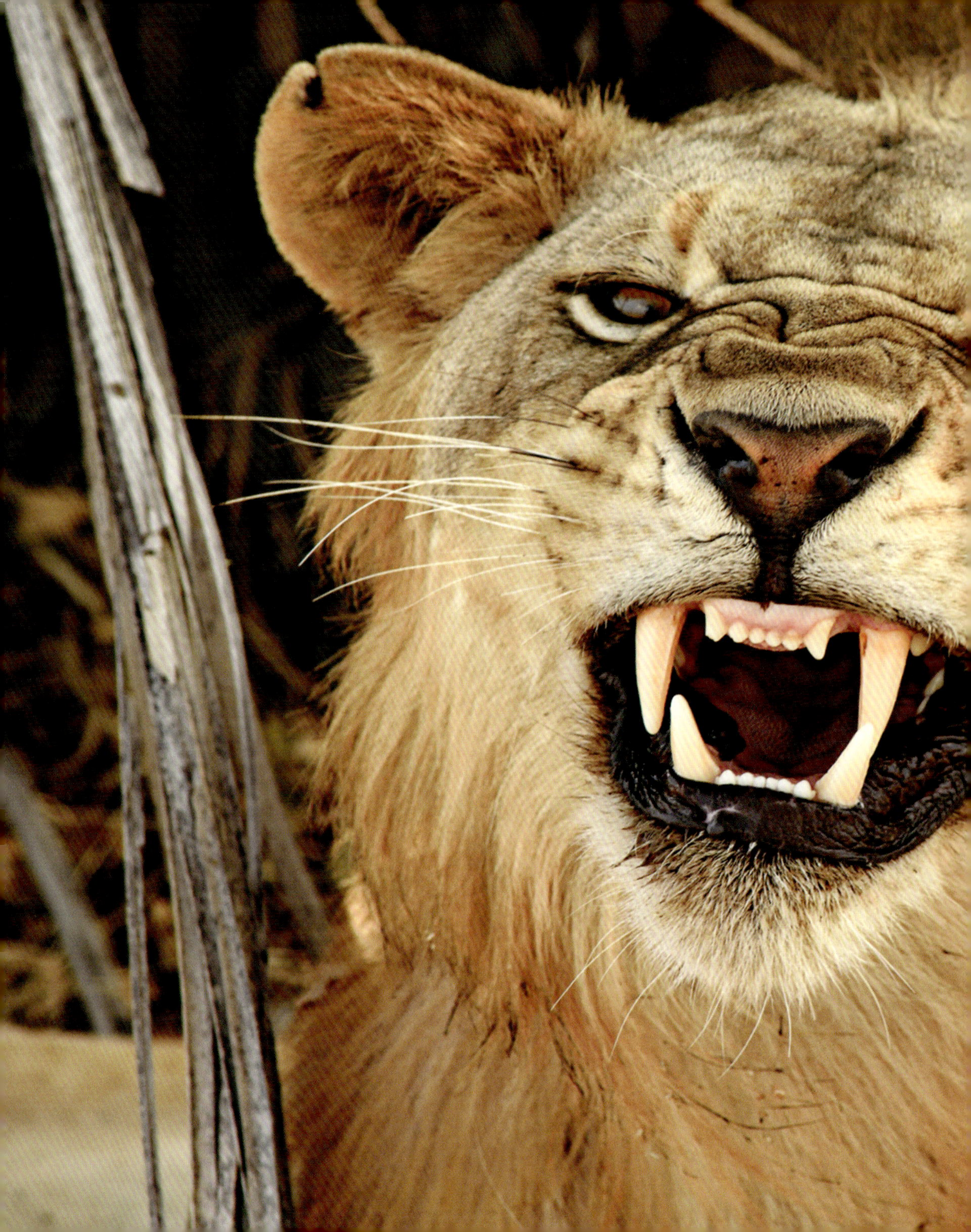

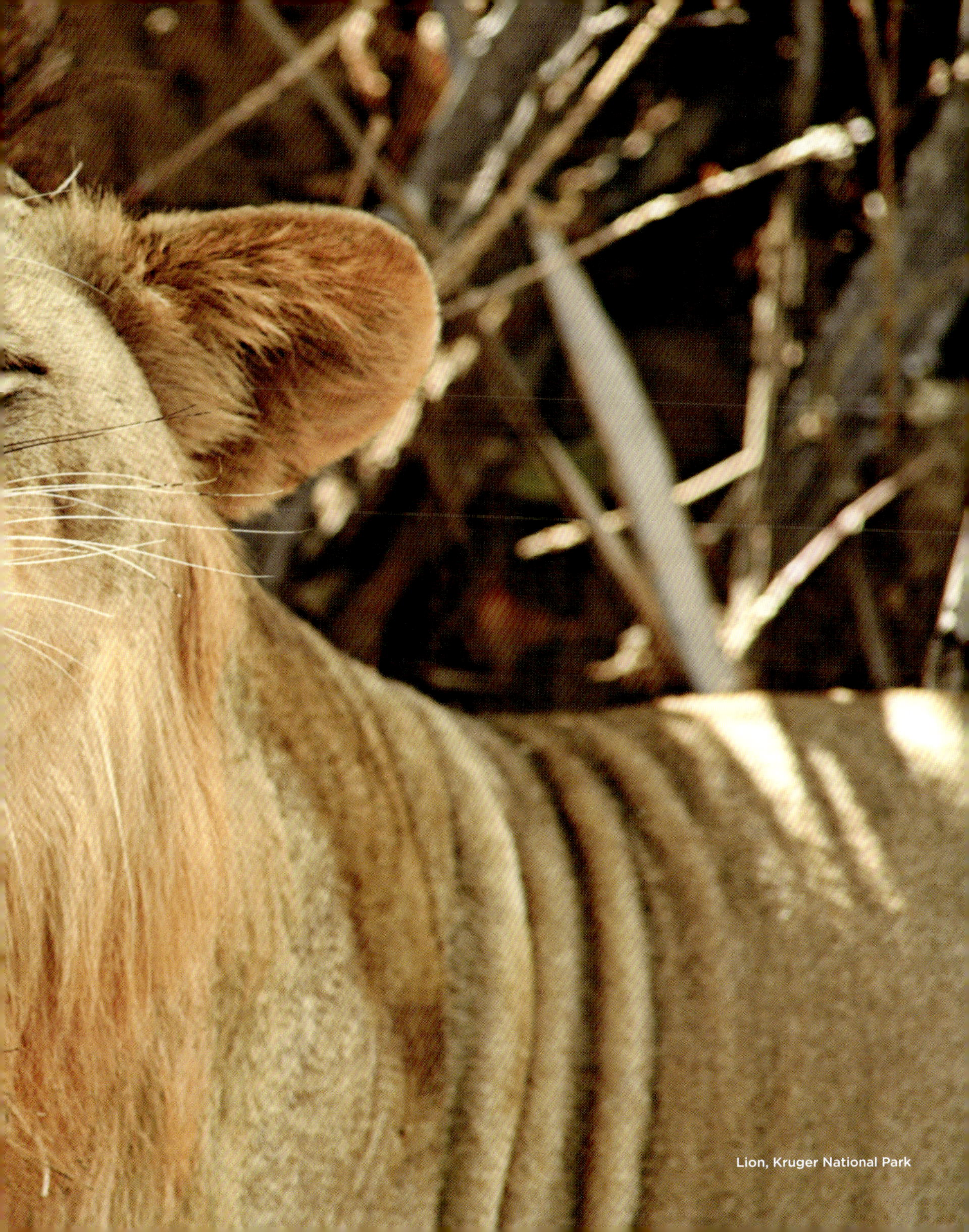

Lion, Kruger National Park

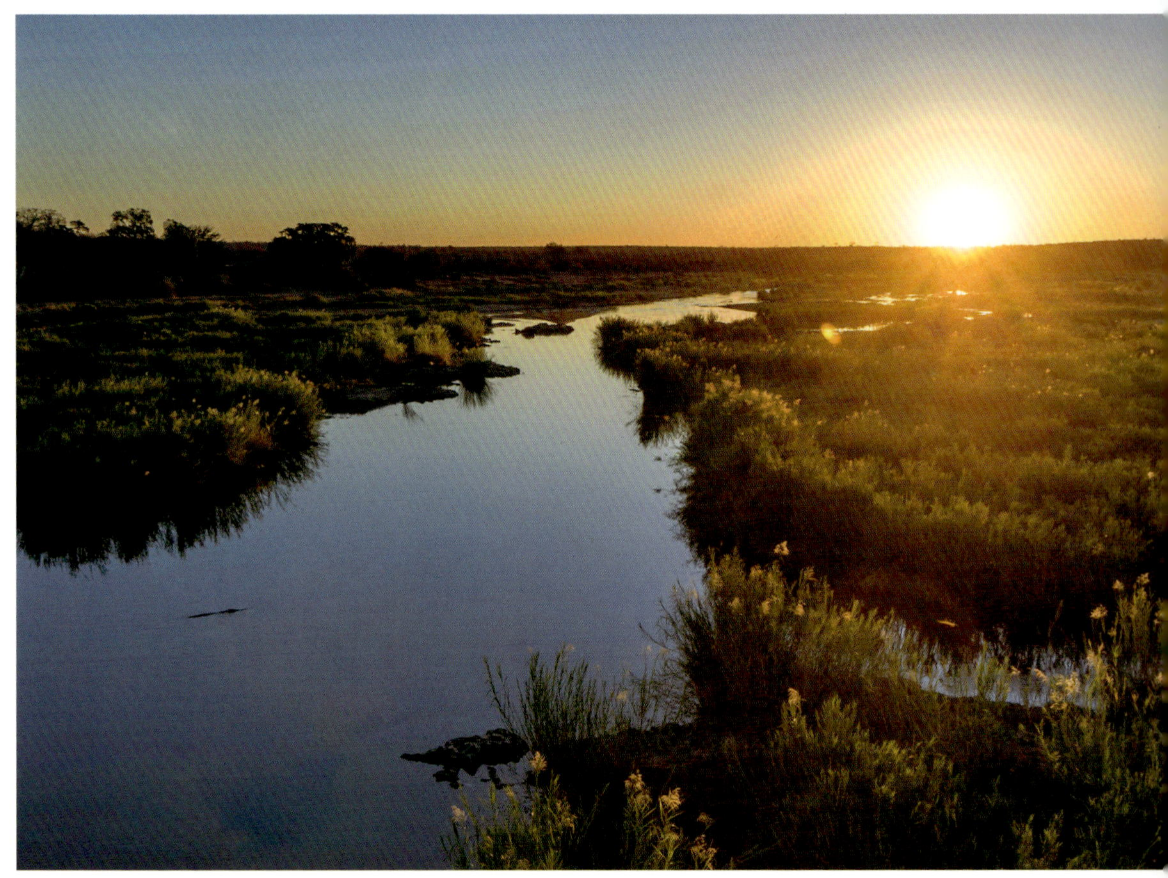

Southern Kruger National Park

Leopard, Kruger National Pa

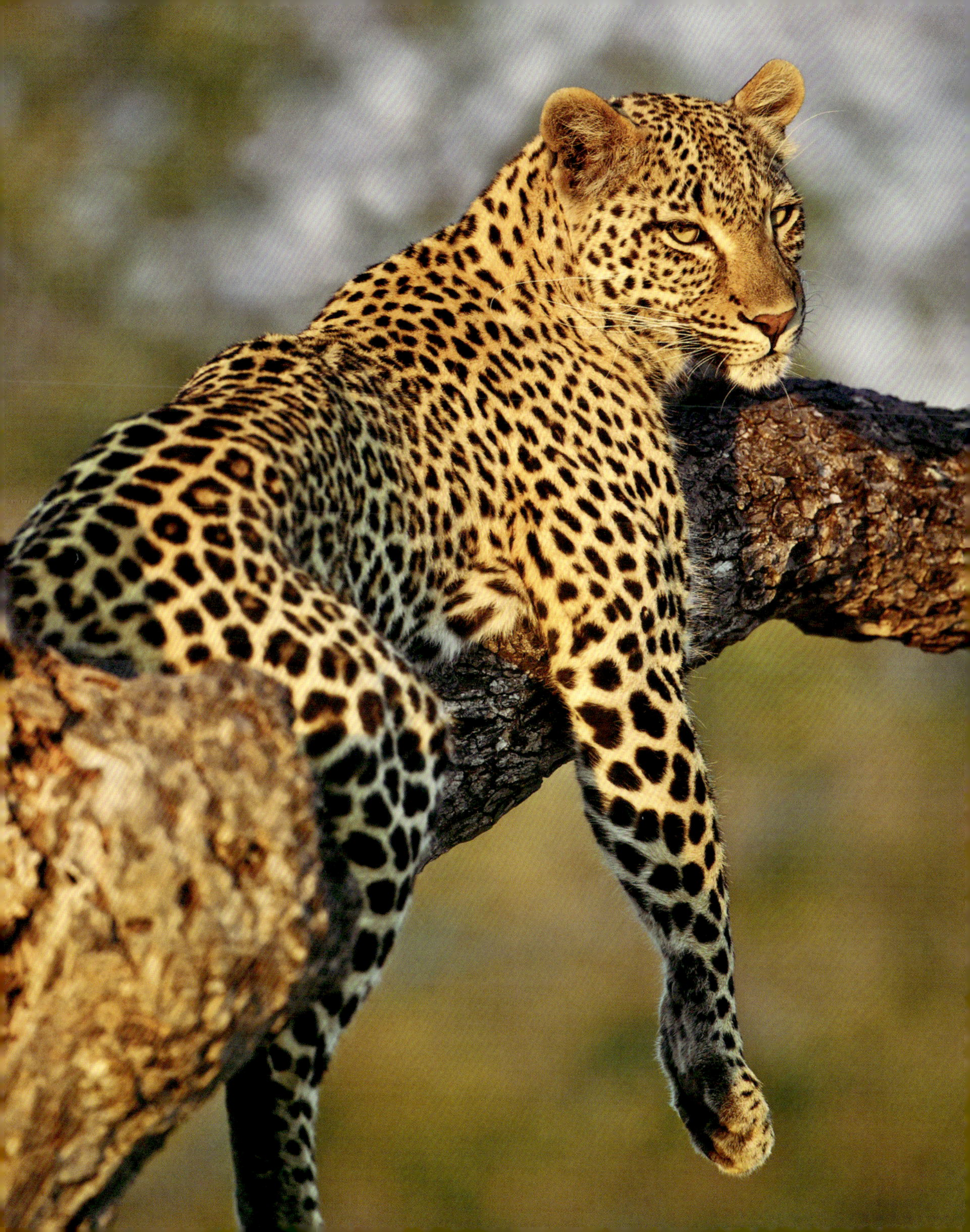

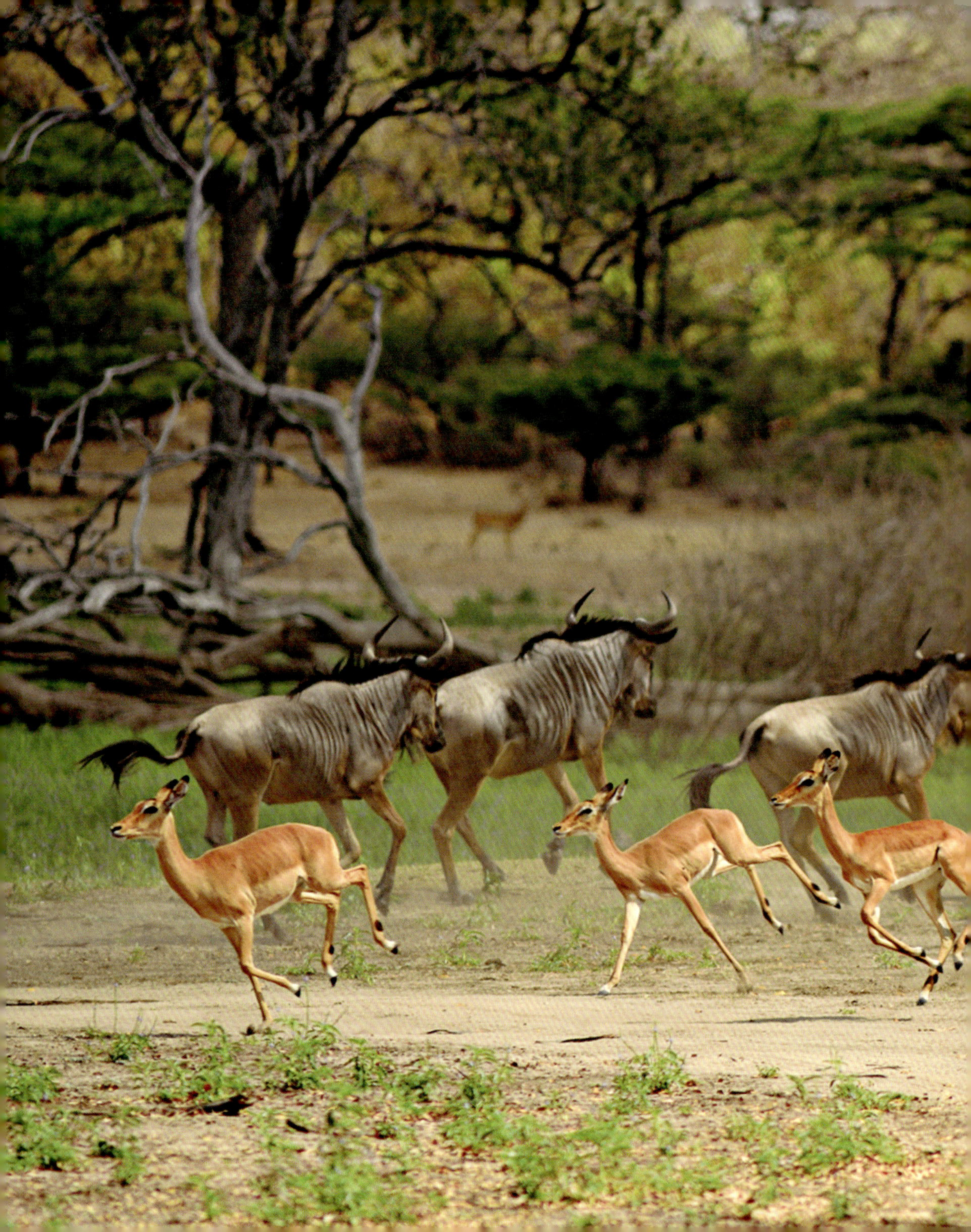

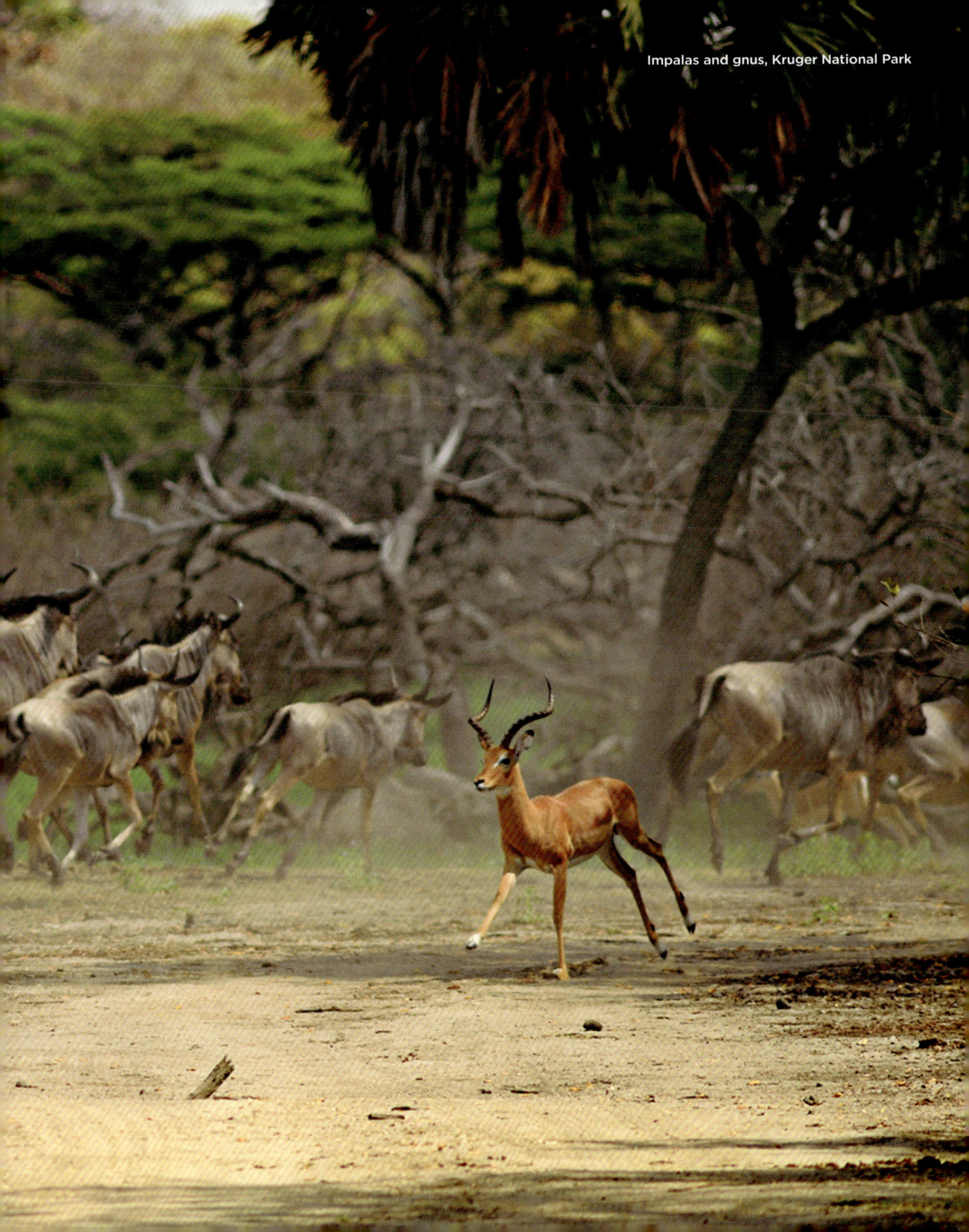
Impalas and gnus, Kruger National Park

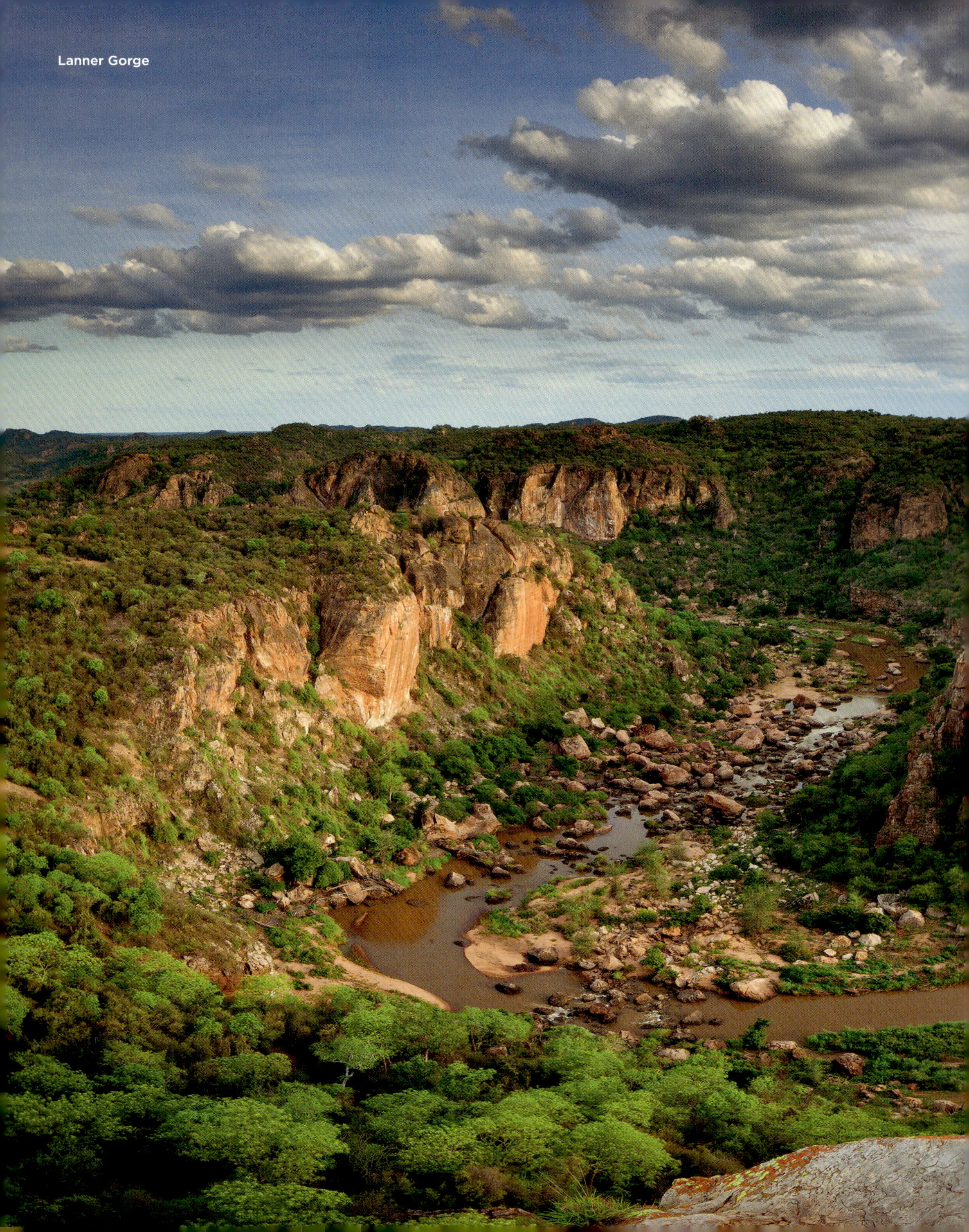

Lanner Gorge

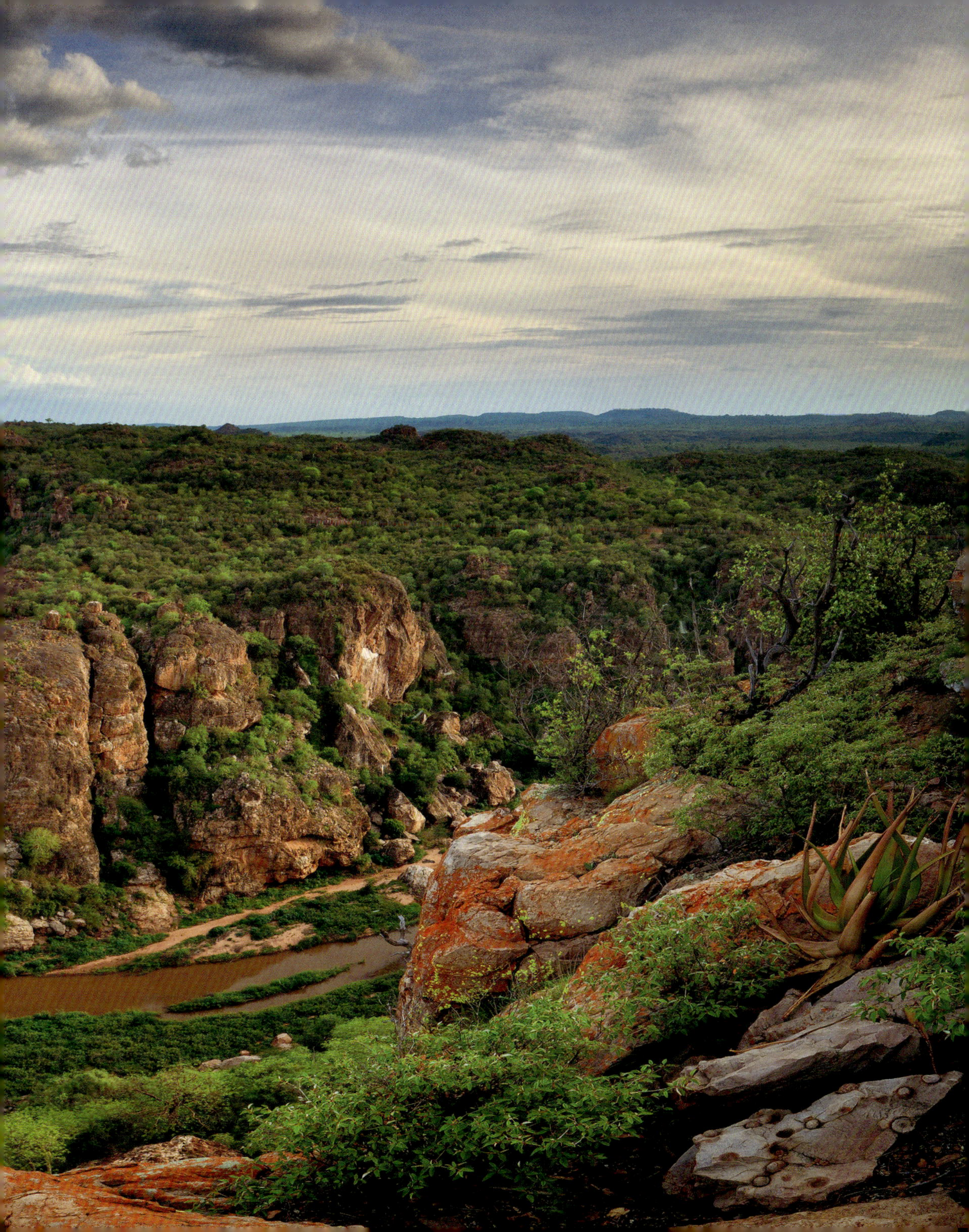

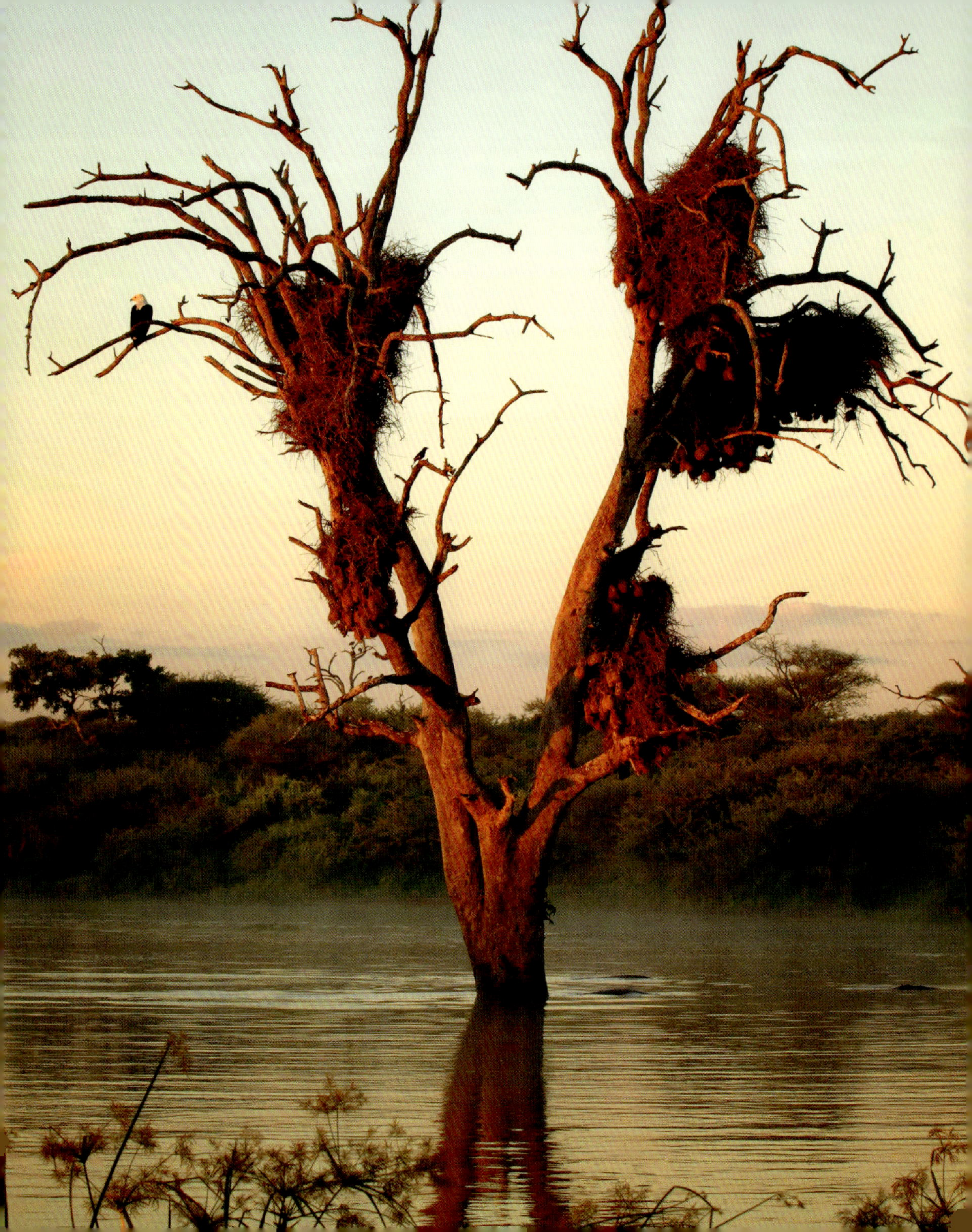

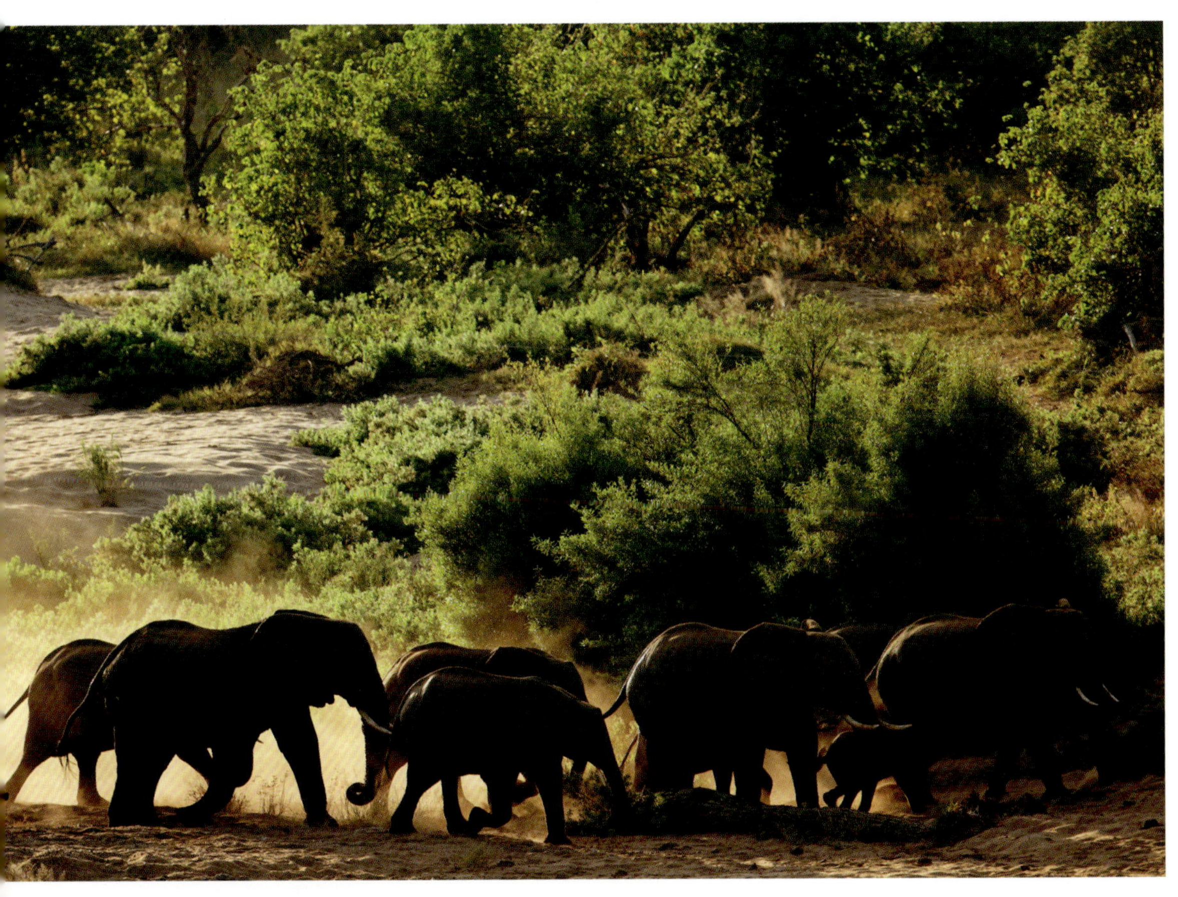

Elephants, Southern Kruger National Park

Sunset Dam, Kruger National Park

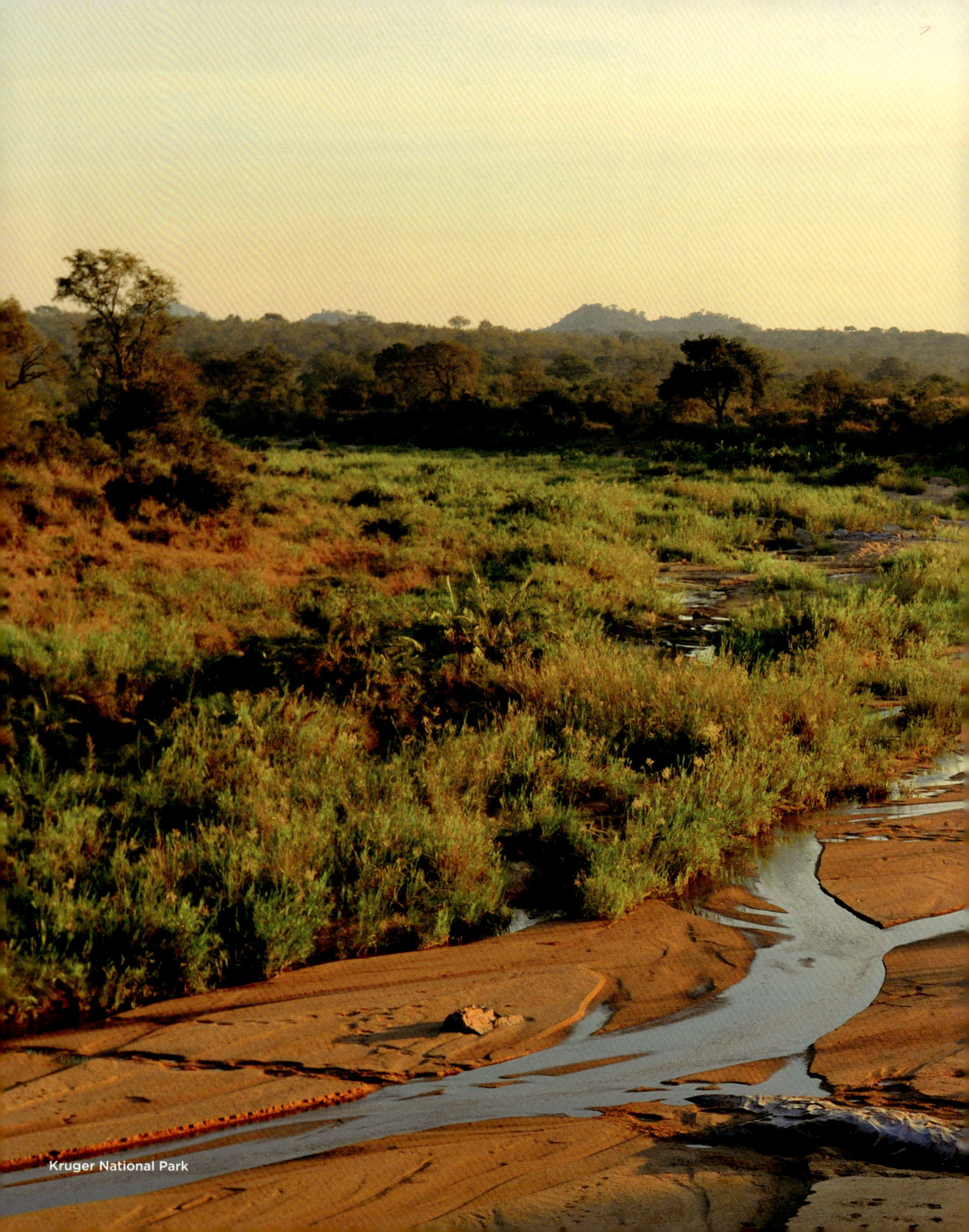

Kruger National Park

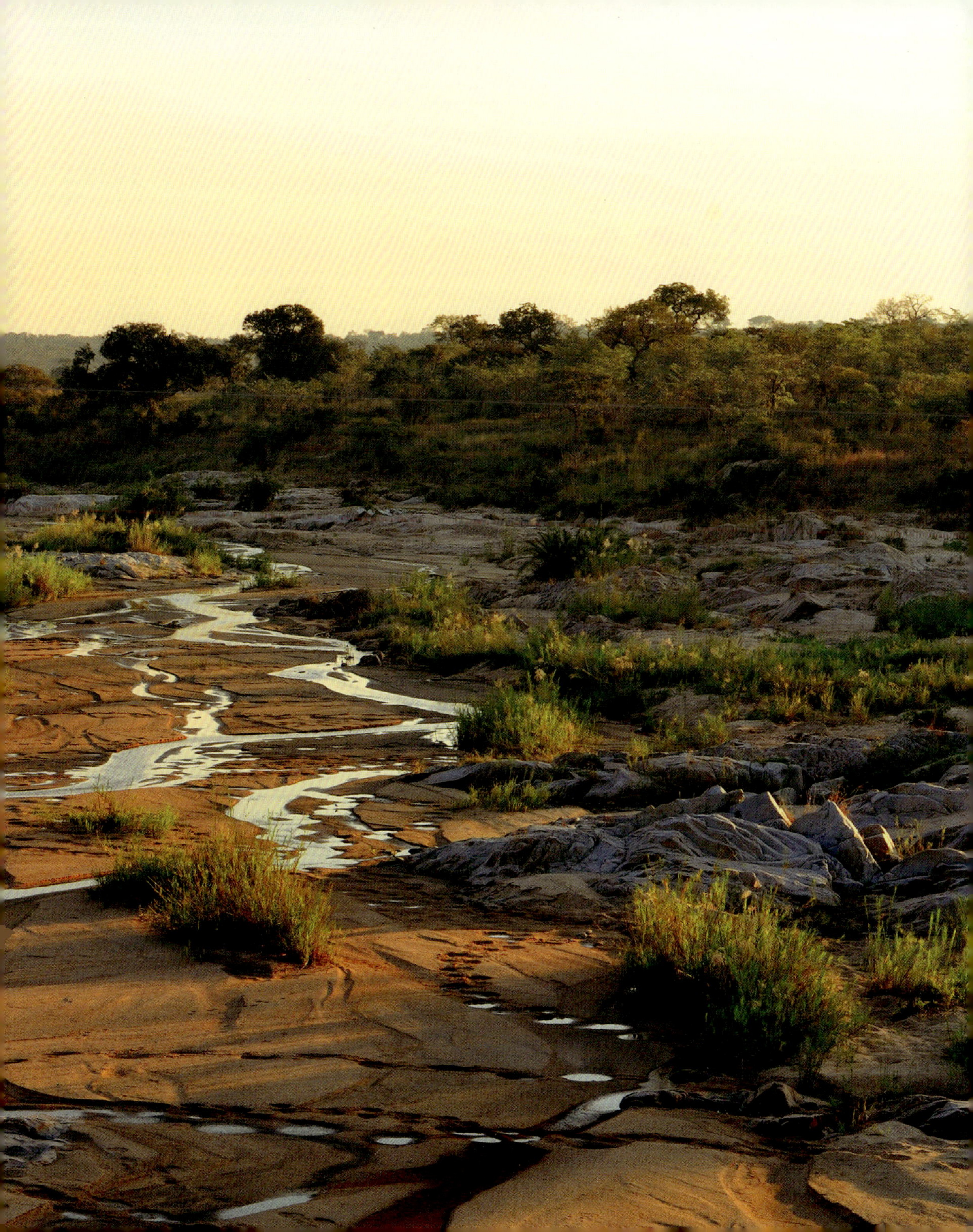

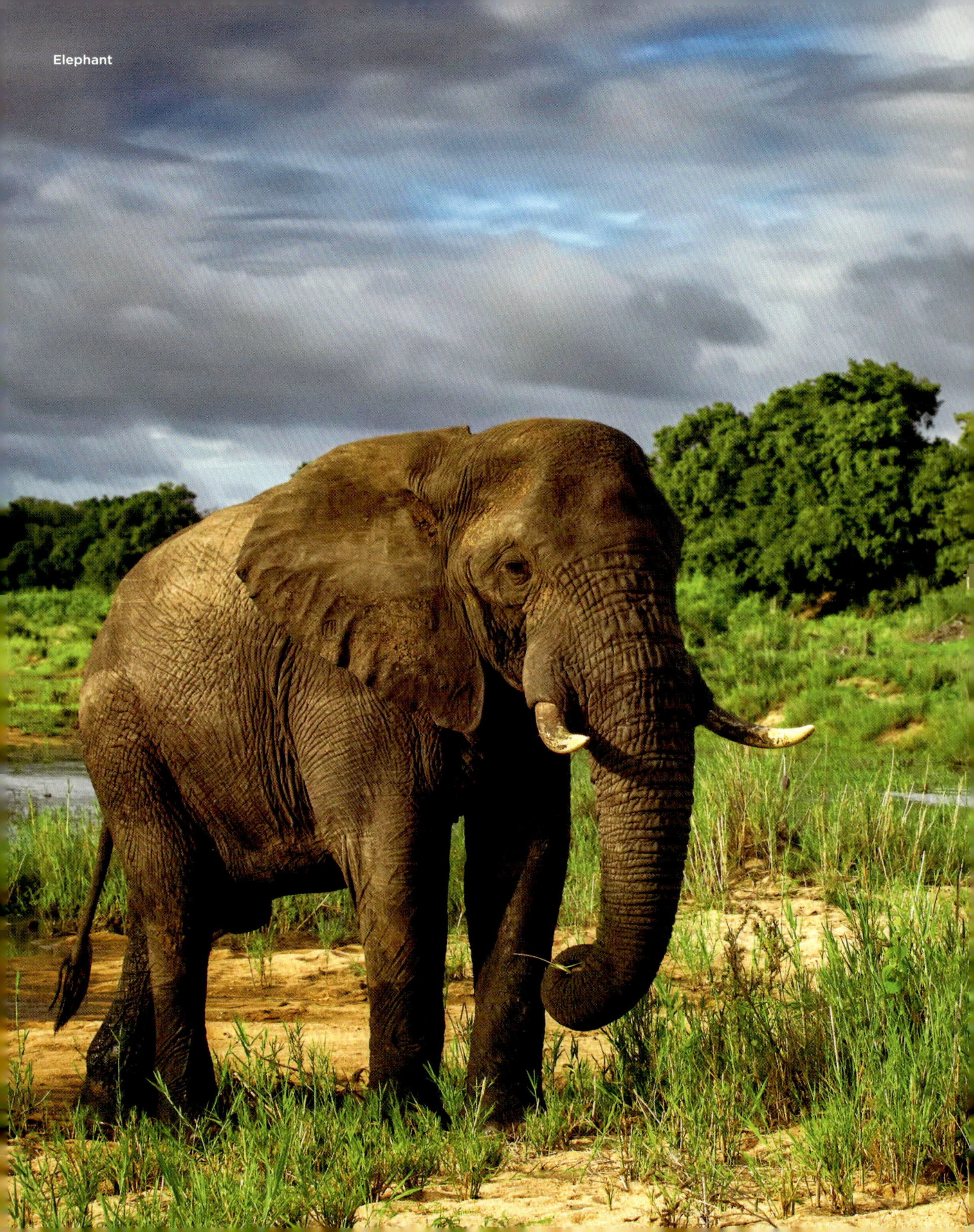
Elephant

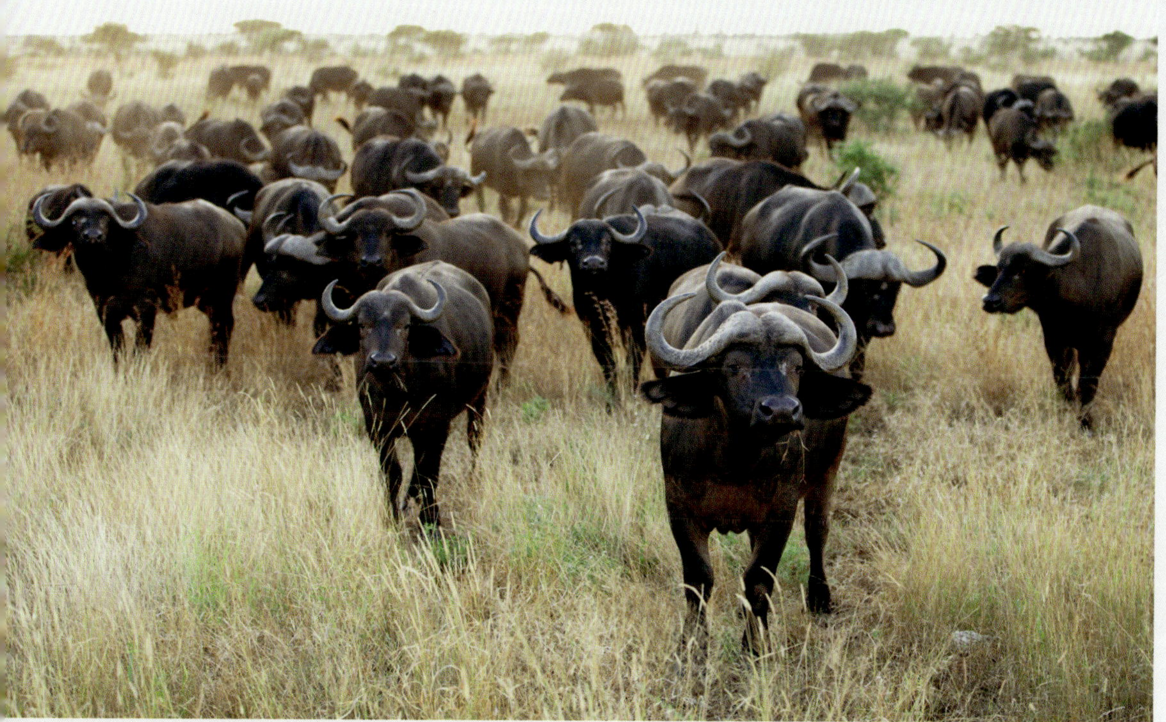

ıffalos

ıe Big Five
ıe "Big Five" are not those wild animals Africa which are the largest in stature, ıt those which used to be the most fficult and dangerous to hunt during g game hunts: Lion, leopard, buffalo, ephant and rhino. The chance to see five in one game park is greatest in a ivate game reserve.

g Five
expression « Big Five » ne désigne pas s animaux d'Afrique qui sont les plus ands par leur stature, mais ceux qui aient autrefois les plus durs et les plus ngereux à chasser : le lion, le léopard, buffle, l'éléphant et le rhinocéros. C'est ns les réserves privées que l'on a le plus chances de tomber nez à nez avec s cinq.

Big Five
Mit den „Big Five" sind nicht jene Wildtiere Afrikas gemeint, die von der Statur her am größten sind, sondern die, die früher bei Großwildjagden am schwierigsten und gefährlichsten zu jagen waren: Löwe, Leopard, Büffel, Elefant und Nashorn. Die Chance alle Fünf in nur einem Wildpark zu Gesicht zu bekommen, ist in einem privaten Wildreservat am größten.

Los Cinco Grandes
Los "Cinco Grandes" no son los animales salvajes de África más grandes en cuanto a estatura se refiere, sino los que solían ser los más difíciles y peligrosos de cazar durante la caza mayor: león, leopardo, búfalo, elefante y rinoceronte. La oportunidad de ver a los cinco en un parque aumenta en una reserva privada de caza.

Big Five
Con il termine "Big Five" non si intende quegli animali selvatici dell'Africa di mole più grande, ma quelli che una volta erano i più difficili e pericolosi da cacciare durante la caccia grossa: leone, leopardo, bufalo, elefante e rinoceronte. La possibilità di vedere tutti e cinque in un parco naturale è maggiore rispetto ad una riserva naturale.

De Big Five
De "Big Five" zijn niet de wilde dieren in Afrika die het grootst in omvang zijn, maar de dieren die vroeger het moeilijkst en gevaarlijkst te bejagen waren tijdens de jacht op groot wild: leeuw, luipaard, buffel, olifant en neushoorn. De kans om alle vijf in een wildpark te zien is het grootst in een particulier wildreservaat.

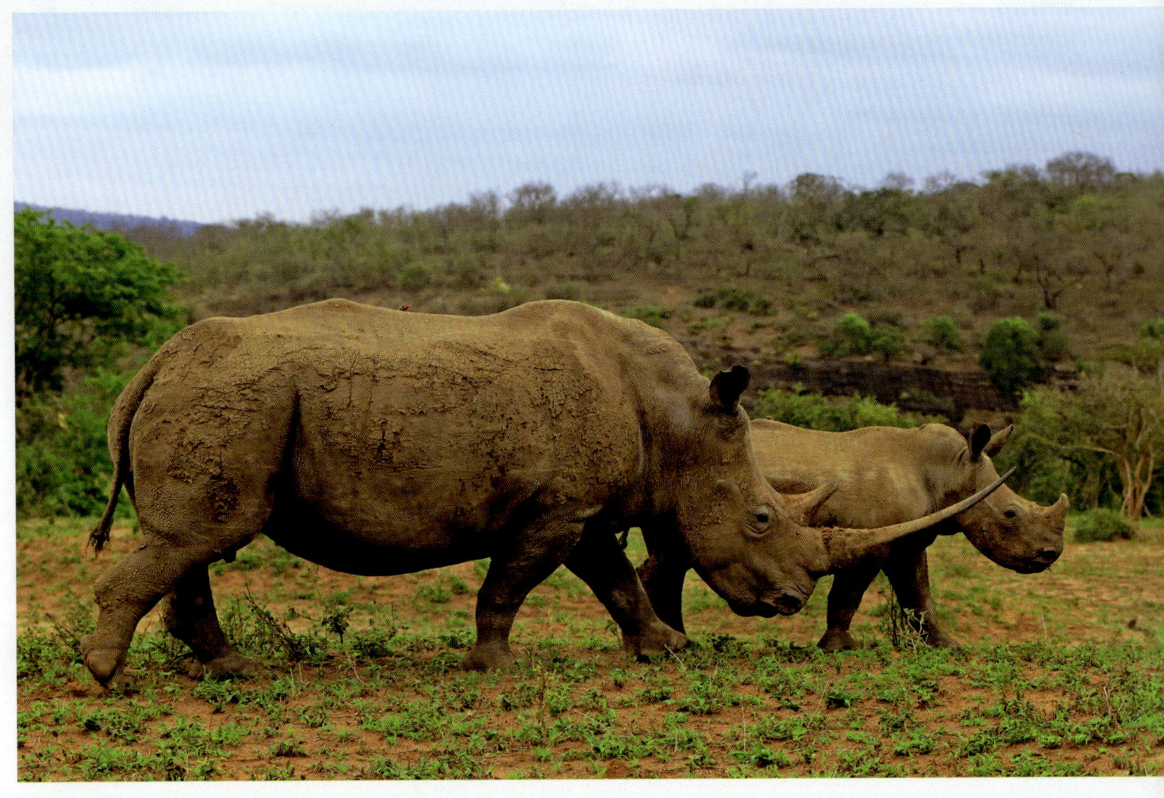

White rhinoceros

Rhinos
Two species of rhinoceros live in southern Africa: the black rhinoceros and the white rhinoceros. Both species are inhabitants of the savannahs and the open landscapes of southern Africa. Black rhinoceroses are loners and much smaller than white rhinoceroses, which live in small groups. The former feed mainly on leaves, branches and bark, which they pluck off with their mouths. The white rhinoceros, on the other hand, with its low-hanging head and broad lips, is perfectly adapted to grass eating. While young white rhinoceroses usually walk in front of their mother, black rhinoceroses always run after their mother, who clears the way for the calf.

Les rhinocéros
Dans le sud de l'Afrique, on trouve deux sortes de rhinocéros : le noir et le blanc. Tous deux habitent la savane et les grands espaces de l'Afrique australe. Les rhinocéros noirs sont solitaires, et sensiblement plus petits que les blancs, qui eux vivent en groupes. Ils se nourrissent principalement de feuilles, de branchages et d'écorces, qu'ils arrachent délicatement avec leur gueule fine. Les rhinocéros blancs, en revanche, avec leur tête basse et leur large gueule, préfèrent brouter l'herbe. Si les jeunes rhinocéros blancs marchent la plupart du temps devant leur mère, les noirs, eux, restent en général derrière elle, qui leur ouvre la voie.

Nashörner
Im südlichen Afrika leben zwei Nashornarten: Spitzmaul- und Breitmaulnashorn. Beide Arten sind Bewohner der Savannen und der offenen Landschaften im südlichen Afrika. Spitzmaulnashörner sind Einzelgänger und deutlich kleiner als Breitmaulnashörner, die in kleinen Gruppen leben. Sie ernähren sich überwiegend von Blättern, Ästen und Rinde, die sie mit ihrem Maul abzupfen. Das Breitmaulnashorn ist im Gegensatz dazu mit seinem tief hängenden Kopf und seinen breiten Lippen hervorragend an das Grasfressen angepasst. Während junge Breitmaulnashörner meist vor dem Muttertier gehen, laufen Spitzmaulnashörner immer hinter ihrer Mutter her, die den Weg für das Kalb frei macht.

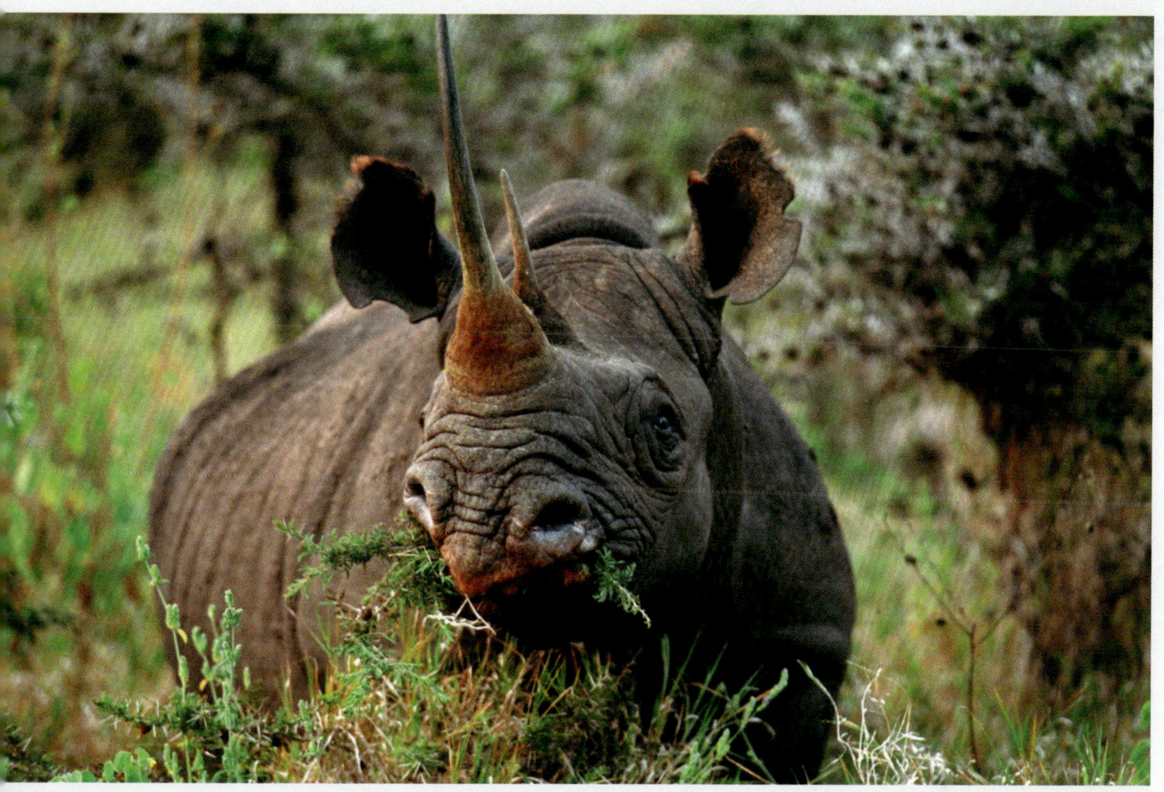

ack rhinoceros

nocerontes
os especies de rinocerontes viven en sur de África: el rinoceronte negro y rinoceronte blanco. Ambas especies bitan en las sabanas y en los paisajes iertos del sur de África. Los rinocerontes gros son solitarios y mucho más queños que los rinocerontes blancos, e viven en grupos pequeños. Se mentan principalmente de hojas, ramas corteza, que arrancan con la boca. El oceronte blanco, en cambio, con la beza baja y los labios anchos, se adapta rfectamente al consumo de hierba. entras que los jóvenes rinocerontes ancos suelen caminar delante de su adre, los rinocerontes negros siempre rren detrás de su madre, la cual despeja camino para la cría.

Rinoceronti
Nell'Africa meridionale vivono due specie di rinoceronte: il rinoceronte nero e il rinoceronte bianco. Entrambe le specie sono abitanti della savana e dei paesaggi aperti dell'Africa meridionale. I rinoceronti neri sono solitari e molto più piccoli dei rinoceronti bianchi, che vivono in piccoli gruppi. Si nutrono principalmente di foglie, rami e cortecce, che strappano con la bocca. Il rinoceronte bianco, invece, con la testa bassa e le labbra larghe, si adatta perfettamente al consumo di erba. Mentre i piccoli di rinoceronti bianchi camminano di solito davanti alla madre, i rinoceronti neri corrono sempre dietro la madre, che spiana la strada al cucciolo.

Neushoorns
In zuidelijk Afrika leven twee soorten neushoorns: de zwarte en de witte neushoorn. Beide soorten zijn bewoners van de savannes en de open landschappen van zuidelijk Afrika. Zwarte neushoorns zijn solisten en veel kleiner dan witte neushoorns, die in kleine groepen leven. Ze voeden zich voornamelijk met bladeren, takken en schors, die ze eraf trekken met hun mond. De witte neushoorn daarentegen is met zijn laaghangende kop en brede lippen perfect aangepast aan het eten van gras. Terwijl jonge witte neushoorns meestal voor hun moeder lopen, lopen zwarte neushoorns altijd achter hun moeder aan, die het pad baant voor het kalf.

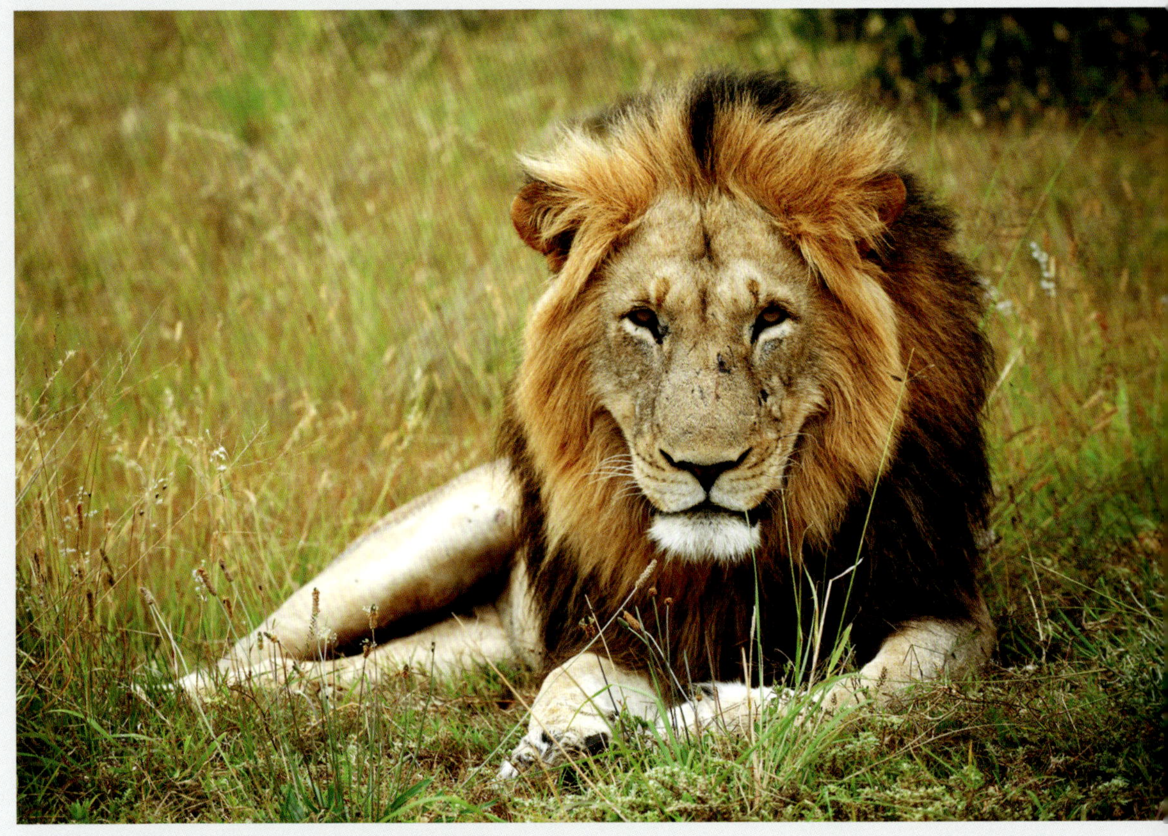

Lion

Lion and Leopard
The "King of Animals" is the largest land predator in Africa. Adult lions reach a shoulder height of well over one meter and a weight of almost 230 kg. However, the more delicate lionesses do most of the hunting. The shy, nocturnal leopards are widespread, but rarely seen in the wild. They have a very good sense of intuition and can swim and climb extraordinarily well. Leopards are able to drag their prey into trees to safeguard them from other predators. Unlike lions, leopards are loners.

Lions et léopards
Le roi des animaux est le plus grand carnivore d'Afrique. Les lions adultes peuvent avoir une hauteur au garrot de plus d'un mètre, et peser près de 230 kg. C'est pourtant surtout les lionnes, plus menues, qui s'occupent de chasser. Craintifs et nocturnes, les léopards sont certes largement répandus, mais rarement visibles en liberté. Dotés d'un excellent odorat, ce sont aussi des nageurs et des grimpeurs hors pair. Les léopards sont capables de hisser leurs proies dans les arbres pour les protéger des autres animaux. Contrairement aux lions, ce sont des animaux solitaires.

Löwe und Leopard
Der König der Tiere ist das größte Landraubtier in Afrika. Ausgewachsene Löwen bringen es auf eine Schulterhöhe von gut über einem Meter und ein Gewich von knapp 230 kg. Die Jagd übernehmen jedoch weitgehend die zierlicheren Löwinnen. Die scheuen, nachtaktiven Leoparden sind zwar weit verbreitet, aber eher selten in freier Wildbahn zu entdecken. Sie besitzen einen sehr gut ausgeprägten Spürsinn und können außerordentlich gut schwimmen und klettern. Leoparden sind in der Lage, ihre Beute auf Bäumen zu schleppen, um sie vor anderen Tieren zu schützen. Anders a Löwen sind Leoparden Einzelgänger.

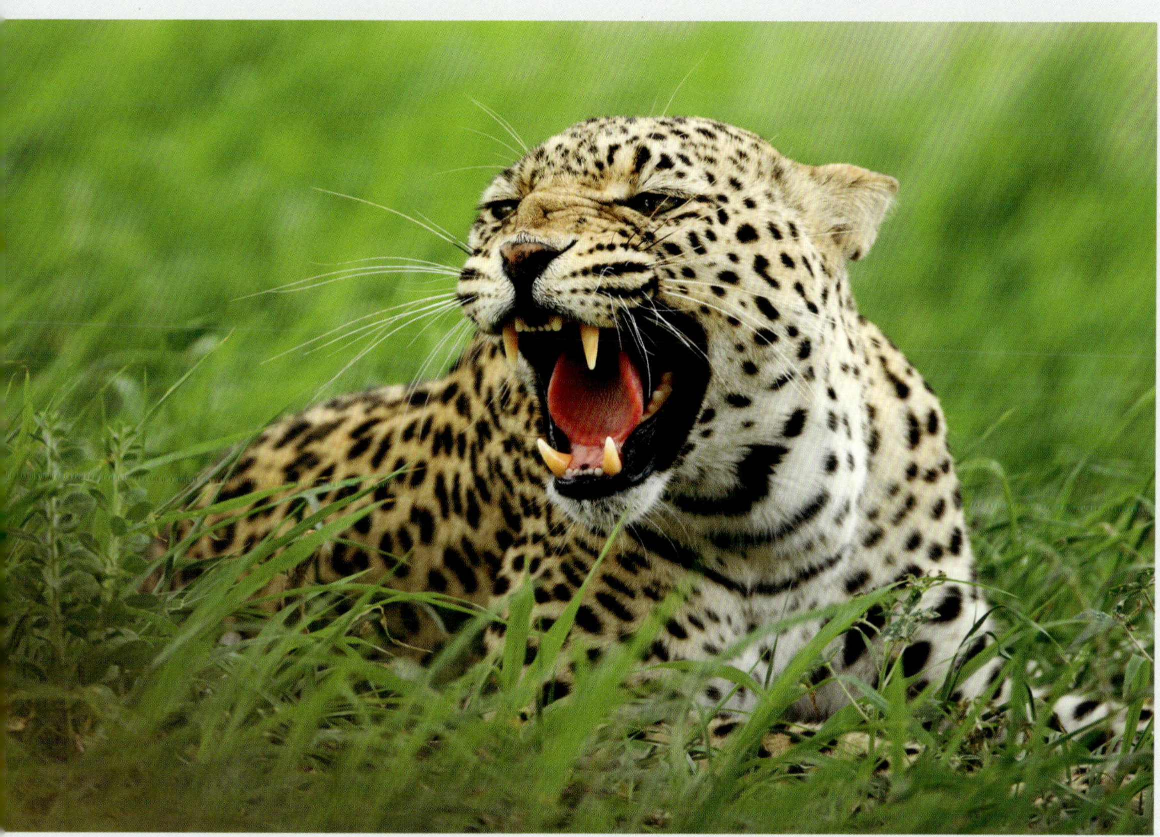

eopard

eón y Leopardo
 rey de los animales es el depredador rrestre más grande de África. Los leones dultos alcanzan una altura de hombros e más de un metro y un peso de casi 30 kg. Sin embargo, las leonas más elicadas hacen la mayor parte de la caza. os tímidos leopardos nocturnos están uy extendidos, pero rara vez se les ve n la naturaleza. Tienen un gran sentido e la intuición y saben nadar y escalar xtraordinariamente bien. Los leopardos ueden arrastrar a sus presas a los árboles ara protegerlas de otros animales. A ferencia de los leones, los leopardos son olitarios.

Leone e Leopardo
Il re degli animali è il più grande predatore terrestre in Africa. I leoni adulti raggiungono un'altezza spalle di oltre un metro e un peso di quasi 230 kg. Tuttavia, sono le leonesse, di statura decisamente più piccola, a occuparsi della caccia. I leopardi, riservati e notturni, sono sì diffusi, ma raramente avvistati allo stato selvatico. Hanno un ottimo senso del fiuto e possono nuotare e arrampicarsi straordinariamente bene. I leopardi sono in grado di trascinare le loro prede sugli alberi per tenere lontano gli altri animali. A differenza dei leoni, i leopardi sono solitari.

Leeuw en luipaard
De koning van de dieren is het grootste roofdier van Afrika. Volwassen leeuwen bereiken een schouderhoogte van ruim een meter en een gewicht van bijna 230 kilo. De fijner gebouwde leeuwinnen nemen het grootste deel van de jacht op zich. De verlegen, 's nachts actieve luipaarden zijn weliswaar wijdverspreid, maar worden in het wild zelden waargenomen. Ze hebben een zeer goed ontwikkelde speurzin en kunnen buitengewoon goed zwemmen en klimmen. Luipaarden kunnen hun prooi de boom in slepen om hem uit de buurt van andere dieren te houden. In tegenstelling tot leeuwen zijn luipaarden solisten.

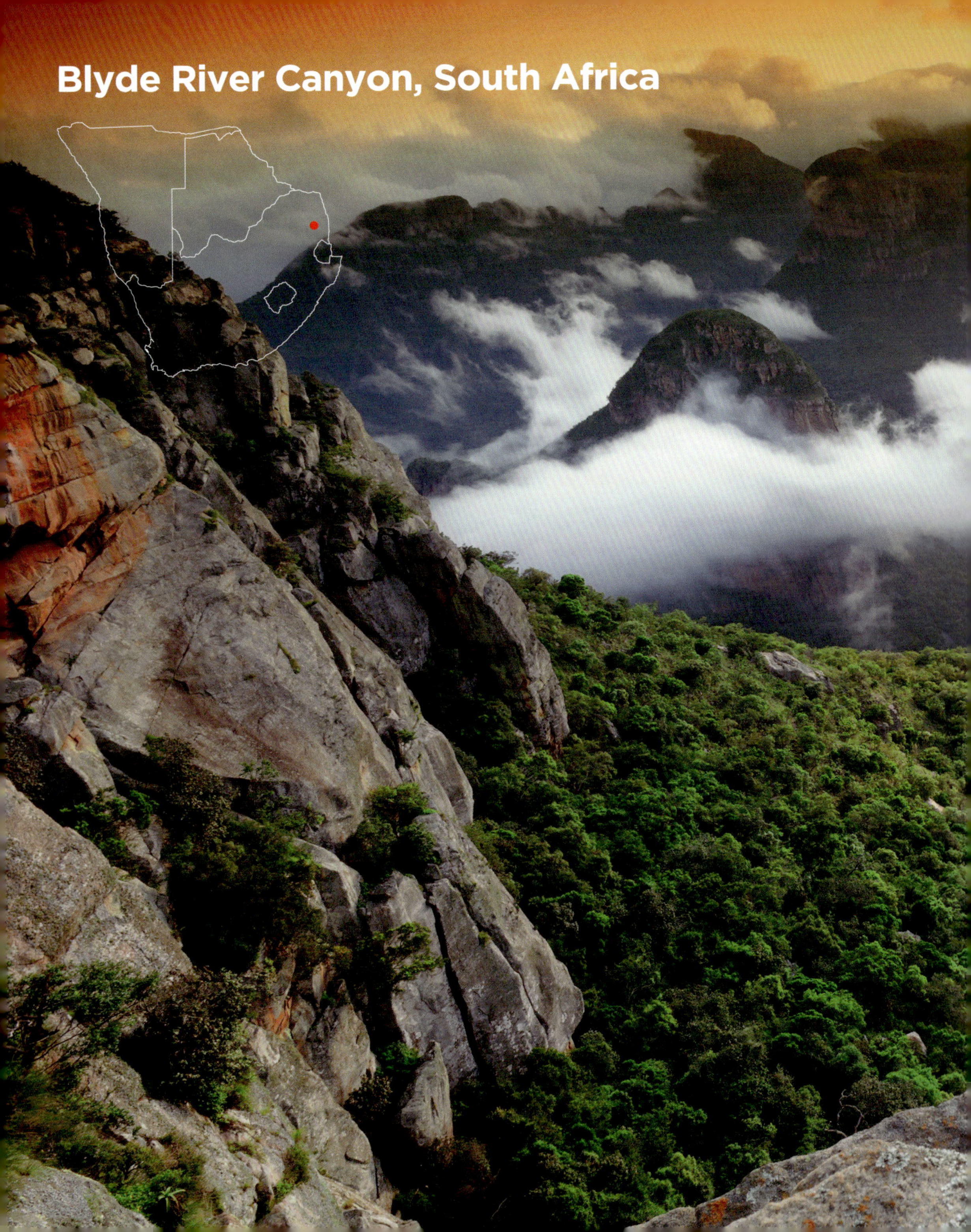
Blyde River Canyon, South Africa

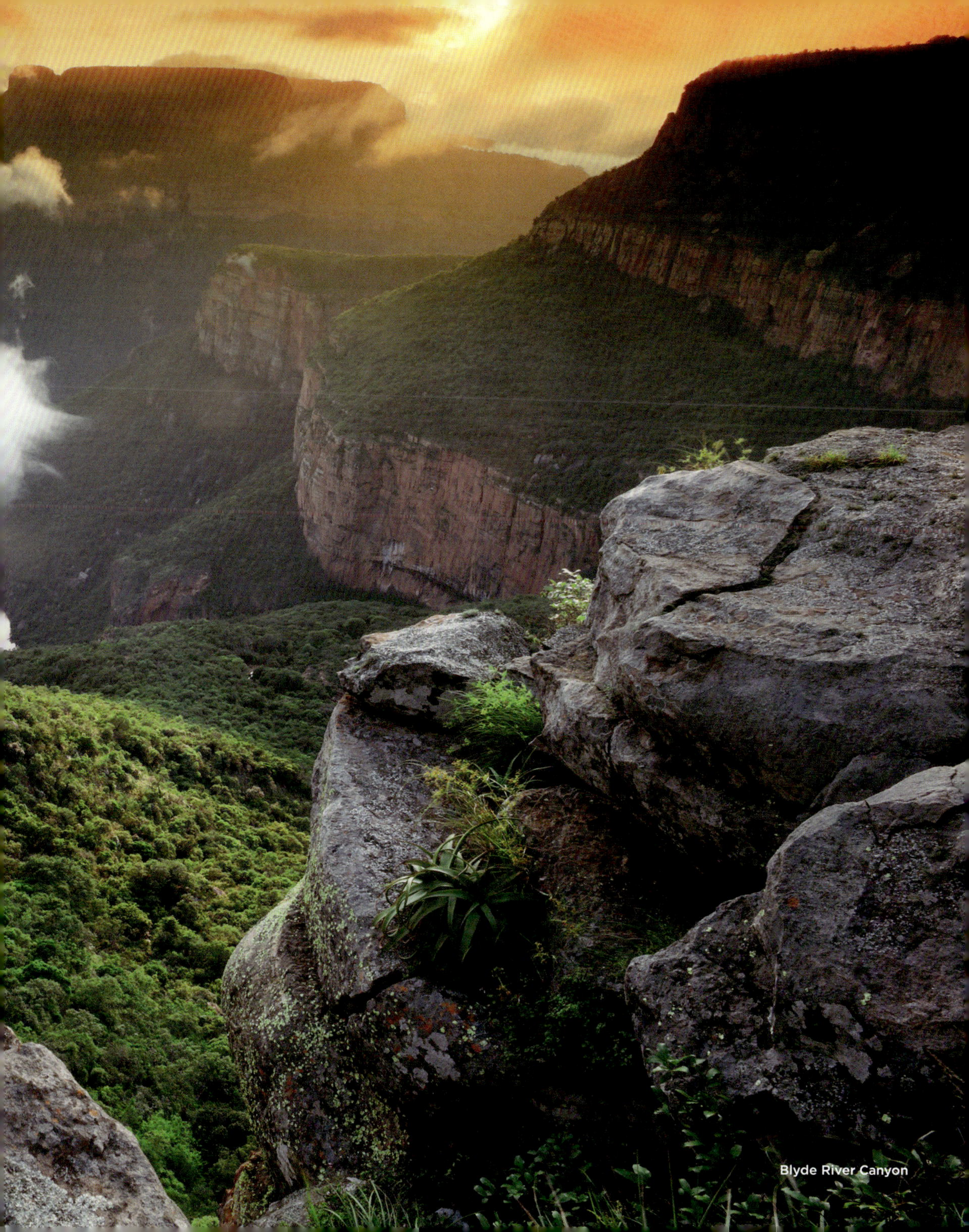
Blyde River Canyon

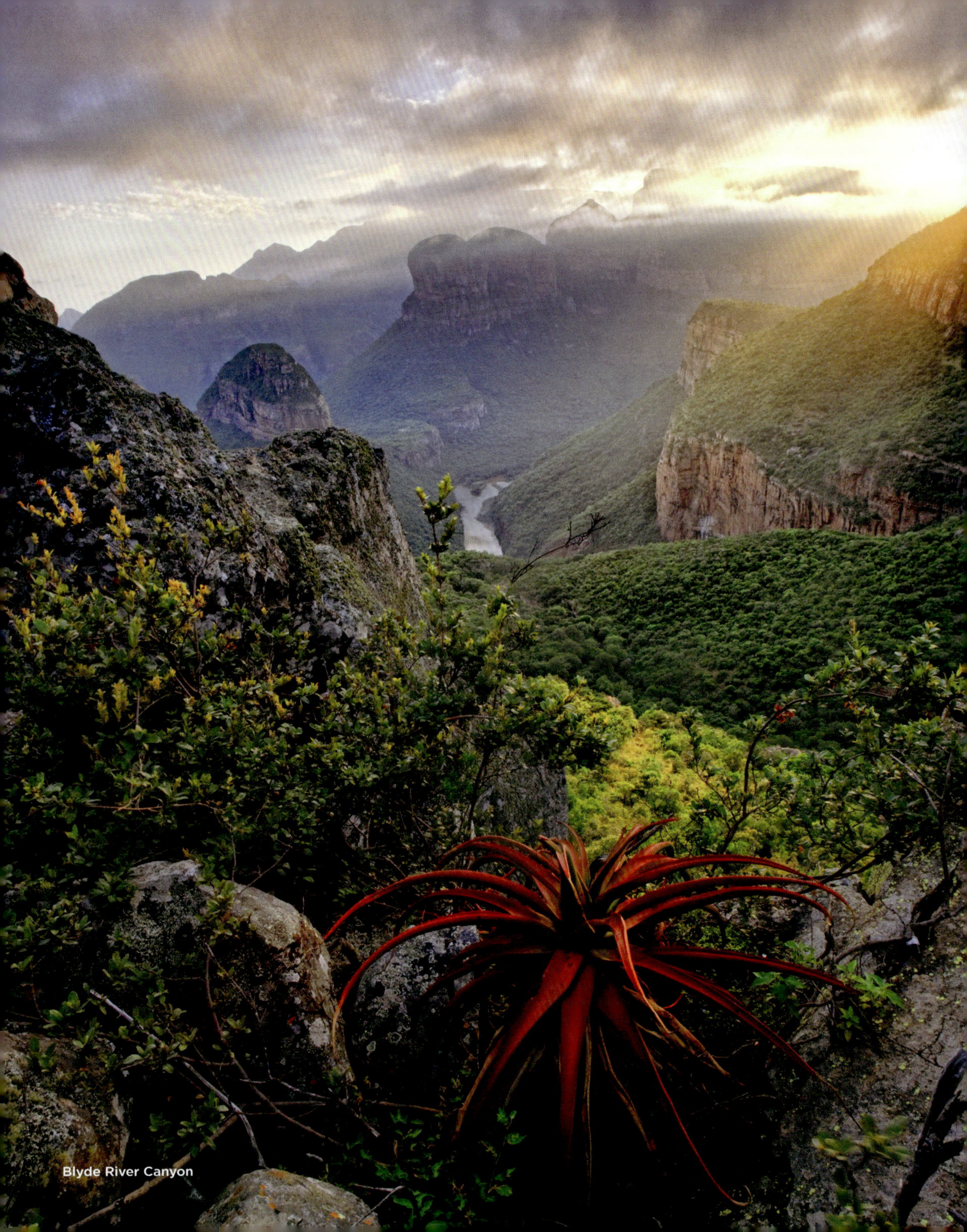

Blyde River Canyon

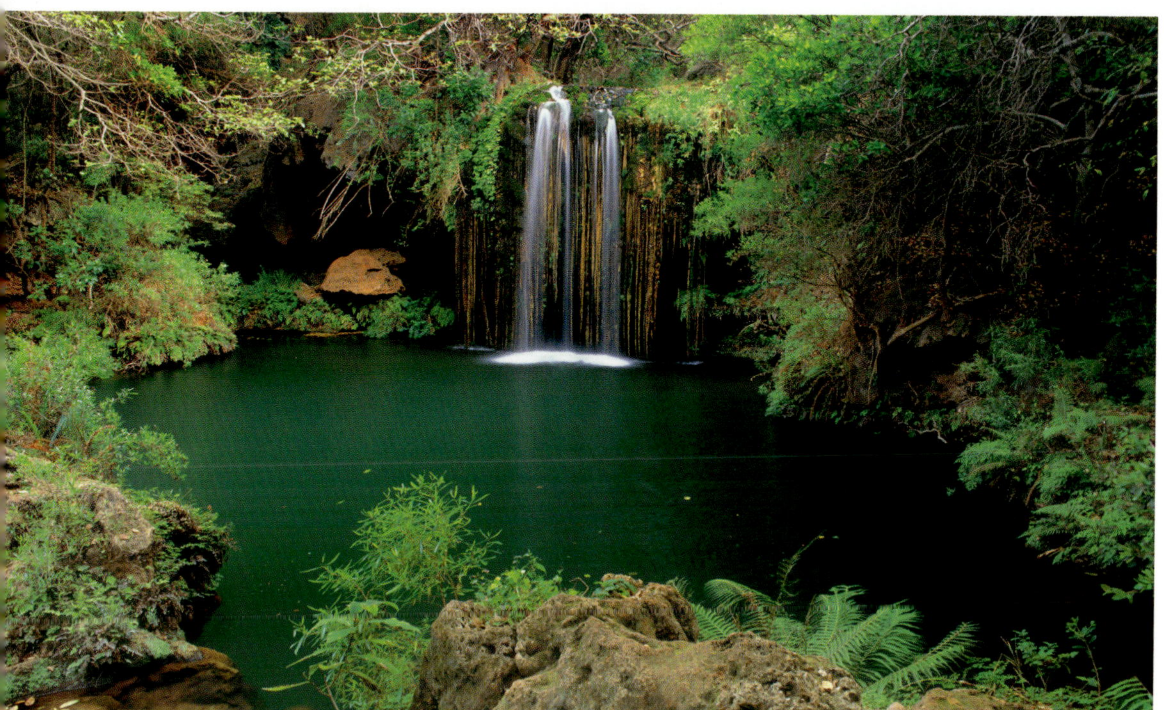

'yde River Canyon

lyde River Canyon
yde River Canyon may be "only" the ird-largest canyon in the world, but it is far the greenest of the big three. The rand Canyon in the US and Fish River anyon in Namibia are larger, but they ature barren rock. This South African anyon is overlaid with greenery, its flanks vered by vegetation. The gigantic gorge 26 km (16 mi) long and up to 800 m 625 ft) deep.

Blyde River Canyon
Der Blyde River Canyon ist zwar „nur" der drittgrößte Canyon der Welt, aber als „grüner Canyon" schafft er Platz eins: Während die vor ihm Platzierten – der Grand Canyon (USA) und der Fish River Canyon (Namibia) – schieren Fels zeigen, liegt der südafrikanische Canyon in Grün gebettet, seine Flanken sind von Vegetation bedeckt. Die gigantische Schlucht ist 26 km lang und bis zu 800 m tief.

Blyde River Canyon
Il Blyde River Canyon è "solo" il terzo canyon più grande del mondo, ma come "canyon verde" si piazza al primo posto: mentre i due canyon che sono ai primi posti, il Grand Canyon (USA) e il Fish River Canyon (Namibia), sono pura roccia, il canyon sudafricano è immerso nel verde e i suoi fianchi sono coperti di vegetazione. La gigantesca gola è lunga 26 km e profonda fino a 800 m.

Blyde River Canyon
Blyde River Canyon, certes, n'est que le oisième canyon du monde par la taille, ais le premier des « canyons verts ». les deux premiers du classement, le rand Canyon du Colorado (États-Unis) les gorges de la Fish River (Namibie) montrent que des murailles nues, ur homologue sud-africain est installé ns une coulée verte et ses parois sont pissées de végétation. Cette gorge gantesque s'étire sur 26 km et atteint une ofondeur de 800 m.

Cañón del río Blyde
Aunque el río Blyde es "sólo" el tercer cañón más grande del mundo, como "cañón verde" ocupa la primera plaza: mientras que los que están situado antes que él – el Gran Cañón (EE.UU.) y el Cañón del río Fish (Namibia) – muestran roca pura , el Cañón de Sudáfrica está enterrado en el verde, sus flancos están cubiertos de vegetación. La garganta gigantesca tiene 26 km de largo y hasta 800 m de profundidad.

Blyde River Canyon
De Blyde River Canyon is "slechts" het op twee na grootste ravijn ter wereld, maar als "groene canyon" staat hij op de eerste plek. Terwijl de twee grotere ravijnen – de Grand Canyon (VS) en de Fish River Canyon (Namibië) – uit kale rotsen bestaan, hult de Zuid-Afrikaanse kloof zich in weelderig groen en zijn de hellingen hier met vegetatie bedekt. De gigantische kloof is 26 km lang en tot wel 800 m diep.

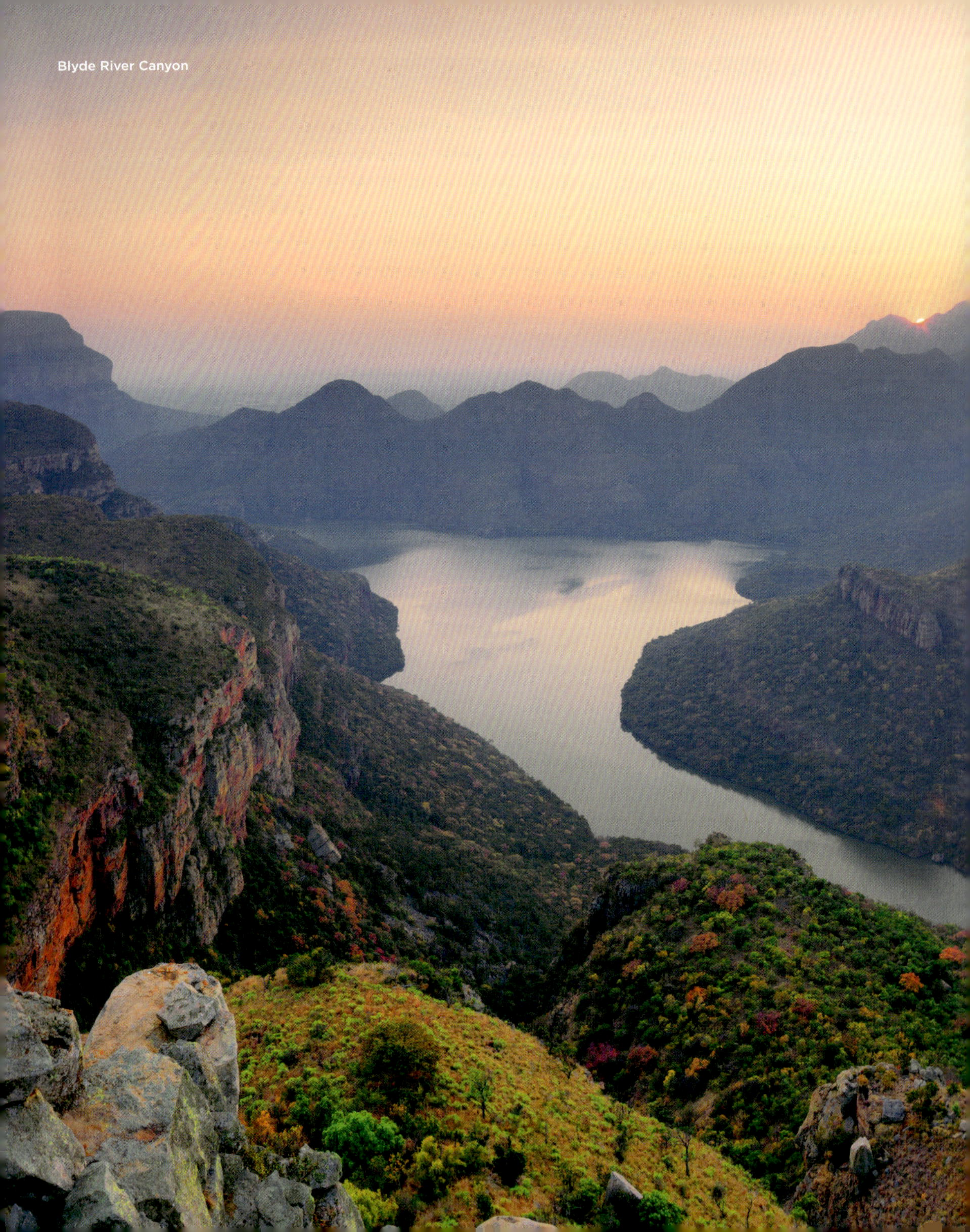
Blyde River Canyon

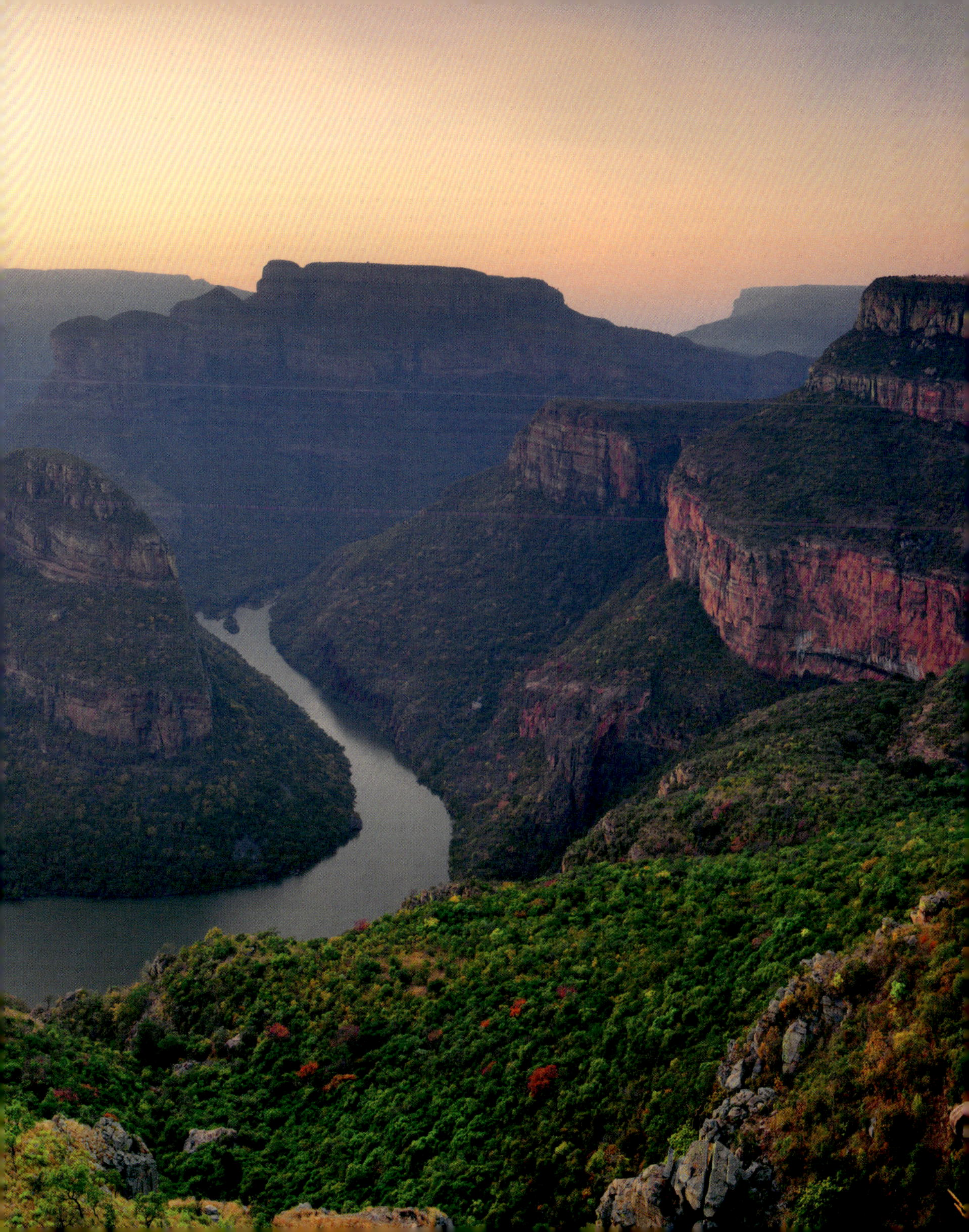

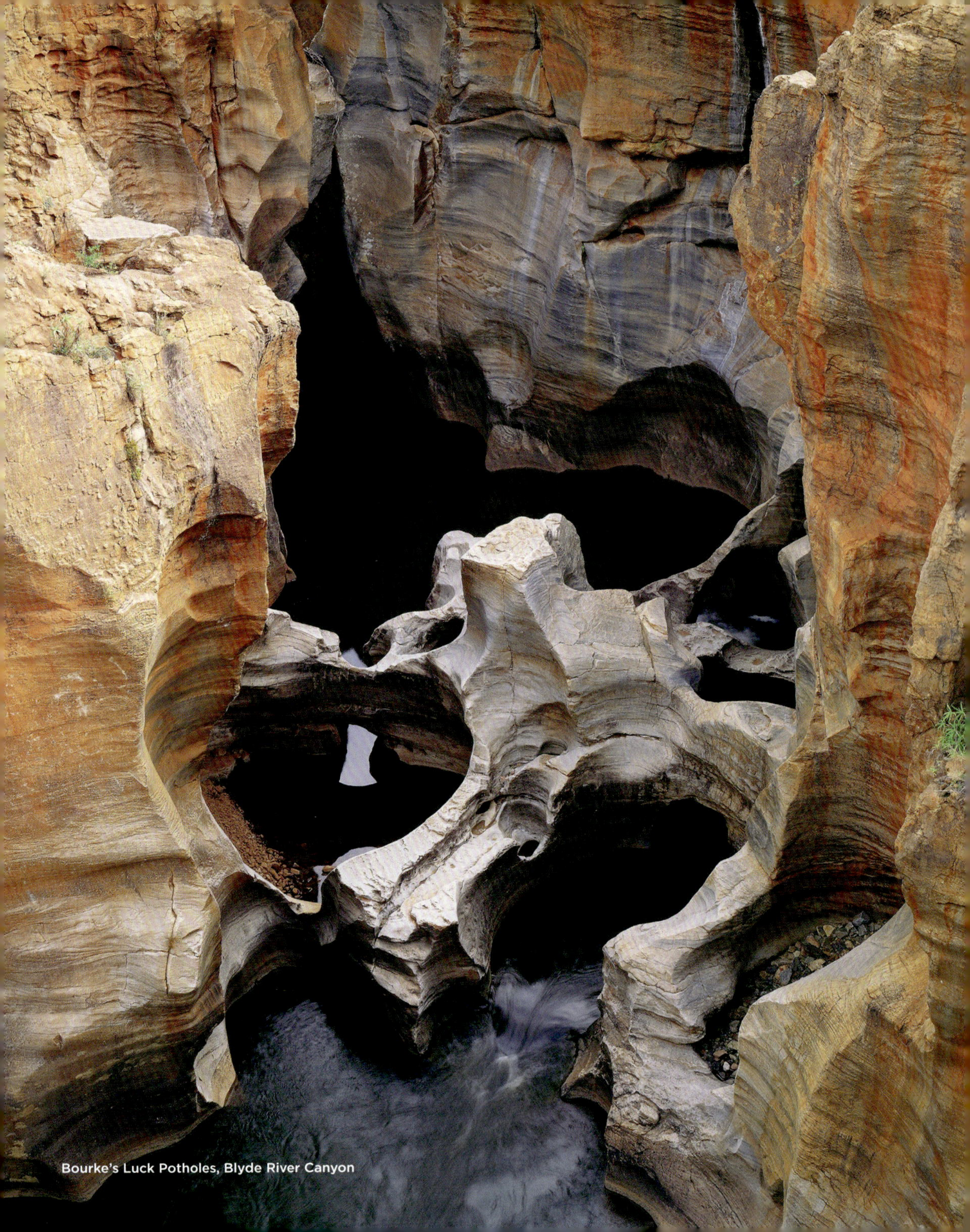

Bourke's Luck Potholes, Blyde River Canyon

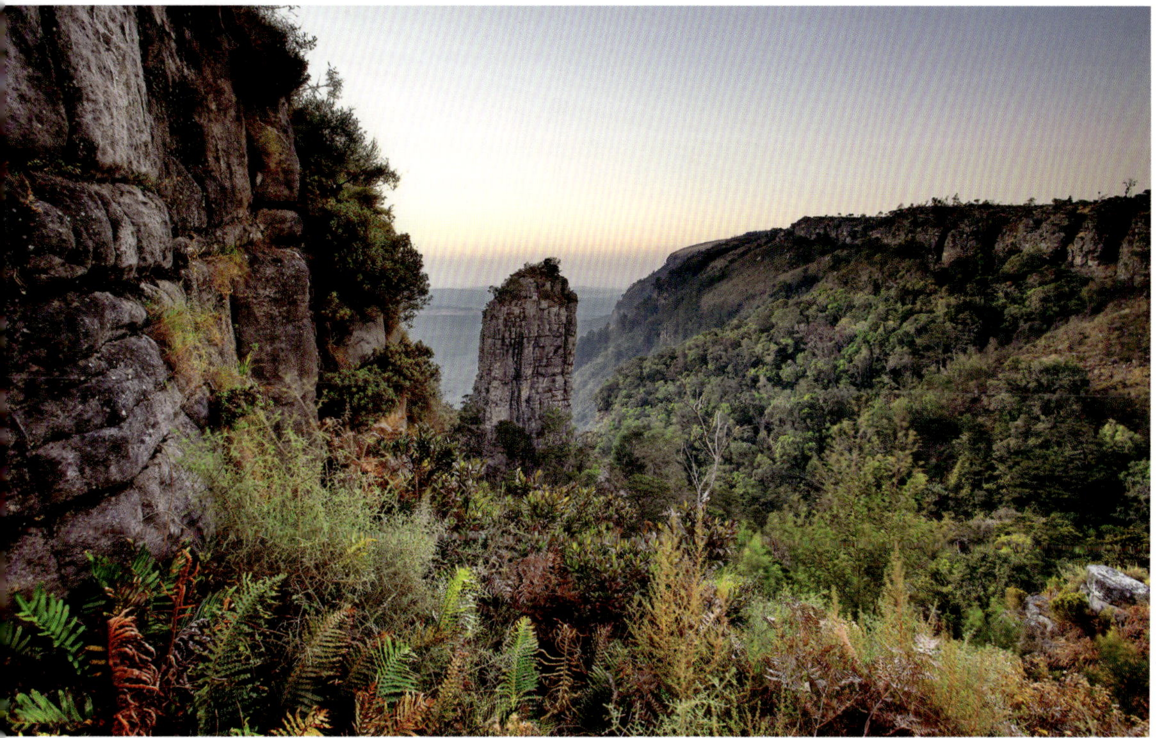

nnacle Rock, Blyde River Canyon

ourke's Luck Potholes
here the Treur River flows into the yde River, the water has created its own asterpiece: Bourke's Luck Potholes. The lindrical erosion patterns in the rock ere caused by the whirlpool action of e water and the debris caught up in e vortex.

Bourke's Luck Potholes
Wo der Treur River in den Blyde River fließt, hat das Wasser ein ausgefallenes Werk geschaffen: die Bourke's Luck Potholes. Diese zylinderförmigen Auswaschungen im Gestein entstanden durch die Strudelbewegungen des Wassers. Geröll, das in die Wirbel gerät, unterstützt die Erosion.

Bourke's Luck Potholes
Dove il fiume Treur si getta nel Blyde, l'acqua ha creato un'opera stravagante: i Bourke's Luck Potholes. Queste erosioni nella roccia di forma cilindrica si formarono a causa dei movimenti a turbine dell'acqua. I detriti che finivano nel vortice provocarono l'erosione.

s Bourke's Luck Potholes
l'endroit où la rivière Treur se jette dans Blyde, l'eau a sculpté dans la roche étonnantes cuvettes, les Bourke's Luck otholes. Ses tourbillons ont façonné ces lindres par érosion, avec l'aide des galets traînés par les remous.

Bourke's Luck Potholes
Donde el río Treur desemboca en el río Blyde, el agua ha creado una obra inusual: Bourke's Luck Potholes. Estas formas cilíndricas erosionadas surgieron en la roca a través del movimiento de vórtice del agua. Las rocas que se meten en el remolino apoyan la erosión.

Bourke's Luck Potholes
Waar de rivier de Treur in de rivier de Blyde stroomt, heeft het water een bizar kunstwerk geschapen: de Bourke's Luck Potholes. Deze cilindervormige uitslijtingen in het gesteente zijn ontstaan door waterkolken. Het gruis dat in deze draaikolken terechtkomt, fungeert als schuurpapier.

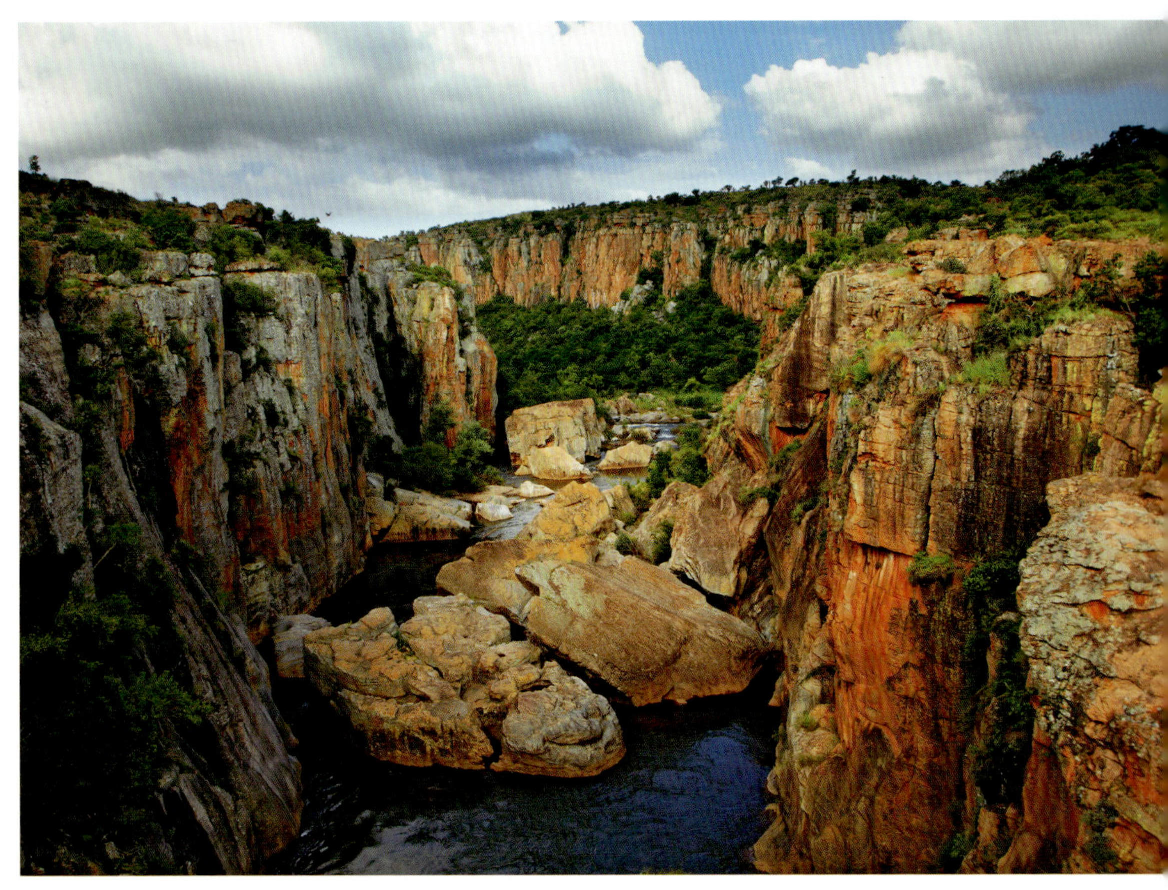

Blyde River Canyon

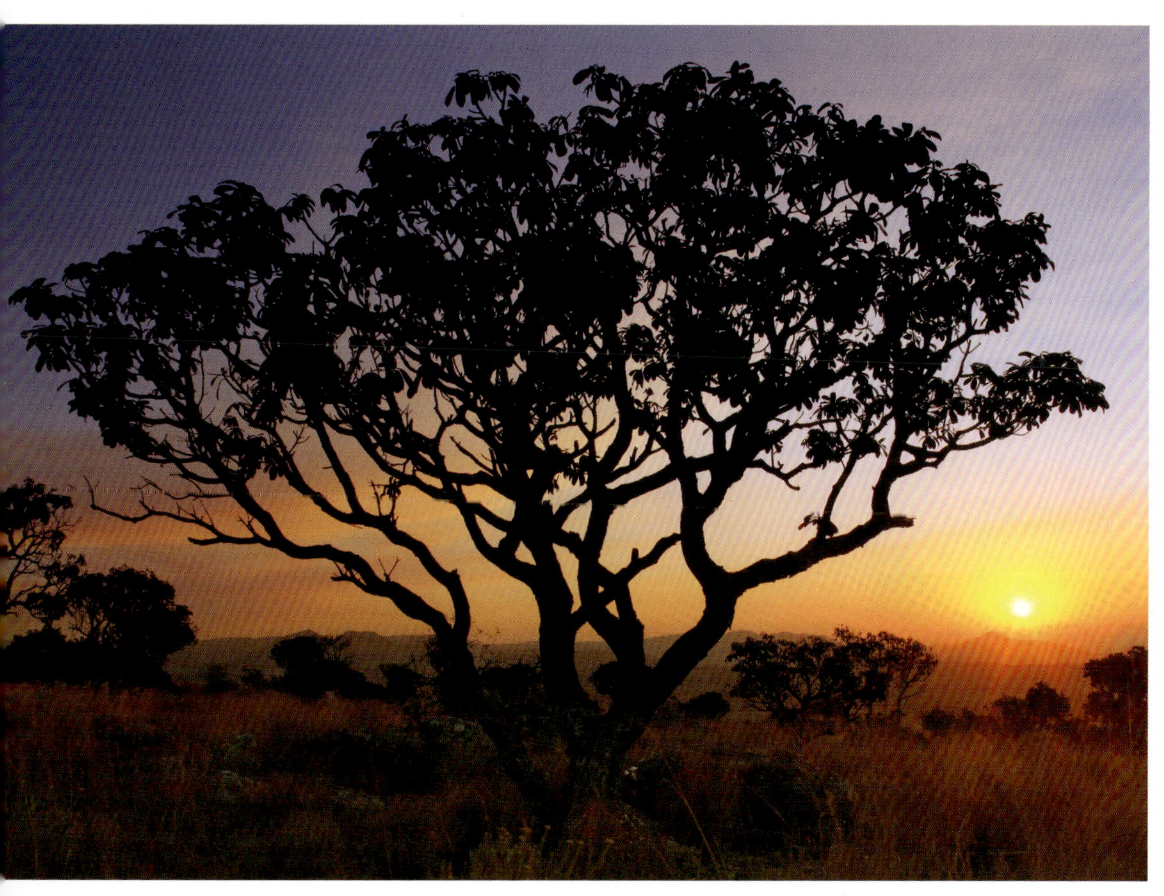

ɩyde River Canyon

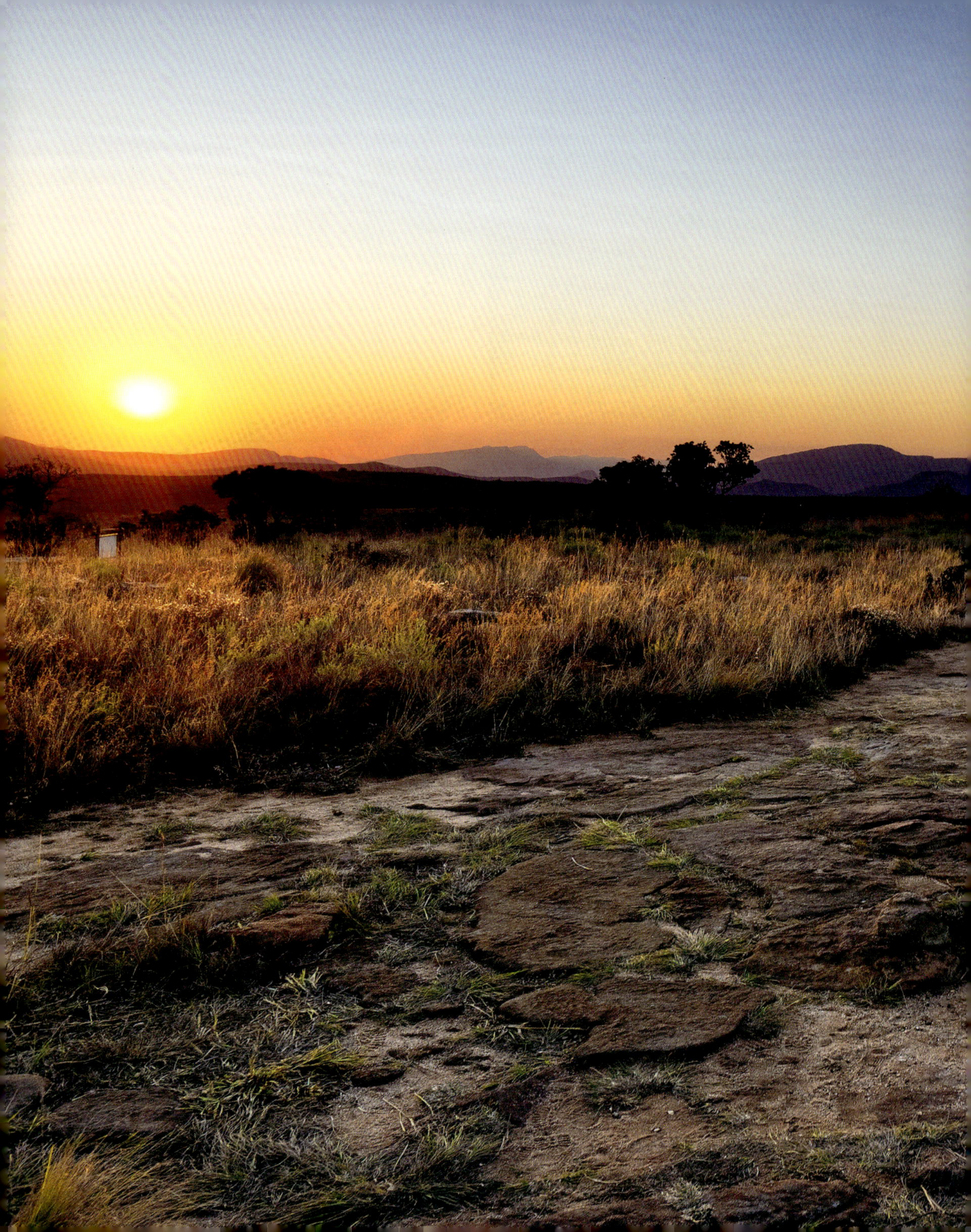

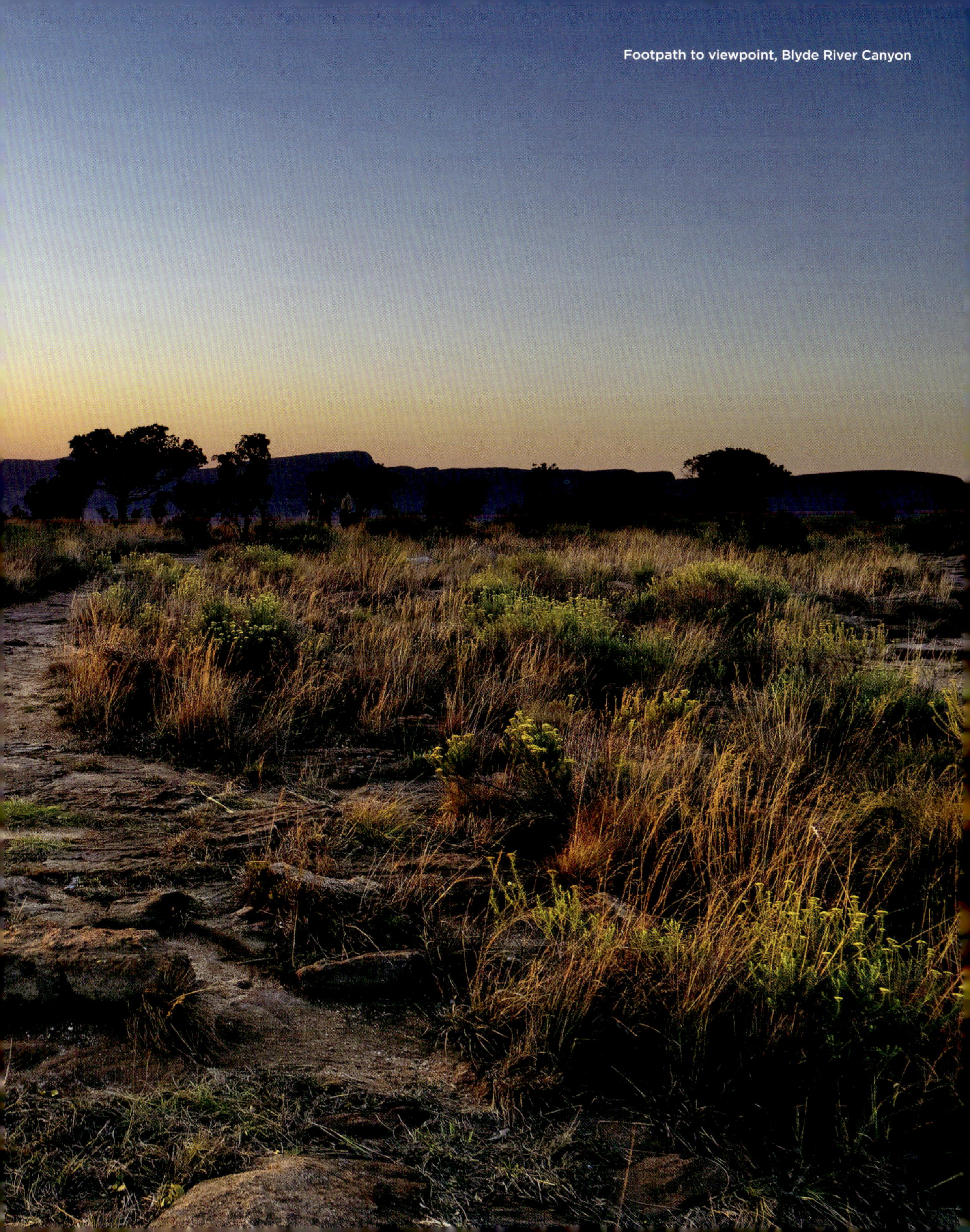

Footpath to viewpoint, Blyde River Canyon

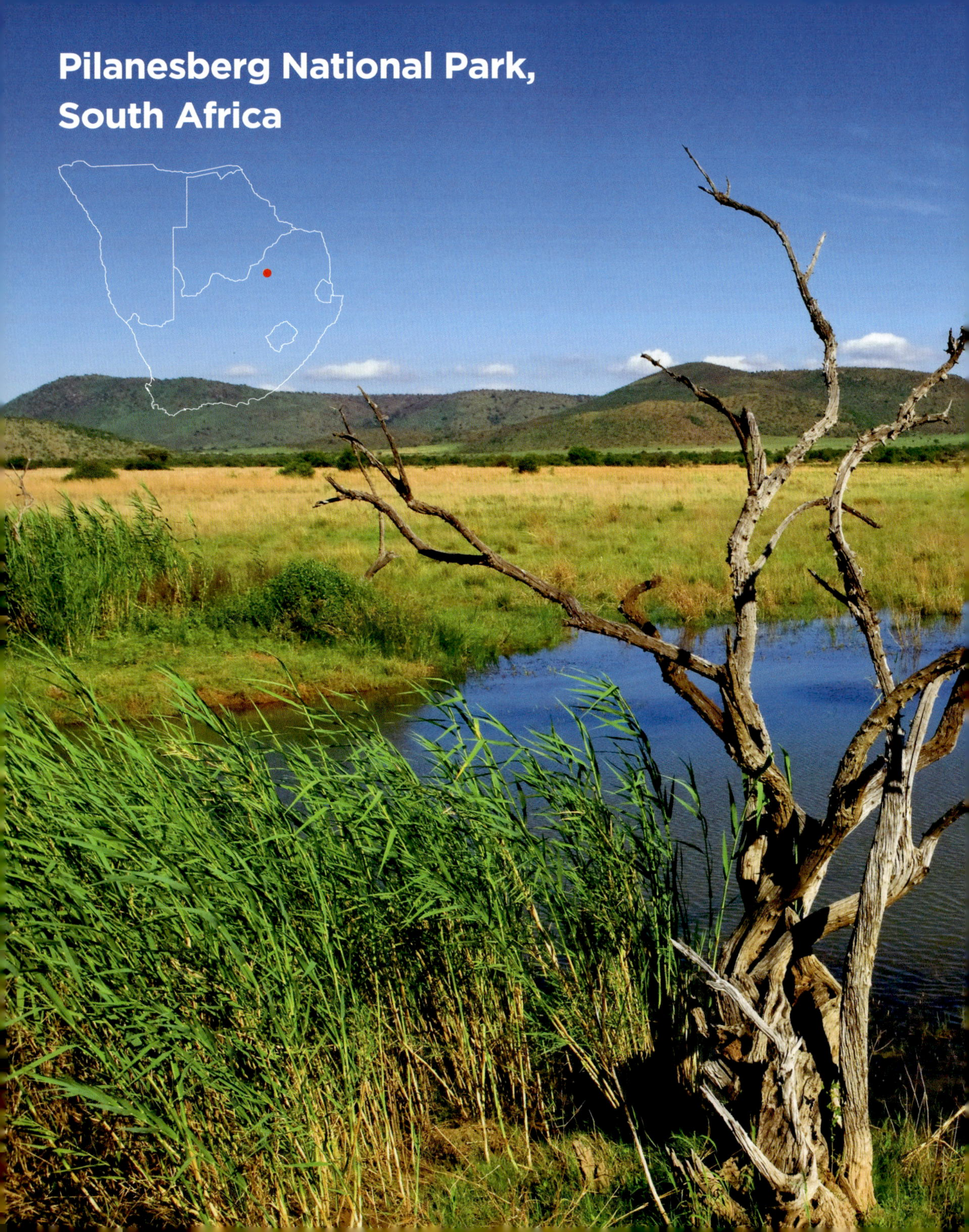
Pilanesberg National Park,
South Africa

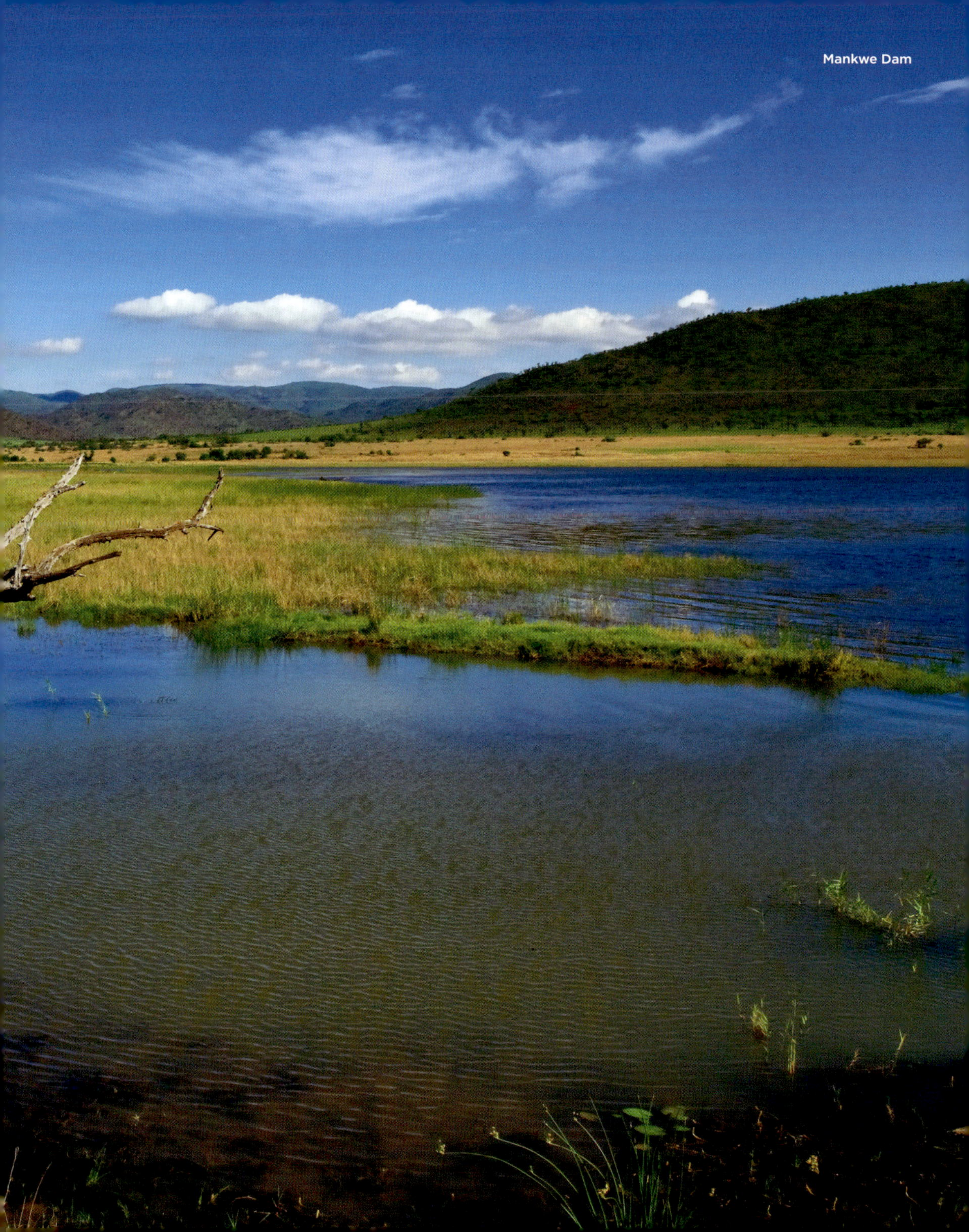
Mankwe Dam

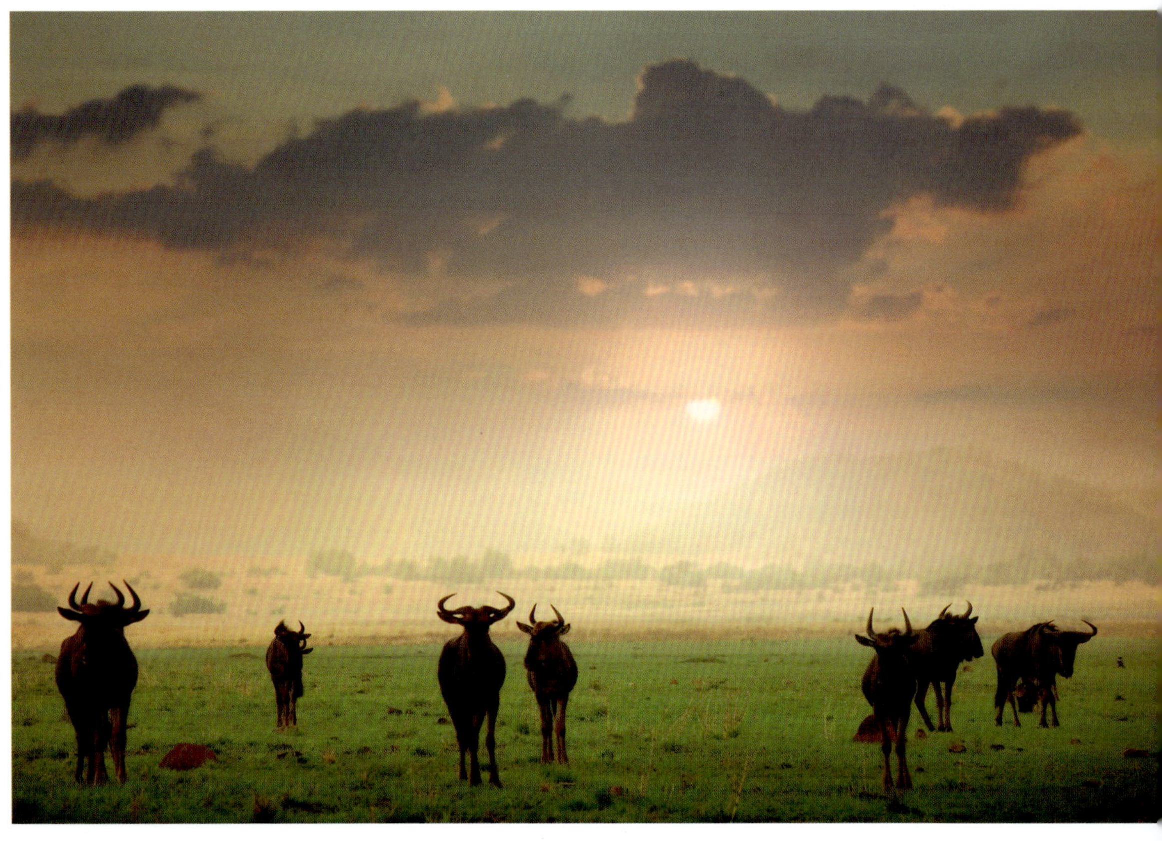

Gnus, Pilanesberg National Park

Pilanesberg National Park
The centre of Pilanesberg National Park is a volcanic crater dating back 1.2 billion years. The park in the North West Province of South Africa is located in the transition zone between the thornbush savanna of the Kalahari and the subtropical plateau of the Lowveld. This makes this park home to an especially diverse range of flora and fauna.

Le parc national du Pilanesberg
Un cratère daté de 1200 millions d'années marque le centre du parc national du Pilanesberg. Le parc, situé dans la province sud-africaine du Nord-Ouest, se trouve à la lisière entre la savane épineuse du Kalahari et le plateau subtropical du Lowveld. Sa flore et sa faune sont par conséquent abondantes et variées.

Pilanesberg-Nationalpark
Das Zentrum des Pilanesberg-Nationalparks bildet ein 1200 Millionen Jahre alter Vulkankrater. Der Park in der Nordwest-Provinz Südafrikas liegt in der Übergangszone zwischen der Dornbuschsavanne der Kalahari und dem subtropischen Plateau Lowveld. Flora und Fauna sind entsprechend divers und vielfältig.

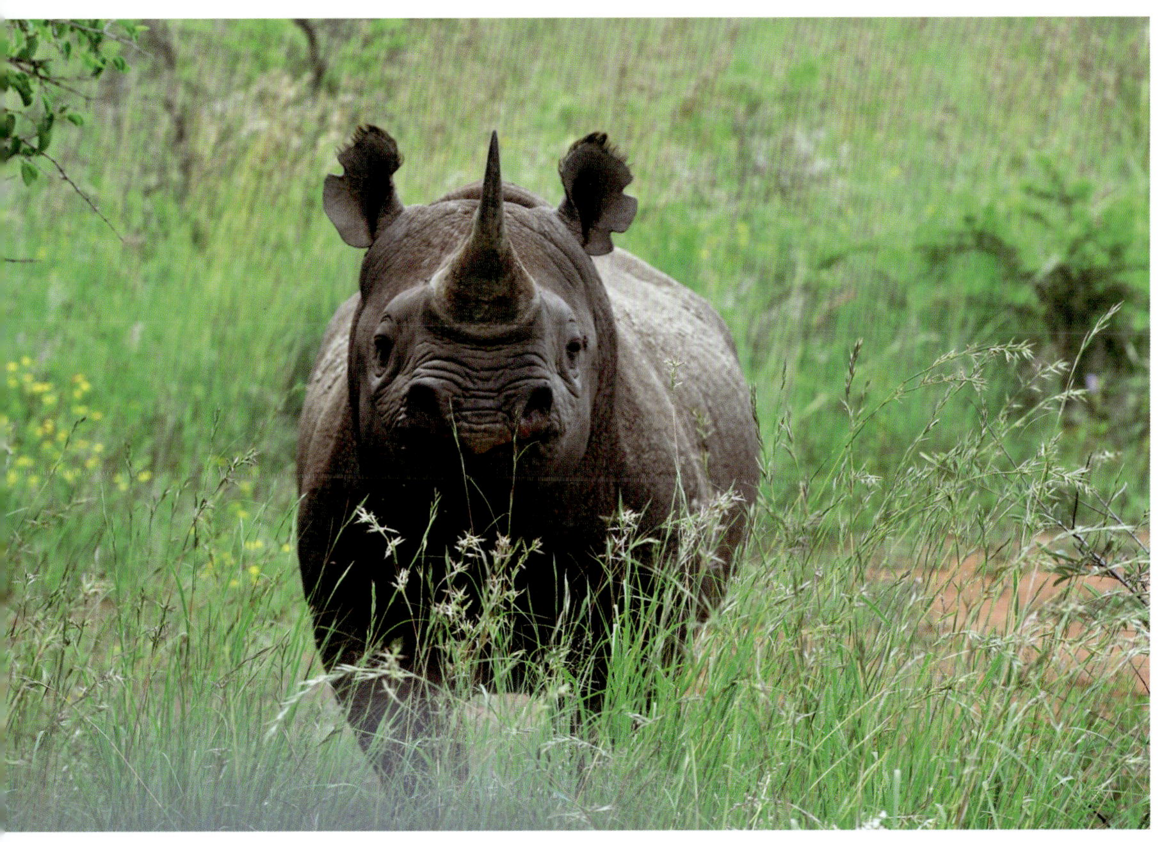

ɿinoceros, Pilanesberg National Park

ırque Nacional Pilanesberg
centro del Parque Nacional de lanesberg es un cráter volcánico de unos ꞉00 millones de años de antigüedad. parque en la provincia del noroeste ꞉ Sudáfrica se encuentra en la zona de ansición entre los montes de sabana del ılahari y la meseta Lowveld subtropical. ı flora y la fauna son por tanto diversas variadas.

Parco Nazionale di Pilanesberg
Un cratere vulcanico di 1200 milioni di anni costituisce il centro del Parco Nazionale di Pilanesberg. Il parco nella provincia nord-ovest del Sudafrica si trova nella zona di passaggio tra la savana di arbusti spinosi del Kalahari e l'altopiano subtropicale di Lowveld. Di conseguenza la flora e la fauna sono diverse e variegate.

Nationale Park Pilanesberg
Het hart van het Nationale Park Pilanesberg wordt gevormd door een 1,2 miljard jaar oude vulkaankrater. Het park in de Zuid-Afrikaanse provincie Noordwest ligt in de overgangszone tussen de doornstruiksavanne van de Kalahari en het subtropische plateau Laagveld. De flora en fauna hier zijn hier dan ook zeer veelzijdig.

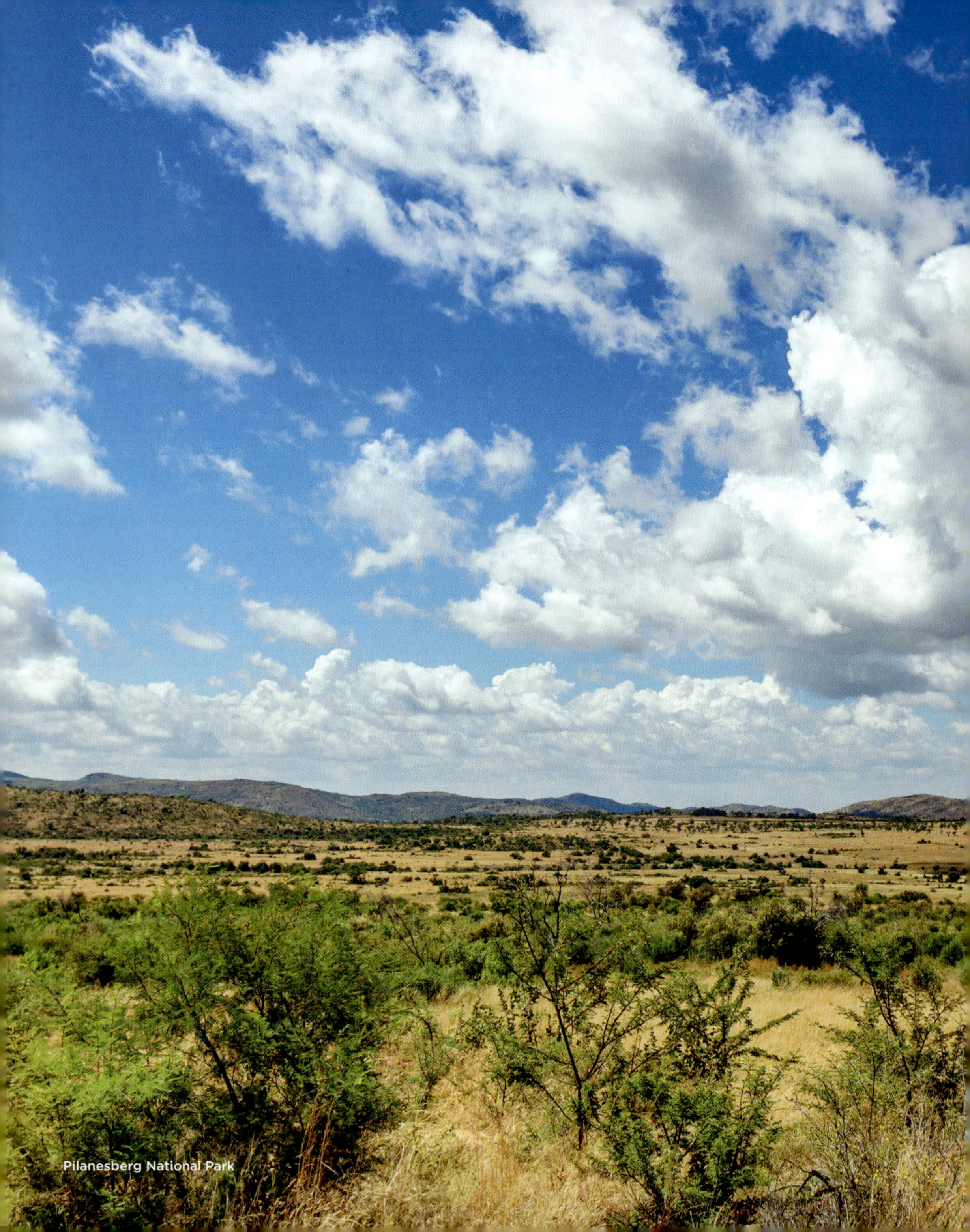

Pilanesberg National Park

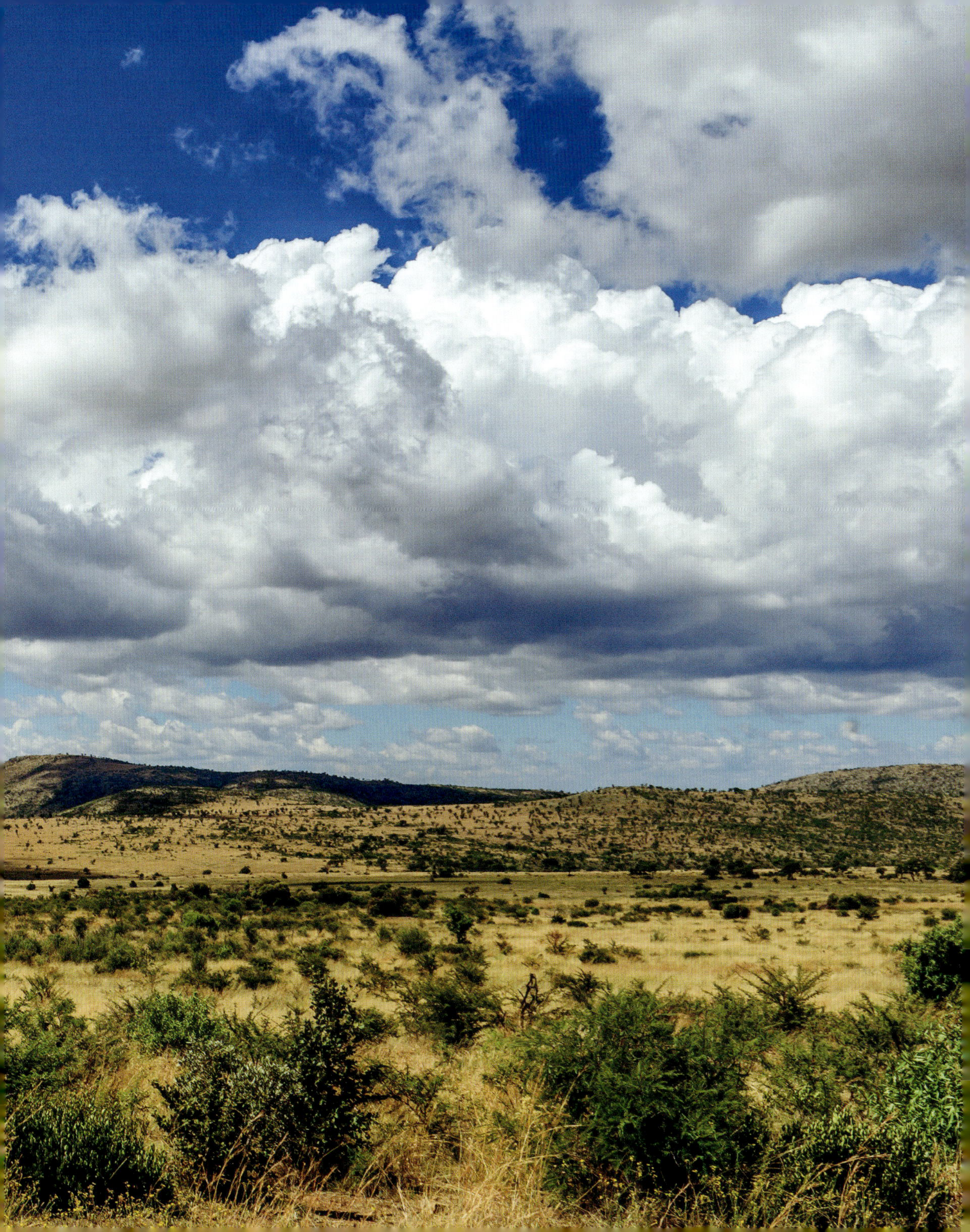

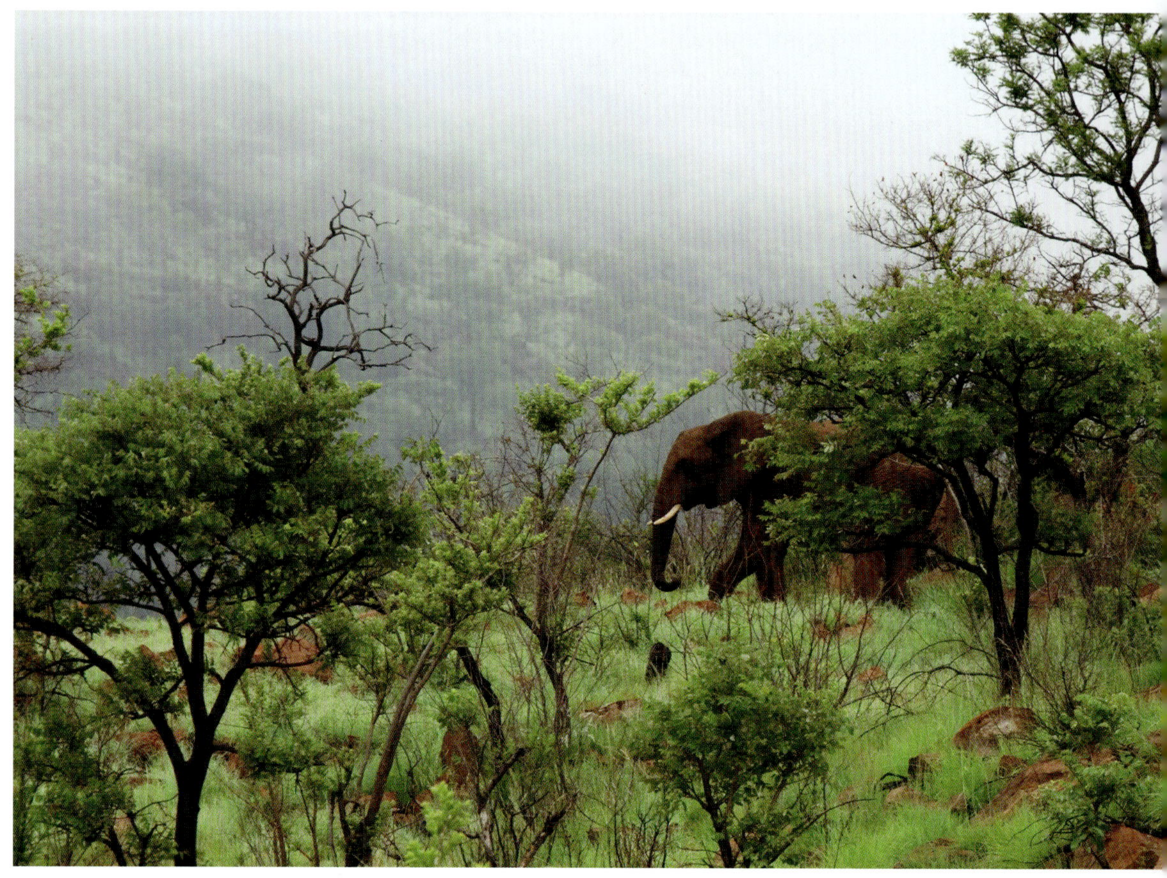

Elephant, Pilanesberg National Park

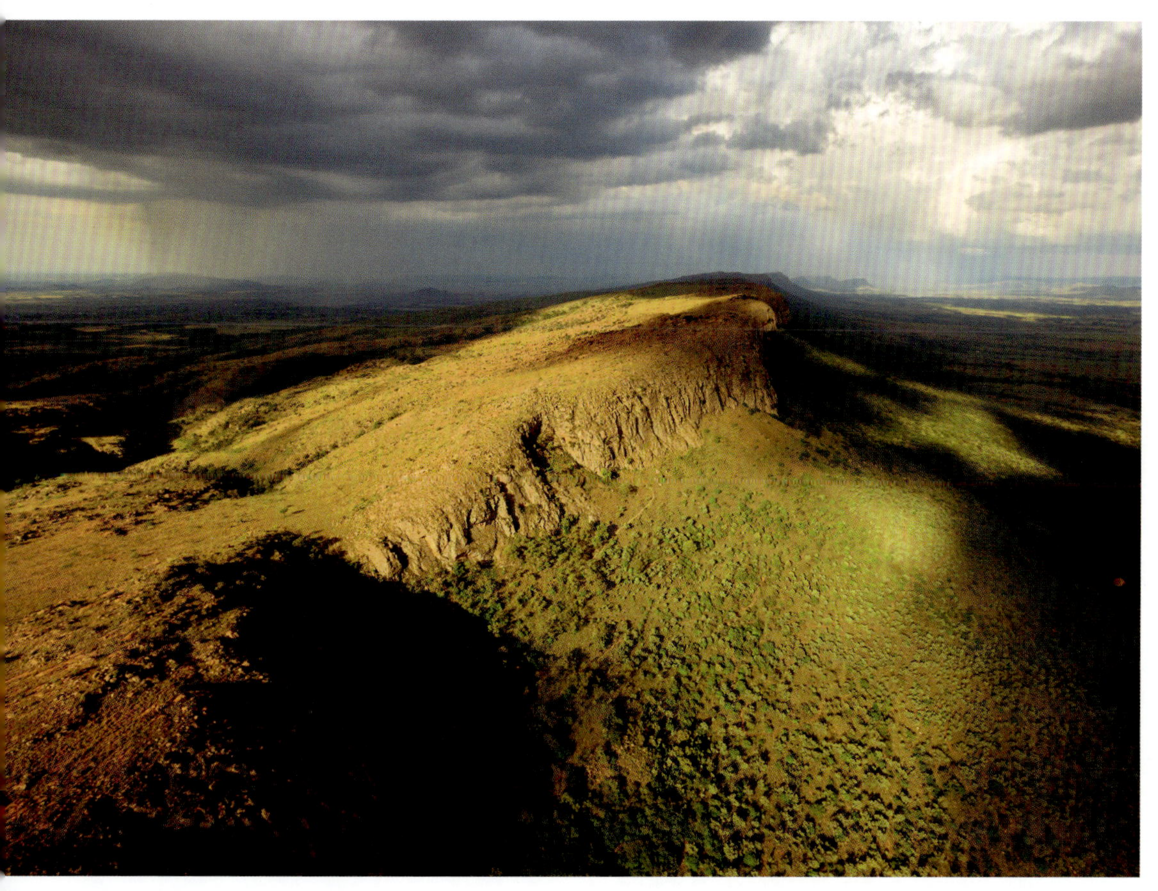

agaliesburg Mountains (1853 m · 6079 ft)

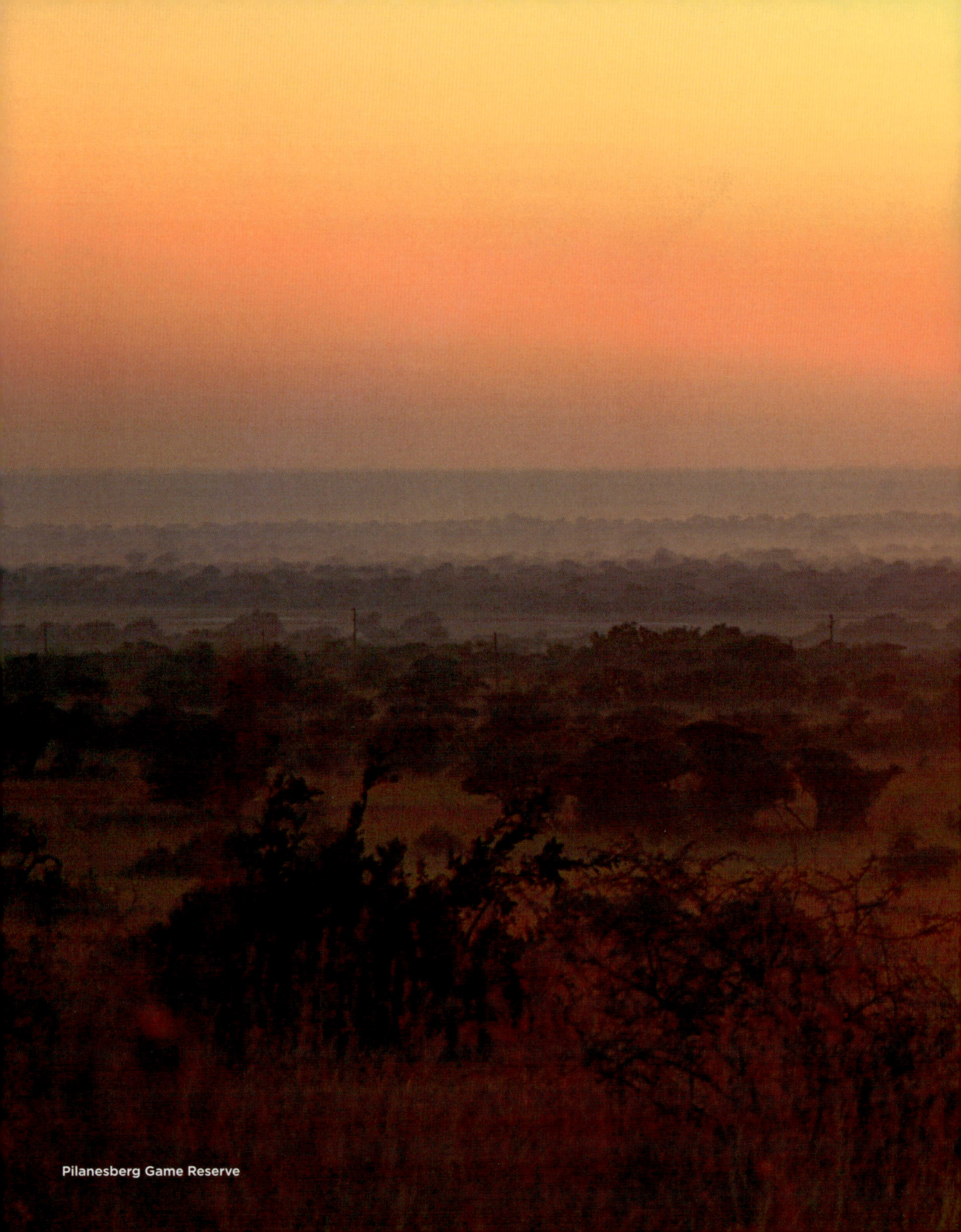

Pilanesberg Game Reserve

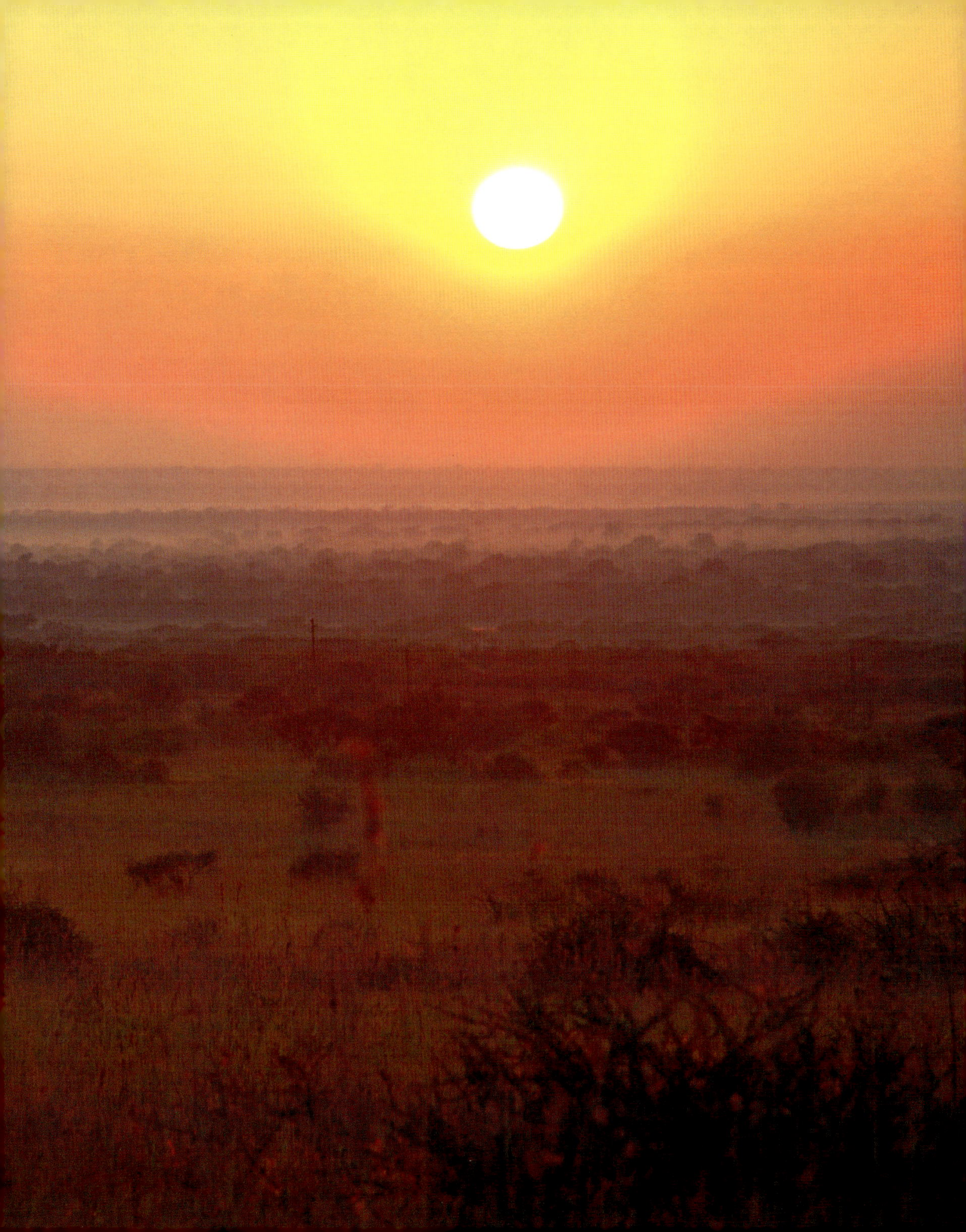

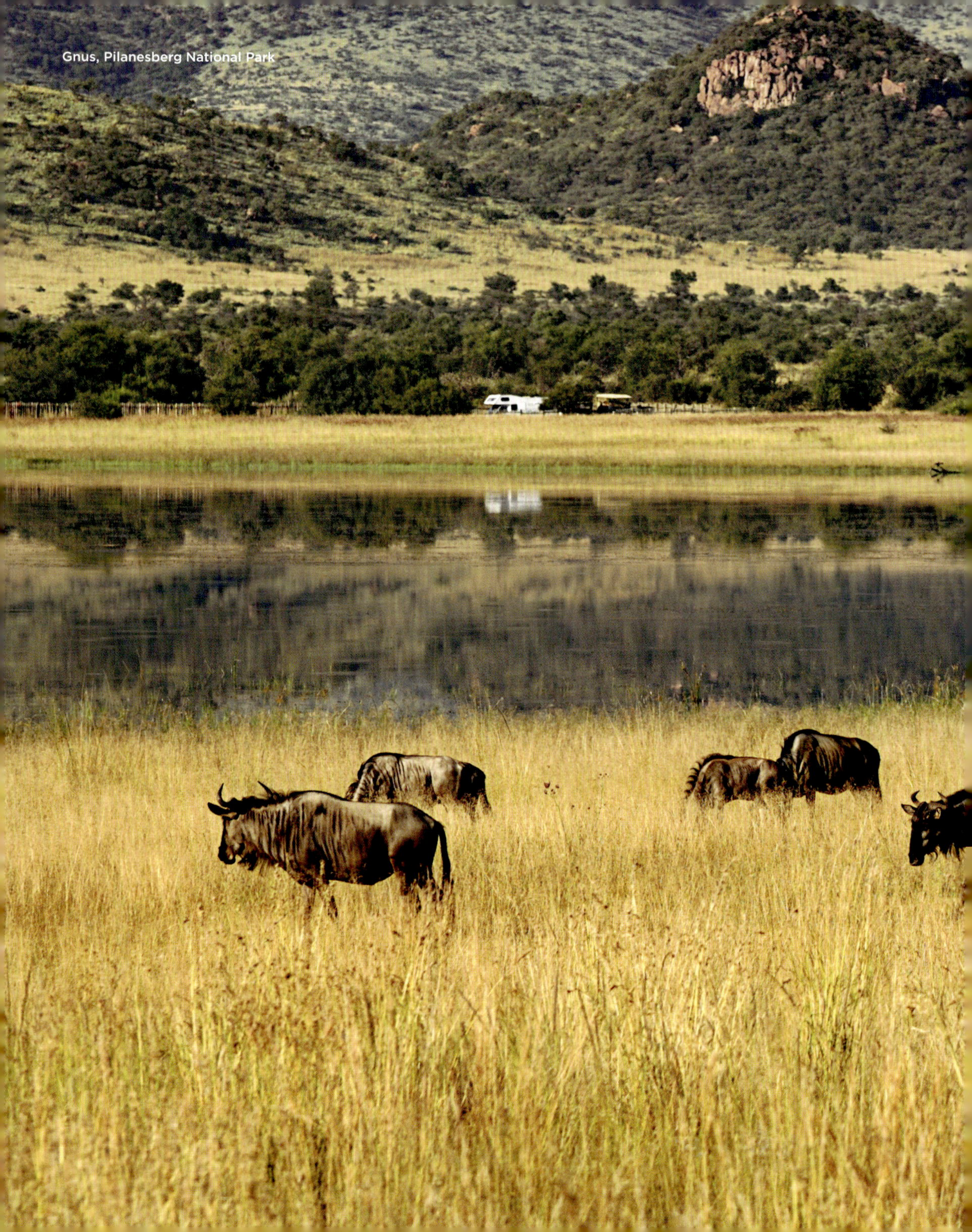

Gnus, Pilanesberg National Park

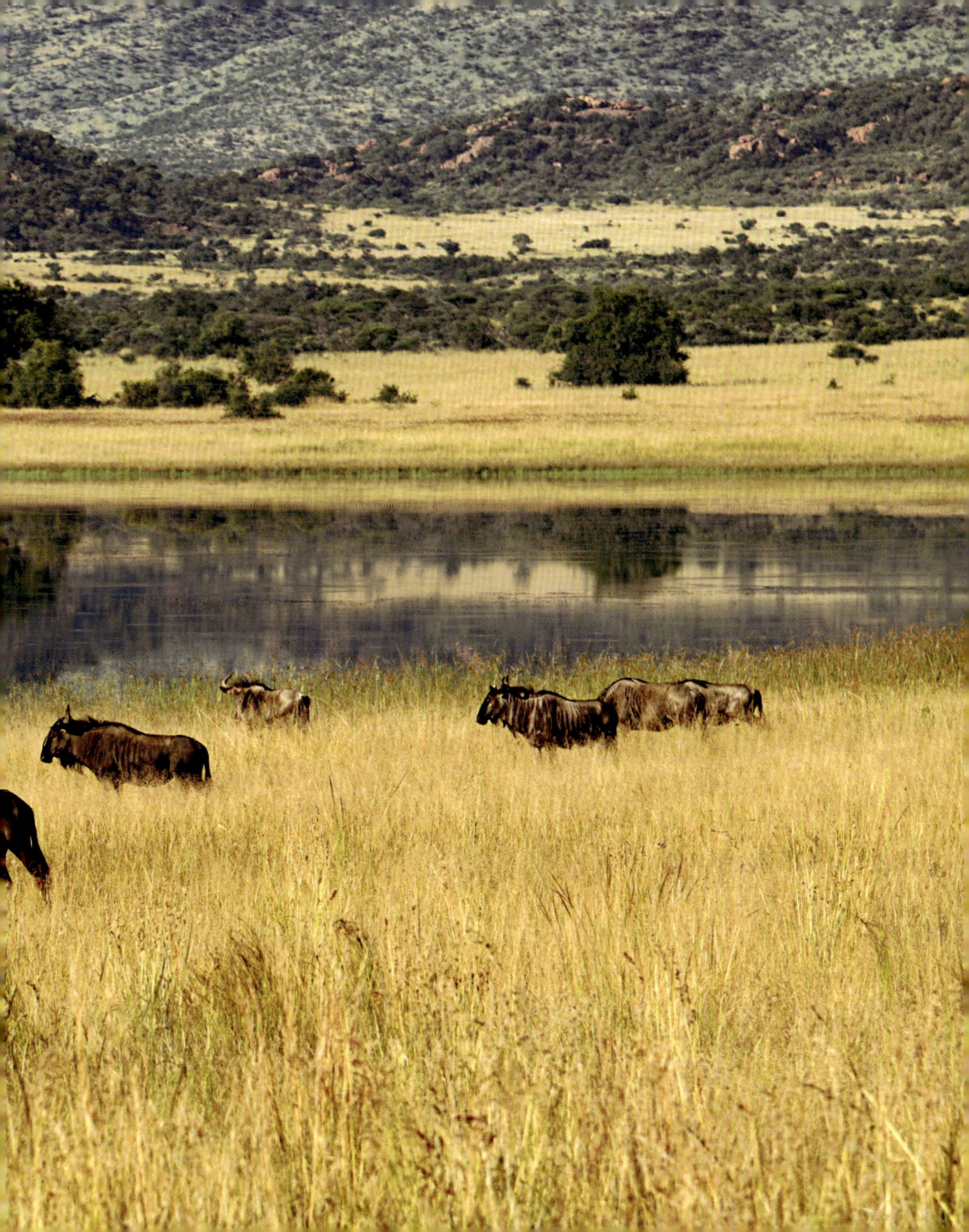

Johannesburg & Pretoria, South Africa

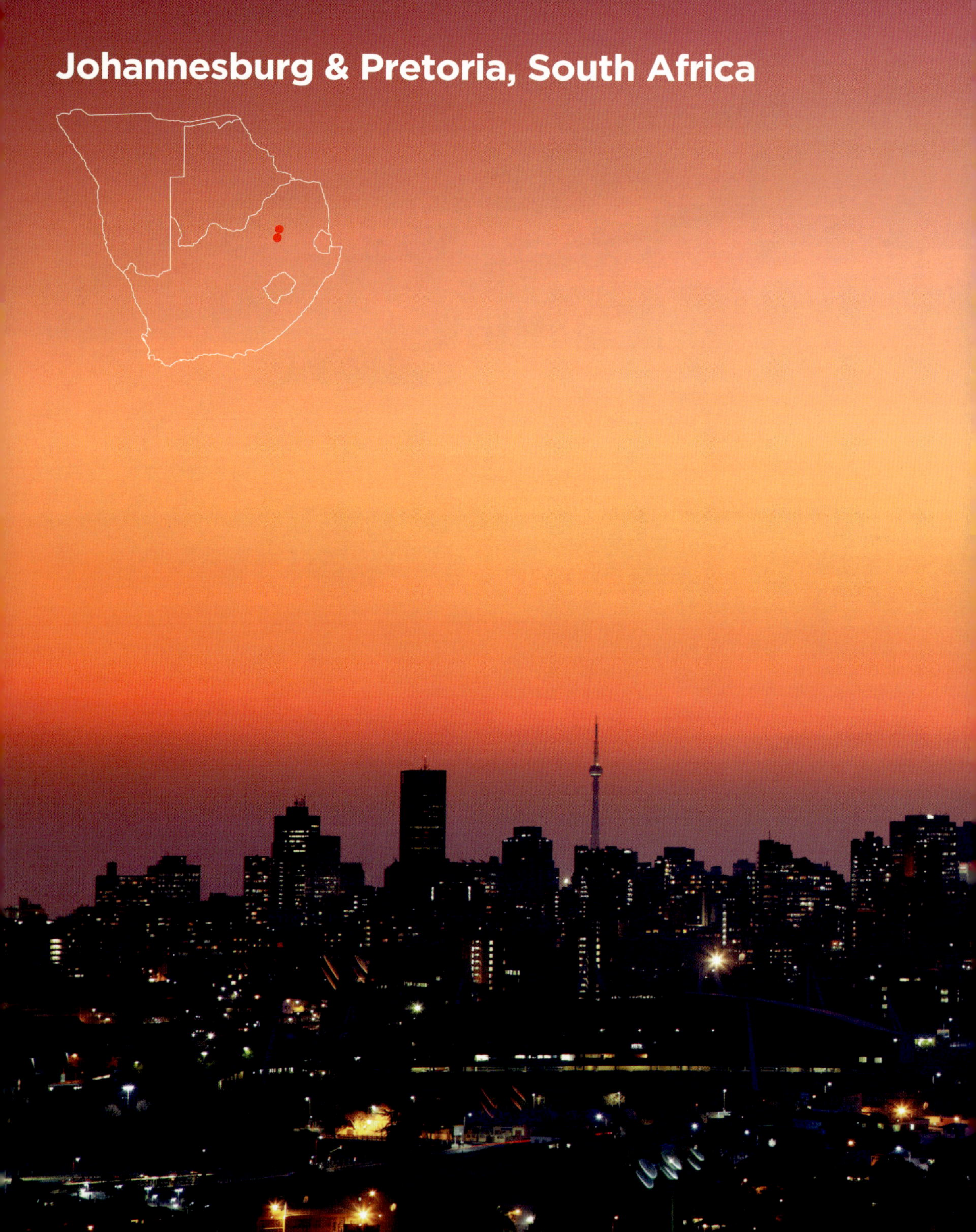

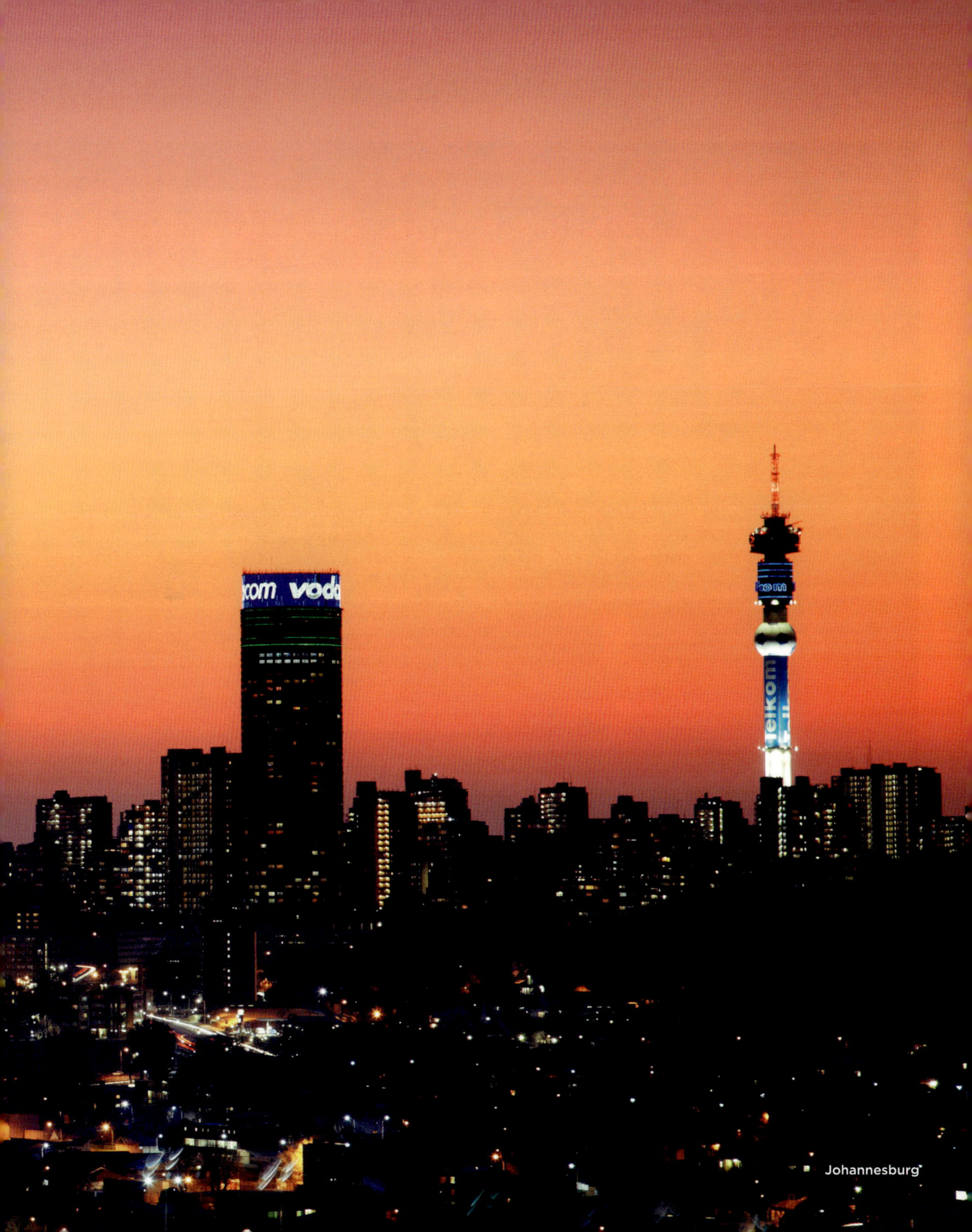

Johannesburg

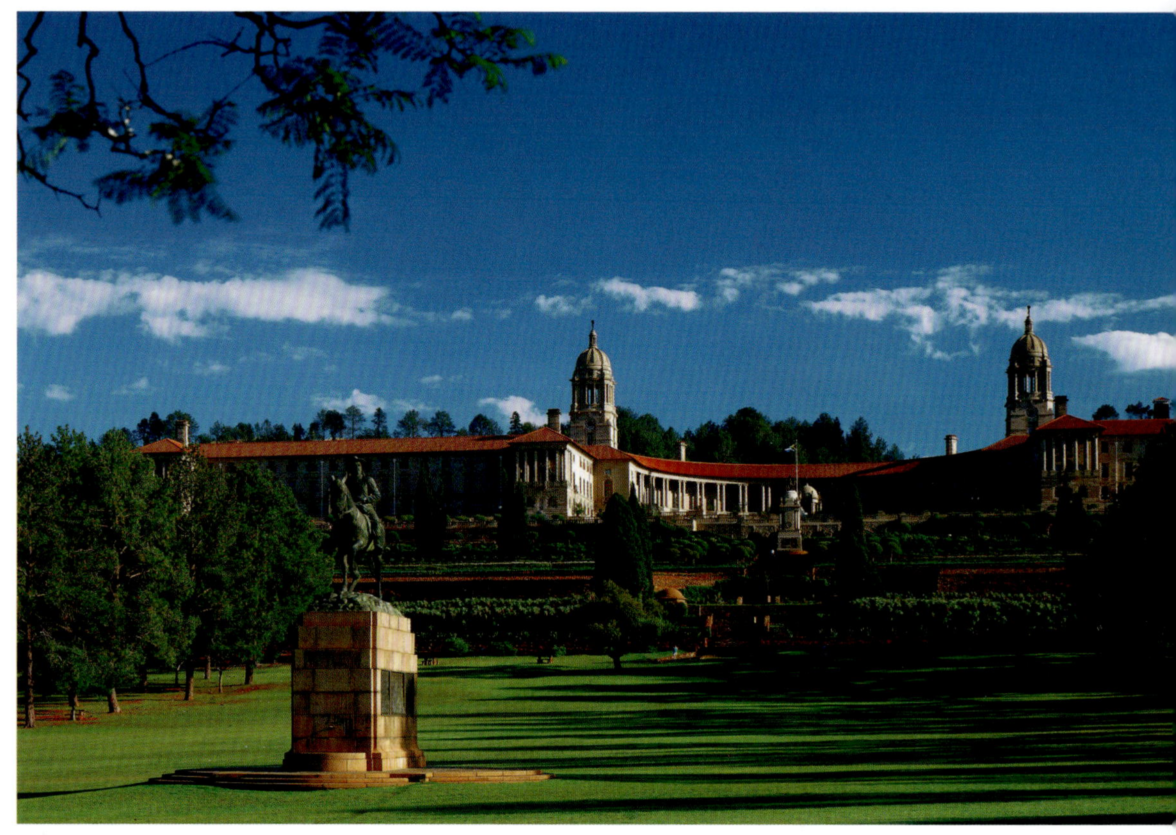

Union Building, Pretoria

Johannesburg and Pretoria
Johannesburg is the third largest city on the African continent, after Cairo and Alexandria. Originally, discoveries of gold deposits propelled the city to a boom towards the end of the 19th century. Pretoria, South Africa's capital, seems a bit more tranquil but still has much to offer, with spacious parks and magnificent colonial buildings around Union Square, as well as modern skyscrapers in the futuristic centre.

Johannesburg et Pretoria
Johannesburg est la troisième plus grande ville du continent africain, après Le Caire et Alexandrie. Grâce à la découverte d'or, vers la fin du XIXe siècle, la ville a connu un véritable essor économique. La capitale de l'Afrique du Sud, Pretoria, est sensiblement plus paisible, mais elle a également beaucoup à offrir : de vastes parcs et des bâtiments coloniaux fastueux, autour de l'Union Square, ou encore des gratte-ciel modernes dans le centre-ville futuriste.

Johannesburg und Pretoria
Neben Kairo und Alexandria ist Johannesburg die drittgrößte Stadt des afrikanischen Kontinents. Erste Goldfunde verhalfen der Stadt gegen Ende des 19. Jahrhunderts zu einem regelrechten Boom. Südafrikas Hauptstadt Pretoria wirkt etwas beschaulicher, hat aber dennoch einiges zu bieten: großzügig angelegte Parks und prunkvolle Kolonialbauten rund um den Union Square sowie moderne Hochhäuser im futuristischen Zentrum.

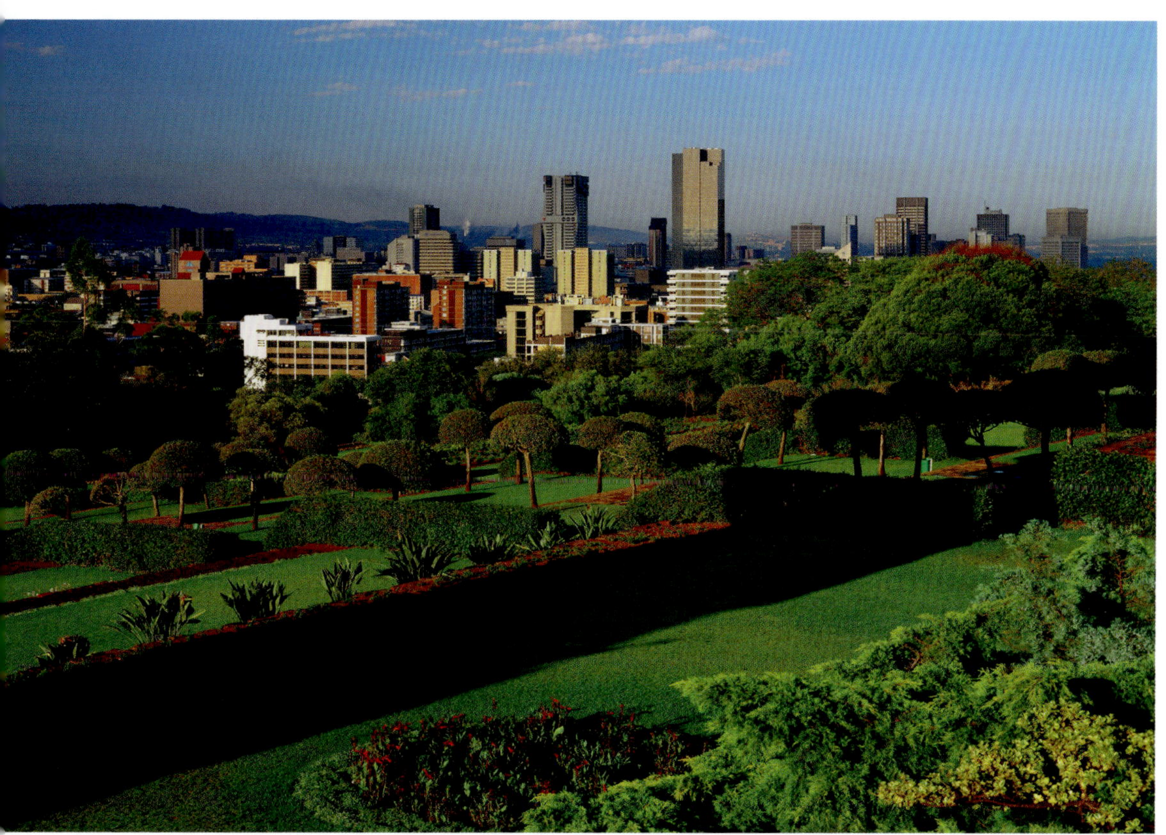

retoria

ohannesburgo y Pretoria
ohannesburgo es la tercera ciudad más rande del continente africano después e El Cairo y Alejandría. Los primeros escubrimientos de oro desencadenaron n la ciudad un verdadero boom hacia nales del siglo XIX. Pretoria, la capital de udáfrica, parece un poco más tranquila, ero todavía tiene mucho que ofrecer: mplios parques y magníficos edificios oloniales alrededor de Union Square, sí como modernos rascacielos en el turista centro.

Johannesburg e Pretoria
Johannesburg è la terza città più grande del continente africano dopo il Cairo e Alessandria. I primi ritrovamenti di giacimenti di oro favorirono un vero e proprio boom verso la fine del XIX secolo. La capitale del Sudafrica, Pretoria, ha un'apparenza un po' più tranquilla, ma ha molto da offrire: grandi parchi e magnifici edifici coloniali intorno a Union Square e moderni grattacieli nel centro futuristico.

Johannesburg en Pretoria
Johannesburg is na Caïro en Alexandrië de grootste stad op het Afrikaanse continent. Door de eerste goudvondsten beleefde de stad tegen het einde van de 19e eeuw een echte opleving. De Zuid-Afrikaanse hoofdstad Pretoria oogt wat rustiger, maar heeft nog genoeg te bieden: ruim aangelegde parken en prachtige koloniale gebouwen rond het Union Square, evenals moderne hoogbouw in het futuristische centrum.

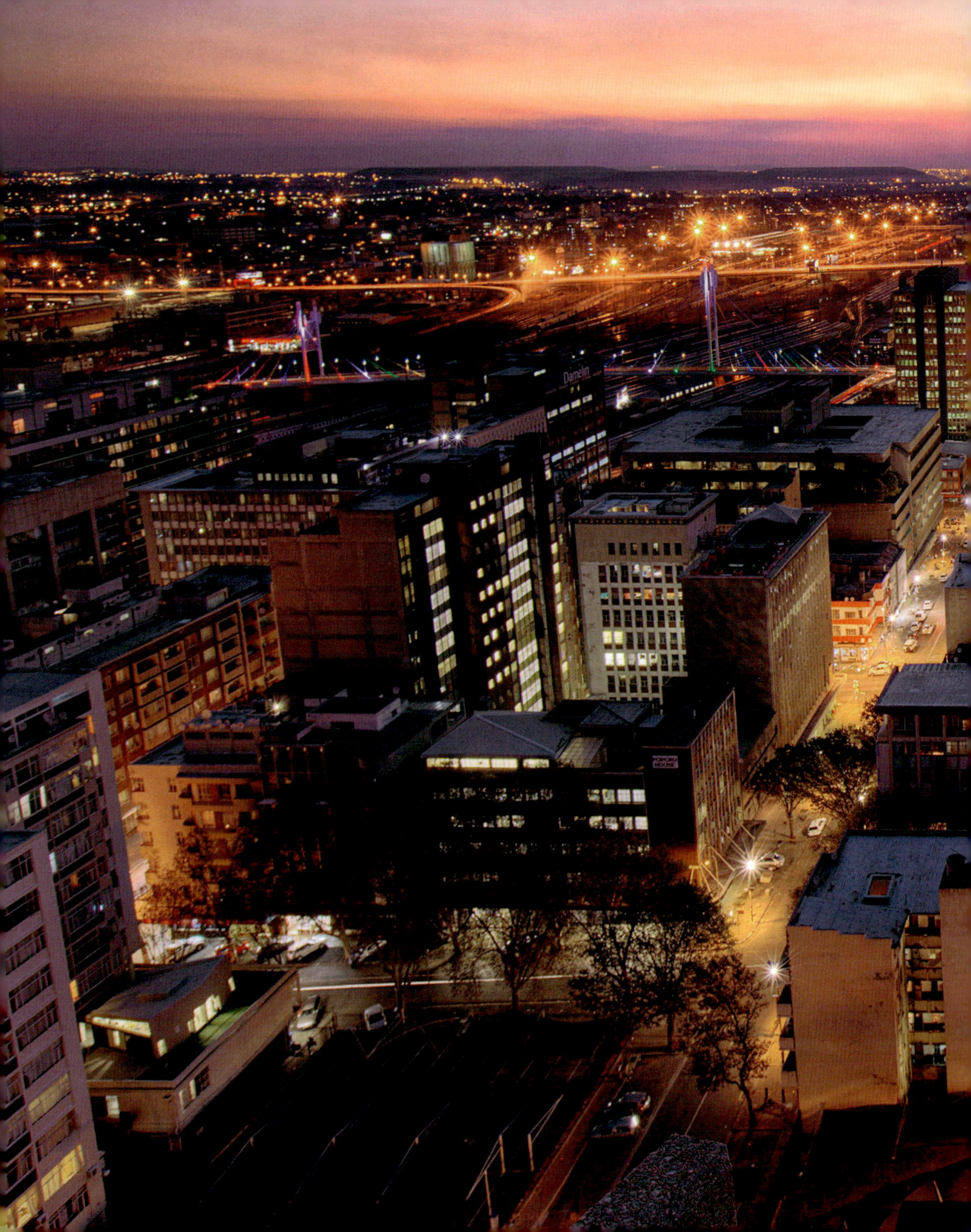
Damelin

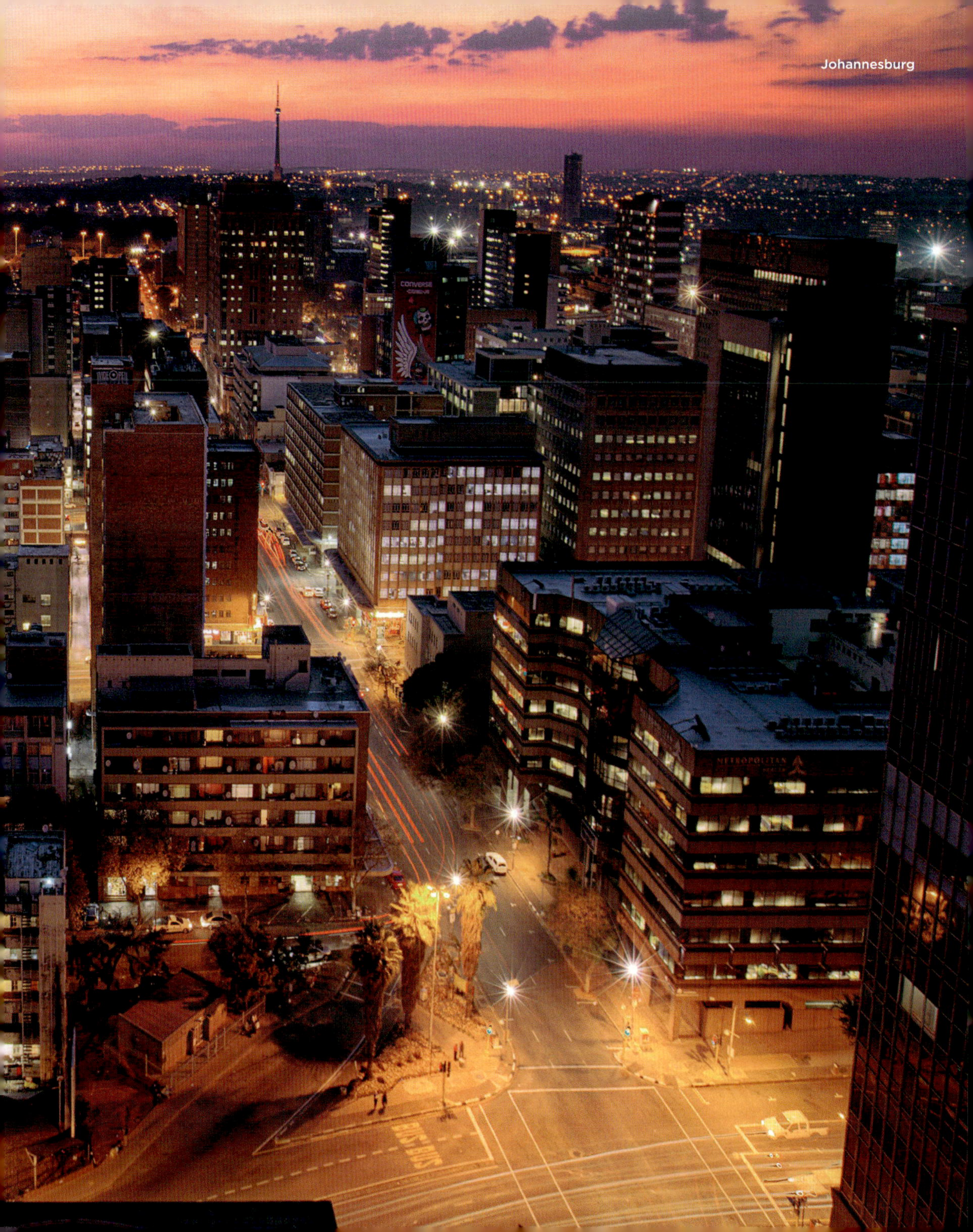

Johannesburg

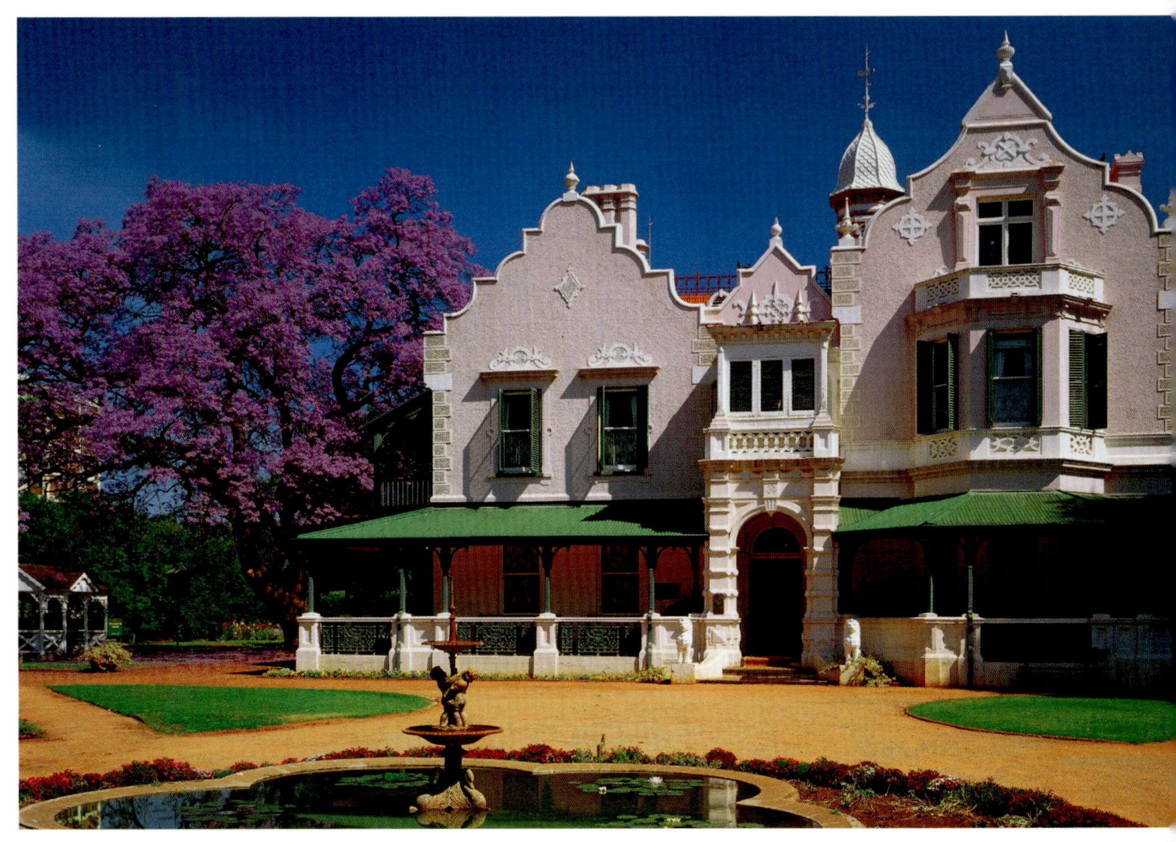

Melrose House, Pretoria

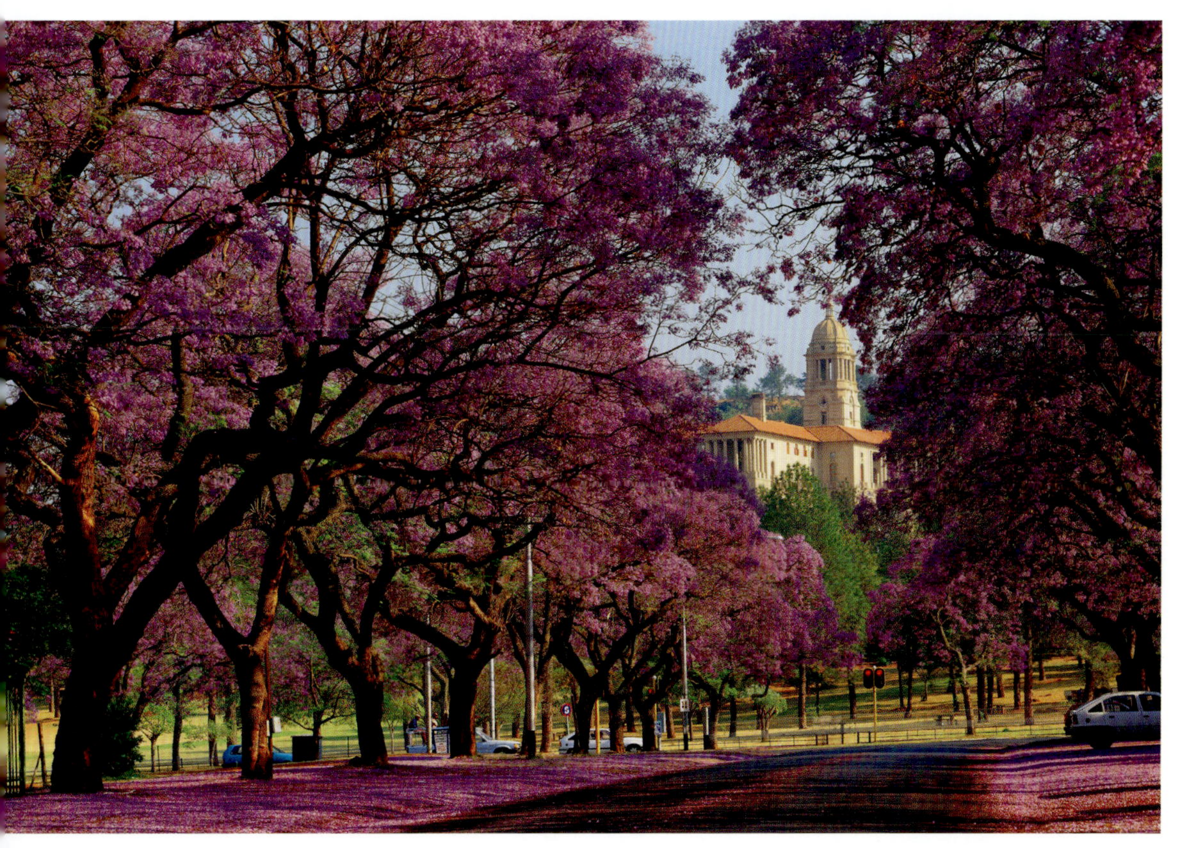

Jnion Building and Jacaranda trees, Pretoria

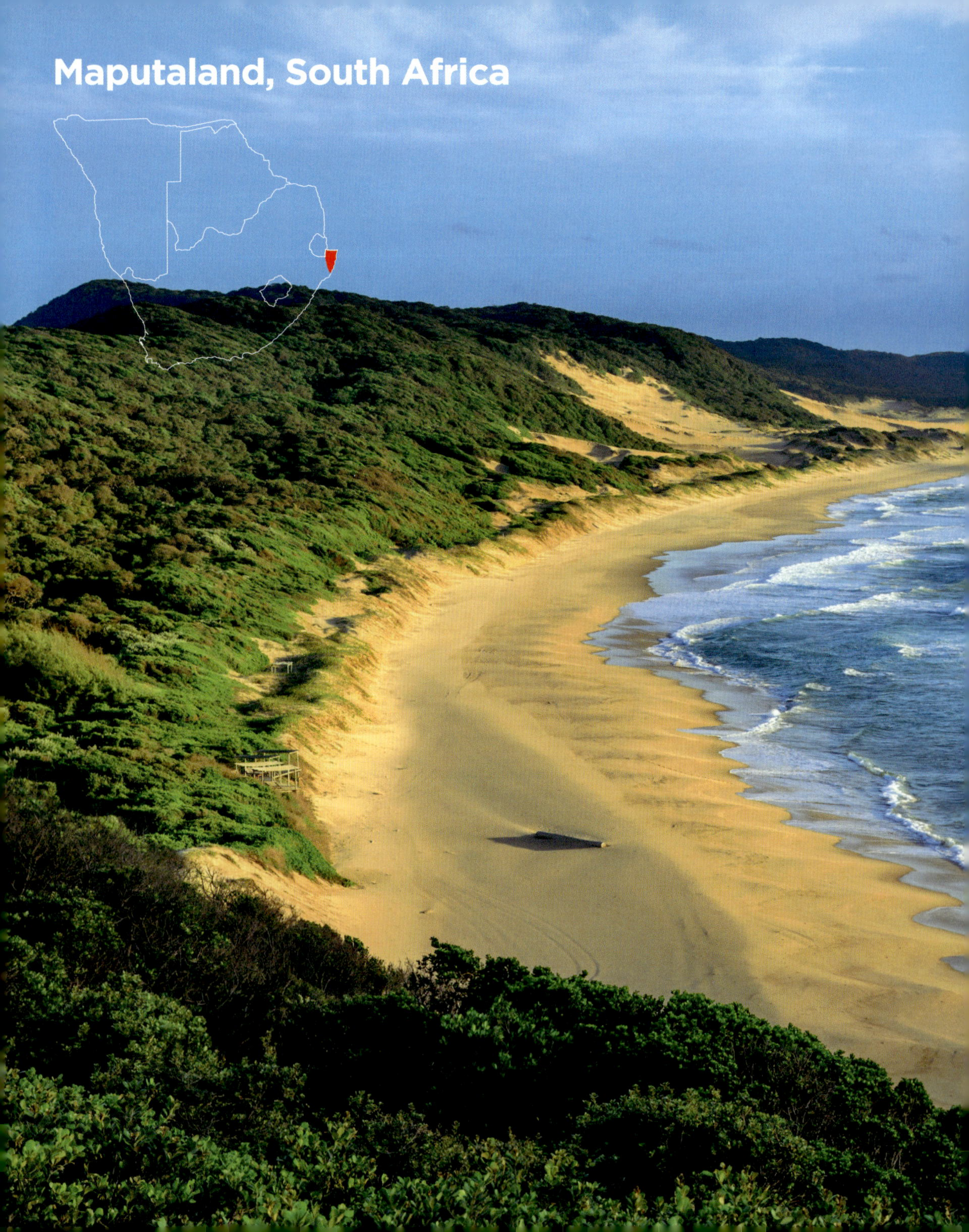

Maputaland, South Africa

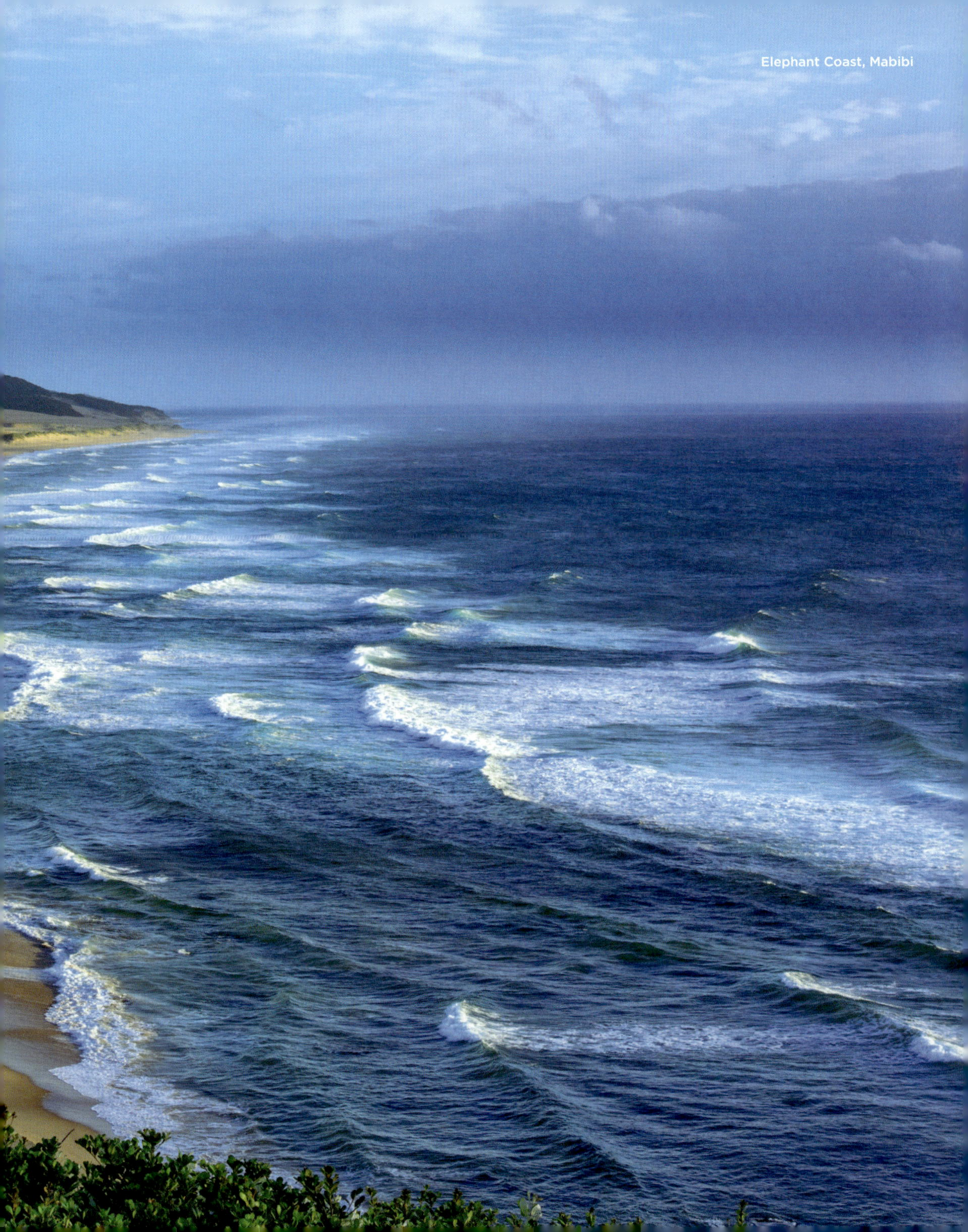

Elephant Coast, Mabibi

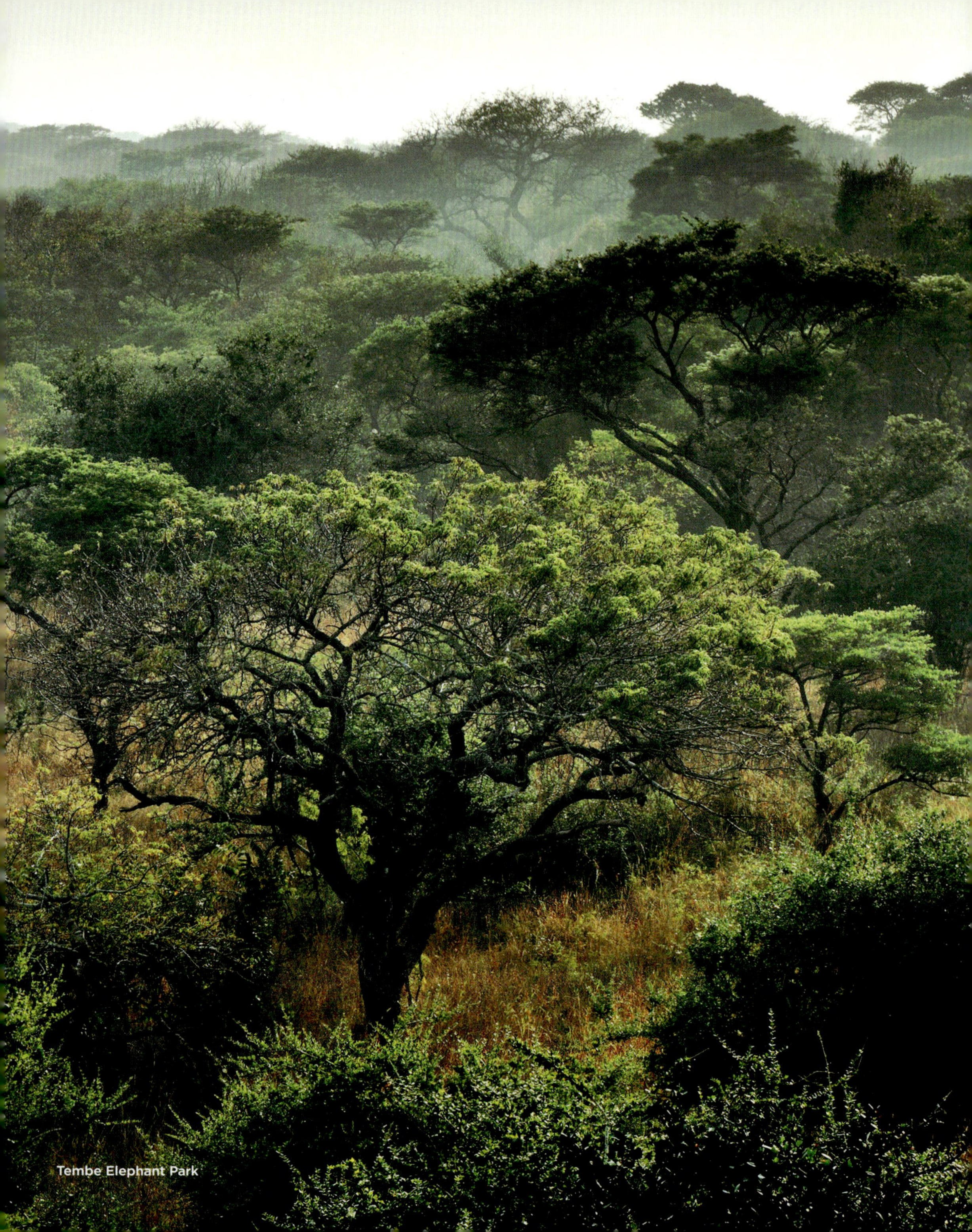
Tembe Elephant Park

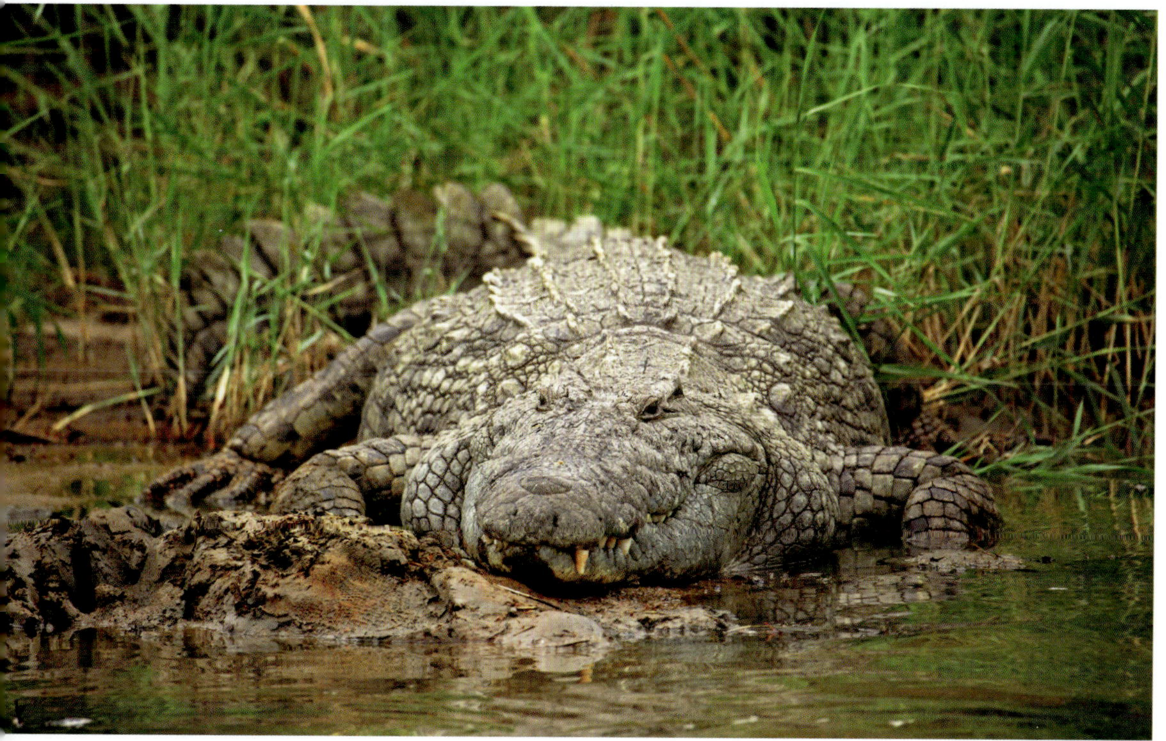

rocodile, iSimangaliso Wetland Park

aputaland
here is much to discover in the tropical orth of the South African province of waZulu-Natal: vast, deserted beaches n the Indian Ocean, little known nature eserves such as the Tembe Elephant Park nd Hluhluwe-Imfolozi Park, as well as the etlands and coastal areas included in the imangaliso Wetland Park.

Maputaland
Es gibt noch Land zu entdecken im tropischen Norden der südafrikanischen Provinz KwaZulu-Natal: weite, menschenleere Strände am Indischen Ozean, wenig bekannte Naturparks, wie der Tembe Elephant Park oder der Hluhluwe-Imfolozi-Park, sowie Feucht- und Küstengebiete, die im iSimangaliso-Wetland-Park unter Schutz gestellt sind.

Maputaland
Nella zona nord tropicale della provincia sudafricana di KwaZulu-Natal esistono ancora terre da scoprire: ampie spiagge spopolate sull'Oceano Indiano, parchi naturali poco conosciuti, come il Tembe Elephant Park o il Parco Hluhluwe-Imfolozi, oltre a zone umide e costiere, che sono sotto protezione nel Parco iSimangaliso Wetland.

e Maputaland
reste des territoires à explorer dans nord tropical de la province sud-ricaine du Kwazulu-Natal : d'immenses ages vides sur l'océan Indien, des parcs aturels peu connus, comme le Tembe ephant Park ou la réserve d'Hluhluwe-mfolozi, mais aussi des zones humides et tières, qui sont protégées dans le parc iSimangaliso-Wetland.

Maputaland
Hay aún tierra por descubrir en el norte tropical de la provincia sudafricana de KwaZulu-Natal: anchas playas desiertas en el Océano Índico, parques naturales poco conocidos, tales como el Parque de Elefantes Tembe o el Parque Hluhluwe-Imfolozi, así como los humedales y las zonas costeras en el Parque del Humedal de iSimangaliso que están protegidos.

Maputaland
In het tropische noorden van de Zuid-Afrikaanse provincie KwaZulu-Natal is er nog onbekend gebied te ontdekken: brede en lege zandstranden aan de Indische Oceaan, minder bekende natuurreservaten als het Olifantenpark van Tembe of het Hluhluwe-Imfolozi-park, en de draslanden en kustgebieden die in het iSimangaliso Wetland Park worden beschermd.

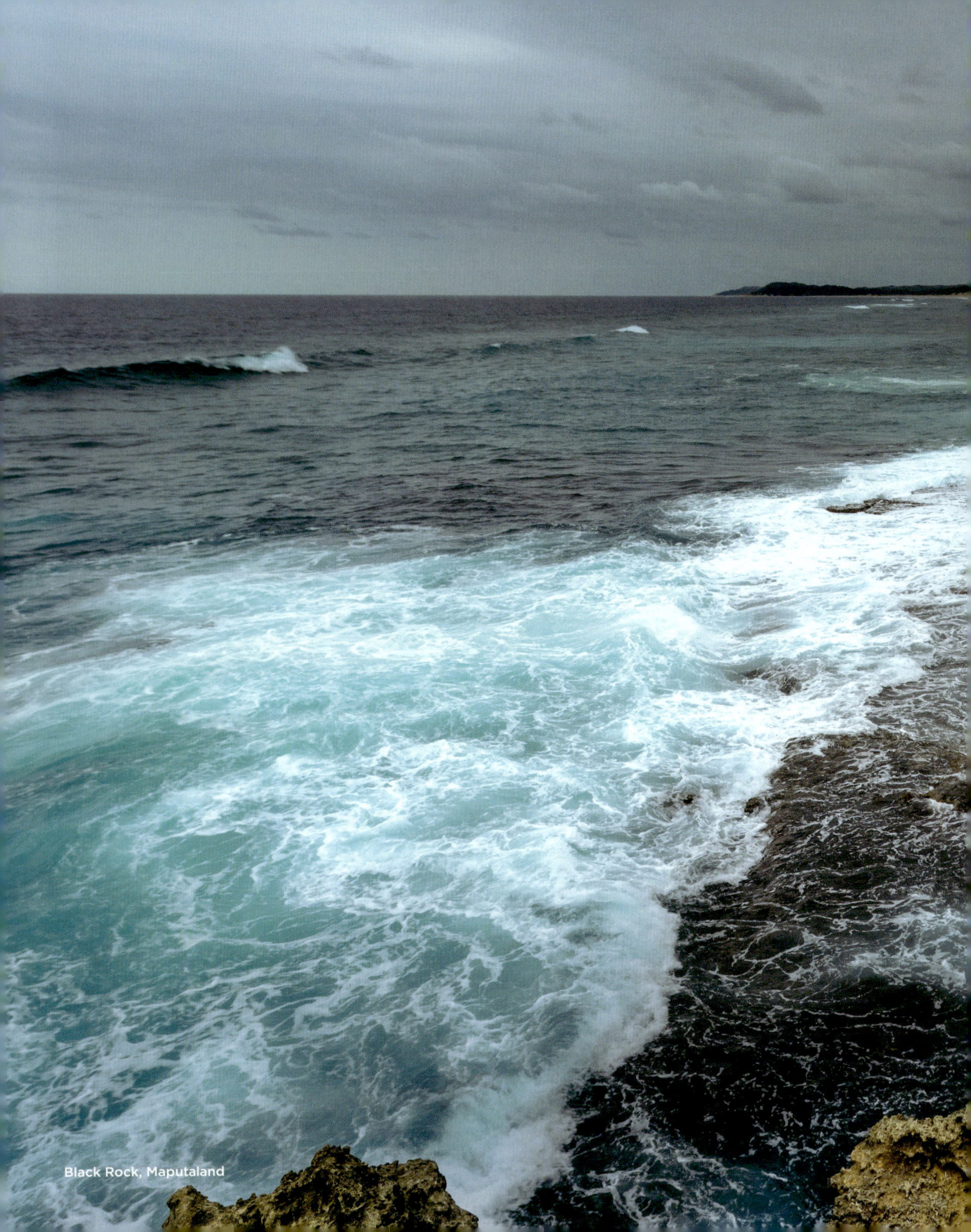
Black Rock, Maputaland

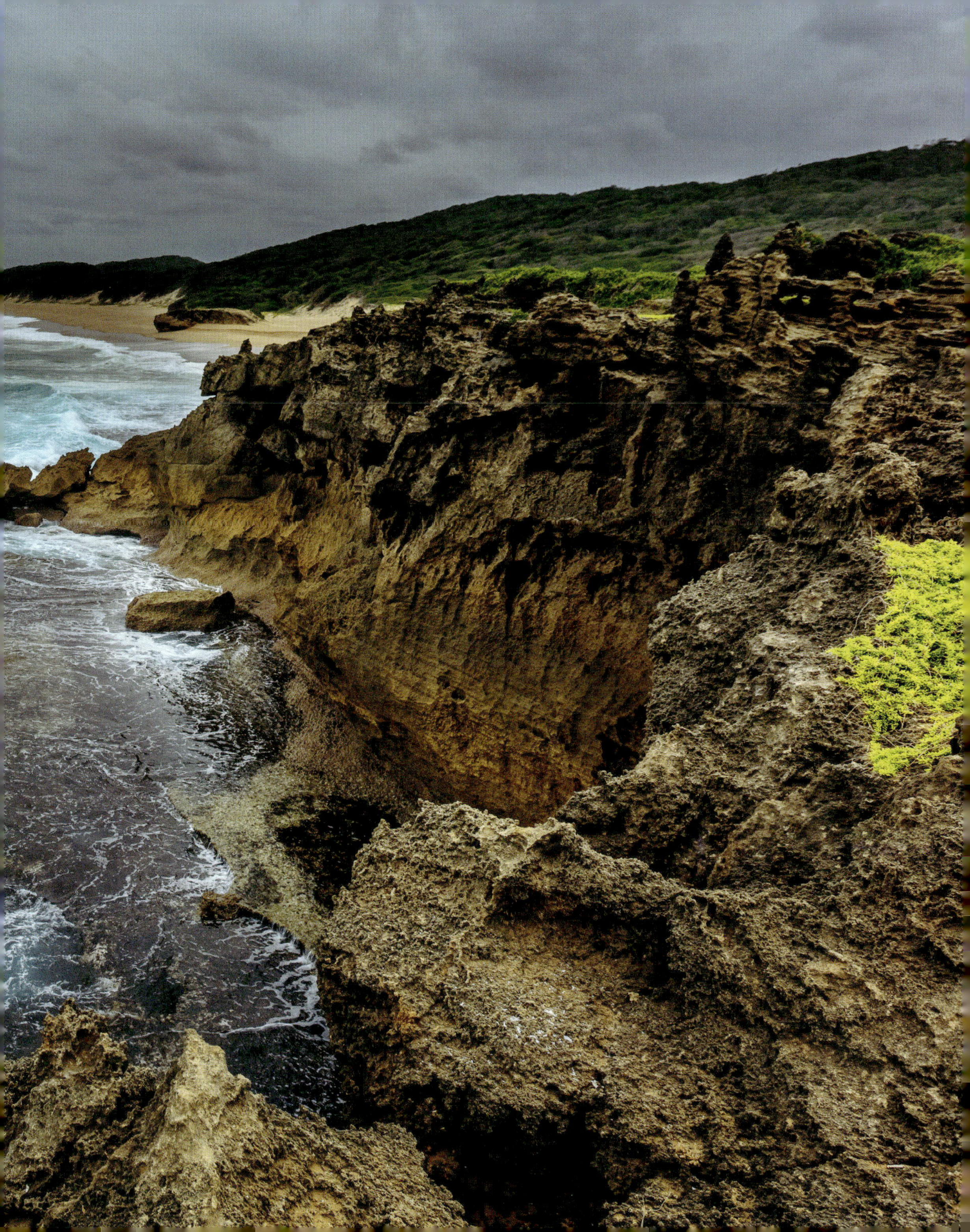

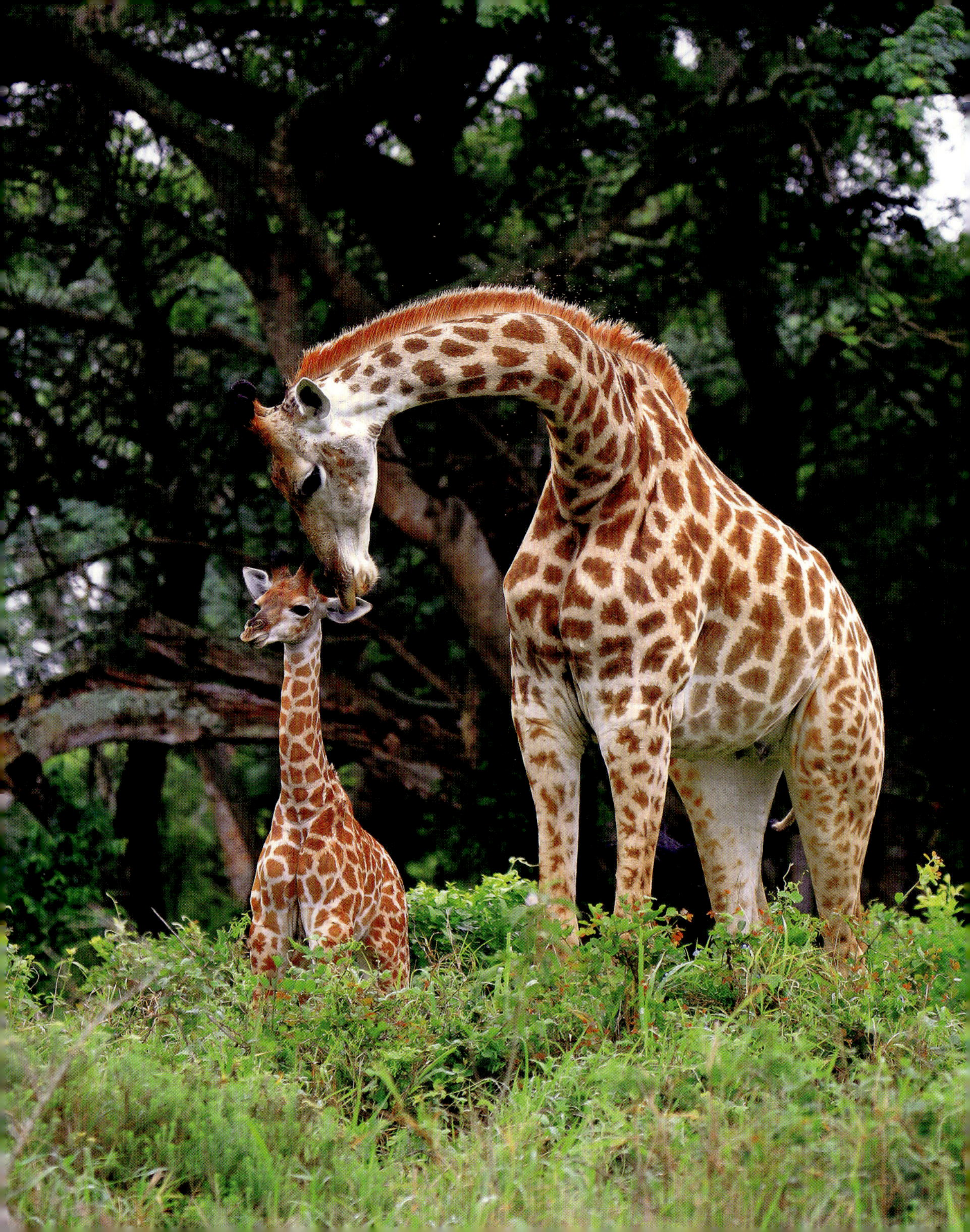

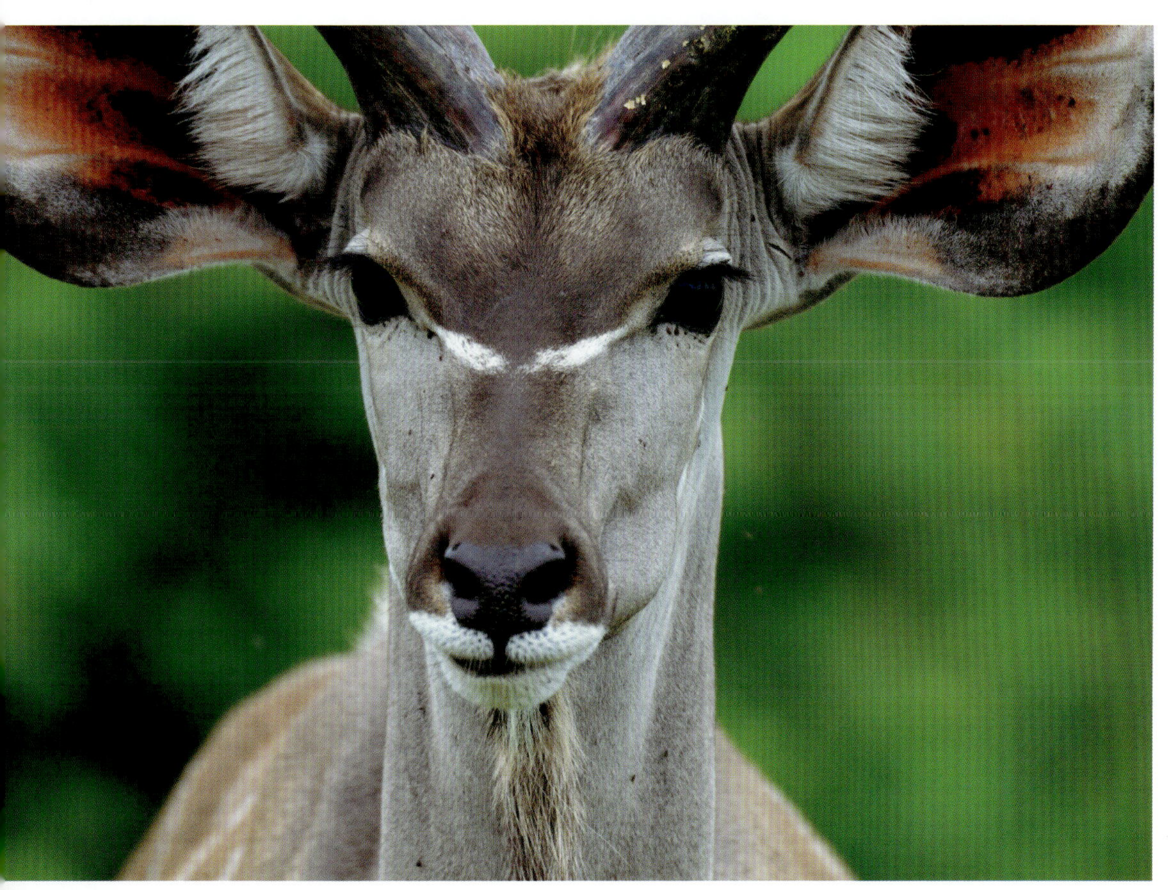

udu, iSimangaliso Wetland Park

outh African giraffes, iSimangaliso Wetland Park

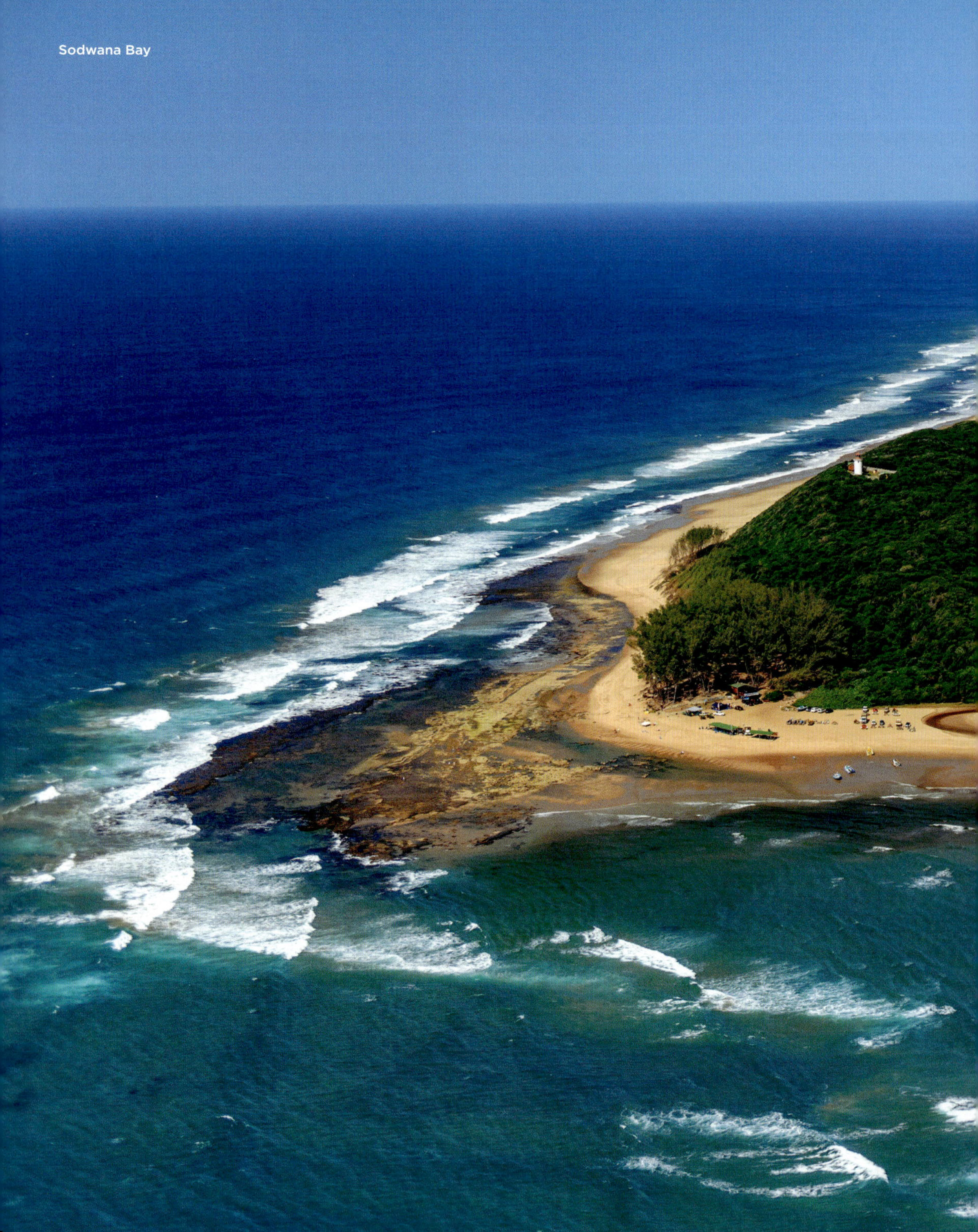

Sodwana Bay

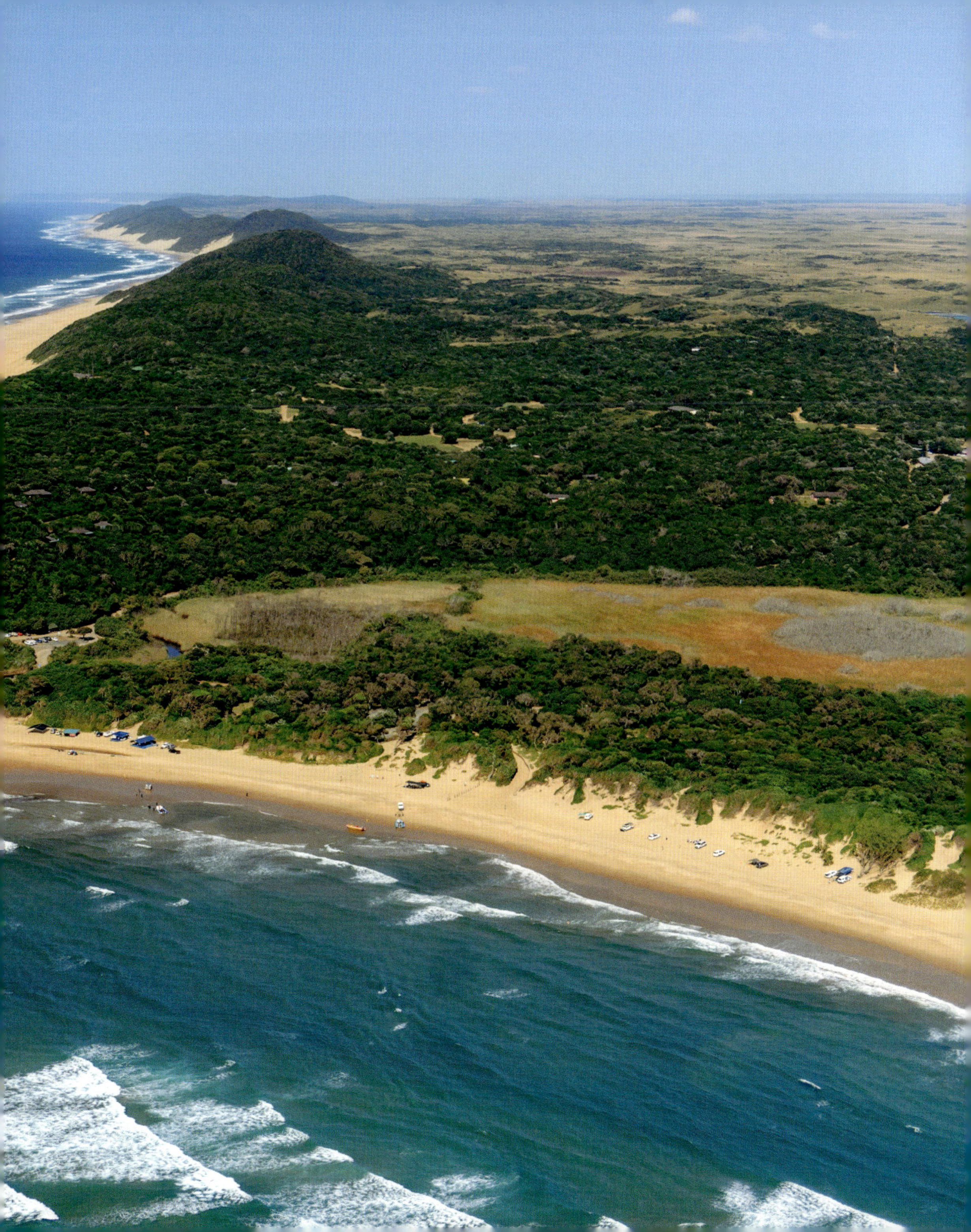

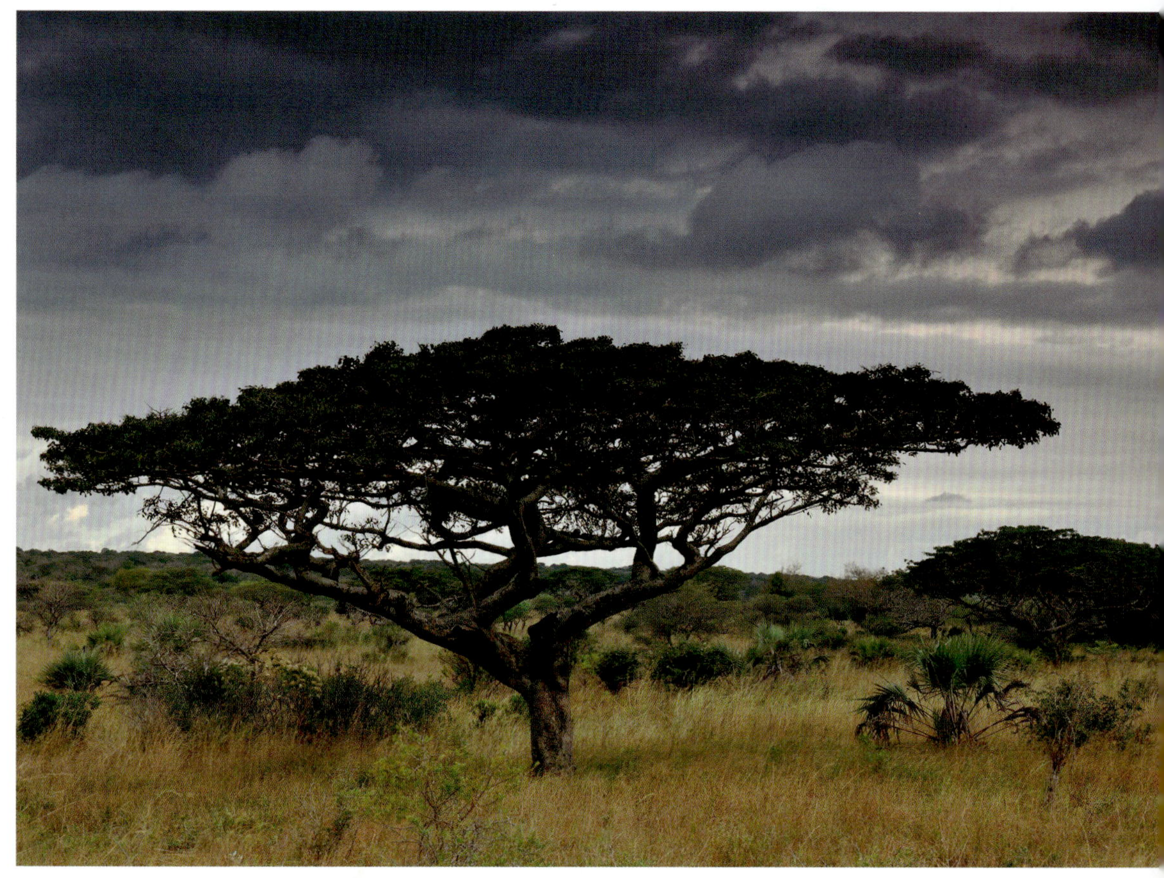

Pod Mahogany tree, Temba Game Reserve

Hippopotamus, iSimangaliso Wetland Pa

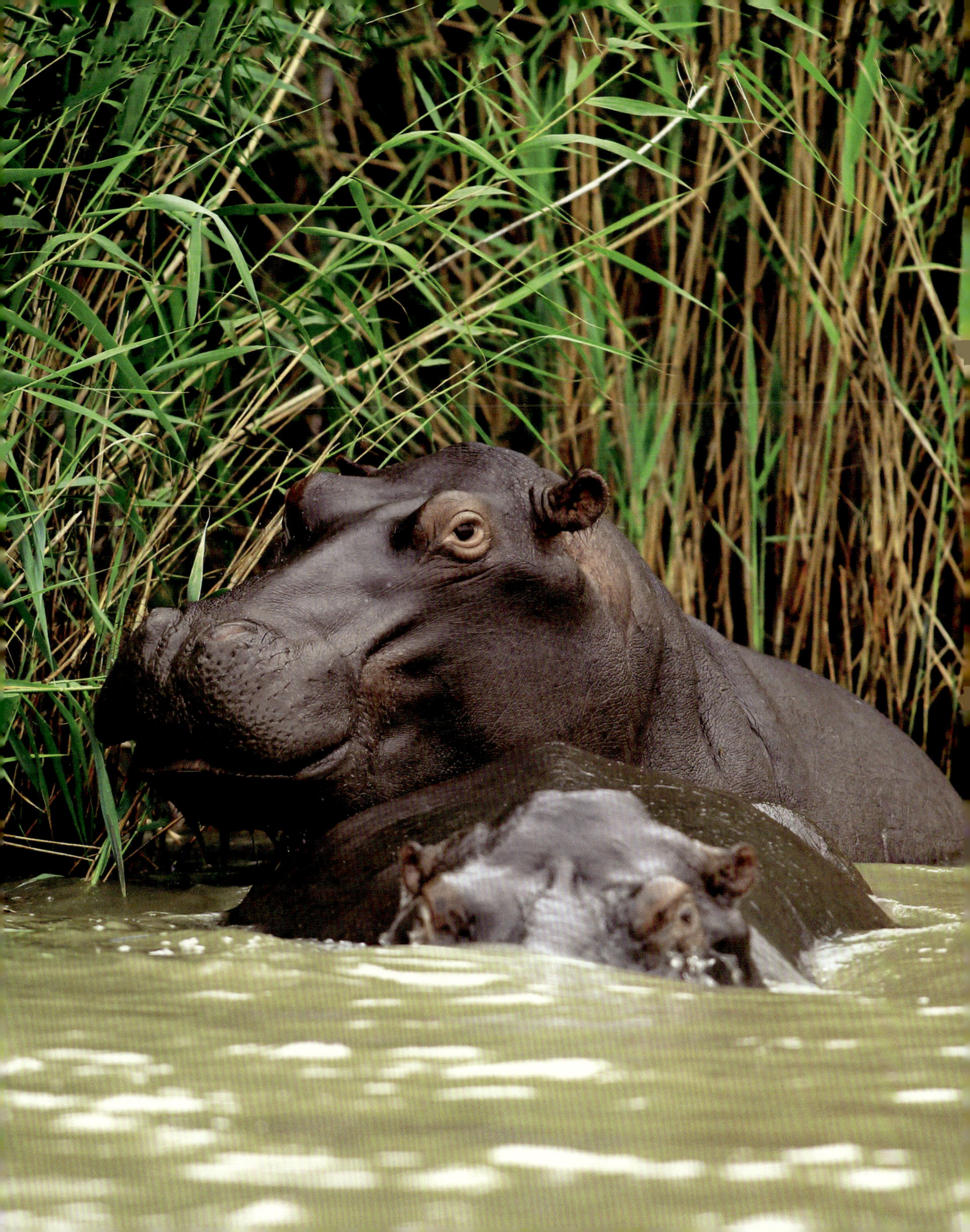

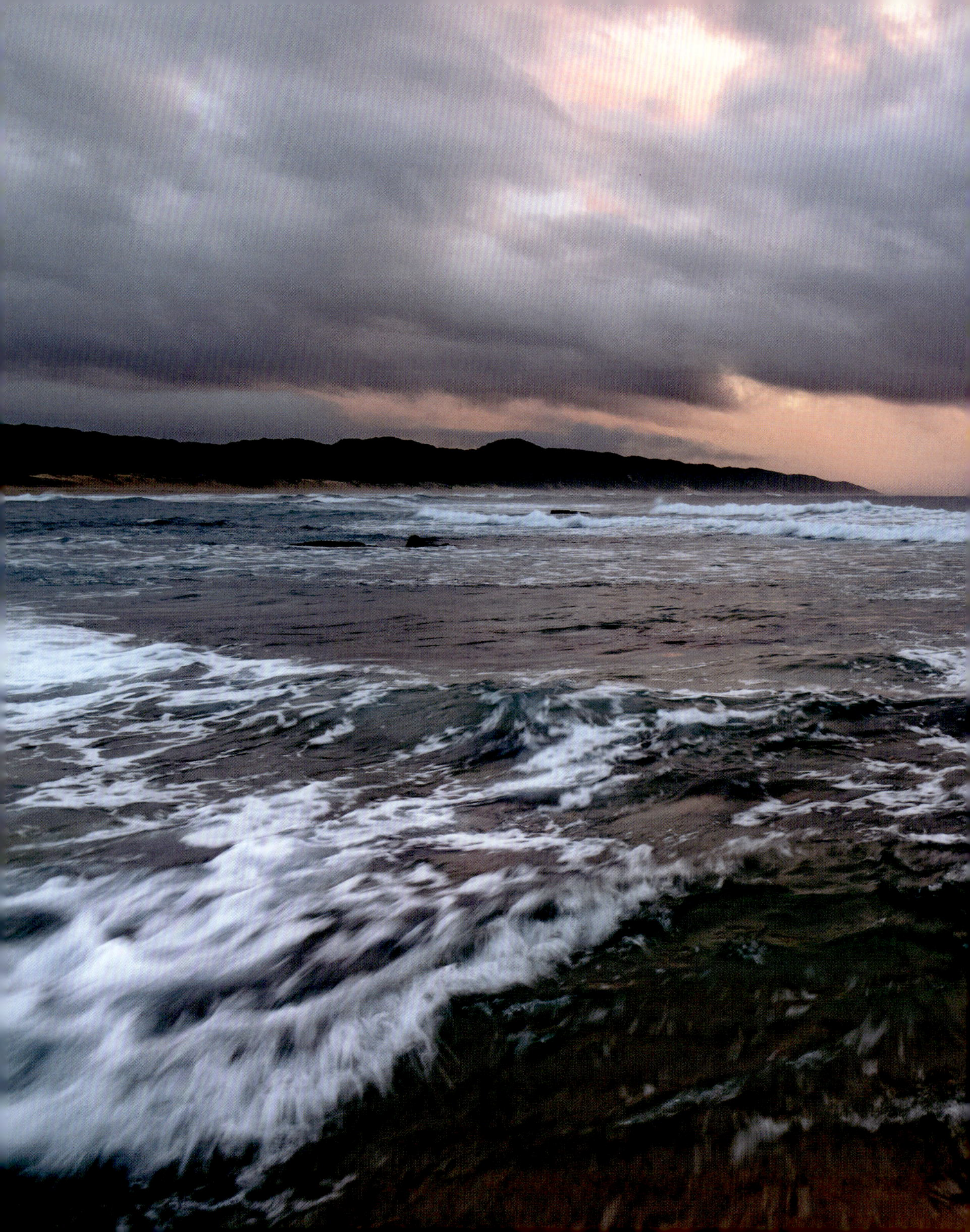

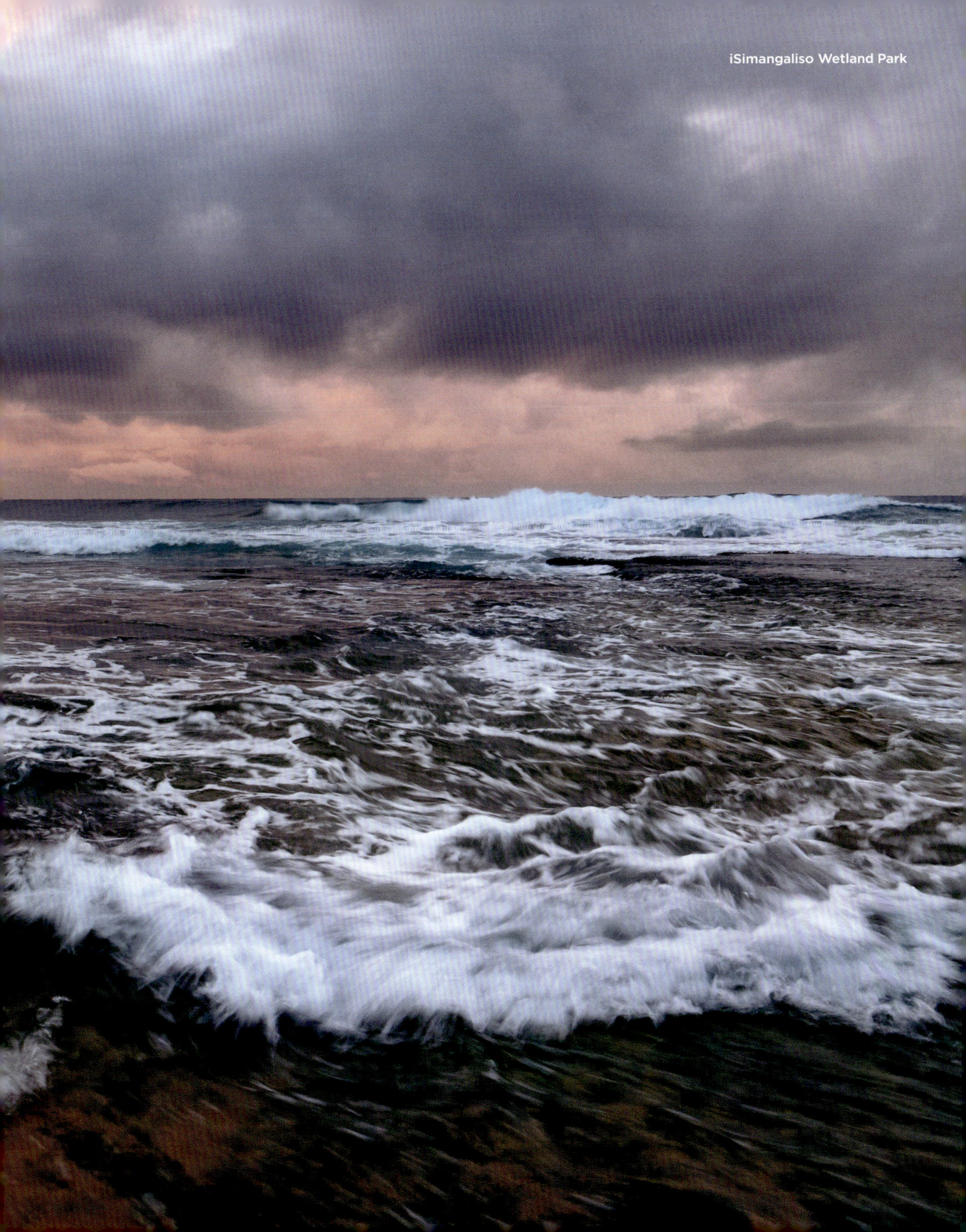

Hluhluwe-Imfolozi Park, South Africa

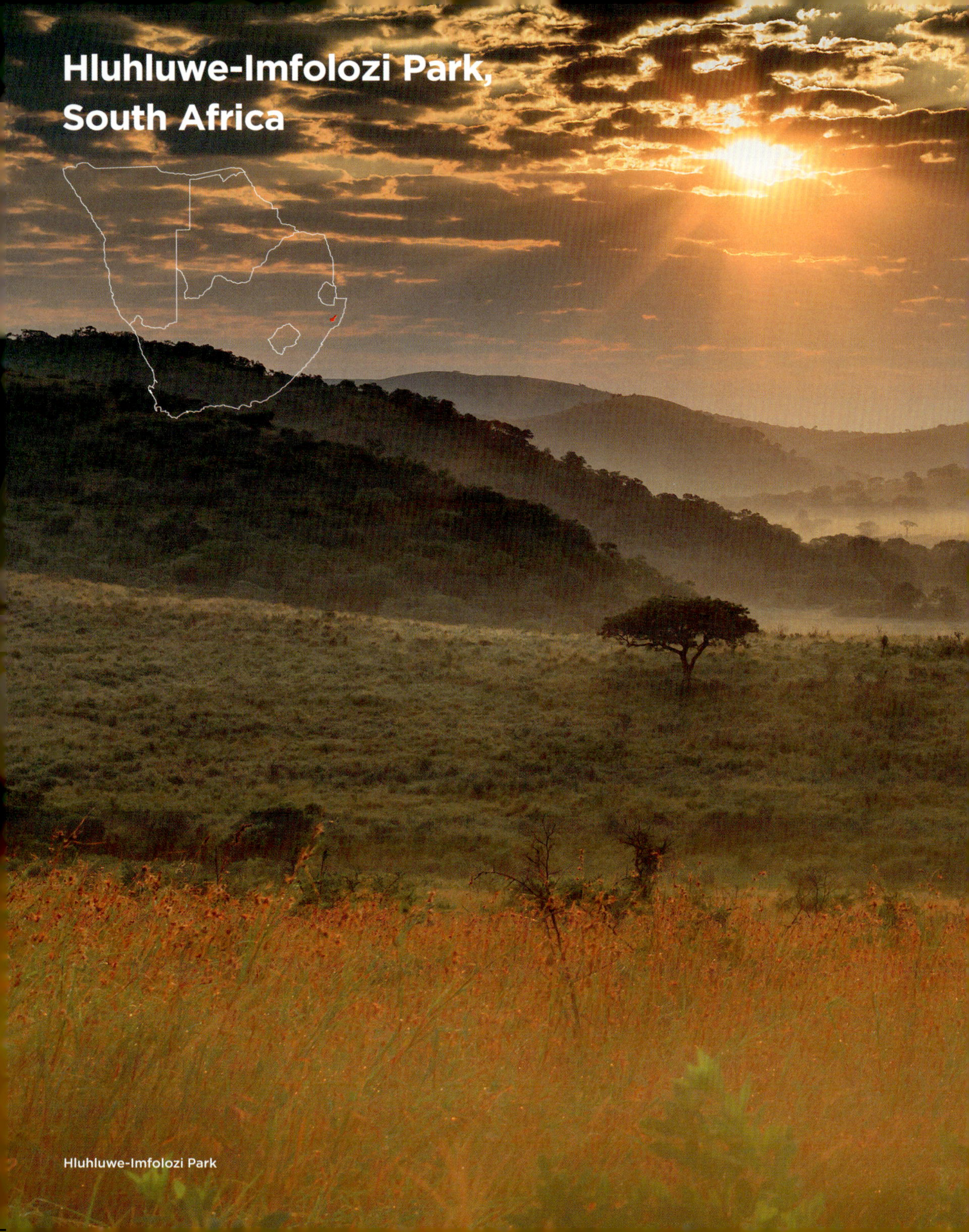

Hluhluwe-Imfolozi Park

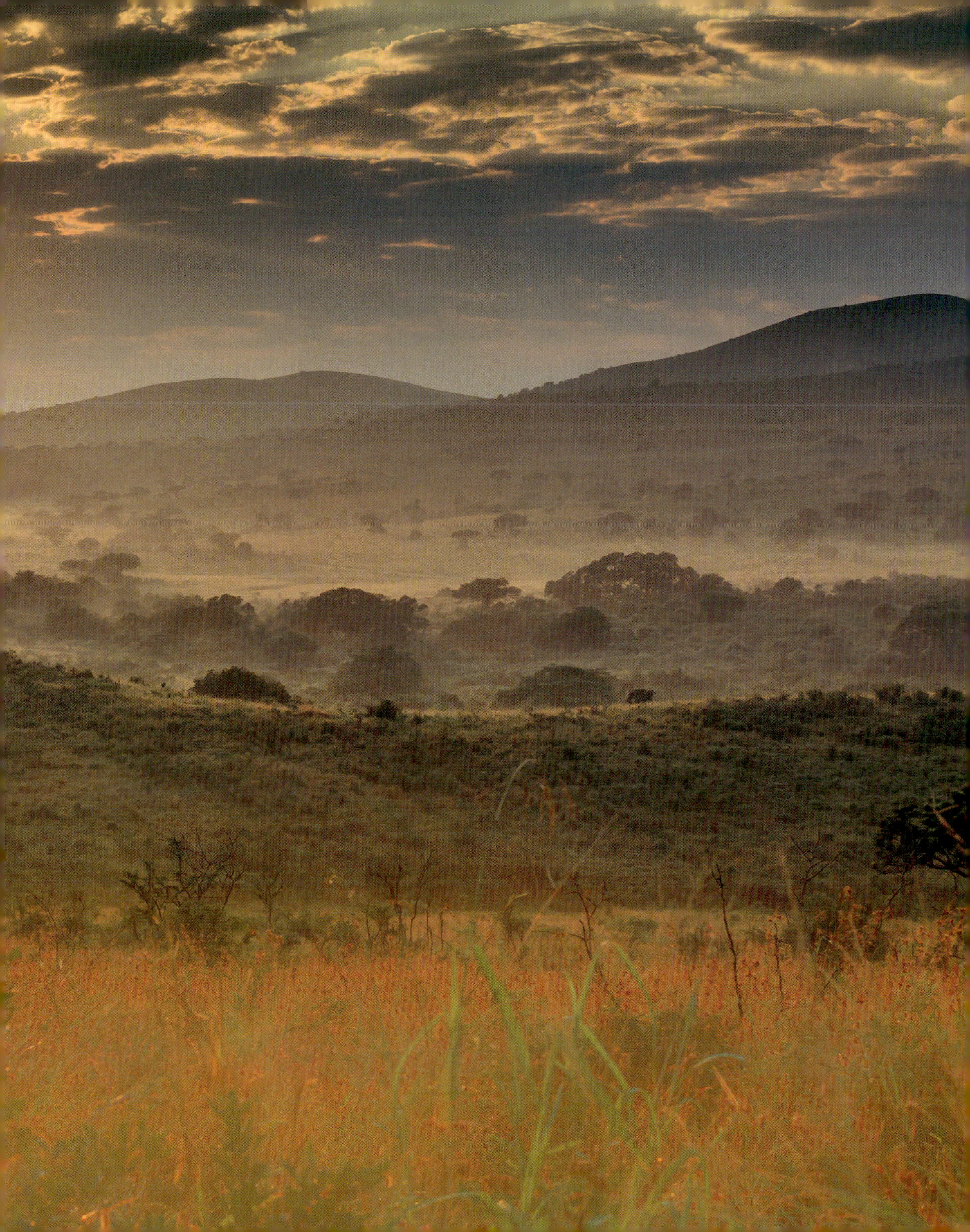

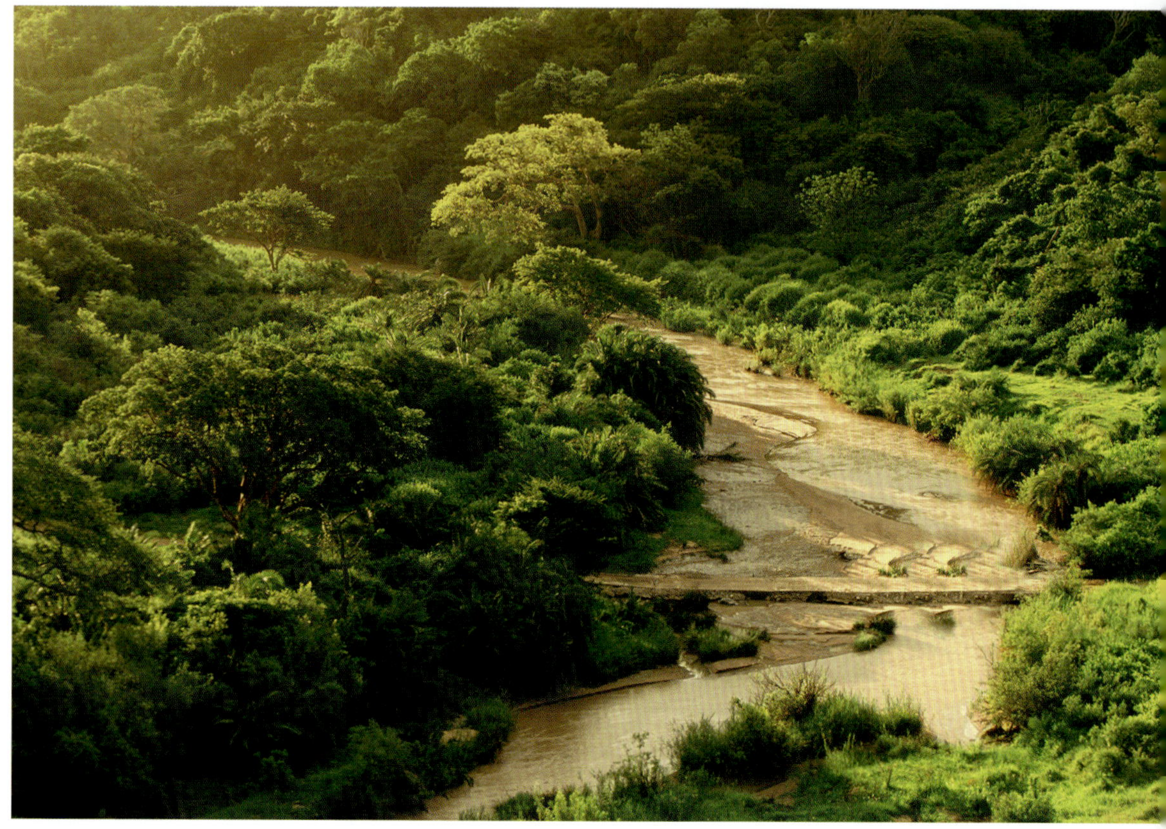

Hluhluwe-Imfolozi Park

Hluhluwe-Imfolozi Park
Originally one of Africa's oldest game reserves, this comparatively small national park covers only 1000 km², with gently undulating hills as far as the eye can see, densely overgrown and crossed by watercourses and offering fantastic views. This diverse landscape is world-famous for its large rhino population and is also home to the Big Five game animals.

La réserve d'Hluhluwe-Umfolozi
Ce parc national relativement petit, avec sa superficie d'environ 1000 km², est l'une des plus vieilles réserves de gibier d'Afrique. Les collines ondulent à perte de vue, couvertes de végétation et entrecoupées de cours d'eau, offrant un panorama de rêve. Ce paysage si varié est connu dans le monde entier pour ses nombreux rhinocéros, et également parce qu'il abrite les Big Five.

Hluhluwe-iMfolozi-Park
Als eines der ältesten Wildreservate Afrikas erstreckt sich dieser vergleichsweise kleine Nationalpark nur über 1000 km². Sanft gewellte Hügel soweit das Auge reicht, dicht bewachsen und von Wasserläufen durchzogen, bieten traumhafte Ausblicke. Diese vielfältige Landschaft ist weltbekannt für ihre hohe Nashornpopulation und zudem Heimat der Big Five.

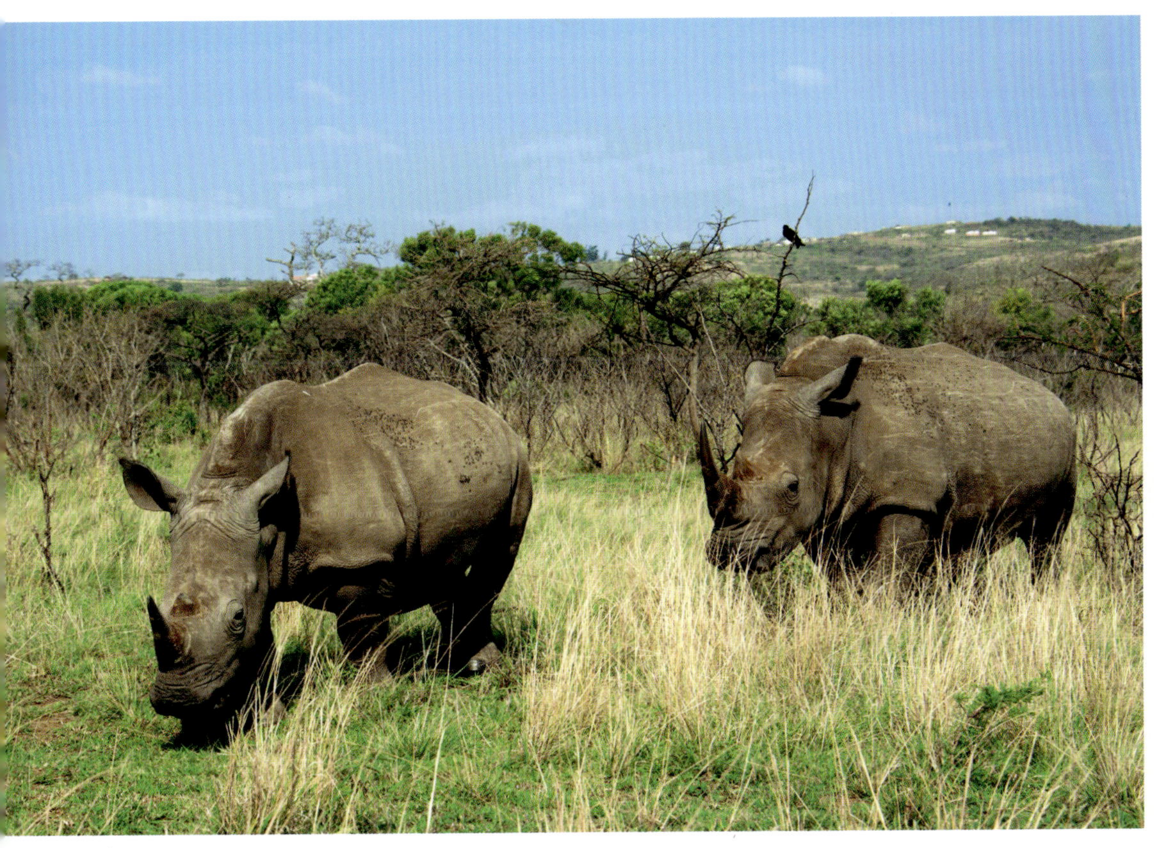

Vhite rhinoceros, Hluhluwe-Imfolozi Park

Parque Nacional Hluhluwe-Imfolozi
Como uno de los parques cinegéticos más ntiguos de África, este parque natural elativamente pequeño se extiende a lo argo de solamente 1000 km², con colinas uavemente onduladas hasta donde lcanza la vista, densamente cubiertas de egetación y atravesadas por cursos de gua, que ofrecen unas vistas fantásticas. Este paisaje diverso es mundialmente onocido por su alta población de inocerontes y también es el hogar de los Cinco Grandes.

Parco Nazionale Hluhluwe-Imfolozi
Questo parco nazionale, una delle più antiche riserve naturali dell'Africa, è relativamente piccolo si estende solo 1000 km², con colline dolcemente ondulate a perdita d'occhio, densamente coltivate e attraversate da corsi d'acqua, che offrono una vista magnifica. Questo ricco paesaggio è famoso in tutto il mondo per la sua alta popolazione di rinoceronti ed è anche dimora dei Big Five.

Hluhluwe-Imfolozipark
Dit relatief kleine nationale park, een van de oudste wildreservaten van Afrika, beslaat slechts 1000 km². Met zijn zacht glooiende heuvels zover het oog reikt, dichte begroeiing en vele waterlopen biedt het fantastische uitzichten. Dit afwisselende landschap is wereldberoemd om zijn grote neushoornpopulatie en herbergt ook de Big Five.

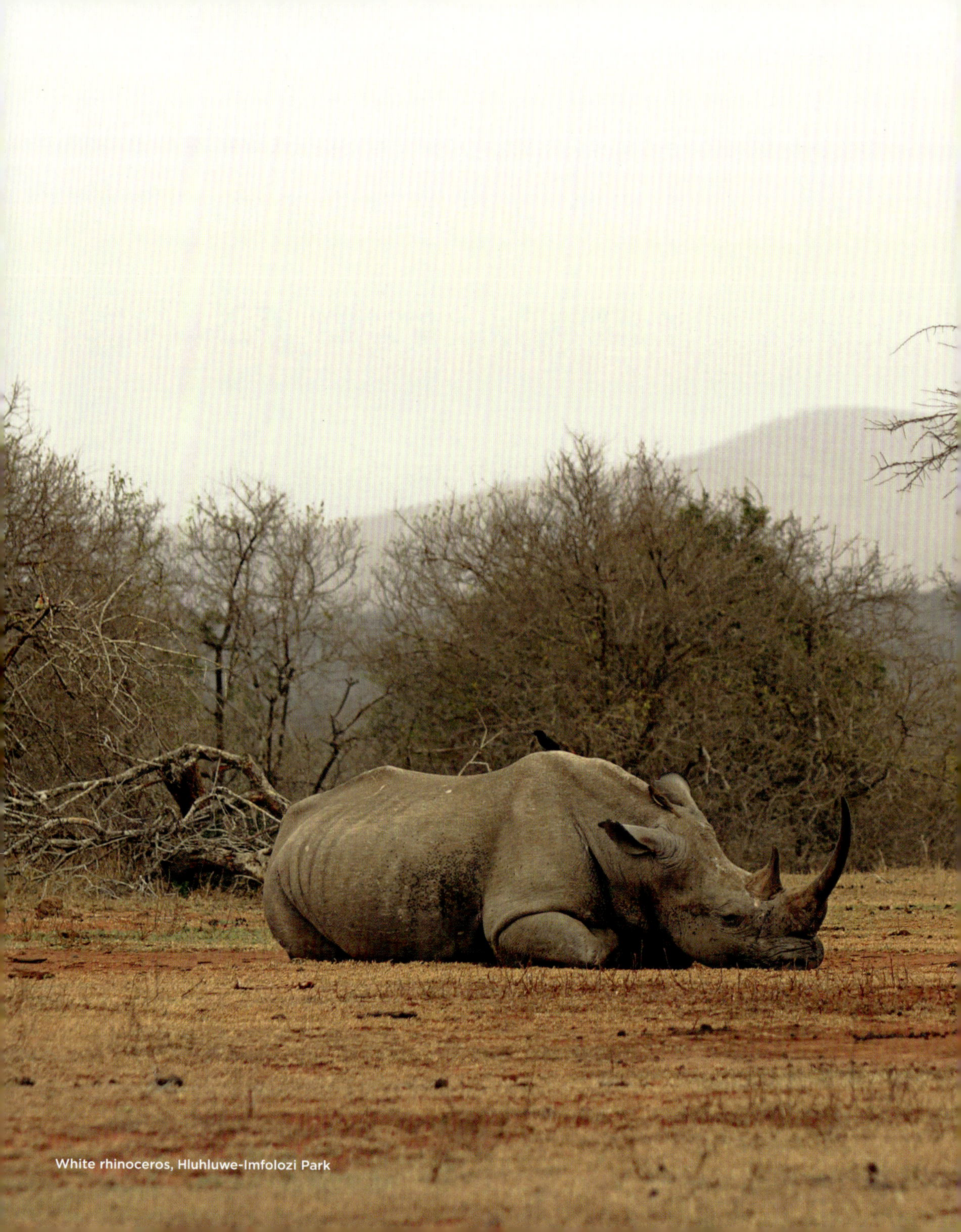

White rhinoceros, Hluhluwe-Imfolozi Park

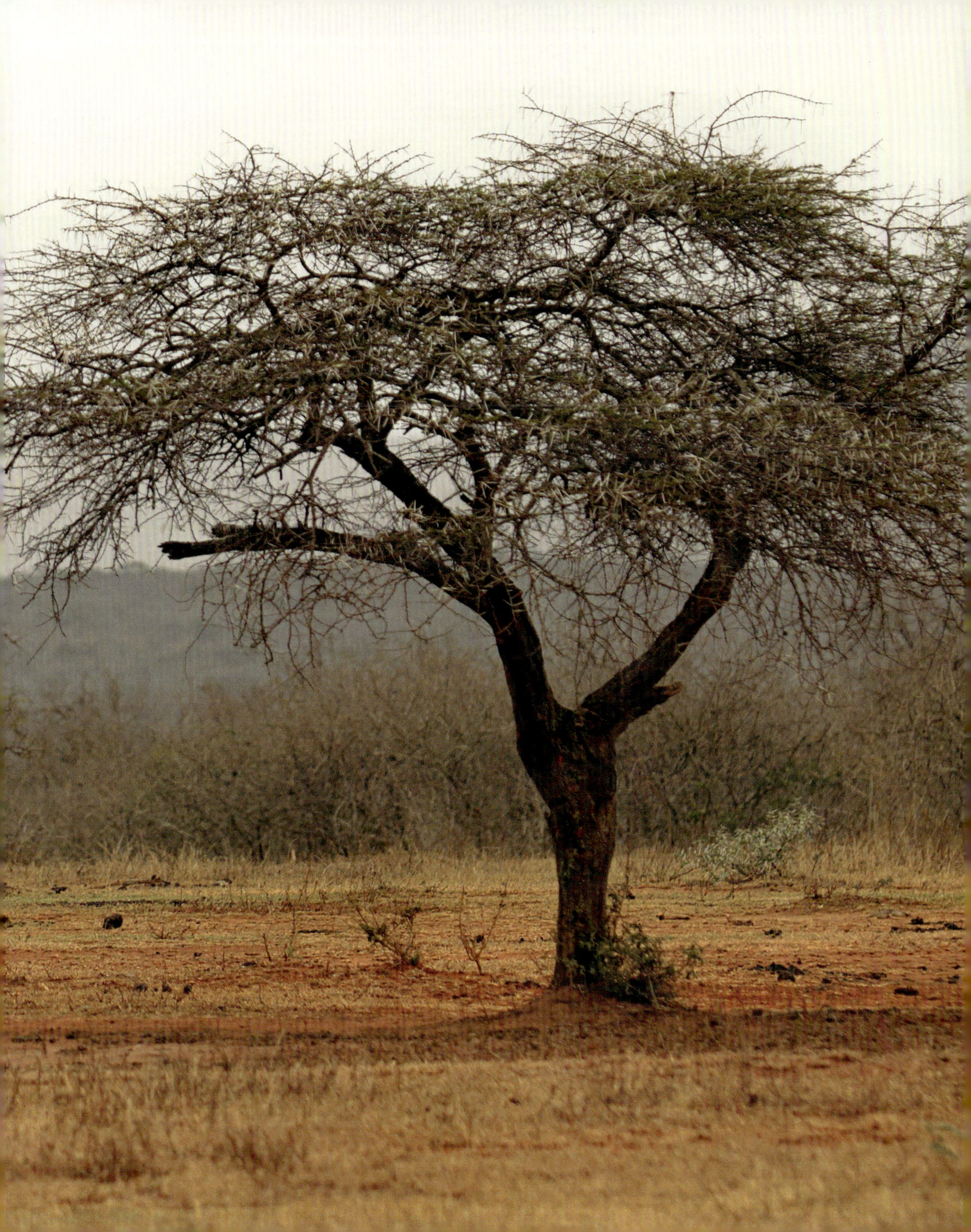

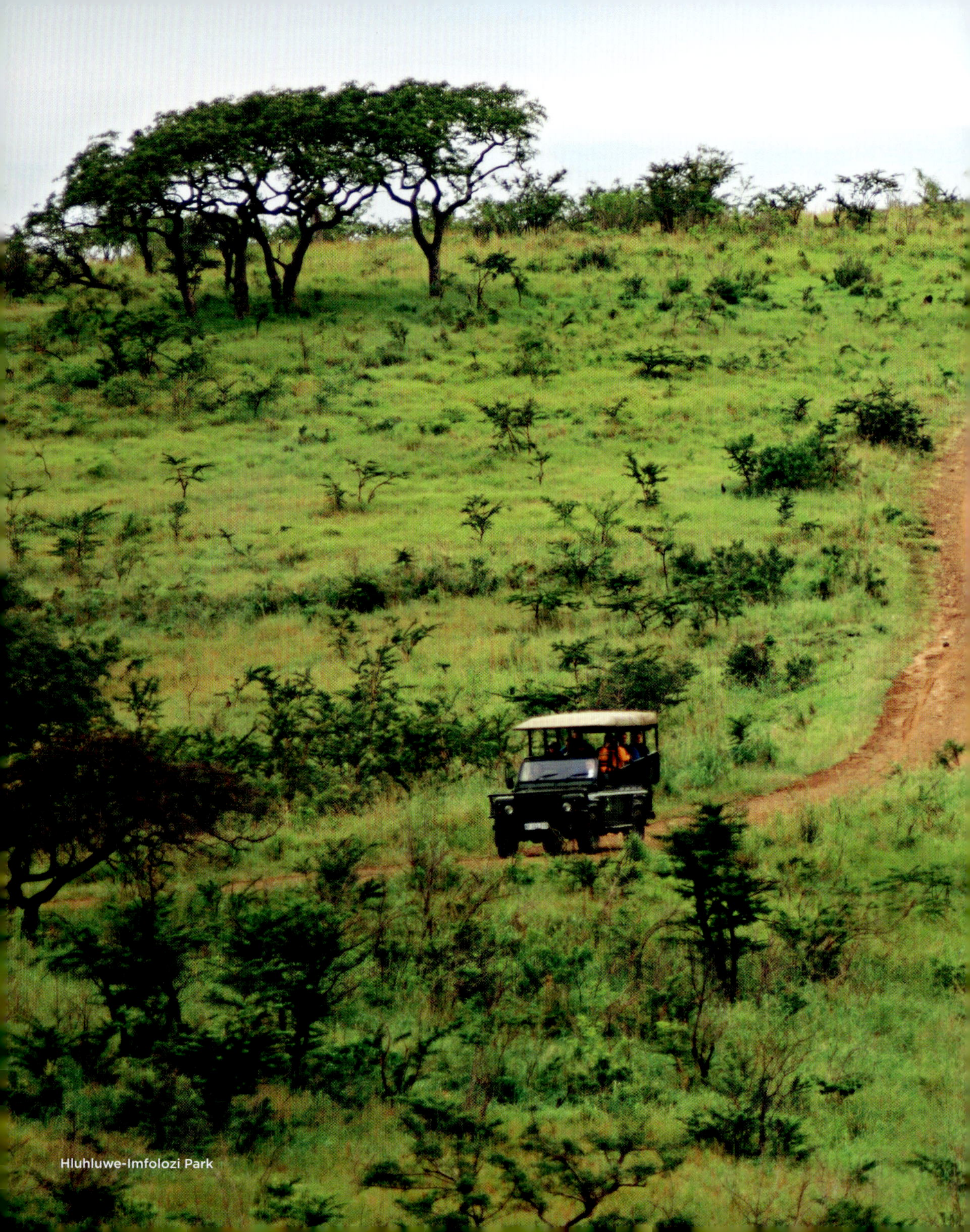

Hluhluwe-Imfolozi Park

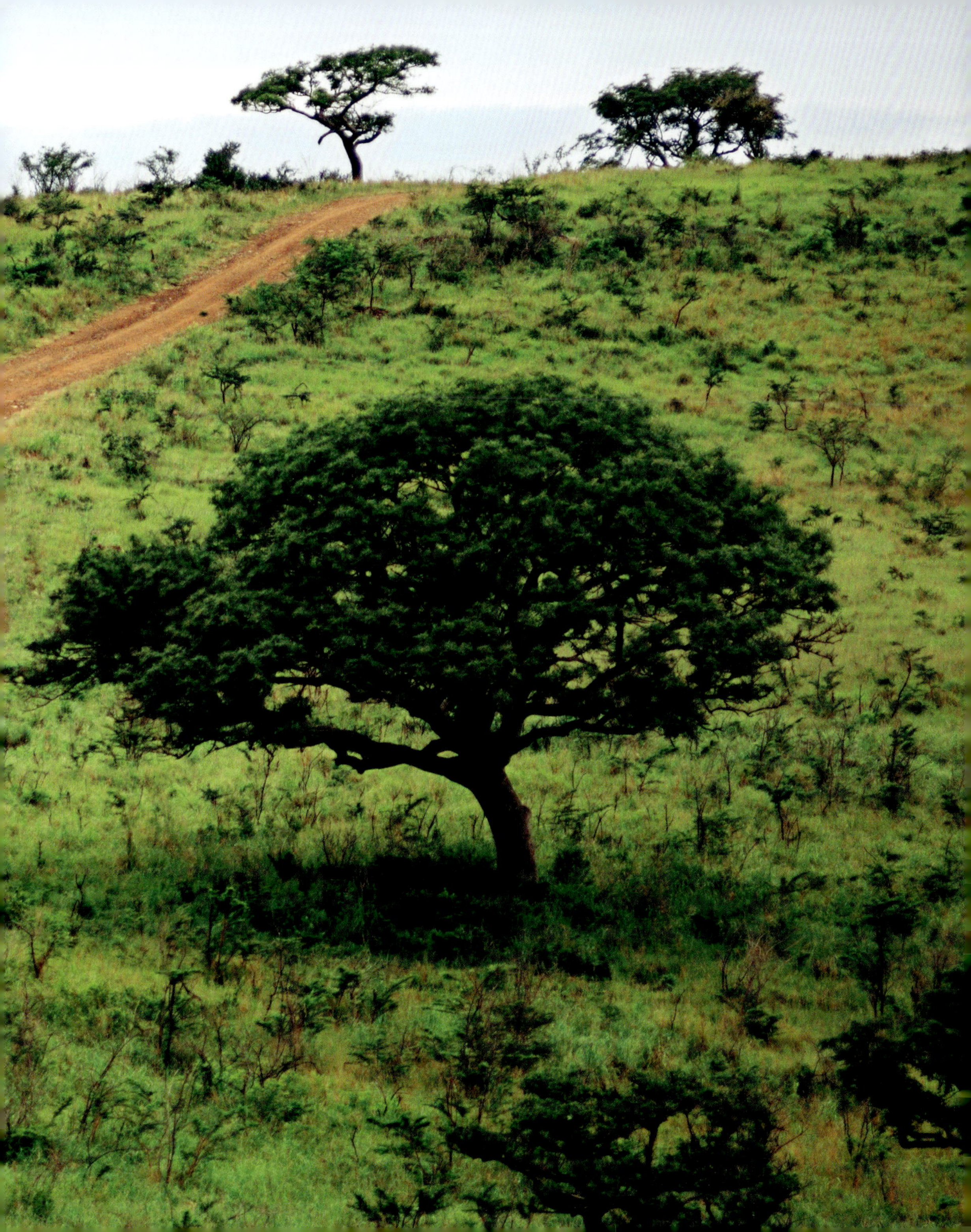

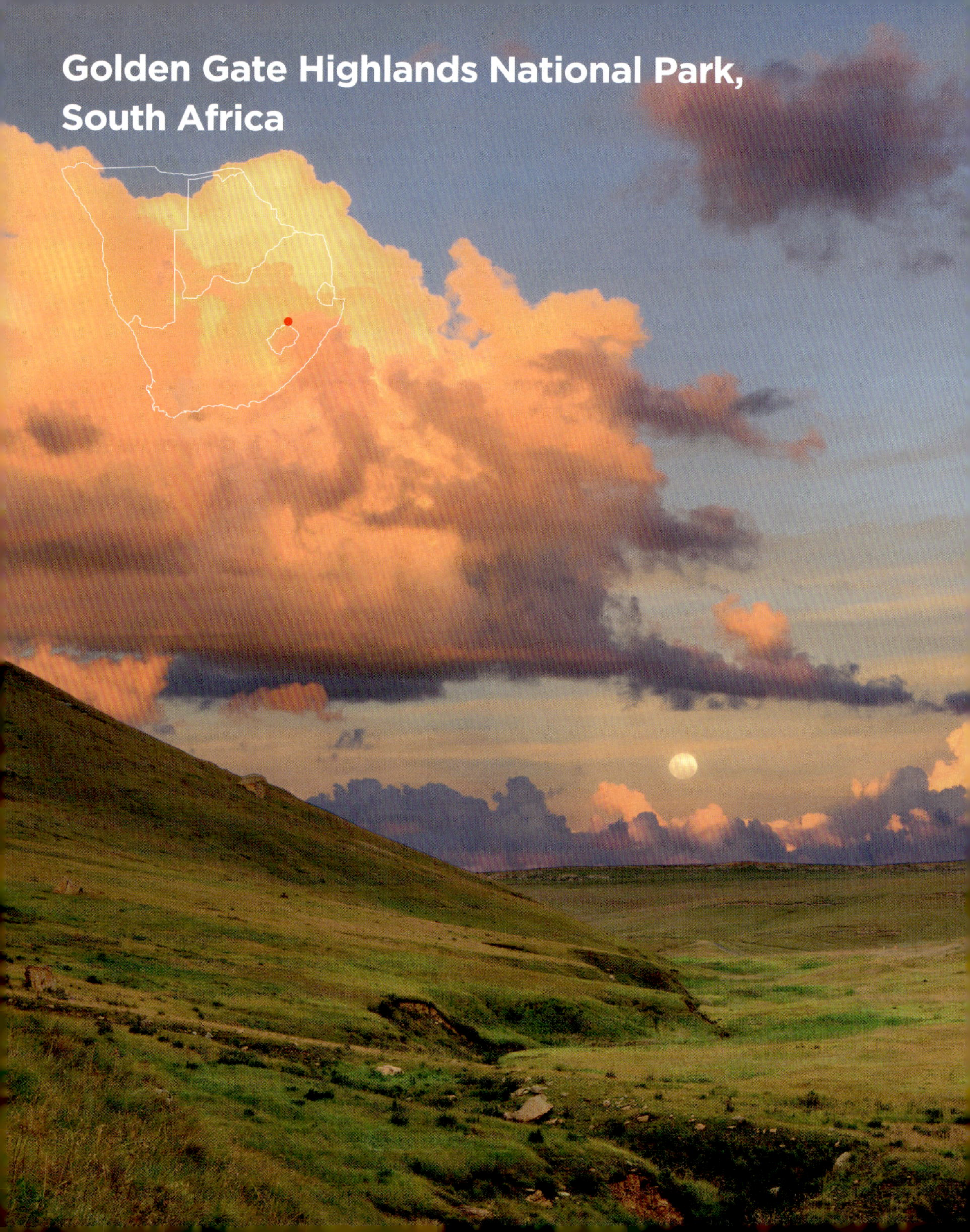
Golden Gate Highlands National Park,
South Africa

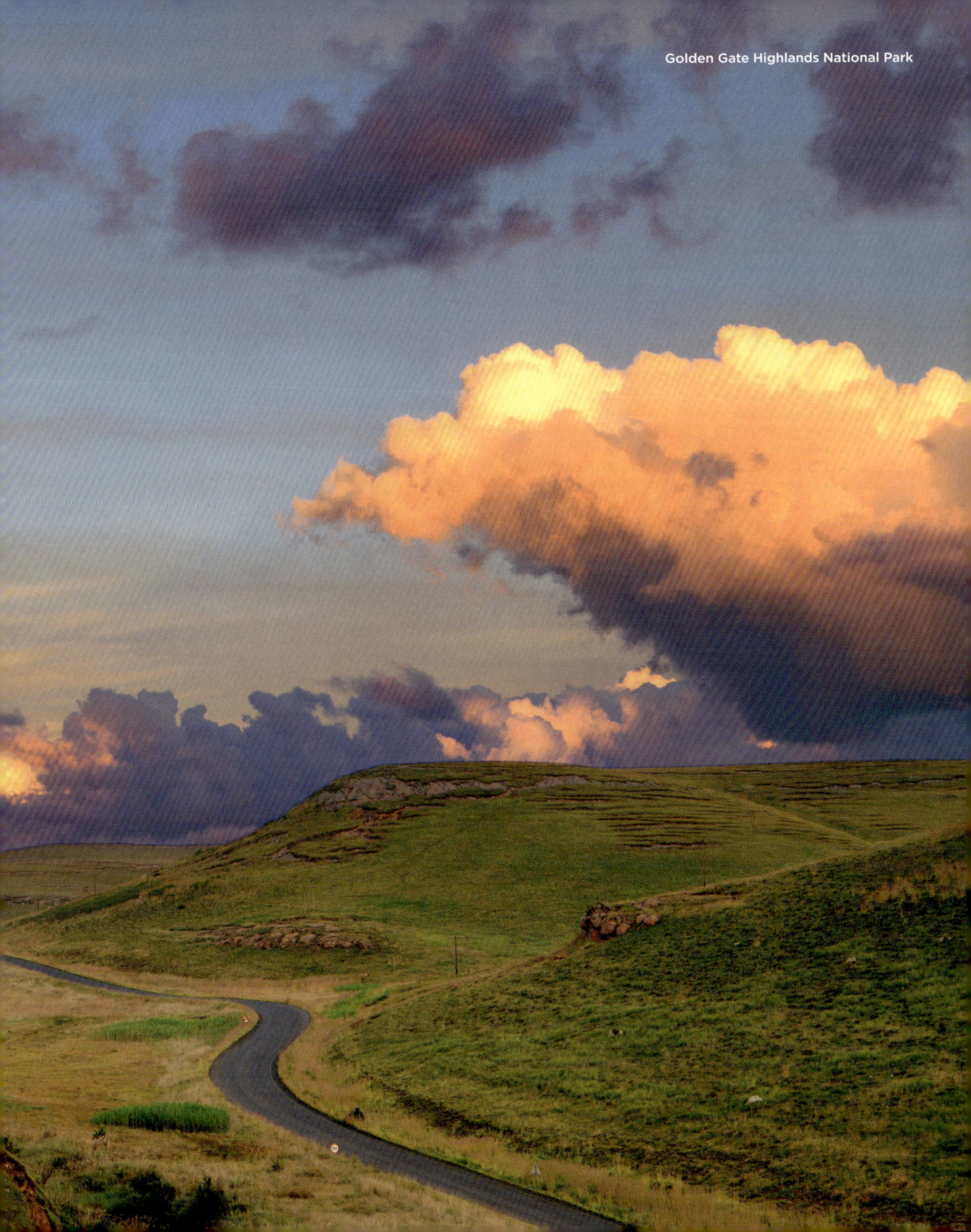
Golden Gate Highlands National Park

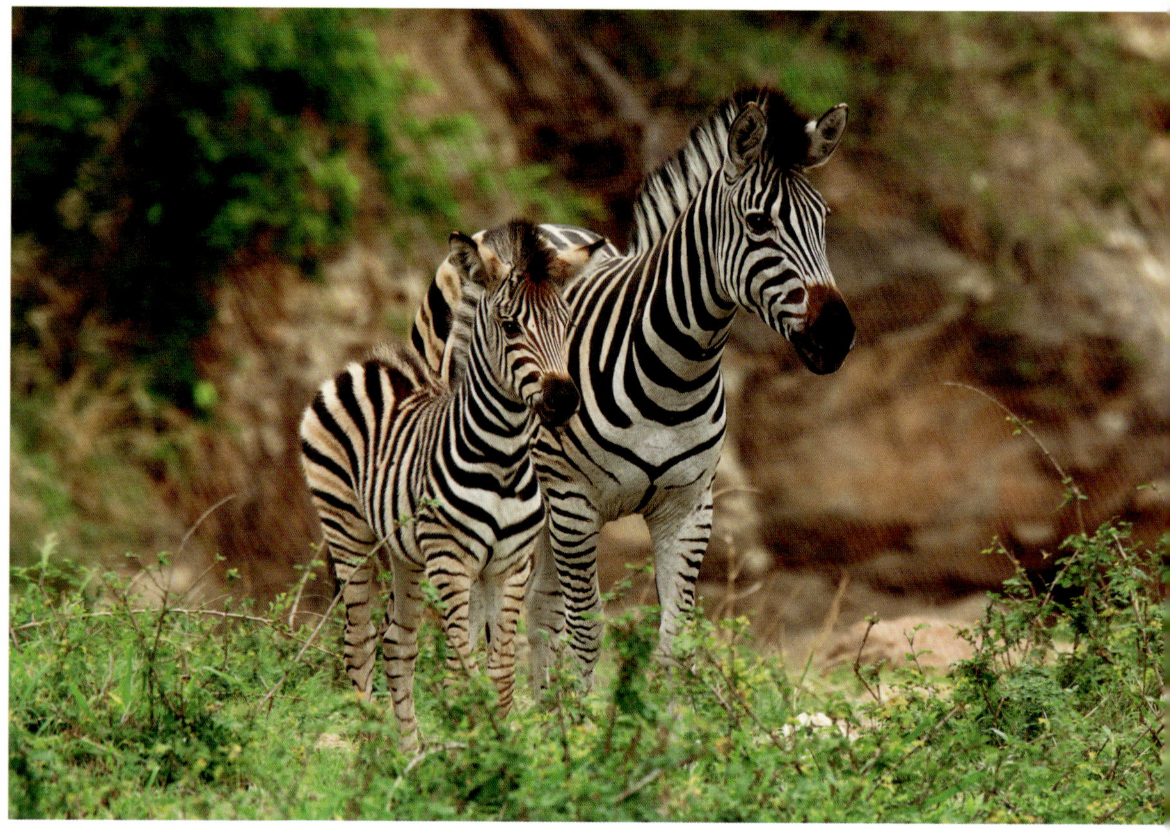

Zebras, Golden Gate Highlands National Park

Golden Gate Highlands National Park
This park is located in the South African province of Free State. Massive sandstone formations, caves, and gorges characterize this relatively small park, having an area of just 117 km^2 (45 mi^2), but it offers other highlights, such as the golden glow of the sandstone rocks as the sun goes down,.

Le parc national des Golden Gate Highlands
Le parc national des Golden Gate Highlands est situé dans la province d'État-Libre, en Afrique du Sud. Les imposantes falaises de grès, les grottes et les gorges définissent les paysages de ce parc relativement petit avec ses 117 km^2. Il n'en offre pas moins des points de vue superbes, comme ses murailles de grès jaune d'or au soleil couchant.

Golden-Gate-Highlands-Nationalpark
Der Golden-Gate-Highlands-Nationalpark liegt in der südafrikanischen Provinz Freistaat. Massive Sandsteinformationen, Höhlen und Schluchten prägen das Bild dieses mit einer Fläche von 117 km^2 relativ kleinen Parks, der aber besondere Highlights bietet: Wenn die Sonne untergeht, leuchten die Sandsteinfelsen goldgelb.

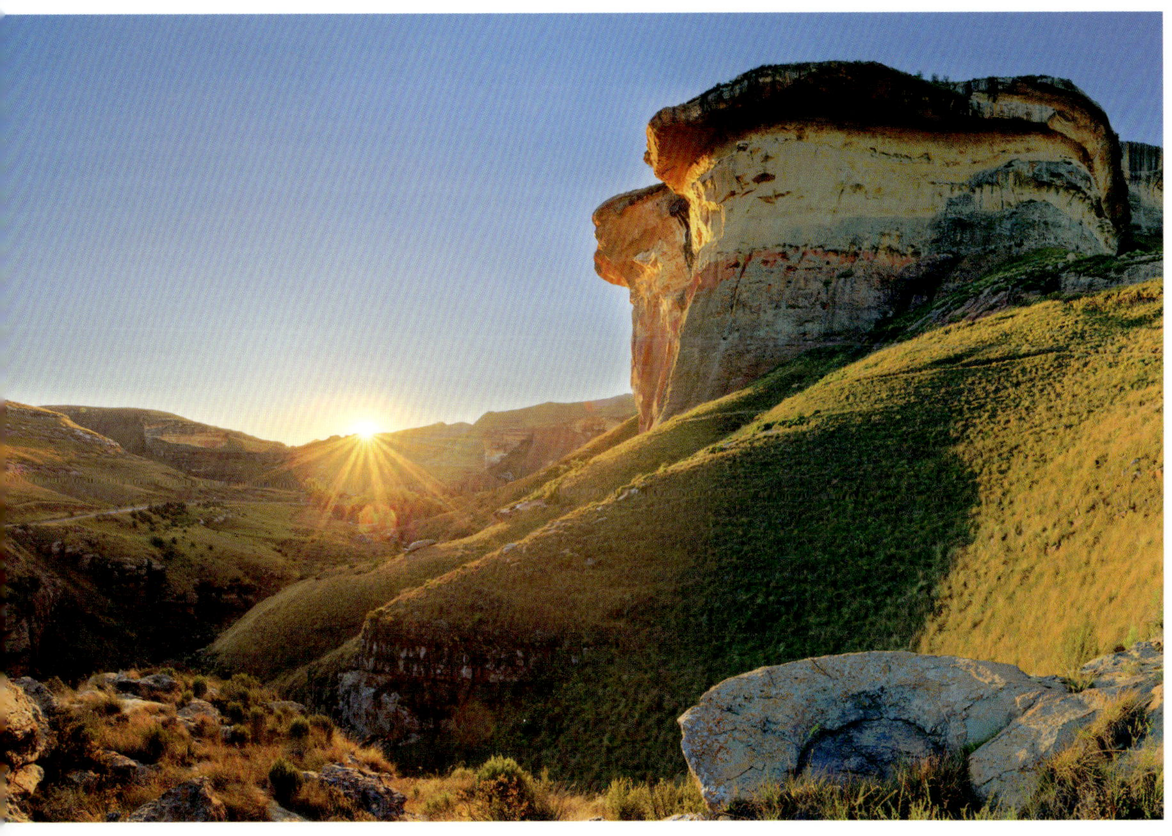

Brandwag Buttress, Golden Gate Highlands National Park

Parque Nacional Golden Gate Highlands
El Parque Nacional Golden Gate Highlands se encuentra en la provincia del Estado Libre de Sudáfrica. Formaciones masivas de piedra arenisca, cuevas y gargantas dan forma a la imagen de este parque relativamente pequeño con una superficie de 117 km^2, pero ofrece particularidades especiales: cuando se pone el sol, los acantilados de arenisca de color amarillo brillan como el oro.

Parco Nazionale Golden Gate Highlands
Il Parco Nazionale del Golden Gate Highlands si trova nella provincia sudafricana di Free State. Massicce formazioni di pietra arenaria, caverne e gole caratterizzano il paesaggio di questo parco relativamente piccolo, con una superficie di 117 km^2, ma che offre dei particolari punti d'interesse: quando il sole tramonta, le rocce di arenaria si illuminano di un colore giallo oro.

Nationaal Park Golden Gate Hoogland
Het Nationaal Park Golden Gate Hoogland ligt in de Zuid-Afrikaanse provincie Vrijstaat. Enorme zandsteenformaties, spelonken en kloven bepalen het landschap van dit park, dat met een oppervlakte van 117 km^2 relatief klein is maar niet minder bijzonder: wanneer de zon ondergaat, krijgen de zandsteenrotsen een goudgele glans.

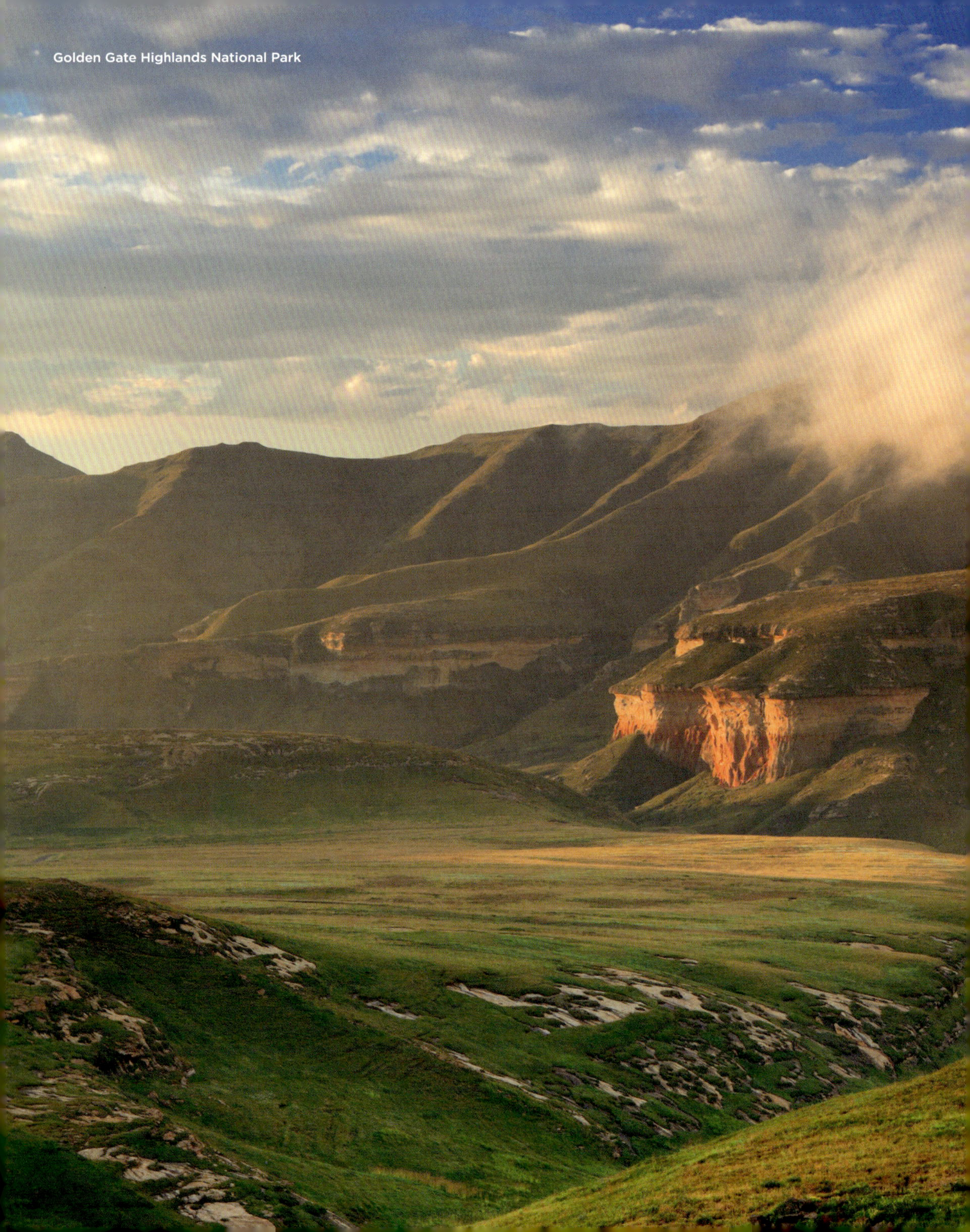

Golden Gate Highlands National Park

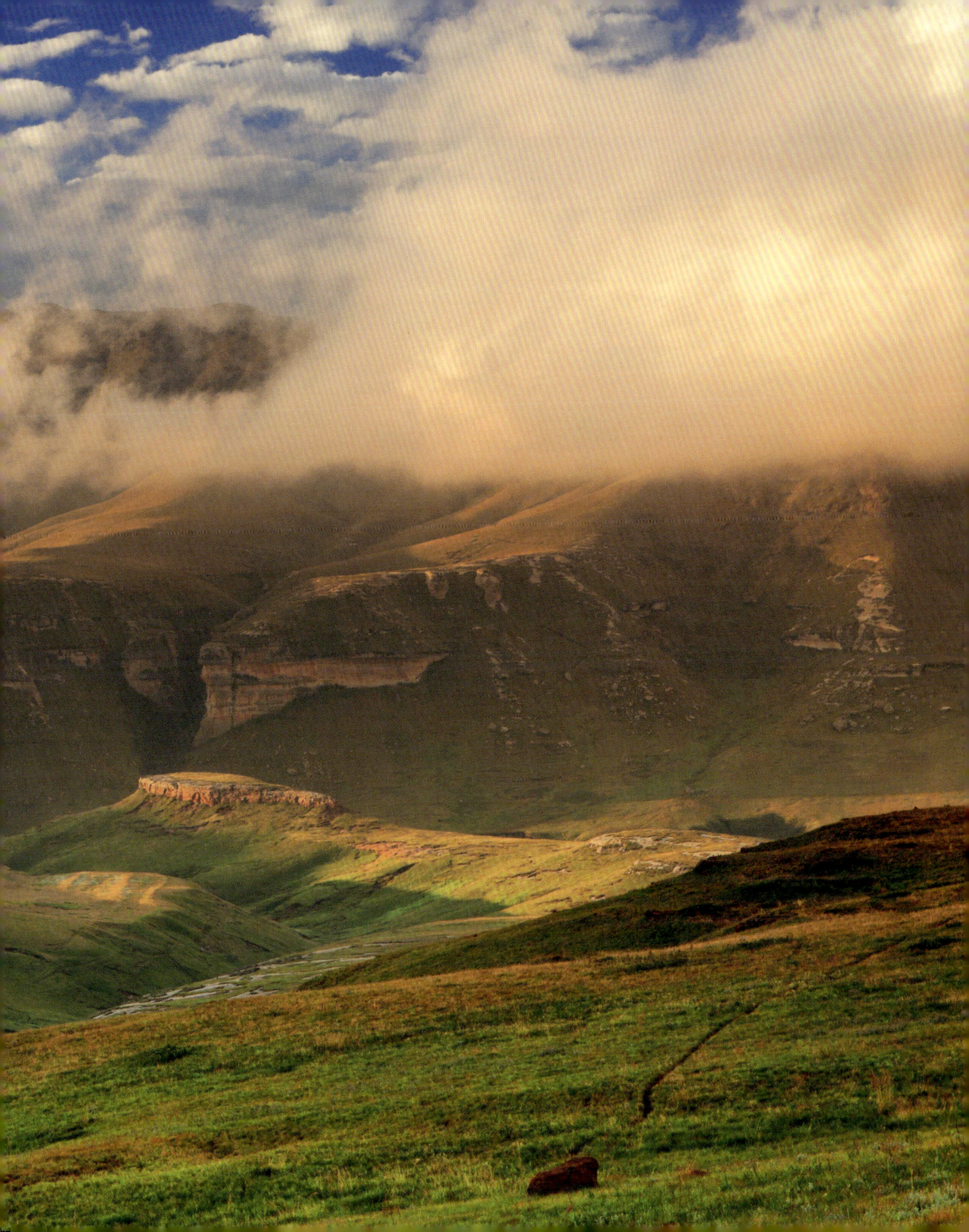

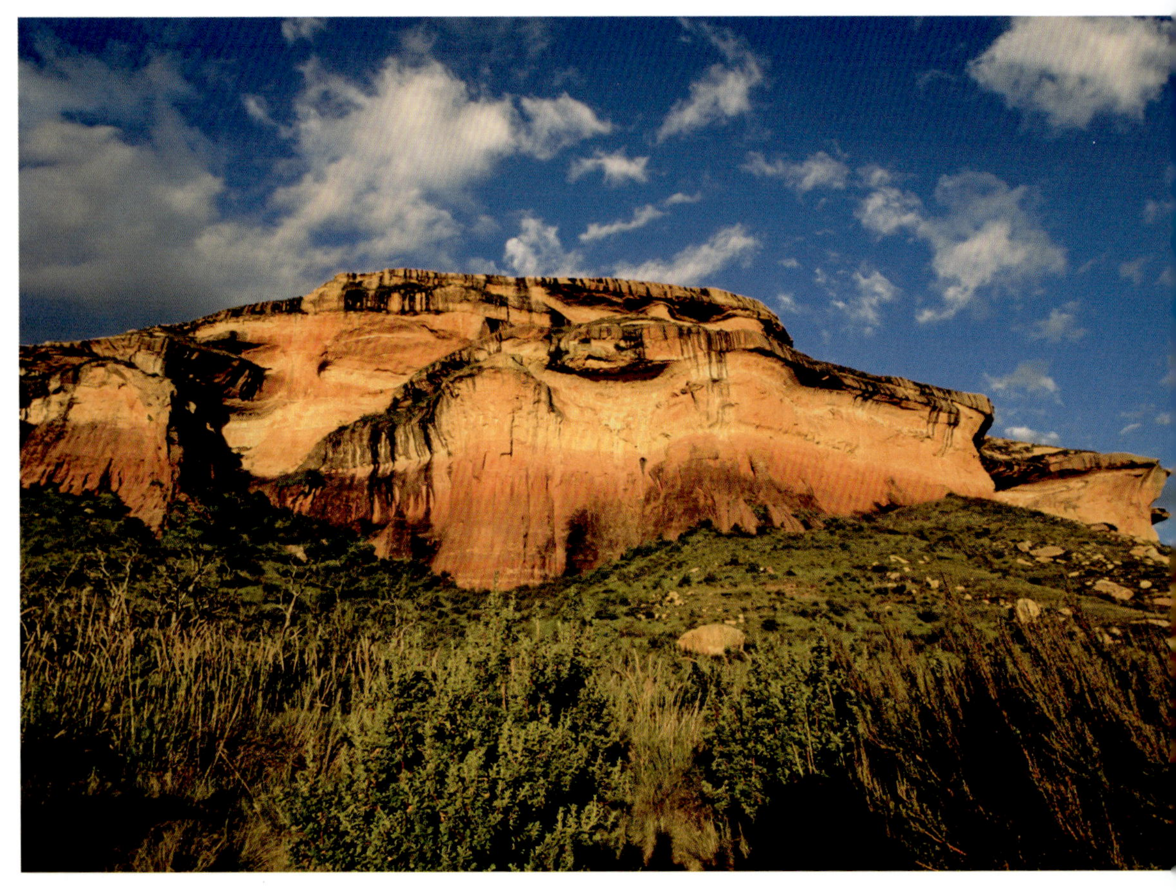

Sandstone cliff, Golden Gate Highlands National Park

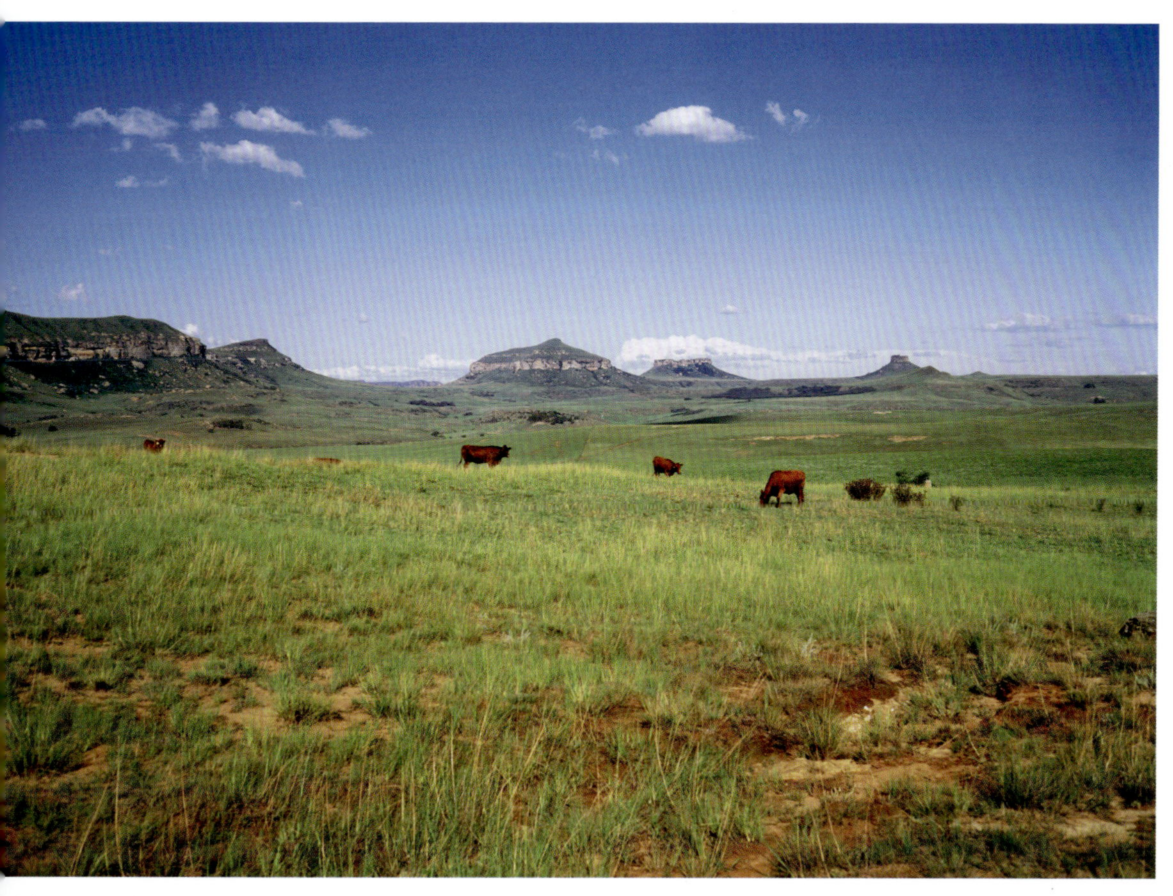

olden Gate Highlands National Park

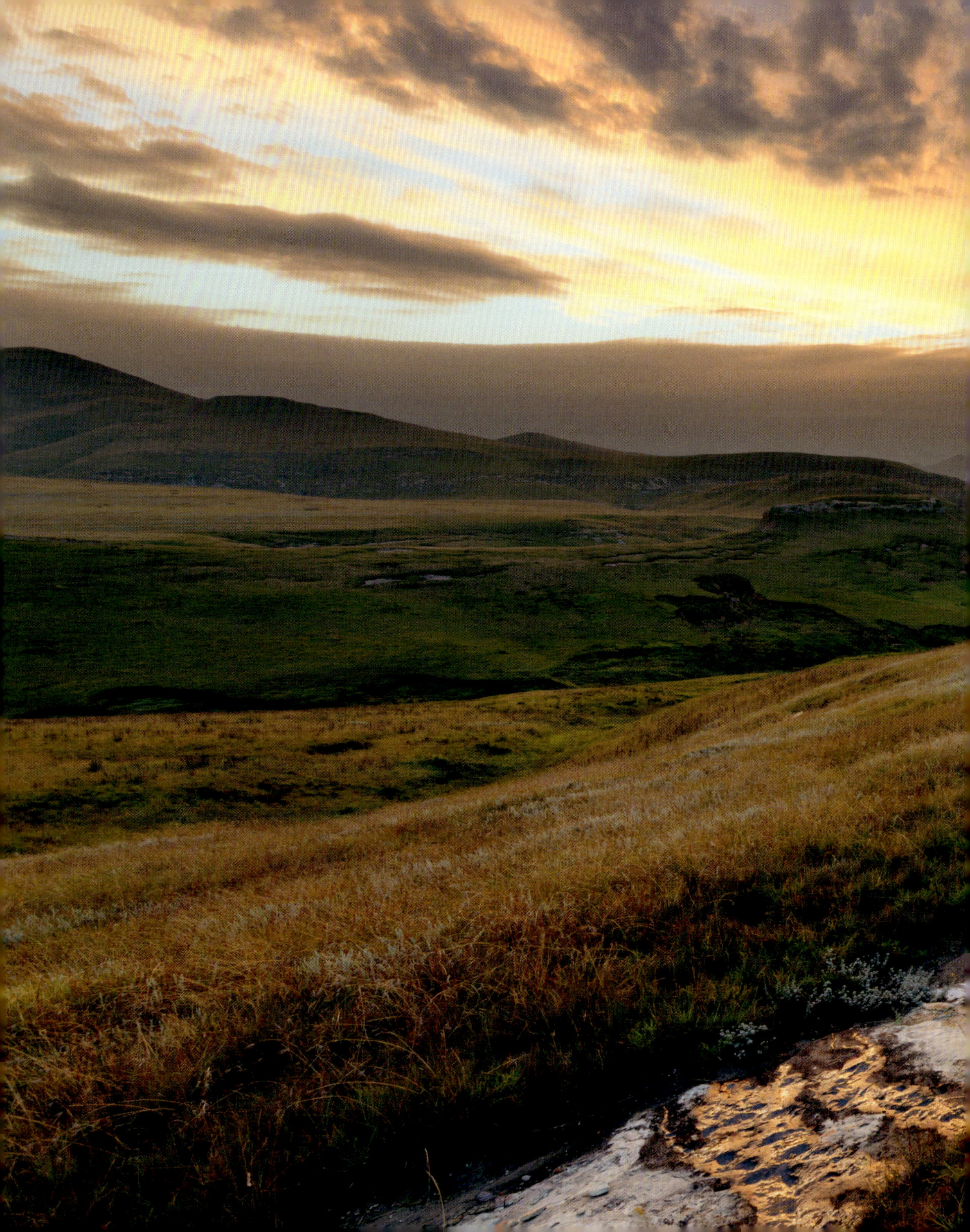

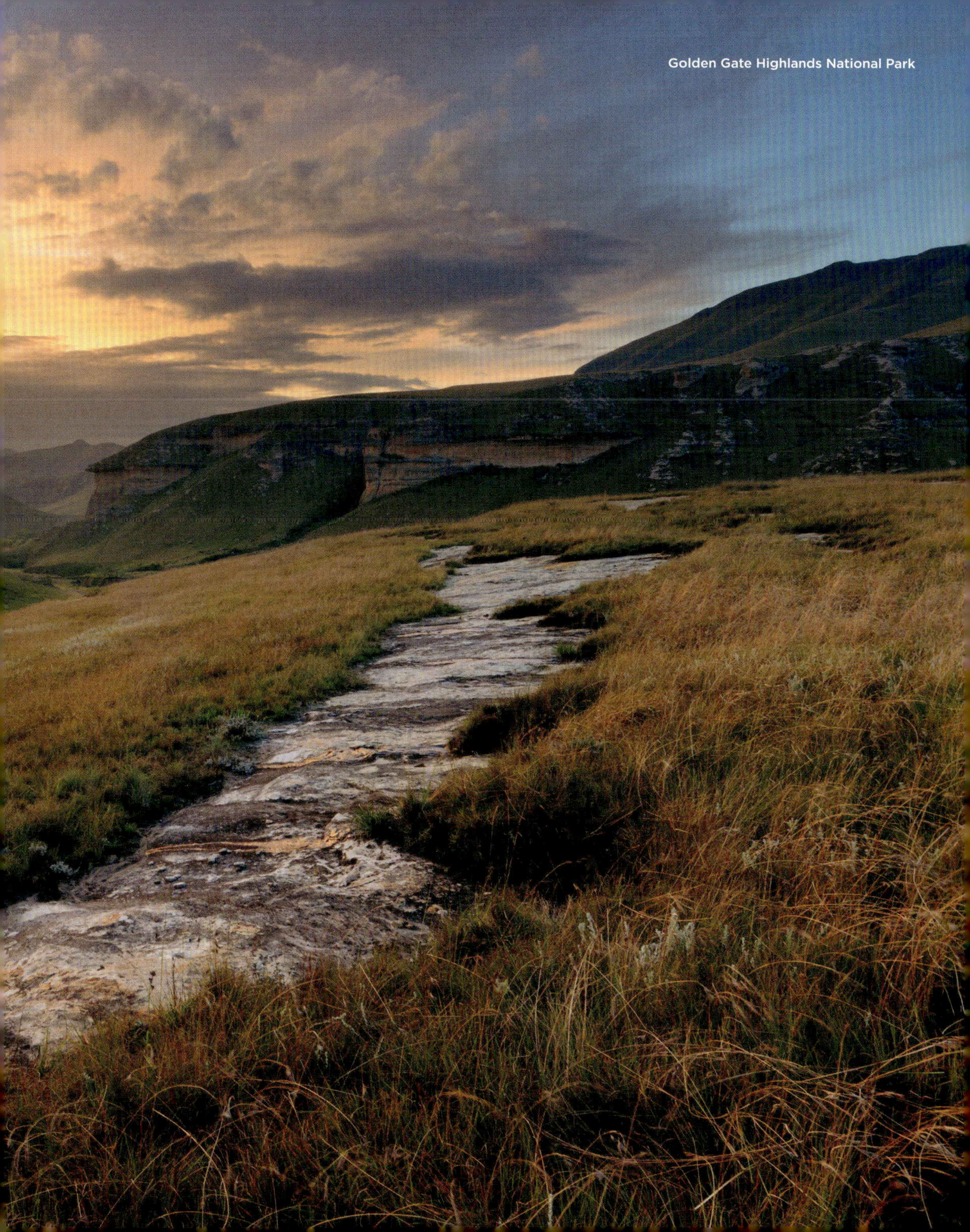

Golden Gate Highlands National Park

Drakensberg Mountains & Durban, South Africa

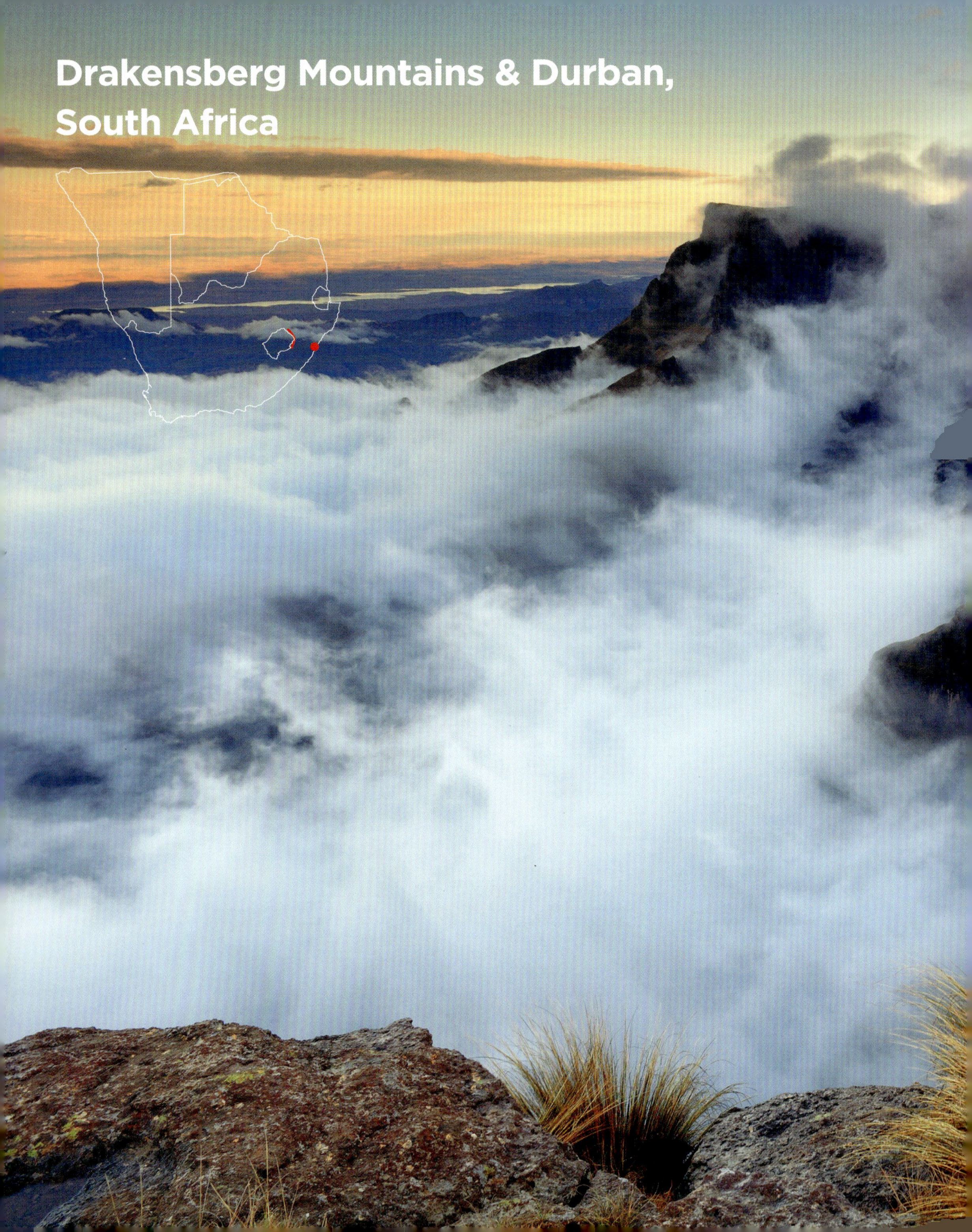

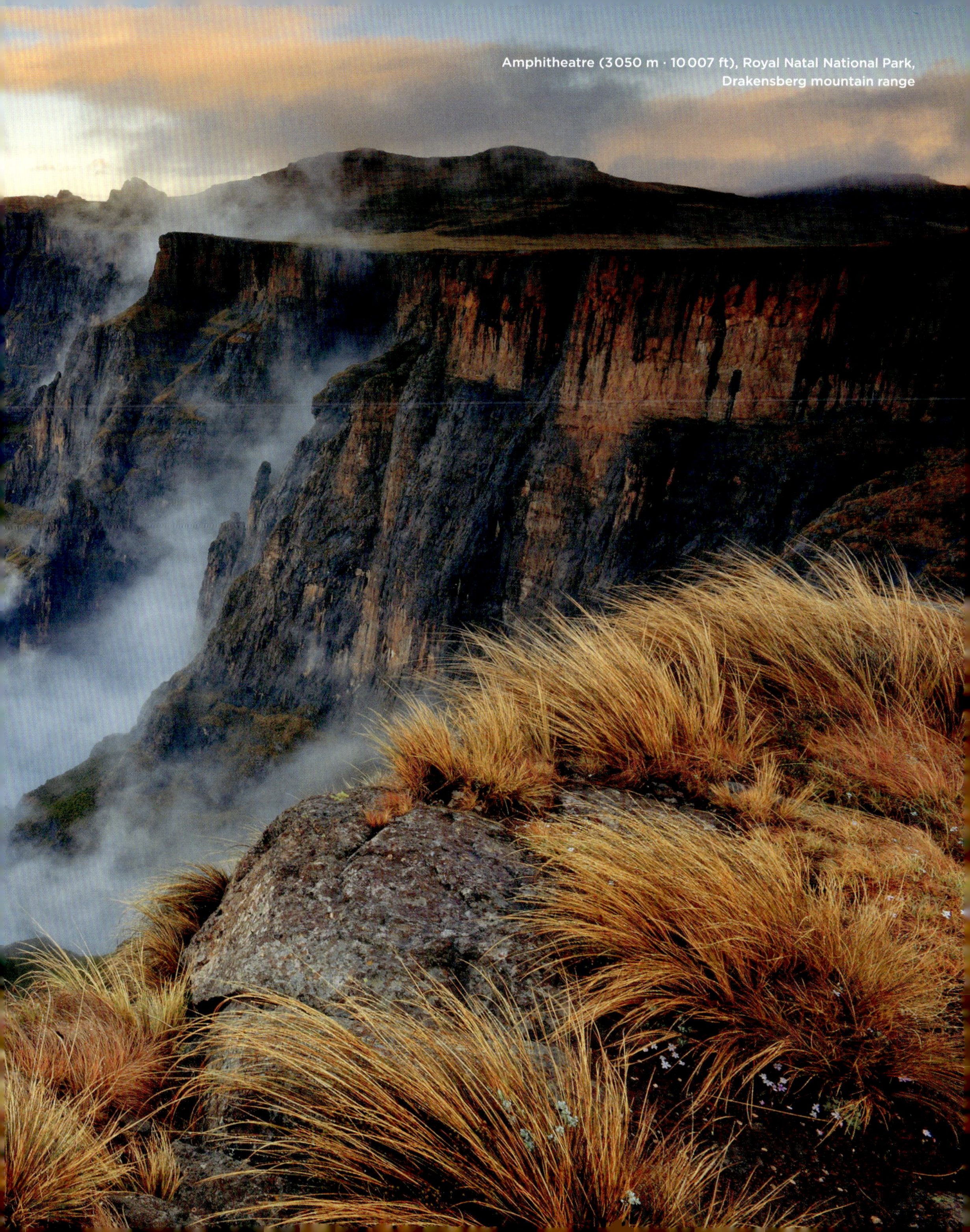

Amphitheatre (3 050 m · 10 007 ft), Royal Natal National Park, Drakensberg mountain range

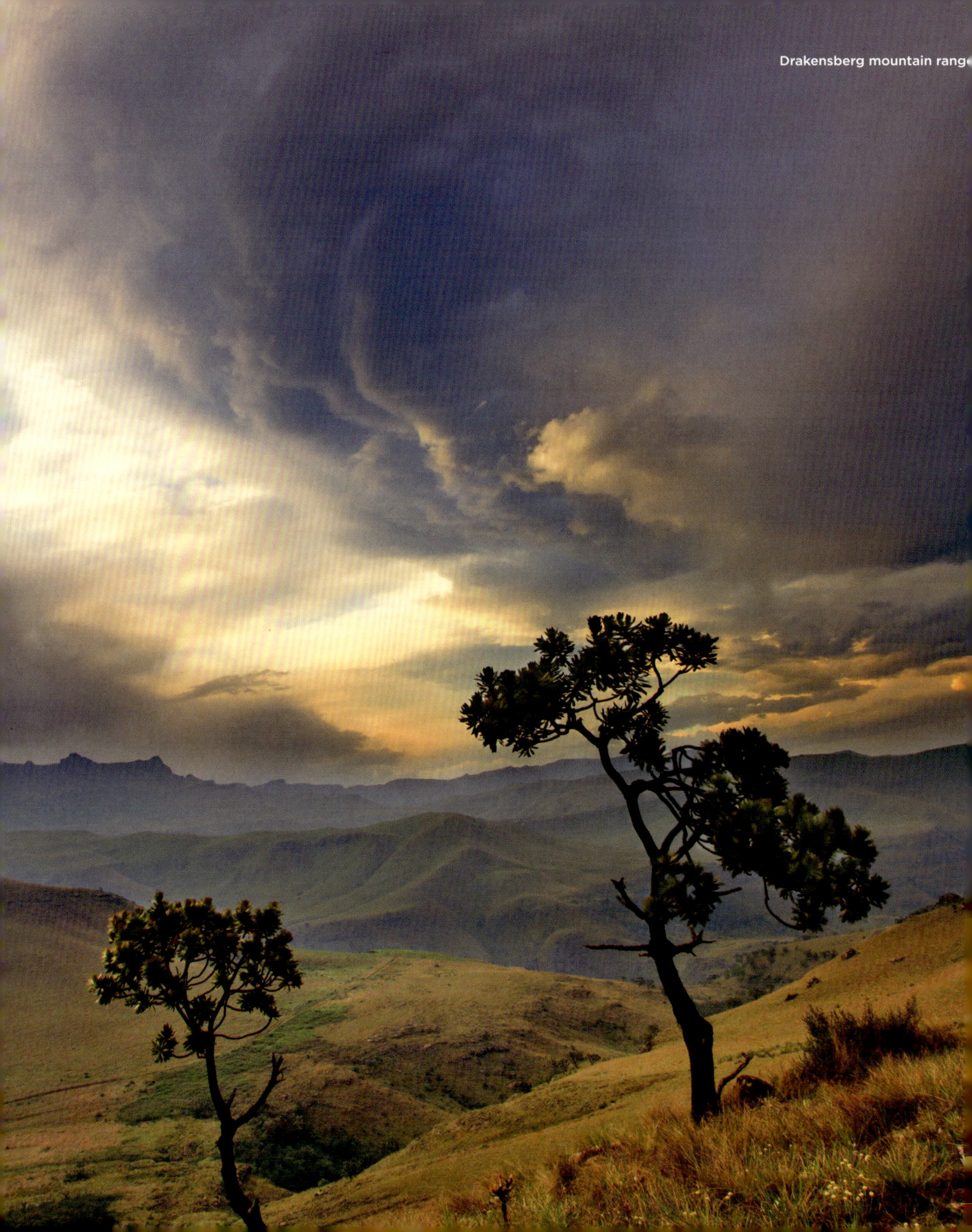

Drakensberg mountain range

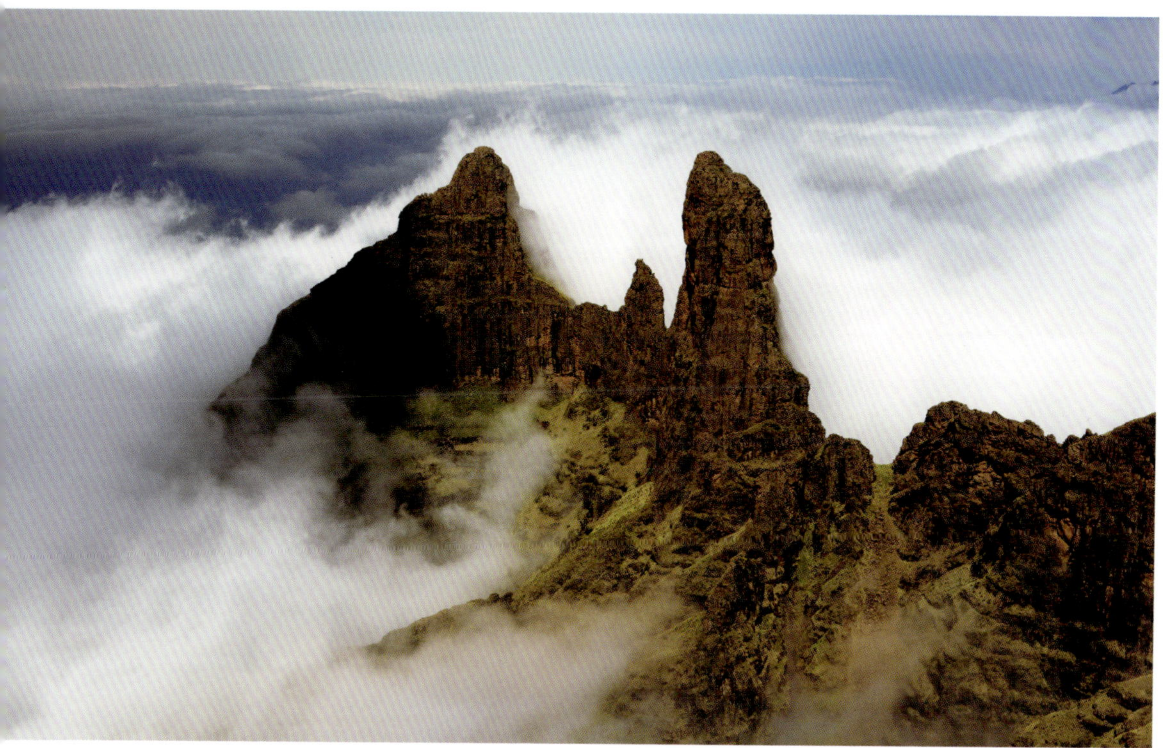

athedral Peak region, Drakensberg mountain range

rakensberg Mountains

he Drakensberg Mountains, which rise to 3482 m (11424 ft), are the highest ountains in southern Africa. The ountain range runs for about 1000 km 21 mi) from the South African province Mpumalanga, over Lesotho to the ovince of East Cape. The mountains are volcanic origin and consist mainly of salt-like rock.

Drakensberge

Die bis zu einer Höhe von 3482 m ansteigenden Drakensberge sind das höchste Gebirge im Süden Afrikas. Der Gebirgszug ist rund 1000 km lang und erstreckt sich von der südafrikanischen Provinz Mpumalanga über Lesotho bis in die Provinz Ostkap. Das Gebirge ist vulkanischen Ursprungs und besteht überwiegend aus basaltartigen Steinen.

Monti dei Draghi

I Monti dei Draghi raggiungono un'altitudine di 3482 m e sono i più alti dell'Africa del Sud. La catena montuosa è lunga circa 1000 km e si estende dalla provincia sudafricana di Mpumalanga attraverso il Lesotho, fino alla provincia del Capo Orientale. La montagna è di origine vulcanica e composta prevalentemente da pietra basaltica.

Drakensberg

Drakensberg, qui culmine à 3482 m, t le plus haut massif d'Afrique du Sud. s'étend sur environ 1000 km et traverse province de Mpumalanga, le Lesotho le Cap-Est. D'origine volcanique, il se mpose en majeure partie de roches saltiques.

Drakensberg

El Drakensberg se eleva hasta una altitud de 3482 m y es la montaña más alta de África del Sur. La cordillera tiene de largo unos 1000 km y se extiende desde la provincia sudafricana de Mpumalanga sobre Lesotho hasta la provincia del Cabo Este. La región es de origen volcánico y se compone principalmente de piedras de basálticas.

Drakensbergen

De Drakensbergen, die tot een hoogte van 3482 m verrijzen, zijn de hoogste van zuidelijk Afrika. De bergketen is circa 1000 km lang en strekt zich van de Zuid-Afrikaanse provincie Mpumalanga via Lesotho tot aan de provincie Oost-Kaap uit. Het gebergte is van vulkanische oorsprong en bestaat grotendeels uit basaltgesteente.

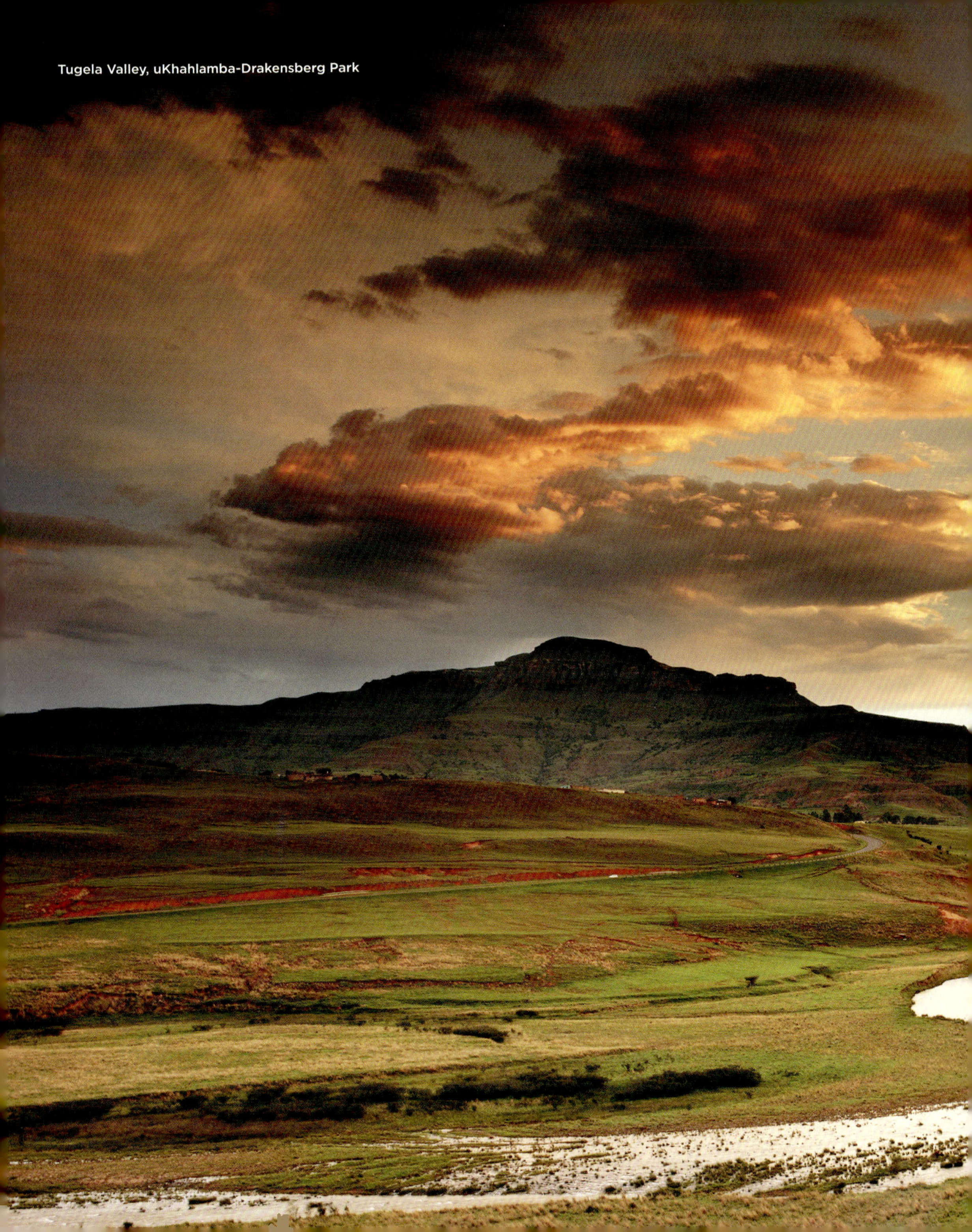

Tugela Valley, uKhahlamba-Drakensberg Park

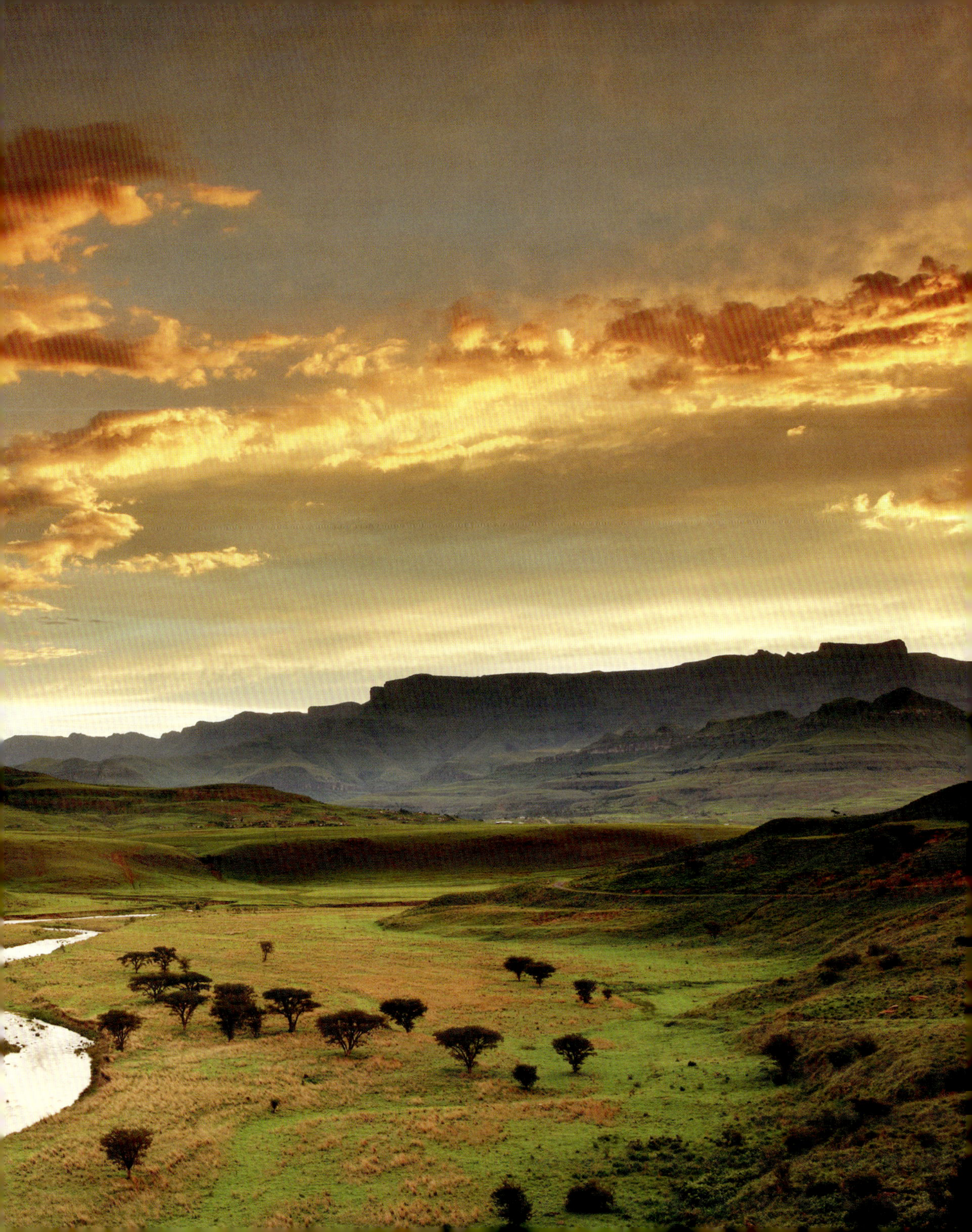

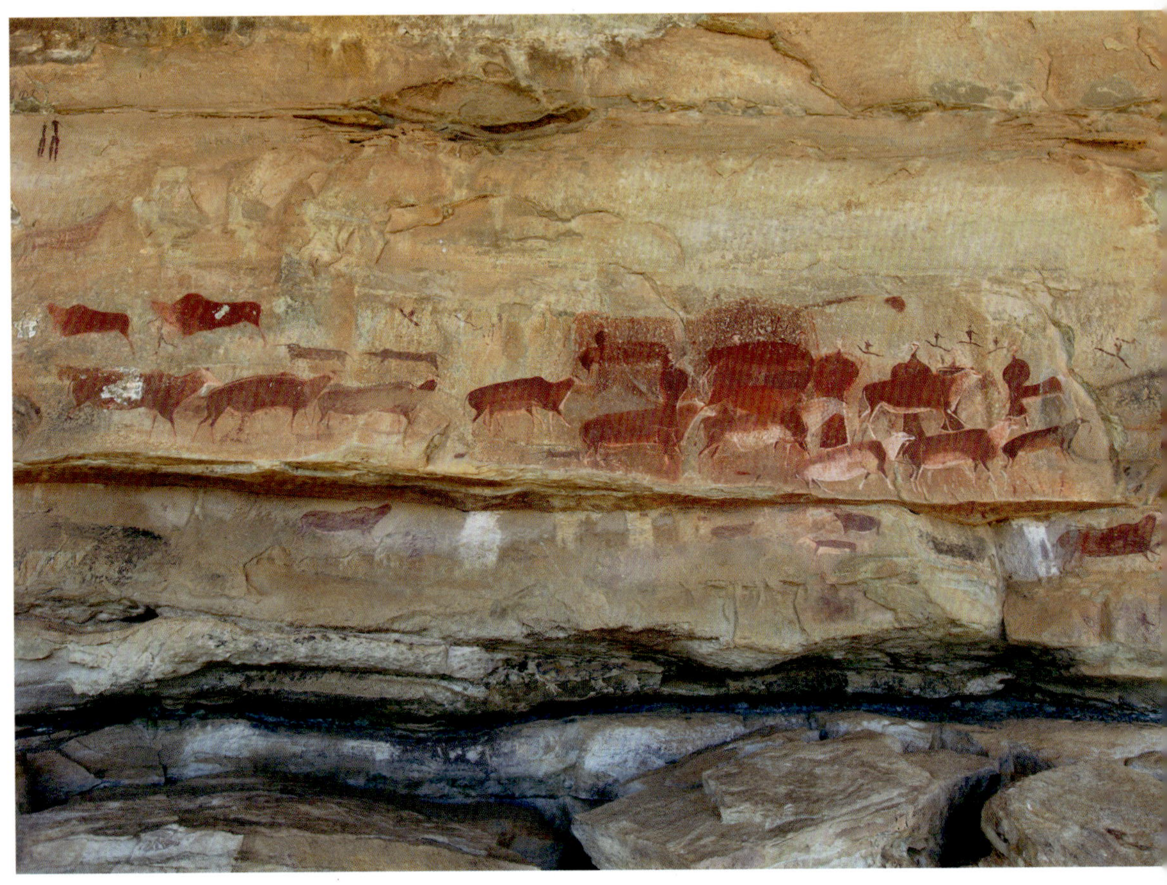

San rock art, Game Pass Shelter, Drakensberg mountain range

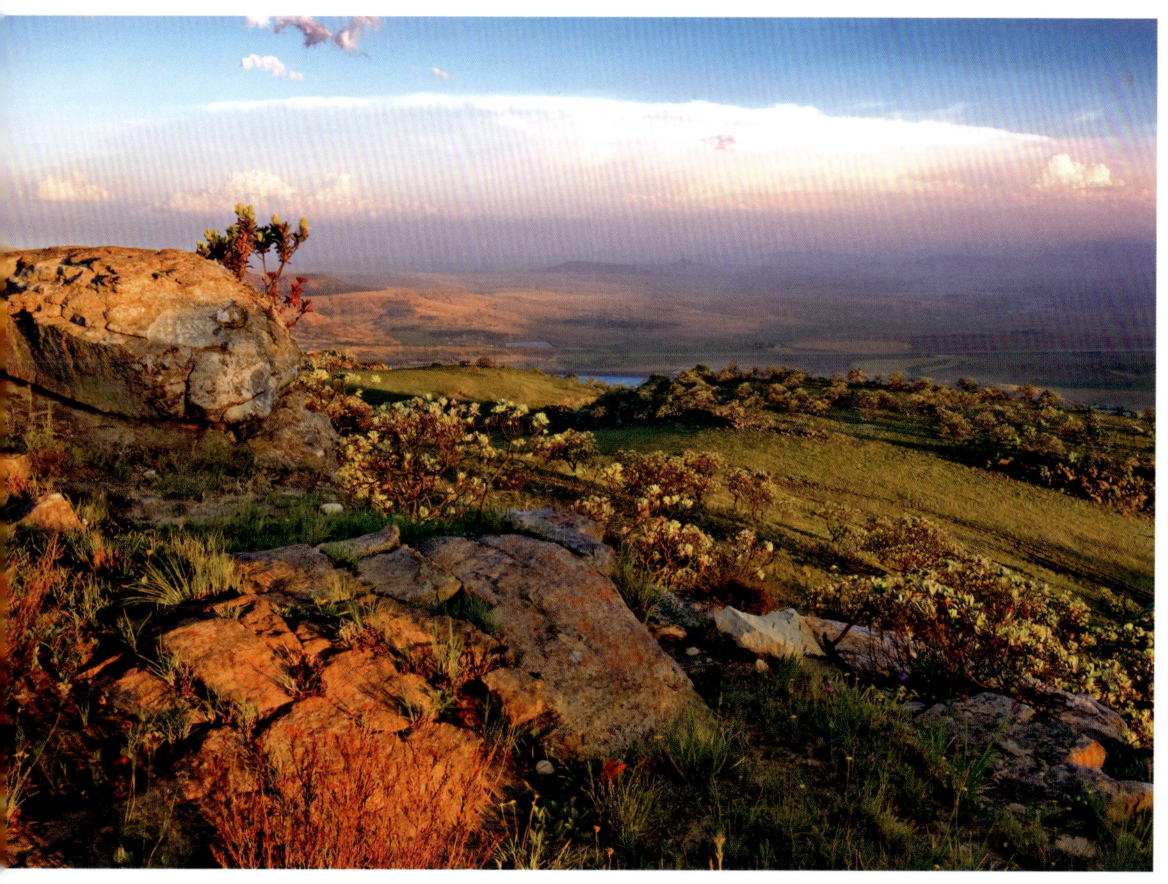

rakensberg mountain range, uKhahlamba-Drakensberg Park

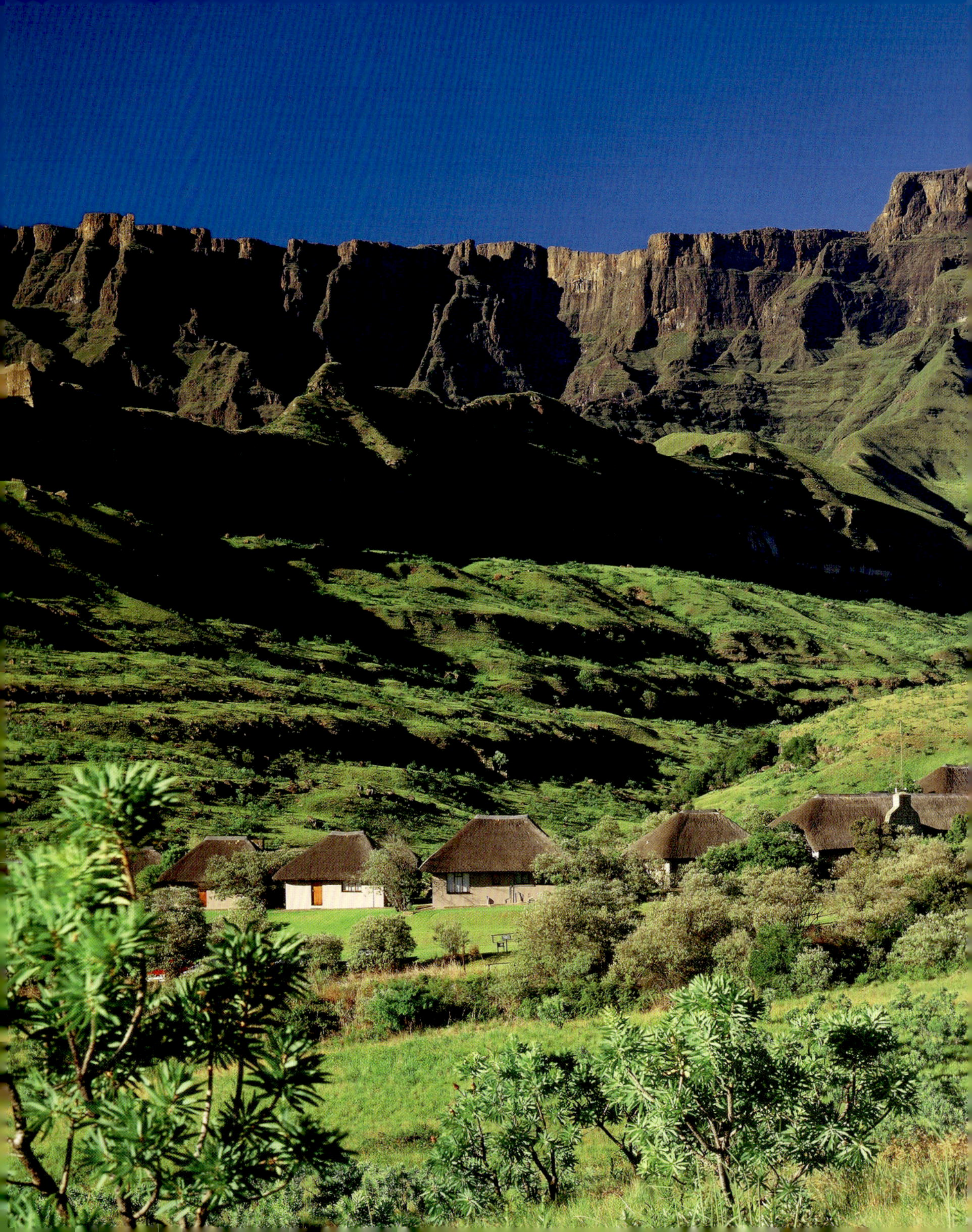

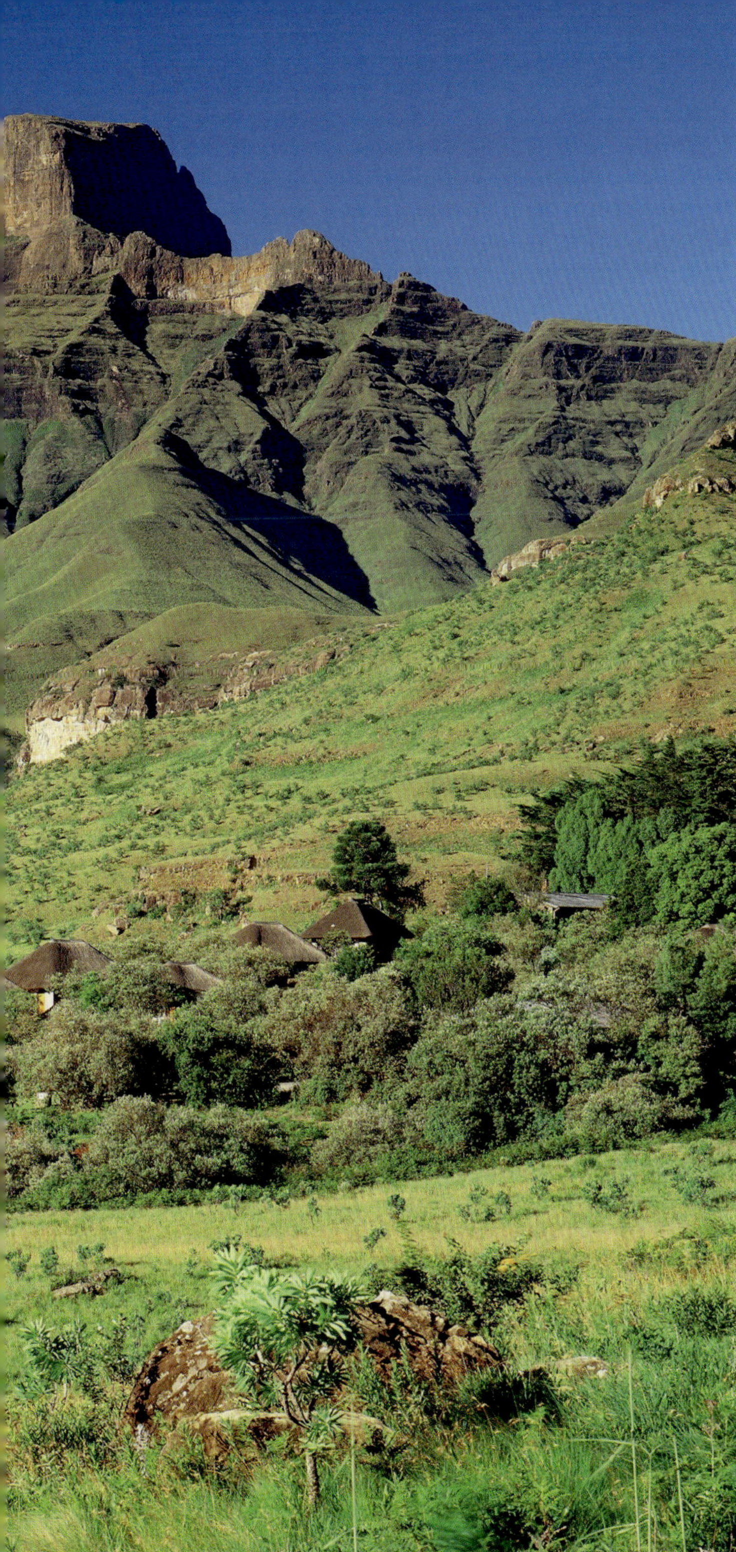

Mont-Aux-Sources (3282 m · 10768 ft), Drakensberg mountain range

Great Escarpment
The Drakensberg Mountains are part of the Great Escarpment of southern Africa. It originated some 180 million years ago, when the primordial continent Gondwana split and the continents began to shift. The Great Escarpment divides the inland highlands from the coastal plain.

Le Grand Escarpement
Le Drakensberg fait partie du Grand Escarpement, dont l'origine remonte à 180 millions d'années. À cette époque, le Gondwana se scinda et les continents entamèrent leur dérive. Le Grand Escarpement s'intercale entre les plateaux intérieurs et le littoral.

Große Randstufe
Die Drakensberge sind Teil der Großen Randstufe im südlichen Afrika. Sie entstand vor rund 180 Millionen Jahren, als der Urkontinent Gondwana sich aufspaltete und die Kontinente begannen, sich zu verschieben. Die Große Randstufe grenzt das Binnenhochland gegen die Küstenebenen ab.

Peldaño de borde grande
Las montañas Drakensberg son parte de la Gran Escarpada (Great Scarpment) en el sur de África. Se originó hace unos 180 millones de años, cuando el supercontinente Gondwana se dividió y los continentes comenzaron a cambiar. Demarca las tierras altas del interior frente a las llanuras costeras.

La Grande Scarpata
I Monti dei Draghi fanno parte della Grande Scarpata nell'Africa meridionale. Nacquero circa 180 milioni di anni fa, quando il continente ancestrale Gondwana si spaccò e i continenti cominciarono a spostarsi. La Grande Scarpata delimita l'altopiano interno dalle pianure costiere.

Namibisch Escarpment
De Drakensbergen maken deel uit van de Namibische plateaurand van zuidelijk Afrika, die circa 180 miljoen jaar geleden ontstond toen het oerlandmassa Gondwana zich opsplitste en de continenten begonnen te verschuiven. De Namibische plateaurand vormt de grens tussen het centrale "hoogveld" van Zuid-Afrika en de kustvlakten.

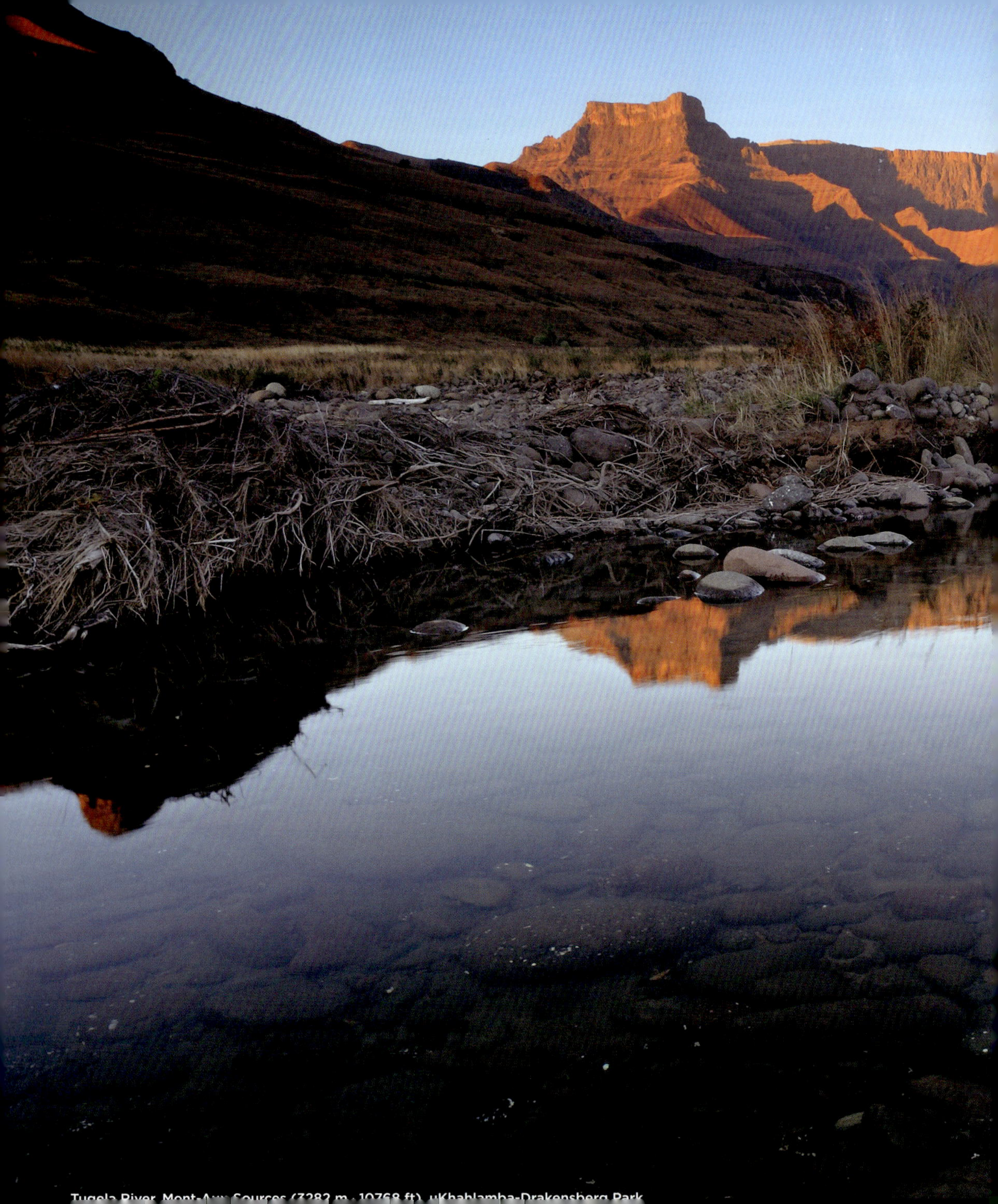

Tugela River, Mont-Aux-Sources (3282 m, 10768 ft), uKhahlamba-Drakensberg Park

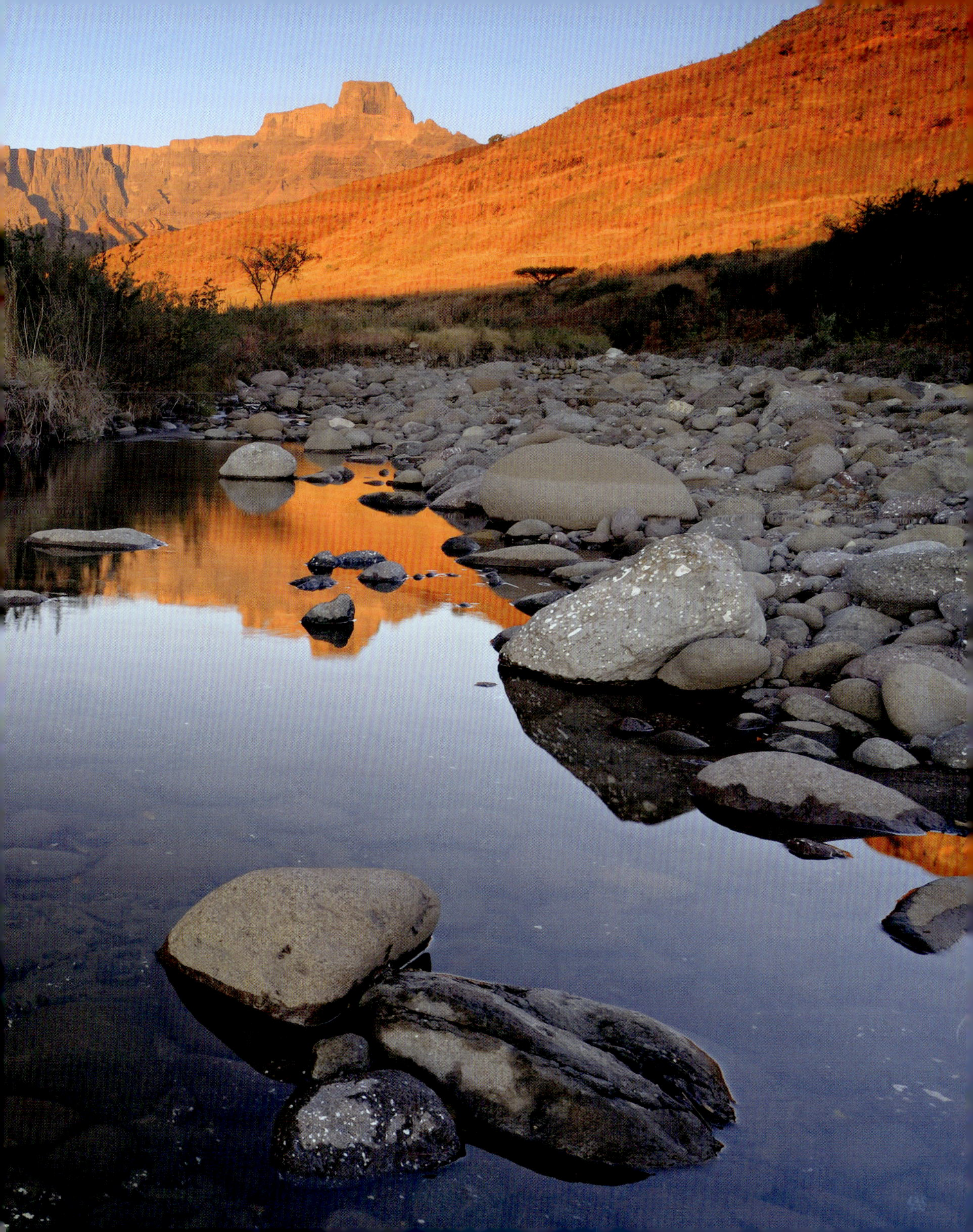

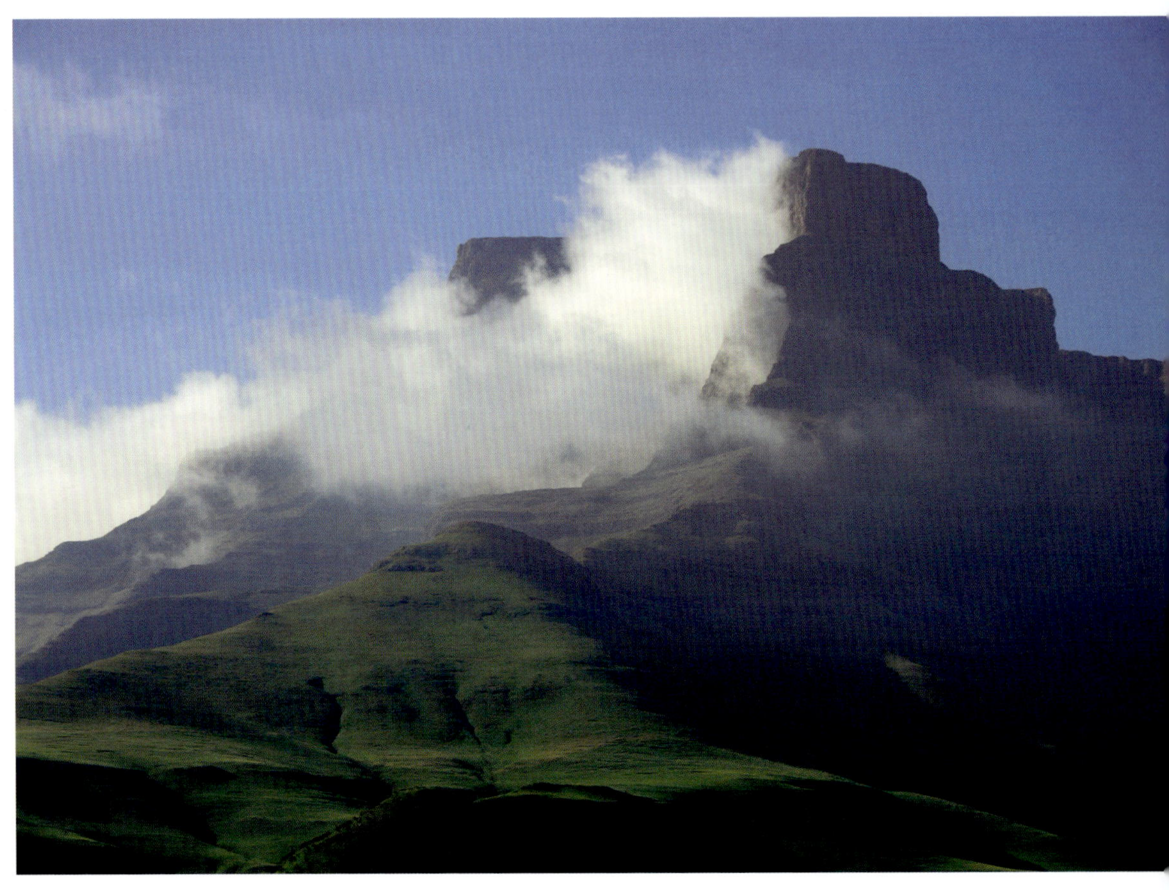

Amphitheatre (3050 m · 10007 ft), Royal Natal National Park,
Drakensberg mountain range

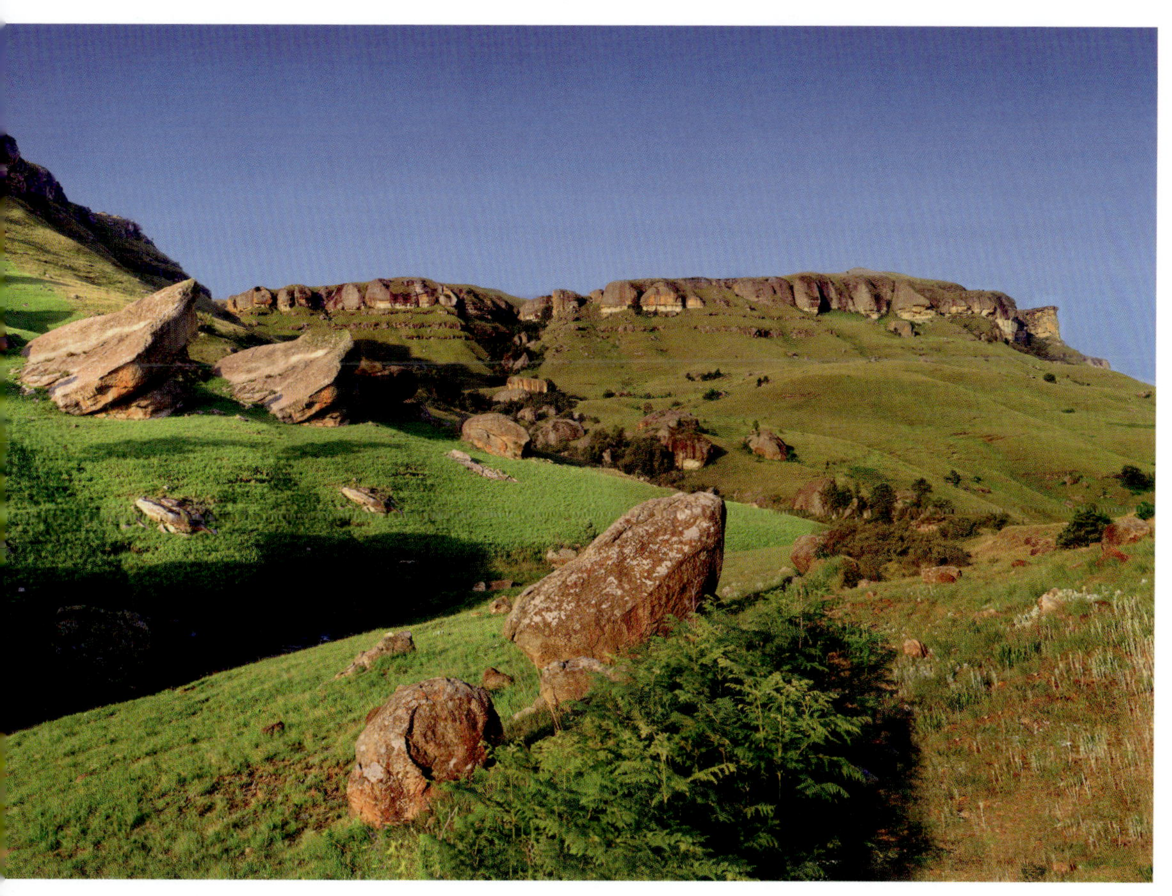

'dlands, KwaZulu-Natal

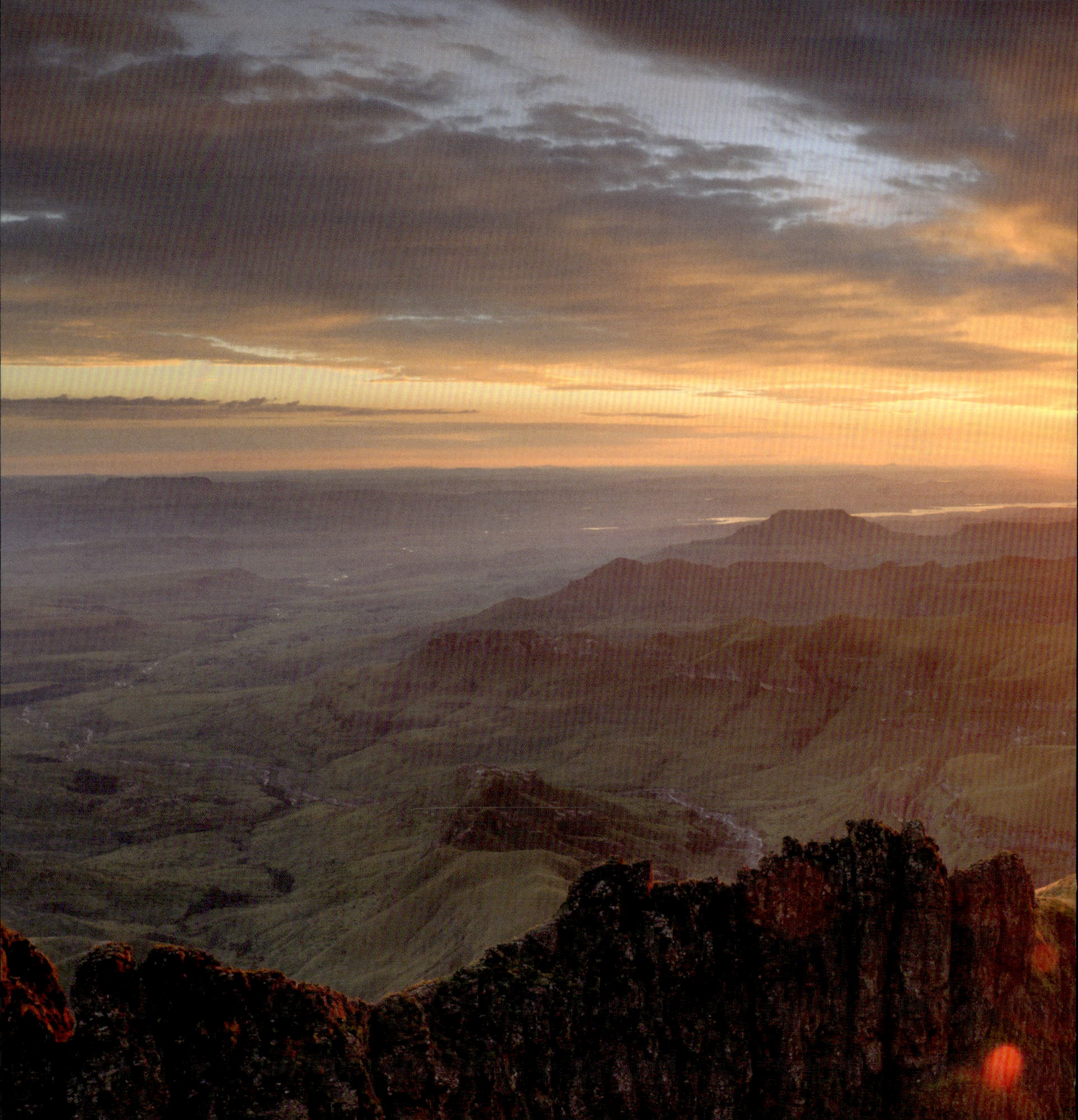

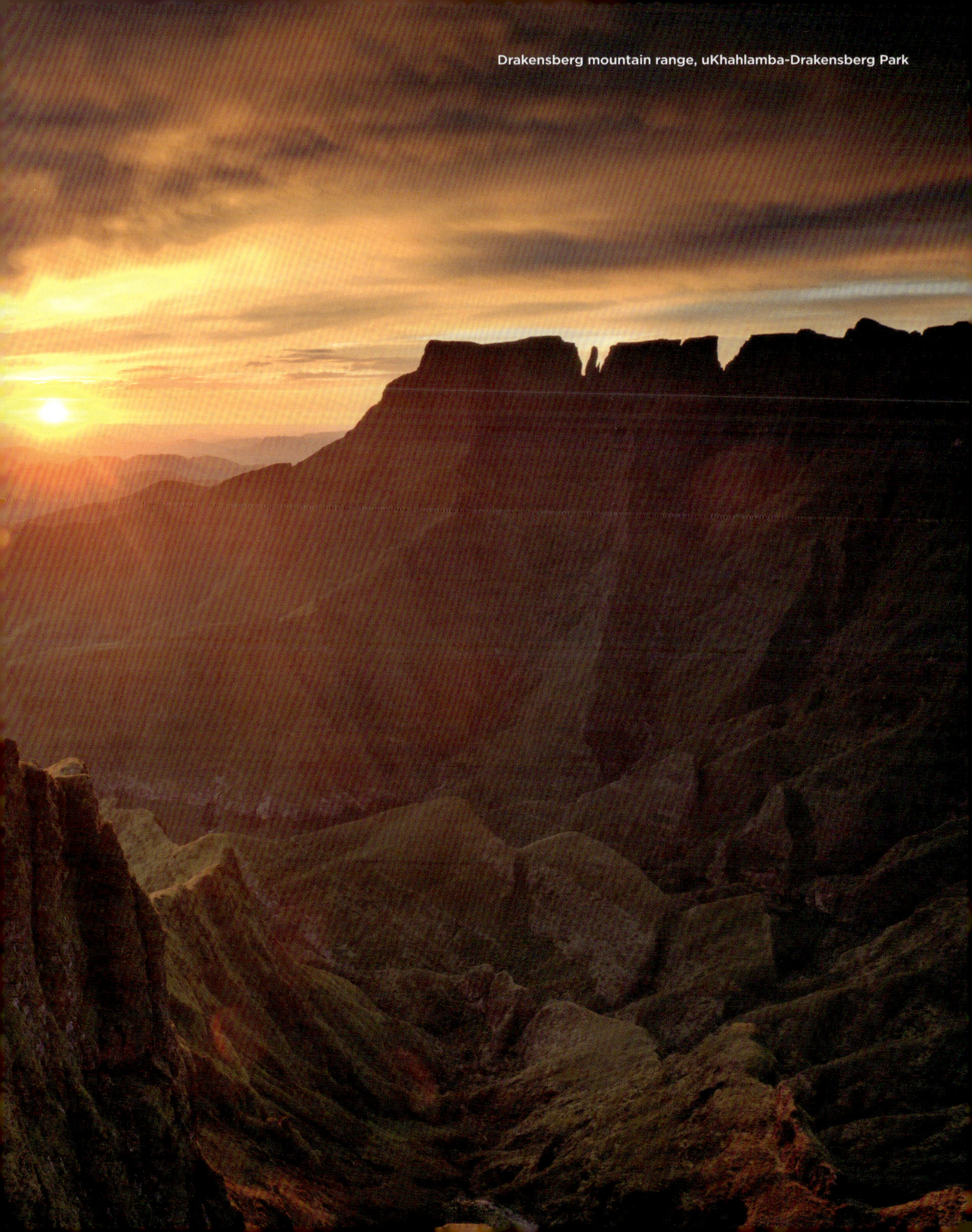

Drakensberg mountain range, uKhahlamba-Drakensberg Park

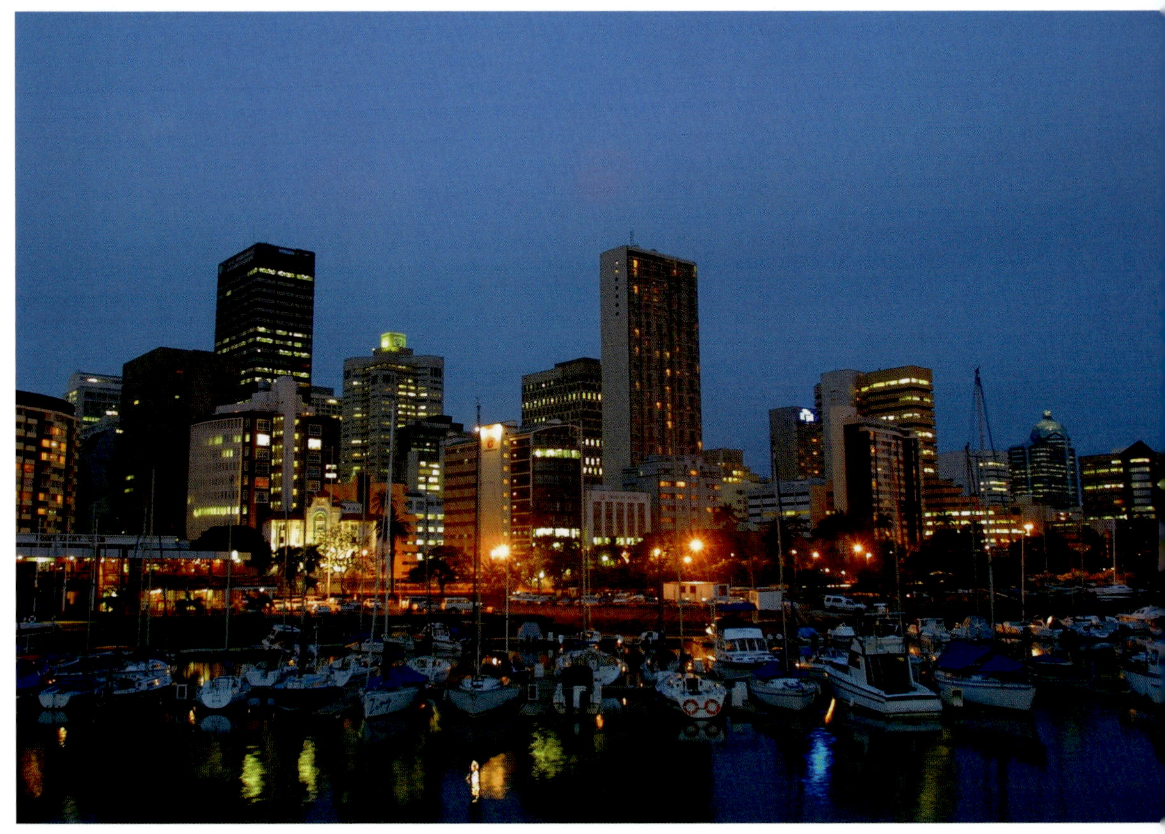

Point Yacht Club, Durban

Durban
The third largest city is also South Africa's most important port city, called "eThekwini" (lagoon) in the Zulu language. The bay of Durban was discovered in 1497 by the Portuguese navigator Vasco da Gama. Today, Durban is an important industrial and financial centre and also a popular holiday destination. About 8 km of the finest sandy beach stretch along the seafront of the metropolis.

Durban
Troisième ville du pays par sa taille, c'est aussi la plus importante ville portuaire d'Afrique du Sud, baptisée « eThekwini » (lagune) en zoulou. Cette baie fut découverte en 1497, par le navigateur portugais Vasco de Gama. Aujourd'hui, Durban est un haut lieu de l'industrie et de la finance, et une destination touristique prisée. Cette grande ville est bordée par une plage de sable fin, longue d'environ 8 km.

Durban
Die drittgrößte Stadt ist zugleich auch die wichtigste Hafenstadt Südafrikas, in der Sprache der Zulu „eThekwini“ (Lagune) genannt. Entdeckt wurde die Bucht von Durban schon 1497 durch den portugiesischen Seefahrer Vasco da Gam Heute gilt Durban als wichtiger Industrie- und Finanzstandort und ist zudem beliebtes Urlaubsziel. Etwa 8 km feinster Sandstrand erstreckt sich entlang der Beachfront der Millionenstadt.

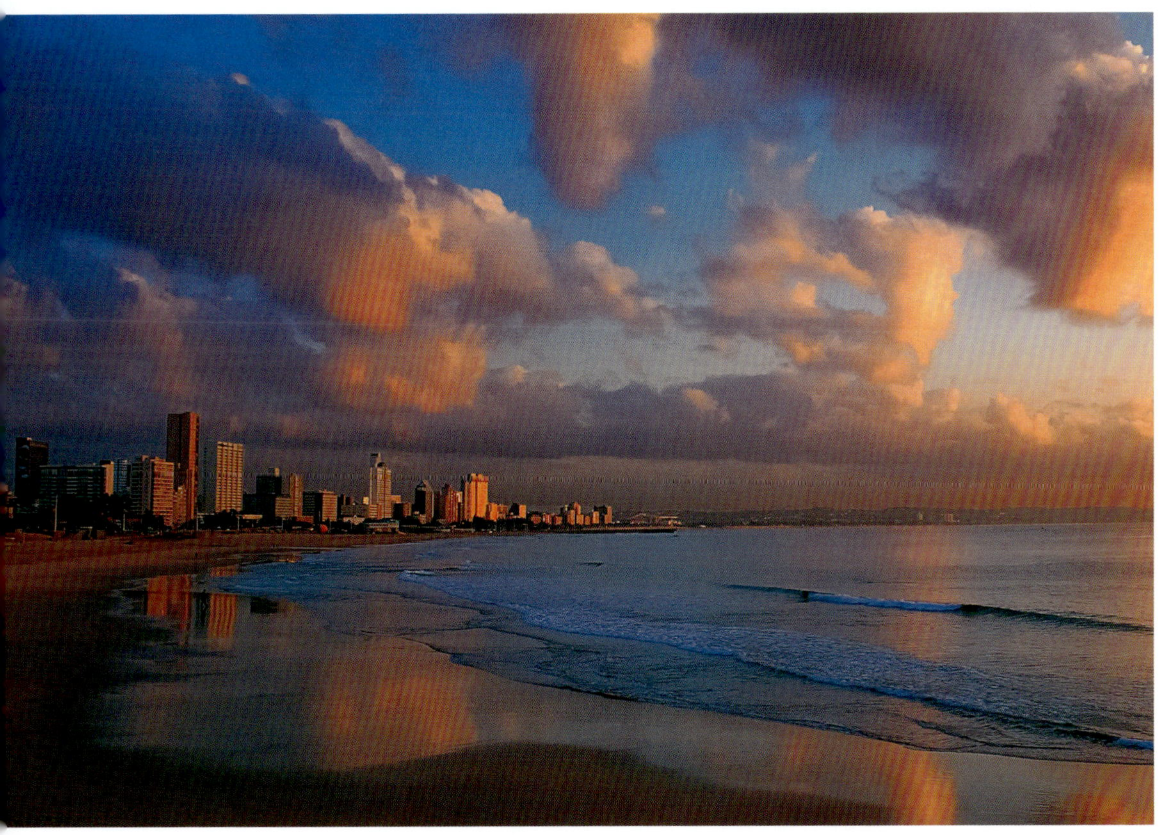

eachfront, Durban

urban

a tercera ciudad más grande es también ciudad portuaria más importante de udáfrica, llamada "eThekwini" (laguna) n lengua zulú. La bahía de Durban fue escubierta en 1497 por el navegante ortugués Vasco da Gama. Hoy en día, urban es un importante centro industrial financiero y es también un popular estinovacacional. Aproximadamente 8 km e la playa de arena más fina se extienden lo largo de la playa frente a la metrópoli.

Durban

La terza città più grande è anche la più importante città portuale del Sud Africa, chiamata "eThekwini" (laguna) in lingua Zulu. La baia di Durban fu scoperta nel 1497 dal navigatore portoghese Vasco da Gama. Oggi, Durban è un importante centro industriale e finanziario ed è anche una popolare destinazione turistica. Circa 8 km di spiaggia di sabbia finissima si estende sul lungomare della metropoli.

Durban

De op twee na grootste stad is meteen de belangrijkste havenstad van Zuid-Afrika en wordt "eThekwini" (lagune) genoemd in het Zoeloe. De baai van Durban werd in 1497 ontdekt door de Portugese zeevaarder Vasco da Gama. Tegenwoordig is Durban een belangrijk industrieel en financieel centrum, evenals een populaire vakantiebestemming. Het strand met heel fijn zand strekt zich zo'n 8 km uit langs de strandzijde van de miljoenenstad.

Augrabies Falls National Park, South Africa

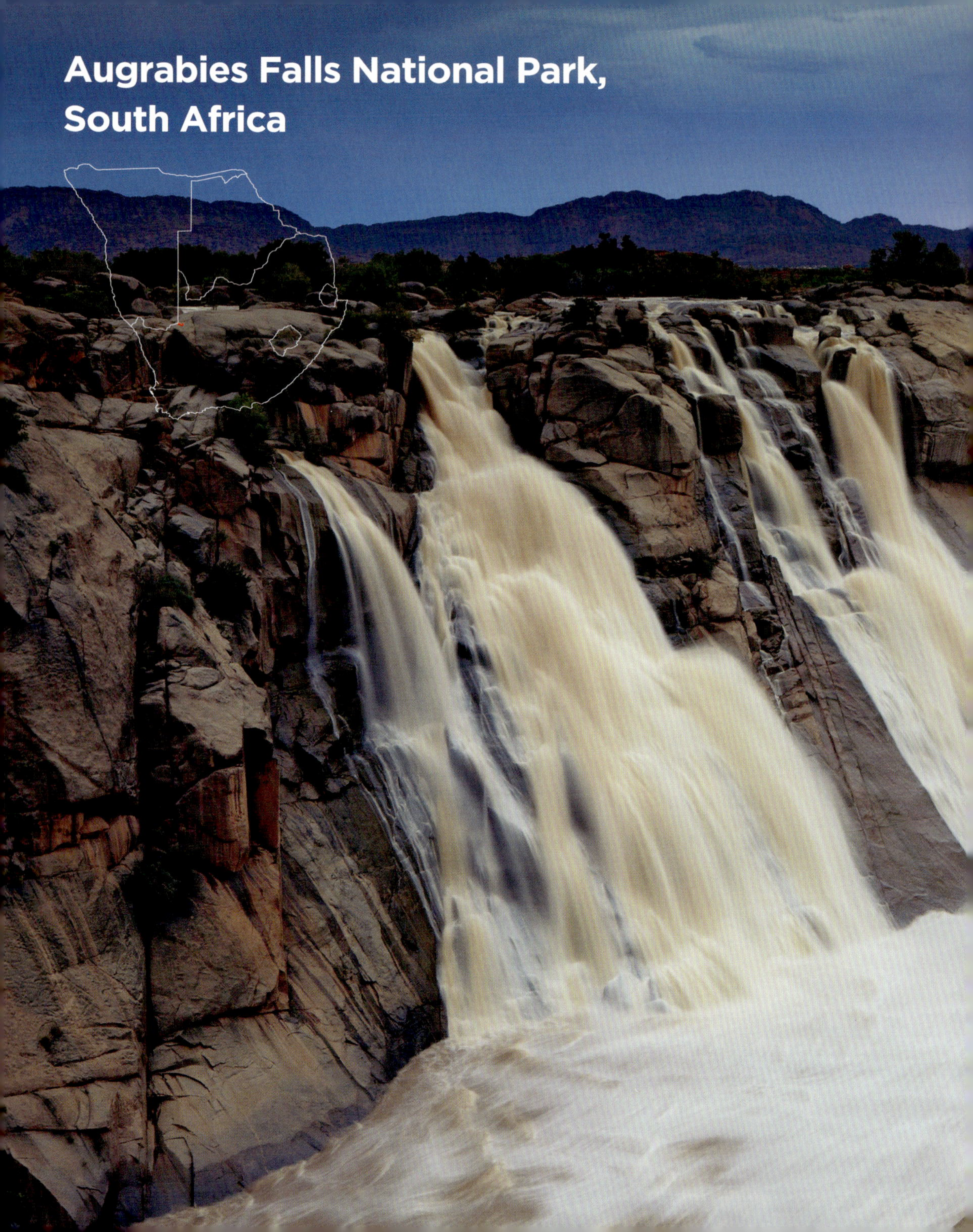

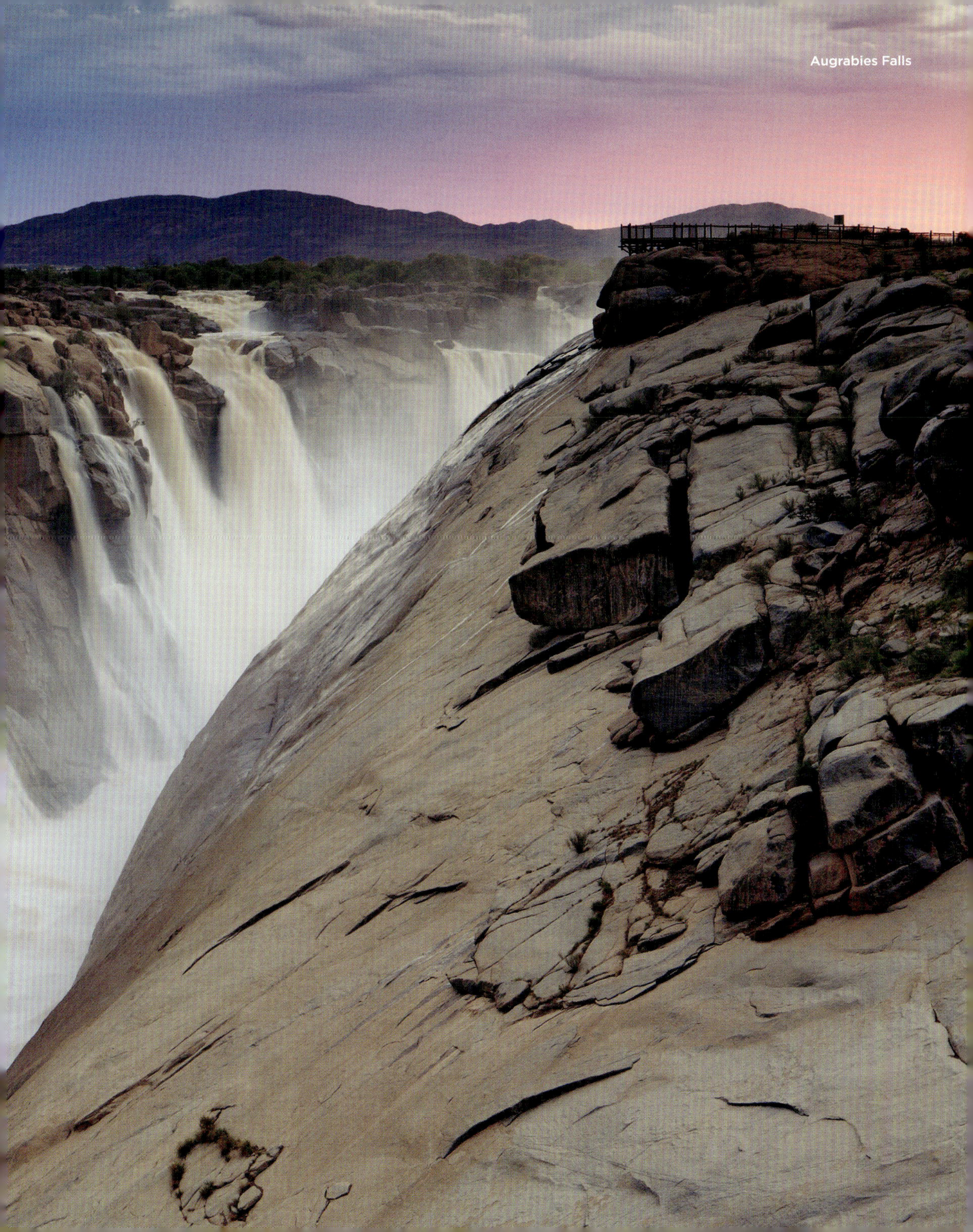
Augrabies Falls

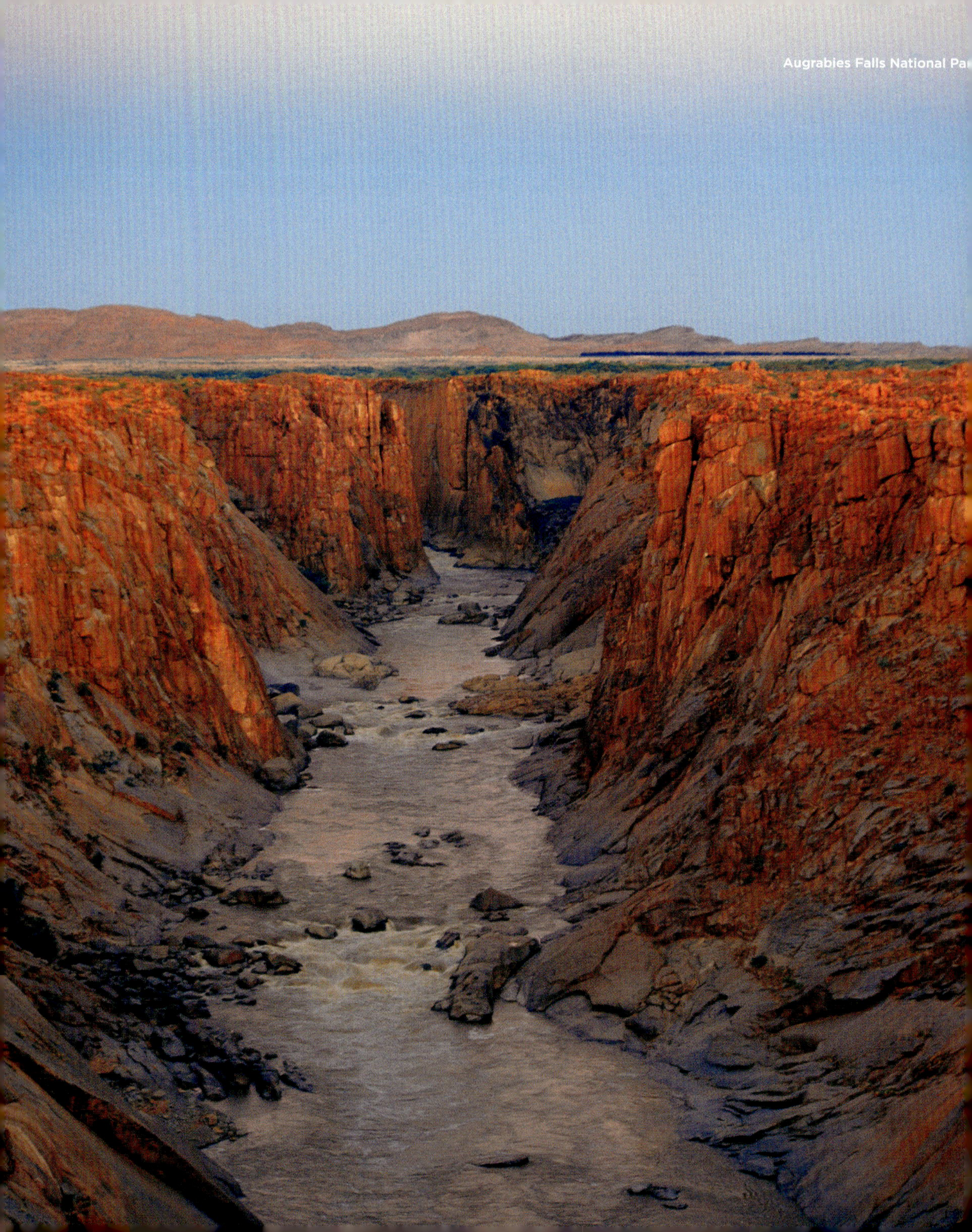

Augrabies Falls National Pa

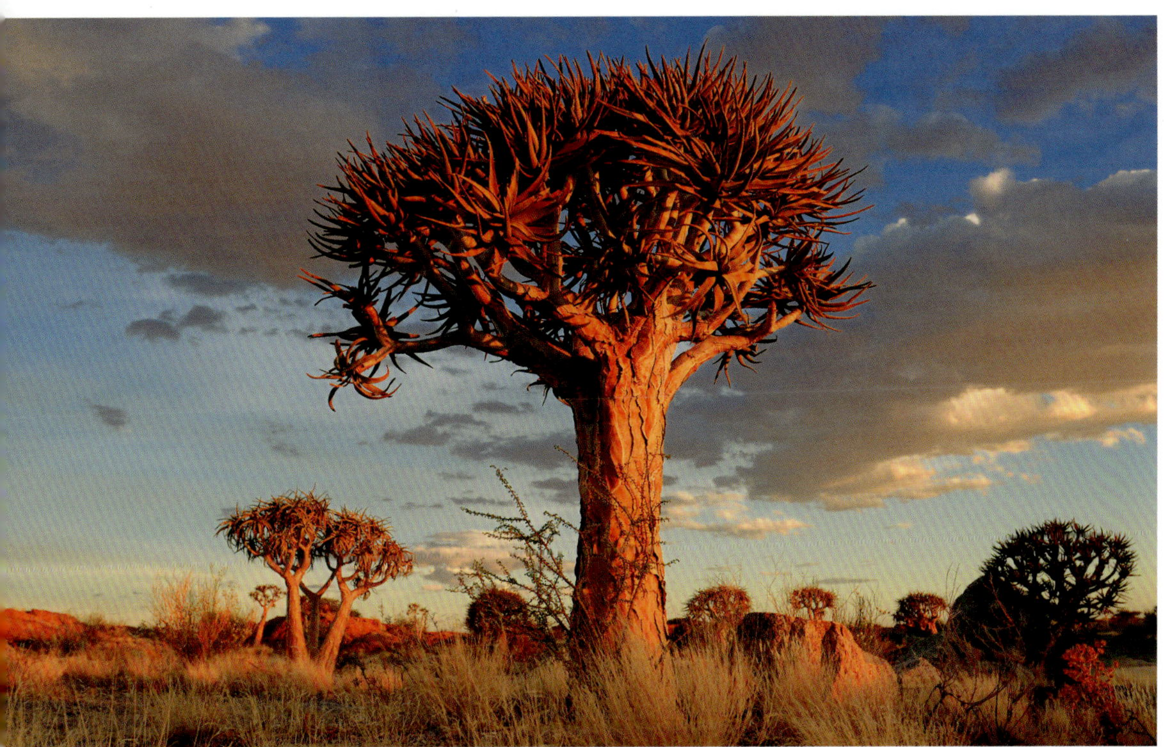

uiver trees, Augrabies Falls National Park

ugrabies Falls National Park
n the San language, "Aukoerebis" means "place of great noise". The noise here is caused by the Orange River, which is 150 m (492 ft) wide at this point and then plunges into the deep in the middle of the desert. The Europeans turned "Aukoerebis" into Augrabies. The waterfall, which gives its name to the national park in the South African province of North Cape, is 191 m (626 ft) high.

e parc national des hutes d'Augrabies
ukoerebis signifie « lieu de grand bruit » ans la langue des Sans. Ce vacarme st produit par le fleuve Orange, large i de 150 m, qui se jette dans le vide en lein milieu du désert. Les Européens ont éformé Aukoerebis en « Augrabies ». La ascade, qui a donné son nom au parc ational situé dans la province du Cap-ord, est haute de 191 m.

Augrabies-Wasserfälle-Nationalpark
„Aukoerebis" bedeutet in der Sprache der San „Ort des großen Lärms". Diesen Lärm verursacht der Oranje. Der Fluss ist an dieser Stelle 150 m breit und stürzt sich mitten in der Wüste in die Tiefe. Aus „Aukoerebis" machten die Europäer „Augrabies". Der Wasserfall, der dem Nationalpark in der südafrikanischen Provinz Nordkap seinen Namen gab, ist 191 m hoch.

Parque Nacional de las Cataratas Augrabies
"Aukoerebis" significa en la lengua de los San „lugar de gran ruido". Ese ruido lo causa el Orange. El río en este punto es de 150 m de ancho y se sumerge en las profundidades del desierto. De "Aukoerebis" los europeos hicieron "Augrabies". La cascada, que dio su nombre al Parque Nacional en la provincia de Cabo Norte de Sudáfrica su nombre, tiene 191 m de alto.

Parco Nazionale delle Cascate di Augrabies
"Aukoerebis" nella lingua San significa "luogo del grande rumore". Questo rumore è causato dall'Orange; il fiume in questo punto è largo 150 m e precipita in mezzo al deserto. "Aukoerebis" divenne per gli Europei "Augrabies". La cascata che dà il nome al parco nazionale nella provincia sudafricana del Capo Settentrionale è alta 191 m.

Nationaal Park Augrabies Falls
In de taal van de San betekent "aukoerebis" de "plek van groot geraas". Dat geraas werd veroorzaakt door de rivier de Oranje, die op deze plek 150 m breed is en zich midden in de woestijn in de diepte stort. De Europeanen verbasterden "aukoerebis" tot "Augrabies", en de waterval die het park in de Zuid-Afrikaanse provincie Noord-Kaap zijn naam gaf, is 191 m hoog.

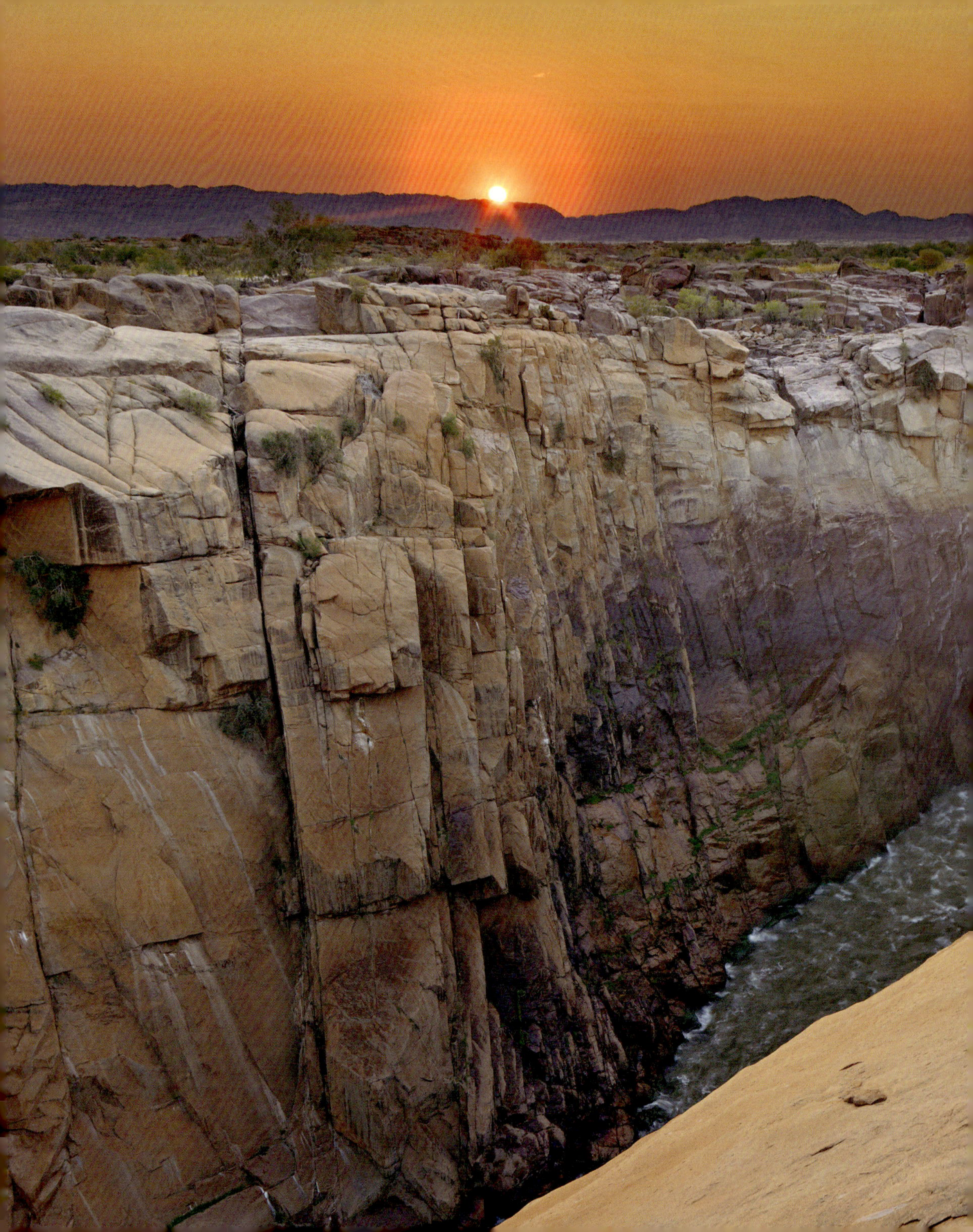

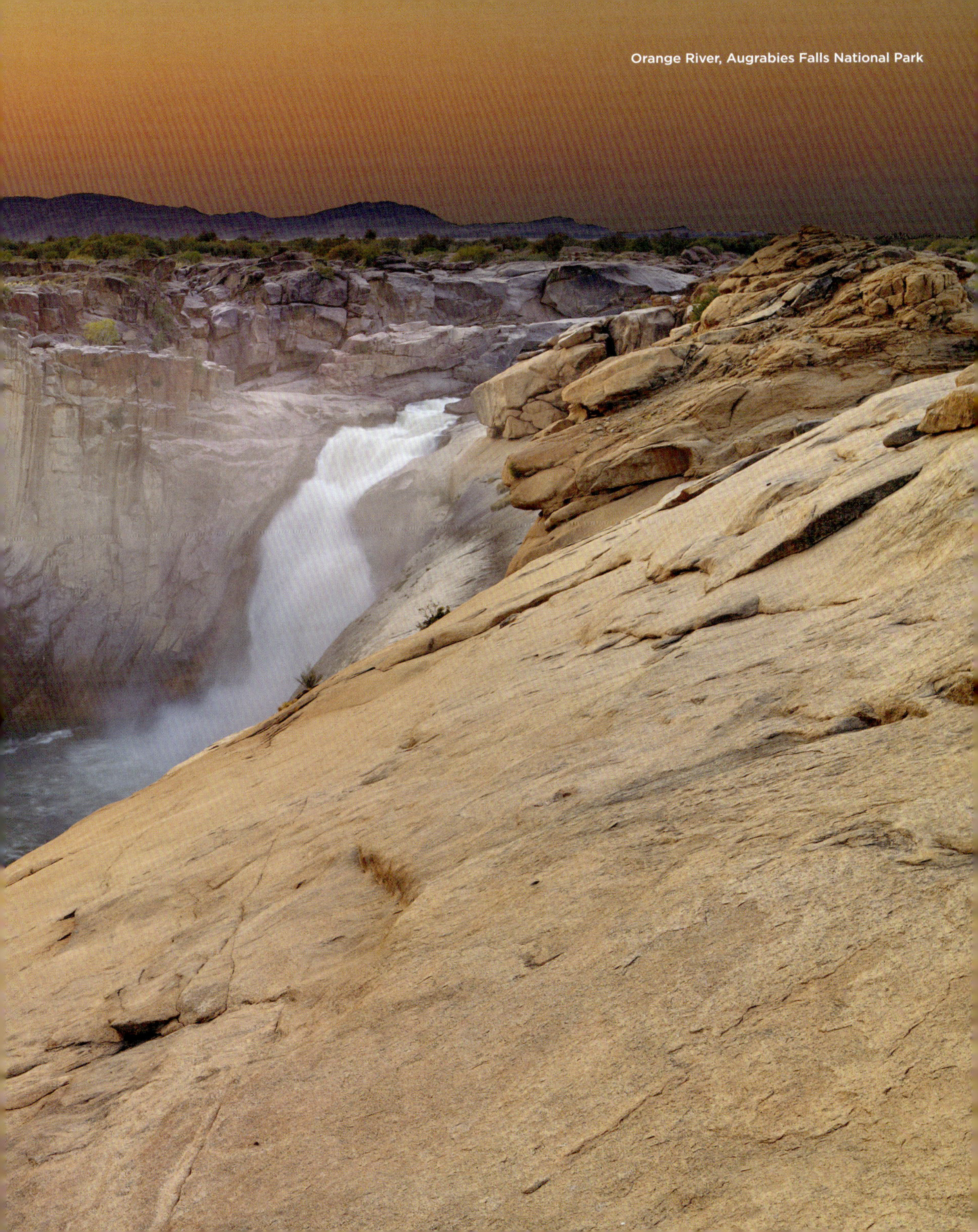
Orange River, Augrabies Falls National Park

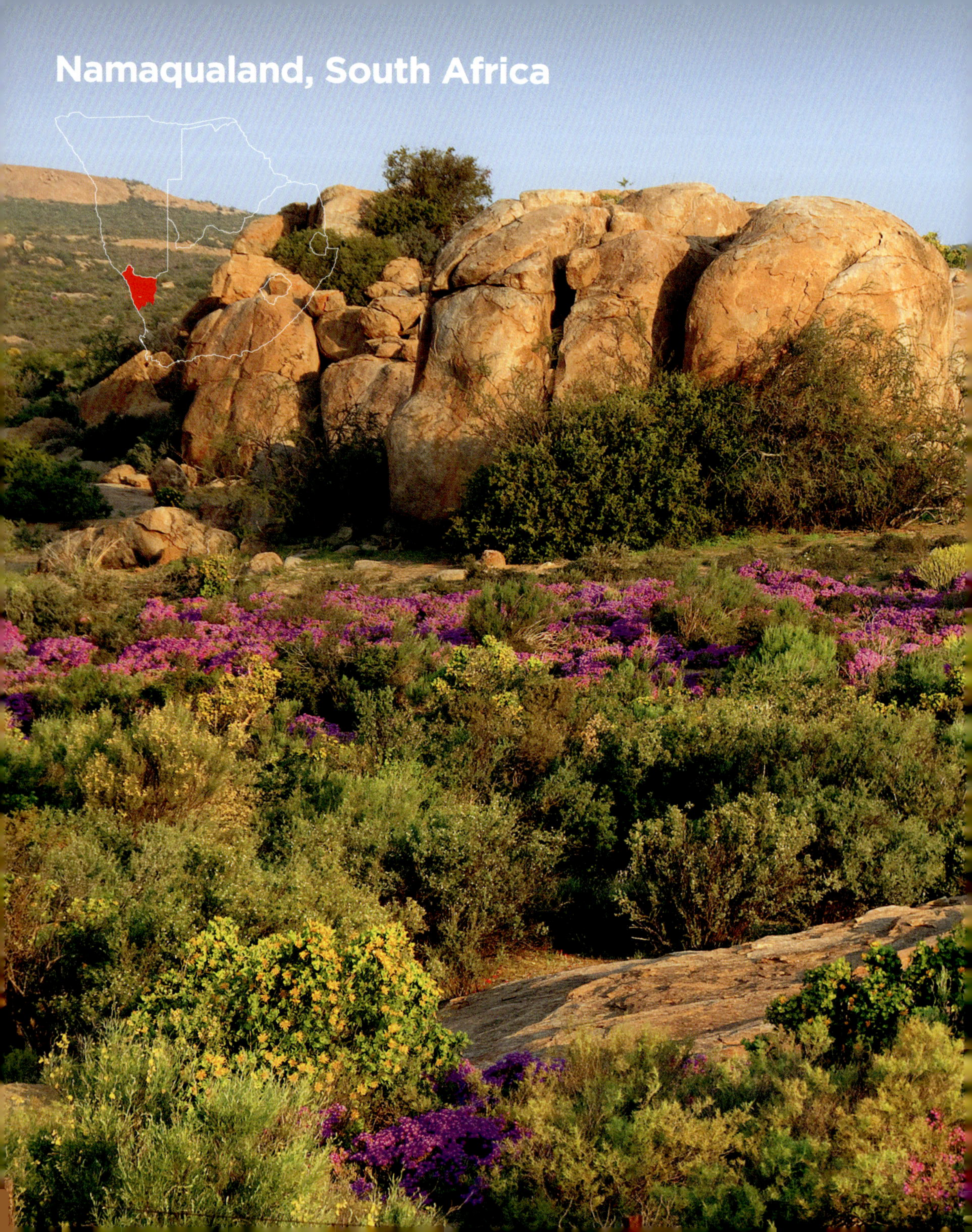
Namaqualand, South Africa

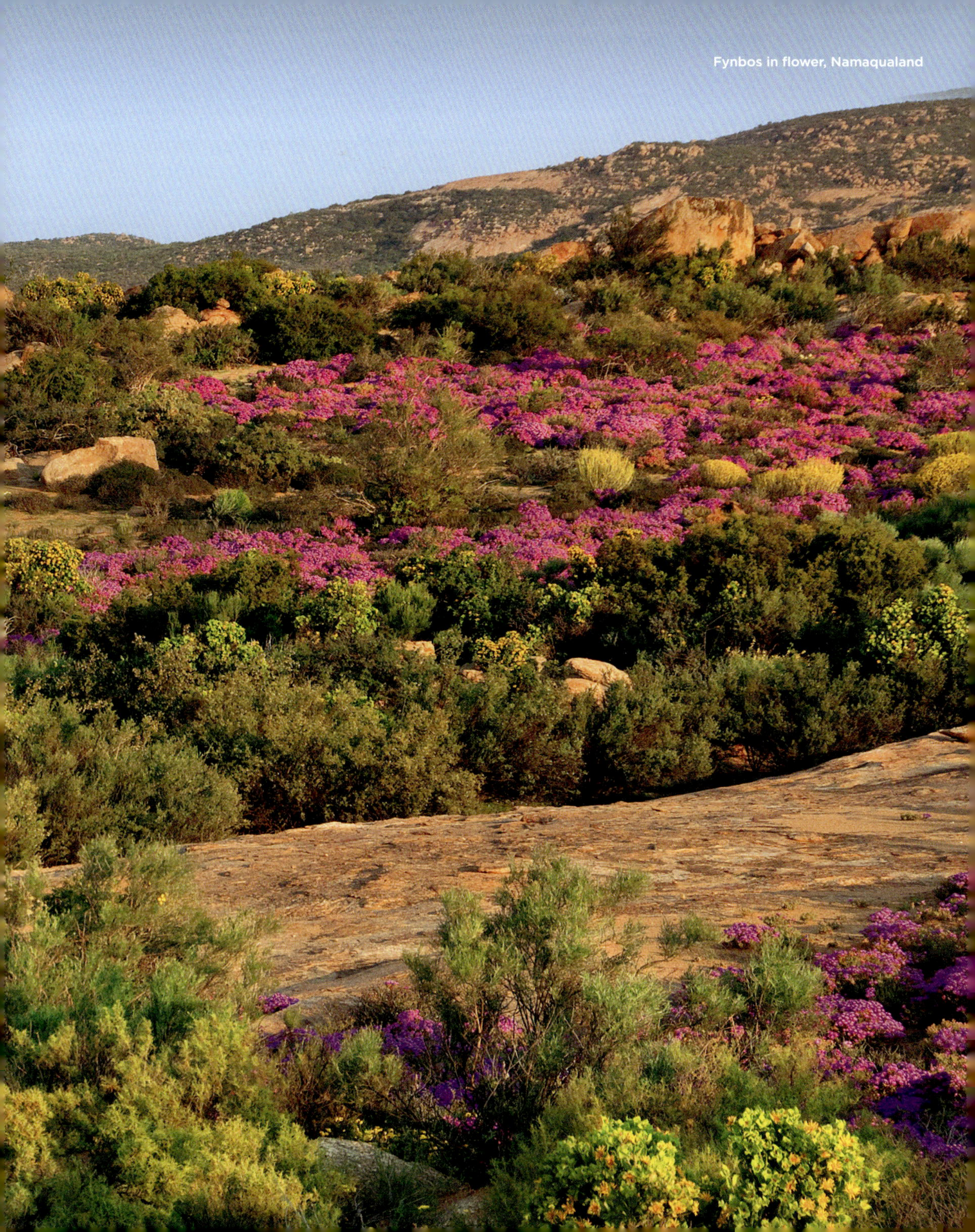
Fynbos in flower, Namaqualand

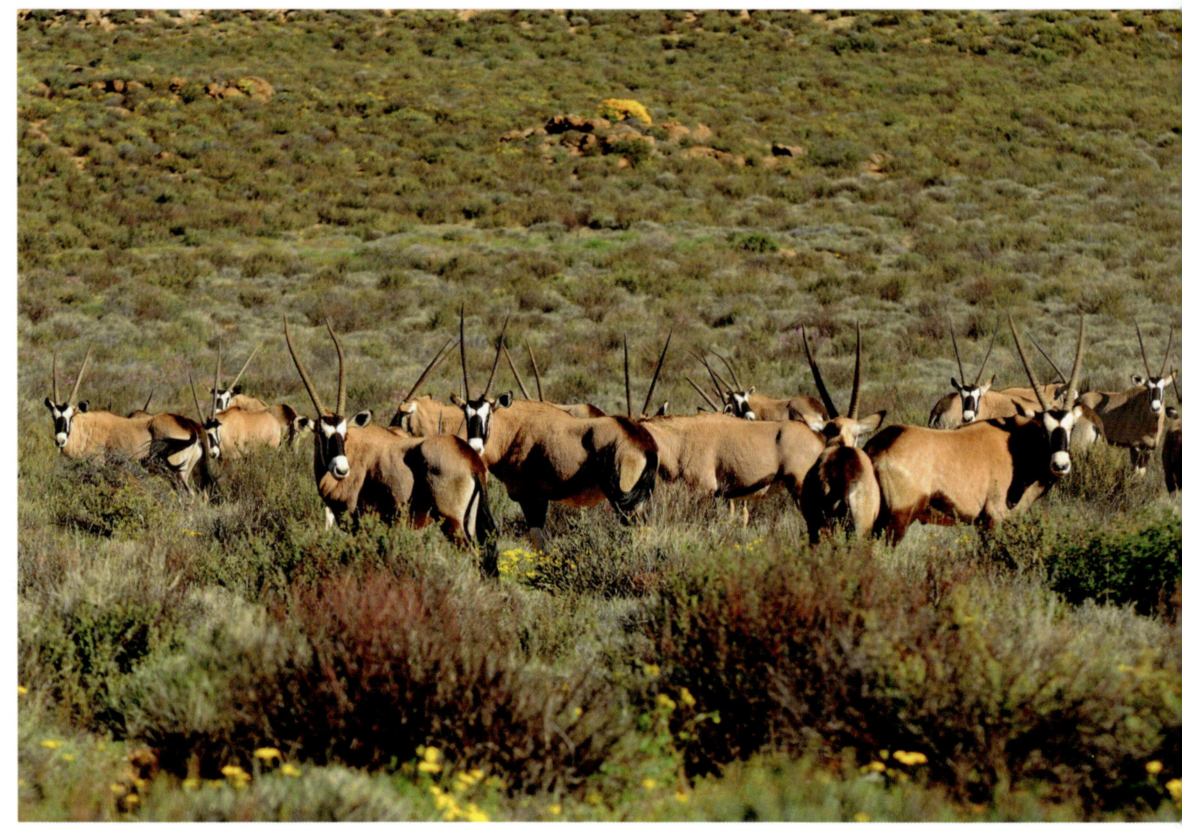

Oryxes, Geocap Nature Reserve

Namaqualand

Namaqualand, in the South African province of North Cape, is home to the Spektakelberg, a mountain rising 826 m (2710 ft). It was named in the 17th century by the first governor of the Cape Colony. Seeing the flower carpet spreading over the desert, he shouted, "What a spectacle!". This spectacle may be seen annually from mid-August to mid-October.

Le Namaqualand

Une montagne haute de 826 m, le Spektakelberg, s'élève au Namaqualand, dans la province sud-africaine du Cap-Nord. Elle a été baptisée par le premier gouverneur de la colonie du Cap. Lorsqu'il vit le tapis de fleurs qui se déployait sur le désert, il s'écria : « Quel spectacle ! » Ce spectacle se reproduit chaque année, de la mi-août à la mi-octobre.

Namaqualand

Im Namaqualand in der südafrikanischen Provinz Nordkap erhebt sich ein 826 m hoher Berg: der Spektakelberg. Er erhielt seinen Namen im 17. Jahrhundert vom ersten Gouverneur der Kapkolonie. Als er den Blütenteppich sah, der sich über der Wüste ausbreitete, rief er: „Was für ein Spektakel!" Dieses Spektakel wiederholt sich alljährlich von Mitte August bis Mitte Oktober.

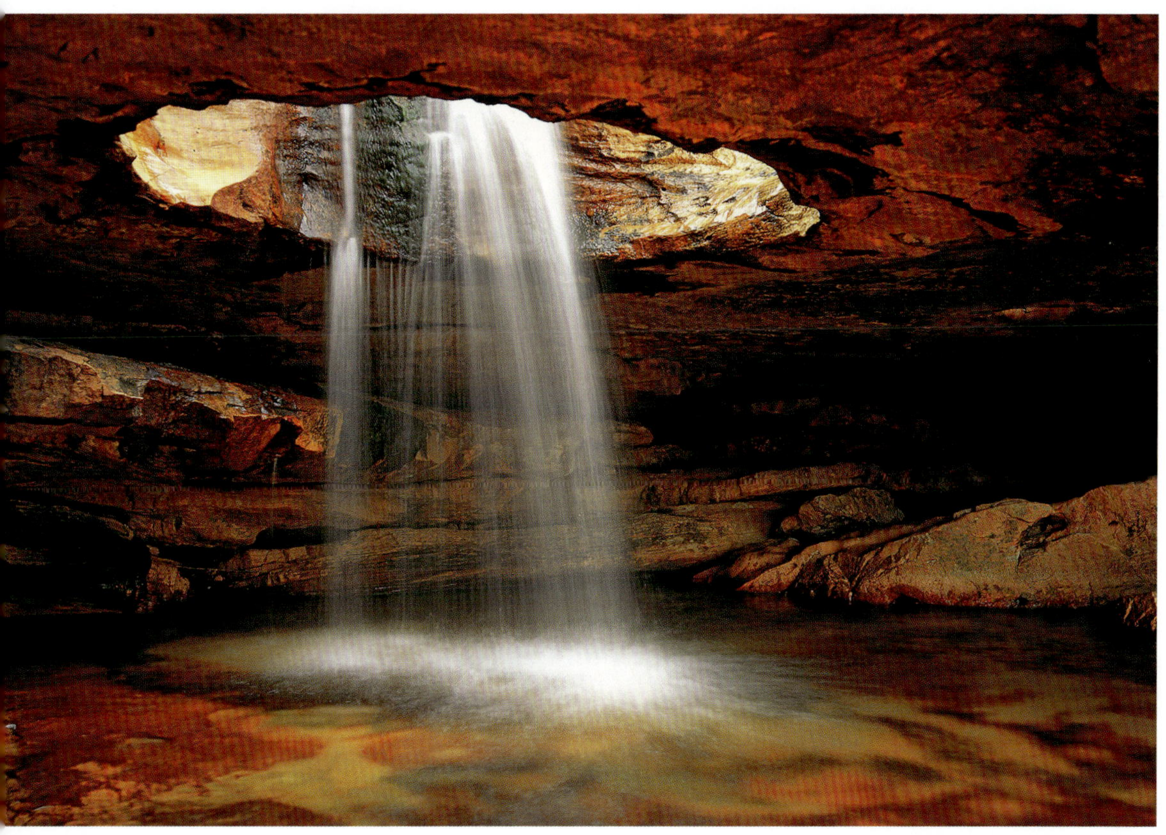

amaqualand

amaqualand

n Namaqualand en la provincia del abo Norte de Sudáfrica se eleva una ontaña de 826 m de altura: la montaña spectáculo. Fue nombrada en el siglo XVII or el primer gobernador de la Colonia el Cabo. Cuando vio la alfombra de ores que se propagaba a través del esierto, exclamó: „¡Qué espectáculo!" ste espectáculo se repite cada año desde ediados de agosto hasta mediados e octubre.

Namaqualand

Nella provincia sudafricana del Capo Settentrionale si trova il Namaqualand, dove si innalza un monte alto 826 m: lo Spektakelberg. Ha preso il nome nel XVII secolo dal primo governatore della Colonia del Capo. Quando vide il tappeto di fiori che si stendeva sul deserto, esclamò: „Che spettacolo!". Questo spettacolo si ripete ogni anno dalla metà di agosto alla metà di ottobre.

Namaqualand

In Namaqualand, in de Zuid-Afrikaanse provincie Noord-Kaap, verrijst de 826 m hoge Spektakelberg, een naam die in de zeventiende eeuw werd geïntroduceerd door de eerste gouverneur van de Kaapkolonie. Toen de gouverneur het bloementapijt zag dat zich in de woestijn uitstrekte, riep hij uit: "Wat een spektakel!" Dit spektakel herhaalt zich jaarlijks van half augustus tot half oktober.

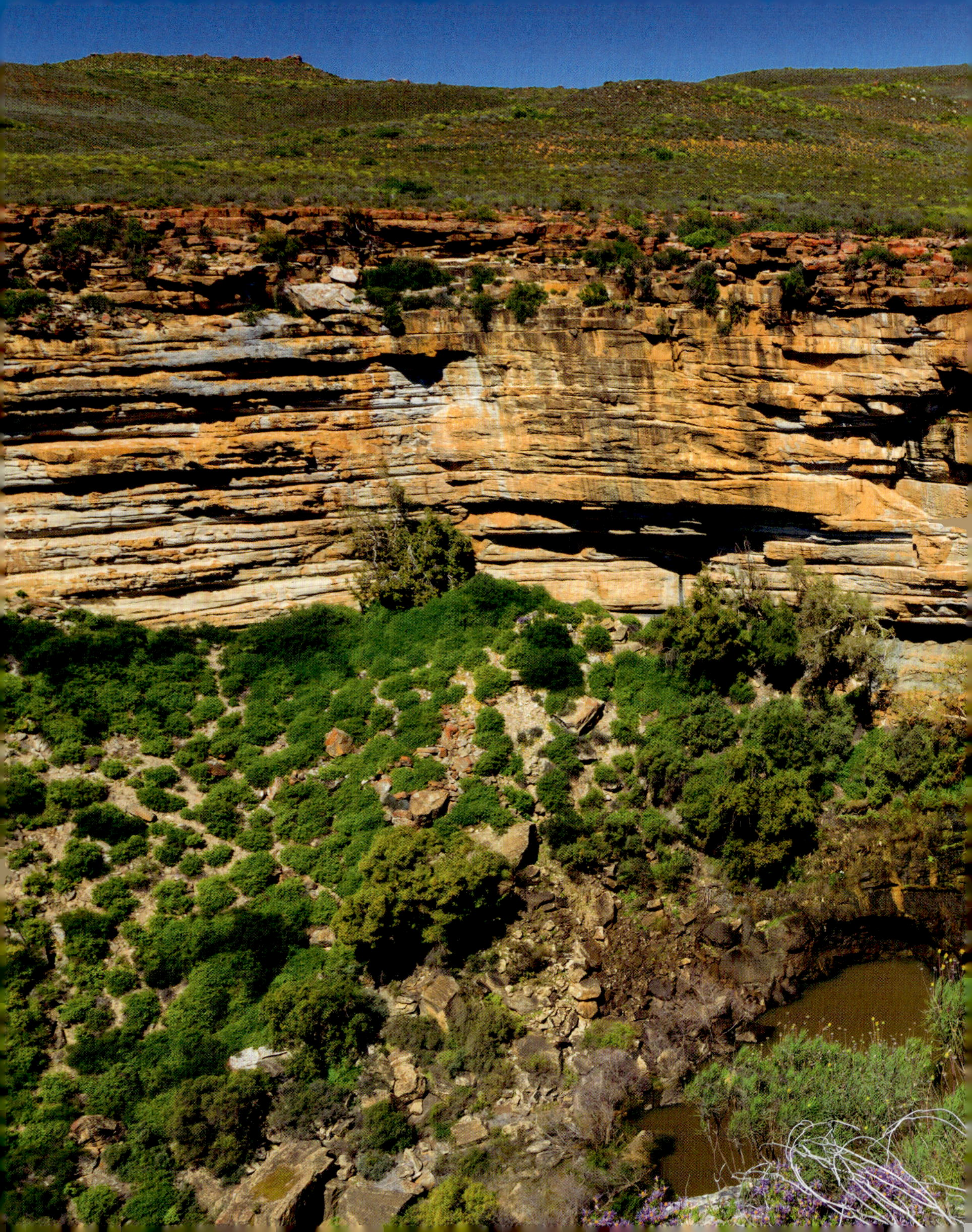

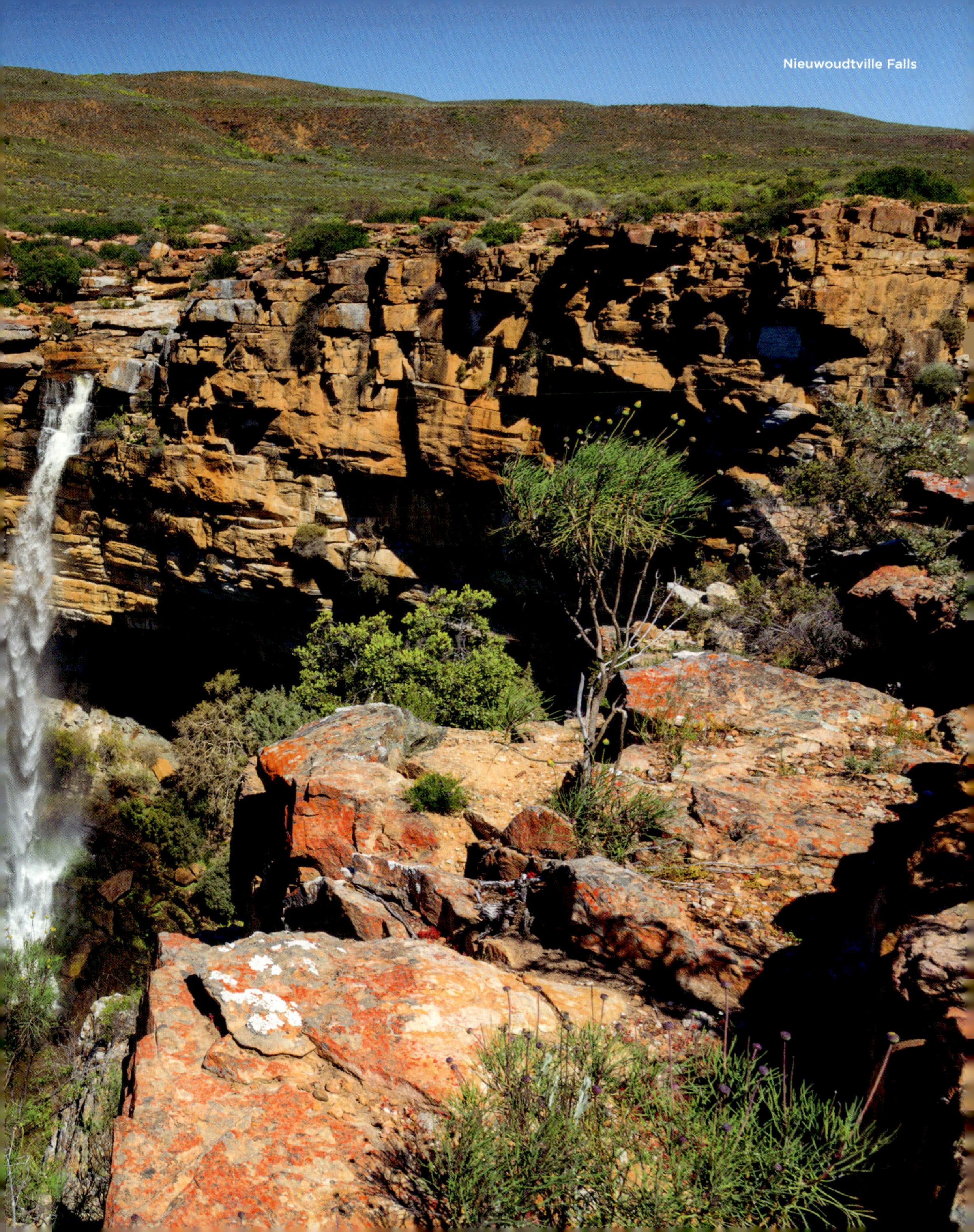
Nieuwoudtville Falls

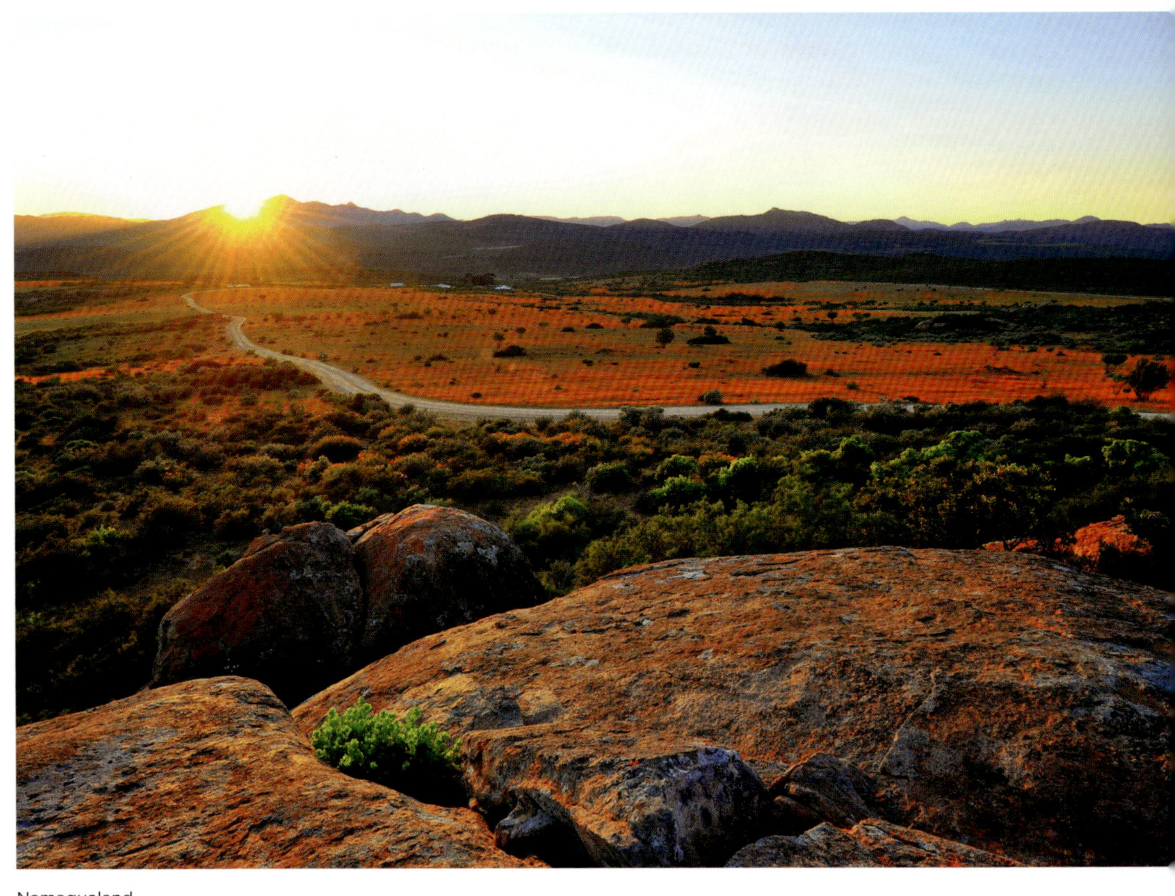

Namaqualand

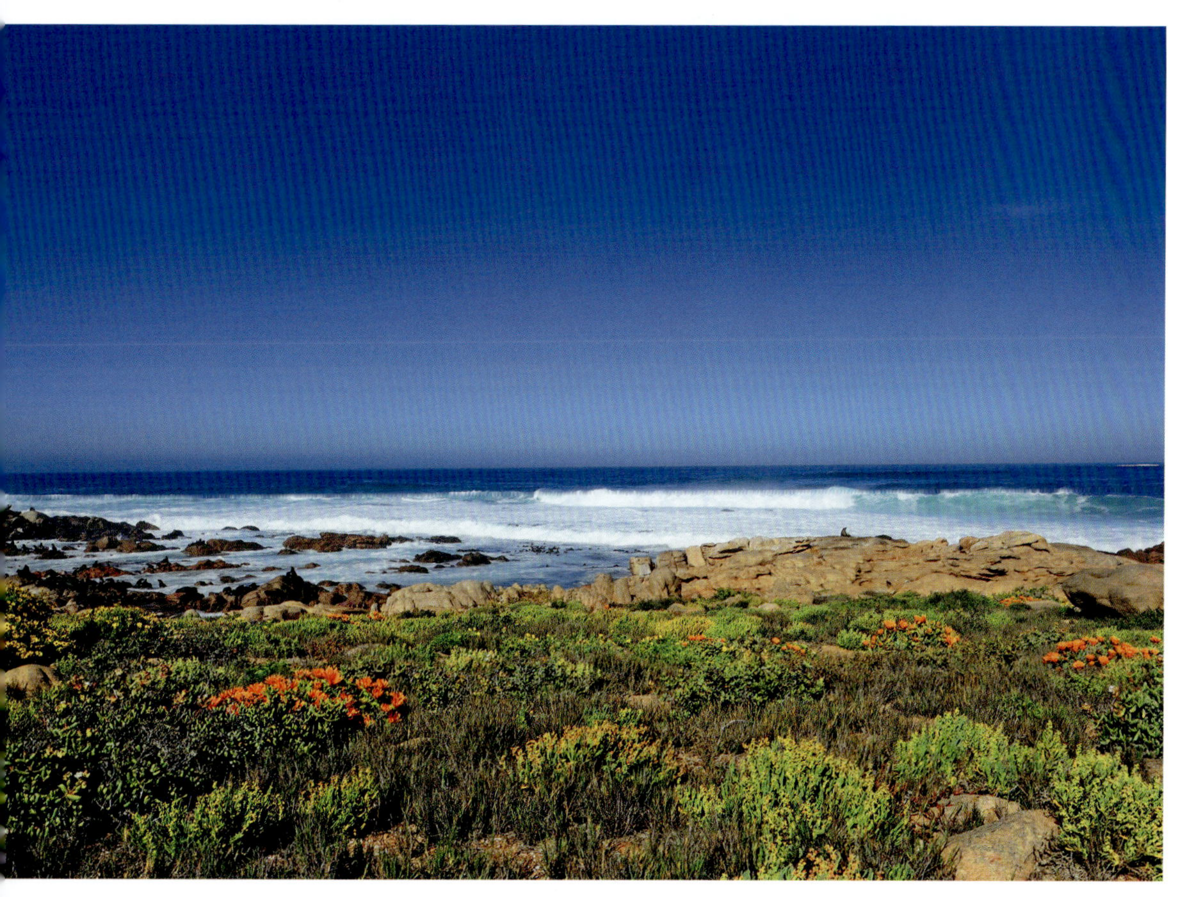

Atlantic Ocean, Namaqualand

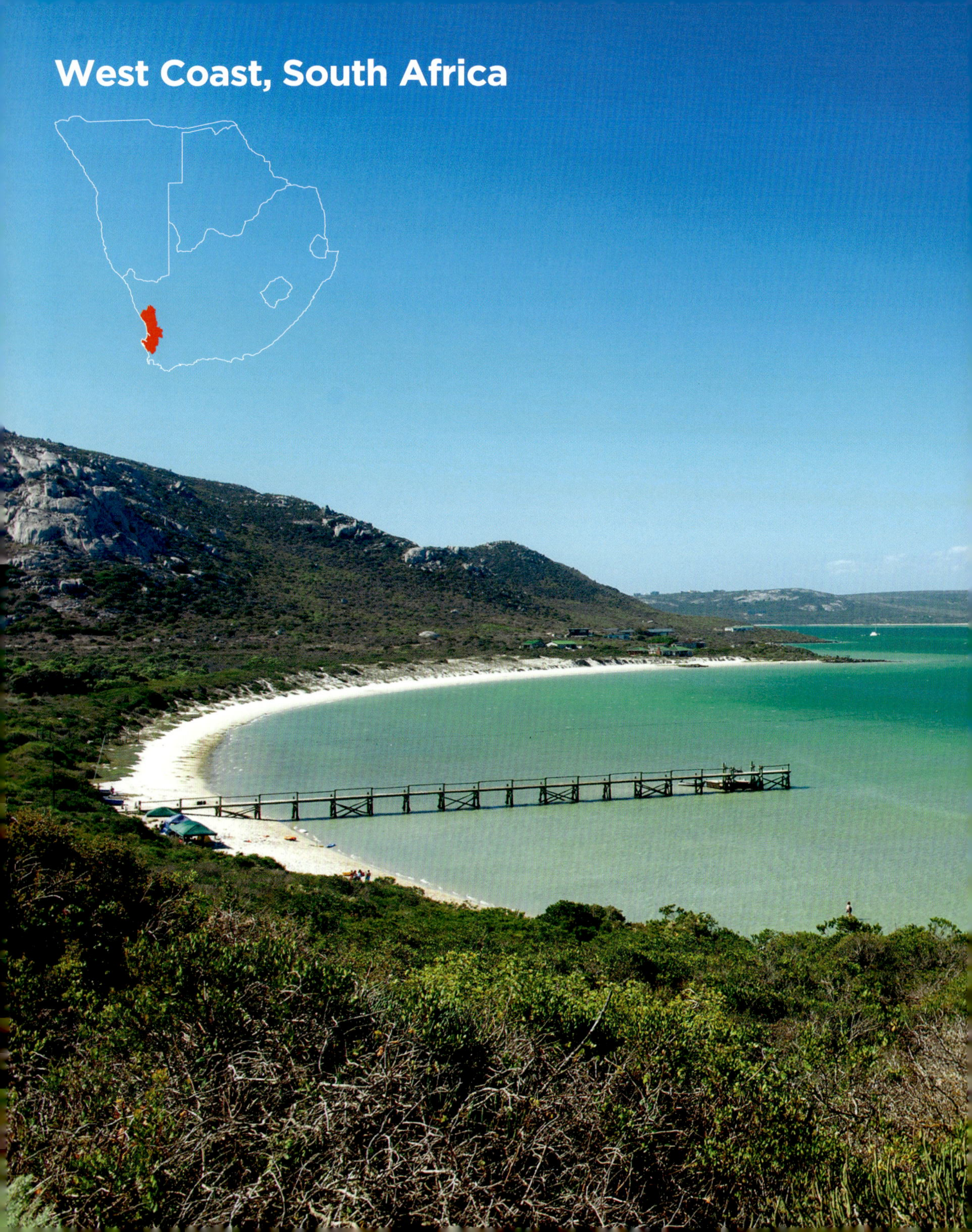
West Coast, South Africa

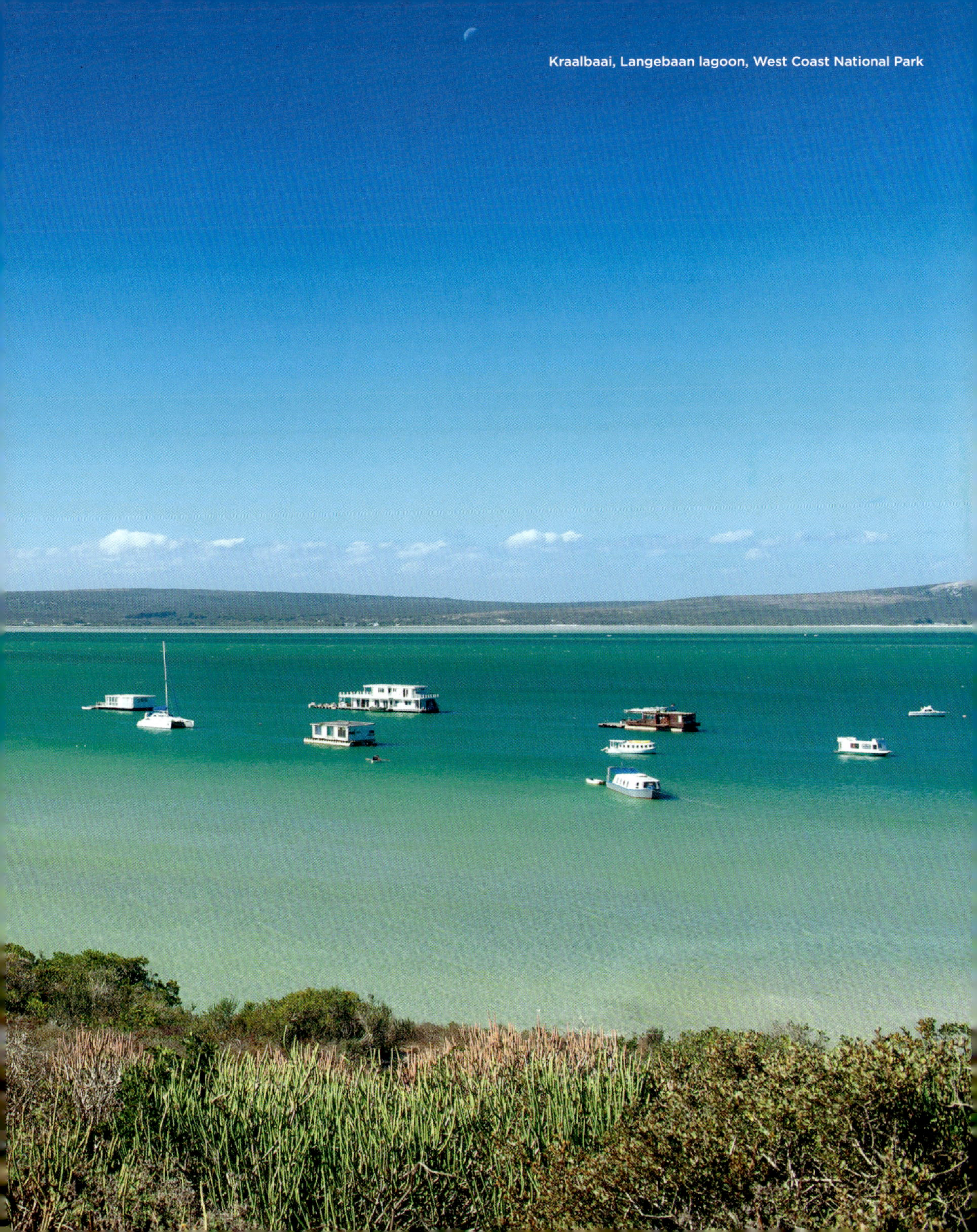
Kraalbaai, Langebaan lagoon, West Coast National Park

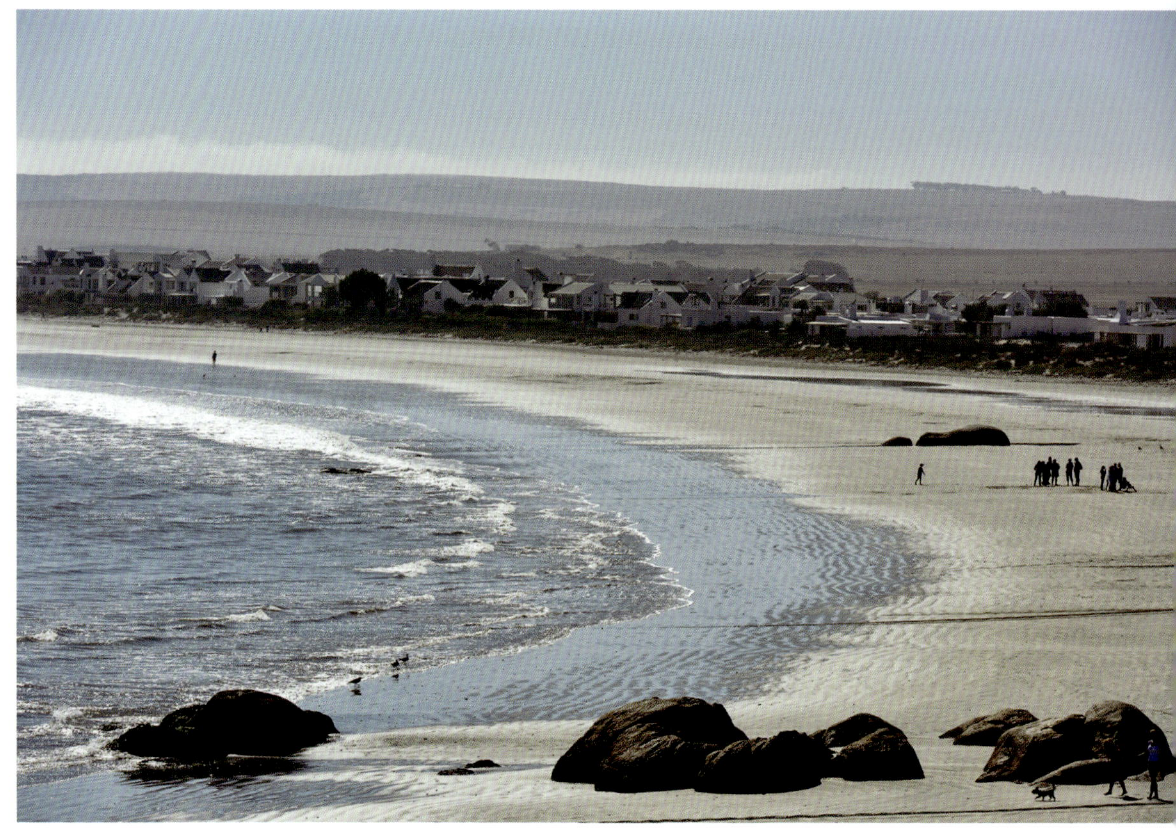

Beach of Paternoster

West Coast
North of Cape Town, the west coast of South Africa stretches to the border with Namibia and is filled with scenic highlights. Despite the Atlantic Benguela Current, which provides a cool and harsh climate, an astonishingly diverse biodiversity has developed here. The beautiful lagoon landscape of the West Coast National Park is lined with millions of wild flowers in spring.

West Coast
Au nord du Cap, la côte ouest sud-africaine s'étend jusqu'à la frontière de la Namibie, avec ses paysages impressionnants. En effet, malgré le courant de Benguela, un courant froid océanique auquel la région doit son climat rigoureux, une biodiversité incroyable a vu le jour ici. Au printemps, les lagunes magnifiques du parc national de West Coast sont recouvertes de millions de fleurs sauvages.

Westküste
Nördlich von Kapstadt erstreckt sich bis zur Grenze Namibias die Westküste Südafrikas voller landschaftlicher Highlights. Denn trotz des atlantischen Benguela-Stroms, der für ein kühles und raues Klima sorgt, hat sich hier eine erstaunlich facettenreiche Artenvielfalt entwickelt. Die traumhafte Lagunenlandschaft des West-Coast-Nationalparks wird im Frühjahr von Millionen Wildblumen gesäumt.

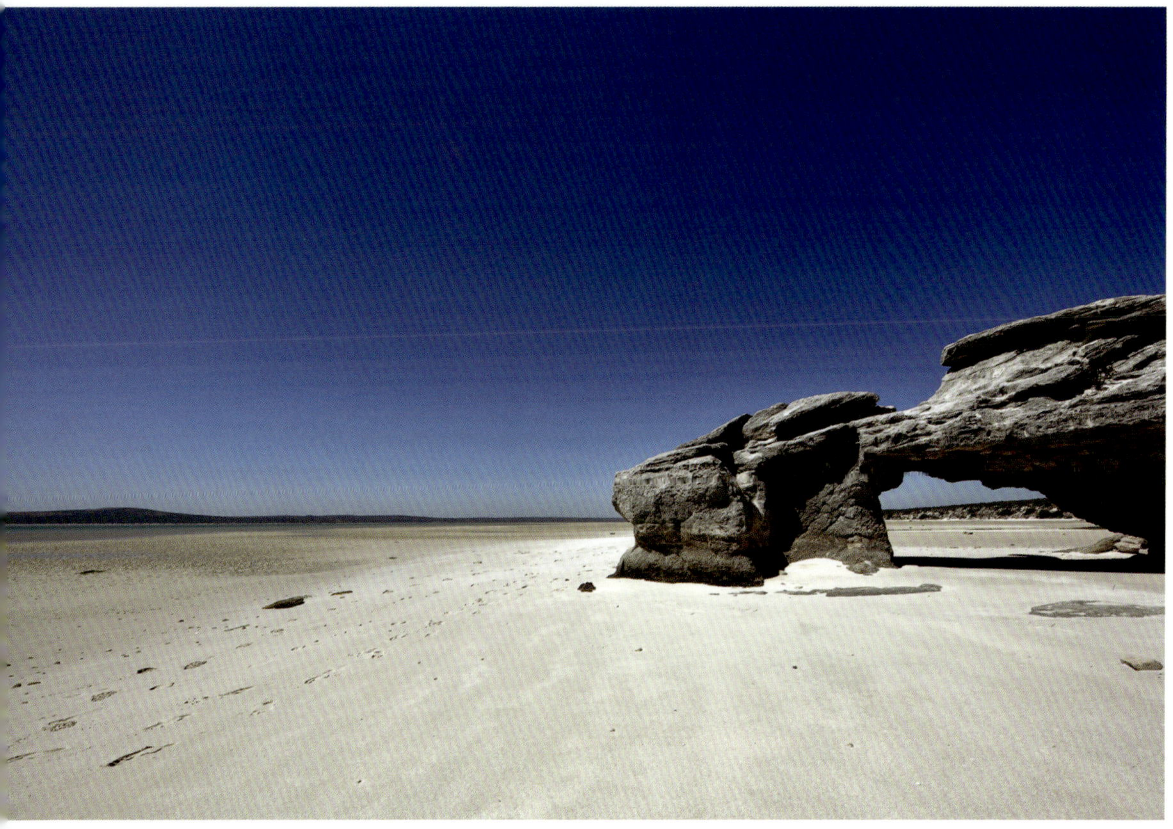

West Coast National Park

Costa Oeste
Al norte de Ciudad del Cabo, la costa oeste de Sudáfrica se extiende hasta la frontera con Namibia, llena de lugares de interés paisajístico. A pesar de la corriente atlántica de Benguela, que proporciona un clima fresco y duro, aquí se ha desarrollado una biodiversidad asombrosamente diversa. El hermoso paisaje lagunar del Parque Nacional de la Costa Oeste está bordeado por millones de flores silvestres en primavera.

Costa occidentale
A nord di Città del Capo, la costa occidentale del Sud Africa si estende fino al confine con la Namibia, ricca di attrazioni paesaggistiche. Nonostante la Corrente atlantica del Benguela porti un clima freddo e rigido, si è sviluppata una biodiversità sorprendentemente diversificata. In primavera, lo splendido paesaggio lagunare del West Coast National Park è adornato di milioni di fiori selvatici.

West Coast
Ten noorden van Kaapstad strekt de westkust van Zuid-Afrika zich vol schilderachtige hoogtepunten uit tot aan de grens met Namibië. Ondanks de Noord-Atlantische drift of stroom, die voor een koel en ruw klimaat zorgt, heeft zich hier een verbazingwekkend diverse soortenrijkdom ontwikkeld. Het prachtige lagunelandschap van het Nationaal Park Westkus is in het voorjaar omzoomd met miljoenen wilde bloemen.

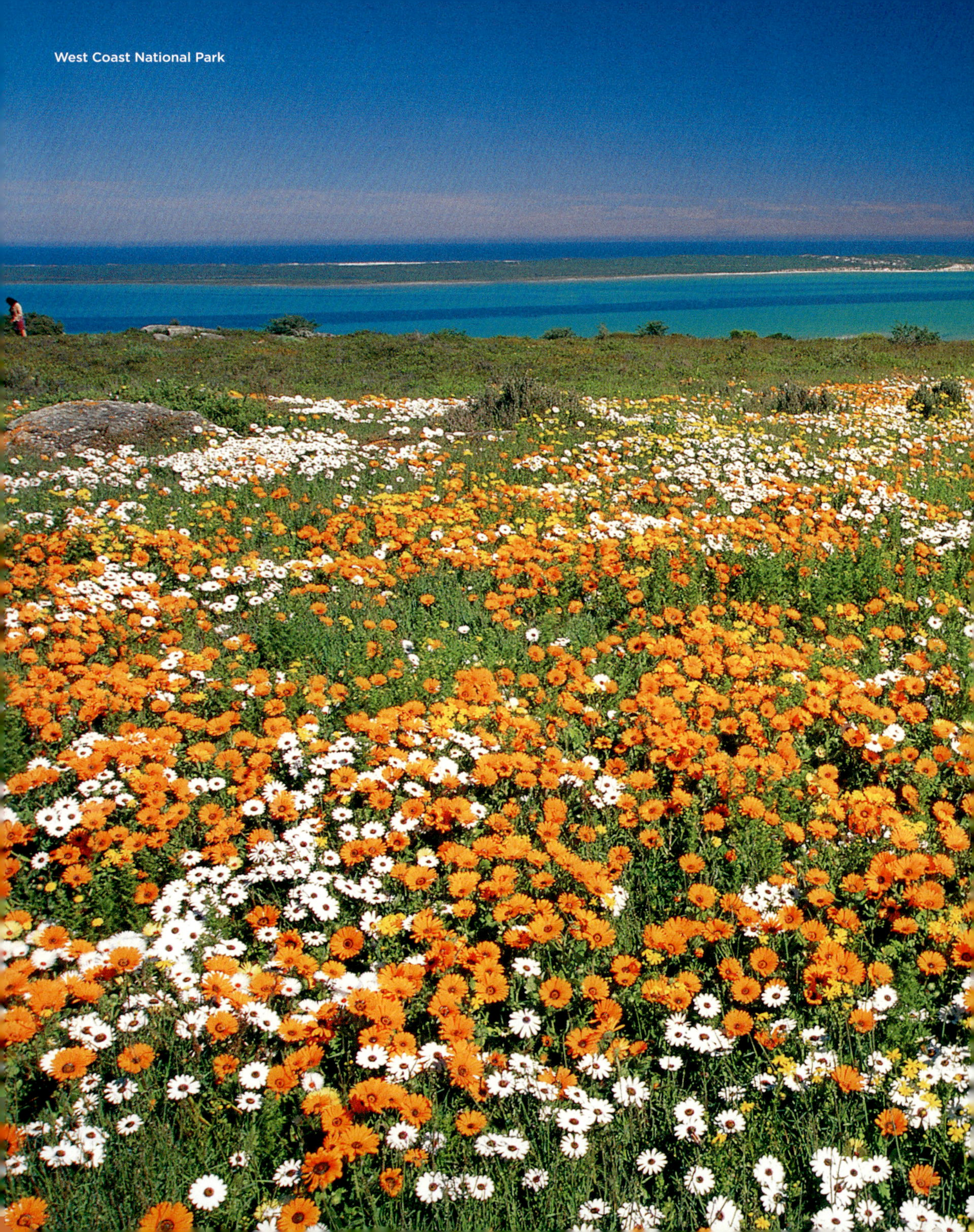
West Coast National Park

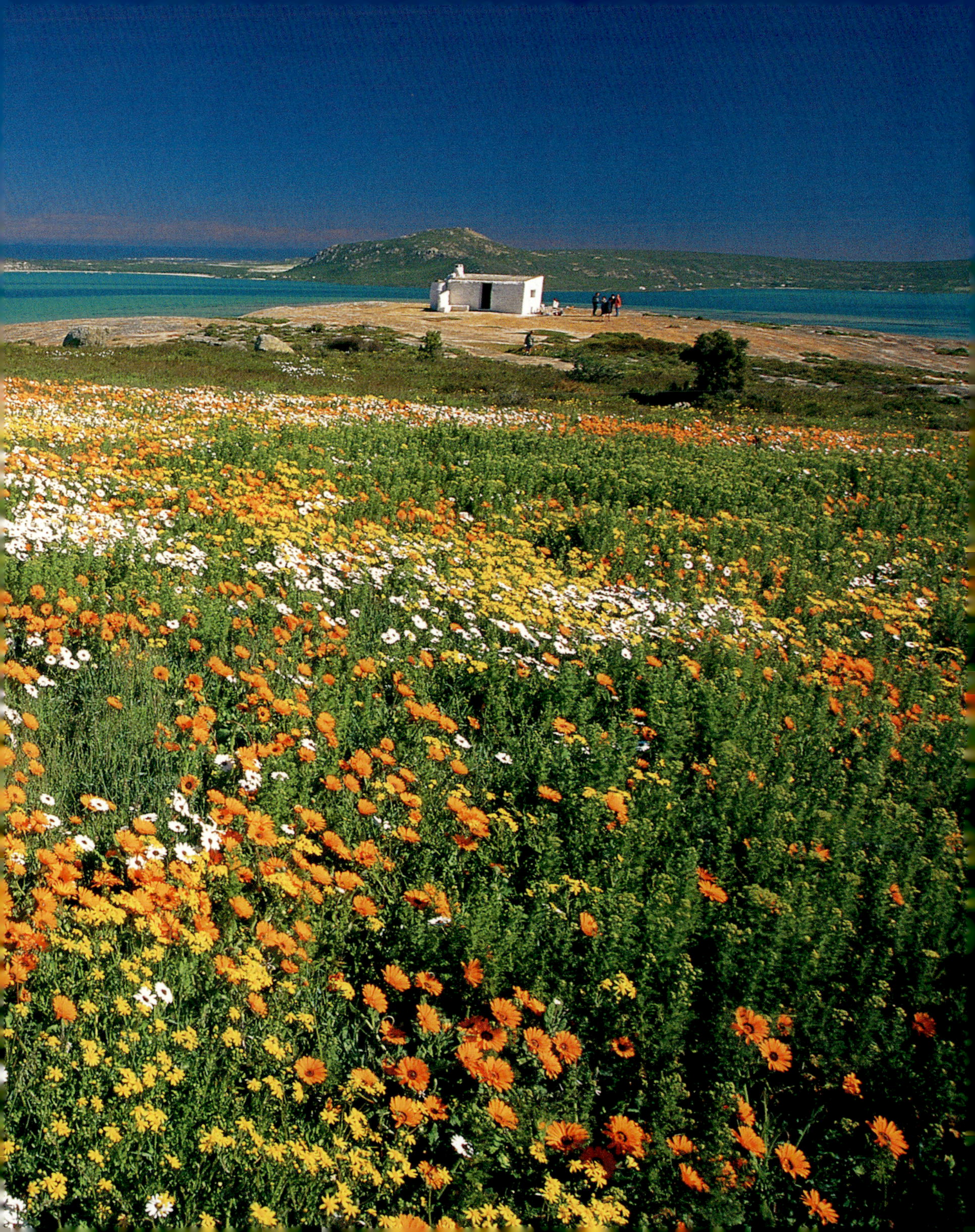

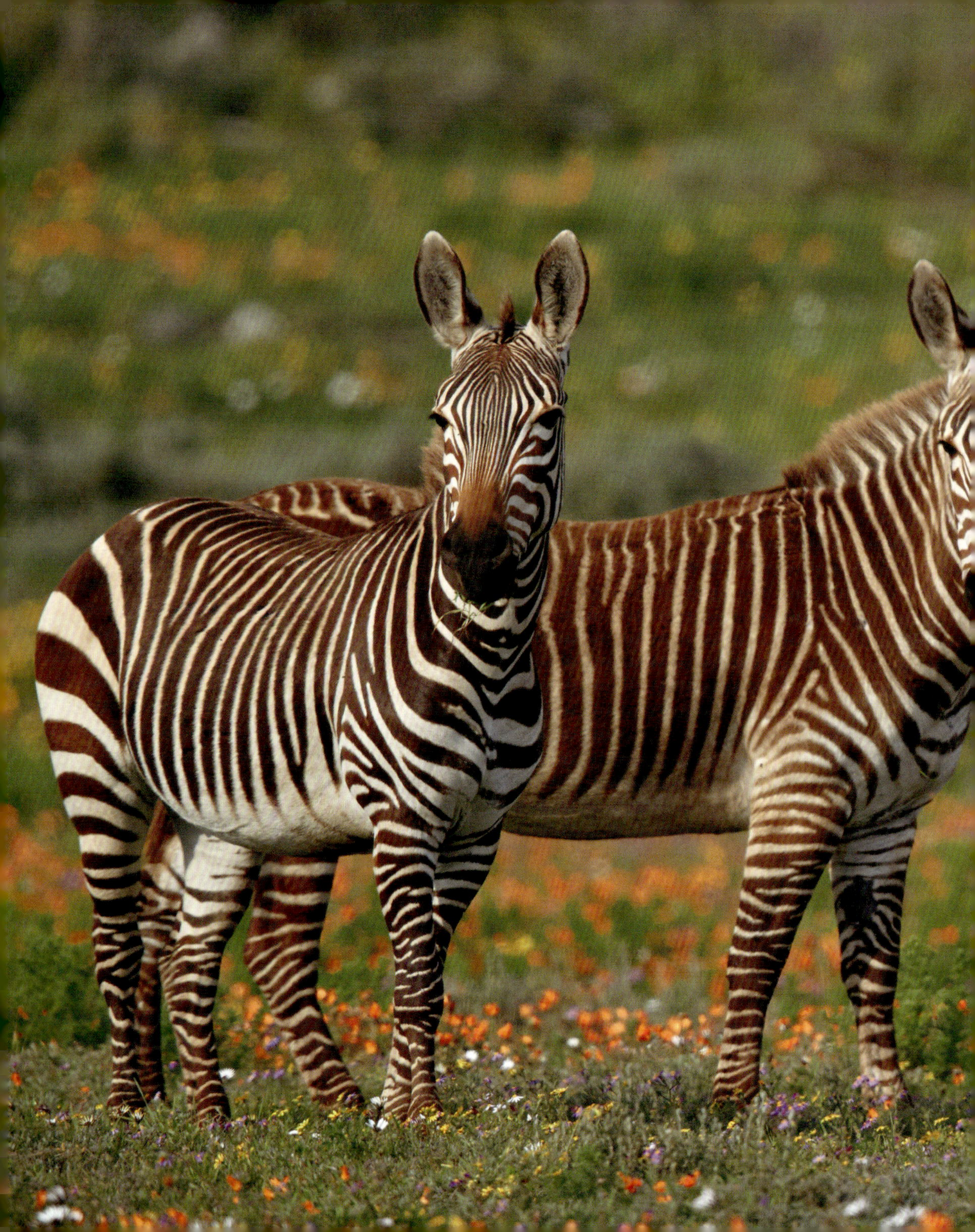

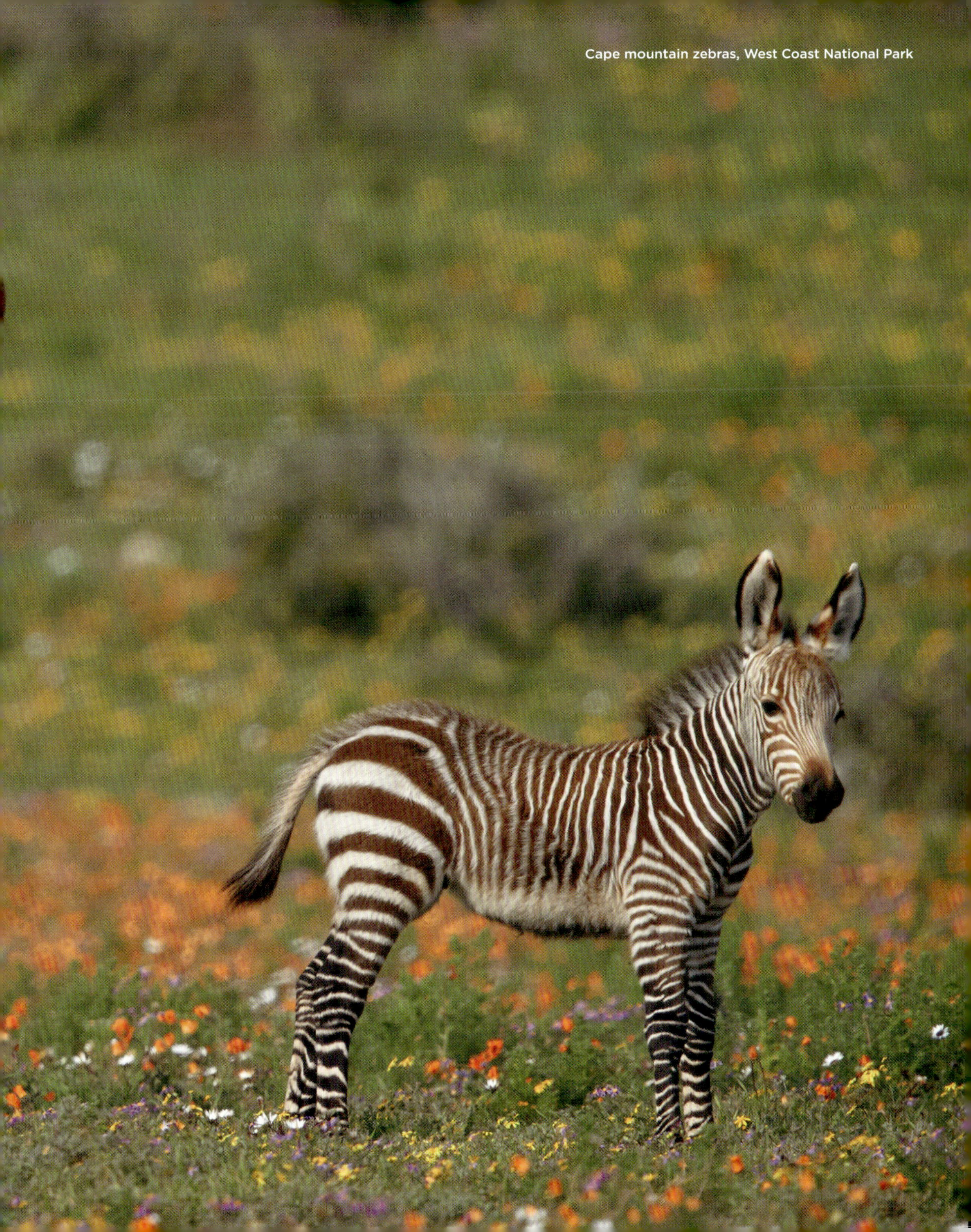
Cape mountain zebras, West Coast National Park

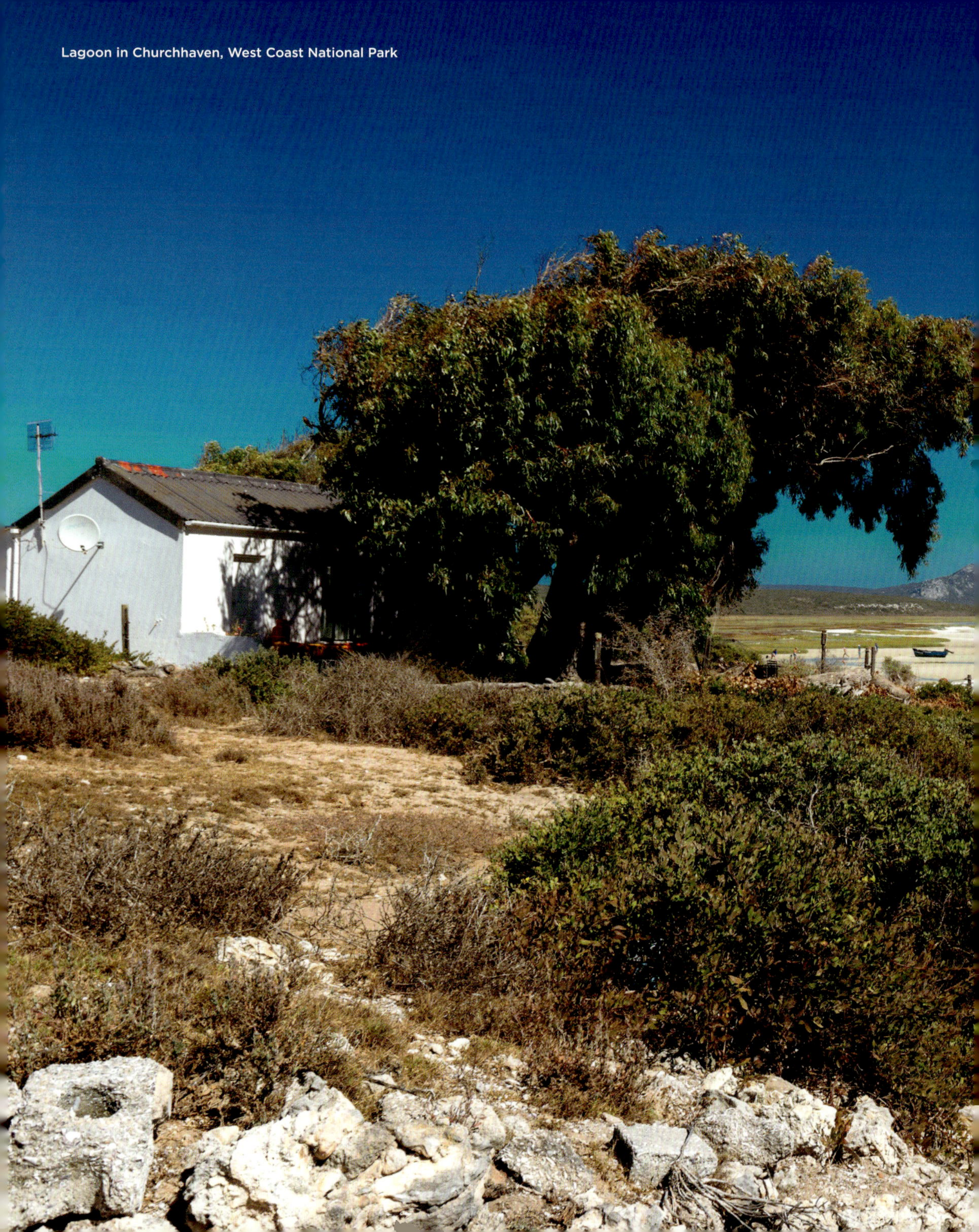
Lagoon in Churchhaven, West Coast National Park

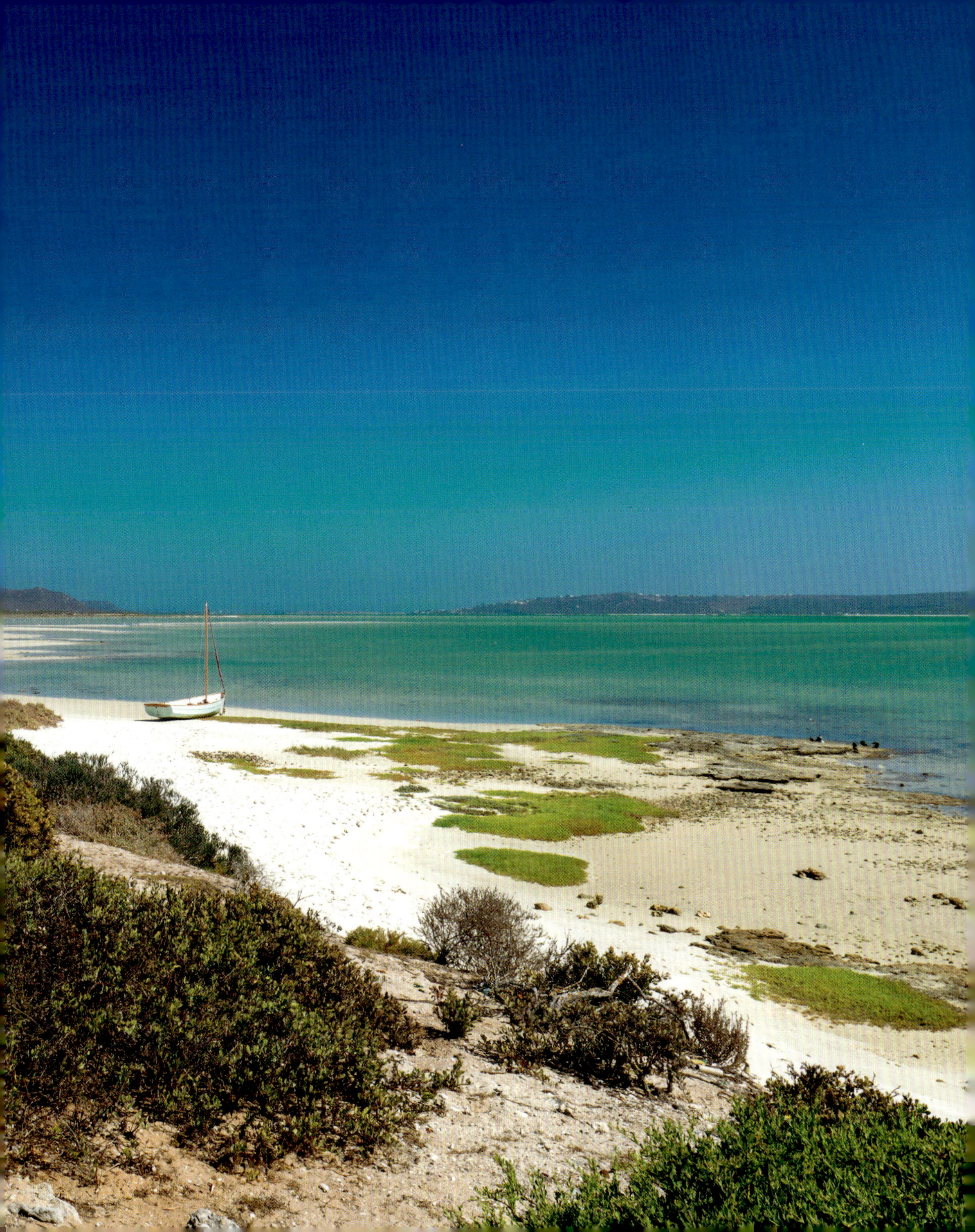

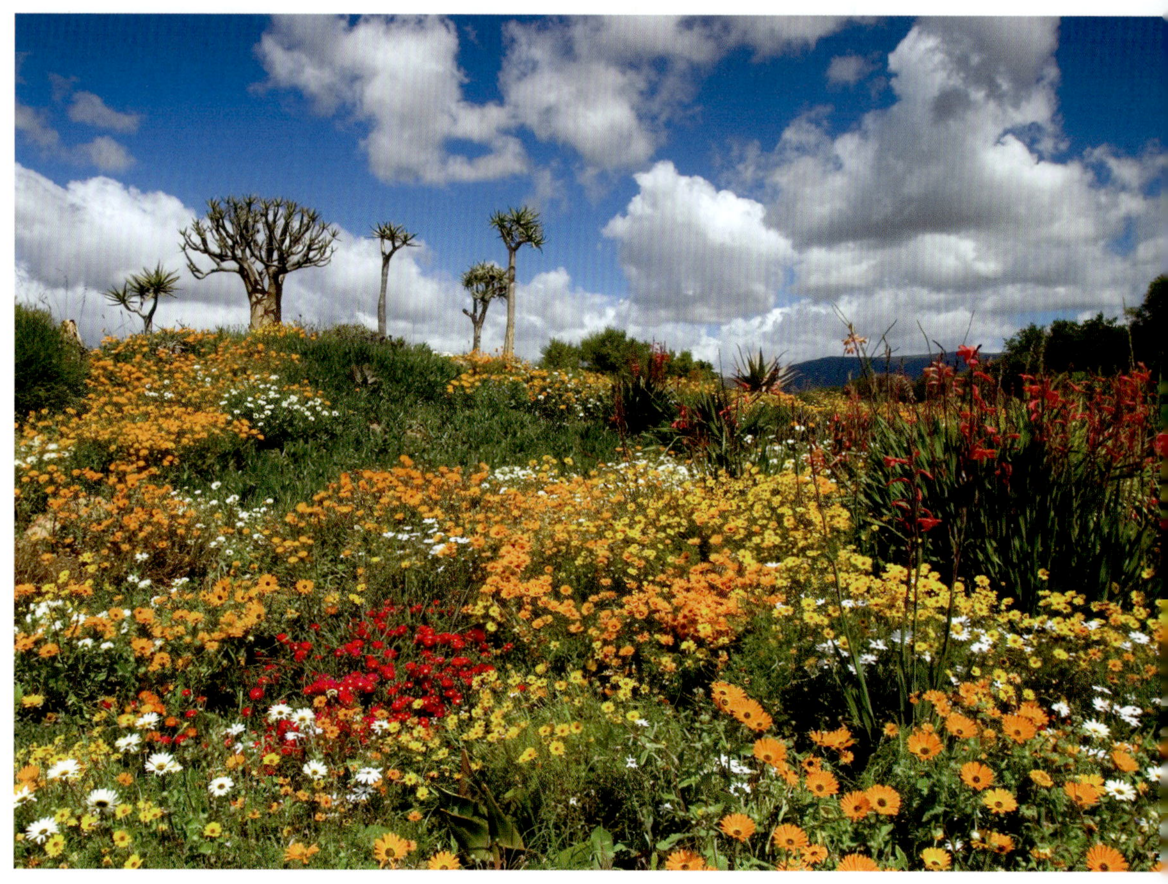

West Coast National Park

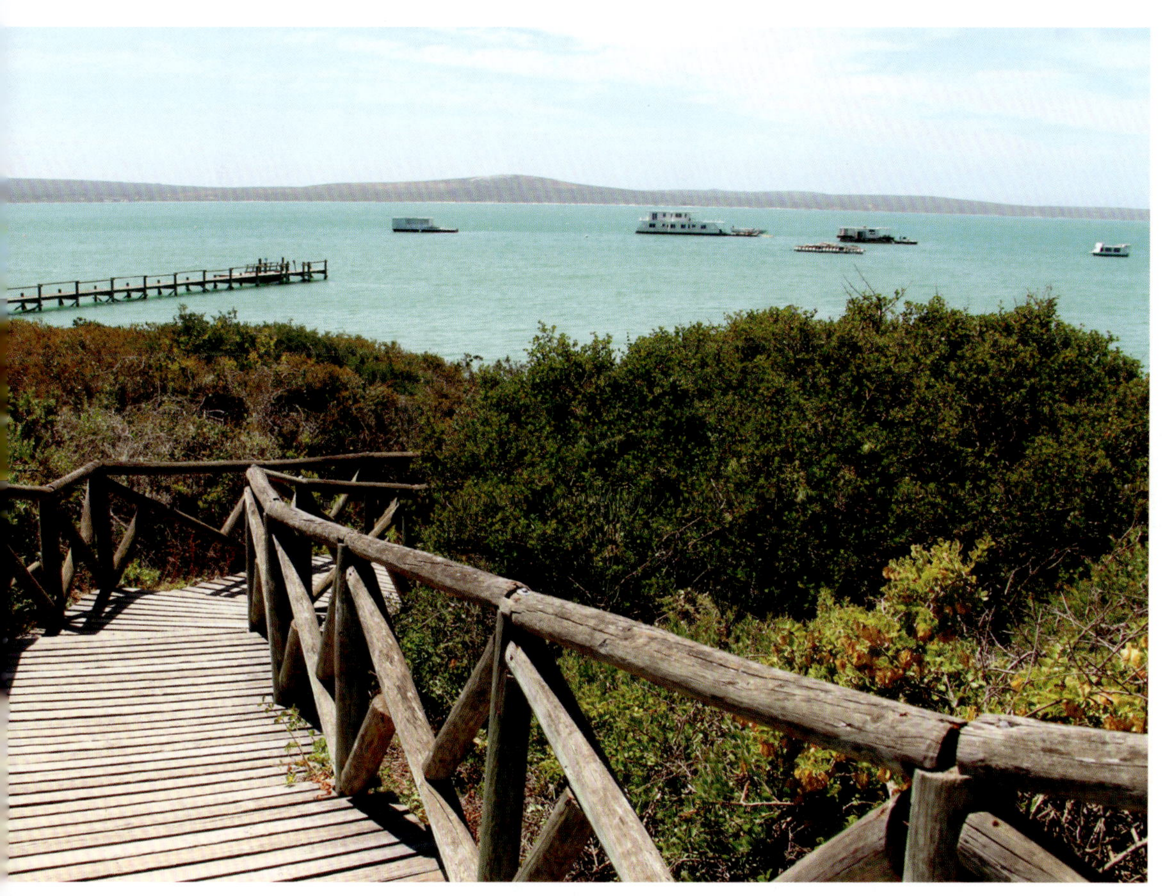

angebaan Lagoon, West Coast National Park

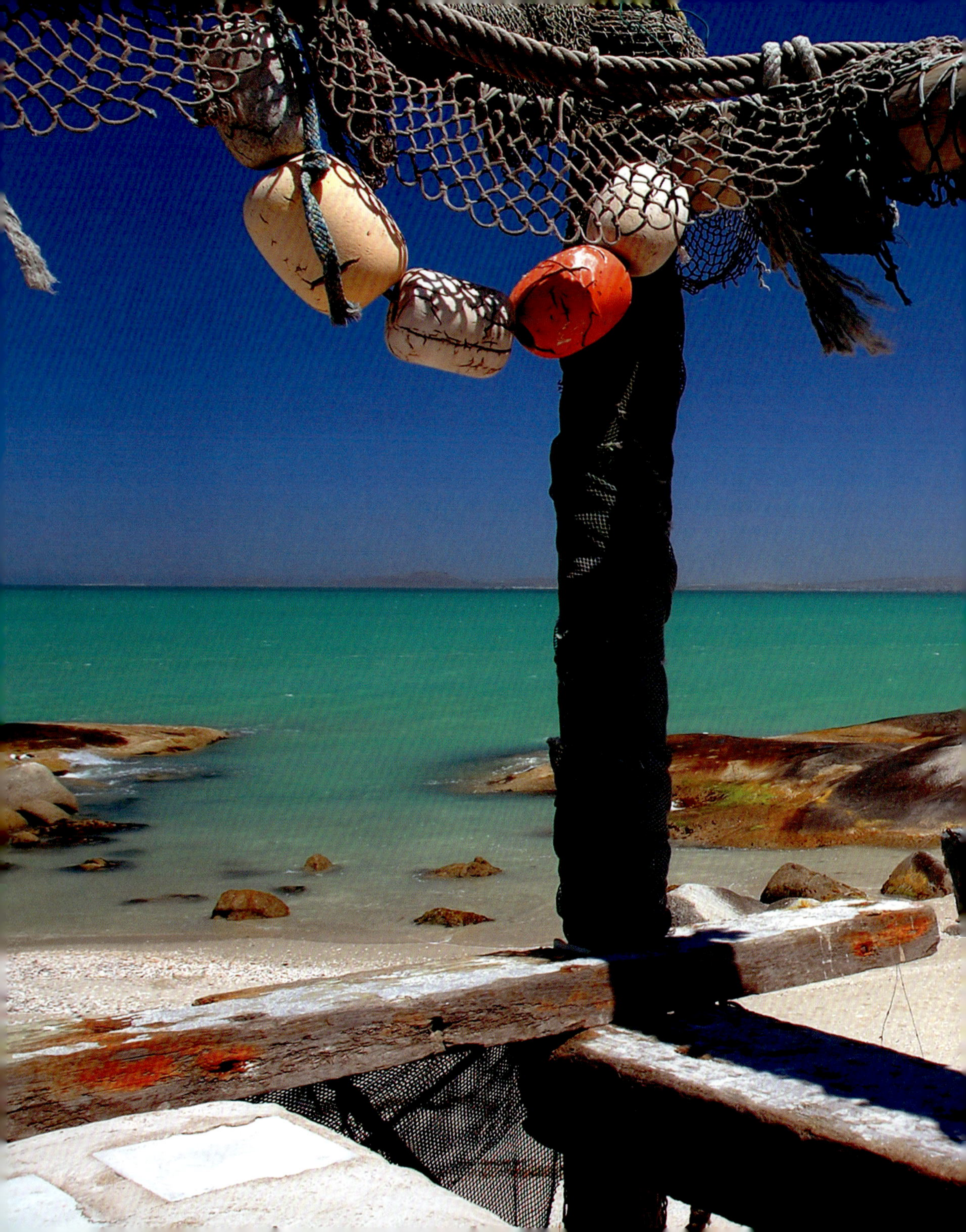

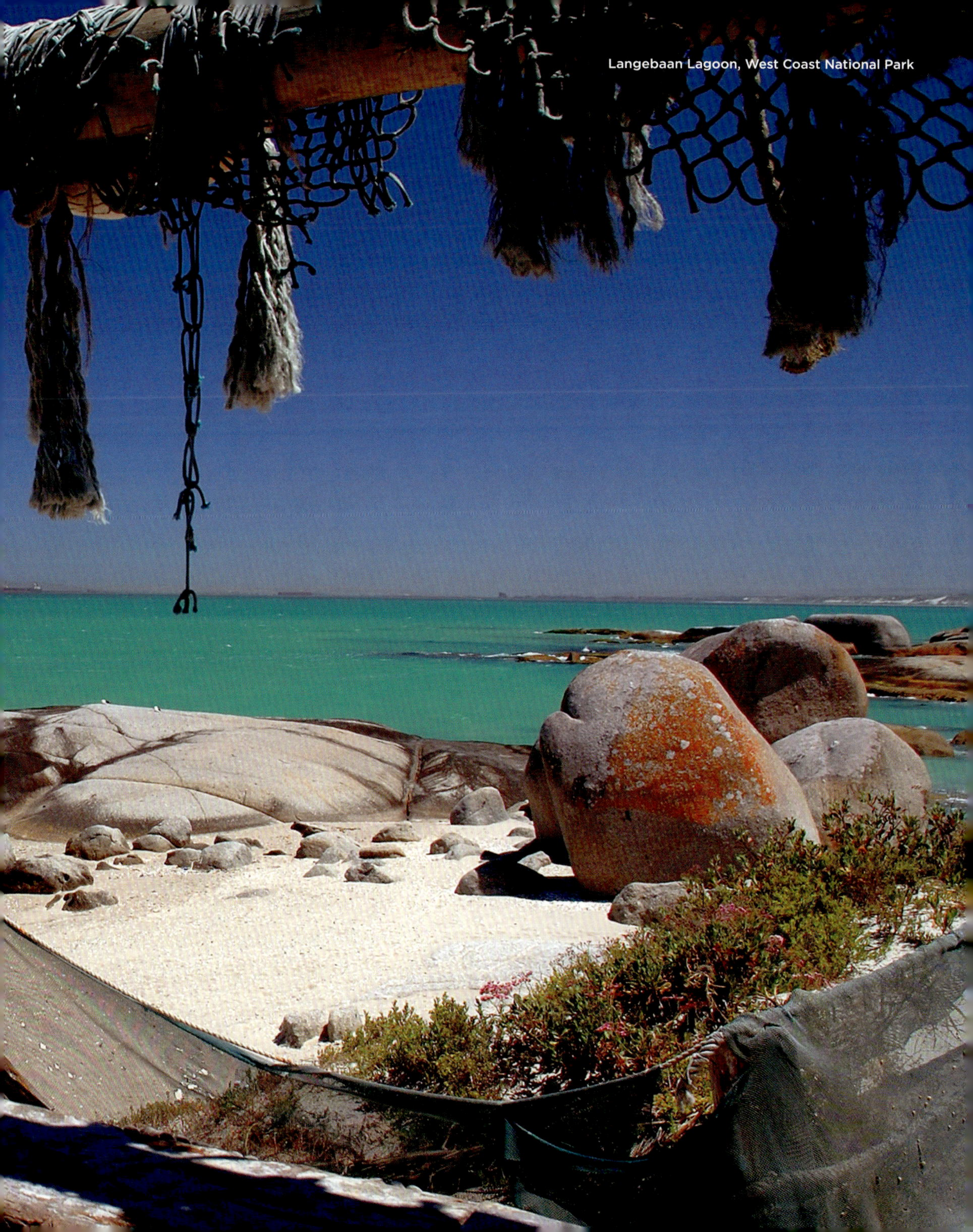

Langebaan Lagoon, West Coast National Park

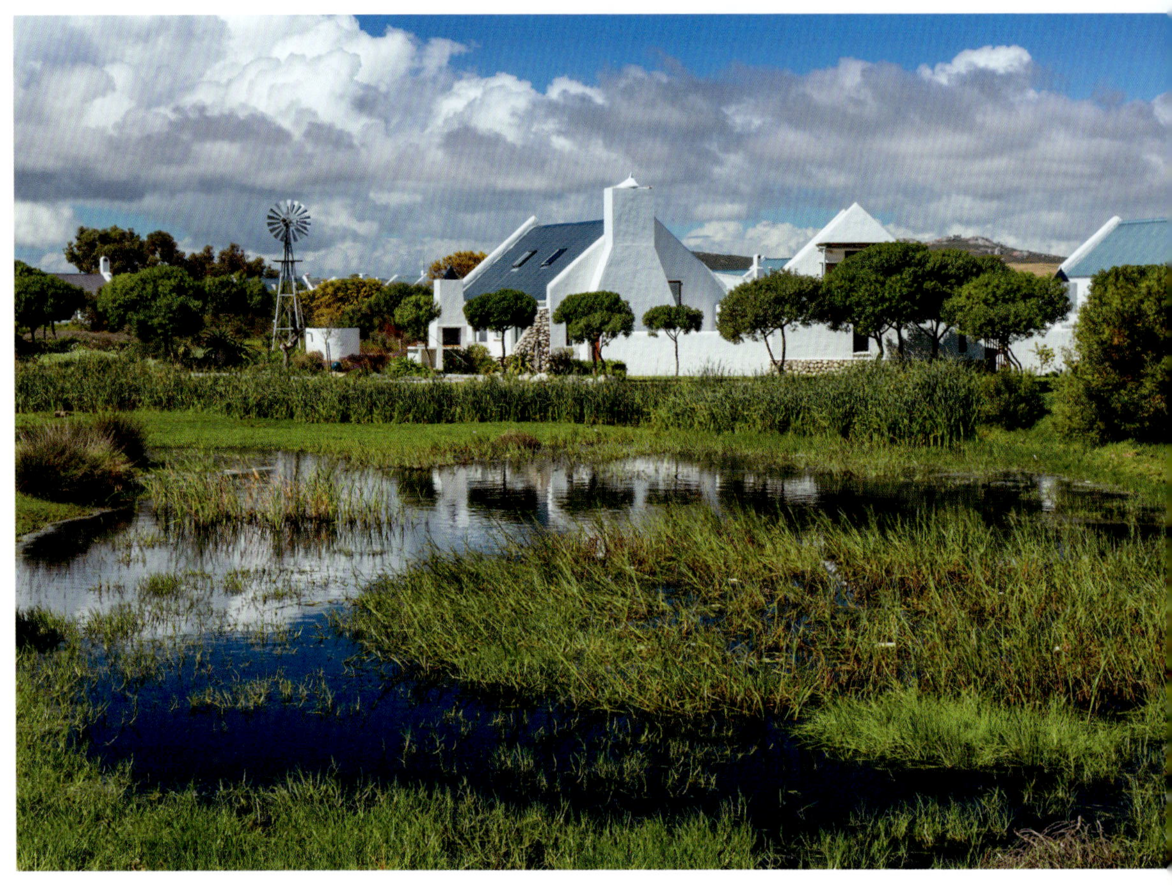
Wetland pool outside Paternoster Village

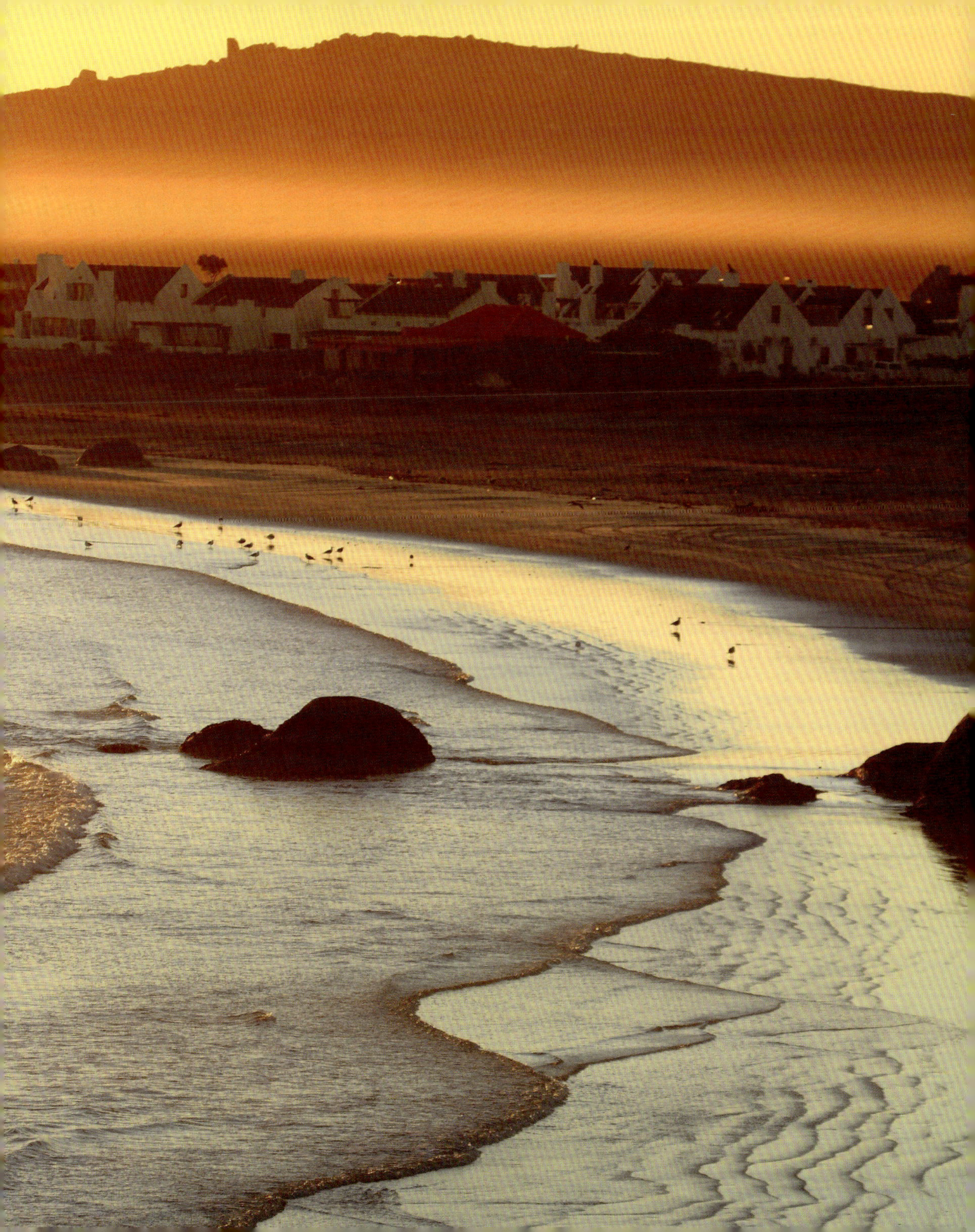

Marine animals
1 Humpback whale
2 Short-beaked common dolphin
3 Great white shark
4 Sperm whale
5 African Penguin
6 Killer whale
7 Southern right whale
8 Seal

Animaux marins
1 Baleine à bosse
2 Dauphin commun
3 Grand requin blanc
4 Grand cachalot
5 Manchot du Cap
6 Orque
7 Baleine australe
8 Otarie à fourrure

Meerestiere
1 Buckelwal
2 Gemeiner Delfin
3 Weißer Hai
4 Pottwal
5 Brillenpinguin
6 Schwertwal
7 Südkaper
8 Seebär

Animales marinos
1 Ballena jorobada
2 Delfín común
3 Tiburón blanco
4 Cachalote
5 Pingüino de El Cabo
6 Orca
7 Ballena franca austral
8 Oso marino

Animali marini
1 Megattera
2 Delfino comune
3 Grande squalo bianco
4 Capodoglio
5 Pinguino del capo
6 Orca
7 Balena franca australe
8 Otaria orsina

Zeedieren
1 Bultrugwalvis
2 Gewone dolfijn
3 Witte haai
4 Potvis
5 Brilpinguïn
6 Orka
7 Zuidkaper
8 Zeebeer

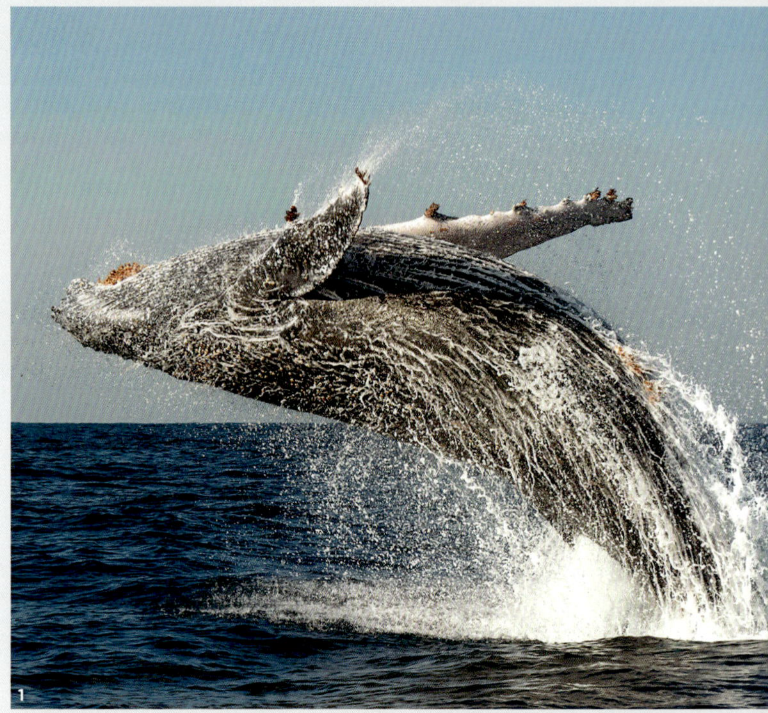
1

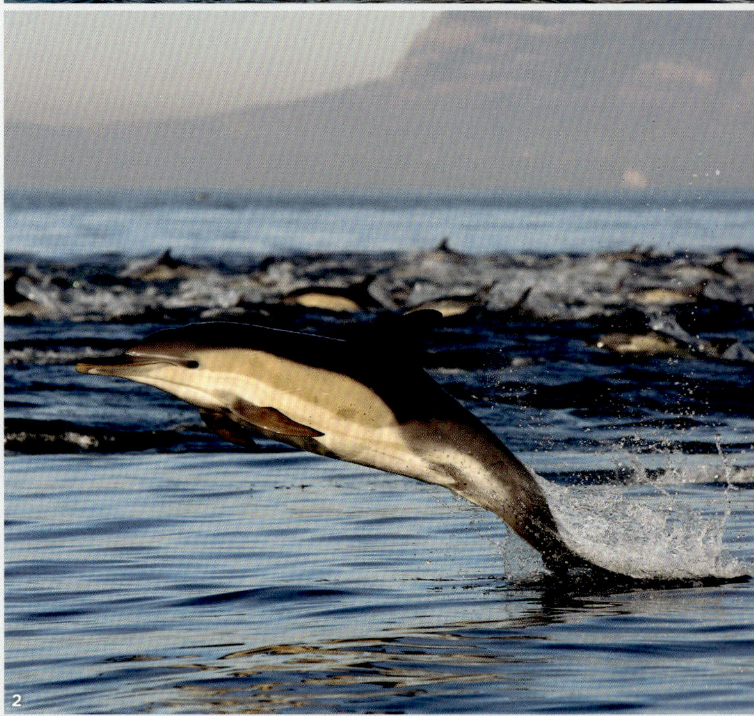
2

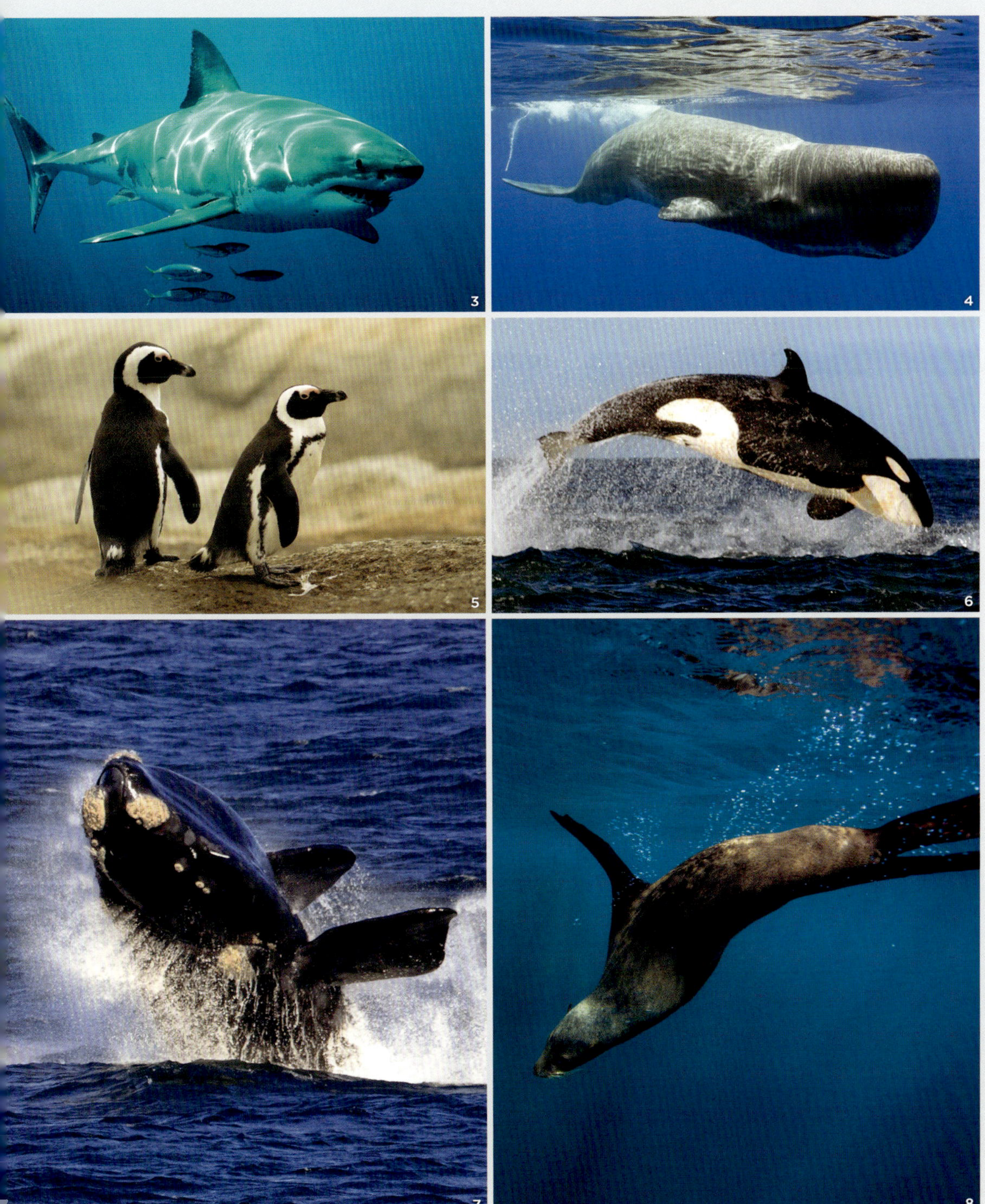
3
4
5
6
7
8

Cederberg Mountains & Tankwa Karoo National Park, South Africa

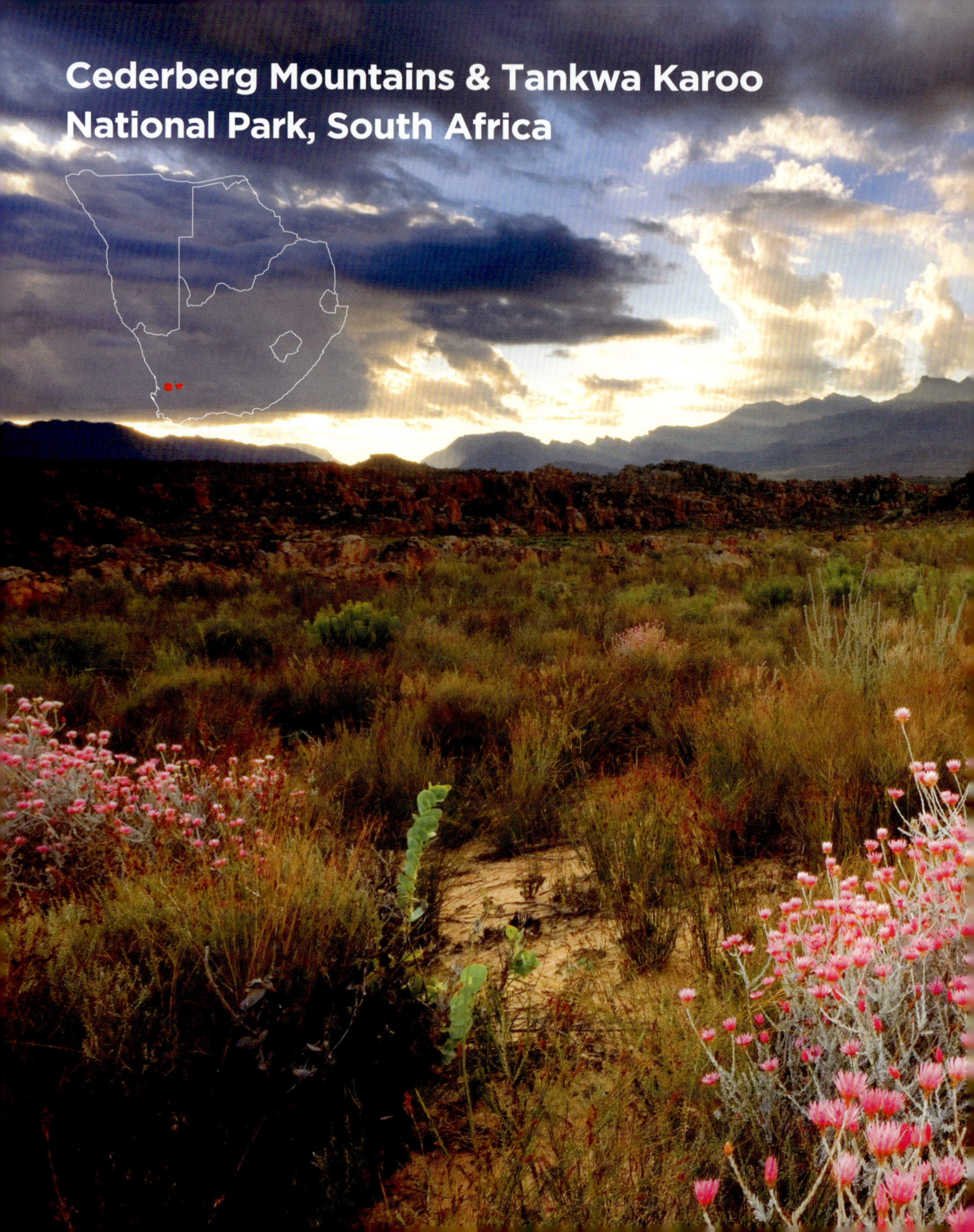

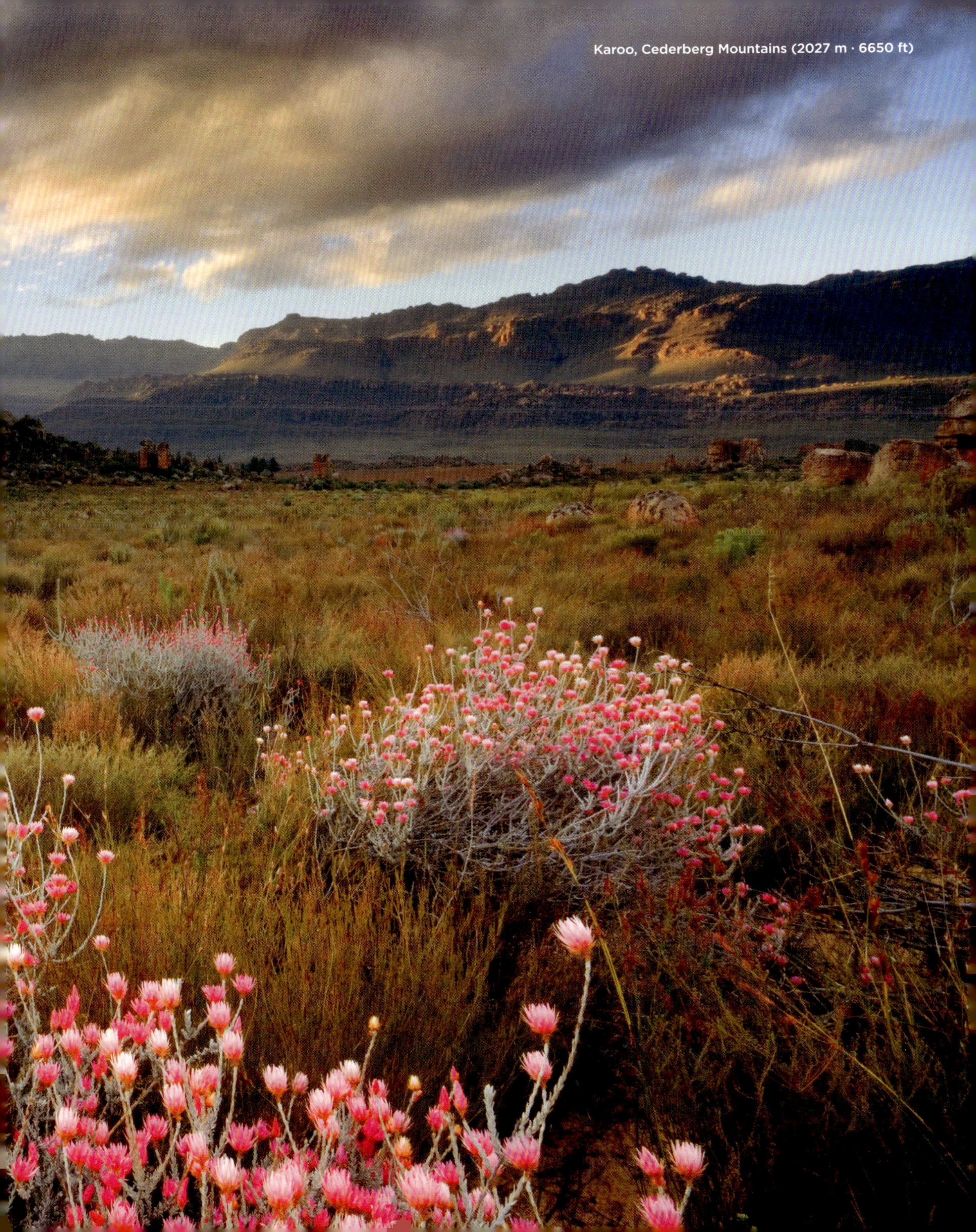
Karoo, Cederberg Mountains (2027 m · 6650 ft)

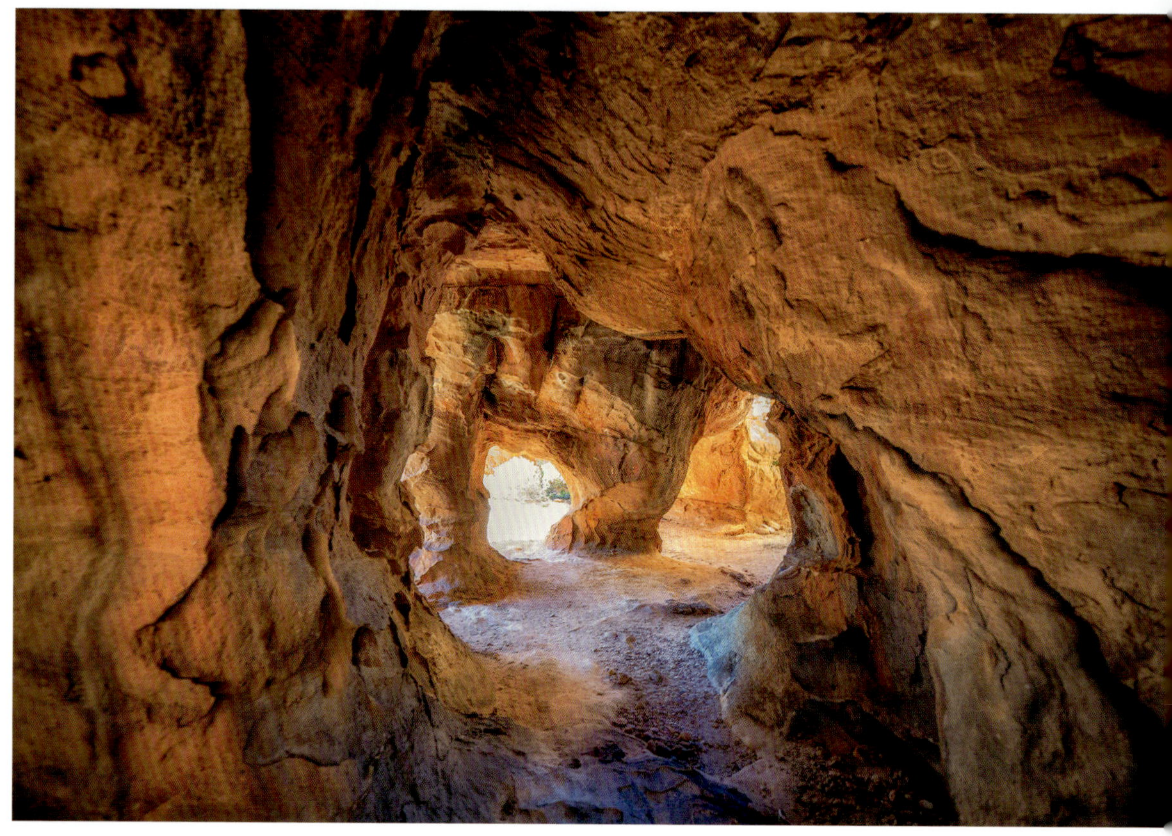

Stadsaal Caves, Cederberg Wilderness Area

Cederberg Mountains
The Cederberg Mountains are located about 200 km (124 mi) north of Cape Town. The mountain range consists of sandstone which has been worn down through erosion into unusual formations. Its highest mountain is the Sneeuberg (2026 m · 6645 ft). In August and September, large areas of the Cederberg Wilderness Area are transformed into a colourful carpet of flowers. As part of the Cape Floristic Region, this natural reserve is also a UNESCO World Heritage Site.

Les montagnes du Cederberg
Ces montagnes se dressent à 200 km au nord du Cap. Ces reliefs gréseux présentent des formations originales. La cime la plus élevée est le Sneeuberg (2026 m). En août et en septembre, d'immenses étendues de la réserve naturelle du Cederberg se métamorphosent en tapis de fleurs multicolores. Cette réserve, qui fait partie de la Région florale du Cap, est inscrite sur la Liste du patrimoine mondial de l'Unesco.

Zederberge
Die Zederberge liegen etwa 200 km nördlich von Kapstadt. Die Gebirgskette besteht aus Sandstein und weist ausgefallene Formationen auf. Ihr höchster Berg ist der Sneeuberg (2026 m). Im August und September verwandeln sich weite Flächen der Cederberg Wilderness Area in bunte Blütenteppiche. Als Teil der Region Cape Floral gehört dieses Naturreservat zum UNESCO-Weltnaturerbe.

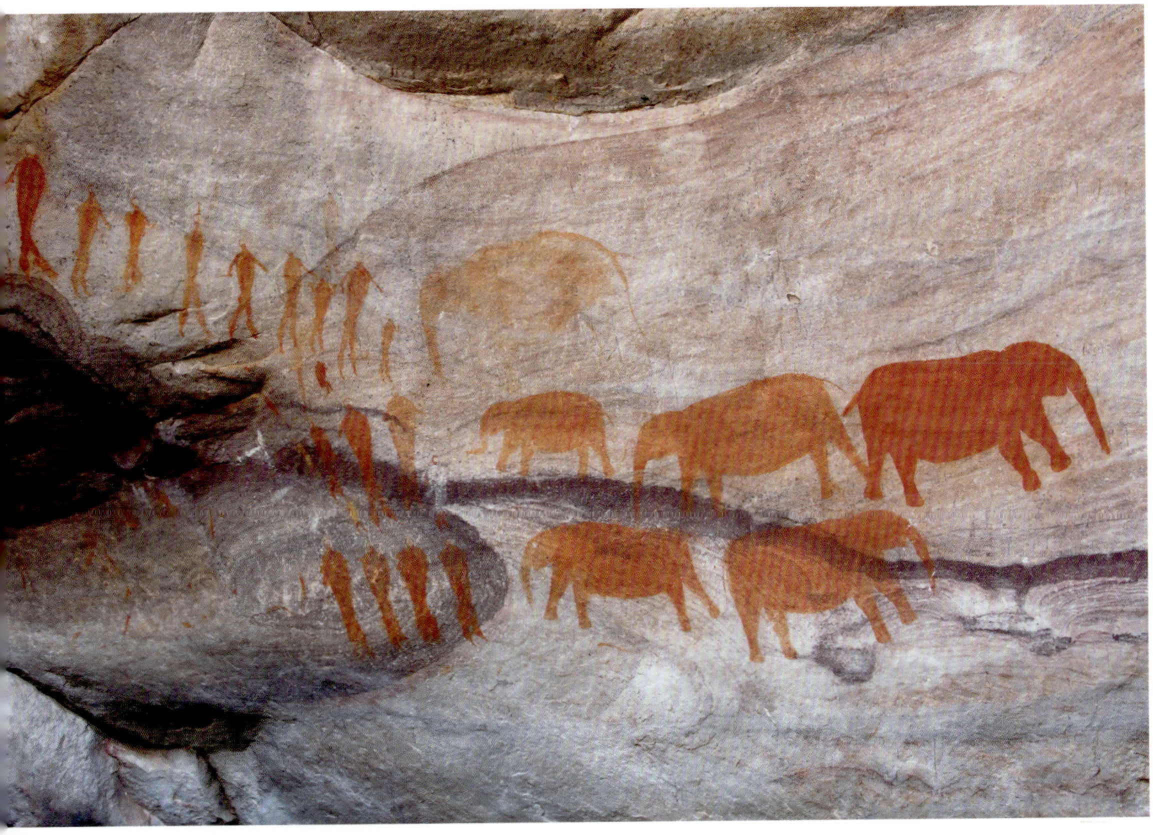

Bushman rock art, Stadsaal Caves, Cederberg Wilderness Area

Cederberg
Las montañas Cederberg se sitúan a 200 km al norte de Ciudad del Cabo. La cordillera se compone de piedra arenisca y tiene formaciones inusuales. Su pico más alto es Sneeuberg (2026 m). En agosto y septiembre, grandes áreas del área silvestre del Cederberg se transforman en alfombras de flores de colores. Como parte de esta región floral del Cabo, esta reserva natural pertenece al Patrimonio de la Humanidad.

Cederberg
I Monti Cederberg si trovano a circa 200 km a nord di Città del Capo. La catena montuosa è composta da pietra arenaria e presenta formazioni stravaganti. Il monte più alto è lo Sneeuberg (2026 m). In agosto e settembre vaste aree della Cederberg Wilderness Area si tramutano in variopinti tappeti di fiori. Come parte della regione di Cape Floral, questa riserva naturale appartiene al patrimonio naturale mondiale dell'UNESCO.

Cederberg
De Cederberg ligt circa 200 km ten noorden van Kaapstad. Het bergmassief bestaat uit zandsteen en bizarre rotsformaties. De hoogste berg van de keten is de Sneeuberg (2026 m). In augustus en september worden de weidse vlakten van de Cederberg Wilderness Area omgetoverd in een bont bloementapijt, een onderdeel van het werelderfgoed Cape Floristic Region.

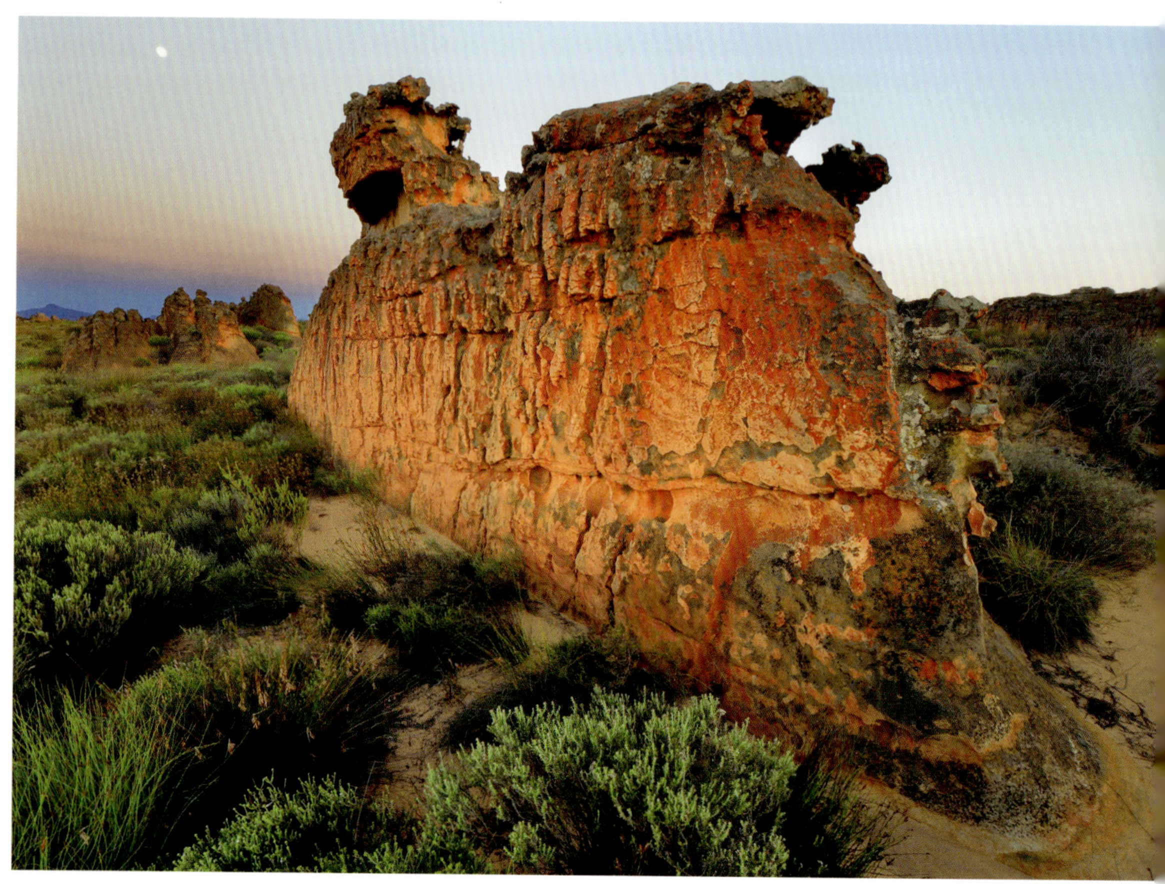

Kagga Kamma Nature Reserve, Cederberg Mountains

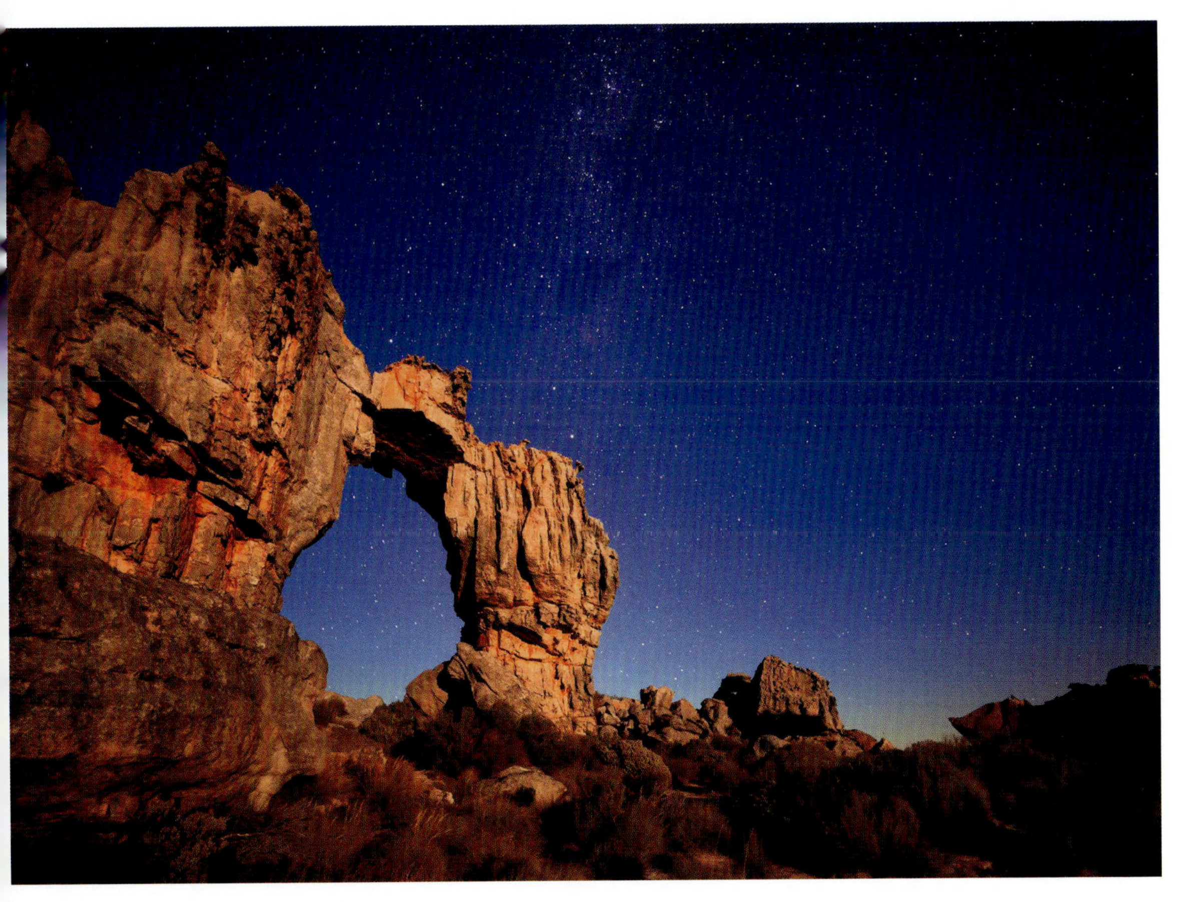

Wolfberg Arch, Cederberg Wilderness Area

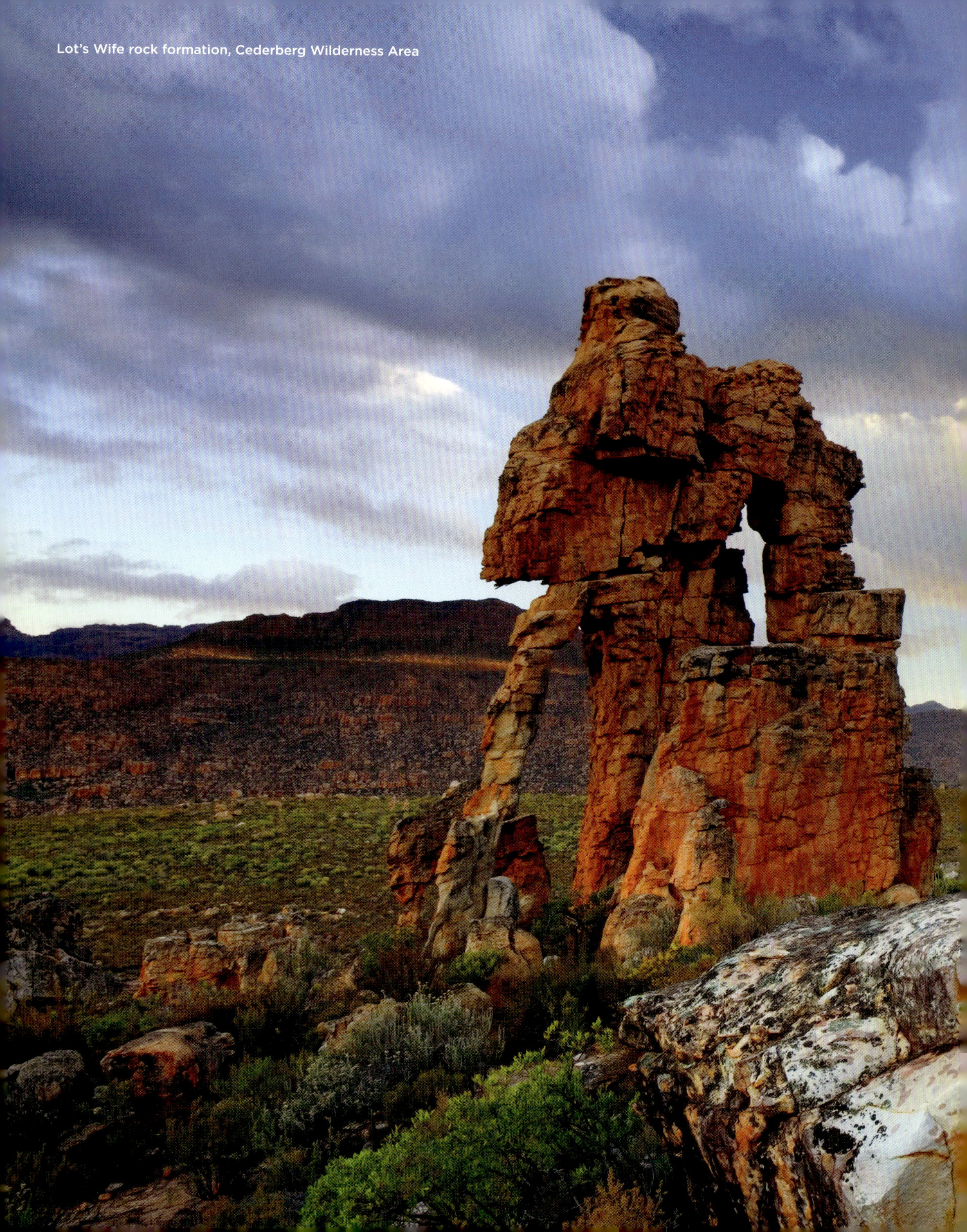

Lot's Wife rock formation, Cederberg Wilderness Area

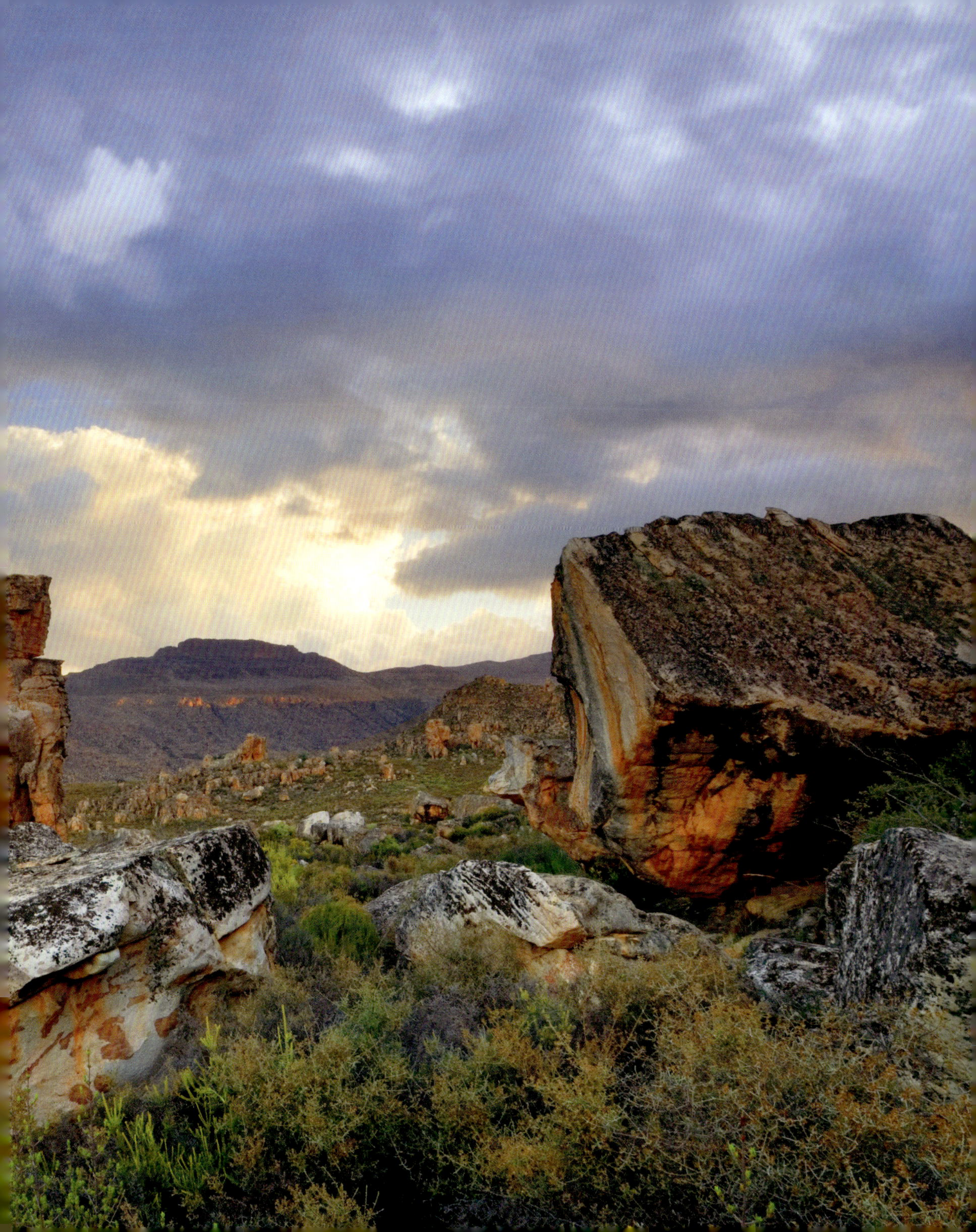

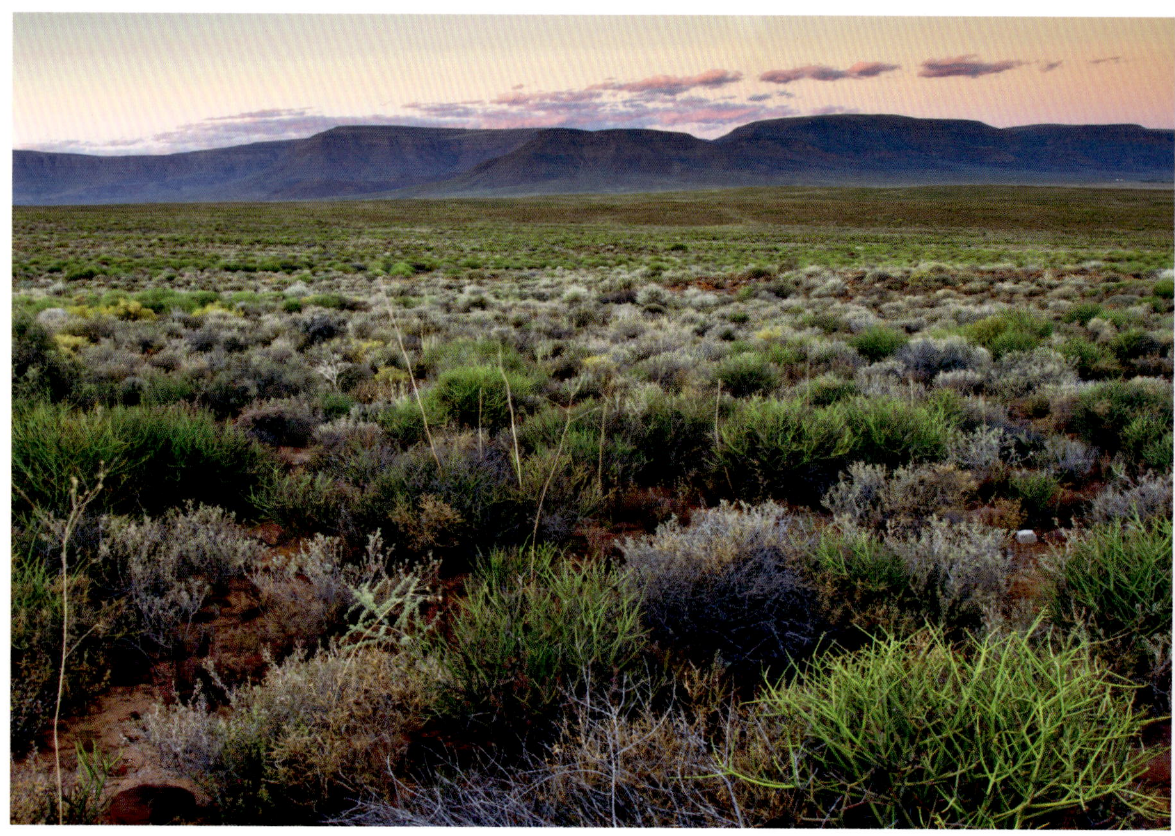

Tankwa Karoo National Park

Tankwa Karoo National Park
Translated, the name Tankwa means "thirsty water". The desert climate in this national park is extremely hot and dry. Surrounded by several mountain ranges, spectacular panoramic views of the endlessly wide plateau are offered. In this wild and pristine landscape, there is little tourist infrastructure.

Le parc national de Tankwa Karoo
Littéralement, le nom Tankwa signifie « eau qui a soif ». Dans ce parc national règne un climat désertique extrêmement chaud et aride. Cet immense haut plateau est entouré de plusieurs chaînes de montagnes et la vue panoramique y est spectaculaire. C'est un paysage sauvage et authentique, presque dépourvu d'infrastructures touristiques.

Tankwa Karoo Nationalpark
Übersetzt heißt der Name Tankwa etwa „durstiges Wasser". Im Nationalpark herrscht extrem heißes und trockenes Wüstenklima. Umgeben von mehreren Gebirgszügen bieten sich spektakuläre Panoramaaussichten auf die endlos weite Hochebene. In der wilden und ursprünglichen Landschaft gibt es kaum touristische Infrastruktur.

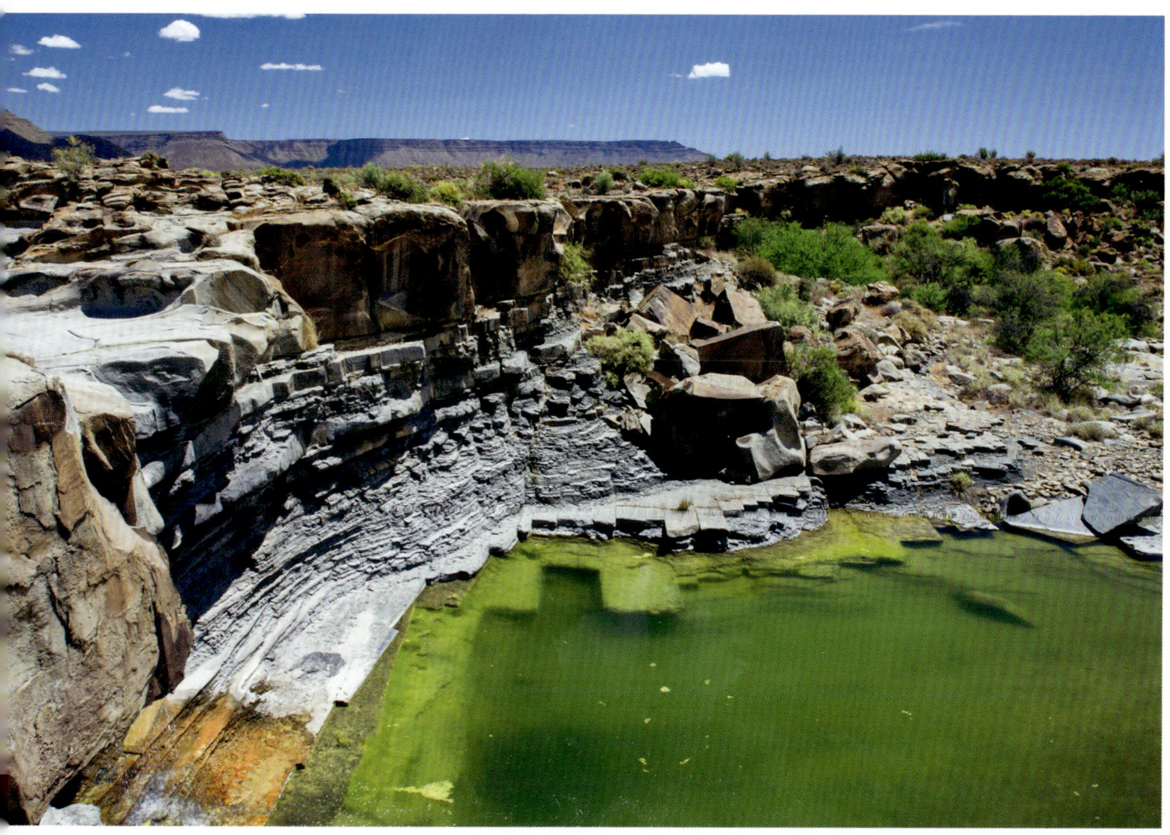

ankwa Karoo National Park

arque Nacional Tankwa Karoo
raducido, el nombre Tankwa significa agua sedienta". El clima desértico en l parque nacional es extremadamente aluroso y seco. Rodeado de varias adenas montañosas, se ofrecen spectaculares vistas panorámicas e la interminable meseta. En el aisaje salvaje y prístino apenas hay fraestructura turística.

Tankwa Karoo National Park
Tradotto, il nome Tankwa significa "acqua assetata". Il clima desertico nel parco nazionale è estremamente caldo e secco. Circondato da diverse catene montuose, offre una spettacolare vista panoramica sull'ampio altopiano. Nel paesaggio selvaggio e incontaminato non è presente quasi nessuna infrastruttura turistica.

Nationaal Park Tankwa Karoo
Vertaald betekent de naam Tankwa "dorstig water". Het woestijnklimaat in dit nationale park is extreem heet en droog. Doordat het is omringd door diverse bergketens biedt het een spectaculair panoramisch uitzicht op de eindeloos brede hoogvlakte. In het ongerepte en wilde landschap is er nauwelijks toeristische infrastructuur.

Cape Winelands, South Africa

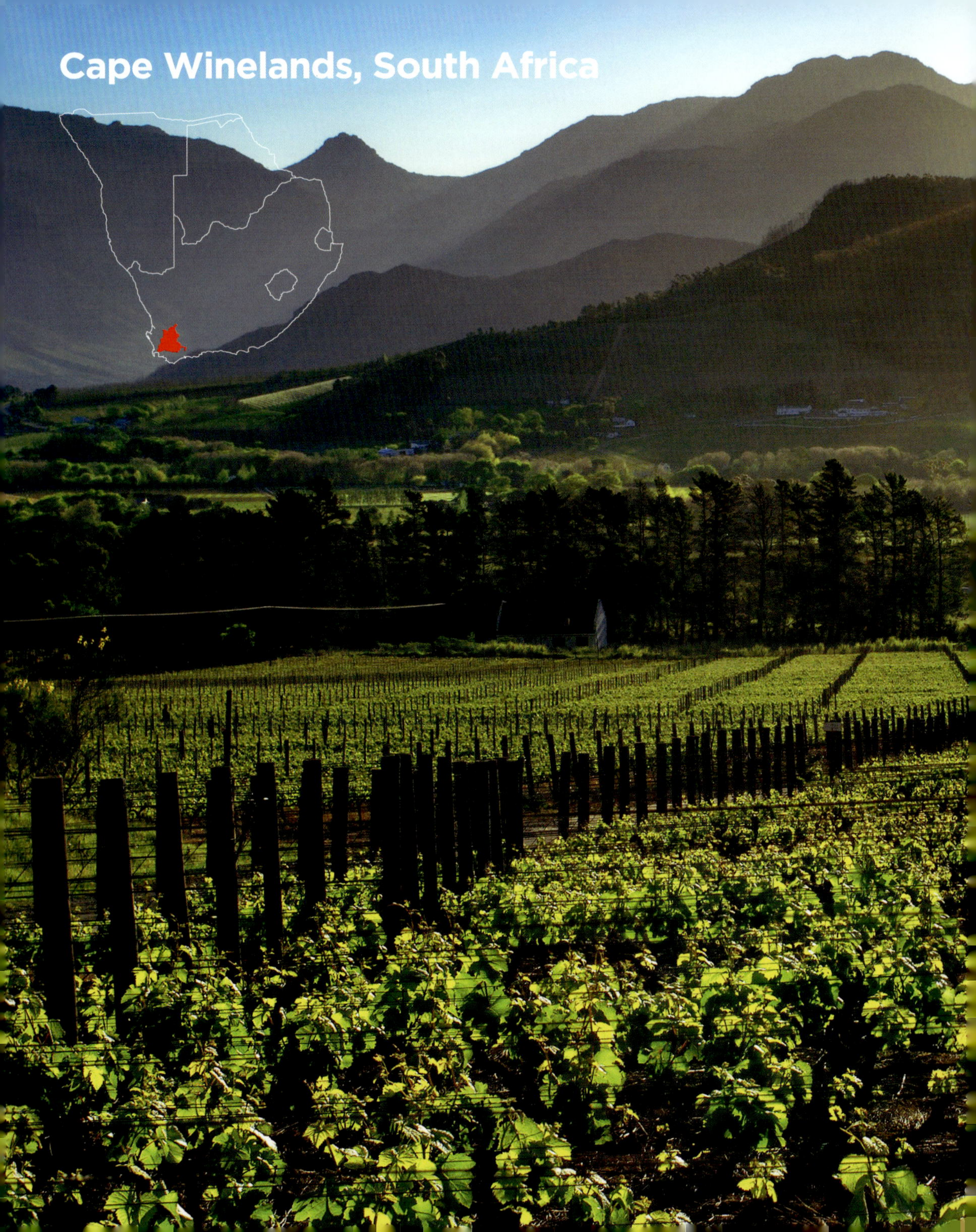

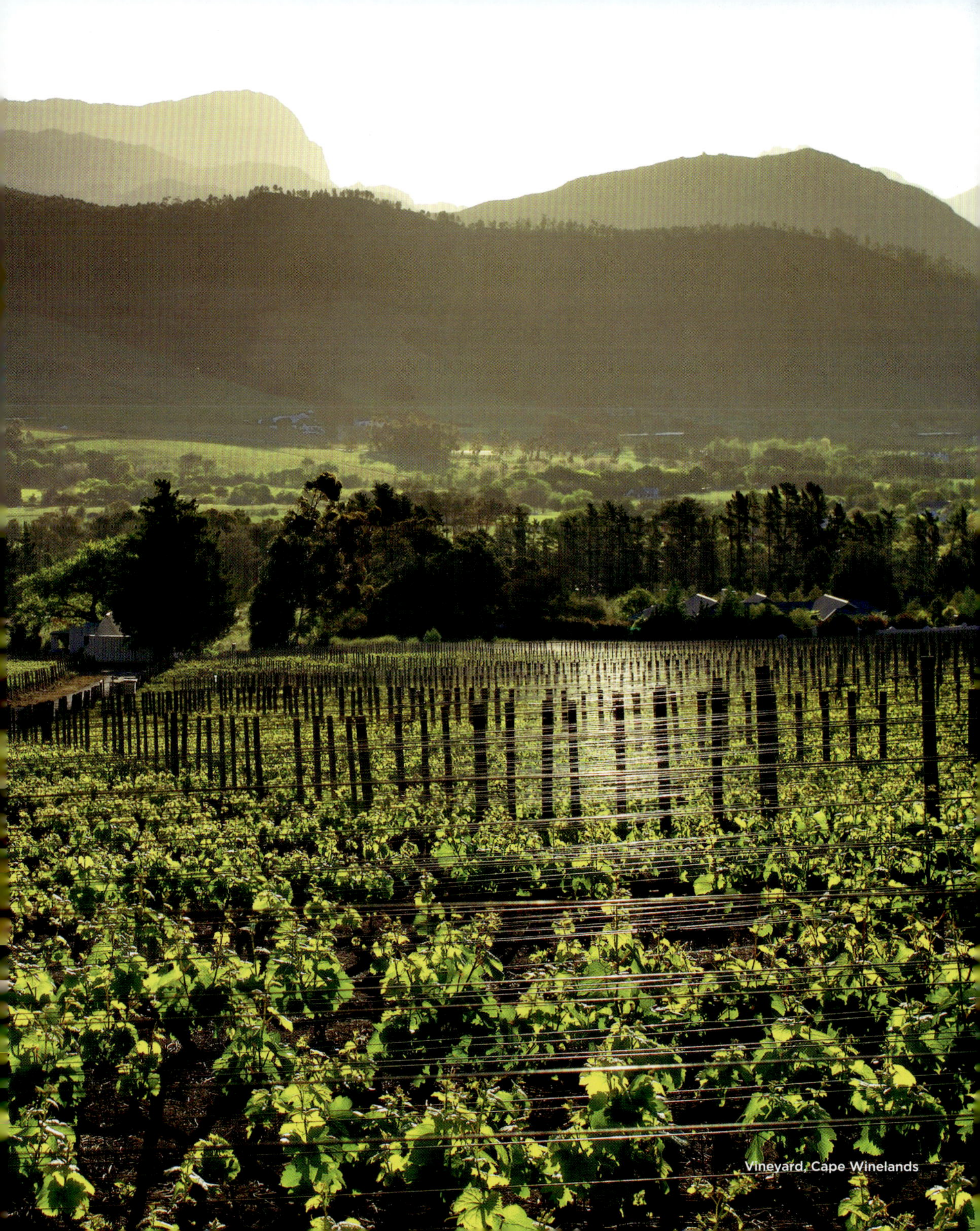

Vineyard, Cape Winelands

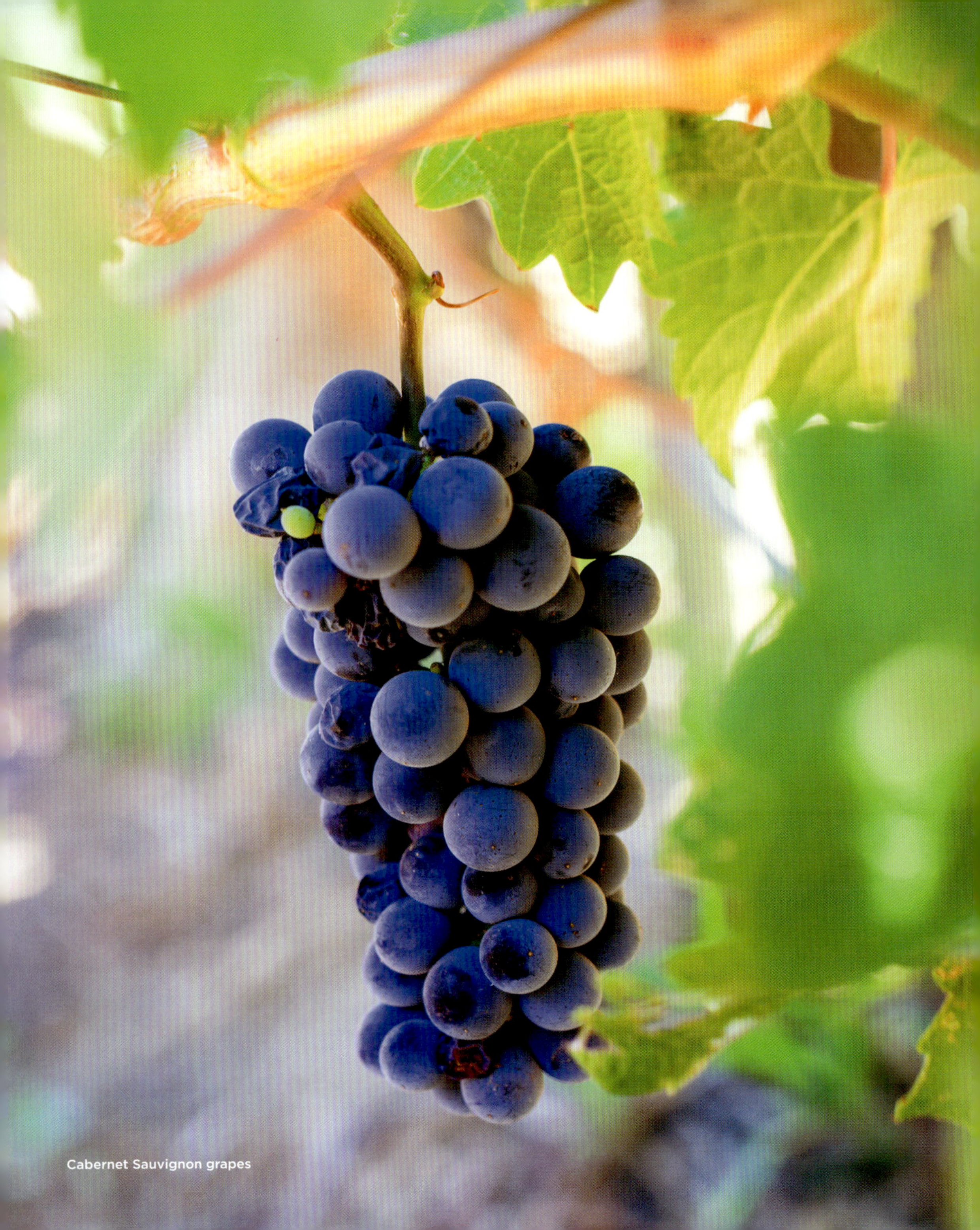

Cabernet Sauvignon grapes

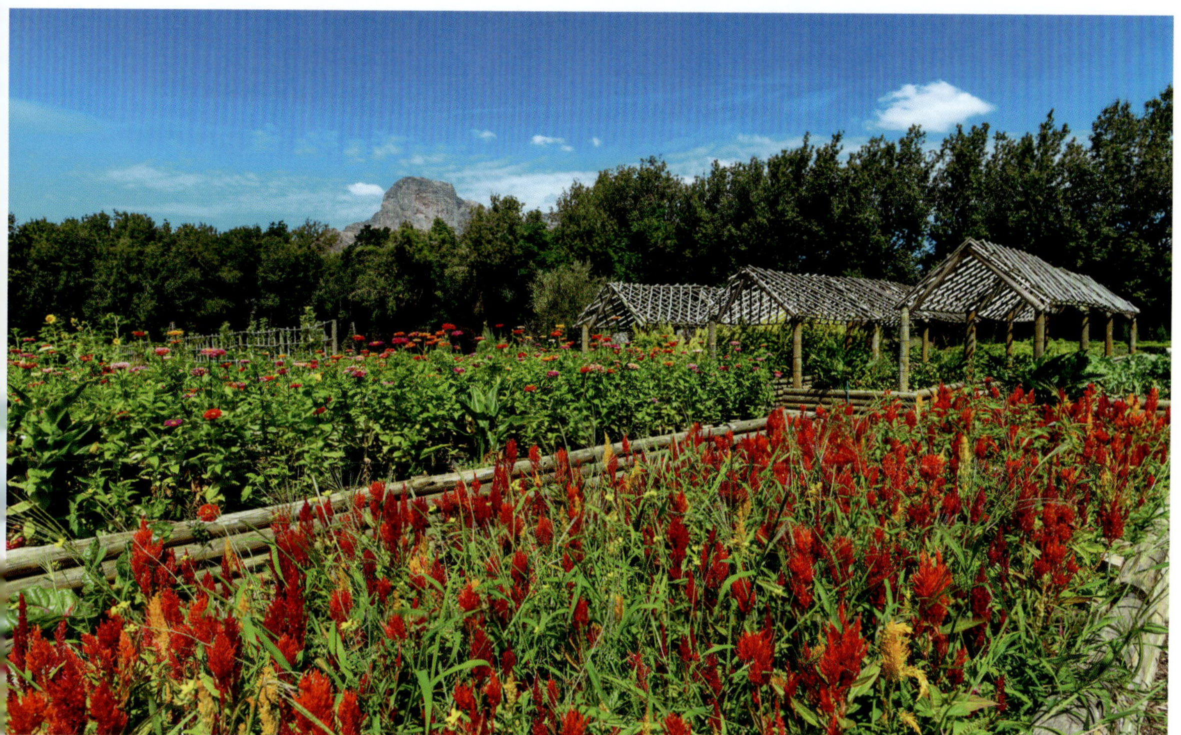

Boschendal Wine Estate, Franschhoek

Cape Winelands
The proximity to the sea in connection with the Mediterranean climate offers perfect cultivation conditions: In South Africa's oldest wine-growing region, the vines grow in numerous valleys protected by massive mountain ranges millions of years old. In the midst of this picturesque landscape lie the towns of Stellenbosch and Franschhoek, with their colonial charm.

Cape Winelands
Die Nähe zum Meer in Verbindung mit dem mediterranen Klima bietet perfekte Anbaubedingungen: In der ältesten Weinbauregion Südafrikas wachsen die Reben in zahlreichen Tälern, geschützt von massiven, Millionen Jahre alten Bergketten. Inmitten dieser malerischen Landschaft liegen die Städte Stellenbosch und Franschhoek mit ihrem kolonialen Charme.

Cape Winelands
La vicinanza al mare e il clima mediterraneo offrono condizioni di coltivazione perfette: nella più antica regione vitivinicola del Sudafrica, le viti crescono in numerose valli protette da massicce catene montuose, vecchie di milioni di anni. In mezzo a questo paesaggio pittoresco si trovano le città di Stellenbosch e Franschhoek con il loro fascino coloniale.

Cape Winelands
La proximité de la mer et le climat méditerranéen offrent des conditions parfaites : dans cette région viticole, la plus ancienne d'Afrique du Sud, les vignes poussent dans de nombreuses vallées, protégées par des chaînes de montagnes imposantes, vieilles de millions d'années. Les villes de Stellenbosch et Franschhoek, avec le charme de leur architecture coloniale, sont nichées au cœur de ce paysage si pittoresque.

Cape Viñedos
La proximidad al mar en relación con el clima mediterráneo ofrece unas condiciones de cultivo perfectas: En la región vitivinícola más antigua de Sudáfrica, las viñas crecen en numerosos valles protegidos por enormes cadenas montañosas de millones de años de antigüedad. En medio de este paisaje pintoresco se encuentran las ciudades de Stellenbosch y Franschhoek con su encanto colonial.

Cape Winelands
De nabijheid van zee in combinatie met het mediterrane klimaat biedt perfecte wijnbouwomstandigheden: in de oudste wijnstreek van Zuid-Afrika groeien de wijnstokken in talrijke valleien die in de beschutting van miljoenen jaren oude, massieve bergketens liggen. In dit pittoreske landschap liggen de steden Stellenbosch en Franschhoek met hun koloniale charme.

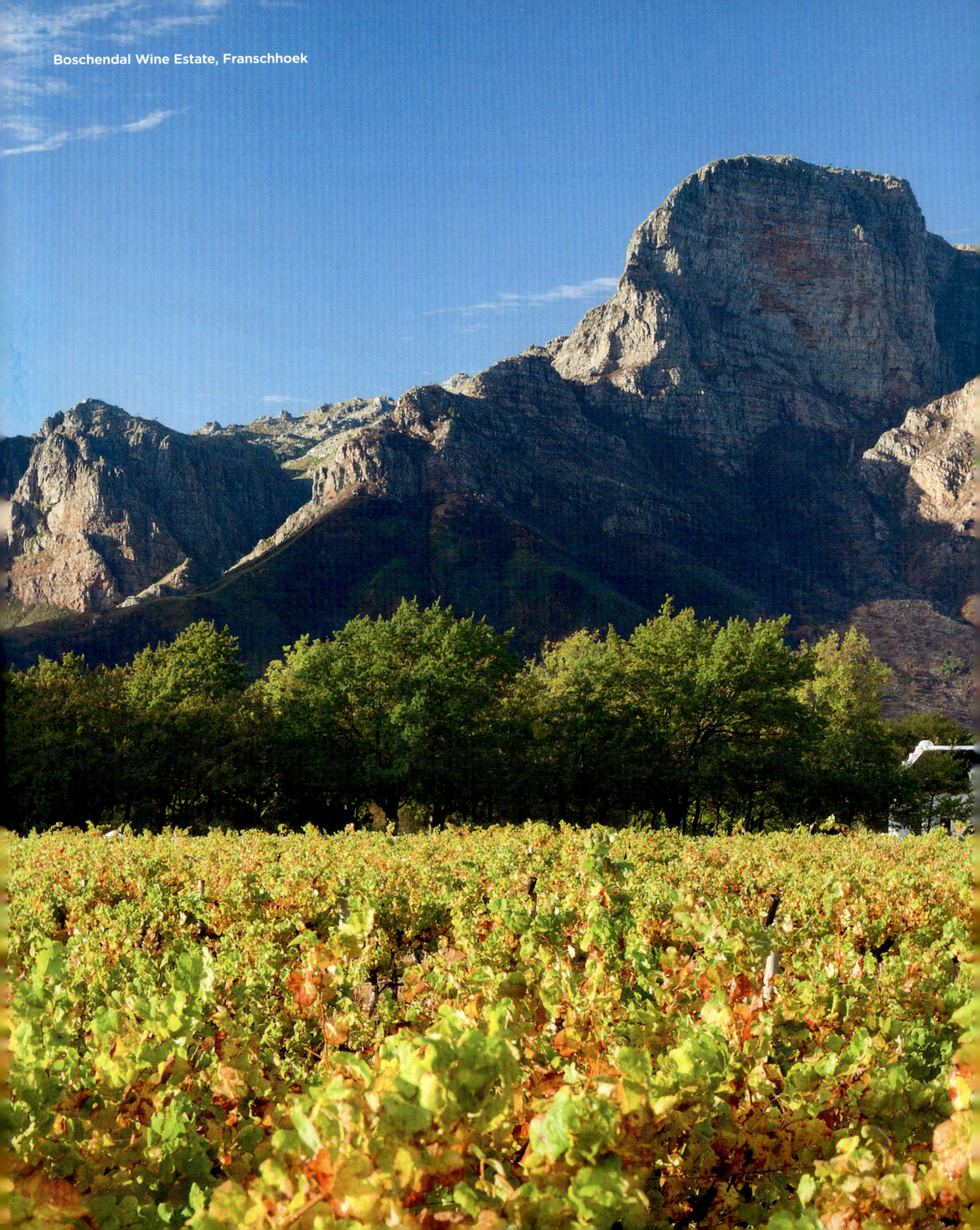
Boschendal Wine Estate, Franschhoek

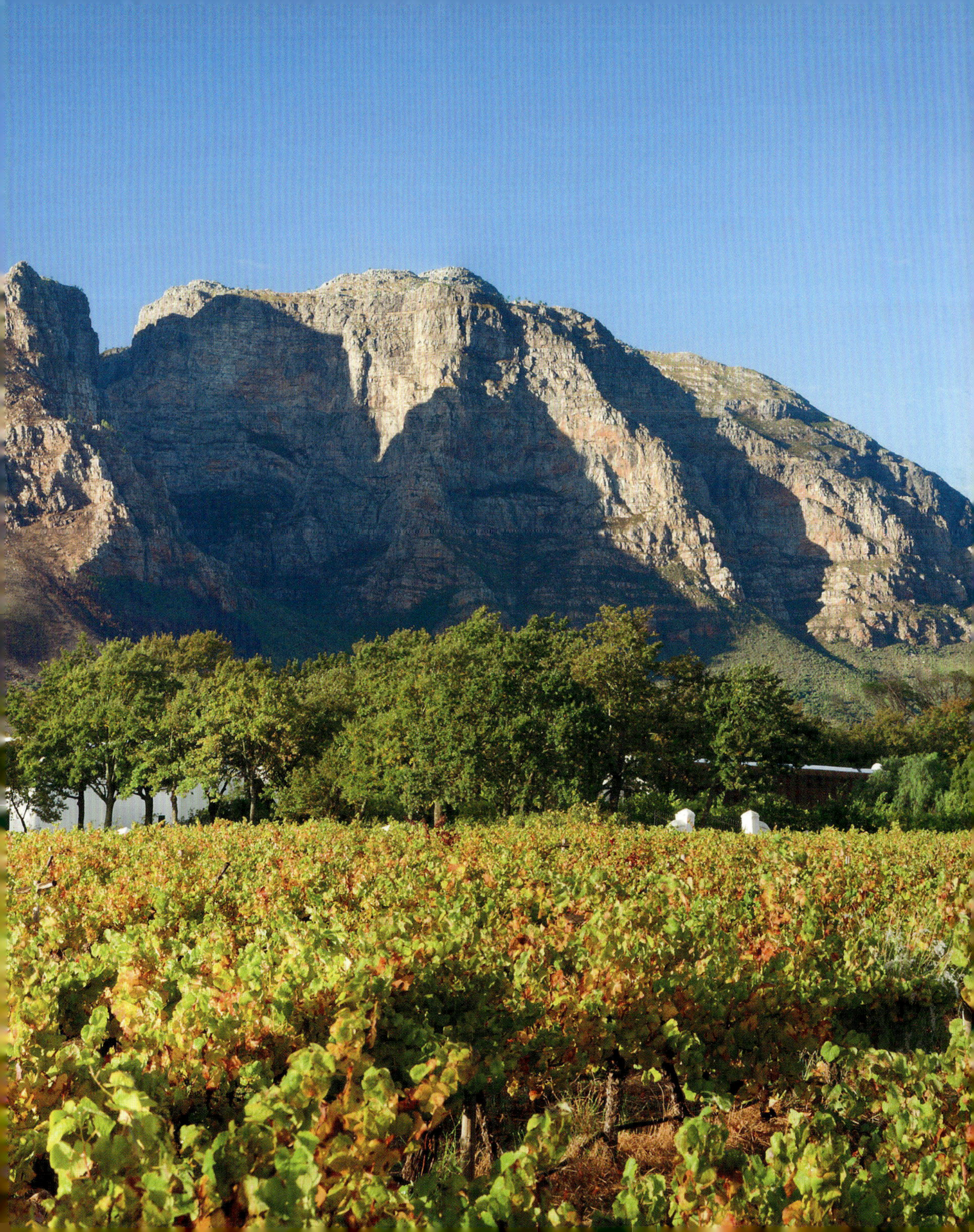

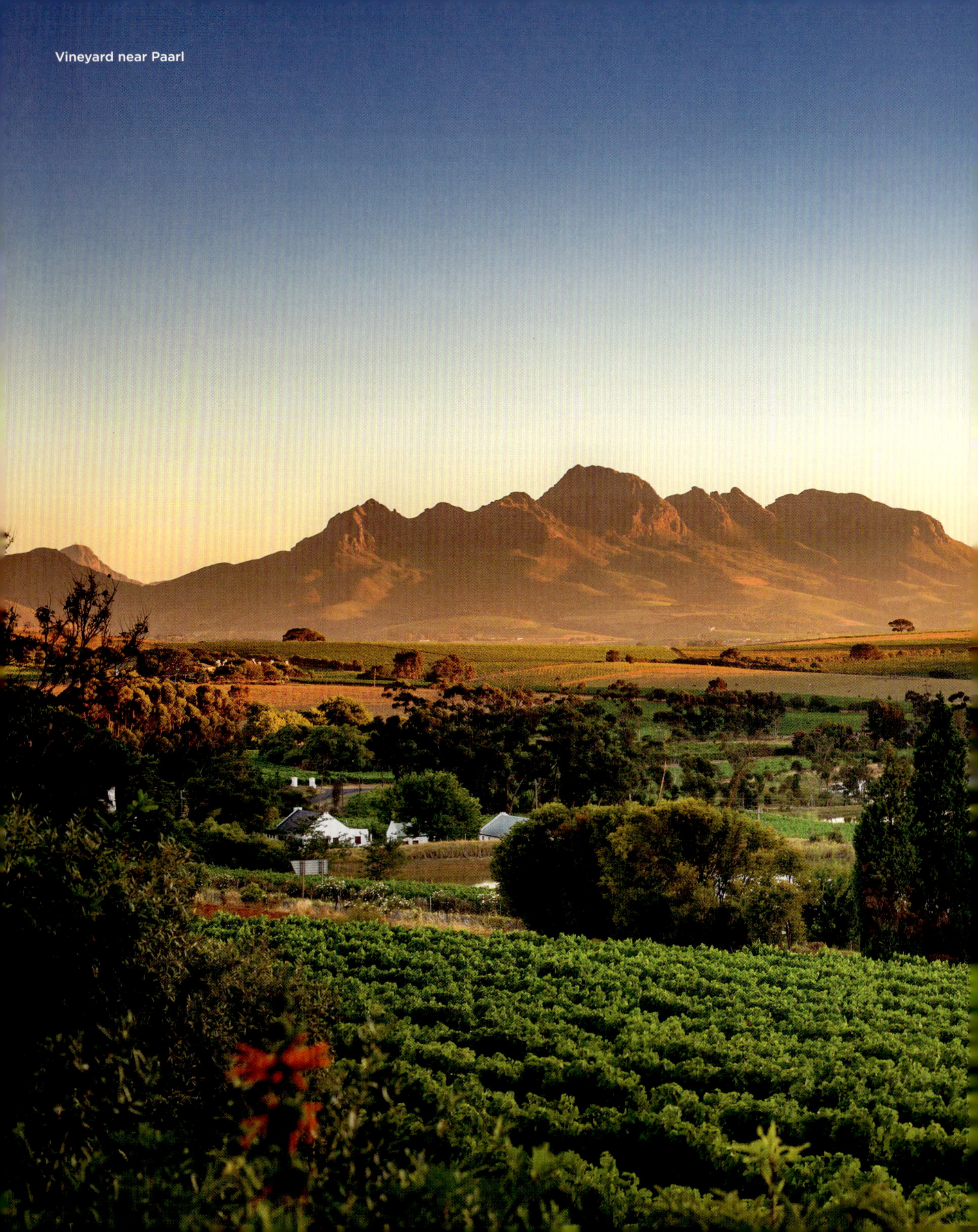
Vineyard near Paarl

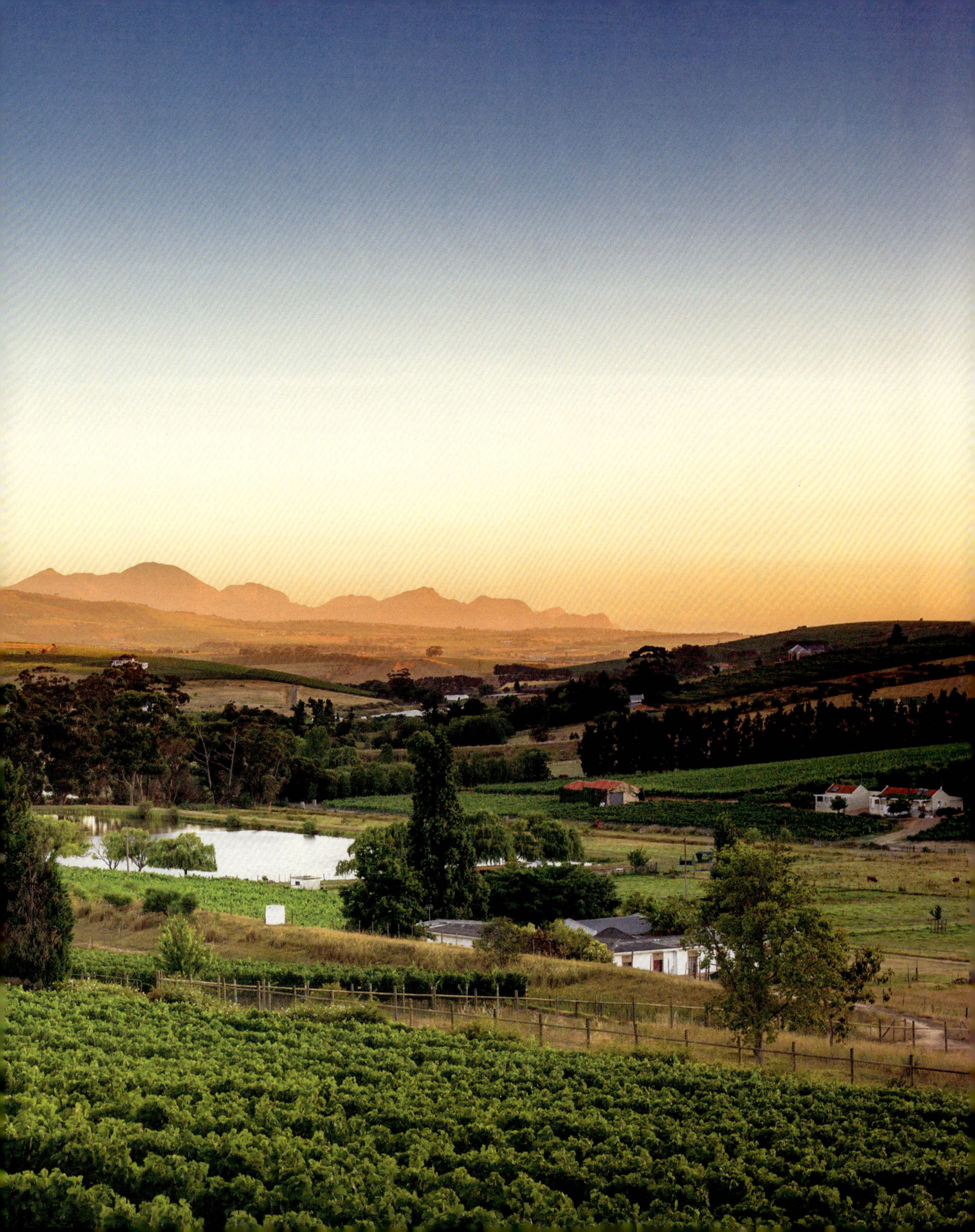

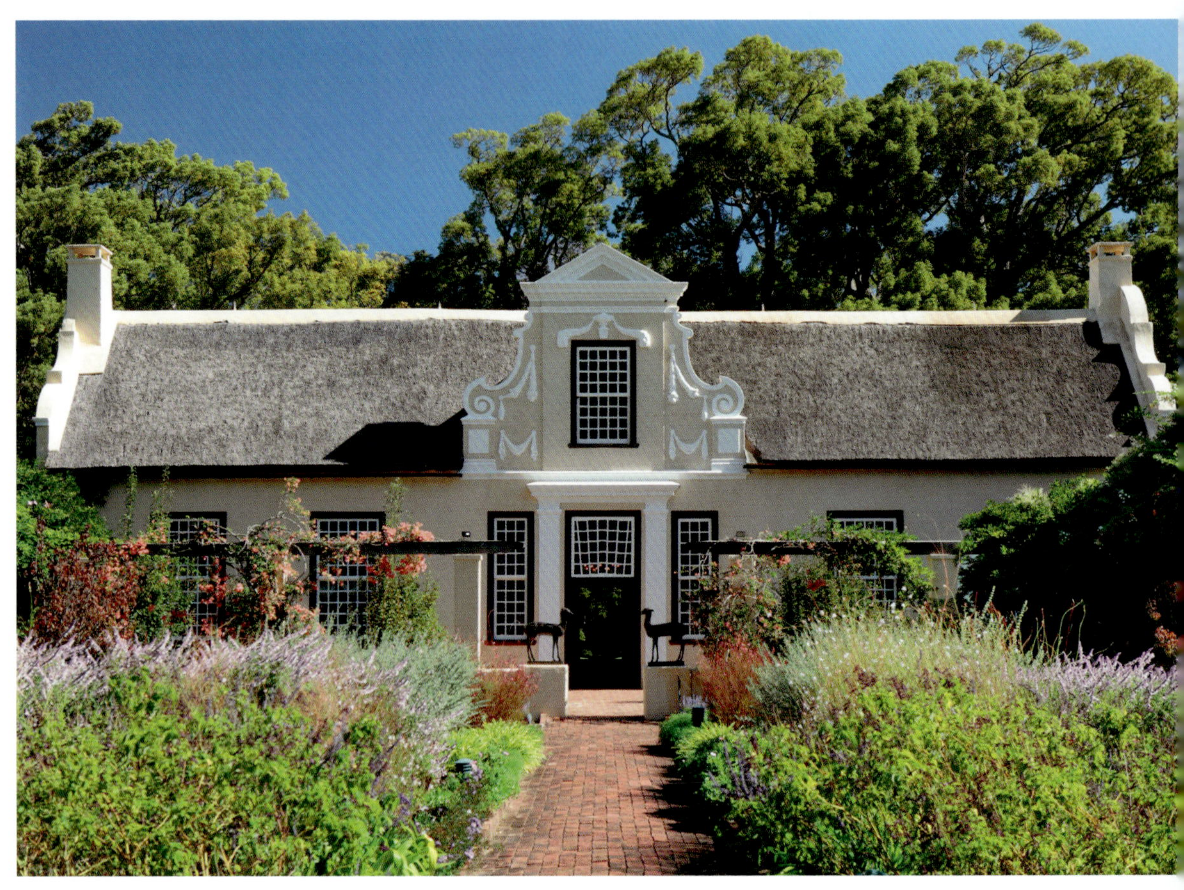

Vergelegen Wine Estate near Somerset West

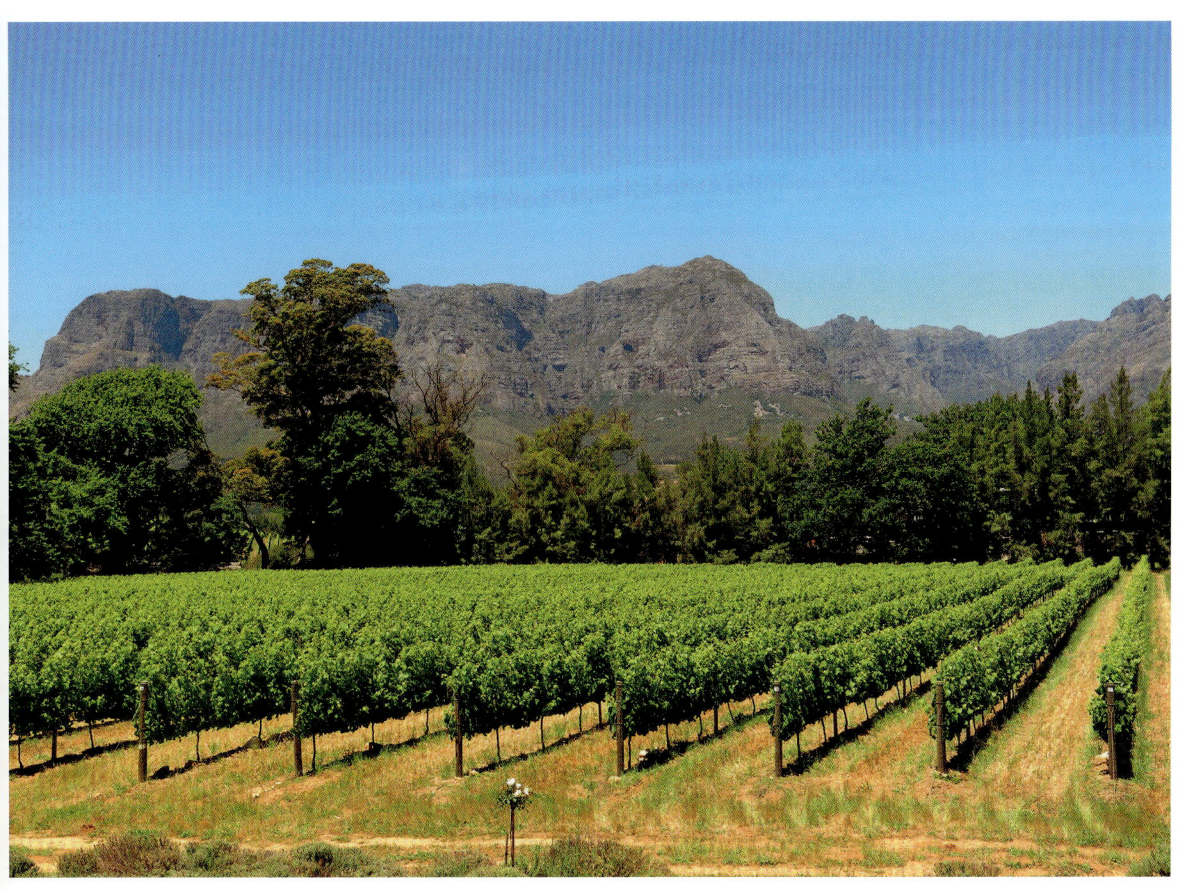

Vineyard, Fraschhoek

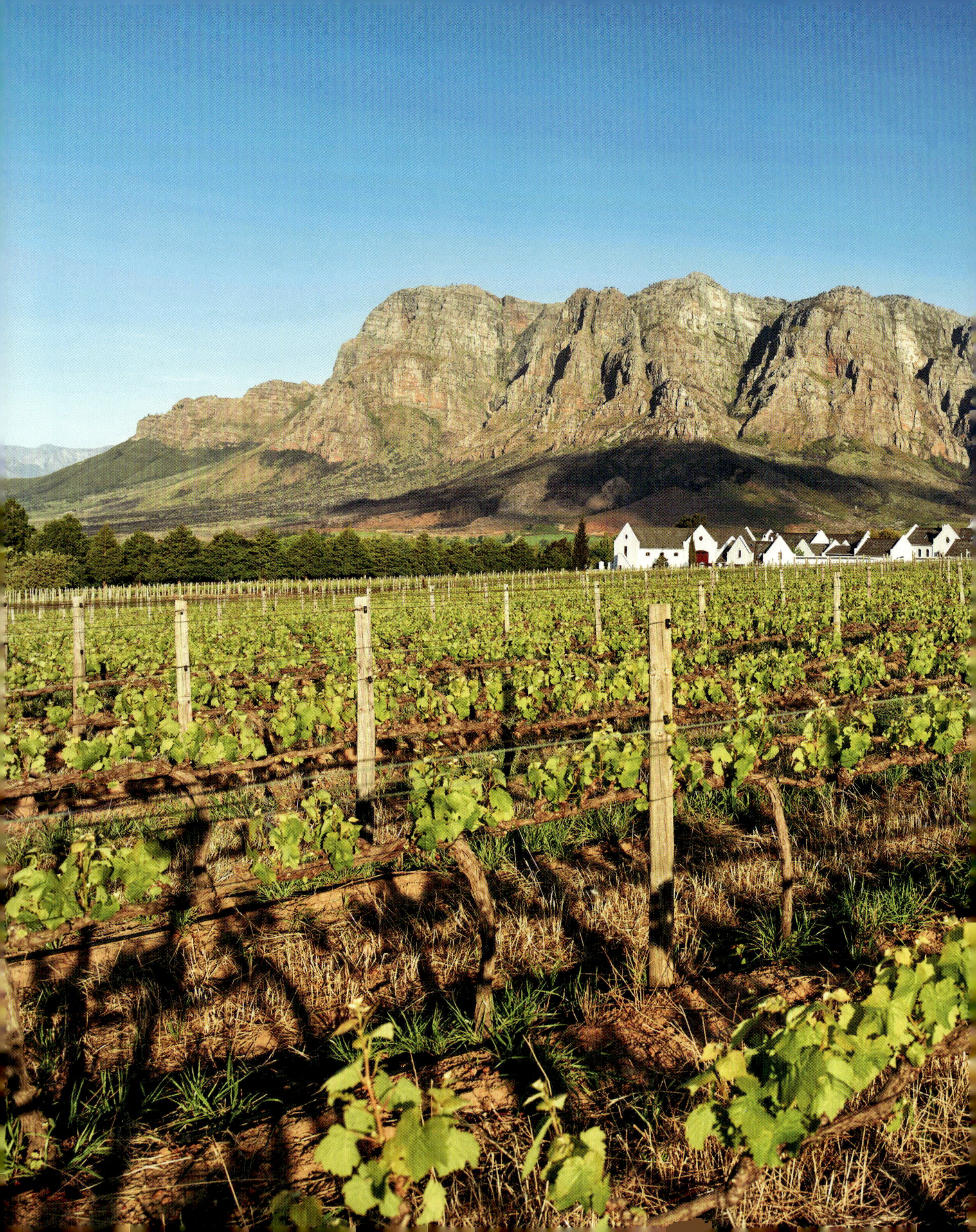

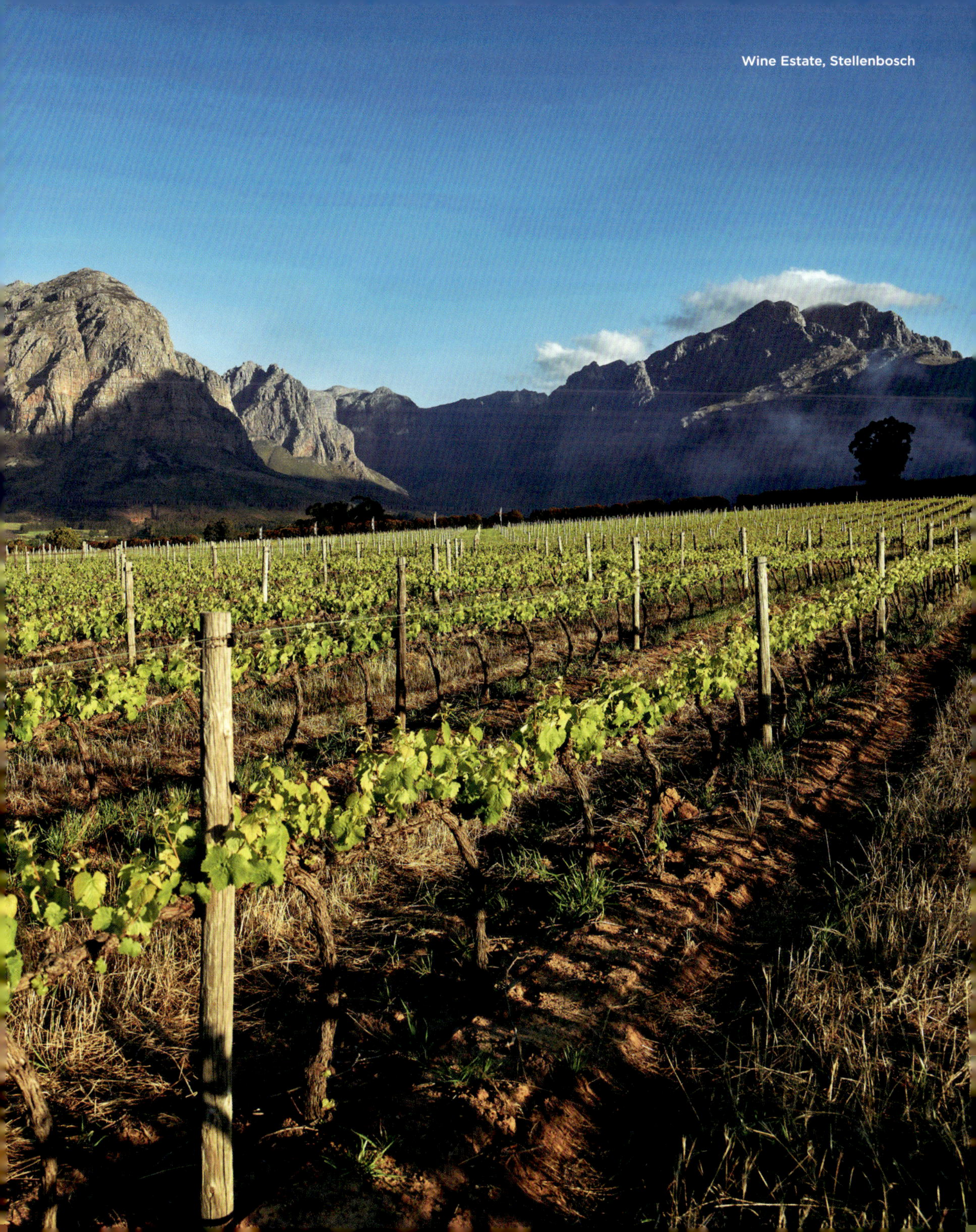
Wine Estate, Stellenbosch

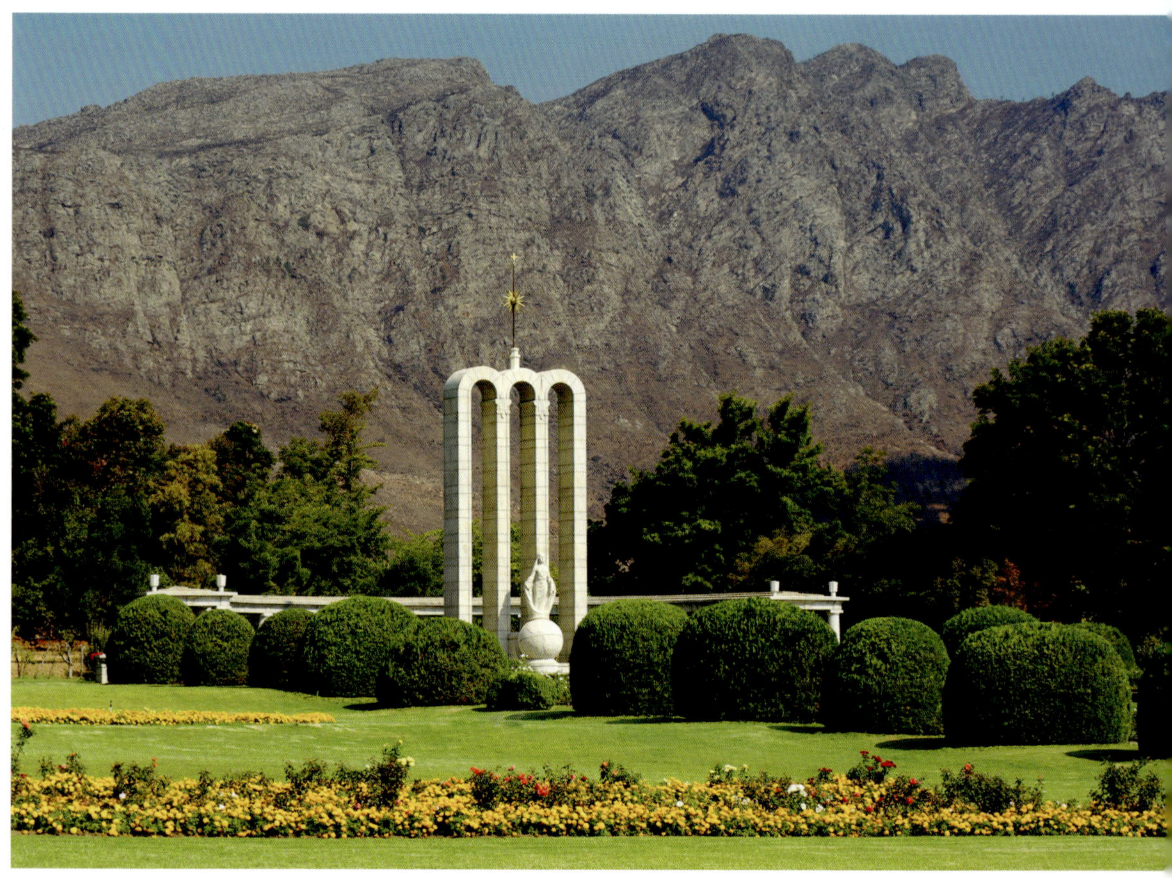

The Huguenot monument, Franschhoek

Vergelegen Wine Estate near Somerset Wes

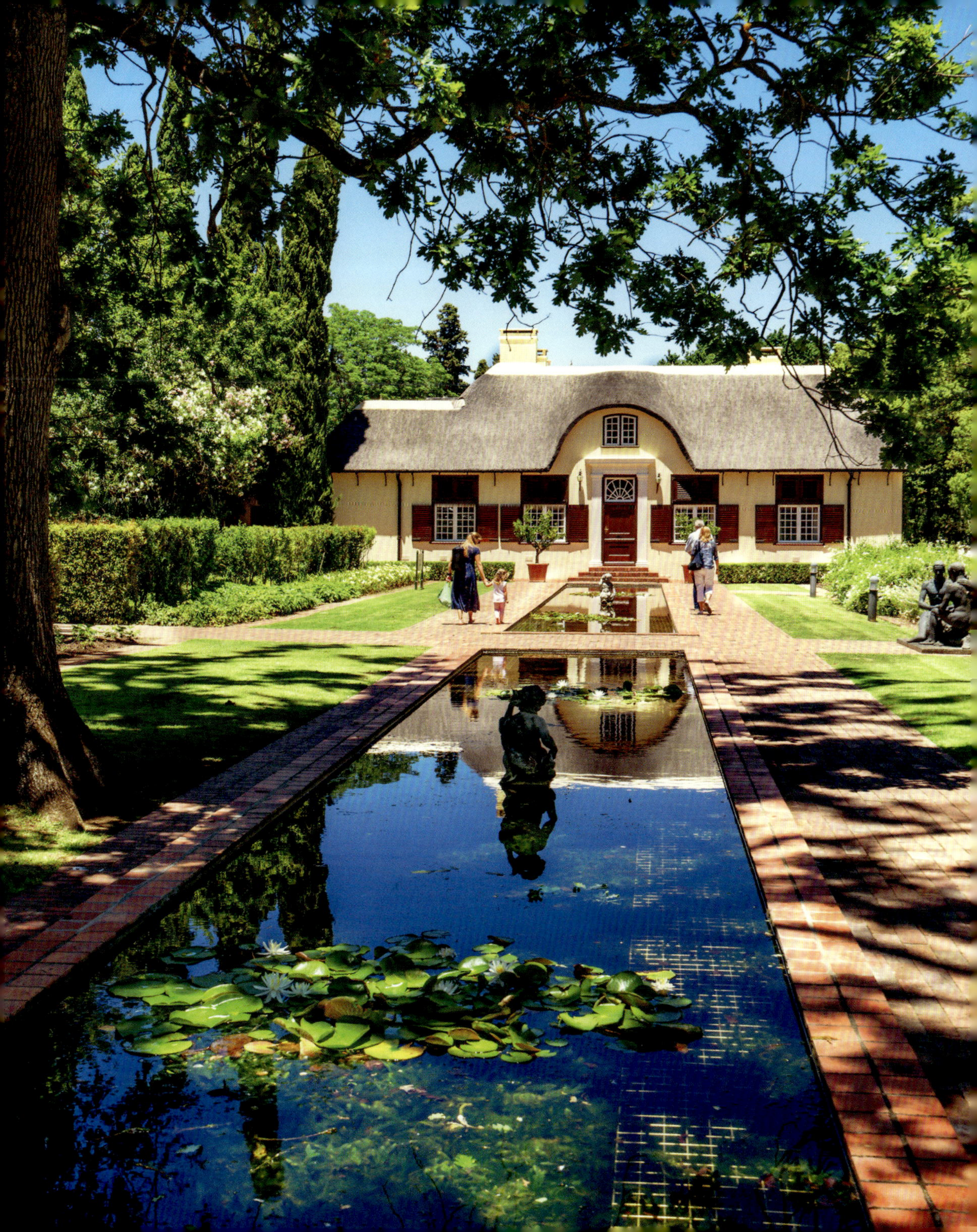

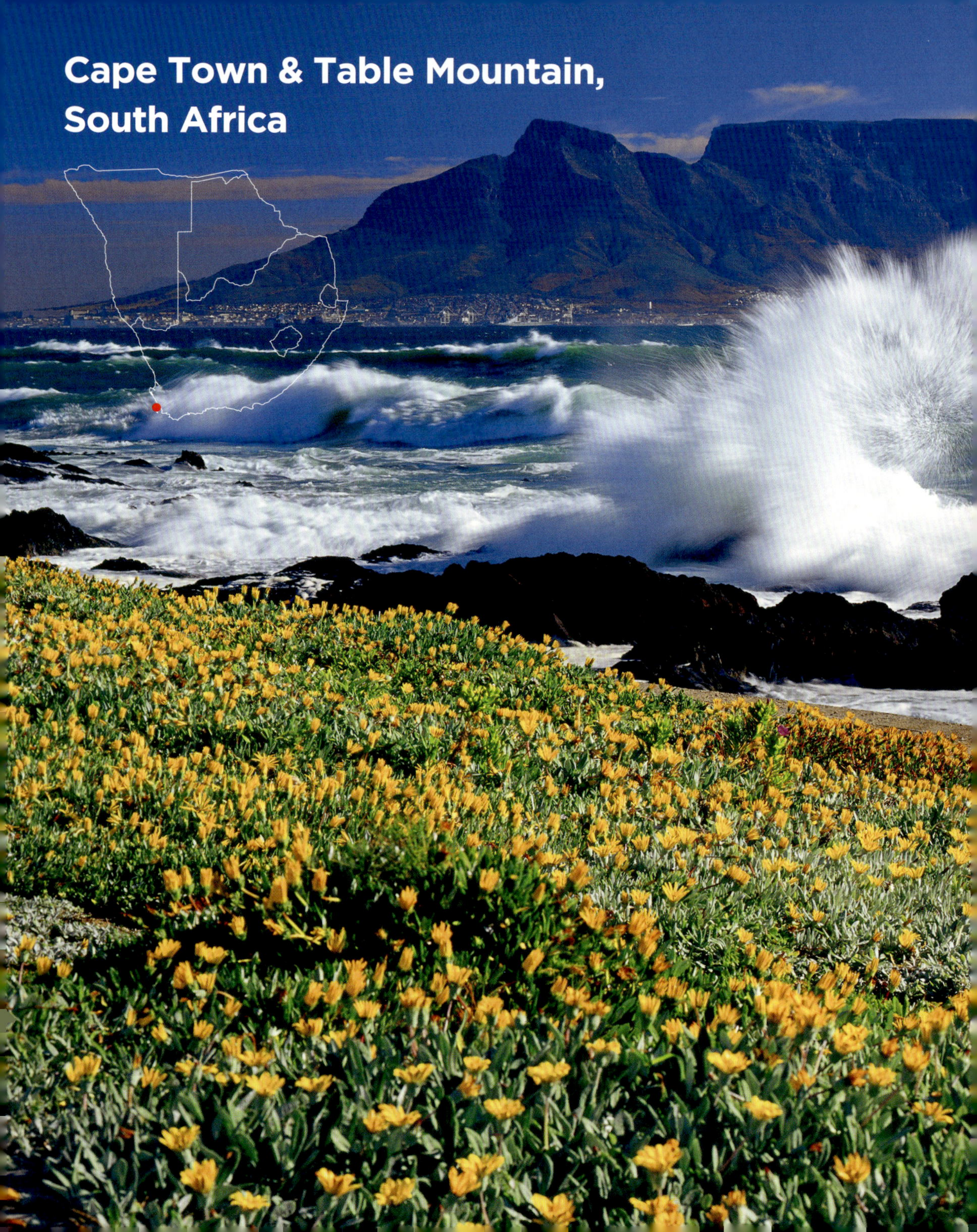

Cape Town & Table Mountain, South Africa

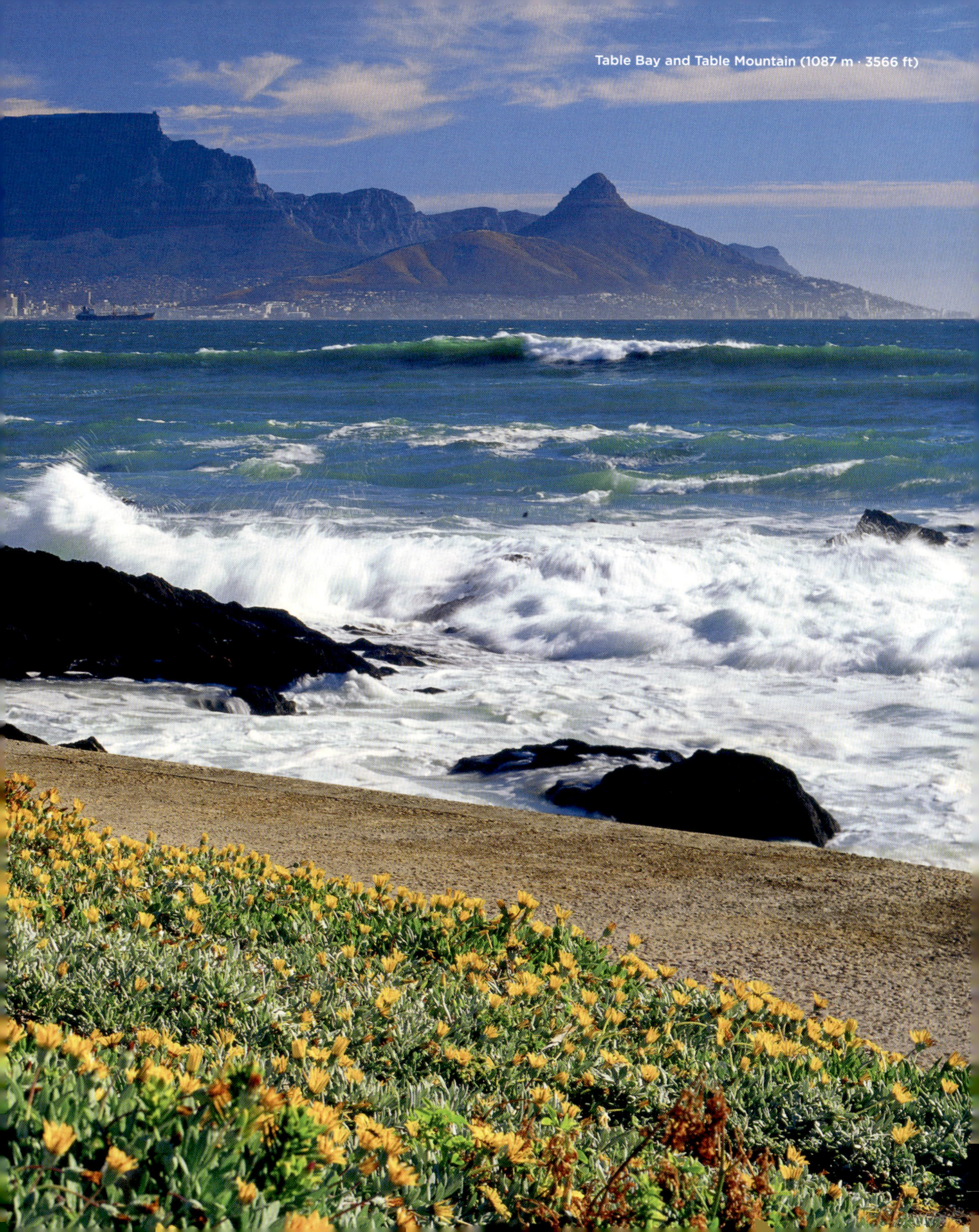
Table Bay and Table Mountain (1087 m · 3566 ft)

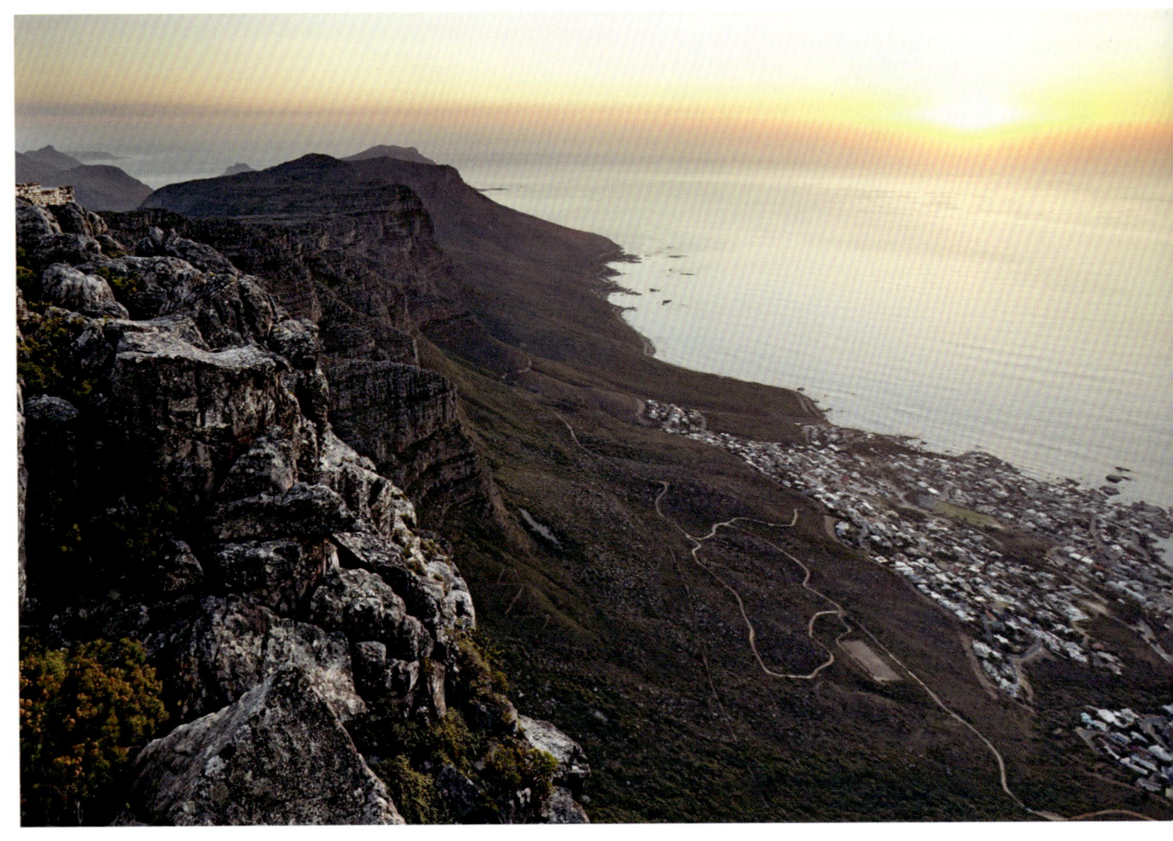

Twelve Apostles, Table Mountain

Cape Town and Table Mountain
Cape Town is the second largest city in South Africa and the capital of the province of Western Cape. The town is beautifully situated alongside Table Bay. Table Mountain (1087 m · 3566 ft) is the main landmark in Cape Town and forms part of the national park of the same name. The Table Mountain range includes Devil's Peak (1000 m · 3280 ft), Lion's Head (668 m · 2191 ft), Signal Hill (350 m · 1148 ft) and the Twelve Apostles (780–800 m · 2559–2624 ft).

Le Cap et la montagne de la Table
Le Cap est la deuxième ville d'Afrique du Sud et la capitale de la province du Cap-Ouest. Elle jouit d'une situation merveilleuse sur la baie de la Table. Elle a pour emblème la montagne de la Table (1087 m), qui se dresse dans le parc du même nom. Ce massif compte Devil's Peak (1000 m), Lion's Head (668 m), Signal Hill (350 m) et les monts des Douze Apôtres (780–800 m).

Kapstadt und der Tafelberg
Kapstadt ist die zweitgrößte Stadt Südafrikas und Hauptstadt der Provinz Westkap. Die Stadt liegt wunderschön direkt an der Tafelbucht. Wahrzeichen Kapstadts ist der Tafelberg (1087 m), der Teil des gleichnamigen Nationalparks ist. Zum Tafelberg-Massiv gehören außerdem Devil's Peak (1000 m), Lion's Head (668 m), Signal Hill (350 m) und die Berge der Zwölf Apostel (780–800 m).

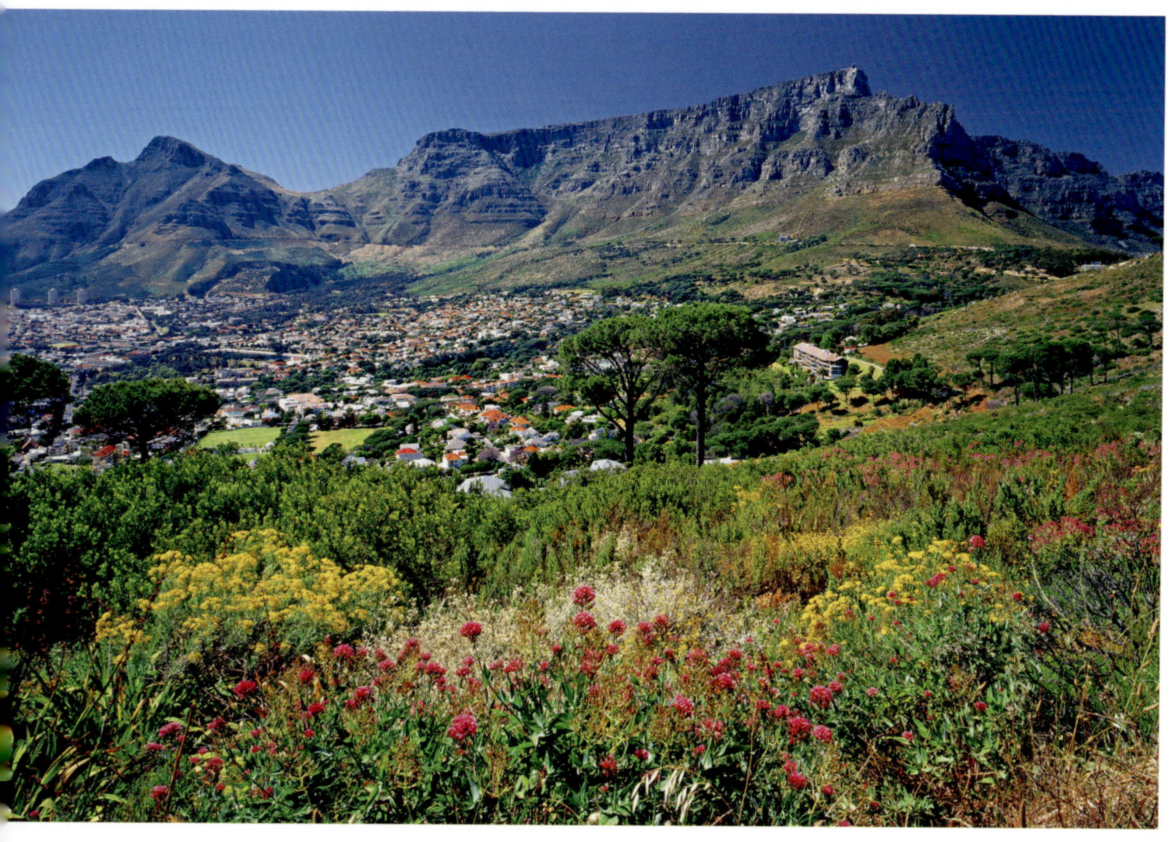

ape Town and Table Mountain (1087 m · 3566 ft) from Signal Hill

udad del Cabo y la Montaña de la Mesa
udad del Cabo es la segunda ciudad ás grande de Sudáfrica y la capital de provincia del Cabo Oeste. La ciudad stá muy bien situada en la bahía de la esa. Un hito en Ciudad del Cabo es la esa (1087 m), que es parte del parque acional del mismo nombre. La montaña la Mesa incluye el Pico del Diablo 000 m), Cabeza de León (668 m), Signal ll (350 m) y las montañas de los Doce póstoles (780–800 m).

Città del Capo e il Tafelberg
Città del Capo è la seconda città più grande del Sudafrica e la capitale della provincia del Capo Occidentale. La città si trova in una posizione meravigliosa direttamente nella baia di Tafel. Simbolo di Città del Capo è il Tafelberg (1087 m), che fa parte del Parco Nazionale omonimo. Al massiccio del Tafelberg appartengono Devil's Peak (1000 m), Lion's Head (668 m), Signal Hill (350 m) e i monti dei Dodici Apostoli (780–800 m).

Kaapstad en de Tafelberg
Kaapstad is de op één na grootste stad van Zuid-Afrika en de hoofdstad van de provincie West-Kaap. De ligging van de stad, direct aan de Tafelbaai, is spectaculair. Hét symbool van Kaapstad is de Tafelberg (1087 m), die deel uitmaakt van het gelijknamige nationale park. Tot het Tafelbergmassief behoren de Duivelspiek (1000 m), de Leeukop (668 m), de Seinheuwel (350 m) en de Twaalf Apostelen-bergen (780–800 m).

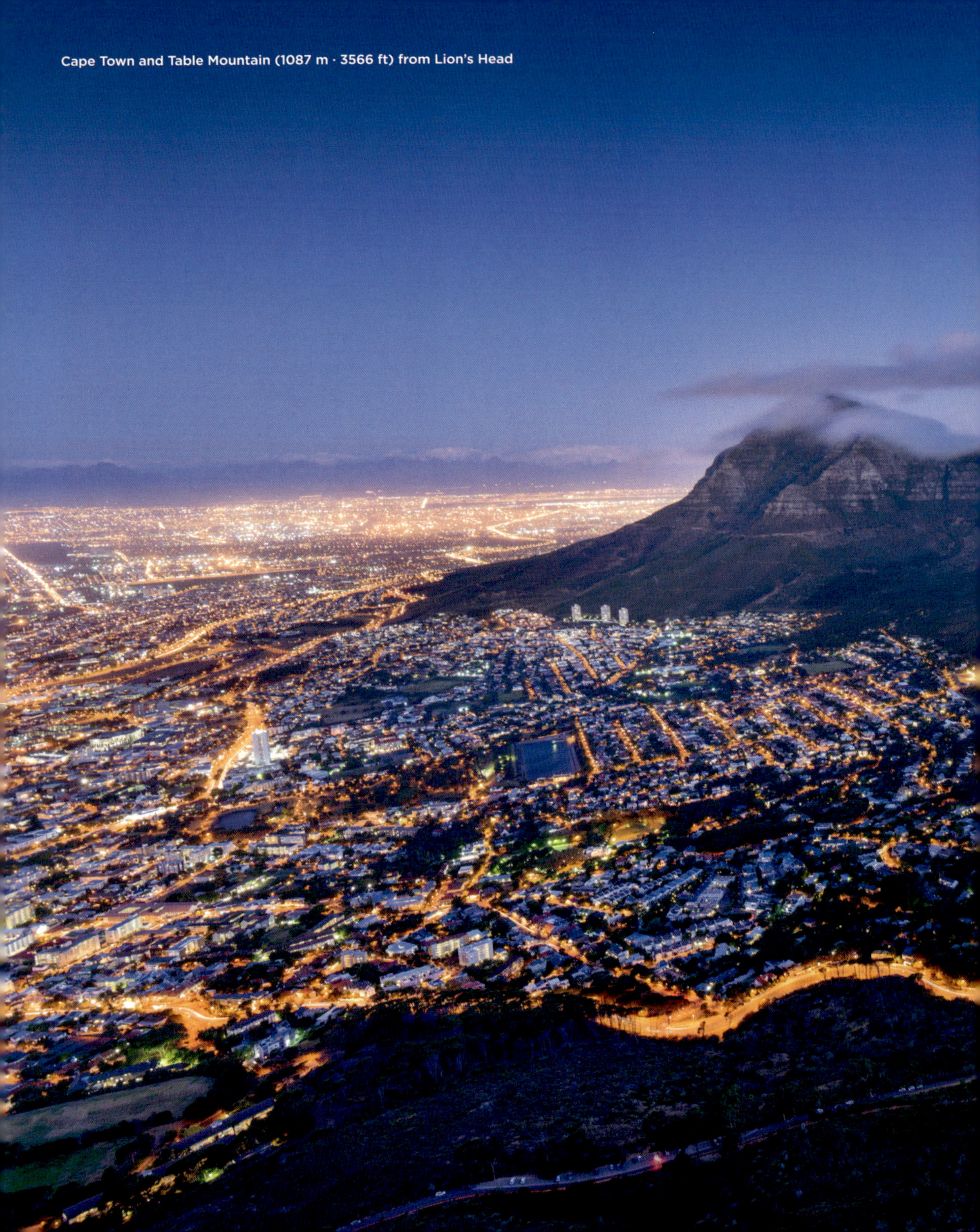
Cape Town and Table Mountain (1087 m · 3566 ft) from Lion's Head

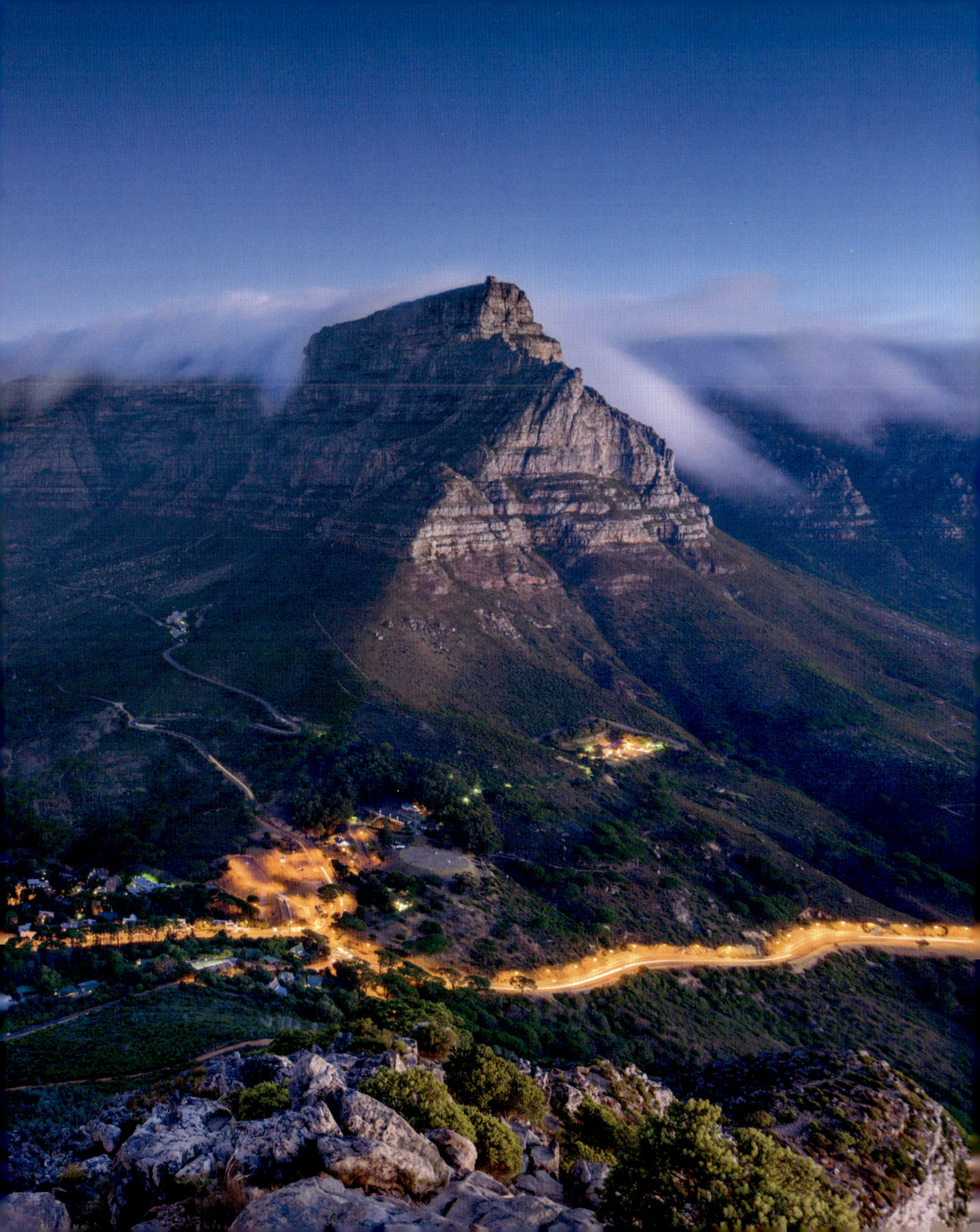

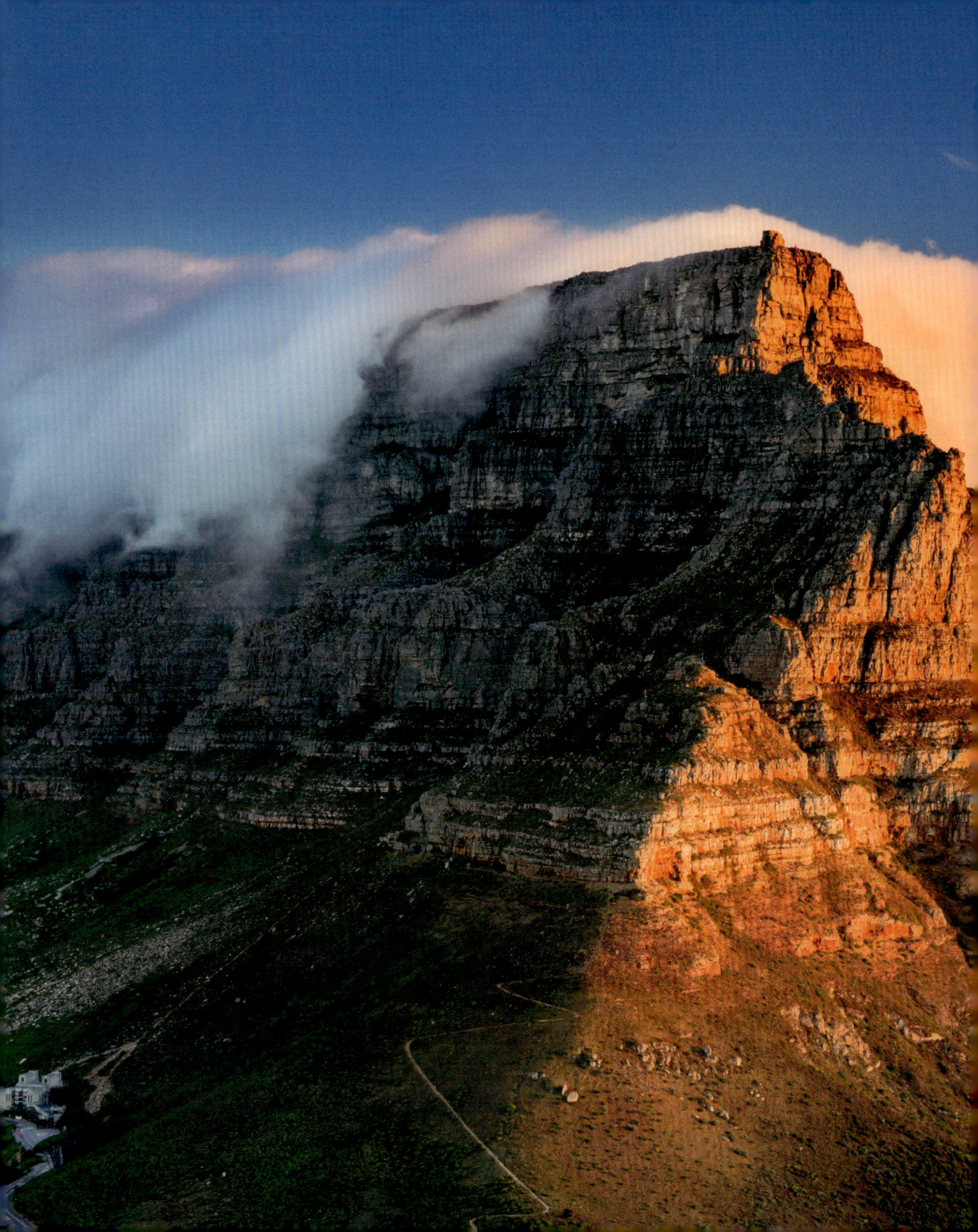

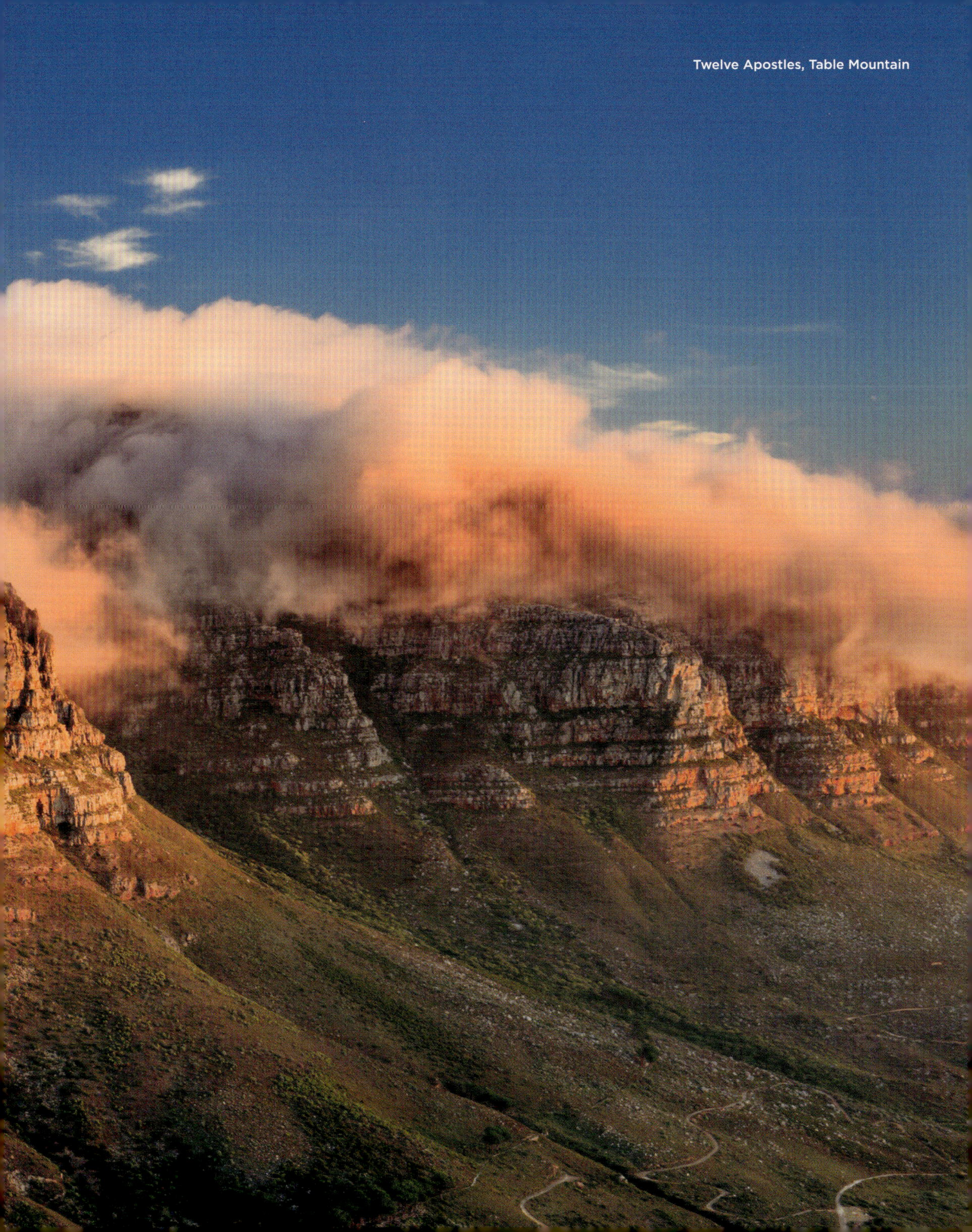
Twelve Apostles, Table Mountain

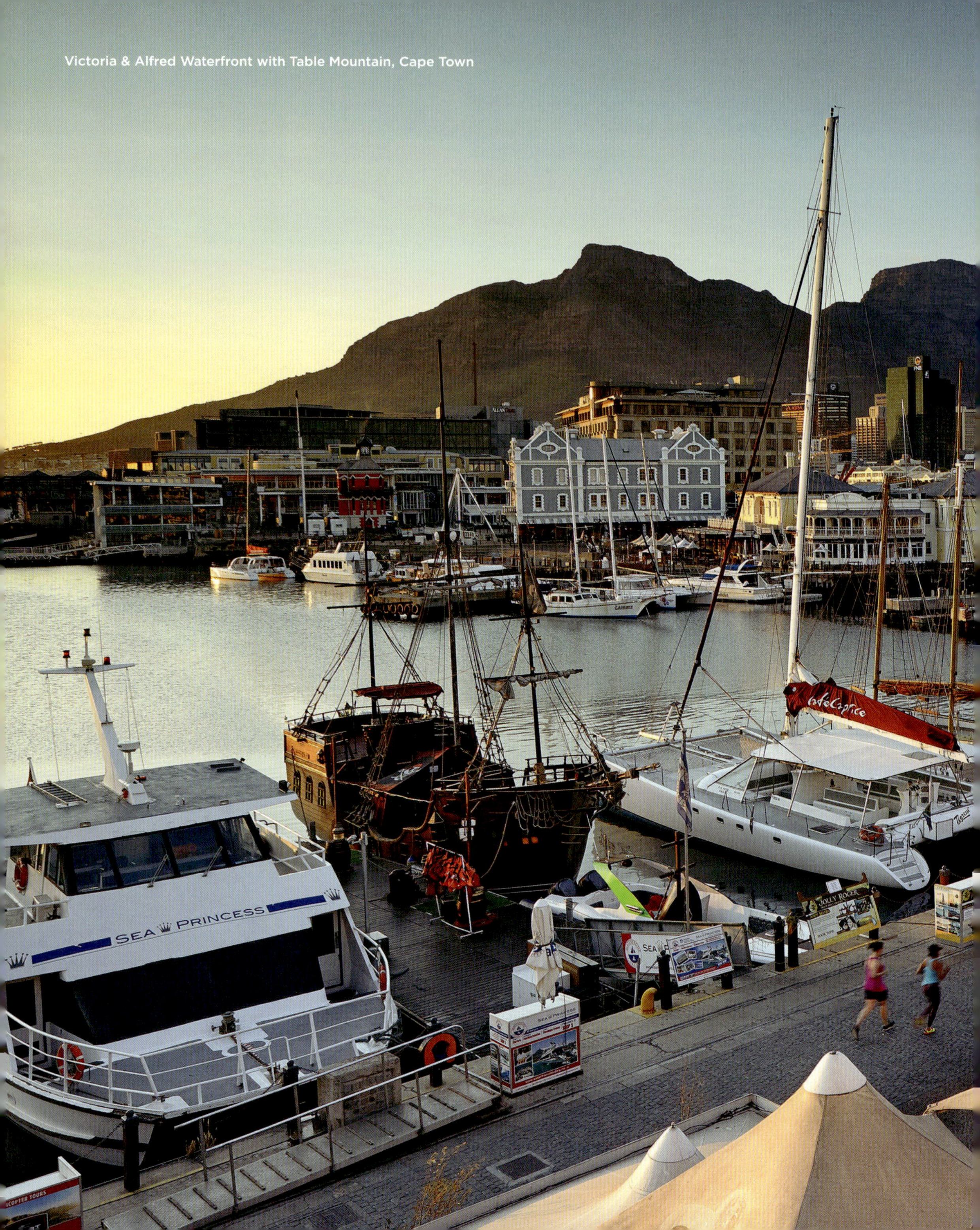

Victoria & Alfred Waterfront with Table Mountain, Cape Town

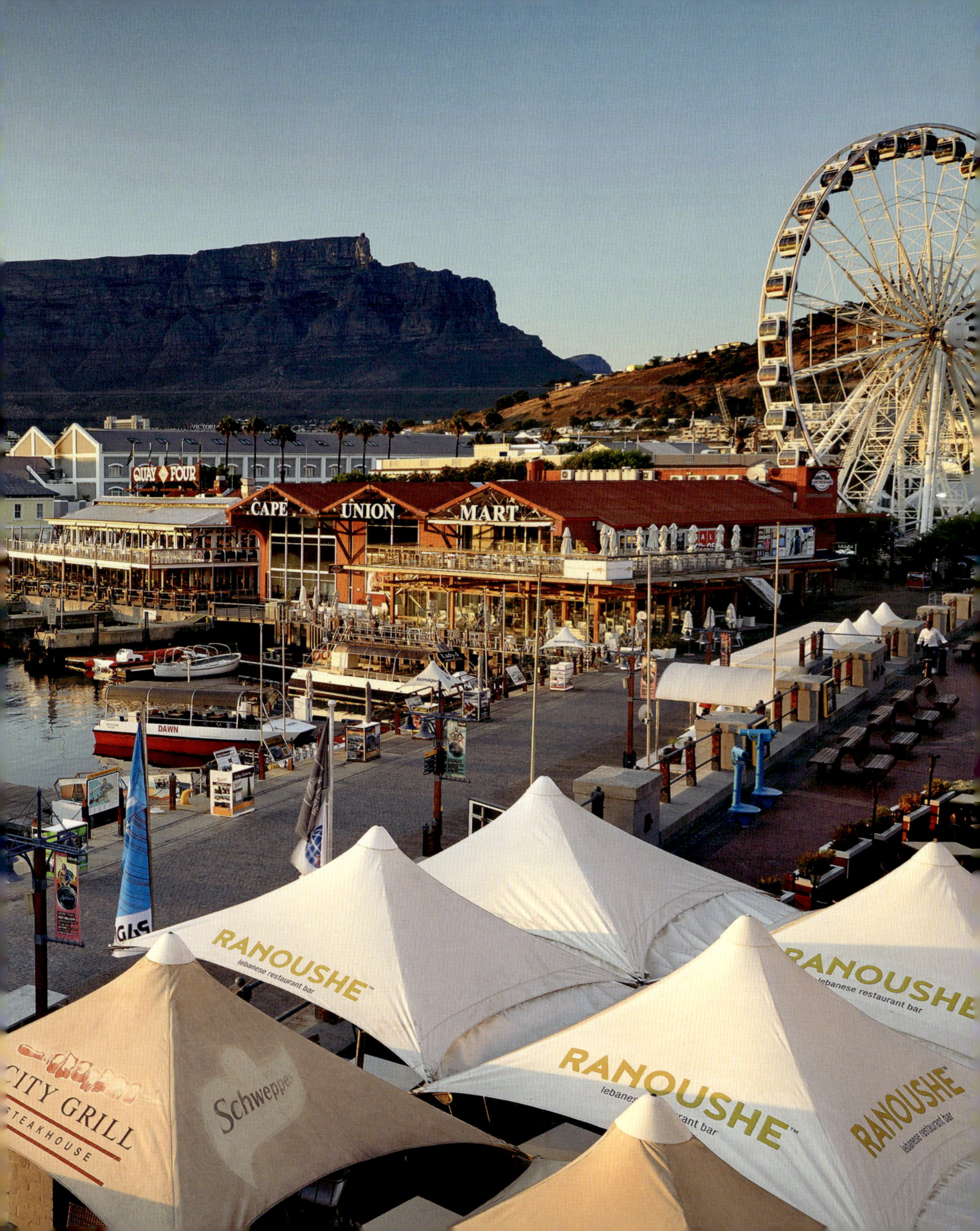
QUAY FOUR
CAPE
UNION
MART
DAWN
RANOUSHE
lebanese restaurant bar
CITY GRILL
STEAKHOUSE
Schweppes

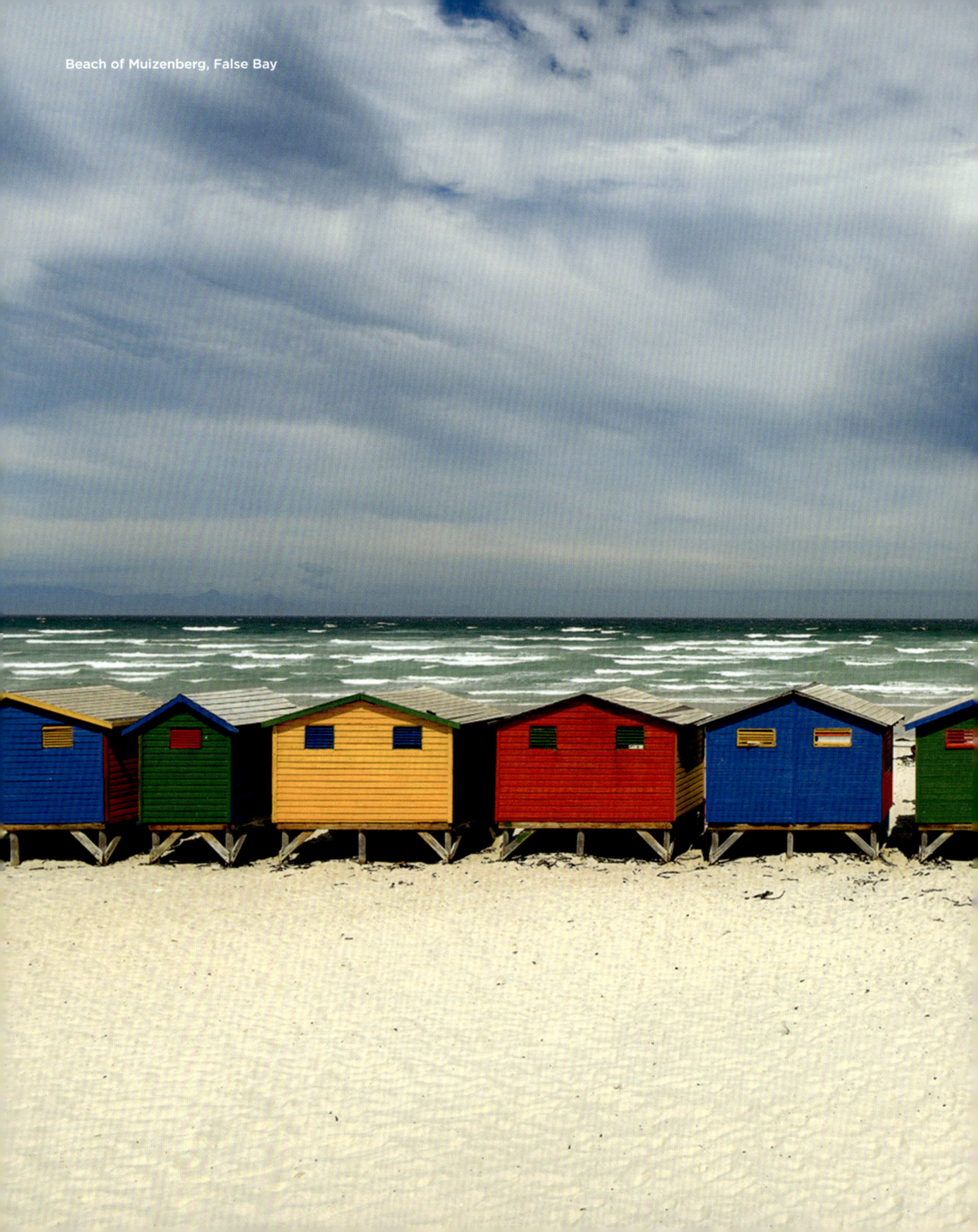

Beach of Muizenberg, False Bay

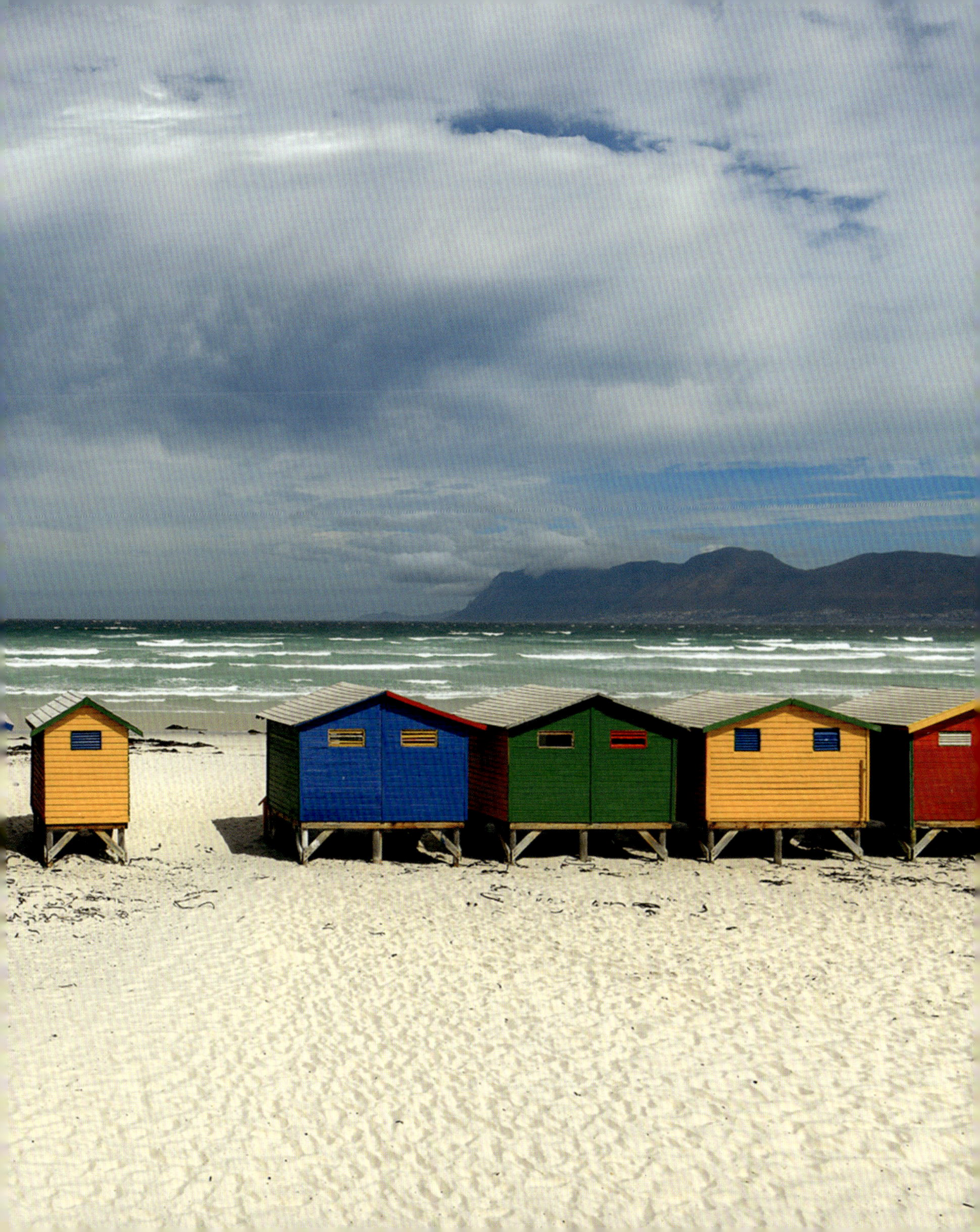

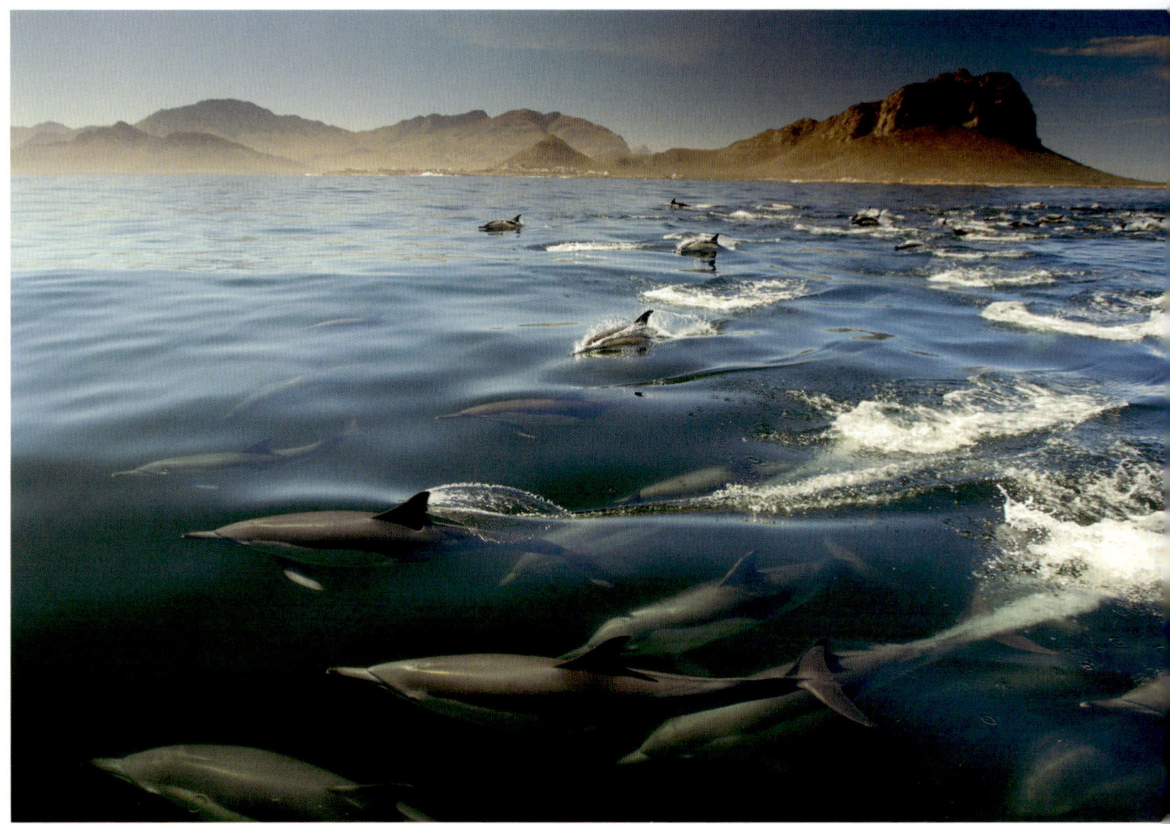

Dolphins, False Bay

Cape of Good Hope
Despite the bays, beaches, and high mountains towering over the sea, it should not be assumed that the sailors of yore had an eye for the beauty of this coast. They feared wicked winds, dangerous currents and sharp rocks lurking under the surface of the water, and so consequently could only breathe freely when they finally had the Cape of Good Hope behind them.

Le cap de Bonne-Espérance
Des baies, des plages, des montagnes surplombant la mer – il est difficile d'imaginer les marins d'autrefois insensibles à la beauté de cette côte. Pourtant ils redoutaient les vents perfides, les courants dangereux, les écueils impitoyables et ne respiraient qu'une fois franchi le cap de Bonne-Espérance.

Kap der Guten Hoffnung
Buchten, Strände, hoch über der See thronende Berge – es ist nicht anzunehmen, dass die Seefahrer früherer Zeiten ein Auge für die Schönheit dieser Küste hatten. Sie fürchteten tückische Winde, gefährliche Strömungen, spitze Felsen unter der Wasseroberfläche und konnten erst aufatmen, wenn sie das Kap der Guten Hoffnung umschifft hatten.

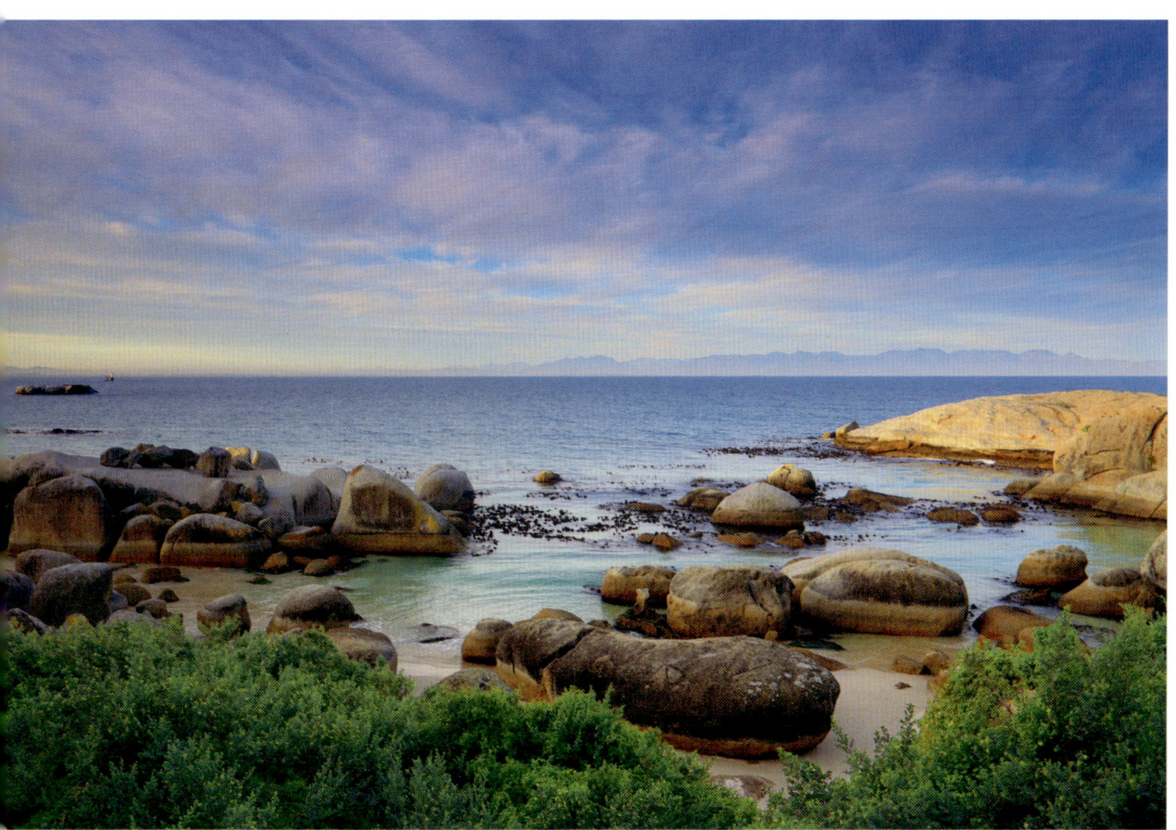

Hout Bay

Cabo de Buena Esperanza
Bahías, playas, montañas que se elevan sobre el mar– no es probable que los marineros de otras épocas tuvieran ganas de admirar la belleza de la costa. Temían los vientos traicioneros, corrientes peligrosas, rocas dentadas por debajo de la superficie del agua y sólo podían respirar cuando habían dado la vuelta al cabo de Buena Esperanza.

Capo di Buona Speranza
Baie, spiagge, montagne che svettano alte sopra il mare: si presume che i navigatori in tempi passati non sapessero apprezzare la bellezza di questa costa. Temevano i venti insidiosi, le correnti pericolose, le rocce appuntite sotto la superficie dell'acqua e potevano solo tirare un sospiro di sollievo quando avevano circumnavigato il Capo di Buona Speranza.

Kaap de Goede Hoop
Baaien, stranden, bergen die hoog boven de zee uittorenen – we mogen niet aannemen dat de eerste zeevaarders oog hadden voor de pracht van deze kust. Zij vreesden de wispelturige wind, de verraderlijke stromingen en de scherpe rotsen onder het wateroppervlak en konden pas opgelucht ademhalen als ze de Kaap de Goede Hoop veilig hadden gerond.

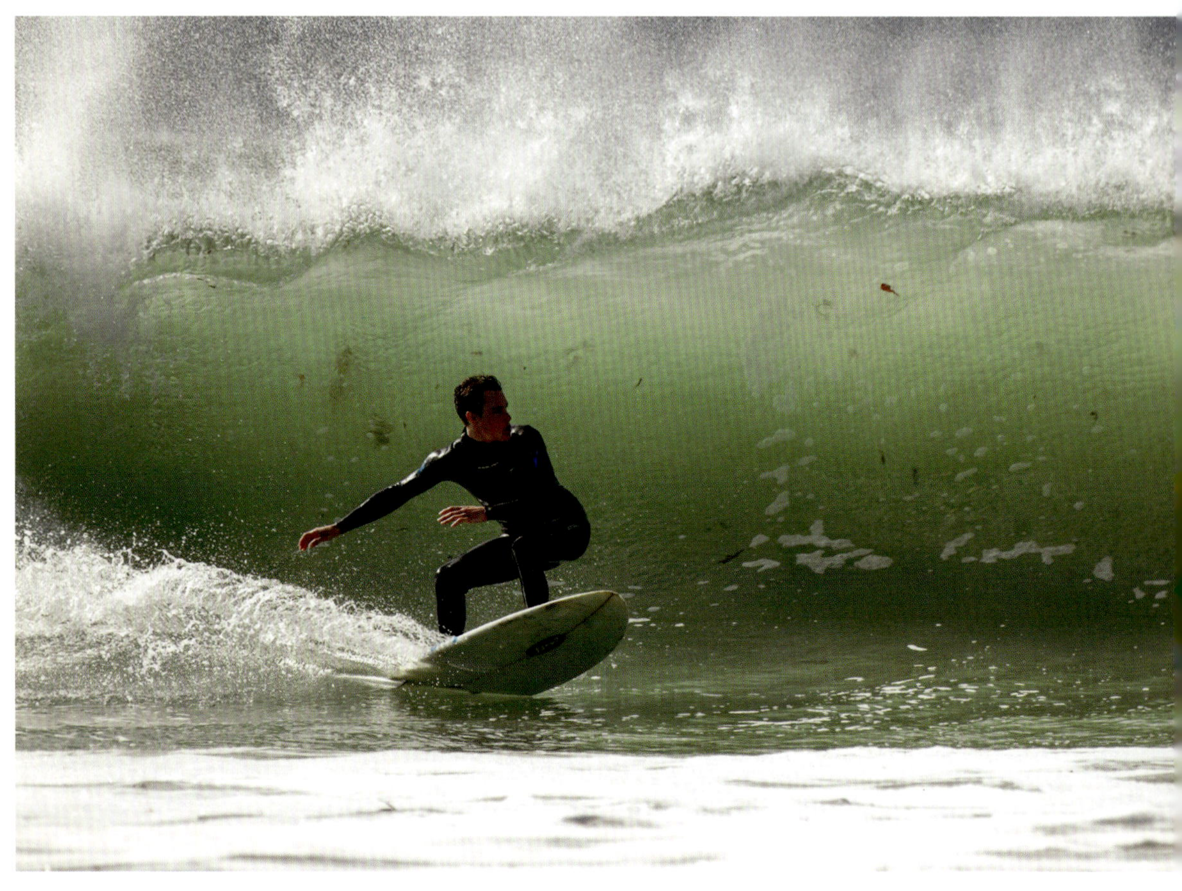

Surfer at the beach of Kommetje, Hout Bay

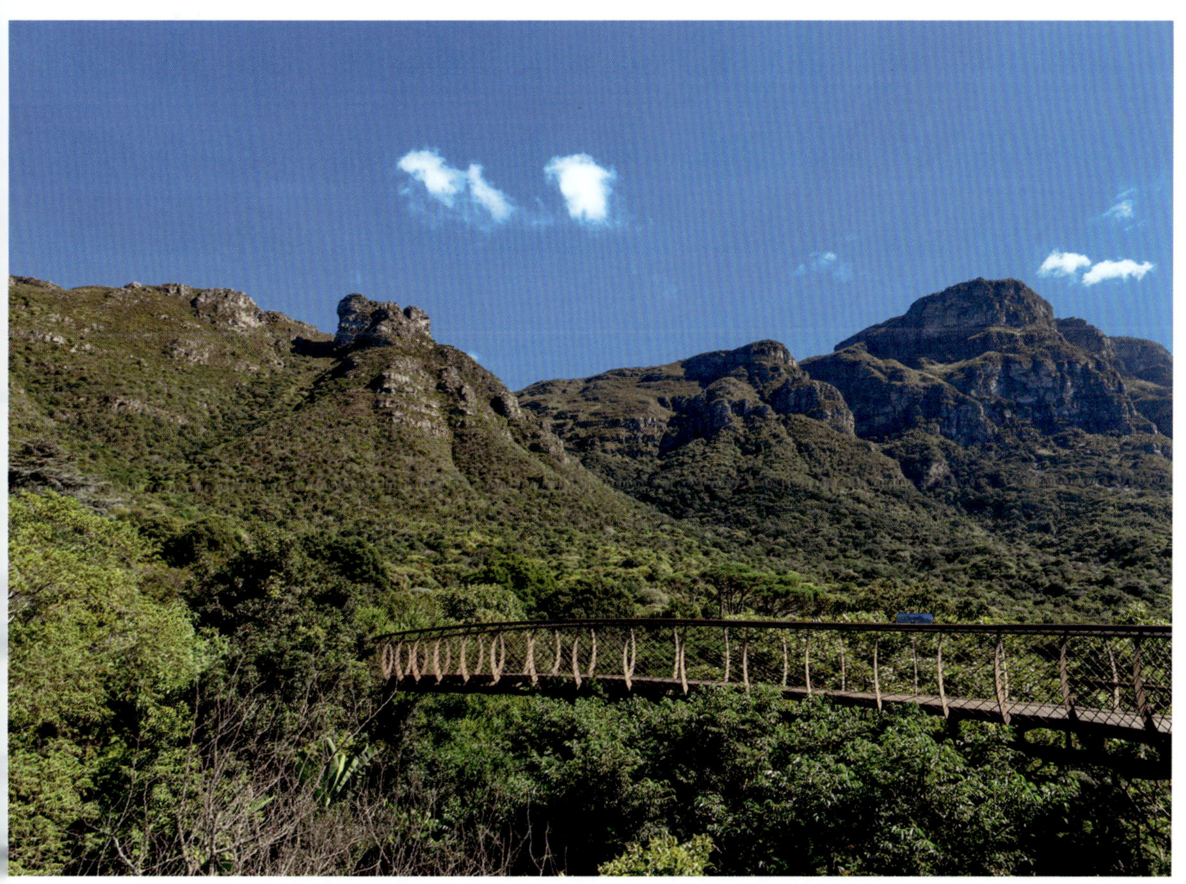

Tree Top Walk at Kirstenbosch Botanical Garden

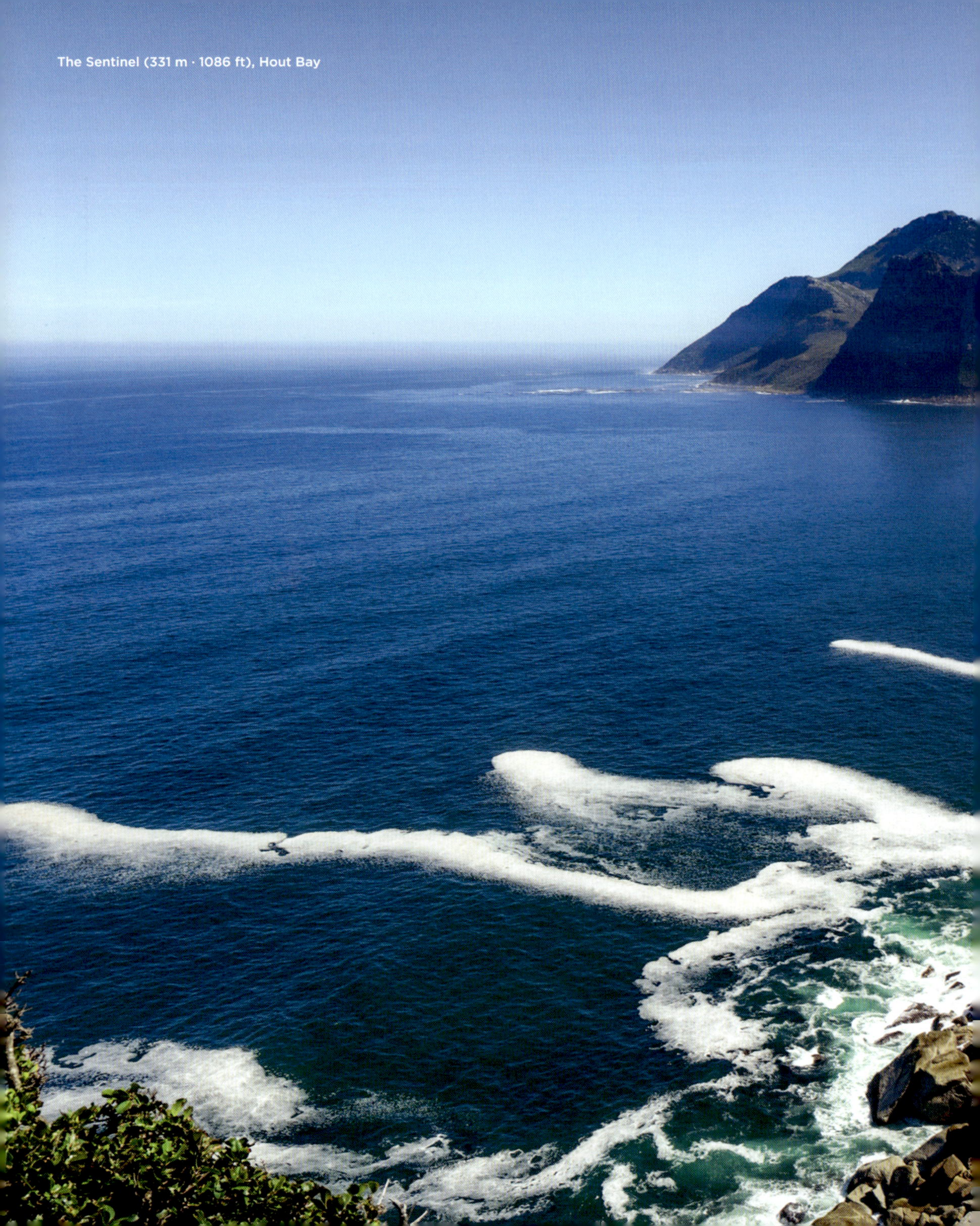
The Sentinel (331 m · 1086 ft), Hout Bay

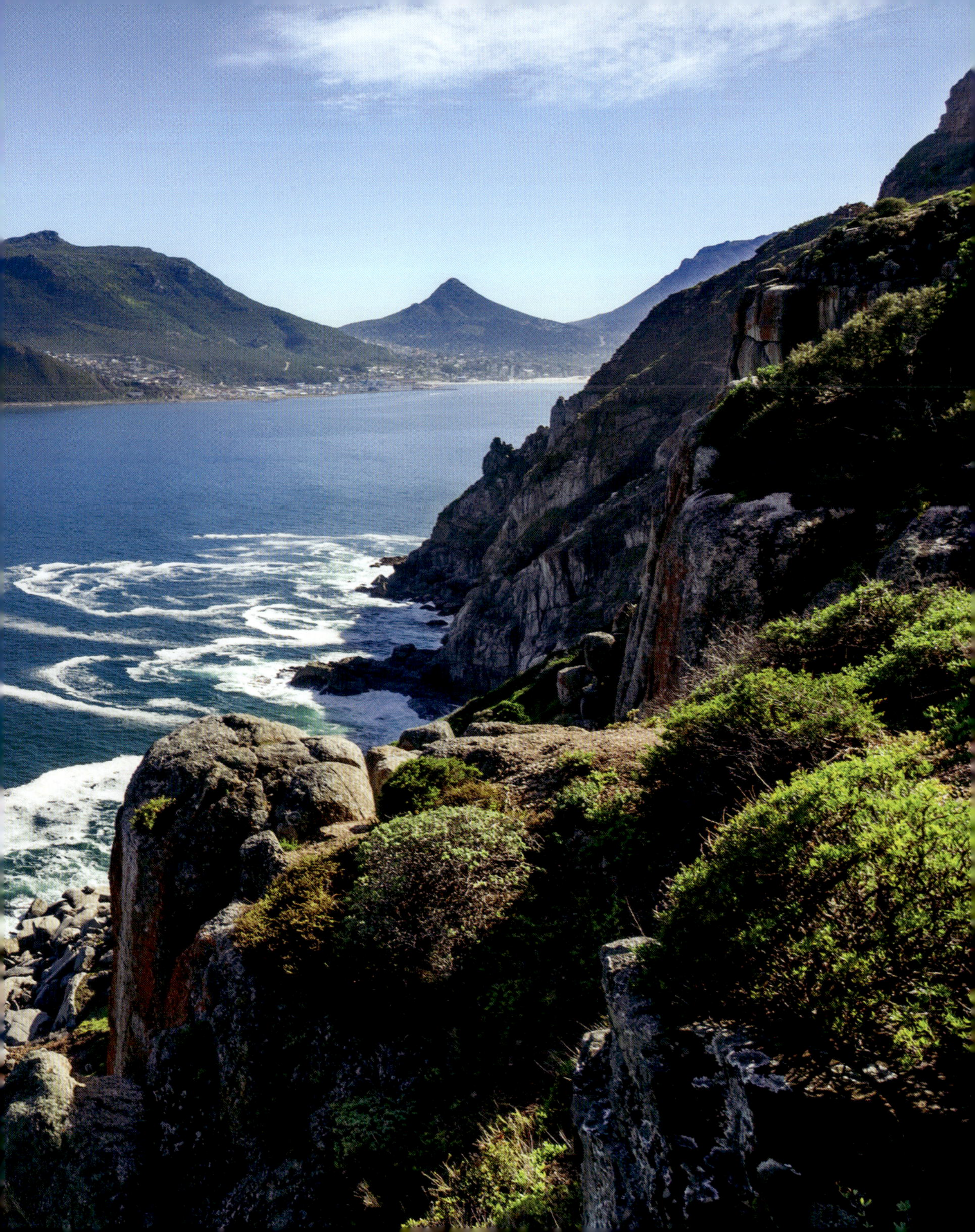

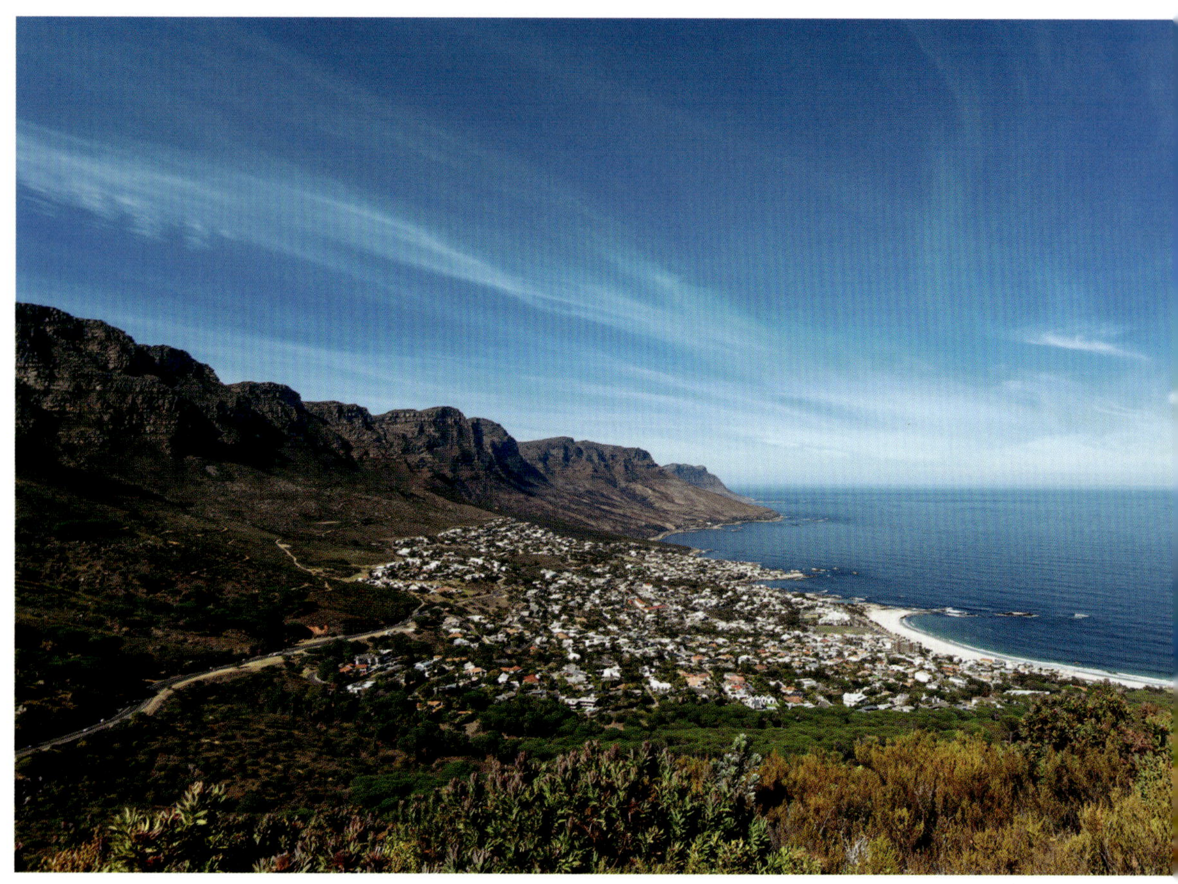

Camps Bay and Twelve Apostles

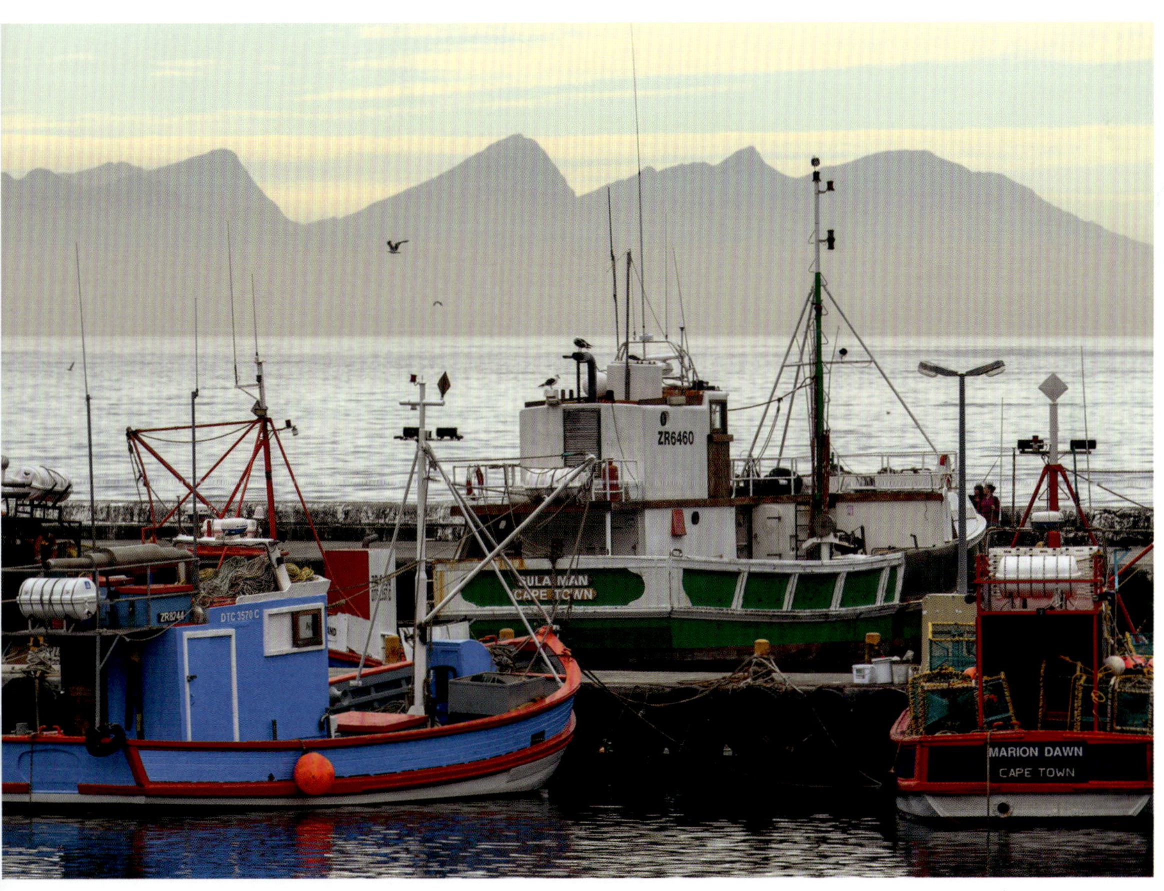

Kalk Bay

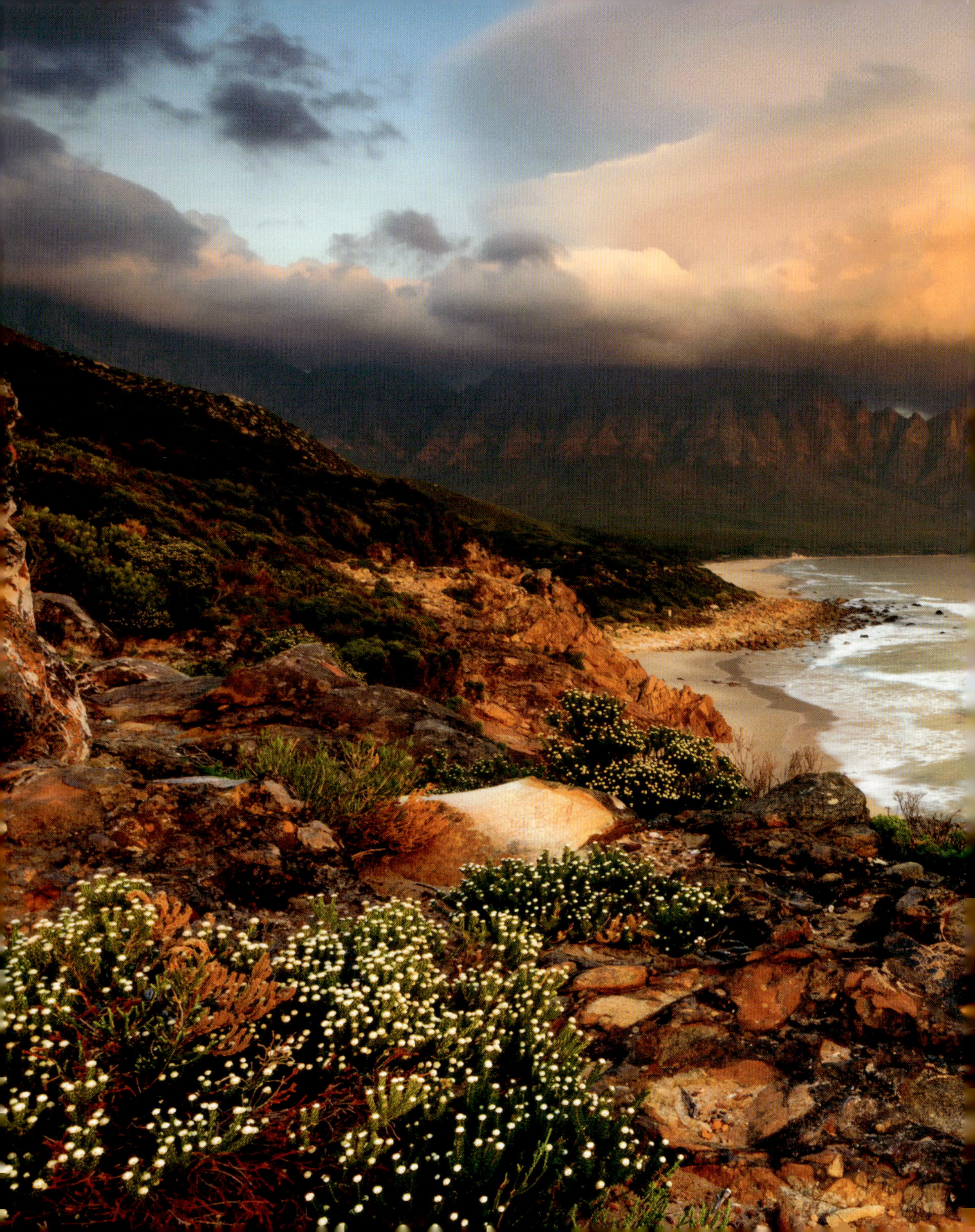

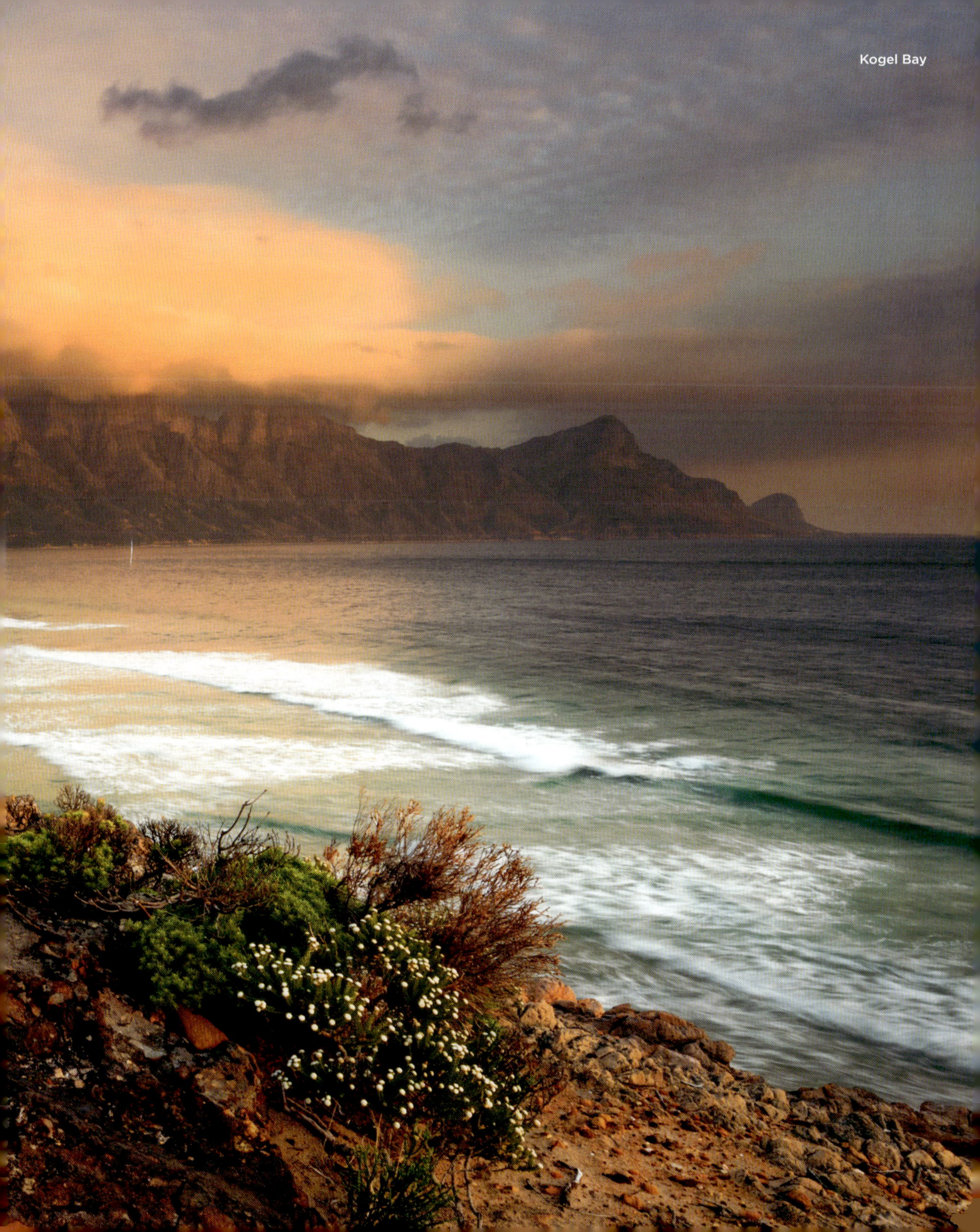

Kogel Bay

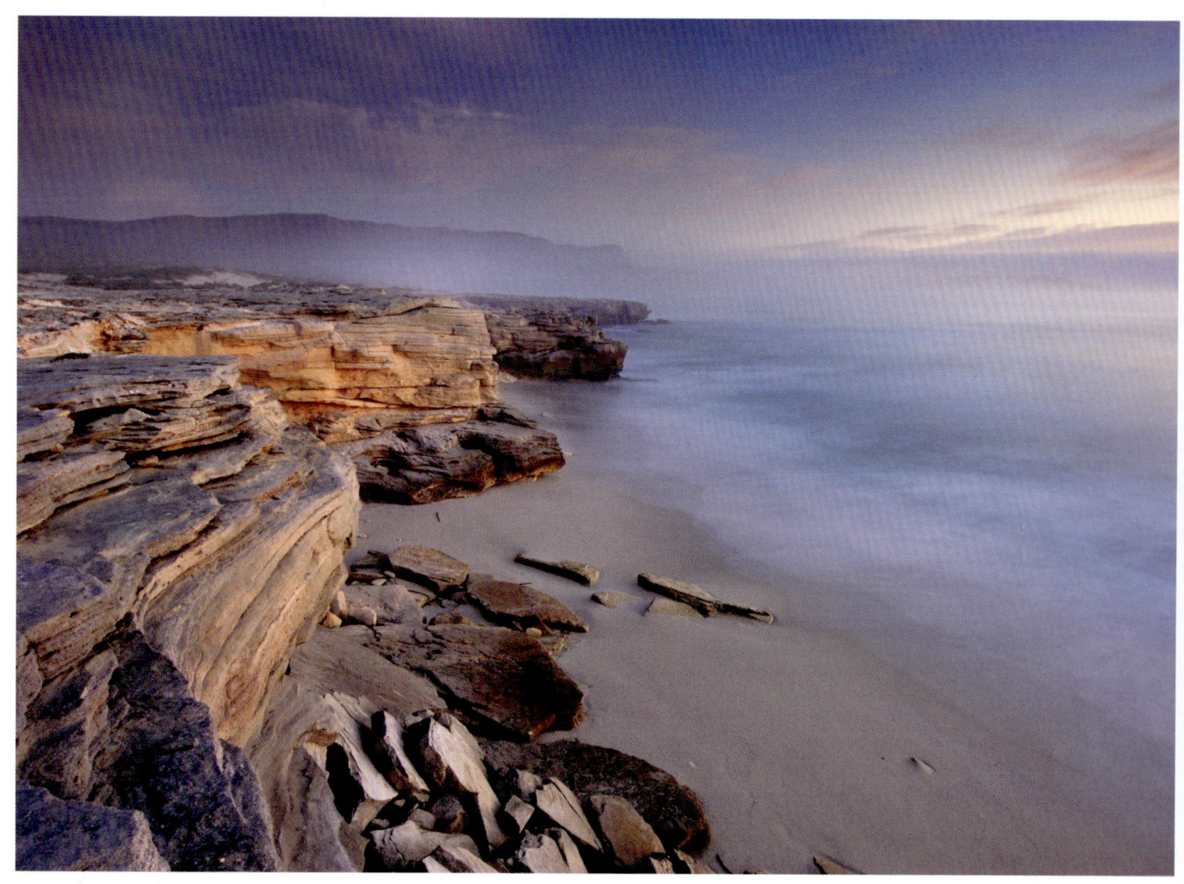

Sandstone cliffs, Western Cape

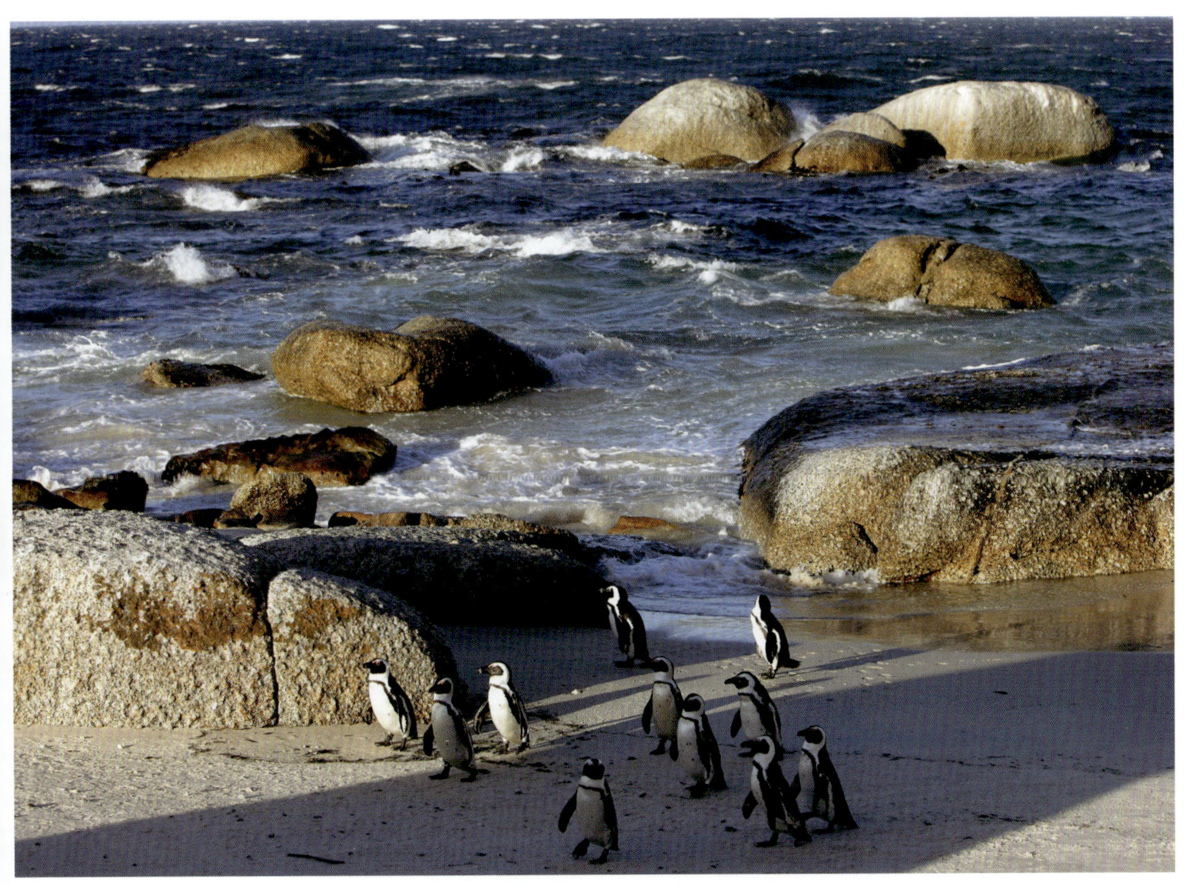

Penguins, Boulders Beach

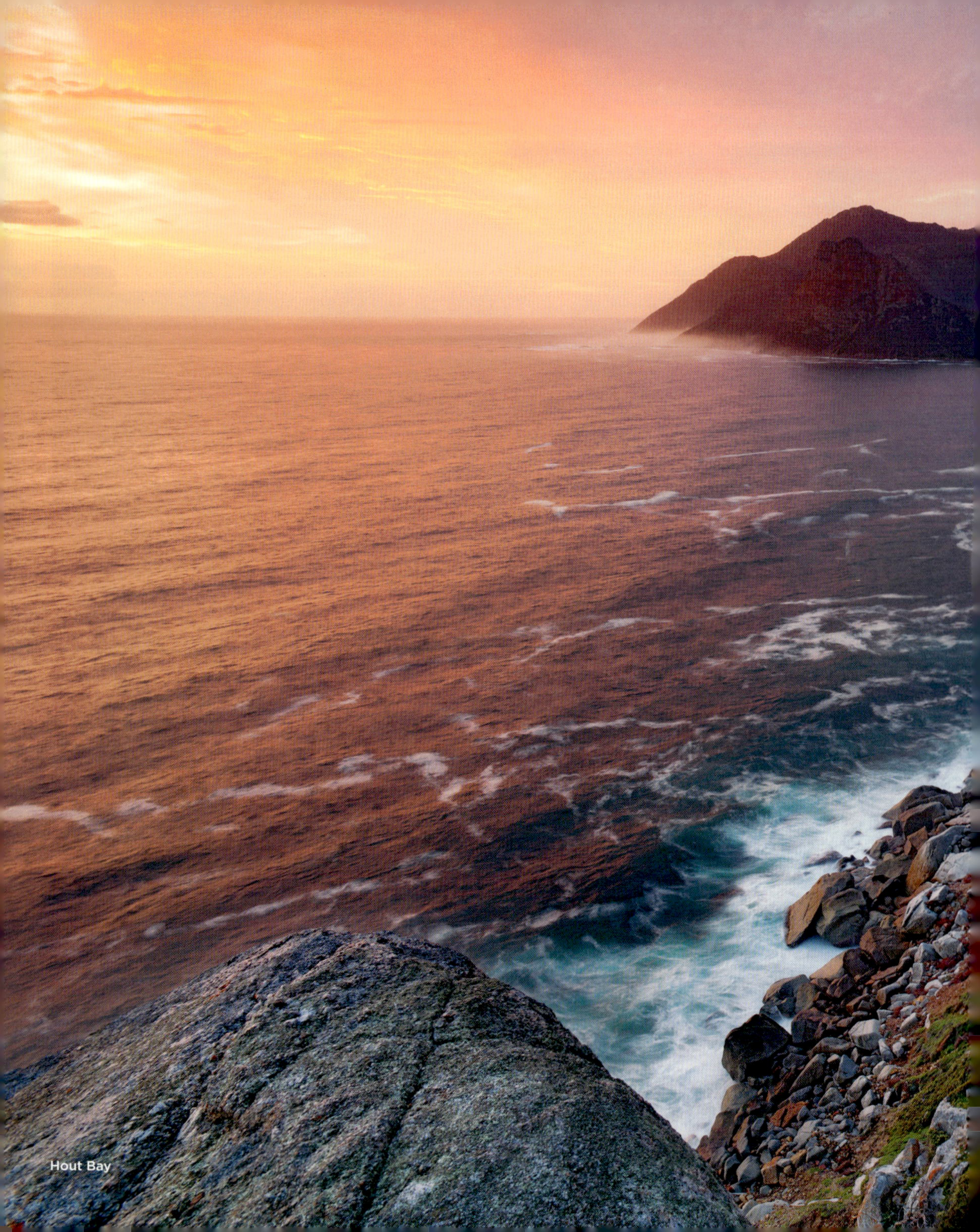

Hout Bay

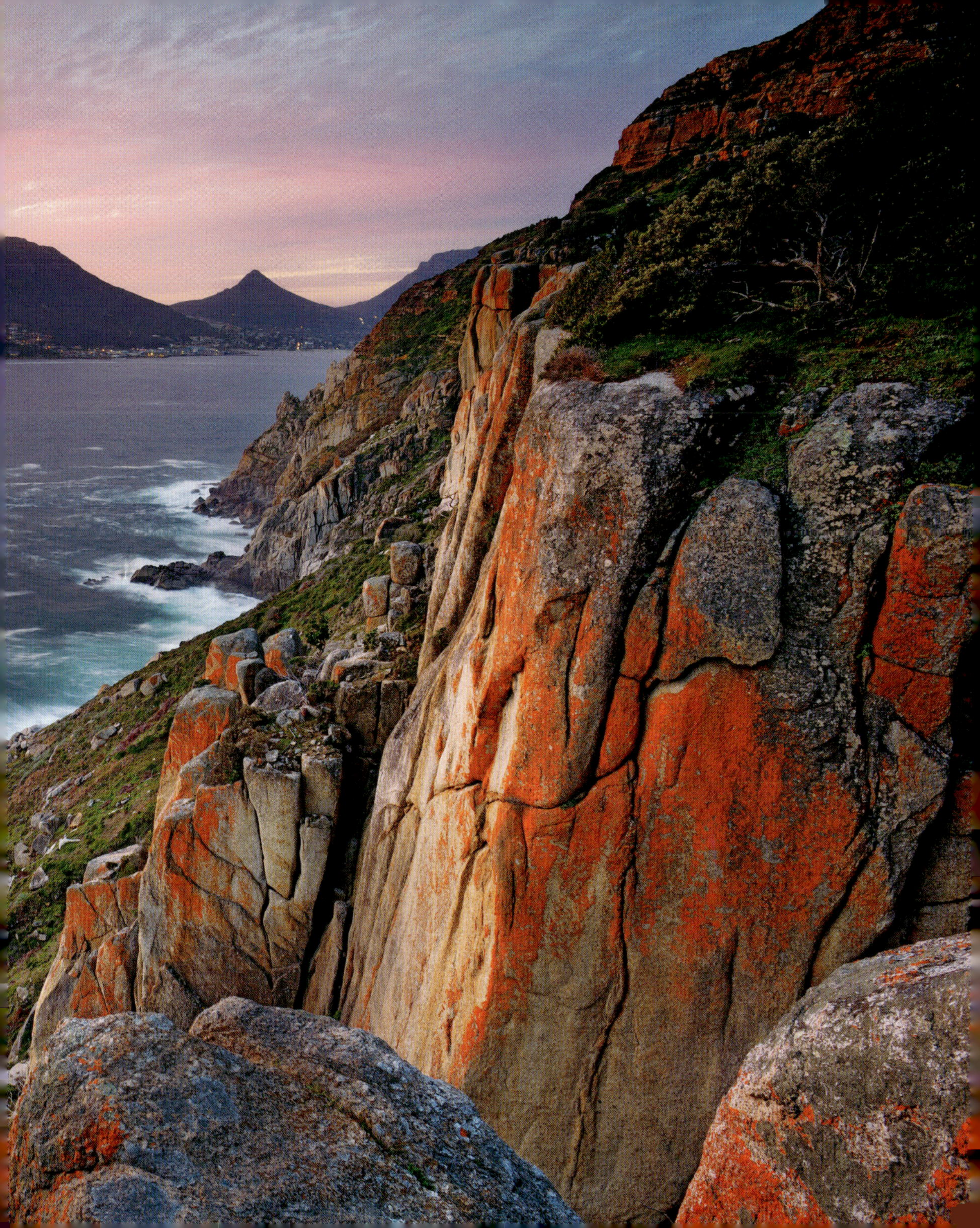

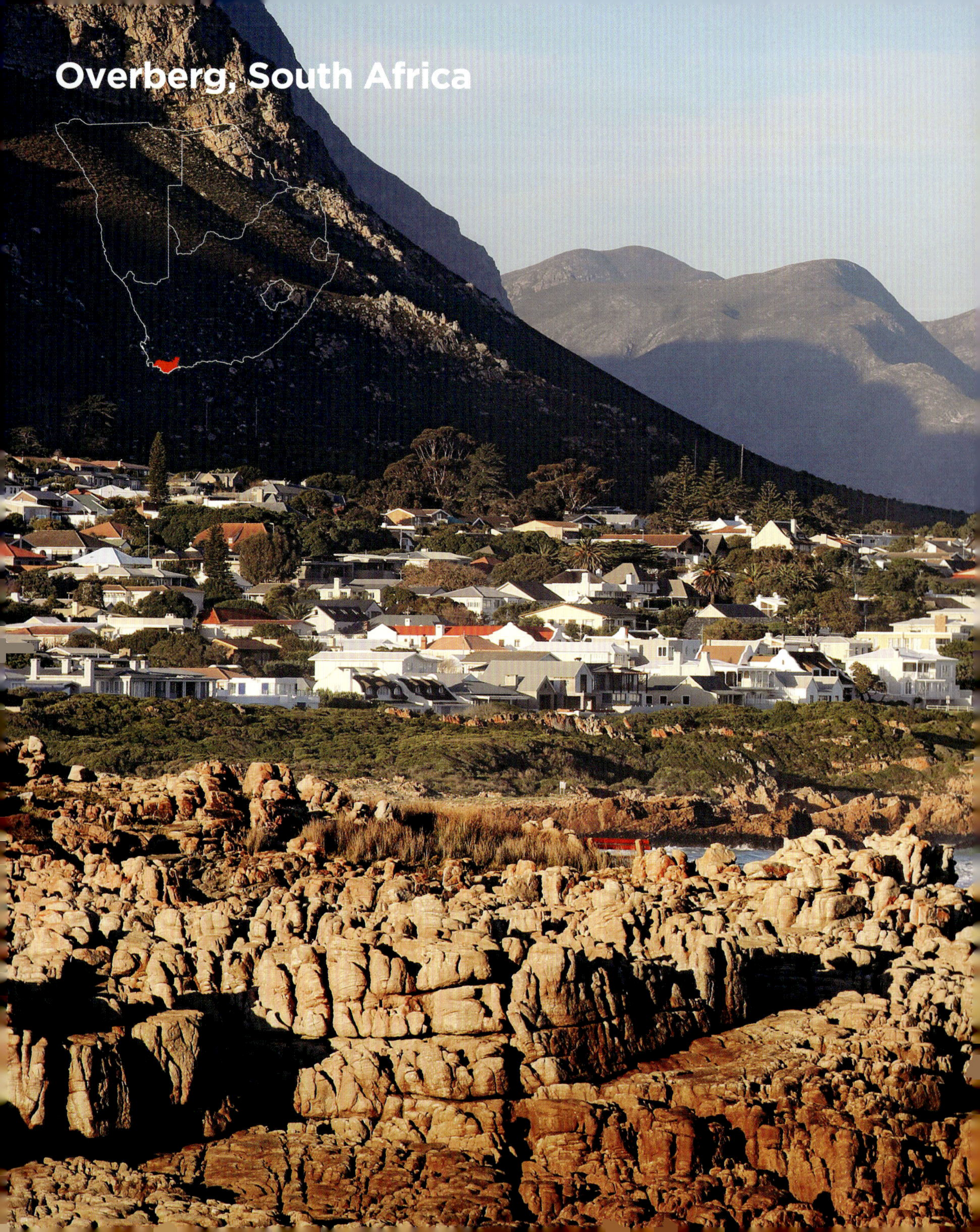
Overberg, South Africa

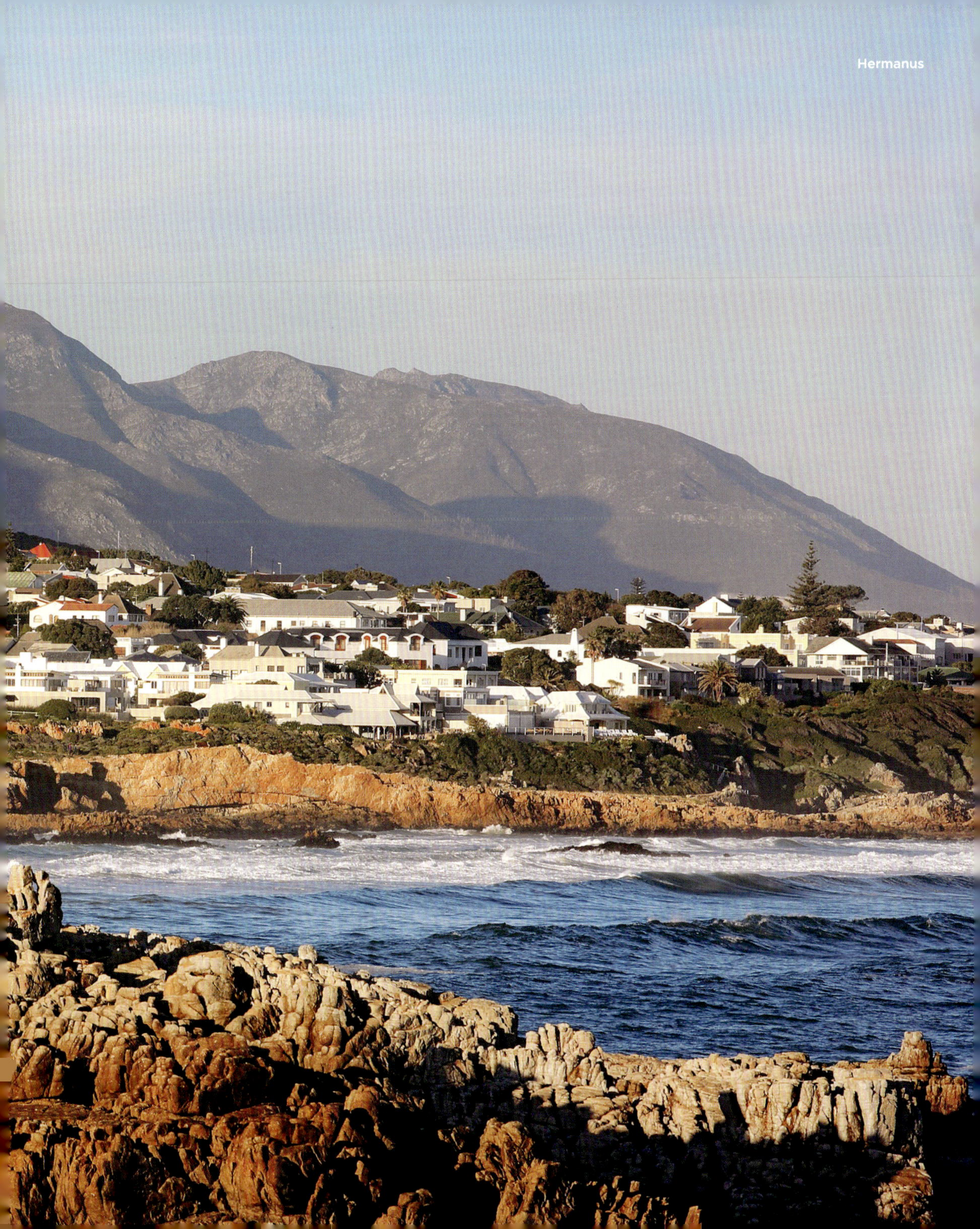

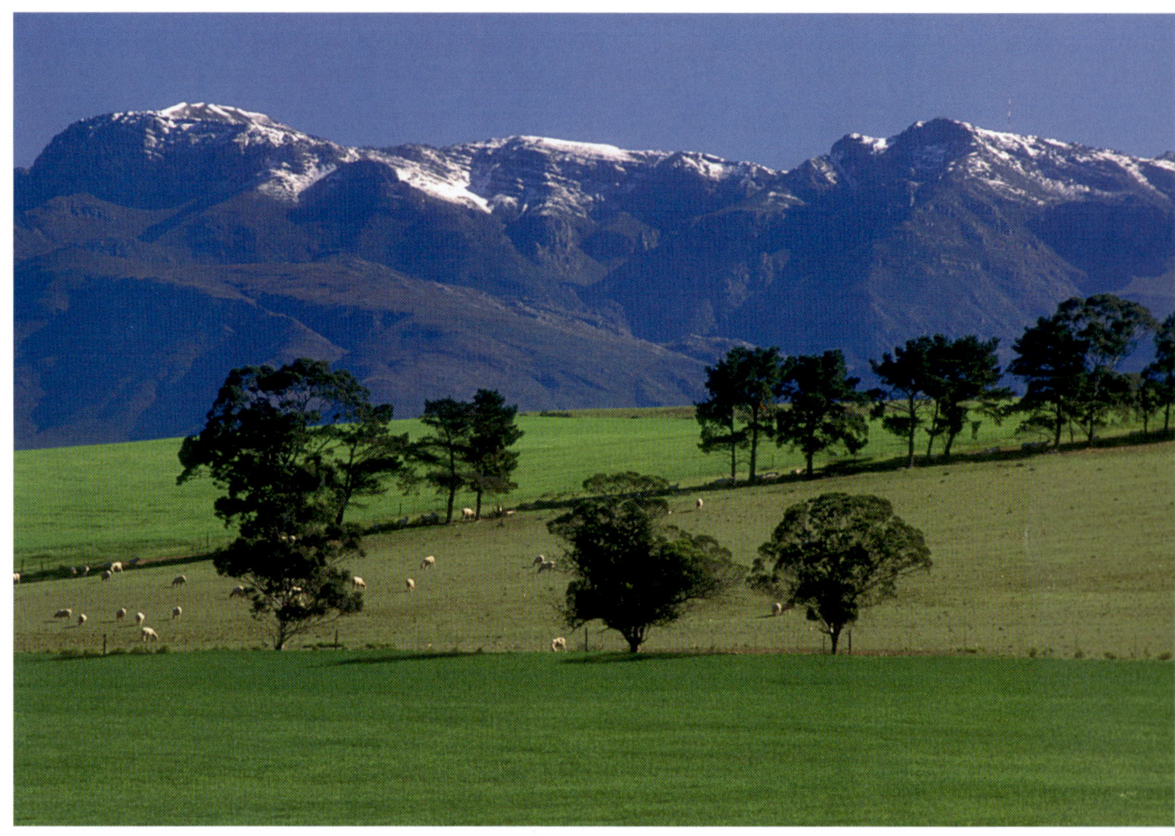

Kogelberg Nature Reserve, Overberg

Overberg
Overberg means "behind the mountain", referring to the mountain range of the Hottentots Holland mountains east of Cape Town. Between June and November, hundreds of whales, up to 18 metres long, move alongside the endless sandy beaches of Walker Bay. The waters off Gansbaai have the highest concentration of white sharks in the world.

Overberg
Overberg signifie littéralement « derrière la montagne », ce qui fait référence aux montagnes de Hottentots Holland, à l'est du Cap. Entre juin et novembre, des centaines de baleines dont la taille peut atteindre jusqu'à 18 m longent les plages interminables de la baie de Walker. Au niveau de Gansbaai se trouve la population de grands requins blancs la plus dense au monde.

Overberg
Overberg bedeutet übersetzt etwa „Hinter dem Berg", gemeint ist der Gebirgszug der Hottentots-Holland-Berge östlich von Kapstadt. Zwischen Juni und November ziehen hunderte, bis zu 18 m lange Wale an den endlosen Sandstränden der Walker Bay entlang. Bei Gansbaai gibt es die höchste Konzentration an weißen Haien weltweit.

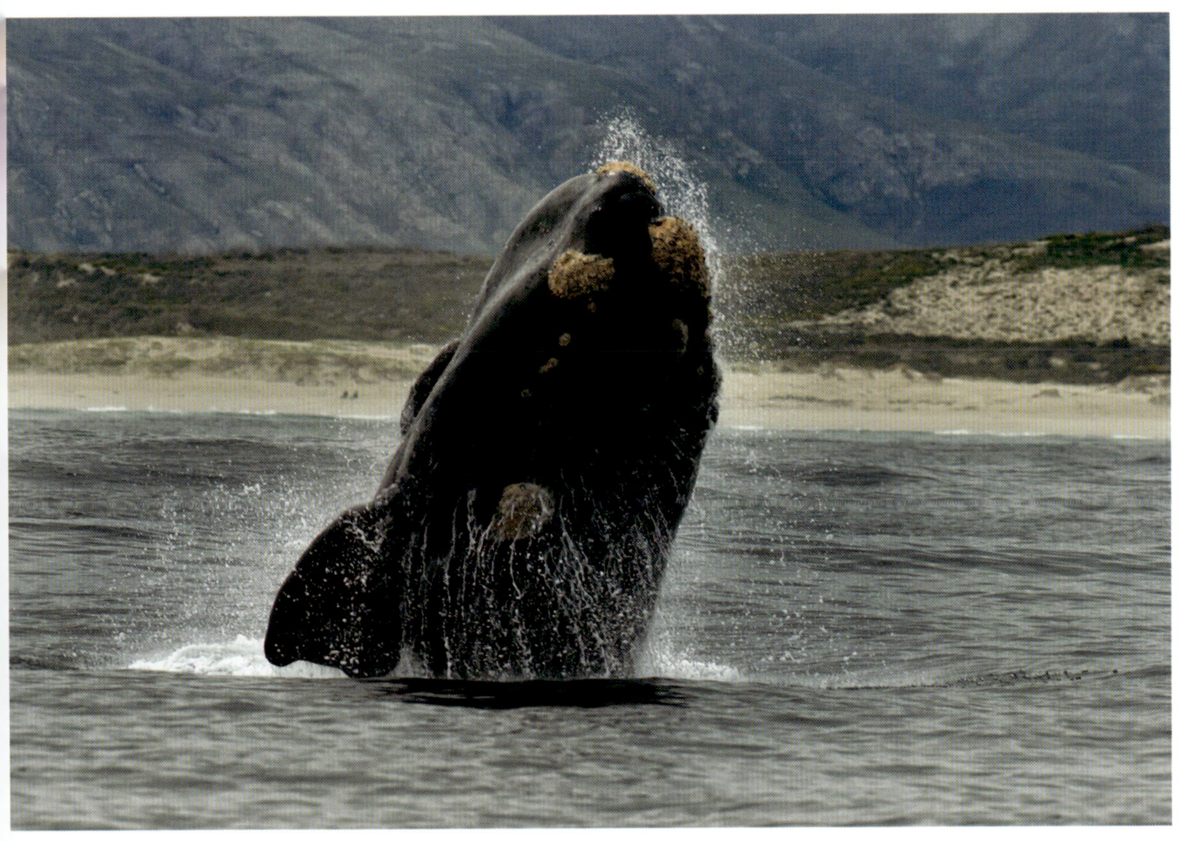

Southern right whale, Walker Bay, Hermanus

Overberg
Overberg significa "detrás de la montaña", es decir, la cordillera de las montañas Hottentots-Holland al este de Ciudad del Cabo. Entre junio y noviembre, cientos de ballenas de hasta 18 metros de largo se mueven a lo largo de las interminables playas de arena de Walker Bay. Gansbaai tiene la mayor concentración de tiburones blancos del mundo.

Overberg
Overberg significa "dietro la montagna", cioè la catena montuosa delle montagne dell'Hottentots-Holland ad est di Città del Capo. Tra giugno e novembre, centinaia di balene, lunghe fino a 18 metri, nuotano lungo le infinite spiagge sabbiose di Walker Bay. Gansbaai ha la più alta concentrazione di squali bianchi al mondo.

Overberg
Overberg betekent "achter de berg", d.w.z. de bergen van Hottentots-Holland ten oosten van Kaapstad. Tussen juni en november trekken honderden walvissen, tot wel 18 meter lang, langs de eindeloze zandstranden van Walker Bay. Gansbaai heeft de hoogste concentratie witte haaien ter wereld.

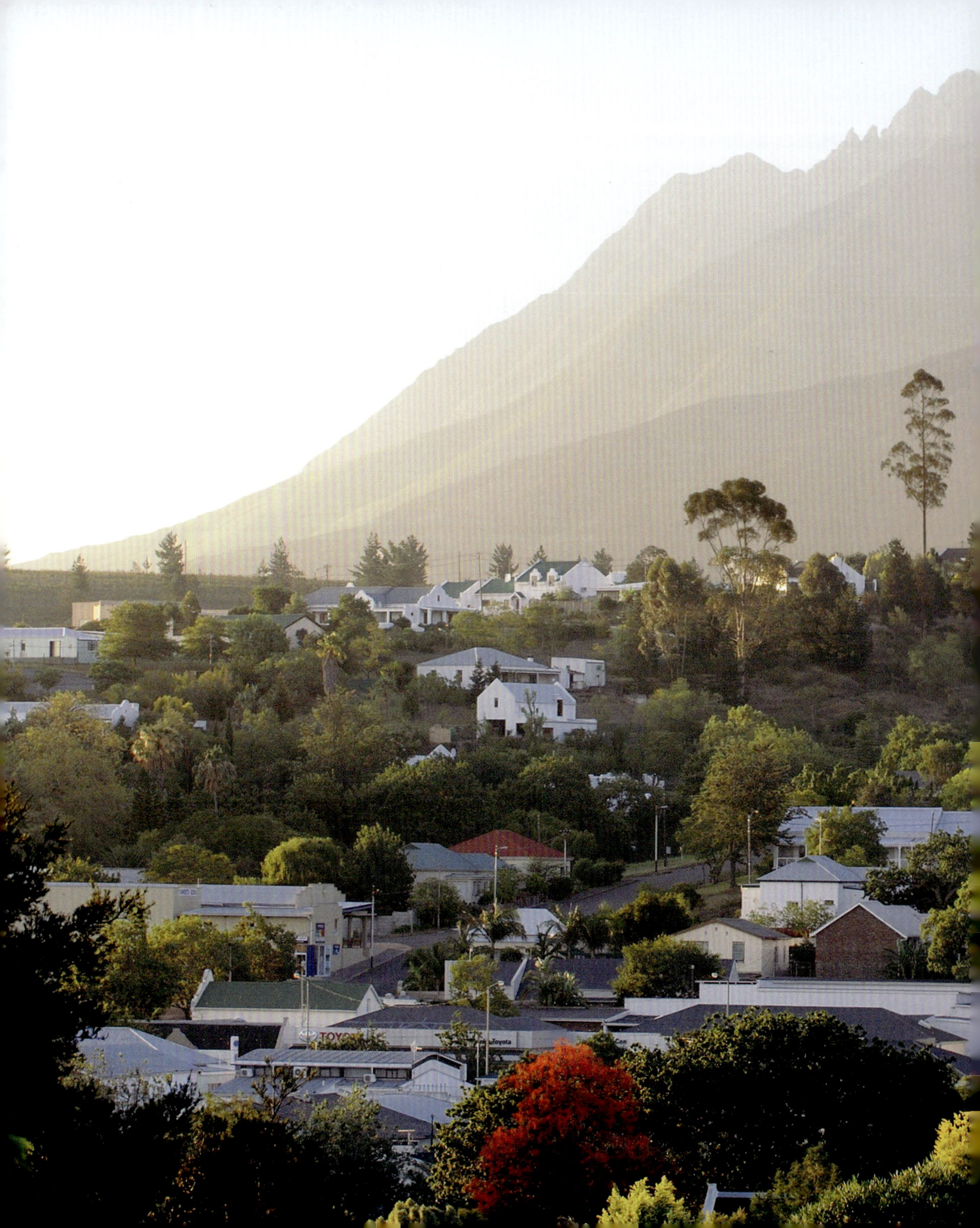

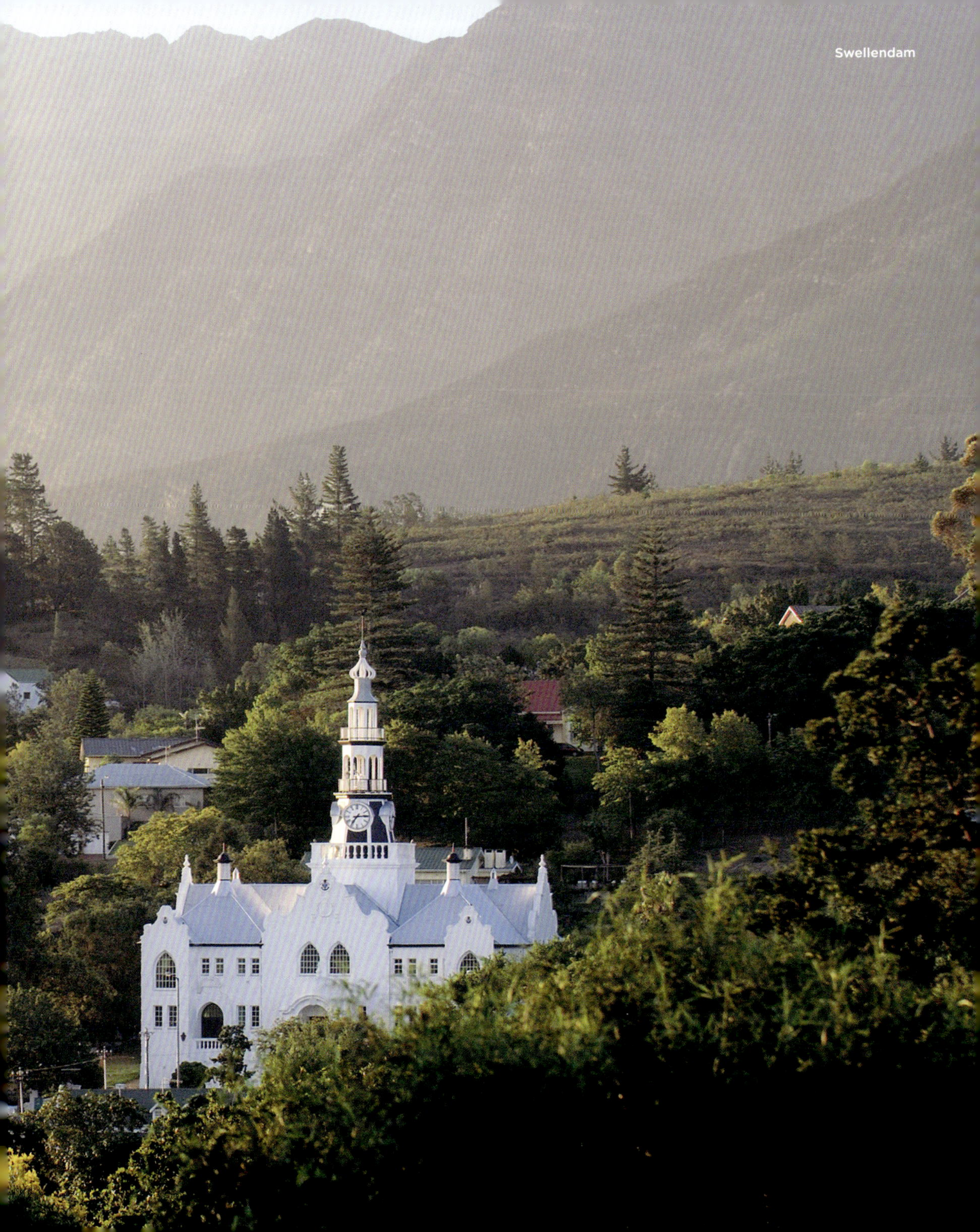

Swellendam

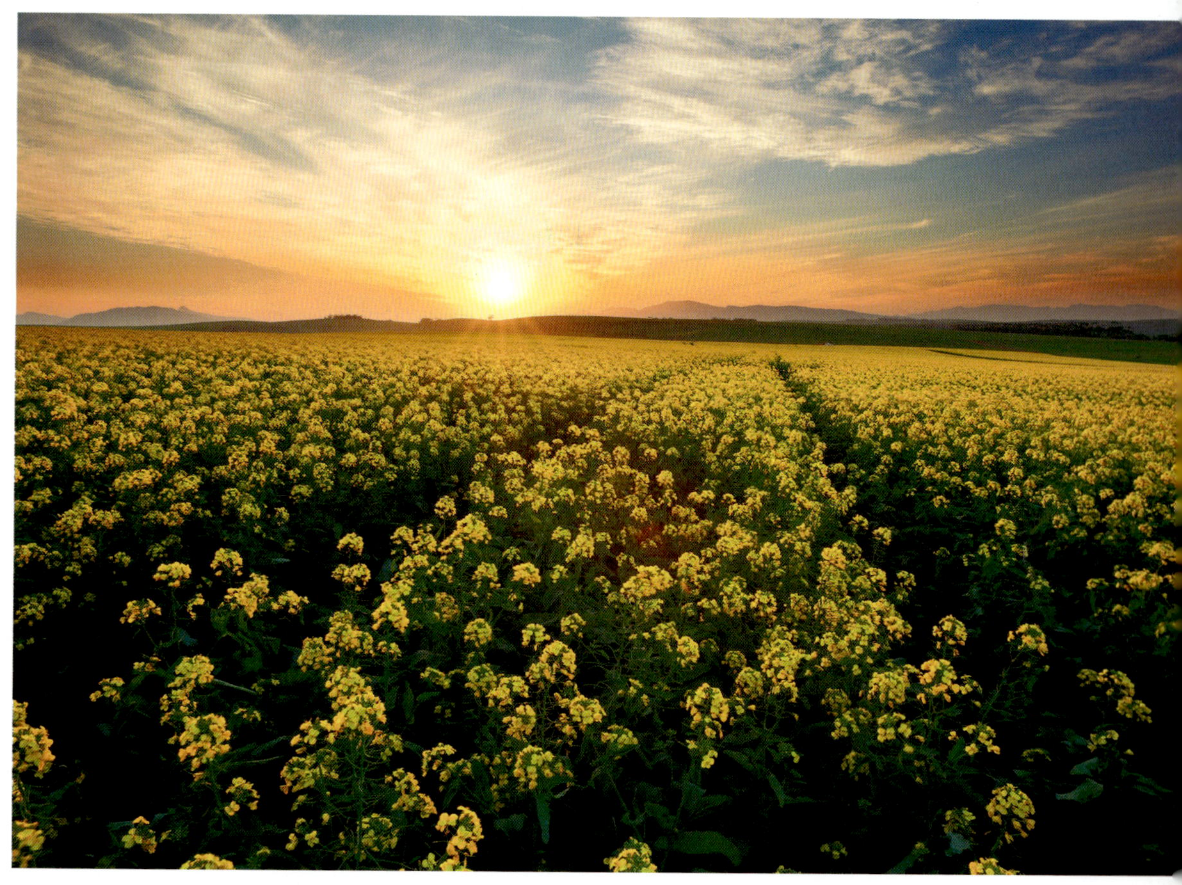

Canola farmland near Caledon, Overberg

Bontebok, Overberg

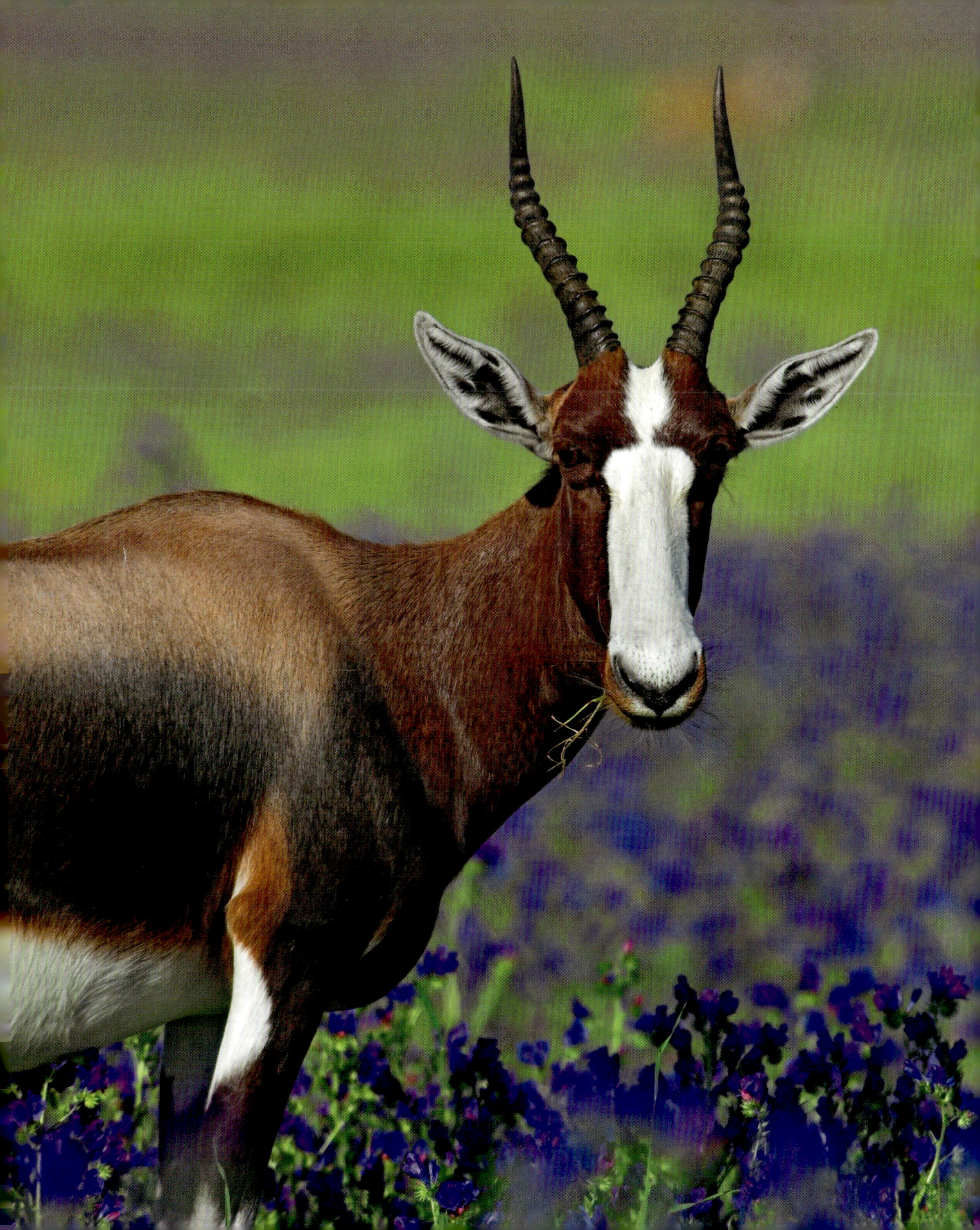

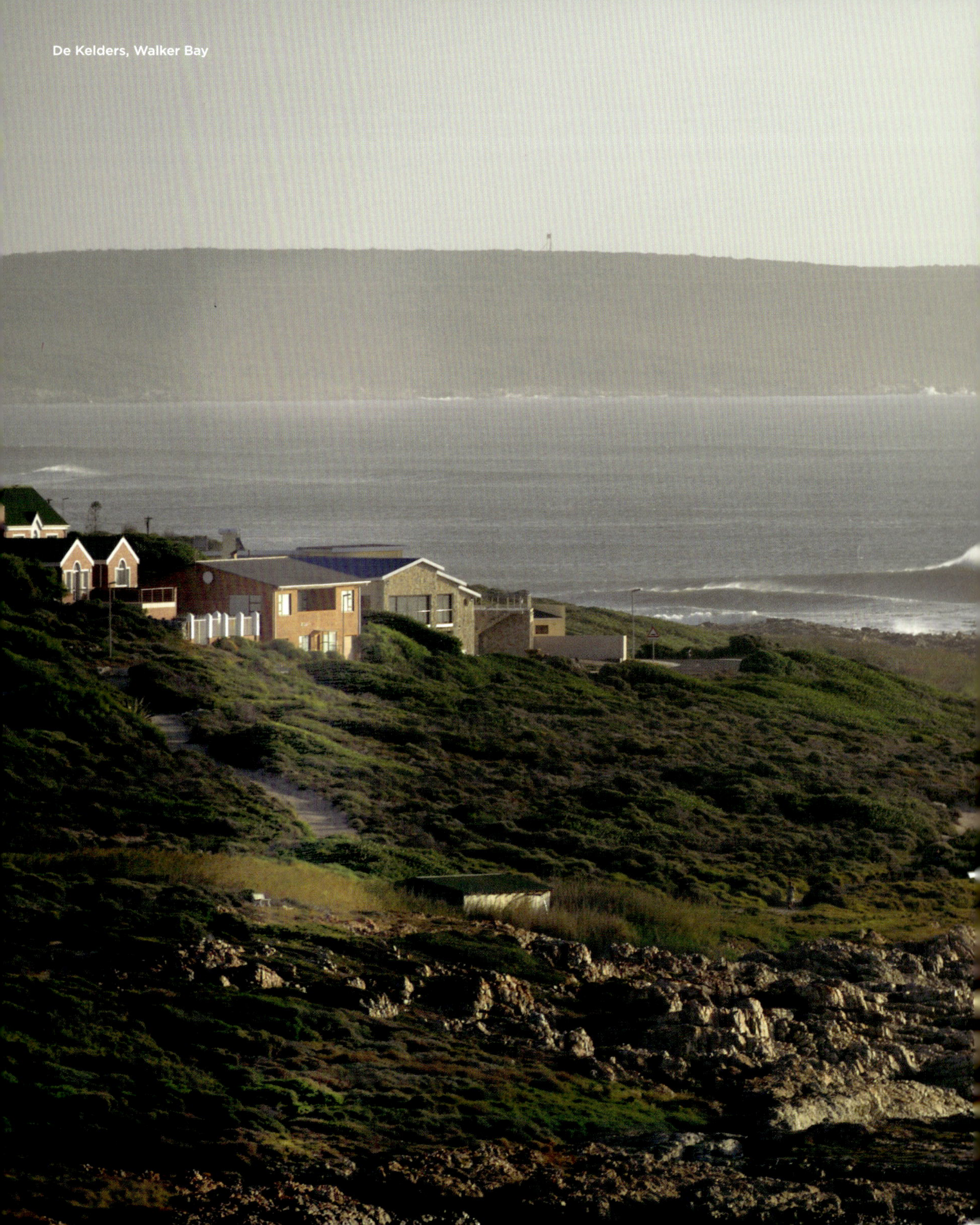

De Kelders, Walker Bay

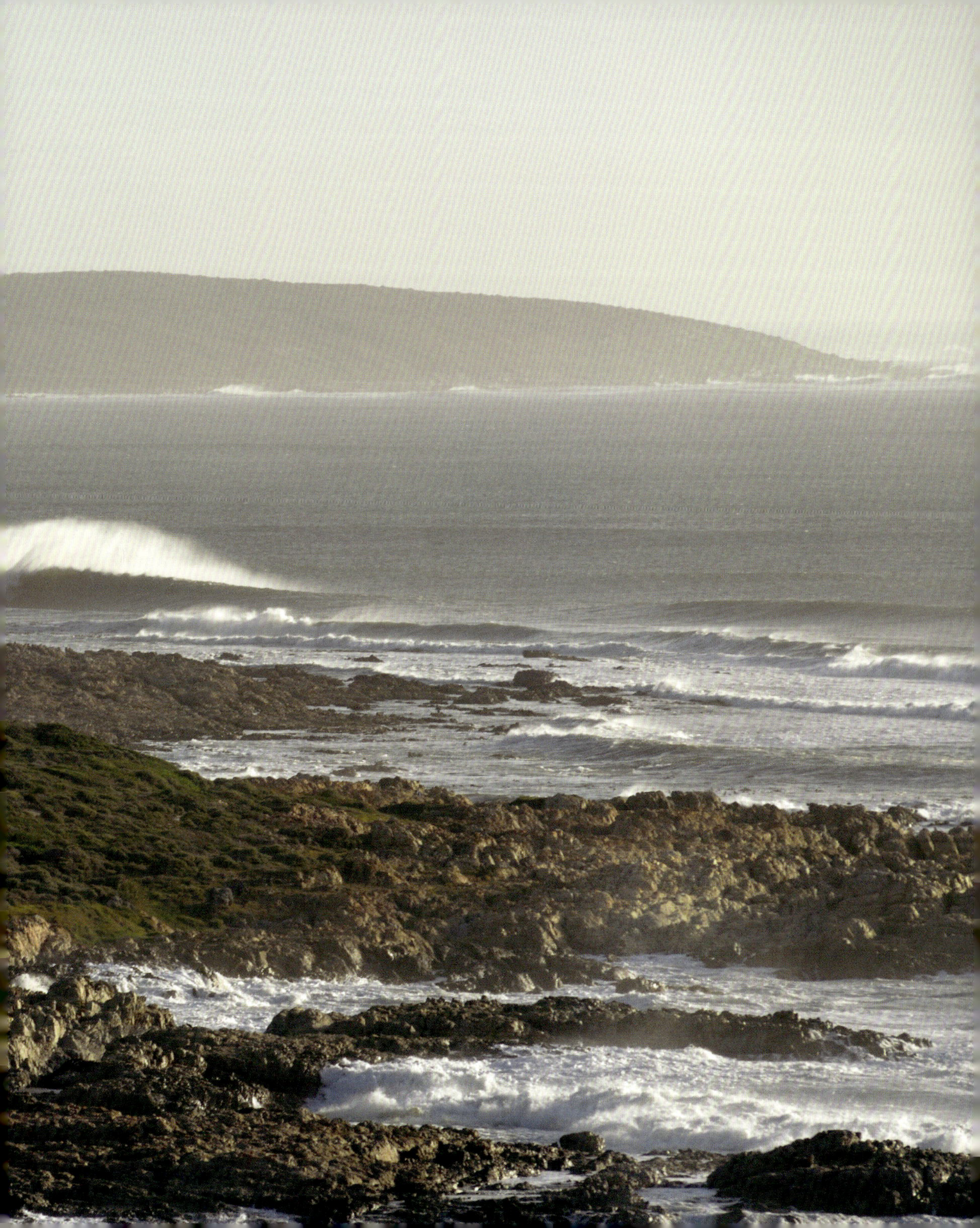

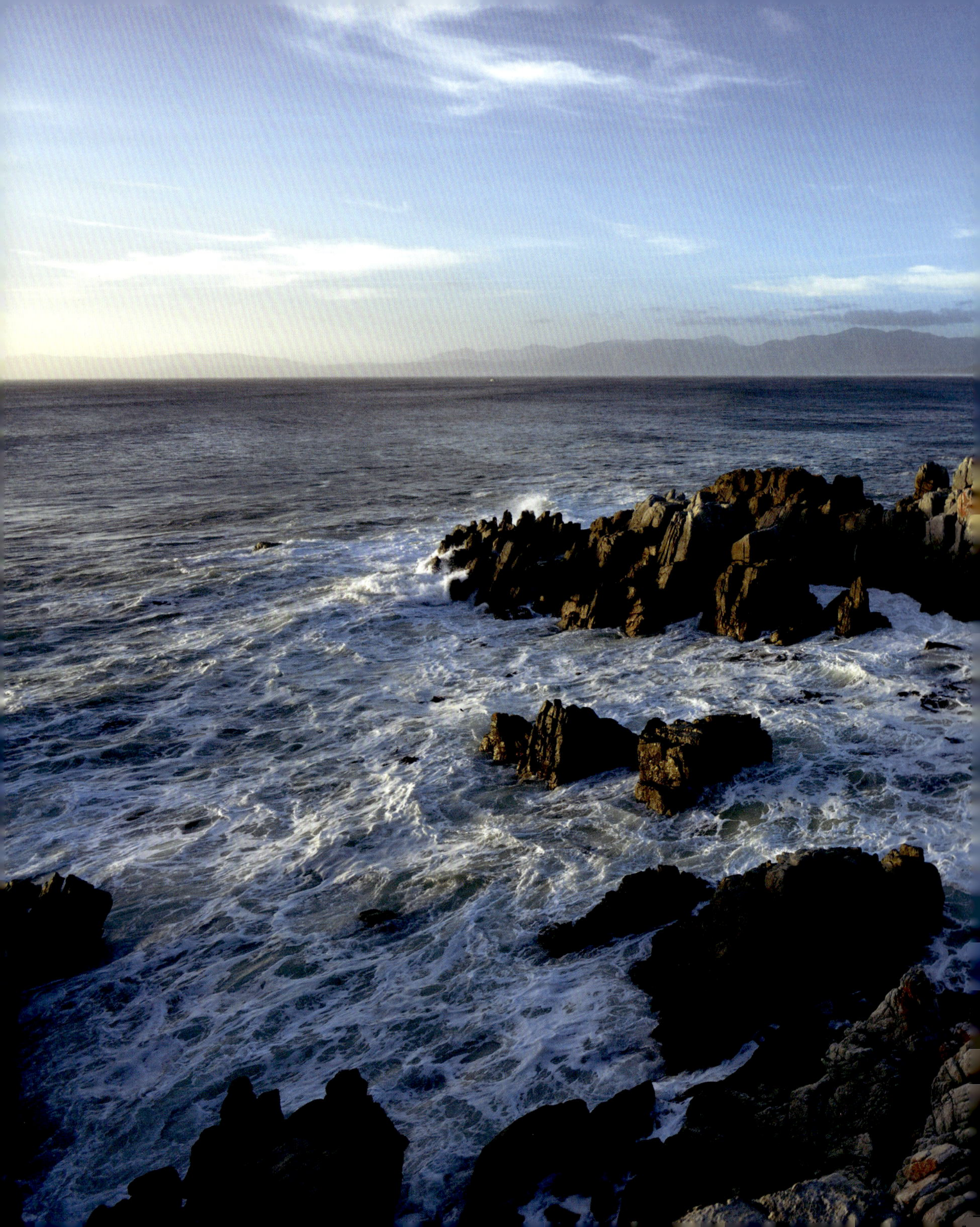

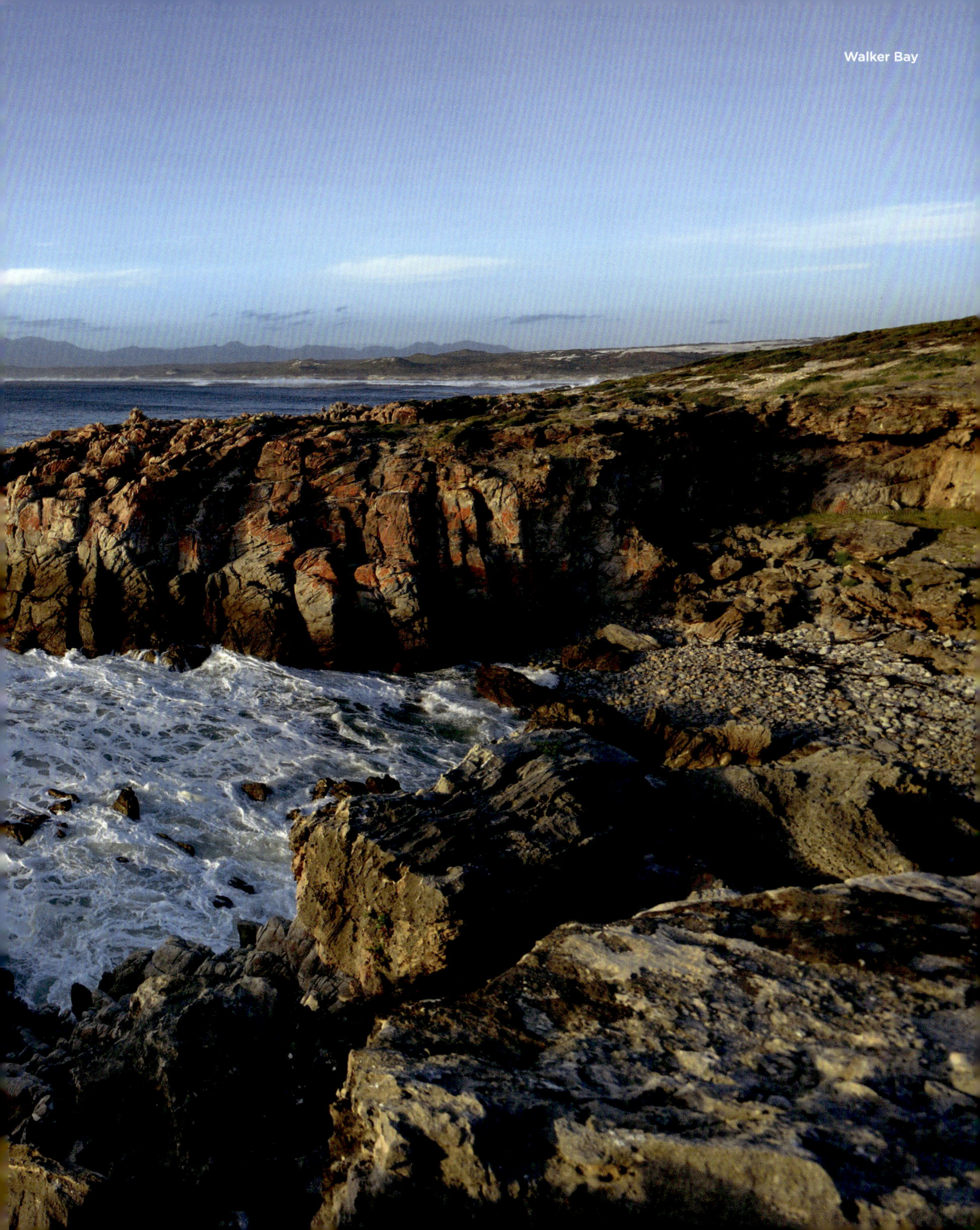
Walker Bay

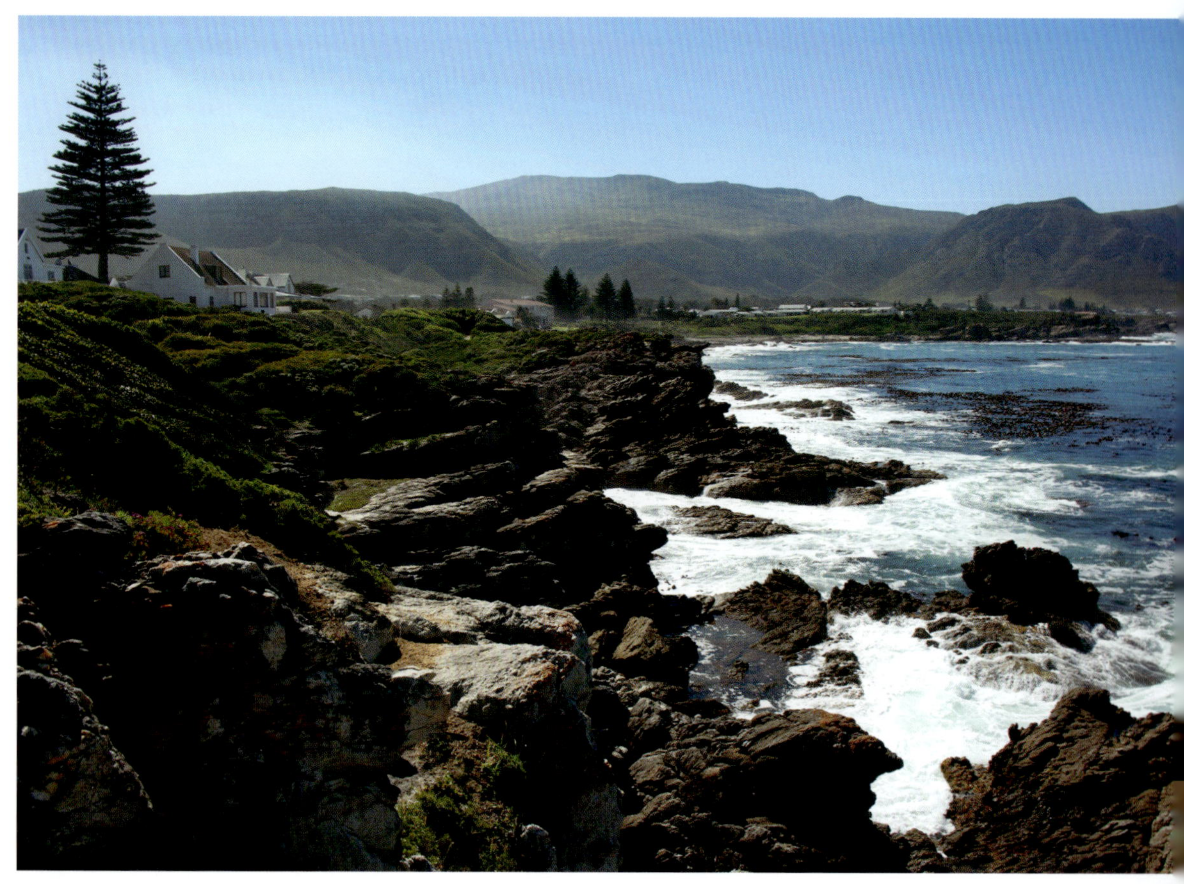

Coast near Hermanus

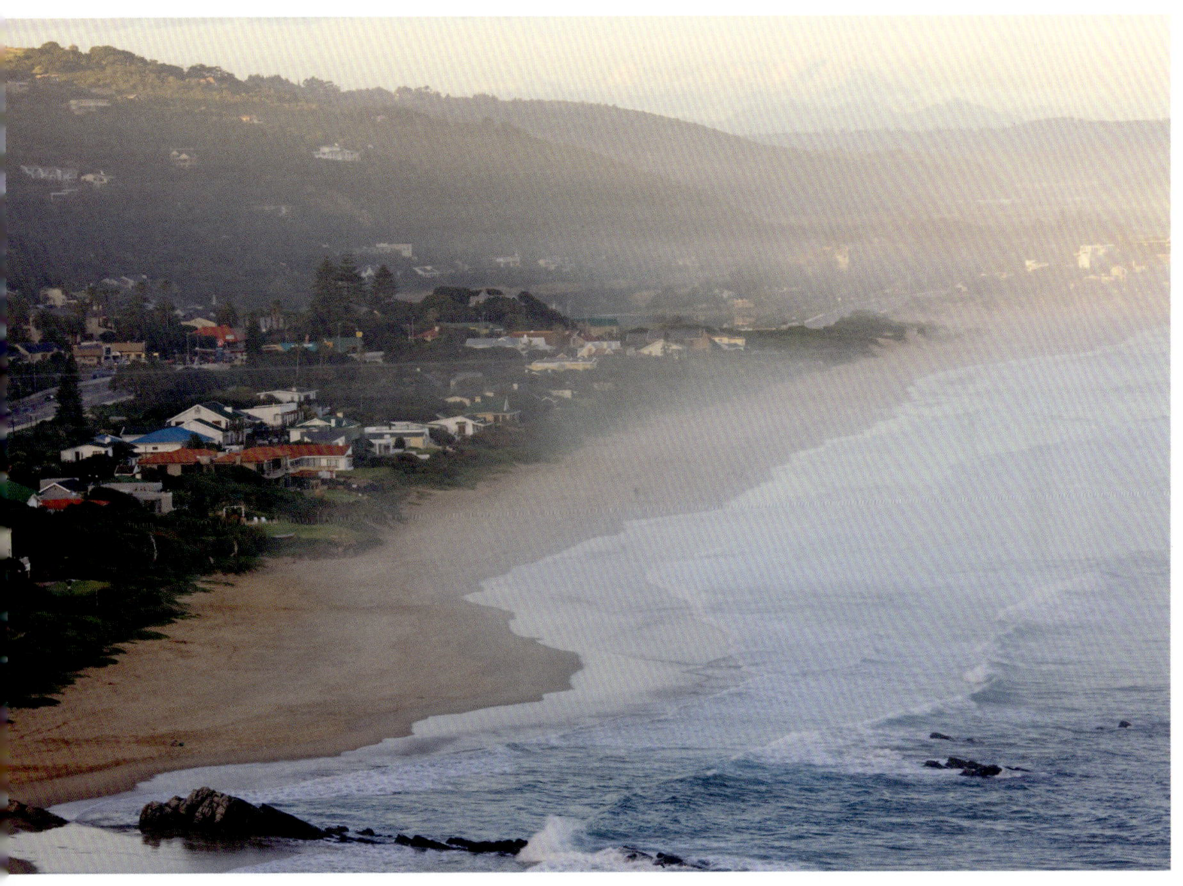

Hermanus

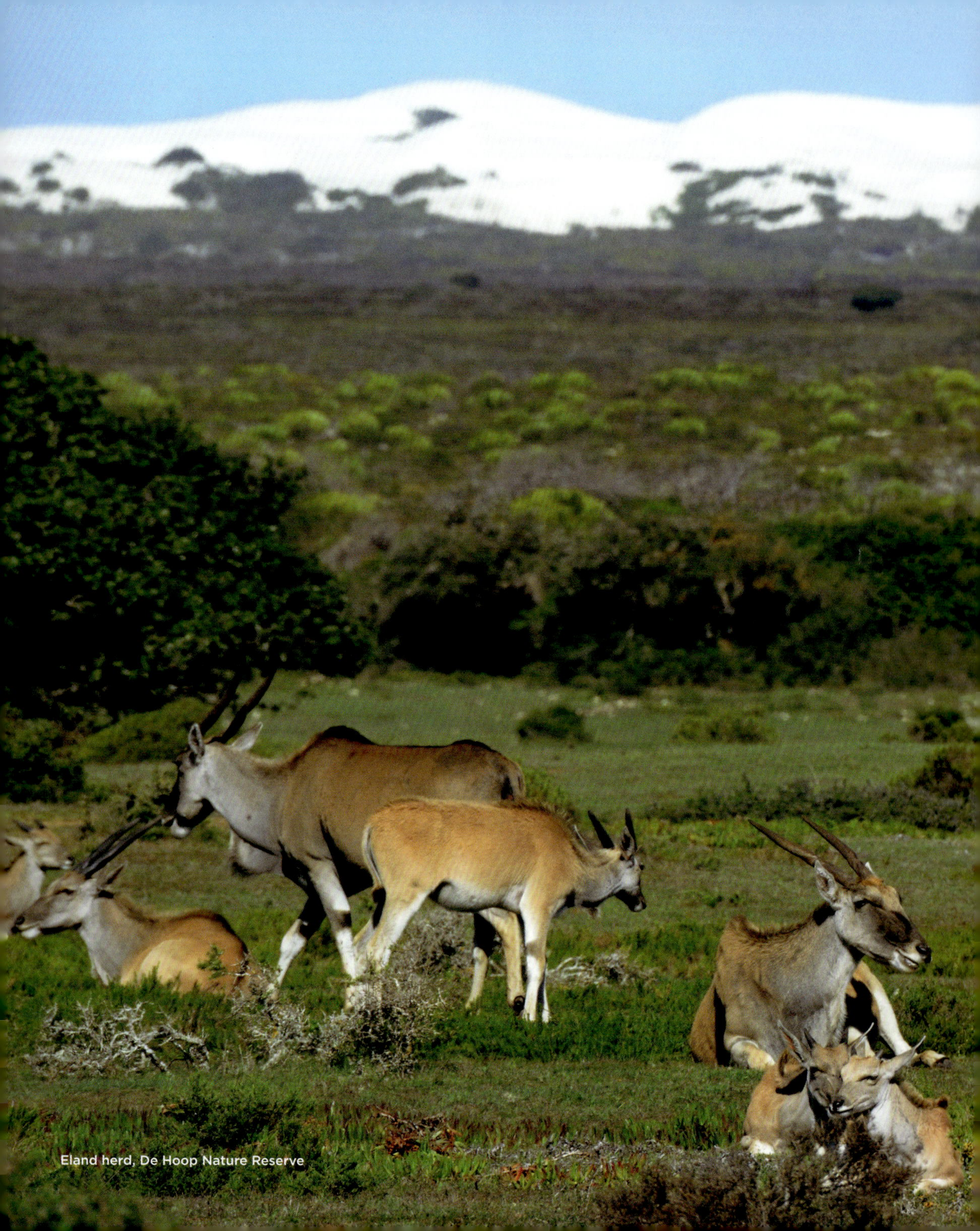

Eland herd, De Hoop Nature Reserve

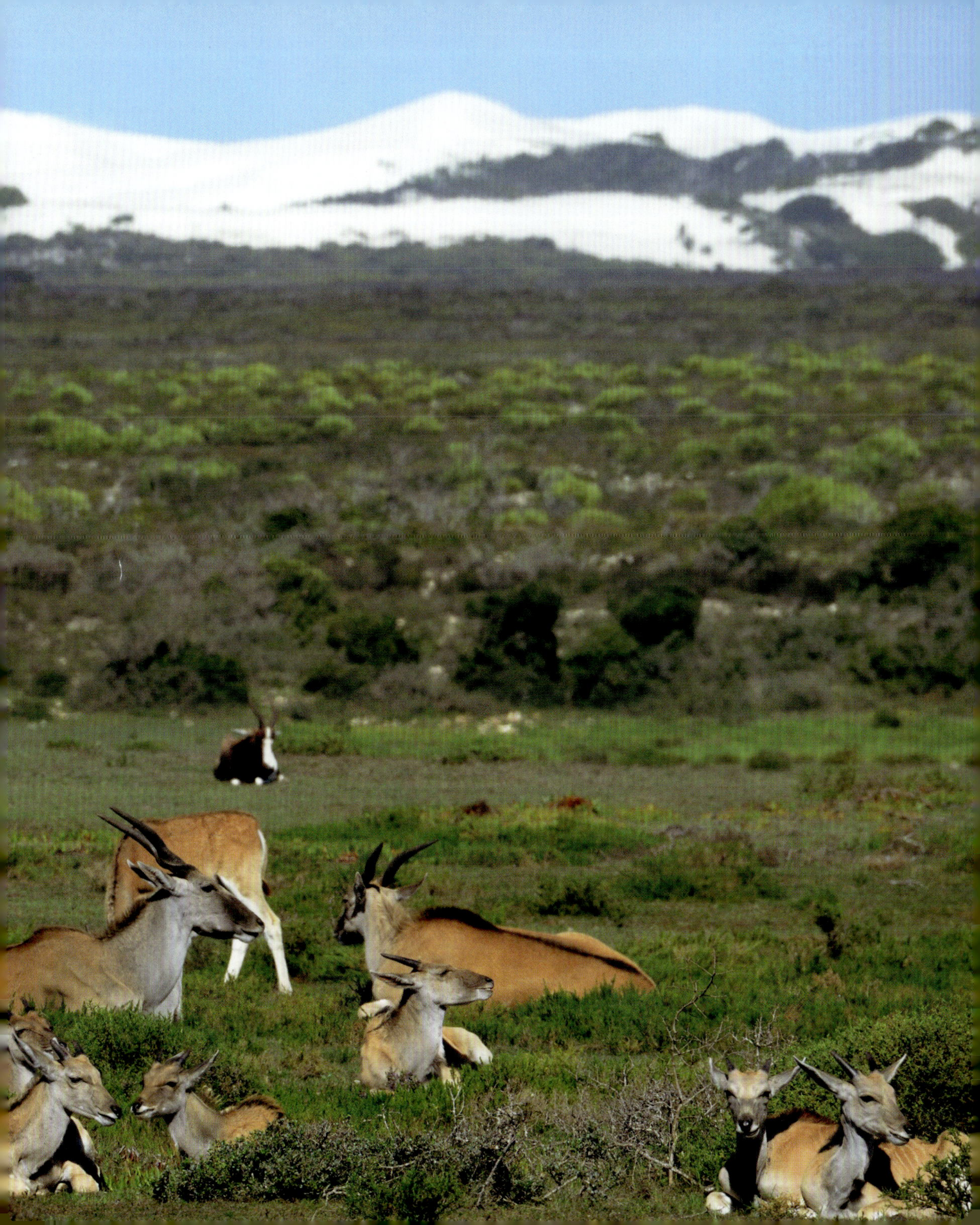

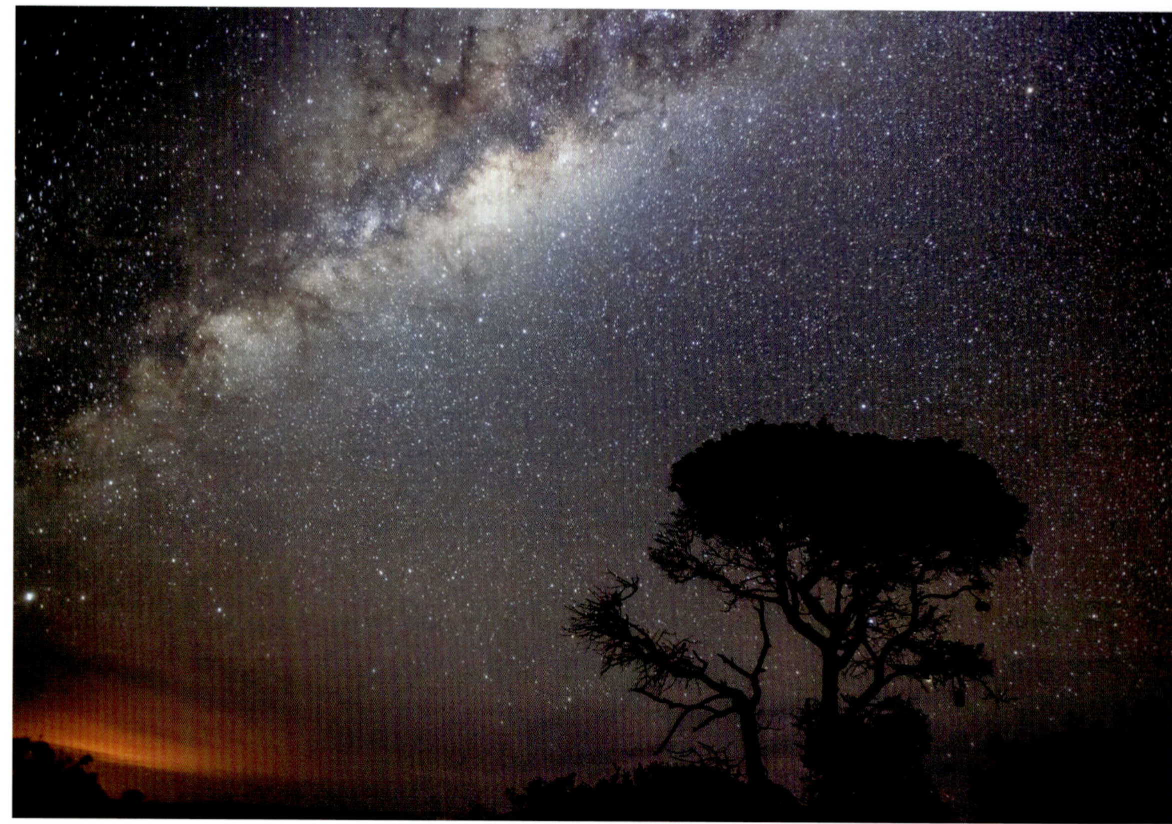

De Hoop Nature Reserve

De Hoop Nature Reserve
The De Hoop Nature Reserve, with its white sand dunes, is a UNESCO World Heritage Site. It is a protected area of fynbos vegetation, with over 1500 plant species.

La réserve naturelle de De Hoop
La réserve naturelle de De Hoop, avec ses dunes de sable blanc, fait partie du patrimoine mondial de l'UNESCO. Elle permet de préserver la végétation du fynbos, soit plus de 1500 espèces de plantes.

De Hoop Nature Reserve
Das Naturschutzgebiet De Hoop Nature Reserve mit seinen weißen Sanddünen zählt zum UNESCO-Weltkulturerbe. Es ist Schutzgebiet der Fynbosvegetation mit über 1500 Pflanzenarten.

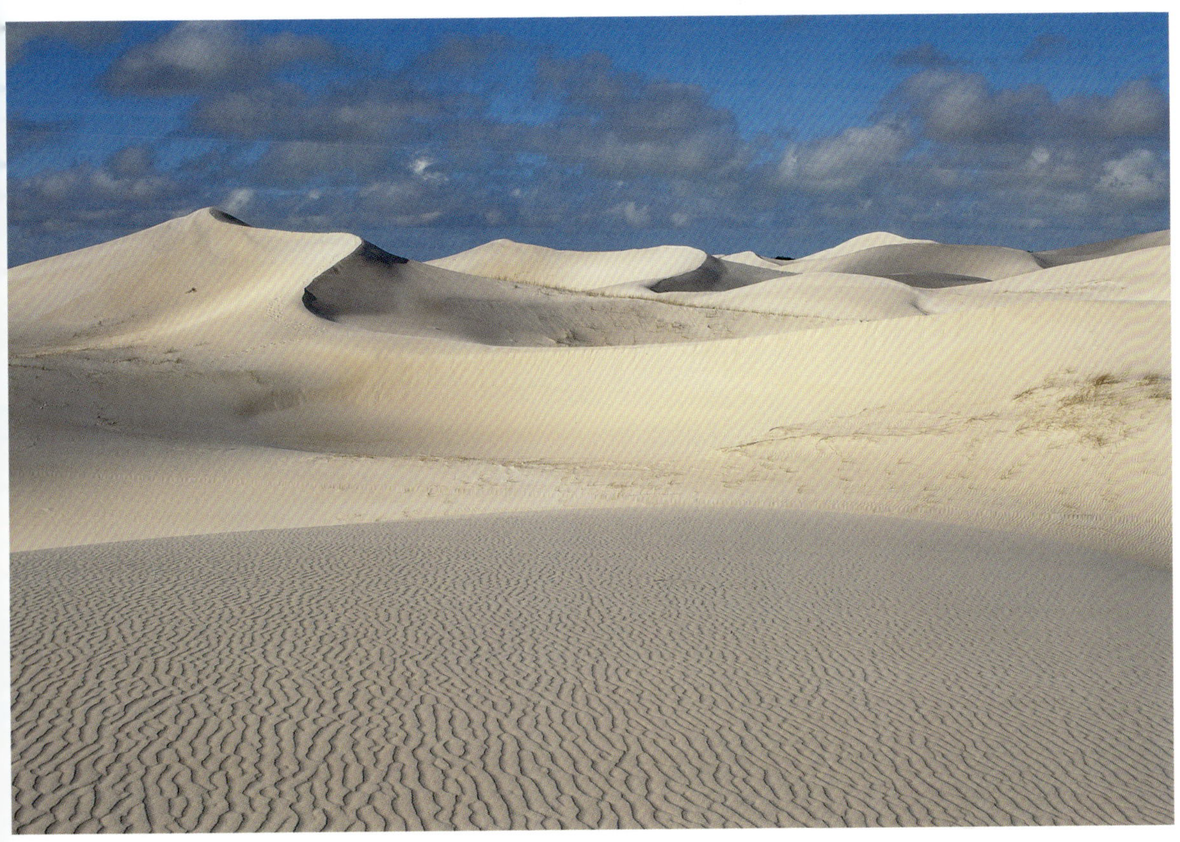

De Hoop Nature Reserve

Reserva Natural De Hoop
La Reserva Natural de De Hoop, con sus dunas de arena blanca, es Patrimonio de la Humanidad de la UNESCO. Es un área protegida de vegetación de fynbos con más de 1500 especies de plantas.

De Hoop Nature Reserve
La Riserva Naturale De Hoop con le sue dune di sabbia bianca è Patrimonio dell'Umanità dell'UNESCO. Si tratta di un'area protetta di vegetazione arbustiva di fynbos con oltre 1500 specie vegetali.

Natuurreservaat De Hoop
Het natuurreservaat De Hoop met zijn witte zandduinen maakt deel uit van het werelderfgoed van Unesco. Het is een beschermd gebied met fynbos-vegetatie en meer dan 1500 plantensoorten.

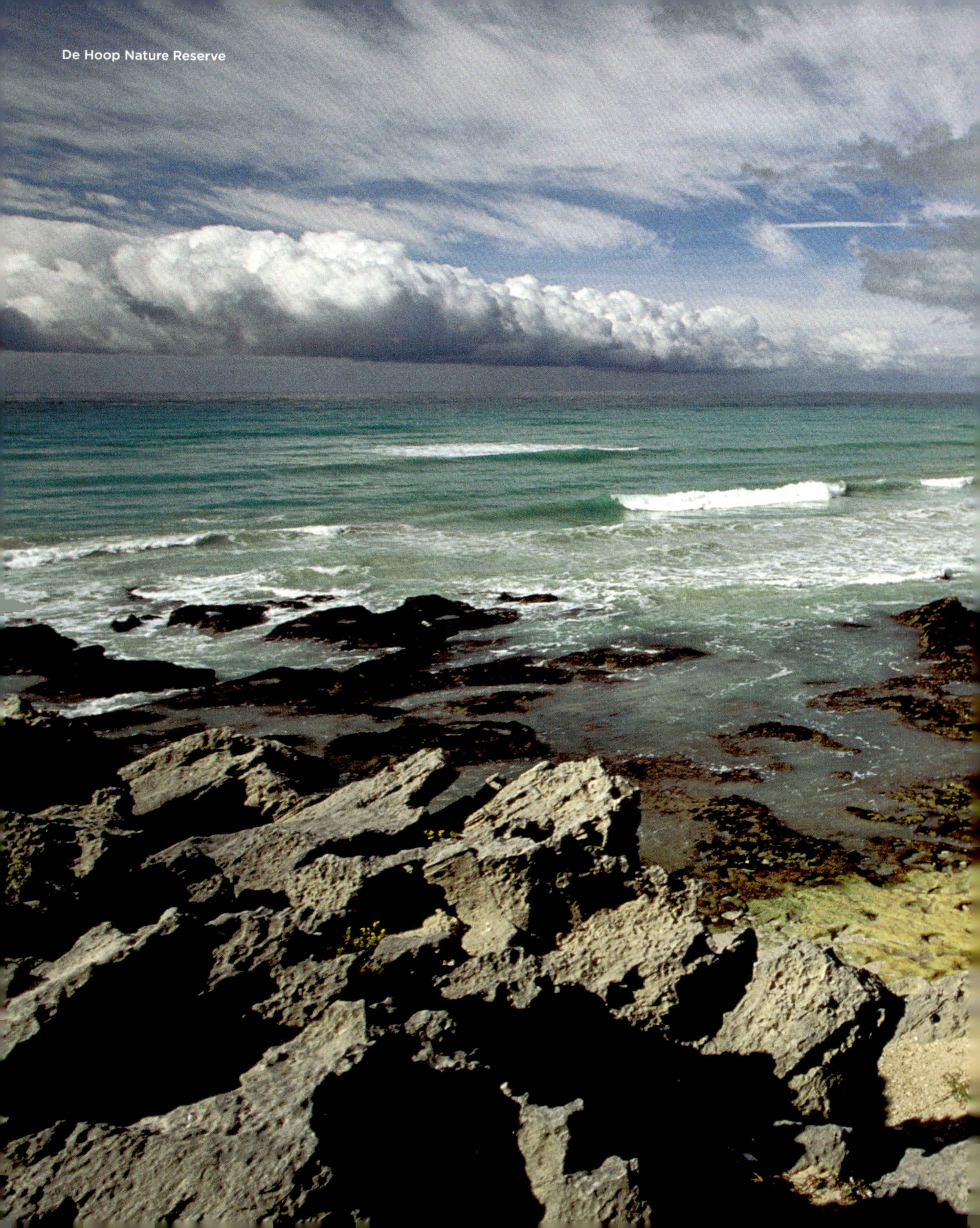

De Hoop Nature Reserve

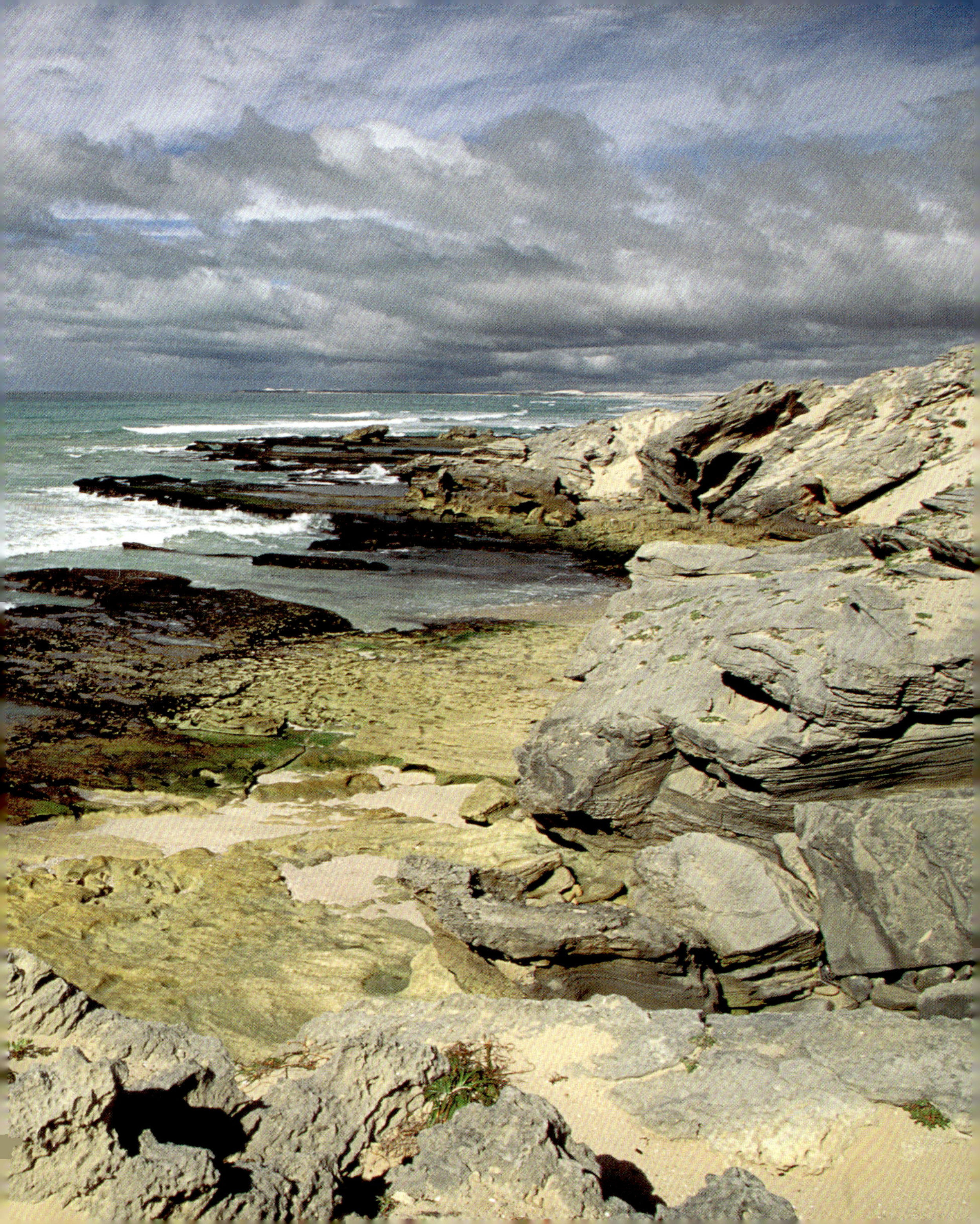

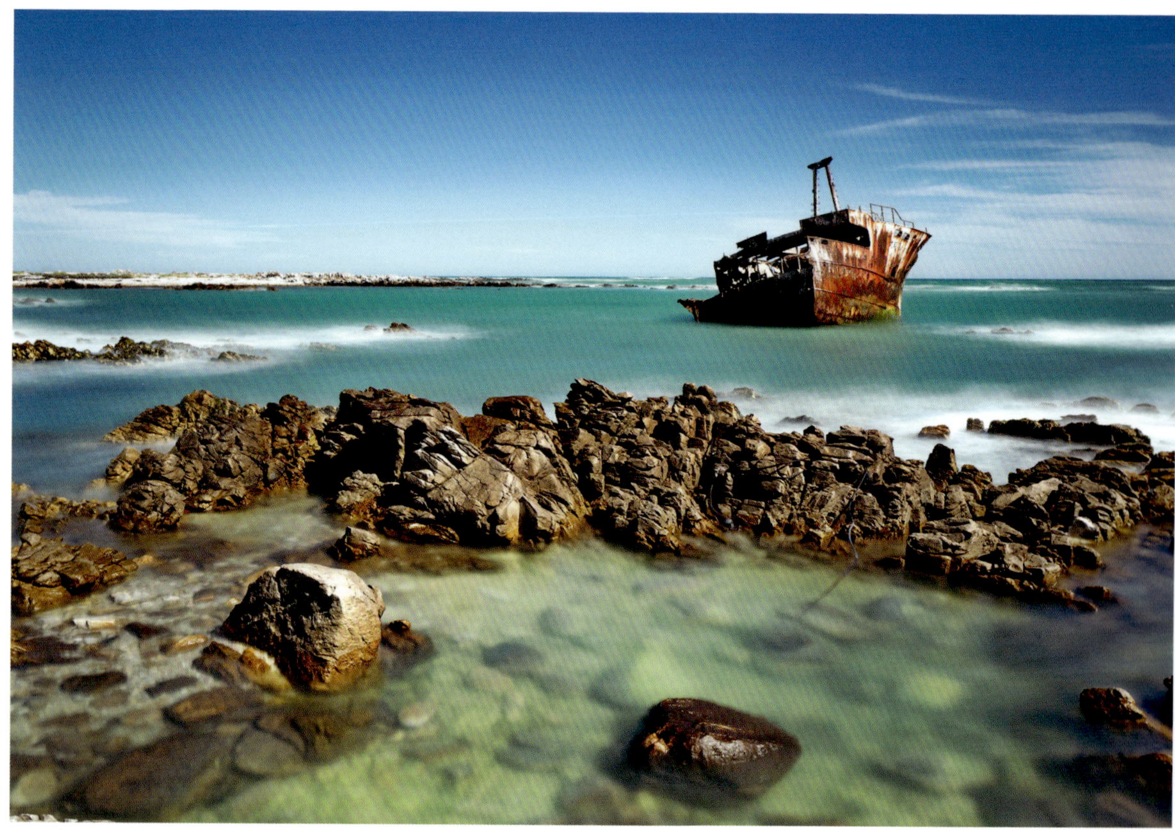

Shipwreck near Cape Agulhas

Cape Agulhas
Cape Agulhas is the southernmost point of Africa. It lies 150 m (492 ft) west of the 20th meridian, and forms the geographical boundary between the Atlantic and the Indian Oceans.

Le cap des Aiguilles
Le cap des Aiguilles est le point le plus au sud de l'Afrique. Il se trouve à 150 m du 20e méridien, qui marque la frontière géographique entre l'océan Atlantique et l'océan Indien.

Kap Agulhas
Kap Agulhas ist der südlichste Punkt Afrikas. Es liegt 150 m westlich des 20. Meridians, der die geografische Grenze zwischen dem Atlantischen und dem Indischen Ozean bildet.

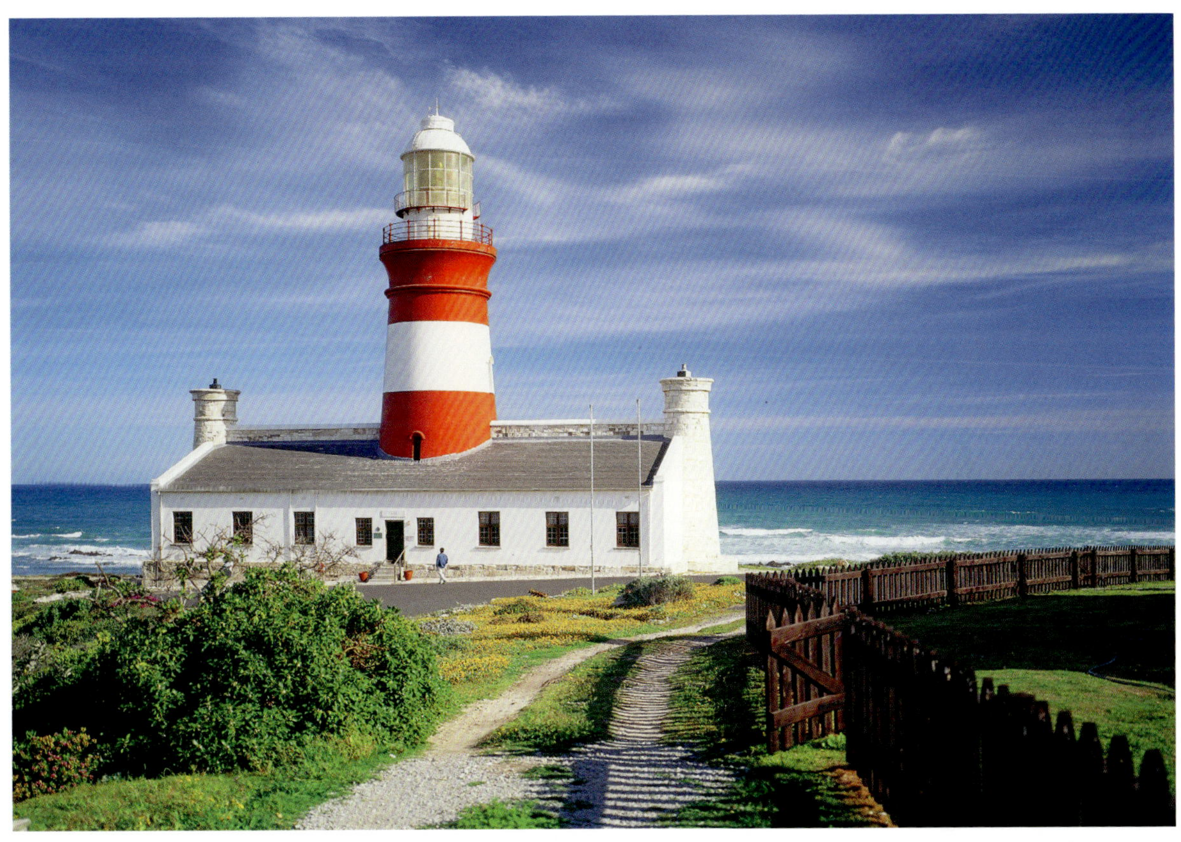

Cape Agulhas

Cabo Agulhas
Cabo Agulhas es el punto más al sur de África. Se encuentra a 150 m al oeste del meridiano 20, que forma la frontera geográfica entre el Atlántico y el Océano Índico.

Cabo Agulhas
Capo Agulhas è il punto più meridionale dell'Africa. Si trova 150 m ad ovest del 20° meridiano, che forma il confine geografico tra l'Atlantico e l'Oceano Indiano.

Kaap Agulhas
Kaap Agulhas is het zuidelijkste punt van het continent Afrika en ligt slechts 150 m ten westen van de 20e meridiaan, de geografische grens tussen de Atlantische en de Indische Oceaan.

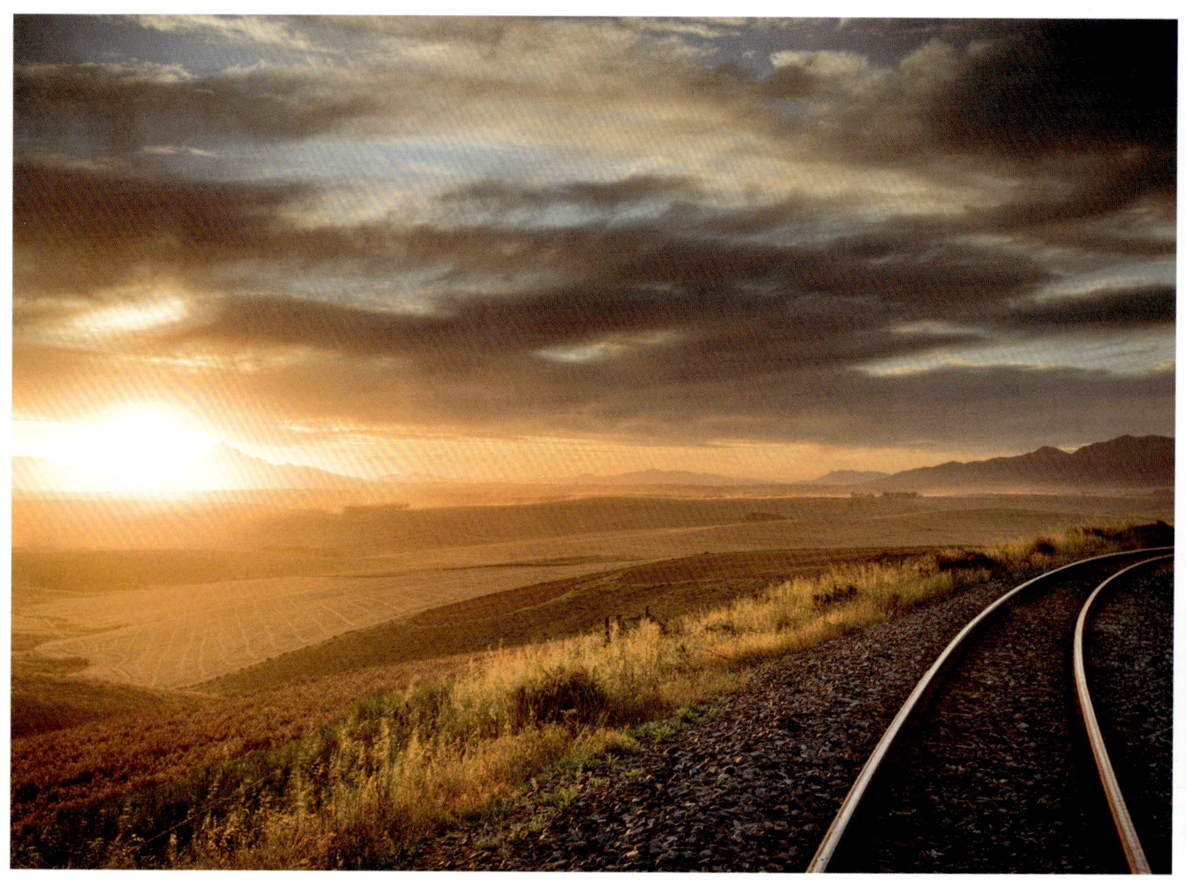

Overberg

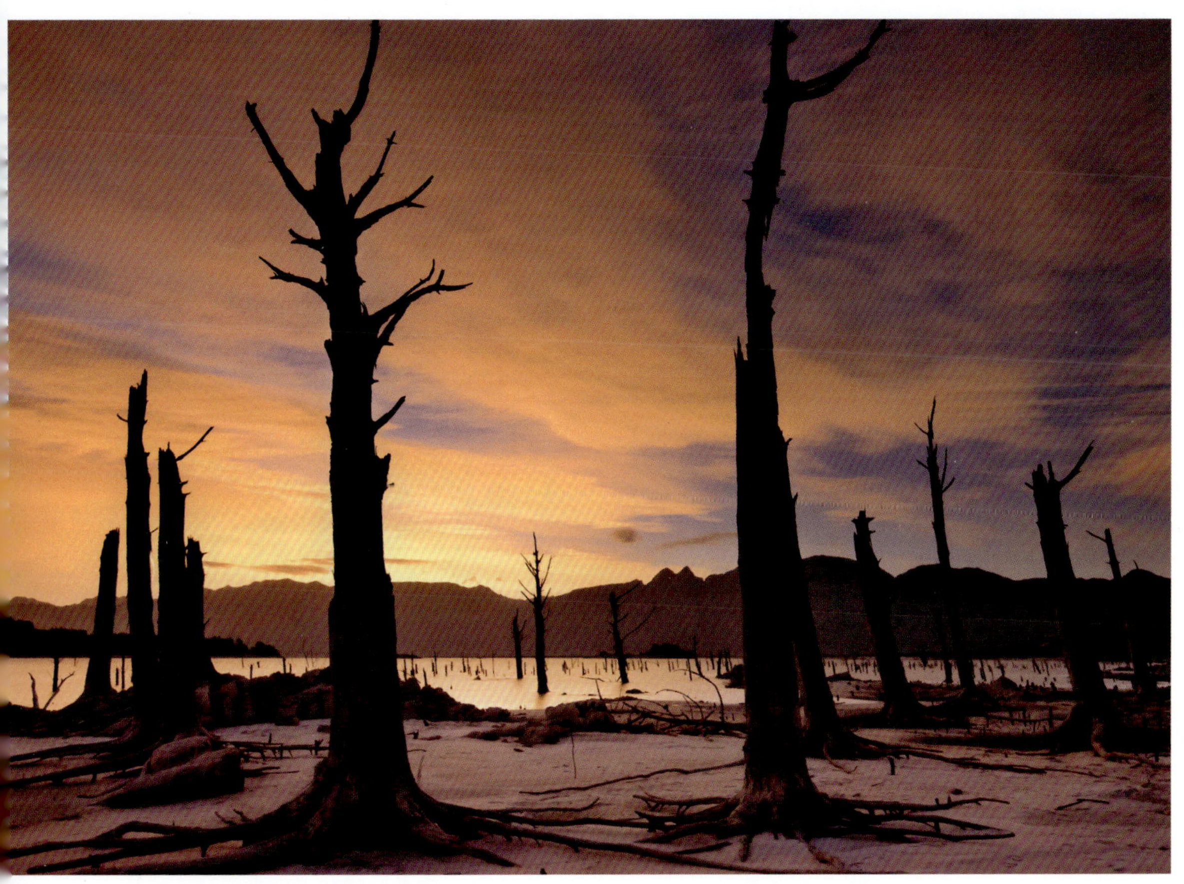

Dead trees on the banks of Theewaterskloof Dam

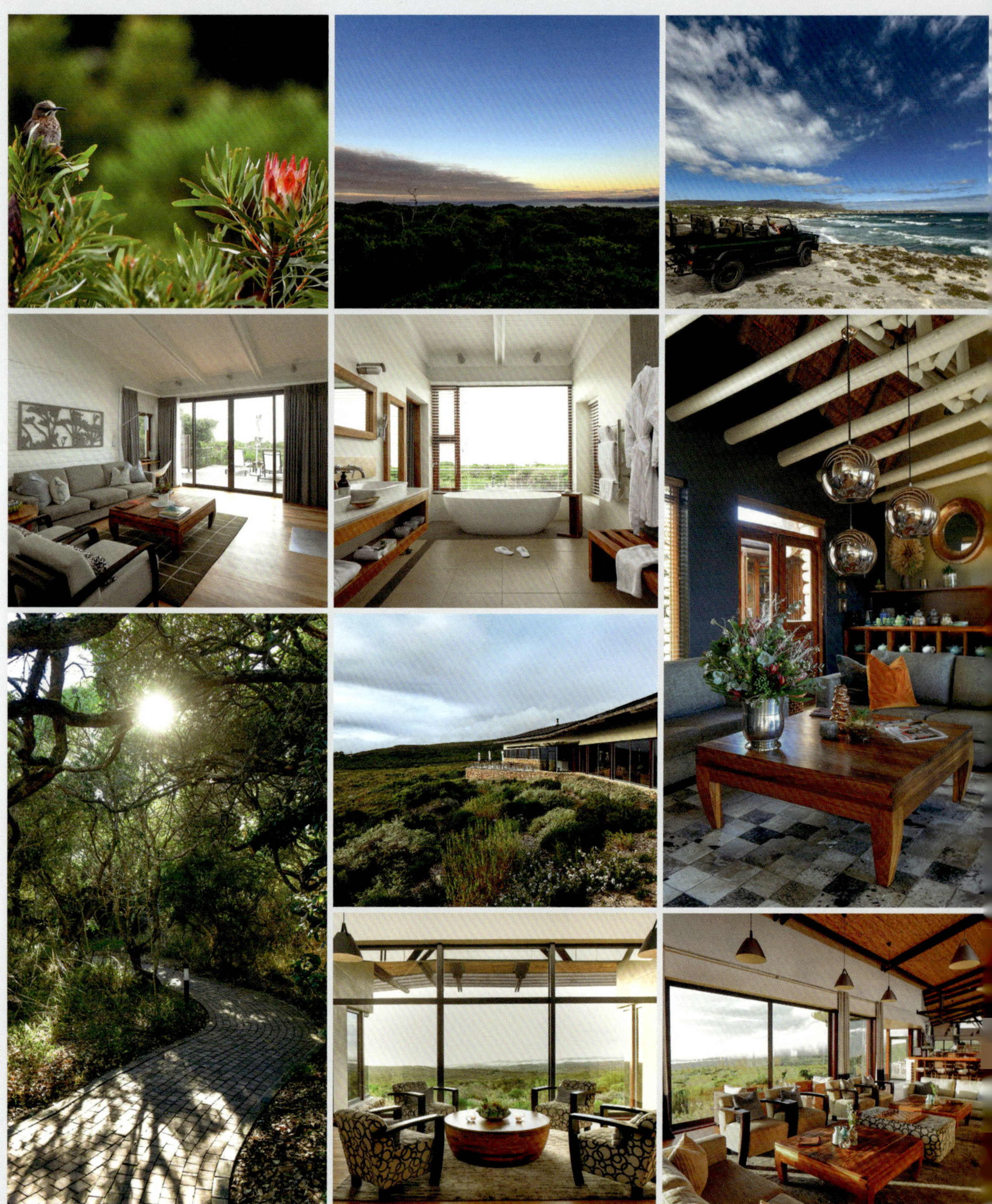

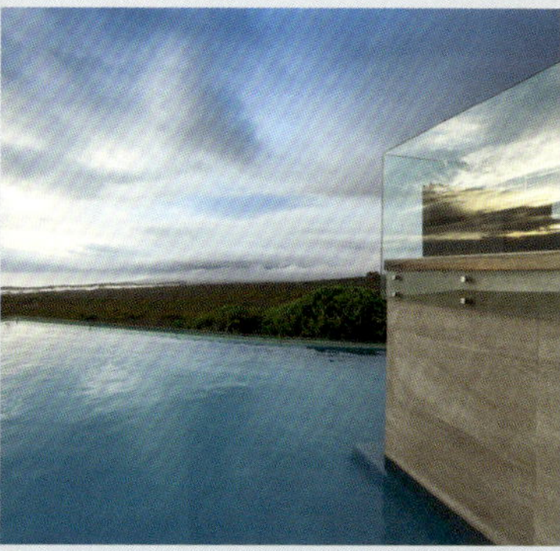

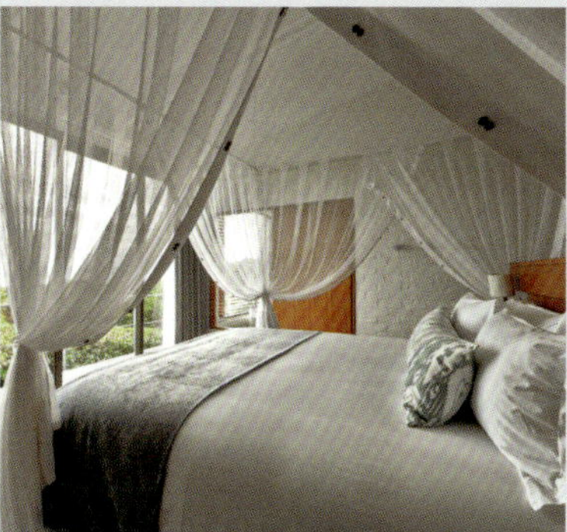

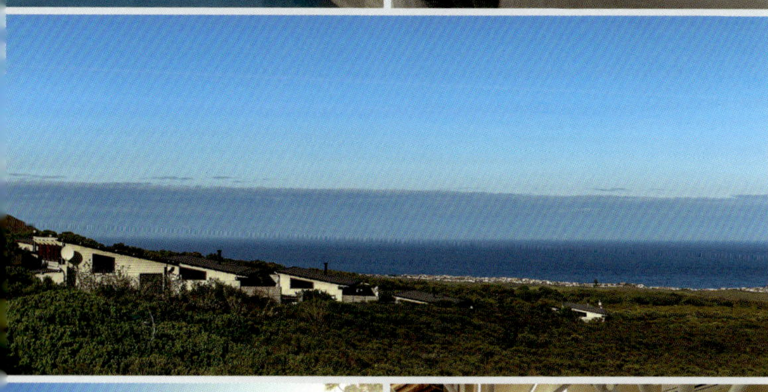

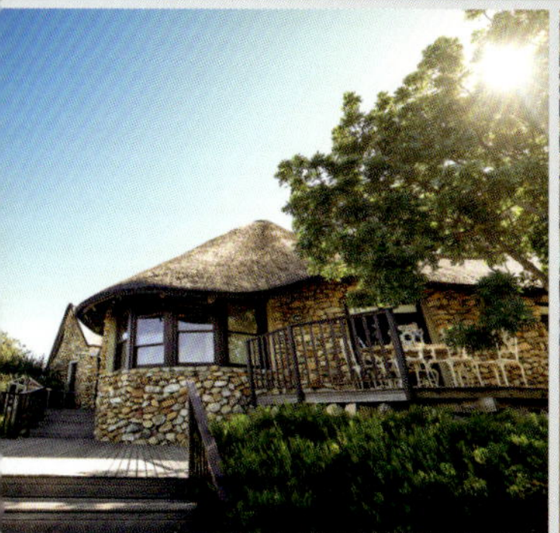

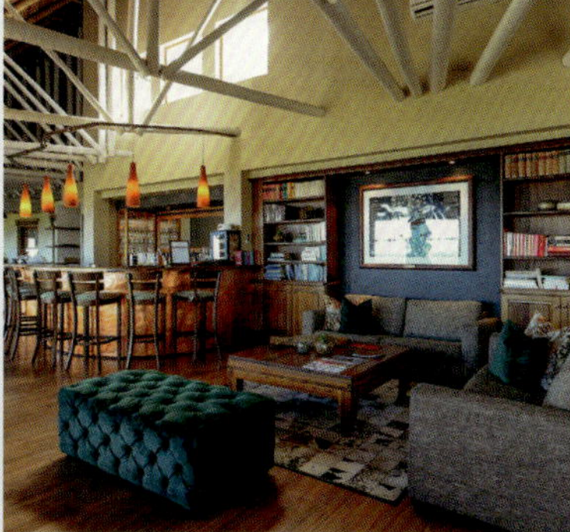

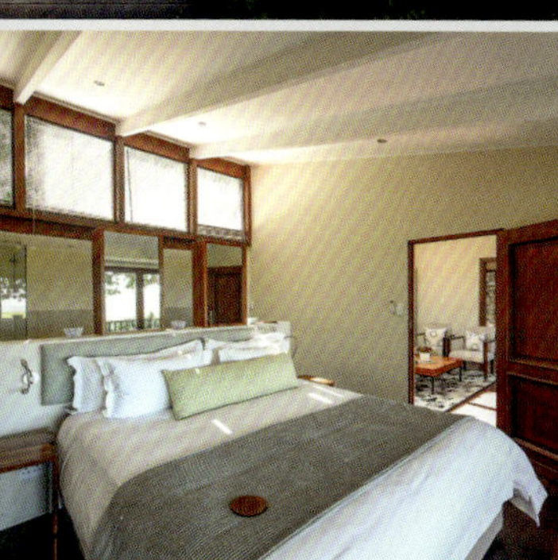

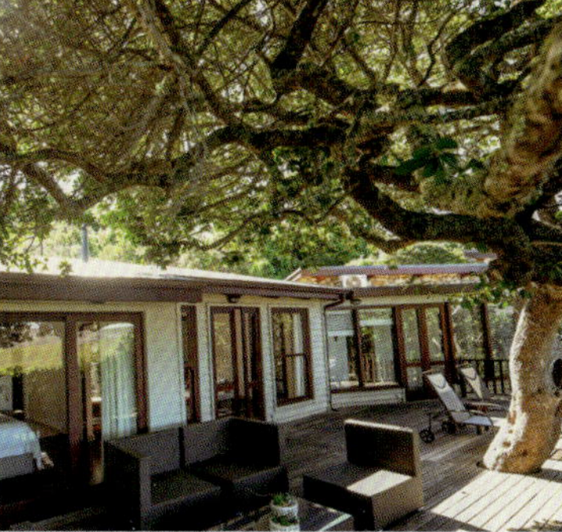

Lodge
Luxury in harmony with nature: Grootbos Private Nature Reserve is nestled between the mountains and the sea. The name *Grootbos* in Afrikaans means "big forest" and can be traced back to the old Milkwood forest on the site. The exclusive accommodations offer breathtaking views over the fynbos-covered plain towards the sparkling Walker Bay.

Lodge
Le luxe en harmonie avec la nature : la réserve naturelle privée de Grootbos est lovée entre les montagnes et la mer. En afrikaans, le nom Grootbos signifie « grande forêt » et renvoie à la forêt ancienne de Milkwoods (Sideroxylon inerme) située sur le terrain. Ces lodges très haut de gamme offrent une vue époustouflante sur les vastes étendues de *fynbos* et l'étincelante baie de Walker.

Lodge
Luxus in Harmonie mit der Natur: Eingebettet zwischen Berge und Meer liegt das Grootbos Private Nature Reserve. Der Name Grootbos bedeutet auf Afrikaans „großer Wald" und ist auf den alten Milkwood Wald auf dem Gelände zurückzuführen. Die exklusiven Unterkünfte bieten eine atemberaubende Aussicht über die mit Fynbos bewachsene Ebene bis hin zur funkelnden Walker Bay.

Lodge
Lujo en armonía con la naturaleza: el Parque Natural Privado de Grootbos está enclavado entre las montañas y el mar. El nombre Grootbos significa "gran bosque" en afrikáans y su nombre se debe al antiguo bosque de Milkwooddel lugar. Los exclusivos alojamientos ofrecen impresionantes vistas sobre la llanura cubierta de fynbos y la chispeante Bahía Walker.

Lodge
Lusso in armonia con la natura: la "Grootbos Private Nature Reserve" è incastonata tra le montagne e il mare. Il nome Grootbos significa "grande foresta" in afrikaans e può essere fatta risalire alla vecchia Milkwood Wald presente latte sul sito. Gli esclusivi alloggi offrono una vista mozzafiato sulla pianura ricoperta di fynbo e sulla luminosa Walker Bay.

Lodge
Luxe in harmonie met de natuur: het Grootbos Private Nature Reserve ligt tussen bergen en zee. De naam Grootbos is terug te voeren op het oude Melkbos op het terrein. De exclusieve accommodaties bieden een adembenemend uitzicht over de met *fynbos* begroeide vlakte tot aan het sprankelende Walker Bay.

Garden Route & Port Elizabeth, South Africa

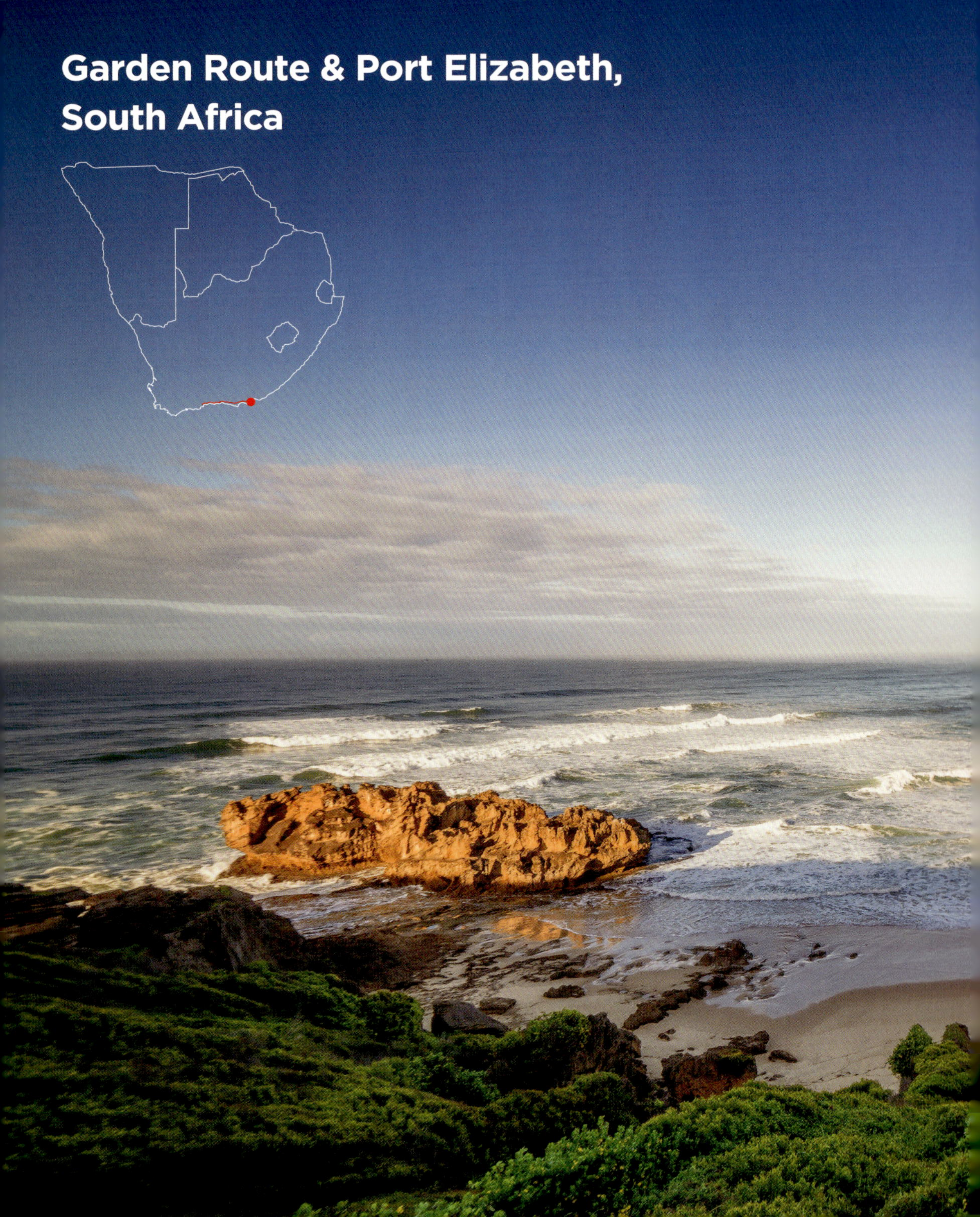

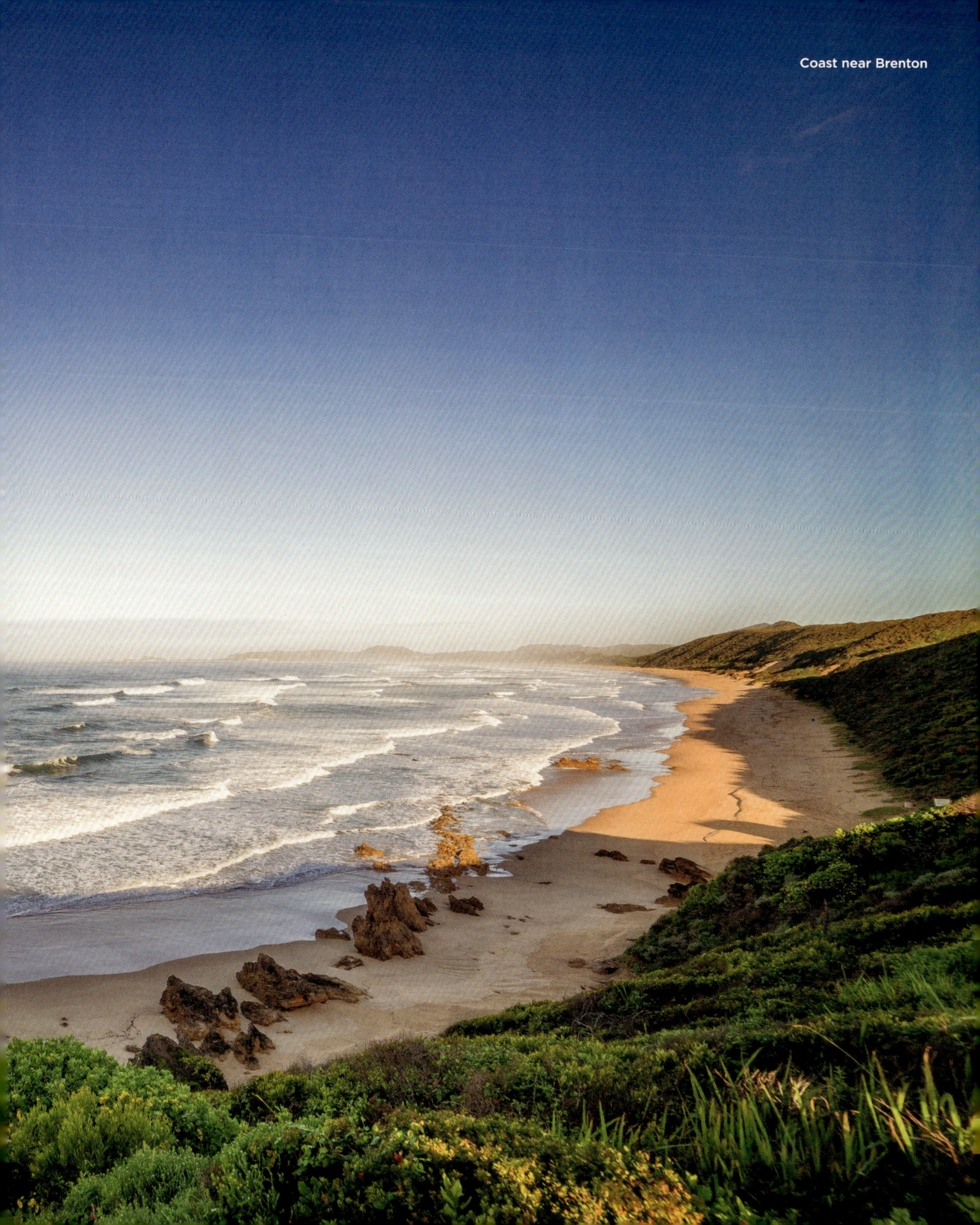

Coast near Brenton

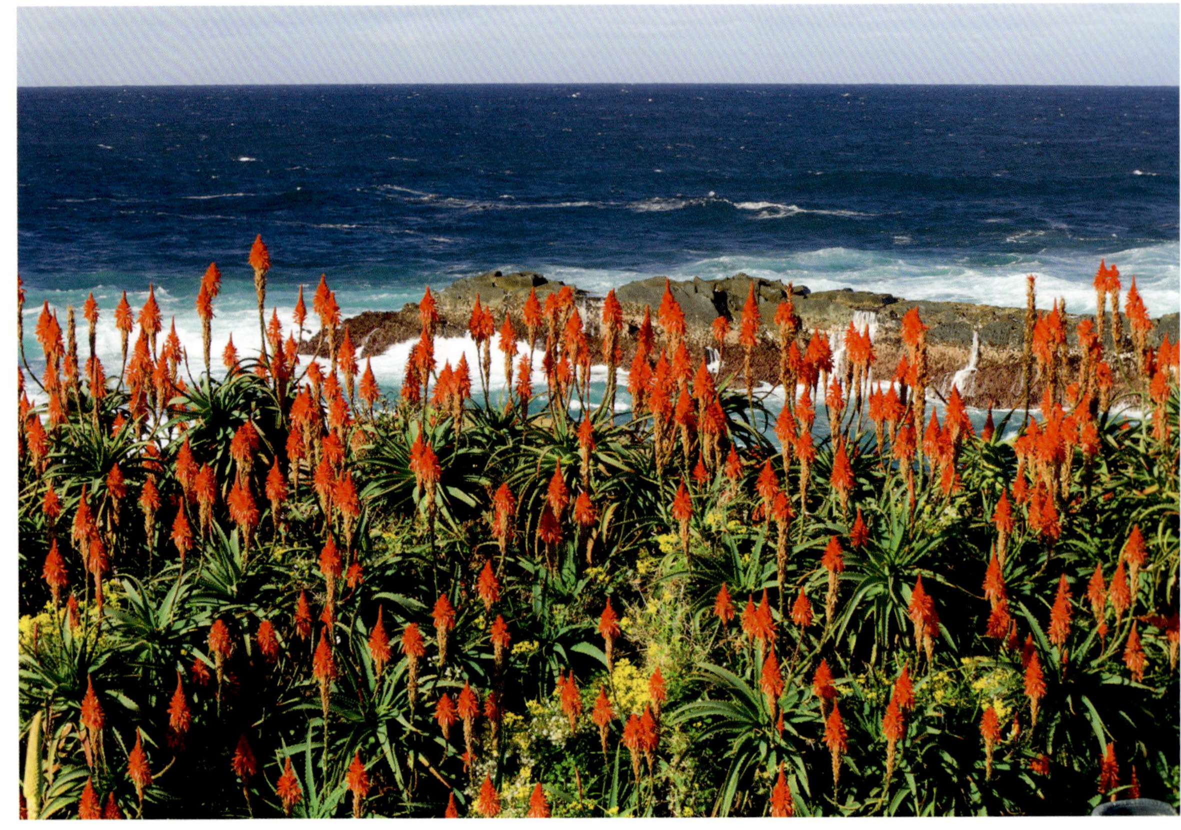

Krantz aloe, Garden Route National Park

Garden Route
The Garden Route follows the coast of the Western Cape and opens up its hinterland. The diversity of the landscape is immense: bays, lagoons, rocky coasts, forests, and hillsides. The Garden Route National Park, which stretches along the coast of the Indian Ocean, was formed by the merger of Wilderness National Park, Knysna National Lake Area, and Tsitsikamma National Park.

Garden Route
La Garden Route suit le littoral du Cap-Ouest et fait découvrir son arrière-pays. Les paysages se révèlent d'une diversité fabuleuse, entre les baies, les lagunes, les falaises côtières, les forêts et les collines. Le parc national de Garden Route, qui longe la côte de l'océan Indien, résulte de la fusion entre le Wilderness National Park, le Knysna National Lake Area et le parc national de Tsitsikamma.

Garden Route
Die Garden Route folgt der Küste des Westkaps und erschließt deren Hinterland. Die landschaftliche Vielfalt ist immens: Buchten, Lagunen, Felsküsten, Wälder, Hügelland. Der Garden-Route-Nationalpark, der sich entlang der Küste des Indischen Ozeans erstreckt, entstand durch die Zusammenlegung des Wilderness National Parks, der Knysna National Lake Area und des Tsitsikamma-Nationalparks.

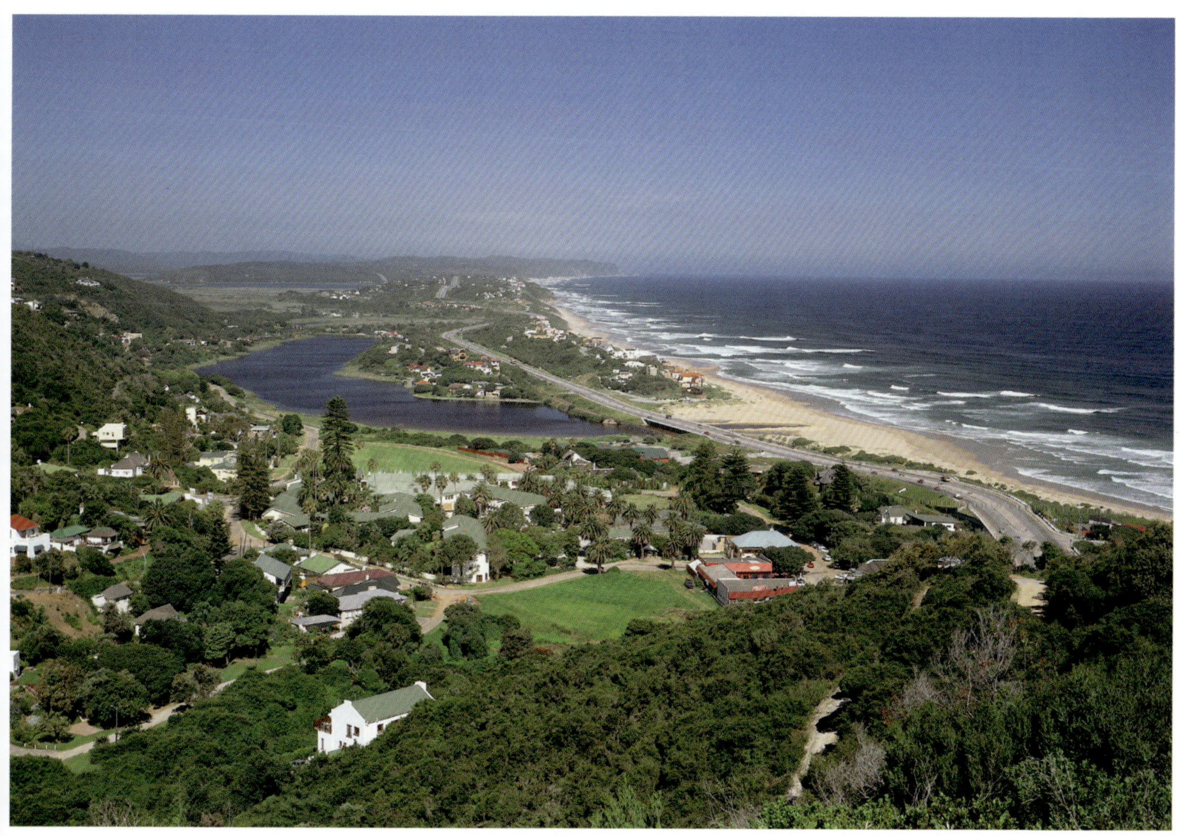

Wilderness

Ruta Jardín
La Ruta Jardín sigue la costa del Cabo Occidental y abre su zona de influencia. La diversidad del paisaje es inmensa: bahías, lagunas, acantilados, bosques, colinas. El Parque Nacional Ruta Jardín, que se extiende a lo largo de la costa del Océano Índico, fue creado por la fusión del Parque Nacional de Wilderness, el Área Nacional Lago Knysna y el Parque Nacional Tsitsikamma.

Garden Route
La Garden Route segue la costa del Capo Occidentale, rendendo accessibile l'entroterra. La sua ricchezza paesaggistica è enorme: baie, lagune, coste rocciose, boschi, colline.Il Parco Nazionale di Garden Route, che si estende lungo la costa dell'Oceano Indiano, è nato dalla fusione del Wilderness National Park, della zona dei laghi di Knysna e del parco nazionale di Tsitsikamma.

Garden Route
De Garden Route loopt langs de kust van West-Kaap en ontsluit het binnenland van deze provincie. Het landschap is hier zeer veelzijdig: baaien, lagunes, rotskusten, bossen en heuvelland. Het Garden Route National Park, dat zich langs de kust van de Indische Oceaan uitstrekt, ontstond door de samenvoeging van het Wilderness National Park, de Knysna National Lake Area en het Nationale Park Tsitsikamma.

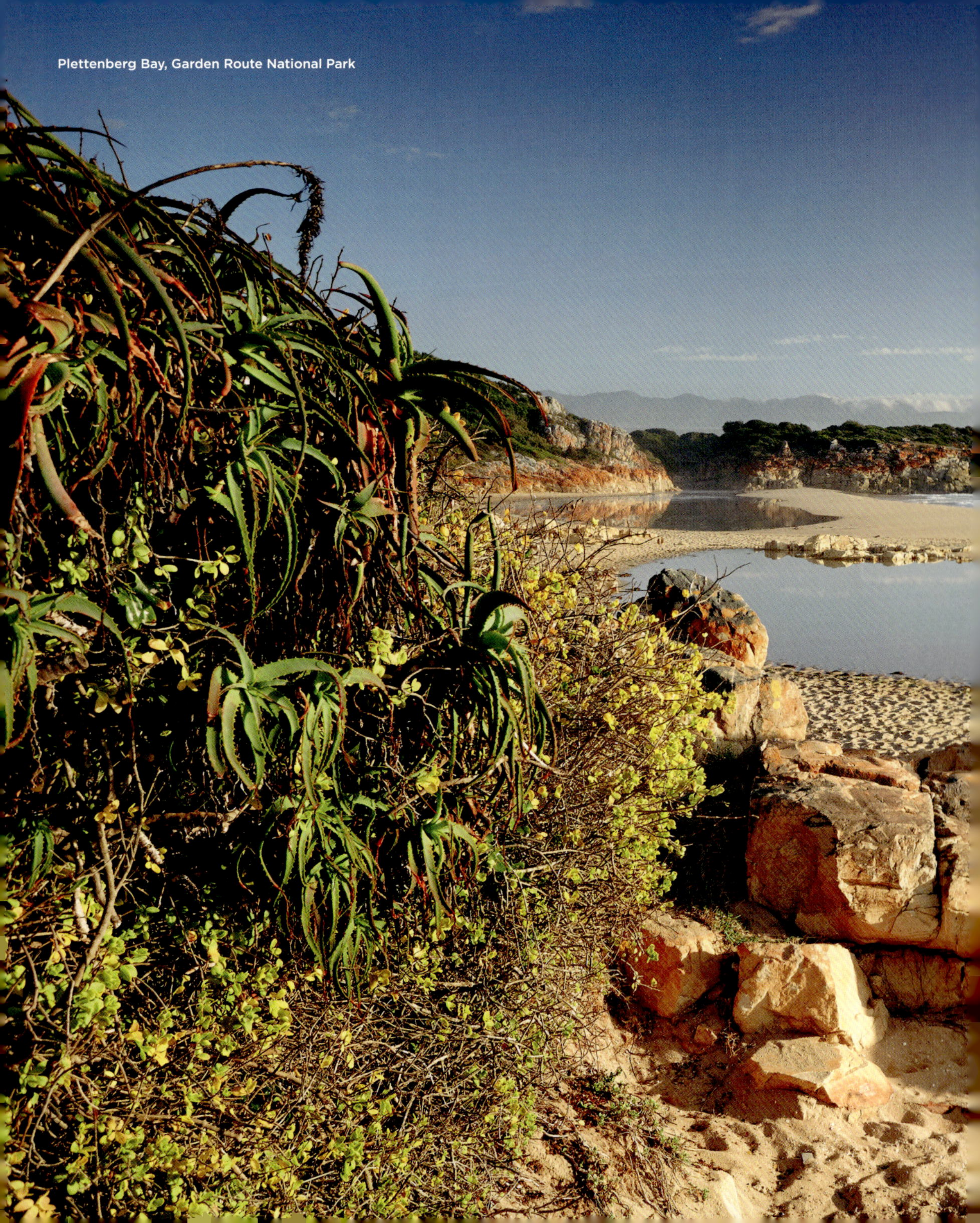
Plettenberg Bay, Garden Route National Park

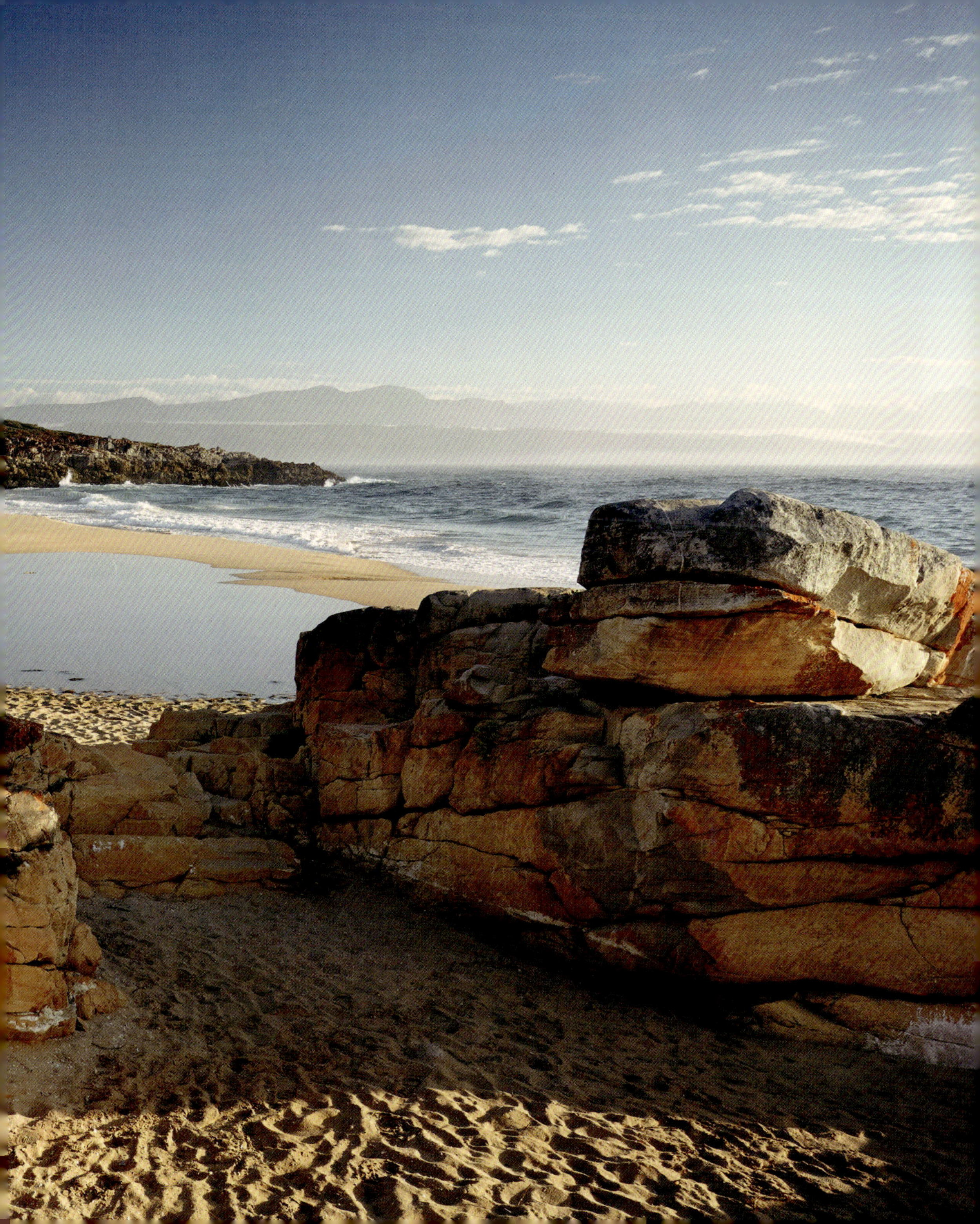

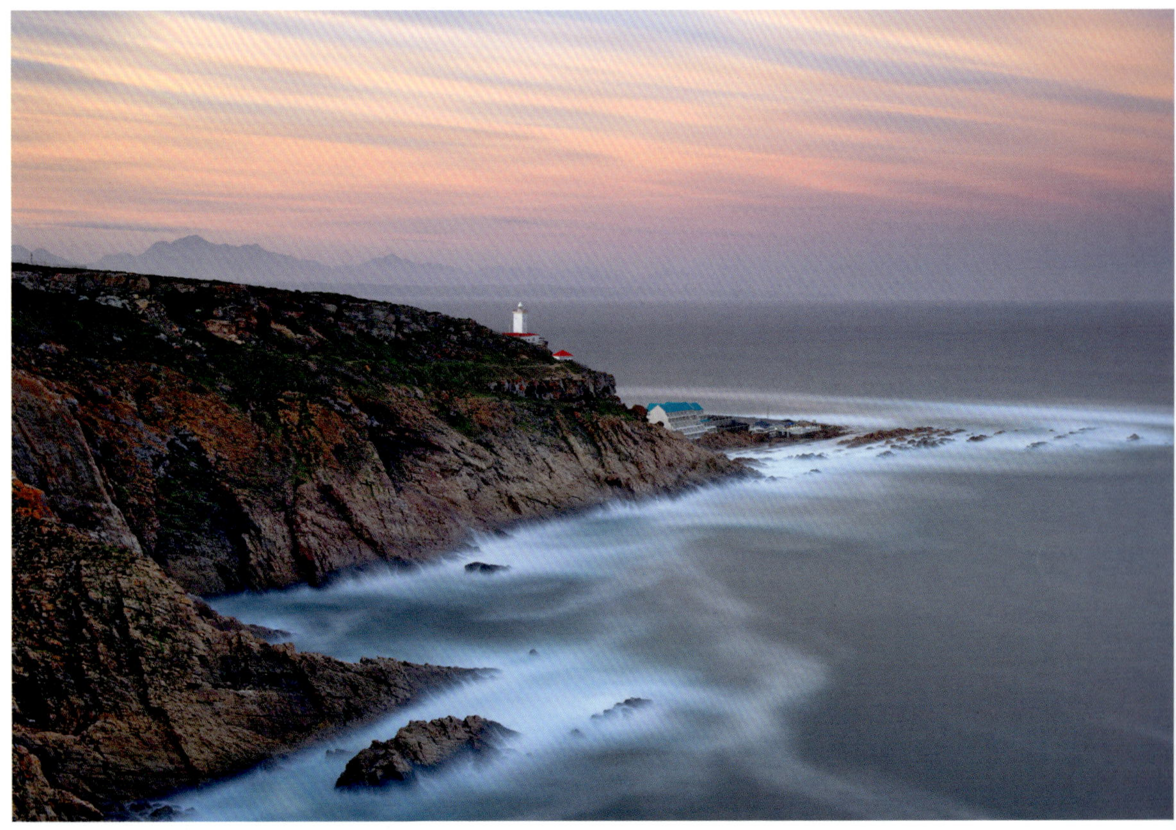

Cape St Blaize Lighthouse, Mossel Bay

Mossel Bay
Since 1864, Cape St Blaize Lighthouse has been guarding Mossel Bay, warning passing ships of the rough rocks which lie just off the sandy beaches of the town bearing the same name. The lighthouse was named by Vasco da Gama after landing at Mossel Bay in 1497 on February 3, the name day of St Blaise.

Mossel Bay
Depuis 1864 le phare du cap Saint-Blaise veille sur la ville de Mossel Bay et sa baie. Il met en garde les navires de passage, qui ne devraient pas se laisser induire en erreur par les jolies plages de sable de Mossel Bay. De terribles écueils les guettent sous l'eau. En 1497, Vasco da Gama jeta l'ancre dans la baie le jour de la Saint-Blaise, ce qui explique le nom du phare.

Mossel Bay
Seit 1864 wacht Cape St Blaize Lighthouse über Stadt und Bucht Mossel Bay und warnt die vorüberfahrenden Schiffe: So anmutig die sandigen Strände von Mossel Bay auch wirken mögen, unter Wasser lauern raue Felsen. Benannt wurde der Leuchtturm nach dem hl. Blasius. An dessen Namenstag landete Vasco da Gama 1497 in der Mossel Bay.

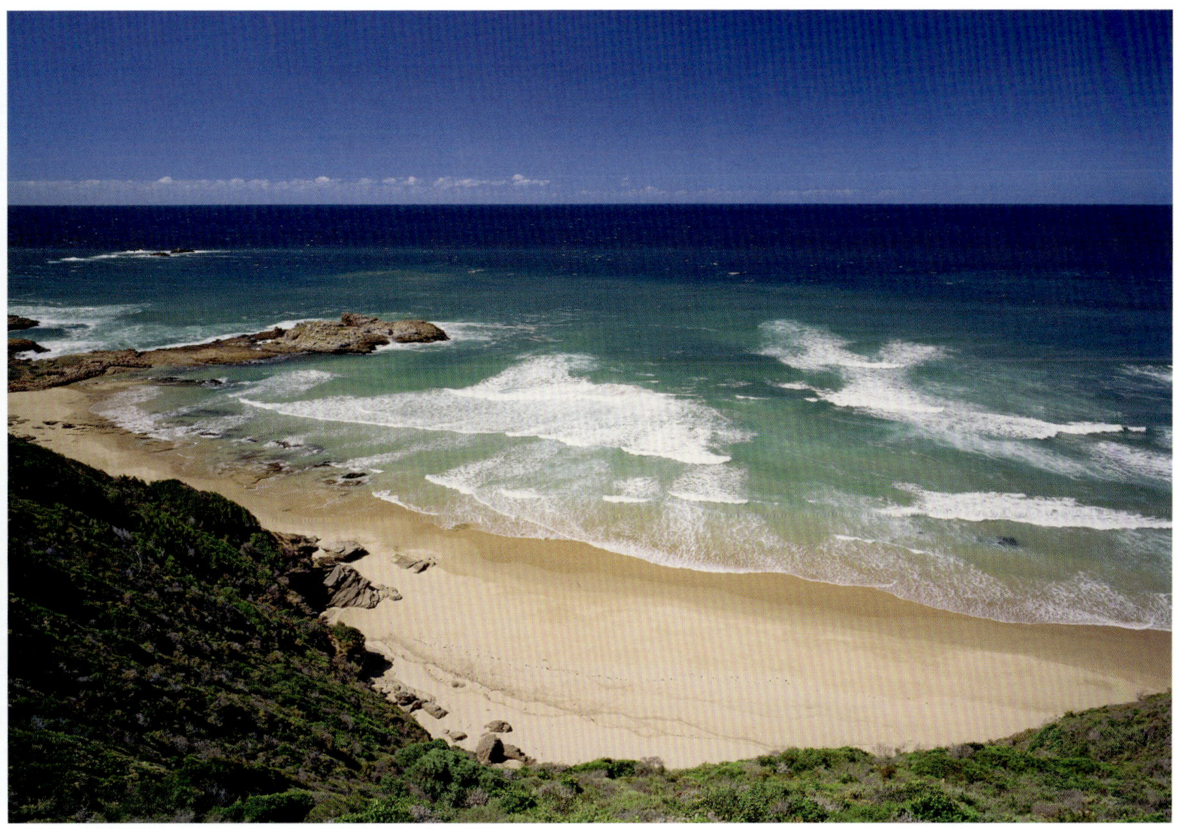

Beach of Brenton-on-Sea

Bahía de Mossel
Desde 1864 el faro de Cabo Saint Blaize vigila la ciudad y la bahía de Mossel y advierte a los barcos: bajo las encantadoras playas de Mossel Bay están las rocas al acecho bajo el agua. Su nombre procede de San Blas. En ese día desembarcó Vasco de Gama en la bahía de Mossel en 1497.

Baia di Mossel
Dal 1864 il faro di Capo St Blaize veglia sulla città e sulla baia di Mossel e avverte le navi che passano di lì: per quanto le spiagge sabbiose della baia di Mossel siano così graziose, sotto l'acqua sono in agguato rocce ruvide. Il faro ha preso il nome da San Biagio. Nel 1497 Vasco da Gama arrivò nella baia di Mossel nel giorno del santo.

Mosselbaai
Sinds 1864 waakt de vuurtoren van Kaap Sint-Blasius over de Mosselbaai en het gelijknamige havenstadje. Het baken waarschuwt voorbijvarende schepen, want de aangename zandstranden van Mosselbaai doen niet vermoeden dat onder het wateroppervlak scherpe rotsen op de loer liggen. De vuurtoren werd vernoemd naar de heilige Sint – Blasius op wiens naamdag Vasco da Gama hier in 1497 aan land ging.

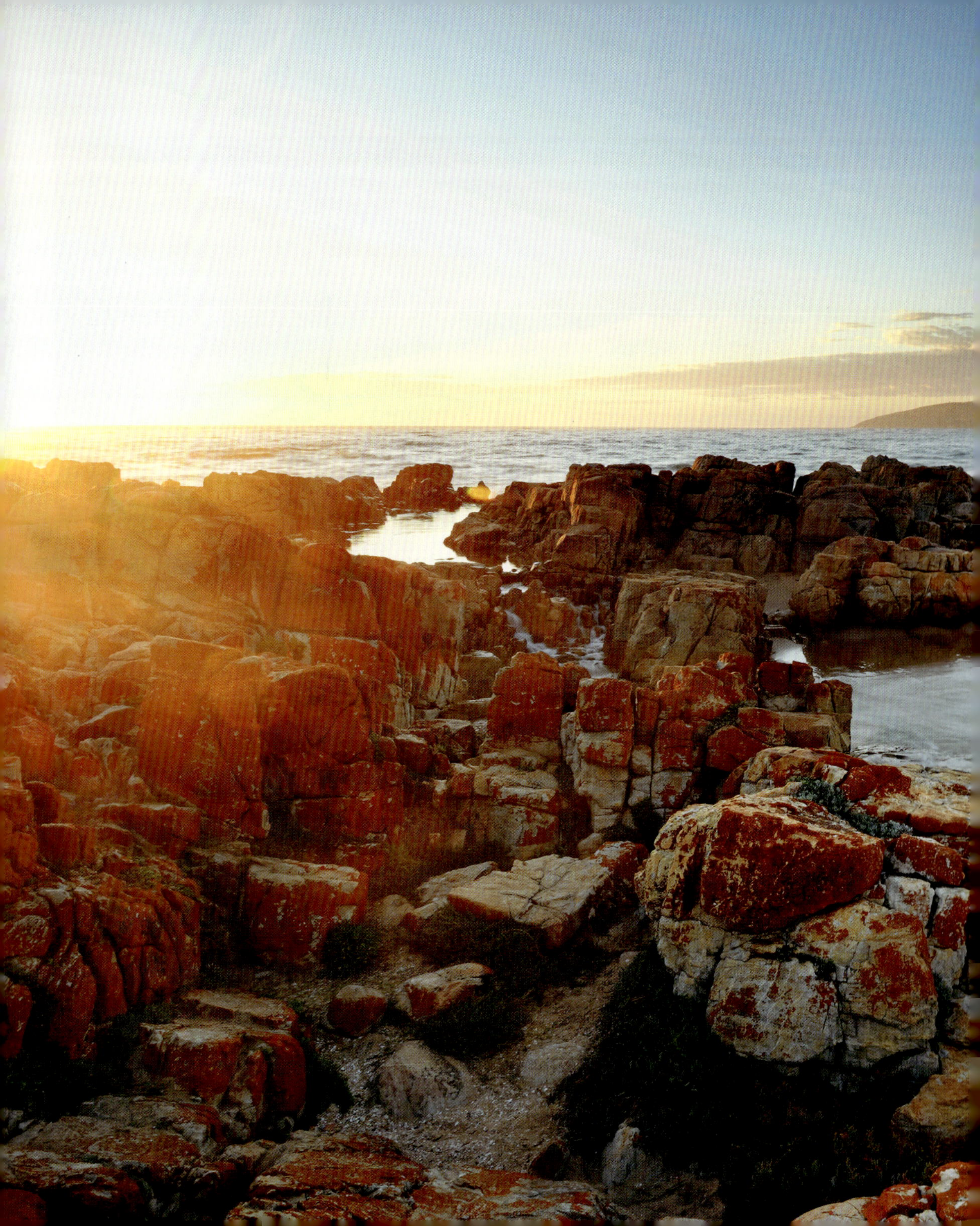

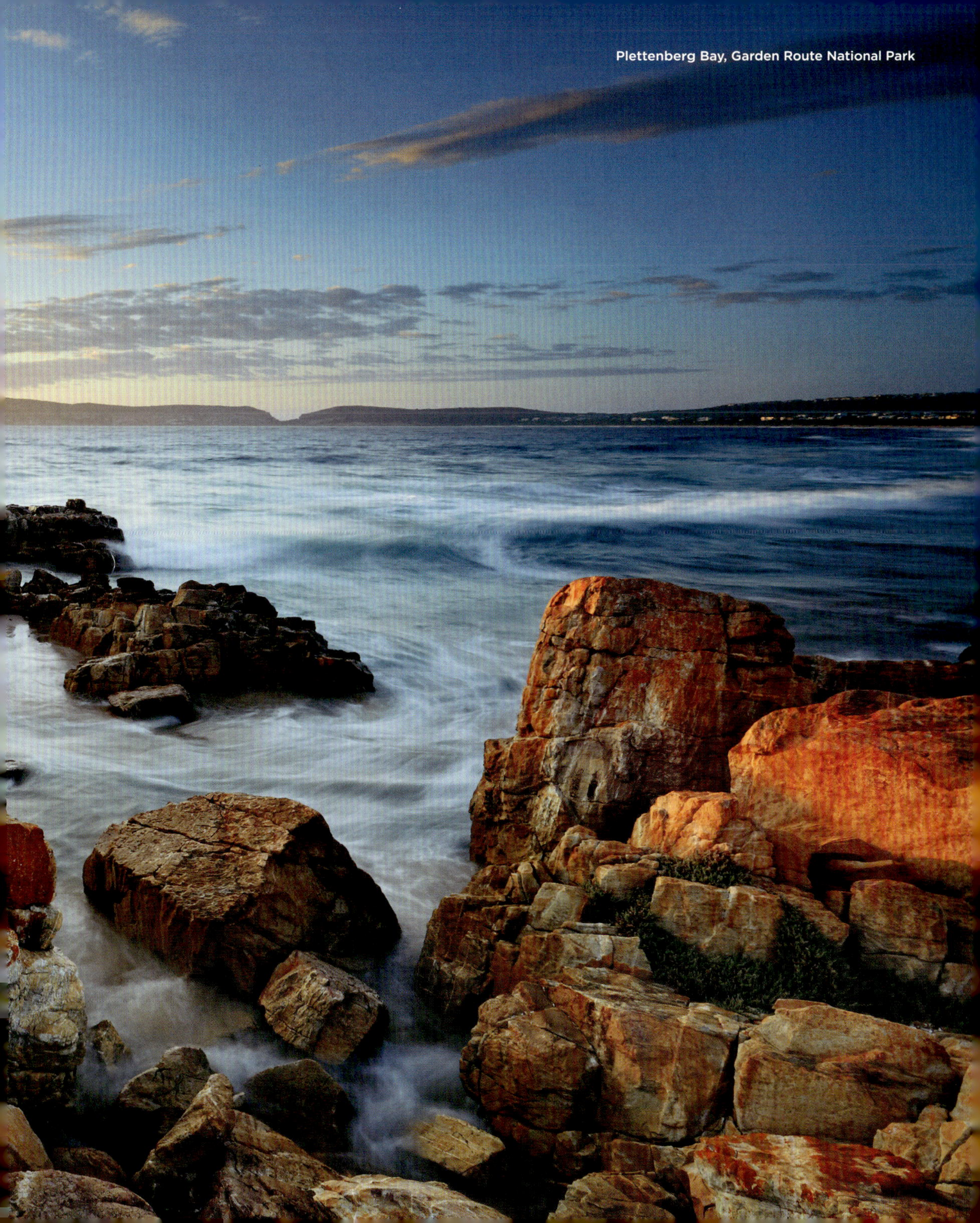
Plettenberg Bay, Garden Route National Park

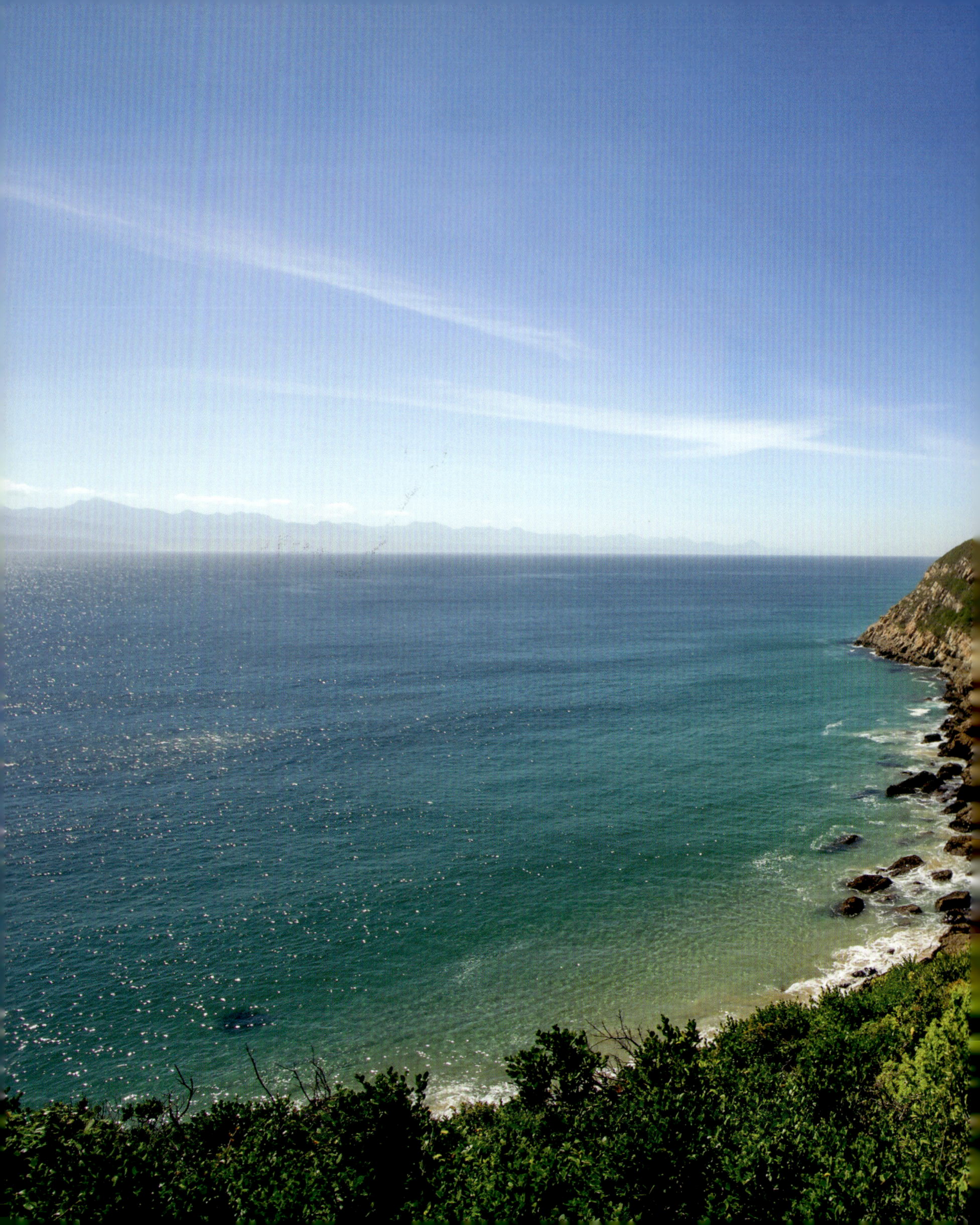

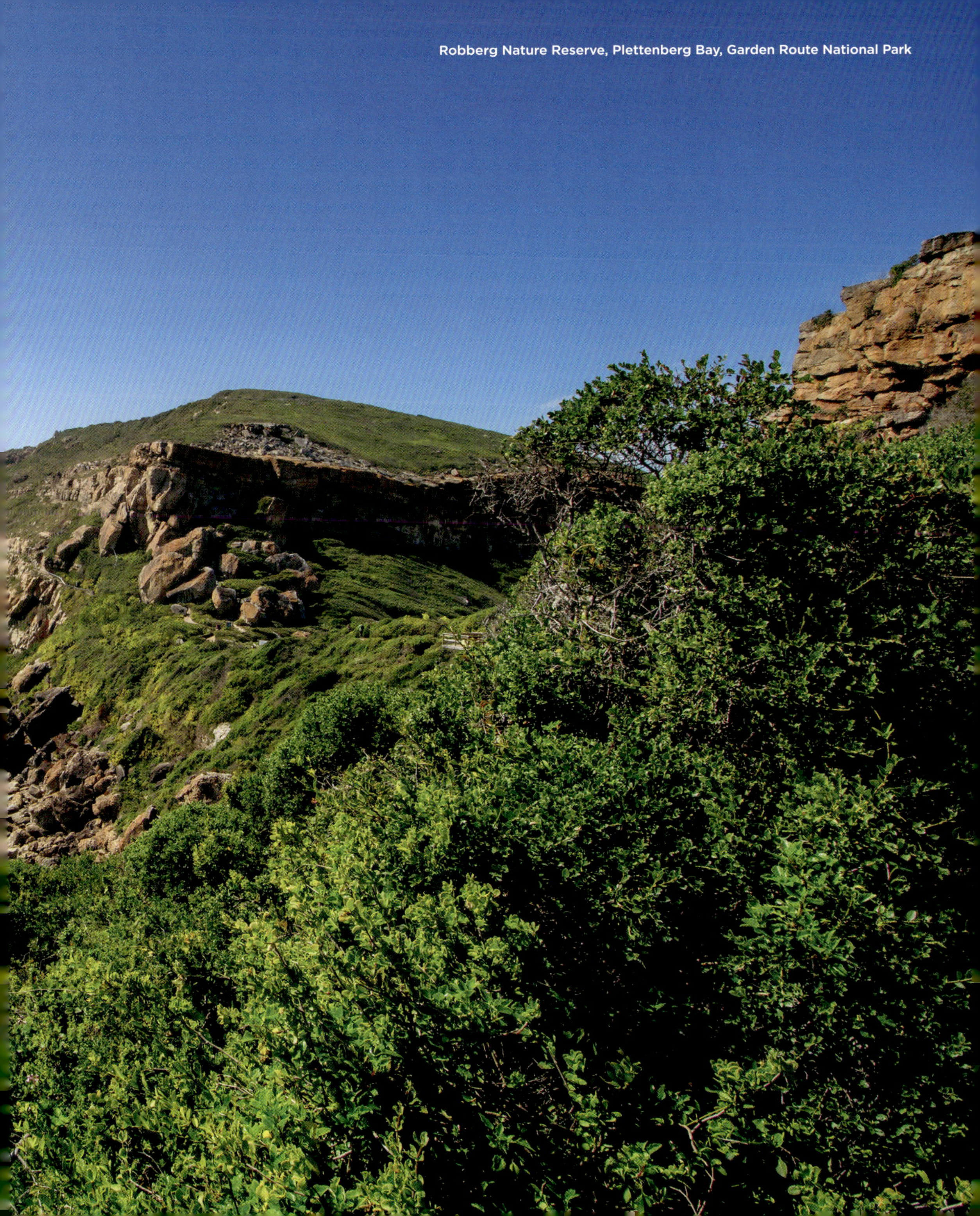
Robberg Nature Reserve, Plettenberg Bay, Garden Route National Park

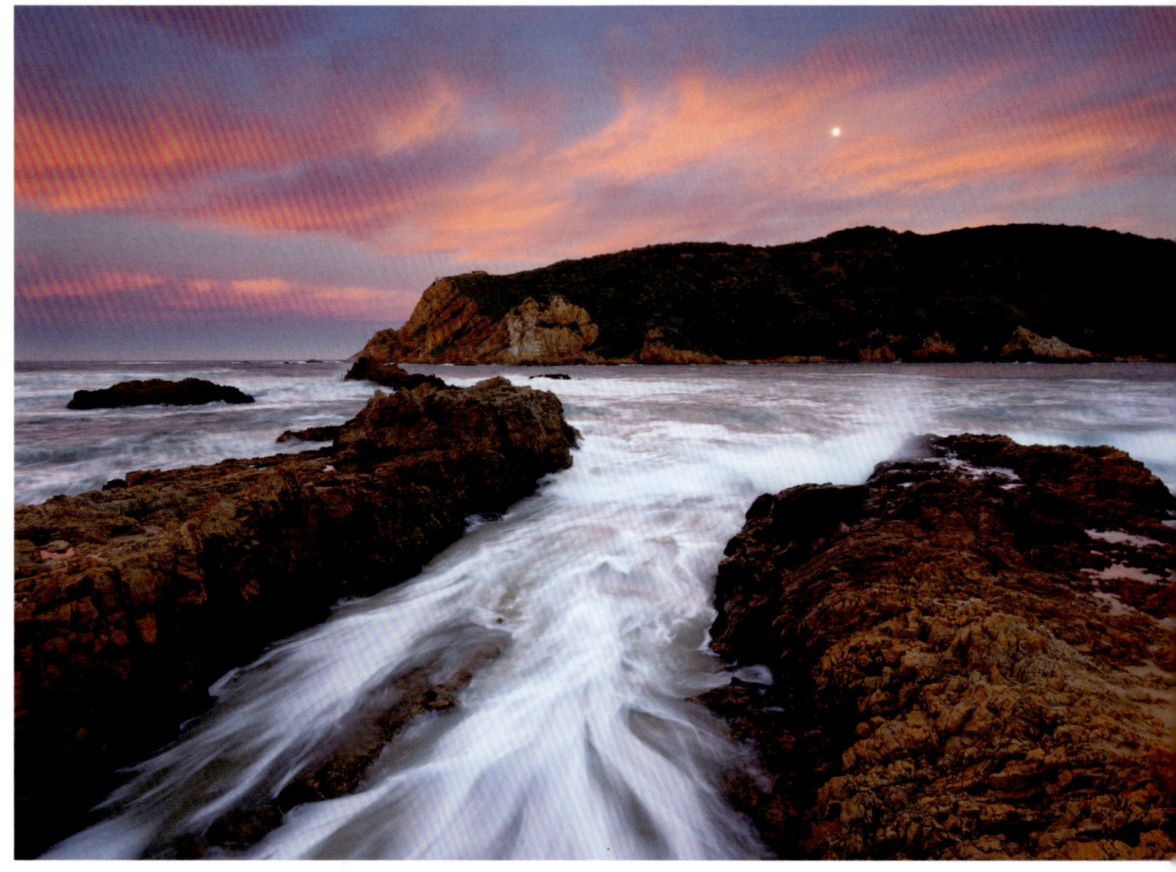

Knysna Heads, Garden Route National Park

Knysna Heads
Two sandstone cliffs known as the Knysna Heads line the entrance from the Indian Ocean into the lagoon where the coastal town of Knysna lies. For seafarers, passing through this narrow, rocky passage is challenging and is, in fact, considered one of the most dangerous passages in the world. Insurance companies even decline coverage for any damage caused to ships trying to pass through this southern *Scylla* and *Charybdis.*

Knysna Heads
Les Knysna Heads sont deux falaises de grès qui bordent le passage entre l'océan Indien et le lagon sur les rives duquel s'est implantée la ville de Knysna. Pour les marins, c'est un redoutable défi. Ce détroit est considéré comme l'un des plus dangereux du monde. Les assureurs déclinent toute responsabilité vis-à-vis des avaries subies ici par les navires.

Knysna Heads
Zwei Sandsteinklippen, die Knysna Heads, säumen den Zugang vom Indischen Ozean in die Lagune, an deren Ufer der Ort Knysna liegt. Für Seefahrer stellt die Fahrt durch die schmale felsige Passage eine Herausforderung dar. Die Einfahrt gilt als eine der gefährlichsten der Welt. Versicherungen übernehmen keine Haftung, wenn hier ein Schiff zu Schaden kommt.

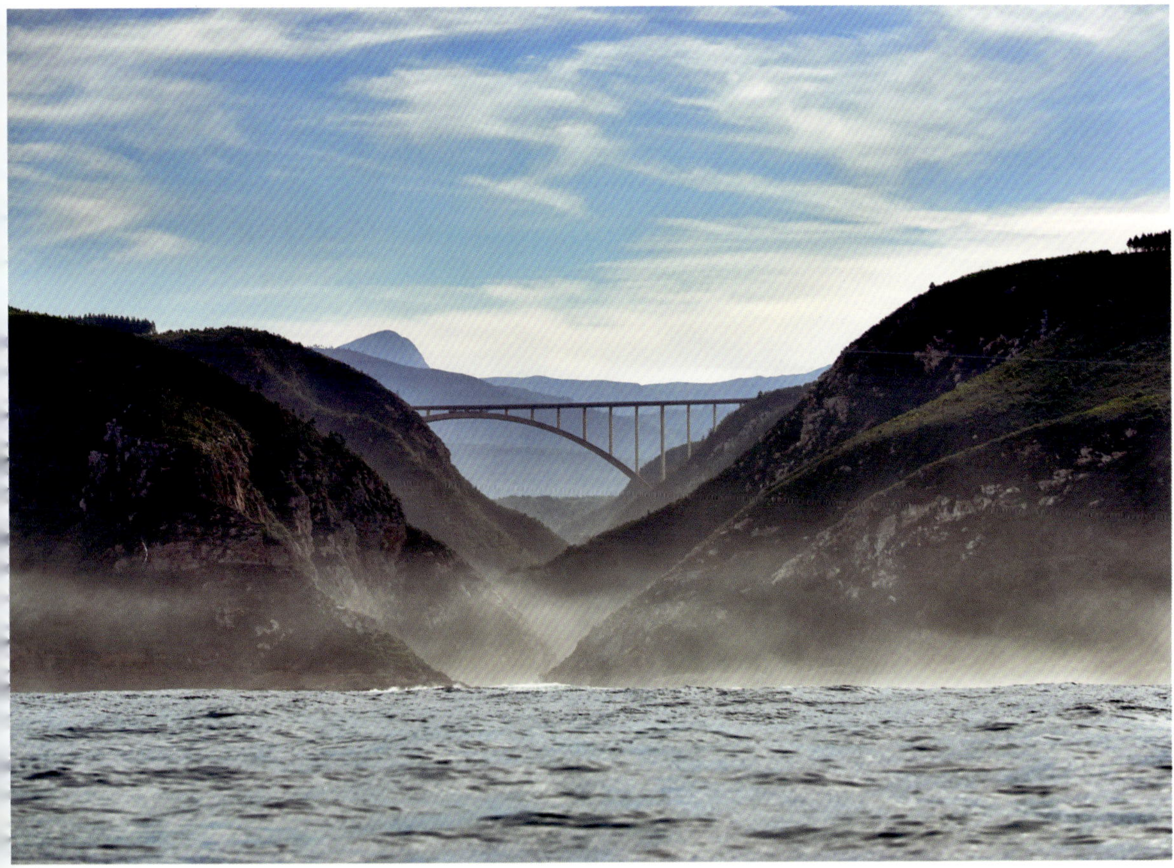

Bloukrans Bridge, Plettenberg Bay, Garden Route National Park

Knysna Heads
Dos acantilados de arenisca, los Knysna Heads, revisten el acceso desde el Océano Índico a la laguna,
en cuyas orillas se sitúa la población de Knysna. El trayecto a través del estrecho paso rocoso es todo un desafío para los marineros. La entrada está considerada como una de las más peligrosas en el mundo. Los seguros no asumen ninguna responsabilidad cuando los barcos sufren daños aquí.

Knysna Heads
I Knysna Heads, due scogli di pietra arenaria, fiancheggiano l'accesso dall'oceano Indiano nella laguna, sulle cui rive si trova la località di Knysna. Per i navigatori il viaggio attraverso lo stresso passaggio roccioso rappresenta una sfida, in quanto l'ingresso è considerato uno dei più pericolosi al mondo. Le compagnie di assicurazione non si assumono responsabilità se qui una nave viene danneggiata.

Knysna Heads
De twee zandsteenklippen Knysna Heads flankeren de toegang vanaf de Indische Oceaan naar een lagune, met aan de oever het plaatsje Knysna. Voor zeelieden is de passage door de smalle geul tussen de klippen een uitdaging: de ingang wordt als een van de gevaarlijkste ter wereld beschouwd en geen verzekering wil eventuele schade tijdens deze vaart vergoeden.

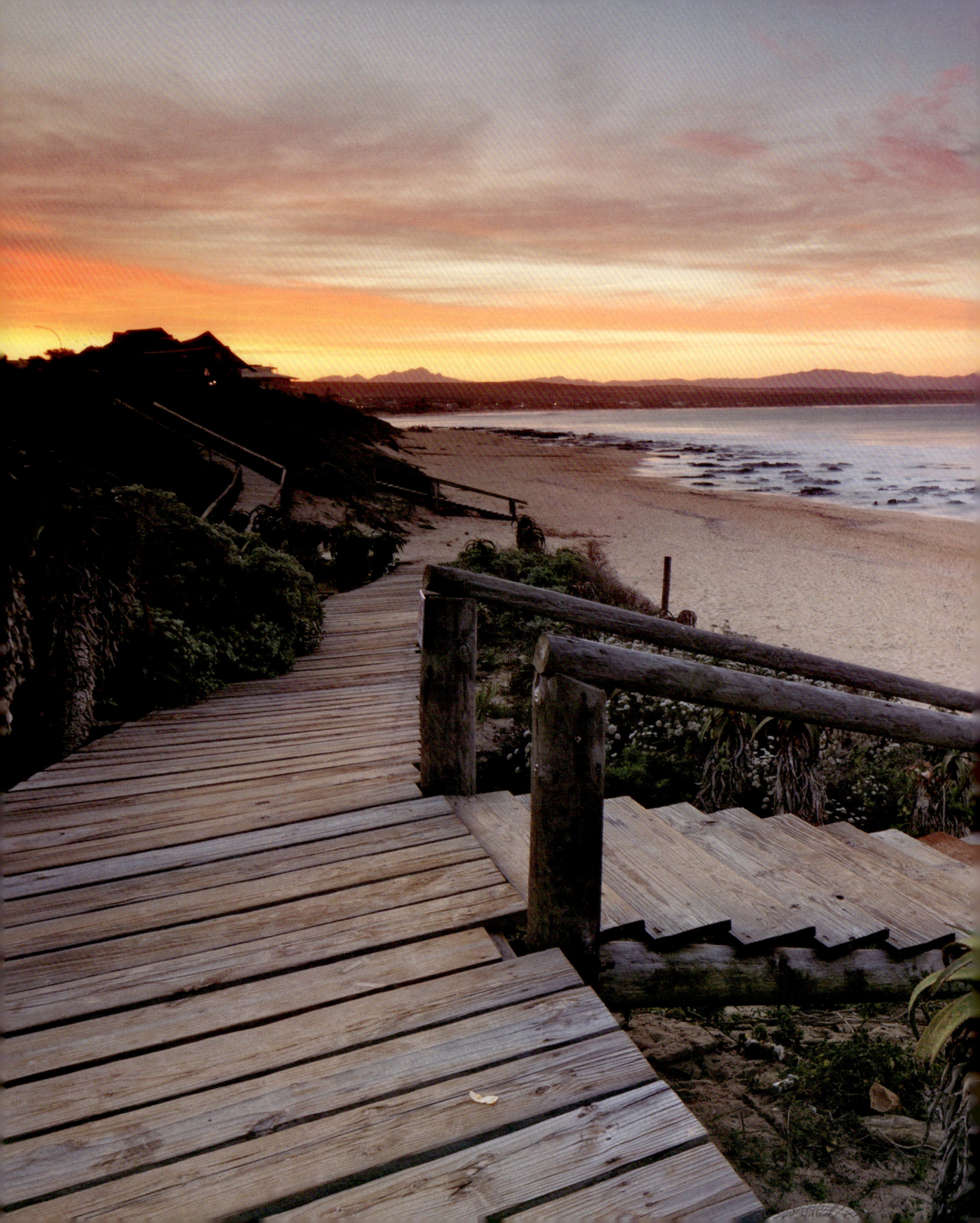

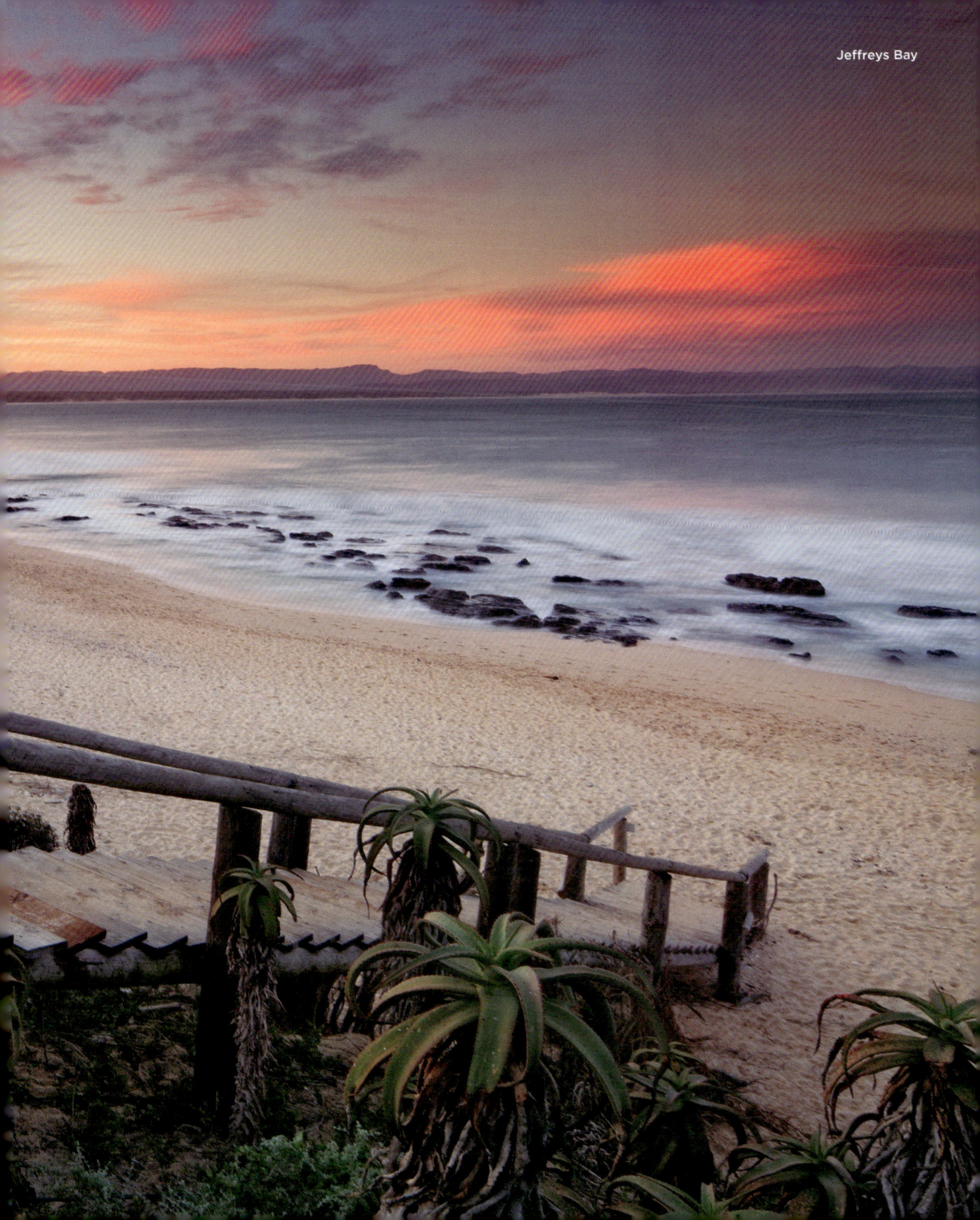
Jeffreys Bay

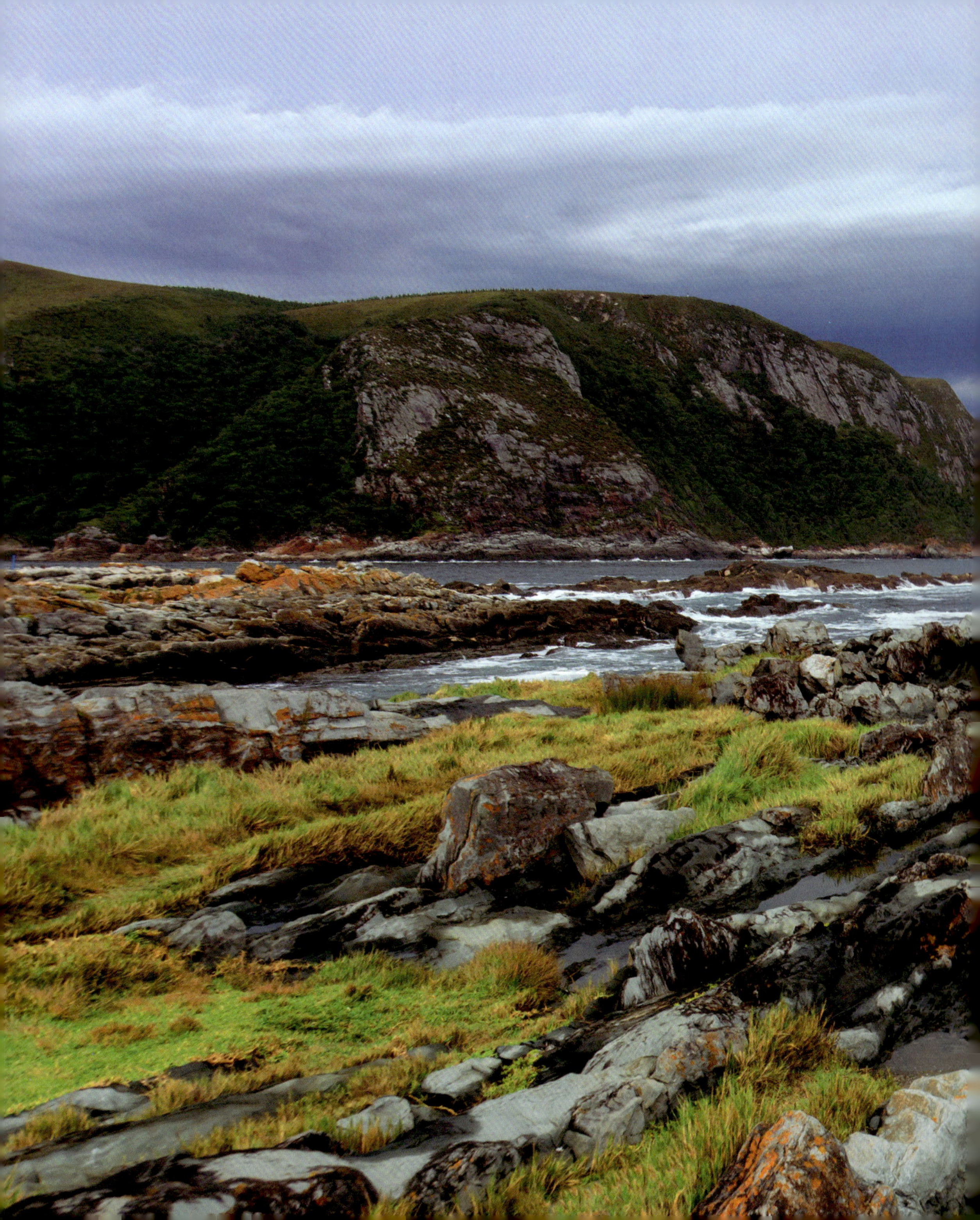

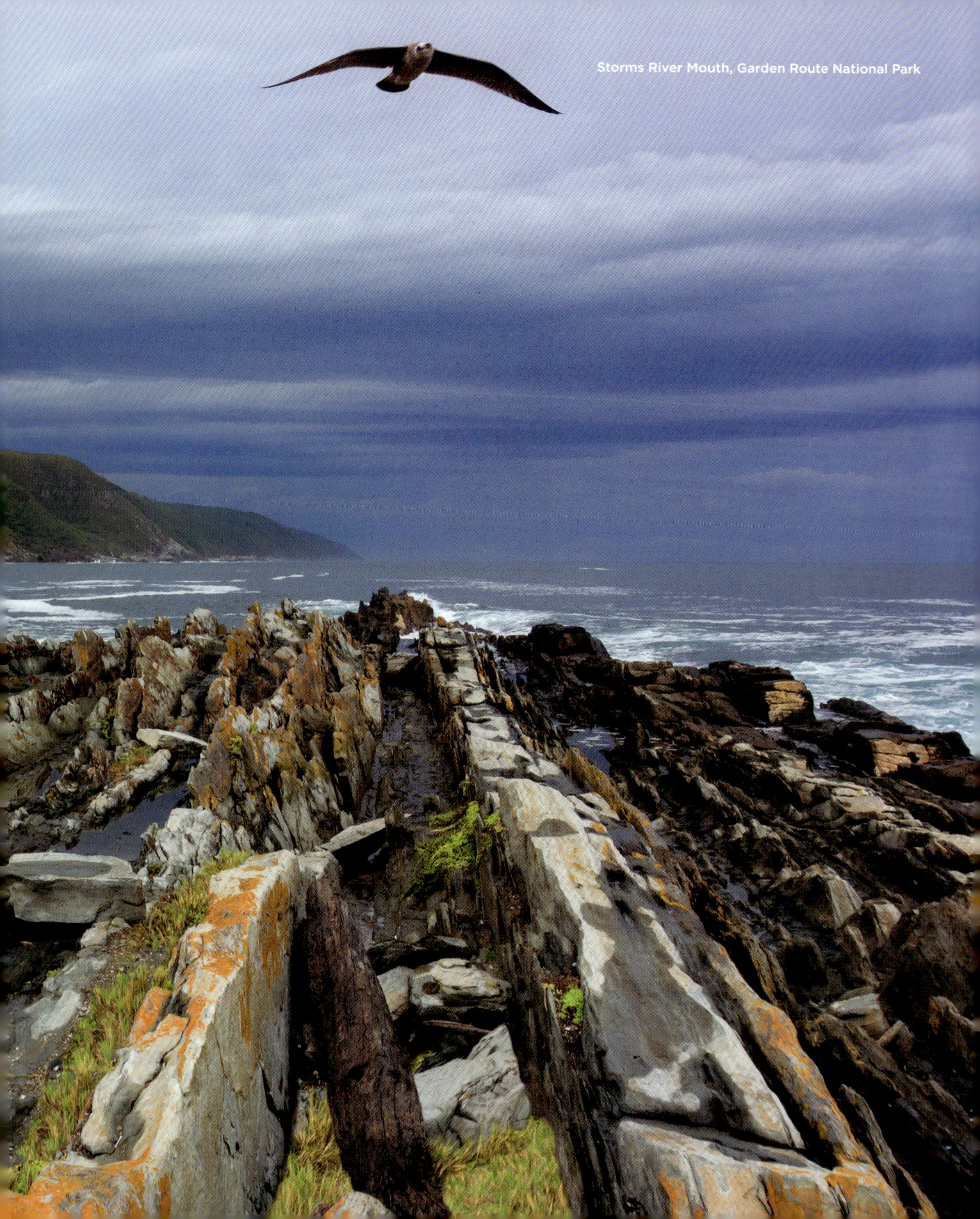
Storms River Mouth, Garden Route National Park

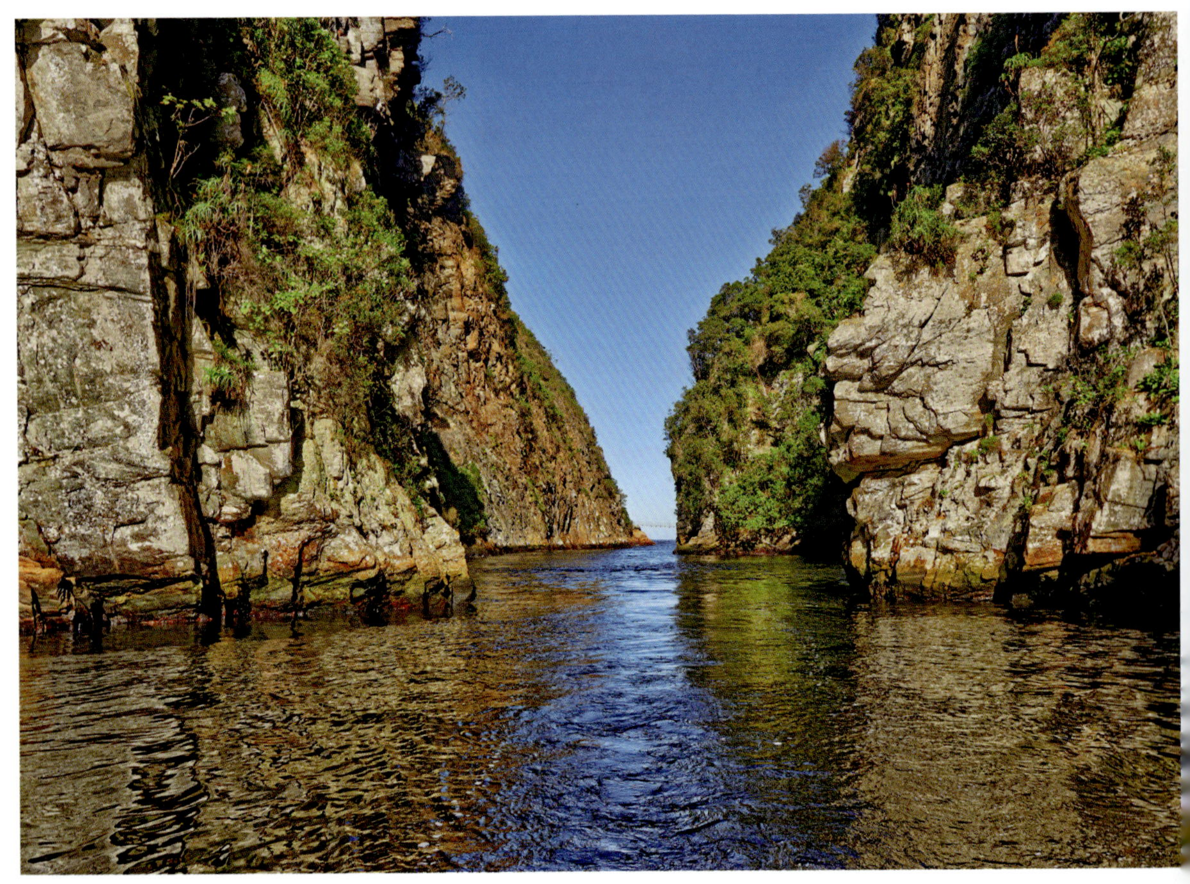

Storms River Mouth, Garden Route National Park

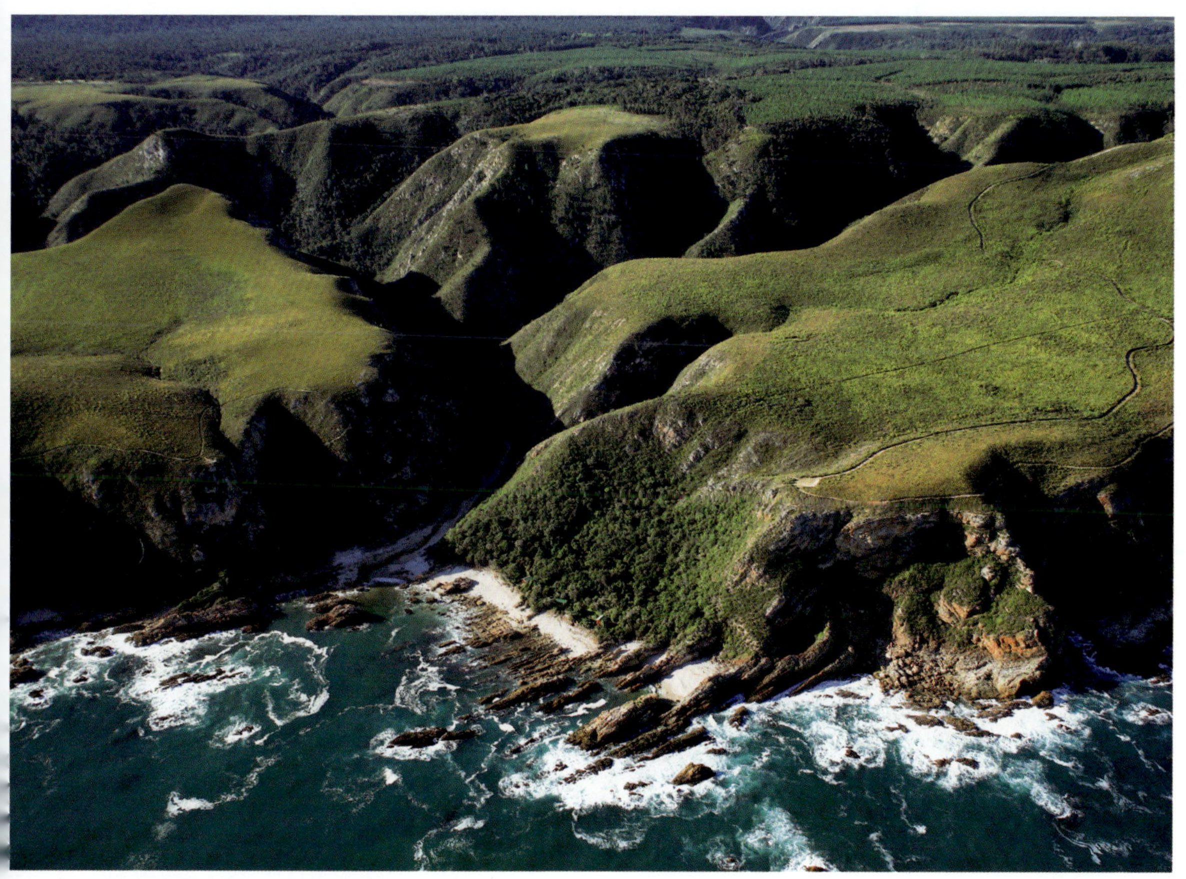

Tsitsikamma National Park, Otter Trail, Garden Route National Park

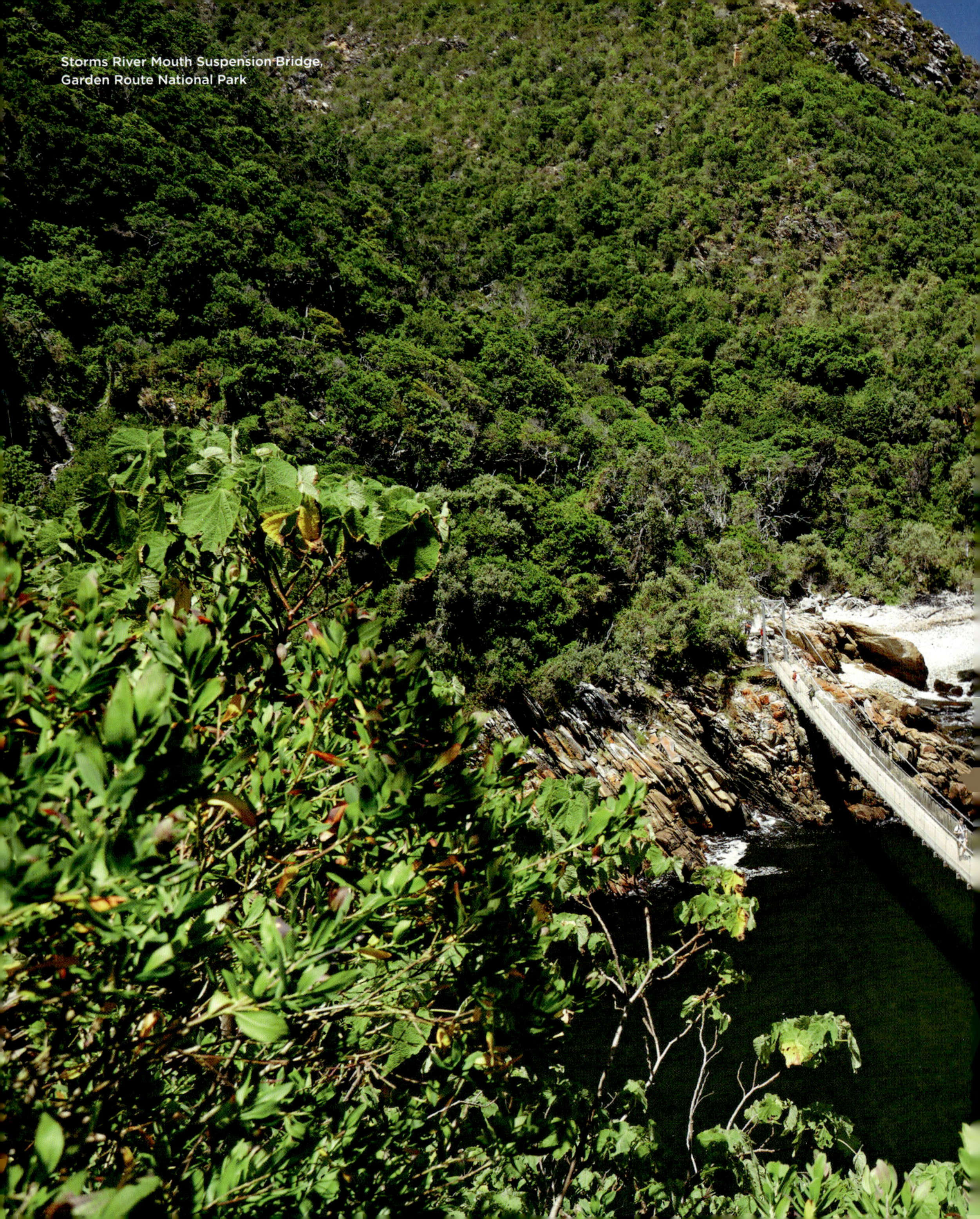

Storms River Mouth Suspension Bridge,
Garden Route National Park

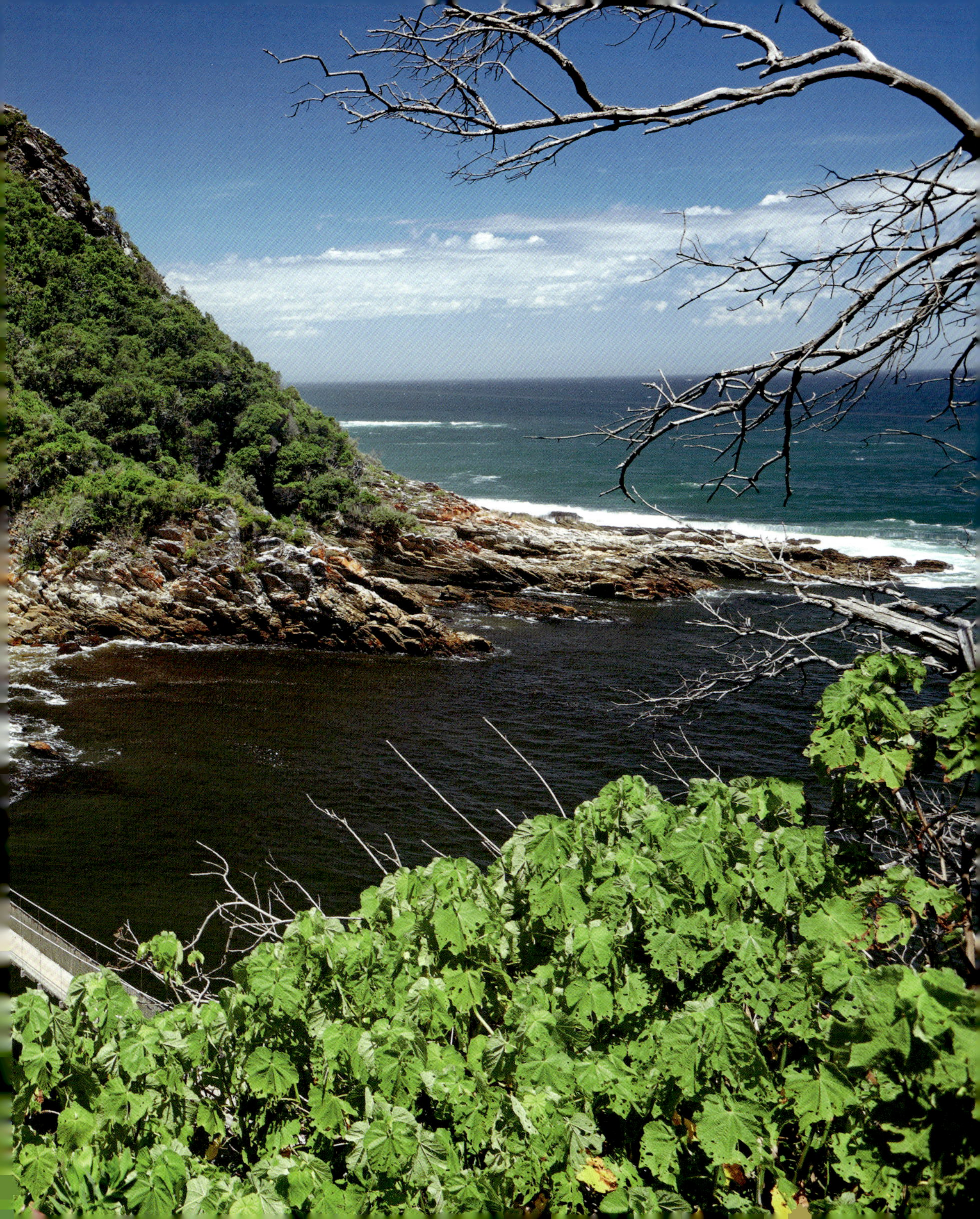

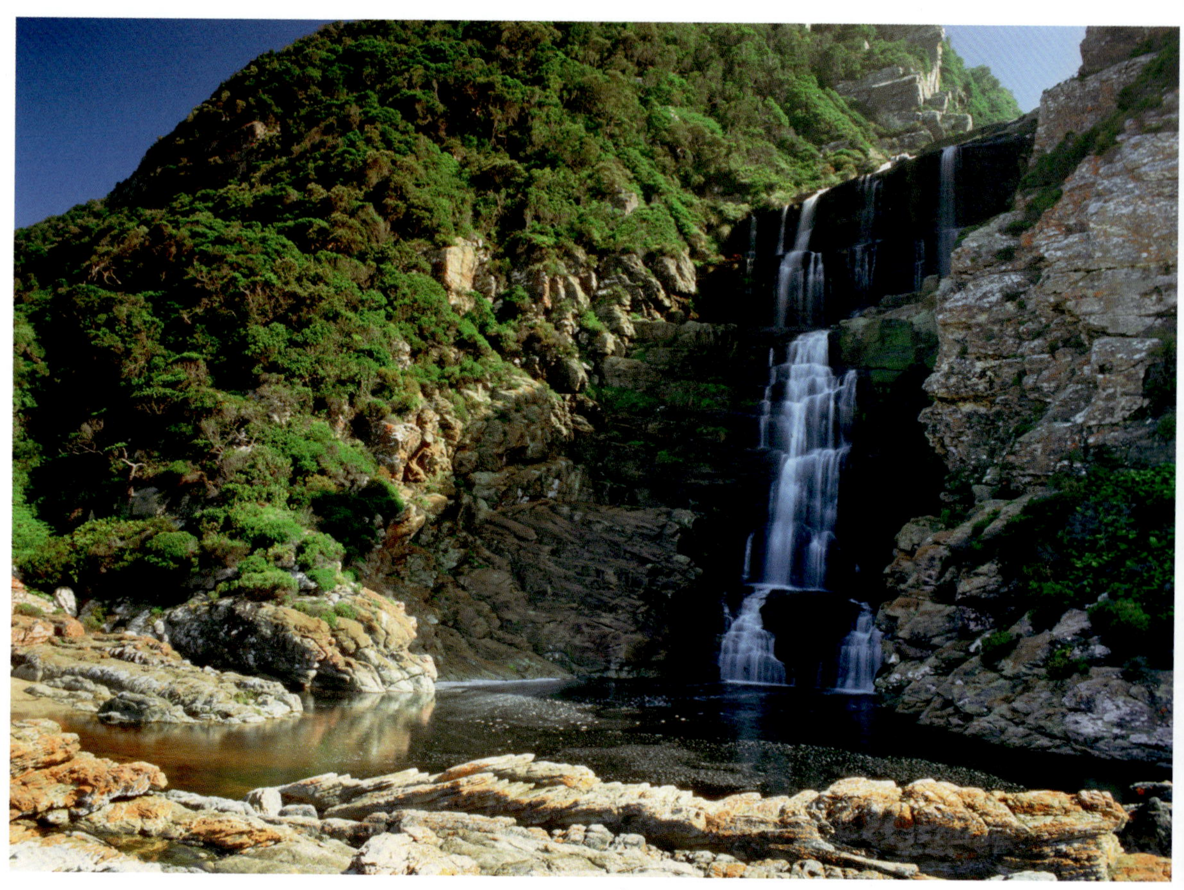

Storms River Mouth Waterfall, Garden Route National Park

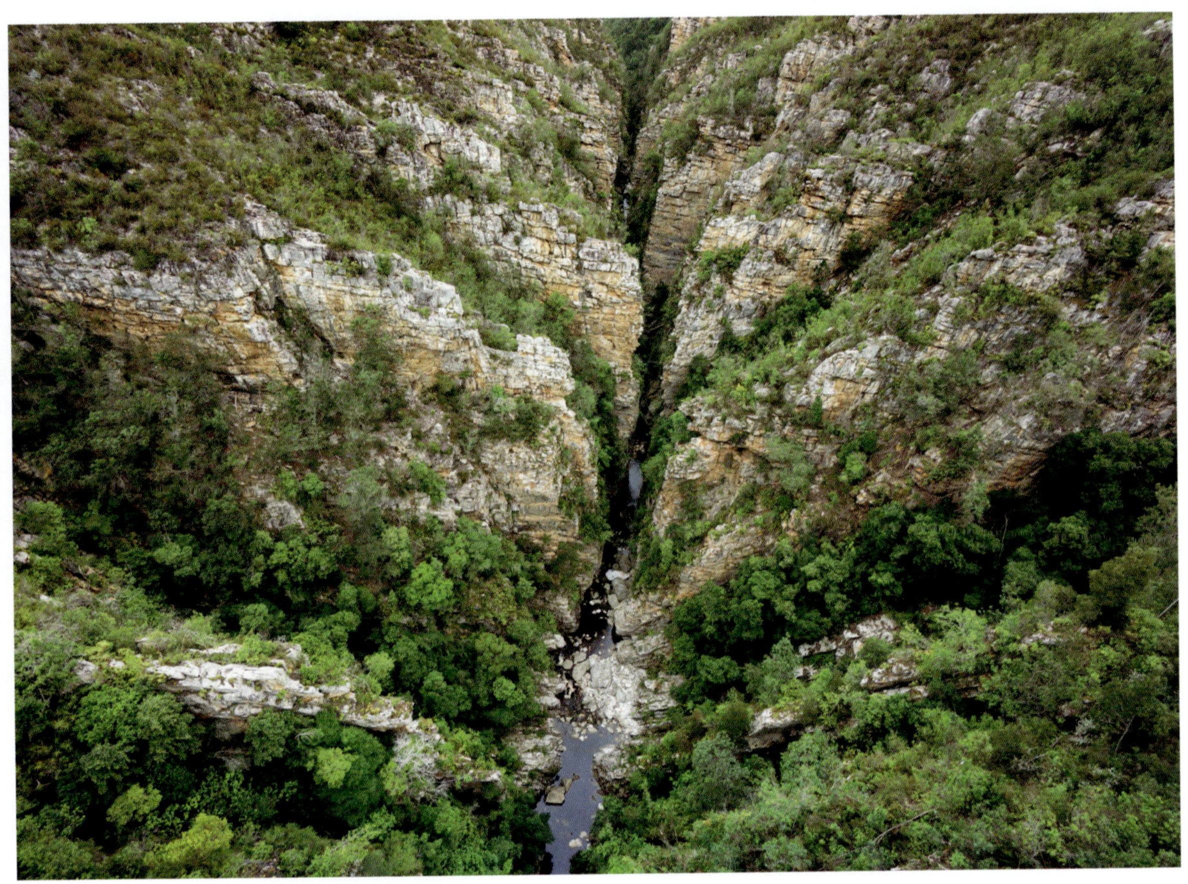

Bloukrans River Gorge, Garden Route National Park

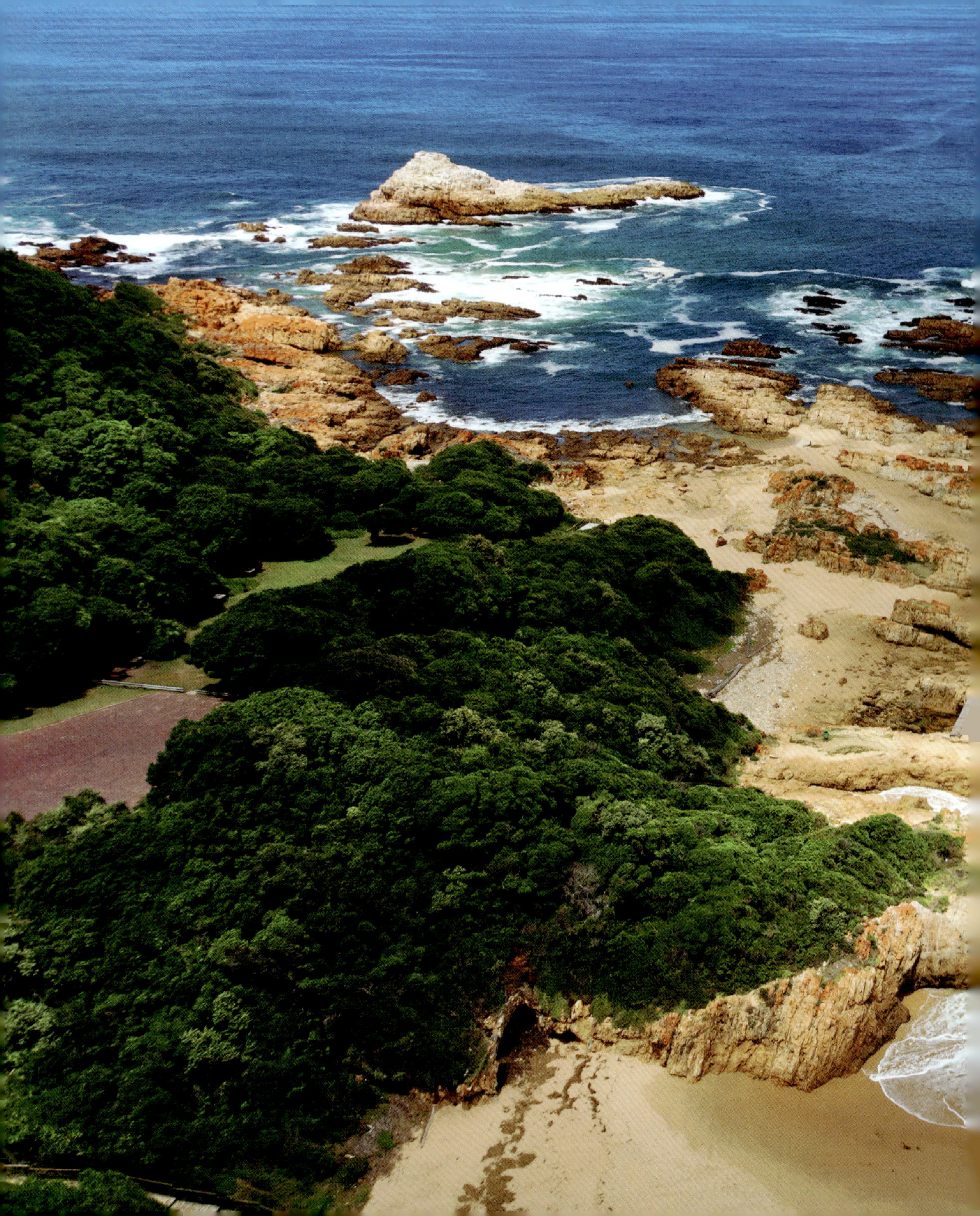

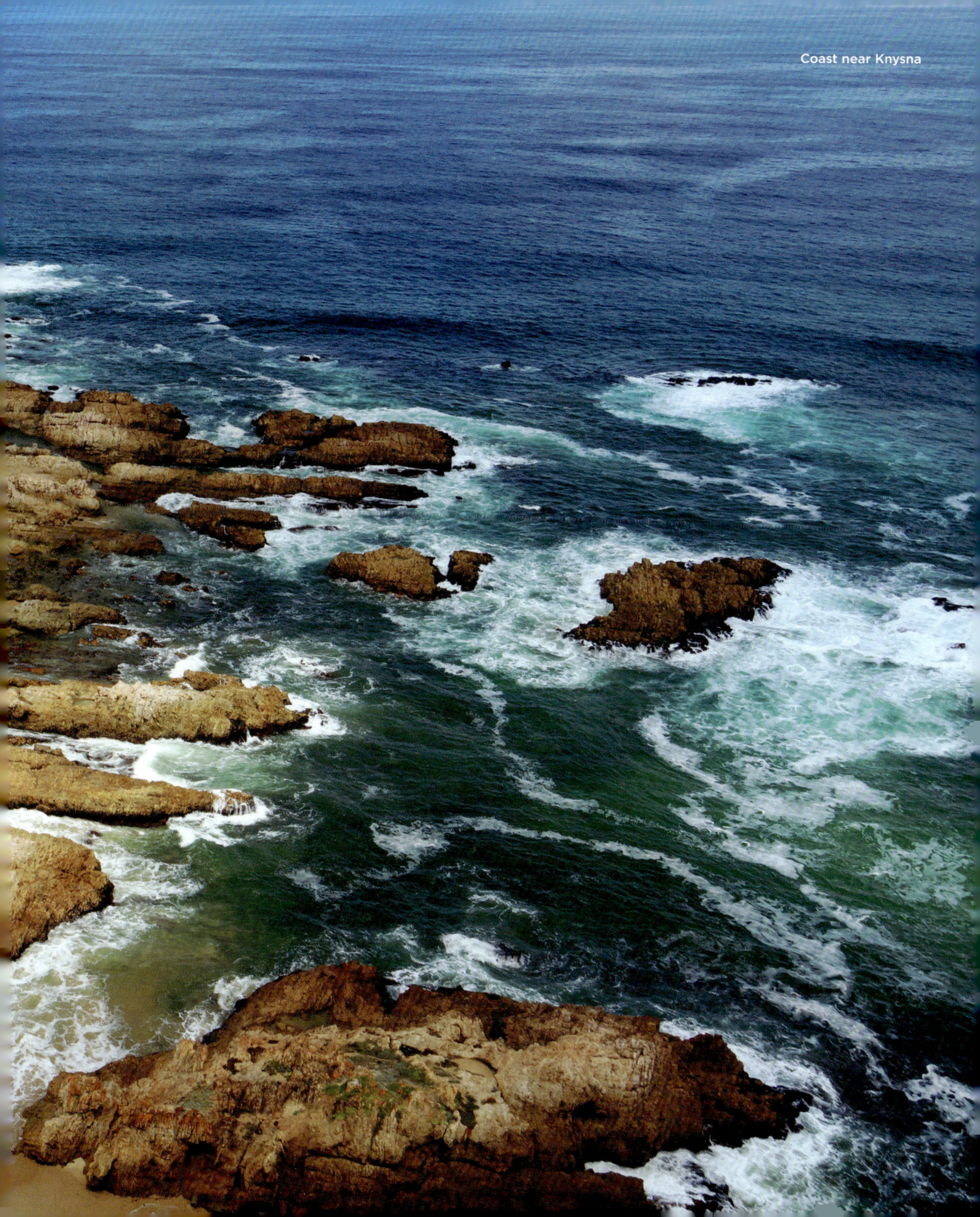
Coast near Knysna

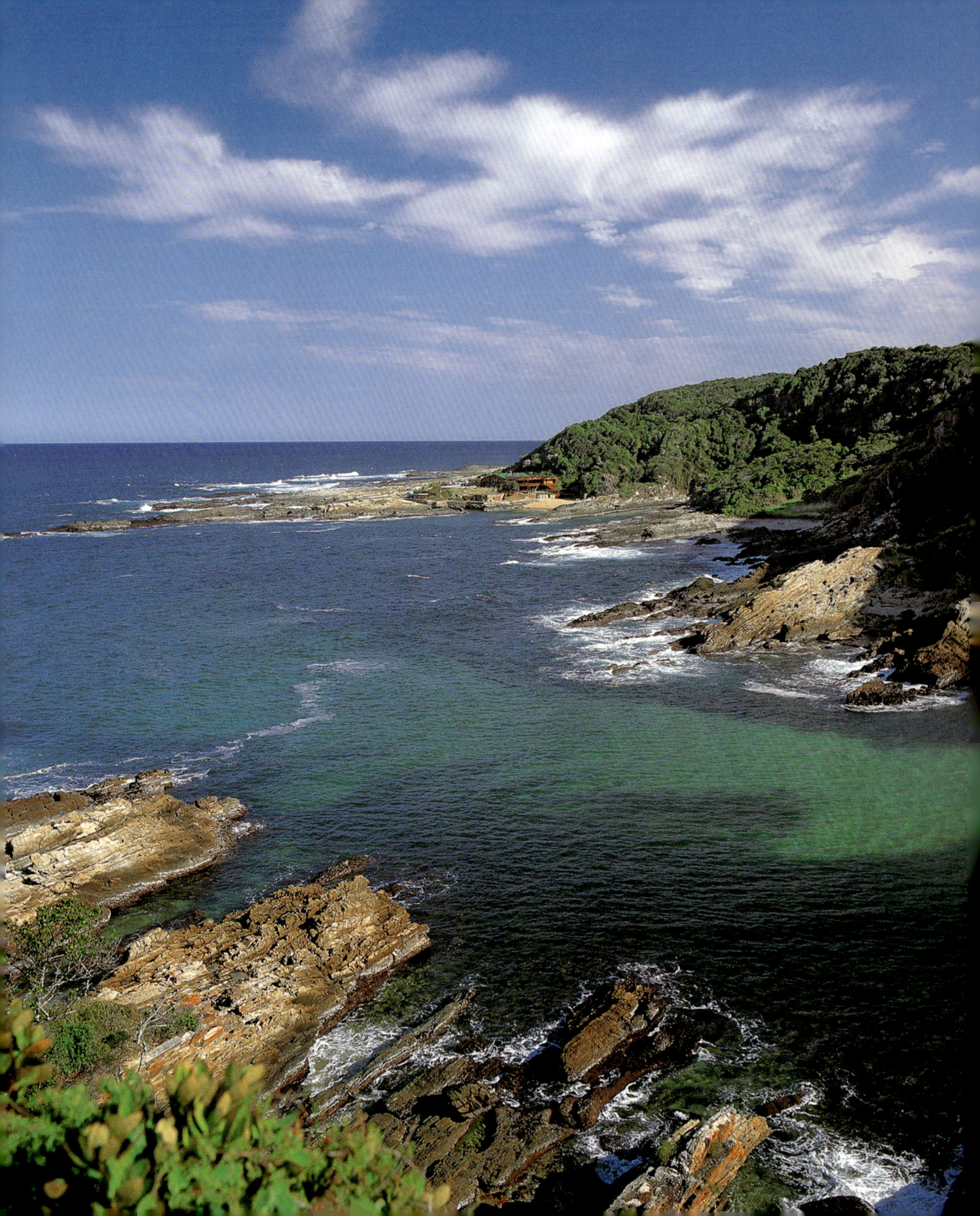

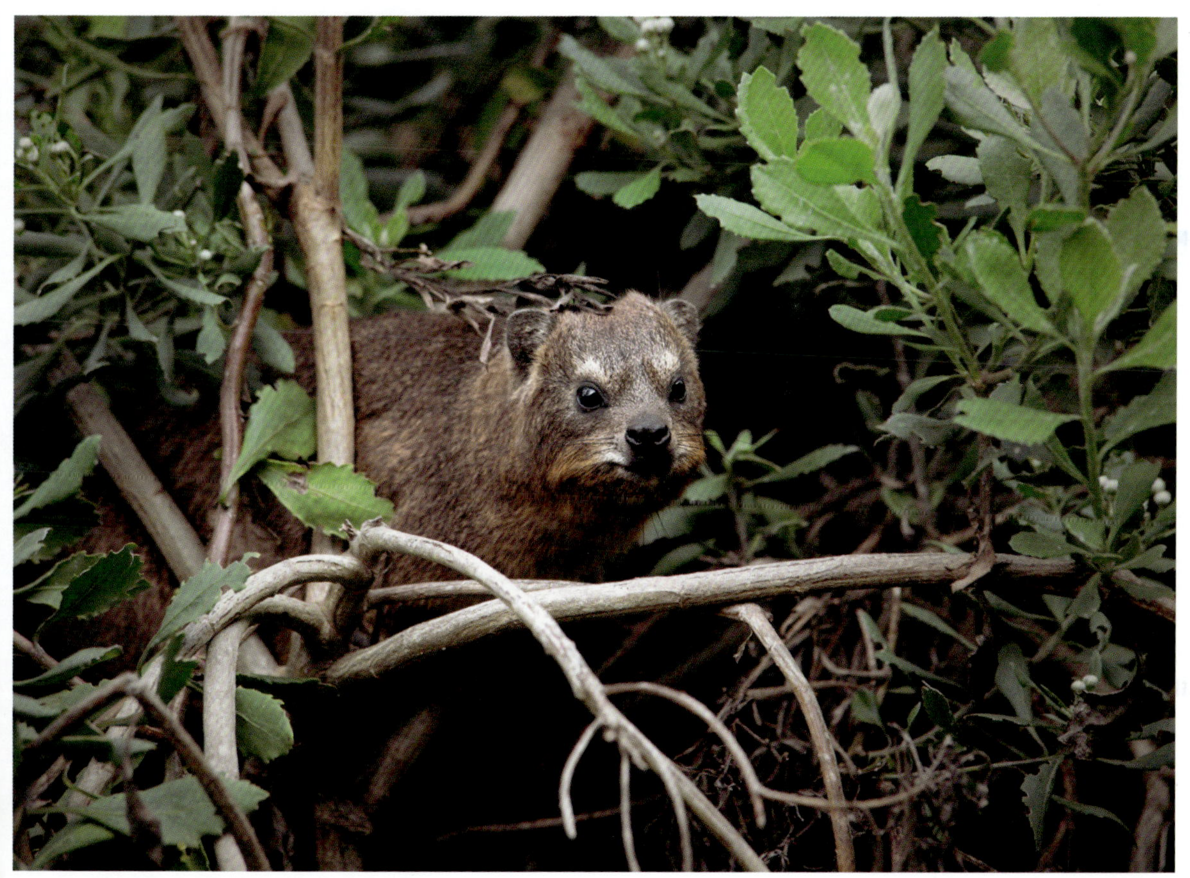

Cape hyrax, Garden Route National Park

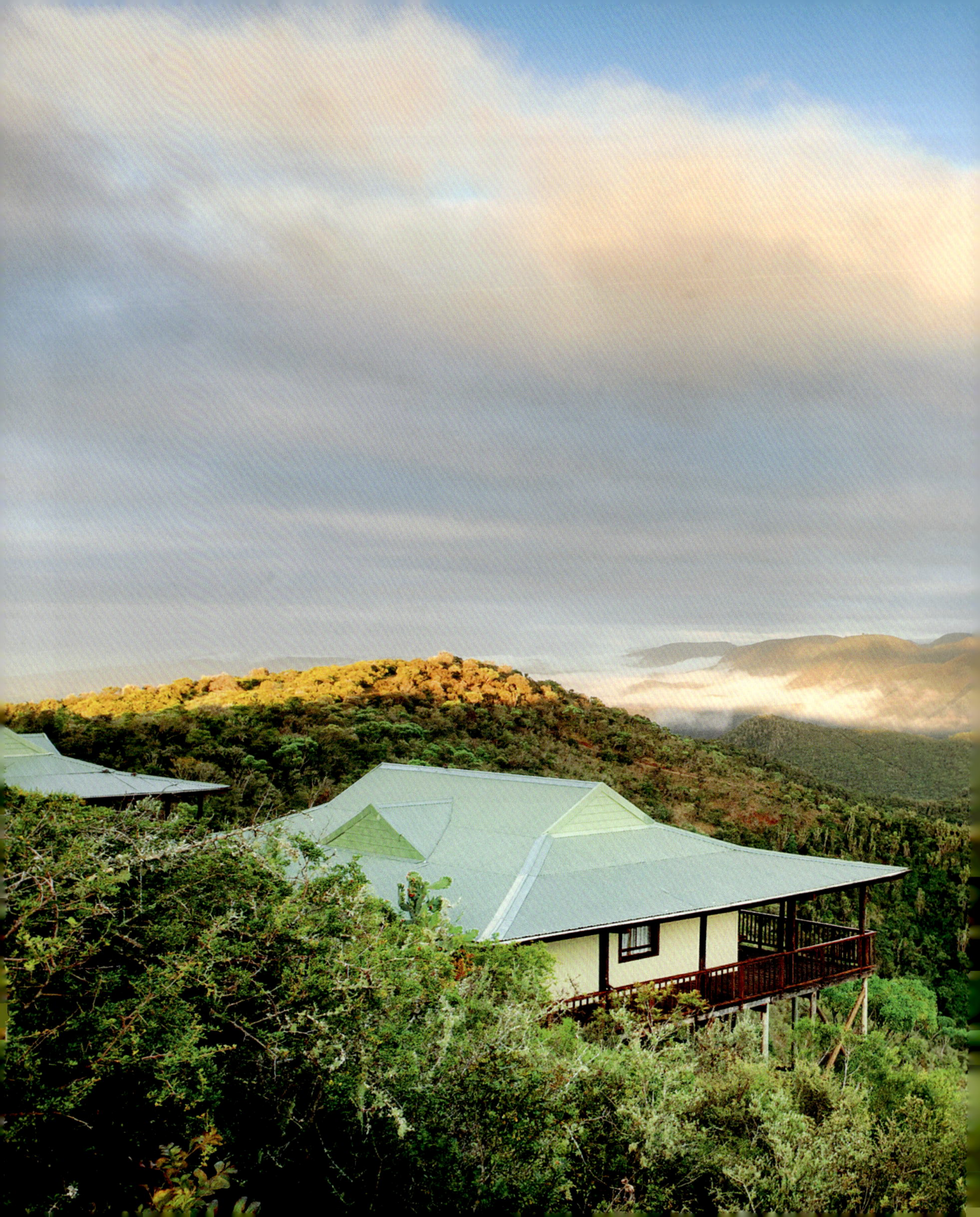

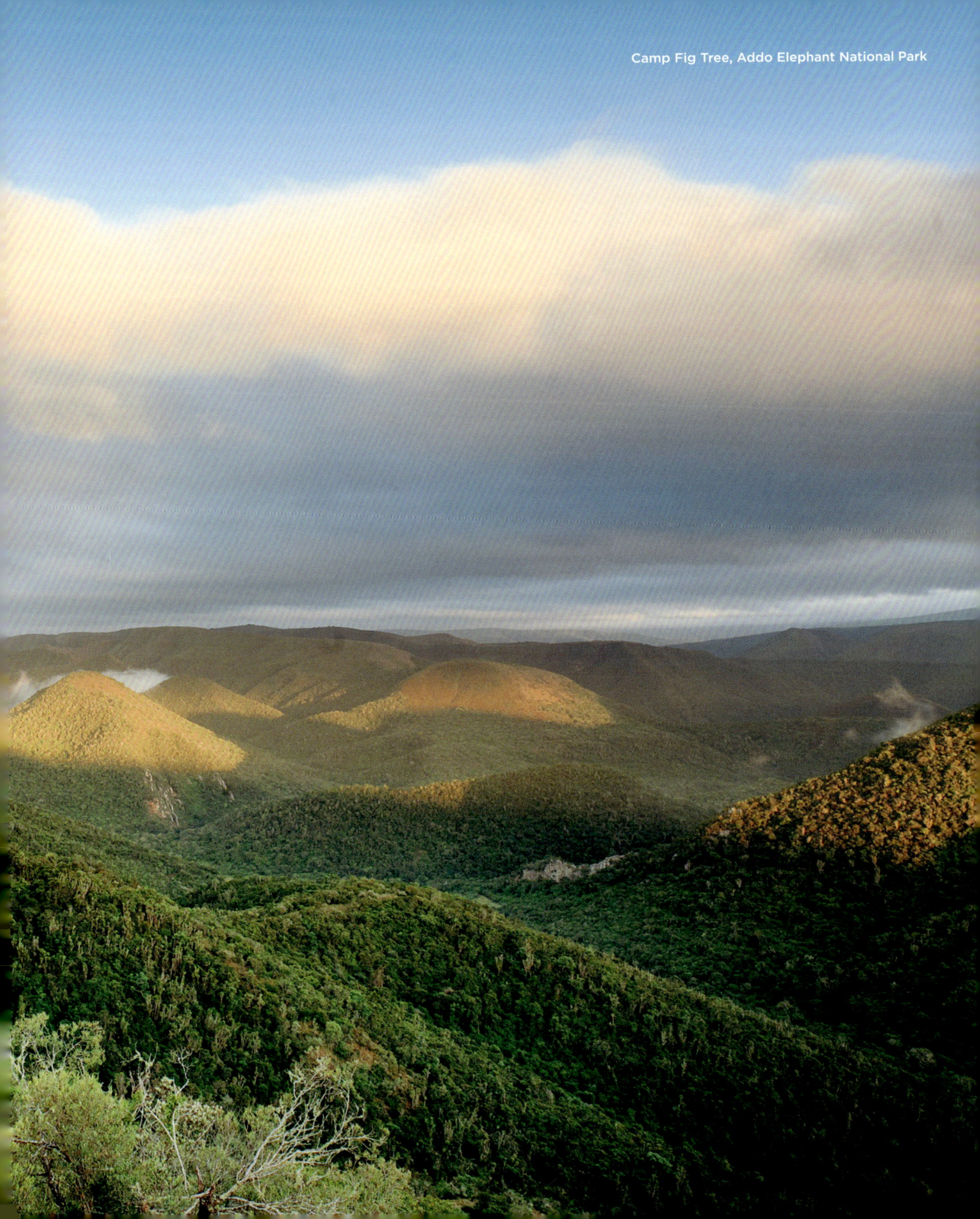

Camp Fig Tree, Addo Elephant National Park

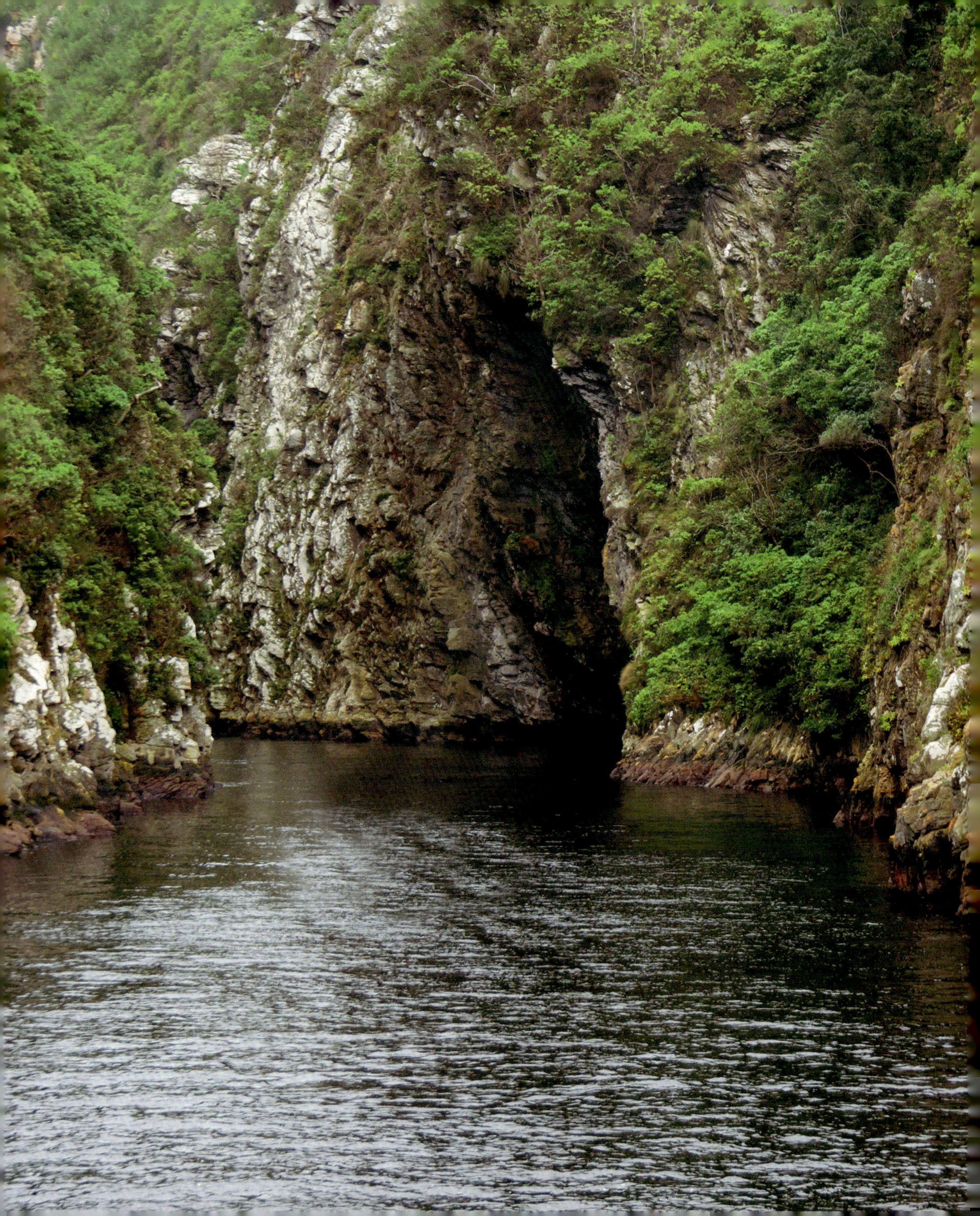

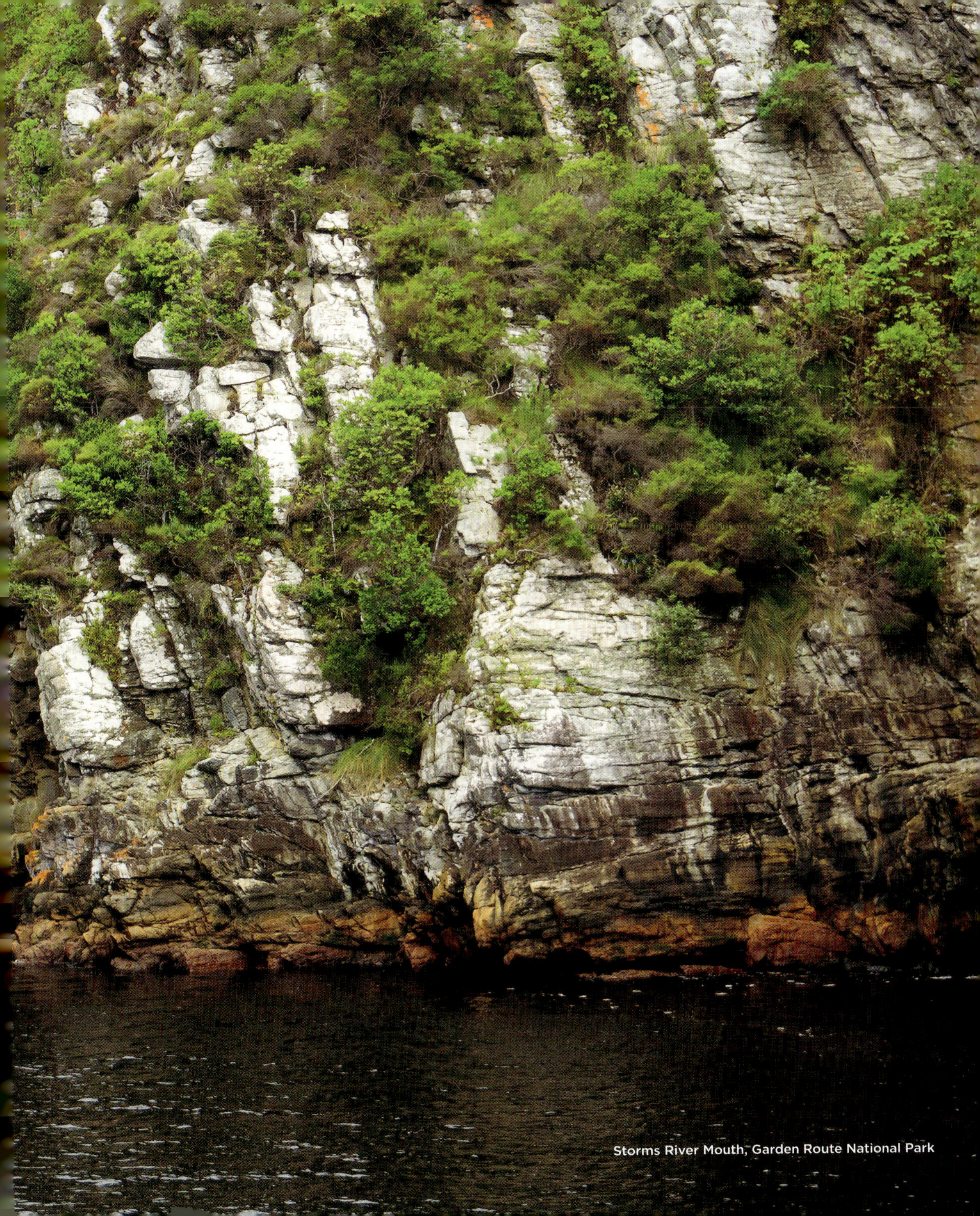
Storms River Mouth, Garden Route National Park

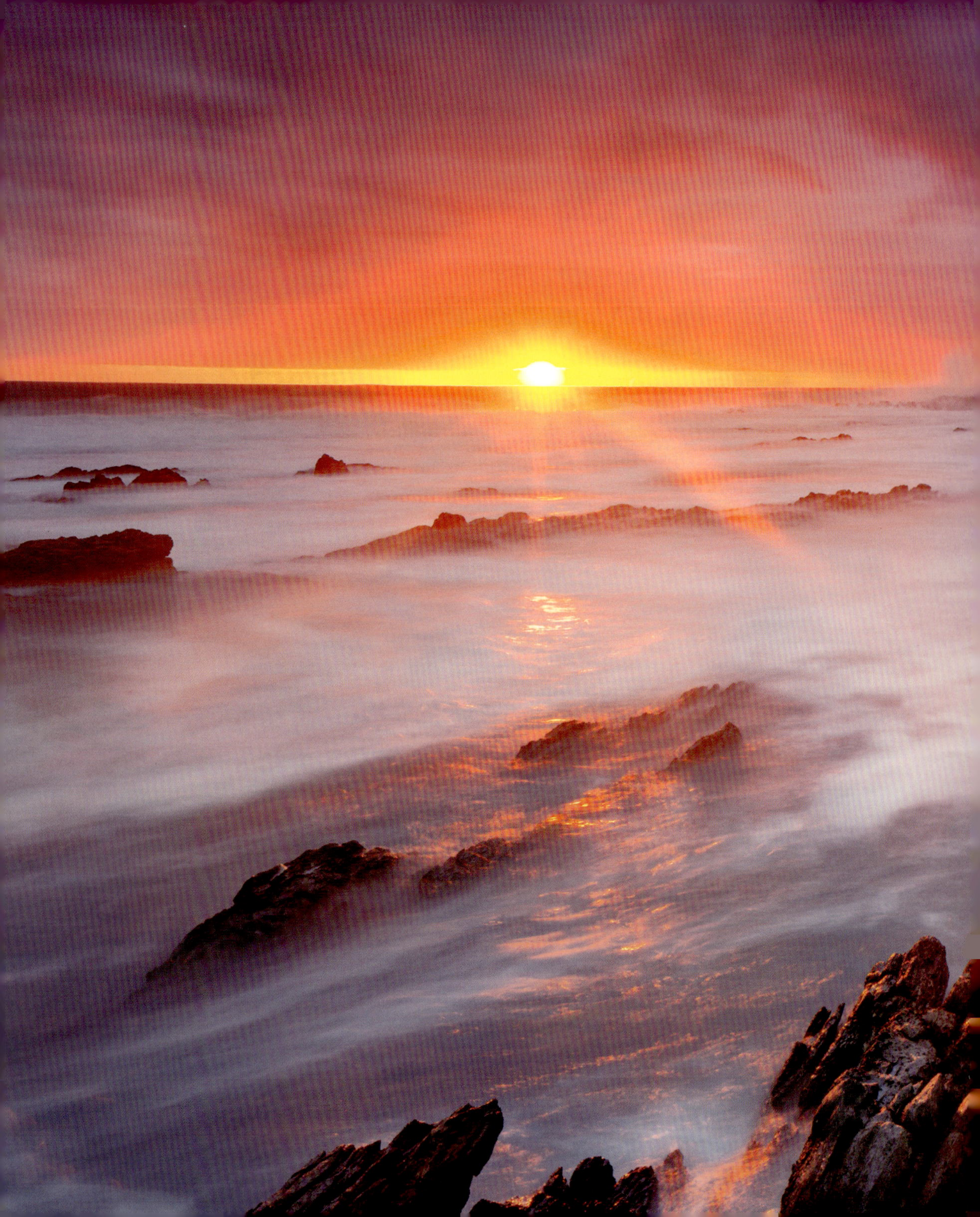

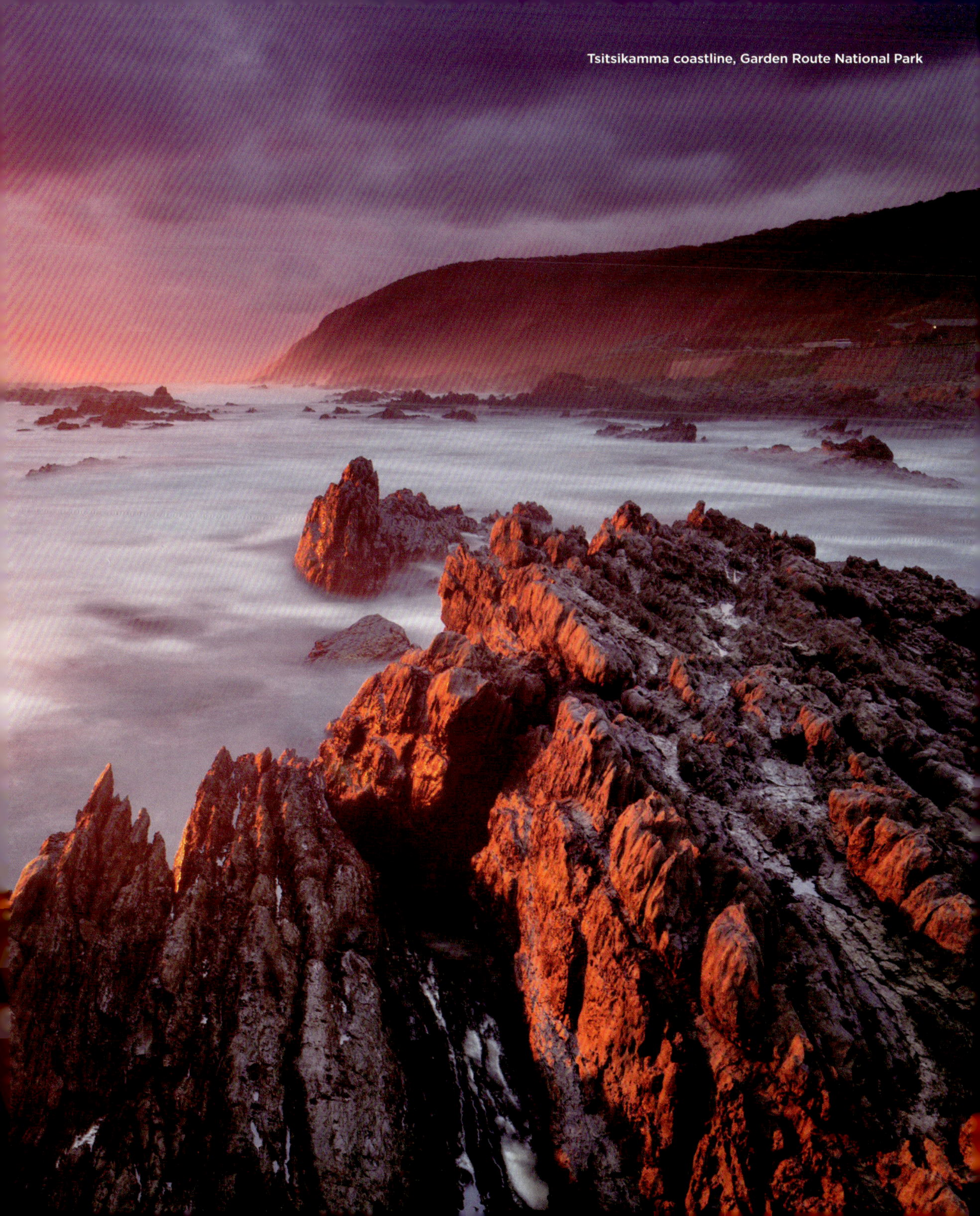
Tsitsikamma coastline, Garden Route National Park

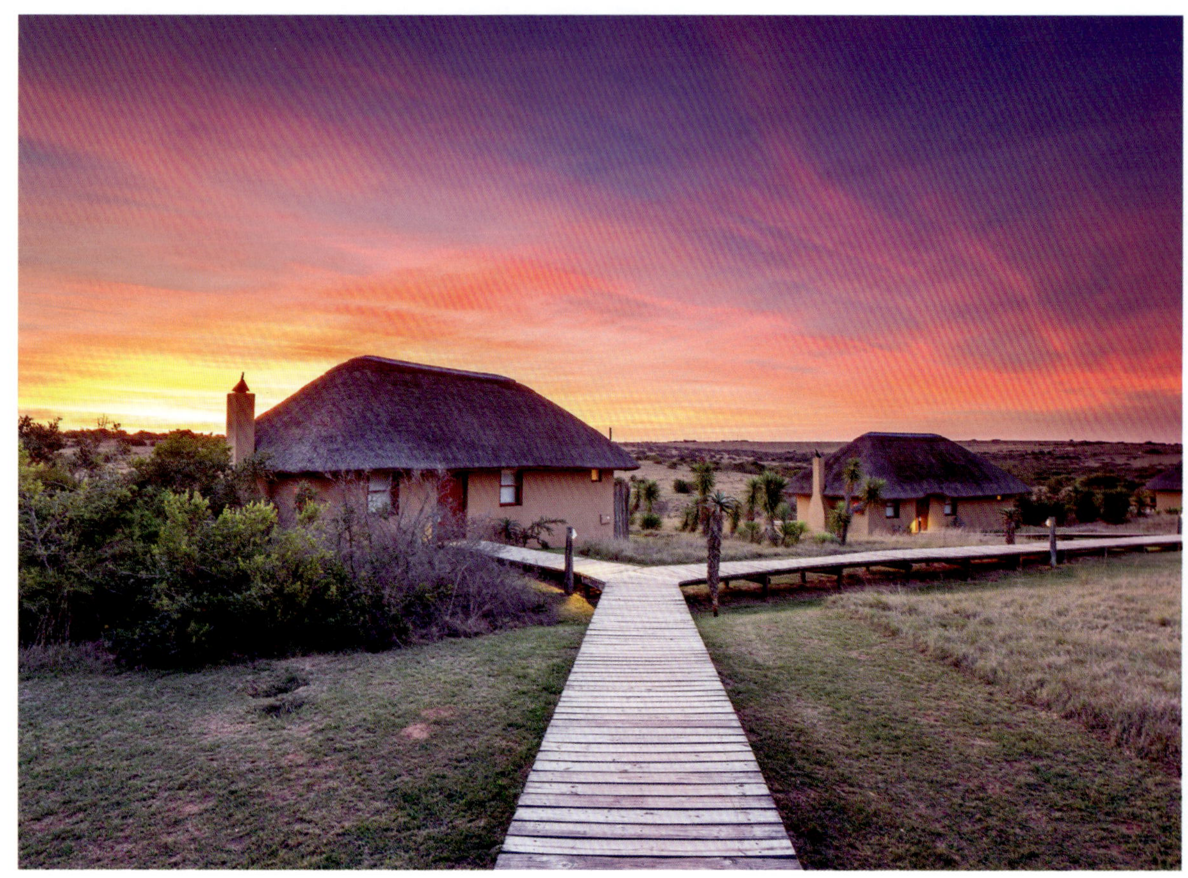

Hlosi Game Lodge, Amakhala Game Reserve

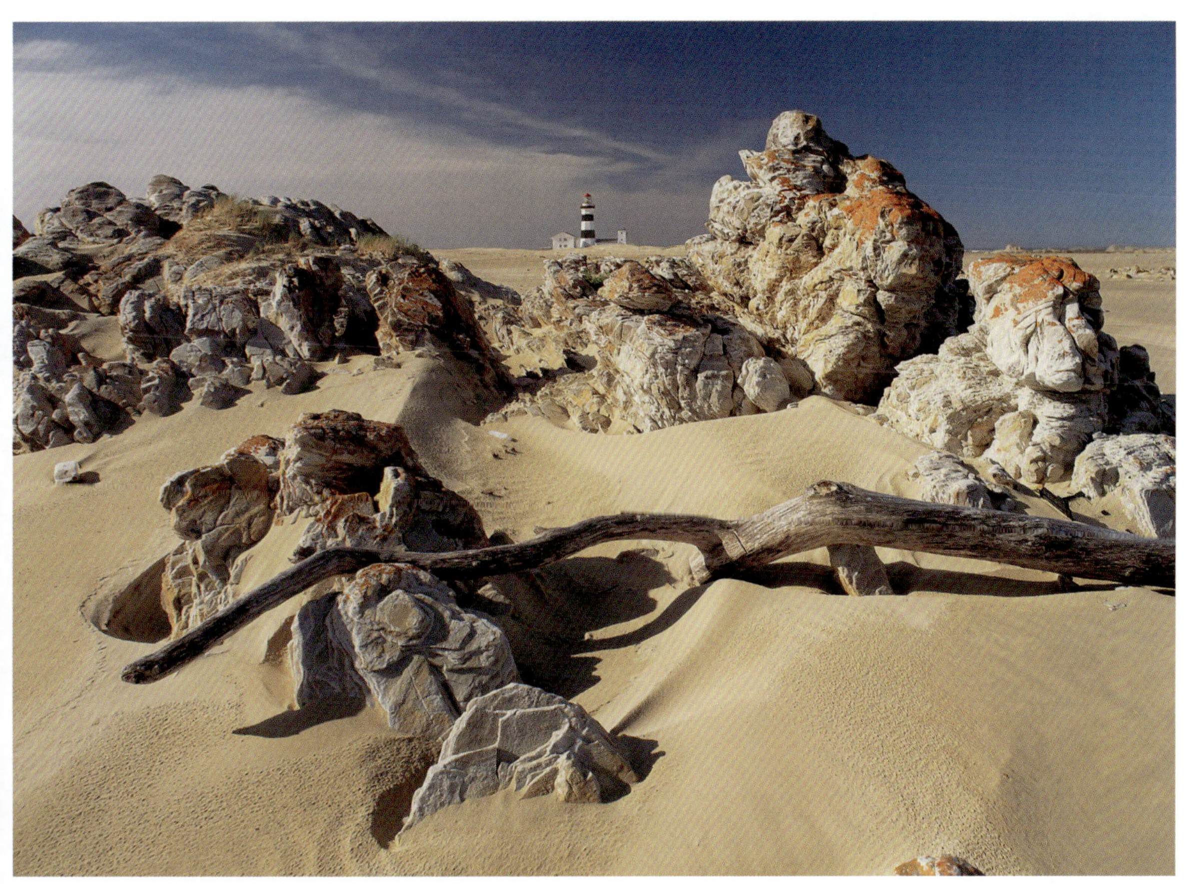

The Cape Recife Nature Reserve, Port Elizabeth

Port Elizabeth
The city on the South African east coast is still relatively young. It was not until 1820 that British emigrants founded this settlement on Algoa Bay. Today, it is an important port city and is also known for its numerous beaches. On the coast one may find whales and rare seabirds. The water temperatures are much more pleasant than further west in the cold Atlantic.

Port Elisabeth
Cette ville de la côte est sud-africaine est encore relativement jeune : ce n'est qu'en 1820 que les Britanniques ont fondé cette colonie dans la baie d'Algoa. Aujourd'hui, c'est une ville portuaire importante, connue également pour ses nombreuses plages. Sur la côte, on trouve des baleines et des espèces d'oiseaux de mer rares. Les eaux y ont une température nettement plus agréable que dans l'Atlantique, plus à l'ouest.

Port Elisabeth
Die Stadt an der südafrikanischen Ostküste ist noch relativ jung. Erst 1820 gründeten britische Auswanderer jene Siedlung an der Algoa Bay. Heute ist sie eine bedeutende Hafenstadt und auch für ihre zahlreichen Strände bekannt. An der Küste findet man Wale und seltene Meeresvögel. Die Wassertemperaturen sind wesentlich angenehmer als weiter westlich im kalten Atlantik.

Puerto Elizabeth
La ciudad en la costa este de Sudáfrica es todavía relativamente joven. No fue hasta 1820 que los emigrantes británicos fundaron este asentamiento en la Bahía de Algoa. Hoy en día es una importante ciudad portuaria y también conocida por sus numerosas playas. En la costa encontrará ballenas y aves marinas raras. Las temperaturas del agua son mucho más agradables que más al oeste en el frío Atlántico.

Port Elisabeth
Questa città sulla costa orientale sudafricana è ancora relativamente giovane. Solo nel 1820 gli emigranti britannici fondarono questo insediamento sulla baia di Algoa. Oggi è un'importante città portuale e conosciuta anche per le sue numerose spiagge. Sulla costa si trovano balene e rari uccelli marini. Le temperature dell'acqua sono molto più piacevoli rispetto a quelle del freddo Atlantico.

Port Elisabeth
De stad aan de Zuid-Afrikaanse oostkust is nog relatief jong. Pas in 1820 stichtten Britse emigranten deze nederzetting op Algoa Bay. Nu is het een belangrijke havenstad die ook bekend is om zijn vele stranden. Aan de kust leven walvissen en zeldzame zeevogels. De watertemperaturen zijn veel aangenamer dan verder naar het westen in de koude Atlantische Oceaan.

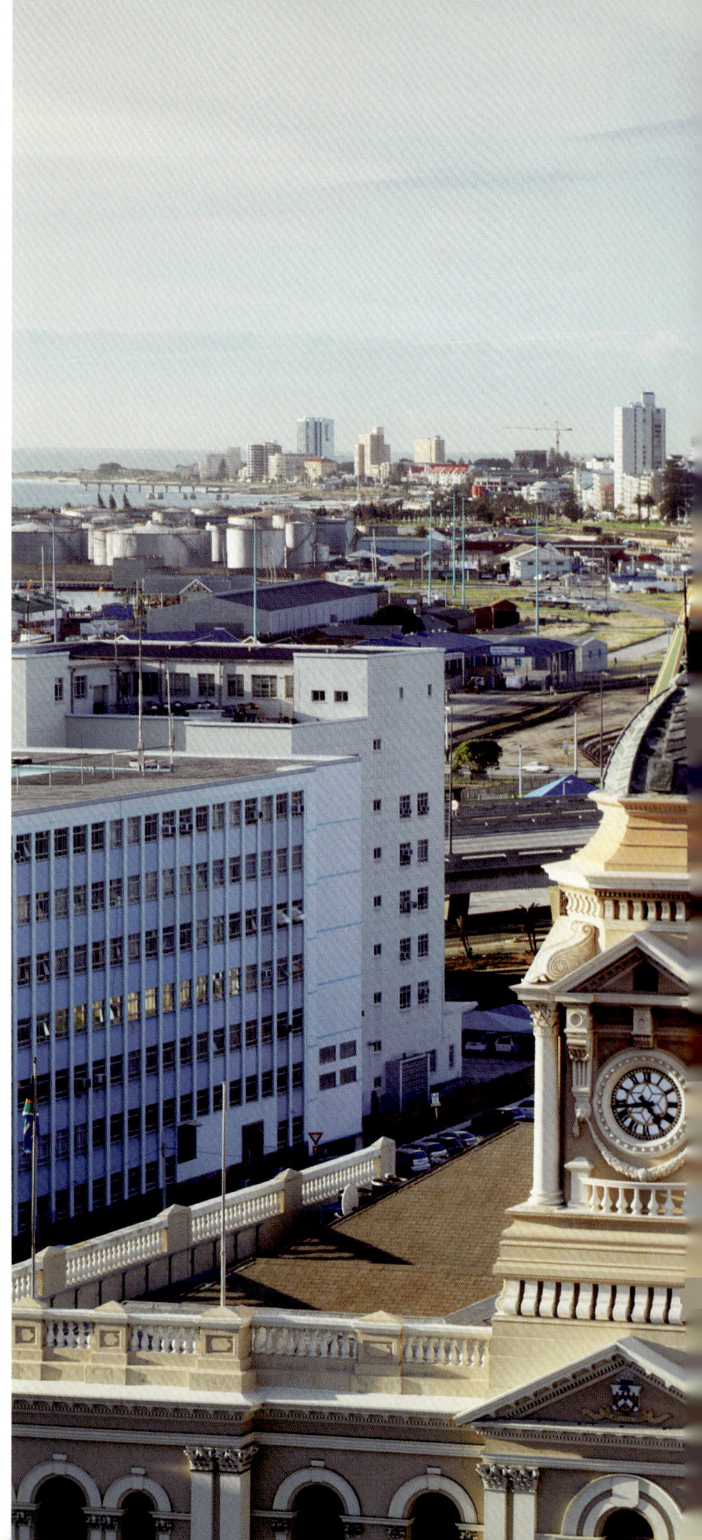

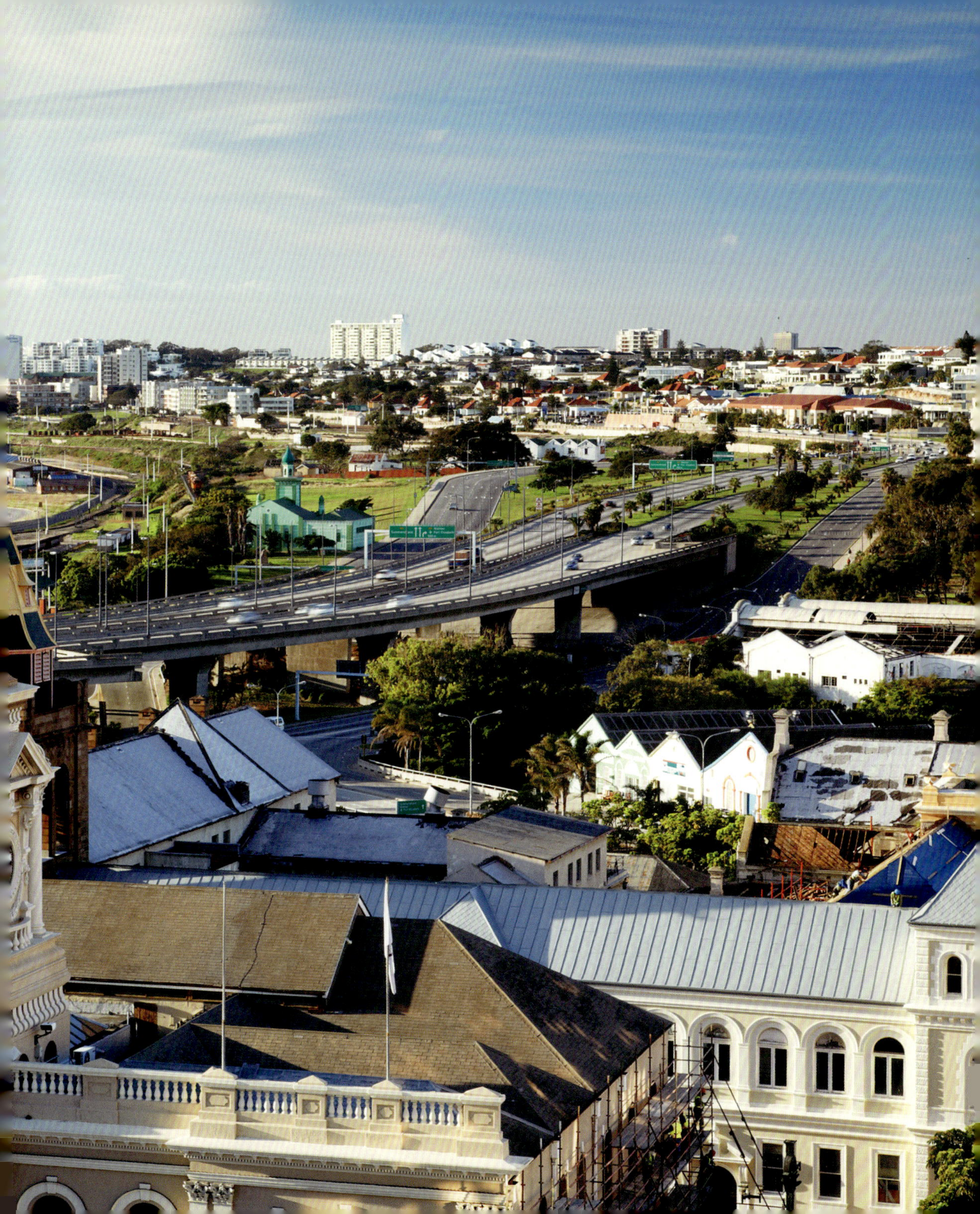

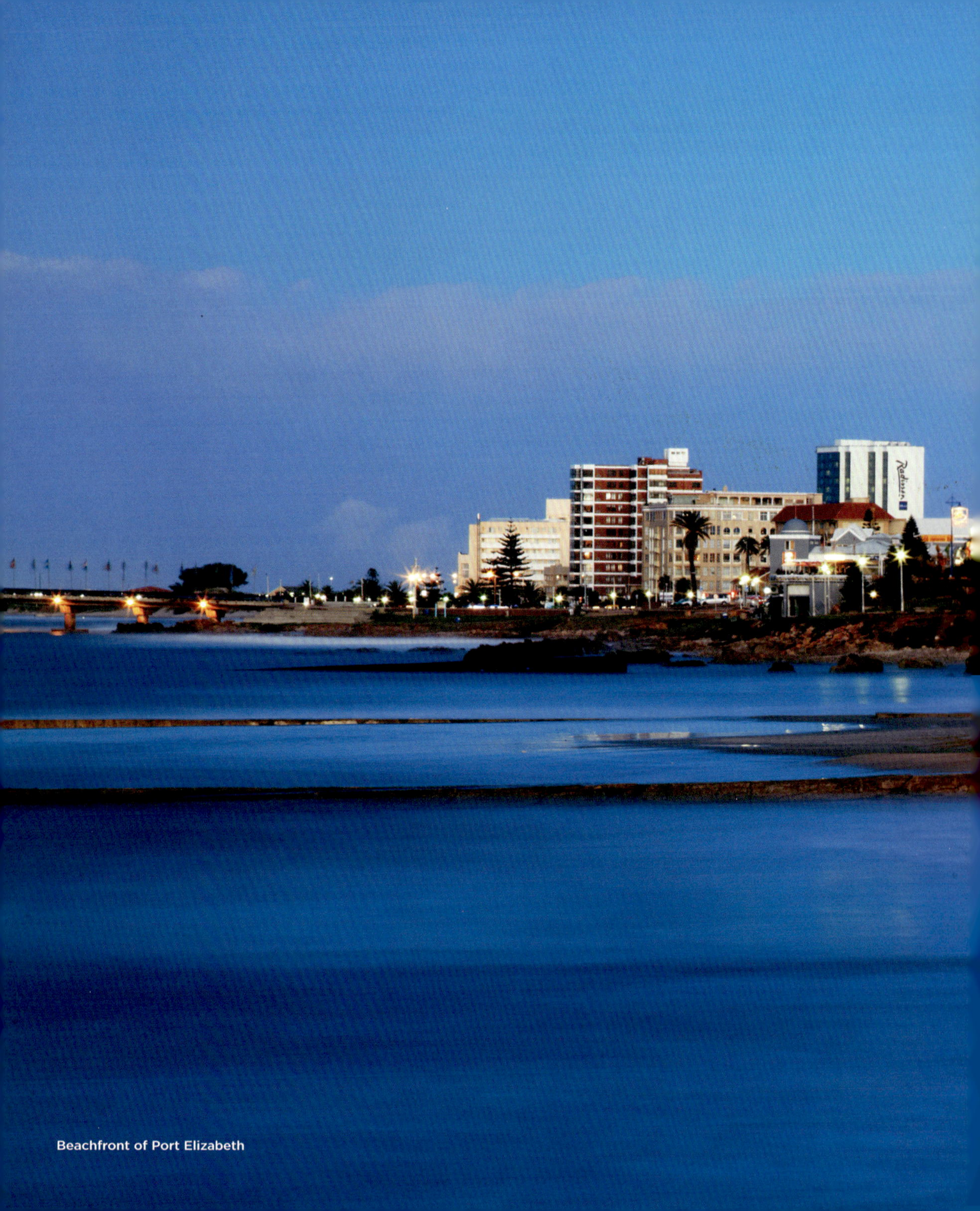
Beachfront of Port Elizabeth

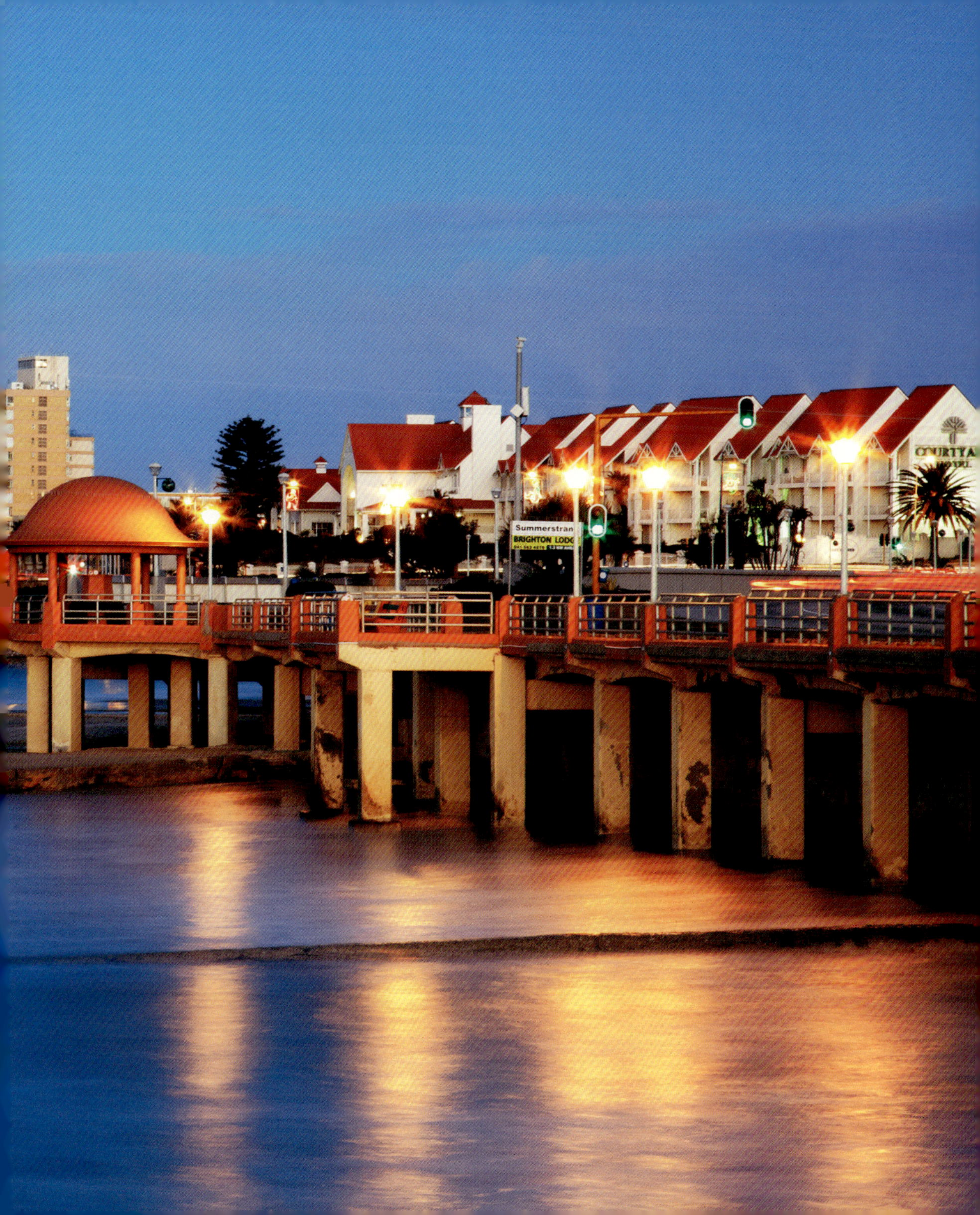
Summerstran
BRIGHTON LODG

Wild Coast, South Africa

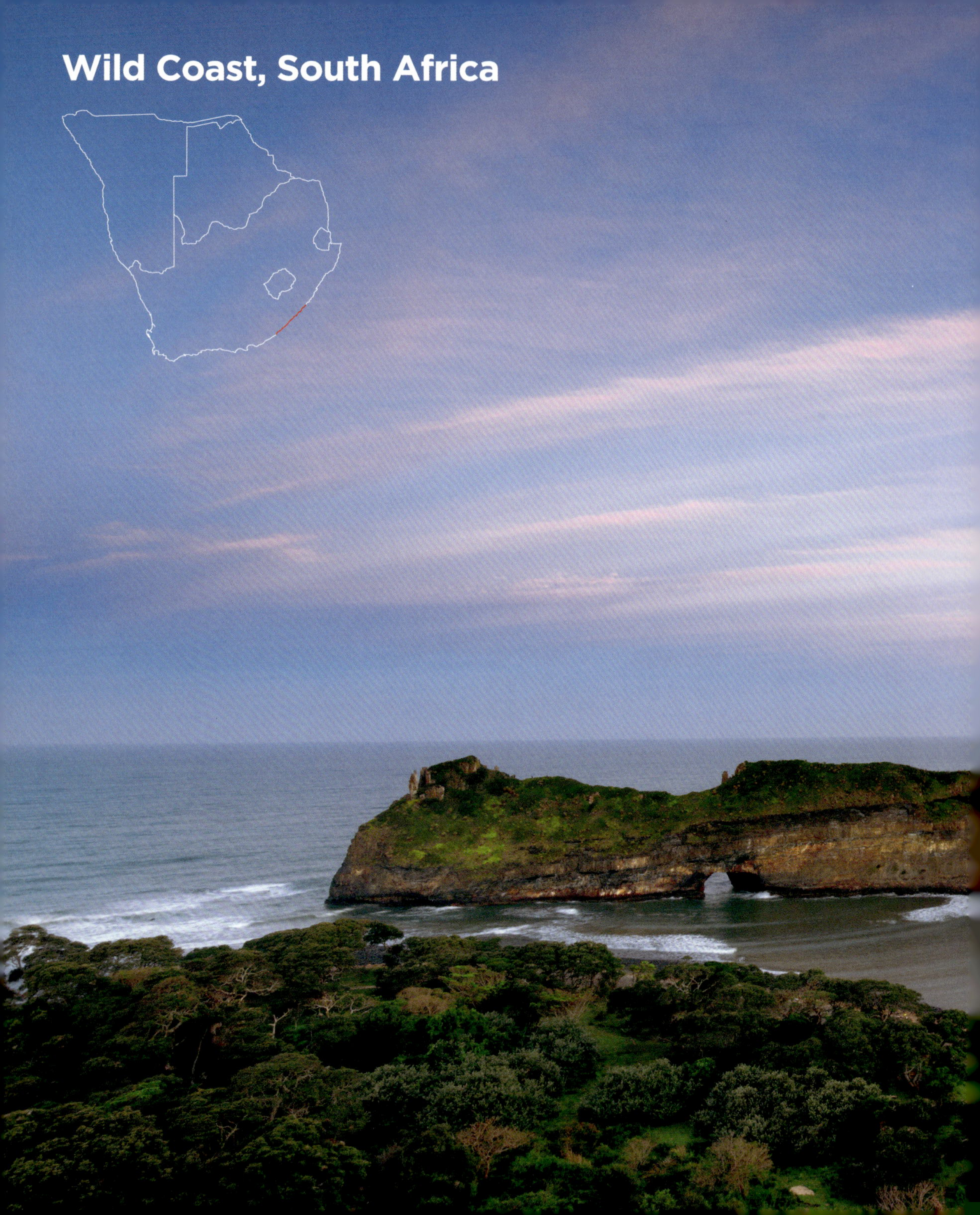

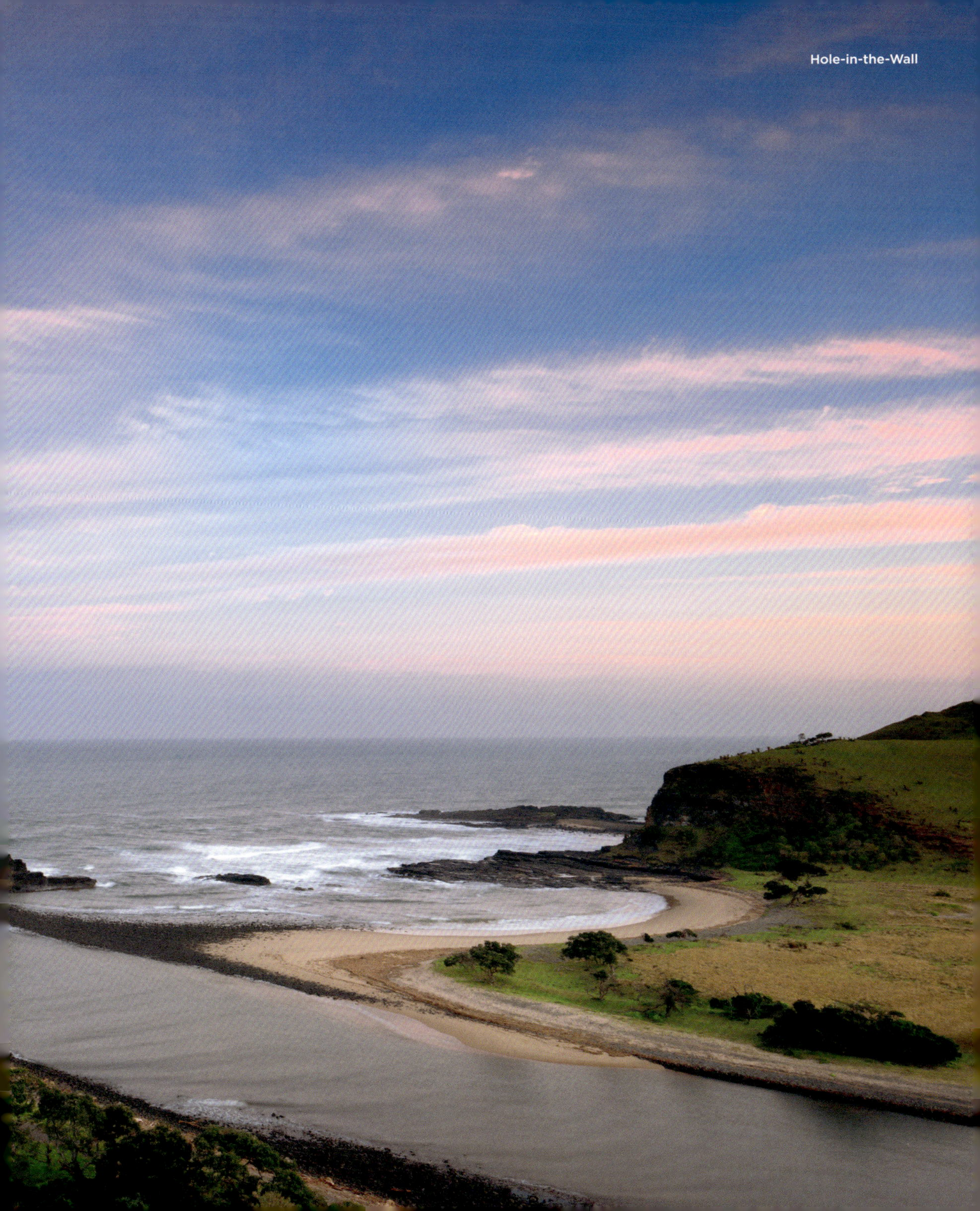
Hole-in-the-Wall

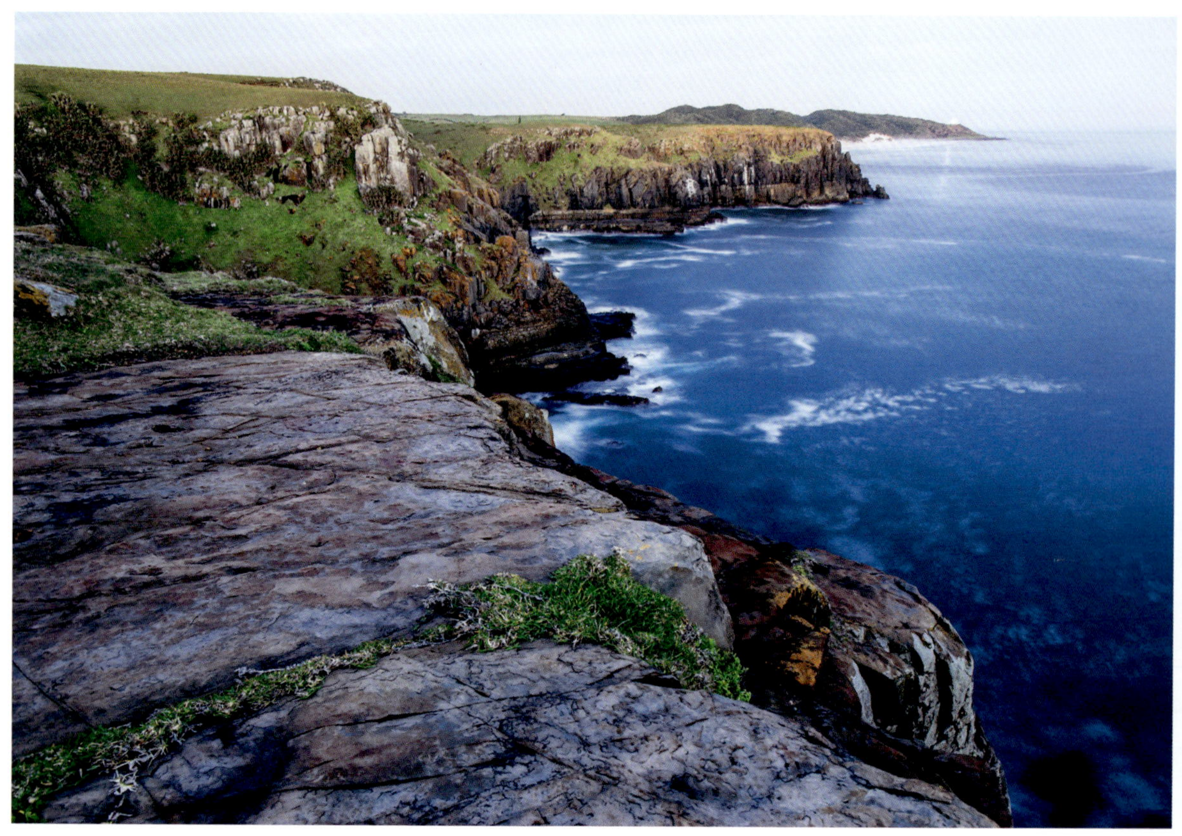

Wild Coast

Wild Coast
Part of the Eastern Cape coast has earned the name "Wild Coast". It runs about 270 km (168 mi) from Buffalo City in the southwest, to the mouth of the Mtamvuna River, near Port Edward, in the northeast. Sandy beaches are found in the south where the rivers flow into the Indian Ocean, whilst in the north the water has carved through the rocks to create impressive ravines.

La Côte Sauvage
Cette Côte sauvage est un pan du littoral dans la province du Cap-Est. Longue de 270 km, elle part de Buffalo City au sud-ouest pour finir à l'embouchure du Mtamvuna près de Port Edward, dans le nord-est. Les fleuves qui rejoignent l'océan Indien dans la partie sud ont donné naissance à des plages de sable, tandis qu'au nord l'eau s'est frayé un chemin à travers les roches et a creusé des gorges impressionnantes.

Wild Coast
Als „Wild Coast" bezeichnet man einen Küstenabschnitt in der südafrikanischen Provinz Ostkap. Die Wild Coast ist rund 270 km lang und erstreckt sich von Buffalo City im Südwesten bis zur Mündung des Mtamvuna bei Port Edward im Nordosten. Wo die Flüsse im südlichen Teil in den Indischen Ozean münden, liegen Sandstrände, im Norden hat das Wasser sich den Weg durch die Felsen gebahnt und beeindruckende Schluchten geschaffen.

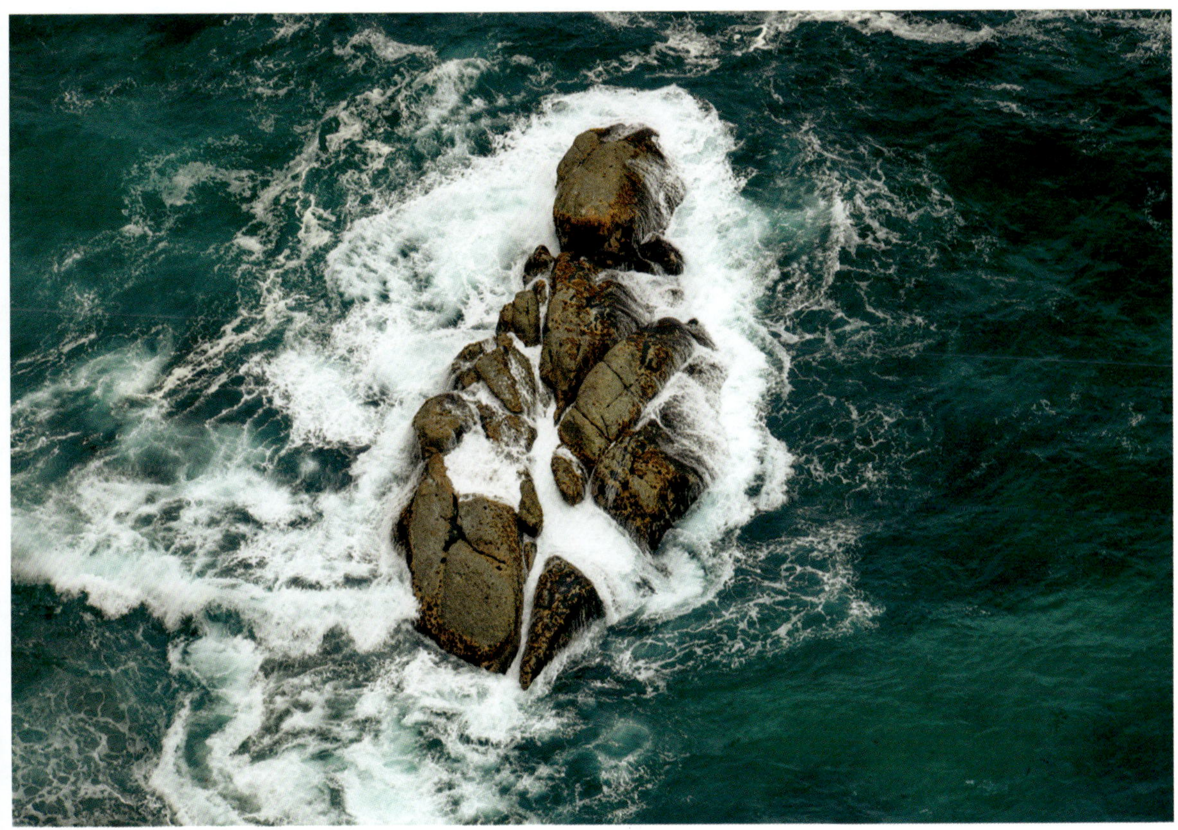

Wild Coast

Costa Salvaje
La "Costa Salvaje" se refiere a un tramo de costa en la provincia del Cabo Oriental de Sudáfrica. La Costa Salvaje tiene de largo 270 km y se extiende desde la ciudad de Buffalo en el suroeste hasta la desembocadura del Mtamvuna en Port Edward en el noreste. Donde los ríos desembocan en la parte sur del Océano Índico, las playas son de arena, en el norte, el agua ha allanado el camino a través de las rocas y los impresionantes cañones creados.

Wild Coast
"Wild Coast" indica un tratto di costa nella provincia sudafricana del Capo Orientale. La Wild Coast è lunga circa 270 km e si estende da Buffalo City nella zona sud-occidentale fino alla foce del fiume Mtamvuna, vicino a Port Edward nel nord-est. Dove i fiumi sfociano nella parte meridionale dell'Oceano Indiano, si trovano spiagge sabbiose, nel nord l'acqua si è scavata un varco tra le rocce creando gole impressionanti.

Wild Coast
Een kustgedeelte van de Zuid-Afrikaanse provincie Oost-Kaap wordt de "Wild Coast" genoemd. De kust is circa 270 km lang en strekt zich uit van Buffalo City in het zuidwesten tot aan de monding van de rivier de Mtamvuna bij Port Edward in het noordoosten. Op plekken langs de kust waar rivieren in de zuidelijke Indische Oceaan uitmonden, zijn er zandstranden; in het noorden heeft rivierwater indrukwekkende kloven in de rotsen uitgesleten.

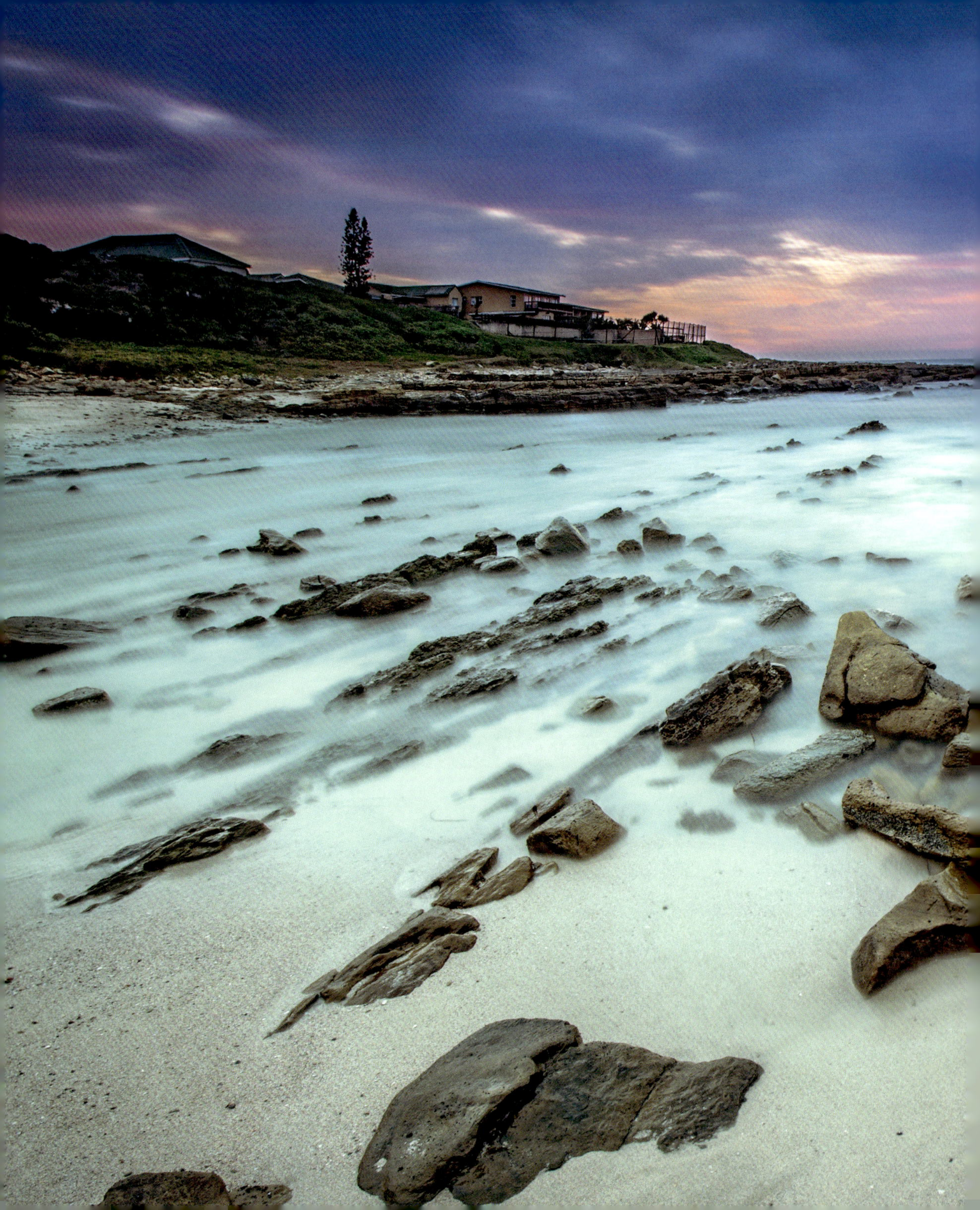

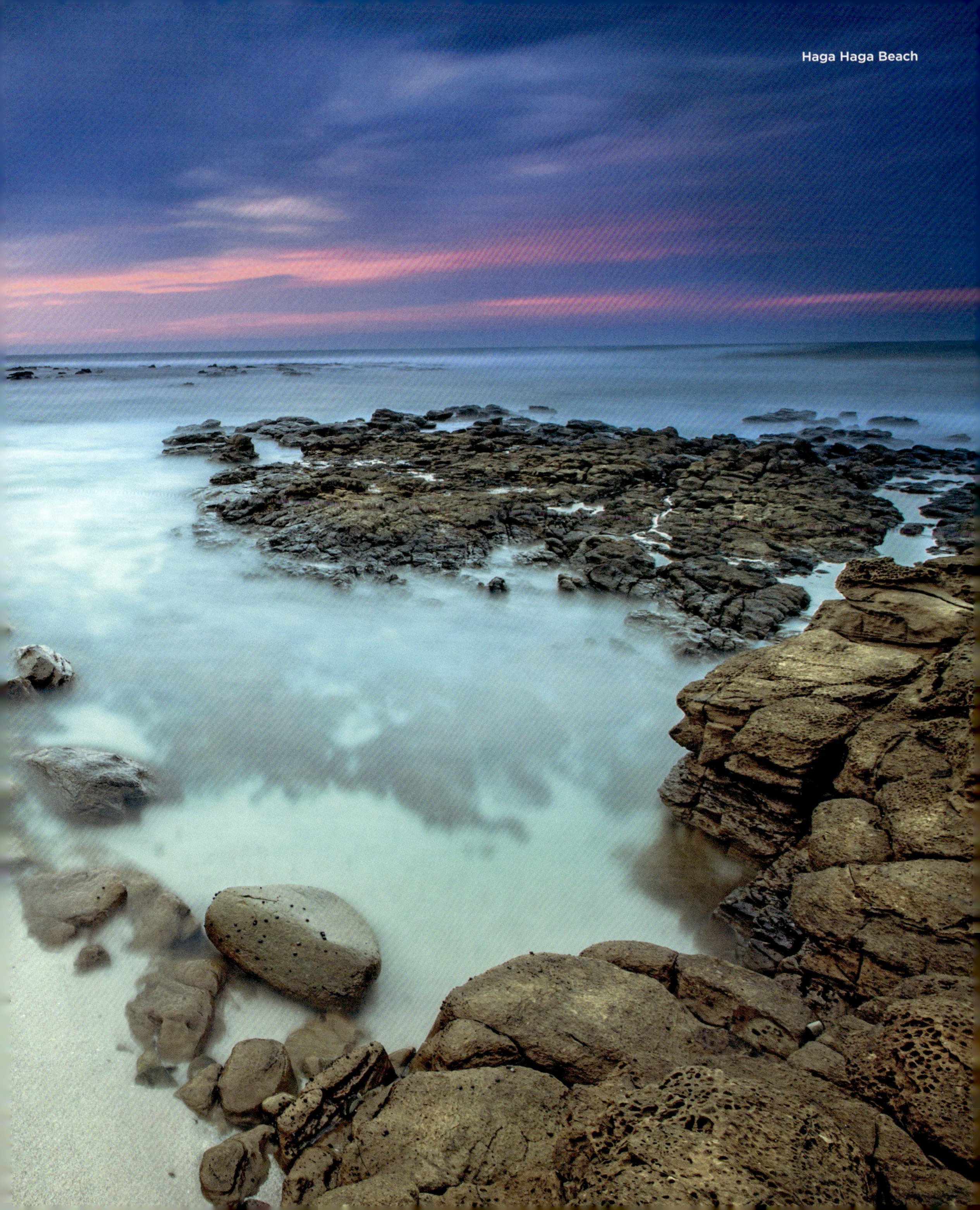
Haga Haga Beach

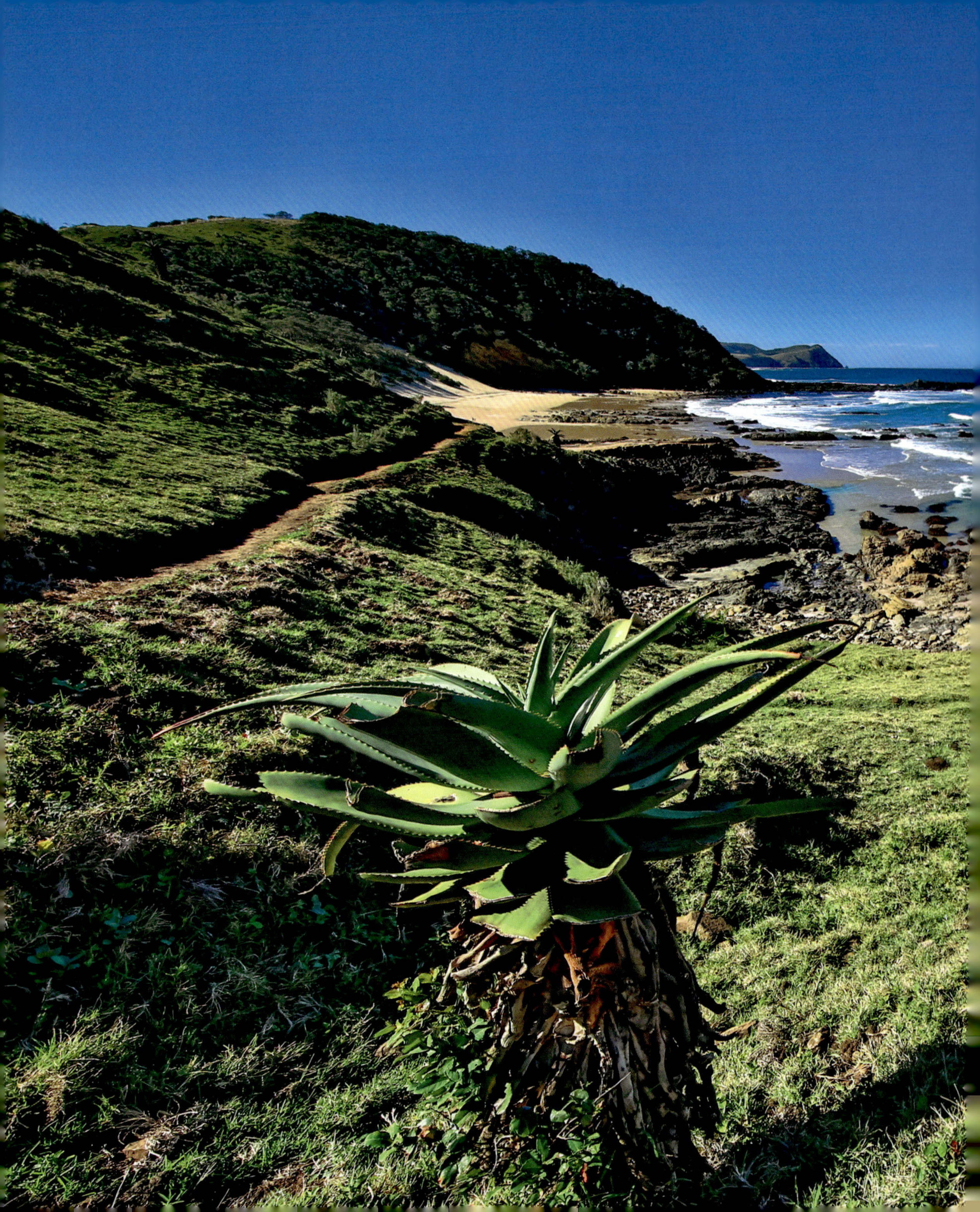

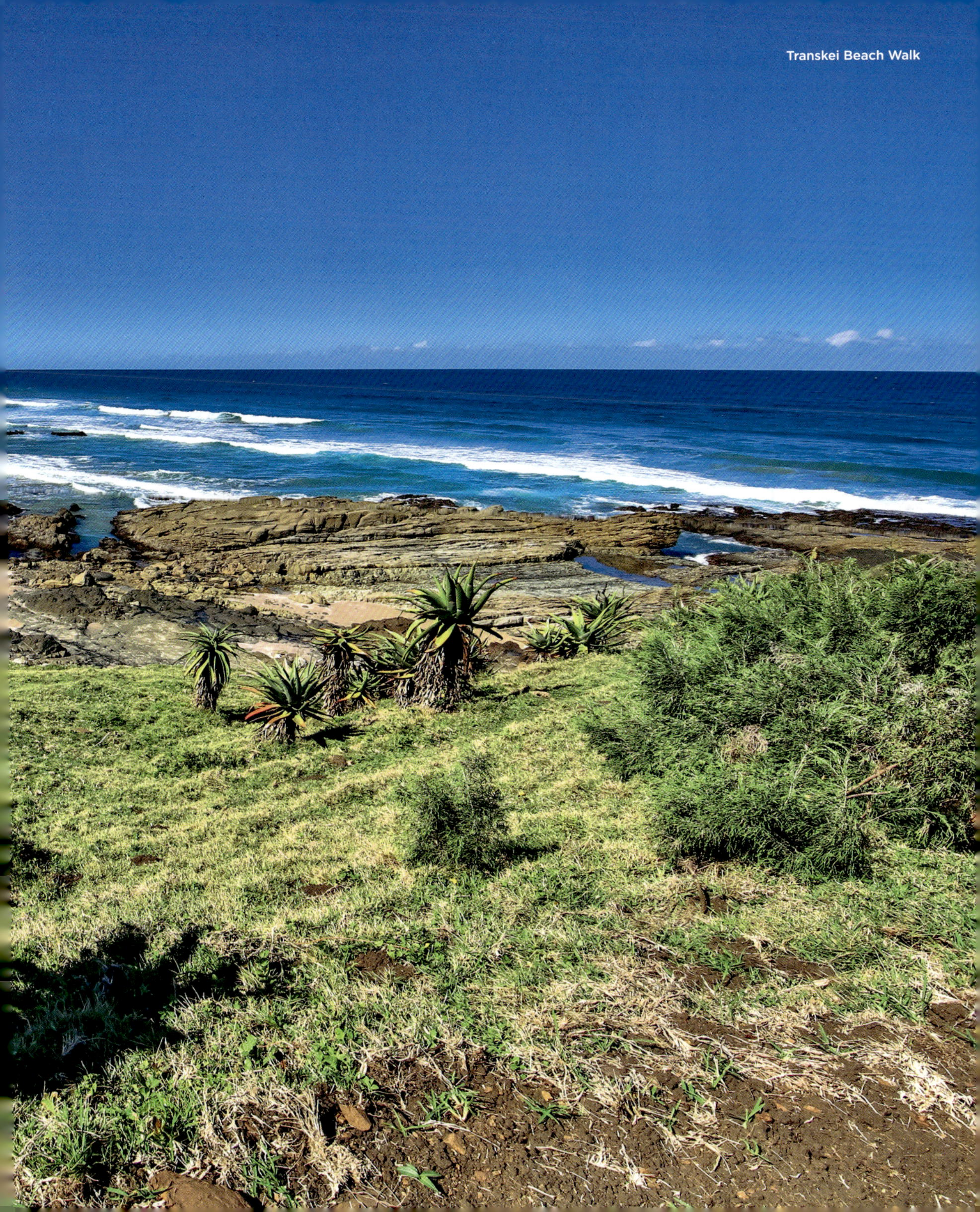

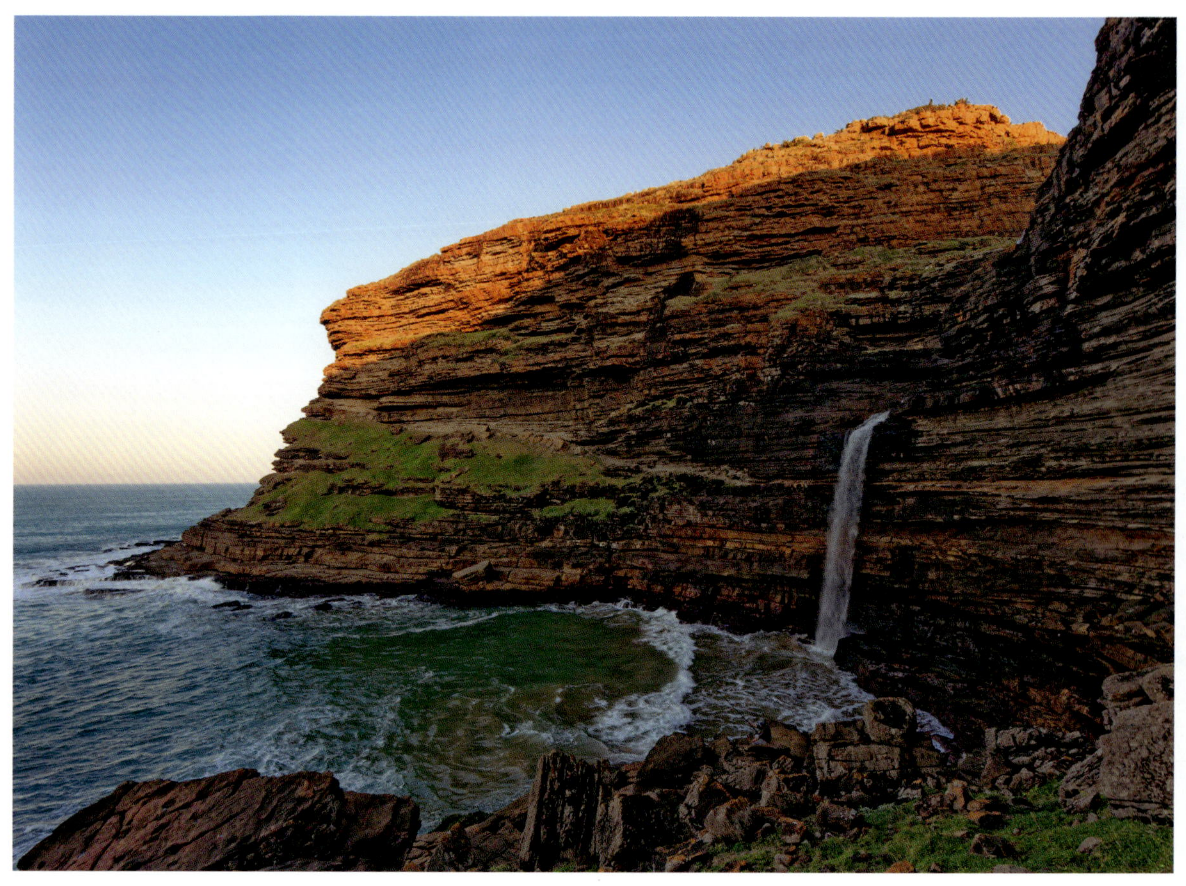

Waterfall Bluff, Pondoland

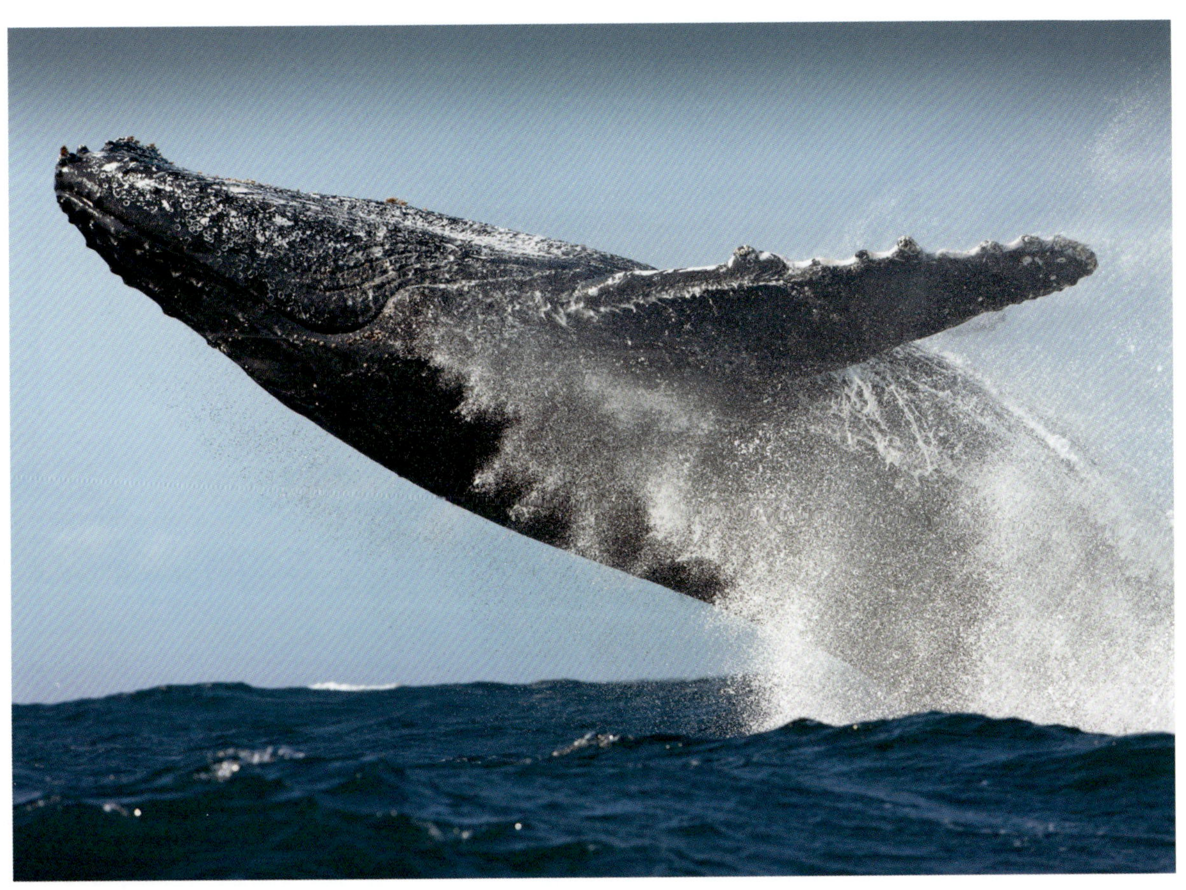

Humpback whale, Wild Coast

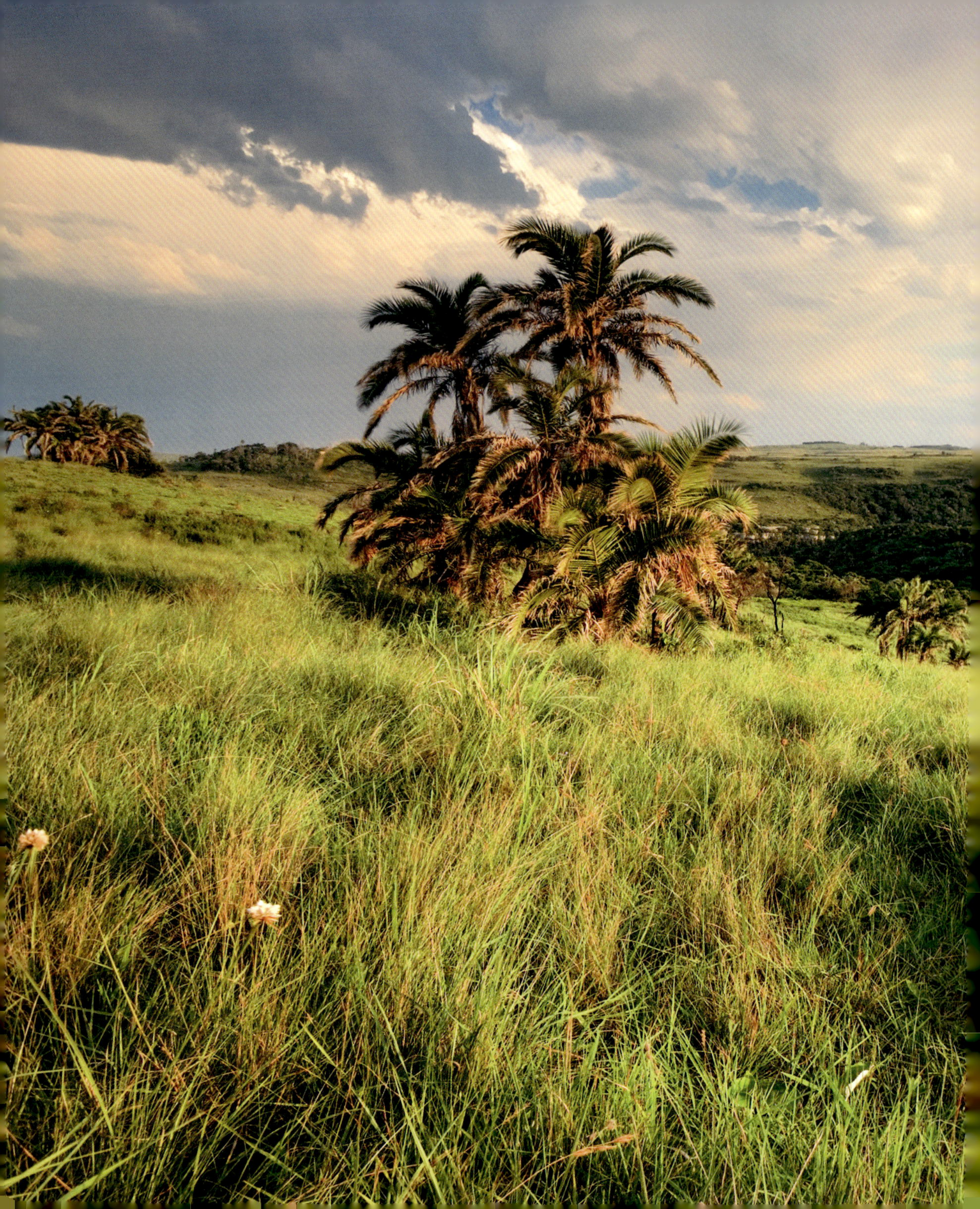

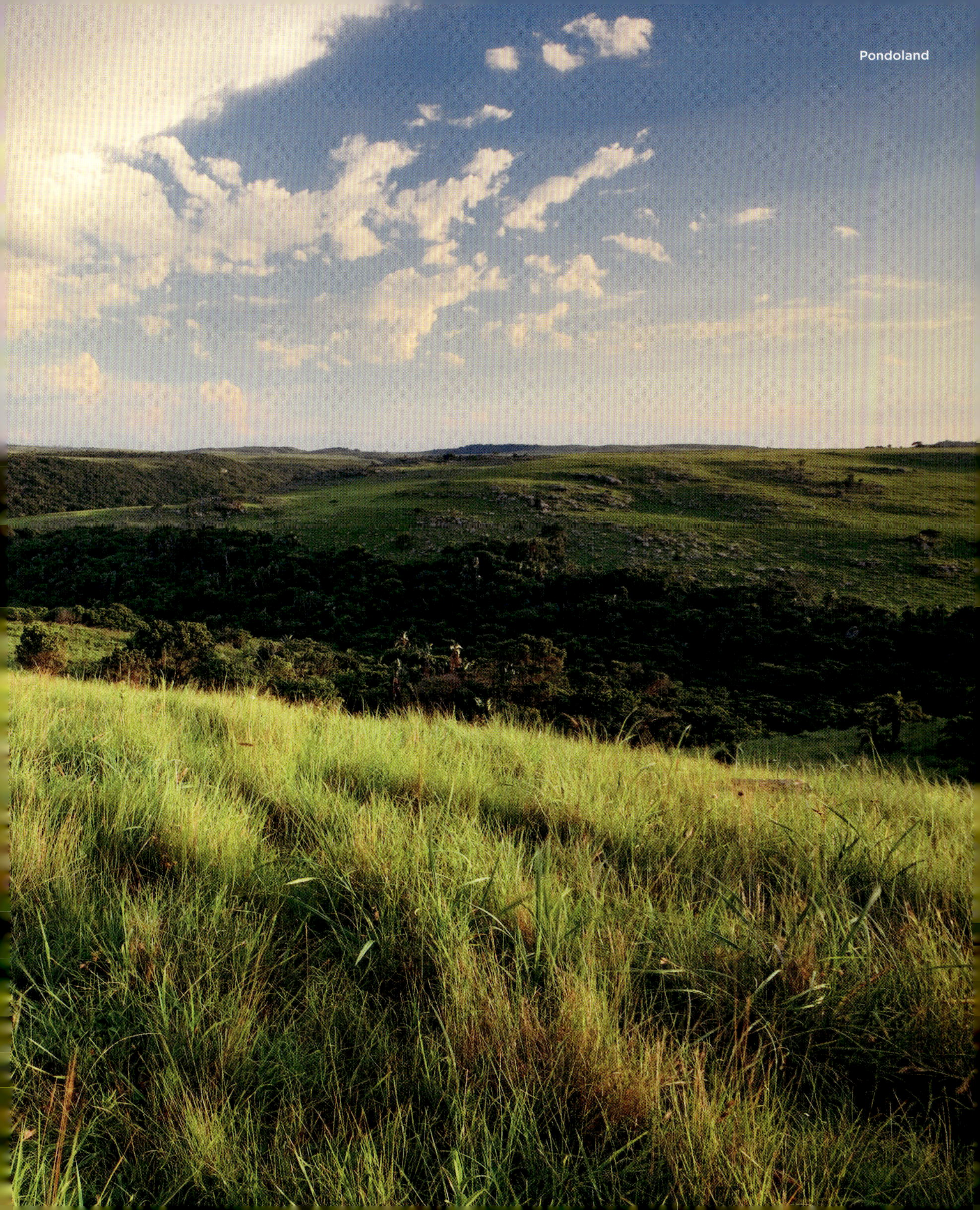
Pondoland

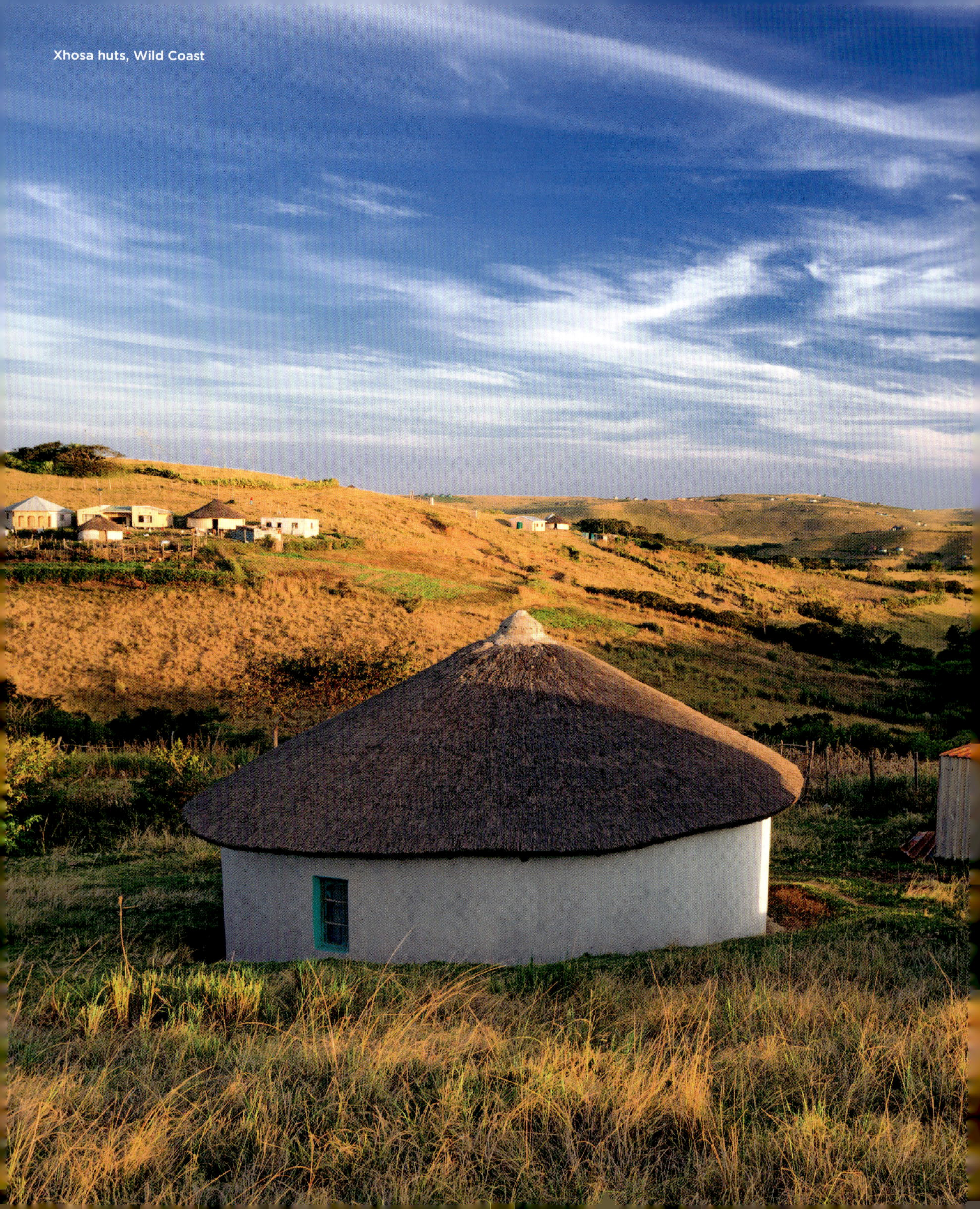
Xhosa huts, Wild Coast

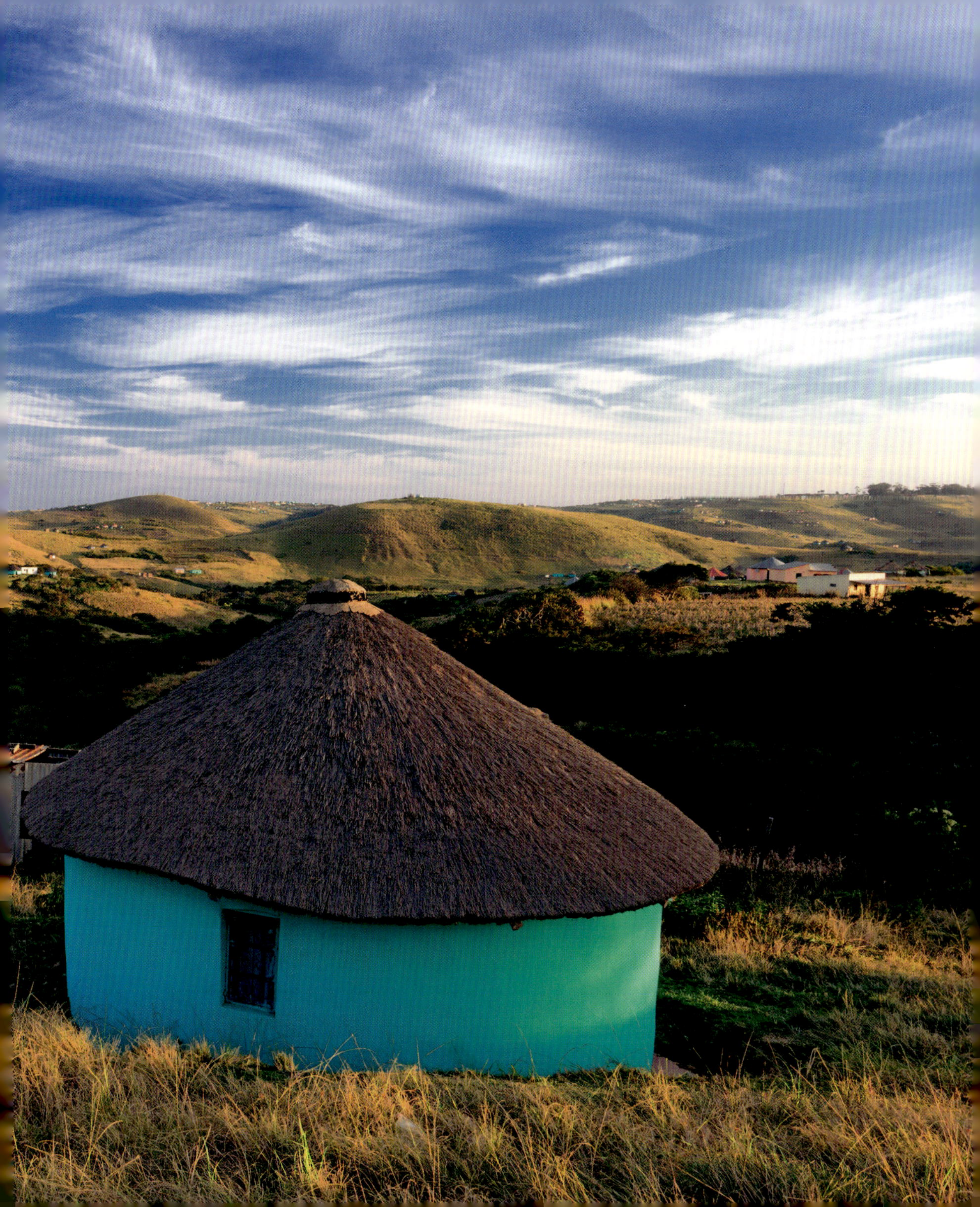

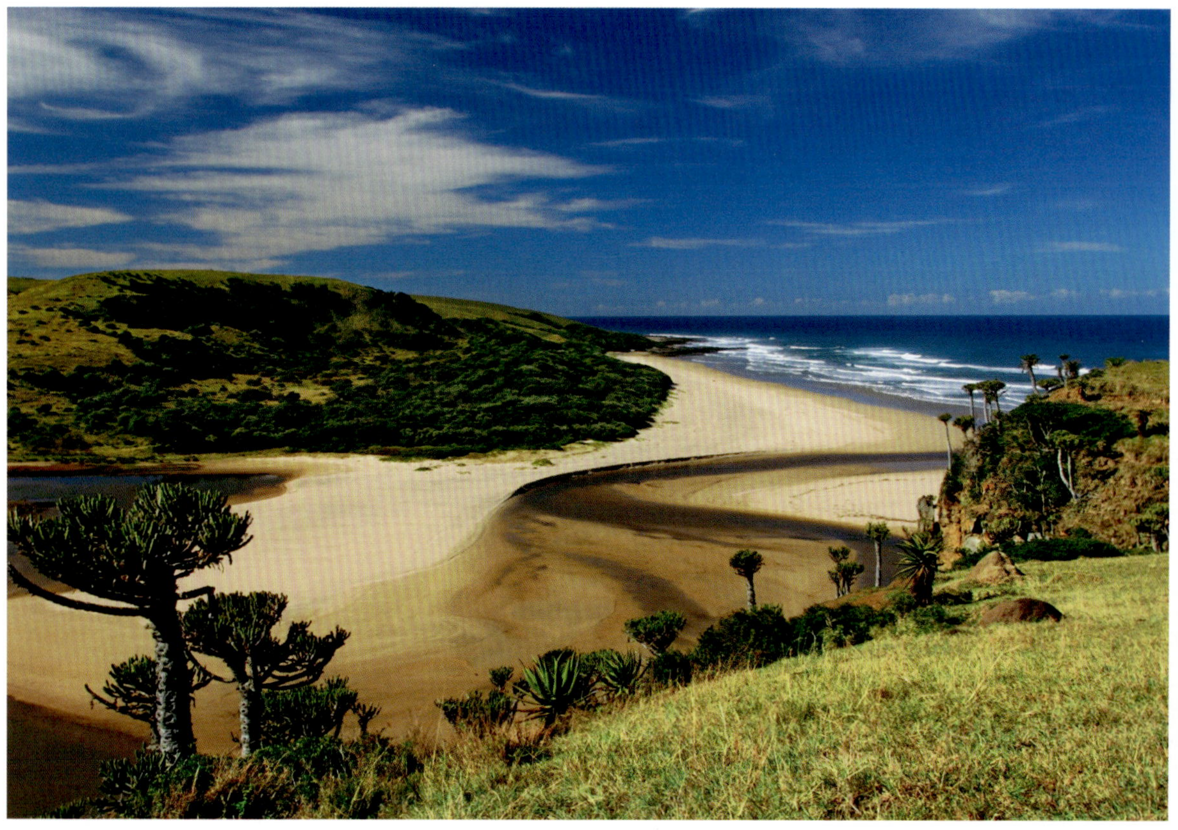

Shixini River

Hole-in-the-Wall
Where did the hole in the wall come from? The scientific answer: the crashing of the waves. The Xhosa tell a different story of a mighty cliff that protected a lagoon by which a beautiful girl lived. She fell in love with one of the half-human, half-sea creature sea-people, but her father did not want to let his daughter go. A huge fish then came and rammed its head through the rock face to clear her way.

Hole-in-the-Wall
Qui a troué cette paroi rocheuse ? Les vagues, répond l'esprit rationaliste. Mais les Xhosas connaissent l'histoire. Cette falaise immense protégeait une lagune où vivait une jeune fille merveilleusement belle. Les gens de la mer, mi-hommes, mi-poissons, la convoitaient, mais le père ne voulait pas laisser partir sa fille. Un poisson gigantesque décida de les aider : en se servant de sa tête comme d'un bélier, il ouvrit une brèche dans la muraille.

Hole-in-the-Wall
Wie das Loch in die Wand kommt? Ein Werk der Wellen, lautet die nüchterne Antwort. Die Xhosa erzählen eine andere Geschichte: Die mächtige Klippe schirmte eine Lagune ab, in der ein wunderschönes Mädchen lebte. Sie hatte das Begehren der Sea People, halb Mensch, halb Wasserwesen, geweckt, aber der Vater wollte seine Tochter nicht ziehen lassen. Ein riesiger Fisch half: Er rammte seinen Kopf durch die Felswand und machte den Weg frei.

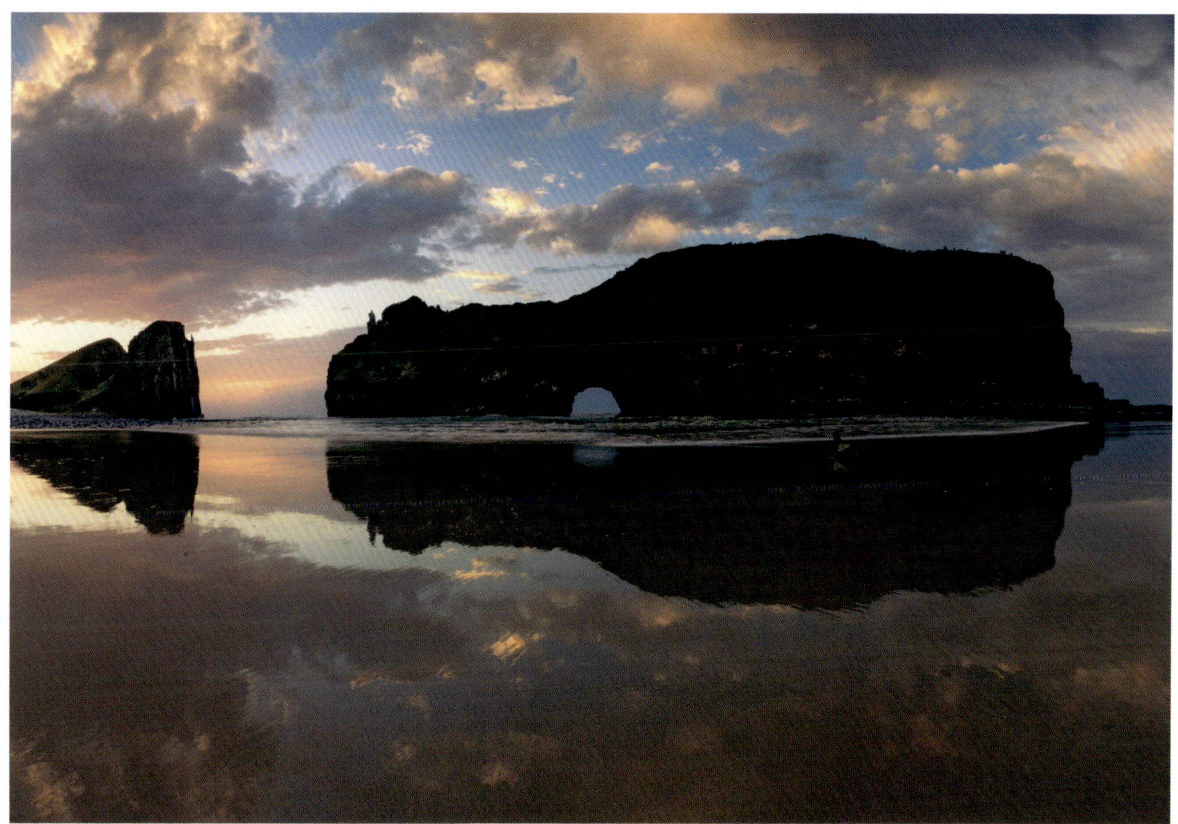

Hole-in-the-Wall

Hole-in-the-Wall
¿De dónde viene el agujero de la pared? Una obra de olas, es la respuesta sobria. Los Xhosa cuentan una historia diferente: el poderoso acantilado blindaba una laguna donde vivía una hermosa niña. Despertaba los deseos de la gente del mar, mitad humana, mitad ser de agua, pero el padre no quería sacar a su hija. Un enorme pez la ayudó: estrelló su cabeza contra una pared de roca y despejó el camino.

Hole-in-the-Wall
Come si è formato il buco nella parete? Un'opera delle onde, è la risposta asciutta. La tribù degli Xhosa racconta un'altra storia: l'imponente scoglio nascondeva una laguna dove viveva una splendida fanciulla, che aveva destato il desiderio dei Sea People, metà uomini e metà creature acquatiche, ma suo padre non voleva lasciar andare la figlia. Venne in aiuto un pesce gigante, che conficcò la sua testa nella parete di roccia e liberò il passaggio.

Hole-in-the-Wall
Hoe het gat in de muur is ontstaan? De kracht van de golven, luidt het eenvoudige antwoord. Maar de Xhosa vertellen een ander verhaal: de machtige klip schermde een lagune af waarin een beeldschoon meisje woonde. Zij wekte de begeerte van het Zeevolk op, dat uit half-menselijke waterwezens bestond. Maar de vader schermde zijn dochter af. Een reusachtige vis ramde daarop zijn kop door de rotswand en maakte de weg vrij.

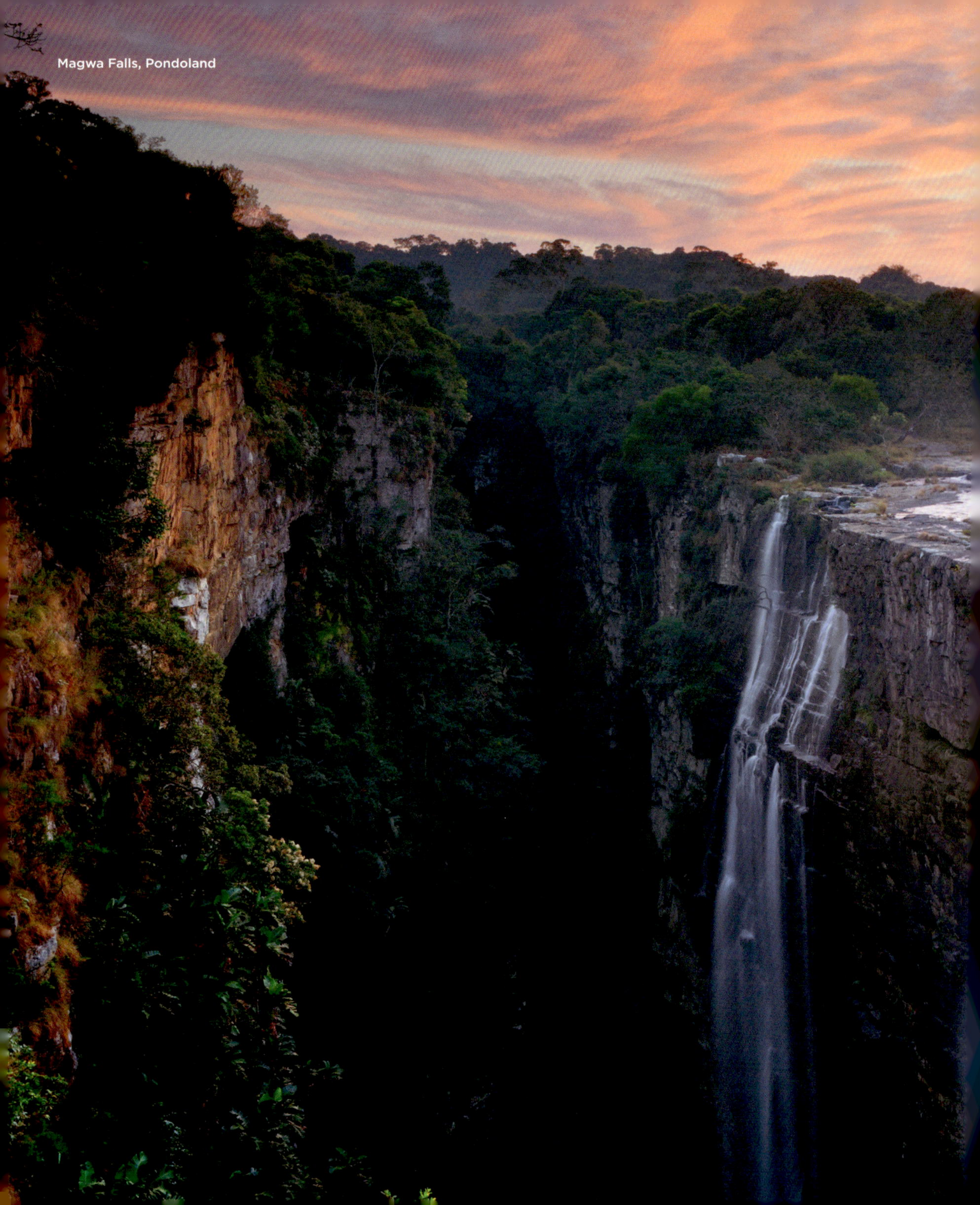
Magwa Falls, Pondoland

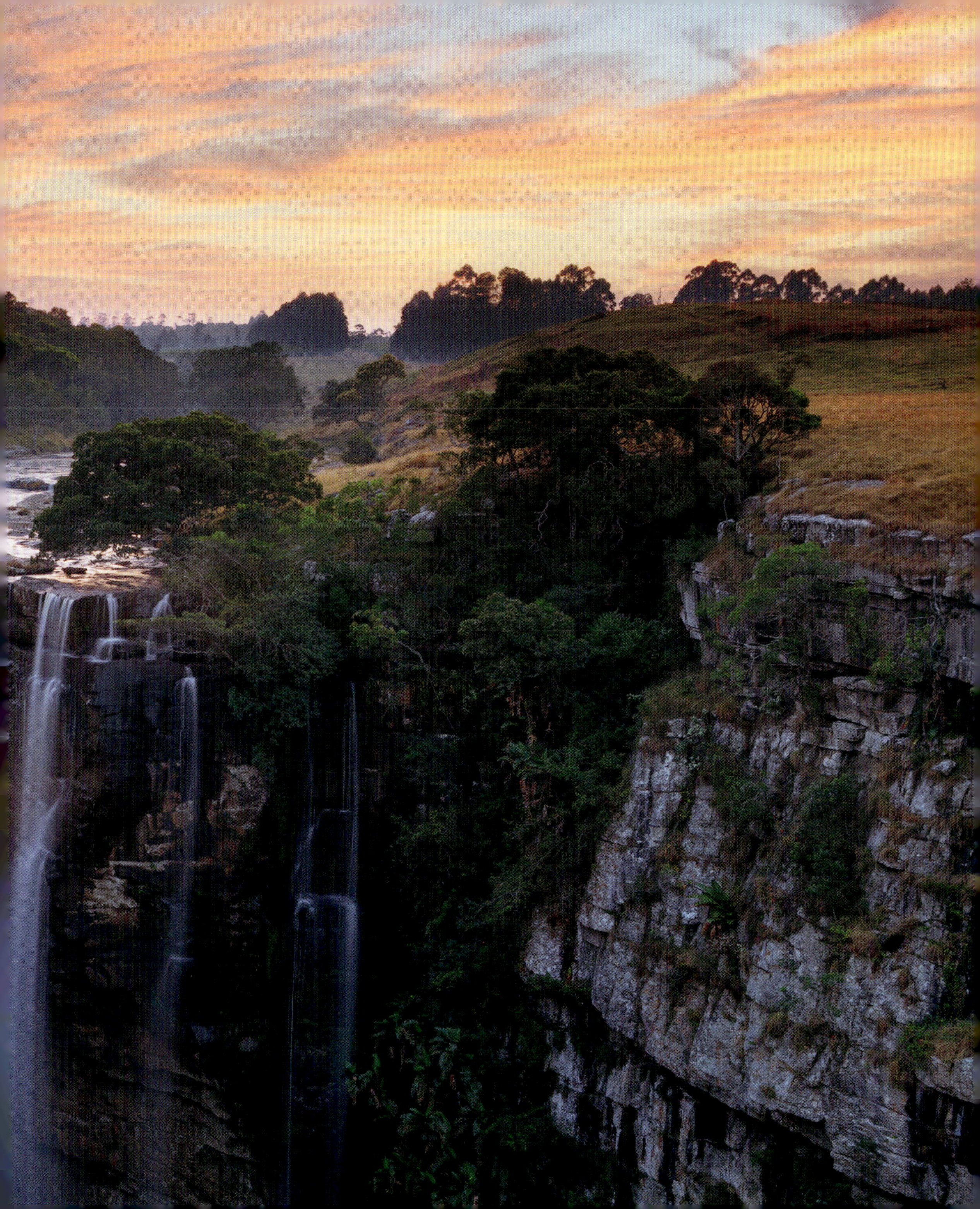

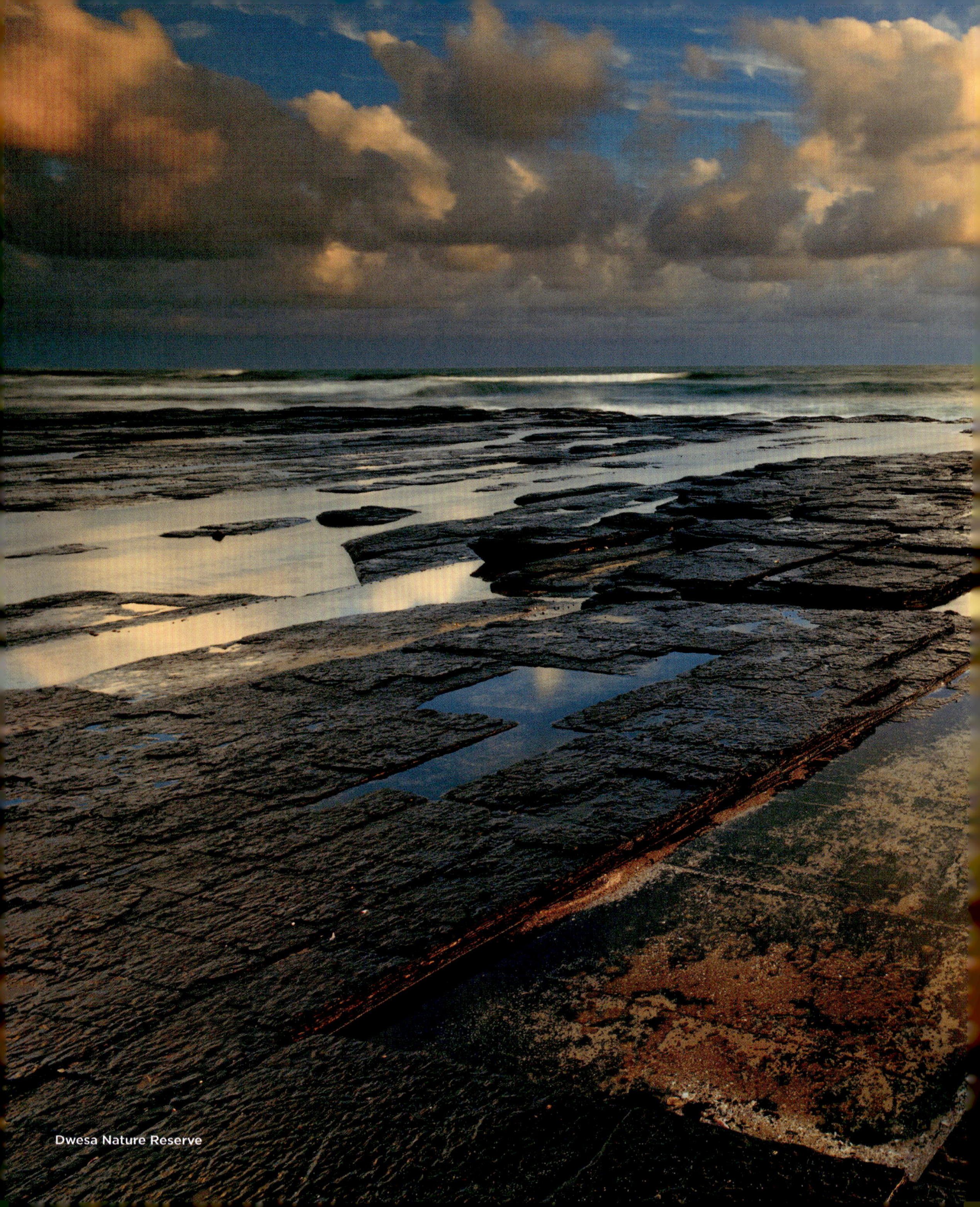

Dwesa Nature Reserve

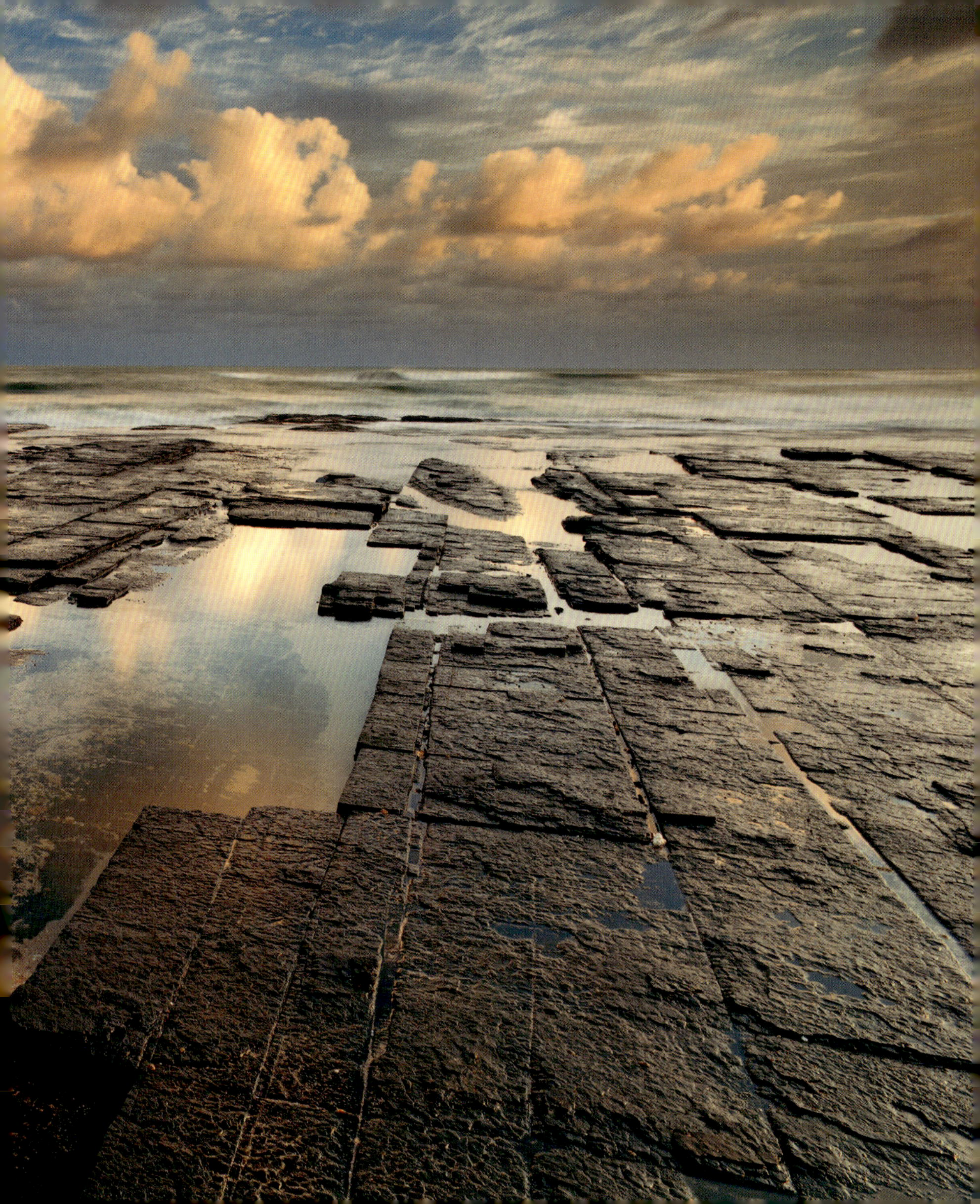

1	Kaokoveld	18
2	Caprivi Strip	32
3	Etosha National Park	40
4	Skeleton Coast	62
5	Damaraland	70
6	Waterberg Plateau National Park	84
7	Namib-Naukluft National Park, Walvis Bay & Windhoek	92
8	Tsau ǁKhaeb National Park (Sperrgebiet) & Lüderitz	116
9	Fish River Canyon	128
10	Chobe National Park & Tsodilo Hills	138
11	Okavango Delta	150
12	Makgadikgadi Salt Pans	166
13	Northern Tuli Game Reserve & Mapungubwe National Park	178
14	Kalahari & Gaborone	188
15	Kgalagadi Transfrontier Park	204
16	Kruger National Park	220
17	Blyde River Canyon	246
18	Pilanesberg National Park	258
19	Johannesburg & Pretoria	270
20	Maputaland	278
21	Hluhluwe-Imfolozi Park	292
22	Golden Gate Highlands National Park	300
23	Drakensberg Mountains & Durban	310
24	Augrabies Falls National Park	328
25	Namaqualand	334
26	West Coast	342
27	Cederberg Mountains & Tankwa Karoo National Park	360
28	Cape Winelands	370
29	Cape Town & Table Mountain	384
30	Overberg	410
31	Garden Route & Port Elizabeth	436
32	Wild Coast	476

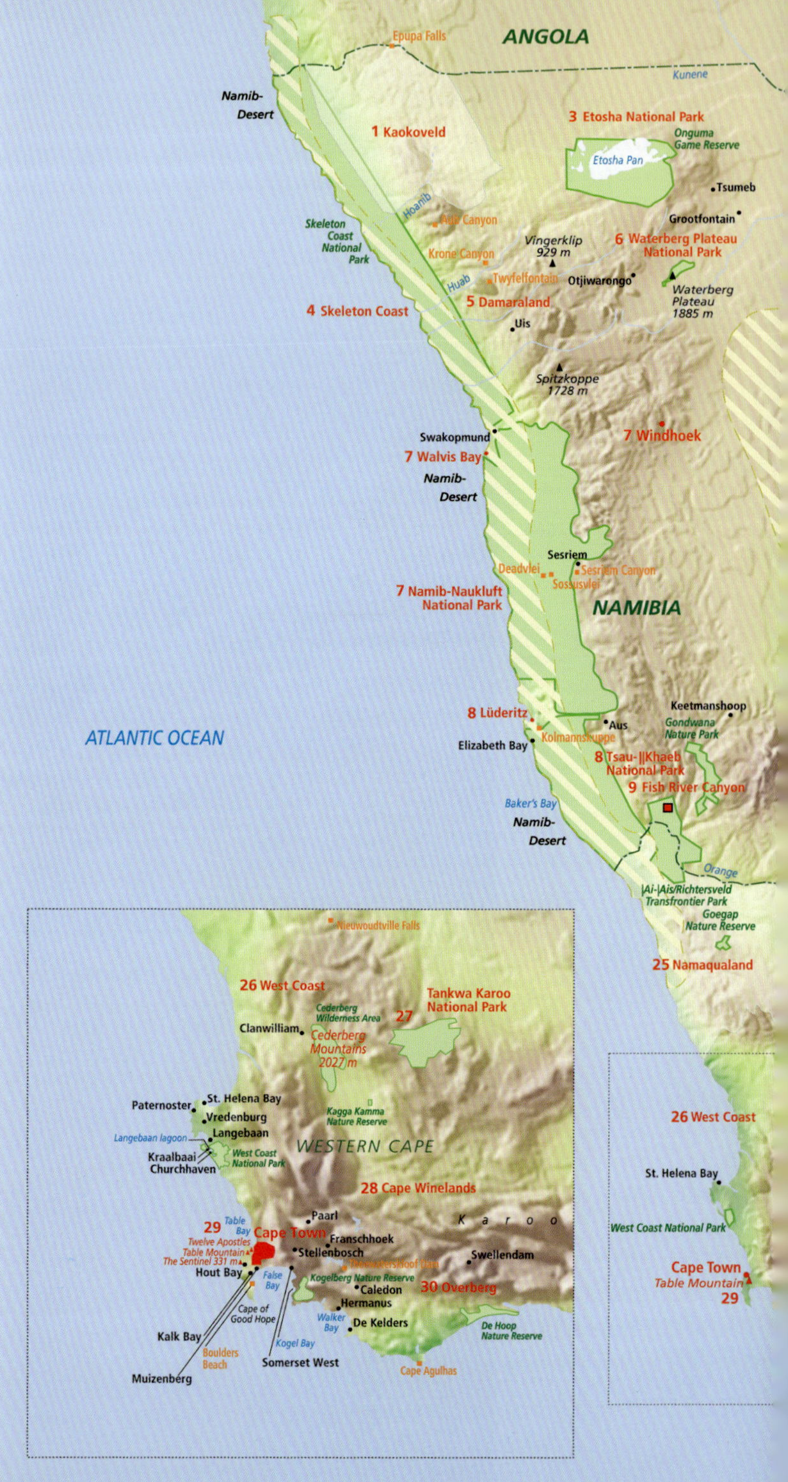

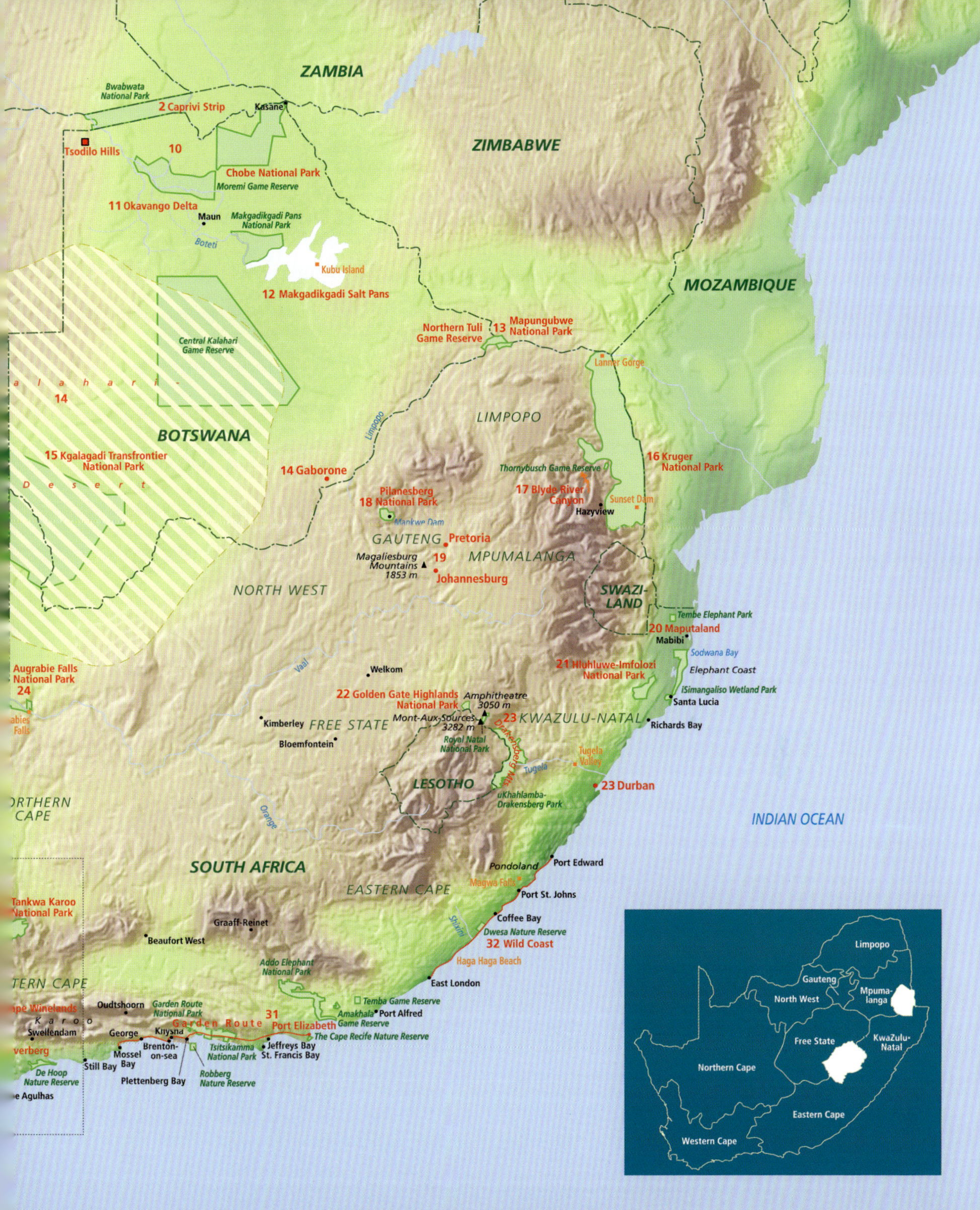

ZAMBIA
ZIMBABWE
MOZAMBIQUE
BOTSWANA
SOUTH AFRICA
INDIAN OCEAN
Bwabwata National Park
2 Caprivi Strip
Kasane
Tsodilo Hills
10
Chobe National Park
Moremi Game Reserve
11 Okavango Delta
Maun
Makgadikgadi Pans National Park
Boteti
Kubu Island
12 Makgadikgadi Salt Pans
Central Kalahari Game Reserve
Northern Tuli Game Reserve
13 Mapungubwe National Park
Lanner Gorge
14
15 Kgalagadi Transfrontier National Park
14 Gaborone
LIMPOPO
Limpopo
16 Kruger National Park
Thornybusch Game Reserve
17 Blyde River Canyon
Sunset Dam
Hazyview
Pilanesberg
18 National Park
Mankwe Dam
GAUTENG
Pretoria
Magaliesburg Mountains 1853 m
19
MPUMALANGA
Johannesburg
NORTH WEST
SWAZI-LAND
Tembe Elephant Park
20 Maputaland
Mabibi
Sodwana Bay
Elephant Coast
21 Hluhluwe-Imfolozi National Park
iSimangaliso Wetland Park
Santa Lucia
Richards Bay
Augrabie Falls National Park
24
Vaal
Welkom
22 Golden Gate Highlands National Park
Amphitheatre 3050 m
Mont-Aux-Sources 3282 m
23 KWAZULU-NATAL
Kimberley
FREE STATE
Bloemfontein
Royal Natal National Park
Drakensberg Mts
Tugela
Tugela Valley
LESOTHO
uKhahlamba-Drakensberg Park
23 Durban
Orange
Pondoland
Port Edward
EASTERN CAPE
Magwa Falls
Port St. Johns
Tankwa Karoo National Park
Graaff-Reinet
Coffee Bay
Beaufort West
Shixini
Dwesa Nature Reserve
32 Wild Coast
Haga Haga Beach
Addo Elephant National Park
East London
Temba Game Reserve
Oudtshoorn
Garden Route National Park
Amakhala Game Reserve
Port Alfred
Garden Route
31 Port Elizabeth
Swellendam
George
Knysna
The Cape Recife Nature Reserve
Brenton-on-sea
Tsitsikamma National Park
Jeffreys Bay
St. Francis Bay
Mossel Bay
Still Bay
De Hoop Nature Reserve
Plettenberg Bay
Robberg Nature Reserve
Limpopo
Gauteng
North West
Mpuma-langa
Free State
KwaZulu-Natal
Northern Cape
Eastern Cape
Western Cape

A
Aardwolf 57
The Abu Elephant Camp 162
Acacia tree 52 f.
Addo Elephant National Park 464 f.
African baobab 178 f., 182, 186 f., 223
African buffalo 160 f.
African clawless otter 55
African Penguin 358
African wild dog 55, 158 f.
African wildcat 55
|Ai-|Ais/Richtersveld Transfrontier Park 128 ff., 134 ff.
Aloidendron dichotomum 192
Amakhala Game Reserve 470
Amphitheatre 310 f., 322
Antelope 58, 60, 91, 424 f.
Atlantic Ocean 341
Aub Canyon 30 f.
Augrabies Falls 328 f.
Augrabies Falls National Park 328–333

B
Baker's Bay 122 f.
Banded mongoose 57
Baobab 170 f., 178 f., 182, 186 f., 223
Bat-eared fox 55
Big Five 240 ff.
Black rhinoceros 243
Black Rock 282
Bloukrans Bridge 449
Bloukrans River Gorge 459
Blue wildebeest 60
Blyde River Canyon 6 f., 246–257
Bontebok 60, 416
Boschendal Wine Estate 373 ff.
Boteti River 166 ff., 172 f., 175
Bottle trees 72
Boulders Beach 407
Bourke's Luck Potholes 252 f.
Brandwag Buttress 303
Brenton 436 f.
Brenton-on-Sea 443
Buffalo 160 f., 226 f., 241
Burchell's zebra 58
Bushman rock art 363
Bwabwata National Park 35, 38

C
Cabernet Sauvignon grapes 372
Caledon 416
Camp Fig Tree 464 f.
Camps 44 f., 50 f., 162, 464 f.
Camps Bay 402
Canyon Lodge 132 f.
Cape Agulhas 430 f.
Cape fox 57
Cape fur seal 106 f., 122 f.
Cape hyrax 463
Cape mountain zebra 348 f.
Cape of Good Hope 396
The Cape Recife Nature Reserve 471
Cape St Blaize Lighthouse 442
Cape Town 384–409
Cape Winelands 370–383
Caprivi-Strip 32–40
Caracal 55
Carnivores 54 f.
Cathedral Peak region 313
Cederberg Mountains 360–369
Cederberg Wilderness Area 362 f., 365 ff.
Central Kalahari Game Reserve 188 f., 197, 200 f.
Chacma baboon 57
Cheetah 55, 181, 190, 222
Chitabe 158
Chobe National Park 138–149
Churchhaven 350 f.
Common duiker 58
Common eland 58
Crocodile 55, 140, 281
Cuando River 32 f.

D
Damaraland 25, 70–83
De Hoop Nature Reserve 424 ff.
De Kelders 418 f.
Deadvlei 96 f.
Desert elephant 24
Desert warthog 58
Diamond Hill 126 f.
Dog 55, 158 f.
Dolomite Camp 51
Dolphin 358, 396
Drakensberg Mountains 310–327
Duiker 58
Durban 326 f.
Dwesa Nature Reserve 494 f.

E
East African oryxes 197
Eland antelope 58, 91, 424 f.
Elbow Rock 119
Elephant 24, 35, 66 f., 73, 138 f., 156 f., 175, 237, 240, 264
Elephant Coast 278 ff.
Epupa Falls 15, 20, 22 f., 28 f.
Etosha National Park 40–53
Etosha Pan 40 f.
Evangelical Lutheran church (Windhoek) 126 f.

F
False Bay 394 ff.
Fish River Canyon 128–137

Flamingo 109
Fox 55, 57
Franschhoek 373 ff., 379, 382
Fynbos 334 f.

G
Gaborone 202 f.
Game Lodge 154 f.
Game Pass Shelter 316
Garden Route 436–475
Garden Route National Park 438, 440 f., 444 ff., 452 ff., 463, 466 ff.
Garub 125
Gemsbok 26, 60, 100
Geocap Nature Reserve 336
Giraffe 16, 42, 38, 58, 145, 284
Gnu 145, 191, 217, 232 f., 260, 268 f.
Golden Gate Highlands National Park 300–309
Gondwana Nature Park 132 f.
Great white shark 358
Greater Kudu 60
Grootbos Private Nature Reserve 435

H
Haga Haga Beach 480 f.
Halfmens 134
Herbivores 58 ff.
Hermanus 410 f., 413, 422 f.
Hippopotamus 38, 60, 149, 288
Hlosi Game Lodge 470
Hluhluwe-Imfolozi Park 292–299
Hoanib 24
Hole-in-the-Wall 476 f., 490 f.
Hout Bay 397 f., 400 f.
Huab River 73
Huguenot monument 382
Humpback whale 358, 485
Hyena 55
Hyrax 60, 463

I
Imbabala 58
Impala 58, 141, 232 f.
Insectivores 56 f.
iSimangaliso Wetland Park 281, 284 f., 288 ff.

J
Jacaranda trees 277
Jackal 55
Jeffreys Bay 450 f.
Johannesburg 270–277

K
Kagga Kamma Nature Reserve 364
Kalahari 188–203
Kalahari Desert 2, 188 ff., 207
Kalk Bay 403
Kaokoveld 15, 18–31,
Karoo 360 f.
Keetmanshoop 192 f.
Kgalagadi Transfrontier Park 191, 194 f., 204–119
Killer whale 358
Kirstenbosch Botanical Garden 399
Klein-Aus Vista 120 f.
Klipspringer 58
Knysna 460 f.
Knysna Heads 448
Kogel Bay 404 f.
Kogelberg Nature Reserve 412
Kolmanskop 124
Kommetje 398
Kraalbaai 342 f.
Krantz aloe 438
Krone Canyon 70 f.
Kruger National Park 220–239
Kubu Island 174
Kudu 46 f., 60, 285
Kunene River 21
KwaZulu-Natal 323

L
Langebaan lagoon 342 f., 353 ff.
Lanner Gorge 234 f.
Leopard 152, 183, 206, 230, 244 f.
Limpopo River 184
Linyanti Marshes 164 f.
Lion 34, 46 f., 148, 212, 228, 244
Lion's Head 388 f.
Lodges 132 f., 154 f., 434 f., 434 f., 470
Lot's Wife rock formation 366 f.
Lüderitz 116–127
Lyre antelope 60

M
Mabibi 278 ff.
Magaliesburg Mountains 265
Magwa Falls 492 f.
Makgadikgadi Pans National Park 166 f., 169, 172 ff.
Makgadikgadi Salt Pans 166–177
Mankwe Dam 258 f.
Mapungubwe National Park 178–187
Maputaland 278–291
Marine animals 358 f.
Meerkat 39, 57
Melrose House (Pretoria) 276
Midlands 323
Milky Way 78, 174 f.
Mmamagwa archaeological site 180

Mongoose 57
Monkey 57
Mont-Aux-Sources 318 ff.
Moremi Game Reserve 163
Moringa trees 49
Mossel Bay 442
Muizenberg 394 f.

N
Namaqualand 334–341
Namib Desert 62 ff.
Namib-Naukluft National Park 4 f., 92–115
Namibian desert elephant 24
Namibian Poison Spurge 70 f.
Ngamiland 164 f.
Nieuwoudtville Falls 338 f.
Nile crocodile 55
Northern Tuli Game Reserve 178–187
Nyala 60

O
Okaukuejo watering hole 48
Okavango Delta 16 f., 150–165
Okavango River 36 f.
Omnivores 56 f.
Onguma Game Reserve 44 f., 50
Onguma Tented Camp 44 f.
Onguma Tree Top Camp 50
Orange River 332 f.
Oribi 60
Oryx 197, 336
Ostriche 213
Otjinjange riverbed 18 f.
Otter Trail 455
Overberg 410–433

P
Pachypodium namaquanum 134
Paternoster 344, 356 f.
Pearl 376 f.
Penguin 358, 407
Pilanesberg Game Reserve 266 f.
Pilanesberg National Park 258–269
Pinnacle Rock 253
Plettenberg Bay 440 f., 444 ff., 449
Pod Mahogany tree 288
Point Yacht Club (Durban) 326
Pondoland 484 ff., 492 f.
Porcupine 57
Port Elizabeth 471 ff.
Pretoria 8 f., 270–277

Q
Quiver trees 130, 192 f., 331

R
Red Dunes 104 f.
Red hartebeest 58
Red-billed oxpeckers 38
Red-billed quelea 168
Rhinoceros 242 f., 260, 295 ff.
Roan antelope 58
Robberg Nature Reserve 444 f.
Rock art 144, 363
Rock hyrax 60
Royal Natal National Park 310 f., 322

S
Sable antelope 58
San rock art 316
Sandstone cliffs 306, 406
Savuti Marsh 148
Seal 106 f., 122 f., 358
The Sentinel 400 f.
Serval 55
Sesriem Canyon 101
Shark 358
Shixini River 490
Short-beaked common dolphin 358
Signal Hill 387
Skeleton Coast 62–69,
Skeleton Coast National Park 62 ff., 66 f.
Sodwana Bay 286 f.
Somerset West 378, 382
Sossusvlei 4, 94 f., 96 f.
South African giraffe 284
South African porcupine 57
Southern right whale 358, 413
Sperm whale 358
Spitzkoppe 76 f., 79, 82
Spotted hyena 55
Springbok 46 f., 58, 208 f.
Stadsaal Caves 362 f.
Stauch, August 124
Steenbok 60
Stellenbosch 380 f.
Storms River Mouth 452 ff., 456 f., 466 f.
Storms River Mouth Waterfall 458
Sunset Dam 236
Suspension Bridge 456 f.
Swakopmund 110 f.
Swellendam 414 f.

T
Table Bay 10 f., 384 f.
Table Mountain 10 f., 384–409
Tankwa Karoo National Park 360–369
Temba Game Reserve 288
Tembe Elephant Park 280
Termite mound 43
Theewaterskloof Dam 433
Thorn tree 204 f.
Thornybusch Game Reserve 224 f.
Transkei Beach Walk 482 f.
Tree Top Walk 399
Tsau ||Khaeb National Park (Sperrgebiet) 116–127
Tsitsikamma coastline 468 f.
Tsitsikamma National Park 455
Tsodilo Hills 144 ff.
Tugela River 320 f.
Tugela Valley 314 f.
Twelve Apostles 386, 390 f., 402
Twyfelfontein 80 f.

U
uKhahlamba-Drakensberg Park 314 f., 317, 320 f., 324 f.
Union Building (Pretoria) 272, 277

V
Vergelegen Wine Estate 378, 382
Vervet monkey 57
Victoria & Alfred Waterfront (Cape Town) 392 f.
Vineyard 370 f., 376 f., 379
Vingerklip 83
Voortrekker Monument 8 f.

W
Walker Bay 413, 418 ff.
Walvis Bay 106 ff.
Warthog 58
Waterberg Mountain 87
Waterberg Plateau 84 ff.
Waterberg Plateau National Park 84–91,
Waterfall Bluff 484
West Coast 342–357
West Coast National Park 342 f., 345 ff.
Western Cape 10 f., 406
Whale 358, 413, 485
White rhinoceros 242, 295 ff.
Wild Coast 476–495
Wilderness 439
Windhoek 112 ff.
Wine Estates 373 ff., 378, 380 ff.
Wolfberg Arch 365

X
Xhosa huts 488 f.

Z
Zebra 12, 46 f., 58, 145, 153, 302, 348

Getty Images
2 Hannes Thirion;8/9 Hannes Thirion; 12 Cedric Favero; 15 CarasDelMundo; 16 Panoramic Images; 20 2630ben/ iStockphoto; 21 Perspectives; 28/29 Hemis. fr RM; 32/33 Franz Aberham; 34 National Geographic Creative; 39 Paul Souders; 40/41 Robert Harding World Imagery; 43 Dennis K Johnson/Lonley Planet Images; 52/53 Buena Vista Images; 62/63 Theo Allofs; 64 Wolfgang Kaehler/ Kontributor; 70/71 Markus Obländer; 74/75 Tiago_Fernandez; 76/77 Mitchell Krog; 78 Alex Saberi; 80/81 Arctic-Images; 83 JTB/UIG; 84/85 infried Schafer; 96/97 Buena Vista Images; 101 Hannes Thirion; 102/103 Hannes Thirion; 109 Juan Carlos Muoz; 128/129 Hannes Thirion; 130 Hannes Thirion; 132/133 Hoberman Collection/Kontributor; 138/139 2630ben; 140 Gaston Piccinetti; 145 Bob Smith; 150/151 Kelly Cheng; 152 Chris Jackson/ Staff; 156/157 Thousandsanimals; 159 Getty Images/National Geographic Magazines; 164/165 Blaine Harrington; 174 Hannes Thirion; 175 Shumba138; 181 Roger de la Harpe; 183 Cameron Spencer/Staff; 184 Roger de la Harpe; 185 Andy Nixon; 186/187 Andy Nixon; 190 Paul Souders; 191 Peter Van Der Byl; 192/193 Matthias Graben; 194/195 Hougaard Malan Photography; 196 Ole Jorgen Liodden/Nature Picture Library; 207 Ann & Steve Toon/robertharding; 231 Larry Dale Gordon/Design Pics; 234/235 mDumbleton; 238/239 MATTES Rene/hemis.fr; 246/247 Hougaard Malan; 248 Mitchell Krog; 250/251 Hougaard Malan Photography; 253 Dewald Kirsten; 256/257 fabio lamanna; 260 Jon Hicks; 262/263 kamira777; 265 Martin Harvey; 278/279 Roger de la Harpe; 282/283 Roger de la Harpe; 286/287 Roger de la Harpe; 290/291 Roger de la Harpe; 300/301 This content is subject to copyright.; 303 HannesThirion; 304/305 Hougaard Malan Photography; 306 Heinrich van den Berg; 308/309 Hougaard Malan Photography; 312 Alta Oosthuizen; 313 Hougaard Malan; 316 Stephen Alvarez; 317 Daleen Loest; 320/321 Emil von Maltitz; 322 Travel_Nerd; 324/325 Emil von Maltitz; 328/329 Hougaard Malan Photography; 336 Guenter Fischer; 341 Shumba138; 359 ea-4; 360/361 Hougaard Malan; 362 Chiara Salvadori; 363 Mike Copeland; 365 Hougaard Malan; 366/367 Hougaard Malan; 376/377 Merten Snijders; 397 Laurent Lhote; 400/401 Jason Edwards; 404/405 Liesel Kershoff; 406 Liesel Kershoff; 407 Paula Bronstein; 432 Liesel Kershoff; 433 Liesel Kershoff; 436/437 Chiara Salvadori; 438 Dirk Bleyer; 442 Hougaard Malan Photography; 446/447 Ben1183; 450/451 Gallo Images; 455 Homebrew Films Company; 458 O. lamany & E. Vicens; 468/469 Sara Winter; 472/473 Ian Trower; 474/475 Ian Trower; 478 Peter Chadwick; 480/481 2630ben; 482/483 wildacad; 484 Hougaard Malan Photography; 486/487 Hougaard Malan; 488/489 Hougaard Malan Photography; 490 Roger de la Harpe; 491 Hougaard Malan Photography; 492/493 Hougaard Malan Photography; 494/495 Hougaard Malan Photography

Markus Hertrich
224/225; 228/229; 232/233; 344; 345; 373; 394/395; 398; 399; 402; 403; 418/419; 420/421; 434; 435; 479

Huber Images
4/5 Fantuz Olimpio; 10/11 Gräfenhain; 36/37 Harscher; 42 Marco Gaiotti; 49 R. Schmid; 69 Andrew Stewart; 72 K. Richard; 73 Harscher; 82 Ritterbach Jürgen; 92/93 Tom Mackie; 94 Harscher; 95 Harscher; 100 Harscher; 104 Jürgen Ritterbach/Huber-Images; 105 C. Dörr; 108 Roberto Moiola; 126/127 Cornelia Dörr; 131 Harscher; 141 Harscher; 158 Jürgen Ritterbach; 170/171 Reiner Harscher; 188/189 Ritterbach; 197 Ritterbach; 200/201 Jürgen Ritterbach; 217 Jürgen Ritterbach; 252 Simeone Giovanni; 272 Giovanni Simeone; 273 Giovanni Simeone/SIME; 276 Giovanni Simeone; 277 Giovanni Simeone; 318/319 Simeone Giovanni; 323 Paolo Giocoso; 372 Justin Foulkes; 374/375 Justin Foulkes; 383 Andrea Armellin; 384/385 Gräfenhain; 387 Gräfenhain; 392/393 Richard Taylor; 431 Giovanni Simeone; 443 Simeone Giovanni; 449 Ritterbach

laif
35 Christian Heeb; 59 Denis-Huot/hemis.fr; 59 Michel Denis-Huot/hemis; 60 Thorsten Milse/robertharding; 61 Ann & Steve Toon/robertharding; 112/113 Christian Kerber; 124 Rene Mattes/hemis.fr; 125 Toma Babovic; 244 Andreas Hub; 464/465 Andreas Hub; 470 Matt Parry/ robertharding

mauritius images
6/7 nature picture library/Hougaard Malan; 18/19 FRIEDRICHSMEIER/ Alamy; 22/23 imageBROKER/ Christian Heinrich; 24 imageBROKER/ Egmont Strigl; 25 imageBROKER/ Christian Heinrich; 26 Greatstock/ Alamy; 27 John Warburton-Lee/Amar Grover; 30/31 roederPhotography; 38 FRIEDRICHSMEIER/Alamy; 44/45 Bill Gozansky/Alamy; 46/47 Westend61/ Gemma Ferrando; 48 Travel Collection/ Hänel, Gerald; 50 Bill Gozansky/Alamy; 51 Cultura/Lost Horizon Images; 54 Minden Pictures/Richard Du Toit; robertharding/ Ann and Steve Toon; imageBROKER/ Malcolm Schuyl/FLPA; Max Allen/Alamy; imageBROKER/Uwe Skrzypczak; Avico Ltd/Alamy; 55 Donovan Klein/Alamy; nature picture library/Ann & Steve Toon; MARKA/Alamy; Dan Barker/Alamy; 56 age fotostock/Gaston Piccinetti; Arterra Picture Library/Alamy; Juergen Sohns/Alamy; nature picture library/ Richard Du Toit; 57 Photoshot Creative/ Anthony Bannister; age fotostock/Bernd Rohrschneider; Ann and Steve Toon/ Alamy; 58 Minden Pictures/Richard Du Toit; McPHOTO/Eva + Helmut Pum; Rene Mattes; nature picture library/Ann & Steve Toon; Juergen Sohns/Alamy; Ann and Steve Toon/Alamy; Minden Pictures/ Richard Du Toit; 59 robertharding/James Hager; Premium Stock Photography GmbH/Alamy; Minden Pictures/Juergen & Christine Sohns; 60 Hemis.fr/GUIZIOU Franck; United Archives; nature picture library/Richard Du Toit; Laura Romin & Larry Dalton/Alamy; age fotostock/Gerard Lacz; 61 nature picture library/Richard Du Toit; PhotoKratky - Wildlife/Nature/ Alamy; Minden Pictures/Richard Du Toit; Minden Pictures/Richard Du Toit; 65 Pete

Niesen/Alamy; 66/67 Minden Pictures/ Theo Allofs; 68 Axiom RF/Robert Postma; 79 Simon Wilkinson/Alamy; 86 Prisma Bildagentur AG/Alamy; 87 dfwalls/ Alamy; 88/89 roederPhotography; 90 imageBROKER/Christian Handl; 91 Armands Pharyos/Alamy; 98/99 imageBROKER/Harry Laub; 106/107 Westend61/Martin Moxter; 110/111 imageBROKER/Markus Obländer; 114/115 imageBROKER/Matthias Graben; 116/117 Scott Hurd/Alamy; 118 Radius Images; 119 Prisma by Dukas Presseagentur GmbH/Alamy; 120/121 roederPhotography; 122/123 nature picture library/Solvin Zankl; 134 Africa Media Online/Ariadne Van Zandbergen; 135 imageBROKER/Markus Obländer; 136/137 age fotostock/Hougaard Malan; 142/143 Sergi Reboredo/Alamy; 144 Kevin Schafer/Alamy; 146/147 Juergen Ritterbach/Alamy; 148 Danita Delimont RF/Paul Souders; 149 Tierfotoagentur/ Fotofeeling; 153 Steve Bloom; 154/155 Travel Collection/Benjamin A. Monn; 160/161 Beverly Joubert; 162 Travel Collection/Benjamin A. Monn; 163 Graham Prentice/Alamy; 166/167 Juergen Ritterbach/Alamy; 168 Minden Pictures/ Vincent Grafhorst; 169 Science Faction/ Seth Resnick; 172/173 Minden Pictures/ Vincent Grafhorst; 176/177 Mint Images/ Frans Lanting; 178/179 Africa Media Online/Roger de la Harpe; 180 age fotostock/Roger de la Harpe; 182 mauritius images/Africa Media Online/Roger de la Harpe; 198/199 Westend61; 202 AfriPics. com/Alamy; 203 Karin Duthie/Alamy; 204/205 robertharding/Ann and Steve Toon; 206 nature picture library/Richard Du Toit; 208/209 Minden Pictures/Richard Du Toit; 210/211 Minden Pictures/Vincent Grafhorst; 212 age fotostock/Claus Brandt; 213 nature picture library/Hougaard Malan; 214/215 Minden Pictures/Richard Du Toit; 216 Minden Pictures/Vincent Grafhorst; 218/219 Minden Pictures/Vincent Grafhorst; 220/221 robertharding/James Hager; 222 Friedrich von Hörsten/Alamy; 223 age/ Colin Marshall; 226/227 Minden Pictures/ Richard Du Toit; 230 imageBROKER/ Dirk Bleyer; 236 Russell Hunter/ Alamy; 237 Nature in Stock/Perry de Graaf; 240 Axiom RF/Robert Postma; 241 Minden Pictures/Richard Du Toit; 242 Minden Pictures/Juergen & Christine Sohns; 243 age fotostock/Gerard Lacz; 245 Minden Pictures/Richard Du Toit; 249 imageBROKER/Michael Krabs; 254 Danita Delimont/David Wall; 255 Prisma/CCO_Photostock_BS; 258/259 Sylvain Oliveira/Alamy; 261 Prisma Bildagentur AG/Alamy; 264 AfriPics. com/Alamy; 266/267 Vicki Wagner/ Alamy; 268/269 robertharding/Peter Groenendijk; 270/271 John Warburton-Lee/Ian Trower; 274/275 Alamy RF/ RooM the Agency; 280 Anka Agency International/Alamy; 281 imageBROKER/ jspix; 284 imageBROKER/Jürgen & Christine Sohns; 285 age fotostock/ Roger de la Harpe; 288 Anka Agency International/Alamy; 289 imageBROKER/ Jürgen & Christine Sohns; 292/293 ClickAlps; 294 Africa Media Online/Roger de la Harpe; 295 United Archives; 296/297 Etienne Volschenk/ Alamy; 298/299 Eric Nathan/Alamy; 302 Photoshot Creative/Roger Tidman; 307 Prisma Bildagentur AG/Alamy; 310/311 mauritius images/age fotostock/ Hougaard Malan; 314/315 mauritius images/David Noton Photography/Alamy; 326 Africa Media Online; 327 Africa Media Online/9-30-04; 330 Images of Africa Photobank/Alamy; 331 Prisma Bildagentur AG/Alamy; 332/333 Minden Pictures/Chris Stenger/ Buiten-beeld; 334/335 nature picture library/RHONDA KLEVANSKY; 337 Africa Media Online/Neil Austen; 338/339 nature picture library/Juan Carlos Munoz; 340 Diversion/Tetsuya Nomura; 342/343 Ulrich Doering/Alamy; 346/347 Images of Africa Photobank/ Alamy; 348/349 robertharding/James Hager; 350/351 Ulrich Doering/Alamy; 352 robertharding/Thorsten Milse; 353 jackie ellis/Alamy; 354/355 Suzanne Long/Alamy; 356 nature picture library/ Juan Carlos Munoz; 357 Photononstop/ Philippe Turpin; 358 Dan Callister/Alamy; Wildestanimal/Alamy; 359 Reinhard Dirscherl/; Westend61/Herbert Meyrl; Prisma/Dirscherl Reinhard; Marie Bärsch; nature picture library/Chris & Monique Fallows; 364 nature picture library/ Lou Coetzer; 368 Minden Pictures/Piotr Naskrecki; 369 nature picture library/ Cheryl-Samantha Owen; 370/371 Alamy RF/Gallo Images; 378 EggImages/ Alamy; 379 Angus McComiskey/Alamy; 380/381 imageBROKER/Christian Vorhofer; 382 Eric Nathan/Alamy; 396 nature picture library/Chris & Monique Fallows; 408/409 nature picture library/ Hougaard Malan; 410/411 paul kennedy/ Alamy; 412 Africa Media Online/Lance van Horsten; 413 nature picture library/ Graham Eaton; 414/415 Peter Titmuss/ Alamy; 416 Pixtal; 417 Minden Pictures/ Martin Woike/ NiS; 422 United Archives; 423 Masterfile RM/Jeremy Woodhouse; 424/425 nature picture library/Tony Phelps; 426 Nick Turner/Alamy; 427 Africa Media Online/Neil Austen; 428/429 age fotostock/Nigel Dennis; 430 Westend61/ Fabian Pitzer; 439 Rudolf Pigneter; 448 nature picture library/Hougaard Malan; 452/453 Catharina Lux; 454 Juergen Ritterbach/Alamy; 459 Catharina Lux; 460/461 Catharina Lux; 462 Africa Media Online/Neil Austen; 463 imageBROKER/ Franziska Ritter; 466/467 Catharina Lux; 471 AfriPics.com/Alamy; 476/477 nature picture library/Hougaard Malan; 485 Reinhard Dirscherl

Schapowalow

386 Richard Taylor/4Corners;
388/389 Justin Foulkes/4Corners;
390/391 Justin Foulkes/4Corners;
440/441 Richard Taylor/4Corners;
444/445 Richard Taylor/4Corners;
456/457 Richard Taylor/4Corners

KÖNEMANN

www.koenemann.com

6, rue du Mail – 75002 Paris
www.victoires.com
Depôt légal : 1er trimestre 2020
ISBN: 978-28099-1777-2

Series Concept: koenemann.com GmbH

Responsible Editors & Picture Editors: Jennifer Wintgens, Markus Hertrich
Text: Christine Metzger, Christina Hertrich, Markus Hertrich
Layout: Regine Ermert
Maps: Angelika Solibieda
Front Cover: Getty Images/2630ben

English, Spanish, Italian & Dutch translations: textcase, koenemann.com GmbH
Translation into French: Virginie de Bermond Gettle, Julie Fillatre

Printed in China by Shyft Publishing / Hunan Tianwen Xinhua Printing Co., Ltd.

ISBN: 978-3-7419-2510-8